P9-DMF-767

FINANCIAL ACCOUNTING

FOURTH EDITION

A CRITICAL APPROACH

JOHN FRIEDLAN

University of Ontario Institute of Technology

The McGraw-Hill Companies

Financial Accounting: A Critical Approach
Fourth Edition

ISBN-13: 978-0-07-040196-9
ISBN-10: 0-07-040196-9

1 2 3 4 5 6 7 8 9 0 TCP 1 9 8 7 6 5 4 3

Printed and bound in Canada

Editorial Director: *Rhondda McNabb*
Sponsoring Editor: *Keara Emmett*
Executive Marketing Manager: *Joy Armitage Taylor*
Developmental Editor: *Chris Cullen*
Supervising Editor: *Cathy Biribauer*
Photo/Permissions Researcher: *Photo Affairs, Inc.*
Senior Editorial Associate: *Christine Lomas*
Copy Editor: *Gillian Scobie*
Proofreader: *Rodney Rawlings*
Production Coordinator: *Lena Keating*
Cover and Interior Design: *Michelle Losier*
Composition: *Aptara®, Inc.*
Cover Photo: *© Matthew Trace*
Printer: *Transcontinental Printing Group*

Photo Credits: Page 1: Courtesy of Cineplex Inc.; page 34: Courtesy of Leon's Furniture Limited; page 101: Courtesy of Rogers Sportsnet; page 187: Courtesy of Indigo Books and Music Inc.; page 251: Courtesy of Loblaw Companies Limited; page 314: Courtesy of the Town of Georgina; page 378: Courtesy of Mountain View Estates Coffee Company; page 439: Courtesy of WestJet Airlines Ltd.; page 515: Courtesy of Dollarama Inc.; page 600: © Toronto Star/GetStock.com; page 667: Courtesy of Onex Corporation; page 706: Courtesy of Stephen MacLeod

Library and Archives Canada Cataloguing in Publication Data

Friedlan, John
Financial accounting : a critical approach / John Friedlan.—4th ed.

Includes index.
ISBN 978-0-07-040196-9
1. Accounting—Textbooks. I. Title.

HF5636.F76 2013 657 C2012-904686-8

ABOUT THE AUTHOR

High atop the peak of the Sulphur Skyline Trail in Jasper National Park, John Friedlan paused to take in the incredible view. It had taken him about two hours to reach the summit and through the mist, at 723 metres above sea level (2,370 feet), he could see patches of snow still clinging to the slopes of the nearby Rocky Mountains, including one called, appropriately, Utopia.

Suddenly, two mountain goats trotted by, searching for salt to lick among the bare rocks above the treeline.

For the award-winning university accounting professor, climbing to the top of a mountaintop ranks pretty close to his own utopia. Friedlan has hiked in some of the world's most scenic elevations, including the Dolomites in Italy, Denali National Park in Alaska, Gros Morne in Newfoundland and Labrador, and Skiddaw and The Fells in England's Lake District.

It is fitting that Friedlan's love of hiking began while completing his PhD in Accounting in Seattle, where he spent his off hours with colleagues climbing in the Cascade Mountains of Washington State. And, just as it takes plenty of determination and persistence to reach the end of a strenuous mountain trail, Friedlan takes a similar approach while teaching his accounting courses to undergraduates at the University of Ontario Institute of Technology in Oshawa, or as a sought-after speaker and consultant while training lawyers.

Friedlan wants his students to look beyond what's right in front of them, to push past the easy start at the trailhead, and to seek out the mysteries and the beauty that financial statements and balance sheets can contain, just as he discovers the beauty of the larkspurs or fireweed wildflowers he photographs on his outdoor excursions.

A Montreal native, Friedlan graduated from McGill University. At first, he wanted to be a scientist, but he turned to business studies at York University in Toronto, completing his MBA, and obtaining his CA designation before pursuing graduate studies on the West Coast.

After two years working as an auditor at the Toronto offices of accounting firm Deloitte, and then in the private sector for Nabisco, Friedlan became a full-time professor at the Schulich School of Business at York University. He was approached to write the first edition of his *Introductory Financial Accounting* textbook in 1997. Three editions later, students at many Canadian university business schools continue to use his books to learn the foundations of accounting.

Friedlan spent many years as an official with the Canadian Institute of Chartered Accountants, where he contributed to the UFE (uniform final examination). He's been interviewed on CTV's *Canada AM* and BNN's predecessor, *Report on Business Television*, and is currently developing an accounting video game.

He lives in Richmond Hill, north of Toronto, with his wife and two teenaged boys, where he enjoys listening to satellite radio, running, and being a hockey dad.

BRIEF
CONTENTS

CONTENTS

CHAPTER 9

Liabilities 515

CHAPTER 10

Owners' Equity 600

OBJECTIVES

Welcome to the fourth edition of *Financial Accounting: A Critical Approach*. I've written the book to provide an accessible and insightful introduction to the nature of accounting information. My goal is to have anyone who studies the book thoroughly become a sophisticated user of financial statements and understand the accounting issues, controversies, and scandals that are reported in the business press. I'm proud that this book is written exclusively by a Canadian author, the only such introductory financial accounting book currently available. As an IFRS (International Financial Reporting Standards) country, the relevance of a Canadian perspective is all the more important. Adaptations of U.S. books are less able to effectively capture the Canadian accounting environment.

The title of the book requires some explanation. The *Critical Approach* to financial accounting guides students to look critically at accounting information. The book emphasizes the importance of accounting information as a decision-making tool but also addresses the limitations, controversies, and problems with accounting and accounting information. Rather than accept the numbers in financial statements at face value, students learn that managers often choose from alternative acceptable ways of accounting for transactions and economic events and that these choices can have economic consequences for an entity's stakeholders and for the entity itself. Students also learn that accounting information provided by an entity can't be all things to all people. The information may be useful to some decision makers, but not to others. Students learn to critically evaluate whether the information is appropriate for the decisions *they* are making.

A conversation with a student a few years back reminds me of the importance of a critical approach to studying accounting. The student, who had transferred from another university, was struggling as he prepared for the mid-term exam. He said that he found the approach I use in introductory financial accounting quite challenging, explaining that at his previous university he was mainly asked to calculate, not to analyze and interpret information. After he left, I wondered how students' careers benefit from learning accounting from mainly a technical or procedural standpoint.

Many accounting textbooks classify themselves as having a "user" or a "preparer" orientation. In my view, these classifications are artificial: a good introductory education in financial accounting requires elements of both. Although the main purpose of this book is to make students literate readers of financial statements (a user orientation), it's difficult to understand financial statements without having some appreciation of how data are entered into an accounting system and converted into the information included in accounting reports. As a result, it's useful for introductory accounting students to understand basic bookkeeping (a preparer orientation). Without this familiarity, students will find it difficult to understand how and why accounting choices made by managers affect the financial statements.

Thus, while *Financial Accounting: A Critical Approach* is not primarily a book about how to do accounting, the "how to" part is fully covered. Chapter 3 explains how transactions and economic events are recorded and the data converted into financial statements. In the context of this book, understanding the procedural aspects of accounting is helpful for understanding the relationship between transactions and economic events and the resulting financial statements.

One of the important features of *Financial Accounting: A Critical Approach* is the use of short decision-oriented "mini-cases." The cases, and an approach for solving them, are first introduced in Chapter 4. Cases with solutions are provided as the Solved Problems in Chapters 4 through 12. Cases for assignment and exam purposes appear in the Appendix to the book. All of the cases place the student in the role of a user or interpreter of financial statements (what I call user-oriented cases). The cases serve three purposes: first, they help develop critical thinking and problem-solving skills; second, they help develop an appreciation of the context-specific nature of accounting; and third, they allow students to get "inside the heads" of preparers and users to understand how perspective affects the preparation and use of financial statements. Accounting comes to life as students are forced to think about alternative ways of accounting for transactions and economic events, and to consider the impact the different alternatives can have on decisions and economic outcomes.

Contemporary Canadian accounting students, accountants, and users of financial statements must function is a very challenging environment. Accounting standards tend to be complex and there are two quite independent sets of standards in use in Canada: International Financial Reporting Standards (IFRS) and Accounting Standards for Private Enterprises (ASPE). At the introductory level, ASPE and IFRS are very similar (as they say, "the devil is in the details"), so there's really not a big impact. I decided the main emphasis in this book would be IFRS because public companies are the most visible, although there are many more private companies, so there will likely be more companies that use ASPE. In places where there are significant differences between the two sets of standards, I've included boxes called "Accounting Standards for Private Enterprises." When using the book, you can be confident that, unless otherwise stated, ASPE and IFRS are the same for purposes of introductory accounting. However, it's important for readers to know that the two sets of standards can result in very significantly different financial statements.

In the fourth edition, I was able to use IFRS financial statements of Canadian companies as they issued their first annual sets of IFRS statements in early 2012. My thanks to the many companies that gave their permission for extracts of their financial statements to be used in the book.

CHANGES TO THE FOURTH EDITION

I've made some significant changes in the fourth edition. The major ones are:

- The learning objectives in each chapter have been expanded so that it's easier to link specific parts of a chapter to a specific learning objective.
- Almost all financial statement examples are from Canadian companies that prepared their statements on an IFRS basis.
- Added balloon comments to some exhibits to explain the key points.
- Chapter 1: Expanded the introduction to IFRS and ASPE.
- Chapter 2: Moved coverage of the qualitative characteristics of useful accounting information to Chapter 2 from Chapter 4 and updated the content to reflect the current IFRS conceptual framework.
- Chapter 4: Clarified the appropriateness of using the percentage-of-completion method for service arrangements. Added a short section that explained multiple deliverable arrangements.
- Chapter 7: Introduced accounting for biological assets and agricultural produce and explained different types of inventory errors and the impact they have on the financial statements.
- Chapter 9: Added a discussion of mortgages.

- Chapter 11: Revised coverage of passive investment to reflect the current/upcoming IFRS standard. Briefly introduced amortized costs, fair value through profit and loss, and fair value through other comprehensive income.
- Chapter 12: Coverage of auditors' opinions has been moved to a chapter appendix here from Chapter 10.

In this edition, I changed the nature of the chapter-opening vignettes. This time, each vignette links the chapter coverage to a Canadian corporation. The vignettes welcome readers to each chapter with an engaging, interesting, and relevant story. They were written by Canadian journalist Ellin Bessner (who is also my wife!). I thank her for her for the hard work and creativity she brought to the task. I hope you find the vignettes interesting and valuable.

In addition, many other minor changes have been added to improve the text. Many of the exercises and problems in the end-of-chapter material have been revised and many new problems and exercises added.

PEDAGOGICAL FEATURES OF *FINANCIAL ACCOUNTING: A CRITICAL APPROACH*

Besides the cases mentioned above, this text is full of other useful pedagogical tools.

- Learning Objectives and Summary of Key Points—The learning objectives at the beginning of each chapter focus students' attention on what they will learn. The summary at the end of each chapter outlines how each learning objective was addressed.
- Key Terms and Glossary—Key terms are printed in bold in the text and are listed with page references at the end of each chapter. The terms are defined in the text and appear with their definitions and a page reference in the glossary at the end of the book.
- Questions for Consideration boxes—Each chapter contains a number of questions for consideration, providing opportunities for students to stop and think about what they have read so far in the chapter. The boxes are designed as critical thinking questions requiring application of the material in the chapter. Solutions to the questions are provided.
- Knowledge Check boxes—Each chapter contains numbered Knowledge Check boxes that give students a chance to stop and check their understanding of key points raised in the chapter. If a student can't answer the questions, they should go back and review the preceding sections. Solutions to the Knowledge Checks are provided on Connect.
- Insight boxes—Throughout the text, commentary on key points is provided in the Insight boxes. These provide additional details concerning the nature and interpretation of accounting information.
- Accounting Standards for Private Enterprises boxes—Where appropriate, these boxes highlight differences between IFRS and ASPE.
- Use of extracts from actual entities' financial statements—Many of the issues, concepts, and points raised in the book are demonstrated through extracts from the financial statements of actual entities, presented as they appeared in the entity's annual report. Students are able to see first-hand the presentation of the topic in a real-world setting.
- Solved Problems—Each chapter provides a detailed problem with a solution. Most of the solved problems are cases that should help students develop their analytical skills.
- Similar Terms list—This unique feature provides a list of accounting terms used in the text compared to other terms with essentially the same meaning that students may encounter in the media, in financial documents, and in accounting practice.
- Using Financial Statements—Each chapter's assignment material provides extensive extracts from an entity's financial statements and a series of questions that provide students with the

opportunity to work with actual financial statement material and to apply the chapter content in a realistic context.

- Assignment material—Each chapter contains a large number of questions, exercises, and problems that provide students with the opportunity to apply the knowledge and skills they have gained from the chapter. All of this material is keyed to the learning objectives in the text.

A NOTE ON COVERAGE

Financial Accounting: A Critical Approach provides considerable depth on a number of topics not normally covered in introductory accounting texts or courses. These topics include revenue recognition, leases, pensions, future income taxes (in an appendix), employee stock options, and consolidated financial statements. Coverage of revenue recognition is intended to introduce the concept of accounting choice and demonstrate the impact of different ways of reporting economic events on the financial statements. The other, more complex, topics are included because they commonly appear in financial statements and often have large dollar amounts associated with them. If students are to make sense of an entire set of statements, they must have some familiarity and comfort with these topics, even if they tend to be complex. Some instructors may prefer not to cover some of the sections on leases, pensions, future income taxes, and investments in other companies. These topics can easily be skipped without having any impact on students' understanding of later chapters.

NAMES OF ENTITIES

Some readers may wonder about the origins of the names given to the entities used in the examples and end-of-chapter material. *Financial Accounting: A Critical Approach* provides names for more than 500 entities throughout the book and most are actual names of places in Canada!

Mc Graw Hill connect™

McGraw-Hill Connect™ is a Web-based assignment and assessment platform that gives students the means to better connect with their coursework, with their instructors, and with the important concepts that they will need to know for success now and in the future.

With Connect, instructors can deliver assignments, quizzes, and tests online. Nearly all the questions from the text are presented in an auto-gradeable format and tied to the text's learning objectives. Instructors can edit existing questions and write entirely new problems, track individual student performance—by question, assignment, or in relation to the class overall—with detailed grade reports, and integrate grade reports easily with Learning Management Systems (LMS) such as WebCT and Blackboard.

By choosing Connect, instructors are providing their students with a powerful tool for improving academic performance and truly mastering course material. Connect allows students to practise important skills at their own pace and on their own schedule. And, equally important, students' assessment results and instructors' feedback are all saved online—so students can continually review their progress and plot their course to success.

Connect also provides 24/7 online access to an eBook—an online edition of the text—to aid students in successfully completing their work, wherever and whenever they choose.

KEY FEATURES OF CONNECT

Simple Assignment Management

With Connect, creating assignments is easier than ever, so you can spend more time teaching and less time managing.

- Create and deliver assignments easily with selectable end-of-chapter questions and test bank material to assign online.

- Streamline lesson planning, student progress reporting, and assignment grading to make classroom management more efficient than ever.
- Go paperless with the eBook and online submission and grading of student assignments.

Smart Grading

When it comes to studying, time is precious. Connect helps students learn more efficiently by providing feedback and practice material when they need it, where they need it.

- Automatically score assignments, giving students immediate feedback on their work and side-by-side comparisons with correct answers.
- Access and review each response; manually change grades or leave comments for students to review.
- Reinforce classroom concepts with practice tests and instant quizzes.

Instructor Library

The Connect Instructor Library is your course creation hub. It provides all the critical resources you'll need to build your course, just how you want to teach it.

- Assign eBook readings and draw from a rich collection of textbook-specific assignments.
- Access instructor resources, including ready-made PowerPoint presentations and media to use in your lectures.
- View assignments and resources created for past sections.
- Post your own resources for students to use.

eBook

Connect reinvents the textbook learning experience for the modern student. Every Connect subject area is seamlessly integrated with Connect eBooks, which are designed to keep students focused on the concepts key to their success.

- Provide students with a Connect eBook, allowing for anytime, anywhere access to the textbook.
- Merge media, animation, and assessments with the text's narrative to engage students and improve learning and retention.
- Pinpoint and connect key concepts in a snap using the powerful eBook search engine.
- Manage notes, highlights and bookmarks in one place for simple comprehensive review.

INSTRUCTOR RESOURCES

Solutions Manual The fully revised Solutions Manual contains in-depth answers and step-by-step solutions for all assignment material included in the text.

Instructor's Manual The thoroughly updated Instructor's Manual includes learning objectives, chapter overviews, classroom icebreakers, active learning techniques, comprehensive lecture notes, writing assignments, and an assignment topic grid related to the coverage in the assignment material.

Computerized Test Bank The test bank contains more than 1,000 questions of the highest quality, varying in style and level of difficulty.

Microsoft® PowerPoint® Presentations With one presentation for every chapter of the text, instructors can guide their students through the text with ease. The slides have been adapted to fit the fourth edition, and the addition of figures and diagrams increases their visual appeal.

SUPERIOR LEARNING SOLUTIONS AND SUPPORT

The McGraw-Hill Ryerson team is ready to help you assess and integrate any of our products, technology, and services into your course for optimal teaching and learning performance. Whether it's helping your students improve their grades, or putting your entire course online, the McGraw-Hill Ryerson team is here to help you do it. Contact your *i*Learning Sales Specialist today to learn how to maximize all of McGraw-Hill Ryerson's resources!

For more information on the latest technology and Learning Solutions offered by McGraw-Hill Ryerson and its partners, please visit us online: **www.mcgrawhill.ca/he/solutions**.

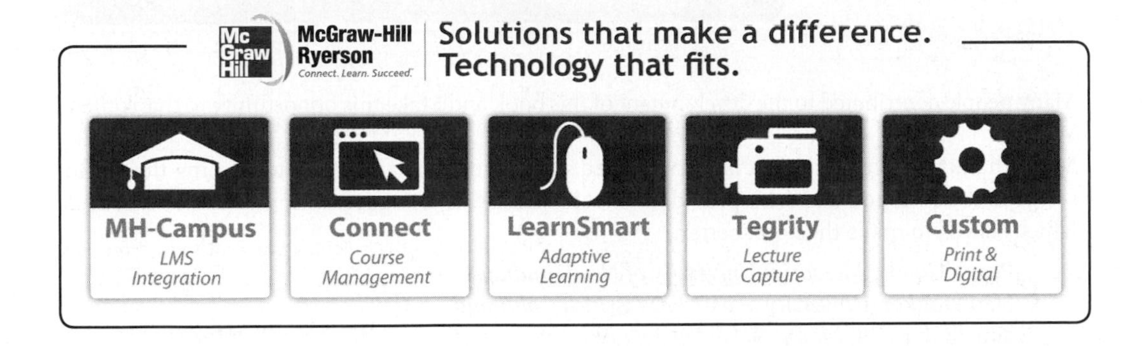

ACKNOWLEDGMENTS

Many people contributed to the development of this book and I take this opportunity to thank them.

Many thanks to faculty reviewers who devoted significant time and effort to reading the manuscript as it developed and who provided valuable comments, suggestions, and criticisms, all of which served to make the book better:

Peggy Coady, *Memorial University of Newfoundland*
Han Donker, *University of Northern British Columbia*
Gurpinder Gill, *Mount Royal University*
Ian Hutchinson, *Acadia University*
Michael Khan, *University of Toronto*
Jaime Morales, *Trent University*
Sandy Qu, *York University*
Shu-Lun Wong, *Memorial University of Newfoundland*

Thanks to Bic Ngo, then a fourth-year accounting student at the University of Ontario Institute of Technology and now with Deloitte & Touche LLP, for the work he did on the solutions, and to Katelyn Menard, currently a student at UOIT for her work on the solutions. Also, thank you to Susan Cohlmeyer of Memorial University of Newfoundland for her technical checks and comments, and to Ellin Bessner for writing the vignettes.

Various instructors assisted in preparing the set of supplements that accompany the book:

Sandy Hilton, *University of British Columbia* (Connect)
Jane Bowen, *University of Ontario Institute of Technology*
(Microsoft® PowerPoint® Presentations)
Lynn de Grace, *McGill University* (Test Bank)
Alla Volodina, *York University* (Instructor's Manual)

I'd like to thank the many companies whose financial statement extracts are presented in the book. It would be very difficult to write a book like this without real-world examples of financial reporting. Also thanks to the companies that are featured in the chapter-opening vignettes.

The staff at McGraw-Hill Ryerson provided outstanding support to help develop and market the book and were a pleasure to work with. Many thanks to the entire team, specifically Keara Emmett, Sponsoring Editor; Chris Cullen, Developmental Editor; and Cathy Biribauer, Supervising Editor. Thanks also to Gillian Scobie and Rodney Rawlings for their work on the copy editing and proofreading, respectively, of this book.

Finally, a special acknowledgment to Professor Al Rosen who helped shape and develop the way I think about and teach accounting. His contribution to this book is significant.

John Friedlan
Faculty of Business and Information Technology
University of Ontario Institute of Technology

CHAPTER 1

The Accounting Environment: What Is Accounting and Why Is It Done?

LEARNING OBJECTIVES

After studying the material in this chapter you will be able to do the following:

LO 1 Define accounting and explain why it's important.

LO 2 Describe the accounting environment and understand that the accounting information an entity presents is affected by the accounting environment.

LO 3 Discuss how the interests of the people who prepare accounting information can conflict with the interests of those who use it.

LO 4 Explain what a critical approach to accounting is.

LO 5 Understand the purpose of accounting standards such as International Financial Reporting Standards (IFRS) and Accounting Standards for Private Enterprises (ASPE) and be familiar with the different sets of accounting standards that are used in Canada.

LO 6 Understand that the main purpose of accounting is to measure economic activity and that accounting measurements can often be difficult and subjective.

When Marvel's *The Avengers* movie opened across North America on the first weekend in May 2012, it earned over $200 million at the box office and set a new record for opening weekend ticket sales.

Cineplex Entertainment

At Cineplex Entertainment's SilverCity Richmond Hill Cinemas, in Ontario, some of that money came from the wallets of moviegoers who shelled out for a premium-priced $16.99 3D ticket so they could experience the action flick in the special UltraAVX auditorium. These theatres offer reserved seating, a Christie Solaria digital projector, a wall to wall screen, 7.1 Dolby digital surround sound, and leatherette high-back rocker seats with moveable arm rests.

But while Cineplex encouraged its customers to "Escape With Us" and sit in the dark to watch Captain America team up with Iron Man, Hulk, Thor, and Black Widow, executives at the company's head office in Toronto were also paying careful attention to a wide range of business information in the world outside that could have an impact on their $1.8 billion company.

For example, the healthy eating trend prompted a switch to canola oil for the popcorn. Concern for the environment has Cineplex using recyclable popcorn bags and food trays, among other green initiatives.

Economic conditions have an effect as well because, according to Pat Marshall, a Cineplex spokesperson, "Our business tends to grow during difficult economic times as people downsize their more expensive out-of-home entertainment offerings and find movies a more affordable form of escapism."

Technological developments are also a factor for Cineplex, because people can now watch movies at home on DVD, or via Netflix or Rogers On Demand, instead of fighting the lineups at the cinema.

"We compete for people's available time and leisure dollars," Marshall acknowledged.

The company is also concerned about clamping down on movie piracy, noting that piracy affects studios' budgets, meaning that they might produce fewer and poorer quality movies.

Then there is government regulation to keep in mind.

Probably some of the people engrossed in watching the blockbuster knew that Cineplex Inc. is also required to follow Ontario Film Review Board admission rules for who can see various movies. While the board rated *The Avengers* PG, for Parental Guidance, Cineplex employees couldn't allow just anyone in to watch *The Hunger Games*. The board gave that movie a 14A classification, meaning that you had to be older than 14 to see it, or else you had to be accompanied by an adult.

Cineplex's Web site says it is "the largest motion picture exhibitor in Canada" with 130 theatres, 1,359 screens, and 10,000 employees, who it calls Cast Members. The company owns several top-tier brands: Cineplex Odeon, Galaxy, Famous Players, Colossus, Coliseum, SilverCity, Cinema City, and Scotiabank Theatres.

Companies like Cineplex also check the business environment to keep up with their competitors, including AMC and Empire Theatres. After careful study of the industry, Cineplex management decided to open a dozen more of its UltraAVX auditoriums across Canada before the summer of 2012.

The stock market also has an impact on the Canadian entertainment powerhouse. The share price on Bay Street for Cineplex stock was worth $31.28 on the Friday that *The Avengers* opened, which is the highest level it had been in a year.

–E.B.

LO 1

WHAT IS ACCOUNTING AND WHY DOES IT MATTER?

I have spent over 30 years in accounting education and I still get excited and passionate when I walk into a classroom to talk about the topic of the day. You may find this strange and surprising: How can anyone get excited about accounting? But there is a lot more to the subject than most people realize. Accounting is dynamic. It requires creativity. It can be controversial. Accounting matters! It's almost impossible to make good business decisions without relevant accounting information, and accounting information can be very relevant to personal decisions people make in their day-to-day lives.

Some of the decisions that both business managers and individuals might use accounting information for are listed in Table 1.1. The details about how many of these decisions are made is what this book is going to explore.

TABLE 1.1

Business and Personal Decisions That Rely on Accounting Information

LO 1

- Determine whether or not to buy a business and how much to pay.
- Calculate the amount of tax to pay.
- Evaluate whether to lend to a prospective borrower, and at what interest rate.
- Assess whether or not you can afford to borrow money.
- Decide if you can afford to go on vacation.
- Determine how to divide family assets in a divorce.
- Find out how much money you have in the bank.
- Determine how to invest money in a retirement savings plan or a tax free saving account.
- Determine bonuses earned by management.
- Evaluate whether to expand your business.
- Assess whether to make a product or to purchase it from an outside supplier.
- Evaluate how well managers have managed a business.
- Assess how well a business has performed.
- Determine if you should donate money to a particular charity. (Has the charity been managed well? Is it using its money effectively?)
- Determine how much a business is worth.
- Evaluate how much regulated businesses should be allowed to charge for their goods and services.
- Evaluate if a government has provided effective and efficient financial management.
- Decide whether to make a major purchase like a computer or car.

Most people don't see accounting as it really is. Consider the following:

- *Accounting isn't a science.* Indeed, it's probably more an art than a science.
- *Accounting isn't precise or exact.* Many estimates have to be made and uncertainty surrounds most accounting numbers.
- *Accounting doesn't provide the "right" answer.* There can be more than one reasonable answer for many accounting situations.
- *Accounting is flexible.*
- *Accounting requires judgment.*

As you work through the material in this book keep these statements in mind. I'm not going to explain them here, but as you learn more about accounting you will gradually come to see that they are true.

What Is Accounting?

LO 1

Let's begin with some definitions. **Accounting** is a system for gathering data about an entity's economic activity, processing and organizing that data to produce useful information about the entity, and communicating that information to people who want to use it to make decisions (see Figure 1.1). The **entity** is an economic unit of some kind, such as a business, university, government, or even a person. Note that data and information aren't the same thing. *Data* are raw, unprocessed facts about an entity's economic activity that are entered into an accounting system. *Information* results from organizing and presenting the data in ways that make it useful for decision making by stakeholders.

FIGURE 1.1 The Accounting System

While this definition of accounting may seem straightforward, it's not. When designing an accounting system, accountants and managers have to make many decisions about what data should be gathered and how it should be organized. Communicating using accounting information presents the same complexities people face with any form of communication. Just as writers choose words to influence readers, accountants can use legitimate, alternative ways of reporting the economic activity of an entity to influence how people perceive financial information.

INSIGHT

Bookkeeping Is *Not* the Same as Accounting

It's important not to confuse accounting and bookkeeping. When most people think of accounting, what they are really thinking of is bookkeeping. For those of you who have taken an "accounting" course in the past, what you may have been studying was *bookkeeping*—the process of recording financial transactions and maintaining financial records. Bookkeeping is part of accounting, but only one part. *Accounting* involves the design and management of information systems, how to account for and report an entity's economic activity, and the analysis and interpretation of financial information.

LO 1

Why Does Accounting Matter?

Accounting matters because it has **economic consequences**—it affects people's wealth—and it can have an impact on the decisions they make. For example, suppose you owned a small business, and you could choose between two legitimate and legal ways to account for a particular transaction. One accounting method will result in paying less tax than the other. Which method would you choose? Almost everyone would choose the one that involves paying the least amount of tax. The economic consequence of your choice is that you keep more money and the government gets less. Choose the other accounting method and the economic consequence is that you have less money.

Does this example surprise you? In reality, accountants and managers can often choose among alternative ways of accounting for transactions and economic events, and often the method chosen has significant economic consequences. Indeed, how an entity accounts for its transactions and economic events can have economic consequences for all the decisions described in Table 1.1. One of the main themes of this book is explaining the choices available to accountants and managers so that you can be a savvy user of accounting information and avoid unexpected negative economic consequences.

LO 1

WHY DO PEOPLE NEED AND WANT ACCOUNTING INFORMATION?

More and better information allows for better decisions. Without information, a "decision" is nothing more than a guess. For example, suppose you wanted to take a vacation over the winter break. You see an advertisement in the newspaper promoting Aruba as a fabulous winter destination. Assuming you have never been to Aruba and know little about it, would you simply accept the advertisement's claims at face value? Most wouldn't. Most people would probably want to find out whether Aruba offered what they wanted from a winter vacation. They might ask friends and relatives if they know anything about Aruba, do research in the library or on the Internet, or consult with expert sources that specialize in travel information, such as a good travel agent or a guide published by an independent company. They would gather information until they were comfortable making a decision. Not all information is equal; in making a decision, you would generally give more weight to the information that is most reliable and most relevant to your needs.

What does a trip to Aruba have to do with accounting? To make good decisions, whether about a winter vacation or a business strategy, people need good information. Every day people make important decisions, both for themselves and on behalf of other entities: individuals decide how to invest their retirement money, bankers decide whether to lend money to struggling businesses. Table 1.1 lists other decisions people have to make.

INSIGHT

The Cost-Benefit Trade-off

While more information leads to better decisions, there are limits. It's usually not possible or worthwhile to collect all the information available on a subject. First, gathering and analyzing information is costly and takes time. At some point the benefit isn't worth the cost. The concept of comparing the benefits of an action with its costs, and of taking the action only if the benefits are greater, is known as the **cost-benefit trade-off**. Information should be collected only if the benefit from it exceeds its cost. (For example, it's probably not worth the cost in time and money to call a university to find out the colour of the carpeting in its lecture halls.) Second, there are limits to the amount of information people can effectively manage and process. Too much information or "information overload" can impair a person's ability to make decisions.

QUESTION FOR CONSIDERATION

Explain why a potential vacationer to Aruba would likely find travel information published by Aruba's government travel department less credible than information provided by an independent travel company.

ANSWER: The objective of the government travel department is to encourage people to visit the island. Its publications will likely emphasize the favourable qualities of the island and downplay or ignore negative ones. In contrast, an independent travel company's objective (if it's truly independent) should be to provide a useful service to its customers that will encourage them to use the company's services again (the company will make more money if it can generate repeat business). As a result, its information is less likely to be biased. This doesn't mean the information provided by Aruba's government travel department wouldn't be useful. It means that a user should recognize the probable bias, and its implications, when assessing the information.

Let's consider an example of how information can improve a business decision. Suppose you were approached by a recent acquaintance who asked you to lend a significant amount of your own money to her business. What would you want to know before you agree? Your first key question would probably be, "Will the company be able to pay back the money borrowed, plus interest?" A second question would be, "If the company were unable to pay me back, what resources does it have that I could take and sell to recover my money?"

This is where accounting comes in. In answer to the first question, accounting information might be helpful in telling you how well the business has performed in the past and how much cash it has been able to generate. This information might help you predict how the business will do in the future. To help answer the second question you might want a list of the resources the business owns and a list of other entities it owes money to so you can see what would be available to you if the loan weren't repaid. You can probably think of more examples. Of course, non-accounting information, perhaps about the people managing the business, might also be helpful in making your decision.

KNOWLEDGE CHECK 1.1

Mc Graw Hill connect

- ❑ What is accounting?
- ❑ What is meant by the statement "accounting has economic consequences"?
- ❑ What is the cost-benefit trade-off? Why is it usually not appropriate to collect all possible information that might be useful in making a decision?
- ❑ Explain the difference between data and information.

THE ACCOUNTING ENVIRONMENT

LO 2

How an entity reports its economic activity in its financial statements or other type of accounting report is influenced by the circumstances under which the activity is occurring. Accounting was created to provide a record of economic activity and information useful in decision making, so it makes sense that accounting should be responsive to the environment and the people using the information. To say that all economic activity should be accounted for in the same way makes no more sense than saying that everyone should live in the same type of house or drive the same type of car. There are different types of houses and cars because people have different needs, dictated by factors around them such as climate, family, wealth, and employment, as well as personal preferences.

Therefore, before we start our examination of accounting information we will explore the accounting environment and consider the factors that can affect how an entity approaches its financial reporting. There are four key components of the accounting environment: overall environment, entities, stakeholders, and constraints. These components are displayed in Figure 1.2 and discussed below.

Environment

The character of a county's institutions influence the way its citizens live their lives. Canada, for example, is a constitutional democracy with a mixed economy and a legal system based on British common law (except for Quebec, which uses the civil code). The environment "umbrella" at the top of Figure 1.2 identifies some of the important factors that establish the structure of a society: political, cultural, economic, competitive, regulatory, and legal parameters. The differences in these between countries help explain why accounting rules vary from country to country.

The Accounting Environment

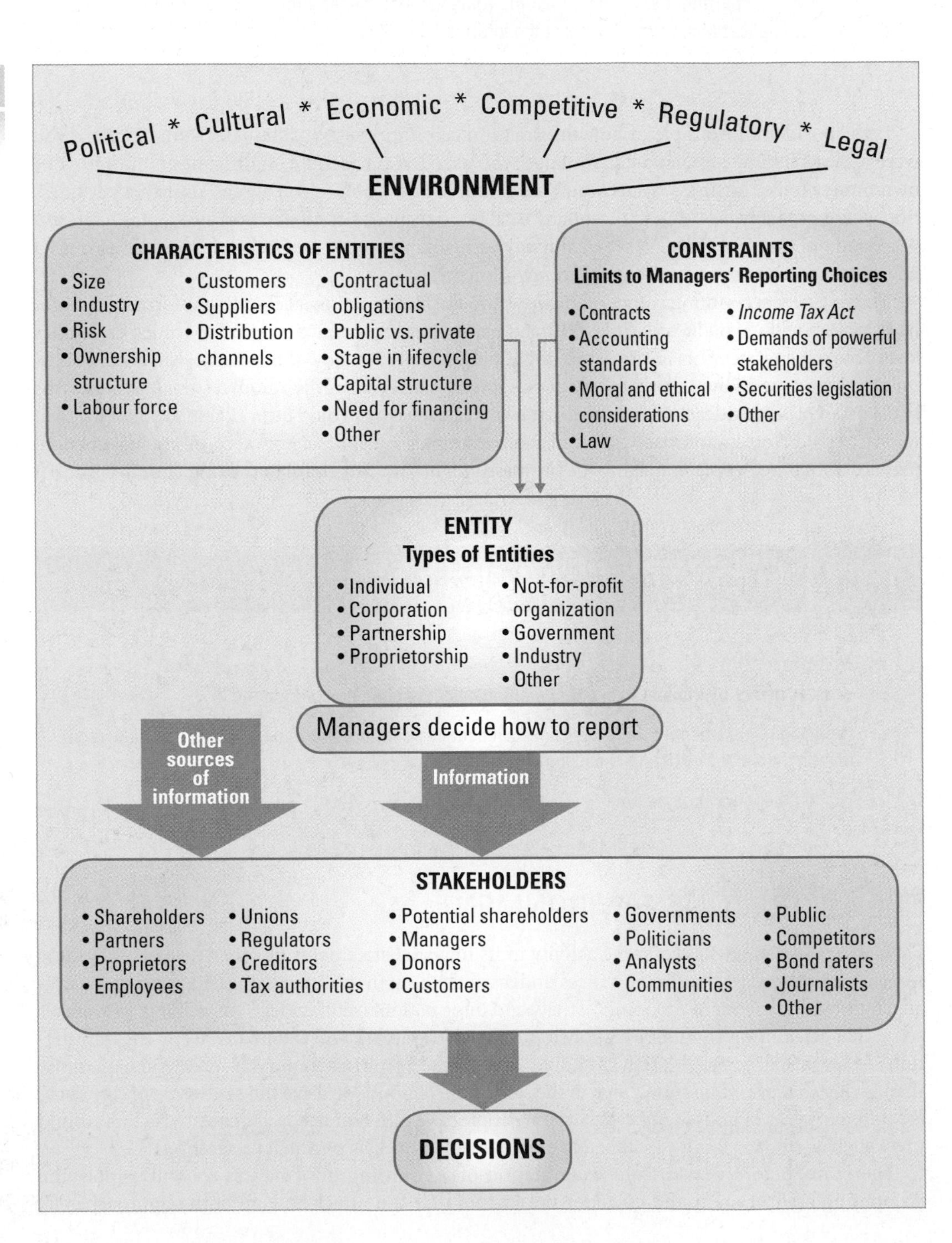

Entities

Entities are at the centre of the accounting environment because stakeholders are looking for information about them and it's the entities that typically provide the accounting information stakeholders need. There are three categories of business entities—corporations, proprietorships, and partnerships—as well as not-for-profit organizations, governments, and individuals. Let's take a brief look at some of the different types of entities.

Corporations A **corporation** is a separate legal entity created under the corporation laws of either Canada, one of the provinces, or some other jurisdiction in the world. Corporations have many of the same rights and responsibilities as individuals. For example, they must file tax returns, can be sued, and can enter into contracts (to borrow money, to provide goods or services to customers, etc.).

Ownership in a corporation is represented by **shares**, and owners of shares are called **shareholders**. Shares are issued to investors when a company is formed, and they can be issued at any time during a corporation's life.

One of the most important features of a corporation is that it provides **limited liability** to its shareholders, which means that shareholders aren't liable for the obligations of the corporation or the losses it suffers. For example, if a corporation borrows money and is unable to repay the loan, the lender can't demand repayment from shareholders. Another attractive feature of corporations is that share ownership is easily transferred without affecting the corporation, which simply carries on business with new owners. For other types of entities a transfer of ownership can be more difficult.

Shares of **public corporations** can be purchased by anyone interested in owning part of the company. The shares are usually traded on a **stock exchange**—a place (physical or virtual) where the shares of publicly traded entities can be bought and sold. Examples of exchanges are the Toronto Stock Exchange (TSX), the TSX Venture Exchange, and the New York Stock Exchange (NYSE).

www.tsx.ca

In contrast, the shares of **private corporations** can't be purchased unless the entity or its shareholders agree. If you set up your small business as a corporation, and you are the sole shareholder, no one could obtain shares unless you wanted to sell them. Most corporations in Canada are private. Examples of Canadian public and private corporations are given in Table 1.2.

Proprietorships A **proprietorship** is an unincorporated business with one owner. Unlike a corporation, a proprietorship isn't a separate legal entity. It doesn't pay taxes; instead, the **proprietor** (the owner of the proprietorship) includes the money made by the proprietorship in his or her personal tax return, along with income from other sources, such as employment. If a proprietorship doesn't meet its obligations any entities that are owed money can attempt to recover it by seizing the proprietor's personal assets, such as his or her house, car, or bank account. An attractive feature of proprietorships is that, unlike corporations, they are easy and inexpensive to set up.

TABLE 1.2 Examples of Public and Private Canadian Corporations

Name of Corporation	Ownership	Type of Business	Web Site
Canadian Tire Corporation	Public	Retail	www.canadiantire.ca
Loblaw Companies Limited	Public	Food distribution	www.loblaw.ca
Research In Motion Limited	Public	Technology	www.rim.com
Royal Bank of Canada	Public	Bank	www.rbc.com
WestJet Airlines Ltd.	Public	Transportation	www.westjet.com
Maple Leaf Sports and Entertainment Limited	Private	Sports and entertainment	www.mlse.com
McCain Foods Limited	Private	Food processing	www.mccain.com
McDonald's Restaurants of Canada Ltd.	Private	Food services	www.mcdonalds.ca
Home Hardware Stores Limited	Private	Retail	www.homehardware.ca
Irving Oil Limited	Private	Fuel oil dealer	www.irvingoil.com

Partnerships A **partnership** is an unincorporated business owned by two or more entities called **partners**. The partners could be people or corporations. A partnership is like a proprietorship except that there is more than one owner. Partnerships don't pay taxes; their earnings are included in the partners' incomes. There are different types of partnerships, some of which provide limited legal liability to the partners. (The different types of partnerships are discussed further in Chapter 10.) Like a proprietorship, a partnership can be relatively easy and inexpensive to set up. However, since it involves more than one entity, it's wise to have a partnership agreement, which adds cost and complexity. The agreement is important, however, as it sets out the rights and responsibilities of the partners.

Not-for-Profit Organizations A large part of the Canadian economy isn't devoted to making money or profit. **Not-for-profit organizations** provide social, educational, professional, religious, health, charitable, and other services in Canadian communities and around the world. Examples are hospitals, charities, religious organizations, unions, clubs, daycare centres, and universities. Not-for-profit organizations are exempt from paying income taxes and can incorporate and provide members with limited liability.

Governments Government plays a major role in the lives of Canadians. The various levels of government in Canada raise and spend hundreds of billions of dollars every year and financial reporting by governments is an important source of accountability.

Mc Graw Hill connect

KNOWLEDGE CHECK 1.2

- ❑ Identify and describe the three types of business entities.
- ❑ Explain the differences between public and private corporations.
- ❑ What is a not-for-profit organization? Provide some examples.

Individuals *Individual* people are also accounting entities as they often have to produce information in quantitative form to meet the demands of everyday life. Consider the following examples:

www.cra-arc.gc.ca

- *Filing an income tax return.* Most Canadians have to file a tax return every year with the **Canada Revenue Agency (CRA)**, the Canadian government agency responsible for administration and enforcement of federal tax laws, which means that information must be accumulated and organized to complete the return.
- *Keeping track of finances.* Accounting software is an easy-to-use accounting system designed to help people organize their finances.
- *Borrowing money from banks.* Banks may request financial information as part of a loan application.
- *Insuring homes and belongings.* To determine the amount of insurance needed, an individual lists his or her personal belongings and estimates a value for them.
- *Preparing budgets.* A student may want to estimate how much it will cost to attend university each year and then plan monthly or weekly spending to ensure that he or she has enough money to meet all financial needs for the year.

www.statcan.gc.ca

Others Although most of the common accounting entities have been identified above, there are other entities that may be of interest to people, depending on their needs. For example, some people may want data on a particular industry. While industries don't prepare financial statements, useful information can sometimes be obtained from sources such as trade associations, industry publications, public interest groups, and Statistics Canada.

Characteristics of Entities

No two entities are identical and, like people, each has characteristics that make it unique. Some characteristics are obvious, for example, an entity's size or industry. Canada has businesses in a vast range of industries, including natural resources, agriculture, finance, manufacturing, technology, hospitality, and retail, to name a few. But even though many companies may operate in an industry, there will still be differences among them. Some are public and others private. They might be large or small, unionized or non-unionized. Each may do business in different markets. Figure 1.2 identifies some characteristics of entities. All these characteristics are important for understanding an entity—what it does, and how it accounts for its economic activity. We will explore many of these as we proceed.

Constraints

How an entity accounts for its economic activity and what information it reports aren't entirely up to the people who prepare the information (although they have a lot of influence over it). Often, the choices available are constrained by contracts, laws, accounting standards, and the information needs and demands of powerful stakeholders. Consider the following examples:

- The *Income Tax Act* defines how certain transactions and economic events must be accounted for in calculating the amount of income tax an entity must pay.
- Corporations must meet the requirements of the law they are incorporated under (such as the *Canada Business Corporations Act*).
- Some entities must agree to follow formal sets of accounting rules such as Accounting Standards for Private Enterprises (ASPE) or International Financial Reporting Standards (IFRS).
- Companies that trade on Canadian stock exchanges must meet the requirements of the securities laws of their province and the rules of the stock exchange.
- Entities often enter voluntarily into contracts with other parties to do their accounting in a certain way.
- Above all, people involved in the accounting and financial reporting process have a responsibility to be ethical.

Stakeholders: Different Users, Different Decisions, Different Information

There are many groups and individuals that might be interested in, or "have a stake in," an entity. These interested parties are called **stakeholders** and they include owners, lenders, taxation authorities, employees, governments, consumers, and regulators (see Figure 1.2). Of course, not every stakeholder will be interested in every entity—some entities will have many stakeholders, others very few. Each stakeholder has his or her own perspective and has specific decisions to make concerning an entity. An owner will be concerned about different things than a lender, who will in turn be concerned about different things than the public, the employees, or the government. Therefore, the information most useful to one stakeholder group might be different from what is most useful to another group.

Many stakeholders don't have direct and unrestricted access to an entity's accounting system or the power to obtain specific information from management, so they have to rely on the information the entity provides. Ideally, each stakeholder would receive information tailored to his or her own needs; usually, however, the information provided is designed for the use of all stakeholders. Let's consider some of an entity's stakeholders and look at how accounting information can be useful to each of them.

Owners Often the owners of a business don't manage it themselves and, thus, aren't involved in its day-to-day affairs (e.g., shareholders of public corporations). When the owners don't manage the business, they need information from it for purposes of evaluating how well their investment is doing, determining if management is doing a good job, assessing the effectiveness of business strategies, considering whether they should sell their interest in the company, or deciding if the managers should be replaced.

Creditors A creditor is a stakeholder because it's owed money, goods, or services. Creditors need information to determine if an entity will be able to pay amounts owed and, in the event it doesn't pay, whether there are assets that might be taken and sold to recover the money owed.

Taxation Authorities In Canada, most individuals and corporations must file a tax return each year. The Canada Revenue Agency (CRA) requires taxpayers to calculate their taxes using methods consistent with the *Income Tax Act*, Canada's federal tax legislation. Provinces also have tax rules that must be followed. The CRA uses accounting information to assess the taxes owed by a business or individual.

Governments Governments use accounting information to decide whether certain entities should receive government support or subsidies. Accounting information can also have a political impact if, for instance, a company attracts the attention of politicians by making what the public perceives as "too much money."

Labour Unions Labour unions are concerned with the interests of their members and attempt to negotiate good wage and benefits packages with employers. Accounting information can provide insights to the union about how much an entity can afford to pay employees.

Communities/Public Interest Groups The lives of people are affected by the entities in their communities. For example, entities can be employers, taxpayers, or polluters. Accounting information provides citizens and community leaders with information regarding the entity and its impact in the community.

Donors to Charities Many Canadians donate money to charities. Donors would like to know that their donations are mainly being used to achieve the goals of the charity and not excessively for administration and fundraising. Accounting information can be useful for assessing whether the money donated will be put to good use.

Why Is It Important to Be Aware of the Accounting Environment?

From this discussion, it should be clear that the accounting environment affects how an entity will and should account for its economic activity. The information needs of stakeholders vary with the accounting environment so no single accounting report can suit all of them. An analogy may be useful in clarifying this point. Suppose your uncle, who is very busy, approaches you to help him choose a new car. What car would you suggest? You might encourage him to buy the car that appeals most to you, in the hope that he will let you borrow it. However, if it's going to be suitable for your uncle you will have to gather relevant information first. You will need to know how much he wants to spend, how big the car should be, and how much importance your uncle places on characteristics such as safety, style, colour, fuel economy, resale value, reliability, and so on. If you don't consider these factors, your uncle might say, "Nice car, but a two-seater sports car doesn't leave any room for the baby," or "I love the Rolls-Royce, but I only make $35,000 a year." In other words, deciding what car to recommend to your uncle involves considering his "environment."

This example illustrates how no single solution will be suitable for all because everyone's needs are different. Accounting is much the same. No one accounting report can provide the information every decision maker needs; accounting information has to be tailored. The people who prepare accounting information can often tailor information to suit needs by choosing among alternative accounting methods. (Sometimes the tailoring is for the benefit of the preparers themselves, as we will see!)

LO 2, 3

Stakeholders versus Preparers

Accounting information has to be thought of from two perspectives: preparers and stakeholders. **Preparers** (or managers of an entity) decide what, how, and when information is to be presented in an entity's financial statements and other accounting reports. Preparers are senior managers such as controllers, chief financial officers, and even chief executive officers, not junior or mid-level employees. To fully appreciate some of the main themes of this book it's essential to recognize that managers aren't neutral. How they prepare accounting reports may have economic consequences. Consider the following examples:

- Managers' bonuses are sometimes based on the numbers contained in accounting reports.
- Managers might own shares in a company so their wealth will be affected by the company's share price.
- Managers might lose their jobs if the company's performance isn't good enough.
- The selling price of a business can be based on accounting information so the owner of a business may benefit from "better" numbers.

There is clearly potential for conflict here. Stakeholders want information that is useful for their decision making. Managers have an interest in supplying useful information, but they are also motivated to act in their own interests to achieve favourable economic consequences for themselves (perhaps resulting in less favourable outcomes for other stakeholders). There is danger for stakeholders because managers have both the motivation and the ability to pursue their own interests using accounting information. They can do this because, by its nature, accounting is flexible, and managers must make choices that can affect the numbers and information in the financial statements. Even constraints don't eliminate flexibility and choice. Widely used accounting rules such as ASPE and IFRS leave managers a great deal of latitude in deciding what, how, and when information is presented in statements.

You shouldn't conclude from this discussion that accounting information isn't reliable or useful. Accounting information is crucial for decision making. What this means is that stakeholders must carefully analyze and interpret the information before reaching a decision. Paul Beeston, then (and now) president of the Toronto Blue Jays Baseball Club, former president and chief operating officer of Major League Baseball, and a Chartered Accountant, characterized the situation well when he said:

> Anyone who quotes profits of a baseball club is missing the point. Under generally accepted accounting principles, I can turn a \$4 million profit into a \$2 million loss, and I can get every national accounting firm to agree with me.[1]

Mr. Beeston's point is that the numbers reported in financial statements can vary depending on the choices the managers make and that a range of numbers can be considered "within the rules." This flexibility exists because the diversity of entities, stakeholders, and entity characteristics, along with the complexity of economic activity, requires flexibility—enough to allow information to be presented in a way that makes sense in the circumstances. Just as one type of car won't meet the needs of all drivers, one way of accounting won't meet the needs of all stakeholders, entities, and transactions. Indeed, it's sometimes difficult to say with certainty what the best way is to account for a transaction or economic event.

The accounting choices managers can make and their economic consequences is a major theme of this book and we will discuss it often.

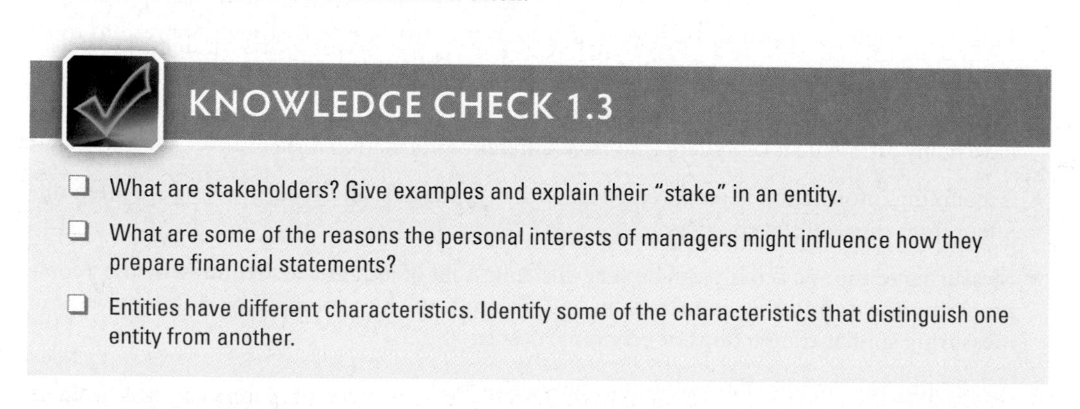

KNOWLEDGE CHECK 1.3

- ❑ What are stakeholders? Give examples and explain their "stake" in an entity.
- ❑ What are some of the reasons the personal interests of managers might influence how they prepare financial statements?
- ❑ Entities have different characteristics. Identify some of the characteristics that distinguish one entity from another.

Mc Graw Hill connect

The apparent conflict between stakeholders and managers creates a need for independent people who can provide assurance about the accounting information managers prepare. People who examine entities' financial information on behalf of external stakeholders are called **external auditors**, and their examination is called an **external audit**. Auditors examine the information in an entity's financial statements, as well as the data supporting it, to provide assurance the statements are fair representations of the entity's underlying economic activity and the accounting has been done in accordance with the designated set of accounting standards. Assurance will be discussed in Chapter 12.

I'll conclude this section with an example of the challenges accountants face. On December 15, 2017 a Toronto Blue Jays fan orders season tickets for the 2018 baseball season. The tickets cost $10,000 and the fan pays a $500 deposit when ordering them. The balance must be paid in full on February 28, 2018. The baseball games will be played from April through October, 2018. When do you think the Blue Jays should report they've sold these season tickets: when the tickets are ordered, December 15, 2017; when they're paid for, February 28, 2018; or when the games are actually played, April through October 2018? Arguments can be made for each of these, and accountants can actually disagree on when to report the sale. But while the accountants are scratching their heads figuring this out, the economic activity—receipt of the deposit, payment in full, and playing of the games—still occurs.

But while the actual economic activity is unaffected by how the Blue Jays do their accounting, how the accounting is done can have economic consequences. When the sale is reported can affect the amount of tax the Blue Jays pay, the size of bonus the sales manager earns, perhaps the terms of a bank loan, and even the price of Rogers Communications Inc.'s (owner of the Blue Jays) shares.

INSIGHT

Accounting, Ethics, and Choice

This discussion of the accounting environment should make clear the potential for significant and frequent ethical dilemmas. Managers, auditors, and accountants continually face choices about what, how, and when information should be presented in an entity's financial statements and other accounting reports. These choices are often difficult and usually aren't a simple matter of being right or wrong. Economic activity is complex and deciding how to account for it requires careful judgment. Managers have an ethical and moral responsibility to provide information that is a reasonable representation of the entity's activity. But it's important to understand that intelligent, ethical, and responsible managers, auditors, and accountants can have legitimate differences of opinion about these things. The "right" answer isn't always obvious!

LO 4

WHAT IS A "CRITICAL APPROACH" TO ACCOUNTING?

You may be wondering what I mean by "a critical approach" in the title of the book. "Critical" refers to critical thinking, which is applying high-level mental skills such as analysis, application, evaluation, explanation, inference, interpretation, judgment, and synthesis to decision making.

This first chapter shows how the world of accounting isn't nearly as straightforward as most people believe. The accounting environment is subtle, sophisticated, and complex. Consider:

- There are different kinds of entities with a wide variety of characteristics, and each entity can have many different stakeholders who have different information needs;
- Accounting information is prepared by an entity's managers, and their interests are often different from those of stakeholders;
- Measuring economic activity can be very difficult. A lot of judgment is required by the people preparing the accounting information, and accounting rules often allow different ways of measuring similar transactions or economic events;
- Accounting information has economic consequences.

These points should make it clear that using accounting information is intellectually very challenging and demanding. One of the crucial lessons is that you, as a user of accounting information, can't just accept the numbers at face value; you will have to apply critical thinking skills to get the full story.

As a final comment, remember that while it's fine to develop strong critical thinking skills, you must have something to think critically about. There is a lot to know in accounting. The challenge is to accumulate the knowledge presented here and develop and apply your critical thinking skills to that knowledge. Figure 1.3 provides a pictorial view of knowledge and critical thinking.

FIGURE 1.3
Knowledge and Critical Thinking

THE RULES OF THE GAME

LO 5

One of the constraints I identified in the discussion of the accounting environment was formal sets of accounting rules or standards. In Canada there are two sets of accounting standards for businesses:

a. **International Financial Reporting Standards (IFRS)** are mandatory for publicly accountable companies, while private companies can choose to use them.[2] IFRS are intended as a single set of globally accepted, high-quality accounting standards. (Canadian companies whose shares are traded on U.S. stock exchanges can choose to use U.S. accounting standards (Research In Motion Limited and Canadian National Railways have chosen to do so).)

b. **Accounting Standards for Private Enterprises (ASPE)** were developed for Canadian private companies. The objective of ASPE is to provide a simplified set of accounting principles that are appropriate for private businesses.

There are no natural laws (like gravity) that define how accounting should be done so it's necessary to create rules of the game, or accounting standards, so preparers and stakeholders can understand what to expect from financial statements. IFRS and ASPE are the principles, conventions, practices, procedures, and rules that define acceptable accounting practices at a particular time. In other words, IFRS and ASPE provide bases for preparing financial statements.

Because accounting standards have been created to meet the information needs of stakeholders, they may differ depending on the characteristics of the entity, the situation, and the jurisdiction. In Canada, both IFRS and ASPE (which are similar but not identical) apply. The United States has its own set of standards, as do other countries.

How can this be? Shouldn't there be just one set of rules for everyone, everywhere? In reality, many things differ from one jurisdiction to another. Consider hockey, which isn't the same wherever it's played. Rules in the National Hockey League differ from those in games played under the authority of the International Ice Hockey Federation (such as the Olympics), for example, the size of the rink, penalties for fighting, calling of icing, and where the goaltender can go behind the net. Rules can also vary between minor professional and amateur leagues. Similarly, while IFRS and ASPE are quite similar, there are differences that can lead to significantly different financial statements.

Also, hockey rules are subject to interpretation and sometimes even controversy. In the course of a game the referee must make judgments about whether to call a penalty, when to blow the whistle, or if a goal has been scored. Similarly, accounting rules have to be interpreted. The same transactions and economic events can sometimes be legitimately accounted for differently, even if a company is following IFRS or ASPE. IFRS and ASPE are both flexible and each requires managers who prepare the financial statements to exercise good judgment. The choices managers make when preparing statements can significantly affect the amounts reported in the financial statements (as the calls a referee does and doesn't make can affect the outcome of a hockey game).

LO 5

International Financial Reporting Standards

In the past, most countries set their own accounting standards and, as a result, each country's standards were different. This approach made sense because each country could set standards that reflected its accounting environment, by addressing the issues facing important industries, for example. In the 1970s, companies were increasingly trying to raise money internationally by listing their shares on international stock exchanges. This created demand for a common set of accounting standards to make it easier for stakeholders in different countries to understand and compare financial statements. In response, accountants in several countries, including Canada, formed the International Accounting Standards Committee (IASC) to develop accounting standards that could be used around the world.

In the 1990s, increasing globalization accelerated the push for international standards and the IASC was replaced by the International Accounting Standards Board (IASB) in London, England, which is responsible for developing IFRS. IFRS are used in over 100 countries around the world, including the countries in the European Union, Brazil, Australia, and New Zealand. IFRS became mandatory in Canada for publicly traded companies in 2011. Standard setters in the United States haven't decided whether to stay with their own domestic standards or adopt IFRS. In the meantime, U.S. standard setters are working with the IASB to harmonize IFRS and U.S. generally accepted accounting principles as much as possible.

LO 5

Accounting Standards for Private Enterprises

Accounting Standards for Private Enterprises (ASPE) arose out of recognition that private companies are different from public ones. Some key differences are:

- Private companies usually have a relatively small number of stakeholders;
- Private companies usually know who the stakeholders are;
- Private company stakeholders are typically more knowledgeable about the entity;
- Private company stakeholders can usually obtain information directly from the company (for example, a shareholder could speak with the president of the company), something that is likely impossible for shareholders of a public company.

ASPE provides high-quality standards that are less detailed and more straightforward to implement, and more cost effective for reporting entities. The Accounting Standards Board (AcSB) in Canada is responsible for setting ASPE. Many jurisdictions around the world have domestic accounting standards that can be used by private companies.

IFRS and ASPE are very similar at a conceptual level as they are both based on the same set of concepts and principles. However, there are differences between the standards and these can result in very different financial statements. Throughout this book I emphasize IFRS. Most of the financial statements that we come across are for public companies, which means that familiarity with IFRS is necessary. However, the vast majority of businesses in Canada are private so an appreciation of ASPE is also needed. In situations where the differences are significant, IFRS will be addressed in the main part of the text and ASPE will be presented in an Insight box.

www.iasb.org
www.cica.ca

Readers who are interested in more information about accounting standards can visit the Web sites of the International Accounting Standards Board (IASB) and the Canadian Institute of Chartered Accountants (CICA).

IFRS and ASPE aren't necessarily the only or best bases for preparing financial statements. The measurements reported in IFRS or ASPE financial statements don't always provide the information a particular stakeholder requires. It's crucial for stakeholders to critically evaluate the relevance of any information for the decisions they have to make. Despite the usefulness of having a set of guidelines and rules for preparing financial statements, IFRS and ASPE aren't without flaws. To be a sophisticated user of financial information, you need to know and understand what IFRS- and ASPE-based information tells you, how it can help you, and what its limitations are.

Who Has to Follow IFRS and ASPE?

LO 5

It's easy to get the impression that all Canadian companies have to follow either IFRS or ASPE. Public companies are required by law to provide audited financial statements prepared in accordance with IFRS.

On the other hand, private companies, partnerships, and proprietorships don't have to follow IFRS or ASPE, although they can choose to. They might use IFRS or ASPE if there are external stakeholders—for example, shareholders who aren't involved in the day-to-day management of the company or creditors—who rely on the financial statements for information. These stakeholders may demand financial statements prepared in accordance with an appropriate and understood set of accounting standards.

If there are no significant external stakeholders a private company might not use IFRS or ASPE to simplify and reduce the cost of preparing financial statements. They might prepare their statements to meet the information needs of managers or owners, or to meet the requirements of the *Income Tax Act*.

A diagram of which standards different types of entities have to follow is provided in Figure 1.4.

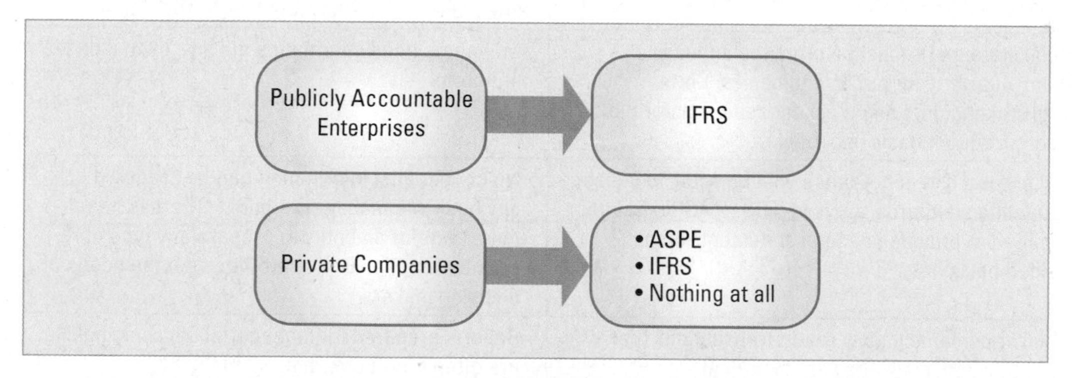

FIGURE 1.4
Who Has to Use What?

PROFESSIONAL ACCOUNTANTS IN CANADA

LO 2

In Canada, there are three groups of professional accountants: Certified General Accountants (CGAs), Certified Management Accountants (CMAs), and Chartered Accountants (CAs). People with any of these designations have demonstrated that they have the knowledge, skills, and abilities required by the professional body, and that they have the expertise to practise accounting. Anyone who hires a professional accountant can be confident that the person will be able to carry out their duties properly. Members of these professional groups have important responsibilities: to act in a professional, ethical, and competent manner at all times and to adhere to the code of conduct of their group.

Becoming a professional accountant isn't easy. Each professional body has its own requirements; but, in general, to earn an accounting designation, you need to

- obtain a university degree
- complete specific course requirements to learn the body of knowledge needed to be an effective practitioner
- pass the examinations administered by the professional body
- obtain experience on the job

LO 1 FINANCIAL VERSUS MANAGERIAL ACCOUNTING

You may have noticed when looking at accounting courses at your school that there are two distinct fields of accounting: financial accounting and managerial accounting. The first, **financial accounting**, provides information to stakeholders who are *external* to an entity. The second subfield is **managerial accounting**, which addresses the information needs and decisions of the stakeholders who are internal to an entity—the managers and other employees. Table 1.3 highlights some of the differences between these two fields and should give you an idea of what to expect in courses focusing on each.

TABLE 1.3 Differences between Financial and Managerial Accounting

	Financial Accounting	Managerial Accounting
Stakeholders	External to the entity. Includes investors, lenders, taxation authorities (such as the Canada Revenue Agency), competitors, and many others. These stakeholders usually don't have direct access to information about the entity and must rely on the entity to provide it.	Internal to the entity. Managers and other employees.
Purpose of information	Used for the decisions of a particular stakeholder. Includes investment decisions, evaluating performance, predicting cash flows, lending/credit decisions, etc.	Used for operating decisions such as price setting, expansion, evaluating which products are successful, and determining the amount of a product that should be produced.
Reporting unit	Financial statements are usually for an entity as a whole.	Information can be very detailed and can be about any aspect of the entity (product, activity, etc.).
Frequency of reporting	Financial statements must be prepared annually at a minimum, quarterly for public companies. Certain external stakeholders might ask for specific information on a more frequent basis (e.g. bank).	Managers need information quickly, even daily or hourly.
Constraints	Usually prepared in accordance with an established set of accounting standards, such as IFRS or ASPE. Entities are required to provide financial statements on a prescribed basis.	No constraints. Information can be prepared on any basis the manager requires. There is no requirement for an entity to prepare any type of report. Information is prepared to meet the needs of decision makers.
Perspective	Financial statements mainly report transactions that have already occurred. They are historical.	Reports prepared for managerial decision making are often future oriented.

LO 6 ACCOUNTING IS FOR MEASUREMENT

Accounting is all about measuring economic activity. The information produced by an accounting system allows stakeholders to measure different attributes of an entity, such as

- performance
- efficiency
- performance of managers, and how much bonus they should receive
- how much it owes lenders
- how much it's worth
- tax obligation

But measurement isn't always straightforward. Some things, of course, are easy to measure and create little controversy: how tall you are, how much you weigh, or whether you did the calculations in a math problem correctly. Other measurements are very subjective and can give rise to a lot of controversy. Consider Olympic competitions in judged sports such as diving, gymnastics, or figure skating. Judges evaluating an athlete's performance don't always agree on scoring or ranking. Over the years there have been suggestions of bias among Olympic judges, and even some full-fledged scandals. It's also difficult to measure things like public opinion on an issue, an employee's job performance, a hospital patient's pain, even the quality of a term paper you wrote.

Accounting involves similar problems. Some things are easy to measure. For instance, there will be little controversy about how much cash an entity has at a certain point in time, or how much a building cost. Other accounting measurements, such as profit (as we'll see in a later chapter), are much more difficult.

Let's look at some examples of how accounting can be used for measuring. Suppose that you have a summer job in a mining town in northern Canada. You expect to earn enough money to pay for next year's tuition and a winter vacation with your friends. But after the first couple of months on the job, you look at your bank balance on the Internet and worry you aren't saving enough. Fortunately, at the start of the summer you had decided to keep track of your spending in an accounting software package. An excerpt from your software for April and May is shown in Table 1.4.

TABLE 1.4

An Example of Basic Data in an Accounting System

Money Spent during the Summer		
Date	**Purpose**	**Amount**
April 1	Rent	$300.00
•	•	•
•	•	•
•	•	•
April 13	Magazines	5.75
April 13	Entertainment	22.50
April 13	Groceries	44.85
•	•	•
•	•	•
•	•	•
May 17	Groceries	45.25
May 18	Entertainment	12.75
May 19	Miscellaneous	14.50
•	•	•
•	•	•
•	•	•
May 31	Clothes	47.99
May 31	Taxi	5.00

The list of transactions in your software is raw data. To be useful, the data have to be processed, organized, and converted into information. Accounting software allows you to classify transactions into categories such as food, entertainment, and rent. Table 1.5 shows an example of how the software could organize the data so that it's easy to see how much money you made, how much you spent and on what, and how much you have left over.

Next, consider how to use the information in Table 1.5. Your concern is that you're not saving enough money, so you might identify ways to reduce your spending. For example, you might go out less often or find less expensive forms of entertainment. You might consider working more hours. Notice that Table 1.5 helps you address your problem but doesn't actually tell you what to do. The decision maker (you, in this case) has to use the information to come up with a solution.

TABLE 1.5

An Example of a Basic Accounting Report

Summary of Earnings and Spending—April and May		
Amount earned (gross pay)	$5,258.88	
Amount withheld*	946.60	
Deposited in the bank (net pay)		$4,312.28
Amounts Spent		
Books, magazines, etc.	75.33	
Clothes	138.25	
Entertainment	221.55	
Groceries	327.58	
Local transportation	45.56	
Miscellaneous	99.98	
Rent	600.00	
Amount spent		1,508.25
Amount saved in April and May		$2,804.03

*Employers are required to withhold money from employees' wages for taxes, employment insurance, and Canada Pension Plan contributions. The amount earned before withholding is called *gross pay*. The amount after deductions is called *net pay*.

A crucial point is that you should organize the data according to what you or some other stakeholder wants to know. Table 1.5 doesn't tell you the type of entertainment you enjoyed, what groceries you bought, or what the miscellaneous items represent, so it might not be detailed enough for you. But if you didn't care how you spent your money, a statement like the one in Table 1.6 might suffice.

TABLE 1.6

An Example of a Basic Accounting Report

Summary of Earnings and Spending—April and May		
Amount earned (gross pay)	$5,258.88	
Amount withheld	946.60	
Deposited in the bank (net pay)		$4,312.28
Amount spent during April and May		1,508.25
Amount saved in April and May		$2,804.03

You should also recognize that your ability to extract information from an accounting system is limited to the data entered into it. That is, you couldn't see how much money you spent on soft drinks if you hadn't recorded soft drink spending separately. There is a cost to a more detailed breakdown of information: it takes more time to enter the data into the software.

This example demonstrates how accounting can organize and summarize data to provide useful information for solving a problem. Let's consider an example that looks at a different perspective on measurement.

Imagine you're a first-year university or college student who has just moved into a new apartment near the campus. You've furnished it with personal belongings and it has appliances supplied by the building's owner. You need to get insurance for the apartment, but how much coverage do you need? You want to have enough to protect your own things as well as things you're responsible for—the building owner's appliances. The insurance company needs to know how much coverage you require and what type, so it can write a policy and set a premium. To estimate the amount of insurance you need, you go through the apartment and make a list of the items you want to insure (your list is shown in Table 1.7).

TABLE 1.7

Items in a Student's Apartment

Inventory of Apartment Contents			
Column 1	**Column 2**	**Column 3**	**Column 4**
Item	**What it cost**	**What it would cost to replace**	**What it could be sold for**
Television	$ 1,100	$ 925	$ 400
Laptop	800	900	300
Furniture	4,225	4,525	2,300
Books	750	875	300
Clothes	1,600	1,950	300
iPhone	175	600	275
Jewellery	500	625	300
Appliances	2,600	3,300	1,800
Art	300	500	500
Other	1,000	1,200	750
Total	**$13,050**	**$15,400**	**$7,225**

Column 1 of Table 1.7 lists the contents of the apartment. You have to assign a value to each item so that you can "sum up" to a total. The total is important because if you don't know the worth of what you want to insure you may buy too little insurance, leaving you without enough coverage in the event of a fire or robbery. If you buy too much insurance you're wasting money on premiums since the insurance company won't pay out more than the amount of the loss. (For example, if you have $50,000 of insurance coverage and everything you own is destroyed in a fire but is worth $10,000, the insurance company will pay you only $10,000.)

So what is the appropriate value to assign to each item? In Table 1.7, three different measurements of value have been given for each item, and are explained as follows:

- Column 2 gives the amount paid for each item.
- Column 3 shows the cost to replace the item with an equivalent new item. (For example, the TV might be a ten-year-old model that is no longer made, so you would have to get something comparable that is available today.)
- Column 4 is the amount each item could be sold for (known as net realizable value).

Notice that the total of each column is different.

All these amounts represent valid measures of the items in your apartment, but which would be appropriate for determining the amount of insurance to purchase? That depends on your needs. If you want the insurance to return you to the situation you were in before the loss, Column 3 would be best (this is called *replacement cost insurance*). For example, if your television were stolen, replacement cost insurance would allow you to obtain an equivalent television. On the other hand, if you simply want compensation for the loss, Column 4 should be used. This would allow you the cash value of the items you lost. So if your ten-year-old television were stolen, your loss would be the market value of an identical ten-year-old TV. (The insurance company wouldn't get estimates of the worth of the specific items but would use a formula to estimate the extent to which they were used, based on the type of item and its age.)

There are two important points to note from the insurance example. First is the importance of measurement. To decide on the amount of insurance needed, you need to come up with a measure of the total value of the items in the apartment. Second, there is often more than one way to measure the same thing. We have easily come up with three ways to measure, in dollars, the "value" of the items in an apartment. Which is best? That question can't be answered in absolute terms. Which is best depends on the situation and the needs of the decision maker.

INSIGHT

While most accounting reports use money as the basis for measurement, it's important to say that it isn't the only basis. Accounting and accountants can provide information in many different ways. For example, accountants might be involved in providing information on the amount of pollution a company produces or the effectiveness of a medical care system (mortality rates, utilization of beds and equipment, etc.). They might help develop measures of customer satisfaction or evaluate whether a government is getting value for the money it spends. These measurements aren't made in terms of money.

QUESTION FOR CONSIDERATION

A few months ago you borrowed $1,000 from an acquaintance and now you don't have the cash to pay back the loan. As repayment you offered some of your personal belongings instead of cash. If the list in Table 1.7 represents your belongings, which measurement basis (which column) would be most appropriate for determining which items the acquaintance could reasonably take?

ANSWER: Column 4, what the items could be sold for, would be most appropriate. Since you owe $1,000, the acquaintance should be given items that would allow her to obtain the equivalent of $1,000 cash. She doesn't have to actually sell the items, as long as they could be sold for $1,000.

Let's briefly consider an example showing a type of measurement problem that accountants face. Suppose you operate a business that offers credit (*credit* means that customers can buy now and pay later). A stakeholder would like to know how much you are currently owed by customers and how much you actually expect to collect. The first question is easy. You look at how much customers have promised to pay but that hasn't been collected yet. As long as your records are up to date, this information will be readily available.

The second question is more challenging. How much you will actually collect depends on future events: customers actually paying. You can't know the answer for sure until some time in the future when a customer either pays or definitely indicates it won't be paying. To provide the information now you'll have to make an estimate, an informed guess. You could base your estimate on a number of things: the proportion of the amount owed that has been collected in the past, your knowledge of your customers, and economic conditions. However, chances are your estimate won't be correct.

In sum, accounting is about measurement. The challenge for accountants is to develop appropriate ways of measuring aspects of economic activity that are difficult or even impossible to observe, and to make those measurements useful for stakeholders. Stakeholders have to realize that accounting measurements are a messy business. Many are inherently imprecise and uncertain, and the best way of measuring is often far from obvious. A large part of this book is devoted to helping you understand the complex nature of accounting measurement.

Solved Problem

BAYTON LTD.—PART 1

Bayton Ltd. (Bayton) operates garbage dumps in western Canada. The company purchases land from private owners, has the land zoned for a garbage dump, and then develops and operates the dump. The planning and development of the dumps is done in close cooperation with the local communities the dump will serve. Bayton doesn't provide garbage collection services; local governments or private contractors do that. The garbage collectors pay a fee to Bayton based on the weight of the garbage dumped.

Bayton is a privately owned corporation with 15 investors living all across Canada. The business is run by a team of professional managers who have considerable experience in the waste management business. Managers are paid a salary plus a bonus based on the company's performance, as measured by its accounting information. The company employs over 500 people, many of whom are unionized. Bayton has borrowed heavily from several banks and other lenders.

Required:

Identify all of the stakeholders in Bayton and explain their "stake" in the company. Not all the stakeholders are explicitly referred to in the scenario. You will have to think about the business situation carefully to identify others. (You may be able to identify stakeholders in addition to those in the Solution.)

Solution:

Stakeholders	Stake
1. Shareholders (owners)	The shareholders are Bayton's owners. Part of their wealth is invested in the company.
2. Lenders	Bayton owes the lenders money. The lenders are concerned about Bayton's ability to repay amounts owed to them.
3. Managers	Managers are interested in keeping their jobs and enhancing their reputations in the job market. In addition, part of the managers' compensation is based on the performance of Bayton.
4. Canada Revenue Agency (CRA)	Bayton Ltd. is a taxpaying entity and the CRA is interested in ensuring it pays its taxes and complies with the *Income Tax Act*.
5. People located in communities where dumps are or will be located	Garbage dumps are often unpopular neighbours. People living near existing dumps want to ensure the dumps are being managed responsibly and that Bayton will be able to carry out its obligations in the future. People living near prospective garbage dumps may want to take steps to prevent a dump from being opened near their homes.
6. Government	Garbage dumps can be politically sensitive issues. Governments want to ensure that Bayton's garbage dumps don't cause political problems.
7. Employees/unions	Bayton Ltd.'s employees rely on the company for their incomes. Unions negotiate contracts with Bayton Ltd. on behalf of their employees.
8. Environmental regulatory agencies	Because of the potential environmental problems associated with Bayton's garbage dumps, many jurisdictions have regulatory agencies responsible for monitoring the company's waste management practices, ensuring compliance with government standards, and reporting to the government and public.
9. Communities	Communities need reliable ways to dispose of their garbage. Bayton provides a solution for these communities.
10. Garbage collection companies	Garbage collection companies require a place to dump the garbage they collect and must pay fees to do so.
11. Environmental groups	Garbage dumps pose potentially serious environmental problems. Improper waste management practices can contaminate land and ground water. Private environmental groups monitor the dumps and the companies operating them.

BAYTON LTD.—PART 2

In 1984, Bayton paid $150,000 ($300 per hectare) for a 500-hectare piece of land it intended to develop into a garbage dump. For various reasons Bayton has not yet developed the land but Bayton's president has stated that it will do so at the appropriate time. Over the last two years there have been two transactions involving the sale of land located near Bayton's property. In the first transaction, which occurred 20 months ago, the land was sold for $825 per hectare. In the second transaction, which occurred three months ago, the land was sold for $730 per hectare.

Recently, a business person made an offer for Bayton's land of $690 per hectare or $345,000. The president of Bayton hired an independent appraiser to estimate the value of the land so he could assess the offer. The appraiser estimated the land was worth between $340,000 and $390,000. Two years ago, for the purpose of calculating property taxes, the local government where the land is located assigned it a value of $290,000. The president himself thinks that Bayton could sell the land for $410,000 if Bayton chose to sell it.

Required:

Identify and explain the different measurements of the value of Bayton's land. Discuss the usefulness of each measurement for determining whether a good price is being offered for the land.

Solution:

There are a number of different measurements available for valuing Bayton's land, none of which represents the actual current value of the land. The measurements are:

Measurement	Explanation	Usefulness
Cost: $150,000	The amount Bayton paid for the land.	Cost isn't useful for determining whether the price being offered is reasonable. There is no relationship between the amount Bayton paid in 1984 and the market value now. Cost isn't useful for most other decisions as well but it would be useful for determining the amount of tax that would have to be paid when the land is sold.
Property tax value: $290,000	The value assigned to the land by the local government for determining the property taxes.	Not very useful. The amount was determined two years ago, which makes it somewhat out of date. Also, it was determined for a very specific purpose and it isn't clear how it was determined, so its usefulness for non-property-tax purposes is difficult to assess.
Bayton's president's estimate: $410,000	The amount that Bayton's president thinks the company can sell the land for.	Could be useful depending on whether the president has good information on which to base his estimate. However, this estimate is the highest of all, which suggests the president may be influenced by his desire to get a high price for the land.
Independent appraiser's estimate: $340,000–$390,000	The price range that an independent appraiser estimated the land is worth.	The appraised value would be useful because it's a somewhat unbiased estimate of the land's current market value. However, the appraiser provided a range rather than an exact amount, which reduces usefulness. Also, the amount is an informed guess; it isn't based on the actual sale of the land.
Sale of nearby land: $412,500 based on the first sale (500 hectares × $825 per hectare) and $365,000 based on the second sale (500 hectares × $730 per hectare).	These amounts are calculated by multiplying Bayton's 500 hectares by the price per hectare paid in the transactions for the nearby land.	The sale prices for the nearby land is potentially useful but with limitations. They are useful because they are market prices for a similar commodity, and one of the transactions occurred fairly recently. However, there are three significant limitations: (1) though recent, the transactions don't necessarily represent the value today because market conditions may have changed; (2) the land may not be similar to Bayton's despite being nearby; and (3) the prices alone don't inform us about the circumstances surrounding the sales (the sellers may have required cash urgently and therefore could not wait to get a higher price).

SUMMARY OF KEY POINTS

LO 1 Accounting is a system for gathering data about an entity's economic activity, processing and organizing the data to produce useful information about the entity, and communicating the information to people who use it to make decisions. Communication is an important but often challenging part of the process. Effective decision making requires information and accounting is a crucial source of information. In addition, accounting matters because it has economic consequences for stakeholders.

LO 2 Accounting doesn't operate in a vacuum. You can't sensibly use or provide accounting information without considering the accounting environment, which includes the social, political, legal, cultural, and economic environment of a society; the types of entities and the characteristics of those entities; the different stakeholders that may have an interest in an entity; and the constraints that limit the accounting choices an entity can make. The diversity of the accounting environment makes it impossible for a single accounting report to be appropriate for all situations. Accounting reports must be tailored to suit the circumstances of an entity's accounting environment.

LO 3 An entity's stakeholders rely on the entity itself to provide accounting information. The managers of an entity who prepare the information aren't neutral. They may be influenced by their personal interests, and these interests may conflict with those of the stakeholders. Managers often have considerable leeway and choice in how they do their accounting, which makes it necessary for stakeholders to exercise a great deal of care to ensure that they are aware of the choices managers made and the economic consequences of those choices.

LO 4 A critical approach to accounting refers to this book's emphasis on critical thinking; applying high-level mental skills such as analysis, application, evaluation, explanation, inference, interpretation, judgment, and synthesis to decision making. Economic activity can be complex so preparers need these skills to prepare accounting information and stakeholders need them to use it effectively.

LO 5 Accounting standards are the principles, conventions, procedures, and rules that define acceptable accounting practices and guide the preparation of financial statements in certain situations. In Canada, International Financial Reporting Standards (IFRS) must be used by public companies whereas private companies can use IFRS or a set of standards called Accounting Standards for Private Enterprises (ASPE). Most Canadian companies are private and not obliged to follow either standard. IFRS and ASPE are flexible and require managers to exercise judgment. The same transactions and economic events can sometimes be legitimately accounted for in different ways. The accounting choices managers make can significantly affect the amounts reported in the financial statements.

LO 6 Accounting is about measurement. Accountants face the challenge of developing appropriate ways of measuring aspects of economic activity that are difficult or even impossible to observe, and making those measurements useful for stakeholders. There are often alternative ways of measuring the same thing and stakeholders must be aware of the methods being used and their economic consequences. Also, stakeholders have to realize that accounting measurements are inherently imprecise and uncertain, and it's often not obvious what is, or if there is, a best way.

KEY TERMS

accounting, p. 3
Accounting Standards for Private Enterprises (ASPE), p. 13
Canada Revenue Agency (CRA), p. 8
corporation, p. 7
cost-benefit trade-off, p. 4
economic consequences, p. 4
entity, p. 3
external audit, p. 12
external auditors, p. 12

financial accounting, p. 16
International Financial Reporting Standards (IFRS), p. 13
limited liability, p. 7
managerial accounting, p. 16
not-for-profit organization, p. 8
partner, p. 8
partnership, p. 8
preparer, p. 10
private corporation, p. 7
proprietor, p. 7
proprietorship, p. 7
public corporation, p. 7
share, p. 7
shareholder, p. 7
stakeholder, p. 9
stock exchange, p. 7

SIMILAR TERMS

The left column gives alternative terms that are sometimes used for the accounting terms introduced in this chapter, which are listed in the right column.

non-profit organization	**not-for-profit organization, p. 8**
stockholder	**shareholder, p. 7**
stock market	**stock exchange, p. 7**

ASSIGNMENT MATERIALS

Questions

Q1-1. Provide a definition of accounting that someone without a business background would understand.

Q1-2. Explain the difference between managerial and financial accounting.

Q1-3. Describe the characteristics and qualities that you think are required by a "good" accountant.

Q1-4. Explain what economic consequences are. Why does accounting have economic consequences?

Q1-5. Explain how accounting information could help you assess whether you could afford to borrow money.

Q1-6. Entities can have many different stakeholders. Explain why the same information may not be suitable or appropriate for all stakeholders.

Q1-7. Explain why the self-interests of preparers of accounting information can affect what information is reported to stakeholders and how it's reported.

Q1-8. Which of an entity's stakeholders do you think is most important? Explain.

Q1-9. Are employees of an entity also stakeholders? Explain.

Q1-10. Pinwana Ltd. is a successful software developer located in Ottawa. The company is owned by Melanie Pinwana. Is the government of Canada a stakeholder in Pinwana Ltd.? Explain.

Q1-11. You are deciding where to go to university. One of the alternatives is a school in another province. What financial information would you want so that you could assess whether you could attend that university? Be specific and explain the purpose of each piece of information you would want.

Q1-12. What is a corporation? What are the attractive features of organizing a business as a corporation?

Q1-13. What is a proprietorship? How does a proprietorship differ from a corporation?

Q1-14. What is a partnership? How does a partnership differ from a corporation and a proprietorship?

Q1-15. What is a publicly owned corporation? How does it differ from a privately owned corporation?

Q1-16. What is a not-for-profit organization? Give two examples. What is the purpose of each of the organizations you identified?

Q1-17. Why is information important for good decisions?

Q1-18. You're looking for a job. You're not completely sure what kind of job you want so you decide to contact several companies in different industries about a variety of jobs. You have prepared a two-page résumé (as recommended by your advisor) but you have modified it for each company and position you're applying for so that it emphasizes the experience, skills, and abilities you think will be most relevant for the prospective employer. All the information in each résumé is factual. You mention your approach to a friend, who says she doesn't think it's ethical to have more than one résumé. How would you respond to your friend?

Q1-19. Explain the cost-benefit trade-off. What are its implications for decision making?

Q1-20. When you make a decision, should you collect all possible relevant information? What limits would you set on the information gathering?

Q1-21. Why is it important for stakeholders to understand that the managers of an entity are responsible for preparing accounting information?

Q1-22. What is an external audit of financial information and why is it important for many stakeholders of an entity?

Q1-23. You are considering buying a small business from the person who currently owns and manages it. The current owner explains that the business is doing great and provides financial statements that support that position. Would you accept the financial statements as given to you? Explain. How could you get some assurance about the information in the statements? Explain.

Q1-24. Which entities must follow ASPE and IFRS? Why would an entity that isn't required to follow ASPE or IFRS do so? If an entity doesn't follow ASPE or IFRS, how would it prepare its financial statements?

Exercises

E1-1. **(Consider the information relevant for making a decision, LO 2)** You meet a stranger on a street corner in Vancouver. She asks you for instructions on the best way to get from Vancouver to Montreal. What would you tell her?

E1-2. **(Challenges with measurement, LO 6)** Consider the situations below and explain whether it would be easy or difficult to measure them:

a. How happy employees of a company are.
b. How much money customers have deposited in accounts at a major bank.
c. How much your car could be sold for.
d. How well you understand the material in your accounting course.

E1-3. **(Factors affecting measurement of a piece of land, LO 6)** You own a piece of undeveloped land on the outskirts of a large city. The land is zoned for agriculture but you purchased the land last year for $1 million with the expectation that it would be rezoned for residential construction. What would be the impact of the following events on the value of the land?

a. The government decides the land is in an ecologically sensitive area and passes a law the it must remain as green space (undeveloped land).
b. The government agrees to rezone the land for residential development.
c. A large land development company begins buying land in the area.

E1-4. **(Considering the stakeholders in a university or college, LO 2)** Consider the university or college you attend. Who are the stakeholders in your institution? Explain the interest or "stake" each has in the university. What types of decisions would each of these stakeholders have to make regarding the university? Explain what type of information would be useful to each of them?

E1-5. **(Assessing the credibility of information, LO 3)** You are looking to buy a new tablet computer. You read an advertisement in a newspaper that describes the company's product as being the best in its class. Based on this advertisement, would you purchase the computer? Why? What additional information would you require to decide whether to buy the company's tablet?

E1-6. **(Assessing the credibility of information, LO 3)** A chain of donut shops claims to have the world's best coffee. Do you believe the claim? Explain. How would one go about determining whether the chain had the world's best coffee?

E1-7. **(Consider the information relevant for making a decision, LO 2)** Your brother has just asked you to lend him $5,000 to help him buy a car. Would you lend him the money? How would you decide? What would you want to know before you made a final decision?

E1-8. **(Consider the information relevant for making a decision, LO 2)** Your cousin is in her last year of high school and is in the process of deciding which university to attend. Since you went through the process just a few years ago she has asked you to advise her on which university to attend. What would you tell your cousin? What questions would you ask her before you could provide an answer?

E1-9. **(Considering different ways of measuring, LO 6)** For each of the following situations, explain which method of valuing the item in question would be most useful:

Measurement method	Explanation of the method
Cost	What you paid for the item.
Replacement cost	What it would cost to replace the item with an identical item in the same condition.
Replacement cost new	What it would cost to replace the item with an identical item that is new.
Net realizable value	What the item could be sold for now.

a. You need to get some money fast and you have nothing in your bank account, so you're thinking of selling your car.
b. An electronics store offers double the difference back if you buy an item at the store and find it offered at another store at a lower price within 90 days of purchase. You find the television you bought available at a competitor for $125 less than what you paid for it
c. Your 2004 Ford Mustang was stolen and you're looking to get another one just like it.
d. Your collector's set of James Bond DVDs was stolen and you want to replace it.
e. Your Elvis Presley poster, signed by Elvis with a personal message to your father, was accidently thrown out by the people cleaning your apartment.

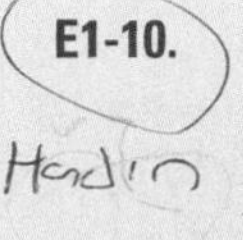

E1-10. **(Consider the different ways of measuring the attributes of a university, LO 6)** There are many attributes of an item you can measure. For a car, you could measure how fast it can go, its gas mileage, the number of doors it has, what you could sell it for, etc. Notice that only one of these measures is stated in terms of money. Now consider the university you attend. Identify six different attributes of your university and explain how you would measure each. How could you use the measurement of each attribute? Which measurement is best? Explain. Which measurements would be easy to make and which would be subjective? Explain. (Don't consider this question only from the perspective of a student.)

E1-11. **(Consider the different ways of measuring the attributes of a restaurant, LO 6)** There are many attributes of an item that you can measure. For a car, you could measure how fast it can go, its gas mileage, the number of doors it has, what you could sell it for, etc. Notice that only one of these measures is stated in terms of money. Now consider your favourite restaurant. Identify six different attributes of a restaurant and explain how you would measure each. How could you use the measurement of each attribute? Which measure is best? Explain. Which measurements would be easy to make and which would be subjective? Explain.

E1-12. **(Consider different ways of organizing information, LO 6)** Your 99-year-old grandfather died recently and left you his beloved library of books. At the time of his death, your grandfather's library contained over 5,000 books. The books had been packed away in boxes, which have been delivered to you. After opening the boxes you realize the books were not organized in any particular way. You decide to build a library in your basement and organize and catalogue the books. What are some of the ways you could organize the library? What are the benefits and limitations of the different ways of organizing the books? What are the benefits of organizing the books at all?

E1-13. **(Cost-benefit analysis, LO 1)** You are considering selling your car and replacing it with a smaller, more fuel-efficient model. The new car will cost you $19,000 including all taxes. Your present car is fairly new, you bought it only six months ago, but you underestimated its operating costs. You estimate you can sell it for $14,700. This car uses 12 litres per 100 kilometres travelled whereas the new one is rated at 8 litres per 100 kilometres. The cost of insuring the new car will be $875 instead of the current $1,025, and you estimate that the cost of servicing the new car will be about $225 instead of $350 per year. You drive approximately 22,000 kilometres per year and you expect to keep the car for five years. The current price of gas is $1.50 per litre. Is it worth it for you to buy the new car? Are there any considerations other than financial ones?

E1-14. **(Cost-benefit analysis, LO 1)** You have the opportunity to buy a licence to operate a food vending cart in a local park. The licence would cost $1,250 per year. You expect to operate the cart each summer for the next four years, at which time you'll graduate from university and move on to other things. You aren't allowed to sell the licence to someone else. You would also have to purchase a cart, which would cost $7,500. You estimate that after four years you would be able to sell the cart for about $1,000. You would have to work 11 hours per day seven days a week from May 15 to September 15. You estimate that on an average day you would be able to sell $350 of food and drinks and that the cost of the food and drinks you sell, along with condiments and other supplies (such as ice, straws, cutlery, cooking fuel) would be $215 per day. In addition, the annual maintenance cost for the cart would be about $900. Should you get into this business? What should you consider beyond the dollar and cents information that was provided? State any assumptions you make.

E1-15. **(Take a first look at an annual report, LO 1, 2, 3, 6)** Choose a Canadian public company. (Your instructor can choose for you or could ask you to make your own choice.) Download the company's annual report from www.sedar.com or from the company's Web site and read through it, especially the section with the financial statements and notes. List seven questions that come to mind while reading the financial statements (or the annual report). Your questions should cover topics such as why particular information is reported or what it means.

Problems

P1-1. **(Consider who should make accounting choices, LO 2, 3, 4, 6)** Figure 1.2 of the accounting environment and the chapter as a whole emphasized that it's the managers of an entity who choose the accounting methods an entity uses. Do you think the managers should have this responsibility or should it belong to someone else? Who else could possibly fulfill this task? Explain your answer fully.

P1-2. **(Explain the reason stakeholders would want information about an entity, LO 2)** Consider the following stakeholders in an entity. Why would each want information about the entity? Explain.

a. The partners in an accounting firm.
b. A company's supplier of inventory. The supplier gives the company up to 60 days to pay for purchases.
c. A member of a labour union.
d. A company's largest competitor.
e. A prospective customer purchasing an expensive piece of equipment from a company. The equipment comes with a five-year warranty.

P1-3. **(Explain the reason stakeholders would want information about an entity, LO 2)** Consider the following stakeholders in an entity. Why would each want information about the entity? Explain.

a. A person considering making a donation to a charity.
b. Members of a community group concerned about pollution by a local factory.
c. A government minister evaluating whether to provide assistance to a business.
d. The head of a labour union preparing for negotiations with management of a company.
e. Canada Revenue Agency (the federal government department responsible for tax collection).

P1-4. **(Explain different stakeholders' interest in an entity, LO 2)** Osoyoos Inc. is a manufacturer of sports equipment. The company is privately owned by the Osoyoos family. Some family members help run the company but most are simply shareholders. Consider the following stakeholders and explain what types of decisions each would have to make about the company:

a. A shareholder who isn't involved in managing the company.
b. The company president.
c. Canada Revenue Agency.
d. A banker who has a major loan to Osoyoos outstanding.
e. The head of the union representing some of Osoyoos's employees.

P1-5. **(Identify the stakeholders in an entity and the decisions they make, LO 2)** Consider the following entities. Identify the stakeholders in each of the entities. What types of decisions would each of these stakeholders want to make? (To answer this question you may have to do some research to find out about each of these entities.)

a. Research In Motion Limited.
b. Government of Canada.
c. Wikipedia.
d. McCain Foods Limited.

P1-6. **(Identify the stakeholders in an entity and the decisions they make, LO 2)** Consider the following entities. Identify the stakeholders in each of the entities. What types of decisions would each of these stakeholders want to make?

a. A local, privately owned convenience store (not part of a chain).
b. A major Canadian bank.
c. A national fast food franchisor.
d. The transit commission of city (the government organization responsible for oversight of public transit).

P1-7. **(Consider the decisions stakeholders make and the nature of the information they require, LO 1, 2)** Consider the following decisions that a stakeholder of an entity might have to make. For each decision, identify the stakeholder who would likely be making the decision and indicate whether the decision would be considered a financial or managerial accounting decision. Remember that the classification as financial or managerial accounting depends on who the decision maker is. Explain your answers.

a. Assess whether a retail chain should expand to a new part of the country.
b. Evaluate whether to lend money to a company.
c. Decide whether to donate to a particular charity.

P1-8. **(Consider the decisions stakeholders make and the nature of the information they require, LO 1, 2)** Consider the following decisions that a stakeholder of an entity might have to make. For each decision, identify the stakeholder who would likely be making the decision and indicate whether the decision would be considered a financial or managerial accounting decision. Remember that the classification as financial or managerial accounting depends on who the decision maker is. Explain your answers.

a. Evaluate whether a company should purchase a part used in the production of its product or make the part itself.
b. Assess whether goods should be sold to a customer on credit or whether cash should be paid on delivery.
c. Determine whether a company should purchase a competitor.

P1-9. **(Consider the information needed to decide whether to invest in a business, LO 1, 2, 6)** A friend of yours has just called with "a great business opportunity." He is planning on purchasing a franchise that offers environmental lawn care services. He thinks that because chemical lawn care products have recently been banned the business is a sure money maker. He says that $25,000 is needed to get the business started and he is going to invest $12,500. He wants to know whether you would like to invest the other half. If you invest you would become part-owner of the business. Would you invest in the franchise? Why or why not? What additional information would you want to have before making a decision?

P1-10. **(Consider the information needed to decide whether to invest in a business, LO 1, 2, 6)** A classmate of yours is thinking of starting a used-textbook business to service your campus. The university bookstore already operates such a business but your classmate thinks the prices are much higher than they should be. He has asked you to become a partner in the business, which he thinks is going to be very successful, by contributing $15,000. The money will be used to rent office space, advertise, and purchase books. Would you invest the $15,000? How would you decide? What additional information would you want to have before making a final decision?

P1-11. **(Consider the information needed to decide whether to invest in a business, LO 1, 2, 6)** Two of your friends own and operate a business that rents bicycles and inline skates at a local lake. They have told you that they want to expand the business but are short of the money needed for the expansion and have asked you to become a partner by investing $8,000. Would you invest the $8,000? How would you decide? What additional information would you want to have before making a final decision?

P1-12. **(Classify and organize information so that it's useful for decision making, LO 1, 6)** Khaleel is a first-year university student who lives in residence at his university. He often finds that he is short of cash. A month may pass and he has no idea where his money went. After suffering with this problem for several months, Khaleel decides to monitor his spending for the next month. He keeps his records using a software package. The summary of Khaleel's spending for the month follows:

Date	Amount	Purpose
February 4	$ 24.50	Starting balance (cash in wallet)
February 4	100.00	Cash from ATM
February 4	12.50	Buy new songs from iTunes
February 6	24.50	Supplies for courses
February 6	6.25	Lunch
February 10	45.75	Concert ticket
February 11	5.25	Laundry
February 12	100.00	Cash from ATM
February 12	18.25	Lunch with Emily
February 15	22.75	Vitamins and ibuprofen
February 16	175.00	New hockey stick
February 17	5.00	Contribution to charity drive
February 19	100.00	Cash from ATM
February 19	22.50	Card and gift for Dad
February 20	1.99	New app for phone
February 20	33.90	Cell phone bill
February 21	15.00	Borrow from Lisa
February 21	23.00	Food/drink for dorm room
February 24	100.00	Cash from ATM
February 24	15.00	Pay Lisa back
February 27	18.75	Celebration after exam
February 28	9.11	Amount remaining in wallet

Required:

Prepare a statement that organizes the information from the month's spending in a useful way. Explain why you organized the information the way that you did. How could you use the information if you were Khaleel?

P1-13. (Classify and organize information so that it's useful for decision making, LO 1, 6) Fatima is a second-year university student. Last year she lived in residence, but this year she has rented a room in a house with a number of friends. As of the end of September, Fatima has $8,000 in her bank account to cover her expenses until the end of May, when she will return home for the summer. Fatima is concerned that she isn't managing her money as well as she could. She has already covered major costs like her tuition for the full year, furniture, and laptop. She decides to monitor her spending for the next month to get an idea of where her money is going. She records her daily spending in a spreadsheet. Her spending summary for October is shown below:

Date	Purpose	Amount
Oct. 1	Rent	$450.00
Oct. 2	Groceries	70.00
Oct. 7	Lunches (for the week)	23.50
Oct. 8	Course book	42.25
Oct. 10	Drinks for party	12.34
Oct. 10	Taxi home from party	9.00
Oct. 14	Lunches (for the week)	18.50
Oct. 15	Medicine	9.90
Oct. 16	Dinner and movie	22.50
Oct. 17	Magazine	5.25
Oct. 17	Dry cleaning	8.75

Oct. 17	Toiletries	15.15
Oct. 17	Groceries	82.00
Oct. 20	Pub night	20.00
Oct. 23	Cell phone	42.75
Oct. 25	Utilities	62.75
Oct. 26	Parents' anniversary gift	25.00
Oct. 26	New running shoes	125.25
Oct. 26	Groceries	75.50
Oct. 28	School supplies	18.65
Oct. 28	Lunches (for the week)	28.90
		$1,167.94

Required:

Prepare a statement that organizes the information from the month's spending in a useful way. Explain why you organized the information the way that you did. How is this information useful? What advice would you give to Fatima?

P1-14. **(Evaluate different ways of measuring the value of a house, LO 6)** Rajiv owns a home in suburban Ottawa. You obtain the following information about the home:

a. Purchase price in 1978	$175,000
b. Selling price of a similar house on another street last year	$625,000
c. Price offered (and turned down) for Rajiv's house two months ago	$575,000
d. What it would cost to rebuild the house (on the same land) if it were destroyed	$235,000

Required:

Explain how each of the measures of the "value" of Rajiv's house could be used by a decision maker. What decision would the person be making? How would the information be useful?

P1-15. **(Evaluate different ways of measuring the value of a vintage automobile, LO 6)** Otto Collector owns a vintage 1925 Ford automobile. You obtain the following information about the car:

a. What Otto paid for the car in 1983	$29,000
b. Selling price of a similar car one year ago	$80,000
c. Price offered (and turned down) by Otto for his car last month	$95,000
d. What the car sold for new in 1925	$800

Required:

Explain how each of the measures of the "value" of Otto's car could be used by a decision maker. What decision would the person be making? How would the information be useful?

P1-16. **(Evaluate different ways of measuring the value of your tablet computer, LO 6)** Six months ago, you purchased the newest version of a popular line of tablet computers. At the time you paid $725 for your unit. Yesterday, you read an ad from a local electronics store that offered the same tablet for $610. You've also learned that your existing unit could be sold (used) for $250. Explain the relevance of each of the measures of your tablet (how each could be used). Which measure do you think is best?

P1-17. **(Consider the usefulness of audited information, LO 1, 2, 3)** For each of the following situations, explain whether and why having an independent review of the information provided—that is, an audit—would be useful. Who would be an appropriate person to conduct the audit?

a. Politicians are concerned that a government agency is misspending money.
b. An airline claims its flights are on time 90% of the time.

c. A farm claims to produce organic vegetables.
d. A graduate university program requests a list of grades a student earned in her undergraduate program.

P1-18. **(Consider the usefulness of audited information, LO 1, 2, 3)** For each of the following situations, explain whether and why having an independent review of the information provided—that is, an audit—would be useful. Who would be an appropriate person to conduct the audit?

a. A charity states that it spends 85% of money raised providing services to the community.
b. An individual files an income tax return with Canada Revenue Agency in which she reports the amount of money her business earned during the previous year.
c. A public corporation predicts that it will double its profit next year.
d. A job applicant submits a résumé to a prospective employer outlining her employment history and educational background.
e. A donut shop advertises that it has the world's best coffee.

P1-19. **(Identify the characteristics of different entities, LO 2, 3)** Identify two distinct entities. These could be corporations, partnerships, proprietorships, not-for-profit organizations, or any other type of entity you are familiar with or can obtain information about. Identify the characteristics of each entity. (You can use the characteristics listed in Figure 1.2.) Explain how the entities differ.

P1-20. **(Identify the characteristics of different entities, LO 2, 3)** Identify two different corporations that are in a similar business. Identify the characteristics of each corporation. (You can use the characteristics listed in Figure 1.2.) Explain how the corporations are similar and how they differ.

P1-21. **(Identify the stakeholders in an accounting partnership, LO 2, 3)** Bricket, Brack, and Bosh (BBB) is a small accounting firm in Oshawa, Ontario. The firm has four partners and ten other employees. All of the partners belong to professional accounting organizations. The firm provides accounting, tax, and consulting services to small- and medium-sized businesses in the community. When the firm does work for clients, the work is often used by third parties such as banks or prospective investors. For example, BBB might audit a client's financial statements, which are then given to the bank as part of a loan application. BBB is also part of a group of independent accounting firms in Ontario that will do work for clients of other firms in the group. For example, if BBB has a client that has an office elsewhere in Ontario, it might use the services of a firm in the group to do necessary work at that office.

Required:

Identify all of the stakeholders in Bricket, Brack, and Bosh and explain their "stake" in the partnership. Not all the stakeholders are explicitly referred to in the scenario. You will have to think about the business situation carefully to identify some of the stakeholders.

P1-22. **(Identify the stakeholders in a not-for-profit organization, LO 2, 3)** Safety House provides shelter and services to homeless and runaway youth in Vancouver. Safety House began in the early 1980s as a group home providing a safe haven to street children in the city but now provides additional services including a telephone support line, outreach programs, substance abuse programs, and other necessary community services. In recent years it has become an advocacy group for children, making government and the public aware of the problems faced by youth, as well as working with government and community social service agencies to improve the lives of children and families. Safety House is managed by people with experience in social services and it employs about 100 people who fill a wide range of roles. Safety House raises money from the public through a variety of fundraising programs and receives a significant amount of money from the provincial government.

Required:

Identify all of the stakeholders in Safety House and explain their "stake" in the organization. Not all the stakeholders are explicitly referred to in the scenario. You will have to think about the situation carefully to identify some of the stakeholders.

P1-23. **(Identify the stakeholders in a private family-owned business, LO 2, 3)** Alder Flats Farms Ltd. is a certified producer of organic fruits and vegetables located near Halifax. Alder Flats is owned by the Sedley family. The land has been in the family's hands for over 100 years, although it's only been an organic producer for the last 15 years. The farm is currently operated by Lars Sedly and two of his sons. One other son and two daughters have an ownership interest in the farm but aren't involved in the day-to-day operation. Each year, at the start of the growing season, Alder Farms borrows money from the bank to finance the purchase of supplies such as seed, fertilizer, and so on. Alder Flats supplies a number of grocery stores and small chains with organic produce throughout the year. In addition, people come and purchase produce directly from the farm. A farm can only use the term "certified organic" if it produces food according to the standards of the certifying body. Farms must be inspected annually by an independent inspector.

Required:

Identify all of the stakeholders in Alder Flats Farms Ltd. and explain their "stake" in the organization. Not all the stakeholders are explicitly referred to in the scenario. You will have to think about the business carefully to identify some of the stakeholders.

ENDNOTES

1. Andrew Zimbalist, *Baseball and Billions*, updated ed. (New York: Basic Books, 1994), p. 62.
2. The CICA defines publicly accountable companies as ones that have issued debt or equity securities that are traded in a public market, that are required to file financial statements with a securities commission, or that provide financial statements for the purpose of issuing any class of securities in a public market.

CHAPTER 2

Financial Statements: A Window on an Entity

LEARNING OBJECTIVES

After studying the material in this chapter you will be able to do the following:

LO 1 Understand the objectives of general purpose financial reporting and the qualitative characteristics of useful financial information as described in the IFRS conceptual framework.

LO 2 Recognize the basic accounting assumptions that are fundamental to contemporary accounting.

LO 3 Identify components that make up a set of general purpose financial statements, understand the information each statement provides, and prepare simple examples of them.

LO 4 Describe and interpret the accounting equation.

LO 5 Explain the nature of assets, liabilities, owners' equity, revenues, and expenses.

LO 6 Differentiate between accrual-basis and cash-basis accounting, and prepare simple income statements using each method.

LO 7 Use financial statement information to assess the liquidity, risk, and profitability of an entity.

His code name? Agent Zero. His drink? A martini, with two olives. His mission? Operation Payless, with a licence to lower prices and save you money.

Sound familiar? You've probably seen the tuxedo-clad secret service agent in an ad for Leon's Furniture, one of the largest retailers of home furnishings in Canada.

Leon's Furniture Limited

From those James Bond look-alike commercials to the cheesy "Ho! Ho! Hold the Payments!" events that air at Christmas time, century-old Leon's is also famous for its "Don't Pay a Cent" policy.

With 75 owned or franchised stores across Canada, and plans to expand into British Columbia, Leon's uses humour to attract an estimated 20 million customers every year, according to the *Toronto Star*.

Customers may laugh when they see the ads, but investors and analysts can see the more serious side of the company when they look closely at the retailer's financial statements, which are released four times a year.

When Stephen MacLeod of BMO Capital Markets pored over the 40 pages of quarterly results released through Canada News Wire on May 14, 2012, he found them fascinating.

The Toronto-based analyst says financial statements might not seem interesting to someone buying a flat-screen television for half of what it would have cost a year earlier. But for stakeholders like him, it's "a good way to find out how businesses really work" and how they are affected by the economy around them.

"It's not so good for the company but they have to do that [sell electronics at lower prices than in 2011] to keep volumes up," MacLeod explained. "You don't think about the fact that the reason it's so cheap is the market is being flooded with these things and Leon's isn't really making a lot of money selling flat-screen TVs anymore."

Leon's reported a drop in its net profit to $8.6 million in the first quarter of the year, down from $10.3 million the year before.

Despite reporting higher overall sales in the three months ending in March, company officials admitted same-store sales were down 0.6 percent because customers weren't buying as many big-ticket items as in 2011. The higher sales came because Leon's opened new superstores in Guelph and Mississauga, Ont., Rosemère, Que., and Regina, Sask.

"The slowdown in the economy which began in 2009 continues to affect our results and we do not see signs of any immediate improvement," said Terry Leon, the president and CEO, in a statement.

To MacLeod, the financial statements and management's discussion and analysis of them are "a reflection of what's really happening out there."

"You can see things that you would read in the newspaper about such as consumer spending, and you might just think it stops there, but you can see how weakening consumer spending comes through in the numbers and you can see how businesses react to different economic conditions by either cutting back on expenses or promoting the products more."

Which is exactly how Leon's announced it planned to meet the challenge.

"To help counter this, we plan an even more robust marketing and merchandising campaign for the balance of 2012," vowed the CEO.

After the financial statements were released to the public, the stock price slid for the rest of that week, reaching $11.22 a share, a level it hadn't touched since 2010.

According to Google Finance, the value of the company's stock (it trades under the ticker symbol LNF on the Toronto Stock Exchange) had actually dropped by more than 9 percent in the first half of 2012.

Despite how the stock performed after the May 2012 financial statements were released, observers actually like Leon's overall financial stability.

"They've done a really good job of managing in a difficult environment and you can't argue with how they run the business when they have a huge stockpile of cash on the balance sheet and they continue to increase the dividend and paid a special dividend, in the middle of one of the worst recessions that people have seen," said MacLeod.

Both MoneySense.com and the *Globe and Mail* agree that the company has been well managed by the grandchildren of the founder, and is a good stock to own.

Which may explain why Terry Leon was able to send out a strong message to investors that they should Ho! Ho! Hold on to the furniture maker as it rides out the rough period.

"Our strong financial position coupled with our experience in adjusting to changing market conditions, provide us with the confidence to adapt to the prevailing economic conditions," said Leon in the statement.

–E.B.

INTRODUCTION

The most familiar products of accounting and accountants are financial statements. The financial statements most people see are those published by public companies whose shares trade on stock exchanges. These companies are required to make this information available and anyone who is interested can easily obtain it.

In this chapter we will explore the components of the financial statement package:

- balance sheet (also called the **statement of financial position**)
- statement of comprehensive income (includes the income statement)
- statement of changes in equity
- statement of cash flows
- notes to the financial statements

The objectives of this chapter are to familiarize you with the financial statement package and begin our investigation of how the information in financial statements can be used for decision making.

The chapter begins with a discussion of the IFRS conceptual framework, which the International Accounting Standards Board (IASB) (the organization responsible for IFRS) has created to provide a foundation for the development for accounting standards. Some of the basic assumptions that underlie all financial reporting are also introduced.

LO 1 THE IFRS CONCEPTUAL FRAMEWORK

Before we dig into the financial statements, it's worth taking a moment to consider the framework within which financial statements are prepared. In Chapter 1, when I introduced the accounting standards used by businesses in Canada, I pointed out that there are no natural laws governing accounting so it's necessary for people to create them. The IASB has developed a conceptual framework that provides a basis for preparing and presenting financial statements. The framework's purpose is to provide a structure for creating new accounting standards and to assist preparers of financial statements when there are no standards for guidance. In this section we'll take a look at two parts of the conceptual framework: the objective of general purpose financial reporting and the qualitative characteristics of useful financial information.

The Objective of General Purpose Financial Reporting

The conceptual framework states that the objective of general purpose financial reporting is to provide useful information about an entity to existing and potential equity investors, lenders, and other creditors in making decisions about providing resources to the entity. The framework explains that these stakeholders need information to help them assess an entity's future net cash flows. The focus of IFRS is quite narrow. There are many stakeholders who aren't equity investors, lenders, or other creditors, and many stakeholders will want to use accounting information for purposes other than assessing future net cash flows.

The framework's focus is probably narrow by necessity. Emphasizing a wider range of stakeholders or purposes for financial statements would make it too difficult to provide useful or coherent information. What's important to recognize is that accounting information prepared in accordance with IFRS isn't tailored for all stakeholders and all uses. If you're not in one of the designated stakeholder groups or have the indicated use for the information, general purpose financial statements may not serve your needs. This doesn't mean that IFRS-based information isn't useful for other stakeholders or uses; it may be. However, it isn't designed for stakeholders and uses outside those specified.

Qualitative Characteristics of Useful Financial Information

The IFRS framework identifies two levels of qualitative characteristics. The **fundamental qualitative characteristics** are required if information is to be useful. These characteristics are relevance and faithful representation. The **enhancing qualitative characteristics** enhance the usefulness of accounting information that's relevant and faithfully represented.

Fundamental Qualitative Characteristics—Relevance and Faithful Representation

Relevance—Information is *relevant* if it influences stakeholder decisions. The framework says that information is relevant if it helps stakeholders make predictions or if it confirms or corrects evaluations they made in the past. For example, lenders want to estimate future cash flows to determine whether an entity will be able to repay a loan. Shareholders may want to predict future earnings as a basis for predicting the stock price of public companies. Shareholders might also want to assess why their earlier predictions about future stock prices were different from the actual amounts.

It's important to note that while accounting information is relevant if it helps make predictions, financial statements aren't themselves predictions. Stakeholders are expected to use financial statements as a basis for making their own predictions. This approach is probably effective for stable and established companies but for new entities and ones experiencing significant change, such as high-tech, Internet, and high-growth companies, the task can be difficult because historical financial statements may not provide a relevant basis for making predictions.

Faithful representation—If you examine a map of Canada, you would expect the provincial boundaries and the locations of cities and towns on the map to be an accurate reflection of where the boundaries and the cities and towns are. Faithful representation refers to the association between underlying information being represented (the actual locations of boundaries and communities) and the representation of that information (the map). Financial statements are a representation of the underlying economic activity of an entity. If the statements are to be representationally faithful they must capture the economic activity of an entity. This means that all the assets, liabilities, revenues, and expenses must be reflected in the statements. According to the framework, accounting information is a faithful representation if it's complete, neutral, and free from error.

- *Complete*—All information required to reflect the underlying economic activity should be provided. The information shouldn't mislead or misrepresent because it isn't complete.
- *Neutral*—Information is neutral or free from bias if it isn't presented in a way that is designed to bias or manipulate stakeholders' decisions.
- *Free from error*—Information should be free of significant errors and omissions. However, this doesn't mean the information has to be perfectly accurate. When financial statements are prepared managers must make many estimates; for example, the amount of accounts receivable outstanding at the end of the year that won't be collected. By their nature estimates are uncertain and so amounts in the financial statements will be different than the actual amounts that occur in the future.

Enhancing qualitative characteristics The enhancing qualitative characteristics improve the usefulness of information that is relevant and faithfully represented. These characteristics may also help managers choose among acceptable alternatives. The enhancing characteristics are:

- **Comparability**—It's easier for stakeholders to make decisions if they can readily compare information about an entity from year to year or compare information about different entities. Comparability is achieved if like transactions are accounted for the same way. If entities use different accounting methods for like transactions, it's difficult to know whether differences in the numbers are due to economic or accounting differences.
- **Verifiability**—Information is verifiable if independent and knowledgeable observers can come up with similar results for measuring an attribute. If a group of people were asked to measure the height and weight of the members of a sports team, it's likely each person would come up with similar results. Measurement of height and weight would be considered verifiable. If the same people were asked to rate the ability of the players on the team, it's likely the results would be more diverse: The measurement of ability isn't as easily verified. In other words, the tallest player on the team is more verifiable than the best player. In an accounting context, the amount of cash on hand is more verifiable than the estimate of accounts receivable that won't be collected.
- **Timeliness**—For information to be useful for decision making it must be available to stakeholders in time to influence their decisions.
- **Understandability**—To be useful, accounting information must be understood by stakeholders. But who is the target audience? Stakeholders range from very unsophisticated readers to highly skilled experts (e.g., financial analysts or pension fund managers). The conceptual framework says that accounting information should be prepared for stakeholders with a reasonable understanding of business and a willingness to study the information. This has implications for the information presented in financial statements because simpler information would have a wider audience, but financial statements directed at more sophisticated stakeholders could be more detailed and complex.

The conceptual framework is important because it provides a structure for accounting. However, the qualitative characteristics described above sometimes conflict, so it's necessary to trade off among them. Also, while the conceptual framework is a centre piece of IFRS, in the event the framework and an accounting standard conflict, the conceptual framework doesn't override the standard. As you read through the rest of the chapter, keep the framework in mind and evaluate whether the goals of the framework are being achieved.

LO 2

BASIC ACCOUNTING ASSUMPTIONS

All contemporary sets of accounting standards have some assumptions in common. These assumptions are described below. Keep these assumptions in mind as you work through the rest of the chapter.

Unit of Measure

The **unit-of-measure assumption** states that the economic activity of an entity can be effectively reported in terms of a single unit of measure, namely money. This is usually the Canadian dollar in Canada, although some Canadian companies, for example Research In Motion Limited, use the U.S. dollar.

A single unit of measure allows diverse information to be aggregated and summarized. Otherwise, it wouldn't be possible to calculate sums like total assets, total liabilities, or net income. It's like adding apples, pears, and oranges together—it can't be done without designating a common unit of measure; in this case, fruit.

There are drawbacks to a single unit of measure:

- Information about the individual items being measured is lost. In the fruit example above, we lose the amount of the different types of fruit when fruit is used as the unit of measure.
- Characteristics not easily measured in terms of dollars aren't accounted for. For example, intellectual and human capital and social costs are typically not reported.
- In Canada, the changing purchasing power of the dollar over time caused by inflation is ignored.

Entity Concept

The **entity concept** assumes that an entity of interest (corporation, partnership, proprietorship, a division of a corporation, etc.) can provide information that is separate from the information of owners or other entities. Transactions and economic events that don't pertain to the entity of interest should be excluded, but this doesn't always occur. For example, in some proprietorships and private corporations, the personal transactions of the owners are included with the entity's business activities. When expenses and revenues that aren't relevant are included in financial statements, stakeholders can come to inappropriate decisions and conclusions.

Going Concern

For accounting purposes, a **going concern** is an entity that will be continuing its operations for the foreseeable future. It's expected to complete its current plans, use its existing assets in the ordinary course of business, and meet its obligations as they come due. In the absence of evidence to the contrary it's normally assumed an entity is a going concern. If the going-concern assumption doesn't apply—for example, because an entity is going out of business or because it's a short-term venture, such as a summer business set up by a student—the approach to financial reporting changes.

Periodic Reporting

The **periodic-reporting assumption** states that meaningful financial information about an entity can be provided for periods of time that are shorter than the entity's life, such as annually or quarterly. Accounting would be much easier if entities only had to prepare financial information at the end of their life because then everything about their activities would be certain—no estimates or accounting policy decisions would be needed. But by waiting until the end of an entity's life, information wouldn't be provided to stakeholders on a timely basis. At a minimum, financial statements are prepared annually. However, some stakeholders, for example banks, may require more frequent reports, and stock exchanges and securities commissions require public companies to produce quarterly reports.

GENERAL PURPOSE FINANCIAL STATEMENTS

LO 3

General purpose financial statements are prepared for use by all stakeholders and aren't necessarily tailored to meet the information needs of any particular stakeholder or purpose. In other words, **general purpose financial statements** are intended for no one in particular and for everyone in general. (The alternative to this are special purpose reports designed for a specific user and/or a specific use.) The focus of the discussion in this chapter will be the general purpose financial statements of Leon's Furniture Limited (Leon's). Leon's has been in the retail furniture business for over 100 years. The Company's 43 corporate and 32 franchise stores can be found in every province across Canada except British Columbia. Its main product lines include furniture, appliances and electronics. Leon's general purpose financial statements are shown in Exhibit 2.1.[1]

Every business prepares a set of general purpose financial statements at least once a year, if for no other reason than the statements must be included with its tax return. It can also produce any number of special purpose reports. The published financial statements of public companies like Leon's are always general purpose and, because Leon's is a public company, must be prepared in accordance with IFRS.

Because general purpose financial statements aren't designed to meet the information needs of every stakeholder in every situation, it's important to consider the information carefully and critically. You must be aware of what the statements do and don't tell to use them effectively. You have to know the strengths and limitations of the information, what questions to ask, and when to look elsewhere for what you need.

LEON'S FINANCIAL STATEMENTS: AN OVERVIEW

LO 3

Financial statements can be intimidating: What do the numbers mean? Where do they come from? What about all this unusual terminology? To familiarize you with financial statements and make you more comfortable looking at those of real companies, the following sections weave a general discussion of each financial statement with an examination of Leon's statements as examples. To begin, here are four points about Leon's statements you may notice when examining Exhibit 2.1:

1. Leon's financial statements are **consolidated**—they aggregate the financial information of more than one corporation into a single set of statements. Consolidated statements are prepared when a corporation controls (owns more than 50 percent of) other corporations and they are intended to give stakeholders information on all the companies in the group. We'll look at consolidated statements in more detail in Chapter 11.
2. Financial statements are presented for more than one year. This reflects the enhancing qualitative characteristic of comparability by providing stakeholders with benchmarks. It's very difficult to make sense of accounting information without something to compare with, such as other companies, the industry, performance in other years, the economy in general, and previous periods for the same entity. As we will discuss, making comparisons using accounting information can be very difficult and misleading, while not making comparisons makes accounting information difficult to interpret. (Normally, companies reporting under IFRS will provide two balance sheets. When companies report under IFRS for the first time, as is the case with Leon's, a balance sheet at the beginning of the comparative year is provided.)

EXHIBIT 2.1 Leon's Furniture Limited's Financial Statements

CONSOLIDATED STATEMENTS OF FINANCIAL POSITION			**2011 ANNUAL REPORT** Consolidated Financial Statements
Leon's Furniture Limited/Meubles Leon Ltée Incorporated under the laws of Ontario	**As at December 31**	As at December 31	As at January 1
($ in thousands)	**2011**	2010	2010
		(Note 22)	(Note 22)
Assets			
Current			
Cash and cash equivalents (Notes 5 and 7)	**$ 72,505**	$ 71,589	$ 58,301
Available-for-sale financial assets (Notes 5 and 19(e))	**149,318**	140,224	112,425
Trade receivables (Note 5)	**28,937**	28,569	31,501
Income taxes receivable	**5,182**	–	–
Inventories	**87,830**	85,423	83,957
Total current assets	**$ 343,772**	$ 325,805	$ 286,184
Other assets	**1,431**	1,574	1,560
Property, plant and equipment, net (Note 8)	**214,158**	201,492	203,653
Investment properties (Note 9)	**8,366**	8,417	8,545
Intangible assets, net (Note 10)	**3,958**	4,902	5,334
Goodwill (Note 10)	**11,282**	11,282	11,282
Deferred income tax assets (Note 17)	**12,372**	13,202	12,598
Total assets	**$ 595,339**	$ 566,674	$ 529,156
Liabilities and Shareholders' Equity			
Current			
Trade and other payables (Notes 5 and 11)	**$ 75,126**	$ 71,724	$ 72,603
Provisions (Note 12)	**11,231**	12,341	11,277
Income taxes payable	–	524	1,958
Customers' deposits	**19,157**	17,198	15,632
Dividends payable (Note 14)	**17,457**	6,310	4,938
Deferred warranty plan revenue	**16,152**	16,882	16,150
Total current liabilities	**$ 139,123**	$ 124,979	$ 122,558
Deferred warranty plan revenue	**19,445**	21,392	22,248
Redeemable share liability (Notes 5 and 13)	**382**	172	383
Deferred income tax liabilities (Note 17)	**10,928**	9,845	8,829
Total liabilities	**$ 169,878**	$ 156,388	$ 154,018
Shareholder's equity attributable to the shareholders of the Company			
Common shares (Note 14)	**$ 20,918**	$ 19,177	$ 17,704
Retained earnings	**404,647**	390,629	357,576
Accumulated other comprehensive income (loss)	**(104)**	480	(142)
Total shareholders' equity	**$ 425,461**	$ 410,286	$ 375,138
	$ 595,339	$ 566,674	$ 529,156

EXHIBIT 2.1 (continued) Leon's Furniture Limited's Financial Statements

CONSOLIDATED INCOME STATEMENTS Years ended December 31 ($ in thousands, except shares outstanding and earnings per share)	**2011**	**2010**
Revenue (Notes 15 and 22)	**$ 682,836**	$ 710,435
Cost of sales	**394,099**	412,379
Gross profit	**$ 288,737**	$ 298,056
Operating expenses (Notes 16 and 22)		
General and administrative expenses	**96,038**	98,684
Sales and marketing expenses	**78,387**	78,221
Occupancy expenses	**32,731**	29,551
Other operating expenses	**6,260**	5,785
	$ 213,416	$ 212,241
Operating profit	**75,321**	85,815
Gain on sale of capital property	**21**	1,236
Finance income	**3,506**	3,134
Profit before income tax	**78,848**	90,185
Income tax expense (Note 17)	**22,182**	26,901
Profit for the year attributable to the shareholders of the Company	**$ 56,666**	**$ 63,284**
Weighted average number of common shares outstanding		
Basic	**69,969,417**	70,371,744
Diluted	**72,305,424**	73,133,906
Earnings per share		
Basic	**$ 0.81**	$ 0.90
Diluted	**$ 0.78**	$ 0.87
Dividends declared per share		
Common	**$ 0.52**	$ 0.32
Convertible, non-voting	**$ 0.20**	$ 0.18

3. Financial statements cover a **fiscal year**—the 12-month period about which an entity provides information. Leon's fiscal year runs from January 1 to December 31. An entity can choose any 12-month period as its fiscal year. For example, Bank of Montreal's is November 1 to October 31.
4. Dollar amounts in the statements are rounded to the nearest thousand dollars. Leon's balance sheet reports cash and cash equivalents of $72,505,000, but because the thousands are dropped, the actual amount of cash and cash equivalents could be anywhere between $72,504,500 and $72,505,500. This presentation makes the statements less cluttered in appearance but assumes that rounding won't affect the decisions of any stakeholders. For example, ignoring the thousands isn't likely to affect whether an investor buys Leon's shares. Some companies round to the nearest million; for example, Air Canada, Rogers Communications Inc., and Royal Bank of Canada.

EXHIBIT 2.1 (continued) Leon's Furniture Limited's Financial Statements

CONSOLIDATED STATEMENTS OF CHANGES IN EQUITY

($ in thousands)	Common Shares	Accumulated Other Comprehensive Income (Loss)	Retained Earnings	Total
At January 1, 2010	$ 17,704	$ (142)	$ 357,576	$ 375,138
Comprehensive income				
Profit for the period	—	—	63,284	63,284
Change in unrealized gains on available-for-sale financial assets arising during the period	—	622	—	622
Total comprehensive income	—	622	63,284	63,906
Transactions with shareholders				
Dividends declared	—	—	(22,492)	(22,492)
Management share purchase plan (Note 13)	1,768	—	—	1,768
Repurchase of common shares (Note 14)	(295)	—	(7,739)	(8,034)
Total transactions with shareholders	1,473	—	(30,231)	(28,758)
At December 31, 2010	$ 19,177	$ 480	$ 390,629	$ 410,286
At January 1, 2011	**$ 19,177**	**$ 480**	**$ 390,629**	**$ 410,286**
Comprehensive income				
Profit for the period	—	—	**56,666**	**56,666**
Change in unrealized (losses) on available-for-sale financial assets arising during the period	—	**(584)**	—	**(584)**
Total comprehensive income	—	**(584)**	**56,666**	**56,082**
Transactions with shareholders				
Dividends declared	—	—	**(36,371)**	**(36,371)**
Management share purchase plan (Note 13)	**1,798**	—	—	**1,798**
Repurchase of common shares (Note 14)	**(57)**	—	**(6,277)**	**(6,334)**
Total transactions with shareholders	**1,741**	—	**(42,648)**	**(40,907)**
At December 31, 2011	**$ 20,918**	**$ (104)**	**$ 404,647**	**$ 425,461**

CONSOLIDATED STATEMENTS OF COMPREHENSIVE INCOME

Year ended December 31 ($ in thousands)	2011	2011 Tax Effect	2011
Profit for the year	**$ 56,666**	**$ —**	**$ 56,666**
Other comprehensive loss, net of tax			
Unrealized (losses) on available-for-sale financial assets arising during the year	**(621)**	**(87)**	**(534)**
Reclassification adjustment for net gains and losses included in net income	**(58)**	**(8)**	**(50)**
Change in unrealized gains on available-for-sale financial assets arising during the year	**(679)**	**(95)**	**(584)**
Comprehensive income for the year	**$ 55,987**	**$ (95)**	**$ 56,082**

Year ended December 31 ($ in thousands)	2010	2010 Tax Effect	2010
Profit for the year	$ 63,284	$ —	$ 63,284
Other comprehensive income, net of tax			
Unrealized gains on available-for-sale financial assets arising during the year	917	144	773
Reclassification adjustment for net gains and losses included in net income	(178)	(27)	(151)
Change in unrealized gains on available-for-sale financial assets arising during the year	739	117	622
Comprehensive income for the year	$ 64,023	$ 117	$ 63,906

EXHIBIT 2.1 (continued) Leon's Furniture Limited's Financial Statements

CONSOLIDATED STATEMENTS OF CASH FLOWS

Years ended December 31 ($ in thousands)	2011	2010
Operating Activities		
Profit for the year	**$ 56,666**	$ 63,284
Add (deduct) items not involving an outlay of cash		
Depreciation of property, plant and equipment and investment properties (Note 16)	**12,705**	15,354
Amortization of intangible assets (Note 16)	**880**	802
Amortization of deferred warranty plan revenue	**(17,271)**	(16,838)
Gain on sale of property, plant and equipment (Note 16)	**(21)**	(1,236)
Deferred income taxes	**2,008**	295
Gain (loss) on sale of available-for-sale financial assets	**35**	(337)
Cash received on warranty plan sales	**14,594**	16,714
	69,596	78,038
Net change in non-cash working capital balances related to operations (Note 20)	**(4,426)**	1,391
Cash provided by operating activities	**65,170**	79,429
Investing Activities		
Purchase of property, plant and equipment (Note 8)	**(24,999)**	(13,567)
Purchase of intangible assets (Note 10)	**64**	(370)
Proceeds on sale of property, plant and equipment (Note 8)	**39**	2,117
Purchase of available-for-sale financial assets	**(569,050)**	(524,414)
Proceeds on sale of available-for-sale financial assets	**559,242**	497,691
Decrease in employee share purchase loans (Note 13)	**2,008**	1,556
Cash used in investing activities	**(32,696)**	(36,987)
Financing Activities		
Dividends paid	**(25,224)**	(21,120)
Repurchase of common shares (Note 14)	**(6,334)**	(8,034)
Cash used in financing activities	**(31,558)**	(29,154)
Net increase in cash and cash equivalents during the year	**916**	13,288
Cash and cash equivalents, beginning of year	**71,589**	58,301
Cash and cash equivalents, end of year	**$ 72,505**	$ 71,589

INSIGHT

Materiality

Materiality is the significance of financial information to stakeholders. Information is material if its omission or misstatement affects the judgment of the information's users. Financial statements should be free of material misstatements or errors, and all material information should be reported in the financial statements or notes because its absence may affect decision making.

What information should be considered material? It's difficult to establish firm rules as materiality is a matter of judgment, and it depends on who will be using the financial statements and for what purpose. Depending on the decision being made, materiality could be very low, even as low as a dollar, and some information about an entity may not even have a dollar amount associated with it but still could be considered material.

Think of materiality from a personal standpoint. If you lost a dollar, it probably wouldn't have any impact on your life. Your behaviour, your plans, and your activities would probably stay the same. But losing $5,000 might have a significant impact. You might have to forgo a vacation, computer equipment, some entertainment, or even your education. The loss of one dollar wouldn't be material; the loss of $5,000 would be.

LO 3, 4, 5

THE BALANCE SHEET (STATEMENT OF FINANCIAL POSITION)

We'll begin our tour of the financial statements with the balance sheet or statement of financial position. The balance sheet provides a summary of an entity's financial position at a point in time. When accountants talk about an entity's financial position they're referring to its assets, liabilities, and owners' equity. We can initially define these elements as follows:

- **Assets** are economic resources that provide future benefits to an entity.
- **Liabilities** are an entity's *obligations*.
- **Owners' equity** is the investment owners have made in the entity.

Information about an entity's financial position can help stakeholders evaluate its financial health, assess its risk, and predict its future cash flows.

A balance sheet is like a photograph—it captures the scene at a particular moment. The scene could be dramatically different the moment before or after the picture is taken. For example, Leon's December 31, 2011 balance sheet reports cash of $72,505,000. It's possible that in early January 2012 Leon's could have spent that cash but the December 31, 2011 balance sheet wouldn't show it.

Look at Leon's balance sheet in Exhibit 2.1 and find these three elements (Leon's calls its owners' equity "shareholders' equity" because it's a corporation and a corporation's owners are called shareholders).

The elements in a balance sheet are organized to conform to the **accounting equation**, which is the conceptual foundation of accounting. The accounting equation is

Assets = Liabilities + Owners' Equity

The left side of the equation represents the assets and the right side represents how those assets were financed. Assets can be financed by **creditors** (entities money is owed to), which results in liabilities, or by owners, resulting in owners' equity.

Leon's balance sheet can be expressed in terms of the accounting equation as follows:

Assets	=	Liabilities	+	Owners' (Shareholders') Equity
$595,339,000		$169,878,000		$425,461,000

Find these amounts in Leon's balance sheet (Exhibit 2.1). The two sides of the equation must always be equal, or in balance, which is why the statement is called the balance sheet. Notice that each of the elements in Leon's balance sheet is broken down into categories called accounts, which provide additional detail about an entity's financial position. For example, one of Leon's asset accounts is cash and cash equivalents, which means that on December 31, 2011, it had $72,505,000 in cash and cash equivalents.

INSIGHT

Accounting Terminology

Accounting terminology is sometimes confusing because different names are given to the same thing. For example, the balance sheet is often called the statement of financial position. Accounting standards are quite flexible when it comes to terminology. The list of Similar Terms at the end of each chapter will help sort things out.

The accounting equation isn't unique to Canada, to IFRS or ASPE, or to any particular method of measuring balance sheet items. It's almost universal. Recall the example in Chapter 1 where the contents of an apartment were valued in three different ways. The accounting equation can accommodate all of these ways, and others, of measuring assets.

All economic events entered into an accounting system are summarized in terms of the accounting equation; that is, each event is recorded based on its effect on assets, liabilities, and owners' equity. The equality between the left side and right side of the equation must be maintained for any event entered into an accounting system. For example, if an entity borrows $500 from a bank, its assets increase by $500 because it has additional cash. It also has a liability or obligation to repay the bank, so liabilities increase by $500 as well. Both sides of the accounting equation have increased by $500, so it remains in balance.

Now let's take a closer look at assets, liabilities, and owners' equity.

Assets

LO 5

We will now expand our definition of assets. According to IFRS an asset must have the following characteristics:

- Provide a future benefit to the entity and it must be probable that the entity will enjoy the benefit. (If there is too much uncertainty about whether the entity will enjoy the benefit, there is no asset.) Note that when accountants speak of an asset having a future benefit they mean it will help the entity generate cash.
- Be controlled by the entity that will obtain the benefits. (This means the entity has the right to use the asset to make money.)
- Be the result of a transaction or event that has already occurred.
- Be measurable.

The definition of an asset doesn't include a requirement for ownership. An entity only has to have control over the benefits of the item. For example, leased items are sometimes classified as assets because they can be used to make money even though they aren't owned.

Table 2.1 explains why some of the assets on Leon's balance sheet meet this definition.

INSIGHT

The Importance of Accounting Definitions

Definitions in accounting are crucial, so it's important to know and understand them. Applying a definition often helps to determine how to deal with an unfamiliar transaction or situation. Throughout the book you will be challenged to apply basic principles to solve accounting problems. It may sometimes feel like you're not prepared to solve a problem, but this is where your critical thinking skills come in.

TABLE 2.1
Why are these assets?

Type of Asset	What is it?	Why is it an asset?
Cash	Money.	Future benefit: Cash can be spent to buy goods and services, pay debts, and pay dividends. Control: Leon's can use the cash however it wishes. Past transaction: Events in the past, such as sales of furniture, gave rise to the cash. Measurable: The amount of cash can be determined by counting.
Trade receivables (many companies call these accounts receivable)	Money owed to Leon's by customers who received goods but haven't paid for them yet.	Future benefit: Right to receive cash in the future. Control: The right to collect the cash belongs to Leon's. Past transaction: Trade receivables arise when goods are sold to customers on credit. Measurable: Measurable, but with uncertainty. The exact amount that will be collected isn't known because some customers may not pay.
Inventories	Merchandise that Leon's has available for sale to customers.	Future benefit: Leon's can sell the inventory to customers and receive cash. Control: Leon's owns the inventory and can determine how, when, where, and at what price to sell it. Past transaction: The inventory was purchased in a transaction with the manufacturer. Measurable: The cost of the inventory can be determined from invoices.
Property, plant, and equipment	Includes land, buildings, equipment, vehicles, and so on that allow Leon's to operate its businesses. Leon's doesn't sell these but uses them to operate the business. Building improvements are costs incurred to improve/renovate stores (paint stores). This explanation will focus on buildings.	Future benefit: A building provides a place to operate a furniture store. Control: Leon's can use the building in any way it deems appropriate (sell, decorate, renovate, rent to others, etc.), limited only by relevant law or contract. Past transaction: A building would have been purchased from a previous owner or built to Leon's specifications. Measurable: The cost of the building can be determined from purchase documents or from construction cost details.

Missing assets: Not everything our intuition might tell us is an asset gets classified as one in the financial statements. For example, Leon's human resources (its employees) and its loyal customers are important to the success of the company but these aren't found on the balance sheet. Because the future benefit associated with customers is difficult to measure and companies don't control their employees, these items don't meet the definition of an asset. Other examples of items that aren't classified as assets when we might think they would be include advertising, trademarks, brand names, and research. The implication of this for the balance sheet is that every asset of an entity may not be captured on it—the balance sheet isn't comprehensive.

Balance sheet measurements: When an asset is acquired, it's recorded at the transaction value—the amount paid. After that, there are different ways to measure assets. For example, inventory is usually reported at its cost; **capital assets** (**property, plant, and equipment** [see Table 2.1] and intangible assets) can be reported, according to IFRS, at cost or fair value; accounts receivable is an estimate of how much the entity expects to collect. We will return to measurement of balance sheet items many times in the book.

Current versus non-current assets: **Current assets** are used up, sold, or converted to cash within one year or one operating cycle. An **operating cycle** is the time it takes from the initial investment made in goods and services until cash is received from customers. Leon's will typically sell/use its inventory within one year, so it's classified as current. Leon's will collect its **trade receivables** (see Table 2.1) within a year, so they're also current. The operating cycle of most businesses is a year or less but there are exceptions; for example, distillers and wineries age some products for more than a year but classify the inventory as current because the operating cycle is greater than one year.

In contrast, assets that won't be used up, sold, or converted to cash within one year or one operating cycle are classified as **non-current**. Leon's property, plant, and equipment are non-current because they will provide benefits for more than one year. Notice that non-current assets aren't specifically identified on Leon's balance sheet. If an asset isn't classified as current it's understood to be non-current.

QUESTION FOR CONSIDERATION

Many companies' balance sheets have an account called prepaid expenses. This can include money spent to pay for an insurance policy in advance. For example, on December 15, 2017, an entity pays $5,000 for insurance coverage for the period January 1, 2018 to December 31, 2018. Use the definition of an asset to explain why this insurance paid for in advance would be reported as an asset on December 31, 2017.

ANSWER: The prepaid insurance is reported as an asset because it meets the definition of an asset:

- Future benefit—the entity has the benefit of insurance coverage during 2018.
- Control—the policy provides the entity with insurance coverage on its property. The entity is entitled to recover any losses covered by the policy.
- Past transaction—the policy was purchased from an insurance company on December 15, 2017.
- Measurable—the amount paid for the policy is stated in the invoice from the insurance company.

Liabilities

LO 5

Liabilities are an entity's obligations to pay money or provide goods or services to suppliers, lenders, customers, and government. According to IFRS, a liability must

- be the result of a past transaction or economic event
- require some kind of economic sacrifice to settle

For example, if an entity borrows money from a bank it has a liability to repay the amount borrowed. The loan is the result of a transaction between the bank and the entity; the entity will have to "sacrifice" cash to repay the loan. Table 2.2 provides a description and explanation of some of Leon's liabilities.

Like assets, liabilities are classified on Leon's balance sheet as current and non-current. **Current liabilities** will be paid or satisfied within one year or one operating cycle. **Non-current liabilities** will be paid or satisfied in more than one year or one operating cycle. As was the case with assets, Leon's doesn't specifically identify non-current liabilities on its balance sheet. If a liability isn't identified as current it's understood to be non-current.

INSIGHT

It's important to understand that the assets, liabilities, and amounts reported on an entity's balance sheet are the result of applying accounting standards. If a different set of rules was used you would get a different balance sheet. Accounting information is a representation of an entity's economic activities. There are many different ways assets, liabilities, and other financial statement elements can be defined and measured, some allowed by IFRS and others not. Balance sheets prepared in accordance with IFRS and ASPE will be different.

TABLE 2.2

Why Are These Liabilities?

Type of Liability	What is it?	Why is it a liability?
Trade and other payables	Amounts owed to suppliers for goods and services purchased on credit. Includes amounts owed to inventory suppliers, utilities, property owners, and employees, to name a few.	Obligation: Pay for goods and services provided by suppliers. Past transaction or economic event: The suppliers have provided the goods and services. Economic sacrifice: In most cases, money must be paid to settle the liabilities.
Customers' deposits	Customers pay in advance for goods to be provided in future.	Obligation: Provide goods and services that have been paid for by customers but not yet delivered. Past transaction or economic event: Payment has been received from customers for goods or services. Economic sacrifice: Goods and services must be provided.
Deferred warranty plan revenue	Amounts paid to Leon's for extended warranty protection on merchandise.	Obligation: Provide warranty service to customers as required. Past transaction or economic event: Customers have purchased extended warranties. Economic sacrifice: Warranty service must be provided (parts and labour).
Dividends payable	Dividends that have been declared by the board of directors but not yet paid to shareholders. (Dividends are payments, usually in cash, by a corporation to its shareholders.)	Obligation: Pay shareholders dividends declared. Past transaction or economic event: Dividend has been declared by the board. Economic sacrifice: Cash must be paid.

LO 7 Using Balance Sheet Information to Analyze Liquidity

The classification of assets and liabilities into current and non-current components is useful for assessing **liquidity**, which is the availability of cash or the ability to convert assets to cash quickly. Liquidity is important to creditors who are expecting to be paid and to potential creditors who are considering extending credit. For example, a banker wants to assess the likelihood that a borrower will be able to repay a loan. Liquidity is also important to shareholders because a company that's unable to meet its obligations is at significant risk of going out of business.

Taken together, current assets and current liabilities provide important information about an entity's liquidity. Current assets minus current liabilities is called **working capital**. The more working capital an entity has, the more current assets there are available to pay current liabilities. Negative working capital means the entity has more current liabilities than current assets and this could indicate liquidity problems, although that isn't always true. Leon's working capital on December 31, 2011 was

$$\text{Working capital} = \text{Current assets} - \text{Current liabilities}$$
$$\$204{,}649{,}000 = \$343{,}772{,}000 - \$139{,}123{,}000$$

On December 31, 2011 Leon's had $204,649,000 more current assets than current liabilities, which suggests it was in good shape to pay its current liabilities. Suppliers could confidently extend credit to Leon's because it has lots of working capital including lots of cash and cash equivalents (investments that are easily converted to cash).

Another way of examining working capital is with a ratio. The ratio of current assets to current liabilities is called the **current ratio**, or **working capital ratio**, and is defined as

$$\text{Current ratio} = \frac{\text{Current assets}}{\text{Current liabilities}}$$

The current ratio gives the relative amount of current assets to current liabilities. The larger the ratio, the more current assets are available to meet current liabilities, which, on the surface at least, means the entity is more able to meet its obligations. Leon's current ratio on December 31, 2011 was

$$\text{Current ratio} = \frac{\text{Current assets}}{\text{Current liabilities}}$$
$$= \frac{\$343{,}772{,}000}{\$139{,}123{,}000}$$
$$= 2.47$$

A current ratio of 2.47 means that for every dollar of current liabilities, Leon's has $2.47 of current assets, which suggests the company should be able to meet its obligations.

To make sense of accounting information it's important to have benchmarks, such as a company's information over a number of years, information for similar firms, or industry averages. For example, Leon's current ratio for the past three years shows an improving current ratio:

Leon's Current Ratio on December 31			
	2011	2010	2009
Current ratio	2.47	2.61	2.34

Comparing Leon's with similar companies is also useful. The Brick Ltd. is another large national Canadian furniture retailer. Table 2.3 provides liquidity information for Leon's and The Brick. Based on the current ratio Leon's liquidity position is stronger than The Brick's because the current ratio is significantly higher.

TABLE 2.3 Liquidity Information for Leon's and The Brick as of December 31, 2011

	Current Assets	Current Liabilities	Working Capital	Current Ratio
Leon's Furniture Limited	$343,772,000	$139,123,000	$204,649,000	2.47
The Brick Ltd.	388,087,000	280,005,000	108,082,000	1.39

There are no universal rules for evaluating ratios. For example, people sometimes learn that a "good" current ratio is 2:1, but different industries have different norms so a current ratio considered acceptable and reasonable in one industry could be a source of concern in another.

Making sense of financial information isn't usually straightforward, and it can require a lot of detective work. The numbers in the financial statements can raise questions, but they will rarely provide answers. Stakeholders must analyze, assess, evaluate, and compare the information in financial statements to make sense of it. Calculating ratios is a part of the analysis and assessment of financial data, but it's often just a first step. After some preliminary investigation, it may be necessary to gather more information.

KNOWLEDGE CHECK 2.1

- Use Exhibit 2.1 to calculate Leon's working capital and current ratio on January 1, 2010.

LO 5

Owners' Equity

Owners' equity is the amount owners have invested in an entity. In terms of the accounting equation, owners' equity represents the amount of the assets financed by the owners. Equivalent terms you may see in a financial statement include the following:

- **shareholders' equity**—owners' equity of a corporation
- **partners' equity**—owners' equity of a partnership
- *owners'* or **proprietors' equity**—owners' equity of a proprietorship

Owners' investments can be direct or indirect. Direct investments are made by purchasing shares of a corporation or units in a partnership, or by contributing money to a proprietorship. The investment is direct because the investors contribute their own assets directly to the entity. These investments are usually cash, but sometimes other assets can be invested. Indirect investment occurs when an entity's net income or profit isn't paid to the owners but is "reinvested" in the business. The investment is indirect because investors don't choose to invest: management or the board of directors decides to keep the profits in the company.

In a corporation's balance sheet, the shareholders' equity section separates direct investments and the reinvestment of net income (see these terms in Leon's balance sheet in Exhibit 2.1):

- Direct investments by shareholders are reported in the common shares account (also called common share capital, share capital, or capital stock). The amount in **common shares** represents the amount of money (or other assets) that shareholders have contributed to the corporation in exchange for shares.
- Reinvested net incomes are accumulated in retained earnings. **Retained earnings** is the sum of all the net incomes a corporation has earned since its inception, less dividends paid (there are some other adjustments but net income and dividends are the main items). **Dividends** are payments, usually in cash, by a corporation to its shareholders. If retained earnings is negative it's referred to as a **deficit**.

On its December 31, 2011 balance sheet (see Exhibit 2.1), Leon's reported shareholders' equity of $425,461,000. This is the total investment shareholders have made in the company. Shareholders have made direct investments by purchasing $20,918,000 in common shares from the company and indirect investments of $404,647,000 in retained earnings. Shareholders' equity also includes −$104,000 of "accumulated other comprehensive income," which we'll discuss later.

LO 7

The Debt-to-Equity Ratio

Another common balance sheet analytical tool is the **debt-to-equity ratio**:

$$\text{Debt-to-equity ratio} = \frac{\text{Liabilities}}{\text{Shareholders' equity}}$$

This ratio is a measure of how an entity is financed—the higher the ratio, the more debt an entity is using relative to equity—and an indication of risk. More debt means more risk because, regardless of whether it's doing well or poorly, the entity must make payments on its debt on time. Debt has a fixed cost associated with it called interest. **Interest** is the cost of borrowing money and is usually calculated as a percentage of the amount borrowed. For example, if an entity borrows \$10,000 at a 10 percent interest rate, the interest cost for the year would be \$1,000 (\$10,000 × 0.10). If an entity doesn't pay the interest and **principal** (the amount originally borrowed), the lenders can take legal action. In contrast, equity is less risky for a business because there are no mandatory payments—the business doesn't have to pay dividends at any time and shareholders can't take any action if they aren't paid.

Leon's debt-to-equity ratio on December 31, 2011 was

$$\text{Debt-to-equity ratio} = \frac{\text{Liabilities}}{\text{Shareholders' equity}} = \frac{\$169{,}878{,}000}{\$425{,}461{,}000} = 0.40$$

The ratio of 0.40 means that Leon's is financed with 40 percent as much liabilities as equity. In other words, for every \$1 invested by shareholders, \$0.40 is supplied by creditors. There has been little change in the ratio for the three years shown; it was at 0.38 and 0.41 at the end of fiscal 2010 and 2009 respectively, which means Leon's debt-to-equity ratio is very stable. A low debt-to-equity ratio is an indication of a strong balance sheet—the entity is low-risk. Things are actually even better than the ratio suggests. Almost all of Leon's liabilities are operational, meaning they are incurred as a result of operating the business (obligations to suppliers, customers, and employees, for example). Leon's has not borrowed any money so it's an attractive candidate for a loan if management decides to borrow for expansion or major capital expenditures.

This isn't to say that financing with debt is a bad thing—in fact, there are some very attractive reasons for doing so. Management must achieve the right balance between debt and equity when deciding how to structure the company's financing. Like the current ratio, average debt-to-equity ratios vary from industry to industry.

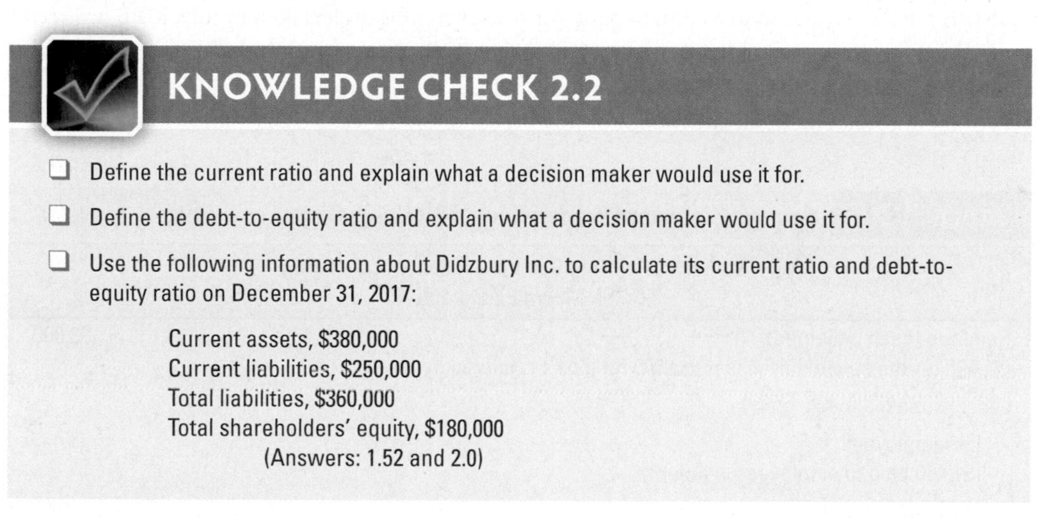

KNOWLEDGE CHECK 2.2

- ☐ Define the current ratio and explain what a decision maker would use it for.
- ☐ Define the debt-to-equity ratio and explain what a decision maker would use it for.
- ☐ Use the following information about Didzbury Inc. to calculate its current ratio and debt-to-equity ratio on December 31, 2017:

  Current assets, \$380,000
  Current liabilities, \$250,000
  Total liabilities, \$360,000
  Total shareholders' equity, \$180,000
  (Answers: 1.52 and 2.0)

THE INCOME STATEMENT

LO 3, 4, 5, 6, 7

If a balance sheet is like a photograph, then an income statement is like a movie: it shows events over a period of time. The **income statement** is a "How did we do?" statement, measuring an entity's economic activity over a period of time, such as a year. Among the uses for an income statement are:

- evaluating the performance of an entity and its management
- predicting future earnings and cash flows
- estimating the value of an entity
- determining the amount of tax that must be paid

The income statement can have significant economic consequences for entities and their stakeholders. For example,

- stock prices often change when a company announces its net income;
- managers' bonuses are often based on net income;
- net income is used to determine income taxes;
- the selling price of a business can be based on net income.

Measuring an entity's economic activity is more challenging than you might think. After all, how can the complex activities of an entity be reasonably reflected in an income statement? This is a question that we'll devote a lot of time to.

LO 6

There are different ways accountants measure an entity's activities. The two most common methods are cash accounting and accrual accounting.

- **Cash accounting** reports the cash flowing into and out of the entity. Under this method, economic performance represents the change in cash over the period.
- **Accrual accounting** measures an entity's economic activity rather than its cash flows.

We'll get a better sense of cash and accrual accounting with an example. Melissa Picard is a student entrepreneur who operates a small business called Melissa's Painting Business (MPB). During July MPB had the following economic activity:

1. MPB started and completed seven painting jobs. It collected $2,500 for these jobs and was still owed $900 by one of its customers. The customer told Melissa she would pay her on August 15. MPB also collected $500 during July for jobs completed during June.
2. MPB paid $1,450 to people hired to paint and owed its employees $250 at the end of July. MPB will pay the amount owed in early August.
3. MPB purchased and used $1,550 of paint for the seven jobs undertaken in July. MPB has credit at the paint store so it didn't pay for any of the paint purchased in July, but it did pay $900 for paint it bought before July.

An income statement for the month of July prepared on the cash basis is shown in Table 2.4.

TABLE 2.4 Income Statement Prepared for MPB Using Cash Accounting

Melissa's Painting Business Income Statement For the Month Ended July 31	
Revenue (cash collected) ($2,500 for the seven July jobs plus $500 for jobs completed in June)	$3,000
Less: Expenses (cash spent)	
For employees ($1,450 paid to employees in July)	(1,450)
For paint ($900 paid for paint purchased in previous months)	(900)
Net income (cash flow)	$ 650

Net income on the cash basis means that MPB had $650 more in cash at the end of July than at the beginning. Of course, MPB still has bills to pay (employees and paint) so Melissa can't spend the $650 any way she'd like. In general, cash accounting is of limited usefulness for many stakeholders' decisions because it provides an incomplete measure of performance and economic activity.

In contrast, accrual accounting attempts to reflect a more complete picture of economic activity by capturing relevant economic events, not just cash flows. For example, it captures sales on credit, whereas cash accounting doesn't. However, accrual accounting is a lot more complicated than cash accounting and requires much more judgment by managers, accountants, and stakeholders.

Two important concepts for measuring income under accrual accounting are:

Revenue (or sales or sales revenue)—economic benefits earned by providing goods or services to customers.

Expenses—economic sacrifices made in a period.

Under these definitions, revenue and expenses can be reported before, after, or at the same time as the related cash flow. A challenge of accrual accounting is determining when revenue and expenses should be reported in the income statement. MPB's income statement for the month of July using accrual accounting is shown in Table 2.5.

TABLE 2.5 Income Statement Prepared for MPB Using Accrual Accounting

Melissa's Painting Business Income Statement For the Month Ended July 31	
Revenue ($2,500 for the six July jobs that were paid for, plus $900 for the July job that wasn't paid for by the end of July)	$3,400
Less: Expenses	
Employees ($1,450 paid for work done by employees in July plus $250 owed for work done in July)	(1,700)
Paint ($1,550 for paint purchased and used in July; this paint won't be paid for until later)	(1,550)
Equipment depreciation	(50)
Net income	$100

On the accrual income statement revenue reflects work done and money earned in July, not cash collected. Even though a customer hasn't paid as of the end of July, the amount is still reported as revenue in July. On the other hand, the money collected for the June job isn't included in July's revenue because it has nothing to do with July's economic activity. The revenue for the June job would have been reported in June's income statement. The expenses include the cost of paint used and the cost of the work done by employees in July, regardless of when these expenses are paid. Expenses are the costs incurred to earn revenue in July. When the cash changed hands doesn't matter.

Expenses in the accrual income statement include $50 for equipment. MPB needs equipment (ladders, trays, scaffolding, etc.) to operate. Unlike paint that gets used up on one job, the equipment contributes to earning revenue over many periods and many jobs. As a result, under accrual accounting a portion of the cost of the equipment is expensed each month to reflect the economic sacrifice or "using up" of the equipment. The term **depreciation** describes the expensing of the cost of capital assets in a period.

The last line on the accrual statement is net income. What does accrual net income mean? It's more difficult to interpret than net income in the cash accounting income statement, where the $650 bottom line simply represents how much more cash MPB had at the end of the month. In the accrual statement net income of $100 means that Melissa's business enjoyed net economic benefits of $100 during July because the economic benefits (revenue) exceeded the economic sacrifices (expenses) by $100. Another way to interpret net income is that it corresponds with an increase in **net assets** (net assets equal assets − liabilities). For MPB, net income of $100 means assets − liabilities increased by $100 in July as a result of its activities. The increase could be due to more cash, more receivables, more of any other asset, or fewer liabilities.

It should be clear, even from this introductory discussion, that accrual accounting can be very tricky. With accrual accounting it's necessary to decide when economic activity occurs—when revenue and expenses happen and should be recorded in the accounting system. Accrual accounting is an important reason why accounting standards are flexible, why there are often valid alternatives for recording transactions and economic events, why judgment is so important in accounting, and why it's possible for managers to comply with accounting standards while pursuing their own interests.

Even though the income statement is always presented separately, it's really just part of the owners' equity section of the balance sheet. We could rewrite the accounting equation to reflect the current year's income statement (this equation ignores direct investments and dividends):

LO 4

Assets	=	Liabilities	+	Owners' equity at the beginning of the period	+	Revenue for the period	−	Expenses for the period
or								
Assets	=	Liabilities	+	Owners' equity at the beginning of the period	+	Net Income for the period		

Notice that net income in a period increases owners' equity, meaning the owners' investment in the entity or the owners' wealth increases. Also, since owners' equity equals assets minus liabilities, net income means net assets have increased.

Examine the two income statements that were prepared for Melissa's Painting Business in Tables 2.4 (cash basis) and 2.5 (accrual basis). Explain why revenue in the two statements is different.

ANSWER: With cash accounting, revenue is the cash collected from customers during a period. In contrast, with accrual accounting revenue represents amounts earned by providing goods and services to customers during the period, regardless of when the cash is collected. The difference between cash and accrual accounting for MPB is the $500 that was collected in July for the job done in June and the $900 owed at the end of July. Revenue on the cash basis includes the $500 from June and excludes the $900 owing at the end of July. Revenue on the accrual basis excludes the $500 from June and includes the $900 owing at the end of July. Both methods include the amounts for jobs completed and paid for in July.

LO 3

Leon's Income Statement

For the year ended December 31, 2011, Leon's reported net income (profit) of $56,666,000 on its income statement (Exhibit 2.1). This means that revenues (economic benefits) exceeded all expenses (economic sacrifices) by $56,666,000 and that shareholder wealth (as reflected by the equity section of the balance sheet) and net assets have increased. But is this amount of net income good news? That question must be answered in relation to benchmarks. Compared with 2010, Leon's 2011 net income decreased by $6,618,000 or about 10.5 percent, so this isn't as good. But how did other similar businesses do? The Brick's net income increased by $88,195,000, which is much better than Leon's, but The Brick had a loss in 2010 (net income was negative) and its net income in 2011 was less than Leon's. So performance has to be assessed in the context of the environment. (Like the balance sheet, the income statement has more than one name. Other names include the statement of income, statement of operations, and the statement of profit and loss.)

Besides net income itself, Leon's statement of income includes important information about how it generated that net income. Consider the following:

- During fiscal 2011, Leon's sold $682,836,000 in goods and services (revenue).
- Leon's reported several different types of expenses for the year ended December 31, 2011:
  - **cost of sales** of $394,099,000—cost of inventory sold (furniture and appliances)
  - general and administrative expenses of $96,038,000—head office costs, wages and salaries depreciation, etc.

- sales and marketing expenses of \$78,387,000—advertising, promotion, sales commissions, etc.
- occupancy expenses of \$32,731,000—cost of operating the stores.
- other operating expenses of \$6,260,000—other costs of operating the business.

These expenses are subtracted from revenue to determine *operating profit*, which is the amount earned from actual business operations—selling furniture and appliances. Operating profit for 2011 was \$75,321,000. Leon's added to its profit for the year by selling capital property at a profit (\$21,000) and by earning finance (interest) income (\$3,506,000). The breakdown of operating expenses is very helpful for analyzing the company's performance. Throughout the book we'll examine different ways of analyzing this type of information.

Because Leon's is a corporation, it must pay taxes. For fiscal 2011, Leon's reports an income tax expense of \$22,182,000, which is deducted in the calculation of net income.

KNOWLEDGE CHECK 2.3

Mc Graw Hill connect

During the summer Hank operated a cart that sold hot dogs and cold drinks. By the end of the summer Hank had collected \$6,500 from customers and paid \$3,300 to suppliers. At the end of the summer he owed suppliers \$500 and was owed \$200 by customers. The depreciation on his cart for the summer was \$800.

- ❑ What was Hank's net income on a cash basis for the summer? (Answer: \$3,200)
- ❑ What was his net income on an accrual basis? (Answer: \$2,100)
- ❑ Why is depreciation an expense under accrual accounting?

Gross Margin and Gross Margin Percentage

LO 7

A very useful tool for analyzing some companies' financial performance is **gross margin**, which is sales less cost of sales. (Leon's calls gross margin "gross profit.") For a retailer, cost of sales is mainly the cost of the inventory it sells. For a manufacturer, cost of sales is the cost of producing the goods it sells. The gross margin is available for covering the other costs of operating the business and for providing profit to the owners. The higher a company's gross margin, the better.

Gross margin can be useful as an analytical tool when expressed as a percentage of sales:

$$\text{Gross margin percentage} = \frac{\text{Gross margin}}{\text{Revenue}} \times 100\%$$

Gross margin percentage is the percentage of each dollar of sales that is available to cover other costs and return a profit to the owners. If a company can increase its gross margin percentage (perhaps by increasing the selling price of its products) without decreasing sales or increasing other costs, its net income will increase. Using the gross margin percentage makes it easier to compare the performance of different entities and the same entity year to year.

www.leons.ca

Leon's gross margin is calculated on its income statement:

Gross margin	=	Revenue	−	Cost of sales
\$288,737,000	=	\$682,836,000	−	\$394,099,000

This means that Leon's sold its products for \$288,737,000 more than what they cost. From this, Leon's gross margin percentage can be calculated:

$$\text{Gross margin percentage} = \frac{\text{Revenue} - \text{Cost of sales}}{\text{Revenue}} \times 100\% = \frac{\text{Gross margin}}{\text{Revenue}} \times 100\%$$

$$= \frac{\$682{,}836{,}000 - \$394{,}099{,}000}{\$682{,}836{,}000} \times 100\% = \frac{\$288{,}737{,}000}{\$682{,}836{,}000} \times 100\%$$

$$= 42.3\%$$

Leon's gross margin percentage in 2011 was 42.3 percent, which means that for every dollar of sales it has $0.423 to apply to costs other than the cost of sales, and to profit. Leon's gross margin percentage in 2010 and 2009 was 42.0 percent and 40.3 percent respectively (try to calculate the 2010 amount yourself), so there's been a steady improvement over the three years. (The gross margin percentage for 2009 isn't prepared in accordance with IFRS whereas the 2010 and 2011 percentages are, so it's not really appropriate to compare; the results are presented only to show how to examine accounting information.) Note that small changes in the gross margin percentage can have a significant impact on performance. If Leon's had had the same gross margin in 2011 as in 2010, the gross margin would have been $866,211 lower (0.3% × $288,737,000). If all other expenses had stayed the same, the profit would have been $2,259,890 lower.

When assessing company performance, it's useful to compare gross margin percentages of similar businesses, but you can't meaningfully compare the gross margin percentages of different types of entities. Also, the percentage can't be calculated for some businesses, such as those offering services, because they don't have cost of sales.

We can compare the gross margins of Leon's and The Brick:

Comparative Gross Margin Percentages			
	2011	2010	2009
Leon's	42.3%	42.0%	40.3%
The Brick	44.2%	43.1%	43.0%

The Brick's gross margin percentage has also improved over the three years by 1.2 percentage points. The Brick's gross margin has been better over the period.

QUESTION FOR CONSIDERATION

In 2011, Leon's gross margin decreased by $9,319,000 whereas its gross margin percentage increased very slightly, by 0.3 percent. What factors could give rise to a furniture chain's gross margin decreasing while its gross margin percentage increases?

ANSWER:

A decrease in gross margin could be due to three factors:

- a decrease in the amount sold
- a decrease in the selling price of the goods sold
- an increase in the amount Leon's pays for the goods it sells

An increase in the gross margin percentage would result from:

- an increase in the selling price of the goods sold
- a decrease in the amount Leon's pays for the goods it sells
- a change in the mix of products Leon's sold during the year, so that it sells more products with higher gross margin percentages

LO 3 THE STATEMENT OF COMPREHENSIVE INCOME

Comprehensive income is an extension of net income. Over the years, accounting standard setters decided to exclude certain types of economic events from the calculation of net income (the items went directly to owners' equity instead). The standard setters later decided there should be a measure that captures all transactions and economic events that involve non-owners and that affect equity (remember that revenue and expenses affect equity). This measure is called **comprehensive income** and is calculated as follows:

Comprehensive income = Net income + Other comprehensive income

Other comprehensive income includes transactions and economic events that involve non-owners and affect equity but are, for various reasons, excluded from the calculation of net income. Examine Leon's statement of comprehensive income in Exhibit 2.1. Notice that the first line of the statement is profit (net income) followed by adjustments that are called "other comprehensive income." Leon's comprehensive income for 2011 is $56,082,000 and other comprehensive income is −$584,000. Leon's provides a separate statement of comprehensive income but some companies combine their income statements and statements of comprehensive income into a single statement called the statements of comprehensive income.

Comprehensive income also affects the equity section of the balance sheet. Normally, other comprehensive income for a period is added to an account called **accumulated other comprehensive income** in the equity section of the balance sheet. The balance in this account on Leon's 2011 balance sheet is −$104,000 (find this amount on Leon's balance sheet in Exhibit 2.1).

THE STATEMENT OF CHANGES IN EQUITY

LO 3, 4

The **statement of changes in equity** shows changes in each account in the equity section of the balance sheet during a period. Each column of the statement corresponds with an account in the equity section of Leon's balance sheet (see Exhibit 2.1). Notice how the statement shows how each equity account changed over the period. The ending balance of each account can be tied to the amounts on the balance sheet.

Let's look at the transactions and economic events that affect Leon's retained earnings. Recall that retained earnings represents indirect investment by the owners of a corporation and equals the sum of an entity's net incomes over its life, less dividends paid. In equation form, changes to retained earnings can be expressed as

Retained earnings at the end of the year	=	Retained earnings at the beginning of the year	+	Net income for the year	−	Dividends declared during the year

Notice that in addition to the effect of net income and dividends, Leon's also shows a reduction in retained earnings as a result of the company buying back shares from investors. We'll discuss repurchases of shares later in the book.

Finally, dividends aren't considered expenses when calculating net income. They are distributions of the shareholders' investment in the business back to the shareholders, not a cost of operating the business, and so aren't included in the calculation of net income. A dividend doesn't affect the overall wealth of a shareholder—it simply moves the wealth from the entity (which the shareholder owns) to the shareholder's bank account. In other words, retained earnings decreases by the same amount shareholders' cash increases.

ACCOUNTING STANDARDS FOR PRIVATE ENTERPRISES

ASPE only requires a **statement of retained earnings**, not a statement of changes in equity. The statement of retained earnings shows the changes in the retained earnings account over the period. ASPE also doesn't require entities to calculate comprehensive income and the equity section of the balance sheet doesn't include the accumulated other comprehensive income account.

THE STATEMENT OF CASH FLOWS

LO 3

They say cash is king! Cash is crucial to the survival and success of any entity. It's needed to pay bills and meet obligations as they come due. While accrual net income is an important indicator of performance, you can't forget cash. Cash and net income aren't the same thing and no matter how large a company's net income, if it doesn't have the cash to meet its obligations it's in serious trouble.

The **statement of cash flows** shows how an entity obtained and used cash during a period and it provides information about how cash was managed. It's an important source of information about an entity's liquidity. The statement of cash flows is another "How did we do?" statement but it measures "how we did" differently than the income statement.

The statement of cash flows reports three types of cash flows. Let's look at each type in detail.

1. **Cash from/used in operations** is the cash an entity generates from or uses in its regular business activities. For Leon's, this is cash collected from selling furniture items and money spent buying inventory and for advertising, employees, rent, utilities, supplies, taxes—any money spent on the day-to-day operation of the business.

   For fiscal 2011, Leon's reported cash from operations (called cash provided by operating activities) of $65,170,000, which means that during this period Leon's regular business activities generated $65,170,000 in cash. This cash could be used for expansion, purchasing property, plant, and equipment, paying dividends, and so on, without having to borrow or sell more shares. Notice that cash from operations is almost $9 million higher than net income in 2011. Remember that under accrual accounting, net income measures economic flows, not cash flows. This means that net income can include amounts that aren't cash flows, whereas cash from operations simply reflects the movement of cash.
2. **Cash from/used in investing activities** is cash spent buying and received from selling property, plant, and equipment; intangible assets; other long-term assets; and investments. Most of Leon's investing activity during 2011 was for the purchase and sale of "available-for-sale financial assets." These are investments in securities such as stocks and bonds of other companies purchased to earn money on cash on hand. Leon's also spent $24,999,000 on property, plant, and equipment. Investing cash flows were also affected by a number of small items (see Exhibit 2.1). Overall, Leon's had a net cash outflow of $32,696,000 for investing activities.
3. **Cash from/used in financing activities** is the cash an entity raises from and pays to equity investors and lenders. It includes cash borrowed or raised by issuing shares and cash paid for loan repayments, share repurchases, and can include dividends and interest paid (the treatment of dividends and interest is an accounting choice under IFRS). During fiscal 2011, Leon's had a net cash outflow from financing activities of $31,558,000, which included $25,224,000 in dividends and $6,334,000 to repurchase common shares from shareholders. There were no cash inflows from financing activities in 2011 or 2010.

Overall, what does Leon's statement of cash flows tell us? During 2011, Leon's generated cash from operations of $65,170,000 that it used to purchase property, plant, and equipment, increase the net amount of available-for-sale financial assets, pay dividends, and repurchase common shares. Leon's also increased its cash holdings by $916,000 (calculated by adding together cash from operations, financing activities, and investing activities) during 2011.

LO 3, 4 THE RELATIONSHIP AMONG THE FINANCIAL STATEMENTS

It may not be clear from the discussion of the individual financial statements, but the statements are closely related. The relationships for Cupar Inc.'s (Cupar) financial statements are shown in Figure 2.1. At the top of Figure 2.1 is Cupar's balance sheet on December 31, 2016. Below it are *flow statements* showing changes during the period: the statement of comprehensive income (including the income statement and the statement of comprehensive income), statement of changes in equity, and statement of cash flows for 2017. At the bottom of Figure 2.1 is Cupar's balance sheet on December 31, 2017. The flow statements capture the changes between the two balance sheets. Thus, the statement of cash flows shows how the balance in the cash account on the balance sheet changed from December 31, 2016 to December 31, 2017. The statements of income and changes in equity provide information on changes in the equity section of the balance sheet from December 31, 2016 to December 31, 2017. The equity section is simplified for ease of use. The arrows in Figure 2.1 show how information flows from one statement to another.

The relationships among the statements are more extensive than cash and equity. Many transactions and economic events involve both the income statement and the balance sheet and any transaction that involves cash is included in the cash flows statement. Figure 2.1 only shows the amounts that are explicitly shown on more than one statement.

FIGURE 2.1 **The Relationship among the Financial Statements**

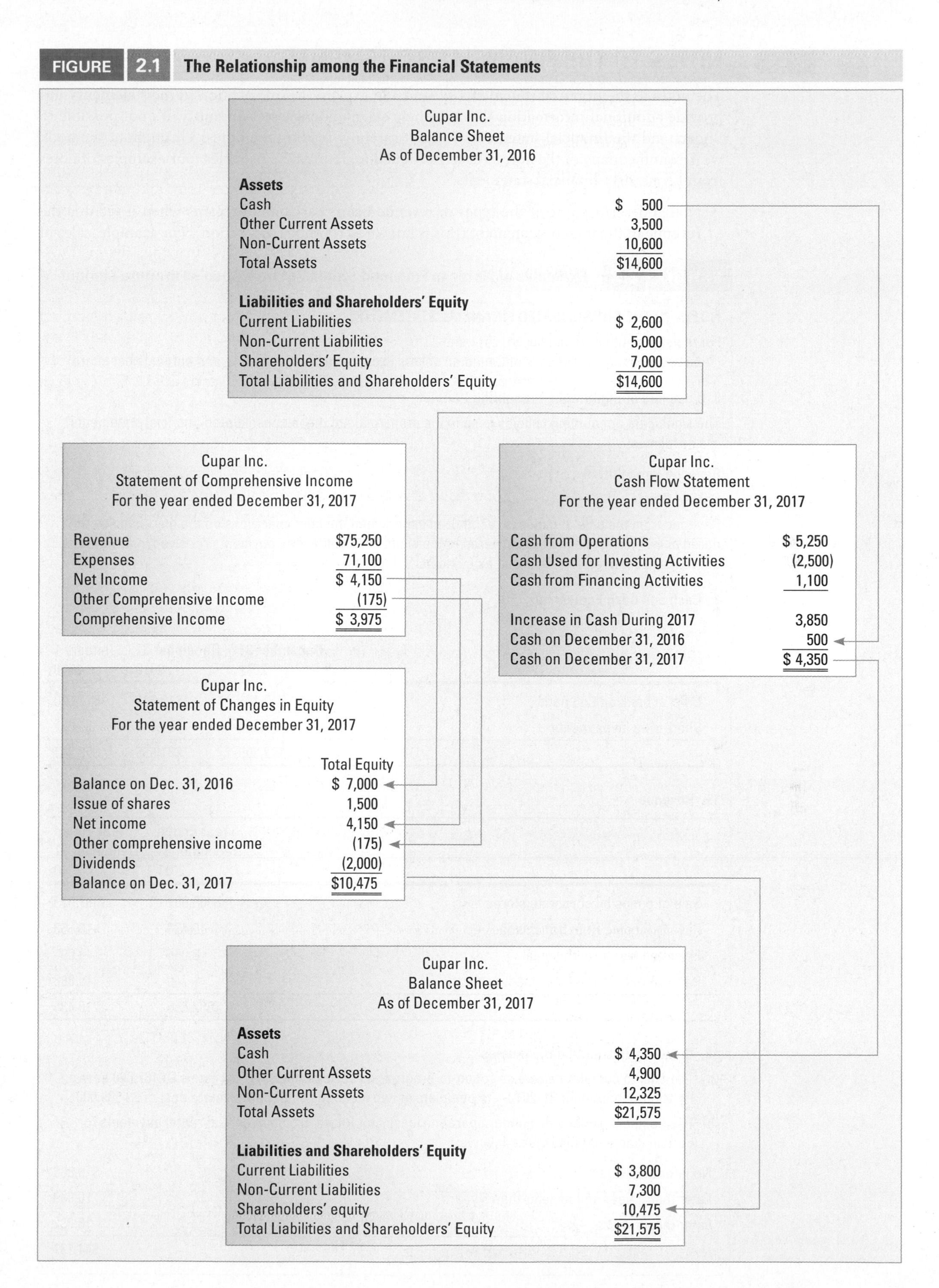

Cupar Inc.
Balance Sheet
As of December 31, 2016

Assets	
Cash	$ 500
Other Current Assets	3,500
Non-Current Assets	10,600
Total Assets	$14,600
Liabilities and Shareholders' Equity	
Current Liabilities	$ 2,600
Non-Current Liabilities	5,000
Shareholders' Equity	7,000
Total Liabilities and Shareholders' Equity	$14,600

Cupar Inc.
Statement of Comprehensive Income
For the year ended December 31, 2017

Revenue	$75,250
Expenses	71,100
Net Income	$ 4,150
Other Comprehensive Income	(175)
Comprehensive Income	$ 3,975

Cupar Inc.
Cash Flow Statement
For the year ended December 31, 2017

Cash from Operations	$ 5,250
Cash Used for Investing Activities	(2,500)
Cash from Financing Activities	1,100
Increase in Cash During 2017	3,850
Cash on December 31, 2016	500
Cash on December 31, 2017	$ 4,350

Cupar Inc.
Statement of Changes in Equity
For the year ended December 31, 2017

	Total Equity
Balance on Dec. 31, 2016	$ 7,000
Issue of shares	1,500
Net income	4,150
Other comprehensive income	(175)
Dividends	(2,000)
Balance on Dec. 31, 2017	$10,475

Cupar Inc.
Balance Sheet
As of December 31, 2017

Assets	
Cash	$ 4,350
Other Current Assets	4,900
Non-Current Assets	12,325
Total Assets	$21,575
Liabilities and Shareholders' Equity	
Current Liabilities	$ 3,800
Non-Current Liabilities	7,300
Shareholders' equity	10,475
Total Liabilities and Shareholders' Equity	$21,575

LO 3

NOTES TO THE FINANCIAL STATEMENTS

The notes to the financial statements expand and explain the information in the statements and provide additional information that may help stakeholders assess an entity. It's not possible to understand the financial statements without carefully reading the notes. Throughout the book we'll examine many of the notes. As an introduction, Exhibit 2.2 provides four examples of notes from Leon's 2011 financial statements:

- Note 3 describes one of the types of revenue Leon's earns and explains when it records the revenue in the income statement (this is known as revenue recognition). For example, sales of

EXHIBIT 2.2 Examples of Notes to Financial Statement from Leon's Furniture Limited

NOTES TO THE CONSOLIDATED FINANCIAL STATEMENTS

For the years ended December 31, 2011 and 2010
(Tabular amounts in thousands of Canadian dollars except shares outstanding and earnings per share)

3. Summary of Significant Accounting Policies

The significant accounting policies used in the preparation of these consolidated financial statements are as follows:

Revenue Recognition

Sale of Goods

Revenue from the sale of goods is recognized either when the customer picks up the merchandise ordered or when merchandise is delivered to the customer's home. Any payments received in advance of delivery are deferred and recorded as customer's deposits.

7. Cash and Cash Equivalents

	As at December 31 2011	As at December 31 2010	As at January 1 2010
Cash at bank and on hand	$ 2,181	$19,642	$ 7,620
Short-term investments	70,324	51,947	50,681
	$72,505	$71,589	$58,301

15. Revenue

	Year Ended December 31 2011	Year Ended December 31 2010
Sale of goods by corporate stores	$663,607	$691,079
Royalty income from franchisees	10,434	10,663
Extended warranty revenue	8,055	8,007
Rental income from investment property	740	686
	$682,836	$710,435

19. Commitments and Contingencies

(a) The cost to complete all construction-in-progress as at December 31, 2011 totals $4,407,000 at two locations (December 31, 2010—to complete at two locations at an approximate cost of $9,609,000).

(b) The Company is obligated under operating leases for future minimum annual rental payments for certain land and buildings as follows:

No later than 1 year	$ 5,860
Later than 1 year and no later than 5 years	19,989
Later than 5 years	18,282
	$44,131

goods to customers occur either when the customer picks up the merchandise or when the merchandise is delivered. The revenue recognition note is part of the summary of significant **accounting policies**, which are the methods, principles, and practices used by an entity to report its financial results. It has been mentioned several times that accounting standards, including IFRS, are flexible and often provide managers with different ways of accounting for a transaction or economic event. This note explains the accounting choices that managers have made and is crucial for understanding the financial statements and the impact of these choices on the amounts reported on the financial statements.

- Note 7 shows that the cash and cash equivalents of $72,505,000 reported on the balance sheet are made up of $2,181,000 in cash and $70,324,000 in short-term investments. The note doesn't describe the types of short-term investments.
- Note 15 shows the different categories of revenue Leon's earns. Most of the revenue comes from sales of goods in the stores it owns. Other revenue comes from royalty income from franchise stores, sale of extended warranties, and rental income.
- Note 19 provides information about Leon's commitments and contingent liabilities. This note provides information that isn't reflected in the financial statements at all. A contingent liability is a possible liability—whether it becomes a liability that is recorded in the balance sheet depends on a future event such as the decision of a judge. A commitment is an agreement to pay for goods and services when they're provided. Note 19(a) explains that the company will have to spend $4,407,000 to complete construction that was in progress on December 31, 2011. Note 19(b) describes the amount of lease payments Leon's has agreed to make.

This section has provided only a brief introduction of the importance of reading and understanding the notes for effectively using an entity's financial statements. At this point I recommend that you obtain the complete annual report of Leon's, or of another company if you prefer, and read through the notes and tie the information to the financial statements themselves. You can obtain the annual reports of Canadian public companies at www.sedar.com.

www.sedar.com

QUESTION FOR CONSIDERATION

You are a loan officer for a major bank and an executive from Leon's has come to ask for a $50,000,000 loan. What information on the balance sheet and statement of cash flows would be of interest to you?

ANSWER: As a banker, your main concern is Leon's ability to repay the loan. You would be interested in whether Leon's has the cash flow to support the interest on the loan and to pay back the principal when it's due. If the interest rate on the loan were 5 percent, Leon's would have to pay the bank $2,500,000 per year in interest. In 2011, Leon's had cash from operations of over $65 million, which easily covers the interest cost. If you were confident that Leon's could continue to generate that much cash from operations each year, you could assume that it would have little trouble paying the interest on the loan. You might also check Leon's debt-to-equity ratio to evaluate the risk of making the loan.

You would also be interested in knowing what other debts Leon's has and when they have to be repaid. The liability section of the balance sheet shows Leon's hasn't borrowed any money, which makes any loan less risky.

USERS OF LEON'S FINANCIAL STATEMENTS

Leon's financial statements give us insights into the identity of some of the stakeholders of the company. From the information in the financial statements, we can surmise that there are a number of stakeholders:

- *Shareholders* Since Leon's is a public company traded on the TSX, shareholders are an important stakeholder group. Some of Leon's shareholders are small investors who don't have access to information other than what is publicly available.

EXHIBIT 2.3

Example of a Balance Sheet Prepared in an Alternative Format—Edleun Group, Inc.

EDLEUN GROUP, INC.
CONSOLIDATED STATEMENTS OF FINANCIAL POSITION

(CDN $000s)	Note	December 31, 2011	December 31, 2010	January 1, 2010
Assets				
Non-current assets				
Property and equipment	5	$ 33,434	$ 18,717	$ –
Goodwill	6	22,940	9,183	–
Definite life intangible assets	6	340	–	
		56,714	27,900	–
Current assets				
Cash and cash equivalents		1,911	8,662	–
Accounts receivable	7	1,589	603	–
Prepaid and other expenses	8	3,606	243	–
Short term investments	9	39	204	–
		7,145	9,712	–
Total Assets		**$ 63,859**	**$ 37,612**	**$ –**
Liabilities				
Non-current liabilities				
Loans payable	10	$ 2,260	$ –	$ –
Deferred tax liability	13	42	34	–
		2,302	34	–
Current liabilities				
Accounts payable and accrued liabilities	11	2,877	1,369	75
Deferred revenue		399	80	–
		3,276	1,449	75
Total Liabilities		**5,578**	**1,483**	**75**
Shareholders' Equity				
Share capital	12	62,931	38,463	–
Equity settled share based compensation	12	1,330	1,089	–
Accumulated deficit		(5,980)	(3,423)	(75)
Total Shareholders' Equity		**58,281**	**36,129**	**(75)**
Total Liabilities and Shareholders' Equity		**$ 63,859**	**$ 37,612**	**$ –**

- *Creditors* Leon's owes over $75 million (trade and other payables) to various suppliers. These suppliers are interested in short-term liquidity (does Leon's have the liquidity to pay?). Some creditors will want to examine the financial statements as part of their assessment of how much credit they will offer Leon's.
- *Canada Revenue Agency* Leon's must file regular tax returns and the general purpose financial statements are required with the filing.

FORMAT OF GENERAL PURPOSE FINANCIAL STATEMENTS

LO 3

There is no one right way to format financial statements. Different formats are possible and allowable under IFRS. An example of an alternative balance sheet format is seen in Exhibit 2.3. Edleun Group Inc. is a Canadian childcare provider. Notice that in contrast to the Leon's balance sheet, non-current assets are at the top of the asset side and current assets at the bottom. On the liabilities and equity side, non-current liabilities appear first, followed by current liabilities, followed by shareholders' equity. It's important to recognize that as long as the information you need is presented, you can reorganize the statements to meet your requirements.

OTHER ACCOUNTING INFORMATION

LO 3

In addition to the general purpose financial statements, accountants can prepare any type of report to satisfy the needs of stakeholders. The only limitations to this are the entity's willingness to provide the information and its availability in the accounting system (an accounting system can provide only information that's entered into it).

Accounting reports that are prepared to meet the needs of specific stakeholders or a specific purpose are called **special purpose reports**. For example, a creditor might want a statement of cash inflows and outflows, along with budgeted cash flows for the next year, to assess the borrower's ability to pay its debts. A property manager might want a statement of revenues from a retailer so that the appropriate amount of rent can be charged, if rent is based on the store's sales. The list of special purposes is endless. Normally, special purpose reports, even by public companies, aren't publicly available and they don't have to be prepared in accordance with IFRS or any other set of standards.

Solved Problem

SNOWFLAKE'S SNOW REMOVAL COMPANY (SSRC)

Stan Snowflake recently started a new business clearing snow from residential driveways. Stan is a construction worker and while he tends to have a lot of work during the spring, summer, and fall, he doesn't usually work during the winter. Stan finds being idle quite frustrating so he decided that a snow removal business would be a good way to make some money and keep busy during the winter. As a result, he organized Snowflake's Snow Removal Company (SSRC), an unincorporated business. SSRC purchased a truck and offered snow removal for $250 for the entire winter, or $50 per month for the five months SSRC would be operating (November through March). In October, 10 people paid for the entire winter. Other people will pay monthly beginning in November. SSRC's balance sheet on October 31 is shown below.

Snowflake's Snow Removal Company
Balance Sheet
As at October 31

Assets		**Liabilities and Owners' Equity**	
Cash	$ 6,300	Bank loan	$ 5,000
Equipment	17,700	Accounts payable	6,500
		Services to be provided	2,500
			14,000
		Owners' equity	10,000
Total assets	$24,000	Total liabilities and owners' equity	$24,000

November and December were very busy for Stan and SSRC. There were a number of snowfalls, two of them quite heavy.

1. SSRC has 75 regular customers, 10 of whom paid in full in October. By the end of December, Stan had collected $5,600 from the customers who agreed to pay each month, and they owed $900. In addition, SSRC received $800 from people who stopped Stan on the street during heavy snowfalls and asked him to clean their driveway.
2. SSRC was so busy that Stan sometimes had to hire someone to help him do shovelling. He paid this person $450 for work done and owed her $100 at the end of December.
3. SSRC paid $700 for gas, oil, and service on the truck.
4. Stan estimates that the monthly depreciation of the truck and other equipment should be $700.

Required:

- Prepare income statements on the cash basis and the accrual basis for the two months ended December 31.
- Use the information from SSRC's balance sheet on October 31 to calculate the following amounts. Discuss the information provided by these results:
  - **a.** working capital
  - **b.** current ratio
  - **c.** debt-to-equity ratio

Solution:

1.

Snowflake's Snow Removal Company Income Statement
For the Two Months Ended December 31
(Prepared using the cash basis)

Revenue (cash collected)	$6,400
($5,600 from customers who pay monthly, plus $800 from people who stopped Stan on the street)	
Less: Expenses (cash spent)	
For employee ($450 paid for work done)	(450)
For oil, gas, and service ($700 for gas, oil, and service)	(700)
Net income (cash flow)	$5,250

Snowflake's Snow Removal Company Income Statement
For the Two Months Ended December 31
(Prepared using the accrual basis)

Revenue	$8,300
($5,600 from customers who pay monthly, plus $900 owed by customers who pay monthly, plus $1,000 for the people who paid in advance [10 customers × $50 per month × 2 months],* plus $800 from people who stopped Stan on the street)	
Less: Expenses	
For employee ($450 paid for work done, plus $100 owed)	(550)
For oil, gas, and service ($700 for gas, oil, and service)	(700)
Equipment depreciation (estimated at $700 monthly)	($1,400)
Net income	$5,650

*Even though customers paid in advance, SSRC earns the money on a monthly basis. Therefore, one-fifth of the advance payments should be recognized each month.

2. a. Working capital = Current assets − Current liabilities
($7,700) = $6,300 − $14,000

b. $\text{Current ratio} = \frac{\text{Current assets}}{\text{Current liabilities}} = \frac{\$6{,}300}{\$14{,}000} = 0.45$

c. $\text{Debt-to-equity-ratio} = \frac{\text{Liabilities}}{\text{Owner's equity}} = \frac{\$14{,}000}{\$10{,}000} = 1.4$

The working capital calculation and current ratio show that SSRC has more current liabilities than current assets. This is a potential problem because if cash wasn't forthcoming in the near future SSRC wouldn't be able to pay the bank or the truck dealer. However, on October 31 this wouldn't have been much of a concern because customers were expected to begin paying in November. The main concern on October 31 would have been signing up enough customers.

The debt-to-equity ratio indicates that SSRC has more liabilities than equity. It's not possible to tell whether this is a problem because there is no benchmark for comparison. However, the more debt an entity has, the more risk it faces. In this case, if SSRC isn't successful (if it didn't have enough paying customers), Stan would still be obliged to pay the bank and the truck dealer. SSRC probably doesn't have any major purchases left to make for the year, so it just has to concern itself with paying operating costs (wages, oil, gas, service) and using the remaining cash flow to pay debts and provide a profit to Stan.

SUMMARY OF KEY POINTS

LO 1 The IASB has developed a conceptual framework that provides a basis for preparing and presenting general purpose financial statements. The framework explains that the objective of financial reporting is to provide information to existing and potential providers of debt and equity investment. The framework identifies two fundamental qualitative characteristics that are required if information is to be useful. These are relevance and faithful representation. The framework also describes four enhancing qualitative characteristics that improve the usefulness of information that is relevant and faithfully represented. These are comparability, verifiability, timeliness, and understandability.

LO 2 There are four basic assumptions that underlie GAAP. The assumptions are: unit of measure, entity, going concern, and periodic reporting.

LO 3 A set of general purpose financial statements includes the balance sheet, the income statement and statement of comprehensive income, the statement of retained earnings/statement of changes in equity, the statement of cash flows, and the notes to the financial statements. The balance sheet summarizes the financial position of the entity—its assets, liabilities, and owners' equity—at a point in time. The income statement provides a measure of economic activity over a period. The statement of changes in equity summarizes changes to equity over a period while the statement of retained earnings summarizes the changes to retained earnings during a period. The statement of cash flows shows how cash during a period was obtained from and used for operating, investing, and financing activities. The notes to the financial statements expand and explain the information in the statements and provide additional information that may be helpful in assessing an entity. General purpose financial statements are designed to suit a broad set of users and uses and are usually prepared according to IFRS (or ASPE).

LO 4 The accounting equation is the conceptual foundation of accounting and is defined as

$$\text{Assets} = \text{Liabilities} + \text{Owners' equity}$$

All economic events entered into an accounting system must be summarized in terms of the accounting equation. The equality of the equation must always be maintained.

LO 5 There are five basic elements in the financial statements: assets, liabilities, owners' equity, revenues, and expenses. Assets are economic resources that provide future benefits to an entity. Liabilities are an entity's obligations to pay debts or provide goods or services. Owners' equity represents the owners' investment in an entity. Owners' investments can be made directly, by contributing assets to the entity, or indirectly, by reinvesting profits. Revenues represent economic benefits earned by providing goods and services to customers. Expenses are economic sacrifices made to earn revenue.

LO 6 The two most commonly used methods of accounting are the cash basis and the accrual basis. Cash accounting records only cash inflows and outflows. Under the cash basis, revenues are recorded when cash is received and expenses are recorded when cash is paid. Accrual accounting attempts to measure economic activity rather than just cash flows. Under the accrual basis, revenues are economic benefits earned by providing goods or services to customers and expenses are economic sacrifices incurred to earn revenue. Accrual accounting is more complicated than cash accounting and it requires judgment by managers, accountants, and stakeholders.

LO 7 Obtaining and examining financial statements is often only the first step in evaluating an entity. Financial statement numbers can be analyzed to obtain additional insights. One of the analytical tools available to stakeholders is ratios. The current ratio (current assets ÷ current liabilities) provides information about an entity's liquidity. The debt-to-equity ratio (debt ÷ equity) gives an indication of an entity's risk, and the gross margin percentage (gross margin ÷ sales) gives an indication of an entity's profitability.

FORMULA SUMMARY

$$\text{Accounting equation: Assets} = \text{Liabilities} + \text{Owners' Equity}$$

$$\text{Working capital} = \text{Current assets} - \text{Current liabilities}$$

$$\text{Current ratio} = \frac{\text{Current assets}}{\text{Current liabilities}}$$

$$\text{Debt-to-equity ratio} = \frac{\text{Liabilities}}{\text{Owners' (shareholders') equity}}$$

$$\text{Gross margin} = \text{Revenue} - \text{Cost of sales}$$

$$\text{Gross margin percentage} = \frac{\text{Gross margin}}{\text{Revenue}} \times 100\%$$

KEY TERMS

accounting equation, p. 44
accounting policies, p. 61
accrual accounting, p. 52
accumulated other comprehensive income, p. 57
asset, p. 44
balance sheet, p. 44
capital assets, p. 46
cash accounting, p. 52
cash from/used in financing activities, p. 58
cash from/used in investing activities, p. 58
cash from/used in operations, p. 58
common shares, p. 50
comparability, p. 37
comprehensive income, p. 56

consolidated financial statements, p. 39
cost of sales, p. 54
creditor, p. 44
current asset, p. 47
current liability, p. 47
current ratio, p. 49
debt-to-equity ratio, p. 50
deficit, p. 50
depreciation, p. 53
dividend, p. 50
enhancing qualitative characteristics, p. 36
entity concept, p. 38
expense, p. 53
faithful representation, p. 37
fiscal year, p. 41
fundamental qualitative characteristics, p. 36
general purpose financial statements, p. 39
going concern, p. 38
gross margin, p. 55
gross margin percentage, p. 55
income statement, p. 51
interest, p. 51
liability, p. 44
liquidity, p. 48
materiality, p. 43
net assets, p. 53
non-current asset, p. 47
non-current liability, p. 47
operating cycle, p. 47
other comprehensive income, p. 57
owners' equity, p. 44
partners' equity, p. 50
periodic-reporting assumption, p. 38
principal, p. 51
property, plant, and equipment, p. 46
proprietor's equity, p. 50
relevance, p. 36
retained earnings, p. 50
revenue, p. 53
shareholders' equity, p. 50
special purpose report, p. 63
statement of cash flows, p. 58
statement of retained earnings, p. 57
statement of changes in equity, p. 57
timeliness, p. 37
understandability, p. 37
unit-of-measure assumption, p. 38
verifiability, p. 37
working capital, p. 48
working capital ratio, p. 49

SIMILAR TERMS

The left column provides alternative terms that are sometimes used for the accounting terms introduced in this chapter. The accounting terms used in the chapter are listed in the right column.

accrual basis of accounting	**accrual accounting, p. 52**
accounts receivable	**trade receivables, p. 47**
amortization	**depreciation, p. 53**
balance sheet	**statement of financial position, p. 35**
capital assets, fixed assets	**property, plant, and equipment, p. 46**
capital stock	**common shares, p. 50**
cash basis of accounting	**cash accounting, p. 52**
cash flow statement	**statement of cash flows, p. 58**
cash from operating activities	**cash from operations, p. 58**
common stock	**common shares, p. 50**
cost of goods sold	**cost of sales, p. 54**
depletion	**depreciation, p. 53**
finance income	**interest income, p. 51**
gross profit	**gross margin, p. 55**
long-term assets, long-lived assets	**non-current asset, p. 47**
operating income	**operating profit, p. 55**

partners' equity (for a partnership)	**owners' equity, p. 44**
sales, sales revenue	**revenue, p. 53**
share capital	**common shares, p. 50**
shareholders' equity (for a corporation)	**owners' equity, p. 44**
statement of earnings, statement of income, statement of profit and loss, statement of operations	**income statement, p. 51**
statement of financial position	**balance sheet, p. 44**
stockholders' equity (for a corporation)	**owners' equity, p. 44**

ASSIGNMENT MATERIALS

Questions

Q2-1. What are the components of a complete package of general purpose financial statements?

Q2-2. Explain the difference between cash and accrual accounting.

Q2-3. Do you think all entities should be required to use the same format for financial statements? Explain.

Q2-4. What are general purpose financial statements? What problems does any individual stakeholder have with using general purpose statements?

Q2-5. Why are the financial statements produced by public companies in Canada considered general purpose financial statements?

Q2-6. The balance sheet has been compared to a photograph. Explain.

Q2-7. Explain why net income calculated using cash accounting can be different from net income calculated using accrual accounting.

Q2-8. Why is cash a crucial asset for an entity to have? What are the consequences of not having enough cash?

Q2-9. Explain each of the following terms in your own words and give an example of each:
a. asset
b. liability
c. owners' equity
d. dividend
e. revenue
f. expense

Q2-10. Define the following accounting measurements and explain how and why they would be used when evaluating an entity:
a. working capital
b. current ratio
c. debt-to-equity ratio
d. gross margin
e. gross margin percentage

Q2-11. Explain why each of the following would be classified as assets on an entity's balance sheet:
a. cash
b. payment to a lawyer for services to be provided later
c. airplane belonging to an airline
d. shares of other corporations owned by the entity

Q2-12. Explain why each of the following would be considered liabilities on an entity's balance sheet:
a. amounts owing to suppliers of inventory
b. advances received from customers for services to be provided in the future
c. bank loan

Q2-13. Under IFRS, money spent on research by companies in the biotechnology, pharmaceutical, high technology, and other industries isn't reported on the balance sheet as an asset. In your opinion, is the money companies spend on research an asset? Explain your thinking. Based on what you read in this chapter, why do you think money spent on research isn't considered an asset according to IFRS? What do you think the implications of this treatment of research costs are for stakeholders?

Q2-14. Explain the difference between common shares and retained earnings in the shareholders' equity section of a corporation's balance sheet.

Q2-15. What is comprehensive income? How does it differ from net income?

Q2-16. Explain the concept of liquidity. Why is evaluating liquidity important?

Q2-17. By law, distillers of Irish whiskey must age the whiskey for a minimum of three years, although the whiskey is often aged for a much longer time. If you were evaluating the liquidity of a distiller of Irish whiskey, how would you deal with the whiskey inventory?

Q2-18. Explain why net income results in an increase in owners' equity.

Q2-19. Explain why paying dividends results in a decrease in retained earnings of a corporation.

Q2-20. Why is knowing an entity's ability to generate cash flow so important to assessing the survival of the entity?

Q2-21. Virtually all entities prepare financial statements on an annual basis. For example, Leon's prepares its statements for a calendar year. Provide three reasons why entities report on an annual basis. In answering, consider the qualitative characteristics of useful financial information described in the IFRS conceptual framework.

Q2-22. It's normal for entities to present financial statements for more than one year rather than for just the most recent year. Provide reasons why it's useful for stakeholders to receive more than one year's financial statements.

Q2-23. Explain why different entities will organize the presentation of their financial statements in different ways (use different formats). For example, why would some companies present a lot of detail in their statements, whereas others might present as little as possible? In answering, consider different users and uses of the statements.

Q2-24. Why is it important for financial statements to have the qualitative characteristics of relevance and faithful representation? If you had to choose between having information that was more relevant but less representationally faithful or information that was more representationally faithful but less relevant, which would you pick? Explain.

Q2-25. What are the enhancing qualitative characteristics of financial information? Explain how these characteristics make information more relevant.

Q2-26. Identify and explain the four assumptions that underlie IFRS.

Q2-27. The requirement of periodic reporting is the source of some of the problems and challenges that contemporary accounting faces. Why do you think this is the case? In responding, consider the discussion in the chapter about the judgment required to decide when revenue and expenses should be recorded.

Q2-28. What unit of measure is typically used in the financial statements of Canadian companies? What are the some of the benefits and drawbacks of using the Canadian dollar as the unit of measure?

Exercises

E2-1. **(Accounting equation, LO 4)** For each of the following independent situations, fill in the shaded area with the appropriate dollar amount.

	Assets	=	Liabilities	+	Owners' Equity
Situation 1	$680,000				$295,000
Situation 2	100,000		40,000		
Situation 3	255,000				89,000
Situation 4			$430,000		620,000

E2-2. **(Accounting equation, LO 4)** For each of the following independent situations, fill in the shaded area with the appropriate dollar amount. You are provided with assets and liabilities on December 31, 2017, owners' equity on January 1, 2017, and revenue and expenses for 2017.

	Assets on Dec. 31, 2017	=	Liabilities on Dec. 31, 2017	+	Owners' Equity on Jan. 1, 2017	+	Revenue in 2017	−	Expenses in 2017
Situation 1	$		$29,000		$110,000		$295,000		$210,000
Situation 2	648,000				213,000		550,000		250,000
Situation 3	245,000		220,000		(50,000)				300,000
Situation 4	32,000		10,000		35,000		65,000		

E2-3. **(Classification of balance sheet accounts, LO 3, 5)** Sheho Bulk Foods Ltd. sells a wide range of foods in bulk to retail and commercial customers. Classify each of the following of Sheho's balance sheet accounts as a current asset, non-current asset, current liability, or non-current liability. Briefly explain your classification:

a. inventory of food products on display in the store
b. accounts payable owed to suppliers; these are usually paid within 60 days of receiving an invoice from the supplier
c. accounts receivable from commercial customers; payment is required within 30 days
d. bins used to store inventory
e. art work in Sheho's president's office
f. a bank loan that the bank can ask the company to repay at any time
g. an account receivable that will be paid by the customer in two years
h. a loan that is to be repaid in full in three years

E2-4. **(Calculate ending retained earnings, LO 3)** On December 31, 2017, Canmore Inc. (Canmore) reported retained earnings of $160,000. For the year ended December 31, 2018, Canmore had net income of $105,000 and paid dividends of $75,000.

Required:

Calculate Canmore's retained earnings on December 31, 2018.

E2-5. **(Prepare a statement of comprehensive income, LO 3)** During the year ended December 31, 2016, Speers Ltd. had revenues of $2,250,000 and expenses of $1,875,000. In addition, the company had other comprehensive income of $37,500.

Required:

Prepare an income statement and a statement of comprehensive income for Speers Ltd. for the year ended December 31, 2016.

E2-6. **(Prepare a statement of comprehensive income, LO 3)** During the year ended August 31, 2017, Vaughn Ltd. had revenues of $25,000,000 and expenses of $16,850,000. In addition, the company had other comprehensive income of $−155,000.

Required:

Prepare an income statement and a statement of comprehensive income for Vaughn Ltd. for the year ended August 31, 2017.

E2-7. **(Calculate ending retained earnings, LO 3)** Minden Corporation was incorporated on August 1, 2015, by five shareholders who each invested $100,000 in cash in exchange for common shares. Minden's year end is July 31. In its first year of business, Minden had net income of $119,500. For its years ended July 31, 2017 and 2018, its second and third years of operation, Minden reported net income of $212,000 and $291,000, respectively. In its first year, Minden didn't pay any dividends, but in fiscal 2017 it paid $55,000 in dividends and in 2018 it paid $175,000 in dividends.

Required:

Calculate Minden's retained earnings on July 31, 2018.

E2-8. **(Classification of cash flows, LO 3)** Schomberg Motors Ltd. is a car dealership that sells new and used cars and offers servicing to customers. Classify each of the following cash flows that Schomberg incurred as operating, financing, or investing activities:

a. sale of a new car to a customer
b. purchase of new van for use as a shuttle for customers leaving their cars for servicing
c. purchase of new cars from the manufacturer for sale to customers
d. deposit paid by a customer for a vehicle that will be delivered next year
e. sale of common shares to an investor to pay for an expansion
f. purchase of a piece of land to build the expanded facility
g. repayment of a bank loan
h. sale of old equipment used for providing service to customers
i. payment of utilities

E2-9. **(Classification of cash flows, LO 3)** Consider the following cash flows incurred by Leon's. Classify each as operating, financing, or investing activities:

a. sale of furniture to customers
b. cash paid to renovate a store
c. purchase of new carpeting for stores
d. sale of old shelving
e. a new bank loan
f. wages paid to employees
g. purchase of furniture for sale in a store
h. payment of a dividend to shareholders
i. purchase of advertising in newspapers promoting merchandise on sale
j. refund to a customer who purchased products that were damaged

E2-10. **(Prepare a balance sheet, LO 3, 5)** You have received the following alphabetical list of balance sheet accounts for Perkins Outfitters Ltd. (Perkins), a retail supplier of outdoor clothing and equipment. Organize the accounts into Perkins' balance sheet as of December 31, 2017.

Accounts receivable	$20,000	Long-term debt (non-current portion)	$100,000
Advances paid by customers for goods to be provided in the future	5,000	Long-term debt-due in less than one year	20,000
Amounts owed to suppliers	95,000	Long-term loan from shareholder	45,000
Bank loan	125,000	Property and equipment	290,000
Cash	8,000	Rent paid in advance	8,000
Common shares	150,000	Retained earnings	141,000
Inventory	175,000	Taxes payable	20,000
Investment in shares of other companies	200,000		

E2-11. **(Complete statements of income and retained earnings, LO 3, 4)** Selkirk Corporation began operations in 2016. Its summarized financial statements are presented below. Fill in the shaded areas to complete the financial statements. Begin your work with 2016 and move forward from there.

	2018	2017	2016
Revenues	$	$265,000	$225,000
Expenses	230,000		155,000
Net income	92,000	75,000	
Retained earnings at the beginning of the year			0
Dividends declared during the year		32,000	15,000
Retained earnings at the end of the year	148,000		55,000
Common shares at the end of the year	105,000	100,000	
Liabilities at the end of the year	165,000		125,000
Assets at the end of the year		347,000	275,000

E2-12. **(Complete statements of income and retained earnings, LO 3, 4)** Sparwood Ltd. began operations in 2015. Its summarized financial statements are presented below. Fill in the shaded areas to complete the financial statements. Begin your work with 2015 and move forward from there.

	2017	2016	2015
Revenues	$	$95,000	$70,000
Expenses	105,500	92,000	
Net income	(3,500)		20,000
Retained earnings at the beginning of the year			0
Dividends declared during the year	6,500		7,000
Retained earnings at the end of the year		10,000	
Common shares at the end of the year	37,000	35,000	
Liabilities at the end of the year	23,000		15,000
Assets at the end of the year		65,000	53,000

E2-13. **(Classification of cash flows, LO 3)** During 2014 Argentia Ltd. entered into the following cash transactions. Classify each transaction as operating, financing, or investing cash flows and indicate whether it's a cash inflow or outflow. Explain your thinking in each case.

a. Inventory is purchased for $100,000.
b. Dividends of $75,000 are paid to shareholders.
c. $500,000 is borrowed from the bank.
d. Office furniture is purchased for $20,000 to furnish the president's office.
e. Four delivery trucks are sold for $22,500.
f. Common shares are sold to investors for $500,000.
g. Payments of $30,000 are collected from customers.
h. Insurance for the next two years costing $8,000 is purchased.

E2-14. **(Prepare a statement of cash flows, LO 3)** You have been provided the following cash flow activities about Arcola Inc. for the year ended December 31, 2017. Organize this information into a statement of cash flows. Use Leon's statement in Exhibit 2.1 as a model. Be sure to provide a reconciliation to the cash balance on December 31, 2017:

• Cash balance on December 31, 2016	$?
• Cash balance on December 31, 2017	19,000
• Cash from operations	184,000
• Dividends paid to shareholders	50,000
• Sale of commons shares to new investors	310,000

- Purchase of investments in other companies 350,000
- Sale of old equipment 25,000
- Purchase of land 175,000

E2-15. **(Prepare a statement of cash flows, LO 3)** You have been provided the following cash flow activities about Dugald Ltd. for the year ended December 31, 2018. Organize this information into a statement of cash flows. Use Leon's statement in Exhibit 2.1 as a model. Be sure to provide a reconciliation to the cash balance on December 31, 2018:

- Cash balance on December 31, 2018 $75,000
- Cash balance on December 31, 2017 ?
- Cash from operations 245,000
- Issue of long-term debt 150,000
- Sale of land 45,000
- Purchase of equipment 210,000
- Repayment of bank loan 85,000

E2-16. **(Classifying items on the financial statements, LO 3, 5)** Name the financial statement (balance sheet, statement of comprehensive income/income statement, statement of changes in equity, statement of cash flows) on which each of the following items would appear. Indicate the part of the statement each item would appear (e.g., assets, expenses, cash from operations, etc.). Some items may appear on more than one statement.

a. Revenue
b. Property and equipment
c. Inventory
d. Cash received from selling common shares to investors
e. Common shares
f. Wage expense
g. Cash spent paying employees
h. Long-term debt
i. Other comprehensive income

E2-17. **(Classifying items on the financial statements, LO 3, 5)** Name the financial statement (balance sheet, income statement, statement of changes in equity, statement of cash flows) on which each of the following items would appear. Indicate the part of the statement each item would appear (e.g., assets, expenses, cash from operations, etc.). Some items may appear on more than one statement.

a. Accounts receivable
b. Retained earnings
c. Cash received from customers paying in advance for services to be provided next year
d. Advertising expense
e. Accumulated other comprehensive income
f. Taxes payable
g. Total assets
h. Cash received from the bank as a loan
i. Credit sales to customers

E2-18. **(Calculation of ratios, LO 7)** Below is a simplified balance sheet for Summerside Inc. (Summerside):

Summerside Inc.
Balance Sheet
As at December 31, 2017

Assets		**Liabilities and shareholders' equity**	
Current assets	$2,250,000	Current liabilities	$1,750,000
Non-current assets	6,250,000	Non-current liabilities	2,500,000
		Shareholders' equity	4,250,000
Total assets	$8,500,000	Total liabilities and shareholders' equity	$8,500,000

Required:

Calculate the following on December 31, 2017 using Summerside's balance sheet. Explain what each amount tells you.

a. working capital
b. current ratio
c. debt-to-equity ratio

E2-19. **(Calculation of ratios, LO 3, 7)** Consider the following alphabetical list of income statement accounts for Sussex Ltd. (Sussex) for the year ended September 30, 2018:

Cost of sales	$ 375,000
Depreciation expense	174,000
Income tax expense	39,000
Interest expense	72,000
Other expenses	75,000
Rent expense	110,000
Salaries, wages, and benefits expense	280,000
Sales	1,525,000
Selling, general, and administrative expenses	201,000

Required:

a. Prepare an income statement for Sussex for the year ended September 30, 2018.
b. What is net income for the year?
c. What is Sussex' gross margin for 2018?
d. What is Sussex' gross margin percentage for 2018?

E2-20. **(Calculation and interpretation of the debt-to-equity ratio, LO 4, 7)** You are provided with the following information from the December 31, 2016 to 2018 balance sheets of Peguis Inc.:

Peguis Inc.
Extracts from Balance Sheets
On December 31

	2018	2017	2016
Current liabilities	$ 259,875	$ 247,500	$ 225,000
Non-current liabilities	1,656,000	1,380,000	1,150,000
Common shares	500,000	500,000	500,000
Retained earnings	1,449,000	1,050,000	750,000

Required:

a. Calculate the debt-to-equity ratio for each year.
b. Describe how the ratio has changed over the three years.
c. Interpret why the change in the ratio took place. What changes in the accounts caused the ratio to change as it did?
d. Explain what the change in the ratio means to Peguis' shareholders.

E2-21. **(Calculation and interpretation of the gross margin percentage, LO 4, 7)** You are provided with the following summarized income statements for Oxdrift Inc. for 2016 to 2018:

Oxdrift Inc.
Summarized Income Statements
For the year ended December 31

	2018	2017	2016
Sales	$247,000	$232,180	$220,571
Cost of goods sold	151,905	147,434	143,371
Gross margin	95,095	84,746	77,200
Other expenses	74,100	67,332	61,760
Net income	$ 20,995	$ 17,414	$ 15,440

Required:

a. Calculate the gross margin percentage for each year.
b. Describe what's happened to the gross margin percentage over the period and explain the implications for net income.
c. What would net income be in 2017 and 2018 if the gross margin percentage in those years was the same as in 2016?

E2-22. **(Prepare income statements using cash and accrual accounting, LO 3, 6)** You have been provided the following information about Kedgwick Company, a small proprietorship, as of the end of its first year of operations. Assume that all supplies were used up at year end.

Cash collected from customers	$8,000
Amounts owing from customers	1,200
Amounts paid to suppliers	4,700
Amounts owing to suppliers	1,100

Required:

Calculate net income on the cash basis and on the accrual basis for Kedgwick Company. Explain why the cash basis and the accrual basis result in different amounts of income.

E2-23. **(Prepare income statements using cash and accrual accounting, LO 3, 6)** You have been provided the following information about Lunenberg Ltd. (Lunenberg) as of the end of its first year of operations.

Cash collected from customers	$413,000
Amounts owing from customers	39,200
Amounts paid to suppliers for business supplies	121,450
Amounts owing to suppliers for business supplies	28,350
Business supplies on hand at the end of the year	9,800
Amounts paid to employees for work done	61,250
Amounts owing to employees for work done	7,700
Advances paid to employees for work that will be done in the future	3,500
Depreciation of assets	14,000
Income taxes paid	26,250

Required:

Calculate net income on the cash basis and on the accrual accounting basis for Lunenberg. Explain why the cash basis and the accrual basis result in different amounts of income.

Problems

P2-1. **(Complete a set of financial statements, LO 3, 4, 5)** Below are three years of balance sheets, income statements, and statements of retained earnings for Auberndale Ltd.

Required:

a. Replace the missing information in the shaded areas with the appropriate amount. Begin your analysis with 2015 and work forward.
b. If you were a banker, would you lend Auberndale Ltd. $5,000,000? Explain your answer. What additional information would you require to make your decision whether to lend? Explain.

Auberndale Ltd.
Balance Sheets
As at December 31
(in thousands of dollars)

	2017	2016	2015
Current Assets			
Cash	$	$	$
Accounts Receivable	22,134	19,992	17,850
Inventory	39,270	31,416	28,560
Prepaid Assets	2,142	714	1,428
Total Current Assets	70,686		50,694
Land	8,925	8,925	8,925
Plant & Equipment	53,550	49,266	
Accumulated Depreciation		(22,134)	(19,278)
Other Assets	3,285	5,850	7,311
Total Non-Current Assets			40,512
Total Assets	$	$	$
Current Liabilities			
Accounts Payable	$21,420	$ 20,703	$16,422
Bank Loan Payable		6,168	2,856
Total Current Liabilities	23,805	26,871	
Mortgage Payable	12,138		15,708
Total Liabilities	35,943		34,986
Shareholders' Equity			
Common Shares			12,138
Retained Earnings		52,452	
Total Shareholders' Equity	74,085	64,740	
Total Liabilities and Shareholders' Equity	$	$105,741	$

Auberndale Ltd.
Income Statement
For the Year Ended December 31
(in thousands of dollars)

	2017	2016	2015
Revenue	$178,500	$160,650	$
Cost of Goods Sold			99,960
Gross Margin		49,980	46,410
Expenses			
Selling	22,134		17,850
Administrative	10,710	9,996	9,639
Depreciation	4,641	3,570	2,856
Interest	1,785	2,712	
Total Expenses		35,913	33,201
Income before Income Taxes	14,280	14,067	
Income Taxes	5,427		4,113
Net Income	$	$	$ 9,096

Auberndale Ltd.
Statement of Retained Earnings
For the Year Ended December 31
(in thousands of dollars)

	2017	2016	2015
Retained Earnings, Beginning of Year	$	$	$ 35,700
Net Income		9,156	
Dividends	786	786	714
Retained Earnings, End of Year	$	$	$

P2-2. **(Preparing an income statement, LO 3, 5)** The junior accountant for Josselin Ltd. was asked to prepare an income statement and statement of comprehensive income for the year ended October 31, 2017. The accountant summarized the accounts he thought were necessary to prepare the statement but isn't sure how to proceed. Use the information provided by the junior accountant to prepare the income statement and statement of comprehensive income (you can combine the statements into one or prepare two separate statements). Note that not all the information provided may be appropriate to use in the income statement.

Accounts receivable	$ 510,000	Other comprehensive income	$ (75,000)
Cash from operations	375,000	Property, plant, and equipment	1,870,000
Cost of sales	2,800,000	Retained earnings	4,356,000
Depreciation expense	224,000	Revenue	5,750,000
Dividends	300,000	Salaries and wages expense	545,000
Income tax expense	300,000	Selling, general, and administrative expense	650,000
Interest expense	185,000	Wages payable	210,000

P2-3. **(Prepare and interpret an income statement, LO 3, 7)** You are provided with the following accounting information for Hanmer Ltd. (Hanmer), a retail electronics store, for the years ended December 31, 2016 and 2017:

	2017	2016
Advertising and promotion expense	$ 250,000	$ 187,500
Cost of inventory sold	850,000	801,000
General and administrative expense	270,000	225,750
Income tax expense	140,625	111,000
Miscellaneous expense	55,000	48,000
Rent expense	43,500	41,250
Salaries, wages, and commissions expense	426,600	337,500
Sales	2,370,000	2,138,250
Utilities expense	11,850	11,400

Required:

a. Prepare income statements for Hanmer for 2016 and 2017.
b. What was Hanmer's gross margin and gross margin percentage each year? In which year do you think Hanmer was more successful? Explain.
c. Suppose Hanmer had the same gross margin percentage in 2017 as it did in 2016. What would its gross margin and net income have been in 2017? Explain the impact of the different gross margin on Hamner's performance.
d. Examine your income statement and explain the change in net income from 2016 to 2017.

P2-4. **(Explaining assets, LO 5)** Consider the following items that Leon's would have and explain why, according to IFRS, each would be considered an asset. If an item isn't an asset, explain why not.

a. computers used by sales people in the stores
b. tables and chairs used for conversations between customers and sales people
c. television promotion for a new product (that's sold at Leon's stores) paid for by the product's producer (not by Leon's)
d. large, brightly lit sign outside the store
e. furniture badly damaged in an in-store accident
f. money owed to Leon's by a senior executive
g. money paid in advance by Leon's for rent on a building housing a store

P2-5. **(Explaining assets, LO 5)** General Motors Corporation (GM) is one of the world's largest automakers. Explain why, according to IFRS, GM would consider each of the following items an asset. If an item isn't an asset, explain why not.

a. partially completed vehicle
b. shares in other companies that GM owns
c. a vehicle that was involved in a collision during testing
d. tools employees use to assemble cars
e. computer equipment and software used by engineers to design new cars
f. the General Motors name
g. amounts owed to GM by dealerships for cars purchased
h. amounts owed to GM by a bankrupt dealership for cars purchased

P2-6. **(Explaining liabilities, LO 5)** General Motors Corporation (GM) is one of the world's largest automakers. Explain why, according to IFRS, GM would classify each of the following items as a liability. If you don't think an item is a liability, explain why not.

a. wages owed to employees
b. amounts withheld from employees' pay for income taxes.
c. commitment made to employees while they are working to provide them with dental care when they retire

d. amounts owed to suppliers of auto parts
e. estimated cost of providing warranty service to people who have purchased GM cars and trucks
f. amount GM is being sued for by an employee who was fired. The lawsuit hasn't been settled or gone to court yet.

P2-7. **(Prepare a balance sheet, LO 3, 4)** Andrea Reed is in her fourth year at a business school in Nova Scotia. Recently, Andrea was asked by her brother Nathan to help him prepare a personal balance sheet. Nathan needed the balance sheet because he was applying for a scholarship at a prestigious art school and the school required the information to help it assess Nathan's financial need. Andrea sat down with Nathan to go over his situation and she obtained the following information:

a. Nathan has $844 in his bank account.
b. Nathan purchased a used car from his uncle three years ago. He paid $4,500 for the car and he thinks he should be able to use it for another two years.
c. Nathan is owed $750 for some decorating he did for a local social group's recent fundraising party.
d. Nathan owes $2,000 to a local bank for a job training program he took a couple of years ago. He must begin to pay back the money once he accepts a full-time job or in five years, whichever comes first.
e. About six months ago, Nathan bought a computer from a local store. The computer cost $1,200 and he paid the seller $700 at the time he purchased it and he must pay $50 a month until the computer is paid for. Nathan expects he will be able to use the computer for four years.
f. Nathan's personal property such as furniture, books, jewellery, etc. cost him about $6,000.

Required:

a. Use the information provided to prepare a balance sheet for Nathan. Provide an explanation for why you classified each item as you did (asset, liability, equity). The difference between assets and liabilities will give you Nathan's equity.
b. How do you think the balance sheet would help the art school assess whether Nathan should receive financial assistance?
c. What additional information do you think the school would want before making a decision to offer financial assistance?

P2-8. **(Prepare a balance sheet, LO 3, 4)** In addition to the information provided in P2-7 you also learn the following about Nathan's assets:

a. Nathan thinks the car could be sold for about $2,200.
b. A friend of Nathan's recently offered him $1,000 for the computer.
c. Nathan is unlikely to receive more than $1,000 for his personal property.

Required:

a. Use the additional information along with the information provided in P2-7 to prepare a revised personal balance sheet for Nathan. Explain the choices you made in preparing the statement.
b. Compare your balance sheet with the one you prepared in P2-7. Which do you think would be more useful to the art school in assessing Nathan's need for financial assistance? Explain.
c. What problems arise when using market values of Nathan's assets instead of the cost? What are some of the benefits of using the cost of the assets? Is the balance sheet prepared using market value information more or less useful than the balance sheet prepared using the cost information?

P2-9. **(Prepare a balance sheet, LO 3, 4)** Louis Davis is a dentist with a practice in a small town in Manitoba. Recently, he separated from his wife and they are currently negotiating how they will divide their assets when their divorce proceedings conclude. As part of the process, Louis' lawyer has asked for a balance sheet for his dental practice to help value it. Louis has asked you to prepare the balance sheet. You gather the following information from Louis:

i. Louis purchased all his equipment eight years ago when he started his practice. The total cost of all the equipment was $100,000. He expects to replace all the equipment in four years.
ii. He purchased furniture and decorations for his office four years ago for $22,000. He expects the furniture and decorations to last for about ten years.
iii. Patients owe Louis $19,000.
iv. Louis owes suppliers $12,000 for goods and services he purchased for his practice.
v. The practice has $4,750 in its bank account.
vi. Louis owes his staff $2,500. This amount will be paid on the next payday, in two weeks.
vii. Louis has a bank loan outstanding for $10,000.
viii. Louis keeps supplies he needs in his practice. The cost of the supplies he currently has on hand is $750.

Required:

a. Use the information provided to prepare a balance sheet for Louis' dental practice. Provide an explanation for why you classified each item as you did (asset, liability, equity). The difference between assets and liabilities will give you Louis' equity.
b. As a judge in this case, how would you use the balance sheet in deciding how to value Louis' practice?
c. What additional information would you as judge might want before deciding how to value Louis' practice?

P2-10. **(Prepare a balance sheet, LO 3, 4)** In addition to the information provided in P2-9, you also learn the following about Louis' assets:

i. Louis thinks that if he closed his practice he could sell his list of patients to another dentist for $125,000.
ii. If Louis tried to sell his equipment he would receive about $25,000.
iii. Louis would be unlikely to receive any money if he tried to sell the furniture and decorations.

Required:

a. Use the additional information along with the information in P2-9 to prepare a revised personal balance sheet for Louis' dental practice. Explain the choices you made in preparing the statement.
b. Compare your balance sheet with the one you prepared in P2-9. Which do you think would be more useful for valuing Louis' practice? Explain.
c. What problems arise when using market values of Louis' assets instead of the cost? What are some of the benefits of using the cost of the assets? Is the balance sheet prepared using market value information more or less useful than the balance sheet prepared using the cost information?

P2-11. **(Prepare income statements using cash and accrual accounting, LO 3, 5, 6)** Joe Krazman is a first-year university student and an excellent tennis player. During the winter semester Joe thought that he could use his tennis ability as a way to make money to pay for his education. He started offering lessons in May and he was successful right from the get-go. During May, he received $3,500 in cash from people who purchased lessons. He's owed another $400 from a couple of people who took lessons but said they would be able to pay him in June. He also received $500 from a family that wanted to guarantee lessons when school ended at the end of June. To ensure that he had a proper location to give lessons he purchased time at his tennis club. During May, he paid the club $1,000 for court time. At the end of May $350 of the amount hadn't been spent, but Joe will be able to use it to purchase time in June. In late May, Joe was so busy he asked a friend to help him out with lessons. He paid the friend $250 during the month and owed him $50 at the end of the month for lessons he gave in May. To generate more business in the summer Joe began advertising in his community newspaper. The ads appeared in May but he hasn't received an invoice yet so they won't be paid until June. Joe was told the ads would cost $75. Joe also spent $150 on supplies such as tennis balls during May.

Required:

Prepare income statements for Joe's business for May using cash and accrual accounting. Explain why the two methods result in different amounts of income. Do you think Joe's business is successful? Explain your answer.

P2-12. **(Prepare income statements using cash and accrual accounting, LO 3, 5, 6)** Hikaru Sulu owns and operates a small carpet cleaning business. During May, he had the following activity:

i. Mr. Sulu charged customers $10,800 for cleaning carpets during May. He collected $8,500 of the amount charged. The remainder is due in June.
ii. Mr. Sulu signed a contract with a condominium association to clean carpets in the complex. Work is to begin in mid-June. Mr. Sulu received a $3,500 deposit for the work.
iii. He collected $2,150 for carpet cleaning he did in March and April.
iv. Mr. Sulu purchased supplies during the month for $1,500. He paid $800 in cash and the remainder must be paid within 60 days. All the supplies purchased during May were used up by month's end.
v. Mr. Sulu paid $1,200 for supplies that he purchased and used in April.
vi. Mr. Sulu's employee received $2,000 for his work. Of that amount, $1,800 was for work done in May and $200 was owed to him at the end of April. Mr. Sulu owes the employee $700 for work done in May.
vii. Mr. Sulu incurred and paid $1,600 for other costs incurred for May.
viii. Mr. Sulu estimates depreciation of $500 for the month on his equipment, tools, and vehicle.

Required:

Prepare income statements for Mr. Sulu's business for May using cash and accrual accounting. Explain why the two methods result in different amounts of income. Which statement do you think gives a better indication of how the business performed? Do you think the business was successful in May? Explain.

P2-13. **(Correcting a balance sheet, LO 3, 4, 5)** A friend of yours recently started a small business and he's prepared a balance sheet at the end of the first year. He's puzzled because the balance sheet doesn't balance and he isn't sure why. Examine the balance sheet below and make any corrections needed. Your friend also said there were a couple of items he didn't know what to do with: deposits from customers (the cash received was included in the cash balance)—$2,000; equipment—$18,000.

Balance Sheet as of September 30

Assets		Liabilities and shareholders' equity	
Cash	$ 8,000	Bank loan	$16,000
Accounts payable	4,200	Accounts receivable	2,400
Inventory	10,000	Common shares	8,000
Cash dividend paid	2,200	Net income	10,400

P2-14 **(Calculation and interpretation of the gross margin percentage, LO 3, 7)** You are examining the 2016 income statement of Ferintosh Pharmacies Ltd., a chain of pharmacies you've invested in. It's a very competitive business and the company recently announced that it's going to become a discount chain in an effort to improve its lackluster performance, indicated by its modest net income.

The new strategy means Ferintosh will cut prices and thereby reduce its gross margin percentage in an effort to increase volume. It will also try to control costs. You're trying to predict the impact of the strategy on next year's net income to decide whether this is a sensible strategy. From your analysis, if Ferintosh's strategy stays the same in 2017, sales will grow by about 3 percent, interest will remain the same, and all other expenses will be at the same proportion of sales as last year. If Ferintosh implements the new strategy, you estimate that its gross margin will decrease by three percentage points but sales will increase by 10 percent. You also conclude that by implementing cost control measures Ferintosh will be able to limit the increase in salary and wages expense to 2 percent and general and administrative to 1.5 percent over 2016 levels. The advertising and promotion and interest expenses wouldn't change. The depreciation expense would increase by 3 percent.

Ferintosh Pharmacies Ltd.
Income Statement
For the year ended December 31, 2016

Revenue	$475,000
Cost of sales	296,875
Gross margin	178,125
Salaries and wages	64,125
General and administrative	66,975
Advertising and promotion	19,000
Depreciation	19,475
Interest	7,125
Income before taxes	1,425
Income tax expense	256
Net income	$ 1,169

Required:

a. Prepare forecasted income statements for 2017 using the existing business strategy and the new discounting strategy.
b. Provide an assessment of the two strategies. Which do you think Ferintosh should pursue? Explain.
c. Explain the difference in gross margin between the two strategies. What amount of sales would be needed for the gross margin in the new strategy to be the same as in the old?

P2-15. **(Calculation and interpretation of the gross margin percentage, LO 3, 7)** The owner of Nipawin Shoes Ltd., Lenore Ryerson, is puzzled. Sales in the store are higher than ever but it's been less profitable in each of the last three years. Lenore admits that competition has been tough and she held more sales in recent years but the store is still busy and people seem willing to buy. She's provided you with Nipawin's summarized income statements for the last three years and has asked you to take a look and see if you can find any answers.

Nipawin Shoes Ltd.
Income Statements
For the year ended December 31

	2017	2016	2015
Sales	$998,250	$938,355	$900,821
Cost of goods sold	379,335	328,424	301,775
Gross margin	618,915	609,931	599,046
Selling, general, and administrative expenses	411,778	382,380	360,328
Interest expense	75,800	76,700	73,125
Income before taxes	131,337	150,851	165,593
Income tax expense	28,894	33,187	36,430
Net income	$102,443	$117,664	$129,163

Required:

Examine the Nipawin's income statements and prepare a report that explains to Lenore why profit is falling despite increasing sales. In your analysis, look at the gross margin and the gross margin percentage. Also consider the comments Lenore made about the business environment her store has been facing and the effect on net income if gross margin in 2017 was the same as in 2015.

P2-16. **(Calculation and interpretation of the current ratio, LO 3, 7)** You have been provided with the following information about two companies:

	Company A	Company B
Cash	$ 90	$ 15
Accounts receivable	375	410
Inventory	200	255
Short-term bank loan	225	170
Accounts payable and accrued liabilities	170	195
Customer deposits	60	60

Required:

a. Calculate the current ratio for each company and the amount of working capital each company has.
b. Which company has a stronger liquidity position? In responding consider the composition of the accounts used to calculate the current ratio in addition to the current ratio itself.

P2-17. **(Calculation and interpretation of the current ratio, LO 3, 7)** You have been provided with the following three years of information about the current assets and liabilities of Ignace Ltd.:

Ignace Ltd.
Current Assets and Current Liabilities
On December 31

	2017	2016	2015
CURRENT ASSETS			
Cash	$ 64,354	$ 44,391	$ 36,567
Inventories	1,957,525	1,852,441	1,743,253
Accounts receivable	432,089	471,029	448,476
Prepaid expenses	43,468	50,573	39,054
Total current assets	$2,497,436	$2,418,434	$2,267,350
CURRENT LIABILITIES			
Bank loans	$ 336,841	$ 530,718	$ 778,646
Accounts payable	981,491	964,736	1,018,505
Dividends payable	48,927	46,748	46,709
Long-term debt coming due	110,525	121,151	54,255
Total current liabilities	$1,477,784	$1,663,353	$1,898,115

Required:

a. Calculate the current ratio for each year.
b. Evaluate the liquidity position of Ignace. Interpret the trend over the three-year period.
c. Examine the information provided and explain why the current ratio changed over the period. In your response consider the changes in the individual accounts.

P2-18. **(Calculation and interpretation of the gross margin percentage, LO 3, 7)** You have been provided with the following three years of information about the current assets and liabilities of Moyie Ltd.:

Moyie Ltd.
Current Assets and Current Liabilities
On December 31

	2017	2016	2015
CURRENT ASSETS			
Cash	$ 3,558	$ 21,286	$ 66,567
Accounts receivable	472,360	415,258	401,269
Inventories	1,577,524	1,352,698	1,245,672
Prepaid expenses	40,145	50,573	39,054
Total current assets	$2,093,587	$1,839,815	$1,752,562
CURRENT LIABILITIES			
Bank loans	$ 868,951	$ 630,215	$ 515,426
Accounts payable	990,545	845,698	775,841
Long-term debt coming due	165,856	121,151	54,255
Total current liabilities	$2,025,352	$1,597,064	$1,345,522

Required:

a. Calculate the current ratio and the amount of working capital at the end of each year.
b. Evaluate the liquidity position of Moyie. Interpret the trend over the three-year period.
c. Examine the information provided and explain why the current ratio changed over the period. In your response, consider the changes in the individual accounts.

P2-19. **(Analyze financial information, LO 7)** Below are the balance sheets and income statements for Penticton Inc. (Penticton) for 2016 and 2017.

Penticton Inc.
Balance Sheets
As of December 31,

	2017	2016		2017	2016
Assets			**Liabilities and shareholders' equity**		
Cash	$ 5,000	$ 10,000	Bank loan	$ 100,000	$ 75,000
Accounts receivable	205,000	175,000	Accounts payable	200,000	150,000
Inventory	264,200	225,000	Deposits from customers for future delivery of goods	42,000	35,000
Long-term receivable—due 2020	60,000	60,000	Long-term debt	250,000	150,000
			Shareholders' equity:		
Property and equipment (net of accumulated depreciation)	720,000	530,000	Common shares	260,000	250,000
Other non-current assets	75,000	100,000	Retained earnings	440,200	413,000
			Accumulated other comprehensive income	37,000	27,000
Total assets	$1,329,200	$1,100,000	Total liabilities and shareholders' equity	$1,329,200	$1,100,000

Penticton Inc.
Income Statements
For the Years Ended December 31

	2017	2016
Revenue	$2,475,000	$1,925,000
Cost of goods sold	1,350,000	1,098,000
Selling, general, and administrative expenses	550,000	495,000
Depreciation expense	120,000	100,000
Interest expense	125,000	120,000
Tax expense	132,000	44,800
Net income	$ 198,000	$ 67,200
Other comprehensive income	10,000	7,500
Comprehensive income	$ 208,000	$ 74,700

Required:

a. Calculate the following for Penticton for 2017 and 2016:
   i. working capital
   ii. current ratio
   iii. debt-to-equity ratio
   iv. gross margin
   v. gross margin percentage

b. Explain why the amounts you calculated in (a) changed from 2016 to 2017.

c. Comment on Penticton's liquidity position on December 31, 2017. As a prospective lender of money to Penticton, what concerns would you have about its current liquidity position?

d. What could Penticton's management do to improve liquidity?

P2-20. **(Understanding the impact of transactions on financial ratios, LO 4, 7)** Determine the effect that each of the following transactions have on Leon's current ratio and debt-to-equity ratio. Indicate whether the transaction increases, decreases, or has no effect on each ratio. On December 31, 2011 Leon's current ratio was 2.47 and its debt-to equity ratio was 0.40.

	Transaction	Effect on the current ratio	Effect on the debt-to-equity ratio
1.	Furniture is sold to customers for cash.		
2.	Leon's borrows $10 million. The loan must be repaid in ten years.		
3.	Cash is paid to settle an account payable		
4.	Inventory is purchased on credit.		
5.	New display cases are purchased on credit. Payment is due 30 days.		
6.	Display cases are purchased for cash		
7.	Employee wages are paid in cash.		
8.	A cash dividend is paid.		
9.	Common shares are sold to investors for cash.		

P2-21. **(Understanding the impact of transactions on financial ratios, LO 4, 7)** Longueuil Ltd. (Longueuil) is a small manufacturer of shirts in Québec. Longueuil recently obtained financing from a local bank for an expansion of the company's facilities.

The agreement with the bank requires that Longueuil's current ratio and debt-to-equity ratio be within ranges stated in the agreement. If the ratios fall outside of these ranges Longueuil would have to repay the new loan immediately. At this time, Longueuil has a current ratio of 2.0 (based on current assets of $700,000 and current liabilities of $350,000) and a debt-to-equity ratio of 1.5 to 1 (based on total liabilities of $900,000 and total equity of $600,000). The chief financial officer of Longueuil is concerned about the effect a number of transactions that will be occurring in the last few days of the year will have on the company's current ratio and debt-to-equity ratio.

Required:

Determine the effect that each of the following transactions will have on the initial current ratio and debt-to-equity ratio. Calculate what each ratio will be after each transaction takes place and state the effect each transaction has on the ratios (increase, decrease, or no effect). Treat each item independently.

	Transaction	Revised current ratio	Effect on the current ratio	Revised debt-to-equity ratio	Effect on the debt- to-equity ratio
	Example: Purchase of equipment for $250,000. The supplier of the equipment must be paid within six months.	1.17	Decrease	1.92 to 1	Increase
1.	$10,000 owed by a customer is collected in cash.				
2.	Sale of common shares to investors for $100,000 cash.				
3.	Declaration and payment of $100,000 of dividends.				
4.	A loan of $100,000 from a bank is arranged and the cash received. The loan must be repaid in 18 months.				
5.	A $50,000 short-term bank loan is repaid.				
6.	Merchandise is sold to a customer for $50,000. The customer must pay in two years. The inventory sold cost $20,000. (This one is tricky. Be sure to consider the effect of the transaction on net income and the resulting impact on equity.)				

P2-22. **(Prepare financial statements from a list of accounts, LO 3, 5)** You have been provided with the following alphabetical list of accounts for Sudbury Ltd. for 2017. Use the information to prepare an income statement, statement of changes in equity, and statement of comprehensive income for the year ended December 31, 2017, and balance sheet as of December 31, 2017. You should be able to figure out how to treat accounts that have names unfamiliar to you by applying your understanding of the financial statements learned in this chapter.

Accounts payable	$31,000	Dividends	$33,000
Accounts receivable	38,000	Income tax expense	21,000
Accounts receivable—due in 2021	15,000	Income taxes payable	4,500
Accrued liabilities	8,000	Interest expense	11,200
Accumulated depreciation	51,000	Interest revenue	1,500
Accumulated other comprehensive income (December 31, 2017)	45,000	Inventory	52,000
Advertising and promotion expense	43,000	Investment in shares of other corporations (current asset)	130,000
Bank loan	27,500	Long-term debt (non-current portion)	100,000
Cash	35,000	Other comprehensive income	25,000
Cash sales	85,000	Other expenses	22,000
Charitable donations	10,000	Other non-current assets	18,800
Common shares	111,000	Prepaid expenses	3,500
Cost of goods sold	120,000	Property, plant, and equipment	260,000
Credit sales	343,800	Research expense	18,800
Current portion of long-term debt	25,000	Retained earnings (January 1, 2017)	89,000
Deposits from customers	9,200	Salaries and wages expense	84,000
Depreciation expense	21,700	Salaries and wages payable	5,500

P2-23. **(Prepare an income statement and balance sheet from a list of accounts, LO 3, 5)** You have been provided with the following alphabetical list of accounts for Thaxted Ltd. for 2017. Use the information to prepare an income statement for the year ended December 31, 2017, and balance sheet as of December 31, 2017. You should be able to figure out how to treat accounts that have names that are unfamiliar to you by applying your understanding of the financial statements learned in this chapter.

Accounts payable	$ 26,250	Income taxes recoverable from government	$ 2,250
Accounts receivable	27,500	Interest expense	70,000
Accrued liabilities	5,000	Interest revenue	500
Accumulated depreciation	375,000	Inventory	42,500
Accumulated other comprehensive income at the end of the year	10,000	Intangible assets	100,000
Advances to employees	1,250	Investments in the shares of other	
Advertising expenses	47,500	corporations (non-current)	60,000
Depreciation expense	115,000	Long-term debt (non-current portion)	700,000
Cash	5,000	Loss on lawsuit	45,000
Cash sales in 2017	112,500	Other comprehensive income	3,250
Charitable donations made	50,000	Other expense	10,000
Common shares	500,000	Other non-current assets	25,000
Cost of sales	187,500	Prepaid insurance	1,000
Credit sales in 2017	725,000	Property, plant, and equipment	1,800,000
Current portion of long-term debt	27,500	Retained earnings at the beginning of the year	366,000
Deposits from customers	1,250		
Dividends	12,500	Selling expenses	67,500
Income tax expense	75,000	Wages expense	110,000
Income taxes payable	3,750	Wages payable	1,750

P2-24. **(Evaluate the format of a balance sheet, LO 3)** Look at the balance sheet shown in Exhibit 2.3. Redo that balance sheet in the more traditional format used by Leon's. How does your statement differ from the one prepared by the company? Which statement is more informative? Should it make any difference to stakeholders how the balance sheet is formatted? Explain.

P2-25. **(Prepare a statement of cash flows, LO 3)** The Pas Ltd. was organized on August 1, 2016 with a cash investment of $1,000,000 by its shareholders. The Pas arranged a mortgage with a local lender for $600,000 and purchased a warehouse for $1,200,000. During its fiscal year ended July 31, 2017, The Pas collected $425,000 in cash from customers, paid $270,000 in cash for operating expenses, and paid $60,000 in cash dividends to its shareholders. At the end of the year it invested $300,000 in the shares of another corporation.

Required:

a. Classify each of the cash flows described above as operating, investing, or financing.
b. Organize the cash flows into a statement of cash flows.
c. Explain what your statement of cash flows tells you that an income statement doesn't.

P2-26. **(Prepare a statement of cash flows, LO 3)** Prelate Ltd. was organized on September 1, 2017 to buy and operate real estate properties. The shareholders started the company with a cash investment of $1,500,000. Prelate arranged a long-term loan with a local bank for $1,100,000 and purchased an office building for $2,100,000. During its fiscal year ended August 31, 2018 Prelate collected $500,000 in rent from tenants, paid $170,000 in cash for operating expenses, and paid $20,000 in cash dividends to its shareholders.

Required:

a. Classify each of the cash flows described above as operating, investing, or financing.
b. Organize the cash flows into a statement of cash flows.
c. Explain what your statement of cash flows tells you that an income statement doesn't.

P2-27. **(Explain whether and why an expenditure is an asset, LO 5)** Consider the following items:

i. A piece of land a company planned to build a warehouse on is determined by a government agency to be toxic and not suitable for construction. The land is no longer considered usable for any purpose.
ii. An electronics retailer spends $225,000 building an expansion to the store so that it can offer a broader range of products to customers.
iii. A dental practice has a list of the names and addresses of its 800 patients.
iv. A survey determines that the logo of an international athletic wear maker is the one best known and respected in the world.
v. A student has paid university tuition totalling $15,000 to study business. The student plans to become a professional accountant in two years and hopes to open his own accounting practice within five years.
vi. A company sends certain employees for training in business and technology to enhance their skills and make them more valuable to the company.

Required:

For each of the items explain whether and why it would be considered the following:
a. an asset by a non-accountant (use your intuition, common sense, and judgment to decide whether the item in question should be considered an asset.)
b. an asset according to IFRS (use the IFRS criteria that were discussed in the chapter.)

P2-28. **(Classify the effect of economic events on cash and accrual income, LO 5, 6)** Consider the following economic events involving Leon's. Indicate whether Leon's would include each item in a calculation of net income using cash accounting and accrual accounting for the year ended December 31, 2016. Provide a brief explanation for your treatment:

	Economic Event	Net income on the cash basis	Net income on the accrual basis
	Example: Leon's sells furniture to a customer for cash.	Yes, because cash is collected from a customer.	Yes, because a sale with a customer has been completed.
a.	Leon's sells furniture to a franchise store. Payment will be made in January 2017.		
b.	Dividends are declared and paid to shareholders in December 2016.		
c.	During 2016 Leon's sells inventory for cash. Leon's hasn't yet paid for the inventory that has been sold.		
d.	A customer pays a deposit in December 2016 goods that will be delivered in February 2017.		
e.	Leon's purchases and pays for stoves in December 2016. The inventory is unsold as of the year-end.		
f.	Leon's depreciates its stores in 2016.		
g.	Leon's pays employees in December 2016 for their work in November.		

P2-29. (Classify the effect of economic events on cash and accrual income, LO 5, 6) Indicate whether each of the following events would be included in a calculation of net income on the cash basis, the accrual basis, or both. Provide a brief explanation for your treatment. Remember that under accrual accounting, inventory is expensed in the period it's sold or used up and sales are recorded when the goods and services are provided to customers:

	Economic Event	Net income on the cash basis	Net income on the accrual basis
	Example: An entity sells merchandise for cash.	Yes, because cash is collected from a customer.	Yes, because a sale with a customer has been completed.
a.	An entity receives a deposit from a customer for services that will be provided next year.		
b.	An entity provides services to a customer this year that were paid for last year.		
c.	Inventory paid for last year is sold to a customer this year.		
d.	Inventory paid for this year is sold this year		
e.	Inventory is purchased on credit this year but is sold by the end of the year		
f.	Inventory is purchased on credit this year but hasn't been sold by the end of the year		

P2-30. (Prepare balance sheets using different asset values, LO 3, 4) In Chapter 1, you were asked to imagine that you were a student needing insurance on your apartment and you examined different ways of valuing the contents of the apartment. We identified three different ways of valuing the contents of the apartment. Table 1.7 from Chapter 1 is reproduced next. All the items on the list are owned by you, except for the appliances, which belong to the building.

Inventory of Apartment Contents			
Column 1	**Column 2**	**Column 3**	**Column 4**
Item	**What it cost**	**What it would cost to replace**	**What it could be sold for**
Television	$ 1,100	$ 925	$ 400
Laptop	800	900	300
Furniture	4,225	4,525	2,300
Books	750	875	300
Clothes	1,600	1,950	300
iPhone	175	600	275
Jewellery	500	625	300
Appliances	2,600	3,300	1,800
Art	300	500	500
Other	1,000	1,200	750
Total	**$13,050**	**$15,400**	**$7,225**

In addition to the above, the following information is available:

Item	Amount
Student loans	$27,500
Loans from parents	5,000
Cash in bank	1,200
Owing from employer	700

Required:

a. Prepare three separate balance sheets using the information in each column above. Make sure to include the "other information" in each balance sheet.
b. Explain the benefits and limitations of each balance sheet to the people who might use them. Make sure to discuss specific stakeholders that might use each balance sheet.
c. Which balance sheet do you think would be appropriate under IFRS?
d. Which balance sheet do you think is best? Explain.

P2-31. (Prepare a personal balance sheet, LO 3, 4, 5) Make a list of your personal assets and liabilities and try to organize them into an accounting balance sheet format. Assign values to the assets and the liabilities. Answer the following questions about your balance sheet:

a. How did you determine your equity in your assets?
b. How did you decide what amount to assign to each asset and liability?
c. Did you include your education among your assets? Why or why not? If your personal balance sheet was being prepared according to IFRS would your education be included as an asset? Explain.

Using Financial Statements

Shoppers Drug Mart Corporation (Shoppers) is the licensor of full-service retail drug stores operating under the name Shoppers Drug Mart® (Pharmaprix® in Québec). The Company has grown to a network of more than 1,180 Shoppers Drug Mart/Pharmaprix stores across Canada. These stores are owned and operated by the Company's licensed associate-owners. The Company also licenses or owns more than 51 medical clinic pharmacies and seven luxury beauty destinations. Shoppers is the leader in Canada's retail drug store marketplace and is the number one provider of pharmacy products and services. It has successfully leveraged its leadership position in pharmacy and its convenient store locations to capture a significant share of the market in front-store merchandise, including over-the-counter medications, health and beauty aids, cosmetics and fragrances, seasonal products, and everyday household essentials. Shoppers is a public company traded on the Toronto Stock Exchange.[2]

Shoppers' consolidated balance sheets and statements of income, comprehensive income, changes in shareholders' equity, and cash flows, along with some extracts from the notes to the financial statements, are provided in Exhibit 2.4.[3] Use this information to respond to questions FS2-1 to FS2-15.

EXHIBIT 2.4 Shoppers Drug Mart Corporation—Extracts from Financial Statements

SHOPPERS DRUG MART

CONSOLIDATED STATEMENTS OF EARNINGS

For the 52 weeks ended December 31, 2011 and January 1, 2011

(in thousands of Canadian dollars, except per share amounts)	Note	2011	2010
Sales		**$ 10,458,652**	$ 10,192,714
Cost of goods sold	9	**(6,416,208)**	(6,283,634)
Gross profit		**4,042,444**	3,909,080
Operating and administrative expenses	10, 11, 13	**(3,131,539)**	(3,011,758)
Operating income		**910,905**	897,322
Finance expenses	12	**(64,038)**	(60,633)
Earnings before income taxes		**846,867**	836,689
Income taxes	14		
Current		**(208,696)**	(238,779)
Deferred		**(24,237)**	(6,059)
		(232,933)	(244,838)
Net earnings		**$ 613,934**	$ 591,851

CONSOLIDATED STATEMENTS OF COMPREHENSIVE INCOME

For the 52 weeks ended December 31, 2011 and January 1, 2011

(in thousands of Canadian dollars)	Note	2011	2010
Net earnings		$ 613,934	$ 591,851
Other comprehensive income (loss), net of tax			
Effective portion of changes in fair value of hedges on interest rate derivatives (net of tax of $nil (2010: $525))	18	–	1,120
Effective portion of changes in fair value of hedges on equity forward derivatives (net of tax of $12 (2010: $205))	18	**(39)**	(521)
Net change in fair value of hedges on interest rate and equity forward derivatives transferred to earnings (net of tax of $163 (2010: $13))	18	**411**	33
Retirement benefit obligations actuarial losses (net of tax of $7,433 (2010: $2,905))	21	**(21,943)**	(8,150)
Other comprehensive loss, net of tax	7	**(21,571)**	(7,518)
Total comprehensive income		**$ 592,363**	$ 584,333

EXHIBIT 2.4 (continued) Shoppers Drug Mart Corporation—Extracts from Financial Statements

CONSOLIDATED BALANCE SHEETS

As at December 31, 2011, January 1, 2011 and January 3, 2010
(in thousands of Canadian dollars)

	Note	December 31, 2011	January 1, 2011	January 3, 2010
Current assets				
Cash		**$ 118,566**	$ 64,354	$ 44,391
Accounts receivable		**493,338**	432,089	470,935
Inventory		**2,042,302**	1,957,525	1,852,441
Income taxes recoverable		–	20,384	–
Prepaid expenses and deposits		**41,441**	68,468	74,206
Total current assets		**2,695,647**	2,542,820	2,441,973
Non-current assets				
Property and equipment	15	**1,767,543**	1,677,340	1,541,841
Investment property	15	**16,372**	12,770	5,884
Goodwill	16	**2,499,722**	2,493,108	2,483,430
Intangible assets	17	**281,737**	272,217	258,766
Other assets		**18,214**	19,678	16,716
Deferred tax assets	14	**21,075**	26,264	28,456
Total non-current assets		**4,604,663**	4,501,377	4,335,093
Total assets		**$ 7,300,310**	$ 7,044,197	$ 6,777,066
Liabilities				
Bank indebtedness	19	**$ 172,262**	$ 209,013	$ 270,332
Commercial paper	19	–	127,828	260,386
Accounts payable and accrued liabilities	18	**1,109,444**	990,244	970,831
Income taxes payable		**26,538**	–	17,046
Dividends payable	24	**53,119**	48,927	46,748
Current portion of long-term debt	20	**249,971**	–	–
Provisions	22	**12,024**	12,562	11,009
Associate interest		**152,880**	138,993	130,189
Total current liabilities		**1,776,238**	1,527,567	1,706,541
Long-term debt	20	**695,675**	943,412	946,098
Other long-term liabilities	23	**520,188**	442,124	386,262
Provisions	22	**1,701**	1,852	1,062
Deferred tax liabilities	14	**38,678**	26,607	25,219
Total long-term liabilities		**1,256,242**	1,413,995	1,358,641
Total liabilities		**3,032,480**	2,941,562	3,065,182
Shareholder's equity				
Share capital	24	**1,486,455**	1,520,558	1,519,870
Treasury shares	24	**(4,735)**	–	–
Contributed surplus	26	**10,246**	11,702	10,274
Accumulated other comprehensive loss	7	**(30,214)**	(8,643)	(1,125)
Retained earnings		**2,806,078**	2,579,018	2,182,865
Total shareholders' equity		**4,267,830**	4,102,635	3,711,884
Total liabilities and shareholders' equity		**$ 7,300,310**	$ 7,044,197	$ 6,777,066

EXHIBIT 2.4 (continued) Shoppers Drug Mart Corporation—Extracts from Financial Statements

CONSOLIDATED STATEMENTS OF CHANGES IN SHAREHOLDERS' EQUITY

For the 52 weeks ended December 31, 2011 and January 1, 2011
(in thousands of Canadian dollars)

	Note	Share Capital	Treasury Shares	Contributed Surplus	Accumulated Other Comprehensive Loss (Note 18 and 21)	Retained Earnings	Total
Balance as at January 1, 2011		$ 1,520,558	$ –	$ 11,702	$ (8,643)	$ 2,579,018	$ 4,102,635
Total comprehensive income		–	–	–	(21,571)	613,934	592,363
Dividends	24	–	–	–	–	(215,671)	(215,671)
Share repurchases	24	(35,576)	(4,735)	–	–	(171,203)	(211,514)
Share-based payments	26	–	–	(1,210)	–	–	(1,210)
Share options exercised	26	1,466	–	(246)	–	–	1,220
Repayment of share-purchase loans		7	–	–	–	–	7
Balance as at December 31, 2011		**$ 1,486,455**	**$ (4,735)**	**$ 10,246**	**$ (30,214)**	**$ 2,806,078**	**$ 4,267,830**
Balance as at January 3, 2010		$ 1,519,870	$ –	$ 10,274	$ (1,125)	$ 2,182,865	$ 3,711,884
Total comprehensive income		–	–	–	(7,518)	591,851	584,333
Dividends	24	–	–	–	–	(195,698)	(195,698)
Share-based payments	26	–	–	1,592	–	–	1,592
Share options exercised	26	655	–	(164)	–	–	491
Repayment of share-purchase loans		33	–	–	–	–	33
Balance as at January 1, 2011		$ 1,520,558	$ –	$ 11,702	$ (8,643)	$ 2,579,018	$ 4,102,635

FS2-1. Examine Shoppers' balance sheet and confirm that the accounting equation equality holds in all three years shown (Assets = Liabilities + Owners' Equity). Show your work.

FS2-2. What were Shoppers' year-ends in the last three fiscal years? Why aren't they the same? Do the different dates cause any problems for stakeholders who want to compare the three years of information Shoppers provides? (To answer, look at the notes to the financial statements.)

FS2-3. On what basis (according to which set of accounting principles) did Shoppers prepare its financial statements? Why does Shoppers provide information for more than one fiscal year?

FS2-4. Find the following information in Shoppers' financial statements:

a. Sales for the year ended December 31, 2011.
b. Operating and administrative expenses for the year ended December 31, 2011.
c. Total assets on December 31, 2011.
d. Long-term debt on December 31, 2011 (look at the current and non-current portion).
e. Inventory on December 31, 2011.
f. Dividends paid on common shares during the year ended December 31, 2011.
g. Dividends declared on common shares during the year ended December 31, 2011.
h. The amount spent on additions to property, plant, and equipment during 2011.
i. Comprehensive income for the year ended December 31, 2011.
j. The amount of accumulated other comprehensive loss on December 31, 2011.
k. Retained earnings on December 31, 2011.

EXHIBIT 2.4 (continued) Shoppers Drug Mart Corporation—Extracts from Financial Statements

CONSOLIDATED STATEMENTS OF CASH FLOWS
For the 52 weeks ended December 31, 2011 and January 1, 2011
(in thousands of Canadian dollars)

	Note	2011	2010[1]
Cash flows from operating activities			
Net earnings		**$ 613,934**	$ 591,851
Adjustments for:			
Depreciation and amortization	13, 15, 17	**296,464**	278,421
Finance expenses	12	**64,038**	60,633
Loss on sale or disposal of property and equipment, including impairments	15, 17	**2,015**	3,880
Share-based payment transactions	26	**(1,210)**	1,592
Recognition and reversal of provisions, net	22	**9,218**	12,160
Other long-term liabilities	23	**296**	18,491
Income tax expense	14	**232,933**	244,838
		1,217,688	1,211,866
Net change in non-cash working capital balances	27	**32,166**	(34,824)
Provisions used	22	**(9,907)**	(9,817)
Interest paid		**(63,853)**	(62,916)
Income taxes paid		**(202,256)**	(276,108)
Net cash from operating activities		**973,838**	828,201
Cash flows from investing activities			
Proceeds from disposition of property and equipment and investment property		**55,459**	60,538
Business acquisitions	8	**(10,496)**	(11,779)
Deposits		**105**	1,534
Acquisition or development of property and equipment	15	**(341,868)**	(415,094)
Acquisition or development of intangible assets	17	**(53,836)**	(56,625)
Other assets		**1,464**	(3,249)
Net cash used in investing activities		**(349,172)**	(424,675)
Cash flows from financing activities			
Repurchase of own shares	24	**(206,779)**	–
Proceeds from exercise of share options	26	**1,220**	491
Repayment of share-purchase loans	24	**7**	33
Repayment of bank indebtedness, net	19	**(36,714)**	(61,319)
Repayment of commercial paper, net	19	**(128,000)**	(133,000)
Revolving term debt, net	20	**152**	(1,298)
Payment of transaction costs for debt refinancing	20	**(575)**	(2,792)
Repayment of financing lease obligations	23	**(2,173)**	(1,436)
Associate interest		**13,887**	9,277
Dividends paid	24	**(211,479)**	(193,519)
Net cash used in financing activities		**(570,454)**	(383,563)
Net increase in cash		**54,212**	19,963
Cash, beginning of the year		**64,354**	44,391
Cash, end of the year		**$ 118,566**	$ 64,354

1. GENERAL INFORMATION

These consolidated financial statements of the Company as at end for the financial year ended December 31, 2011 include the accounts of Shoppers Drug Mart Corporation, its subsidiaries, and the Associate-owned stores that comprise the majority of the Company's store network. The financial year of the Company consists of a 52 or 53 week period ending on the Saturday closest to December 31. The current financial year is the 52 weeks ended December 31, 2011. The comparative financial year is the 52 weeks ended January 1, 2011. The Company has also presented the consolidated balance sheet as at January 3, 2010, the Company's date of transition to international Financial Reporting Standards ("IFRS").

EXHIBIT 2.4 (continued) Shoppers Drug Mart Corporation—Extracts from Financial Statements

2. BASIS OF PREPARATION

(a) Statement of Compliance

These consolidated financial statements have been prepared in accordance with Canadian Generally Accepted Accounting Principles ("Canadian GAAP"). These consolidated financial statements also comply with International Financial Reporting Standards ("IFRS") as issued by the International Accounting Standards Board ("IASB").

(b) Use of Estimates and Judgments

The preparation of these consolidated financial statements in conformity with IFRS requires management to make certain judgments, estimates, and assumptions that affect the application of accounting policies and the reported amounts of assets and liabilities and disclosure of contingent assets and liabilities at the date of these consolidated financial statements and the reported amounts of revenues and expenses during the reporting period.

10. OPERATING AND ADMINISTRATIVE EXPENSES

During the financial year ended January 1, 2011, the Company recognized an expense of $10,282 in operating and administrative expenses related to the settlement of a long-standing legal dispute related to a commercial arrangement with one of the Company's ancillary businesses.

11. EMPLOYEE BENEFITS EXPENSE

Employee benefits expense, recognized within operating and administrative expenses, is as follows:

	Note	2011	2010
Wages and salaries		**$ 1,391,430**	$ 1,325,489
Statutory deductions		**164,528**	155,721
Expense related to pension and benefits	21	**6,130**	6,059
Share-based payment transactions	26	**2,135**	12,618
		$ 1,564,223	$ 1,499,887

12. FINANCE EXPENSES

The components of the Company's finance expenses are as follows:

	2011	2010
Finance expense on bank indebtedness	**$ 5,907**	$ 5,642
Finance expense on commercial paper	**1,702**	4,269
Finance expense on long-term debt	**52,626**	50,961
Finance expense on financing leases	**6,859**	4,757
	67,094	65,629
Finance expense capitalized	**(3,056)**	(4,996)
	$ 64,038	$ 60,633

The amount of finance expense capitalized is based on the Company's weighted average cost of borrowing and is attributed to those items of property and equipment which meet the definition of a qualifying asset. A qualifying asset is defined as an asset that requires a substantial period of time to get ready for its intended use or sale.

EXHIBIT 2.4 (continued) Shoppers Drug Mart Corporation—Extracts from Financial Statements

15. PROPERTY AND EQUIPMENT AND INVESTMENT PROPERTY

	Properties Under Development	Land	Buildings	Equipment, Fixtures and Computer Equipment	Leasehold Improvements	Assets under Financing Leases (Note 23)	Total
Cost							
Balance at January 1, 2011	$ 72,035	$ 70,411	$ 206,472	$ 1,135,805	$ 1,179,795	$ 83,082	$ 2,747,600
Additions:							
– Asset acquisitions	9,979	–	–	–	–	43,952	53,931
– Development	9,990	3,688	25,738	168,204	131,667	–	339,287
Transfers	(20,662)	6,147	8,791	752	320	–	(4,652)
Computer software transfers from intangible assets	–	–	–	1,330	–	–	1,330
Disposals	–	(14,768)	(26,958)	(23,563)	(20,337)	–	(85,626)
Retirements	–	–	–	534	–	–	534
Balance at December 31, 2011	**$ 71,342**	**$ 65,478**	**$ 214,043**	**$ 1,283,062**	**$ 1,291,445**	**$ 127,034**	**$ 3,052,404**
Depreciation							
Balance at January 1, 2011	$ –	$ –	$ 16,102	$ 655,467	$ 355,523	$ 11,446	$ 1,038,538
Depreciation for the financial year	–	–	11,542	140,537	92,423	4,965	249,467
Transfers	–	–	(216)	375	(123)	–	36
Computer software transfers from intangible assets	–	–	–	(18)	–	–	(18)
Disposals	–	–	(3,103)	(19,792)	(11,807)	–	(34,702)
Retirements	–	–	–	(182)	–	–	(182)
Balance at December 31, 2011	**$ –**	**$ –**	**$ 24,325**	**$ 776,387**	**$ 436,016**	**$ 16,411**	**$ 1,253,139**
Impairment losses							
Balance at January 1, 2011	$ –	$ –	$ –	$ 16,257	$ 15,465	$ –	$ 31,722
Impairment loss	–	–	–	–	–	–	–
Balance at December 31, 2011	**$ –**	**$ –**	**$ –**	**$ 16,257**	**$ 15,465**	**$ –**	**$ 31,722**
Net book value							
At December 31, 2011	**$ 71,342**	**$ 65,478**	**$ 189,718**	**$ 490,418**	**$ 839,964**	**$ 110,623**	**$ 1,767,543**

FS2-5. Find the following information in Shoppers' financial statements:

a. Net income for the year ended December 31, 2011.
b. Cost of goods sold for the year ended December 31, 2011.
c. Other comprehensive income for the year ended December 31, 2011.
d. Cash on December 31, 2011.
e. Share capital on December 31, 2011.
f. Total liabilities on December 31, 2011.
g. Total current assets on December 31, 2011.
h. Cash from operations for the year ended December 31, 2011.
i. The amount of cash spent during the year ended December 31, 2011 for business acquisitions.
j. The amount spent during the year ended December 31, 2011 repurchasing its own shares.

EXHIBIT 2.4 (continued) Shoppers Drug Mart Corporation—Extracts from Financial Statements

17. INTANGIBLE ASSETS

	Note	Prescription Files	Customer Relationships	Computer Software	Computer Software under Development	Other	Total
Cost							
Balance at January 1, 2011		$ 129,803	$ 43,600	$ 211,162	$ 52,412	$ 8,824	$ 445,801
Additions							
– purchases		–	7,136	1,381	–	696	9,213
– development		–	–	–	44,624	–	44,624
– business acquisitions	8,15	4,184	–	–	–	–	4,184
Transfers	16	–	–	74,260	(75,337)	(253)	(1,330)
Disposals		–	–	–	(24)	–	(24)
Balance at December 31, 2011		**$ 133,987**	**$ 50,736**	**$ 286,803**	**$ 21,675**	**$ 9,267**	**$ 502,468**
Amortization							
Balance at January 1, 2011		$ 49,675	$ 9,959	$ 108,463	$ –	$ 5,487	$ 173,584
Amortization for the financial year		14,697	3,732	27,932	–	804	47,165
Transfers		–	–	11	–	(29)	(18)
Balance at December 31, 2011		**$ 64,372**	**$ 13,691**	**$ 136,406**	**$ –**	**$ 6,262**	**$ 220,731**
Net book value at December 31, 2011		**$ 69,615**	**$ 37,045**	**$ 150,397**	**$ 21,675**	**$ 3,005**	**$ 281,737**

20. LONG-TERM DEBT

	Face Value as at December 31, 2011	Maturity	December 31, 2011	January 1, 2011	January 3, 2010
Medium-term notes					
Series 2 Notes – 4.99%	$ 450,000	June 2013	**$ 449,298**	$ 448,704	$ 447,977
Series 3 Notes – 4.80%	250,000	January 2012	**249,971**	249,305	248,640
Series 4 Notes – 5.19%	250,000	January 2014	**249,081**	248,632	248,183
			948,350	946,641	944,800
Less: current portion of long-term debt			**(249,971)**	–	–
			698,379	946,641	944,800
Revolving term facility	$ 725,000	December 2015	**152**	–	1,298
Less: financing costs			**(2,856)**	(3,229)	–
			(2,704)	(3,229)	1,298
Total long-term debt			**$695,675**	$ 943,412	$ 946,098

As at December 31, 2011, $9,598 (2010: $137,053) of the $725,000 (2010: $750,000) revolving term facility was utilized as follows: drawings on the revolving term facility $152 (2010: $nil), $9,446 (2010: $9,053) relating to letters of credit and trade finance guarantees and $nil (2010: $128,000) relating to commercial paper issued by the Company. As at January 3, 2010, the revolving term facility was $800,000 and was utilized as follows: $8,322 related to letters of credit and trade finance guarantees and $261,000 relating to commercial paper issued by the Company.

EXHIBIT 2.4 (continued) Shoppers Drug Mart Corporation—Extracts from Financial Statements

24. SHARE CAPITAL

Share Capital and Contributed Surplus

Authorized

Unlimited number of common shares

Unlimited number of preferred shares, issuable in series without nominal or par value

Outstanding

	2011		2010	
	Number of Common Shares	**Stated Value**	Number of Common Shares	Stated Value
Beginning balance	**217,452,068**	**$ 1,520,558**	217,431,898	$ 1,519,870
Shares issued for cash	**109,729**	**1,220**	20,170	491
Shares repurchased in cash	**(5,086,200)**	**(35,576)**	–	–
Repayment of share purchase loans	–	**7**	–	33
Exercise of share options	–	**246**	–	164
Ending balance	**212,475,597**	**$ 1,486,455**	217,452,068	$ 1,520,558

Dividends

The following table provides a summary of the dividends declared by the Company:

Declaration Date	Record Date	Payment Date	Dividend per Common Share
February 10, 2011	March 31, 2011	April 15, 2011	$ 0.250
April 27, 2011	June 30, 2011	July 15, 2011	$ 0.250
July 21, 2011	September 30, 2011	October 14, 2011	$ 0.250
November 9, 2011	December 30, 2011	January 13, 2012	$ 0.250
February 11, 2010	March 31, 2010	April 15, 2010	$ 0.225
April 28, 2010	June 30, 2010	July 15, 2010	$ 0.225
July 22, 2010	September 30, 2010	October 15, 2010	$ 0.225
November 9, 2010	December 31, 2010	January 14, 2011	$ 0.225

On February 9, 2012, the Board of Directors declared a dividend of 26.5 cents per common share payable April 13, 2012 to shareholders of record as of the close of business on March 30, 2012.

FS2-6. Find the following information in the notes to Shoppers' financial statements:

a. The amount paid to employees in wages and salaries during fiscal 2011.
b. The amount of interest (finance expense) expensed for long-term debt during fiscal 2011.
c. The carrying amount (net book value) of buildings on December 31, 2011.
d. The amount of depreciation expenses on equipment, fixtures, and computer equipment during fiscal 2011.
e. The carrying amount (net book value) of customer relationships on December 31, 2011.
f. The number of common shares outstanding on December 31, 2011.
g. The interest rate on the Series 4 medium-term notes and the amount outstanding on December 31, 2011.

FS2-7. Use Shoppers' financial statements to respond to the following:

a. Calculate the amount of working capital on December 31, 2011, January 1, 2011, and January 3, 2010.
b. Calculate the current ratio on December 31, 2011, January 1, 2011, and January 3, 2010.
c. By how much did working capital change between the end of fiscal 2011 and the end of fiscal 2010?
d. What does the information you calculated in (a) to (c) above tell you about Shoppers' liquidity?

FS2-8. Use Shoppers' financial statements to respond to the following:

a. Calculate the debt-to-equity ratio on December 31, 2011, January 1, 2011, and January 3, 2010.
b. Do you see a pattern in how the ratio changed over the three years?
c. Explain why the debt-to-equity ratio changed from the beginning of fiscal 2010 to the end of fiscal 2011.
d. Interpret Shoppers' debt-to-equity ratio. What does it tell you about the financial position of the company?

FS2-9. Use Shoppers' financial statements to respond to the following:

a. Calculate the gross margin for fiscal 2011 and 2010.
b. Calculate the gross margin percentage for fiscal 2011 and 2010.
c. Interpret your calculations in (a) and (b) above. What do they tell you about Shoppers' performance? What additional information would you want to do a more thorough evaluation of Shoppers' gross margin?

FS2-10. Note 10 to Shoppers' financial statements explains that a $10,282,000 expense pertaining to a legal dispute is included in operating and administrative expenses for the year ended January 1, 2011. Is this information useful? How would it affect a stakeholder's ability to interpret the financial statements?

FS2-11. Examine Note 15 to Shoppers' financial statements, which describes its property and equipment, and Note 17 on intangible assets, and respond to the following questions:

a. Describe the different categories of property and equipment Shoppers has. What do these assets contribute to Shoppers' business?
b. Describe the different categories of intangible assets Shoppers has.
c. What's the difference between property and equipment and intangible assets?
d. How much land did Shoppers dispose of in fiscal 2011?
e. What amount did Shoppers expense for property and equipment in fiscal 2011?
f. How much did Shoppers amortize for intangibles in total in fiscal 2011 and how much did it amortize for prescription files?

FS2-12. Examine Note 20 to Shoppers' financial statements entitled Long-Term Debt and respond to the following questions:

a. How much long-term debt did Shoppers have on December 31, 2011? How much of the long-term debt was current? Why is it valuable to know the portion of long-term debt that's current?
b. How much of the Series 2 medium-term notes was outstanding on December 31, 2011? What is the interest rate on the Series 2 notes and when do they mature?
c. What is the available amount of Shoppers revolving term credit facility? How much of the credit facility was used as of December 31, 2011? (Be sure to read the text at the bottom of the note.) Why is the amount used different from the amount reflected in the financial statements for the facility (this is a hard question!)?
d. How does the information in the note help you evaluate Shoppers' financial position better than having only the information on the balance sheet?

FS2-13. One of the intangible assets that Shoppers describes in Note 17 is "prescription files." It records these as assets when it purchases other pharmacies to operate under the Shoppers Drug Mart banner. Explain why the prescription files are considered an asset? Apply the asset criteria to answer.

FS2-14. List five questions you would ask Shoppers' management if you were considering lending money to the company. Your questions should pertain to information that you can't obtain from the financial statements.

FS2-15. Compare Shoppers' balance sheet with Leon's. Describe how the composition of assets differs between the two companies. Given the different industries these two companies are in, do the differences make sense? Explain. In answering this question it may be helpful for you to calculate on a percentage basis what each asset represents as a proportion of total assets.

ENDNOTES

1. Extracted from Leon's Furniture Limited's 2011 audited financial statements.
2. Adapted from Shoppers Drug Mart Corporation's Web site at http://www.shoppersdrugmart.ca/english/corporate_information/about_us/index.html.
3. Extracted from Shoppers Drug Mart Corporation's 2011 financial statements.

Practise and learn online with Connect. Connect resources include additional and interactive study exercises, videos, and practice quizzing, as well as additional material you won't find in the printed text.

CHAPTER

3

The Accounting Cycle

LEARNING OBJECTIVES

After studying the material in this chapter you will be able to do the following:

LO 1 Describe the purpose and nature of accounting information systems and the accounting cycle.

LO 2 Analyze transactions and economic events and prepare financial statements using an accounting equation spreadsheet.

LO 3 Describe how financial statements are affected by the way managers choose to record transactions and economic events.

LO 4 Differentiate between the different types of adjusting journal entries and understand their purposes.

LO 5 Analyze transactions and economic events, record them using journal entries, post entries to T-accounts, and prepare and use the trial balance to prepare financial statements.

LO 6 Explain the purpose of closing journal entries and describe how to prepare them.

At 6:30 p.m. at Rogers Sportsnet's studios in Toronto on an early May evening in 2012, anchor Hazel Mae checked her script pages while the theme for the all-sports network's flagship news show, *Connected*, played across nearly 100,000 television screens in Canada.

Rogers Sportsnet

Mae stood at the news desk amidst the splashy blue, red and grey "Transformers"-style graphics and the rousing music composed by *Canada's Got Talent* judge Stephan Moccio.

When Rogers relaunched its Sportsnet brand in the fall of 2011, they hired Mae, a Canadian, back from her high-profile broadcasting job with MLB in New York to helm the supper hour *Connected*. On this evening, she led with these top stories: Milos Raonic losing his Madrid Open tennis match to Roger Federer, the Toronto Blue Jays 5–2 victory over the Athletics in Oakland, and a preview of that night's NHL Stanley Cup playoff game between Washington and New York.

The final lineup of the show is a result of a continuous cycle that goes on in the Sportsnet newsroom all day and night. There, journalists are constantly watching feeds of live sporting events from around the world, and recording the raw data about scores and game highlights. They process the information in the form of broadcast style scripts that they type into a writing program used by many news organizations around the world.

The producers decided what information would be most useful to their viewers, who are mainly male sports fans. Many of those stories later became the content that the audience sees in the first part of the *Connected* show, in the scripts that Mae reads off her teleprompter.

The flow of sports news is constantly changing: when someone hits a home run in a ball game or when, for example, Washington Capitals star Alexander Ovechkin gave an interview about an imminent game. Often, while the anchor is already live on air a journalist in the newsroom can enter the updated information as a new script, which will be approved and can quickly be added into the show's lineup.

This constant updating of the sports news process happens again a few hours later, for the late night *Connected* newscast, which runs at 9:30 p.m.

The accounting cycle has a similar process, but instead of marking down wins and losses, accounting systems record transactions such as amounts on invoices and cheques. Much like the production underway in the Sportsnet newsroom, accounting cycles record data collected over a fixed period, usually over a three-month quarter.

Similarly, accountants who prepare a trial balance also have to make adjustments for new information, before they produce a final set of financial statements for that period.

Sportsnet's Mae does have one benefit that most accountants don't usually get: she has her hair and makeup done each afternoon, and gets a stylish wardrobe supplied by Z Zegna.

–E.B.

INTRODUCTION

In Chapter 2, the different financial statements were introduced. In this chapter, we examine the mechanics of accounting—how transactions and other economic events are recorded in an accounting system, and how the raw data are organized, processed, and converted into information that's useful to stakeholders.

Recording and processing transactions and economic events are essential parts of accounting. They provide the raw data used to produce the information needed by managers and stakeholders for decision making. But remember, the mechanics of accounting—bookkeeping—isn't accounting; it's only part of it. Some readers may wonder if they need to know the mechanics of accounting if they don't want to be accountants. It's a good question. Users of accounting information don't have to be expert bookkeepers, but it's useful to understand how accounting works to understand the relationship between managers' accounting choices—their decisions about how to record transactions and economic events—and the impact of those choices on financial statements. This will help you become an effective and sophisticated user of financial statements.

Some students find a focus on accounting procedures attractive because there is little judgment, analysis, or evaluation required. These students are comfortable solving problems that have right answers. But that isn't learning accounting!

LO 1 THE ACCOUNTING CYCLE: INTRODUCTION

The **accounting cycle** is the process of entering transaction and economic event data into an accounting system and then processing, organizing, and using it to produce information, such as financial statements. It's very difficult to understand and use data that aren't organized in a useful way. For example, you wouldn't know anything about your spending habits unless you recorded every purchase, organized each one by category, and determined the totals.

Figure 3.1, Panel A, provides an overview of an accounting system's role in capturing raw data, processing it, and producing financial statements and other financial information. Let's look at

FIGURE 3.1

Panel A—Overview of an Accounting Information System

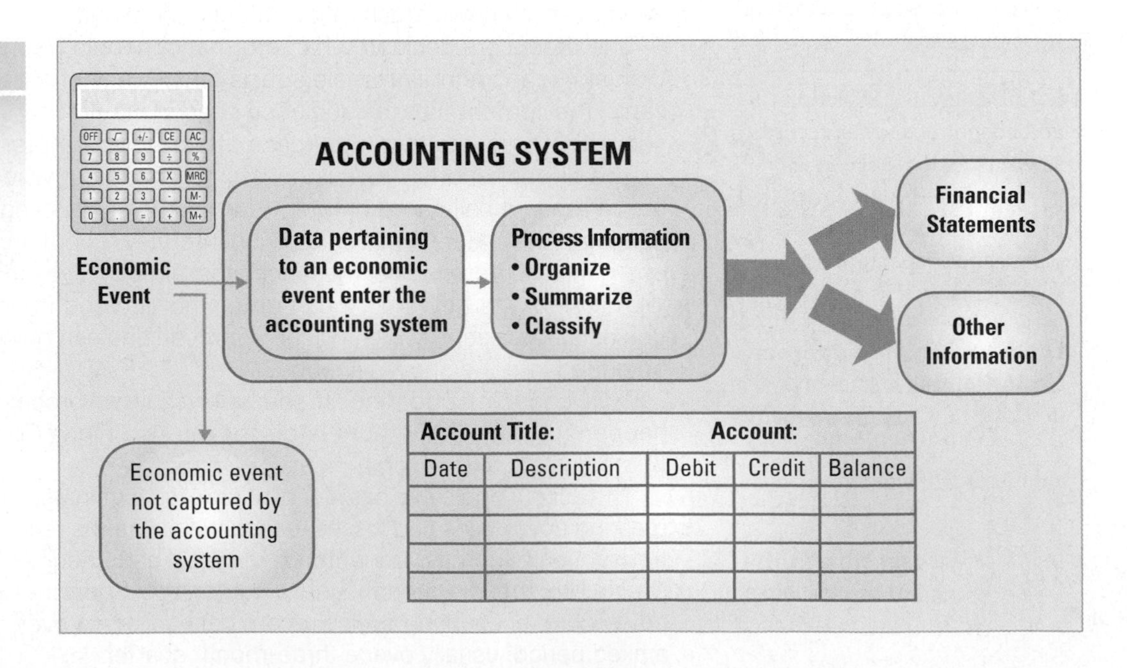

each step of the process. An entity is continuously involved in economic events. In many cases these are transactions with other entities, such as buying and selling assets, incurring and settling liabilities, and supplying goods and services to customers. Some economic events affect an entity but aren't the result of transactions involving it, for example, decisions by competitors and governments, technological changes, and economic conditions.

An accounting system is designed to capture relevant economic events affecting the entity. A relevant event must be entered into the accounting system in some way—it doesn't happen automatically—and judgment is required to decide if, when, and how the event is recorded. Figure 3.1, Panel A, shows that accounting systems aren't designed to capture all economic events. It's key that the accounting system gathers relevant data for providing information to meet the decision-making needs of the stakeholders and the reporting requirements of the entity.

In Canada, most entities base financial reporting on transactions that have already occurred. Once recorded, transaction values usually stay at that amount. For instance, if an entity buys a piece of land for $2,000,000, it's recorded at $2,000,000 and usually remains at that amount for as long as it's owned. If the value of the land increases, in most cases the increase wouldn't be recorded.

An accounting system is conceptually similar to a newspaper's editorial process (see Figure 3.1, Panel B). Each day the editors assign reporters to cover stories. Many newsworthy events take place in the world every day and it isn't possible to cover them all, so a newspaper will cover the stories the editors think are most relevant to its readers. If a story isn't covered, it can't appear in the newspaper.

This makes newspapers and financial reporting similar in two respects. First, a newspaper is a general purpose report—all readers get the same newspaper regardless of their interests or information needs, and it's designed for a wide range of readers. Second, newspapers have a "point of view"—they aren't neutral. The stories covered, how they are written, and the paper's editorial perspective all reflect the viewpoints of the publisher, editors, columnists, and reporters, and they are intended to influence, for example, the social or political agenda in a community. Similarly, financial statements are prepared from the managers' point of view. The accounting choices they make may be intended to have economic consequences for stakeholders; for example, by increasing managers' bonuses, deferring taxes, or affecting the selling price of a business.

Just as newspapers can't give a complete picture of what's going on in the world, so too accounting systems can't give a complete picture of the entity. Accounting systems can only provide information about transactions and economic events that have been entered into the system and organized in a way that makes them accessible.

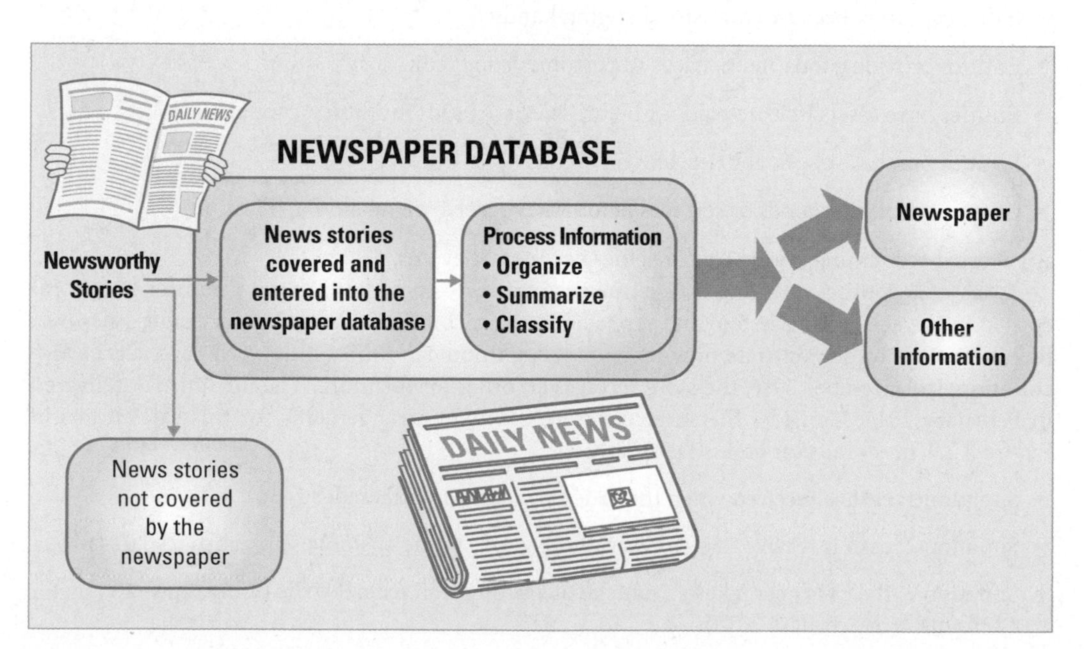

FIGURE 3.1 (continued) Panel B—Overview of a Newspaper Editorial Process

INSIGHT

Thinking of a Career in Accounting?

Many students enter university with the ambition of becoming professional accountants. Careers in accounting are challenging, satisfying, and rewarding, but to "make it" it's necessary to have the skills and abilities accountants require for success. The accounting profession believes that to be successful, accountants must be creative, comfortable with ambiguity, good critical thinkers and problem solvers, and they must possess strong quantitative, interpersonal, and communication skills, both written and oral.

Some students are attracted to accounting for the wrong reasons: they like the certainty, straightforwardness, and "right answers" of bookkeeping. Technical skills are important (as an accountant you have to know how to "do accounting") but that's only a small part of the skill set. So as you proceed through your introductory financial accounting course and ponder your career choices, keep in mind the things that accountants think are important for success in the profession.

LO 3 ACCRUAL ACCOUNTING

In Chapter 2, I introduced accrual accounting as a method for measuring economic activity rather than using cash flows. Accountants believe that accrual accounting provides more relevant information to stakeholders than cash accounting does. Contrasting the two methods is a good way to explain accrual accounting. With cash accounting, an economic event is recorded only when cash is exchanged: a sale is recorded when the customer pays cash, an expense when cash is paid to a supplier. Cash doesn't have to be exchanged when an economic event is recorded (although it may) with accrual accounting: inventory purchased on credit is recorded as an asset and the obligation to pay the supplier is recorded as a liability. With accrual accounting, revenues and expenses can be recorded before, after, or at the same time cash changes hands. (Remember from Chapter 2 that revenue is economic benefits earned by providing goods or services to customers and expenses are economic sacrifices made or costs incurred to earn revenue.)

If you think about it, a cash system provides incomplete information about an entity's activity. Consider the following situations where economic activity is occurring but a cash system wouldn't capture it because cash isn't changing hands:

- Entities provide goods and services to customers on credit.
- Entities have assets that are paid for before they are used (inventory, capital assets).
- Entities purchase goods and services on credit.
- Customers pay for goods or services before they receive them.

An accrual accounting system captures these economic events.

A key concept in accounting is **revenue recognition**—the point in time when revenue is recorded in the accounting system and reported in the income statement. Let's consider sales by a furniture store to demonstrate how revenue recognition can differ under cash and accrual accounting. In December 2016, the store receives an order for furniture. The furniture is delivered in February 2017. Consider the three different payment arrangements for this sale shown in Figure 3.2. The store's year-end is December 31:

- Situation 1: cash is received when the order is placed (in December 2016).
- Situation 2: cash is received on delivery of the goods to the customer (in February 2017).
- Situation 3: the customer takes advantage of a promotion whereby she doesn't have to pay for 12 months (in February 2018).

FIGURE 3.2 **Cash versus Accrual Accounting**

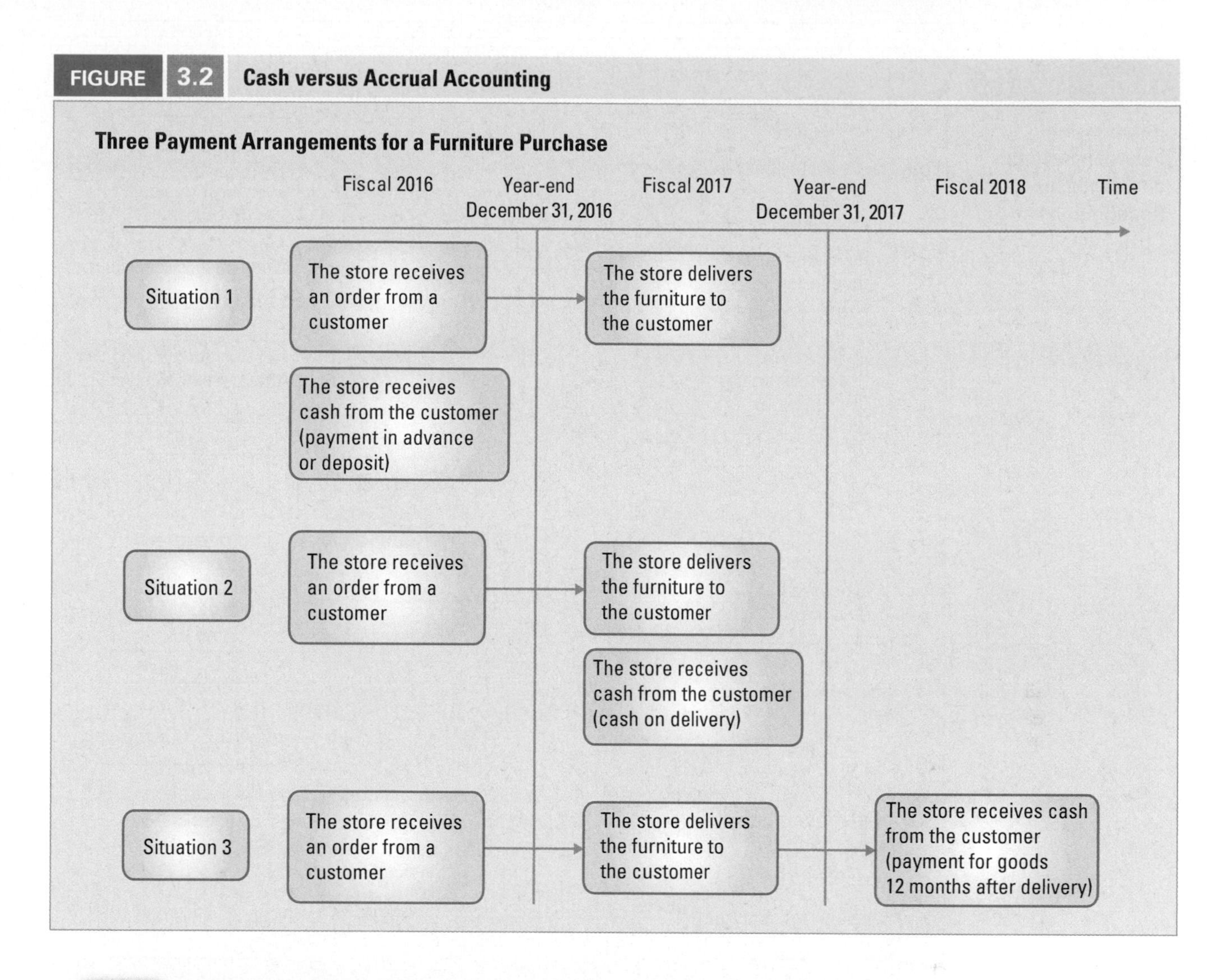

INSIGHT

A Question of Timing

Sooner or later all transactions and economic events are reflected in the financial statements; it's mainly a matter of when. But the "when" matters a lot because it can have economic consequences for stakeholders and can influence their decisions. Under accrual accounting it can be a matter of judgment when revenues and expenses are reported in the income statement.

Preparing financial statements only at the end of an entity's life would be much simpler because, over the life of an entity, accrual accounting and cash accounting provide the same results—there would be no decisions about when to recognize revenue and expenses. Indeed, many accounting scandals and controversies happen because financial statements are prepared periodically—monthly, quarterly, or annually—and judgment is often required in determining which period an economic event belongs to.

In the fifteenth and sixteenth centuries, periodic income statements weren't important. At that time, many business opportunities were short-term ventures. Investors put money into a venture, like a trade voyage to the New World. The organizers purchased the necessary items, including a ship. At the end of the venture everything was sold off and the proceeds distributed among the investors. Income measurement during the trade voyage wasn't necessary and profit just meant you received more than you invested. As business became more complex, it was no longer possible or appropriate to sell all of a company's resources from time to time. But because stakeholders want to know how the entity is doing, the need for periodic statements of performance arose.

FIGURE 3.3

Relationship between Revenue and Expense Recognition and Cash Flow

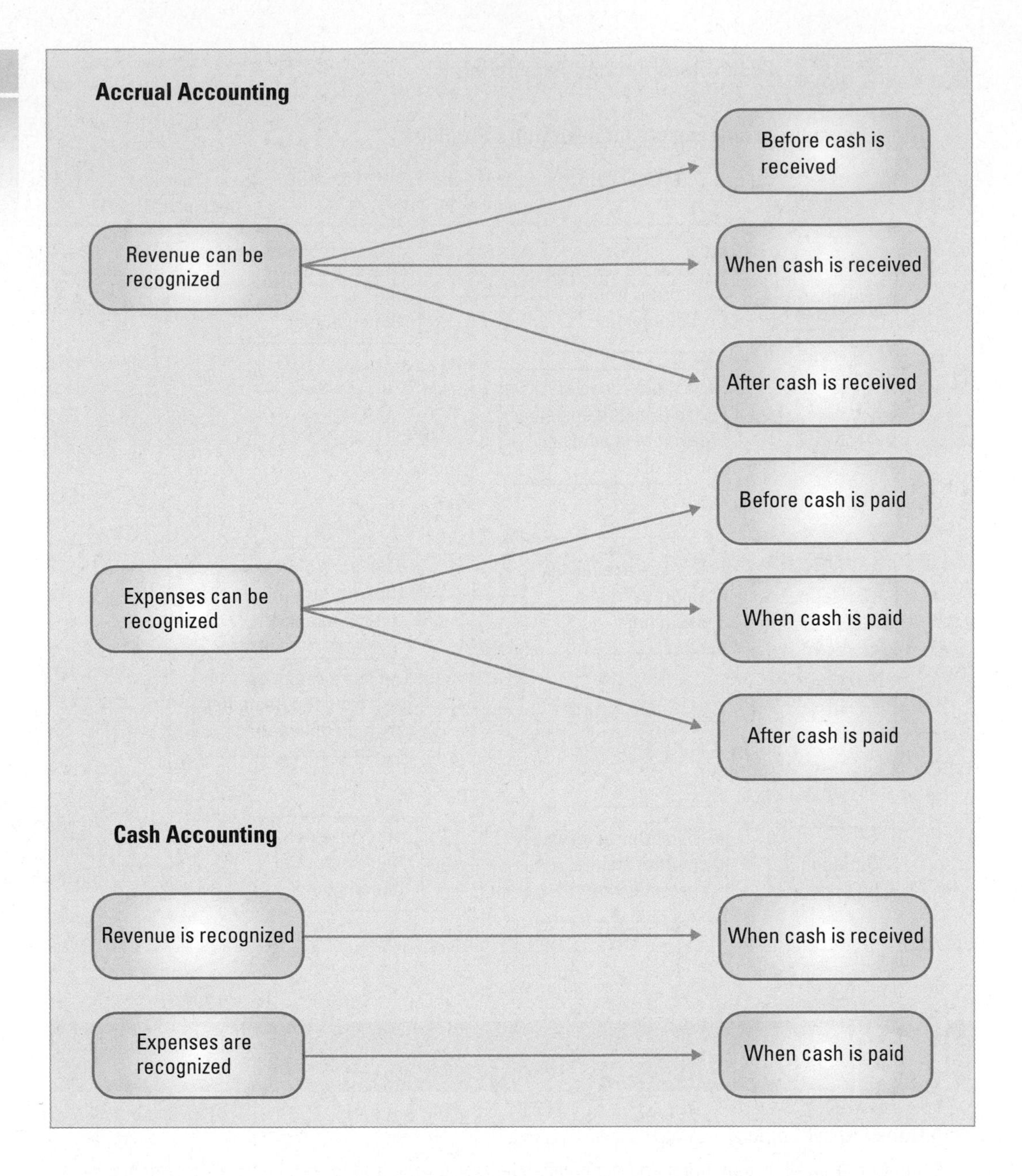

Delivery of goods to customers is typically (but not always) the economic event that triggers revenue recognition under accrual accounting, so the store would recognize revenue in fiscal 2017 in all three situations, regardless of when the cash is received. With cash accounting, the sale would be recognized when cash is received, which is at a different time in each of the three situations.

A similar story exists for expenses. Under accrual accounting, accountants try to *match* expenses to revenue. With **matching**, expenses are recognized (recorded) in the same period as the revenue they helped earn is recognized. For the furniture store's sale, the cost of the furniture sold would be expensed in the same period the revenue from the sale is recorded, regardless of when the store paid for the furniture. Associating economic benefits (revenues) and economic costs (expenses) is necessary if profit is to be a meaningful measure of performance. Figure 3.3 summarizes the relationship between revenue and expense recognition and cash flow under cash and accrual accounting.

While accrual accounting may provide more relevant information to stakeholders in many situations, it also requires judgment, which is subjective. With cash accounting, it's obvious when a sale should be recognized—cash is received. With accrual accounting, it isn't always obvious. Revenue is recognized when an entity enjoys an economic benefit, *but* someone has to decide when the benefit occurs. We will explore in Chapter 4 how managers decide when to recognize revenue and how to match expenses. For now, understand that revenue recognition and matching aren't always straightforward and can require the exercise of judgment.

THE ACCOUNTING CYCLE: TRANSACTIONAL ANALYSIS

LO 2

We are now going to examine the mechanics of accounting—the process of recording data about transactions and economic events in an accounting system and converting it into useful information like financial statements. At the heart of the process is the accounting equation introduced in Chapter 2:

Assets = Liabilities + Owners' equity

Every economic event is analyzed in terms of the accounting equation to determine the impact it has on each element of the equation. The equality of the equation must be maintained with each entry to an accounting system. I will demonstrate the full accounting cycle in a straightforward, conceptual, and compact way using an *accounting equation spreadsheet.* The spreadsheet method clearly lays out the effect of transactions and economic events on the accounting equation and the process by which economic activity gets turned into financial statements. I will also develop an approach to the accounting cycle that is a representation of the way accounting systems are structured in practice. Both of these methods apply the **double-entry bookkeeping** system in which each transaction or economic event is recorded in at least two places in the accounts. This system is necessary to keep the accounting equation in balance.

The Accounting Equation Spreadsheet and Journal Entries

In an accounting equation spreadsheet, transactions and economic events are recorded to reflect their impact on the accounting equation. For example, if an entity borrows $10,000 from the bank, our analysis is that assets increase by $10,000 (the entity has more cash) and liabilities increase by $10,000 (money is owed to the bank). The effect could be shown in the following way:

Assets	=	Liabilities	+	Owners' equity
+$10,000 (Cash increases)		+$10,000 (Bank loan increases)		

This represents a very basic accounting equation spreadsheet; each column represents one of the elements of the accounting equation and a row represents a transaction. To do this type of analysis, you must answer each of the following questions:

1. Which elements of the accounting equation are affected—assets, liabilities, and/or owners' equity, including revenues and expenses?
2. How are the accounts affected—does the amount of each element increase or decrease?
3. By how much has each element increased or decreased?

Let's do some transactional analyses using this basic spreadsheet. You should review the definitions of the financial statement elements (assets, liabilities, owners' equity, revenue, expenses) before proceeding. Consider the following transactions for Cheticamp Ltd. (Cheticamp):

- Sells shares to investors for $50,000 cash.
- Purchases inventory and promises to pay the supplier $3,000 in 30 days.
- Provides services to a customer worth $1,100. The customer agrees to pay in 60 days.

- Collects $500 owed by a customer.
- Pays $2,000 owed to a supplier.
- Receives $2,500 from a customer for goods that will be delivered next month.

1. Cheticamp sells shares to investors for $50,000 cash.

Assets	=	Liabilities	+	Owners' equity
+$50,000 (Cash increases)	=		+	+$50,000 (Common shares increases)

Explanation: Cheticamp received $50,000 from the investors so cash, an asset, increases. By purchasing shares, the investors have made an equity investment in Cheticamp, so owners' equity increases.

2. Cheticamp purchases inventory and promises to pay the supplier $3,000 in 30 days.

Assets	=	Liabilities	+	Owners' equity
+$3,000 (Inventory increases)	=	+$3,000 (Accounts payable increases)	+	

Explanation: Cheticamp has received some inventory, which is an asset because it can be sold to earn revenue. It didn't pay cash, but promised to pay in 30 days, so there is a liability to pay the supplier.

3. Cheticamp provides services to a customer worth $1,100. The customer agrees to pay in 60 days.

Assets	=	Liabilities	+	Owners' equity
+$1,100 (Accounts receivable increases)	=		+	+$1,100 (Revenue increases, Owners' equity increases)

Explanation: Services are provided to a customer, which represents an increase in revenue and an increase in owners' equity. The customer has agreed to pay in 60 days, which is an asset because it represents the right to receive the customer's money. Remember that revenue is reported on the income statement but it's part of owners' equity. When revenue increases, owners' equity increases at the same time.

4. Cheticamp collects $500 owed by a customer.

Assets	=	Liabilities	+	Owners' equity
+$500 (Cash increases) −$500 (Accounts receivable decreases)	=		+	

Explanation: This transaction converts one asset into another. The entity received cash from a customer so assets increase. But assets also decrease because the customer has fulfilled its obligation to pay Cheticamp, which decreases accounts receivable.

5. Cheticamp pays $2,000 owed to a supplier.

Assets	=	Liabilities	+	Owners' equity
−$2,000 (Cash decreases)	=	−$2,000 (Accounts payable decreases)	+	

Explanation: Cheticamp has fulfilled its obligation to a supplier by paying an amount owing so accounts payable decrease. The obligation is paid in cash so cash decreases.

6. Cheticamp receives $2,500 from a customer for goods that will be delivered next month.

Assets	=	Liabilities	+	Owners' equity
+$2,500 (Cash increases)	=	+$2,500 (Unearned revenue increases)	+	

Explanation: Cheticamp has received cash in advance for providing goods to the customer. Cash increases since the cash was received, but since the goods haven't been provided to the customer, it isn't appropriate in most cases to recognize revenue. Instead, Cheticamp has a liability to provide $2,500 worth of goods to the customer in the future.

In practice, an entity creates separate categories called **accounts** to reflect the different types of assets, liabilities, and owners' equity it has. Instead of a single column for each element of the accounting equation, there will be many columns under each element, each representing a separate account. For example, an entity might have asset accounts for cash, accounts receivable, inventory, furniture, land, and any other assets the managers specify. The number and type of separate accounts an entity maintains are determined by the information managers need and want to have to meet their managerial and financial reporting needs. A larger number of accounts provides more detailed information but at the cost of making the accounting system more complicated and more expensive to set up and run.

Cheticamp's transactions could be represented in a more detailed spreadsheet that breaks down assets, liabilities, and owners' equity into the different accounts (note that decreases in accounts are shown in parentheses):

	Assets			=	Liabilities		+	Owners' equity			
Transaction	Cash	Accounts receivable	Inventory		Accounts payable	Unearned revenue		Common shares	Retained earnings	Revenue	Expenses
1.	$50,000	$	$		$	$		$50,000	$	$	$
2.			3,000		3,000						
3.		1,100								1,100	
4.	500	(500)									
5.	(2,000)				(2,000)						
6.	2,500					2,500					

LO 5

Before moving on to a detailed example, I'm going to introduce the method for entering transactions and economic events into an accounting system that is used in practice—journal entries. A **journal entry** describes how a transaction or economic event affects the accounting equation. A spreadsheet isn't very practical for an entity with large numbers of transactions in a year and hundreds or thousands of different asset, liability, and equity accounts. A journal entry accomplishes exactly the same thing as an entry to an accounting equation spreadsheet, but in a different format. The journal entry format showing the three key pieces of information appears below:

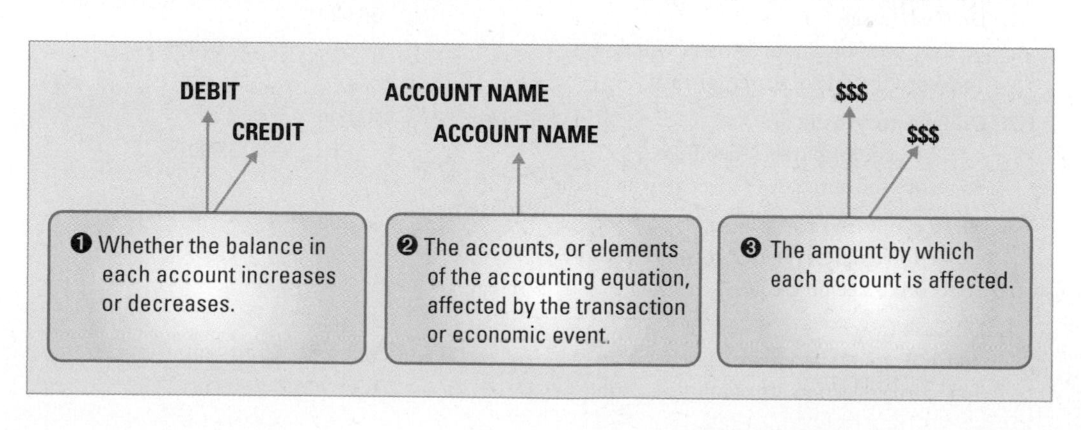

Account names in a journal entry correspond to the column headings on the spreadsheet. The terms **debit** and **credit** indicate whether the balance in the account has increased or decreased. These terms have very precise meanings in accounting and are defined as follows:

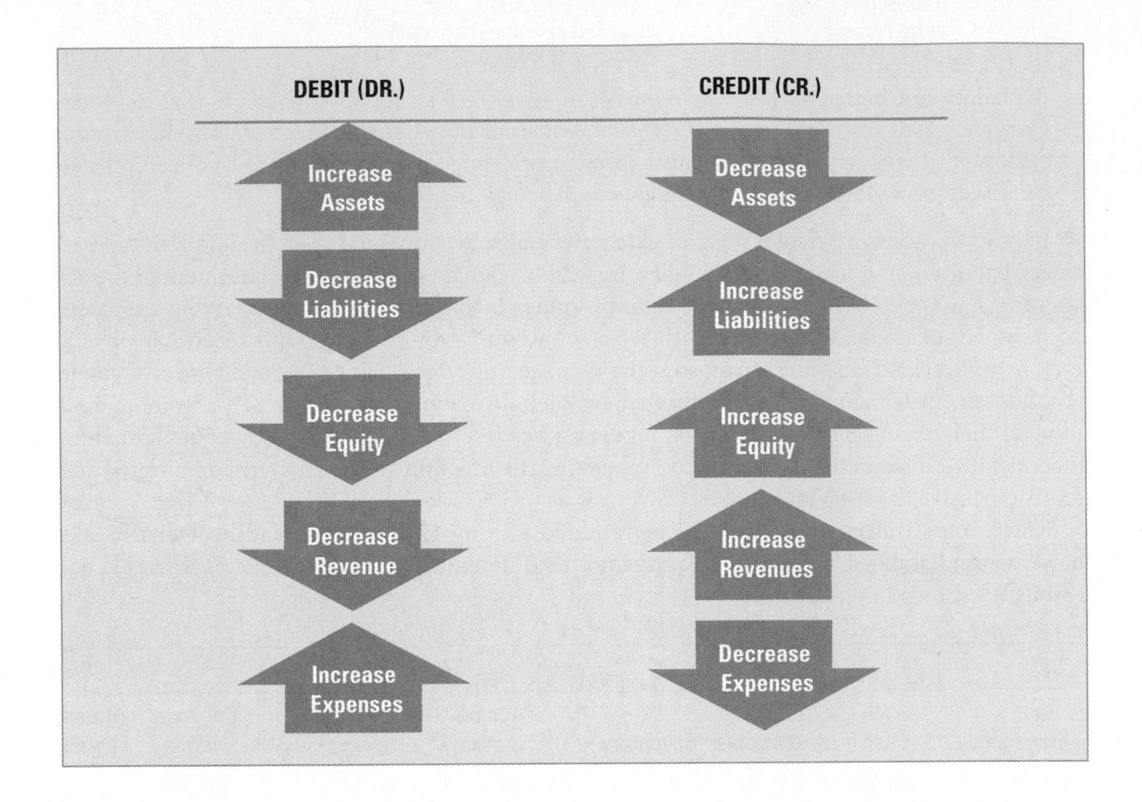

At first, these terms may be confusing and cumbersome to work with. As you work with journal entries, what they mean will become second nature to you. In a journal entry, the debits must equal the credits; if they don't, the accounting equation won't balance.

Now we'll repeat the transactional analysis of six events that was done above for Cheticamp, only this time using journal entries. Notice that after each journal entry a brief explanation is provided.

1. Sells shares to investors for $50,000 cash.
2. Purchases inventory and promises to pay the supplier $3,000 in 30 days.
3. Provides services to a customer worth $1,100. The customer agrees to pay in 60 days.
4. Collects $500 owed by a customer.
5. Pays $2,000 owed to a supplier.
6. Receives $2,500 from a customer for goods that will be delivered next month.

	Dr.	Cr.
1. Dr. Cash (asset +)	50,000	
Cr. Common shares (owners' equity +)		50,000
To record the sale of shares for cash		
2. Dr. Inventory (asset +)	3,000	
Cr. Accounts payable (liabilities +)		3,000
To record the purchase of inventory on credit		
3. Dr. Accounts receivable (asset +)	1,100	
Cr. Revenue (revenue +, owners' equity +)		1,100
To record a sale on credit		
4. Dr. Cash (asset +)	500	
Cr. Accounts receivable (assets −)		500
To record collection of accounts receivable		

5. Dr. Accounts payable (liabilities −)	2,000	
Cr. Cash (assets −)		2,000
To record payment to a supplier		
6. Dr. Cash (asset +)	2,500	
Cr. Unearned revenue (liabilities +)		2,500
To record the deposit for goods to be delivered in future		

Notice that after each account name, the type of account (asset, liability, owners' equity, revenue, expense) and the direction of the change are shown. You may find this helpful for finding errors and making sure that your journal entries make sense.

Entering a transaction or economic event is a crucial step in the accounting process. Judgment must be exercised to determine if a transaction or event should be recorded, when it should be recorded, and how it should be accounted for (which elements of the accounting equation and specific accounts should be affected). Entries that occur frequently become routine and can be made by bookkeepers or clerks. However, an accountant must oversee the entry process to ensure that routine entries are done properly and that new and different transactions and economic events are correctly analyzed and interpreted.

INSIGHT

Debits and Credits

It's easy to fall into the trap of assigning qualities to debits and credits; for example, credits are good, debits are bad. While the term "credit" has positive connotations in ordinary language, it doesn't share that positive meaning in an accounting context. In accounting, a credit means a decrease of an asset or an expense account or an increase to a liability, equity, or revenue account. A debit means an increase to an asset or an expense account or a decrease in a liability, equity, or revenue account. From the perspective of a journal entry, a debit amount is in the left-hand column and a credit amount is in the right-hand column. Also, the credit entry is indented.

KNOWLEDGE CHECK 3.1

A hot dog vendor operates a cart in an urban park. Prepare journal entries for the following transactions:

- ❑ The vendor sells food items to customers during a day for $425 cash.
- ❑ The vendor purchases a supply of condiments for $300 cash.
- ❑ The vendor pays $250 on his bank loan.

The Accounting Cycle—Example

LO 2, 5

Let's use the accounting equation spreadsheet and journal entries in a realistic business setting. In June 2017, two friends from business school, Filomena and Teresa, decide to open a small restaurant near the campus. They develop a business plan and set to work opening their restaurant, called Strawberries. They organize the business as a corporation for tax and legal liability purposes. They will use July and August to ready the restaurant and will open for business on September 1. Filomena and Teresa design their restaurant's accounting system to provide information needed to prepare tax returns and to evaluate the restaurant's performance. Thus, the accounting system will process mainly transactional information and historical costs. Filomena and Teresa will use this accounting equation spreadsheet:

	Assets					=	Liabilities		+	Shareholders' equity			
Transaction	Cash	Accounts receivable	Food, drinks, and supplies inventory	Prepaid rent	Renovations, equipment, and furniture		Bank loan	Accounts payable		Common shares	Retained earnings	Revenue	Expenses
Balance													
Transaction													
Balance													

The very top line of the spreadsheet states the accounting equation in the familiar format, with the difference that owners' equity is called shareholders' equity because Strawberries is a corporation and the owners of a corporation are called shareholders. Under each accounting equation element—asset, liability, and shareholders' equity—you find the various accounts making up the element. A transaction or economic event affecting an account will appear as a dollar amount in that account's column. Account decreases are shown in brackets. Note that only one column has been provided for each of revenue and expenses. In practice, separate accounts would exist for each type of revenue and expense. The income statement details are shown later.

To record transactions in the spreadsheet, we follow these procedures:

- The row just under the account headings shows the balance in each account before the transaction under consideration is recorded in the spreadsheet.
- The transaction under discussion will be recorded in the next row and given a number for easy reference. This line is highlighted.
- The bottom row gives the balance in each account after the transaction is recorded. This row is the sum of the balance before the current transaction and the current transaction and that amount that will be carried forward to the next transaction.

For each transaction, the journal entry is also provided.

The transactional analysis requires answering the following questions for each transaction and economic event (these are the same steps we examined earlier with step 2 as an additional step):

1. Which elements of the accounting equation are affected—assets, liabilities, and/or owners' equity, including revenues and expenses?
2. Which specific asset, liability, owners' equity, revenue, and expense accounts have been affected?
3. How are the accounts affected—does the amount of each account increase or decrease?
4. By how much has each specific asset, liability, owners' equity, revenue, and expense account increased or decreased?

Strawberries Transactions

1. On June 7, 2017, Filomena and Teresa set up a corporation called Strawberries Inc. They each contribute $20,000 to the corporation and receive 1,000 shares of Strawberries Inc. in return.

	Assets					=	Liabilities		+	Shareholders' equity			
Transaction	Cash	Accounts receivable	Food, drinks, and supplies inventory	Prepaid rent	Renovations, equipment, and furniture		Bank loan	Accounts payable		Common shares	Retained earnings	Revenue	Expenses
Balance													
1	$40,000									$40,000			
Balance	$40,000									$40,000			

1. Dr. Cash (asset +) 40,000
   Cr. Common shares (shareholders' equity +) 40,000
   To record the sale of shares for cash

Strawberries' cash (an asset) has increased by $40,000 because of Filomena and Teresa's contributions. The shares they received represent their ownership interest in Strawberries and result in an increase to common shares of $40,000. Notice that the journal entry corresponds to entries on the spreadsheet: $40,000 debit to cash corresponds to $40,000 added to the cash column, $40,000 credit to common shares corresponds to $40,000 added to the common shares column. Also notice that the debits equal the credits in the journal entry, and in the spreadsheet the accounting equation is in balance because $40,000 was added to both sides.

2. Filomena and Teresa realize they need more cash and take out a bank loan for $20,000 on July 4. Interest of $150 is due at the end of each month, beginning in September. Strawberries must begin paying back the loan in one year.

	Assets					=	Liabilities		+	Shareholders' equity			
Transaction	Cash	Accounts receivable	Food, drinks, and supplies inventory	Prepaid rent	Renovations, equipment, and furniture		Bank loan	Accounts payable		Common shares	Retained earnings	Revenue	Expenses
Balance	$40,000									$40,000			
2	$20,000						$20,000						
Balance	$60,000						$20,000			$40,000			

2. Dr. Cash (asset +) 20,000
   Cr. Bank loan (liability +) 20,000
   To record the $20,000 bank loan

The bank loan increases Strawberries' cash by $20,000 and creates a liability of $20,000—Strawberries owes the bank $20,000. As a result of the loan, cash and bank loan each increase by $20,000. The cost of borrowing the money, the interest, isn't recorded because under accrual accounting the cost of using money occurs with the passage of time. An interest expense will be recorded only after Strawberries has had the use of the money for a period of time.

3. Filomena and Teresa sign a two-year lease for space in a shopping centre and agree to pay $1,250 per month in rent beginning in September. Rent must be paid on the first day of each month with the first three months' rent due upon signing the lease. Filomena writes a cheque for $3,750.

	Assets					=	Liabilities		+	Shareholders' equity			
Transaction	Cash	Accounts receivable	Food, drinks, and supplies inventory	Prepaid rent	Renovations, equipment, and furniture		Bank loan	Accounts payable		Common shares	Retained earnings	Revenue	Expenses
Balance	$60,000						$20,000			$40,000			
3	($3,750)*			$3,750									
Balance	$56,250			$3,750			$20,000			$40,000			

*Brackets indicate a decrease in the account balance.

3. Dr. Prepaid rent (asset +) 3,750
   Cr. Cash (asset −) 3,750
   To record the prepayment of three months' rent

The $3,750 payment is an asset because it provides a future benefit—the right to use the location for three months (September through November). This asset is called prepaid rent. As a result, cash decreases by $3,750 and prepaid rent increases by $3,750.

The payment is treated as cash even though it was by cheque because a cheque is equivalent to cash. When a cheque is cashed the amount is removed from the bank account of the cheque writer. Also, even though the lease is for two years, only the amount paid is recorded as an asset. The right to use the location for two years at an agreed-upon price isn't recorded, even though having the lease is a benefit to Strawberries. This type of future benefit isn't usually classified as an asset according to IFRS.

4. Filomena and Teresa do some renovations costing $15,000, all of which is paid in cash.

	Assets					=	Liabilities		+	Shareholders' equity			
Transaction	Cash	Accounts receivable	Food, drinks, and supplies inventory	Prepaid rent	Renovations, equipment, and furniture		Bank loan	Accounts payable		Common shares	Retained earnings	Revenue	Expenses
Balance	$56,250			$3,750			$20,000			$40,000			
4	($15,000)				$15,000								
Balance	$41,250			$3,750	$15,000		$20,000			$40,000			

4. Dr. Renovations, equipment, and furniture (asset +) 15,000
   Cr. Cash (asset −) 15,000
   To record the cost of renovating the restaurant

The renovations are an asset because they will contribute to the environment of the restaurant—after all, a restaurant's ambiance is part of the attraction of dining out. The renovations were paid for in cash so cash decreases by $15,000 and renovations, equipment, and furniture increase by $15,000.

5. On August 10, Teresa buys equipment, furniture, dishes, and other necessary materials for $25,000. Half of the amount is paid in cash. The remainder must be paid to the supplier in 90 days.

	Assets					=	Liabilities		+	Shareholders' equity			
Transaction	Cash	Accounts receivable	Food, drinks, and supplies inventory	Prepaid rent	Renovations, equipment, and furniture		Bank loan	Accounts payable		Common shares	Retained earnings	Revenue	Expenses
Balance	$41,250			$3,750	$15,000		$20,000			$40,000			
5	($12,500)				$25,000			$12,500					
Balance	$28,750			$3,750	$40,000		$20,000	$12,500		$40,000			

5. Dr. Renovations, equipment, and furniture (asset +) 25,000
   Cr. Cash (asset −) 12,500
   Cr. Accounts payable (liability +) 12,500
   To record the purchase of equipment and furniture

This transaction affects more than two accounts because the items were purchased partly for cash and partly on credit. As a result, cash decreases by $12,500, the amount paid to the supplier, and there is a liability—accounts payable—to pay the supplier $12,500 in 90 days. Accounts payable are amounts owed to suppliers for goods or services purchased on credit and are usually current liabilities.

The items purchased are non-current assets because they will help Strawberries earn revenue over several years by providing the equipment to prepare meals, the dishes to serve meals on, and so on. They won't be used up, sold, or converted to cash within one year. The assets purchased are recorded at their cost of $25,000. The amount recorded is the full economic sacrifice made to acquire the assets; it doesn't matter that the full amount isn't paid in cash at the time of purchase.

INSIGHT

Valuing Capital Assets

For the most part, capital assets (which for Strawberries are renovations, equipment, and furniture) are reported at cost. If the market value increases after it's purchased, no change is recorded. Under IFRS, companies can choose to value capital assets at fair value (the amount the asset could be sold for now), although research shows that few companies do. If an entity uses cost as the basis for valuing capital assets, the amounts reported on the balance sheet doesn't provide any information about their market value.

6. As opening day approaches, Strawberries hires a server and kitchen help, who will begin work when Strawberries opens. The restaurant purchases non-perishable food items and supplies for $900 and pays using its debit card. (A **debit card** allows a customer to pay for goods and services by transferring money directly from the customer's bank account to the vendor's bank account. Payment by debit card is equivalent to payment by cash.)

	Assets					=	Liabilities		+	Shareholders' equity			
Transaction	Cash	Accounts receivable	Food, drinks, and supplies inventory	Prepaid rent	Renovations, equipment, and furniture		Bank loan	Accounts payable		Common shares	Retained earnings	Revenue	Expenses
Balance	$28,750			$3,750	$40,000		$20,000	$12,500		$40,000			
6	($900)		$900										
Balance	$27,850		$900	$3,750	$40,000		$20,000	$12,500		$40,000			

6. Dr. Food, drinks, and supplies inventory (asset +)	900	
Cr. Cash (asset −)		900
To record the purchase of inventory		

The purchase reduces Strawberries' cash by $900 and increases the food, drinks, and supplies inventory by $900. These purchases will contribute to meals for customers, so they are assets, and they will become expenses when they are used. The inventory is recorded at its cost.

The hiring of employees isn't recorded because they haven't done any work yet and Strawberries hasn't paid them. If the employees had worked or Strawberries had paid them, an entry would have been required. Under IFRS, these executory contracts aren't usually recorded in the accounting system. (An **executory contract** is an exchange of promises in which one party promises to supply goods or services and the other party promises to pay for them, but neither side has fulfilled its side of the bargain.)

7. During September, Strawberries purchases $12,000 of food and drinks to serve to customers. The food and drinks are paid for by debit card.

	Assets					=	Liabilities		+	Shareholders' equity			
Transaction	Cash	Accounts receivable	Food, drinks, and supplies inventory	Prepaid rent	Renovations, equipment, and furniture		Bank loan	Accounts payable		Common shares	Retained earnings	Revenue	Expenses
Balance	$27,850		$900	$3,750	$40,000		$20,000	$12,500		$40,000			
7	($12,000)		$12,000										
Balance	$15,850		$12,900	$3,750	$40,000		$20,000	$12,500		$40,000			

7. Dr. Food, drinks, and supplies inventory (asset +)	12,000	
Cr. Cash (asset −)		12,000
To record the purchase of food and drinks during September (In practice, each purchase of food and drinks would require a separate journal entry, but for the purpose of the example all purchases are recorded in a single entry)		

The food and drinks are classified as inventory because they will be used to prepare meals for customers. They will be expensed when used. Under accrual accounting, inventory is an asset until it's sold. Under a cash accounting system, the purchase of food and drinks would be expensed when paid for. Cash decreases and food, drinks, and supplies inventory increases by $12,000.

8. During September, Strawberries had sales of $17,900. Of these, $17,200 was for meals served in the restaurant and paid for by cash, credit card, or debit card and $700 was for a faculty party that was catered. Payment for the party is due in the middle of October.

	Assets					=	Liabilities		+	Shareholders' equity			
Transaction	Cash	Accounts receivable	Food, drinks, and supplies inventory	Prepaid rent	Renovations, equipment, and furniture		Bank loan	Accounts payable		Common shares	Retained earnings	Revenue	Expenses
Balance	$15,850		$12,900	$3,750	$40,000		$20,000	$12,500		$40,000			
8	$17,200	$700										$17,900	
Balance	$33,050	$700	$12,900	$3,750	$40,000		$20,000	$12,500		$40,000		$17,900	

8. Dr. Cash (asset +)	17,200	
Dr. Accounts receivable (asset +)	700	
Cr. Revenue (shareholders' equity +, revenue +)		17,900
To record sales for the month of September		

All sales during the month are recorded as revenue. The amount owed for catering is an asset because it represents cash that will be received in the future, so $700 is recorded as accounts receivable, the usual account name for amounts owed by customers.

It isn't always obvious when revenue should be recorded. For example, when did Strawberries enjoy an economic benefit from catering the faculty party? When the order was received, when the event was catered, or when the cash was collected? Arguments can be made in support of each. Under IFRS and accrual accounting, it isn't necessary to wait until cash is received to record a sale. On the other hand, IFRS encourage caution in deciding when to record a sale. If revenue is recorded too soon the financial statements could be unreliable. For example, if the faculty party was cancelled at the last minute and Strawberries had recorded the revenue when the order was received, revenue that never happened would be reported. In contrast, the only logical time to recognize revenue for the people who eat at Strawberries is when they pay at the end of their meals.

Although the $17,900 of sales was recorded on a single line on the spreadsheet and in a single journal entry, in fact a separate line would be added for each individual sale or each day's sales.

9, 10. At the end of September, Strawberries paid $525 for utilities and $925 in wages to its employees.

	Assets					= Liabilities		+ Shareholders' equity			
Transaction	Cash	Accounts receivable	Food, drinks, and supplies inventory	Prepaid rent	Renovations, equipment, and furniture	Bank loan	Accounts payable	Common shares	Retained earnings	Revenue	Expenses
Balance	$33,050	$700	$12,900	$3,750	$40,000	$20,000	$12,500	$40,000		$17,900	
9	($525)										($525)*
10	($925)										($925)**
Balance	$31,600	$700	$12,900	$3,750	$40,000	$20,000	$12,500	$40,000		$17,900	($1,450)

*Utilities expense
**Wages expense

9, 10. Dr. Utilities expense (shareholders' equity −, expenses +) 525
Dr. Wage expense (shareholders' equity −, expenses +) 925
Cr. Cash (asset −) 1,450
To record the utilities and wages expenses for the month of September

The utilities and wage payments are costs of operating the restaurant in September and represent expenses for the month. Since these expenses were paid in cash, cash decreases by $1,450. Notice in the spreadsheet that expenses are recorded as negative amounts (in brackets). This is done because expenses reduce shareholders' equity. Notice that both expenses were recorded as part of a single journal entry. Each expense could have also been recorded with a separate journal entry.

11. At the end of September, Strawberries pays the bank $150 interest for the loan.

	Assets					= Liabilities		+ Shareholders' equity			
Transaction	Cash	Accounts receivable	Food, drinks, and supplies inventory	Prepaid rent	Renovations, equipment, and furniture	Bank loan	Accounts payable	Common shares	Retained earnings	Revenue	Expenses
Balance	$31,600	$700	$12,900	$3,750	$40,000	$20,000	$12,500	$40,000		$17,900	($1,450)
11	($150)										($150)*
Balance	$31,450	$700	$12,900	$3,750	$40,000	$20,000	$12,500	$40,000		$17,900	($1,600)

*Interest expense

11. Dr. Interest expense (shareholders' equity −, expenses +) 150
Cr. Cash (asset −) 150
To record the interest expense for the month of September

The interest cost is a $150 expense. Cash decreases by $150 since it was paid in cash. If Strawberries hadn't made the interest payment at the end of September, it would still be recorded as an expense. Under accrual accounting, expenses are any costs incurred to earn revenue during the period, regardless when cash is paid. If Strawberries had the use of the bank's money during September but didn't pay the interest by the end of the month, it should record an interest expense in September and record a liability called interest payable (instead of a decrease in cash).

12. One of Strawberries' major operating costs is the food, drinks, and supplies used in preparing meals. At the end of September, Teresa counted the food, drinks, and supplies inventory and found that there were items on hand costing $1,000. Because Strawberries had $12,900 of food, drinks, and supplies available during September and there was $1,000 left in inventory at the end of the month, this means that $11,900 ($12,900 − $1,000) was used.

	Assets					=	Liabilities		+	Shareholders' equity			
Transaction	Cash	Accounts receivable	Food, drinks, and supplies inventory	Prepaid rent	Renovations, equipment, and furniture		Bank loan	Accounts payable		Common shares	Retained earnings	Revenue	Expenses
Balance	$31,450	$700	$12,900	$3,750	$40,000		$20,000	$12,500		$40,000		$17,900	($1,600)
12			($11,900)										($11,900)*
Balance	$31,450	$700	$1,000	$3,750	$40,000		$20,000	$12,500		$40,000		$17,900	($13,500)

*Food, drinks, and supplies expense

12. Dr. Cost of sales (shareholders' equity −, expenses +) 11,900
Cr. Food, drinks, and supplies inventory (asset −) 11,900
To record the cost of food, drinks, and supplies used to provide meals to customers

An expense of $11,900 reflects the cost of food, drinks, and supplies used to earn revenue during September and the amount of food, drinks, and supplies inventory decreases by $11,900. By expensing the $11,900 we are *matching* the cost of the meals served to the revenue earned from providing those meals.

13. When Filomena paid $3,750 to the shopping centre owner, the amount was recorded as an asset: prepaid rent. At the end of September, Strawberries has used up part of that asset. An asset that is used or consumed becomes an expense (another example of matching). This means that the $1,250 ($3,750 ÷ 3) cost of September's rent can be matched to revenues earned in September. One month of prepaid rent has been used up, so prepaid rent is reduced by $1,250 and there is a $1,250 rent expense for September. The remaining $2,500 balance in prepaid rent represents the right to use the space in the shopping centre in October and November, so it's still an asset.

	Assets					=	Liabilities		+	Shareholders' equity			
Transaction	Cash	Accounts receivable	Food, drinks, and supplies inventory	Prepaid rent	Renovations, equipment, and furniture		Bank loan	Accounts payable		Common shares	Retained earnings	Revenue	Expenses
Balance	$31,450	$700	$1,000	$3,750	$40,000		$20,000	$12,500		$40,000		$17,900	($13,500)
13				($1,250)									($1,250)*
Balance	$31,450	$700	$1,000	$2,500	$40,000		$20,000	$12,500		$40,000		$17,900	($14,750)

*Rent expense

13. Dr. Rent expense (shareholders' equity −, expenses +) 1,250
Cr. Prepaid rent (asset −) 1,250
To record the rent expense for September

14. During September, Strawberries will have consumed some of its renovations, equipment, and furniture while operating its business. The renovations have future benefit as long as the restaurant occupies that particular location. As the lease period expires, so do the benefits associated with the renovations. The equipment and furniture will eventually wear out, break down, or become obsolete.

	Assets					=	Liabilities		+	Shareholders' equity			
Transaction	Cash	Accounts receivable	Food, drinks, and supplies inventory	Prepaid rent	Renovations, equipment, and furniture		Bank loan	Accounts payable		Common shares	Retained earnings	Revenue	Expenses
Balance	$31,450	$700	$1,000	$2,500	$40,000		$20,000	$12,500		$40,000		$17,900	($14,750)
14					($1,042)								($1,042)*
Balance	$31,450	$700	$1,000	$2,500	$38,958		$20,000	$12,500		$40,000		$17,900	($15,792)

*Depreciation expense

14. Dr. Depreciation expense (shareholders' equity −, expenses +) 1,042
Cr. Renovations, equipment, and furniture (asset −) 1,042
To record the depreciation of renovations, equipment, and furniture

The renovations will be depreciated over two years, the period of Strawberries' lease. It isn't possible to determine the renovations' contribution to revenue each month, so we simply depreciate an equal amount of the cost each month: $625 ($15,000 ÷ 24 months). Depreciating an equal amount of the cost of an asset each period is called **straight-line depreciation**. Managers have some opportunity to exercise judgment here. If, for example, Strawberries has the option to renew its lease for another two years, the managers could argue for depreciating over four years rather than two.

The equipment and furniture are handled in the same way. However, these assets can be moved to other locations, so their useful lives aren't limited to the term of the lease and an assumption must be made about how long they will provide benefits to Strawberries. We will assume that the useful life of the equipment and furniture is five years (this is a simplification because it's likely the individual assets have a variety of useful lives) and depreciate it using the straight-line method over 60 months. The depreciation expense for September for the equipment and furniture is $417 ($25,000 ÷ 60 months). Therefore, the depreciation expense for September is $1,042 ($625 + $417) and renovations, equipment, and furniture decreases by $1,042.

INSIGHT

Depreciation

Depreciation (or amortization) allocates the cost of a capital asset to expense over its useful life. It's also another example of matching. Since property, plant, and equipment (PPE) help an entity earn revenue, its cost should be matched to the revenue it helps earn. Instead of expensing the cost of PPE all at once, for example when it's disposed of at the end of its life, some of the cost is expensed each period. This type of matching can be hard to do; after all, how do chairs, ovens, or paint on a wall contribute to revenue? Still, the job has to be done, so accountants or managers estimate how long capital assets will be used (useful life) and choose a method for depreciating the cost.

Depreciation provides no information whatsoever about the change in the market value of capital assets. It's just the allocation of the cost to expense.

15. At the end of September, Filomena and Teresa decide to declare and pay a dividend of $0.50 per share, or $1,000 ($0.50 × 2,000 shares). They didn't pay themselves salaries in September, but they could have.

	Assets					=	Liabilities		+	Shareholders' equity			
Transaction	Cash	Accounts receivable	Food, drinks, and supplies inventory	Prepaid rent	Renovations, equipment, and furniture		Bank loan	Accounts payable		Common shares	Retained earnings	Revenue	Expenses
Balance	$31,450	$700	$1,000	$2,500	$38,958		$20,000	$12,500		$40,000		$17,900	($15,792)
15	($1,000)										($1,000)		
Balance	$30,450	$700	$1,000	$2,500	$38,958		$20,000	$12,500		$40,000	($1,000)	$17,900	($15,792)

15. Dr. Retained earnings (shareholders' equity −)	1,000	
Cr. Cash (asset −)		1,000
To record the payment of a dividend of $0.50 per share		

Retained earnings decreases when dividends are paid because some of the shareholders' investment is being returned to them. (Remember from Chapter 2 that retained earnings is the accumulated earnings of a business over its life, less dividends paid, and represents an indirect investment in the company by the owners.) Cash decreases by $1,000 because the dividend is paid in cash.

We have now accounted for all the transactions and other economic events that affected Strawberries in September 2017. All the activity is summarized in a single spreadsheet in Table 3.1. The table provides a separate account for each type of expense rather than aggregating all expenses into a single account. The beauty of the accounting equation spreadsheet for learning purposes is in how it simplifies preparation of the financial statements. The second row of the spreadsheet

TABLE 3.1 Complete Accounting Equation Spreadsheet for Strawberries Inc.

	Assets					=	Liabilities	
Transaction	**Cash**	**Accounts receivable**	**Food, drinks, and supplies inventory**	**Prepaid rent**	**Renovations, equipment, and furniture**		**Bank loan**	**Accounts payable**
1	$40,000							
2	$20,000						$20,000	
3	($3,750)			$3,750				
4	($15,000)				$15,000			
5	($12,500)				$25,000			$12,500
6	($900)		$900					
7	($12,000)		$12,000					
8	$17,200	$700						
9	($525)							
10	($925)							
11	($150)							
12			($11,900)					
13				($1,250)				
14					($1,042)			
15	($1,000)							
Balance	**$30,450**	**$700**	**$1,000**	**$2,500**	**$38,958**		**$20,000**	**$12,500**

provides the names of the balance sheet and income statement accounts and the bottom row provides the amounts in each account at the end of the period. All you have to do to prepare the balance sheet and income statement is to reorganize the information into an appropriate format. The statements for Strawberries are provided in Table 3.2.

Another attractive feature of the spreadsheet is that it's easy to see how the different ways of accounting for transactions and economic events affect the financial statements. For example, if we wanted to see how depreciating the equipment and furniture over 10 years instead of five would affect net income, we would just change the amount recorded for entry 14 and recalculate. If the equipment and furniture were depreciated over 10 years, the expense would be \$208 per month (\$25,000 ÷ 120 months), the total depreciation expense for September would be \$833 (\$625 + \$208), and net income would be \$2,317, almost 10 percent more than our original calculation.

Notice that dividends aren't included in the calculation of net income. Net income is the amount left for the owners after all other stakeholders (such as employees, lenders, and suppliers) have been considered, so payments of dividends aren't included. Also, the ending balance in the retained earnings account in Table 3.1 isn't the same as the amount on the balance sheet. If you add the balances in the revenue and expense accounts to retained earnings you will get the correct amount. (This process will be discussed later in this chapter in the section on closing entries.)

QUESTION FOR CONSIDERATION

Why does net income (revenue and expenses) affect retained earnings?

ANSWER: Revenue represents economic benefits earned by an entity from providing goods and services to customers, and expenses are the economic sacrifices incurred to earn those benefits. Together, they represent the net benefit or sacrifice for the entity, which belongs to the owners. As a result, when an entity has net income, the owners' interest in the entity increases, which is reflected in the equity section, specifically in retained earnings, of the balance sheet. If an entity suffers a loss, equity decreases.

+	Shareholders' equity								
	Common shares	**Retained earnings**	**Sales**	**Cost of sales**	**Rent expense**	**Wages expense**	**Utilities expense**	**Depreciation expense**	**Interest expense**
	$40,000								
			$17,900						
							($525)		
						($925)			
									($150)
				($11,900)					
					($1,250)				
								($1,042)	
		($1,000)							
	$40,000	**($1,000)**	**$17,900**	**($11,900)**	**($1,250)**	**($925)**	**($525)**	**($1,042)**	**($150)**

TABLE 3.2 Balance Sheet and Income Statement for Strawberries Inc.

Strawberries Inc.
Balance Sheet
As of September 30, 2017

Assets		**Liabilities and Shareholders' equity**	
Cash	$30,450	Bank loan	$20,000
Accounts receivable	700	Accounts payable	12,500
Food, drinks, and supplies inventory	1,000	Total liabilities	32,500
Prepaid rent	2,500	**Shareholders' equity**	
Renovations, equipment, and furniture	38,958	Common shares	40,000
		Retained earnings	1,108
		Total Shareholders' equity	41,108
Total Assets	$73,608	Total Liabilities and Shareholders' equity	$73,608

Strawberries Inc.
Income Statement
For the Month Ended September 30, 2017

Sales		$17,900
Expenses		
Cost of sales	$11,900	
Rent	1,250	
Depreciation	1,042	
Wages	925	
Utilities	525	
Interest	150	
Total expenses		15,792
Net income		$ 2,108

Now that we have prepared Strawberries' balance sheet and income statement, what do we do with them? What do they tell us? In general, financial statements raise questions rather than provide definite answers. Strawberries' financial statements must be used with special care because they provide information for only the first month of operations. Nonetheless, a number of questions can be asked and observations made.

1. How well has Strawberries Inc. done? With only the first month's performance and nothing to compare it with, it's difficult to say. Perhaps if we had information about how restaurants do when they first begin operations, we would have a better idea. After Strawberries has been operating for a few years, we could compare its performance with other years or other restaurants. A stakeholder must be very cautious when making comparisons using the accounting information of different entities. Nonetheless, it isn't possible to make sense of accounting information without some benchmarks or bases for comparison.
2. We can do some analyses that suggest that Strawberries has done reasonably well in its first month:
   - It has "turned a profit" of $2,108, which is a good start. It's very difficult to succeed in the restaurant business.
   - The net income of $2,108 represents a return on equity of about 5 percent on Filomena and Teresa's $41,108 equity in Strawberries (return on equity = net income ÷ shareholders' equity = $2,108 ÷ $41,108). **Return on equity (ROE)** is a measure of the profitability of an entity and its effectiveness in using the assets provided by the owners to generate net income.
   - Strawberries' profit margin ratio (net income ÷ sales) is almost 12 percent, meaning that for every dollar of sales it earns $0.12. The **profit margin ratio** is a measure of how effective the entity is at controlling expenses and reflects the amount of income earned for each dollar of sales.

TABLE 3.3 Strawberries Inc.'s Cash Flow

Strawberries Inc. **Cash Flow Statement** **For the Month Ended September 30, 2017**		
Cash inflows		
Shareholders	$40,000	
Bank	20,000	
Sales	17,200	
Total cash inflows		$77,200
Cash outflows		
Renovations, furniture, and equipment	27,500	
Inventory	12,900	
Rent	3,750	
Utilities	525	
Wages	925	
Interest	150	
Dividends	1,000	
Total cash outflows		46,750
Net cash flow		$30,450

However, as I already pointed out, it's very difficult to draw conclusions from these statements without benchmarks or bases for comparison.

3. Why does Strawberries have so much cash? The new restaurant borrowed $20,000 from the bank, yet it has more than that amount in cash on September 30. It owes $12,500 to the restaurant supply company that it must repay in two months, so at this point it has the cash to meet that obligation. Should Strawberries reduce its bank loan? Or do Teresa and Filomena have plans for the money? Perhaps major purchases are still required. Certainly some of the cash will be needed to buy more food inventory.

4. While Strawberries seems to have a large cash balance, starting up and operating for a month consumed a lot of cash. Table 3.3 shows Strawberries' cash flow since it was incorporated. This statement was prepared by organizing the transactions in the cash column of the accounting equation spreadsheet.

   The cash flow situation isn't nearly as favourable if you remember that $60,000 of this cash came from the bank and the owners. If we ignore these inflows, net cash flow is negative (cash inflows from sales − cash outflows = $17,200 − $46,750 = $−29,550), meaning Strawberries spent $29,550 more than it took in to get the restaurant up and running and for operating it in September.

   Also, cash from operations (cash from or used by an entity's regular business activities) is −$1,050, which means that business operations used more cash than was generated. Cash from operations for Strawberries is shown in Table 3.4. This statement is also prepared using the cash column in Table 3.1. For this statement, it's necessary to identify the operating cash flows and ignore non-operating ones (investment by owners, loans, purchases of equipment). At this point, negative cash from operations isn't a problem because of the large cash balance. Ultimately, the main business activities of Strawberries must produce positive cash flows if the restaurant is to succeed.

5. Strawberries' large cash balance means that it can easily pay the accounts payable as well as purchase inventory, and it will generally be able to pay its debts as they come due. Strawberries' current ratio is 1.07 to 1 (current assets ÷ current liabilities = $34,650 ÷ $32,500), not usually considered to be very high. But the bank loan doesn't have to be paid for almost a year, suggesting that the low current ratio isn't a significant problem yet.

TABLE 3.4 Strawberries Inc.'s Cash from Operations

Strawberries Inc. Cash from Operations For the Period Ended September 30, 2017		
Cash inflows from sales		$17,200
Cash outflows		
Inventory	12,900	
Rent	3,750	
Utilities	525	
Wages	925	
Interest	150	18,250
Net cash flow		($ 1,050)

6. The income statement doesn't tell us much about how Strawberries will perform in the future. The encouraging performance in the first month may be due to curiosity by local people, who may not come back. Alternatively, next month may be even better as more people learn about the new restaurant. It isn't possible to predict what will happen based on the first month's performance of a restaurant.

   One of the limitations of general purpose financial statements is that they are prepared mainly on the basis of events that have already happened so they don't tell us very much about the future. Transactions-based statements can sometimes be a starting point to predict the future. However, in the case of new entities such as Strawberries, or even for established entities facing significant change, the statements may not be very helpful for this.

KNOWLEDGE CHECK 3.2

- ❑ What is depreciation and why are capital assets depreciated?
- ❑ What is the profit margin ratio and what does it mean?
- ❑ Describe the effect (increase or decrease) that debits and credits have on asset, liability, owners' equity, revenue, and expense accounts.

LO 4

ADJUSTING ENTRIES

An entry into an accrual accounting system is usually triggered by a transaction—an exchange between the entity and an external party. In the Strawberries example most of the entries represented exchanges with outside parties (bankers, suppliers, and customers). But some economic events affecting an entity aren't transactions, and these events must also be recorded in the accounting system; entries 12, 13, and 14 for Strawberries are examples. Entries to an accrual accounting system that aren't triggered by exchanges with outside entities are called **adjusting entries**. At the end of each reporting period, managers identify economic changes during the period that haven't been captured by the accounting system and make adjustments. Adjusting entries aren't required in a cash accounting system because recording is triggered only by the exchange of cash, which must involve an outside entity.

Adjusting entries are necessary in accrual accounting because the recognition of revenues and expenses doesn't always correspond with cash flows. In Strawberries' case, Filomena signed a two-year lease in July and paid rent in advance for September, October, and November. As a result of that exchange, we recorded an asset called prepaid rent. At the end of September, some

TABLE 3.5 Four Types of Adjusting Entries

Type	Situation	Examples	Entry made in the current or previous period (Transactional Entry)	Entry made at the end of the current period (Adjusting Entry)	Entry made in the next period (Transactional Entry)
Deferred expense/ prepaid expense	Cash is paid before the expense is recognized	Prepaid insurance Prepaid rent Capital assets	Dr. Asset Cr. Cash	Dr. Expense Cr. Asset	No entry
Deferred revenue	Cash is received before revenue is recognized	Deposits Subscriptions Advances Gift cards	Dr. Cash Cr. Liability	Dr. Liability Cr. Revenue	No entry
Accrued expense/ accrued liability	Expense is recognized before cash is paid	Wages Utilities Interest payable	No entry	Dr. Expense Cr. Liability	Dr. Liability Cr. Cash
Accrued revenue/ accrued asset	Revenue is recognized before cash is received	Interest earned Royalties earned	No entry	Dr. Asset Cr. Revenue	Dr. Cash Cr. Asset

of that prepaid rent had been used up so we reduced the amount of prepaid rent and recorded a rent expense. This event didn't involve an exchange with another entity but the consumption of the prepaid rent had to be reflected in the accounting records.

Before we discuss adjusting entries in detail, note the following:

1. Adjusting entries are required because revenues and expenses can be recognized at times other than when cash is exchanged.
2. Every adjusting entry involves a balance sheet account and an income statement account.
3. Every adjusting entry is associated with a transactional entry that is recorded before or after the adjusting entry. A **transactional entry** is a journal entry triggered by an exchange with another entity.
4. Adjusting entries are required only when financial statements are prepared.
5. Adjusting entries never involve cash. If cash is part of the entry, it isn't an adjusting entry.

There are four types of adjusting entries. They are summarized in Table 3.5.

INSIGHT

Earnings Management

Managers are responsible for preparing an entity's accounting information, whether prepared in accordance with IFRS, ASPE, or some other basis, and they are often able to choose how to account for, disclose, and present information about transactions and economic events. These choices can significantly affect the numbers in the financial statements and the information disclosed in the statements and the notes, which in turn can have significant economic consequences for stakeholders. Managers' use of accounting choices to achieve their own objectives is called **earnings management**. Although the term suggests a focus on net income, it also applies to choices made that affect any amounts reported in the financial statements, such as assets or liabilities, or disclosure in the notes.

We have already touched on how managers can manage earnings; for example, by choosing accounting policies, such as how to recognize revenue or depreciate capital assets, and in making accounting estimates such as the useful life of capital assets, the amount of accounts receivable that won't be collected, or the amount of sales that will be returned. This Insight box is intended to introduce the concept of earnings management and to put it on your radar screen as you work through the book. Each chapter will explain managers' opportunities to use accounting's inherent flexibility to make choices that affect the information reported in the financial statements and that may impose economic consequences for you.

TYPES OF ADJUSTING ENTRIES

1. Deferred Expense/Prepaid Expense Entities often purchase assets providing benefits for more than one period, including insurance policies, equipment, buildings, and patents. The terms **deferred expense** and **prepaid expense** refer to assets acquired in one period but not expensed, at least in part, until a later period or periods. This adjusting entry reduces the amount of the asset reported on the balance sheet and recognizes an expense for the portion of the asset that has been consumed in the period.

On January 5, 2017, Dahlia Ltd. (Dahlia) purchases three years of insurance coverage for $9,000 cash. The insurance covers the period January 1, 2017 to December 31, 2019. Dahlia's year-end is December 31.

When Dahlia purchases the insurance, it makes the following journal entry:

Dr. Prepaid insurance (asset +)	9,000	
Cr. Cash (asset −)		9,000
To record the purchase of insurance for the period January 1, 2017 to December 31, 2019		

This is a transactional entry because an exchange has taken place between Dahlia and the insurance company. The insurance is set up as an asset because the three years of coverage is a future benefit.

On December 31, 2017, an adjusting entry is needed because one year of the insurance coverage has been used up and should be expensed. The balance sheet on December 31, 2017 would report $6,000 of prepaid insurance for the remaining two years of coverage and there would be an insurance expense of $3,000 on the 2017 income statement to reflect the cost of insurance for the year. With no adjusting entry, Dahlia's balance sheet would report $9,000 of prepaid insurance, implying three years of available coverage when there are only two, and expenses in 2017 would be understated by $3,000. On December 31, 2017, Dahlia would make this adjusting entry:

Dr. Insurance expense (expenses +, shareholders' equity −)	3,000	
Cr. Prepaid insurance (asset −)		3,000
To record the cost of insurance used in the year ended December 31, 2017 ($9,000 ÷ 3 years of coverage = $3,000)		

This is an adjusting entry because it isn't triggered by an exchange with another entity. It's assumed that the cost of the insurance is the same each year so the same adjusting entry is required on December 31, 2018 and 2019 to reflect the cost of insurance coverage and reduce the balance in the prepaid insurance account each year. The accounting impacts of the adjusting entries are shown in Figure 3.4.

Figure 3.4 shows the amount of prepaid insurance decreasing as the coverage is used up over time and each year's expense matches the asset account's decrease. At the end of the life of the insurance policy on December 31, 2019, the amount of prepaid insurance on the balance sheet is zero.

If Dahlia's insurance policy came into effect on July 1, 2017 and ran until June 30, 2020, the adjusting entry would be a bit different. It would reflect that on December 31, 2017, half a year's insurance had been used and that the expense was $1,500 ($3,000 ÷ 2):

Dr. Insurance expense (expenses + shareholders' equity −)	1,500	
Cr. Prepaid insurance (asset −)		1,500
To record the cost of insurance used from July 1, 2017 to December 31, 2017 ([$9,000 ÷ 3 years of coverage] × 1/2 year = $1,500)		

Depreciation of capital assets is another type of this adjusting entry. Capital assets such as buildings, vehicles, machinery, computers, and furniture help earn revenue over more than one period so the cost must be expensed over the asset's life.

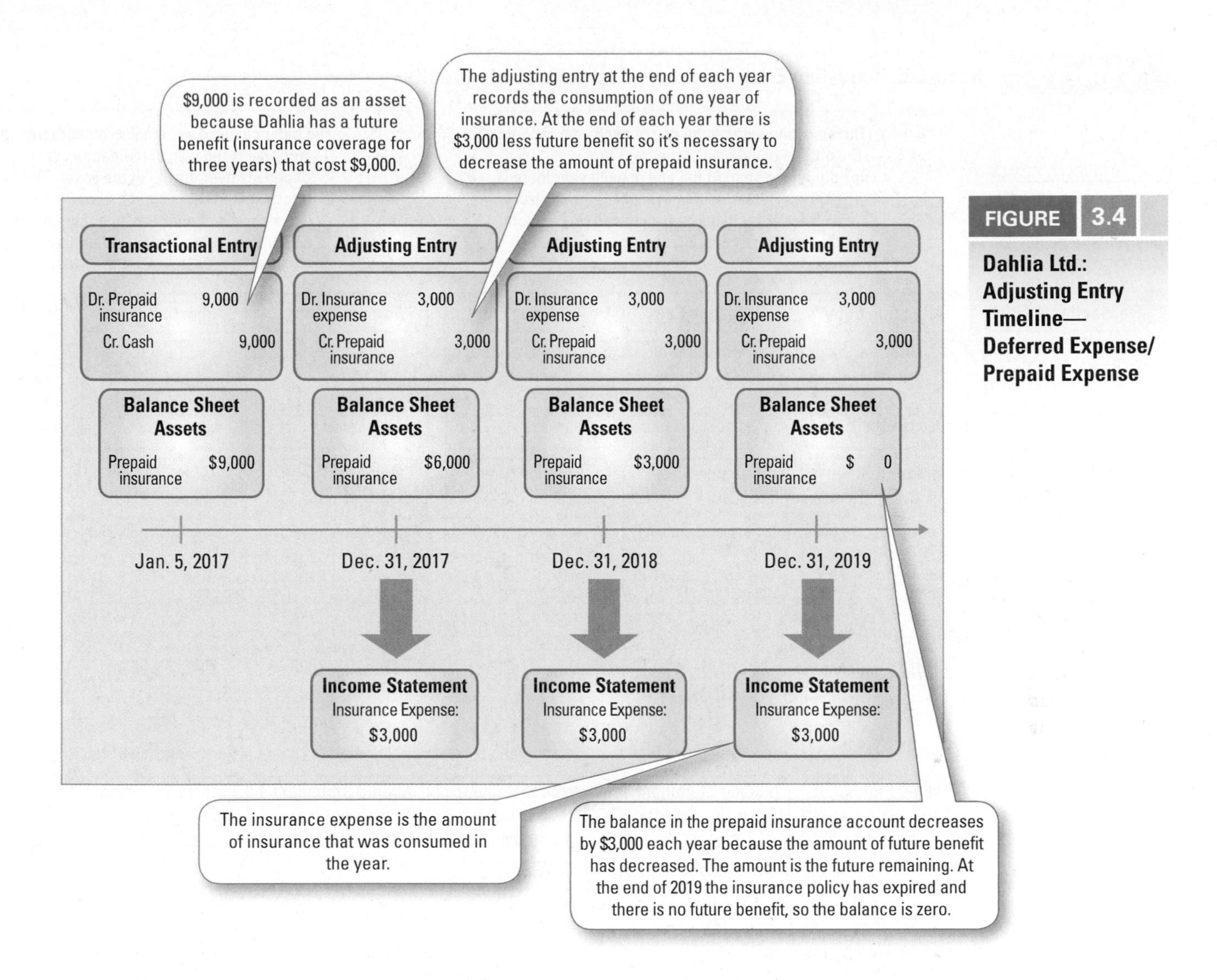

FIGURE 3.4

Dahlia Ltd.: Adjusting Entry Timeline—Deferred Expense/ Prepaid Expense

On January 2, 2017, Kaslo Ltd. (Kaslo) purchased a new delivery truck for $50,000 cash. Management estimates the truck will have a useful life of five years. Kaslo depreciates its trucks on a straight-line basis, which means it will expense an equal amount of the cost in each year of the truck's life. This adjusting entry would be recorded at the end of each year:

Dr. Depreciation expense (expenses +, shareholders' equity −)	10,000	
Cr. Accumulated depreciation (contra asset +)		10,000

Adjusting entry to record depreciation of the truck
(Cost of the asset ÷ estimated useful life = $50,000 ÷ 5 years = $10,000 per year)

The truck account isn't credited directly for the period's depreciation; the credit is made to accumulated depreciation. The accumulated depreciation account is referred to as a **contra-asset account**, which accumulates amounts deducted from a related asset. This makes information about the cost of an asset readily available from the accounting system, which can be important for various reasons, including for tax purposes. The balance in the accumulated depreciation account isn't meaningful by itself, but, taken together, the cost of a capital asset less its accumulated depreciation gives the asset's **carrying amount**.

The accounting impact of the adjusting entries on Kaslo's financial statements is shown in Figure 3.5. Notice that the balance in the truck account itself remains at $50,000 all the time. The accumulated depreciation account increases by $10,000 each year. The amount of annual depreciation expense is $10,000 per year while the carrying amount of the truck decreases by $10,000 each year.

FIGURE 3.5 Kaslo Ltd.: Adjusting Entry Timeline—Depreciation of a Truck

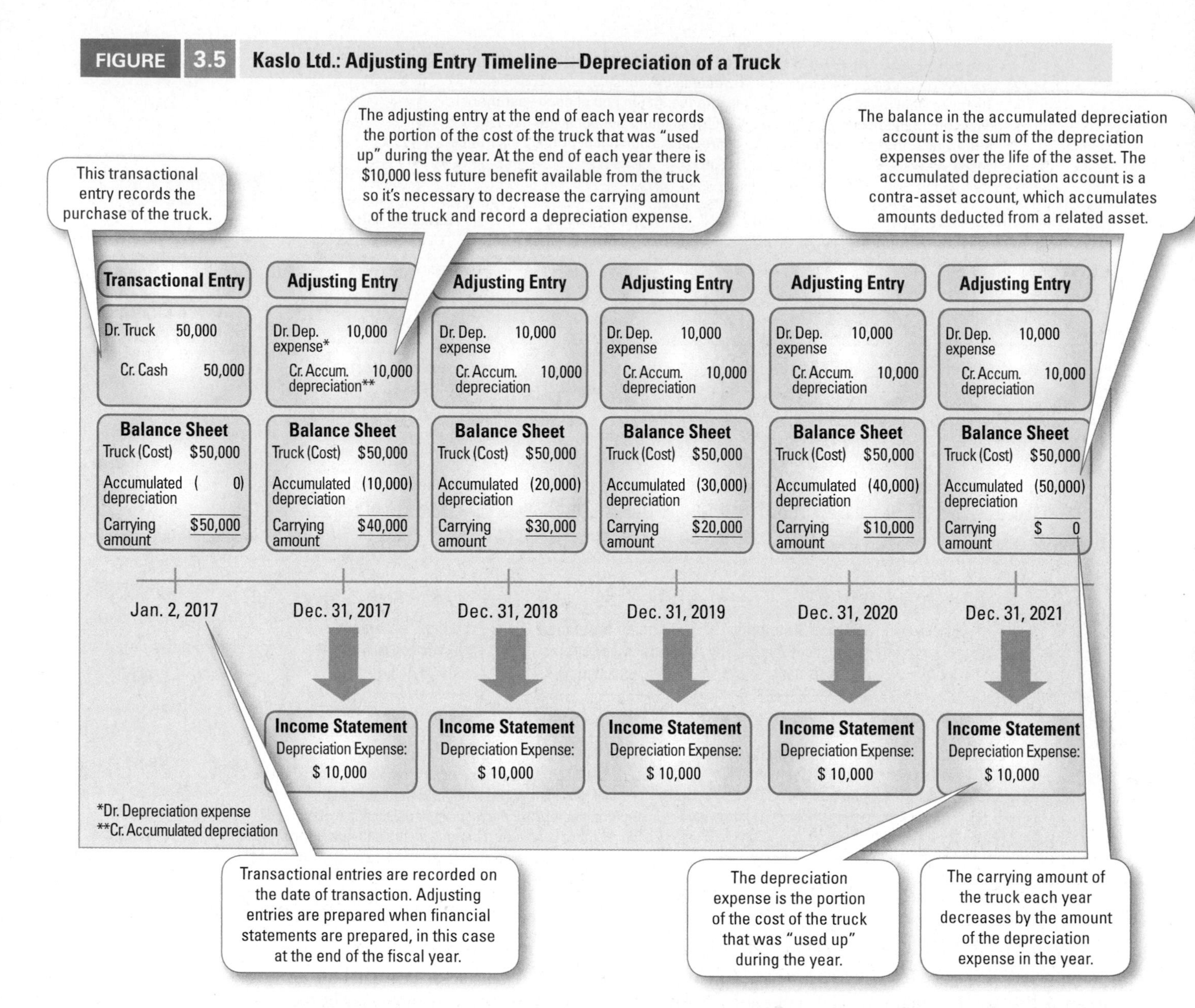

KNOWLEDGE CHECK 3.3

Return to the Dahlia Ltd. example where Dahlia purchased its three-year insurance policy on July 1, 2017 for $9,000.

- ❑ What adjusting journal entries would be required on December 31, 2019 and 2020?

2. Deferred Revenue Sometimes an entity receives payment for goods or services before it recognizes the revenue. For example, a fan purchases tickets to a concert months before the show or a customer pays a deposit for delivery of goods some time later. If the entity recognizes revenue when the concert is performed or the goods are delivered, it would record a liability when payment is received. The liability represents the obligation to provide the good or service the customer paid for. An adjusting entry is necessary when the revenue is recognized and the obligation is fulfilled.

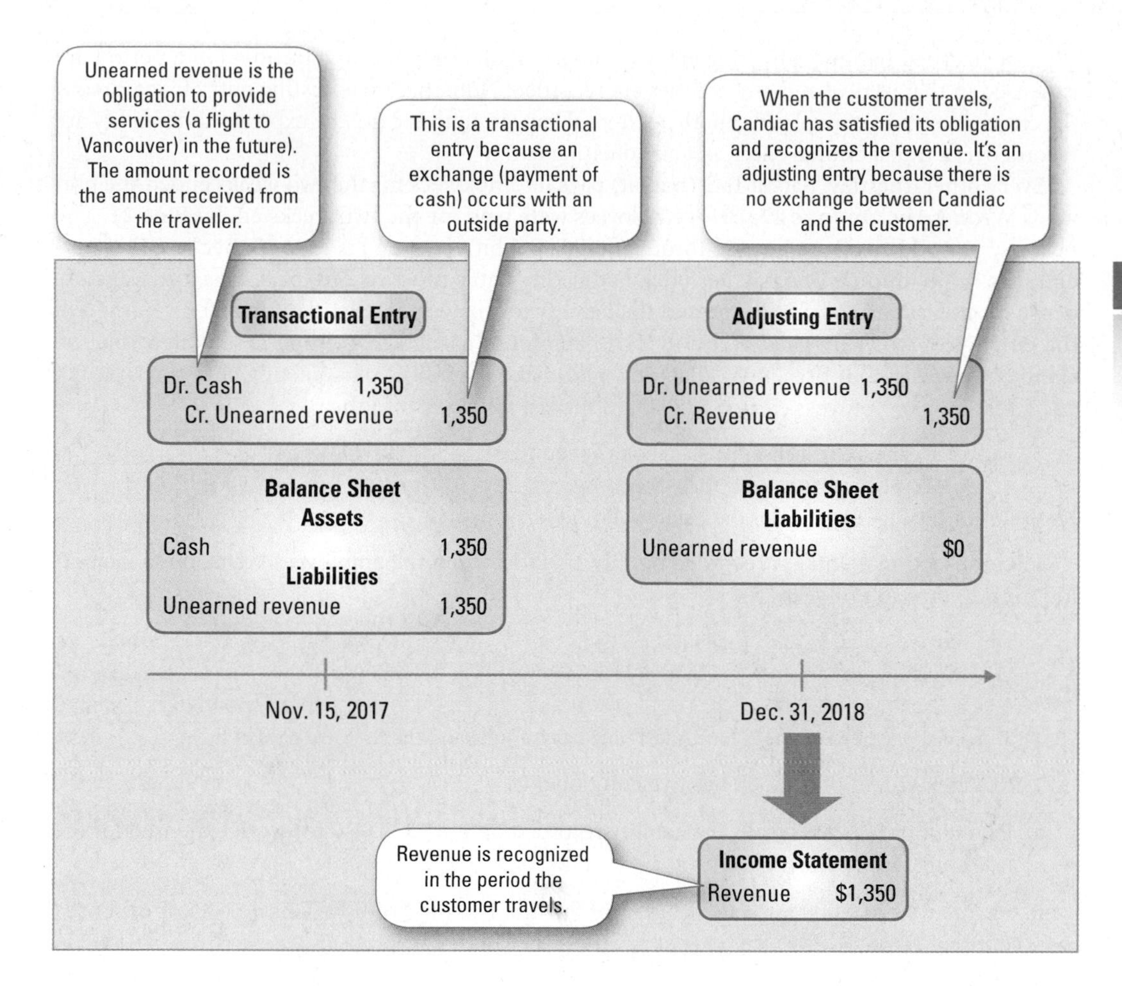

FIGURE 3.6

Candiac Airlines Inc.: Deferred Revenue Adjusting Entries

On November 15, 2017, a traveller purchased a ticket for a January 18, 2018 flight from St. John's to Vancouver on Candiac Airlines Ltd. (Candiac) for $1,350. Candiac's year-end is December 31. When the passenger bought the ticket, Candiac made the following journal entry.

Dr. Cash (asset +)	1,350	
Cr. Unearned revenue (liability +)		1,350
To record cash received for a flight from St. John's to Vancouver on January 18, 2018		

This is a transactional entry because it involves an interaction with an outside entity, the traveller. When Candiac received the payment, revenue wasn't recognized because it hadn't provided the transportation. The unearned revenue liability represents Candiac's obligation to provide the trip on January 18, 2018. The amount is the payment received from the customer. **Unearned revenue** is a liability that is recorded when cash is received before revenue is recognized. When the traveller takes the trip, Candiac recognizes the revenue by making the following adjusting entry:

Dr. Unearned revenue (liability −)	1,350	
Cr. Revenue (revenue +, shareholders' equity +)		1,350
To record revenue earned		

This is an adjusting entry because it doesn't involve an outside entity. The accounting impact of this example is shown in Figure 3.6.

3. Accrued Expense/Accrued Liability This adjusting entry is needed when an entity has incurred an expense but an external event such as receipt of an invoice hasn't triggered the recording of the expense and related liability. An **accrued expense** is an expense recognized in the financial statements before a cash payment is made or an external event triggers an entry. Recognition of the expense gives rise to an **accrued liability** to pay for the expense. The accrued expense/accrued liability adjusting entry ensures that all costs of doing business in a period are expensed in that period and all liabilities are recorded. Note that no adjusting entry is required if the entity received an invoice or another external trigger. In that case, the expense and liability are recorded as a transactional entry, not an adjusting entry.

Every other Tuesday, Babbit Inc. (Babbit) pays its employees for the two weeks ended the previous Wednesday. On June 27, 2017, employees were paid for the two weeks ended June 21. The next pay period runs from June 22 through July 5. Babbit's year-end is June 30. Because the year-end falls in the middle of a pay period, an adjusting entry must record, or *accrue*, the wage expense for the last nine days of June and the liability for the wages owed on June 30. Even though the employees won't be paid until July 11, the amount earned from June 22 through June 30 should be expensed in fiscal 2017. Babbit would make the following adjusting entry on June 30, 2017, assuming employees earned $22,500 in the last nine days of June:

Dr. Wage expense (expenses +, shareholders' equity −)	22,500	
Cr. Accrued wages payable (liabilities +)		22,500
To accrue wage expense for the last nine days of June		

The transactional entry is recorded on July 11, 2017 when the employees are paid for the period June 22 through July 5:

Dr. Accrued wages payable (liabilities −)	22,500	
Dr. Wage expense (expenses +, shareholders' equity −)	10,000	
Cr. Cash (assets −)		32,500
To record payment of wages for the last nine days of June and the first five days of July		

The cash payment of $32,500 has two components:

a. Payment of $22,500 fulfills the liability recorded on June 30, 2017 for work expensed for the last nine days of June.

b. Payment of $10,000 for wages earned in the first five days of July. This amount is expensed in fiscal 2018.

The July 2017 entry is a transactional entry because paying employees triggers it. The balance sheet and income statement effects of this scenario are summarized in Figure 3.7.

QUESTION FOR CONSIDERATION

A sports fan buys tickets for a game. The game will be played in six months, which is in the team's next fiscal accounting year. When the fan purchases the ticket, the team records the following journal entry:

Dr. Cash	*200*	
Cr. Unearned revenue		*200*

The team recognizes revenue from its games when the games are actually played. Explain why an adjusting entry is necessary to recognize revenue when the game is played.

ANSWER: The exchange between the fan and the team occurs when the fan pays for the tickets. There is no exchange between the fan and the team when the game is actually played so an adjusting entry is required to recognize revenue in that period.

4. Accrued Revenue/Accrued Asset **Accrued revenue** is revenue recognized before cash is received. The adjusting entry is required when an entity has earned revenue but there was no exchange with another entity to trigger the recording of it. A receivable (an asset) is also recorded to reflect the coming payment. For example, interest and royalties earned in a period might not be

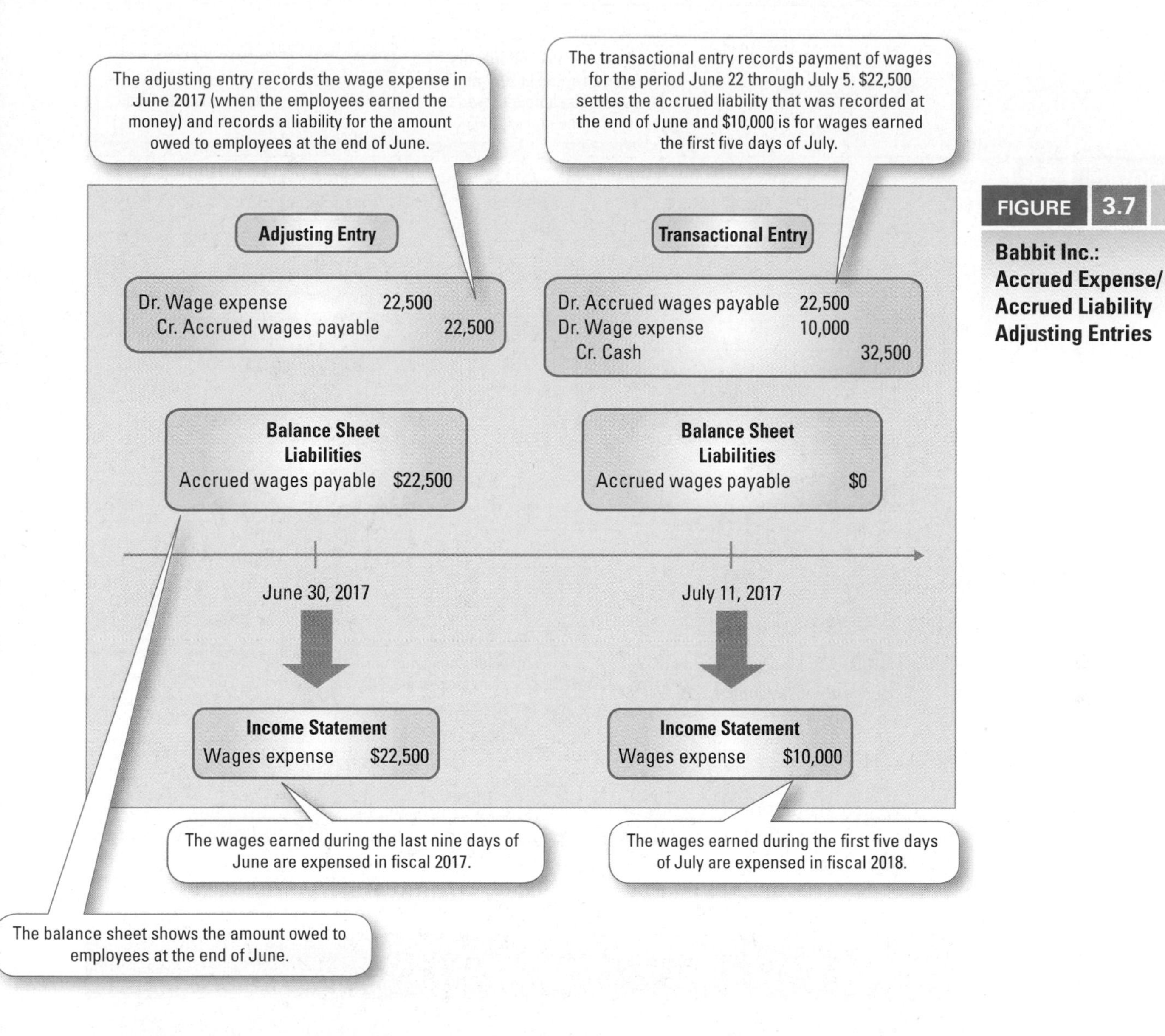

FIGURE 3.7
Babbit Inc.: Accrued Expense/ Accrued Liability Adjusting Entries

paid until a later period. An adjusting entry records the revenue in the period it's earned. This adjusting entry is recorded before the transactional entry.

Jalobert Ltd. (Jalobert) is a real estate company that owns a shopping mall in western Canada. Retail tenants pay rent based on the size of the store plus 2 percent of annual sales. The rent based on sales must be paid within 90 days of the end of the year. For the year ended December 31, 2017, Jalobert estimates that rent based on sales will be about $2,000,000. Jalobert would recognize this revenue in fiscal 2017, since it pertains to space used in 2017, by recording the following adjusting entry:

Dr. Rent receivable (asset +)	2,000,000	
Cr. Rent revenue (revenue +, shareholders' equity +)		2,000,000
To record accrual of rent revenue during 2017		

When payment is received on March 31, 2018, Jalobert would record the following transactional entry (we'll assume all the payments arrive at the same time and the $2,000,000 estimate was accurate):

Dr. Cash (asset +)	2,000,000	
Cr. Rent receivable (asset −)		2,000,000
To record cash received for rent revenue earned in 2017		

FIGURE 3.8

Jalobert Ltd.: Accrued Revenue/ Accrued Asset Adjusting Entries

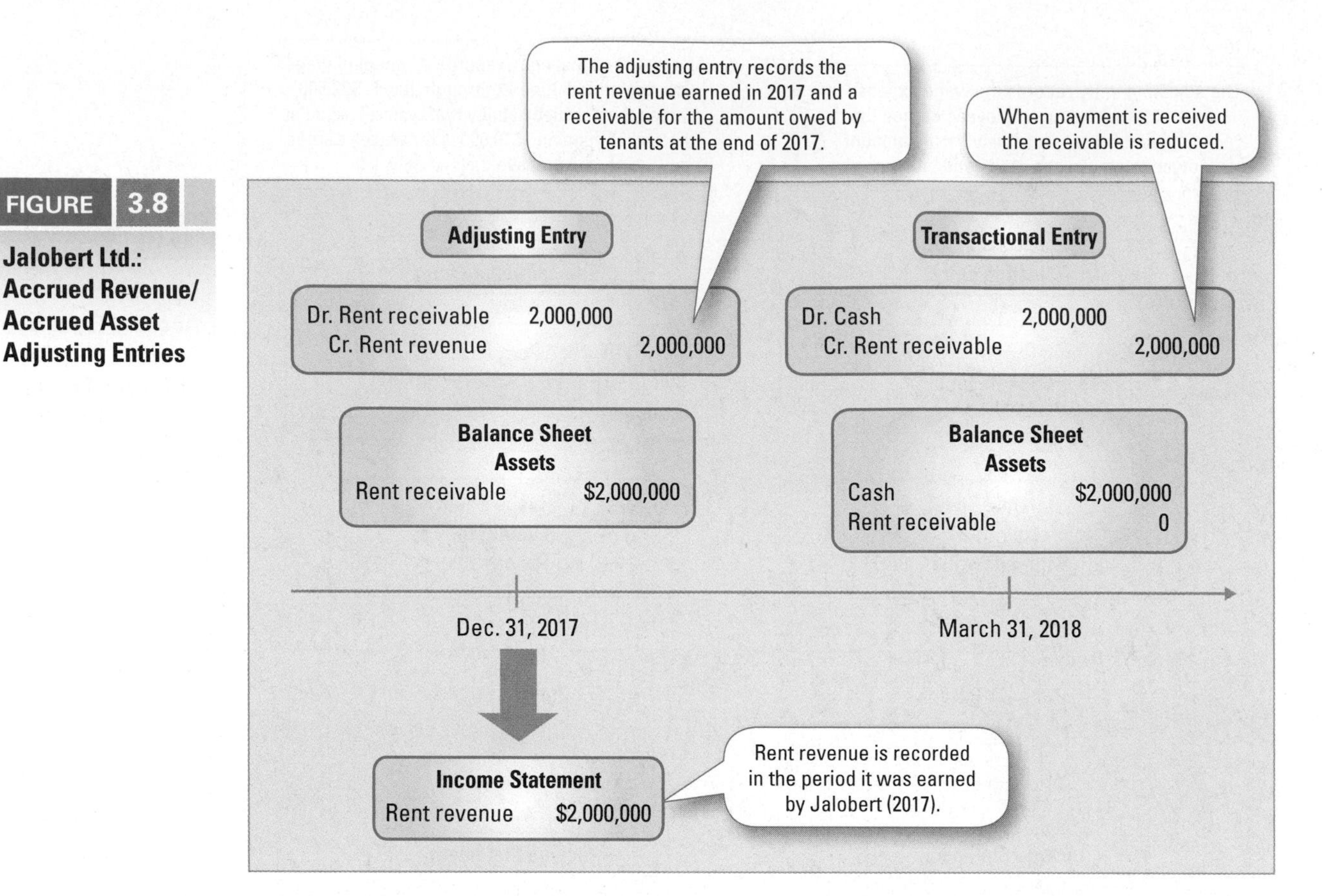

If the actual amount of revenue isn't the same as the estimate, Jalobert would make the correction in 2018. The effects on the balance sheet and income statement of this adjustment are summarized in Figure 3.8.

Accounting Estimates

Adjusting entries and accrual accounting often require **accounting estimates** because the actual amounts aren't known when financial statements are prepared. In the Jalobert example, the amount of rent revenue earned from sales by the retail stores in the mall would be estimated when preparing the December 31, 2017 financial statements because the actual amount wouldn't be known until payment was received in March 2018. Estimates are imprecise because they are really educated guesses; it's very unlikely an estimate and the actual amount will be exactly the same. Most numbers in the financial statements rely to some extent on estimates.

Managers are responsible for making the estimates needed to prepare the financial statements and this requires judgment. Managers can use the inherent uncertainty in estimates to pursue their own interests and objectives, such as maximizing their bonuses, satisfying lenders so they keep lending money, and maximizing profits to keep investors happy.

LO 5 THE FULL ACCOUNTING CYCLE, BEGINNING TO END

The accounting equation spreadsheet is a useful learning tool but not very practical for real-world use. A spreadsheet is difficult to manage if there are many accounts or transactions. In this section, I explain how the mechanics of the accounting cycle operates in practice. We will work through the steps shown in Figure 3.9, using Strawberries Inc. as the example.

FIGURE 3.9 The Accounting Cycle

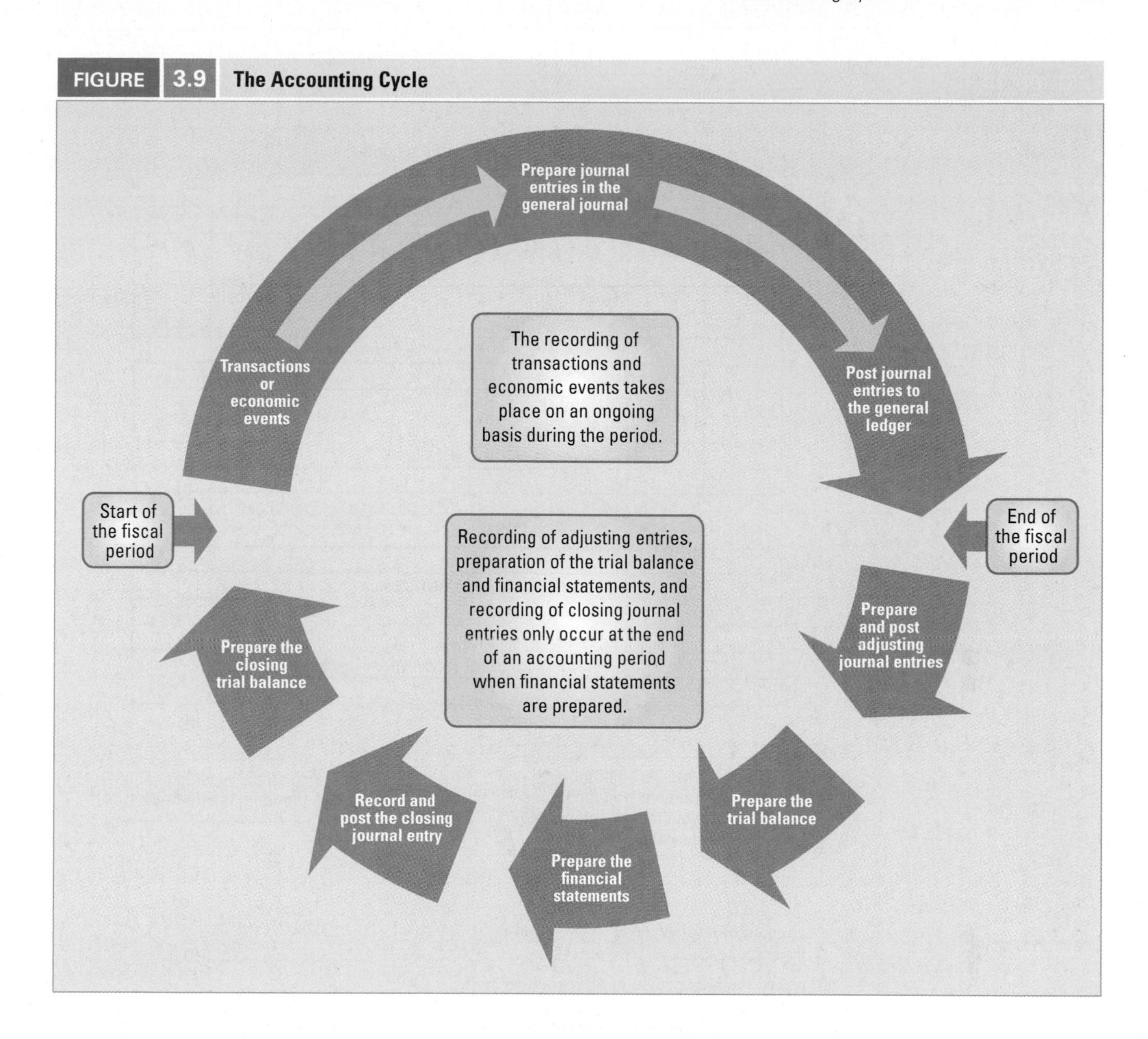

Preparing Journal Entries

As described earlier, a transaction or other economic event is initially recognized in the accounting system by a journal entry. These are recorded in the **general journal**, a chronological record of the entries to the accounting system also referred to as the book of original entry because events are first recorded in the accounting system there. The entries can be written in an actual book but it's more likely an accounting software package. An example of a general journal is given in Figure 3.10, which shows three of Strawberries' journal entries.

Strawberries recorded the following transactional journal entries up to September 30, 2017. (These are the same entries that were developed earlier):

1. Dr. Cash (asset +)	40,000	
Cr. Common shares (shareholders' equity +)		40,000
To record the sale of shares for cash		
2. Dr. Cash (asset +)	20,000	
Cr. Bank loan (liability +)		20,000
To record the $20,000 bank loan		

FIGURE 3.10
The General Journal

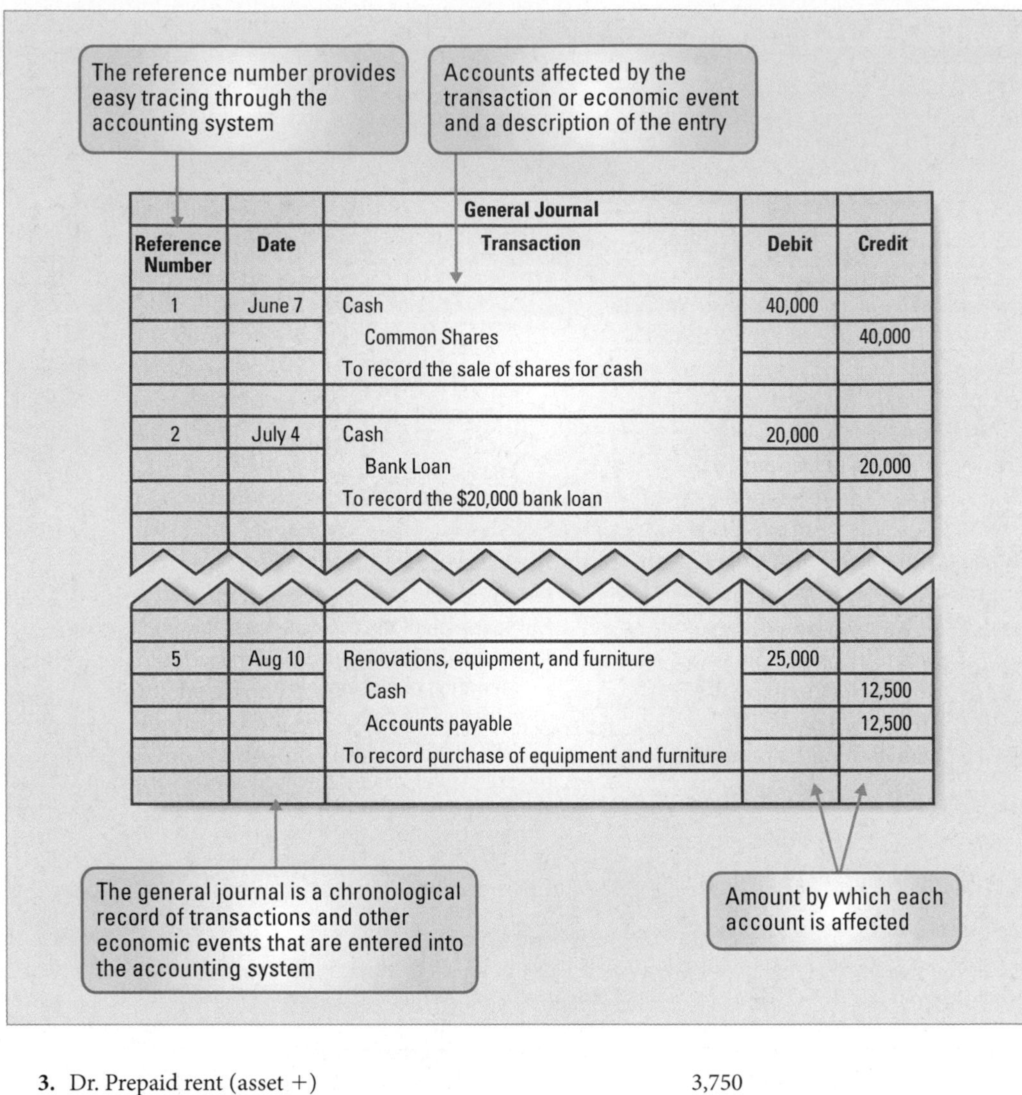

Reference Number	Date	General Journal Transaction	Debit	Credit
1	June 7	Cash	40,000	
		Common Shares		40,000
		To record the sale of shares for cash		
2	July 4	Cash	20,000	
		Bank Loan		20,000
		To record the $20,000 bank loan		
5	Aug 10	Renovations, equipment, and furniture	25,000	
		Cash		12,500
		Accounts payable		12,500
		To record purchase of equipment and furniture		

	Debit	Credit
3. Dr. Prepaid rent (asset +)	3,750	
Cr. Cash (asset −)		3,750
To record the prepayment of three months' rent		
4. Dr. Renovations, equipment, and furniture (asset +)	15,000	
Cr. Cash (asset −)		15,000
To record the cost of renovating the restaurant		
5. Dr. Renovations, equipment, and furniture (asset +)	25,000	
Cr. Cash (asset −)		12,500
Cr. Accounts payable (liability +)		12,500
To record the purchase of equipment and furniture		
6. Dr. Food, drinks, and supplies inventory (asset +)	900	
Cr. Cash (asset −)		900
To record the purchase of inventory		
7. Dr. Food, drinks, and supplies inventory (asset +)	12,000	
Cr. Cash (asset −)		12,000
To record the purchase of food and drinks during September		
8. Dr. Cash (asset +)	17,200	
Dr. Accounts receivable (asset +)	700	
Cr. Sales (shareholders' equity +, revenue +)		17,900
To record sales for the month of September		

9, 10.	Dr. Utilities expense (shareholders' equity –, expenses +)	525	
	Dr. Wage expense (shareholders' equity –, expenses +)	925	
	Cr. Cash (asset –)		1,450
	To record the utilities and wages expenses for the month of September		
11.	Dr. Interest expense (shareholders' equity –, expenses +)	150	
	Cr. Cash (asset –)		150
	To record the interest expense for the month of September		
12.	Dr. Retained earnings (shareholders' equity –)	1,000	
	Cr. Cash (asset –)		1,000
	To record the payment of a dividend of $0.50 per share		

Posting Journal Entries to the General Ledger

The next step in the accounting cycle is posting the journal entry to the general ledger. The **general ledger** is a record of all the entity's accounts. **Posting** a journal entry to the general ledger is the process of transferring each line of a journal entry to the corresponding account in the general ledger. Imagine the general ledger as a book in which each page represents a different account: a page for cash, a page for inventory, a page for sales, etc. Whereas a journal entry shows which accounts a transaction or economic event affects, a general ledger account shows the activity in each account over time. In the accounting equation spreadsheet, each column represents a general ledger account.

Accounting textbooks use **T-accounts** to represent general ledger accounts. The name "T-account" reflects its shape, as you can see in the T-account shown in Figure 3.11. Note the following:

- Each T-account corresponds to a general ledger account. The name of the account is written on the horizontal line at the top.
- The vertical line separates the debits and credits made to the account—debits on the left, credits on the right.
- The beginning balance, the balance in the account at the start of the period, is shown between the horizontal lines at the top of the T-account.
- The ending balance is shown below the horizontal line at the bottom.
- A debit balance at the beginning or end of the period is recorded on the left side of the vertical line. A credit balance at the beginning or end of the period is recorded on the right side.
- When a journal entry is posted to the T-accounts, debits are recorded on the left side of the vertical line and credits on the right side. If an account typically has a debit balance (assets, expenses), credits are subtracted from debits to calculate the ending balance. For accounts typically having a credit balance (liabilities, equity, revenue), debits are subtracted from credits.

Account Name	
Beginning Balance	
Debits	Credits
Ending Balance	

FIGURE 3.11
The T-Account

The posting process is shown schematically in Figure 3.12.

T-accounts showing the postings of Strawberries transactions are given in Figure 3.13. The number on the left side of each line in each T-account corresponds to the number of the journal

FIGURE 3.12

The Posting Process

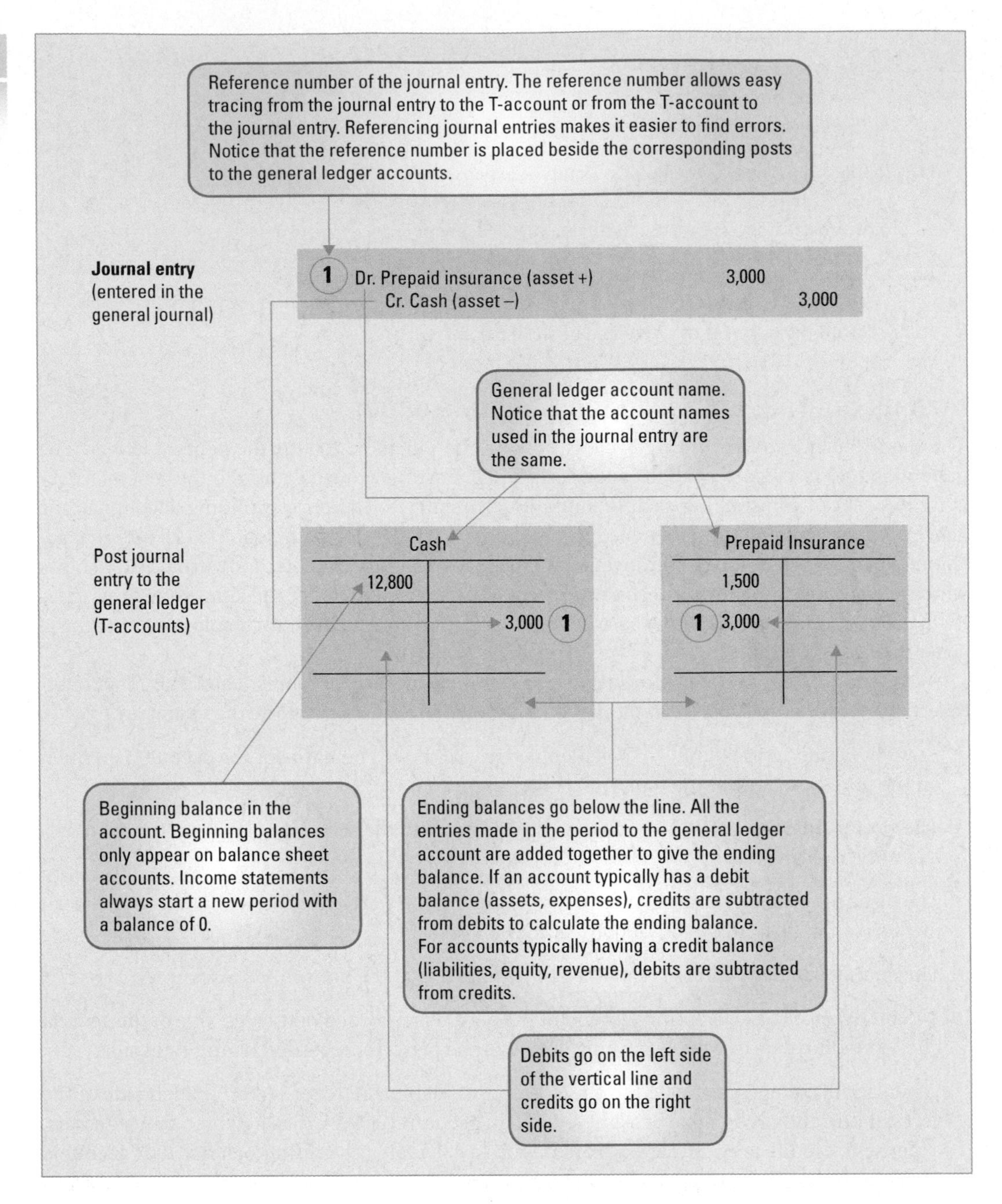

entry. This cross-referencing is important because it makes it easy to trace back from the general ledger account to the journal entry. The opening balance in all accounts is zero because Strawberries just started up. For ongoing businesses, opening amounts in the balance sheet T-accounts would be the ending amount from the previous period. Ending balances aren't shown in Figure 3.13 because we still have to make the adjusting and closing journal entries.

LO 4, 5

Preparing and Posting Adjusting Journal Entries

Preparing journal entries and posting them to the general ledger is ongoing during a reporting period. The remaining steps in the accounting cycle occur at the end of a period when the entity prepares financial statements. At that time, the managers examine the general ledger accounts and determine the adjusting entries that must be made. Many adjusting entries are automatic because they have to be made each period. Other adjustments don't occur regularly and managers

FIGURE 3.13 T-Accounts for Strawberries Inc.: Pre-adjusting Entry Postings to T-Accounts

Cash

	Debit	Credit
Bal	0	
1	40,000	
2	20,000	
3		3,750
4		15,000
5		12,500
6		900
7		12,000
8	17,200	
9		525
10		925
11		150
15		1,000

Accounts receivable

	Debit	Credit
Bal	0	
8	700	

Food, drinks, and supplies inventory

	Debit	Credit
Bal	0	
6	900	
7	12,000	

Prepaid rent

	Debit	Credit
Bal	0	
3	3,750	

Renovations, equipment, and furniture

	Debit	Credit
Bal	0	
4	15,000	
5	25,000	

Accumulated depreciation

	Debit	Credit
Bal		0

Bank loan

	Debit	Credit
Bal		0
2		20,000

Accounts payable

	Debit	Credit
Bal		0
5		12,500

Common shares

	Debit	Credit
Bal		0
1		40,000

Retained earnings

	Debit	Credit
Bal		0
15	1,000	

Sales

	Debit	Credit
Bal		0
8		17,900

Cost of sales

	Debit	Credit
Bal	0	

Rent expense

	Debit	Credit
Bal	0	

Wages expense

	Debit	Credit
Bal	0	
10	925	

Depreciation expense

	Debit	Credit
Bal	0	

Interest expense

	Debit	Credit
Bal	0	
11	150	

Utilities expense

	Debit	Credit
Bal	0	
9	525	

must be careful to make sure these are also recorded. Strawberries' adjusting journal entries are shown below and the posting of them to the T-accounts are shown in bold in Figure 3.14.

	Dr.	Cr.
12. Dr. Cost of sales (shareholders' equity –, expenses +)	11,900	
Cr. Food, drinks, and supplies inventory (asset –)		11,900
To record the cost of food, drinks, and supplies used to provide meals to customers		
13. Dr. Rent expense (shareholders' equity –, expenses +)	1,250	
Cr. Prepaid rent (asset –)		1,250
To record the rent expense for September		
14. Dr. Depreciation expense (shareholders' equity –, expenses +)	1,042	
Cr. Accumulated depreciation—renovations, equipment, and furniture (asset –)		1,042
To record the depreciation of renovations, equipment, and furniture		

Preparing the Trial Balance

A **trial balance** lists all the accounts in the general ledger with their balances. It ensures that the debits equal the credits and it provides a summary of the balances in each account. Unequal

FIGURE 3.14 T-Accounts for Strawberries Inc.: Post-adjusting Entry Postings to T-Accounts

Cash		
Bal	12,800	
1	40,000	
2	20,000	
3		3,750
4		15,000
5		12,500
6		900
7		12,000
8	17,200	
9		525
10		925
11		150
15		1,000
Bal	30,450	

Accounts receivable		
Bal	0	
8	700	
Bal	700	

Food, drinks, and supplies inventory		
Bal	0	
6	900	
7	12,000	
12		**11,900**
Bal	1,000	

Prepaid rent		
Bal	0	
3	3,750	
13		**1,250**
Bal	2,500	

Renovations, equipment, and furniture		
Bal	0	
4	15,000	
5	25,000	
Bal	40,000	

Accumulated depreciation		
Bal		0
14		**1,042**
Bal		1,042

Bank loan		
Bal		0
2		20,000
Bal		20,000

Accounts payable		
Bal		0
5		12,500
Bal		12,500

Common shares		
Bal		0
1		40,000
Bal		40,000

Retained earnings		
Bal		0
15	1,000	
Bal	1,000	

Sales		
Bal		0
8		17,900
Bal		17,900

Cost of sales		
Bal	0	
12	**11,900**	
Bal	11,900	

Rent expense		
Bal	0	
13	**1,250**	
Bal	1,250	

Wages expense		
Bal	0	
10	925	
Bal	925	

Depreciation expense		
Bal	0	
14	**1,042**	
Bal	1,042	

Interest expense		
Bal	0	
11	150	
Bal	150	

Utilities expense		
Bal	0	
9	525	
Bal	525	

debits and credits mean that there is an error that must be corrected. However, equal debits and credits don't mean that the accounting has been done properly. It simply means that all journal entries and postings to the general ledger accounts were balanced. Errors such as missing or duplicated journal entries or incorrect amounts or accounts will provide a balanced trial balance but incorrect financial statements. For example, if an entity purchases land and promises to pay in one year, the correct entry would debit land (asset) and credit payables (liability). If the accountant incorrectly debited cash instead of land, the debits and credits would balance but the account balances wouldn't be correct.

When preparing a trial balance, the accounts with debit balances in the general ledger (T-accounts) are placed in the left column of the trial balance, and accounts with credit balances are placed in the right column. Several trial balances are sometimes prepared at the end of a period, including before and after preparation of the adjusting entries and after the closing entry has been posted. Each trial balance helps ensure that the posting of the journal entries balances at each step.

Strawberries' trial balance is shown in Table 3.6. This trial balance was prepared after the adjusting journal entries had been entered and posted to the appropriate ledger accounts.

TABLE 3.6 **Strawberries Inc. Pre-closing Trial Balance**

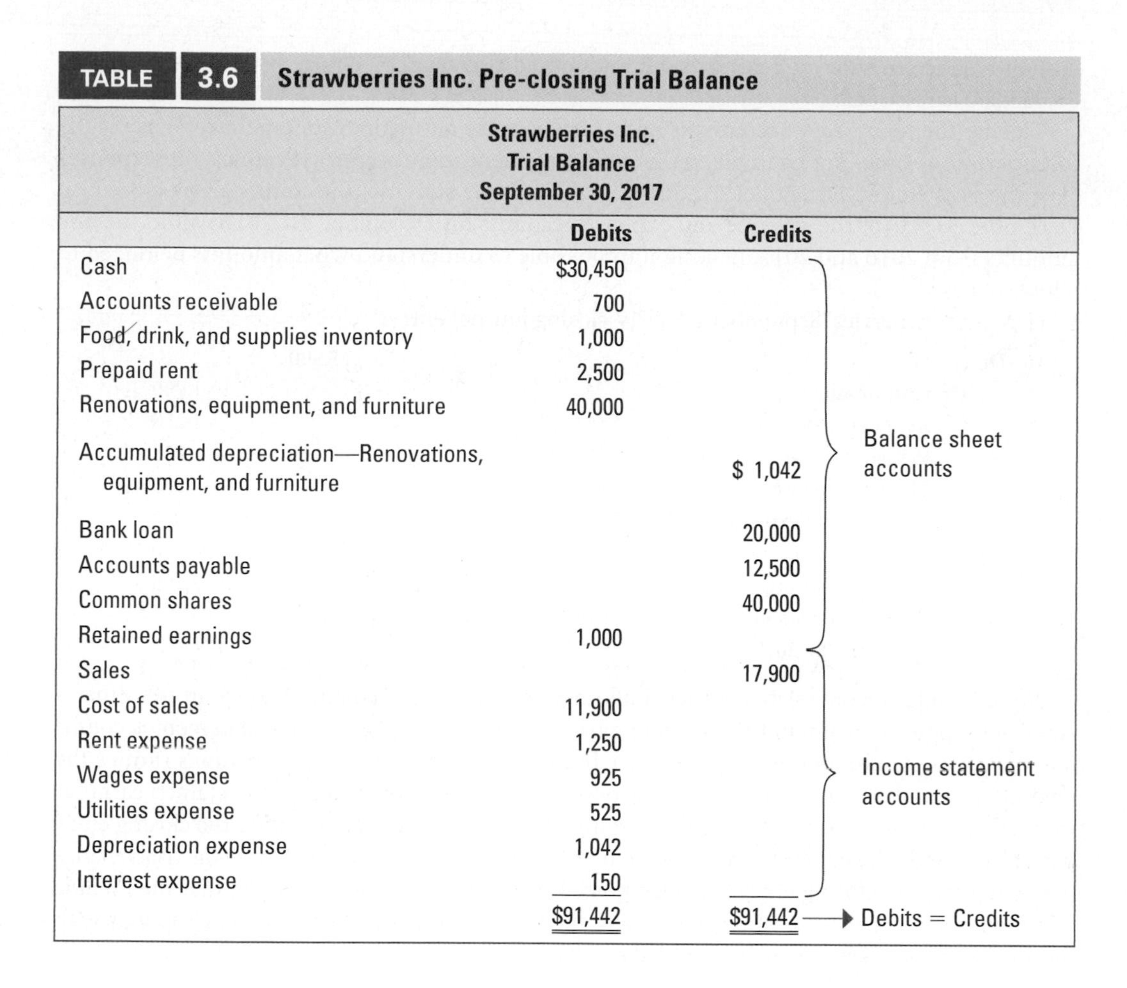

Strawberries Inc. Trial Balance September 30, 2017			
	Debits	**Credits**	
Cash	$30,450		Balance sheet accounts
Accounts receivable	700		
Food, drink, and supplies inventory	1,000		
Prepaid rent	2,500		
Renovations, equipment, and furniture	40,000		
Accumulated depreciation—Renovations, equipment, and furniture		$ 1,042	
Bank loan		20,000	
Accounts payable		12,500	
Common shares		40,000	
Retained earnings	1,000		
Sales		17,900	Income statement accounts
Cost of sales	11,900		
Rent expense	1,250		
Wages expense	925		
Utilities expense	525		
Depreciation expense	1,042		
Interest expense	150		
	$91,442	$91,442	→ Debits = Credits

Preparing the Financial Statements

The trial balance provides all the information required to prepare the balance sheet and income statement. To prepare these statements, the accounts in the trial balance have to be aggregated and organized into the format desired by the managers. (Trial balances will include every account an entity has whereas financial statements aggregate accounts. For example, an entity will have separate ledger accounts for each bank account but the balance sheet will only show a single cash amount.) At this point, retained earnings on the year-end balance sheet isn't known because the income statement accounts haven't been closed (closing entries are described in the next section). Strawberries' balance sheet and income statement can be found in Table 3.2.

Preparing and Posting Closing Journal Entries

LO 4, 6

The next step in the accounting cycle is preparing the closing journal entry, which sets all the income statement accounts to zero and transfers those amounts to owners' equity (retained earnings for corporations and owners' capital accounts for partnerships or proprietorships). All accounts on the income statement are **temporary accounts** because at the end of each period they are reset to zero and aren't carried forward to the next period. (In contrast, balance sheet accounts, which are called **permanent accounts**, carry forward from one period to the next.) The process of setting the income statement accounts to zero is called *closing* and is accomplished with **closing journal entries**. This simply involves recording a journal entry that is equal but opposite in amount to the ending balance in each income statement account with "the other side of the entry" going to owners' equity/retained earnings. For example, if there is a $1,000,000 ending balance in sales, a debit to sales and a credit to owners' equity/retained earnings of $1,000,000 is recorded.

Closing the temporary accounts is necessary because an income statement reports results for a period of time. For example, an income statement might report revenues and expenses "For the Year Ended December 31, 2016." If the income statement accounts aren't closed on December 31, 2016, the revenue and expense accounts on December 31, 2017 would include amounts from 2016 and 2017, making it impossible to understand what amounts belonged to which year.

Here is Strawberries' September 30, 2017 closing journal entry:

16. Dr. Sales	17,900	
Cr. Cost of sales		11,900
Cr. Rent expense		1,250
Cr. Wages expense		925
Cr. Utilities expense		525
Cr. Depreciation expense		1,042
Cr. Interest expense		150
Cr. Retained earnings		2,108

To close income statement accounts to retained earnings for the period ended September 30, 2017

Notice that for income statement accounts on Strawberries' trial balance there is an entry that is equal and opposite in amount to the ending balance. As a result, the income statement accounts have balances of zero and the balances have been "transferred" to retained earnings (notice the credit to retained earnings is equal to Strawberries' net income for the period—retained earnings increases by the amount of net income). Figure 3.15 shows the T-accounts after the closing entry has been posted (closing posts are shown in bold). The post-closing trial balance (the trial balance prepared after the closing entry has been posted) is shown in Table 3.7. Notice that the income statement accounts all have zero balances and the balance in retained earnings corresponds with the amount on the September 30, 2017 balance sheet.

INSIGHT

Accounting Software

Some students may have been exposed to accounting software packages that don't seem to have the accounting cycle components described here. In fact, all the features discussed are present; they're just hidden in the background. Accounting software is designed to be user-friendly for non-accountants. For example, you might input information by completing an electronic form that doesn't require a journal entry. These software packages allow users to examine electronic versions of journals, ledgers, and trial balances.

Mc Graw Hill connect

KNOWLEDGE CHECK 3.4

- ☐ Identify and explain the four types of adjusting journal entries.
- ☐ Explain what accrued expenses and accrued revenue are.
- ☐ What is a contra-asset account?
- ☐ What are closing journal entries and why are they necessary?

FIGURE 3.15 T-Accounts for Strawberries Inc.: Post-closing Entry Postings to T-Accounts

Cash

	Debit	Credit
Bal	12,800	
1	40,000	
2	20,000	
3		3,750
4		15,000
5		12,500
6		900
7		12,000
8	17,200	
9		525
10		925
11		150
15		1,000
Bal	30,450	

Accounts receivable

	Debit	Credit
Bal	0	
8	700	
Bal	700	

Food, drinks, and supplies inventory

	Debit	Credit
Bal	0	
6	900	
7	12,000	11,900
12		
Bal	1,000	

Prepaid rent

	Debit	Credit
Bal	0	
3	3,750	
13		1,250
Bal	2,500	

Renovations, equipment, and furniture

	Debit	Credit
Bal	0	
4	15,000	
5	25,000	
Bal	40,000	

Accumulated depreciation

	Debit	Credit
Bal		0
14		1,042
Bal		1,042

Bank loan

	Debit	Credit
Bal		0
2		20,000
Bal		20,000

Accounts payable

	Debit	Credit
Bal		0
5		12,500
Bal		12,500

Common shares

	Debit	Credit
Bal		0
1		40,000
Bal		40,000

Retained earnings

	Debit	Credit
Bal		0
15	1,000	
16		**2,108**
Bal		1,108

Sales

	Debit	Credit
Bal		0
8		17,900
Bal		17,900
16	**17,900**	
Bal		0

Cost of sales

	Debit	Credit
Bal	0	
12	11,900	
Bal	11,900	
16		**11,900**
Bal	0	

Rent expense

	Debit	Credit
Bal	0	
13	1,250	
Bal	1,250	
16		**1,250**
Bal	0	

Wages expense

	Debit	Credit
Bal	0	
10	925	
Bal	925	
16		**925**
Bal	0	

Depreciation expense

	Debit	Credit
Bal	0	
14	1,042	
Bal	1,042	
16		**1,042**
Bal	0	

Interest expense

	Debit	Credit
Bal	0	
11	150	
Bal	150	
16		**150**
Bal	0	

Utilities expense

	Debit	Credit
Bal	0	
9	525	
Bal	525	
16		**525**
Bal	0	

INSIGHT

Memorization

This is a challenging time to be studying accounting. Standards are changing rapidly as the world aligns itself with IFRS, and ASPE has been created in Canada for private companies. This rapidly changing world means that learning today's sets of rules may not prepare you to be an effective user of accounting information in the future. If you are only able to memorize rules, your knowledge may be obsolete very quickly. But if you understand accounting and can interpret rules, you will be much better positioned to adjust when the rules change.

TABLE 3.7 Strawberries Inc. Post-closing Trial Balance

Strawberries Inc. Trial Balance September 30, 2017			
	Debits	**Credits**	
Cash	$30,450		Balance sheet accounts
Accounts receivable	700		
Food, drink, and supplies inventory	1,000		
Prepaid rent	2,500		
Renovations, equipment, and furniture	40,000		
Accumulated depreciation—Renovations, equipment, and furniture		$ 1,042	
Bank loan		20,000	
Accounts payable		12,500	
Common shares		40,000	
Retained earnings		1,108	
Sales		0	Income statement accounts
Cost of sales	0		
Rent expense	0		
Wages expense	0		
Utilities expense	0		
Depreciation expense	0		
Interest expense	0		
	$74,650	$74,650	→ Debits = Credits

Solved Problem

Child First Safety Ltd. (CFS) is a small business that provides safety advice and equipment to parents and daycare centres wanting a safe, childproofed environment for infants and toddlers. The company has been in business for approximately two years. CFS is 100 percent owned and operated by Yehuda Bigalli. Yehuda has never been much of a bookkeeper and his accounting system has tended to be a bag of business receipts, invoices, cancelled cheques (a cheque that has been cashed and returned by the bank), and so on. Last year, an accountant friend organized the information and prepared financial statements. Yehuda used these for calculating his taxes and showing his bank. This year, Yehuda comes to you for help instead. He gives last year's (October 31, 2017) balance sheet (Table 3.8) along with the information in the bag.

You organize and summarize the data in the bag and determine the following:

1. On November 1, 2017, CFS purchased a two-year insurance policy for $3,000 cash. The policy goes into effect immediately.
2. During the year CFS sold safety equipment and advisory services to customers for $199,000: $140,000 for cash, the remainder on credit.
3. CFS purchased $65,000 of inventory during the year. All purchases were on credit.
4. CFS paid $62,000 during the year to suppliers for inventory purchases.
5. On November 15, 2017, CFS purchased a used car for $12,000 in cash. Yehuda uses the car for service calls and deliveries instead of using his personal vehicle. He estimates the car will last for four years.
6. During the year, CFS paid Yehuda and a part-time sales person $70,000 in salary and commission.

TABLE 3.8 Child First Safety Ltd. October 31, 2017 Balance Sheet

Child First Safety Ltd. Balance Sheet As of October 31, 2017			
Assets		**Liabilities and Shareholder's Equity**	
Current assets		**Current liabilities**	
Cash	$ 12,800	Bank loan	$ 15,000
Accounts receivable	22,000	Accounts payable	49,000
Inventory	52,000	Taxes payable	5,000
	86,800	Unearned revenue	3,000
			72,000
Non-current assets		**Shareholder's equity**	
Property and equipment	24,000	Common shares	15,000
Accumulated depreciation	(8,000)	Retained earnings	15,800
	16,000		30,800
Total assets	$102,800	Total liabilities and shareholder's equity	$102,800

7. During the year, CFS collected $45,000 from customers for purchases they had made on credit.
8. On October 31, 2018 CFS paid interest of $900 for the year on its bank loan.
9. On October 31, 2018 CFS repaid $2,000 of its bank loan.
10. During the year, CFS incurred other expenses of $20,000, all paid in cash.
11. CFS paid a dividend of $15,000 on September 15, 2018.
12. During the year, CFS paid the $5,000 in taxes payable that was owing to the federal and provincial governments on October 31, 2017.
13. In November 2017, CFS supplied $3,000 of equipment to a large daycare centre. The daycare centre had paid in advance for the equipment in October 2017. The payment was reported as unearned revenue on the October 31, 2017 balance sheet.
14. At the end of fiscal 2018, CFS owed the part-time sales person $1,500 in salary and commissions. The amount owing will be paid in mid-November 2018.
15. Depreciation of property and equipment is $6,000, including the used car that was purchased on November 15, 2017.
16. The cost of the safety equipment sold during the year was $72,000.
17. CFS will have to pay $6,700 in income taxes for the 2018 fiscal year. No payments had been made with respect to the 2018 fiscal year as of October 31, 2018.

Required:

A. Use an accounting equation spreadsheet to record the economic activity for CFS during fiscal 2018. Make sure you include the adjusting and closing entries. Prepare the balance sheet as of October 31, 2018 and the income statement and the statement of retained earnings for the year ended October 31, 2018. Also discuss CFS' performance for the year ended October 31, 2018.

OR

B. Use the information provided about CFS to do the following:

a. Prepare all necessary transactional journal entries for the year ended October 31, 2018 and post each journal entry to the appropriate T-account.

TABLE 3.9 Child First Safety Ltd. Completed Spreadsheet

		Assets						=	Liabilities	
Transaction	**Type of entry**	**Cash**	**Accounts receivable**	**Inventory**	**Prepaid insurance**	**Property and equipment**	**Accumulated depreciation**		**Bank loan**	**Accounts payable**
Beginning Balance		12,800	22,000	52,000	0	24,000	(8,000)		15,000	49,000
1	Transactional	(3,000)			3,000					
2	Transactional	140,000	59,000							
3	Transactional			65,000						65,000
4	Transactional	(62,000)								(62,000)
5	Transactional	(12,000)				12,000				
6	Transactional	(70,000)								
7	Transactional	45,000	(45,000)							
8	Transactional	(900)								
9	Transactional	(2,000)							(2,000)	
10	Transactional	(20,000)								
11	Transactional	(15,000)								
12	Transactional	(5,000)								
13	Adjusting									
14	Adjusting									
15	Adjusting						(6,000)			
16	Adjusting			(72,000)						
17	Adjusting									
18	Adjusting				(1,500)					
Pre-closing Balance		7,900	36,000	45,000	1,500	36,000	(14,000)		13,000	52,000
19	Closing									
Ending Balance		7,900	36,000	45,000	1,500	36,000	(14,000)		13,000	52,000

c. Prepare and post adjusting journal entries to their appropriate T-accounts.

d. Prepare a trial balance as of October 31, 2018.

e. Prepare a balance sheet for CFS as of October 31, 2018 and an income statement and statement of retained earnings for the year ended October 31, 2018.

f. Prepare the closing journal entry and post the closing entry to the appropriate T-accounts.

g. Prepare a trial balance as of October 31, 2018 after the closing entry has been prepared.

h. Discuss CFS' performance for the year ended October 31, 2018.

Solution—Approach A—Accounting Equation Spreadsheet

Table 3.9 provides the completed spreadsheet for the year ended October 31, 2018. Most of the entries should be clear, but note the following points:

- The first line of the spreadsheet, which is called "beginning balance," contains the values on the balance sheet on October 31, 2017. Remember that balance sheet accounts are permanent, so the ending balances in last year's balance sheet are the beginning balances in this year's. The income statement accounts all have beginning balances of zero because they are closed each year to retained earnings.
- The depreciation expense in item 15 is the portion of the cost of property and equipment that is expensed in fiscal 2018. The depreciation of the property and equipment is accumulated in a separate contra-asset account.

Liabilities (cont.)			+	Shareholder's equity									
Salaries payable	Taxes payable	Unearned revenue		Common shares	Retained earnings	Sales	Cost of sales	Insurance expense	Salaries expense	Depreciation expense	Other expenses	Tax expense	Interest expense
0	5,000	3,000		15,000	15,800								
						199,000							
									(70,000)				
													(900)
											(20,000)		
					(15,000)								
	(5,000)												
		(3,000)				3,000							
1,500									(1,500)				
										(6,000)			
							(72,000)						
	6,700											(6,700)	
								(1,500)					
1,500	6,700	0		15,000	800	202,000	(72,000)	(1,500)	(71,500)	(6,000)	(20,000)	(6,700)	(900)
					23,400	(202,000)	72,000	1,500	71,500	6,000	20,000	6,700	900
1,500	6,700	0		15,000	24,200	0	0	0	0	0	0	0	0

- Item 18 is tricky because the question doesn't specifically state that part of the prepaid insurance has to be expensed at year-end. This is typical of adjusting entries. Because adjusting entries are generated within the entity, the accountant or bookkeeper has to examine the accounts and decide when an adjusting entry is necessary.
- The balance sheet, income statement, and statement of retained earnings are shown in Table 3.11, following Approach B. The discussion of CFS' performance can also be found in Approach B.

Solution—Approach B

Prepare Journal Entries

		Dr.	Cr.
1.	Dr. Prepaid insurance (asset +)	3,000	
	Cr. Cash (asset −)		3,000
	To record the purchase of insurance for two years		
2.	Dr. Cash (asset +)	140,000	
	Dr. Accounts receivable (asset +)	59,000	
	Cr. Sales (revenue +, shareholders' equity +)		199,000
	To record sales for the year		
3.	Dr. Inventory (asset +)	65,000	
	Cr. Accounts payable (liability +)		65,000
	To record the purchase of inventory on credit		

		Dr.	Cr.
4.	Dr. Accounts payable (liability −)	62,000	
	Cr. Cash (asset −)		62,000
	To record the payment to suppliers for inventory purchased		
5.	Dr. Property and equipment (asset +)	12,000	
	Cr. Cash (asset −)		12,000
	To record the purchase of a car		
6.	Dr. Salaries expense (expenses +, shareholder's equity −)	70,000	
	Cr. Cash (asset −)		70,000
	To record salaries paid		
7.	Dr. Cash (asset +)	45,000	
	Cr. Accounts receivable (asset −)		45,000
	To record collection of accounts receivable		
8.	Dr. Interest expense (expenses +, shareholder's equity −)	900	
	Cr. Cash (asset −)		900
	To record the payment of interest on the bank loan		
9.	Dr. Bank loan (liability −)	2,000	
	Cr. Cash (asset −)		2,000
	To record payment of principal on the bank loan		
10.	Dr. Other expenses (expenses +, shareholder's equity −)	20,000	
	Cr. Cash (asset −)		20,000
	To record the payment of other expenses		
11.	Dr. Retained earnings (shareholder's equity −)	15,000	
	Cr. Cash (asset −)		15,000
	To record the payment of a dividend		
12.	Dr. Taxes payable (liability −)	5,000	
	Cr. Cash (asset −)		5,000
	To record the payment of taxes payable		

Post Journal Entries to the General Ledger

T-accounts are shown in Figure 3.16. For each balance sheet T-account, the beginning balance is the amount in the account on October 31, 2017. Remember that income statement accounts don't have beginning balances because they were set to zero on October 31, 2017, when the temporary accounts were closed.

Prepare and Post Adjusting Journal Entries

At the end of the period, the accounts are examined and any necessary adjusting entries are made. The adjusting entries are then posted to the corresponding general ledger accounts. The adjusting journal entries are shown below and posting of the adjusting entries to the T-accounts is shown in bold in Figure 3.17.

		Dr.	Cr.
13.	Dr. Unearned revenue (liability −)	3,000	
	Cr. Sales (revenue +, shareholder's equity +)		3,000
	Adjusting entry to record recognition of revenue on merchandise paid for in advance		
14.	Dr. Salaries expense (expense +, shareholder's equity −)	1,500	
	Cr. Salaries payable (liability +)		1,500
	Adjusting entry to accrue salaries owed but not paid		
15.	Dr. Depreciation expense (expenses +, shareholder's equity −)	6,000	
	Cr. Accumulated depreciation (contra-asset +)		6,000
	Adjusting entry to record the depreciation of property and equipment		

FIGURE 3.16 T-Accounts for Child First Safety Ltd.: Pre-adjusting Entry Postings to T-Accounts

Cash

	Debit	Credit
Bal	12,800	
1		3,000
2	140,000	
4		62,000
5		12,000
6		70,000
7	45,000	
8		900
9		2,000
10		20,000
11		15,000
12		5,000

Accounts receivable

	Debit	Credit
Bal	22,000	
2	59,000	
7		45,000

Inventory

	Debit	Credit
Bal	52,000	
3	65,000	

Prepaid insurance

	Debit	Credit
Bal	0	
1	3,000	

Property and equipment

	Debit	Credit
Bal	24,000	
5	12,000	

Accumulated depreciation

	Debit	Credit
Bal		8,000

Bank loan

	Debit	Credit
Bal		15,000
9	2,000	

Accounts payable

	Debit	Credit
Bal		49,000
3		65,000
4	62,000	

Salaries payable

	Debit	Credit
Bal		0

Taxes payable

	Debit	Credit
Bal		5,000
12	5,000	

Unearned revenue

	Debit	Credit
Bal		3,000

Common shares

	Debit	Credit
Bal		15,000

Retained earnings

	Debit	Credit
Bal		15,800
11	15,000	

Sales

	Debit	Credit
Bal		0
2		199,000

Cost of sales

	Debit	Credit
Bal	0	

Insurance expense

	Debit	Credit
Bal	0	

Salaries expense

	Debit	Credit
Bal	0	
6	70,000	

Depreciation expense

	Debit	Credit
Bal	0	

Other expenses

	Debit	Credit
Bal	0	
10	20,000	

Tax expense

	Debit	Credit
Bal	0	

Interest expense

	Debit	Credit
Bal	0	
8	900	

16. Dr. Cost of sales (expenses +, shareholder's equity −) 72,000
Cr. Inventory (asset −) 72,000
Adjusting entry to record cost of sales

17. Dr. Tax expense (expenses +, shareholder's equity −) 6,700
Cr. Taxes payable (liability +) 6,700
Adjusting entry to record income tax expense and accrue the liability for income taxes

18. Dr. Insurance expense (expenses +, shareholder's equity −) 1,500
Cr. Prepaid insurance (asset −) 1,500
Adjusting entry to record insurance used during the year

FIGURE 3.17 T-Accounts for Child First Safety Ltd.: Adjusting Entry Postings to T-Accounts

Cash		
Bal	12,800	
1		3,000
2	140,000	
4		62,000
5		12,000
6		70,000
7	45,000	
8		900
9		2,000
10		20,000
11		15,000
12		5,000
Bal	7,900	

Accounts receivable		
Bal	22,000	
2	59,000	
7		45,000
Bal	36,000	

Inventory		
Bal	52,000	
3	65,000	
16		**72,000**
Bal	45,000	

Prepaid insurance		
Bal	0	
1	3,000	
18		**1,500**
Bal	1,500	

Property and equipment		
Bal	24,000	
5	12,000	
Bal	36,000	

Accumulated depreciation		
Bal		8,000
15		**6,000**
Bal		14,000

Bank loan		
Bal		15,000
9	2,000	
Bal		13,000

Accounts payable		
Bal		49,000
3		65,000
4	62,000	
Bal		52,000

Salaries payable		
Bal		0
14		**1,500**
Bal		1,500

Taxes payable		
Bal		5,000
12	5,000	
17		**6,700**
Bal		6,700

Unearned revenue		
Bal		3,000
13	**3,000**	
Bal		0

Common shares		
Bal		15,000
Bal		15,000

Retained earnings		
Bal		15,800
11	15,000	
Bal		800

Sales		
Bal		0
2		199,000
13		**3,000**
Bal		202,000

Cost of sales		
Bal	0	
16	**72,000**	
Bal	72,000	

Insurance expense		
Bal	0	
18	**1,500**	
Bal	1,500	

Salaries expense		
Bal	0	
6	70,000	
14	**1,500**	
Bal	71,500	

Depreciation expense		
Bal	0	
15	**6,000**	
Bal	6,000	

Other expenses		
Bal	0	
10	20,000	
Bal	20,000	

Tax expense		
Bal	0	
17	**6,700**	
Bal	6,700	

Interest expense		
Bal	0	
8	900	
Bal	900	

Prepare the Trial Balance

TABLE 3.10 Child First Safety Ltd. Trial Balance

Child First Safety Ltd. Trial Balance October 31, 2018			
	Debits	**Credits**	
Cash	$ 7,900		Balance sheet accounts
Accounts receivable	36,000		
Inventory	45,000		
Prepaid insurance	1,500		
Property and equipment	36,000		
Accumulated depreciation		$ 14,000	
Bank loan		13,000	
Accounts payable		52,000	
Salaries payable		1,500	
Taxes payable		6,700	
Unearned revenue		0	
Common shares		15,000	
Retained earnings		800	
Sales		202,000	Income statement accounts
Cost of sales	72,000		
Insurance expense	1,500		
Salaries expense	71,500		
Depreciation expense	6,000		
Other expenses	20,000		
Tax expense	6,700		
Interest expense	900		
	$305,000	$305,000	→ Debits = Credits

Preparing the Financial Statements

The balances in the trial balance are used to prepare the financial statements, which are shown in Table 3.11. The financial statements are prepared before the closing entry because once the closing entry is made, the balances in the income statement accounts will be zero. However, preparing the statements before the closing entry is made means that the ending balance in retained earnings isn't known from the trial balance.

TABLE 3.11 Child First Safety Ltd. Balance Sheet, and Income Statement and Statement of Retained Earnings

Child First Safety Ltd.
Balance Sheet
As of October 31, 2018

Assets		**Liabilities and Shareholder's Equity**	
Current assets		**Current liabilities**	
Cash	$ 7,900	Bank loan	$ 13,000
Accounts receivable	36,000	Accounts payable	52,000
Inventory	45,000	Salaries payable	1,500
Prepaid insurance	1,500	Taxes payable	6,700
	90,400		73,200
Non-current assets		**Shareholder's equity**	
Property and equipment	36,000	Common shares	15,000
Accumulated depreciation	(14,000)	Retained earnings	24,200
	22,000		39,200
Total assets	$112,400	Total liabilities and shareholder's equity	$112,400

Child First Safety Ltd.
Income Statement and Statement of Retained Earnings
For the Year Ended October 31, 2018

Sales		$202,000
Cost of sales		72,000
Gross margin		130,000
Expenses		
Salaries expense	$71,500	
Depreciation expense	6,000	
Insurance expense	1,500	
Interest expense	900	
Other expenses	20,000	
Total expenses		99,900
Income before taxes		30,100
Income tax expense		6,700
Net income		23,400
Retained earnings at the beginning of the year		15,800
Dividends		(15,000)
Retained earnings at the end of the year		$ 24,200

FIGURE 3.18 T-Accounts for Child First Safety Ltd.: Closing Entry Postings to T-Accounts

Cash

	Debit	Credit
Bal	12,800	
1		3,000
2	140,000	
4		62,000
5		12,000
6		70,000
7	45,000	
8		900
9		2,000
10		20,000
11		15,000
12		5,000
Bal	7,900	

Accounts receivable

	Debit	Credit
Bal	22,000	
2	59,000	
7		45,000
Bal	36,000	

Inventory

	Debit	Credit
Bal	52,000	
3	65,000	
16		72,000
Bal	45,000	

Prepaid insurance

	Debit	Credit
Bal	0	
1	3,000	
18		1,500
Bal	1,500	

Property and equipment

	Debit	Credit
Bal	24,000	
5	12,000	
Bal	36,000	

Accumulated depreciation

	Debit	Credit
Bal		8,000
15		6,000
Bal		14,000

Bank loan

	Debit	Credit
Bal		15,000
9	2,000	
Bal		13,000

Accounts payable

	Debit	Credit
Bal		49,000
3		65,000
4	62,000	
Bal		52,000

Salaries payable

	Debit	Credit
Bal		0
14		1,500
Bal		1,500

Taxes payable

	Debit	Credit
Bal		5,000
12	5,000	
17		6,700
Bal		6,700

Unearned revenue

	Debit	Credit
Bal		3,000
13	3,000	
Bal		0

Common shares

	Debit	Credit
Bal		15,000
Bal		15,000

Retained earnings

	Debit	Credit
Bal		15,800
11	15,000	
19		**23,400**
Bal		24,200

Sales

	Debit	Credit
Bal		0
2		199,000
13		3,000
Bal		202,000
19	**202,000**	
Bal		0

Cost of sales

	Debit	Credit
Bal	0	
16	72,000	
Bal	72,000	
19		**72,000**
Bal	0	

Insurance expense

	Debit	Credit
Bal	0	
18	1,500	
Bal	1,500	
19		**1,500**
Bal	0	

Salaries expense

	Debit	Credit
Bal	0	
6	70,000	
14	1,500	
Bal	71,500	
19		**71,500**
Bal	0	

Depreciation expense

	Debit	Credit
Bal	0	
15	6,000	
Bal	6,000	
19		**6,000**
Bal	0	

Other expenses

	Debit	Credit
Bal	0	
10	20,000	
Bal	20,000	
19		**20,000**
Bal	0	

Tax expense

	Debit	Credit
Bal	0	
17	6,700	
Bal	6,700	
19		**6,700**
Bal	0	

Interest expense

	Debit	Credit
Bal	0	
8	900	
Bal	900	
19		**900**
Bal	0	

Prepare and Post Closing Journal Entries

The closing journal entry for the year ended October 31, 2018 is

		Debit	Credit
19.	Dr. Sales	202,000	
	Cr. Cost of sales		72,000
	Cr. Insurance expense		1,500
	Cr. Salaries expense		71,500
	Cr. Depreciation expense		6,000
	Cr. Other expenses		20,000
	Cr. Tax expense		6,700
	Cr. Interest expense		900
	Cr. Retained earnings		23,400
	To close income statement accounts to retained earnings		

T-accounts after the closing entry has been posted are presented in Figure 3.18.

Post-closing Trial Balance

The post-closing trial balance is in Table 3.12.

TABLE 3.12 Child First Safety Ltd. Trial Balance

Child First Safety Ltd. Post-closing Trial Balance October 31, 2018			
	Debits	**Credits**	
Cash	$ 7,900		Balance sheet accounts
Accounts receivable	36,000		
Inventory	45,000		
Prepaid insurance	1,500		
Property and equipment	36,000		
Accumulated depreciation		$ 14,000	
Bank loan		13,000	
Accounts payable		52,000	
Salaries payable		1,500	
Taxes payable		6,700	
Unearned revenue		0	
Common shares		15,000	
Retained earnings		24,200	
Sales		0	Income statement accounts
Cost of sales	0		
Insurance expense	0		
Salaries expense	0		
Depreciation expense	0		
Other expenses	0		
Tax expense	0		
Interest expense	0		
	$126,400	$126,400	→ Debits = Credits

How Did Child First Safety Ltd. (CFS) Do?

Since we have put these financial statements together on behalf of Yehuda, who doesn't seem too knowledgeable about the accounting information, we should probably give him some insights into what they say. We should warn Yehuda that the financial statements don't provide clear-cut answers to questions about an entity's situation, but they do raise flags for further investigation.

1. As was the case with Strawberries Inc., our ability to analyze the performance of CFS is hampered by the absence of comparable income statement data. We do have the October 31, 2017 balance sheet for making comparisons between balance sheet accounts.
2. It can be difficult to evaluate the financial statements of an entity when the owner also manages the entity. One reason is that owner-managers are free to pay themselves any amount they choose and the payments can take different forms, including salary, dividends, and loans. Remember that only salary reduces net income so different combinations of payments will result in different net incomes. Often, an important objective of owner-managers of private corporations is to minimize the overall tax burden on themselves and their corporation.
3. Without knowing his share of the salaries expense, we can't make a conclusive statement about how well-paid Yehuda was this year, but it appears he had a reasonably good year. If we assume that his share of the salaries expense was $45,000 (probably a reasonable assumption since the sales person

was a part-time employee), Yehuda took home $60,000 in salary and dividends ($45,000 in salary + $15,000 in dividends). In addition, his business made money, so that also added to his wealth.

4. At first glance, CFS' liquidity position seems adequate. Its current ratio has been stable for the two years available (1.23 in 2018, 1.21 in 2017). We would need to compare these current ratios with other, similar businesses to get some perspective on the adequacy of this current ratio. Of some concern is the low amount of cash and receivables (current assets that are cash or will be cash very soon) relative to the liabilities that will require cash very soon (accounts payable, salaries payable, and taxes payable). If sales slow down, there may be a cash problem since the sale of inventory generates cash. However, CFS' liquidity position was similar a year ago and the company seems to have managed.
5. CFS generated a return on equity of about 67 percent (net income ÷ average shareholders' equity), a very good return on investment. The profit margin for the year is 11.6 percent. This ratio is difficult to assess without some comparative data from similar businesses.
6. Compared with October 31, 2017, the amount of inventory on hand on October 31, 2018, has decreased, while the amount of accounts receivable has increased. Without comparable income statements to tell us how sales changed from fiscal 2017, it's difficult to interpret these changes. For example, the increase in accounts receivable could be due to higher sales, more generous credit terms being offered to customers to attract more business, customers paying more slowly than last year, or other reasons.

SUMMARY OF KEY POINTS

LO 1 Producing accounting information requires an accounting system that captures raw data and organizes, summarizes, and classifies it into a form that is useful for decision making. The information produced by an accounting system is limited by the data entered into it. The accounting cycle is the process by which data about economic events are entered into an accounting system, processed, organized, and used to produce information, such as financial statements.

LO 2 The accounting equation spreadsheet is used to demonstrate the full accounting cycle in a straightforward, conceptual, and compact way. The spreadsheet clearly lays out how transactions and economic events affect the accounting equation and how the economic activity ultimately gets turned into financial statements. Each column in the spreadsheet represents an account in the entity's records and each transaction or economic event is recorded on a separate row. Each entry to the spreadsheet must maintain the accounting equation. The ending balance in each column provides the information needed to prepare the balance sheet and income statement.

LO 3 Managers often have choices for how to record and report transactions and economic events. The choices managers make will affect the accounting numbers that are reported, which in turn may affect how the statements are interpreted and the decisions stakeholders make.

LO 4 Accrual accounting attempts to measure the economic activity of an entity. An entry into an accrual accounting system is usually triggered by a transaction—an exchange between the entity and an external party. Sometimes, economic changes affecting the entity aren't triggered by transactions. Entries not triggered by exchanges with outside entities are called adjusting entries.

There are four types of adjusting entries:

1. Deferred expense/prepaid expense—cash is paid before an expense is recognized
2. Deferred revenue—cash is received before revenue is recognized
3. Accrued expense/accrued liability—an expense is recognized before cash is paid
4. Accrued revenue/accrued asset—revenue is recognized before cash is received

LO 5 The journal entry is the method used in practice to enter economic events into the accounting system. Whenever a relevant transaction or economic event occurs, a journal entry is recorded. During the period, journal entries are posted to T-accounts (general ledger accounts). At the end of the period adjusting entries are recorded and posted to T-accounts, the trial balance is prepared, and financial statements made. Finally, the closing journal entry is recorded and posted to T-accounts.

LO 6 At the end of each period the balances in the income statement, or temporary accounts, must be set to zero and the balances in those accounts transferred to owners' equity/retained earnings in the balance sheet. The balances in the income statement accounts are set to zero so they can accumulate information about transactions and economic events that pertain only to the new period. This process is achieved by a closing journal entry.

FORMULA SUMMARY

$$\text{Return on equity} = \text{Net income} \div \text{Average shareholders' equity}$$

$$\text{Profit margin ratio} = \text{Net income} \div \text{Sales}$$

KEY TERMS

account, p. 109
accounting cycle, p. 102
accounting estimate, p. 132
accrued expense, p. 129
accrued liability, p. 129
accrued revenue, p. 130
adjusting entry, p. 124
carrying amount, p. 127
closing journal entry, p. 139
contra-asset account, p. 127
credit, p. 110
debit, p. 110
debit card, p. 115
deferred expense, p. 121
double-entry bookkeeping, p. 107
earnings management, p. 125
executory contract, p. 115
general journal, p. 133
general ledger, p. 135
journal entry, p. 109
matching (matching concept), p. 106
permanent accounts, p. 139
posting, p. 135
prepaid expense, p. 126
profit margin ratio, p. 122
return on equity (ROE), p. 122
revenue recognition, p. 104
straight-line depreciation, p. 119
T-account, p. 135
temporary accounts, p. 139
transactional entry, p. 125
trial balance, p. 137
unearned revenue, p. 129

SIMILAR TERMS

The left column gives alternative terms that are sometimes used for the accounting terms introduced in this chapter, which are listed in the right column.

deferred expense, deferred charge, deferred cost, deferred debit	**prepaid expense, p. 126**
nominal account	**temporary accounts, p. 139**
deferred revenue	**unearned revenue, p. 129**

ASSIGNMENT MATERIALS

Questions

Q3-1. Explain why much more judgment is required with accrual accounting than with cash accounting.

Q3-2. What are closing journal entries and why are they necessary? When do closing entries have to be prepared?

Q3-3. In 2017, Taymouth Inc. reported net income of $100,000. What would be the effect on retained earnings on Taymouth's 2017 balance sheet and on its 2018 income statement if it didn't record a closing journal entry at the end of 2017?

Q3-4. Explain why adjusting entries are necessary in accrual accounting but not required when the cash basis of accounting is used.

Q3-5. Explain the difference between transactional journal entries and adjusting journal entries.

Q3-6. Identify the four types of adjusting entries and explain why each type is necessary.

Q3-7. For each type of adjusting entry explain the impact on assets, liabilities, owners' equity, revenue, expenses, and net income if the required adjusting entry wasn't made.

Q3-8. When do adjusting entries have to be made? Explain.

Q3-9. What do the terms *debit* and *credit* mean?

Q3-10. What is a contra-asset account? Why are contra-asset accounts used?

Q3-11. When a dividend is declared and paid by a corporation, a debit is made to retained earnings. Explain why.

Q3-12. A company sells merchandise on credit to a customer for $1,000. What is the impact on the balance sheets of the selling company and the customer? Explain.

Q3-13. Explain the difference between permanent and temporary accounts.

Q3-14. Consider the steps of the accounting cycle (recording of transactional and adjusting journal entries, posting of entries, preparation of the trial balance, and recording and posting of closing entries). Which step or steps requires the most judgment? Explain.

Q3-15. Why aren't dividends treated as an expense?

Q3-16. What effect do revenue and expenses have on equity? Explain why.

Q3-17. If cash increases when a debit is made to the cash account, why does the bank credit your account when you make a deposit?

Q3-18. What is an executory contract? How do IFRS usually account for executory contracts?

Q3-19. Identify and explain the four things that must be known when a transaction is to be entered into an accounting system.

Q3-20. Why do entities divide assets, liabilities, and owners' equity into sub-accounts rather than accumulating data simply as assets, liabilities, and owners' equity?

Q3-21. How should an entity determine the number of accounts it should keep in its general ledger?

Q3-22. Why can managers sometimes choose among alternative ways of accounting for transactions and economic events when accrual accounting is used? What are the implications of these choices on the financial statements and to the users of financial statements?

Q3-23. Figure 3.1 (Panel A) shows that not every economic event affecting an entity is entered into the entity's accounting system. What do you think are the implications for financial statements and stakeholders of not having every economic event recorded in the accounting system?

Q3-24. Figure 3.1 (Panel A) shows that not every economic event affecting an entity is entered into the entity's accounting system. Give three examples of economic events that might affect an entity but not be recorded in the entity's accounting system.

Q3-25. Identify and explain the steps of the accounting cycle.

Q3-26. What are T-accounts? Why are they used?

Q3-27. What does "posting" journal entries to the general ledger mean? Why are journal entries posted to the general ledger?

Q3-28. What is a trial balance and what is its purpose? Why doesn't a trial balance guarantee that your accounting is "correct"?

Q3-29. Why is it useful to cross-reference journal entries to the posting to the general ledger account (T-account)?

Q3-30. Explain how information recorded in the general journal (using journal entries) is organized differently from the information in the general ledger (posted from the general journal).

Q3-31. Explain how bookkeeping is different from accounting.

Exercises

E3-1. **(Types of events, LO 4)** For each of the events listed below, indicate whether the event represents a transactional entry, an adjusting entry, or no entry in the accounting system. Assume the accounting system is designed to collect information on an accrual basis.

a. Depreciation of equipment.
b. Collection of accounts receivable from a customer.
c. A customer uses a gift card to purchase merchandise at a store.
d. Recognition of revenue for work done in the current period but paid for in the previous period.
e. Hiring of a new vice-president of finance.
f. Purchase of inventory on credit from a supplier.
g. Earning of interest on an investment. The interest won't be paid until next year.
h. A customer pays currently for work to be done next year.
i. Sale of land to a buyer in exchange for a promise to pay $1,000,000 in cash in two years.
j. Payment of a dividend to shareholders.
k. Expensing the cost of an insurance policy that was paid for last year.

E3-2. **(Creating transactions and economic events from accounting equation effects, LO 2, 5)** Below are pairs of changes that affect elements of the accounting equation. Give an example of a transaction or economic event that reflects each:

a. Asset increases, asset decreases
b. Asset increases, liability increases
c. Asset increases, shareholders' equity increases
d. Asset increases, revenue increases
e. Liability decreases, asset decreases
f. Asset decreases, expense increases
g. Liability decreases, revenue increases
h. Asset decreases, shareholders' equity decreases
i. Liability increases, expense increases
j. Asset decreases, revenue decreases (this one's a bit tricky)

E3-3. **(Preparing closing entries using spreadsheets and journal entries, LO 2, 4, 6)** Below is a summarized income statement for St. Bruno Inc.

St. Bruno Inc.
Income Statement for the Year Ended December 31, 2017

Revenue	$5,125,000
Expenses	3,225,000
Net income	$1,900,000

a. Prepare a spreadsheet and make the entry that is necessary to close the temporary accounts. Assume the balance in retained earnings on December 31, 2016 was $13,750,000.
b. Prepare the journal entry necessary to close the temporary accounts.
c. Explain why closing entries are necessary and when they should be recorded.
d. What would be the effect on net income in 2018 if St. Bruno Inc. forgot to prepare the closing entry in 2017?

E3-4. **(Preparing closing entries using spreadsheets and journal entries, LO 2, 4, 6)** Below is Lashburn Ltd.'s summarized income statement for the year ended August 31, 2016, its first year in business.

Lashburn Ltd.
Income Statement for the Year Ended August 31, 2016
(in thousands of dollars)

Sales		$225,720
Cost of sales		76,200
Gross margin		149,520
Expenses		
Selling and marketing	$22,740	
General and administrative	15,450	
Research and development	9,675	
Depreciation	9,420	
Interest	4,500	
Other	3,315	65,100
Income before taxes		84,420
Income taxes		30,390
Net income		$ 54,030

a. Prepare a spreadsheet and make the entries necessary to close the temporary accounts.
b. Prepare the journal entry necessary to close the temporary accounts.
c. Explain why closing entries are necessary and when they should be recorded.
d. What would be the effect on net income in 2017 if Lashburn Ltd. forgot to prepare a closing entry in 2016?

E3-5. **(Impact of transactions on the accounting equation, LO 2, 5)** For each of the following transactions or economic events, indicate the impact on the elements of the accounting equation (whether each element increases, decreases, has no net effect, or there is no impact):
a. Purchase of equipment; supplier agrees to be paid in one year.
b. Depreciation of a building.
c. Collection of an amount owed by a customer.
d. Repayment of a bank loan.
e. Repair services received and paid for in cash.
f. Property insurance for the next fiscal year purchased for cash.
g. A magazine subscriber pays in advance for a new subscription.
h. Employees are owed wages at the end of the year.
i. An investor earns interest on an investment; the amount is unpaid at the end of the year (consider from the investor's perspective).

E3-6. **(Recognizing the effects of debits and credits, LO 5)** Indicate whether each of the following would be treated as a debit or a credit in a journal entry.
a. Increase in equipment.
b. Increase in unearned revenue.
c. Decrease in accounts receivable.
d. Increase in revenues.
e. Increase in advertising expense.
f. Increase in common shares.
g. Decrease in depreciation expense.
h. Decrease in accrued liabilities.

E3-7. **(Recognizing the effects of debits and credits, LO 5)** Indicate whether each of the following would be treated as a debit or a credit in a journal entry.
a. Decrease in cost of goods sold
b. Decrease in bonds payable.

c. Decrease in land.
d. Decrease in retained earnings.
e. Increase in inventory.
f. Decrease in revenues.
g. Increase in accounts payable.
h. Increase in tax expense.

E3-8. **(Identifying different types of adjusting entries, LO 4)** Refer to Table 3.5, which summarizes the different types of adjusting journal entries. For each of the following transactions involving Beulah Ltd. (Beulah), identify the type of adjusting entry required as a result of the event. Explain the reason for your choice. Beulah's year-end is December 31.

	Type	Situation
Example	Deferred expense/ prepaid expense	Beulah purchased new computer equipment. The estimated life of the equipment is four years.
a.	________	During the period, Beulah has $20,000 of supplies inventory available to use. At the end of the period, $3,000 is still on hand.
b.	________	In late December, Beulah purchases advertising on a local TV station. As of early January, Beulah hasn't paid or received an invoice for the advertising.
c.	________	Beulah pays two years' rent in advance.
d.	________	Beulah sells gift cards to customers.
e.	________	Beulah's senior managers earn bonuses for their excellent performance for the year just ended. The bonuses will be paid in February.
f.	________	Beulah earns a royalty from another company for every product the company sells. As of the year-end, Beulah hasn't received payment.
g.	________	Beulah borrows money during the year. Interest doesn't have to be paid until the next year.

E3-9. **(Recording transactions using an accounting equation spreadsheet, LO 2)** Set up an accounting equation spreadsheet and enter each of the following economic events into it.

a. A car is purchased for $25,000 cash.
b. A car is purchased for $15,000 cash and $10,000 financed through the dealer.
c. A corporation sells common shares to investors for $100,000.
d. A corporation pays $1,000,000 in dividends to shareholders.
e. A corporation declares dividends of $1,000,000. The dividends will be paid in 30 days.
f. A corporation pays $1,000,000 of dividends that were previously declared.
g. A company sells goods to a customer for $300 cash. The goods cost $200. (*Hint:* The company records the reduction in inventory and cost of sales at the time the sale is recorded.)
h. A company sells goods to a customer for $300. The goods cost $200. The customer promises to pay in 30 days. (*Hint:* The company records the reduction in inventory and cost of sales at the time the sale is recorded.)
i. A company collects $1,000 that is due from a customer.

E3-10. **(Recording transactions using journal entries, LO 5)** For each of the events described in Exercise E3-9, prepare the journal entry necessary to record the event. Create a T-account for each account you use and post the journal entries to the appropriate T-accounts.

E3-11. **(Recording transactions using an accounting equation spreadsheet, LO 2)** Feldstein and Partners (Feldstein) is a firm of accountants. Set up an accounting equation spreadsheet and enter each of the following independent economic events into the spreadsheet:

a. Feldstein completed an engagement for a client and sent an invoice for $5,000. The client is required to pay within 30 days.
b. Feldstein exchanges real estate owned by the partnership for a building. The real estate and building are each worth $425,000.
c. Feldstein pays $2,500 owed to a supplier of stationery.
d. Feldstein admitted a new partner to the partnership. The new partner paid $50,000 for an ownership interest.
e. Feldstein borrows $18,000 from the bank.
f. During the month, Feldstein's employees earned $25,000 in salaries and wages. The amount owing will be paid early next month.
g. Feldstein hires a new accountant for the upcoming busy season. The new person will join the firm in two weeks.
h. Feldstein receives a $7,000 deposit from a client for services that will be provided next year.
i. Feldstein collects $3,700 owed by a client.
j. Feldstein donates $1,500 to a local charity.

E3-12. **(Recording transactions using journal entries, LO 5)** For each of the events described in Exercise E3-11, prepare the journal entry necessary to record the event. Create a T-account for each account you use and post each journal entry to the appropriate T-accounts.

E3-13. **(Explaining journal entries, LO 4, 5)** Provide a description of the event represented by each of the following journal entries.

a.	Dr. Equipment	2,000,000	
	Cr. Cash		2,000,000
b.	Dr. Accounts receivable	20,000	
	Cr. Revenue		20,000
c.	Dr. Cash	7,500,000	
	Cr. Common shares		7,500,000
d.	Dr. Land	350,000	
	Cr. Notes payable		350,000
e.	Dr. Salary expense	8,500	
	Cr. Salary payable		8,500
f.	Dr. Unearned revenue	10,000	
	Cr. Revenue		10,000
g.	Dr. Accounts payable	15,000	
	Cr. Cash		15,000
h.	Dr. Insurance expense	2,500	
	Cr. Prepaid insurance		2,500
i.	Dr. Interest receivable	25,000	
	Cr. Interest revenue		25,000

E3-14. **(Explaining journal entries, LO 4, 5)** Provide a description of the event represented by each of the following journal entries.

a.	Dr. Equipment	1,100,000	
	Cr. Cash		350,000
	Cr. Notes payable		750,000
b.	Dr. Cash	2,500	
	Cr. Bank loan		2,500
c.	Dr. Cash	1,500,000	
	Dr. Long-term receivable	3,500,000	
	Cr. Land		5,000,000

d. Dr. Prepaid rent	5,000	
Cr. Cash		5,000
e. Dr. Retained earnings	210,000	
Cr. Dividend payable		210,000
f. Dr. Patent	250,000	
Cr. Common shares		250,000
g. Dr. Cash	35,000	
Cr. Revenue		25,000
Cr. Unearned revenue		10,000
h. Dr. Warranty expense	72,500	
Cr. Warranty liability		72,500

E3-15. **(Recreating journal entries from T-account data, LO 5)** Use the information from the T-accounts below to create the related journal entries. Provide an explanation for each journal entry.

Cash	
❷ 8,000	
	11,000 ❹
❺ 25,000	
	21,000 ❻
❼ 75,000	

Accounts receivable	
❶ 10,000	8,000 ❷

Inventory	
❸ 15,000	4,000 ❽

Equipment	
❻ 52,000	

Bank loan	
	75,000 ❼

Accounts payable	
❹ 11,000	15,000 ❸
	31,000 ❻

Common shares	
	25,000 ❺

Revenue	
	10,000 ❶

Cost of goods sold	
❽ 4,000	

E3-16. **(Recreating journal entries from T-account data, LO 5)** Use the information from the T-accounts below to create the related journal entries. Provide an explanation for each journal entry.

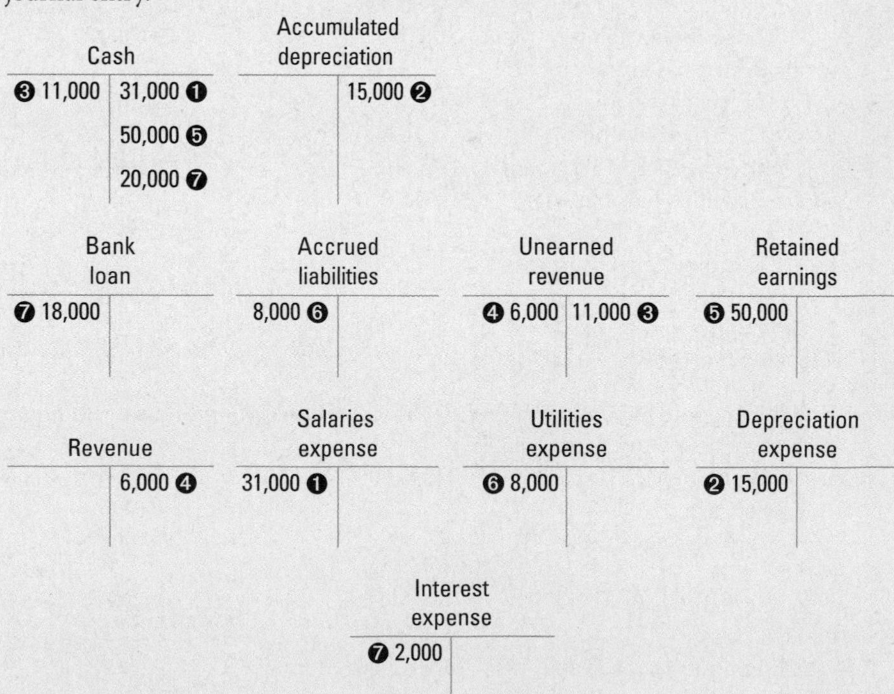

E3-17. **(Recording economic events in an accounting equation spreadsheet and preparing financial statements, LO 2, 4, 5, 6)** Fitness For All Ltd. is a new health club operating in a suburb of Winnipeg. The following transactions take place in September and October 2017:

i. September 1: Fitness For All Ltd. is incorporated. The owner pays $125,000 for 5,000 shares of company stock.
ii. September 3: Fitness For All Ltd. signs a three-year lease for space for the club. The owner pays $3,000 cash in rent for October and November.
iii. September 3–20: Renovations on the location are carried out at a cost of $20,000 cash. The expected useful life of the renovations is three years.
iv. September 21: Equipment worth $125,000 is purchased from a supplier. Fitness For All Ltd. pays $75,000 in cash and promises to pay the remainder in six months. The estimated life of the equipment is five years.
v. September 25: Supplies are purchased on credit for $5,000.
vi. During September and October: Memberships to the club are sold to 300 people at $350 per person per year. Members pay 50 percent immediately and promise to pay the remainder in 30 days. Fitness for All Ltd. records revenue when a new member joins.
vii. During September and October: Employees are paid wages of $10,000. At the end of October, Fitness For All Ltd. owes employees $1,200.
viii. During September and October: Utilities costing $2,000 are paid.
ix. During September and October: Fitness For All Ltd. pays $2,700 toward the supplies purchased on credit on September 25.
x. During September and October: Fitness For All Ltd. collects $30,000 owed by members.
xi. During September and October: $3,900 of supplies is used.

Required:

a. Use an accounting equation spreadsheet to record the transactions that occurred during September and October.
b. Record all necessary adjusting entries (depreciation, rent, supplies, and wages).
c. Record the closing entry.
d. Prepare the balance sheet as of October 31, 2017 and an income statement and statement of retained earnings for the period ending October 31, 2017.

E3-18. **(Cash versus accrual accounting, LO 2, 4, 5)** Saanich Ltd. operates a new fitness centre in a large city. As a grand opening promotion, Saanich offered a three-year membership for $600. To take advantage of the promotion, members had to pay at the time they signed up. Two hundred people took advantage of the offer. The fitness centre opened on January 1, 2017 and all memberships begin on that day.

a. Under cash accounting, how much revenue should Saanich report for the year ended December 31, 2017? Explain.
b. Under accrual accounting, how much revenue should Saanich report for the year ended December 31, 2017? Explain.
c. What is the impact of each method of accounting on the balance sheet on December 31, 2017?
d. Which method of accounting provides a more relevant/useful measure of revenue?

E3-19. **(Recording adjusting entries, LO 2, 4, 5)** Record the journal entries needed for the following adjustments:

a. Depreciation expense of $25,000.
b. Accrual of $5,000 of interest revenue.
c. Accrual of $10,000 consulting expense.
d. Recognition of $6,000 of revenue initially recorded as unearned.

E3-20. **(Recording adjusting entries, LO 2, 4, 5)** You are the accountant for Nedelec Ltd. (Nedelec). For each of the following situations, prepare the required adjusting entries. Also show the related transactional entries and the date the entries would be made. Assume a December 31 year-end. This question can be done using an accounting equation spreadsheet or journal entries.

a. On September 12, Nedelec loaned $25,000 to a senior executive. The loan, plus interest of $750, must be paid on March 1 of the next year.
b. Nedlec pays its salaried employees monthly, on the 15th of the month. On December 31 it owed its employees $4,500.
c. On July 10, Nedlec received a $10,000 deposit for services that were to be provided over the next 10 months, beginning on August 1. The services provided are worth the same amount each month.
d. On November 2, Nedlec purchased $32,000 of merchandise it required for a customer order to be completed in the next year. On December 31, Nedlec discovered that $5,000 of this merchandise had been stolen.
e. On June 30, Nedlec purchased a building for $10,000,000. The estimated life of the building is 25 years.

E3-21. **(Recording adjusting entries, LO 2, 4, 5)** You are the accountant for Rolla Inc. (Rolla). For each of the following situations, prepare the necessary adjusting entries. Also show the related transactional entries and the date the entries would be made. Assume a July 31 year-end. This question can be done using an accounting equation spreadsheet or journal entries.

a. During the year, Rolla earned $5,000 per month in royalty revenue from another company that has rights to use one of Rolla's patents. The full amount for the year must be paid on December 31.
b. On February 15, Rolla paid a supplier a $100,000 advance for materials it will receive over the next six months. As of July 31, 60 percent of the materials had been received. As of the end of July, none of the materials received had been used.
c. As of July 31, Rolla estimates that it owes $5,000 to its natural gas supplier for gas used in July. The company won't be billed until September 8.
d. During the year, Rolla sold gifts cards to customers for $50,000. At the end of the year, $20,000 of the gift cards haven't been redeemed.
e. On March 1, Rolla borrowed $100,000 from the bank. The annual interest cost of the loan is $7,000 per year. Interest must be paid on the last day of February each year the loan is outstanding.
f. On December 1, Rolla purchased a one-year insurance policy for $12,000.

E3-22. **(Recording adjusting entries, LO 4, 5)** The account balances before and after the adjusting entries have been made are presented below for a number of accounts. For each account, prepare the adjusting entry that gave rise to the change in the account balance and provide an explanation for each entry.

Account	Balance before adjusting entry	Balance after adjusting entry
a. Accumulated depreciation	$250,000	$320,000
b. Deposits from customers	20,000	15,000
c. Interest receivable	0	4,000
d. Interest payable	0	5,000
e. Prepaid insurance	16,000	10,000
f. Supplies inventory	30,000	16,000
g. Utilities payable	0	9,000

E3-23. (Understanding the relationship between closing entries and the income statement, LO 6) Below is the closing journal entry prepared by Charny Ltd. on December 31, 2016. Use the closing journal entry to prepare Charny Ltd.'s income statement for the year ended December 31, 2016.

Dr. Sales	650,000	
Dr. Interest revenue	3,000	
Cr. Retained earnings		112,000
Cr. Wage expense		125,000
Cr. Advertising expense		35,000
Cr. Depreciation expense		25,000
Cr. Cost of goods sold		225,000
Cr. Selling and administrative expense		32,000
Cr. Interest expense		12,500
Cr. Rent expense		18,000
Cr. Income tax expense		59,000
Cr. Miscellaneous expense		9,500

E3-24. (Evaluating the effect not recording adjusting entries has on net income, LO 4, 5) For each of the following situations, indicate whether not recording the necessary adjusting entry will result in (i) an overstatement of net income (net income is higher than it would otherwise be), (ii) an understatement of net income (net income is lower than it would otherwise be), or (iii) no effect on net income. Briefly explain your conclusion.

a. Depreciation expense isn't recorded.
b. Interest is earned on a bond but the cash won't be received until next year. The interest earned isn't recorded.
c. A company receives a deposit from a customer for services that will be provided in the following year. When the services are provided in the following year, the company doesn't make an adjusting entry.
d. A company purchases a two-year insurance policy on the first day of the year and records the purchase as prepaid insurance. At the end of the year, no adjustment is made to reflect the portion of the policy that was consumed.
e. An entry to record interest on a loan that isn't payable until next month isn't recorded.
f. Wages are earned by employees in the last week of the year but won't be paid until next year. The wages earned aren't recorded.

E3-25. (Evaluating the effect that not recording adjusting entries has on financial statement elements, LO 4, 5) For each of the items described in E3-24, indicate how not recording the necessary adjusting entry will affect the following financial statement elements: assets, liabilities, owners' equity, revenues, and expenses. Will the impact be (i) an overstatement of each element, (ii) an understatement of each element, or (iii) no effect on each element? Briefly explain your conclusions.

E3-26. (Using an accounting equation spreadsheet to determine the opening balance in an account, LO 2) The chief financial officer of Afton Ltd. (Afton) is trying to determine the amount of cash the company had on hand one month ago on March 1, 2017. The company's computer system has lost the information. Use an accounting equation spreadsheet and the following information to determine the information the CFO requires. Afton Ltd. had a cash balance of $125,000 on March 31, 2017.

a. On March 15, Afton purchased equipment costing $100,000 by paying $20,000 in cash and promising to pay the remainder in 90 days.
b. On March 20, Afton made payments of $10,000 on its bank loan.
c. During March, Afton had sales of $175,000. $25,000 of the sales were for cash, the rest on credit.

d. During March, Afton collected $110,000 from customers who had made credit purchases and paid suppliers $90,000.
e. During March, Afton paid employees $32,000 for work done during the month.
f. During March, Afton received $4,500 in deposits from customers for goods to be provided later in the year.
g. During March, Afton paid $8,000 for other expenses.

E3-27. **(Using an accounting equation spreadsheet to determine missing information, LO 2)** Use an accounting equation spreadsheet and the following information to determine the amount of credit sales to customers that occurred during November 2016:
a. On November 1, 2016, the balance in the accounts receivable account was $350,000.
b. During November 2016, $410,000 was collected from customers.
c. The balance in the accounts receivable account on November 30, 2016 was $380,000.

E3-28. **(Using an accounting equation spreadsheet to determine missing information, LO 2)** Use an accounting equation spreadsheet and the following information to determine the amount paid to suppliers during June 2017:
a. On June 1, 2017, the balance in the accounts payable account was $150,000.
b. During June 2017, there were credit purchases from suppliers of $760,000.
c. The balance in the accounts payable account on June 30, 2017 was $180,000.

E3-29. **(Determining missing information, LO 2, 5)** Use the following information to calculate ending balance in accounts receivable.

• Accounts receivable at the beginning of the period	$20,000
• Revenue for the period (there are no cash sales)	150,000
• Cash collected—accounts receivable	152,000

E3-30. **(Correcting errors, LO 2, 3, 5)** Hixon Ltd. (Hixon) has been having problems with its bookkeeper. Recently, errors have been observed in the bookkeeper's work. Examine each of the following items and make any journal entry necessary to correct the entries originally made. This question can also be answered using an accounting equation spreadsheet.
a. Hixon took delivery of $15,000 inventory. The bookkeeper debited the cost of sales and credited accounts payable.
b. Hixon sold shares to investors for $200,000. The bookkeeper debited cash and credited revenue for $200,000.
c. Hixon purchased four computers for $10,000. The bookkeeper debited computer expense and credited cash for $10,000.
d. Hixon received a $3,000 payment from a customer for goods previously delivered. The bookkeeper debited cash and credited revenue.

E3-31. **(Correcting errors, LO 2, 3, 5)** Examine the accounting errors described in Exercise E3-30. For each error, explain the impact the error (and failure to correct the error) would have on net income, total assets, total liabilities, and total shareholders' equity at the time the incorrect entry was made.

E3-32. **(Correcting errors, LO 2, 3, 5)** Levack Ltd. (Levack) has been having problems with its bookkeeper. Recently, errors have been found in the bookkeeper's work. Examine each of the following items and make any journal entry necessary to correct the entries originally made. This question can also be answered using an accounting equation spreadsheet.
a. Levack arranged a $175,000 bank loan. The bookkeeper debited cash and credited revenue.
b. Levack paid $15,000 rent for the next three months. The bookkeeper debited rent expense and credited cash.

c. Levack paid a dividend to shareholders of $50,000. The bookkeeper debited dividend expense and credited cash for $50,000.
d. Levack repaid $100,000 of its long-term debt. The bookkeeper debited interest expense and credited cash.

E3-33. **(Correcting errors, LO 2, 3, 5)** Examine the accounting errors described in Exercise E3-32. For each error, explain the impact the error (and failure to correct the error) would have on net income, total assets, total liabilities, and total shareholders' equity at the time the incorrect entry was made.

E3-34. **(Preparing a balance sheet and income statement using a trial balance, LO 5)** Below is Kuskonook Inc.'s (Kuskonook) December 31, 2017 trial balance, which was prepared before the closing journal entry was recorded. Use the trial balance to prepare Kuskonook's balance sheet as of December 31, 2017 and the income statement for the year ended December 31, 2017. The accounts in the trial balance are listed alphabetically.

Kuskonook Inc.
Trial Balance
December 31, 2017

Account	Debit	Credit
Accounts payable and accrued liabilities	$	$ 200,000
Accounts receivable	125,000	
Accumulated depreciation		825,000
Bank loan payable		150,000
Cash	25,000	
Common shares		1,250,000
Cost of sales	2,445,000	
Depreciation expense	250,000	
Dividends payable		18,000
Income tax expense	350,000	
Income taxes payable		15,000
Intangible assets	1,000,000	
Interest expense	180,000	
Interest payable		12,000
Inventory	224,000	
Loan receivable	48,000	
Long-term loan receivable	110,000	
Note payable		2,100,000
Note payable—current portion		300,000
Other expenses	182,000	
Prepaid assets	18,000	
Property, plant, and equipment	5,825,000	
Retained earnings		808,000
Revenue		6,650,000
Salaries and commissions expense	950,000	
Salaries and commissions payable		29,000
Selling, general, and administrative expense	725,000	
Unearned revenue		100,000
	$12,457,000	$12,457,000

E3-35. **(Prepare a closing journal entry and a post-closing trial balance, LO 6)** Use the information from the trial balance in E3-34 to prepare the closing journal entry and post-closing trial balance for Kuskonook Inc. for its December 31, 2017 year-end.

E3-36. **(Record information in a simple spreadsheet and prepare a balance sheet, LO 2, 4)** In September 2017, Denis Sonin had a great idea to make some money. He decided he would sell holiday items in the local mall in the two months before Christmas. He set up a proprietorship he called Denis's Great Gifts, opened a bank account in the proprietorship's name, and deposited $10,000 of his savings into the account. He borrowed $7,000 from his grandmother, which he also deposited into the bank account, promising her that he would repay the money by the end of January. On October 15, he came to terms with the mall manager to rent a small store in a good location for two months ending December 31. He paid the rent of $2,000 for the two months in full on October 15. Next, Denis purchased tables, shelving, and the other materials he needed to operate his store for $3,000. He spent as little money as possible on these items because he wanted to provide the merchandise to customers at low prices and that meant keeping the store simple. In the last week of October, Denis purchased merchandise to stock the store. He bought books, Christmas decorations, and other low-cost items he thought would be popular. In total, Denis purchased merchandise costing $22,000. He paid the various suppliers $10,000 in cash and agreed to pay the rest in 30 days. He also purchased an advertisement in the community newspaper for $500 that would run in the first week of November. He paid for the advertisement on October 29.

Required:

a. Use an accounting equation spreadsheet to record the economic activity of Denis's Great Gifts.
b. Use the information from your spreadsheet to prepare a balance sheet for Denis as of October 31.

E3-37. **(Record transactions and prepare income statements, LO 2, 5)** Refer to the information in E3-36. Denis operated Denis's Great Gifts until December 31. In the two months, he sold merchandise to customers for $52,000, all in cash, except for $1,200 that was owed by one customer. He sold all the inventory he originally purchased in October ($22,000) plus most of an additional $10,000 of inventory he purchased in early December. At the end of December, there was about $600 of inventory unsold. As of the end of December, he owed one of his suppliers $1,750. He paid the sales people he hired $3,000 in cash for their work and owed them $400 on December 31. He also incurred an additional $1,500 in advertising costs, all of which had been paid for as of the end of December. At the end of December, he also owed about $500 for utilities and other miscellaneous costs that were incurred during November and December.

Required:

a. Prepare income statements for Denis's Great Gifts for the period ending December 31 on the cash basis and on the accrual basis. (To do this question, you will also have to complete the spreadsheet required in E3-36.)
b. Explain why the two income statements are different.
c. Prepare a balance sheet as of December 31, 2017.
d. Assess the performance of Denis' business using the statements you prepared. Also discuss any issues surrounding Denis' inventory on December 31.

Problems

P3-1. **(Prepare adjusting entries, LO 2, 4, 5)** For each of the following situations, provide the necessary adjusting entries for Hanover Ltd. (Hanover) for the year ended June 30, 2017. (These situations are tricky. When preparing each adjusting entry, compare what is recorded in the accounting system before you make your entry with what you think should be in the accounting system. Your adjusting entry should take the accounting system from "what is" recorded to "what should be" recorded.)

a. On January 2, 2017, Hanover purchased a two-year insurance policy for $15,000 cash. The transactional journal entry debited Insurance Expense for $15,000 and credited cash for $15,000.
b. On April 1, 2017, Hanover received $25,000 for goods that it would produce and deliver to a customer. Hanover delivered $5,000 of the goods each month beginning in May 2017. Hanover recorded the transaction by debiting cash for $25,000 and crediting revenue for $25,000.
c. On March 1, 2017, Hanover invested $100,000 of surplus cash in a one-year investment certificate that paid 0.5 percent per month. The $100,000 initial investment plus the interest of $6,000 are to be paid on February 28, 2018. On March 1, 2017, Hanover recorded the investment by debiting Investments for $100,000 and crediting cash for $100,000. It also debited interest receivable for $6,000 and credited interest revenue for $6,000.

P3-2. **(Prepare adjusting entries, LO 2, 4, 5)** For each of the following situations, provide the necessary adjusting entries for Landis Inc. for the year ended December 31, 2016. (These situations are tricky. When preparing each adjusting entry, compare what is recorded in the accounting system before you make your entry with what you think should be in the accounting system. Your adjusting entry should take the accounting system from "what is" recorded to "what should be" recorded.)

a. On April 1, 2016, Landis Inc. paid $25,000 cash for the right to use a vacant lot to store some of its equipment for the next two years. The transactional journal entry debited prepaid rent for $25,000 and credited cash for $25,000.
b. On November 1, 2016, Landis Inc. received $10,000 as an advance for services to be rendered in 2017. Landis Inc. recorded the transaction by debiting cash for $10,000 and crediting revenue for $10,000.
c. On July 2, 2016, Landis Inc. purchased equipment with a five-year life for $50,000. Landis Inc. debited equipment expense and credited cash to record the transaction.

P3-3. **(The effect of different lease arrangements on the financial statements, LO 3, 4, 5)** Liscomb Consulting is a partnership of business consultants located in Halifax. The company has been successful since it began business five years ago and the partners have decided to move into new offices. On August 20, 2016, the partners came to terms with a property owner and signed a three-year lease for space at a prestigious address. Liscomb occupied its new offices on September 1, 2016. Monthly rent is $1,000. For each situation below, show what would appear on Liscomb's balance sheet and income statement if these statements were prepared on September 1, 2016 and on September 30, 2016. For each situation, show all journal entries prepared in August and September 2016. Indicate whether each journal entry is a transactional or adjusting entry. Consider each situation separately.

a. On August 20, 2016, Liscomb pays the property owner rent for September and agrees to pay each month's rent on the first day of the month (so October's rent is due on October 1).
b. The property owner agrees to allow Liscomb to pay its rent in arrears so that the rent is due on the first day of the next month (so September's rent is due October 1, and so on).
c. The property owner agrees to allow Liscomb to pay its rent on the 15th of each month. The first month's rent is paid on August 20 (so the payment on September 15 is for October).

d. The property owner agrees to allow Liscomb to pay its rent on the 15th of each month. The first month's rent is paid on September 15 (so the payment on September 15 is for September).

P3-4. **(The effect of different lease arrangements on the financial statements, LO 3, 4, 5)** Kashabowie Properties Ltd. (Kashabowie) owns and operates several commercial real estate properties in Halifax. On August 20, 2017, Kashabowie signed a three-year lease with a consulting firm for space in one of its buildings. Monthly rent is $1,000. For each situation below, show what would appear on Kashabowie's balance sheet and income statement if these statements were prepared on September 1, 2017 and on September 30, 2017. For each situation, show all journal entries prepared in August and September 2017. Indicate whether each journal entry is a transactional or adjusting entry.

a. On August 20, 2017, Kashabowie receives the $1,000 rent payment for September. The lease agreement requires the consulting firm to pay each month's rent on the first day of the month (so October's rent is due on October 1).
b. Kashabowie agrees to allow the consulting firm to pay its rent in arrears so that its rent is due on the first day of the next month (so September's rent is due October 1 and so on).
c. Kashabowie agrees to allow the consulting firm to pay its rent on the 15th of each month. The first month's rent is paid on August 20 (so the payment on September 15 is for October).
d. Kashabowie agrees to allow the consulting firm to pay its rent on the 15th of each month. The first month's rent is paid on September 15 (so the payment on September 15 is for September).

P3-5. **(Accounting for gift cards, LO 2, 4, 5)** Cayley Gifts Limited is a chain of gift stores. Cayley sells gift cards that can be redeemed at any of its stores. You are provided with the following information about Cayley's gift cards for the year ended January 31, 2017:

Unredeemed amount on February 1, 2016	$110,000
Gift card purchases during fiscal 2017	370,000
Gift card redemptions during fiscal 2017	325,000

Required

a. What amount should Cayley report for unredeemed gift cards on January 31, 2017?
b. How should this amount be reported in the financial statements (which statement)? Explain why it should be reported this way.
c. Suppose that in the past, 5 percent of Cayley's gift cards were never redeemed. How would that affect the amount you report for unredeemed gift cards? What happens to the money customers pay for unredeemed gift cards? Are unredeemed gift cards good or bad for Cayley?

P3-6. **(Determining missing information, LO 2, 4, 5)** Use the following information to calculate ending balance in accounts receivable. (This is a tricky question. All the information is relevant. Set up T-accounts or a spreadsheet to help.)

• Accounts receivable at the beginning of the period	$75,000
• Revenue for the period (there are no cash sales)	400,000
• Unearned revenue at the beginning of the period	10,000
• Unearned revenue at the end of the period	15,000
• Cash collected—accounts receivable	355,000
• Cash collected—unearned revenue	12,000

P3-7. **(Understanding the effect of errors on the elements of the accounting equation, LO 4, 5)** For each of the following situations, indicate whether assets, liabilities, equity, revenues, and expenses are overstated (too high), understated (too low), or unaffected by the error in the June 30, 2016 financial statements. Briefly explain why the effects occur and state any assumptions you make.

a. On January 3, 2016, a company purchased a new delivery truck for $35,000. The company estimates that the truck will be used for five years. No adjusting entry was made at year-end.
b. On June 15, 2016, a sports fan purchased season tickets for her city's hockey team's games for $6,000 cash. The hockey season begins in October and the team recognizes its revenue when the hockey games are played. The bookkeeper credited revenue for $6,000 when the cash was received.
c. On June 30, 2016, no entry was made to reflect water use during June. The water bill won't be received until late August. In June 2015, the company used $5,000 worth of water and the manager estimates that about the same amount of water was used this year.
d. On September 1, 2015, a company borrowed $1,000,000 from a private lender. The interest rate on the loan is six percent per year. Interest must be paid on August 31 and February 28 of each year. The loan principal must be paid in full on August 31, 2020. No adjusting entry was made by the borrower for the loan and interest on June 30, 2016.
e. On April 17, 2016, a $7,970 cash expenditure for land was recorded as $9,770.

P3-8. **(Understanding the effect of errors on the elements of the accounting equation, LO 4, 5)** For each of the following situations, indicate whether assets, liabilities, equity, revenues, and expenses are overstated (too high), understated (too low), or unaffected by the error in the December 31, 2017 financial statements. Briefly explain why the effects occur and state any assumptions that you make.
a. On January 3, 2017, a three-year insurance policy was purchased for $9,000 cash. The bookkeeper debited prepaid insurance for $9,000 when the policy was purchased. No adjusting entry was made at year-end.
b. On December 15, 2017, $400 was received from a customer paying in advance for lawn care services that were going to be provided in 2018. The bookkeeper credited revenue for $400 when the cash was received.
c. On December 31, 2017, no entry was made to reflect the use of electricity during the month of December. The bill for electricity won't be received until late February. In December 2016, the company used $2,000 of electricity and management estimates that about the same amount was used this year.
d. On September 1, 2017, the company invested $1,000,000 in government bonds that pay interest on September 1 and March 1 of each year. The interest rate is 5 percent per year. No adjusting entry was made.
e. On July 17, 2017, a $5,750 cash expense for casual labour was recorded as $7,570.

P3-9. **(Effect of transactions on financial ratios, LO 2, 5)** For each of the following transactions, indicate whether it increases, decreases, or has no effect on the following financial ratios: current ratio, debt-to-equity ratio, profit margin ratio, and return on equity. Assume the current ratio and debt-to-equity ratio are greater than one and the profit margin ratio and return on equity are less than one before each of the entries is considered. Consider each transaction independently.
a. Purchase land for $25,000 cash.
b. Borrow $10,000 from the bank for five years.
c. Sale of services for cash.
d. An expense incurred; payment to be made in a month
e. Sale of common shares for cash.

P3-10. **(Effect of transactions on financial ratios, LO 2, 5)** For each of the following transactions, indicate whether it increases, decreases, or has no effect on the following financial ratios: current ratio, debt-to-equity ratio, profit margin ratio, and return on equity. Assume the current ratio and debt-to-equity ratio are greater than one and the profit margin ratio and return on equity are less than one before each of the entries is considered. Consider each transaction independently.
a. Collection of an amount owed by a customer.
b. An expense paid in cash.

c. Payment of an amount owed to a supplier
d. Declaration and payment of a dividend.

P3-11. **(Effect of adjustments on financial ratios, LO 4, 5)** For each of the following adjusting entries, state whether the entry increases, decreases, or has no effect on the following financial ratios: current ratio, debt-to-equity ratio, profit margin ratio, and return on equity. Assume the current ratio and debt-to-equity ratio are greater than one and the profit margin ratio and return on equity are less than one before each of the adjusting entries is considered. Consider each entry independently.

a. Dr. Depreciation expense	10,000	
Cr. Accumulated depreciation		10,000
b. Dr. Unearned revenue	5,000	
Cr. Revenue		5,000
c. Dr. Interest receivable	2,000	
Cr. Interest revenue		2,000
d. Dr. Utilities expense	500	
Cr. Accrued utility expense payable		500
e. Dr. Rent expense	1,000	
Cr. Prepaid rent		1,000

P3-12. **(Effect of adjustments on financial ratios, LO 2, 4, 5)** Examine the adjusting entries provided in Exercise P3-11. Indicate the impact (overstated, understated, no effect) that *not* making each of the entries would have on the following financial ratios: current ratio, debt-to-equity ratio, profit margin ratio, and return on equity. Assume that the current ratio and debt-to-equity ratio are greater than one and the profit margin ratio and return on equity are less than one before each of the adjusting entries is considered.

P3-13. **(Impact of economic events on net income, LO 4, 5)** Woking Ltd. is a landscaping company operating in Quebec. For each of the following, explain how much revenue or expense should be reported on the income statement for the month of July. Also explain the impact on the balance sheet at the end of July:

a. At the beginning of July, Woking had $2,000 of supplies on hand and at the end there was $900. During the month, Woking purchased an additional $3,900 of supplies.
b. On July 15, a customer paid a $2,000 deposit for landscaping in his backyard. The total cost of the work will be $15,000. Woking will begin work on the project in August. The next payment on the project will be made when work begins.
c. On April 1, Woking paid $14,000 to rent specialized equipment for seven months, through October.
d. During the month, Woking paid $2,500 in cash to cover various expenses. $500 of the amount was for services used in June.
e. In June, a customer paid $5,000 for some design work. Woking began work on the project in early July and by the end of the month the job was 60 percent completed.
f. During July, Woking's employees earned $3,000. At the end of July, Woking owed the employees $600. During July, the employees received $3,500 in payments for wages.

P3-14. **(Using the accounting equation spreadsheet to record transactions and prepare financial statements, LO 1, 2, 4, 6)** Paul Byrne is a first-year student in a business program in Toronto. Toward the end of the academic year, he was approached by a friend who offered to sell him his hot dog vending cart. The friend was finishing his university studies and was going to be starting a permanent job in the summer, so he no longer needed the cart. Paul thought about the offer for a few days and decided to buy the cart. He thought that it would be a way to make money to finance his education and learn how to manage a business at the same time.

Paul operated his business from late April, when the weather started to warm up, to early September, when it was time to get back to school. Paul was so busy running the business, he had no time to keep any accounting records. So on September 10, after he had put away the cart until the next year, he sat down with all the data he had carefully collected throughout the summer about his business and placed in a shoebox. From the information in the shoebox, he obtained the following:

a. On April 1, Paul opened a bank account in the name of his company Paul's Dogs. He deposited $2,000 from his bank account into the account. Paul decided he would operate the business as a proprietorship. (Remember, in a proprietorship the owners' equity section of the balance sheet includes only a single account called owner's equity or owner's capital. This is different from a corporation, where there will be a common shares account and a retained earnings account.)
b. Paul purchased the cart from his friend on April 8 for $1,500. He gave his friend $1,000 in cash and promised to pay him the rest at the end of the summer. The cart was already four years old and Paul's friend said it should be good for another three or four years, after which time it would probably be junk.
c. Paul took the cart to a repair shop. He had the cart painted, serviced, and repaired. Paul paid the shop $300 in cash.
d. Paul went to city hall and obtained a licence to operate his cart in the city. The license cost $250 and Paul paid with his debit card. The licence is valid for two years and expires at the end of the next calendar year.
e. During the summer, Paul sold hot dogs and drinks for $15,750 cash.
f. In late August, Paul was asked to bring his cart to a softball tournament where he would be the official supplier of hot dogs to participants. The agreement was that Paul would keep track of the hot dogs and drinks he handed out to the players and send a bill to the tournament organizers. At the end of the tournament, Paul sent a bill to the organizers for $1,115. The organizers said they would pay on September 20.
g. During the summer, Paul bought hot dogs, buns, drinks, condiments, napkins, plastic cutlery, paper plates, and other supplies for $8,525. All of these items were paid for in cash.
h. At the end of the summer, Paul had about $750 in non-perishable items stored in his basement at home (he had used $7,775 of the supplies he had bought).
i. On several days during the summer, Paul was unable to operate the cart himself. On those days, he hired his brother to do it. During the entire summer, Paul paid his brother $375 cash. As of today, Paul still owes him $75.
j. During the summer, Paul incurred $1,000 in other expenses. All of these were paid in cash.
k. On August 15, Paul withdrew $1,500 from the business to pay for tuition and other school-related items.
l. On September 5, Paul paid his friend the $500 he owed him.

Required:

a. Enter each of the transactions into an accounting equation spreadsheet. You can use a computer spreadsheet program or create a spreadsheet manually, although the computer spreadsheet will probably be easier because you will be able to correct mistakes more easily. Create a separate column on the spreadsheet for each account. Be sure to include adjusting entries for depreciation of the cart and expensing of the licence.
b. Provide explanations for each of your entries. You should explain why you have treated the economic events as you have (that is, why you have recorded an asset, liability, etc.).
c. Prepare a balance sheet as of September 10 and an income statement for the period ended September 10 from your spreadsheet. Make sure to make a closing entry.
d. Explain why the financial statements you have prepared would be useful to Paul.
e. If Paul asked you for some feedback on his business from examining the financial statements, what would you be able to tell him?

P3-15. **(Following the steps of the accounting cycle, LO 1, 4, 5, 6)** Use the information provided in Problem P3-14 about Paul's Dogs to do the following:

a. Prepare all necessary journal entries until September 10. Provide an explanation for each journal entry.
b. Prepare T-accounts and post each journal entry to the appropriate T-account.
c. Prepare and post adjusting journal entries to their appropriate T-accounts. Adjusting entries are needed for the cart and the license.
d. Prepare a trial balance as of September 10.
e. Prepare a balance sheet for Paul's Dogs as of September 10 and an income statement covering the period until September 10.
f. Prepare the closing journal entry and post the closing entry to the appropriate T-accounts.
g. Prepare a trial balance as of September 10 after the closing entry has been prepared.
h. Explain why the financial statements you have prepared would be useful to Paul.
i. If Paul asked you for some feedback on his business from examining the financial statements, what would you be able to tell him?

P3-16. **(Using the accounting equation spreadsheet to record transactions and prepare financial statements, LO 1, 2, 4, 6)** Ernest Fung is a recent business school graduate and budding entrepreneur. Ernest thinks that hot, fresh, and delicious cookies available all day long on university campuses is a surefire way to make money. Ernest had been toying with this idea for a couple of years and recently he finalized what he thinks is the perfect chocolate chip cookie recipe. His friends think the cookies are the best they ever tasted. Ernest has also developed a couple of other equally delicious varieties of cookies. Ernest wants to test his business idea so he decides to incorporate a company called Cookie Dough, Inc. (Cookie) and arranges to set up a shop in the food court on the university campus.

It's now December 27, 2017 and Cookie has closed for the winter break. Ernest has been working almost continuously since Cookie opened its doors. He's had no time to keep any accounting records and he's asked you to "pull things together" for him. After summarizing the data Ernest provided, you have the following information for 2017:

i. July 4: Ernest incorporates Cookie and contributes $20,000 in cash in exchange for Cookie shares.
ii. August 1: Signs a two-year lease with the university for a small space in the food court. Monthly rent is $1,000. In addition, Cookie must pay 2 percent of sales in additional rent at the end of the year. No rent is required for August. Cookie writes a cheque for $3,000 for rent for September through November.
iii. August 4: Purchases a cookie oven, refrigerator, display cases, cash register, and other required items from a distributor for $22,000. Pays $12,000 in cash and agrees to pay the remainder on February 15, 2018. Ernest estimates that all the equipment will have a useful life of five years. Cookie begins using the equipment on September 1.
iv. August 10: Cookie arranged a $20,000 loan from David Dragon, a rich investor who likes to invest in new small businesses. The interest rate on the loan is 9 percent, payable on December 31 of each year. $10,000 of the loan must be repaid on August 1, 2018 and the remainder on August 1, 2019.
v. During August: Renovates and repairs the shop. A contractor is paid $7,000 in cash.
vi. October 1: Cookie purchases a one-year insurance policy for $1,600.
vii. December 1: Cookie writes a $3,000 cheque to the university for rent for December through February.
viii. December 18: Caters a holiday party for one of the faculties. Bills the faculty $300 and expects to be paid in early January.
ix. During 2017: Purchases ingredients for cookies, drinks, etc. for $18,000. On December 27, there is inventory on hand that cost $800.

x. During 2017: Sells cookies and drinks to customers for $42,000. All sales were for cash.
xi. During 2017: Pays employees $11,200. As of the end of December, employees are owed $500.
xii. During 2017: Pays utilities of $1,200. Utilities are paid in full to the end of December.
xiii. During 2017: Cookie incurred other expenses amounting to $9,500. All were paid in cash.
xiv. During 2017: Ernest took $5,000 to meet his personal needs.

Required:

a. Record Cookie's economic activity for the period in an accounting equation spreadsheet. Don't forget the adjusting entries. You can use a computer spreadsheet program or create a spreadsheet manually. Create a separate column on the spreadsheet for each account. State and explain any assumptions you make.
b. Provide explanations for each of your entries. You should explain why you have treated the economic events as you have (that is, why you have recorded an asset, liability, etc.).
c. Prepare a balance sheet as of December 31, 2017 and an income statement for the period ended December 31, 2017 from your spreadsheet. Make sure to make the closing entry.
d. Compare Cookie's net income with the amount of cash that was generated by the business. Which is a better indicator of how Cookie did? Why are they different? (When looking at the cash flow, consider the cash flows after Ernest made his initial $20,000 investment.)
e. If Ernest asked you to evaluate Cookie's financial situation using the financial statements, what would you be able to tell him?

P3-17. **(Following the steps of the accounting cycle, LO 1, 4, 5, 6)** Use the information provided in Problem P3-16 about Cookie Dough, Inc. (Cookie) to do the following:

a. Prepare all necessary journal entries until December 31, 2017. Provide an explanation for each journal entry.
b. Prepare T-accounts and post each journal entry to the appropriate T-accounts.
c. Prepare and post adjusting journal entries to their appropriate T-accounts. Adjusting entries are needed for the equipment, insurance, rent, and interest.
d. Prepare a trial balance as of December 31, 2017.
e. Prepare a balance sheet as of December 31, 2017 and an income statement for the period ended December 31, 2017. Prepare the closing journal entry and post the closing entry to the appropriate T-accounts.
f. Prepare a trial balance as of December 31, 2017, after the closing entry has been prepared.
g. Compare Cookie's net income with the amount of cash that was generated by the business. Which is a better indicator of how Cookie did? Why are they different? (When looking at the cash flow, consider the cash flows after the owners made their initial $20,000 investment.)
h. If Ernest asked you to evaluate Cookie's financial situation using the financial statements, what would you be able to tell him?

P3-18. **(Using the accounting equation spreadsheet to record transactions and prepare financial statements, LO 1, 2, 4, 6)** Superstar Ice Rinks Inc. (SIR) is a privately owned company owned by a group of investors headed by James T. Kirk, a retired professional hockey player. SIR owns three arenas in suburban areas near a large Canadian city, which it rents out to hockey leagues and individuals for recreational use. SIR's arenas also have a pro shop and food and beverage service.

SIR's balance sheet for June 30, 2016, the company's year-end, follows. SIR uses its financial statements for tax purposes, to show to the holders of the long-term debt that was used to finance the purchase of the arenas, and for the shareholders, particularly those who aren't involved in management.

Superstar Ice Rinks Inc.
Balance Sheet
As of June 30, 2016

Assets		**Liabilities and Shareholders' Equity**	
Cash	$ 1,987,500	Bank loan	$ 225,000
Accounts receivable	62,500	Accounts payable	181,250
Inventory	210,000	Wages payable	21,250
		Taxes payable	115,000
Property, plant, and equipment	18,750,000	Interest payable	31,250
Accumulated depreciation	(4,875,000)	Unearned revenue	1,218,750
		Current portion of long-term debt	937,500
		Long-term debt	7,326,250
		Common shares	4,706,250
		Retained earnings	1,372,500
	$16,135,000		$16,135,000

It's now July 2017. SIR needs to prepare its financial statements for the year ended June 30, 2017. You have obtained the following information about the fiscal year just ended:

i. During fiscal 2017, SIR purchased an existing arena for $4,750,000. The purchase was financed by $1,875,000 of new long-term debt, SIR shares worth $1,253,000 given to the previous owners of the arena, and the remainder in cash.
ii. During fiscal 2017, SIR earned $5,820,000 in revenue from renting ice. In addition, the pro shop and restaurant earned $1,725,000 in revenue. Of these amounts, $625,000 was on credit provided by SIR. During the year, $614,000 was collected from customers who purchased on credit.
iii. Leagues renting ice time for the entire season are required to pay a deposit in May. The deposit is then recognized as revenue over the year as the ice is used by the league. In May 2017, SIR collected $1,310,000 in deposits from leagues. Deposits are for leagues that play from September through April.
iv. SIR has a $250,000 line of credit from a local bank. A line of credit means SIR can borrow up to $250,000 without additional approval from the bank.
v. During the year, SIR paid employees $1,062,000 in cash, including the amount owing at the end of fiscal 2016. During the year employees earned $1,076,000.
vi. During fiscal 2017, SIR repaid $937,500 of its long-term debt. Next year, SIR must repay $1,125,000 of the debt.
vii. During fiscal 2017, SIR paid lenders $563,000 in interest, including interest owed at the end of the previous year. No interest is owing at the end of fiscal 2017.
viii. During the year, SIR purchased goods for sale in the pro shops and restaurants for $756,000, all purchased on credit. Suppliers were paid $750,000 during the year.
ix. SIR purchased other goods and services (fuel for the Zamboni, utilities, maintenance, etc.) during the year, costing $1,969,000, also on credit. These creditors received payments of $1,938,000 during the year.
x. The products sold in the pro shops and food and drink sold in the restaurants during the year cost $765,000.
xi. SIR incurred additional expenses during the year that cost $375,000 and were paid for in cash.
xii. During the year, SIR paid the taxes it owed at the end of fiscal 2016. It also paid $64,000 in instalments on its 2017 income taxes. SIR estimates that it owes an additional $42,000 in income taxes for 2017.
xiii. Depreciation for the year was $1,563,000.
xiv. During the year, SIR traded ice time with a market value of $26,000 for services worth the same amount.

Required:

a. Enter each of the transactions onto an accounting equation spreadsheet. You can use a computer spreadsheet program or create a spreadsheet manually. Create a separate column on the spreadsheet for each account. Make sure you prepare all adjusting entries and the closing entry. Indicate whether each entry is a transactional entry, an adjusting entry, or a closing entry.
b. Provide explanations for each of your entries. You should explain why you have treated the economic events as you have (that is, why you have recorded an asset, liability, etc.).
c. Prepare a balance sheet as of June 30, 2017 and an income statement for the year ended June 30, 2017 from your spreadsheet.
d. SIR's non-management shareholders have asked you to analyze the company's financial position and performance. Write a report analyzing the information you prepared.

P3-19. **(Following the steps of the accounting cycle, LO 1, 4, 5, 6)** Use the information provided in Problem P3-18 about Superstar Ice Rinks Inc. (SIR) to do the following:

a. Prepare all necessary journal entries for fiscal 2017. Provide an explanation for each journal entry.
b. Prepare T-accounts and post each journal entry to the appropriate T-accounts.
c. Prepare and post adjusting journal entries to their appropriate T-accounts.
d. Prepare a trial balance as of June 30, 2017.
e. Prepare a balance sheet for SIR as of June 30, 2017 and an income statement covering the period until June 30, 2017.
f. Prepare the closing journal entry and post the closing entry to the appropriate T-accounts.
g. Prepare an after-closing trial balance as of June 30, 2017.
h. SIR's non-management shareholders have asked you to analyze the company's financial position and performance. Write a report analyzing the information you prepared.

P3-20. **(Using the accounting equation spreadsheet to record transactions and prepare financial statements, LO 1, 2, 5, 6)** Majestic Trucking Inc. (Majestic) is a small trucking company that carries freight between centres in central Canada and the northeastern United States. The Mozart family of Cobourg owns Majestic, but professional managers manage it. One member of the Mozart family serves as the chair of the board of directors. No other family members are actively involved with Majestic.

Majestic's balance sheet for December 31, 2016, the company's year-end, is shown below. Majestic uses its financial statements for tax purposes, to show to the holders of the long-term notes that the company issued to finance the purchase of some of its trucks, and to provide information to the shareholders.

Majestic Trucking Inc.
Balance Sheet
As of December 31, 2016

Assets		**Liabilities and Shareholders' Equity**	
Cash	$ 77,340	Accounts payable	$ 42,220
Accounts receivable	81,500	Taxes payable	15,000
Prepaid insurance	18,000	Wages payable	10,000
Current assets	176,840	Customer deposits	27,000
Capital assets	465,000	Interest payable	11,900
Accumulated depreciation	(201,700)	Current liabilities	106,120
		Long-term notes payable	140,000
		Common shares	80,000
		Retained earnings	114,020
	$440,140		$440,140

It is now January 2018. Majestic needs to prepare its financial statements for the year ended December 31, 2017. You have obtained the following information about the fiscal year just ended:

i. Shipping revenue for the year was $1,065,225. Majestic gives credit to all its customers and there were no cash sales during the year.
ii. Majestic purchased $275,000 worth of fuel during the year. All purchases were on credit. At the end of 2017, Majestic hadn't been billed for an additional $10,000 of fuel that it purchased.
iii. Majestic incurred maintenance costs of $125,000 during 2017. At the end of 2017, Majestic owed mechanics $8,000. (The $8,000 owed is included in the $125,000.)
iv. Majestic paid wages and bonuses of $475,000 to employees. At December 31, 2017, Majestic owed employees $27,500.
v. During the year, Majestic collected $1,075,000 from customers.
vi. Majestic paid its fuel suppliers $250,000 during 2017.
vii. During the year, Majestic paid the taxes it owed at the end of 2016. It also paid $11,000 in instalments on its 2017 income taxes. It's estimated that Majestic owes an additional $12,000 in income taxes for 2017.
viii. The deposits reported on the 2016 balance sheet pertained to customers who were perceived to be high risk to whom Majestic wasn't prepared to offer credit. These customers were required to give deposits against shipping to be done during 2017. These customers used shipping services during 2017 in excess of the amount of the deposits. Majestic decided in 2017 to offer credit to these customers. The deposits are not included in the other revenue recognized in the year.
ix. Members of the Mozart family sometimes used Majestic employees for personal work at their homes and cottages. Usually, the work was done on weekends and the employees were paid at overtime rates. Majestic pays the employees' wages for the work done for the family members and accounts for the cost as a wage expense. The wages paid for work done on behalf of Mozart family members was $11,000.
x. During 2017, Majestic purchased a new truck for $98,000 in cash.
xi. Depreciation expense for 2017 was $48,000.
xii. Prepaid insurance pertains to insurance on its truck fleet and premises. During 2017, Majestic used $15,000 of insurance that was recorded as prepaid on December 31, 2016. In late 2017, it purchased and paid for insurance for 2018. The insurance cost $21,000.
xiii. During the year, Majestic paid $11,900 in interest to the holders of the long-term notes. Interest is paid annually on January 2. In addition to the interest payment, Majestic paid $20,000 on January 2, 2017 to reduce the balance owed on the long-term notes. The interest rate on the notes is 8.5 percent.
xiv. Majestic paid $75,000 in cash for other expenses related to operating the business in fiscal 2017.
xv. Majestic paid dividends of $55,000 to shareholders.

Required:

a. Enter each of the transactions onto an accounting equation spreadsheet. You can use a computer spreadsheet program or create a spreadsheet manually, although the computer spreadsheet will probably be easier because you will be able to correct mistakes more easily. Create a separate column on the spreadsheet for each account. Make sure you prepare all adjusting entries and the closing entry to the spreadsheet. Indicate whether each entry to the spreadsheet is a transactional entry, an adjusting entry or a closing entry.
b. Provide explanations for each of your entries. You should explain why you have treated the economic events as you have (that is, why you have recorded an asset, liability, etc.).
c. Prepare a balance sheet as of December 31, 2017 and an income statement for the year ended December 31, 2017 from your spreadsheet.

d. The North American economy is booming and there is a lot of work for shipping companies like Majestic. However, the competition is fierce and success and failure are defined by how efficient a company is and how well it services its customers. Majestic's managers would like to upgrade its fleet by adding two new trucks and making significant improvements to its existing vehicles. Based on your examination of the statements, what can you tell about Majestic that would be useful to your decision to lend it $125,000? Also, list five questions you might ask Majestic's management that would help you use the financial statements more effectively.

P3-21. **(Following the steps of the accounting cycle, LO 1, 4, 5, 6)** Use the information about Majestic Trucking Inc. (Majestic) provided in Problem P3-20 to do the following:

a. Prepare all necessary transactional journal entries for the year ended December 31, 2017. Provide an explanation for each journal entry.
b. Prepare T-accounts and post each journal entry to the appropriate T-accounts.
c. Prepare and post adjusting journal entries to the appropriate T-accounts.
d. Prepare a trial balance as of December 31, 2017.
e. Prepare a balance sheet for Majestic as of December 31, 2017 and an income statement and statement of retained earnings for the year ended December 31, 2017.
f. Prepare the closing journal entry and post the closing entry to the appropriate T-accounts.
g. Prepare a trial balance as of December 31, 2017, after the closing entry has been prepared.
h. The North American economy is booming and there is a lot of work for shipping companies like Majestic. However, the competition is fierce and success and failure are defined by how efficient a company is and how well it services its customers. Majestic's managers would like to upgrade its fleet by adding two new trucks and making significant improvements to its existing vehicles. Based on your examination of the statements, what can you tell about Majestic that would be useful to your decision to lend it $125,000? Also, list five questions you might ask Majestic's management that would help you use the financial statements more effectively.

P3-22. **(Using the accounting equation spreadsheet to record transactions and prepare financial statements, LO 1, 2, 5, 6)** Wilfred Fong is the owner and operator of Appliance Town Ltd. (ATL), Denzil's largest independent household appliance store. ATL supplies appliances to retail customers as well as to builders of the many new homes and apartments that are going up in the community. Sales to builders have grown substantially in the last year. ATL has been in business for five years and Wilfred has been happy with its performance.

ATL's balance sheet for August 31, 2016, the company's year-end, is shown below. Wilfred uses the financial statements mainly for tax purposes and to show the holders of the long-term notes.

Appliance Town Ltd.
Balance Sheet
As of August 31, 2016

Assets		**Liabilities and Shareholder's Equity**	
Cash	$ 60,000	Accounts payable	$ 530,000
Accounts receivable	246,000	Taxes payable	40,000
Inventory	893,000	Interest payable	17,000
Prepaids	28,000	Long-term notes payable	200,000
Furniture and fixtures	380,000	Common shares	220,000
Accumulated depreciation	(80,000)	Retained earnings	520,000
	$1,527,000		$1,527,000

It is now mid-September 2017. ATL needs to prepare its financial statements for the year ended August 31, 2017. The following information has been obtained about the fiscal year just ended:

i. ATL purchased appliances from suppliers for $1,700,000. All purchases were made on credit.
ii. Sales during the year were $2,700,000. Cash sales were $1,550,000. The remainder was on credit, mainly to builders.
iii. The cost of the appliances sold during fiscal 2017 was $1,490,000.
iv. ATL paid salaries and commissions to employees of $400,000. On August 31, 2017, employees were owed $15,000 by ATL.
v. ATL collected $750,000 during the year from customers who purchased on credit.
vi. ATL paid suppliers $1,200,000 for appliances it purchased on credit.
vii. During the year, ATL paid the taxes it owed at the end of fiscal 2016. During fiscal 2017, ATL paid $30,000 in instalments on its 2017 taxes. At year-end, it's estimated that ATL owes an additional $24,000 in taxes.
viii. ATL accepted $20,000 in deposits from customers who wanted a guarantee that their appliances would be delivered when they needed them. The deposits pertained to a particularly hard-to-get appliance. ATL expects the appliances will be delivered in early November 2017.
ix. Beginning July 1, 2017, ATL pays $8,000 a month for the rent of its store. The terms of the lease require that rent be paid six months in advance on January 1 and July 1 of each year. Before July 1, 2017, ATL paid $7,000 a month in rent. In addition, the new lease requires that ATL must pay 2 percent of annual sales to the property owner 60 days after the year-end (this wasn't required under the old lease).
x. Wilfred recently redecorated his kitchen at home. He took a refrigerator, stove, and microwave that cost $9,000 from the store and installed them in his new kitchen.
xi. During 2017, ATL purchased new capital assets (furniture and fixtures) for $50,000 cash.
xii. Depreciation expense for 2017 is $44,000.
xiii. During the year, ATL paid $17,000 in interest to the holders of the long-term notes. Interest is paid annually on September 1. In addition to the interest payment, ATL paid $40,000 on September 1, 2016 to reduce the balance owed on the long-term notes. The interest rate on the notes is 8.5 percent.
xiv. ATL paid $450,000 in cash for other expenses related to operating the business in fiscal 2017.

Required:

a. Enter each transaction onto an accounting equation spreadsheet. Create a separate column on the spreadsheet for each account. Make sure you prepare all adjusting entries and the closing entry to the spreadsheet. Indicate whether each entry to the spreadsheet is a transactional entry, an adjusting entry or a closing entry.
b. Provide explanations for each of your entries. You should explain why you have treated the economic events as you have (that is, why you have recorded an asset, liability, etc.).
c. Prepare a balance sheet, an income statement, and a statement of retained earnings from your spreadsheet.

For P3-24.

	Assets					=	**Liabilities**		
Transaction	Cash	Royalty revenue receivable	Prepaid rent	Property, plant, and equipment	Accumulated depreciation		Accounts payable	Unearned revenue	Wages payable
Balance before adjusting entries	$52,000	$0	$3,000	$40,000	($14,000)		$8,000	$14,000	$ 0
Balance after adjusting entries	$52,000	$10,000	$1,000	$40,000	($22,000)		$8,000	$6,000	$4,000

d. Wilfred is considering expanding ATL to include a wider range of products. Wilfred has approached you about purchasing common shares of ATL to help finance the expansion. Based on your examination of the financial statements, what can you tell about ATL that would be useful to your decision to invest? Also, list five questions you might ask Wilfred that would help you use the financial statements more effectively.

P3-23. **(Following the steps of the accounting cycle, LO 1, 4, 5, 6)** Use the information about Wilfred's Appliance Town Ltd. (ATL) provided in Problem P3-22 to do the following:

a. Prepare all necessary transactional journal entries for the year ended August 31, 2017. Provide an explanation for each journal entry.
b. Prepare T-accounts and post each journal entry to the appropriate T-accounts.
c. Prepare and post adjusting journal entries to their appropriate T-accounts.
d. Prepare a trial balance as of August 31, 2017.
e. Prepare a balance sheet for ATL as of August 31, 2017 and an income statement and statement of retained earnings for the year ended August 31, 2017.
f. Prepare the closing journal entry and post the closing entry to the appropriate T-accounts.
g. Prepare a trial balance as of August 31, 2017, after the closing entry has been prepared.
h. Wilfred is considering expanding ATL to include a wider range of products. Wilfred has approached you about purchasing common shares of ATL to help finance the expansion. Based on your examination of the statements, what can you tell about ATL that would be useful to your decision to invest? Also, list five questions you might ask Wilfred that would help you use the financial statements more effectively.

P3-24. **(Reconstructing adjusting entries, LO 2, 4, 5)** See the spreadsheet for P3-24 and below. The spreadsheet provides the balances in Takhini Inc.'s accounts on December 31, 2017, before and after the adjusting entries have been made.

Required:

Reconstruct the adjusting entries that were made to Takhini Inc.'s spreadsheet on December 31, 2017.

P3-25. **(Reconstructing adjusting entries, LO 2, 4, 5)** See the spreadsheet for P3-25. The spreadsheet provides the balances in Smithers Inc.'s accounts on May 31, 2017, before and after the adjusting entries have been made.

Required:

Reconstruct the adjusting entries that were made to Smithers Inc.'s spreadsheet on May 31, 2017.

P3-26. **(Evaluating the effect that not recording adjusting entries has on financial statements, LO 3, 4, 5)** For each of the following economic events, indicate the effect that *not* recording the necessary adjusting entry associated with the transaction described at year-end would have on the financial statements. Indicate whether not recording the required adjusting entry would result in:

i. an overstatement of assets, liabilities, owners' equity, or net income,
ii. an understatement of assets, liabilities, owners' equity, or net income, or
iii. no effect on assets, liabilities, owners' equity, or net income.

+	Shareholders' equity						
	Common shares	Retained earnings	Services revenue	Royalty revenue	Rent expense	Wage expense	Depreciation expense
	$10,000	$12,000	$58,000	$ 0	$5,000	$16,000	$ 0
	$10,000	$12,000	$66,000	$10,000	$7,000	$20,000	$8,000

For P3-25.

Transaction	Assets					=	Liabilities		
	Cash	Inventory	Prepaid insurance	Property, plant, and equipment	Accumulated depreciation		Accounts payable	Salaries payable	Unearned revenue
Balance before adjusting entries	$50,000	$325,000	$25,000	$120,000	($44,000)		$78,000	$ 0	$55,000
Balance after adjusting entries	$50,000	$145,000	$15,000	$120,000	($69,000)		$78,000	$12,000	$20,000

Provide explanations for your conclusions and state any assumptions you make. Assume a December 31 year-end. To respond, you will need to determine the required journal entry.

a. On July 15, equipment costing $100,000 is purchased.
b. An investment in a long-term government bond pays interest on March 31 and September 30 of each year. (Respond from the perspective of the entity investing in the bond.)
c. On May 15, a company purchases a two-year insurance policy for $5,000. Coverage begins on July 1. (Respond from the perspective of the company buying the insurance policy.)
d. On May 15, a company purchases a two-year insurance policy for $5,000. Coverage begins on July 1. (Respond from the perspective of the company issuing the insurance policy.)
e. During the last week of December, employees earn $5,000 in wages. The wages won't be paid until next year. (Respond from the perspective of the company paying the wages.)

P3-27. **(Evaluating the effect that not recording adjusting entries has on financial statements, LO 3, 4, 5)** For each of the following economic events, indicate the effect that *not* recording the necessary adjusting entry associated with the transactional entry at year-end would have on the financial statements. Indicate whether not recording the required adjusting entry would result in:

i. an overstatement of assets, liabilities, owners' equity, or net income,
ii. an understatement of assets, liabilities, owners' equity, or net income, or
iii. no effect on assets, liabilities, owners' equity, or net income.

Provide explanations for your conclusions and state any assumptions you make. Assume a December 31 year-end. To respond, you will need to determine the required journal entry.

a. A travel company sells packaged vacations to customers in advance and recognizes revenue when the customer departs on the vacation. (Respond from the travel company's perspective
b. An investment in a long-term corporate bond pays interest on March 31 and September 30 of each year. (Consider this from the perspective of the entity issuing the bond.)
c. On October 1, a tenant pays $12,000 to cover six months' rent beginning October 1. The tenant records the payment as prepaid rent. (Respond from the tenant's perspective.)
d. A retail store pays a percentage of its sales as rent to the property owner. The payment is made three months after its year-end, when the financial statements are released. (Respond from the property owner's perspective.)
e. A retail store pays a percentage of its sales as rent to the property owner. The payment is made three months after its year-end, when the financial statements are released. (Respond from the retail store's perspective.)

P3-28. **(Understanding the effect of different estimates on net income, LO 4)** In 2017, Otis Knight opened a small business that he called The Corner Coffee Cart. The Corner Coffee Cart sells a variety of coffee-based beverages from a portable cart. Otis purchased the cart for $12,000 cash when he began the business. All of The Corner Coffee Cart's transactions with suppliers and customers are for cash. At the end of 2017, Otis decided he wanted to get an idea about how well The Corner Coffee Cart performed in its first year. He assembled the following information:

i. Sales to customers $22,000
ii. Cost of providing coffee to customers $13,000

Liabilities *cont.*		+	Shareholders' equity							
Interest payable	Loan payable		Capital stock	Retained earnings	Revenue	Cost of goods sold	Insurance expense	Salaries expense	Interest expense	Depreciation expense
$ 0	$58,000		$50,000	$55,000	$258,000	$ 0	$ 0	$78,000	$ 0	$ 0
$6,000	$58,000		$50,000	$55,000	$293,000	$180,000	$10,000	$90,000	$6,000	$25,000

From this information Otis concluded that he had made $9,000, which he was satisfied with. A friend who had recently taken an accounting course told Otis that his profit of $9,000 wasn't correct because he didn't depreciate the coffee cart. Otis asked his friend to help him calculate the "correct" amount of profit based on the friend's knowledge of accounting.

Required:

a. Why did Otis' friend tell Otis that his measure of profit wasn't correct without a depreciation expense for the cart? Do you agree with this?
b. If Otis assumes that the useful life of the cart is six years and he depreciates the cost of the cart using the straight-line method (an equal amount is expensed each year), what would The Corner Coffee Cart's net income for 2017 be? Assume that the cart wouldn't have any value at the end of its life.
c. Calculate The Corner Coffee Cart's net income assuming the cost of the cart is depreciated over three years. Calculate net income assuming the cost of the cart is depreciated over ten years. Assume straight-line depreciation in both cases.
d. What is the difference in The Corner Coffee Cart's net income using the three different periods for depreciating the cart in (b) and (c)?
e. How is your evaluation of how The Corner Coffee Cart performed during 2017 affected by using different periods for depreciating the cart?
f. Assume that the different periods used for depreciating the cart simply represent different reasonable estimates of the cart's useful life. Is the actual performance of The Corner Coffee Cart really different even though the net income under each estimate is different? Explain.
g. What is the "correct" number of years over which to depreciate the cart?

P3-29. **(Problems interpreting an income statement, LO 3, 4)** Mishra's Textbooks Ltd. (MTL) buys and sells used textbooks to university students. MTL is located in a strip mall just off a university campus. Arjun Mishra formed MTL in April 2016. It's now May 2017 and MTL has just completed its first year of operation. Arjun's bookkeeper has prepared an income statement for the year based on cash paid and received during the year:

Mishra's Textbooks Ltd.
Income Statement
For the Year Ended April 30, 2017

Revenue		$410,000
Expenses		
	Cost of books	199,000
	Rent	14,000
	Wages	42,000
	Utilities	5,000
	Advertising	11,000
	General and administrative	15,000
	Furniture and fixtures	25,000
Net income		$ 99,000

Arjun is pleased with MTL's performance for its first year with net income of $99,000, but he's concerned that everything hasn't been done correctly, so he'd like you to have a look at it. You talk with Arjun and his bookkeeper and obtain the following information:

- Revenue includes a $50,000 bank loan and $100,000 contributed by Arjun when the corporation was formed.
- Of the used books purchased from students, $109,000 were sold during the year. The rest are on hand and available for sale in the future.
- The furniture and fixtures were required to set up the store and include shelving, counters, computers, signs, and so on. Arjun estimates the furniture and fixtures will have useful lives of about five years.
- At the end of the year, MTL owed employees $1,100.
- When reviewing the inventory on hand at the end of the year, Arjun realized that about $5,000 of the books were obsolete and couldn't be resold.
- The rent expense includes $2,000 paid in advance for May and June 2017.
- The bank loan was arranged on May 1, 2016 and carries an interest rate of 8 percent. The annual interest payment was paid on May 1 (after the year-end).
- MTL received $10,000 from the student association of a college to provide it with certain used textbooks. MTL is to deliver the books in August 2017 and must refund the money if the order isn't fulfilled. MTL hasn't begun acquiring the books yet.

Required:

a. Use the information provided to revise the income statement so that net income is determined on an accrual basis. Also prepare a balance sheet as of April 30, 2017.
b. Explain to Arjun the difference between the two income statements and what each one tells him.
c. Evaluate MTL's performance and financial position using the information you've prepared.

Using Financial Statements

Reitmans (Canada) Limited (Reitmans) is a retailer in the women's clothing sector. It operates over 900 stores under seven different banners across Canada. The flagship Reitmans chain is the largest ladies' apparel specialty chain in Canada. Other banners are Smart Set, Penningtons, Addition Elle, RW & CO., Thyme Maternity, and Cassis. Reitmans also sells apparel online. The family-run company was founded in 1926 by Herman and Sarah Reitman in Montreal. Reitmans' stock trades on the TSX under the symbols RET and RET-A.

Reitmans' consolidated balance sheets, statements of earnings and comprehensive income, and retained earnings, along with extracts from the notes to the financial statements, are provided in Exhibit 3.1.[1] Use this information to respond to questions FS3-1 to FS3-9.

FS3-1. Examine Reitmans' balance sheets. Which accounts do you think would require adjustments at the year-end? Explain.

FS3-2. Reitmans includes among its current liabilities $22,278,000 for "Deferred revenue." Notes 3(1) and 13 provide additional information about this account.

a. When does Reitmans recognize revenue from sales in its stores?
b. Deferred revenue arises from two sources. Describe the transactions that give rise to each. How much deferred revenue is attributable to each source?
c. Why is deferred revenue reported as a liability? What obligation does Reitmans have? How is the liability satisfied? What does Reitmans sacrifice by fulfilling the liability?
d. A customer purchases a $100 gift card at a Reitmans store. What journal entry would be made to record the purchase? (Alternative approach: Use an accounting equation spreadsheet to record an increase in deferred revenue.)
e. A customer purchases $155 of goods at a Reitmans store using a $100 gift card and paying the remainder in cash. What journal entry would Reitmans make to record the sale? (Alternative approach: Use an accounting equation spreadsheet to record a decrease in deferred revenue.)

EXHIBIT 3.1 Reitmans (Canada) Limited: Extracts from the Financial Statements

REITMANS (CANADA) LIMITED
BALANCE SHEETS
(in thousands of Canadian dollars)

	January 28, 2012	January 29, 2011	January 31, 2010
ASSETS			
CURRENT ASSETS			
Cash and cash equivalents (note 5)	**$196,835**	$230,034	$228,577
Marketable securities	**71,442**	70,413	48,026
Trade and other receivables	**3,033**	2,866	2,926
Derivative financial asset (note 6)	**751**	–	–
Income taxes recoverable	**4,735**	–	–
Inventories (note 7)	**78,285**	73,201	63,127
Prepaid expenses	**11,902**	12,491	11,010
Total Current Assets	**366,983**	389,005	353,666
NON-CURRENT ASSETS			
Property and equipment (note 8)	**184,221**	193,064	208,362
Intangible assets (note 9)	**17,057**	13,841	9,964
Goodwill (note 10)	**42,426**	42,426	42,426
Deferred income taxes (note 11)	**23,174**	21,021	18,313
Total Non-Current Assets	**266,878**	270,352	279,065
TOTAL ASSETS	**$633,861**	$659,357	$632,731
LIABILITIES AND SHAREHOLDERS' EQUITY			
CURRENT LIABILITIES			
Trade and other payables (note 12)	**$ 63,875**	$ 64,093	$ 54,684
Derivative financial liability (note 6)	**1,505**	–	–
Deferred revenue (note 13)	**22,278**	19,834	18,122
Income taxes payable	**–**	5,998	4,677
Current portion of long-term debt (note 14)	**1,474**	1,384	1,300
Total Current Liabilities	**89,132**	91,309	78,783
NON-CURRENT LIABILITIES			
Other payables (note 12)	**11,110**	10,180	9,105
Deferred revenue (note 13)	**–**	2,384	2,686
Deferred lease credits	**17,317**	19,011	20,609
Long-term debt (note 14)	**8,573**	10,047	11,431
Pension liability (note 15)	**14,877**	13,626	11,865
Total Non-Current Liabilities	**51,877**	55,248	55,696
SHAREHOLDERS' EQUITY			
Share capital (note 16)	**39,890**	29,614	25,888
Contributed surplus	**5,158**	6,266	5,164
Retained earnings	**439,067**	468,777	461,845
Accumulated other comprehensive income (note 16)	**8,737**	8,143	5,355
Total Shareholders' Equity	**492,852**	512,800	498,252
TOTAL LIABILITIES AND SHAREHOLDERS' EQUITY	**$633,861**	$659,357	$632,731

EXHIBIT 3.1 (continued) Reitmans (Canada) Limited: Extracts from the Financial Statements

REITMANS (CANADA) LIMITED
STATEMENTS OF EARNINGS
(in thousands of Canadian dollars except per share amounts)

	For the years ended	
	January 28, 2012	**January 29, 2011**
Sales	**$1,019,397**	$1,059,000
Cost of goods sold (note 7)	**363,333**	350,671
Gross profit	**656,064**	708,329
Selling and distribution expenses	**547,367**	528,676
Administrative expenses	**46,878**	55,511
Results from operating activities	**61,819**	124,142
Finance income (note 19)	**5,562**	4,505
Finance costs (note 19)	**1,509**	845
Earnings before income taxes	**65,872**	127,802
Income taxes (note 11)	**18,333**	38,817
Net earnings	**$ 47,539**	$ 88,985
Earnings per share (note 20):		
Basic	**$ 0.72**	$ 1.33
Diluted	**0.72**	1.32

2. BASIS OF PRESENTATION

d) Estimates, Judgments and Assumptions

The preparation of the financial statements in accordance with IFRS requires management to make judgments, estimates and assumptions that affect the application of accounting policies and the reported amounts of assets, liabilities, the disclosure of contingent assets and contingent liabilities at the date of the financial statements and reported amounts of revenues and expenses during the period. These estimates and assumptions are based on historical experience, other relevant factors and expectations of the future and are reviewed regularly. Revisions to accounting estimates are recognized in the period in which the estimates are revised and in any future periods affected. Actual results may differ from these estimates.

3. SIGNIFICANT ACCOUNTING POLICIES

The accounting policies set out below have been applied consistently to all periods presented in these financial statements.

1) Revenue

Revenue is recognized from the sale of merchandise when a customer purchases and takes delivery of the merchandise. Reported sales are net of returns and estimated possible returns and exclude sales taxes.

Gift cards sold are recorded as deferred revenue and revenue is recognized when the gift cards are redeemed. An estimate is made of gift cards not expected to be redeemed based on the terms of the gift cards and historical redemption patterns.

Loyalty points and awards granted under customer loyalty programs are recognized as a separate component of revenue, and are deferred at the date of initial sale. Revenue is recognized when the loyalty points and awards are redeemed and the Company has fulfilled its obligation. The amount of revenue deferred is measured based on the fair value of loyalty points and awards granted, taking into consideration the estimated redemption percentage.

EXHIBIT 3.1 (continued) Reitmans (Canada) Limited: Extracts from the Financial Statements

12. TRADE AND OTHER PAYABLES

	January 28, 2012	January 29, 2011	January 31, 2010
Trade payables	**$26,155**	$16,457	$15,148
Non-trade payables due to related parties	**56**	66	90
Other non-trade payables	**10,553**	11,817	4,437
Personnel liabilities	**23,053**	31,457	30,615
Payables relating to premises	**14,398**	13,630	12,630
Provision for sales returns	**770**	846	869
	74,985	74,273	63,789
Less non-current portion	**11,110**	10,180	9,105
	$63,875	$64,093	$54,684

The non-current portion of trade and other payables, which is included in payables relating to premises, represents the portion of deferred rent to be amortized beyond the next twelve months.

13. DEFERRED REVENUE

Deferred revenue consists of the following:

	January 28, 2012	January 29, 2011	January 31, 2010
Loyalty points and awards granted under loyalty programs	**$10,979**	$10,984	$10,142
Unredeemed gift cards	**11,299**	11,234	10,666
	22,278	22,218	20,808
Less amounts expected to be redeemed in the next twelve months	**22,278**	19,834	18,122
Deferred revenue—non-current	**$ –**	$ 2,384	$ 2,686

22. PERSONNEL EXPENSES

	For the years ended	
	January 28, 2012	January 29, 2011
Wages, salaries and employee benefits	**$248,208**	$251,702
Expenses related to defined benefit plans	**1,490**	1,341
Share-based compensation costs	**1,120**	1,990
	$250,818	$255,033

23. CREDIT FACILITY

At January 28, 2012, the Company had unsecured operating lines of credit available with Canadian chartered banks to a maximum of $125,000 or its US dollar equivalent. As at January 28, 2012, $52,187 (January 29, 2011—$60,888) of the operating lines of credit were committed for documentary and standby letters of credit.

FS3-3. Calculate the following ratios for Reitmans for 2011 and 2012:

a. profit margin
b. return on equity
c. current ratio
d. debt-to-equity ratio
e. gross margin

FS3-4. Prepare the closing journal entry that Reitmans would make on January 28, 2012. (Alternative approach: Set up an accounting equation spreadsheet using Reitmans' financial statements and record the closing entry Reitmans would make on January 28, 2012.)

FS3-5. How much does Reitmans report for trade and other receivables on January 28, 2012? Why do you think the amount of trade and other receivables is so small?

FS3-6. How much does Reitmans report for property and equipment on January 28, 2012? What do you think these assets are? Why do you think Reitmans needs to have so much invested in property and equipment (in answering consider the nature of the business and the resources it needs to operate)?

FS3-7. You are a supplier who has recently been approached by Reitmans' management to replace an existing supplier. Assess Reitmans' liquidity. Would you be prepared to provide credit to Reitmans? Explain your decision.

FS3-8. Read note 2.d) to Reitmans' financial statements. Explain why it's necessary for Reitmans to make judgments, estimates, and assumptions when preparing its financial statements. Provide examples from the information about Reitmans in Exhibit 3.1.

FS3-9. How much does Reitmans report for trade and other payables on its January 28, 2012? Who does Reitmans owe money to? Describe the circumstances that explain why money would be owed to these entities.

ENDNOTES

1. Extracted from Reitmans (Canada) Limited's 2012 annual report.

Practise and learn online with Connect. Connect resources include additional and interactive study exercises, videos, and practice quizzing, as well as additional material you won't find in the printed text.

CHAPTER 4

Income Measurement and the Objectives of Financial Reporting

LEARNING OBJECTIVES

After studying the material in this chapter you will be able to do the following:

LO 1 Explain and apply criteria for revenue recognition.

LO 2 Describe the critical-event and gradual approaches of recognizing revenue.

LO 3 Explain the effects that different approaches to recognizing revenue have on the income statement and on financial ratios.

LO 4 Describe how multi-deliverables are accounted for.

LO 5 Describe expense recognition and the matching principle.

LO 6 Recognize how to account for gains and losses.

LO 7 (a) Explain how the constraints, economic facts surrounding a transaction or economic event, and managers' objectives of financial reporting affect the accounting choices made by an entity.
(b) Explain the reasons for, economic consequences to stakeholders of, and limitations to flexible accounting rules that give managers the opportunity to choose how they account for transactions and economic events.

LO 8 Apply an approach to solving accounting choice problems.

Fans of the MTV reality show *Jersey Shore* lined up for hours inside the Indigo bookstore at Toronto's Eaton Centre on a dark winter night. It was February 28, 2011. Suddenly, a smiling, tanned woman strode up to Indigo's specially prepared stage, wearing a tight black dress and high-heeled black shoes. It was Jenni Farley, better known as JWOWW from the hit television series. She was in town to sign copies of her new book *The Rules According to JWOWW*.

Courtesy Indigo Chapters Inc.

Farley's fans recognized her immediately as the tough chick from the cast of *Jersey Shore*. Her book dispenses advice on relationships, fitness, and finding a "mint guy." Customers clutched copies of the hardcover edition of the book, which Farley signed with a pink Sharpie, while her long-time screen boyfriend Roger Matthews sat in a chair beside her and watched the frenzy.

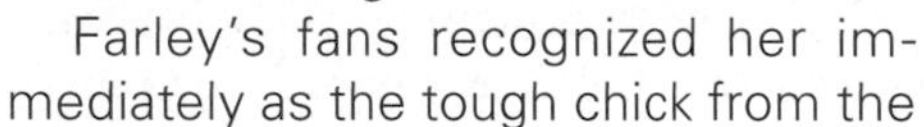

"Out of all your flirting tips, which is your favourite and can you try it on me?" begs one interviewer in an Indigo video posted on YouTube. Farley bursts out laughing but firmly declines.

The moment when eager fans paid $19.99 to buy Farley's hardcover book at the store's cash registers, Indigo's corporate accounting system recognized the sale as revenue.

Those *Jersey Shore* fans who couldn't come down to see Farley in person, perhaps because they were too busy working out at the gym, tanning, or doing laundry, but still wanted to buy the hardcover book, could do it online through the company's Web site, www.chapters.indigo.ca.

But unlike at the bricks and mortar store, Indigo accountants classify the e-commerce sale as revenue not at the moment when it is paid for, but only when the book is actually shipped out.

That's when, according to Indigo's 2011 annual report, "the substantial risks and rewards of ownership pass to the customer."

Buying the book was a little cheaper for some of Indigo's one million *irewards* members, who pay a $35 annual fee to belong, and receive discounts on books they buy during a 12-month period. Indigo's accounting system acknowledges purchases of *irewards* cards based on a formula that spreads the income out over the life of the card.

Indigo also sells a digital version of JWOWW's book that can be downloaded, so customers can read the book on their own mobile devices, including on Kobo e-readers, for $12.99. Indigo helped develop the popular Kobo devices, but sold the company to a Japanese e-commerce firm in early 2012 for US$315 million.

Whether in person, online, or on a mobile tablet using an app, sales of Farley's book helped Canada's largest book and toy and gift retailer act like one of Farley's favourite Gorilla Juice Heads (a big, muscular guy on steroids). For the first time since Indigo was founded in 1996, the company reported revenue of over $1 billion in 2011, up 5 percent from the year before.

–E.B.

INTRODUCTION

We have now covered the fundamentals of accounting. In Chapters 1 to 3, we explored the accounting environment, became familiar with financial statements, and learned the basics of the accounting cycle. We can now begin our exploration of accounting information in depth. In the remainder of the book we will examine how economic events are reported (and not reported) in financial statements.

In the first part of this chapter, we will explore revenue and expense recognition. The term *recognition* refers to revenues and expenses appearing in the income statement. There are different ways of recognizing revenues and expenses, and the methods chosen can affect the amounts reported in an entity's financial statements. Different recognition methods also affect many accounting and financial ratios—tools stakeholders often use to analyze financial statements. Managers must decide which methods to choose (remember from Chapter 1 that managers decide how to report accounting information). Chapter 4 provides some explanation of why alternative acceptable accounting methods are allowed, as well as some implications of allowing managers to choose the methods used.

The second part of this chapter examines the objectives of financial reporting. This material will help you understand factors influencing the accounting choices managers make and incentives encouraging them to pursue self-interests. Most often, managers make accounting choices that are within the rules (such as IFRS or ASPE). But because the rules often allow managers to choose among acceptable alternatives, they can satisfy their own interests and still meet the rules. It's understandable that some readers may be uncomfortable with the ethical implications of this situation, but it's the reality of accounting. This material isn't intended to be a guide or encouragement to misuse accounting information. It's meant to help you understand and avoid being deceived by accounting information. For better or for worse, empirical evidence and casual observation suggest that when people have choices, the choices they make are the ones that are best for them. This applies in accounting too.[1]

However, an entity's managers are still responsible for supplying relevant and reliable information to stakeholders. This responsibility must be carried out to the highest ethical standards. Failure to do so has significant consequences for the economy, society, and stakeholders. Accounting scandals at Enron, WorldCom, Nortel, and Tyco have highlighted how managers can use accounting information unethically as well as what the consequences of unethical behaviour are. Some accounting controversies aren't clear violations of accounting rules but raise questions about management's intent when making accounting choices.

LO 1 REVENUE RECOGNITION

When revenue recognition was introduced in Chapter 3 we learned that under accrual accounting, revenue is economic benefits earned by providing goods or services to customers. But it isn't always obvious when an economic benefit "happens," so someone has to decide what the economic event is that triggers revenue recognition. *When* revenue is recognized and *how* expenses are matched to revenue significantly affect the amounts reported in the financial statements, the value of financial ratios, and possibly a person's perception of how an entity is performing. Once you determine that revenue should be recognized, the journal entry to record it is straightforward:

Dr. Cash (asset +) or Accounts receivables (asset +)	xxx	
or Unearned revenue (liabilities −)		
Cr. Revenue (revenue +, owners' equity +)		xxx
To record revenue		

When revenue is recognized, an income statement account for revenue is credited and a balance sheet account is debited. The entry to the balance sheet either increases assets (usually accounts receivable or cash) or decreases liabilities (often unearned revenue). This is a very important point. For there to be revenue, there has to be a corresponding increase in assets or decrease in liabilities. If assets don't increase or liabilities don't decrease, there is no revenue.

Conceptually, earning revenue is a continuous process. Any activity by an entity to make a good or service available or valuable to customers represents economic benefit or revenue. For example, when Leon's Furniture Limited advertises, trains staff, displays merchandise in the store, or a salesperson spends time with a customer, economic value is created because Leon's merchandise is more attractive and available to customers. From an accounting standpoint, it's difficult to measure this continuous process so methods are required for reporting revenue in the income statement in a logical and rational way.

Accountants have devised two approaches for recognizing revenue. Each applies to different types of transactions—they aren't substitutes for one another. The first, the **critical-event approach**, identifies a point in the earnings process as the appropriate time to recognize revenue. That point is called the critical event. When the critical event occurs, 100 percent of the revenue is recognized. Before it occurs, there is no revenue, and when it occurs all the revenue is recognized. Examples of critical events include delivery of goods to customers and collection of payment. The critical-event approach applies when goods are sold to a customer or a service is provided on a one-time basis (for example, having a computer repaired).

The second approach recognizes revenue gradually over a period of time; for example, services provided over a period, construction contracts, or interest earned, which occurs continuously over time. We can call this approach of recognizing revenue little by little over time the **gradual approach**.

The Critical-Event Approach

LO 1, 2

IFRS provides five criteria for identifying the critical event for recognizing revenue on the sale of goods. The earliest point when all the criteria are met is when revenue should be recognized:

1. Significant risks and rewards of ownership have been transferred from the seller to the buyer.
2. The seller has no involvement or control over the goods sold.
3. Collection of payment is probable.
4. The amount of revenue can be reasonably measured.
5. Costs of earning the revenue can be reasonably measured.

We can call the first two *performance* criteria, meaning the seller has done most or all of what it's supposed to do to be entitled to payment and the buyer has accepted the goods. Most of the time, but not always, performance has occurred when a customer purchases merchandise and takes delivery. Performance might not have occurred on delivery if, for example

- The buyer has to resell the merchandise before the seller gets paid.
- The seller has to install the goods and installation is a significant part of the purchase.

The third criterion is collectability. If payment isn't probable or if the seller can't make a reasonable estimate of how much won't be collected, revenue shouldn't be recognized. This doesn't mean the seller must expect to collect 100 percent of amounts owed. If the uncollectible amount can be estimated, revenue can be recognized and an expense recorded for the uncollected amount.

Criteria four and five deal with measurability. For revenue to be recognized the entity must be able to estimate the amount it has earned and the costs incurred to earn it. Often costs are incurred after the critical event and these must be recorded in the same period as the revenue. For example, warranty costs are incurred after the customer takes delivery of the merchandise. If the seller isn't able to estimate the warranty costs then revenue recognition should be delayed until the end of the warranty period.

These are the criteria according to IFRS. But remember, we are examining financial reporting with a critical eye so it's important not to think of these as the best or only possible criteria for recognizing revenue. We could probably come up with other ways that would suit the information needs of some stakeholders.

The criteria provide guidance to managers, but they aren't hard and fast rules. They require interpretation and judgment. Business transactions don't always fit into convenient categories. After all, at what point have the "significant risks and rewards of ownership" been transferred? For criteria four and five, what does "reasonably" mean? And when does collection become probable? These fairly vague terms provide flexibility for choosing when to recognize revenue. We will see later that this vagueness serves a purpose.

The criteria are fairly *conservative* because they tend to delay revenue recognition until fairly late in the revenue-generating process. This reduces the uncertainty surrounding the numbers in the financial statements, making the information more meaningful and reliable. Unreliable financial statement numbers aren't very useful for decision making. On the other hand, waiting until there is no uncertainty may not be useful either because stakeholders will receive the information too late to influence their decisions. For there to be no uncertainty, revenue would have to be recognized very late—in most cases long after cash is collected and any post-transaction obligations (such as warranties) have been resolved. The IFRS criteria tend to reduce uncertainty but they don't eliminate it.

I will add one more criterion: the critical event selected should provide a reasonable and fair representation of the entity's activities, given the needs of the stakeholders. This means that after deciding on a revenue recognition point based on the criteria the manager should assess whether the choice is reasonable and fair. If the manager believes the choice may be misleading or confusing, an alternative should be considered. As a matter of ethics, this criterion is pervasive and overriding. Remember that accounting information must, above all, provide useful information about an entity so stakeholders can make informed decisions. As our discussion proceeds, we will refer mainly to the first five criteria. However, this sixth criterion should always be kept in mind.

Mc Graw Hill connect

KNOWLEDGE CHECK 4.1

- ❑ What two approaches have accountants devised for recognizing revenue?
- ❑ What are the five criteria for recognizing revenue under IFRS? Explain each criterion.
- ❑ What is the "sixth" criterion for revenue recognition and why is it so important?

QUESTION FOR CONSIDERATION

Evarts Ltd. (Evarts) is a retail store that sells clothing to men and women. Evarts has been in business for 15 years. Customers pay by cash or major credit card at the time they purchase and take their merchandise. Unused merchandise can be returned within 15 days. On occasion, Evarts replaces or repairs goods that are damaged or that customers are otherwise dissatisfied with beyond the 15 day return period. Evarts recognizes its revenue when the customer pays and takes the merchandise. Use the revenue recognition criteria to support when Evarts recognizes its revenue.

ANSWER: When the customer pays and takes the merchandise all the revenue recognition criteria are clearly met. The amount of revenue is known since the customer has paid the agreed price. Most costs have been incurred by that time. The cost of the merchandise sold is known, as well as any other costs directly associated with the sale, such as the salesperson's commission. There are some uncertainties about costs, such as the cost of replacements and repairs, as well as of returns. However, these costs are likely small and, given the length of time Evarts has been in business, can be reasonably estimated. Collection isn't an issue since the customer pays when the goods are taken. The risks and rewards of ownership have transferred because the customer has the clothes and can use them as he or she chooses. Any damage is the responsibility of the customer. Evarts has no control over the clothes at all. While Evarts will accept responsibility for manufacturer's defects and certain repairs, it won't take goods back if a garment became stained or torn as a result of use by the customer. Notice that there are uncertainties (returns, exchanges, repairs) when Evarts recognizes its revenue, but these are normal, reasonable, and can be estimated.

Some Critical Events

LO 1, 2

Let's look at some of the critical events used in practice. Strictly speaking, the criteria apply only to goods because there are no risks and rewards to transfer with services. However, I will include services that are provided all at once (for example, air transportation, haircuts, dry cleaning, and so on) in this discussion.

Delivery Delivery occurs when the buyer takes possession of the goods or receives the service (in a single exchange) being sold. Most retail, manufacturing, and service businesses use delivery as their critical event. There is too much uncertainty before delivery (it's usually unclear whether an exchange will take place), and recognizing revenue after delivery delays recognition beyond the transfer of the risks and rewards of ownership. However, there are exceptions, as we will see. Exhibit 4.1 shows the revenue recognition notes for four Canadian companies in four different industries that use delivery as their critical event.

Indigo Books & Music Inc. is Canada's largest book retailer. As you would expect, Indigo recognizes revenue from in-store sales when customers make their purchases. Online sales are recognized when the goods are shipped. For its online business, the five criteria are met on shipment because (a) the customer has paid (typically by credit card) so collection is assured, (b) the amount of revenue is known (the product ordered has a price), (c) the cost of the product shipped along with associated costs (e.g., shipping costs) are known, (d) the risks and rewards of ownership have transferred, and (e) the merchandise is available to the customer to use and enjoy, and Indigo has no involvement or control since the product ordered has been sent to the customer. There are some uncertainties at shipment; for example, customers may return goods, wrong items might be shipped, and goods might be lost or damaged in transit. These costs can be estimated (Indigo has lots of experience in this business), so revenue can be reasonably recognized when the goods are shipped.

Kinross Gold Corporation is a gold mining company. It recognizes its revenue on delivery to customers. The note provides a general explanation of the conditions that allow for revenue recognition and specifically notes that at delivery the rights and obligations of ownership must be transferred and there is a reasonable expectation of collection.

High Liner Foods Incorporated is a Canadian processor and marketer of seafood products. High Liner recognizes its revenue when risks and rewards have been transferred to customers, which is usually on delivery.

WestJet Airlines Ltd. provides air transportation services. It recognizes its revenue when passengers actually travel, even though many people pay for their tickets in advance of their flight dates. This is consistent with the revenue recognition criteria, since at the time of the journey WestJet provides what the passenger purchased. The other criteria are also met at this point: customers usually pay in advance so collection and the amount of revenue is known and the costs of operating the flight can be determined (wages, fuel, meals, etc.). WestJet records the following journal entry when a passenger books a trip:

Dr. Cash (asset +)	xxx	
Cr. Advance ticket sales (liabilities −)		xxx
To record the purchase of a ticket in advance		

And this entry when the passenger travels:

Dr. Advance ticket sales (liabilities −)	xxx	
Cr. Revenue (revenue +, owners' equity +)		xxx
To recognize revenue		

Completion of Production The revenue recognition criteria can be met as soon as the product is produced, even if it hasn't been delivered to the customer, if the sale of the product is assured and the costs of selling and distributing it are minor. An example is a bill-and-hold arrangement, in which a customer orders merchandise but requests delivery at a later date (perhaps because of a lack of storage space). The seller can recognize the revenue when the goods are produced if certain conditions are met, including: the buyer takes title to the goods and accepts billing, and if the goods are on hand and ready for delivery. The cost of goods sold

EXHIBIT 4.1 Revenue Recognition: Critical Events[2,3]

Indigo Books & Music Inc. (Retailer)

Revenue

The Company recognizes revenue when the substantial risks and rewards of ownership pass to the customer. Revenue is measured at the fair value of consideration received or receivable by the Company for goods supplied, net of sales discounts and returns, and is inclusive of amounts invoiced for shipping. Return allowances are estimated using historical experience. Revenue is recognized when: the amount can be measured reliable; it is probable that economic benefits associated with the transaction will flow to the Company; the costs incurred or to be incurred can be measured reliably; and the criteria for each of the Company's activities (as described below) have been met.

Retail and Kobo sales

Revenue for retail and Kobo customers is recognized at the time of purchase.

Online sales

Revenue for online customers is recognized when the product is shipped.

Kinross Gold Corporation

xv. Metal sales

Metal sales includes sales of refined gold and silver, which are generally physically delivered to customers in the period in which they are produced, with their sales price based on prevailing spot market metal prices. Revenue from metal sales is recognized when all the following conditions have been satisfied:

- The significant risks and rewards of ownership have been transferred;
- Neither continuing managerial involvement to the degree usually associated with ownership, nor effective control over the goods sold, has been retained;
- The amount of revenue can be measured reliably;
- It is probable that the economic benefits associated with the transaction will flow to the Company; and
- The costs incurred or to be incurred in respect of the transaction can be measured reliably.

These conditions are generally met when the sales price is fixed and title has passed to the customer.

High Liner Foods Incorporated (Food processing company)

Revenue recognition

The Company recognizes sales in income when the risks and rewards of the underlying products have been substantially transferred to the customer, usually on delivery of the goods. The Company experiences very few product returns and collectability of its invoices is consistently high.

WestJet Airlines Ltd. (Air transportation service provider)

(extracted from WestJet's 2011 audited financial statements prepared in accordance with IFRS)

(d) Revenue recognition

(i) Guest

Guest revenues, including the air component of vacation packages, are recognized when air transportation is provided. Tickets sold but not yet used are reported in the consolidated statement of financial position as advance ticket sales.

is expensed when the revenue is recognized, even though the inventory is still in possession of the seller. Exhibit 4.2 provides the revenue recognition note for Supremex Income Fund, a manufacturer of envelopes and related products. The note explains the conditions Supremex must meet to recognize revenue before goods are delivered to the customer.

Revenue Recognition after Delivery In some situations, revenue recognition is delayed until after goods have been delivered or services provided to customers. Delay is appropriate if the risk and rewards of ownership haven't transferred at the time of deliver or if there are significant uncertainties about costs, revenue, or collection. Remember, the appropriate time to recognize

EXHIBIT 4.2[4]

Supremex Inc: Bill-and-Hold Arrangement

www.supremex.com/en/index.asp

Revenue recognition

2. SIGNIFICANT ACCOUNTING POLICIES

Revenue recognition

Revenue is measured at the fair value of the consideration received or receivable, net of estimated returns and discounts, and alter eliminating intercompany sales.

Revenue from the sale of goods is recognized when the following criteria are met:

- The risks and rewards of ownership, including managerial involvement, have been transferred to the buyer;
- The amount of revenue can be measured reliably;
- The receipt of economic benefits is probable; and
- Costs incurred or to be incurred can be measured reliably.

In addition to the above general principles, the Company applies specific revenue recognition for bill and hold transactions. When customers request a bill and hold, revenue is recognized when the customer is invoiced for goods that have been produced, packaged and made ready for shipment. These goods are shipped within a specified period of time and are segregated from other inventory, the risk of ownership of the goods is assumed by the customer, and the terms and collection experience on the related billings arc consistent with all other sales.

revenue is the moment that all of the criteria are met. Following are some examples of uncertainties that could delay recognizing revenue until after delivery:

- *Warranty costs* A **warranty** is a promise by a seller or producer of a product to correct specified problems with the product. If a company isn't able to make a reasonable estimate of its warranty costs it should wait until the end of the warranty period to recognize revenue. For example, a company gives a two-year warranty on a product that relies on a new technology. If the company can't make a reasonable estimate of the cost of providing the warranty service at the time of delivery, revenue recognition should be deferred until the warranty period ends because the costs required to earn the revenue can't be reasonably measured.
- *Returns* If a company can't estimate the amount of goods customers will return it should wait until the end of the return period to recognize revenue. For example, a company allows a new customer the right to return merchandise for 180 days. If the company isn't able to estimate the returns, revenue recognition should be delayed because the amount of revenue is unknown (estimated returns are deducted from sales).
- *Cash collection* The third criterion requires a reasonable expectation that payment will be received. If a reasonable estimate of the amount that will be collected isn't possible, collection becomes the critical event. For example, a business that sells on credit to high-risk customers (customers who have a high likelihood of not paying) might delay recognizing revenue until cash is collected.

For each of these cases, it's important to understand that delaying revenue recognition results from too much uncertainty. If reasonable estimates can be made of warranty costs, returns, or uncollectible amounts, it's appropriate to recognize revenue at delivery.

Let's look at an example of recording revenue after delivery. Roblin Ltd. recently began marketing a new product that comes with an 18-month parts and service warranty. The product uses a new technology and the company is unable to estimate the cost of the warranty. As a result, Roblin has decided to recognize revenue at the end of the warranty period. During 2016, Roblin sold $250,000 of the new product to customers for $400,000 and recorded the following entry:

Dr. Accounts receivable (assets +)	400,000	
Cr. Deferred gross margin (liabilities +)		150,000
Cr. Inventory (asset −)		250,000
To record shipment of goods to a customer		

Notice that this entry has no impact on the income statement. The amount owing by the customer is recorded (accounts receivable), but no revenue is recognized. The inventory is removed from the books since it has been shipped. The deferred gross margin is reported as a liability (something like unearned revenue) and represents the difference between the cost of the inventory and its selling price (this entry is necessary so the account receivable can be recognized without recognizing revenue). When the customers pay the amount owing, Roblin would record the following entry:

Dr. Cash (assets +)	400,000	
Cr. Accounts receivable (asset −)		400,000
To record receipt of payment		

Notice there is still no effect on the income statement. During the warranty period Roblin incurs costs for servicing the new product. The costs aren't expensed as incurred but reduce the deferred gross margin:

Dr. Deferred gross margin (liabilities −)	40,000	
Cr. Cash (asset −)		40,000
To record the cost of warranty service (the credit could also be to accounts payable or parts inventory)		

At the end of the warranty period when the uncertainty about the warranty costs has been resolved, Roblin would make this entry:

Dr. Deferred gross margin (liabilities −)	110,000	
Dr. Cost of sales (expenses +, owners' equity −)	250,000	
Dr. Warranty expense (expenses +, owners' equity −)	40,000	
Cr. Revenue (revenue +, owners' equity +)		400,000
To recognize revenue		

It's only at this point, when all the revenue criteria are met, that the income statement is affected. The revenue and expenses are recognized at the same time. This entry may be a bit confusing but what it's doing is eliminating the deferred gross margin liability (which netted revenue and expenses from the sale) and recognizes the component pieces (revenues and expenses) on the income statement. Entries for recognition on cash collection or the end of the sales return period would be similar to these.

Another business arrangement where revenue is recognized after delivery is a **consignment sale**. In a consignment sale a producer/distributor transfers merchandise to another entity (the seller), which agrees to try to sell the merchandise. The seller pays the producer/distributor only when the goods are sold and any unsold merchandise can be returned to the producer/distributor. The producer/distributor recognizes revenue only when the seller sells the merchandise because the producer/distributor retains the risks and rewards of ownership until that time. Art galleries selling the work of artists operate on this principle, as the rights and risks of ownership of the art piece remain with the artist until the gallery sells the piece to a third party or returns it to the artist.

It's important to remember that the critical event selected for a transaction must meet all five revenue recognition criteria (if IFRS is a constraint). The earliest point when all five criteria are met is when revenue should be recognized. However, it's not always obvious when that point is. In some situations there may not be just one possible critical event. Circumstances surrounding a transaction may be ambiguous, allowing people to legitimately interpret the facts in different ways to support different critical events. When there is more than one possible critical event the entity's choice will be influenced by the entity's accounting environment—characteristics of the entity (industry, type of transactions, risk, etc.), constraints, stakeholder needs, and interests of the manager's (see Figure 1.2). Regardless of these other factors, the critical event selected must be supported by the revenue recognition criteria or whatever accounting standards are being followed.

LO 3 Why Does It Matter When a Company Recognizes Revenue?

We can use an example to see the effects on the income statement of using different critical events for recognizing revenue. Escuminac Manufacturing Ltd. (Escuminac) makes sophisticated heavy equipment on a special-order basis to meet the specifications of each customer. Customers usually order equipment well in advance of when they need it and it's common practice in this industry for a manufacturer to store equipment it makes for several months before it's delivered. Customers usually make a payment to Escuminac when the contract to produce equipment is signed and then pay at milestones specified in the contract. In 2017 through 2019, the following dollar amounts of equipment were produced and delivered:

	2017	2018	2019
Produced by Escuminac	$10,000,000	$12,000,000	$8,000,000
Delivered to customers	$7,500,000	$11,500,000	$9,000,000

Now let's look at Escuminac's financial results for the years 2017 to 2019. Two sets of income statements have been prepared and are shown in Table 4.1. The first set assumes production is the critical event for recognizing revenue and the second set assumes delivery is the critical event. Both statements assume the cost of producing the equipment, called *production expenses* in Table 4.1, is 60 percent of the revenue. These costs are expensed when the revenue is recognized, as required by matching. In addition, there are $3,000,000 of other costs, such as executive salaries, cost of support staff, and so on, that are expensed in the period the work is done. The example ignores income taxes.

The numbers in each set of income statements are different. In 2017, revenue is $10,000,000 using production as the critical event versus $7,500,000 using delivery. Net income in 2017 is $1,000,000, using production as the critical event and zero using delivery. Revenue and net income in 2018 and 2019 are also different with each critical event. The gross margin percentage is the same across years and critical events because it's assumed that production expenses were a constant percentage (60 percent) of revenue. The profit margin percentage differs across years and critical events because other expenses are a constant $3,000,000 per year.

TABLE 4.1 Income Statements for Escuminac Manufacturing Ltd.

	1. Revenue recognized when the equipment is produced			2. Revenue recognized when the equipment is delivered			
	2017**	2018	2019	2017	2018	2019	2020
Revenue*	$10,000,000	$12,000,000	$8,000,000	$7,500,000	$11,500,000	$9,000,000	$2,000,000
Production expenses	6,000,000	7,200,000	4,800,000	4,500,000	6,900,000	5,400,000	1,200,000
Gross margin	4,000,000	4,800,000	3,200,000	3,000,000	4,600,000	3,600,000	800,000
Other expenses (assumed)	3,000,000	3,000,000	3,000,000	3,000,000	3,000,000	3,000,000	0
Net income	$ 1,000,000	$ 1,800,000	$ 200,000	$ 0	$ 1,600,000	$ 600,000	$ 800,000
Financial Ratios							
Gross margin percentage	40.0%	40.0%	40.0%	40.0%	40.0%	40.0%	40.0%
Profit margin percentage	10.0%	15.0%	2.5%	0.0%	13.9%	6.7%	40.0%

*Results for 2020 are included for completeness since some of the equipment produced in 2019 wasn't delivered until 2020. No "other expenses" are reported in 2020 for comparability. Over the term of the contracts the amount of revenue, expenses, and net income reported aren't affected by the critical event chosen, but the timing of these elements is affected.

**Below are sample calculations for the amounts shown in the table. Calculations are shown for 2017 when revenue is recognized when the equipment is produced.
production expenses = 60% × revenue = 60% × $10,000,000 = $6,000,000
gross margin = revenue − production expenses = $10,000,000 − $6,000,000 = $4,000,000
other expenses = $3,000,000 (fixed amount)
net income = gross margin − other expenses − $4,000,000 − $3,000,000 = $1,000,000
gross margin percentage = gross margin/revenue − $4,000,000 ÷ $10,000,000 = 0.40 = 40%
profit margin = net income ÷ revenue = $1,000,000 ÷ $10,000,000 = 0.10 = 10.0%

The critical event used will also affect many of Escuminac's other financial ratios. For example, the current ratio (current assets ÷ current liabilities) will be different because the amount of accounts receivable, inventory, and liabilities will differ, as will the debt-to-equity ratio (debt ÷ equity).

Now we can consider some crucial questions. Which critical event for recognizing Escuminac's revenue is best? Which one reports the "right" amount of revenue? How do these different critical events affect Escuminac's stakeholders?

First, recognizing revenue on production or delivery are both potentially reasonable alternatives for Escuminac, depending on the details of the contracts between the company and its customers. Escuminac's business terms are an example of the bill-and-hold arrangement described earlier. Accounting standards provide guidance for recognizing revenue in situations like this, but ultimately managers and accountants must use professional judgment to interpret the terms of the contract and apply the accounting standard. Which critical event is *best* is a question that can't be answered. Assuming that both can be supported by the revenue recognition criteria, the best or most appropriate critical event depends on the environment—the stakeholders, the managers, and the facts underlying the entity's economic transactions.

Which critical event reports the *right* amount of revenue and income? This is another question with no correct answer. The two critical events are different ways of measuring the same underlying economic activity. Both try to capture complex economic activity that occurs over time in a simple way. A critical event is a convenient way of overcoming the difficulty of measuring revenue as it's earned in an economic sense but it's also artificial. It's also important to remember that Escuminac is the same regardless of which critical event is selected: an entity's accounting choices don't change the underlying economic activities being reported.

The final question is, how are stakeholders affected by these alternative critical events? Using the 2017 data, here are some examples of the economic consequences for Escuminac's stakeholders of the different critical events:

- If the president's bonus is based on net income, her bonus will be higher if production is the critical event.
- Escuminac may pay less tax if revenue is recognized on delivery.
- Unionized employees might feel more confident about seeking wage increases if production is the critical event.

Indeed, many different contracts and agreements rely on accounting numbers, which makes accountants' measurement of things like revenue very important. So while an accounting choice doesn't affect an entity's underlying economic activity, it may have economic consequences for stakeholders.

More subtle is the effect the choices may have on the perceptions of stakeholders. Does a more "rosy" income statement make a company more attractive to investors and lenders? Do higher revenues and higher net incomes make stakeholders think managers have done a better job, even if the difference in the numbers is due to accounting choices, not real economic differences?

In summary, here are some of the important issues to keep in mind while you think about the Escuminac example:

1. An income statement doesn't show you what revenue or net income would have been under alternative critical events. That means the income statement you receive shapes your perceptions of the entity.
2. The managers choose the critical event for recognizing revenue. This means the self-interest of management (e.g. possibility of a higher bonus) can affect its choice.
3. The economic activity of an entity isn't affected by how or when it recognizes revenue. Regardless of which critical event Escuminac chooses, the same amount of equipment was produced each year, the same amount of equipment was delivered each year, and the same amount of cash was collected each year. What is affected is how the activities are accounted for and reported, and the different choices may have different economic consequences for stakeholders.

QUESTION FOR CONSIDERATION

Suppose you are an investor who is interested in investing in a manufacturing company. Examine the two sets of income statements provided for Escuminac Manufacturing Ltd. in Table 4.1 and choose which set of statements represent a better investment. Explain your choice.

ANSWER: Were you fooled? The two financial statements represent exactly the same company, at exactly the same time, in exactly the same circumstances. The underlying economic activity of Escuminac isn't affected by the critical event chosen even though it affects how that economic activity is represented in the financial statements.

Google Inc.

LO 3

Now let's look at a real example of how different revenue recognition methods can affect a company's financial statements. Google Inc. (Google) is well known as the company that offers free online search services. In 2004, Google became a public company by offering its shares to investors (the shares were sold by the company itself and by its shareholders). When a company "goes public" it must file a document called a **prospectus** with the securities regulator. This is a legal document providing detailed information about a company offering its securities for public sale.

On July 12, 2004, Google filed a prospectus with the Securities and Exchange Commission (SEC) (the securities regulator in the United States). The income statements in that prospectus can be found in Panel A of Exhibit 4.3. Notice that for the year ended December 31, 2003, Google's revenue was $961,874,000, cost of revenues was $121,794,000, and net income was $105,648,000. Just two weeks later on July 26, 2004, Google filed an amended prospectus with the SEC. The income statements from that prospectus can be seen in Panel B of Exhibit 4.3. For the year ended December 31, 2003 Google's revenue had increased to $1,465,934,000 and cost of revenues had increased to $625,854,000. Net income was unchanged. In the space of two weeks, Google's revenue increased by over $500,000,000, an increase of over 50 percent! What happened? A colossal error? An obvious fraud? No, it's nothing but accounting at work.

The dramatic change was the result of a change in how Google recognized its revenue. One of the ways Google makes money is by placing ads for advertisers on other entities' Web sites. Each time a Web user clicks on an ad, Google is entitled to payment from the advertiser and then must make a payment to the owner of the Web sites where the ad appeared. Suppose Google gets $1 each time an ad is clicked and pays $0.80 of it to the Web publisher on whose site the ad appears. For each click on the ad, how much revenue should Google recognize? Should it recognize $1 of revenue and $0.80 of expense for the payment? (This is called the gross method because the amount reported as revenue is the full amount owed by the advertiser.) Or should it simply recognize $0.20 in revenue? (This is the net method because the amount reported as revenue is the net amount earned by Google after deducting the amount owed to the Web publisher.)

In its July 12, 2004 prospectus, Google used the net method for recognizing its revenue, whereas in the July 26 prospectus it switched to the gross method. By making this change, revenues and cost of revenues increased by the same amount (this is why net income didn't change). No explanation was given. A possible reason is that Google wanted to use the same accounting method as its competitor, Yahoo. The key point is that Google's income statement looks quite different as a result of the change. While there is no effect on net income, there are significant effects on revenues, expenses, and financial ratios such as profit margin. In the July 12, 2004 prospectus, Google's profit margin percentage for 2003 was 11.0 percent ($105,648,000/$961,784,000) while in the July 26, 2004 prospectus the profit margin percentage was 7.2 percent ($105,648,000/$1,465,934,000).

It's crucial to recognize that Google is the same company in the two prospectuses. Suddenly having an extra $500,000,000 of revenue changed nothing; Google's underlying economic activity is exactly the same. What has changed is the accounting representation of that economic activity.

EXHIBIT 4.3

Google Inc.: Income Statements

Panel A—From the prospectus issued July 12, 2004

GOOGLE INC.
CONSOLIDATED STATEMENTS OF INCOME
(IN THOUSANDS, EXCEPT PER SHARE AMOUNTS)

	Year Ended December 31		
	2001	**2002**	**2003**
Net revenues	$86,426	**$347,848**	**$961,874**
Costs and expenses:			
Cost of revenues	14,228	**39,850**	**121,794**
Research and development	16,500	31,748	91,228
Sales and marketing	20,076	43,849	120,328
General and administrative	12,275	24,300	56,699
Stock-based compensation (1)	12,383	21,635	229,361
Total costs and expenses	75,462	161,382	619,410
Income from operations	10,964	**186,466**	**342,464**
Interest income (expense) and other, net	(896)	(1,551)	4,190
Income before income taxes	10,068	184,915	346,654
Provision for income taxes	3,083	85,259	241,006
Net income	$ 6,985	**$ 99,656**	**$105,648**

Extract from the notes to the financial statements:

Google AdSense is the program through which the Company distributes its advertisers' text-based ads for display on the Web sites of the Google Network members. The Company recognizes as revenues the fees charged advertisers net of the portion shared with its Google Network members under its AdSense program.

Panel B—From the prospectus issued July 26, 2004

GOOGLE INC.
CONSOLIDATED STATEMENTS OF INCOME
(IN THOUSANDS, EXCEPT PER SHARE AMOUNTS)

	Year Ended December 31		
	2001	**2002**	**2003**
Net revenues	$86,426	**$439,508**	**$1,465,934**
Costs and expenses:			
Cost of revenues	14,228	**131,510**	**625,854**
Research and development	16,500	31,748	91,228
Sales and marketing	20,076	43,849	120,328
General and administrative	12,275	24,300	56,699
Stock-based compensation (1)	12,383	21,635	229,361
Total costs and expenses	75,462	253,042	1,123,470
Income from operations	10,964	**186,466**	**342,464**
Interest income (expense) and other, net	(896)	(1,551)	4,190
Income before income taxes	10,068	184,915	346,654
Provision for income taxes	3,083	85,259	241,006
Net income	$ 6,985	**$ 99,656**	**$ 105,648**

Extract from the notes to the financial statements:

Google AdSense is the program through which the Company distributes its advertisers' text-based ads for display on the Web sites of the Google Network members. In accordance with Emerging Issues Task Force ("EITF") Issue No. 99-19, Reporting Revenue Gross as a Principal Versus Net as an Agent, the Company recognizes as revenues the fees it receives from its advertisers. This revenue is reported gross primarily because the Company is the primary obligor to its advertisers.

Source: Extracted from Google Inc.'s July 12, 2004 and July 26, 2004 prospectuses.

Why Do Managers Have So Much Choice?

LO 3

The discussions of Escuminac Manufacturing Ltd. and Google Inc. might make you wonder why managers are given so much power over reporting the information in financial statements. Can't rules be established to limit choices and effectively capture economic reality? Wouldn't it be easier if there was just one way to recognize revenue? Accounting standard setters and regulators often try to restrict or eliminate the accounting choices available to managers by issuing accounting standards that entities adhering to IFRS or ASPE must observe. However, while eliminating choice may make all financial statements consistent in when they recognize revenue, a consistent critical event may not result in comparable statements. Not all sale transactions are identical and the terms of sale can vary enough that the same critical event wouldn't make sense for every sale. For example, consider a producer who ships goods on consignment to the customer. The customer only pays if it sells the goods, which can be returned to the producer at any time without penalty. In another transaction the producer ships the goods to the customer on a final-sale basis. The goods can't be returned for any reason and must be paid for in full within 30 days. Does it make sense to use the same critical event in both cases? The transactions are different and the financial statements would probably be more informative if different critical events are used.

In theory, allowing choice for recognizing revenue and other accounting issues is sensible because the economic activities of the Canadian and world economies are too complex for precisely defined accounting rules that suit every situation. The challenge with accounting choice is ensuring that the people preparing financial statements provide the information most useful to stakeholders instead of focusing on their own interests. This is an ethical challenge faced by accountants and other financial professionals.

Consider this analogy. When preparing a résumé for a potential employer you would presumably try to highlight your strengths and downplay your weaknesses. You wouldn't add false university degrees or work experience, but you would certainly organize the information and describe your accomplishments in ways that would put you in the best light. Further, if you were applying for several quite different jobs (perhaps in accounting, marketing, and finance), you might even prepare a different résumé for each job, with each one highlighting attributes most appropriate for that job.

Is it dishonest to give different résumés to different prospective employers if the information in each is truthful? Given the many ways a résumé can be written and organized, how would you describe the "right" way to prepare one? Should there be international rules dictating how every résumé should be prepared? In many ways preparing financial statements is the same. Most people have an honest desire to provide useful and relevant information to people using financial statements or résumés. At the same time, anyone preparing either of those documents will want to put him or herself in a good light. Without strict rules about the right way to prepare financial statements or résumés, a lot of power and judgment is given to the preparers. Strict rules reduce the power of and need for judgment by preparers, but it doesn't necessarily result in better, more useful information for users.

The Gradual Approach to Recognizing Revenue

LO 2

The gradual approach recognizes revenue bit by bit over the entire earnings process rather than when a particular critical event occurs. The gradual approach is consistent with the conceptual nature of the revenue-earning process because it reflects earnings as a continuous rather than a one-time event. I mentioned earlier that recording revenue gradually isn't practical in most situations, but there are situations where the gradual method is practical and necessary for providing useful information to stakeholders. In these situations, the gradual approach isn't an *alternative* to the critical event approach; rather, it's the appropriate approach.

We have already considered an example of the gradual approach to revenue recognition. In Chapter 3, we examined how adjusting journal entries are made to accrue interest earned on investments such as bonds and bank accounts. These adjusting entries, called the accrued revenue/accrued asset type, are made so that the income statement will reflect interest earned to date even though cash hasn't been received and isn't owed as of the financial statement date. With this type of revenue, there is no critical event triggering revenue recognition. Instead, the revenue is recognized in the same way it's earned, gradually over time.

The gradual approach is appropriate for delivery of services and long-term construction projects such as dams and large buildings. With a long-term contract, a single project takes place in more than one reporting period. If the critical-event approach is used, revenues and earnings would tend to be more erratic because economic activity occurring in more than one period would be reported at one point in time. Also, since the revenue recognition criteria usually lead to later rather than earlier revenue recognition, the early years of long-term contracts would have no revenue or income and the final year would have it all. As a result, stakeholders would not be receiving timely information about the entity's economic activity.

The Percentage-of-Completion Method A gradual-approach method used for recognizing revenue on service and long-term contracts is known as the **percentage-of-completion method**, which spreads revenues and expenses associated with a contract over the contract's life. This approach reduces the erratic reporting of revenues and earnings and provides useful economic information to stakeholders on a timelier basis.

To use the percentage-of-completion method it's necessary to have a way of determining how much revenue to recognize in each period. One approach is to use the passage of time. This makes sense for service contracts that are provided over time. This approach is used for extended warranties that are purchased for consumer products. These extended warranties provide protection for products beyond what a manufacturer provides. For example, Leon's Furniture Limited offers extended warranties on its appliances and electronics. Customers pay for these warranties when they purchase the merchandise but Leon's recognizes the revenue evenly over the term of the warranty. Exhibit 4.4 provides the liabilities side of Leon's balance sheet and the relevant note

EXHIBIT 4.4 Leon's Furniture Limited: Revenue Recognition—Percentage of Completion[5]

CONSOLIDATED STATEMENTS OF FINANCIAL POSITION

Leon's Furniture Limited/Meubles Leon Ltée Incorporated under the laws of Ontario	**As at December 31**	As at December 31	As at January 1
Liabilities and Shareholders' Equity			
Current			
Trade and other payables (Notes 5 and 11)	**$ 75,126**	$ 71,724	$ 72,603
Provisions (Note 12)	**11,231**	12,341	11,277
Income taxes payable	–	524	1,958
Customers' deposits	**19,157**	17,198	15,632
Dividends payable (Note 14)	**17,457**	6,310	4,938
Deferred warranty plan revenue	**16,152**	16,882	16,150
Total current liabilities	**$139,123**	$124,979	$122,558
Deferred warranty plan revenue	**19,445**	21,392	22,248
Redeemable share liability (Notes 5 and 13)	**382**	172	383
Deferred income tax liabilities (Note 17)	**10,928**	9,845	8,829
Total liabilities	**$169,878**	$156,388	$154,018
Shareholders' equity attributable to the shareholders of the Company			
Common shares (Note 14)	**$ 20,918**	$ 19,177	$ 17,704
Retained earnings	**404,647**	390,629	357,576
Accumulated other comprehensive income (loss)	**(104)**	480	(142)
Total shareholders' equity	**$425,461**	$410,286	$375,138
	$595,339	$566,674	$529,156

Revenue Recognition

Extended Warranty

The Company recognized extended warranty plan revenue on a straight-line basis over the contract period. The service costs associated with warranty obligations are expensed as incurred.

to the financial statements. Notice that Leon's has a current and non-current liability called "Deferred warranty plan revenue." This represents the amount customers have paid Leon's for warranties but for which they haven't yet received the service.

Another common method is to estimate the revenue earned based on the proportion of total costs incurred on the contract. You can do this by using the ratio of the actual costs incurred on the project during the period to the project's total estimated costs. Thus, the revenue recognized in a period is

$$\text{Revenue for the period} = \frac{\text{Cost incurred during the period}}{\text{Total estimated costs for the project}} \times \text{Estimated revenue for the project}$$

Note that it's necessary to estimate total revenues as well as total costs for the project when calculating the revenue that should be recognized in a period. In practice, the percentage-of-completion method is more complicated because the estimated total costs will vary from period to period. You could determine the percentage of completion in other ways; for example, the proportion of the physical work to be done (miles of a highway project completed) or achievement of specified milestones. The percentage-of-completion method is shown schematically in Figure 4.1.

If the Percentage-of-Completion Method Isn't Appropriate To use the percentage-of-completion method, it's necessary to estimate the total costs that will be incurred over the contract, the amount of revenue that will be earned, and the percentage of the project that has been completed on the financial statement date. There also has to be a reasonable expectation of payment. If any of these requirements isn't met, IFRS requires entities to use the **cost-recovery**, or **zero-profit**, method. With this method, revenue in a period is recognized up to the amount of costs incurred during the period (except for the last year of the project). In the final year of the contract, the remaining revenue and expenses and all the profit are reported. In other words, no profit is reported until the final year of the contract (because revenue always equals expenses in the other years).

ACCOUNTING STANDARDS FOR PRIVATE ENTERPRISES

In Canada, when the percentage-of-completion method can't be used, Canadian GAAP for Private Enterprises requires entities to use the **completed-contract method,** which recognizes revenue in full when a contract is completed. No revenue is reported until the contract is complete, and all expenses on the contract are deferred until the revenue is recognized, when they are expensed and matched to the revenue.

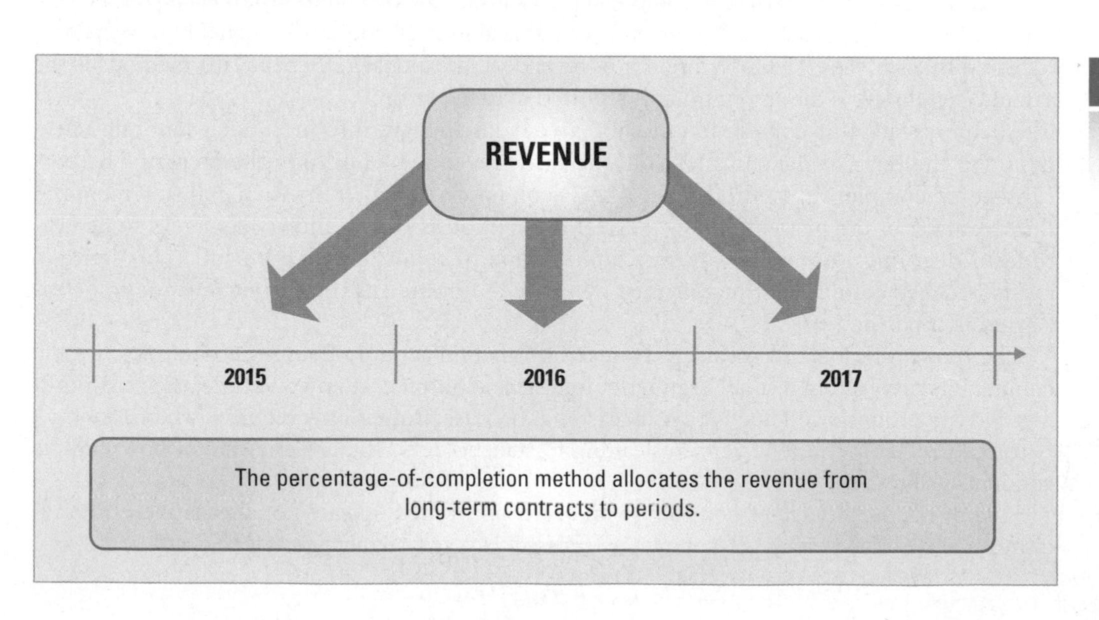

FIGURE 4.1
The Percentage-of-Completion Method

TABLE 4.2 Judique Construction Corporation: Amount of Revenue Recognized Using Percentage-of-Completion Method

	Column A	Column B	Column C	Column D	
Year	Cash payments by Hallam to Judique	Judique's estimated annual cost of building the factory	Percentage of project completed each year based on estimated costs	Amount of revenue recognized each year Calculated as: $\frac{\text{Year's cost}}{\text{Total estimates cost}} \times$ Total revenue	
2017	$ 5,000,000				
2018	$10,000,000	$ 9,000,000	18.75%*	$14,062,500	$\left(\frac{\$9,000,000}{\$48,000,000} \times \$75,000,000\right)$
2019	$10,000,000	$18,000,000	37.50%*	$28,125,000	$\left(\frac{\$18,000,000}{\$48,000,000} \times \$75,000,000\right)$
2020	$10,000,000	$21,000,000	43.75%*	$32,812,500	$\left(\frac{\$21,000,000}{\$48,000,000} \times \$75,000,000\right)$
2021	$40,000,000				
Total	$75,000,000	$48,000,000	100%	$75,000,000	

*The percentage of the project completed each year = $\frac{\text{Year's cost (Column B)}}{\text{Total estimate cost (total of Column B)}}$

Example of the Percentage-of-Completion and Zero-Profit Methods Let's look at an example comparing the percentage-of-completion and zero-profit methods. On December 15, 2017, Judique Construction Corporation (Judique) entered into a three-year contract to build a factory for Hallam Corp. (Hallam). Hallam agreed to pay $75,000,000 for the factory, from which Judique would pay all construction costs. Hallam paid $5,000,000 when it signed the contract and agreed to pay $10,000,000 on July 2 of each of the next three years. The final $40,000,000 is to be paid six months after the factory is completed. The expected completion date is August 1, 2020. Table 4.2 shows Judique's estimated annual costs and the amount of revenue that would be recognized each year using the percentage-of-completion method. Judique's year-end is December 31. It's important to recognize that cash flows and revenue and expense flows don't have to correspond. Revenue is recognized based on the proportion of the job that has been completed, not when payment is received.

Table 4.3 shows summarized income statements under the two methods for each year. For the zero-profit method, the amount of revenue recognized in 2018 and 2019 is equal to the expenses incurred in each year. The total amount of revenue and expense under the two methods is the same. What differs is the amount that is reported in each period.

The percentage-of-completion method gives some insight into Judique's economic activity. Over the term of the contract, Judique earns revenue by building the factory. The percentage-of-completion method reflects this economic activity in the financial statements. A disadvantage of the percentage-of-completion method is that it allows managers some latitude in deciding how much revenue and income to report in each period. This latitude exists because complex estimates must be made to obtain the amount of revenue to be reported in a period.

The zero-profit method doesn't give much information about Judique's economic activity. If a company is involved in a small number of long-term contracts at any one time, the zero-profit method can produce wild fluctuations in earnings because profit is only reported when a contract is completed. This could be very misleading to stakeholders who are unaware of how Judique conducts its business.

Finally, the percentage-of-completion and zero-profit methods are not alternatives. IFRS requires the use of percentage-of-completion unless it isn't reasonably possible to do so.

TABLE 4.3 Judique Construction Corporation: Percentage-of-Completion versus Zero-Profit Methods for Accounting for Long-Term Contracts

Judique Construction Corporation Income Statements (thousands of dollars)										
	Percentage-of-Completion Method					Zero-Profit Method				
	2017	2018	2019	2020	Total	2017	2018	2019	2020	Total
Income Statements										
Revenue	$0	$ 14,062.5	$28,125.0	$32,812.0	$75,000.0	$0	$9,000.0	$18,000.0	$48,000.0	$75,000.0
Expenses	0	9,000.0	18,000.0	21,000.0	48,000.0	0	9,000.0	18,000.0	21,000.0	48,000.0
Net income	$0	$ 5,062.5	$10,125.0	$11,812.5	$27,000.0	$0	$ 0	$ 0	$27,000.0	$27,000.0

INSIGHT

Percentage-of-Completion versus Completed-Contract Methods for Tax Purposes

In Canada, the *Income Tax Act* allows companies to use the completed-contract method for tax purposes on contracts of less than 24 months, otherwise the percentage-of-completion method must be used. There is a tax advantage of using the completed-contract method because it delays payment of taxes until a contract is completed. The following example shows the tax benefit of the completed-contract method.

In 2017, Joynt Corp. (Joynt) signs a contract to renovate an office building. The work will be completed over three fiscal years beginning in July 2017 and finishing in May 2019. Joynt estimates that half the work will be done in 2018 and a quarter in each of 2017 and 2019. Joynt will be paid $900,000 for the job and will incur expenses of $360,000. Joynt's year-end is December 31 and it has a tax rate of 20 percent. Summarized income statements are shown in Table 4.4. If Joynt uses the percentage-of-completion method, it will report income in each of the three years and will have to pay taxes of $27,000 in 2017 and 2019 and $54,000 in 2018. If it uses the completed-contract method, it pays no tax in 2017 and 2018 because it doesn't report any income in those years, but it will pay $108,000 in taxes in 2019. Joynt pays the same amount of tax over the three years but it defers $81,000 of taxes until 2019 without any penalty by using the completed-contract method. This frees up a significant amount of cash for other purposes.

TABLE 4.4 Tax Benefits of Using the Completed-Contract Method

Joynt Corp. Income Statements						
	Percentage-of-Completion Method			Completed-Contract Method		
	Years Ended			Years Ended		
	2017	2018	2019	2017	2018	2019
Revenue	$225,000	$450,000	$225,000	$0	$0	$900,000
Expenses	90,000	180,000	90,000	0	0	360,000
Taxes	27,000	54,000	27,000	0	0	108,000
Net income	$108,000	$216,000	$108,000	$0	$0	$432,000

connect

KNOWLEDGE CHECK 4.2

- ❑ What is the gradual approach to recognizing revenue?
- ❑ How do you determine the percentage of a project that has been completed?
- ❑ Under what circumstances is the zero-profit method used?
- ❑ Plato Inc. (Plato) recently entered into a three-year contract to build a small office building for a growing law firm. The law firm will pay Plato $7,000,000 for the building. Plato is required to pay all costs. Plato estimates its total cost of construction will be $5,200,000 with costs of $1,700,000 in the first year, $2,500,000 in the second year, and $1,000,000 in the third year. Assuming that Plato's cost estimates are correct, how much revenue will it recognize in each year of the contract using (1) the percentage-of-completion method and (2) the zero-profit method?

LO 4

MULTIPLE DEVLIVERABLE ARRANGEMENTS

Sometimes when a person or company buys something they get several things. Consider:

- Buy a new car and you get a warranty.
- Sign up for a three-year wireless package and get a free phone.
- Purchase some new software and get technical support for a year and a free upgrade.

In each case, the customer is getting more than one thing, or more than one deliverable, and in principal the amount of revenue should be split among each of the components purchased. For example, consider the purchase of software. When a software package is sold for $100 the producer could record the following journal entry:

Dr. Accounts receivable	$100	
Cr. Revenue		$75
Cr. Unearned revenue		$25

The unearned revenue would then be recognized over the period that it's earned. The revenue from the technical support would be recognized over the period that the support is available to the customer. Accounting for multiple deliverables is conceptually straightforward but can be challenging. To be able to break revenue into separate components, it's necessary to determine an appropriate value for each. In many cases, a fair value for all the components isn't available. For example, our software producer might not know what the market value of the technical support is since it's not sold independent of the software.

If the fair values can be determined, they form the basis of determining the amount of revenue to recognize for each component. So in the case of the software, if the manufacturer determines that the fair value of the software is $90, the support $20, and the upgrades $10 (notice that the bundle costs less than the fair value of the individual components), the selling price of $100 is allocated on a proportional basis:

Revenue from sale of software = $100 × $90 ÷ $120 = $75

Revenue from sale of support = $100 × $20 ÷ $120 = $16.67

Revenue from sale of upgrades = $100 × $10 ÷ $120 = $8.33

If it's not possible to come up with reasonable measures of the fair values of the separate deliverables, then the revenue is recognized on the bundle as a whole and a critical event must be determined for the entire package.

EXPENSE RECOGNITION

LO 5

In accrual accounting, a key concept for determining income is matching. According to the matching concept, expenses are reported on the income statement in the same period as the revenue those expenses helped earn. The order is important: *expenses* are matched to *revenues*. First, revenue is recognized and then the costs incurred to earn that revenue are expensed. This process is generally the reverse of actual economic activity. Usually, an entity first incurs the costs that will help generate revenues and then earns the revenue.

Matching makes sense, at least for some uses and users of accounting information. If the purpose of an income statement is to provide information about the economic activity (as opposed to cash flow) and performance of an entity, it makes sense to associate economic costs and benefits. If an entity sells a cell phone and the managers want to know how much better off it is because of the sale, it makes sense to subtract the cost of the phone, along with any other costs of selling it, from the revenue earned. Accrual accounting requires all costs to be matched to the revenue—regardless of whether cash was paid before, at the same time as, or after the revenue is recognized.

In a perfect accrual accounting world, all costs would be matched to the related revenues. Practically speaking, it can't be done—many costs are difficult to match. Consider the costs a clothing store incurs to sell a pair of pants. The cost of the pants and the salesperson's commission are easy to match to the revenue from the sale. It's more difficult to match salespeople's hourly wages, rent and utilities for the store, advertising, furniture and fixtures in the store, and the manager's salary. These are necessary costs of running the business, but what's their connection to the revenue from the sale of a single pair of pants? The fact is it's difficult to make a connection and therefore to match these costs to specific revenues.

When it's difficult or impossible to reasonably match costs to specific revenues, accountants don't try to force a match. Instead, these costs are expensed in the period they are incurred. Employees' wages, rent, utilities, and advertising are expensed when the employees do their work, when the space and utilities are used, and when the advertising is done. Costs expensed in the period they are incurred are called **period costs**. Costs that can be matched to specific revenues are called **product costs** and are expensed when the revenue they help generate is recognized. Product costs are usually accumulated in inventory on the balance sheet (or in some other balance sheet account) until the revenue is recognized. Some costs, like depreciation, are matched to revenue but usually no one is really sure what the relationship is between the amount expensed and the revenue earned. Note that the distinction between product costs and period costs isn't always clear, so certain types of cost won't always be treated the same way by different entities.

Costs that have not yet been incurred must be estimated so they can be matched to revenues. For example, bad debts, returns, and warranty costs are usually incurred after revenue is recognized. Let's look at these situations in more detail:

- The bad-debt expense is an estimate of the amount owed by customers that won't be collected. Under accrual accounting, bad debts are a cost of selling on credit and should be expensed in the period the related sale is made.
- When merchandise is returned, it represents revenue that never happened. As a result, an estimate of returns should be accrued in the period the related revenue is recognized.
- Warranty costs should be accrued when the revenue from the product or service under warranty is recognized.

The difficult part of accounting for these costs is estimating how much they will be. Managers rely on historical information and their knowledge of the business and products to come up with estimates.

There is an important caveat about matching under IFRS. While matching is a fundamental accrual accounting concept, it's secondary to the definition of an asset. When we match expenses to revenues we're asking the question: "Is this an expense that helped earn revenue in the current period?" Implied in this question is, if there isn't an expense, then there has to be an asset. For example, suppose a company spends $100 in a period; if the amount isn't an expense, it has to be an asset (the debit has to be to expense or assets, there's no other alternative). IFRS requires that an expenditure can only be capitalized as an asset if it meets the definition of an asset (that is, that the asset criteria from Chapter 2 are satisfied). So, if the company spends $100 that didn't help it earn revenue in the period and doesn't meet the definition of an asset, the expenditure must be an expense.

Finally, with all this talk about matching it's important to remember that not all stakeholders or uses of accounting information benefit from matching. For example, recognizing expenses as early as possible, regardless of matching, reduces the amount of income tax an entity has to pay. Lenders might be more interested in cash flow information for assessing the liquidity of the entity, again regardless of matching. Always keep in mind that the usefulness of information to stakeholders has to be assessed. As a result, it shouldn't be said that a well-matched set of financial statements is the best way to present accounting information to all stakeholders or in all situations.

INSIGHT

Important Accounting Concepts—Recognition

Throughout this chapter we have discussed the term "recognition" in the context of revenues and expenses. **Recognition** has a more general meaning in accounting: it refers to when any financial statement element—asset, liability, equity, expense, or revenue—is recorded. There are three conditions that must be met for an element to be recognized:

- The item under consideration meets the definition of an element—in other words, it meets the definition of an asset, liability, equity, revenue, or expense, whatever the case may be.
- It's probable that the economic cost or benefit associated with the element will occur. This means, for example, that an entity will probably enjoy the benefit associated with an asset.
- The element can be measured.

LO 6

GAINS AND LOSSES

A gain or loss arises when an entity sells an asset that's not sold in the ordinary course of business for an amount that's different from its carrying amount. For example, if an airline sells old aircraft or a bookstore sells furniture and fixtures or old computers, a gain or a loss could arise.

Let's consider some possibilities for a company that owns land with a carrying amount of $500,000:

1. If the land was sold for $600,000, a gain of $100,000 would be reported on the income statement (selling price − carrying amount = $600,000 − $500,000 = $100,000).
2. If the land was sold for $425,000, a loss of $75,000 would be reported (selling price − carrying amount = $425,000 − $500,000 = − $75,000). The journal entries to record the gain and loss would be

1. Dr. Cash	600,000	
Cr. Gain on sale of land (income statement)		100,000
Cr. Land		500,000
To record the gain on the sale of land		
2. Dr. Cash	425,000	
Dr. Loss on sale of land (income statement)	75,000	
Cr. Land		500,000
To record the loss on the sale of land		

In both cases, the land account is credited for $500,000, its carrying amount. The difference between the amount received and the cost of the land is the gain or loss. I have limited the examples here to the sale of land—an asset that isn't depreciated. Gains and losses also arise when assets that are depreciated are sold; we'll examine these in Chapter 8. In the meantime, consider the following points about gains and losses:

1. The sale of incidental assets giving rise to gains and losses are presented differently in the income statement than the sale of inventory. When the sale of an incidental asset occurs, the proceeds from the sale and the cost of the asset sold are shown net—only the gain or loss is shown. When inventory is sold, the revenue and cost of the inventory are shown separately (revenue − cost of sales).
2. It's important for gains and losses to be reported separately from revenues and expenses. Because gains and losses arise from the sale of assets that aren't the entity's main business, including them in revenues and expenses can be confusing and misleading to stakeholders. For example, a gain included in revenue will make revenues from the entity's main business activities greater than they really are, making it more difficult to predict future revenues or evaluate performance.
3. The amount of a gain or loss is affected by the accounting choices that affect the asset. Different accounting choices result in different carrying amounts and different gains and losses.
4. Proceeds from the sale of assets shouldn't be affected by the carrying amount. The amount a buyer pays for an asset is based on its economic value to the buyer, not its carrying amount on the seller's books. Sellers may be affected by the accounting effect of a potential sale because they may be concerned about the impact of the gain or loss on net income.

Exhibit 4.5 provides an example of how gains and losses are reported on the income statement. In its 2011 annual report, Supremex Inc. reported losses of $400,165 in 2011 and $340,169 in 2010 from the disposal of property, plant, and equipment. Notice how the losses are shown separately (gains would be shown the same way). The exact presentation of gains and losses can vary from entity to entity but they should always be presented separately.

EXHIBIT 4.5 Supremex Inc.: Gains and Losses[6]

www.supremex.com

Supremex Inc.

CONSOLIDATED STATEMENTS OF EARNINGS

Years ended December 31	Notes	2011 $	2010 $
Revenue		**143,892,199**	153,124,398
Operating expenses	7, 20	**96,209,379**	102,935,634
Selling, general and administrative expenses	20	**18,144,751**	17,000,754
Operating earnings before amortization, write-down, loss on disposal of property, plant and equipment, acquisition costs and restructuring expenses		**29,538,069**	33,188,010
Amortization and write-down of property, plant and equipment	8,9	**4,397,561**	6,661,624
Amortization of intangible assets	10	**6,163,900**	6,163,900
Amortization of deferred compensation		–	315,079
Loss on disposal of property, plant and equipment		**400,165**	340,169
Acquisition costs	5	–	152,070
Restructuring expenses	13	**1,089,401**	2,054,519
Operating earnings		**17,487,042**	17,500,649
Financing charges	15	**5,974,751**	4,720,981
Earnings before income taxes		**11,512,291**	12,779,668
Income tax expense	16	**3,197,417**	2,961,850
Net earnings		**8,314,874**	9,817,818

LO 7 THE OBJECTIVES OF FINANCIAL REPORTING

Providing relevant information to stakeholders is why financial accounting exists. There can be different reasonable accounting treatments for many transactions and economic events, even under IFRS. The discussion of revenue recognition in this chapter highlights this idea. But how do managers decide which accounting methods to choose? Managers' choices are influenced by two factors: the information needs of stakeholders and their own self-interests, two factors that often conflict. The accounting choice that provides the "best" information to stakeholders (or at least to particular stakeholders) won't always be the one that best satisfies the managers' interests, which include maximizing their compensation, job security, increasing share price or the apparent value of the business, and so on.

Ideally, self-interest should not play a role in the accounting choices a manager makes, but given human nature, self-interest can be a factor. In fact, there is considerable evidence that managers' accounting choices are influenced by self-interest (look at all the accounting scandals, for example). Given this reality, awareness of managers' motivation and ability to craft accounting information to serve their own interests and the economic consequences this behaviour can have on stakeholders is essential to any accounting education. Factors affecting accounting choice are shown in Figure 4.2. This figure builds on the accounting environment that was developed in Figure 1.2, and integrates managers' motivations, the constraints they face, and the objectives of financial reporting to show the financial statement effects of managers' motivations.

Manager self-interest is an important element in accounting choice, but even without this motivation, managers still have choices to make. There are many different stakeholders, each with different information needs, and an entity can prepare only one set of general purpose financial statements so some stakeholders might not be completely satisfied. (An entity can produce any number of special purpose reports but these are prepared only for powerful stakeholders who can demand information tailored to their needs.)

Let's consider an example of how the purpose of a set of financial statements can affect accounting choices. Ellin Bamboo owns and operates a small business, and its financial statements are prepared primarily for tax purposes. If choosing one accounting treatment over another reduces the amount of tax the company has to pay, it makes sense to use the tax-lowering treatment. This isn't illegal, dishonest, or unethical. If the Canada Revenue Agency allows you to choose among alternatives, choosing the ones that work best for you makes sense. For example, if Ms. Bamboo can use the completed-contract method of revenue recognition for her business's long-term contracts, she should.

If Ms. Bamboo decides to sell her business, prospective buyers would want to examine the financial statements as part of their assessment of the business. Would the financial statements prepared for tax purposes be appropriate for this? No, because the financial statements prepared using the completed-contract method could misstate the economic activity of the business. The completed-contract method delays recognition of activity until a contract is completed, and that may understate the company's revenue and income. These financial statements may not fairly and reasonably reflect Ms. Bamboo's business even though they are perfectly acceptable for tax purposes. If they were used to set the price for Ms. Bamboo's business, it's possible that Ms. Bamboo wouldn't receive a fair price for the business.

This example demonstrates that one set of financial statements may not satisfy all financial reporting objectives. Because an entity can prepare only one set of general purpose financial statements, some stakeholders may have to be satisfied with statements that haven't been tailored to their specific needs. A manager's accounting choices will affect the usefulness of the financial statements to those stakeholders and may have economic consequences for them. Figure 4.2 lists some of the objectives of financial reporting that an entity can have. We'll look at these in detail next.

KNOWLEDGE CHECK 4.3

- ❑ Identify and explain the two factors that influence managers' accounting choices. Why do these two factors often conflict?
- ❑ What are some factors limiting the choices that managers can make?

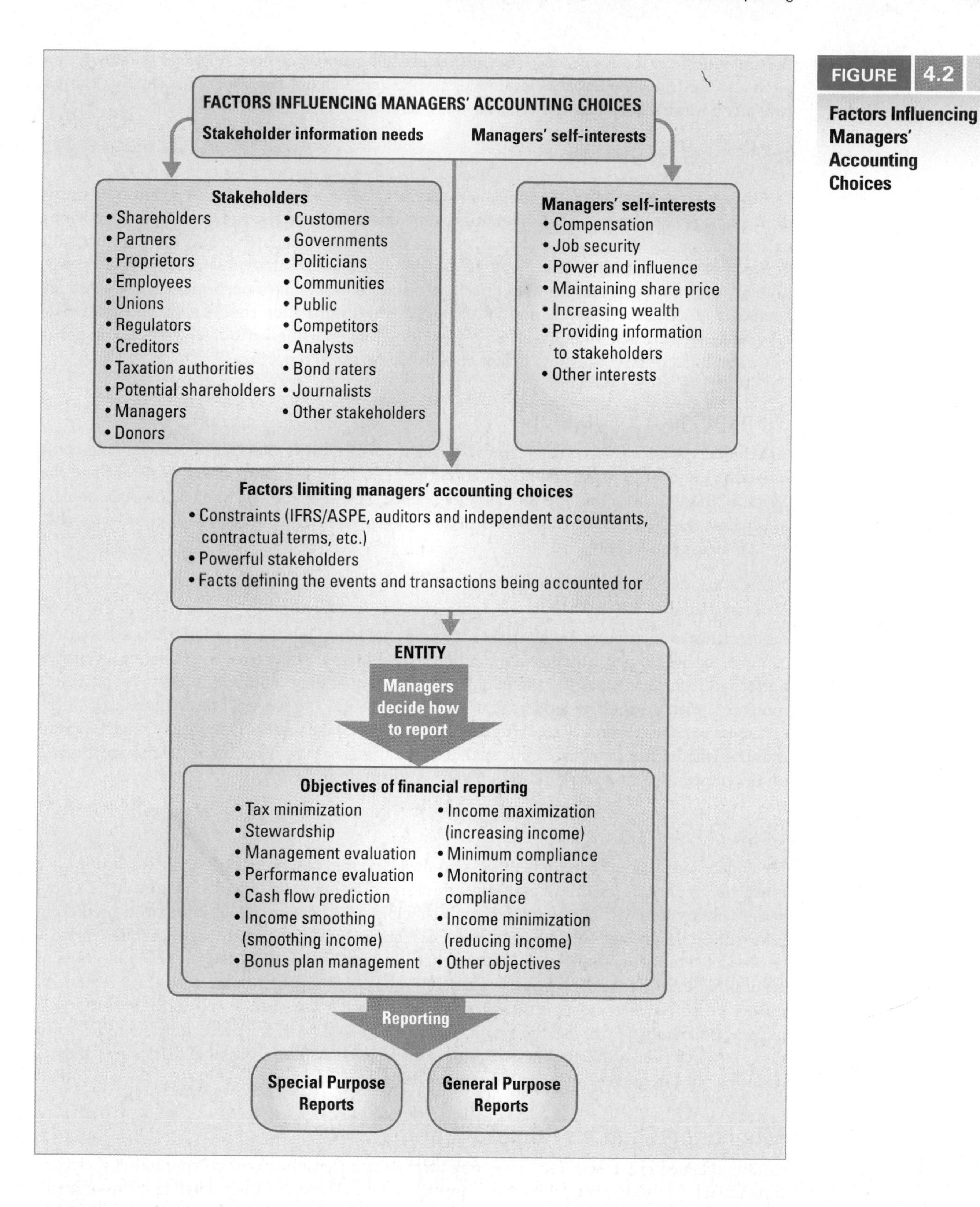

FIGURE 4.2 Factors Influencing Managers' Accounting Choices

Tax Minimization

Accounting information is used to determine the tax an entity pays and a business's general purpose financial statements must be filed with its tax return. (In the case of partnerships or proprietorships, the general purpose financial statements must be filed along with the tax returns of the partners or proprietor.) *Tax minimization* means a taxpayer works within the tax laws to defer taxes or pay as little as possible. Pursuing this objective makes good economic sense because it keeps cash in the hands of the entity for as long as possible. An entity's accounting choices affect the amount of tax it pays because the policies used in general purpose financial statements are often also used for tax purposes. Because tax savings are often not permanent but simply deferred to a later period, this objective is also called tax deferral.

Stewardship

Stewardship is responsibility for someone else's resources. For example, when an entity's owners don't manage it, managers act as stewards of the owners' resources. Stewardship relationships exist for all public companies and many private ones, between charities and their donors, and between governments and citizens. A stewardship objective is satisfied when reports to stakeholders inform them about how resources entrusted to others have been managed—have they been used efficiently, effectively, and satisfactorily? This information should allow the stakeholders to understand easily what has taken place during the reporting period. Stewardship is specifically identified in IFRS as an important objective of financial reporting.

Management Evaluation

Stakeholders often want to evaluate the performance of an entity's managers. Financial statements satisfying this objective provide information that reflects both the managers' decisions and the effects of those decisions on the entity's performance. The information should allow stakeholders to separate the effects of management's decisions from the effects of luck and other factors beyond management's control.

Performance Evaluation

Performance evaluation is similar to management evaluation but with a broader scope because it captures the overall performance of the entity. Stakeholders are interested in evaluating an entity's performance for many reasons: shareholders assess whether they should continue to invest, invest more, or divest; prospective lenders assess whether an entity is a worthwhile credit risk; or workers assess whether the entity can afford wage increases. Stakeholders of a charity might want to evaluate whether the organization is spending an appropriate proportion of the money it raises on the cause, rather than on fundraising and administration.

Cash Flow Prediction

Many decisions that stakeholders make are future oriented and an entity's future cash flows are especially important for this. Knowledge of future cash flows can help a lender evaluate a borrower's ability to pay back the interest and principal on a loan, assist an investor in predicting future dividends, or help a prospective buyer of a business evaluate whether the purchase price is reasonable. Predicting future cash flows is explicitly identified in IFRS as one of the objectives of accounting information. However, information presented in accordance with IFRS in general purpose financial statements is historical—it reflects what *has already happened*, not what *will happen*. Stakeholders can use the financial statements as a basis for predicting the future cash flows but they need additional information to do so, such as future-oriented disclosures and accounting policies that correlate with future cash flows.

Monitoring Contract Compliance

Entities often enter into contracts requiring them to meet certain terms and conditions, including ones intended to limit the actions management can take. These are often stated in terms of financial statement numbers. For example, a lending agreement may require a borrower to maintain its current ratio above, or its debt-to-equity ratio below, a specified amount. Failure to meet these requirements could mean repaying or renegotiating the loan. Contracts include covenants restricting the behaviour of an entity so that, for example, a lender isn't exposed to unforeseen risks when making a loan, such as the entity taking on additional debt. When contract terms and conditions are based on financial statement numbers, the financial statements serve as tools for monitoring entity compliance with the terms of the contract.

Earnings Management

The objectives listed to this point look at things from the perspective of the stakeholders' information needs. In a perfect accounting world, those needs would be met. However, managers might not want to fully cooperate with the needs of stakeholders. Instead, they might want stakeholders to evaluate performance favourably or make rosy predictions of future cash flows. This is where earnings management comes in; managers can use the flexibility in accounting to try to influence the decisions of stakeholders or affect the economic consequences to different stakeholders.

Earnings management was introduced in Chapter 3, where I explained that managers, if given choices among *acceptable* alternative ways of accounting, will likely choose the ways that satisfy their own interests. This discussion of earnings management doesn't include fraud—just legitimate ways managers can use the available accounting choices to their advantage. Also remember that the term "earnings management" applies to accounting choices by managers to affect *any* financial statement numbers with the intent of satisfying their self-interests.

As you proceed through this section, remember that managing earnings through accounting choices has no impact on the underlying economic activity of the entity. Production, sales, expenditures, and collections are all assumed to be unaffected by the accounting methods used. However, different accounting choices may have economic consequences for stakeholders (different choices may affect the distribution of wealth among stakeholders by affecting, for example, the amount of tax the entity pays, the bonuses managers receive, or the price the entity is sold for). In addition, it's also possible to manage earnings by timing transactions, which may have an impact on economic activity as well as have economic consequences.

Now we will look at some of the reasons why managers manage their accounting information.

Managing Earnings to Reduce Income It may come as a surprise but there are situations in which managers want to report lower earnings and make the entity not look so good. Companies in politically sensitive businesses may find themselves under pressure from politicians and citizens if they make "too much money." Managers can ease this pressure by making accounting choices that reduce what might otherwise be seen as excessive profits. Reducing income might also be a good strategy when an entity is looking for government support or subsidies. Lower reported earnings could also influence the outcome of labour negotiations by convincing workers and unions to accept lower wage settlements. Tax minimization is also a motivation for reducing income.

On an ongoing basis, income can be reduced by recognizing revenue late in the earnings cycle and recognizing expenses early. Managers can significantly lower earnings in a particular period by taking a **big bath**, which is expensing a significant amount of assets in the current period that normally would have been depreciated or otherwise expensed in future periods. The benefit of a big bath is that while net income is lowered in the current period, it will be higher in future periods. Income will be higher in the years after a big bath because there are fewer expenses as they were recorded in the big-bath year. Big baths are sometimes seen when a company replaces its management. The new management blames poor current performance on the previous management, takes a big bath, and then takes the credit when earnings subsequently improve (even though the improvement is due, in part at least, to the bath).

Even not-for-profit organizations can benefit from this strategy. Although they don't operate to make a profit and, therefore, don't report earnings, they do report surpluses or deficits that reflect the amount by which their "revenues" are greater than or less than their "expenses." If the revenues of a not-for-profit organization exceed its expenses by a large amount, contributors might doubt the organization's need and make their donations elsewhere.

Managing Earnings to Increase Income At the other end of the spectrum are managers who make accounting choices that increase reported income. Situations in which managers might want to report higher earnings include the following:

- Influencing the stock price of publicly traded companies. There is a well-established relationship between earnings and stock prices, and managers might believe reporting higher earnings will have a positive effect on stock price.

- Making accounting choices to increase the income of a private company before it's sold to increase the selling price. Accounting information is crucial for determining the selling price and managing earnings may increase the amount of money sellers receive.
- Managing accounting information to increase the likelihood of receiving a loan. Improved financial ratios may influence the risk assessment of the entity by lenders.
- Influencing stakeholders' perceptions about how well the entity and its managers are performing.
- Making accounting choices to increase their bonuses.
- Avoiding violating the terms of debt or other kinds of contractual agreements.

Managing Earnings to Smooth Income Earnings that fluctuate from period to period can indicate risk, and many managers prefer to avoid having stakeholders believe that their companies are risky investments. Research shows that the stock prices of public companies benefit from having smooth earnings. To reduce the perception of risk managers might take steps to smooth earnings over time.

It's important to understand that managers may be undermining the objectives of stakeholders by managing earnings. By their accounting choices managers might make an entity look less risky and, as a result a prospective lender might overestimate future cash flows, underestimate risk, and thereby make a loan that it might not have made otherwise. Thus, by managing earnings, managers undermine the cash flow prediction objective of the prospective lender but help themselves achieve their objective of obtaining new financing.

Managing earnings is complex. Stakeholders have to be aware that managers have the ability to manage earnings and keep in mind the impact that different choices can have on financial statements.

Minimum Compliance

Managers sometimes provide only the minimum amount of information necessary to comply with reporting requirements. Minimum reporting requirements are defined in various pieces of federal and provincial legislation. All corporations are subject to the requirements of the *Canada Business Corporations Act* or the equivalent provincial corporations act. Public companies must also meet the requirements of the relevant provincial securities act and of any stock exchange the company's securities trade on. Relevant accounting standards also apply.

Some public companies will pursue minimum compliance if they are concerned about competitors getting information or if they aren't concerned about any negative stock market reactions to supplying limited information. Private companies may prepare minimum compliance statements if the shareholders are active in the entity and, therefore, have other sources of information or if there are special purpose reports for other stakeholders. By providing as little information as they are allowed, managers make it difficult for stakeholders to effectively evaluate an entity and make good decisions.

Is Accounting Information Relevant, Reliable, and Useful?

After reading this discussion of the different objectives of financial reporting, especially earnings management, you might conclude that accounting information can't be relied on or used for decision making. This isn't true. Accounting information is an absolutely essential source of information for most decisions regarding an entity and it would be a mistake to ignore it. The message you should take is that accounting information must be analyzed and interpreted carefully before decisions are made. Understanding the nature of accounting information and the motivations of managers will help make you a more sophisticated user whose decisions are less likely to be affected by managers' accounting choices.

It's also important to recognize that accounting isn't different from other business disciplines or, for that matter, any other form of communication. Take advertising for example. When a company advertises a product it tries to make it attractive and desirable to consumers. Advertisers highlight the positive aspects and minimize or even ignore the negative ones. Sometimes advertising is considered misleading but most of the time it isn't. It's the responsibility of consumers to do their research to assure themselves they are getting what they bargained for. Accounting is no different.

INSIGHT

Can You Tell What Managers' Motivations Are?

A lot has been made of the importance of managers' motivations and objectives for understanding their financial reporting. To understand how an entity approached its financial reporting it's necessary to know the objectives of the managers. Unfortunately, managers aren't likely to be forthcoming about what their objectives of financial reporting are. They will support their accounting choices by referencing relevant accounting rules and the economic facts surrounding the transaction. It may be possible to infer what manager's objectives are, but you can never tell for sure.

Reporting Impact

The objective of financial reporting chosen by an entity's managers can have a significant impact on the financial statements. The table below gives an indication of how managers with particular objectives in mind would approach the preparation of financial statements. The table isn't comprehensive but gives an idea of how different objectives might affect financial reporting.

Objective	Reporting Approach
Tax minimization	Recognize revenue as late as possible and recognize expenses as early as possible while complying with *Income Tax Act.*
Cash flow prediction	Choose accounting policies that correlate current earnings with future cash flows and provide extensive disclosure of information about future cash flows. Provide forecasts (not part of IFRS).
Minimum compliance	Provide the minimum amount of information in the financial statements and notes required by any constraints.
Performance evaluation	Associate economic costs and economic benefits. Separate items that are unusual, less likely to occur in future, and not the result of managerial decisions.
Stewardship	Provide historical, reliable information that will allow stakeholders to see how managers have managed entity resources over the reporting period.

QUESTION FOR CONSIDERATION

Which objective of financial reporting is most important?

ANSWER: There is no "most important" objective of financial reporting. This question must be assessed in the context of each individual entity. For a small private company with few external stakeholders demanding information, income tax minimization is probably the most important objective. For a company urgently requiring a loan the most important objective is providing information that increases the likelihood of obtaining the loan—perhaps by reporting higher net income or providing detailed cash flow forecasts. For senior managers with a net income-based bonus plan the most important objective might be receiving a large bonus. From a stakeholder's perspective the most important objective is the one that satisfies that stakeholder's information needs.

LO 6 CAN MANAGERS DO WHATEVER THEY WANT?

One could get the impression from our discussion that managers are completely unconstrained when they prepare their financial statements and that they can do whatever they want to accomplish their accounting objectives. This isn't true. There are, in fact, forces that limit managers' accounting choices:

- accounting standards (IFRS, ASPE)
- laws (tax, securities, corporations laws)
- independent accountants and auditors who act on behalf of stakeholders to assess the accounting choices made by the managers
- contract terms
- the information demands of powerful stakeholders who may dictate accounting treatments and disclosures
- facts surrounding the economic event or transaction being accounted for

Note that not every constraint applies to every entity. For example, not all entities must follow IFRS or have contractual constraints. Only public companies have to adhere to securities laws and only corporations have to follow the corporations act.

Even companies not constrained by IFRS aren't really free to do whatever they want. Remember that accounting is a means of communication. If the people receiving the accounting information can't understand it, then it serves no purpose. Imagine receiving a set of financial statements prepared in a language you didn't understand!

Sometimes powerful stakeholders can make reporting demands on an entity. If an entity needs a loan a banker can demand special reports that meet the specific information needs of the bank. The entity isn't required to meet the demands of the bank, but the bank isn't required to lend money. Another example of a powerful stakeholder is a corporation's shareholder who owns a large proportion of the shares and, thus, may be able to demand special purpose reports that provide information not available in the general purpose report. A shareholder who controls the majority of the shares may be able to establish the objectives of the corporation and the accounting policies it uses. In contrast, a small shareholder in a public company wouldn't be able to obtain information beyond what was in the general purpose financial statements.

The economic circumstances of transactions can also limit the choices managers have. Consider a vendor selling hot dogs for cash from a mobile cart on the street. No matter what the vendor's reporting objectives are, it's hard to imagine recognizing revenue at a time other than when a hot dog is exchanged for cash. On the other hand, in the case of Escuminac Manufacturing Ltd. there were two viable alternatives for recognizing revenue presented and other alternatives could be identified, especially if IFRS weren't a constraint. An entity not constrained by IFRS may have more accounting alternatives to choose from, but there still has to be a link between the economic circumstances and the choice made.

While constraints may reduce or eliminate choice in some circumstances it's rarely possible to limit completely by law or by contract all or even most of the accounting choices managers have. The economy is far too complex and dynamic to have rules for every possible situation.

LO 8 SOLVING ACCOUNTING CHOICE PROBLEMS

So far this chapter has examined two important accounting topics: revenue and expense recognition and the objectives of financial reporting. In this section these two topics are linked in a problem-solving technique designed to help you understand how managers make accounting choices and how stakeholders can both use and be limited by the information provided to them by entities.

Constraints, Facts, and Objectives

Before looking at the problem-solving approach, let's examine the factors that guide the accounting choices made by entities and that will form the central analytical tool for making these choices. The accounting choices made by managers are affected by three factors:

1. the *constraints* that formally limit the choices available to managers
2. the *facts* surrounding the transaction or economic event being accounted for
3. the *objectives* of financial reporting

The constraints, facts, and objectives that impact accounting choices are shown schematically in Figure 4.3.

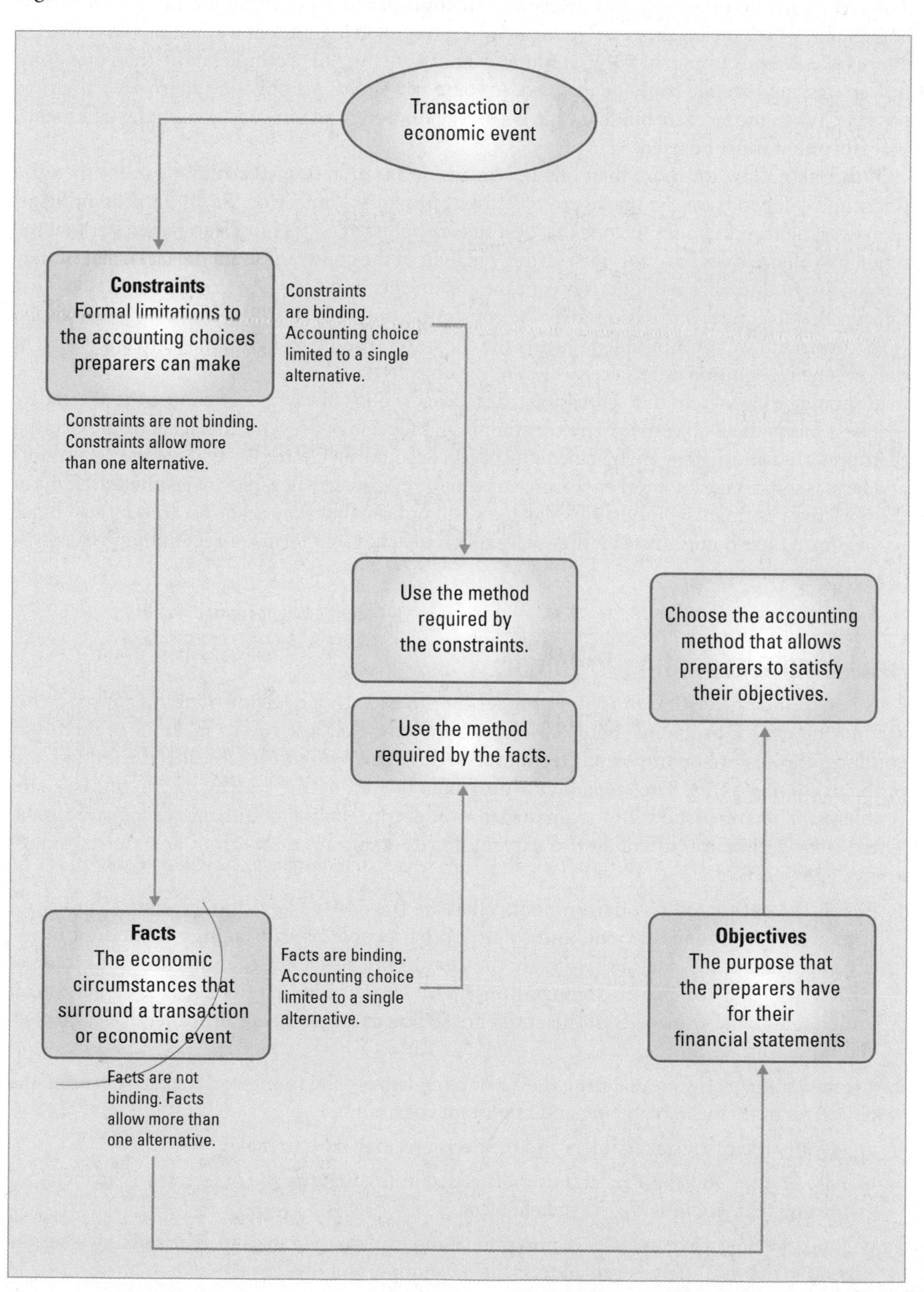

FIGURE 4.3 **The Impact of Constraints, Facts, and Objectives on Accounting Choices**

Constraints are specific external limitations on the accounting choices managers can make. They include legal requirements, IFRS, ASPE, or the terms of contracts. Constraints can eliminate choice by requiring that a particular economic event or transaction be treated in only one way, or they can limit choice by reducing the set of alternatives; for example, IFRS limit the choices available for recognizing revenue. If the constraints limit or eliminate choice there is little purpose in considering alternatives that violate the constraints because they can't be used. If the constraints require a specific method then that method must be used—no further evaluation is necessary. If there are no constraints, or if the constraints allow more than one alternative, then the facts can be examined.

The *facts* are the economic circumstances surrounding a transaction or economic event. The facts must be interpreted to determine an appropriate accounting method. They can be ambiguous, which means they can legitimately be interpreted in different ways to support different alternatives. For example, in the Escuminac Manufacturing Ltd. example, more than one point for recognizing revenue could be justified. In some fact situations only one alternative might be possible. When the facts are binding (that is, they support one and only one accounting treatment), that treatment must be used.

If the facts allow for more than one treatment for a transaction or economic event then the final choice depends on the managers' *objectives* of financial reporting. From the remaining alternatives managers choose the one that best suits the objectives. It's crucial to remember that the remaining alternatives have survived scrutiny in light of the constraints and the facts; that is, they are consistent and acceptable in terms of the constraints and facts. Any recommendation that satisfies the objectives *must* also satisfy the constraints and the facts. For example, if we have an IFRS constraint, we must be able to justify the choice of revenue recognition method in terms of the revenue recognition criteria regardless of the objectives.

It should be clear from this discussion that managers don't always get to choose the alternative that best meets their objectives. The constraints and facts may prevent managers from selecting their preferred alternative. Being able to justify an accounting choice in terms of the constraints and facts is important for another reason: an accounting choice will rarely be justified in terms of the objectives of financial reporting. Managers will not say that they made an accounting choice to maximize their bonus. Instead, they will explain the choice in terms of accounting concepts—in terms of the facts.

Analyzing Accounting Problems

The constraints, facts, and objectives model can be used in a decision-making approach for accounting choice problems. Short cases and problems that ask you to make or evaluate accounting choices are an important technique used in this book to teach critical thinking and problem solving skills. The steps below provide a technique for addressing these cases and problems. The steps show how a manager would approach accounting-choice situations. These steps will be modified later to explain how to approach cases from an external stakeholder's perspective.

1. Assess the entity and its environment. What are the entity's key characteristics (industry, size, ownership, management, and so on)? What problems is it facing? What are the entity's crucial success factors (what are the keys to the entity's success)? How does it make money (if it's a for-profit organization)? This step is important because it helps you understand what the needs of the entity are so you can determine the objectives of financial reporting.
2. Create a framework for analyzing the accounting issues. The framework helps determine the objectives of financial reporting and important constraints:
    a. Identify the main stakeholders and the decisions they have to make.
    b. Based on the stakeholders and uses discussed in (a), identify the objectives of financial reporting that would serve the stakeholders.
    c. Rank the objectives in order of importance and explain the ranking. (The ranking is necessary so that the analysis can address the most important objective.)

d. Consider the accounting implications of the objectives, given your main objective(s). That is, you must understand how the objectives will affect accounting choices.

e. Identify any constraints that can limit or eliminate accounting choices.

Managers rank the objectives from their own perspective. They decide what is most important for the entity (and perhaps for themselves). This step is crucial because it provides a basis for deciding among alternative accounting methods.

3. Identify the accounting issues. Some of the accounting problems an entity faces are clear. Other problems may be hidden and only detected through analysis and inference.
4. Rank the issues in order of importance and emphasize the more important ones in your analysis. More time and effort should be spent on the issues that are more complex and have the greatest impact on the entity.
5. Analyze each accounting problem:
   a. Identify possible alternative accounting treatments.
   b. Eliminate alternatives that violate the constraints. If the constraints allow only a single alternative, then the analysis is complete because the accounting treatment is determined by the constraints.
   c. Analyze each alternative to determine whether the facts support it. This means you must use information about the transaction or economic event and relevant accounting rules/principles/concepts to provide support for the alternative. If an alternative can't be supported, it must be rejected. For example, analyzing a revenue recognition problem for an entity constrained by IFRS means applying the revenue recognition criteria. If the facts allow only for a single alternative then the analysis is complete because the accounting treatment is determined by the facts, even if the treatment isn't useful for achieving the objectives.
   d. If any alternatives remain, choose the one that best suits the objective or objectives of financial reporting identified and ranked in step 2.
6. Link the solution for each accounting problem back to the framework by explaining why the solution addresses the main objectives. Sometimes you won't be able to provide a solution that serves the objective. That's okay. Explain why you weren't able to satisfy the objective.

When you work on cases there are some additional points to remember:

- Play your role. Understand what the role means so you can play it effectively. You could be asked to play the role of advisor to management or the board of directors, various stakeholder groups, arbitrator (a person who helps resolves disputes between parties), external auditor, or auditor for the Canada Revenue Agency. Write your response in role.
- State your assumptions. It's never possible to have all the information. Time, cost, and limitations on a person's ability to process information prevent this. As a result, it's necessary to make assumptions—to fill in the blanks—when information is missing. It's very important to recognize when you are making assumptions and to state them explicitly. Knowing when assumptions are being made and identifying what they are isn't always easy—it takes skill and practise to do it well.
- Cases rarely have one right answer. However, not having one right answer doesn't mean all answers are right—there are many wrong answers. The quality of a response depends on the weightings given to various factors, the assumptions made, and the interpretation of events. It's also possible to come up with a reasonable recommendation that is poorly supported. The quality and usefulness of a recommendation lie in the support provided for it, not in the recommendation itself.

When you are asked to play the role of an external stakeholder the approach is a bit simpler. It isn't necessary to consider all stakeholders and their objectives. As an external stakeholder you are only interested in your own objectives and information needs. Otherwise, the approach is the same as for all other roles.

The following solved problem shows an application of this decision-making approach. This solved problem and the one in Chapter 6 take a manager's (preparer's) perspective. The solved problems in Chapters 5, 7, 8, 9, 10, 11, and 12 take a user's perspective.

Solved Problem

Pizzazz Pizza Parlours Ltd. (PPPL) is a small chain of take-out/delivery pizza shops located in Atlantic Canada. The Pizzazz family owns the chain and until recently it was managed by several members of the family. Many other family members are passive shareholders who aren't involved in managing PPPL, including some who rely on the dividends from the company for their incomes.

In early fiscal 2017 PPPL underwent a number of organizational and strategic changes. First, the family decided that instead of only owning pizza parlours themselves, PPPL would sell franchises to people interested in owning their own business. In a franchise arrangement an individual or company (the franchisee) would approach PPPL about purchasing the right to operate a Pizzazz Pizza Parlour in a particular area. The franchisee would pay PPPL a fee for the rights to own and operate a Pizzazz Pizza shop. The franchisee would also pay PPPL a percentage of the revenue it earned selling pizzas and buy certain supplies from PPPL. PPPL would help the franchisee find a good location; help it set up the shop; provide centralized purchasing, advertising, and order taking from customers; and provide business advice, training, and policy manuals.

The family members who were running the business realized they weren't qualified to manage the business they envisioned. As a result, PPPL's board of directors, which is made up mostly of members of the Pizzazz family, hired as president a person with many years of experience in the pizza industry. The new president signed an employment contract that entitles him to a salary plus a bonus based on net income. Some Pizzazzes remained as part of the new management team. One of the first actions taken by the new president was to arrange a large bank loan to finance the expansion of the company.

As of PPPL's year-end on August 31, 2017 PPPL's new strategy was developing nicely. Fourteen Pizzazz Pizza Parlour franchises had been sold, of which eight were already operating. The remaining six were expected to open by the end of December 2017. Franchises sell for $70,000 each. A franchise owner pays PPPL $5,000 when the franchise agreement is signed, $15,000 when the restaurant opens, and $10,000 per year for five years on the anniversary of the opening of the pizza parlour. In addition, franchisees pay PPPL a royalty of 5 percent of sales and are required to purchase certain ingredients from PPPL or designated suppliers.

PPPL's 2017 fiscal year has just ended and it hasn't yet determined how to recognize revenue on the franchises it sells. You have been asked by PPPL's board of directors to prepare a report that responds to the following questions:

Required:

1. What businesses is PPPL in? How does it make its money? What do you think are crucial success factors for PPPL's franchise business?
2. Who are the likely stakeholders of PPPL's financial statements? For what purposes will these stakeholders want the financial statements?
3. From the perspective of the board of directors of PPPL (which we will assume is responsible for approving major accounting policies used by PPPL), what are the possible objectives of financial reporting? Your response to question 2 should help answer this question. Which objective of financial reporting do you think is most important? Explain. How would you rank the remaining objectives? Are there any conflicts among the objectives?
4. Are there any constraints that limit the accounting choices that PPPL can make?
5. What are some possible alternatives for when PPPL could recognize the revenue from the sale of franchises? (You should be able to identify at least three different revenue recognition points.)
6. Do any of the revenue recognition points you identified in question 5 violate the constraints? Which of the alternatives are supported by the facts? Apply the IFRS revenue recognition criteria to answer.
7. For each revenue recognition alternative you identify, calculate the amount of franchise fee revenue that would be recognized in the years ended August 31, 2017 and 2018.
8. Which revenue recognition method would you recommend PPPL use to recognize franchise fee revenue? Explain.

Solution:

1. PPPL is in three businesses:
   a. It owns and operates pizzerias making money by selling pizzas to customers.
   b. It sells franchise rights to people interested in operating their own Pizzazz Pizza Parlour, making money from the franchise fees and royalties paid by the franchisees.
   c. It supplies ingredients to the franchised pizzerias, possibly making money by selling the ingredients at a profit.

   For the franchise business, the crucial success factors include:

   - Having strong management to run the company, especially during this period of strategic change. Strong management is crucial because the Pizzazz family doesn't feel it has the ability to manage the expansion of the business on its own.
   - Availability of financing for the franchising program. The franchise business requires cash because the pizzerias open before most of the cash is received from the franchises. For the expansion to continue successfully, credit must be available as required.
   - Capable people with adequate resources to buy and operate the franchises. The franchises must be successful so money will be available to pay debts and royalties to PPPL and to help attract new franchisees in the future.
   - PPPL must successfully promote its name so that people will have a preference for eating Pizzazz Pizzas.

2. Possible stakeholders and uses of PPPL's financial statements:

Possible stakeholders	**Decisions that will be assisted by the financial statements and how the information will help stakeholders make the decisions**
Pizzazz family members	Pizzazz family members will have a number of uses that could be helped by financial statements: • They will want to evaluate the performance of the new president. Since the president's bonus is based on net income they will want the income statement to reflect the president's accomplishments. • Pizzazz family members, especially those who depend on PPPL for their incomes, will want information that allows them to assess the performance of PPPL and evaluate the amount of cash that will be available to pay dividends. • Family members who aren't involved in management will want information for stewardship purposes. • The board of directors may want to show the Pizzazz family members that PPPL is performing well.
Lenders and potential lenders	• Existing lenders will want to assess whether their loans are safe and check whether any restrictions (such as current-ratio or debt-to-equity ratio restrictions) have been violated. • Additional loans might be required if the franchising program continues. Potential lenders will want to assess PPPL's ability to generate the cash flows necessary to make interest and principal payments. They will also be interested in the market value of available collateral that could be sold if PPPL were unable to pay back the loan. Potential lenders would want to know the terms of existing loans such as amounts already borrowed, the interest rate, repayment schedule, and collateral pledged to other lenders. • The company will want the financial statements to indicate to lenders that existing loans are and future loans would be secure, and that any restrictions have not been violated.
Canada Revenue Agency (CRA)	• The CRA will want to ensure PPPL complies with the *Income Tax Act*. • From PPPL's perspective, the company will want to pay as little tax as possible and still comply with the *Income Tax Act*.

New president of PPPL	• The president receives a bonus based on net income so he will want to see high net income. • From PPPL's perspective, the company would want the president to receive a fair bonus that reflects his contribution to the performance of the company.
Prospective franchise owners	• Prospective franchise owners may want to assess the financial position of PPPL to obtain some confidence the company is financially solid. If a franchise is purchased, but PPPL is unable to support it, the franchise owners' investment suffers. Prospective franchise owners may want information about cash flows, the number of franchises sold and being negotiated, expansion plans, and information on the performance of operating franchises. PPPL is under no obligation to provide its financial statements to prospective franchisees unless it chooses to do so as part of its effort to sell franchises. • From PPPL's perspective, the company will want to give prospective franchise owners confidence it will be able to support its franchises and that a PPPL franchise is a good investment.
Suppliers	• Major suppliers may want assurances that PPPL will be able to pay for goods and services purchased. They will be interested in cash flows and liquidity. • From PPPL's perspective, the company will want to assure suppliers that it's able to meet its obligations to pay for supplies. PPPL is under no obligation to provide its financial statements to suppliers, unless it chooses to do so.

3. From the analysis of the stakeholders and uses of accounting information a number of possible objectives emerge. Based on our analysis of the crucial success factors in part (1), the important stakeholders from PPPL's perspective are:
   - prospective lenders, because additional loans will be required if PPPL continues to sell franchises;
   - new franchise owners, who are key to PPPL's expansion strategy; and
   - the president of PPPL, who has been hired to implement the new business strategy.

   Of these three, the president is most important because PPPL's board chose him to lead the company in this phase of its development. To lose him at this stage would probably be a serious blow to PPPL's new strategy. A good president will be able to effectively manage the relationship with the bank and help attract good franchise owners.

   Therefore, the objective of financial reporting should be ensuring that the financial statements reflect management performance and adequately compensate the president for his accomplishments—that is, the objective of management evaluation. The board would probably want to make sure that the net income of PPPL was a reasonable reflection of the president's actions so that he would receive a bonus he and the board felt was fair. The needs of lenders would probably be satisfied by the statements used for management evaluation along with supplementary information on cash flows. While people who buy franchises are important stakeholders, PPPL would probably not be making financial statement information available to them.

   Members of the Pizzazz family are also important and powerful stakeholders but their needs must be considered secondary to the stakeholders who are important to expanding PPPL. The board could provide special purpose reports to members of the family to satisfy their information needs.

   Everything else being equal, all businesses want to pay as little tax as possible, and PPPL's need for cash makes the objective of tax minimization even more important. However, the need for strong management makes tax minimization a secondary objective.

   Major suppliers could request financial information if they are to provide credit terms. It's possible PPPL may not need to provide this information

   Note that there are conflicts among the objectives. In particular, the tax minimization objective, which suggests lower net income, conflicts with the management evaluation objective, which suggests "fair" or net income that is representative of the entity's underlying economic activity.

Comment: *This ranking isn't the only one or the best one. Other rankings are possible, reasonable, and supportable. However, any proposed ranking must be supported.*

Comment: *Had we examined the objectives from the perspective of the president of PPPL rather than from that of the board of directors, the primary objective might have been bonus maximization rather than management evaluation. The president's self-interest might have had a stronger influence since he would have been making accounting choices that directly affected his personal wealth.*

4. There don't appear to be any statutory constraints stated in the question. PPPL is a private company and therefore its reporting responsibilities are limited. Some stakeholders, such as the bank, the shareholders who aren't involved in management, and prospective franchise owners, may prefer audited ASPE or IFRS-based financial statements. (PPPL could use ASPE as it isn't public or IFRS if it wanted to.) For purposes of preparing tax returns, PPPL will have to comply with the *Income Tax Act*. The lending agreement with the bank may have minimum requirements for accounting ratios, such as the current ratio or the debt-to-equity ratio, but without any information about these ratios it's not possible to make a reasonable assumption regarding specific amounts. Given the number of external stakeholders of the financial statements we will assume that IFRS will be a constraint.
5. Possible points for recognizing revenue from the sale of franchises include when
   - a franchise agreement is signed with a new franchise owner,
   - a franchised Pizzazz Pizza Parlour opens,
   - cash is collected from a franchise, or
   - full payment is received from a franchise.
6. Since it's assumed that IFRS will be followed, each revenue recognition point must be evaluated in relation to the IFRS revenue recognition criteria:
   - *When a franchise agreement is signed with a new owner of a franchise.* At the time of signing, PPPL has considerable work to do to help the new franchisee to get the shop up and running. It seems clear that PPPL hasn't fulfilled its obligations so risks and rewards of ownership haven't really transferred at this point. On the other hand, a binding agreement is in place and the franchisee would have difficulty backing out of the deal if PPPL fulfilled its obligations. The amount of revenue is known when the contract is signed because the amount is specified in the contract. Costs are uncertain because PPPL still has work to do providing assistance to the franchisee. These costs may be fairly predictable, although at this stage PPPL has a limited history to base its estimates on and each new location may have unique aspects that affect PPPL's costs. Collection is a potential problem because payment depends on the success of the franchises and PPPL has no track record for evaluating how successful the franchised pizzerias will be so it's not clear how much will actually be collected from the franchisees. This alternative doesn't meet the revenue recognition criteria.
   - *When a franchised Pizzazz Pizza Parlour opens.* PPPL has probably met the performance criteria as of this point since once a pizza parlour is open most of what PPPL agreed to has been done (though there are ongoing responsibilities). In addition, the franchise owner has an operating business at this point so one could argue that the risks and rewards of ownership are with the owners of the franchise restaurant. The amount of revenue is specified in the franchise agreement. Most costs are probably known at this time, although some cost uncertainty likely exists regarding the cost of the support that must be provided to the franchisee (especially given that PPPL is new to the franchising business), which may make estimating future costs difficult. Of course, at some point the support provided by PPPL can be considered paid for by the franchisees' royalties rather than from the initial franchise fee. Collection of the amounts owing is still an open question. At the time the pizza parlour opens the franchise will have paid $20,000 of the $70,000 franchise fee. The fact that PPPL is new to the business makes it difficult to estimate the amount that won't be collected. This alternative meets the five criteria provided that a reasonable estimate of the amounts that won't be collected from the franchises can be made.

- *When cash is collected from a franchise.* Restaurants are a notoriously risky business and franchises can fail. There is added concern in this case because PPPL doesn't have a track record of running a franchise operation. As a result, collection isn't a foregone conclusion. Waiting until cash is in hand is conservative but not unreasonable because collection may prove to be unpredictable. Except for the payment received when the franchise agreement is signed, recognizing revenue when cash is received meets the five criteria. The $5,000 received when the contract is signed would probably have to be deferred until the pizza parlour opened because if the opening doesn't go as planned PPPL might have to return the initial payment.
- *When full payment is received from a franchise.* This method is very conservative. It requires that there be significant and unpredictable costs in the later years of the contract, or that PPPL had not earned the revenue once a restaurant opened. The most likely reason for delaying revenue recognition for this long would be for tax purposes, something not allowed under the *Income Tax Act*.

Comment: *Observe from this analysis that reasonable arguments can be made for at least two of the revenue recognition points (opening and cash collection), because the facts surrounding the franchise arrangements are ambiguous and subject to interpretation. This is why managers often face situations where justifiable alternatives exist.*

7. Amount of revenue that would be recognized in the years ended August 31, 2017 and 2018, using each revenue recognition point:

- When a franchise agreement is signed with a new owner of a franchise

Revenue in 2017: $980,000 (14 stores × $70,000 per store)
Revenue in 2018: $0

- When a franchised Pizzazz Pizza Parlour opens

Revenue in 2017: $560,000 (8 × $70,000)
Revenue in 2018: $420,000 (6 × $70,000)

- When cash is collected from a franchise (except for the payment on signing of the franchise agreement, which must be recognized when the franchise restaurant opens)

Revenue in 2017: $160,000 (8 × $20,000)
Revenue in 2018: $200,000 (6 × $20,000 + 8 × $10,000)

- When full payment is received from a franchise

Revenue in 2017: $0
Revenue in 2018: $0

8. The analysis above supports using either the opening of a Pizzazz Pizza Parlour or collection of cash as acceptable points to recognize revenue. Because there is more than one alternative available after the constraints and the facts are addressed, consider the objectives of financial reporting. To satisfy the primary objective, management evaluation, revenue should be recognized when a franchised Pizzazz Pizza Parlour opens. While cash collection is a significant uncertainty in PPPL's earnings process, using cash collection as the basis for evaluating and rewarding the president would likely undermine the incentive value of the bonus plan because the bonus would be significantly delayed. While recognizing revenue when the store opens might make the president less selective in choosing franchise owners (he may focus more on making sure the franchises open rather than making sure that the franchisees are able to pay their debts), the disincentives override this problem. When a restaurant opens, the president has done his job of expanding the chain. At this point, the franchise owners have made a significant financial investment and would likely work hard to make sure that their restaurants succeed.

Comment: *This is one possible solution to this case. Other rankings of objectives, evaluations of alternatives, and recommendations are possible and acceptable provided they are well supported.*

SUMMARY OF KEY POINTS

LO 1 To recognize revenue in a logical and rational manner we need criteria to guide the choice. Under IFRS the following five criteria are used to recognize revenue for the sale of goods:

1. Significant risks and rewards of ownership have been transferred from the seller to the buyer.
2. The seller has no involvement or control over the goods sold.
3. Collection of payment is reasonably assured.
4. The amount of revenue can be reasonably measured.
5. The costs required to earn the revenue can be reasonably measured.

These criteria provide guidance to managers, but they are open to interpretation and require judgment. Additionally, overriding any criterion requires that the revenue recognition point selected provide a reasonable and fair representation of the entity's activities, given the needs of the people who are using the accounting information.

LO 2 Accountants have devised two approaches for recognizing revenue: the critical-event approach and the gradual approach. Under the critical-event approach an entity chooses a "critical event" in the earnings process that it considers an appropriate time to recognize revenue. When this critical event occurs 100 percent of the revenue is recognized. Under the gradual approach revenue is recognized gradually over a period of time. The gradual approach, often used by entities providing services or for long-term contracts, provides useful and timely information to stakeholders about long-term contracts.

LO 3 There are different ways and times that revenues and expenses can be recognized and the methods chosen can affect the amount of revenue, expense, and net income an entity reports. Different revenue and expense recognition methods also affect financial ratios. Even though the financial statements are affected by using different revenue and expense recognition methods, the underlying economic activity of the entity is the same regardless of the methods chosen.

LO 4 Sometimes a single transaction provides more than one good and/or service to customers. In these multi-deliverable arrangements the amount of revenue should be split among each of the components purchased based on the fair value of the components.

LO 5 Accrual accounting requires that costs be matched to revenue—meaning expenses should be recognized in the same period as the revenue those expenses helped earn is recognized—whether the cash flow occurs before, at the same time, or after the revenue is recognized. Not all costs are easy to match to revenue. Costs expensed in the period they are incurred are period costs. Costs matched to specific revenues are product costs. Product costs are expensed when the revenue they help generate is recognized.

LO 6 A gain or loss arises when an entity sells an asset it doesn't sell in the ordinary course of business for an amount that is different from its carrying amount. Gains arise when the proceeds from the sale are greater than the carrying amount and losses arise when the proceeds are less than the carrying amount. Gains and losses are reported separately from revenues and expenses, and are shown net on the income statement.

LO 7 Managers can often choose from a number of reasonable accounting treatments for transactions and other economic events, even under IFRS. Flexible accounting rules are needed because of the complexity of economic activity. Constraints, facts, and objectives relevant to the situation influence mangers' choice of accounting methods. Managers are influenced by their need to provide information to stakeholders and by their own self-interests.

LO 8 Managers must choose an appropriate accounting treatment when there are alternatives. Relevant constraints, facts, and objectives must be considered, and the problem-solving approach incorporating the following steps should be applied:

1. Assess the entity and its environment.
2. Create a framework for analyzing the accounting issues.

3. Identify the accounting problems.
4. Rank the problems in order of importance and emphasize the more important problems in the analysis.
5. Analyze the accounting problems.
6. Make a recommendation and explain why the recommendation is consistent with the main objectives.

KEY TERMS

big bath, p. 211
completed-contract method, p. 201
consignment sale, p. 194
cost-recovery method, p. 201
critical-event approach, p. 189
gradual approach, p. 189
percentage-of-completion method, p. 200
period costs, p. 205
product costs, p. 205
prospectus, p. 197
recognition, p. 206
warranty, p. 193
zero-profit method, p. 201

ASSIGNMENT MATERIALS

Questions

Q4-1. Can a single set of financial statements satisfy all objectives of financial reporting? Explain.

Q4-2. Which objective of financial reporting is most important? Explain.

Q4-3. Explain the difference between period and product costs. How is each type of cost accounted for?

Q4-4. Explain the accounting term "revenue recognition."

Q4-5. How is the balance sheet affected when revenue is recognized? Explain your answer and give examples.

Q4-6. Explain why, under accrual accounting, revenue isn't always recognized when cash is received.

Q4-7. Do you think it's good or bad that entities have flexibility in choosing when to recognize revenue? Explain.

Q4-8. Why does it make sense to use the percentage-of-completion method for long-term service contracts instead of choosing a critical event?

Q4-9. What effects do the objectives of financial reporting have on when an entity recognizes revenue? Explain.

Q4-10. What are constraints, facts, and objectives? How does each affect the accounting methods an entity uses? Why does each have to be considered when making an accounting choice?

Q4-11. Explain the matching concept. Give some examples of matching. Why is matching important for financial accounting? Why is matching sometimes difficult to do in practice?

Q4-12. Explain why recognizing revenue and expenses in different ways has no effect on the underlying economic activity of an entity.

Q4-13. Why can it be difficult for accountants to determine when revenue should be recognized under accrual accounting?

Q4-14. Why is determining when to recognize revenue more difficult under accrual accounting than under cash accounting?

Q4-15. Distinguish between the percentage-of-completion and the zero-profit (cost recovery) methods of revenue recognition. Which method requires the exercise of more judgment by managers? Explain.

Q4-16. Do you think that the managers of entities should be responsible for selecting the accounting methods and estimates they use, or should that responsibility be given to an independent third party? Explain your view. Make sure you consider both sides of the argument.

Q4-17. Do you think accounting would be more useful and relevant if only a single method of revenue recognition were allowed, such as when cash is collected or when the goods or services are provided to the customer? Explain.

Q4-18. Identify and explain the five revenue recognition criteria.

Q4-19. Does it matter how and when a company recognizes its revenue? Explain.

Q4-20. Under what circumstances should the zero-profit (cost recovery) method of revenue recognition be used instead of the percentage-of-completion method?

Q4-21. What are gains and losses on the sale of assets? How do they arise? How are gains and losses reported in the financial statements?

Q4-22. Why are gains and losses usually shown separately from revenues and expenses from ordinary business activities? What are the implications to the users of the financial statements if gains and losses are included in revenues and/or expenses?

Q4-23. Identify and explain the two factors that influence the accounting choices that are made by the managers who prepare the financial statements.

Q4-24. Why does self-interest play a role in accounting choice? Should it, in an ideal world? Explain.

Q4-25. Explain what each of the following objectives of financial reporting means:

a. Tax minimization
b. Management evaluation
c. Minimum compliance
d. Cash flow prediction
e. Stewardship
f. Earnings management

Q4-26. What does it mean when accountants refer to recognizing revenue when a "critical event" occurs?

Q4-27. Name some products that are sold in a "bundle." What are the challenges accountants face in recognizing revenue if they want to unbundle the products being offered?

Exercises

E4-1. **(Classifying period and product costs, LO 5)** Azilda Toy Ltd. develops, manufactures, markets, and distributes a broad range of toys and games for children, from newborns to teenagers. The principal markets for Azilda's products are Canada, the United States, and Australia, where Azilda markets and distributes both company-developed and licensed products. In addition to sales in these countries, Azilda's products are marketed in more than 50 countries worldwide. For each of the costs described below, state whether you would treat the cost as a product cost or a period cost. Explain your choices.

a. Plastic, wood, metal, and other materials that are used to produce toys.
b. Commissions paid to salespeople who sell toys to distributors and retailers.
c. Salaries paid to head office staff and senior executives.
d. Electricity and other utilities used in the manufacturing plant.
e. Depreciation of equipment used to manufacture toys.
f. Amounts paid to trucking companies for delivering toys to customers.
g. Cost of designing new toys.
h. Cost of packaging for toys.
i. Television and print advertising to promote the entire line of Azilda Toy Ltd.'s toys.

E4-2. **(Identify reasonable methods for determining the proportion of a long-term contract that has been completed, LO 2)** For each of the following long-term projects, provide a basis for estimating the percentage of the job that has been completed. The discussion in the text used the percentage of total estimated cost incurred during a year as the percentage completed. For this exercise identify bases other than cost for estimating the percentage completed.

a. Construction of a 50 kilometre stretch of highway;
b. Contract to remove contaminated earth from a factory site where toxic waste has been dumped for many decades;
c. Contract to overhaul of a large shipping vessel.

E4-3. **(Recording journal entries for recording revenue at different critical events, LO 1, 2, 5)** Feeder Computer Systems Design Ltd. (Feeder) designs and installs computer networks for commercial customers. In December 2016, Feeder signed a contract with Magyar Telecommunications Ltd. (Magyar) to design and install a new network for Magyar's production centre in Winnipeg. Magyar's year-end is December 31. The following events pertain to the contract with Magyar:

i. December 13, 2016: The contract between Feeder and Magyar is signed. Magyar will pay $750,000 for the system and the system will cost Feeder $450,000 to design, produce, and install. The contract provides an 18-month warranty to make any repairs or adjustments required. Magyar will pay within 90 days of completion of the installation of the system.
ii. October 15, 2017: Installation of the system is completed.
iii. December 12, 2017: Warranty work costing $22,500 is performed.
iv. January 8, 2018: Feeder receives payment in full from Magyar.
v. April 15, 2018: Warranty expires.

Required:

Prepare the journal entries required for the above events assuming the following:

a. Revenue is recognized when the contract is signed.
b. Revenue is recognized when installation of the system is complete.
c. Revenue is recognized when cash is collected.
d. Revenue is recognized when the warranty period expires.

E4-4. **(Identifying the objectives of financial reporting, LO 7, 8)** For each of the following entities, identify the objectives of financial reporting that the entity's managers might have. In answering, consider who the stakeholders might be and which stakeholder(s) would be most important to the managers. Explain how the objectives of financial reporting would influence the accounting choices made by the managers.

a. A private company with a large labour union that is preparing for negotiations with the union.
b. An accounting firm partnership that uses accounting income to determine the amount of tax the partners pay and the compensation the partners receive.
c. A private corporation that repairs commercial vehicles. The company has one shareholder who is also president of the company. The company urgently needs cash.

d. A public company planning to borrow a large amount of money to finance an expansion.
e. A not-for-profit golf club. Membership fees, green fees, dining room charges, and pro shop sales are used to operate the club. Club members are elected to sit on the board of directors of the club.

E4-5. **(Identifying the objectives of financial reporting, LO 7, 8)** For each of the following entities, identify the objectives of financial reporting that the entity's managers might have. In answering, consider who the stakeholders might be and which stakeholder(s) would be most important to the managers. Explain how the objectives of financial reporting would influence the accounting choices made by the managers.
a. A family-owned corporation that is planning to sell shares to the public and become a public company that is traded on a stock exchange.
b. A municipal government.
c. A public company that has been adversely affected by international competition and that is trying to receive subsidies from government.
d. A charity that raises money to buy and distribute food to hungry children around the world.
e. A private corporation that provides consulting services to restaurants. The company has one shareholder who is also president of the company. The company has a small bank loan and no other major creditors.

E4-6. **(Determining when to recognize revenue, LO 1, 2, 4)** For each of the following situations use the IFRS revenue recognition criteria to determine when revenue should be recognized. Explain your reasoning.
a. A person buys a chocolate donut and a large coffee with double milk and double sugar at a Tim Hortons.
b. A symphony lover buys a series package for the Masterworks Gold and Diamond Series performed by the Vancouver Symphony Orchestra. The series has ten performances over the year from September through May. The symphony lover pays the full price of the series before the series begins and receives tickets for all the performances when he pays.
c. A customer purchases an extended warranty from Leon's when she buys a new 60 inch plasma television. The extended warranty provides two years of coverage for the set beyond the end of the one-year manufacturer's warranty. (Coverage is for the second and third years the customer owns the TV.)
d. A software development company sells a computer graphics program. The company provides 18 months of 24/7 telephone and internet support for the software.

E4-7. **(Determining when to recognize revenue, LO 1, 2)** For each of the following situations, use the IFRS revenue recognition criteria to determine when the interest revenue should be recognized. Explain your reasoning.
a. A lender makes a loan to a borrower with an excellent credit rating. Interest is paid annually and the principal must be paid in full in three years.
b. A lender makes a loan to a borrower. The borrower is now suffering serious financial problems and hasn't made interest payments for several months. Collection of interest and principal from this borrower is in doubt.
c. A lender makes a five-year loan to a borrower. The borrower has a solid credit history and needed the loan to help finance expansion. The expansion hasn't gone according to plan and the company has been short of cash. The borrower has made all required payments to date but usually late, often for as long as 90 days. The borrower has stated that it expects to make all payments on a timely basis but cash flow information suggests the cash crisis is deepening and isn't likely to improve for the foreseeable future.

E4-8. **(Determining when to recognize revenue, LO 1, 2)** Happy Snacks Ltd. (HSL) is a distributor of snack products to various retail stores in Toronto. HSL establishes agreements with stores whereby it places racks in the stores that display HSL's products. HSL is responsible for stocking and maintaining the racks. The retail merchant doesn't pay for the snacks until they are sold to a customer and earns a commission for any snacks sold. Each week an HSL representative visits the stores to replenish the racks and count the number of units that have been sold. The merchant pays HSL monthly for any snacks sold during the month, less commission. The merchant is responsible for snacks that are lost, stolen, or damaged during the month.

Required:

When should Happy Snacks recognize the revenue from the sale of snacks?

E4-9. **(Determining when to recognize revenue, LO 1, 2)** Victory Health Club Inc. allows people to join its health and fitness club by either buying a lifetime membership or paying annually. A lifetime membership entitles the member to use club facilities for the member's life. Members who pay annually can use the facilities for 12 months after a membership is purchased.

Required:

How should the revenue be recognized from the sale of memberships where the member pays monthly and from the sale of lifetime memberships?

E4-10. **(Determining when to recognize revenue, LO 1, 2)** In late December 2017 Kakisa Inc. made a large shipment of goods to a new customer. Kakisa had been in negotiations with the customer for some time and the final agreement was an important step in its planned expansion into western Canada. The agreement was unusual in that it allowed the customer to return any and all of the goods shipped at any time up until March 1, 2018. The customer isn't required to pay for the goods until March. Kakisa recognizes its revenue when goods are delivered to the customer and normally provides 30 days to pay. Kakisa's year-end is December 31.

Required:

How should Kakisa recognize the revenue from the sale to the new customer?

E4-11. **(Determining when to recognize revenue, LO 1, 2)** Daphne's Catering Ltd. (DCL) provides catering services to people living in Saskatoon. DCL can provide meals for groups as small as two and as large as 500. In November 2016, DCL was approached by the executive director of a national accounting organization to cater a gala dinner at the organization's annual convention to be held in August 2017. The parties signed a contract in December 2016 in which they agreed DCL would cater the function for a minimum of 250 people at a price of $110 per person (if fewer than 250 people attend, the organization will pay for 250). The organization paid a non-refundable $5,000 deposit at the time the contract was signed. An additional $15,000 was paid on May 1, 2017. The dinner was held successfully on August 15, 2017, with 297 guests attending. The balance owing was paid to DCL on August 31, 2017. DCL's year-end is December 31.

Required:

a. What are some of the possible points at which DCL could recognize the revenue from the gala dinner?
b. Which revenue recognition points can you support with the IFRS criteria? Explain.

E4-12. **(Determining when to recognize revenue, LO 1, 2)** Charter Airways Ltd. is the charter division of a large national airline. On July 1, 2017 Charter entered an agreement with a major league professional sports team to fly the team and its staff to its 40 away games for a payment of $2,800,000 made in two equal instalments on September 1, 2017 and January 15, 2018. The team's season runs from September through April. The contract is non-cancellable and Charter Airways will keep the $2,800,000 if for any reason the team chooses not to use the flights. In addition, as part of the contract, Charter Airways agreed to display the team's logo on their planes until the end of the contract.

Required:

When should Charter Airways recognize the revenue from the agreement with the sports team? Charter Airways' year-end is December 31.

E4-13. **(Determining when to recognize revenue, LO 1, 2)** Quesnel Ltd. owns patents for number of important drugs used in the treatment of cancer. Quesnel has been unable to meet the global demand for some of its products so it licenses its patents to foreign drug manufacturers. If Quesnel's management is satisfied that a foreign producer can meet its standards for production of a drug, it signs an agreement with it. A typical agreement requires the foreign producer to pay a non-refundable fee of $1,000,000 to Quesnel at the time the contract is signed plus a royalty of $10 for each unit of the drug that is produced and sold. The royalty must be paid within 30 days of the end of each month.

Required:

Explain how Quesnel should recognize the revenue from the licensing agreement. Consider the revenue from the initial fee and the royalty separately. Use the revenue recognition criteria to support your answer.

E4-14. **(Determining when to recognize revenue, LO 1, 2)** In September 2018, Badger Corp. shipped a large quantity of merchandise to a third-party warehouse for storage. The merchandise is to be shipped to customers in October 2018. Normally, Badger Corp. ships merchandise directly to its customers, but because of pending labour problems at Badger's facility the goods were shipped to the third-party warehouse. (The customers were unwilling to accept the merchandise in advance.) The third-party warehouse has assumed responsibility for shipping the merchandise to the customers when required and is responsible for any loss or damage. Badger Corp. continues to be responsible for collecting amounts from customers and providing any required customer support. Badger Corp. normally recognizes revenue on shipment to customers. Badger Corp. has agreed to pay the third party warehouse $50,000 for its services.

Required:

When should Badger recognize the revenue for the goods shipped to the third party warehouse? Explain your answer.

E4-15. **(Determining when to recognize revenue, LO 1, 2)** Alma Books Ltd. (Alma) is a national chain of bookstores. Alma earns revenue in several different ways:

a. Sale of books and magazines to customers in its stores—customers pay cash or use debit or credit cards (Visa or MasterCard) to pay for their purchases.
b. Online sales—customers can browse for books on the company's Web site and make purchases online using a credit card or PayPal. Alma ships the order as soon as it's available. Customers sometimes have to wait if an item isn't in stock.
c. Loyalty program—customers pay $20 per year for membership and receive discounts on their in-store or online purchases. Membership is for one year from the date of purchase.
d. Sale of gift cards—the cards, which can value from $5 to $500, allow customers to purchase items in the store or online without using their own cash. There are no service charges associated with the cards.

Required:

Use the five IFRS revenue recognition criteria to determine when revenue should be recognized for each source of revenue. Explain your reasoning.

E4-16. **(Calculating revenue using the percentage-of-completion and zero-profit methods, LO 2)** Sahtlam Ltd. (Sahtlam) is a small construction company in northern Ontario. Sahtlam recently signed a contract to build a new town hall in one of the region's larger cities. Sahtlam will receive $25,000,000 from the city for building the town hall and will have to pay the costs of construction from that amount.

Construction will begin in September 2017 and is expected to be completed in March 2019. Sahtlam's year-end is December 31. Sahtlam estimates that construction costs in each year will be:

	2017	2018	2019	Total
Estimated costs	$3,500,000	$9,000,000	$4,400,000	$16,900,000

The city paid $7,000,000 when the contract was signed and will pay $6,000,000 on January 1, 2018, 2019, and 2020.

Required:

Calculate the amount of revenue and expense that Sahtlam would recognize in each year of the contract using the percentage-of-completion and zero-profit methods. Assume the actual costs incurred equal the estimated costs.

E4-17. **(The effect of using different ways of estimating the proportion of a long-term contract that has been completed on the amount of revenue recognized, LO 2, 3)** Wekusko Ltd. (Wekusko) is a large construction engineering company. In 2016, Wekusko was awarded a contract to build a small hydroelectric generating plant adjacent to an aluminum smelting plant. The aluminum company decided that it would be cheaper to generate its own power than to buy power from a supplier, so it is having a generating plant built. Wekusko will receive $31,000,000 to build the dam, from which it must pay the costs of construction. Information regarding the yearly progress of the contract measured in different ways is provided below:

	2016	2017	2018	2019	Total
Costs	$4,000,000	$6,500,000	$8,000,000	$2,500,000	$21,000,000
Percentage completed in each year as estimated by an independent engineering expert	12%	38%	40%	10%	100%
Labour hours worked	10,000	25,000	50,000	18,000	103,000

Required:

Wekusko's new vice-president of finance understands that there are different ways to calculate the percentage-of-completion of a project. The vice-president has asked you to calculate the amount of revenue that would be recognized in each year of the contract using three different methods of estimating the percentage completed:

a. Costs incurred.
b. Percentage completed in each year as estimated by an independent engineering expert.
c. Labour hours worked.

The vice-president would also like you to explain how he should choose among the three methods and which method would provide the best indication of the progress of the project to external stakeholders.

E4-18. **(Understanding the impact of self-interest on decision making, LO 7)** Strathroy Ltd. (Strathroy) is a publicly traded newspaper publishing company. The newspaper industry has faced difficult times in recent years with declining circulation and advertising revenue, in part caused by competition from the Internet and other information sources. As a public company Strathroy has many different stakeholders with different goals and objectives for using the financial statements. The following are some of Strathroy's stakeholders:

a. Leaders of a union about to negotiate a new contract for its members.
b. A large supplier of newsprint negotiating a long-term contract to supply newsprint.
c. The CEO of the company who is paid a bonus based on the company's performance.

d. A financial analyst preparing a report for investors on Strathroy. The analyst's employer does investment banking work for Strathroy.
e. Strathroy's shareholders, including 40 percent of the shares that are owned by members of the family that founded the business 75 years ago.

Required:
Different stakeholders of an entity will view the entity's goals and objectives in different ways, in part (at least) influenced by their personal goals and objectives (self-interests). For each of the stakeholders listed above explain what the stakeholder would want to accomplish in its dealings with Strathroy. Explain how the interests of the identified stakeholder could conflict with the interests of other stakeholders.

E4-19. **(Accounting for gains and losses, LO 6)** For each of the following land sales, prepare the journal entry that would be recorded and indicate the amount of the gain or loss that would be reported. Assume that in each case the sale of land isn't a main business activity of the entity.
a. Land costing $500,000 is sold for $410,000.
b. Land costing $1,300,000 is sold for $4,000,000.
c. Land costing $1,800,000 is sold for $1,800,000.

E4-20. **(Accounting for gains and losses, LO 6)** Calculate the missing amounts (indicated by a question mark) using the information provided:

	Carrying amount of land	Gain (loss) on sale of land	Selling price of land
a.	$115,000	$27,000	$?
b.	?	(85,000)	610,000
c.	?	0	250,000
d.	47,000	(15,000)	?
e.	?	122,000	380,000

E4-21. **(Explaining and understanding different roles that accounting problems can be viewed from, LO 7, 8)** Listed below are some of the roles that someone addressing accounting problems can have. The role can affect how the role-player approaches and analyzes an accounting problem. For each role listed below, explain the perspective the role brings to the analysis. (Example: An auditor for the Canada Revenue Agency examines accounting information to ensure an entity complies with the *Income Tax Act* and, as a result, pays an appropriate amount of tax.) In answering, consider the entity the person in the role is working for and the objectives of that entity, and apply these factors to explain how the role-player would approach providing advice on accounting problems.
a. Arbitrator. (An arbitrator is a person who helps resolve disputes between parties. In an accounting setting an arbitrator might be asked to resolve disagreements over the accounting choices an entity made when, for example, the selling price of the entity is based on net income.)
b. Advisor to the buyer of a business when the price of the business is based on net income.
c. Advisor to the board of directors of the company.
d. External auditor.
e. Advisor to a prospective lender.
f. Advisor to a major shareholder who isn't involved in the day-to-day management of the entity.

E4-22. **(Choosing when to recognize revenue according to the objectives of financial reporting, LO 1, 2, 7)** Pisquid Ltd. (Pisquid) is a manufacturer of kitchen furniture. In November 2015, Pisquid received an order for 15,000 sets of specially designed furniture from a large retail chain. The contract guarantees the price the retailer will pay and the quantity it will buy from Pisquid. The furniture is to be delivered monthly, in equal quantities each month, beginning in March 2016 and continuing through August 2017. The retail chain is to pay Pisquid within 45 days of receiving each shipment. Because Pisquid had excess capacity in its plant when the contract was signed it decided to manufacture the full order as soon as it could. Pisquid began producing the furniture in January 2016 and completed making the 15,000 sets in November 2016.

Required:

a. Identify the different possible critical events that could be used to recognize revenue.
b. Which critical event would you recommend for recognizing revenue to satisfy the purposes of each of the following objectives? Explain. (In answering, don't consider the constraints and the facts.)
   i. Tax minimization
   ii. Evaluation of management by outside shareholders
   iii. Income smoothing
   iv. Managing earnings to increase income
   v. Cash flow prediction
c. Which of the revenue recognition methods that you identified in (a) satisfy the IFRS revenue recognition criteria? Explain.

E4-23. **(Accounting for sale of multiple products, LO 1, 2, 4)** Bedeque Wireless Inc. provides wireless communications all over Canada. A customer who signs up for a three-year plan with Bedeque receives a free phone. A typical plan would cost $35 per month (plus applicable taxes and charges). The phone the customer would receive has a retail price of $450. A similar Bedeque plan without the phone costs $25 per month.

Required:

a. Describe the different products Bedeque is selling.
b. What are possible alternative ways of recognizing the revenue on the package purchased by the customer?
c. How much revenue would be recorded at the inception of the contract and monthly under each of the alternatives you identified in part (b) above?

E4-24. **(Assessing different ways of recognizing revenue, LO 1, 2, 7)** Valhalla Furniture Emporium Ltd. (Valhalla) sells poor-quality furniture at low prices. Customers take delivery of their furniture after making a down payment of 10 percent of the selling price. The customers agree to pay the balance owing in 36 equal monthly payments. Valhalla repossesses between 40 percent and 60 percent of the furniture sold because customers default on their payments. Repossessed furniture can be resold if it requires only minor repairs and cleaning. Some repossessed furniture is unsalable and must be disposed of.

Required:

a. What are the possible points at which Valhalla could recognize revenue?
b. Explain what reporting objectives each revenue recognition point would satisfy?
c. Which revenue recognition points can you support with the IFRS criteria?

Problems

P4-1. **(Choosing a revenue recognition point to achieve an objective of financial reporting, LO 1, 2, 3, 7, 8)** For each of the following independent situations, recommend how you would want to recognize revenue if your reporting objective was to minimize taxes. Support your answer. (To respond you should identify alternative points for recognizing revenue and choose the one that best satisfies the objective of minimizing taxes *and* can be reasonably supported.)

a. A construction company signs a contract to build a warehouse for a food distribution company. The project is to take 18 months from the signing date and the company will receive $10,000,000. At the company's fiscal year-end 60 percent of the project has been completed.
b. An investment company purchases shares of publicly traded companies for its portfolio. During the year the market value of the portfolio increases from $2,300,000 to $3,745,000. None of the shares were sold during the year.
c. A national bus company sells passes allowing passengers unlimited travel on the company's buses for 60 days from the day the pass is first used. Passes must be purchased at least 90 days before they are first used. Once purchased, the passes aren't refundable.
d. A law firm charges $10,000 per year to clients who wish to have legal advice available to them 24 hours a day, seven days a week. (The $10,000 fee is simply for the privilege of having a lawyer available all the time. These clients then have to pay the lawyer's hourly rate for the advice given.)

P4-2. **(Evaluating when to recognize revenue to try to achieve an objective of financial reporting, LO 1, 2, 3, 7, 8)** For each of the following independent situations, recommend how you would want to recognize revenue if you were the president of the company and you wanted to provide stakeholders information about how the company is performing. Support your answer. (To respond, you should identify alternative points for recognizing revenue and choose the one that best satisfies the objective of performance evaluation *and* can be reasonably supported.)

a. A construction company signs a contract to build a warehouse for a food distribution company. The project is to take 18 months from the date the contract is signed and the company will receive $10,000,000. At the company's fiscal year-end 60 percent of the project has been completed.
b. An investment company purchases shares of publicly traded companies for its portfolio. During the year, the market value of the portfolio increases from $2,300,000 to $3,745,000. None of the shares were sold during the year.
c. A national bus company sells passes allowing passengers unlimited travel on the company's buses for 60 days from the day the pass is first used. Passes must be purchased at least 90 days before they are first used. Once purchased, the passes aren't refundable.
d. A law firm charges $10,000 per year to clients who wish to have legal advice available to them 24 hours a day, seven days a week. (The $10,000 fee is simply for the privilege of having a lawyer available all the time. These clients then have to pay the lawyer's hourly rate for the advice given.)

P4-3. **(Determining when to recognize revenue, LO 1, 2, 7, 8)** Canadian Equipment Ltd. makes electronic equipment used in mining exploration. The existing owners are in the process of finalizing the sale of the company to some international buyers. The selling price of the company will be based, in part, on Canadian Equipment's income before taxes for the year ended December 31, 2017. The financial statements are being finalized but there is an outstanding sale transaction and the buyer and seller can't agree on the appropriate accounting. In the last week of December 2017, Canadian Equipment shipped a $4 million order to a new customer. The items sold come with a six month warranty. This is the standard warranty offered to all customers. The product is a standard item with only minor modifications to meet the needs of the customer. The order was scheduled to be shipped in early January but because of an opening in the production schedule Canadian Equipment was able to complete the order several weeks early. Once the order was completed, it was shipped to the customer. The customer agreed to accept early delivery before Canadian Equipment shipped the order. The cost of the order was $2.5 million. The goods were received by the customer on December 31, 2017. Canadian Equipment recognized revenue when the good were delivered, as is its normal policy.

Required:

Prepare a report to the parties analyzing how the revenue should be recognized on the sale. The buyer and seller have agreed to accept your recommendation on the appropriate treatment. Provide full support for your recommendation.

P4-4. **(Determining when to recognize revenue, LO 1, 2, 4, 7)** Kynocks Systems Management Corp. is a public company that produces and sells computer network systems and support services for those systems. Customers can buy hardware and support separately or in bundles. For example, Kynocks recently sold a network system, training, and five years of service for $2 million. If purchased separately the network would have cost $1.5 million, the training $125,000, and the service $750,000. The training is provided over six months after the installation of the network.

Required:

a. Identify alternative ways of recognizing revenue and indicate how much revenue would be recognized each year under each of the alternatives.
b. Explain which objectives of financial reporting would be served by each alternative.
c. Indicate which alternative could be supported by the revenue recognition criteria.
d. Which method would you recommend Kynocks use for the four-year contract?

P4-5. **(Determining when to recognize revenue, LO 1, 2, 4, 7)** Noggle Engineering Services provides support for telecommunications networks. The company is relatively new and recently began offering long-term service contracts. A client can sign a three-, four-, or five-year contract for maintenance and support for its network. For example, a new client signed a four-year contract for maintenance and support. The contract requires the client to pay $5,000 on the first day of each year for the term of the contract. Noggle provides 24/7 rapid-response service whenever needed by the client. Based on experience and its knowledge of the industry, Noggle's management expects that as a network gets older more service will be required and the cost of providing service will increase. Management estimates that for the four-year contract 15 percent of the costs will be incurred in the first year, 20 percent in the second year, 30 percent in the third year, and 35 percent in the fourth year.

Required:

a. Identify alternative ways of recognizing revenue and indicate how much revenue would be recognized each year under each of the alternatives.
b. Explain which objectives of financial reporting would be served by each alternative.
c. Indicate which alternative could be supported by the revenue recognition criteria.
d. Which method would you recommend Noggle use for the four-year contract.

P4-6. **(Determining when to recognize revenue, LO 1, 2)** *Good Health Magazine* (GHM) is a monthly publication devoted to healthful living. The magazine is published monthly and can be purchased at newsstands for $5 a copy. The publisher delivers the magazine to newsstands at the beginning of the month and will accept up to 20 percent of an order as returns. From experience, GHM can make fairly good estimates of returns. Readers can also subscribe to the magazine for one, two, or three-year periods. With a subscription GHM mails the magazine to the subscriber each month, after payment in full for the subscription is received. The subscription price per copy is substantially lower than the newsstand price. GHM promises to refund any unused portion of the subscription. Historically, about 5 percent of customers ask for a refund.

Required:

Explain how GHM should recognize its revenue. Consider newsstand and subscription revenue separately. Be sure to use the revenue recognition criteria to support your answer.

P4-7. **(Observing the effects of different revenue recognition methods on financial ratios, LO 1, 2, 3, 5, 7)** On July 15, 2016, Tidnish Vessel Refitters Ltd. (Tidnish) signed a contract to refit a 25-year-old supertanker to meet new environmental standards and operate more efficiently. Tidnish has provided you with the following information about the contract:

i. Tidnish expects the refitting to take three years.
ii. Tidnish will receive $20,000,000 for the refitting. Tidnish will receive payments on the following schedule:
    - $4,000,000 when the contract is signed.
    - $4,800,000 on June 1, 2017.
    - $8,000,000 on February 1, 2018, the expected completion date of the project.
    - $3,200,000 on July 15, 2019.
iii. The total cost of the refitting is expected to be $12,800,000. Costs will be incurred as follows:
    - 2016: $0
    - 2017: $8,000,000
    - 2018: $4,800,000
    - 2019: $0
iv. Other costs associated with the contract are $1,600,000 in each of 2017 and 2018. These costs are treated as period costs in the calculation of income.
v. Tidnish's year-end is July 31.

Required:

a. Calculate revenue, expenses, gross margin, and net income for each year using the following revenue recognition methods:
    i. Percentage-of-completion based on costs incurred
    ii. Zero-profit
    iii. Cash collection (*Hint:* Match refurbishing costs based on the proportion of cash collected in each year.)
b. Calculate the gross margin percentage and the profit margin percentage for each year.
c. Does it matter how Tidnish accounts for its revenue from the refitting contract? To whom does it matter and why?
d. Is the actual economic performance of Tidnish affected by how it accounts for the revenue from the refitting contract? Explain.

P4-8. **(Observing the effects of different revenue recognition methods on financial ratios, LO 1, 2, 3, 5, 7)** Thorsby Construction Ltd. (Thorsby) recently received a contract to do long-needed repairs on the major bridges leading to a large city. The bridges have stress fractures and other evidence of deterioration and the municipal and provincial government agreed to jointly finance repairs. The repairs to all the bridges are expected to take three years. Thorsby will receive $52.5 million in total for the work. A payment of $10.5 million will be made when the contract is signed on July 15, 2017 and $13.3 million on June 1, 2018. Thorsby will receive $21 million when the work is complete, expected to be in May 2019. A final payment of $7.7 million is to be made 90 days after the repairs are complete. Thorsby's year-end is July 31.

Thorsby expects to incur the following costs during each fiscal year for the work:

2017	2018	2019	2020	Total
$0	$21,000,000	$12,600,000	$0	$33,600,000

In addition, Thorsby expects to incur $4,200,000 in additional costs in each of fiscal 2018 and 2019. These costs will be treated as period costs in the calculation of income.

Required:

a. Calculate revenue, expenses, gross margin, and net income for each year using the following revenue recognition methods:
    i. Percentage-of-completion based on costs incurred
    ii. Zero-profit
    iii. Cash collection (*Hint:* Match construction costs based on the proportion of cash collected in each year.)

b. Calculate the gross margin percentage and the profit margin percentage for each year.
c. Does it matter how Thorsby accounts for its revenue from the repairs contract? To whom does it matter and why?
d. Is the actual economic performance of Thorsby affected by how it accounts for the revenue from the repairs contract? Explain.

P4-9. **(Observing the effects of different revenue recognition methods on financial ratios, LO 1, 2, 3, 5, 7)** Antler Manufacturing Ltd. (Antler) is a newly formed company specializing in the production of high-quality machine parts. Paul Wayne incorporated Antler on the understanding it would receive a large contract from his previous employer, Pocologan Inc. (Pocologan), to manufacture parts. Antler has rented the space and equipment it needs to operate. During Antler's first year of operations, the following transactions and economic events take place:

i. January 3, 2017: Paul Wayne contributes $1,000,000 cash in exchange for 100,000 common shares in Antler.
ii. January 5, 2017: Antler borrows $500,000 from Pocologan. The loan carries an interest rate of 10 percent per year. No interest or principal needs to be paid until 2020.
iii. January 8, 2017: Antler rents space and equipment to operate the business. Rent of $400,000 for two years is paid.
iv. January 10, 2017: Antler signs the contract with Pocologan. The contract requires that Antler manufacture and deliver $8,000,000 in parts over the period July 1, 2017 to December 31, 2019. The contract requires payment by Pocologan within 90 days of each delivery by Antler. The selling price of all parts is specified in the contract. Antler begins production of the parts immediately. Pocologan operates a just-in-time inventory system, which requires that Antler be ready to deliver parts within three hours of being notified by Pocologan that parts are required. As a result, Antler is required to keep an adequate supply of parts on hand to meet demand.
v. During 2017, Antler produced and delivered parts, and collected cash in the following amounts:

Selling price of parts produced during 2017	$2,800,000
Cost of parts produced during 2017	$1,680,000
Selling price of parts delivered to Pocologan during 2017	$1,800,000
Cost of parts delivered to Pocologan during 2017	$1,080,000
Cash collected from Pocologan during 2017	$1,050,000
Cost of parts that were paid for by Pocologan during 2017	$630,000

vi. All costs incurred to produce the parts were purchased on credit. Of the $1,680,000 incurred to produce parts in 2017, $1,520,000 had been paid by December 31, 2017.
vii. During 2017, Antler incurred additional costs of $420,000, all on credit. As of December 31, 2017, $350,000 of these costs had been paid. Because these costs were not directly related to the production of parts, Antler plans to expense them in full in 2017. This amount doesn't include the amount paid for rent and the interest expense.
viii. Antler has a December 31 year-end.

Required:

a. Use an accounting equation spreadsheet or journal entries and T-accounts to record the transactions and economic events that occurred in 2017 for Antler. Complete this process separately for the following critical events for recognizing revenue:
   i. Production
   ii. Delivery
   iii. Collection of cash

b. Prepare Antler's income statement for 2017 and its balance sheet as of December 31, 2017 using each of the three critical events (production, delivery, and collection of cash). Your income statements should show revenue, cost of goods sold, gross margin, other expenses, and net income.
c. Calculate the gross margin percentage, profit margin percentage, current ratio, and the debt-to-equity ratio for 2017 for each critical event.
d. Which method of revenue recognition gives the best indication of Antler's performance and liquidity? Explain.
e. Does it matter how Antler recognizes revenue? To whom does it matter and why?
f. Is the actual economic performance of Antler affected by how it recognizes revenue? Explain.

P4-10. **(Observing the effects of different revenue recognition methods on financial ratios, LO 1, 2, 3, 7)** Kinkora Manufacturing Ltd. (Kinkora) is a newly formed company specializing in the production of a new type of pizza oven. Adam Daniel organized Kinkora on the understanding that it would receive a large contract for pizza ovens from his previous employer, Cascumpec Inc. (Cascumpec), which was planning to renovate its chain of pizza restaurants. Cascumpec is one of the largest pizza restaurant chains in central Canada. Kinkora has rented the space and equipment it needs to operate its business. During Kinkora's first year of operations, the following transactions and economic events took place:

- July 3, 2018: Adam Daniel contributes $200,000 cash in exchange for 100,000 common shares in Kinkora.
- July 5, 2018: Kinkora borrows $400,000 from Cascumpec. The loan carries an interest rate of 10 percent per year. No interest or principal must be paid until 2022.
- July 8, 2018: Kinkora rents space and equipment to operate the business. Rent of $150,000 for two years is paid.
- July 10, 2018: Kinkora signs the contract with Cascumpec. The contract requires that Kinkora manufacture and deliver $2,000,000 in pizza ovens over the period January 1, 2018 to June 30, 2021. The contract requires that Cascumpec pay within 90 days of delivery by Kinkora. The selling price of the pizza ovens is specified in the contract. Kinkora begins production of the pizza ovens immediately.
- During 2018 Kinkora produced and delivered pizza ovens, and collected cash in the following amounts:

Selling price of ovens produced during 2018	$1,300,000
Cost of ovens produced during 2018	650,000
Selling price of ovens delivered to Cascumpec during 2018	800,000
Cost of ovens delivered to Cascumpec during 2018	400,000
Cash collected from Cascumpec during 2018	460,000
Cost of ovens that were paid for by Cascumpec during 2018	230,000

- All costs incurred to produce the ovens were purchased on credit. Of the $650,000 incurred to produce ovens in 2018, $580,000 had been paid by June 30, 2018.
- During 2018, Kinkora incurred additional costs of $190,000, all on credit. As of June 30, 2018, $160,000 of these costs had been paid. Because these costs were not directly used in the production of ovens, Kinkora plans to expense them in full in fiscal 2018. This amount excludes the amount paid for rent and the interest expense.
- Kinkora has a June 30 year-end.

Required:

a. Use an accounting equation spreadsheet or journal entries and T-accounts to record the transactions and economic events that occurred in 2018 for Kinkora. Complete this process separately for the following critical events for recognizing revenue:
   i. Production
   ii. Delivery
   iii. Collection of cash
b. Prepare Kinkora's income statement for the year ended June 30, 2018 and its balance sheet as of June 30, 2018 using each of the three critical events (production, delivery, and collection of cash). Your income statements should show revenue, cost of goods sold, gross margin, other expenses, and net income.
c. Calculate the gross margin percentage, profit margin percentage, current ratio, and the debt-equity ratio for fiscal 2018 for each critical event.
d. Which method of calculating the ratios in (c) gives the best indication of Kinkora's performance and liquidity? Explain.
e. Does it matter how Kinkora recognizes revenue? To whom does it matter and why?
f. Is the actual economic performance of Kinkora affected by how it recognizes revenue? Explain.

P4-11. **(Recognizing revenue in a bill and hold arrangement, LO 1, 4)** Wandby Inc. (Wandby) makes plastic lawn furniture. Many of the company's products are generic styles that are sold to distributors and retailers across North America. The company also designs and produces furniture to customers' specifications. In 2017, Wandby entered into a number of arrangements with customers whereby orders were produced but not shipped to customers as of the end of the year. Each arrangement is a bit different and management isn't sure when revenue should be recognized in each case. Provide a report to management explaining when you think revenue should be recognized for each arrangement (whether revenue should be recognized on production, delivery, or some other point). Wandby's year-end is December 31.

a. Wandby received a large order from a regular customer for a line of custom furniture it has purchased for many years. The furniture is needed to restock the customer's distribution centre in advance of spring sales. Normally, the customer wants the order delivered by the end of December but this year asked Wandby to delay shipment pending completion of renovations of the distribution centre. The customer estimates delivery will occur in early February. Wandy agreed to the arrangement and completed production of the furniture on December 19. The furniture has been packed and prepared for shipping with the customer's name and address, and has been set aside in a secure area of the warehouse. The customer agreed to pay for the goods within 30 days of the completion of production and an invoice has been mailed.
b. To use excess capacity on one of its production lines, Wandby contacted an established customer about pre-ordering furniture it has been ordering for a number of years. The customer agrees, but at the end of the year it isn't ready to take delivery because it already has an adequate supply of the product. The goods are to be shipped sometime in the next six to eight months, if and when they are needed. The customer will pay the market price at the time. Wandby has completed production of the products and they have been packaged and are awaiting delivery to the customer.
c. In October, Wandby received a firm order for a standard line of furniture. The customer paid a 30 percent deposit on the final price to ensure delivery. The customer wants the products delivered in mid-February. Since the furniture is a standard product, it will produce the order close to the delivery date, probably in late January or early February.

P4-12. **(Evaluating when to recognize revenue, LO 1, 2)** Wear It Again Sam sells good-quality used clothing. People with wardrobe items they no long want or need can bring it to the Wear It Again Sam store where it will be sold on the person's behalf.

The customer and the store manager agree on a selling price for the clothing items and they are displayed in the store. Items are displayed in the store for three months. In the first month at the agreed price, in the second month at a 30 percent discount, and in the third month at a 60 percent discount. If an item is unsold after three months the owner can pick it up or it's given to charity. If the item sells, the person receives 50 percent of the selling price and Wear It Again Sam keeps 50 percent. About 15 percent of the time, an item of clothing is sold but the person doesn't come in collect her money.

Required:

When should Wear It Again Sam recognize revenue on the sale of clothes and how much should it recognize? Explain your answer. Don't forget the money that isn't collected.

P4-13. **(Evaluating when to recognize revenue, LO 1, 2)** Fair Jewellers is a retail jewellery store. Fair offers a lay-away program allowing customers to make a down payment on an item in the store. The store holds the item for the customer until it's paid in full. Customers are required to pay in full within 180 days of the down payment. Customers don't have to sign a formal agreement to pay for or purchase the selected item. If the customer fails to pay in full, the customer loses the down payment. If the merchandise is lost, damaged, or destroyed, Fair must either refund the down payment or provide replacement merchandise. In the past, about 8 percent of customers didn't complete the purchase and lost their payments.

Required:

When should Fair Jewellers recognize revenue from the lay-away sales? Also address how Fair should account for the deposits that are lost. Explain your answers.

P4-14. **(Evaluating when to recognize revenue and the objectives of financial reporting, LO 1, 2, 5, 7)** In September 2017, the sole shareholder of Molanosa Ltd. (Molanosa) agreed to sell 100 percent of the shares of the company to Winona Ltd. The terms of the sale require Winona to pay the shareholder $1 million when the deal closes on February 15, 2018 plus two times net income for the year ended December 31, 2017. Winona also agreed to pay an additional $100,000 if net income for 2017 exceeds $200,000. You are Winona's CFO and you have just received Molanosa's financial statements for 2017, which shows net income for the year of $207,900. Further investigation showed that in late December 2017, Molanosa made a $20,000 shipment of goods to a new customer. Molanosa had been in negotiations with the new customer for some time and the final agreement was an important step in its planned expansion into western Canada. The terms of the sale are unusual in that they allow the customer to return any and all of the goods shipped at any time up until March 1, 2018. The customer isn't required to pay for the goods until March 31, 2018. Molanosa normally recognizes revenue when goods are delivered to the customer and normally provides 30 days to pay. Molanosa recognized the sale to the new customer in 2017.

Required:

Prepare a report to Winona's CFO analyzing Molanosa's sale to the new customer. Your report should include an evaluation of the appropriateness of Molanosa's accounting for the sale and an assessment of why it might have entered into this transaction and why it might have accounted for it this way.

P4-15. **(Considering when to recognize expenses, LO 4, 5, 7)** Duthil Ltd. is a small public company that publishes a variety of newsletters and magazines. The CEO and founder of Duthil owns 35 percent of the shares of the company with the remainder owned by public investors. Duthil makes money through the sale of subscriptions and individual issues of its magazines and newsletters (revenue is recognized when a publication is mailed to a subscriber or an individual issue is sold) and through the sale of advertising in the publications. In late 2017, Duthil conducted a campaign to increase subscriptions. The company engaged a telemarketing firm to call potential subscribers in the desired demographic group. The cost of the campaign was $66,000. As a result of the campaign, several hundred new subscriptions were obtained. The subscriptions will begin in fiscal 2018 and will generate about $75,000 for the year. All the new subscriptions are for one year but management expects that approximately 50 percent of those subscriptions will be renewed for the next year, and then for each year after that approximately 75 percent of the subscribers will renew. Duthil's year-end is December 31.

Required:

a. Who are Duthil's stakeholders and what use do they have for the financial statements?
b. What objectives of financial reporting might Duthil's management consider when preparing the financial statements? Explain.
c. How would you recommend the objectives be ranked? Explain.
d. Prepare a report to Duthil's management explaining how to account for the costs incurred to increase the number of subscribers. In your answer, be sure to consider your responses to (a), (b), and (c) above. Also consider whether the costs incurred should be classified as assets or expenses when incurred, and if considered assets when incurred, over what period the asset should be expensed. Explain your response.

P4-16. **(Evaluating objectives of financial reporting and recommending how to recognize revenue, LO 1, 2, 7)** Notigi Mines Ltd. (Notigi) is a mining venture that recently began operations in northern Manitoba. The mine has been under development for the last two years and will produce its first shipments of refined metal before the end of the current fiscal year. Two senior executives who have extensive mining experience manage the mine. The mine is owned by a syndicate of 20 investors, mainly professionals such as accountants, doctors, lawyers, and dentists who live in various parts of western Canada.

Notigi extracts ore from the ground and ships it to another company for processing into refined metal. The processing company then returns the refined metal to Notigi for sale and shipment to buyers. Notigi has already entered into long-term contracts with several buyers to purchase virtually all of the mine's production at prices specified in the contract. Any production not covered by the long-term contracts can easily be sold at prevailing prices in the open market.

Required:

a. What do you think Notigi's objectives of accounting might be? Explain.
b. How would you rank the objectives? Explain.
c. When would you recommend that revenue be recognized on the sale of the refined metal? Explain your recommendation. Make sure that you consider the constraints, facts, and objectives in your answer.

P4-17. **(Evaluating objectives of financial reporting and recommending how to recognize revenue, LO 1, 2, 7)** Chetwynd Renovations Ltd. (Chetwynd) is a recently formed company that renovates commercial and industrial properties in southern British Columbia. Chetwynd specializes in repairing damage cause by fire, floods, and other disasters. Chetwynd is a private company with five shareholders: Alex and Evan, brothers who operate the company, and three of their cousins, who live in different parts of the world. Alex and Evan have worked in the construction and renovation industries for several years and they feel they have the expertise to run a company of their own. The three cousins supplied about 70 percent of the cash Chetwynd needed to get started, with the remainder borrowed from the bank. Most of the money raised has been spent.

In December 2017, Chetwynd won a contract to renovate a building in Richmond, B.C. that had suffered significant damage in a fire. This will be Chetwynd's first large job. The renovations will take about 18 months to complete and work is scheduled to begin in early January 2018. Chetwynd will receive $5.88 million to do the renovations. The contract specifies the following payment schedule:

• On commencement of work	$ 300,000
• On the first day of each month beginning with the month after work begins ($210,000 per month for 18 months)	3,780,000
• On completion of the renovations	1,200,000
• 90 days after completion	600,000
• Total	$5,880,000

From this amount, Chetwynd will have to pay the costs of the renovation, which it estimates to be about $4,500,000. Construction costs are expected to be incurred evenly over the 18 months. Chetwynd's year-end is December 31.

Required:

a. What do you think Chetwynd's objectives of accounting might be? Explain.
b. How would you rank the objectives? Explain.
c. What different revenue recognition methods could Chetwynd consider for the warehouse project? How much revenue would be recognized in 2017, 2018, and 2019 under the different methods you identified? Show your work.
d. When would you recommend that revenue be recognized on the renovation project? Explain your recommendation. Make sure that you consider the constraints, facts, and objectives in your answer.

P4-18. **(Considering when to recognize revenue, LO 1, 2, 7, 8)** Teslin Inc. (Teslin) is a medium-sized manufacturer of plastic storage containers. Teslin is a private corporation that is owned entirely by a single shareholder, Rima Ishtiaque. Ms. Ishtiaque isn't involved in the day-to-day management of Teslin but she speaks regularly with Teslin's president, Mr. Krajden. Mr. Krajden is compensated with a salary plus a bonus based on Teslin's net income.

On October 1, 2017 Teslin signed a $1,000,000 contract with the Government of Canada to design and manufacture storage containers for all the tax dollars it collects from Canadians. The storage containers must be delivered by April 1, 2019. The government will pay $250,000 on April 1, 2018, $250,000 on January 15, 2019, and the balance 30 days after all the containers have been delivered. Teslin plans to begin production of the containers in early 2018. Teslin plans to ship 10 percent of the contracted containers per month beginning in September 2018. The contract stipulates that Teslin pay a penalty of $20,000 per week if the containers aren't completely delivered by April 1, 2018. Teslin had to borrow $300,000 from the bank to finance the project. Teslin expects to earn $225,000 from this contract.

You have been hired by Mr. Krajden to provide advice to him on how to recognize revenue on the contract with the government. Teslin's year-end is December 31.

Required:

a. Who are the possible users of Teslin's financial statements and what use do they have for the statements?
b. What objectives of financial reporting would you suggest that Mr. Krajden consider when preparing Teslin's financial statements? Explain.
c. How would you advise Mr. Krajden to rank the objectives? Explain.
d. What critical events for recognizing the revenue on the government contract can you identify? Explain.
e. When would you recommend that Teslin recognize the revenue on the contract? Make sure to consider the constraints, facts, and objectives when responding.

P4-19. **(Evaluating when a partnership of lawyers should recognize revenue, LO 1, 2, 3, 5, 7)** Elnora and Partners is a recently formed a partnership of lawyers. The partnership has ten partners (all of whom are practising lawyers) and 15 associate lawyers (lawyers who work for the partnership but who aren't partners), along with 12 other employees. The partnership's financial statements will be used to determine the following:

- The amount of income tax each partner pays (remember, partners, not the partnership, pay income tax).
- The amount of money paid to each partner, based on the net income of the partnership.
- The amount a new partner pays to join the partnership and the amount a departing partner is paid for his or her partnership interest. In addition, the financial statements are provided to the bank because the partnership has a large line of credit available to it.

The partnership's September 30 year-end has just passed and the managing partner of the firm has asked for your advice about how to recognize revenue. The managing partner provides you with the following information on how the partnership generates revenue:

i. Some clients are billed at the completion of a case, based on the number of hours lawyers worked on the case. (Each lawyer has an hourly billing rate.) Lawyers keep track of the time they spend on each case and report the number of hours each month to the accounting department, which keeps track of the hours spent on each case by each lawyer. The amount actually billed to a client may differ from the actual charges generated by the lawyers who worked on the case. (That is, the amount billed may differ from the number of hours worked multiplied by the hourly billing rate.) The final amount billed is based on the judgment of the partner in charge of the case. Clients have 60 days from receipt of their bill to pay.
ii. Some clients pay only if their cases are successful. The partnership receives a percentage of the settlement if the client wins the case. It can be difficult to determine whether a client will win a case and the amount that will be received if the client does win. These cases can take years to resolve.
iii. Some clients pay amounts called retainers, which are amounts paid to the partnership before services are provided. The retainer is used to pay for legal services as they are provided. If the amount of retainer isn't used by the end of the year, the remaining amount is applied against future years' legal services.
iv. Clients who wish to have legal advice available to them 24 hours a day, seven days a week, pay a fee of $10,000 per year for the service. (The $10,000 fee is simply for the privilege of having a lawyer available all the time. These clients also have to pay the lawyer's hourly rate for the advice given.)

Required:

a. What are the possible objectives of financial reporting? Explain each objective that you identify. Are there any conflicts among the objectives? Explain.
b. Rank the objectives in order of importance. Explain your ranking.
c. When should the partnership recognize its revenue? Explain your recommendations fully. Make sure you discuss constraints, facts, and objectives in your answer.

P4-20. **(Selecting and justifying revenue recognition alternatives to suit the objectives of financial reporting, LO 2, 3, 5, 7)** Graphite Discount Building Supplies Limited (Graphite) is a chain of large building supply stores. Graphite sells building supplies to individuals and small contractors and builders. Until recently, Graphite was a division of another company, but the previous owner decided to sell Graphite because it wasn't in its core business. Graphite had been profitable, but the profits were small and it was consuming too much of senior management's time. A group of 25 business people purchased Graphite. None of the new owners will be involved in the day-to-day management of Graphite, but some will sit on the board of directors. The new owners paid cash for Graphite. The new owners also agreed to pay the previous owner an amount equal to 10 percent of Graphite's net income for each of the next three years (including 2017) as reported in Graphite's audited general purpose financial statements. The board of directors hired a new management team to operate Graphite. The managers will receive performance-based bonuses, in part based on net income as reported in the general purpose financial statements.

It's now mid-January 2018. Graphite is preparing its financial statements for the year ended December 31, 2017. The chair of the board of directors of Graphite has asked you to provide advice on a number of outstanding accounting issues. After the board has discussed your recommendations, they will be given to Graphite's management team for implementation. The following are the issues you have been asked to address.

a. Graphite implemented a policy that requires customers to pay an annual membership fee to shop at its stores. The annual fee is payable when the customer "joins" and on each anniversary of joining. The fee gives a customer the right to shop at Graphite's stores and benefit from the discounts it offers. A customer has the right to cancel the membership at any time and receive a full refund of the membership fee. The fee is refundable in full at any time during the year, regardless of whether the customer has purchased anything in the store. If a customer requests a refund, he or she is not allowed to rejoin for one year. Management estimates that about 40 percent of its customers will request refunds each year.
b. Graphite's business with most customers is transacted in cash or on credit cards. Graphite offers credit terms to builders and contractors, allowing them up to 90 days to pay. Graphite has made special credit arrangements with a small number of struggling home builders. Graphite has extended credit terms to these struggling builders even though sales of the homes they are building have been slower than expected. In these cases, Graphite has agreed to accept payment each time a builder sells one of its homes.
c. During the year, Graphite launched a major advertising campaign to increase awareness of its stores and products. Management wanted to raise the profile of the Graphite chain in the minds of customers and potential customers so that people would think of Graphite when they needed hardware and building supplies. Costs of the campaign included television, radio, and newspaper advertising and sponsorship of community events.

Required:

Prepare the report requested by Graphite's board of directors. Your report should:

i. Identify the likely users of the financial statements and describe the uses they will have for the statements.
ii. Identify and explain the possible objectives of financial reporting and rank the objectives. (You should respond from the perspective of an advisor to Graphite's board of directors. Recognize that different stakeholders could have different objectives. For example, the objectives of the managers may not be the same as the board.)
iii. Are there any constraints that limit the accounting choices that Graphite can make?
iv. Identify and discuss reasonable alternative treatments for each accounting issue and make a recommendation about how Graphite should account for each issue. Your discussion and recommendations should consider any relevant constraints, facts, and objectives.

Using Financial Statements

ROGERS COMMUNICATIONS INC.

Rogers Communications Inc. (Rogers) is a diversified Canadian communications and media company engaged in three primary lines of business. Rogers Wireless is Canada's largest wireless voice and data communications services provider and the country's only national carrier operating on the world standard GSM, HSPA+, and LTE technology platforms. Rogers Cable is a leading Canadian cable services provider, offering cable television, high-speed Internet access, and telephony products for residential and business customers. Rogers Media is Canada's premier group of category-leading broadcast, specialty, sports, print and online media assets, with businesses in radio and television broadcasting, televised shopping, sports entertainment, and magazine and trade journal publication. Rogers' common stock trades on the TSX and NYSE.[7]

Rogers' consolidated balance sheets and statements of income, along with extracts from the notes to the financial statements and the management discussion and analysis, are provided in Exhibit 4.6.[8] Use this information to answer questions FS4-1 to FS4-11.

FS4-1. When customers sign contracts for wireless services with Rogers, they often receive a "free" phone. Are these phones really free? Explain how the phones are paid for if customers don't pay for them when they are received. What possible ways could Rogers recognize revenue on packages that include a free phone and three-year service contract? What would be the impact of the different ways on the income statement? Which would you recommend? Explain why.

FS4-2. Read note 2(s) to Rogers' financial statements called "Use of Estimates." Why do you think this note is included in the statements? How does it help stakeholders? What does the note caution stakeholders? Do you think Rogers' financial statements would be more useful if there were no estimates? Explain. What are some estimates Rogers' management would have to make with respect to revenue and revenue recogniton?

EXHIBIT 4.6 Rogers Communications Inc.: Extracts from Financial Statements

CONSOLIDATED STATEMENTS OF INCOME

(IN MILLIONS OF CANADIAN DOLLARS, EXCEPT PER SHARE AMOUNTS)

Years ended December 31,	**2011**	2010
Operating revenue	**$ 12,428**	$ 12,142
Operating expenses:		
Operating costs (*note 5*)	**7,787**	7,571
Integration, restructuring and acquisition costs (*note 8*)	**70**	40
Depreciation and amortization (*notes 12 and 13*)	**1,743**	1,639
Impairment of assets (*note 13*)	**–**	11
Operating income	**2,828**	2,881
Finance costs (*note 6*)	**(738)**	(768)
Other income (expense), net	**1**	(1)
Share of the income of associates and joint ventures accounted for using the equity method, net of tax	**7**	2
Income before income taxes	**2,098**	2,114
Income tax expense (*note 9*)	**535**	612
Net income for the year	**$ 1,563**	$ 1,502

EXHIBIT 4.6 (continued) Rogers Communications Inc.: Extracts from Financial Statements

CONSOLIDATED STATEMENTS OF FINANCIAL POSITION

(IN MILLIONS OF CANADIAN DOLLARS)

	December 31, 2011	December 31, 2010	January 1, 2010
ASSETS			
Current assets:			
Cash and cash equivalents	**$ –**	$ –	$ 378
Accounts receivable	**1,574**	1,443	1,289
Other current assets (*note 11*)	**322**	315	277
Current portion of derivative instruments (*note 18*)	**16**	1	4
	1,912	1,759	1,948
Property, plant and equipment (*note 12*)	**9,114**	8,437	8,136
Goodwill (*note 13*)	**3,280**	3,108	3,011
Intangible assets (*note 13*)	**2,721**	2,591	2,640
Investments (*note 14*)	**1,107**	933	715
Derivative instruments (*note 18*)	**64**	6	78
Other long-term assets (*note 15*)	**134**	147	113
Deferred tax assets (*note 9*)	**30**	52	84
	$ 18,362	$ 17,033	$ 16,725
LIABILITIES AND SHAREHOLDERS' EQUITY			
Current liabilities:			
Bank advances	**$ 57**	$ 45	$ –
Accounts payable and accrued liabilities	**2,085**	2,133	2,066
Income tax payable	**–**	238	147
Current portion of provisions (*note 16*)	**35**	21	14
Current portion of long-term debt (*note 17*)	**–**	–	1
Current portion of derivative instruments (*note 18*)	**37**	67	80
Unearned revenue	**335**	329	335
	2,549	2,833	2,643
Provisions (*note 16*)	**38**	62	58
Long-term debt (*note 17*)	**10,034**	8,654	8,396
Derivative instruments (*note 18*)	**503**	840	1,004
Other long-term liabilities (*note 19*)	**276**	229	177
Deferred tax liabilities (*note 9*)	**1,390**	655	291
	14,790	13,273	12,569
Shareholders' equity (*note 21*)	**3,572**	3,760	4,156
	$ 18,362	$ 17,033	$ 16,725

EXHIBIT 4.6 (continued) Rogers Communications Inc.: Extracts from Financial Statements

2. SIGNIFICANT ACCOUNTING POLICIES:

(d) Revenue recognition:

The Company's principal sources of revenues and recognition of these revenues for financial statement purposes are as follows:

(i) monthly subscriber fees in connection with wireless and wireline services, cable, telephony, Internet services, rental of equipment, network services and media subscriptions are recorded as revenue on a pro rata basis as the service is provided;

(ii) revenue from airtime, data services, roaming, long-distance and optional services, pay-per-use services, video rentals and other sales of products are recorded as revenue as the services or products are delivered;

(iii) revenue from the sale of wireless and cable equipment is recorded when the equipment is delivered and accepted by the independent dealer or subscriber in the case of direct sales. Equipment subsidies related to new and existing subscribers are recorded as a reduction of equipment revenues upon activation of the equipment;

(iv) installation fees and activation fees charged to subscribers do not meet the criteria as a separate unit of accounting. As a result, in Wireless, these fees are recorded as part of equipment revenue and, in Cable, are deferred and amortized over the related service period. The related service period for Cable ranges from 26 to 48 months, based on subscriber disconnects, transfers of service and moves. Incremental direct installation costs related to reconnects are deferred to the extent of deferred installation fees and amortized over the same period as these related installation fees. New connect installation costs are capitalized to PP&E and amortized over the useful lives of the related assets;

(v) advertising revenue is recorded in the period the advertising airs on the Company's radio or television stations; is featured in the Company's publications; or is displayed on the Company's digital properties;

(vi) monthly subscription revenues received by television stations for subscriptions from cable and satellite providers are recorded in the month in which they are earned;

(vii) The Toronto Blue Jays Baseball Club's ("Blue Jays") revenue from home game admission and concessions is recognized as the related games are played during the baseball season. Revenue from radio and television agreements is recorded at the time the related games are aired. The Blue Jays also receive revenue from the Major League Baseball Revenue Sharing Agreement which distributes funds to and from member clubs, based on each club's revenues. This revenue is recognized in the season in which it is earned, when the amount is estimable and collectibility is reasonably assured;

(viii) discounts provided to customers related to combined purchases of Wireless, Cable and Media products and services are charged directly to the revenue for the products and services to which they relate; and

(ix) awards granted to customers through customer loyalty programs are considered a separately identifiable component of the sales transactions and, as a result, are deferred until recognized as operating revenue when the awards are redeemed by the customer and the goods or services are provided by the Company. The portion allocated to the award credit is estimated based on the fair value of the right to the future goods and services. The amount of revenue recognized is based on the number of award credits redeemed relative to the total number of award credits that are expected to be redeemed.

The Company offers certain products and services as part of multiple deliverable arrangements. The Company divides multiple deliverable arrangements into separate units of accounting. Components of multiple deliverable arrangements are separately accounted for provided the delivered elements have stand-alone value to the customers and the fair value of any undelivered elements can be objectively and reliably determined. Consideration for these units is measured and allocated amongst the accounting units based upon their fair values and the Company's relevant revenue recognition policies are applied to them. The Company recognizes revenue to the extent that it is probable that the economic benefits will flow to the Company and the revenue can be reliably measured.

Unearned revenue includes subscriber deposits, cable installation fees and amounts received from subscribers related to services and subscriptions to be provided in future periods.

(e) Subscriber acquisition and retention costs:

Except as described in note 2(d)(iv) as it relates to cable installation costs, the Company expenses the costs related to the acquisition or retention of subscribers as incurred.

(s) Use of estimates:

The preparation of financial statements requires management to make judgements, estimates and assumptions that affect the application of accounting policies and the reported amounts of assets, liabilities, revenue and expenses. Actual results could differ from these estimates.

EXHIBIT 4.6 (continued) Rogers Communications Inc.: Extracts from Financial Statements

4. SEGMENTED INFORMATION:

OPERATING SEGMENTS:

Management reviews the operations of the Company by business segments. Effective January 1, 2011, the results of the business segments were reclassified to reflect the change in strategy as described in note 2(b). These business segments are the primary operating segments and are described as follows:

(a) Wireless—This segment provides retail and business voice and data wireless communications services.

(b) Cable—This segment provides cable television, cable telephony and high speed Internet access and telephony products primarily to residential customers. The Cable business consists of the following three subsegments:

(i) Cable Operations segment which provides cable services, high speed Internet service and Rogers Home Phone;

(ii) RBS segment offers local and long-distance telephone, enhanced voice and data services, and IP access to medium and large Canadian businesses and governments; and

(iii) Video segment operates a DVD and video game sale and rental business.

(c) Media—This segment operates the Company's radio and television broadcasting operations, televised shopping, consumer, trade and professional publications, sports entertainment and digital media properties.

(a) Information by reportable segments is as follows:

	Year ended December 31, 2011					Year ended December 31, 2010				
	Wireless	Cable	Media	Corporate items and eliminations	Consolidated totals	Wireless	Cable	Media	Corporate items and eliminations	Consolidated totals
Operating revenue	**$ 7,138**	**$ 3,796**	**$ 1,611**	**$ (117)**	**$ 12,428**	$ 6,973	$ 3,785	$ 1,461	$ (77)	$ 12,142
Operating costs*	**4,102**	**2,184**	**1,431**	**(5)**	**7,712**	3,800	2,359	1,330	18	7,507
	3,036	**1,612**	**180**	**(112)**	**4,716**	3,173	1,426	131	(95)	4,635
Integration, restructuring and acquisition costs	**16**	**39**	**14**	**1**	**70**	5	23	12	–	40
Stock-based compensation expense*	**10**	**9**	**9**	**36**	**64**	12	7	10	21	50
Settlement of pension obligations*	**2**	**5**	**3**	**1**	**11**	–	–	–	–	–
Other items, net*	**–**	**–**	**–**	**–**	**–**	5	5	4	–	14
	$ 3,008	**$ 1,559**	**$ 154**	**$ (150)**	**4,571**	$ 3,151	$ 1,391	$ 105	$ (116)	4,531
Depreciation and amortization	**674**	**843**	**63**	**163**	**1,743**	648	807	60	124	1,639
Impairment of assets	**–**	**–**	**–**	**–**	**–**	–	–	11	–	11
Operating income (loss)	**2,334**	**716**	**91**	**(313)**	**2,828**	2,503	584	34	(240)	2,881

EXHIBIT 4.6 (continued) Rogers Communications Inc.: Extracts from Financial Statements

(c) Product revenue:

Revenue is comprised of the following:

	December 31, 2011	December 31, 2010
Wireless:		
Postpaid	**$ 6,275**	$ 6,229
Prepaid	**326**	297
Network revenue	**6,601**	6,526
Equipment sales	**537**	447
	7,138	6,973
Cable:		
Cable Operations:		
Television	**1,904**	1,835
Internet	**927**	848
Telephony	**478**	507
	3,309	3,190
RBS	**405**	452
Video	**82**	143
	3,796	3,785
Media:		
Advertising	**838**	763
Circulation and subscription	**303**	234
Retail	**263**	265
Blue Jays	**164**	156
Other	**43**	43
	1,611	1,461
Corporate items and intercompany eliminations	**(117)**	(77)
	$ 12,428	$ 12,142

Extract from Rogers' Management Discussion and Analysis

Summarized Wireless Subscriber Results

Years ended December 31, (Subscriber statistics in thousands, except ARPU, churn and usage)	**2011**	2010	Chg
Postpaid			
Gross additions	**1,449**	1,330	119
Net additions	**269**	319	(50)
Total postpaid retail subscribers[1]	**7,574**	7,325	249
Monthly churn	**1.32%**	1.18%	0.14%
Average monthly revenue per user ("ARPU")[2]	**$ 70.26**	$ 72.62	$ (2.36)
Prepaid			
Gross additions	**845**	731	114
Net additions	**109**	147	(38)
Total prepaid retail subscribers	**1,761**	1,652	109
Monthly churn	**3.64%**	3.18%	0.46%
ARPU[2]	**$ 16.02**	$ 16.10	$ (0.08)
Blended ARPU[2]	**$ 60.20**	$ 62.62	$ (2.42)
Blended average monthly minutes of usage	**466**	478	(12)

EXHIBIT 4.6 (continued) Rogers Communications Inc.: Extracts from Financial Statements

Subscriber Churn

Subscriber churn is calculated on a monthly basis. For any particular month, subscriber churn for Wireless and Cable represents the number of subscribers deactivating in the month divided by the aggregate number of subscribers at the beginning of the month. When used or reported for a period greater than one month, subscriber churn represents the sum of the number of subscribers deactivating for each period incurred divided by the sum of the aggregate number of subscribers at the beginning of each period incurred.

Average Revenue per User

ARPU is calculated on a monthly basis. For any particular month, ARPU represents monthly revenue divided by the average number of subscribers during the month. In the case of Wireless, ARPU represents monthly network revenue divided by the average number of subscribers during the month. ARPU, when used in connection with a particular type of subscriber, represents monthly revenue generated from those subscribers divided by the average number of those subscribers during the month. When used or reported for a period greater than one month, ARPU represents the monthly average of the ARPU calculations for the period. We believe ARPU helps to identify trends and to indicate whether we have been successful in attracting and retaining higher value subscribers.

FS4-3. New customers to Rogers' cable service pay installation and activation fees at the outset of their contracts. How does Rogers account for these fees? Explain why this treatment does or doesn't make sense.

FS4-4. How many different ways does Rogers make money? How does it recognize the revenue for each way?

FS4-5. Some Rogers Wireless customers purchase prepaid services. For example, a prepaid wireless customer will pay in advance for airtime and her phone will work as long as there is money in the account. How much revenue did Rogers recognize in 2011 for prepaid wireless services? How does Rogers recognize revenue on services customers pay for in advance? What journal entry would Rogers record when a customer prepays for airtime? How should Rogers account for prepaid services if the services are never used? Should it be recognized as revenue and if so, when? Would your answer change if amounts paid in advance expire after a period of time?

FS4-6. Read Note 2(d)(ix) to Rogers' financial statements. What are loyalty programs and why do companies offer them to customers? Who pays for the "free" goods and services a customer receives from a loyalty program and how/when are they paid for? How does Rogers account for amounts paid for goods and services that pertain to loyalty awards that will received later? What journal entry does Rogers make when a purchase is made that has loyalty benefits associated with it? What challenges and difficulties does Rogers face in accounting for the amount that should be reported on the balance sheet pertaining to future loyalty benefits?

FS4-7. Examine note 4 to Rogers' financial statements and respond to the following questions:

a. What is segmented financial information and why do you think it's provided (consider how it will help you as a stakeholder)?
b. What segments does Rogers provide information about?
c. How much sales and revenue did Rogers earn from each segment in 2010 and 2011? How much operating income was reported for each segment each year? What is the operating profit margin percentage for each segment in each year? Evaluate the performance of each segment.
d. Do you think it would make sense for Rogers to dispose of the segment that generates the lowest amount of operating income or the lowest amount of operating income margin? Explain.

FS4-8. How do the Toronto Blue Jays (which Rogers owns) recognize revenue from home-game admissions? Explain by referring to the revenue recognition criteria why this treatment makes sense. If a fan purchases Blue Jays season tickets in December 2016 for the 2017 baseball season, what journal entry would be recorded at the time of the purchase?

FS4-9. Explain how Rogers recognizes the following types of revenue. Explain why the treatments used are consistent with IFRS:

a. Advertising revenue purchased on a Rogers' radio station;
b. Amounts received from non-Rogers cable and satellite service providers (e.g. Bell, Shaw, Videotron) for providing Rogers-owned specialty channels to their subscribers (e.g., Sportsnet);
c. Hardware sold to retailers and directly to customers.

FS4-10. How much unearned revenue does Rogers report on its December 31, 2011 balance sheet? What does the amount represent? Why is it considered a liability? What does an increase in unearned revenue mean for Rogers' cash flow?

FS4-11. Examine the extract from Rogers' Management Discussion and Analysis called "Summarized Wireless Subscriber Results." How many new postpaid subscribers did Rogers add in 2011? How many subscribers did it lose? What was the net increase in subscribers? What is the monthly churn rate? Why do you think this is an important statistic in the wireless industry? What are the benefits of a low churn rate? What can wireless companies do to reduce the churn rate? What is average revenue per user (ARPU)? Why is this an important statistic in the wireless industry? How did ARPU change from 2010 to 2011? What is the financial statement impact of this change? What steps could Rogers take to increase the ARPU?

ENDNOTES

1. For a fascinating look at how people respond to incentives, see the book *Freakonomics* by Steven D. Levitt and Stephen J. Dubner, published in 2005 by HarperCollins.
2. Extracted from 2012 annual audited financial statements of Indigo Books & Music Inc. and from the 2011 annual audited financial statements of Kinross Gold Corporation, and High Liner Foods Incorporated.
3. WestJet Airlines Ltd. information is extracted from its 2011 annual audited financial statements, which are prepared in accordance with International Financial Reporting Standards.
4. Extracted from Supremex Inc.'s 2011 annual report.
5. Extracted from Leon's Furniture Limited's 2011 annual report.
6. Extracted from Supremex Inc.'s 2011 annual report.
7. Extracted from Rogers Communications Inc.'s 2011 annual report. Used with permission of Rogers Communications Inc. All rights reserved.
8. Ibid.

CHAPTER

5

Cash Flow, Profitability, and the Cash Flow Statement

LEARNING OBJECTIVES

After studying the material in this chapter you will be able to do the following:

LO 1 Explain the importance of cash flow and distinguish cash from operations and net income.

LO 2 Describe the cash cycle.

LO 3 Describe how an entity's cash affects how its business operates.

LO 4 Explain the three categories of cash flow reported in the cash flow statement and identify the types of transactions that apply to each category.

LO 5 Read and interpret the cash flow statement.

LO 6 Explain how manager decisions can affect cash flow information and how accrual accounting policy choices affect the cash flow statement.

—Loblaw Companies Ltd.

In March 2012, Loblaw Companies Limited, Canada's largest food retailer and a leading provider of drugstore, general merchandise, and financial products and services, sliced its way into the Guinness World Records® book.

Staff at over 250 of its stores simultaneously cracked open the most ever wheels of Parmigiano Reggiano cheese. They carried out this feat under the strict supervision of the contest judges and some producers of the iconic cheese who'd flown in from Italy.

Using special cutting tools to beat the record of 176 wheels set in 2008 by U.S. rival Whole Foods, apron-clad Loblaw employees cracked open an impressive 305 wheels. Stores from Halifax to Brossard, Que., to Goderich, Ont., participated in splitting the 34-kilogram rounds of Parmesan, including the Loblaws® at Maple Leaf Gardens* store in downtown Toronto.

If the distinctive cheese is one of Italy's best-known symbols, the same could be said for the Loblaws® at Maple Leaf Gardens,* considered by many to be part of Canada's cultural heritage.

Built before the Second World War, the art deco former arena at 60 Carlton Street in Toronto was home until 1999 to the Toronto Maple Leafs hockey team. It was where screaming girls once fainted at concerts by Elvis Presley and the Beatles. It's now been designated a National Historic Site.

At the November 2011 official opening of the food store, Galen G. Weston, executive chairman, said that the renovation project is supposed to "breathe new life into this iconic Canadian landmark," according to a company news release.

Calling it the "crown jewel of food stores," Loblaw executives were banking on attracting some of the chain's 14 million weekly shoppers to see the Toronto facility's artfully preserved hockey mementoes, including the dot on the floor in Aisle 25 where centre ice used to be. They were also hoping customers will come for the retail sensory experience, such as the 5.4-metre-tall Wall of Cheese, the 50 varieties of cupcakes displayed at the Patisserie window, and the open, elevated kitchen with 14 in-house chefs.

Maple Leaf Gardens is one of the most high-profile business ventures for Loblaw Companies Limited. And it required a lot of upfront investment even before the doors officially opened November 30.

Aside from the $5 million Loblaw agreed to pay for renovating the site (Ryerson University owns it), the company needed money to design the inside of the flagship store, pay consultants, fill it with inventory, and hire and train staff, including the 14 chefs and the dietician. So where did the money come from to do this?

In 2011, Loblaw reported in its annual report that the company had $1.8 billion in cash flow from operations. That means it generated more money selling groceries in its 1,026 stores than it cost them to do business. It also had cash and cash equivalents and short-term investments in the bank of $1.72 billion, which helps it pay its bills during the year.

Will earning that world record with Parmesan cheese help Loblaw's bottom line? Only time will tell.

But the company, which was originally started in 1919, over a full decade before Maple Leaf Gardens was built, can now boast of having two entries in the Guinness tally sheets: as of July 2008, the company also held the recording for having baked the largest Naan bread in the world, weighing in at 9.5 kilograms.

Loblaw employs 135,000 people at its stable of 22 different banners, including nofrills®, Fortinos®, Provigo®, Atlantic Superstore®, T&T, and Zehrs Markets®.

*Reg'd TM. Lic'd use.

Watch the video of the world record cheese-cracking event here: www.thegridto.com/life/food-drink/video-loblaws-cuts-the-cheese.

–E.B.

LO 1 INTRODUCTION—CASH IS KING!

Cash is king. If an entity has enough cash it can pay its bills and weather any storm. Without it, business quickly grinds to a halt. If an entity is short of cash, suppliers may stop supplying and employees may stop working. Remember, it's cash, not income or revenue, that pays the bills.

In the first four chapters of this book, most of our attention has been on developing an understanding of accrual accounting. Accrual measures provide important information about an entity. But, make no mistake, you ignore cash and cash flow at your peril. A business can survive quite nicely without showing a profit, provided it has adequate cash inflows or reserves. But an entity that can't generate enough cash, regardless of how profitable it is, will eventually find itself in trouble because it will be unable to meet its financial obligations. Clearly, focusing only on earnings can give a misleading picture of how an entity is doing.

In this chapter, we will explore the importance of cash flow and liquidity. We will discuss the cash cycle, the process of investing in resources that will generate cash for the entity. Most of the chapter will be devoted to understanding and interpreting the cash flow statement. (We won't cover preparing the cash flow statement.)

LO 2 THE CASH CYCLE

Being in business costs money. An entity usually has to spend money before collecting cash from customers. There is almost always a lag between the expenditure of cash and the receipt of cash. For example, when Leon's opens a new furniture store it must buy, build, or rent an appropriate building; design, decorate, and equip it; stock it with merchandise; hire and train employees; and so on. Once operating, the store continually purchases merchandise and puts it on display, pays employees, and so on. Even a relatively simple business like selling hot dogs on the street requires an upfront investment for equipment and supplies before business begins. The cycle of investing cash in resources, providing goods or services to customers using those resources, and collecting cash from customers is called the **cash cycle**. The cash cycle is shown in Figure 5.1.

It's important to notice in Figure 5.1 that an entity expends cash to purchase resources before it collects any cash from customers. Also notice that the cash cycle is partially

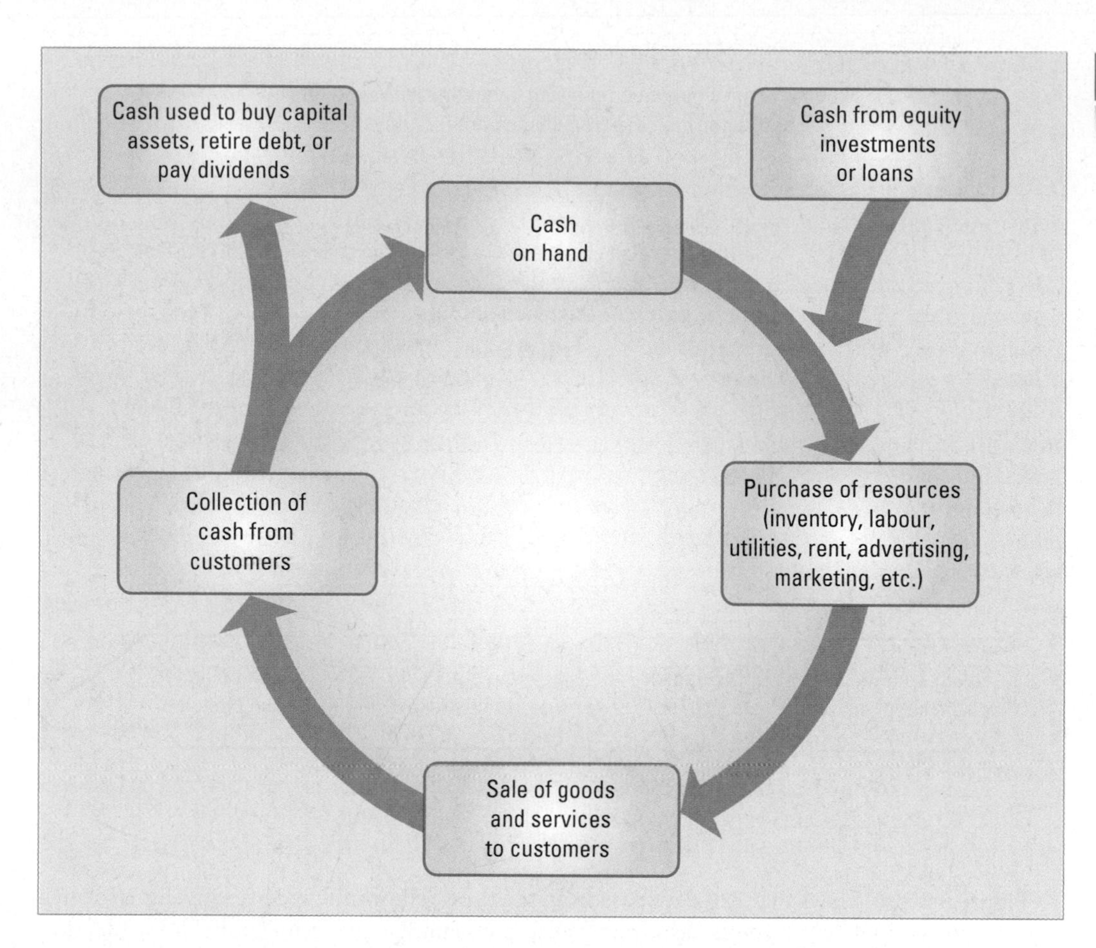

FIGURE 5.1

The Cash Cycle

self-sustaining—the cash generated from customers finances the purchase of new resources that will produce future sales. Cash also enters the cycle from equity investments and loans. These cash injections may be needed, for example, when business expands or the cost of inputs increase. Cash leaves the cycle to repay loans, buy capital assets, and pay dividends to shareholders.

The cash cycle in Figure 5.1 shows all investment, including capital assets, needed to operate a business. A shorter-term view of the cash cycle ignores capital assets and focuses on the investment of cash in operating inputs such as inventory and accounts receivable. The delay between the expenditure of cash and the receipt of cash is called the **cash lag**. We'll examine the cash lag by looking at an example using some numbers (see Figure 5.2). First, here are some relevant definitions:

- **inventory conversion period**—average length of time between receiving inventory from a supplier and selling it to a customer
- **payables deferral period**—average number of days between receipt of goods or services from a supplier to payment of the supplier
- **receivables conversion period**—average length of time between delivery of goods to a customer and receipt of cash
- **inventory self-financing period**—average number of days between the date inventory is paid for by the entity and the date it's paid for by a customer

LO 1, 2

Yellowknife Corp. (Yellowknife) is a distributor of outdoor clothing and equipment. It purchases merchandise from different manufacturers and sells it to retailers. From Figure 5.2, we can see Yellowknife's inventory conversion period (180 days), receivables conversion period (40 days), payables deferral period (30 days), and inventory self-financing period (190 days).

FIGURE 5.2

The Cash Lag for Yellowknife Corp.

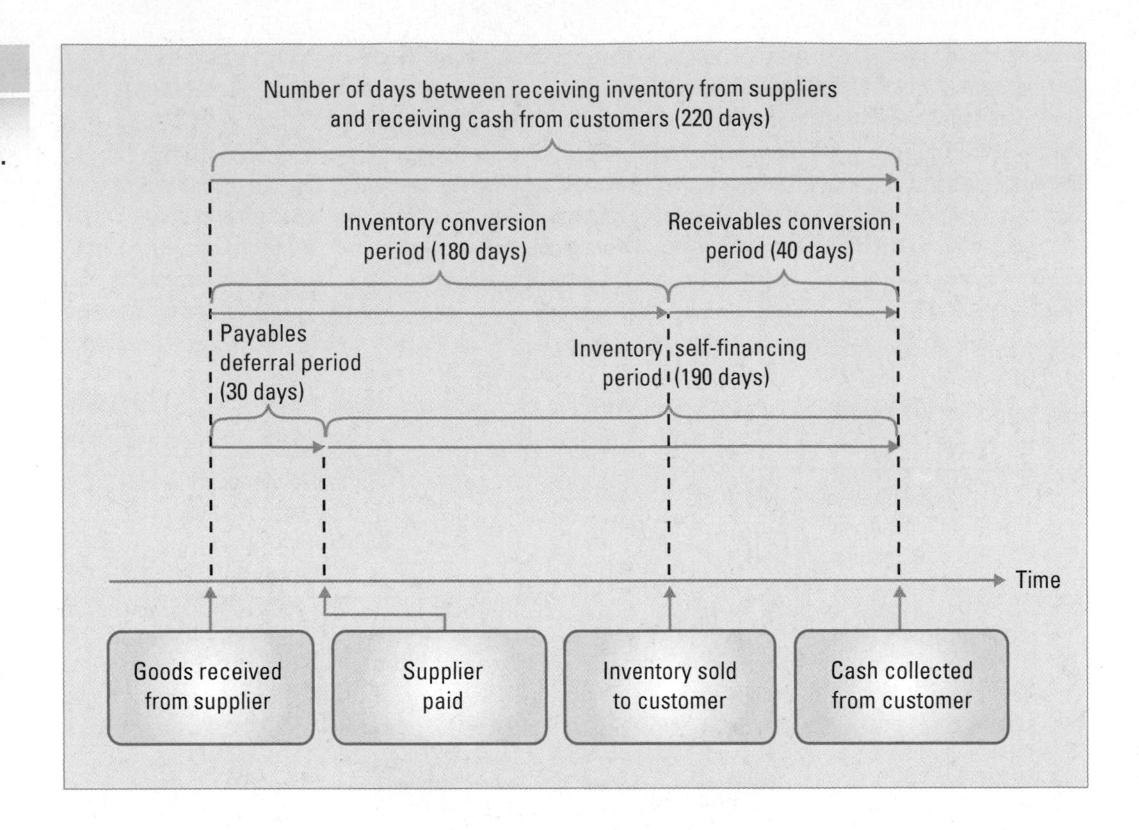

Figure 5.2 also shows that 220 days pass from the time Yellowknife receives inventory from a manufacturer to when it receives cash from a customer. For 30 days, Yellowknife doesn't have to pay for its inventory—suppliers finance the purchases by providing credit. For the remaining 190 days, Yellowknife's cash is tied up in inventory (inventory self-financing period). This means that Yellowknife must use cash on hand, borrow money, or get money from owners to pay for its inventory. The more inventory Yellowknife carries or the longer it has to self-finance, the more cash it needs. Similarly, the longer customers take to pay for purchases, the more cash is tied up. Yellowknife could free up cash if its suppliers gave it more time to pay, it sold the inventory more quickly, or customers paid sooner.

If Yellowknife runs out of cash, business will stop because employees, suppliers, and creditors can't be paid. An entity might have a bright future but to get there it has to survive its present. When examining an entity's financial statements, it's necessary to consider the cash it has on hand, the cash it can obtain from external sources, and its ability to generate cash from business activities. We'll look at some tools for examining liquidity later in the chapter.

INSIGHT

The Length of the Cash Lag

The cash lag varies from business to business and depends on many factors. Credit terms with suppliers and customers vary—the less time suppliers give an entity to pay and the more time an entity gives its customers, the longer the lag. The nature of the business is important. Companies with lengthy manufacturing processes will have money tied up in inventory for a longer time than wholesalers of fresh fruits and vegetables that have to sell inventory very quickly. The cash lag for many service businesses will be short because there isn't any inventory to contend with. Understanding how long an entity has its cash tied up in operations is crucial to understanding its ability to generate the cash it needs to operate.

If the future were perfectly predictable, few entities would face liquidity problems. Liquidity problems occur because things don't always go according to plan. For example, a clothing store manager must order merchandise months before the clothes will be sold. When making buying decisions, the manager must predict customers' tastes and demand and economic conditions to ensure that she has the appropriate merchandise, in the right quantities, to sell at the right price. But many things can go wrong. If there is a downturn in the economy or the manager didn't buy the right styles, sales won't meet expectations and the store will have less cash coming in than expected and more cash will be tied up in the unsold inventory. Even so, creditors, including the suppliers of the merchandise, have to be paid.

KNOWLEDGE CHECK 5.1

Ushta Ltd. manufactures auto parts. The company purchases materials from suppliers and stores them in a warehouse, holding them for an average of 30 days before using them in the manufacturing process. The manufactured parts are held for an average of 15 days until they are sold and shipped to customers. Ushta pays its suppliers 40 days after receiving the goods, and customers pay 30 days after delivery. Calculate the following for Ushta and explain the cash implications of the inventory self-financing period:

- ❑ payables deferral period
- ❑ inventory conversion period
- ❑ receivables conversion period
- ❑ inventory self-financing period
- ❑ number of days between receiving inventory from suppliers and receiving cash from customers

Growing businesses often face liquidity problems. Expansion and growth are positive times for businesses, but poor planning and excessive optimism can lead to cash shortages. Consider a successful restaurant that decides to expand. Expansion requires upfront capital costs to renovate the new space and purchase furniture, fixtures, and equipment. Ongoing operating costs will increase with expansion as well: additional rent, increased utilities costs, more staff, and more inventory. What happens if customers don't come to the new location in the numbers expected? Many of the higher operating costs still have to be paid. If loans were obtained to finance the upfront costs, interest must be paid. If cash inflows are inadequate to meet the cash requirements of the business, financial distress could result.

Example: Cash Flow Scenarios at Peabody Corp.

LO 1, 3

Let's look at an example demonstrating the cash flow problems an entity can face and the differences between earnings and cash flow. Peabody Ltd. (Peabody) began operations on January 1, 2017. Peabody purchases various types of candy in bulk from producers, packages the candy, and sells it to corporate customers. The corporate customers use the packaged candy as gifts for customers, suppliers, and employees. Peabody must maintain an inventory of candy and packaging to fill customer orders quickly. The following information is available about Peabody's operation:

- All inventory purchases are for cash because suppliers aren't ready to extend credit to the new company.
- Customers have up to 90 days to pay for their purchases. Assume that customers always pay in the quarter after they make their purchases.
- Inventory on hand at the start of a quarter is based on management's forecast of sales for the quarter. All purchases of inventory are made on the first day of each quarter.
- Markup on Peabody's product is 100 percent. (Candy costing Peabody $100 is sold to customers for $200.)

- Operating costs, other than the cost of product sold, are $12,000 per quarter. These costs are paid in cash during the quarter.
- Shareholders contributed $40,000 in cash when the company was organized.
- Inventory costing $16,000 was purchased when operations began.
- Sales by quarter for 2017 were:

1st Quarter	2nd Quarter	3rd Quarter	4th Quarter	Total sales in 2017
$20,000	$24,000	$27,500	$31,500	$103,000

Peabody's quarterly income statements for 2017 are shown in Table 5.1. Information about Peabody's inventory purchases and accounts receivable is shown in Table 5.2.

The income statements show that Peabody suffered a loss of $2,000 in the first quarter, broke even in the second quarter, and made profits in the third and fourth quarters. For the entire year, Peabody made a small profit of $3,500. Table 5.2 shows that Peabody's sales are growing and so is the amount of inventory it has on hand. This is an important point—as sales increase, more inventory has to be carried to meet customer demand, and more inventory means more cash is required to purchase it. Accounts receivable represents cash owed to Peabody but not available now. As it does for inventory, growth means more accounts receivable and more cash tied up.

TABLE 5.1 Peabody Ltd.: Quarterly Income Statements for 2017

Peabody Ltd. Quarterly Income Statements for 2017					
	1st Quarter	2nd Quarter	3rd Quarter	4th Quarter	Total 2017
Sales	$20,000	$24,000	$27,500	$31,500	$103,000
Cost of sales	10,000	12,000	13,750	15,750	51,500
Other costs	12,000	12,000	12,000	12,000	48,000
Net income	$ (2,000)	$ 0	$ 1,750	$ 3,750	$ 3,500

TABLE 5.2 Peabody Ltd.: Inventory Information for 2017

Peabody Ltd. Inventory and Accounts Receivable Information for 2017					
	1st Quarter	2nd Quarter	3rd Quarter	4th Quarter	Total 2017
Inventory					
Beginning inventory	$ 0	$ 6,000	$ 7,200	$ 8,250	$ 0
+ Purchases	16,000	13,200	14,800	16,950	60,950
− Cost of sales (inventory sold)	10,000	12,000	13,750	15,750	51,500
= Ending inventory	$ 6,000	$ 7,200	$ 8,250	$ 9,450	$ 9,450
Accounts Receivable					
Beginning accounts receivable	$ 0	$20,000	$24,000	$27,500	$ 0
+ Sales	20,000	24,000	27,500	31,500	103,000
− Collections	0	20,000	24,000	27,500	71,500
= Ending accounts receivable	$20,000	$24,000	$27,500	$31,500	$ 31,500

Now let's consider Peabody's cash flow statements for 2017. These are provided in Table 5.3.

Peabody's cash flow statements tell a different story than the income statements. During 2017, Peabody expended considerably more cash than it collected, and at year-end most of the $40,000 it began operations with was gone. In every quarter, cash flow was negative, and for the entire year Peabody had negative cash flow of $37,450. In contrast, net income was $3,500. Why the difference? As a new business, Peabody had to buy a large amount of inventory, but the buildup in inventory isn't reflected in net income because only goods sold are expensed in an accrual income statement. However, the buildup of inventory did use cash. In addition, Peabody gives customers 90 days to pay. If it had required cash payment on delivery, there would have been an additional $31,500 in cash at the end of 2017—the amount of accounts receivable at year-end. The fact that Peabody couldn't buy on credit lengthened the inventory self-financing period and made things worse.

If a stakeholder focused on the income statement and ignored the cash flow statement, Peabody's performance looks positive despite the fact that it had just about run out of cash. If, in late 2017, Peabody had had to make a $5,000 cash payment, it couldn't have. This highlights how earnings and cash flow can differ dramatically, and how important it is to pay attention to both.

Now let's look at Peabody again to see how cash is affected under two different operating scenarios about inventory purchases and credit terms offered to customers. The income statements are unaffected in both new scenarios.

LO 3

Scenario 1: Peabody decides it needs more variety in inventory and buys $1,000 more inventory per quarter. Inventory information is shown in Table 5.4 and quarterly cash flow information in Table 5.5.

Under this scenario, Peabody runs out of cash in the fourth quarter and actually has negative cash of $1,450 at the end of the year. The cash shortfall occurs because there is $4,000 more cash invested in inventory at the end of 2017 than under the original scenario. Suppliers are paid in cash, so Peabody would have needed a source of money, perhaps from the owners or a bank loan, to pay them.

TABLE 5.3 Peabody Ltd.: Quarterly Cash Flow Statements and Cash Flow Balances for 2017

Peabody Ltd.
Quarterly Cash Flow Statements for 2017 and Quarterly Cash Balances

	1st Quarter	2nd Quarter	3rd Quarter	4th Quarter	Total 2017
Collections*	$ 0	$20,000	$24,000	$27,500	$ 71,500
Disbursements**	28,000	25,200	26,800	28,950	108,950
Net cash flow	(28,000)	(5,200)	(2,800)	(1,450)	(37,450)
Beginning cash balance	40,000	12,000	6,800	4,000	40,000
Ending cash balance	$12,000	$ 6,800	$ 4,000	$ 2,550	$ 2,550

*Collections equal the amount of sales in the previous quarter. Assume 100 percent of amounts are collected.
**Disbursements equal the amount spent purchasing inventory plus $12,000 per month in other costs.

TABLE 5.4 Peabody Ltd.: Inventory Information for 2017

Peabody Ltd.
Inventory Information for 2017—Scenario 1

	1st Quarter	2nd Quarter	3rd Quarter	4th Quarter	Total 2017
Beginning inventory	$ 0	$ 7,000	$ 9,200	$11,250	$ 0
+ Purchases	17,000	14,200	15,800	17,950	64,950
− Cost of sales (inventory sold)	10,000	12,000	13,750	15,750	51,500
= Ending inventory	$ 7,000	$ 9,200	$11,250	$13,450	$13,450

Note: Accounts receivable information is the same as in Table 5.2.

TABLE 5.5 Peabody Ltd.: Quarterly Cash Flow Statements and Cash Flow Balances for 2017—Scenario 1

Peabody Ltd.
Quarterly Cash Flow Statements for 2017 and Quarterly Cash Balances—Scenario 1

	1st Quarter	2nd Quarter	3rd Quarter	4th Quarter	Total 2017
Collections*	$ 0	$20,000	$24,000	$27,500	$71,500
Disbursements**	29,000	26,200	27,800	29,950	112,950
Cash flow	(29,000)	(6,200)	(3,800)	(2,450)	(41,450)
Beginning cash balance	40,000	11,000	4,800	1,000	40,000
Ending cash balance	$11,000	$ 4,800	$ 1,000	$ (1,450)	$ (1,450)

*Collections equal the amount of sales in the previous quarter. Assume 100 percent of amounts are collected.
**Disbursements equal the amount spent purchasing inventory plus $12,000 per month in other costs.

TABLE 5.6 Peabody Ltd.: Accounts Receivable Information for 2017—Scenario 2

Peabody Ltd.
Accounts Receivable Information for 2017—Scenario 2

	1st Quarter	2nd Quarter	3rd Quarter	4th Quarter	Total 2017
Beginning accounts receivable	$ 0	$ 6,667	$ 8,000	$ 9,167	$ 0
+ Sales	20,000	24,000	27,500	31,500	103,000
Collections*	13,333	22,667	26,333	30,167	92,500
= Ending accounts receivable	$ 6,667	$ 8,000	$ 9,167	$10,500	$ 10,500

Note: Inventory information is the same as in Table 5.2.
*Collection in a quarter equals two-thirds of the sales in that quarter plus accounts receivable at the beginnings of the quarter (the uncollected portion of accounts receivable from the previous quarter is collected in the current quarter).

TABLE 5.7 Peabody Ltd.: Quarterly Cash Flow Statements and Cash Flow Balances for 2017

Peabody Ltd.
Quarterly Cash Flow Statements for 2017 and Quarterly Cash Balances—Scenario 2

	1st Quarter	2nd Quarter	3rd Quarter	4th Quarter	Total 2017
Collections*	$13,333	$22,667	$26,333	$30,167	$ 92,500
Disbursements**	28,000	25,200	26,800	28,950	108,950
Cash flow	(14,667)	(2,533)	(467)	1,217	(16,450)
Beginning cash balance	40,000	25,333	22,800	22,333	40,000
Ending cash balance	$25,333	$22,800	$22,333	$23,550	$ 23,550

*Two-thirds of a quarter's sales are collected during the quarter and the remainder is collected in the next quarter. (For the 1st Quarter 2/3 × $20,000 = $13,333 is collected.) Assume 100 percent of amounts are collected.
**Disbursements equal the amount spent purchasing inventory plus $12,000 per month in other costs.

LO 3

Scenario 2: Peabody allows customers 30 days (instead of 90) to pay for their purchases. As a result, two-thirds of a quarter's sales are collected during the quarter and the remainder is collected in the next quarter. Accounts receivable information is shown in Table 5.6 and quarterly cash flow information in Table 5.7.

Because it collects amounts owed by customers much more quickly in this scenario, Peabody ends 2017 with $23,550 in cash (compared with $2,550 in the original scenario).

LO 1, 2, 3

Here are some important points to take from this discussion:

- Cash and net income can be dramatically different. Each provides useful but different information. (A lot more will be said about this issue later in the chapter and throughout the book.)
- The cash cycle and the cash lag are important concepts for understanding the cash and liquidity positions of entities.
- As businesses grow, they usually need more cash to fund operations.
- Many factors and events can affect an entity's liquidity. Scenarios 1 and 2 were management decisions, but often the circumstances are out of management's control, for example, declining sales (caused by a recession or changing consumer tastes), customers who don't pay or take too long to pay, or unexpected expenditures.
- It's management's responsibility to manage an entity's cash and liquidity. An external stakeholder must monitor the entity to ensure it has adequate cash and liquidity to survive and operate successfully.

THE CASH FLOW STATEMENT: OVERVIEW

LO 4

The discussions of the cash cycle and the differences between cash and accrual accounting lead to an important conclusion: financial statement users need to pay attention to cash and cash flow. Cash flow information is found in a set of general purpose financial statements in the **cash flow statement**. It's also known as the statement of cash flows or the statement of changes in financial position.

The cash flow statement is necessary because the income statement doesn't give a complete picture of an entity's resource flows. The income statement reports economic flows but doesn't distinguish liquidity. This means that an income statement treats a cash expense the same as a non-cash expense (such as depreciation) or a cash sale the same as a credit sale. The income statement also doesn't reflect financing transactions or investment in long-term assets. The cash flow statement helps fill these gaps by providing information about the changes in an entity's cash position.

We'll use Thomson Reuters Corporation's (Thomson Reuters) statement of cash flow and related notes in Exhibit 5.1 as the focus of our discussion. (Thomson Reuters describes itself as the world's leading source of intelligent information for businesses and professionals. It combines industry expertise with innovative technology to deliver critical information to leading decision makers in the financial and risk, legal, tax and accounting, intellectual property and science and media markets, powered by the world's most trusted news organization. Thomson Reuters shares are listed on the Toronto and the New York Stock Exchanges). First we need to know what accountants mean by "cash" in the cash flow statement. Notice at the bottom of Thomson Reuters' statement of cash flows the term "Cash and cash equivalents." This is more than just cash in the bank. Cash and cash equivalents include the following:

- Cash on hand and cash in bank accounts.
- Short-term liquid investments—investments easily converted to a known amount of cash, with little risk that the amount of cash to be received will change. Short term usually means investments maturing within three months. Examples include guaranteed investment certificates, term deposits, commercial paper, money market funds, and government treasury bills. Equity investments aren't included because their market values fluctuate.
- Bank overdrafts used for short-term cash management purposes. (A **bank overdraft** occurs when you take more money from your bank account than you have. For example, if an entity has \$20,000 in its bank account and it writes cheques for \$30,000, the account is overdrawn by \$10,000. The \$10,000 overdraft is recorded as a liability.) Some entities use overdrafts to allow them to meet short-term cash requirements. When bank overdrafts are included in the definition of cash and cash equivalents, the amount of the overdraft is subtracted from cash and short-term liquid investments to determine the amount of cash and cash equivalents an entity has.

EXHIBIT 5.1 Thomson Reuters Corporation: Cash Flow Statements and Related Information[1]

THOMSON REUTERS CORPORATION
CONSOLIDATED STATEMENT OF CASH FLOW

	(millions of U.S. dollars)	Notes	Year ended December 31, 2011	2010
	Cash provided by (used in):			
	OPERATING ACTIVITIES			
	Net (loss) earnings		**(1,392)**	933
	Adjustments for:			
	Depreciation		**438**	457
	Amortization of computer software		**659**	572
	Amortization of other identifiable intangible assets		**612**	545
	Goodwill impairment		**3,010**	–
Cash from operations	Net gains on disposals of businesses and investments		**(388)**	(26)
	Deferred tax	22	**(202)**	(205)
	Other	26	**139**	440
	Changes in working capital and other items	26	**(279)**	(38)
	Operating cash flows from continuing operations		**2,597**	2,678
	Operating cash flows from discontinued operations		**–**	(6)
	Net cash provided by operating activities	26	**2,597**	2,672
	INVESTING ACTIVITIES			
	Acquisitions, net of cash acquired	27	**(1,286)**	(612)
	Proceeds from other disposals, net of taxes paid		**415**	26
Investing activities	Capital expenditures, less proceeds from disposals	26	**(1,041)**	(1,114)
	Other investing activities		**49**	8
	Investing cash flows from continuing operations		**(1,863)**	(1,692)
	Investing cash flows from discontinued operations		**56**	–
	Net cash used in investing activities	26	**(1,807)**	(1,692)
	FINANCING ACTIVITIES			
	Proceeds from debt	18	**349**	1,367
	Repayments of debt	18	**(648)**	(1,683)
	Net borrowings under short-term loan facilities		**400**	5
Financing activities	Repurchases of common shares	23	**(326)**	
	Dividends paid on preference shares		**(3)**	(3)
	Dividends paid on common shares	23	**(960)**	(898)
	Other financing activities		**(39)**	(7)
	Net cash used in financing activities		**(1,227)**	(1,219)
	Translation adjustments on cash and cash equivalents		**(5)**	(8)
	Decrease in cash and cash equivalents		**(442)**	(247)
	Cash and cash equivalents at beginning of period	10	**864**	1,111
	Cash and cash equivalents at end of period	10	**422**	864

Supplemental cash flow information is provided in note 26.

	2011	2010
Interest paid	**(399)**	(393)
Interest received	**9**	7
Income taxes paid	**(511)**	(243)

Amounts paid and received for interest are reflected as operating cash flows. Interest paid is net of debt-related hedges.

Amounts paid and received for taxes are reflected as either operating cash flows or investing cash flows depending on the nature of the underlying transaction.

The related notes form an integral part of these consolidated financial statements

EXHIBIT 5.1 (continued) Thomson Reuters Corporation: Cash Flow Statements and Related Information

THOMSON REUTERS CORPORATION
CONSOLIDATED INCOME STATEMENT

(millions of U.S. dollars, except per share amounts)	Notes	Year ended December 31, 2011	2010
Revenues		**13,807**	13,070
Operating expenses	5	**(9,997)**	(10,061)
Depreciation		**(438)**	(457)
Amortization of computer software		**(659)**	(572)
Amortization of other identifiable intangible assets		**(612)**	(545)
Goodwill impairment	17	**(3,010)**	–
Other operating gains (losses), net	6	**204**	(16)
Operating (loss) profit		**(705)**	1,419
Finance costs, net			
Net interest expense	7	**(396)**	(383)
Other finance (costs) income	7	**(15)**	28
(Loss) income before tax and equity method investees		**(1,116)**	1,064
Share of post tax earnings in equity method investees		**13**	8
Tax expense	8	**(293)**	(139)
(Loss) earnings from continuing operations		**(1,396)**	933
Earnings from discontinued operations, net of tax		**4**	–
Net (loss) earnings		**(1,392)**	933

THOMSON REUTERS CORPORATION

Notes to Consolidated Financial Statements

(unless otherwise stated, all amounts are in millions of U.S. dollars)

NOTE 1: SUMMARY OF BUSINESS AND SIGNIFICANT ACCOUNTING POLICIES

Cash and cash equivalents

Cash and cash equivalents comprise cash on hand, demand deposits and investments with an original maturity at the date of purchase of three months or less.

NOTE 10: CASH AND CASH EQUIVALENTS

	December 31, 2011	2010
Cash		
Cash at bank and on hand	**249**	359
Cash equivalents		
Short-term deposits	**25**	158
Money market accounts	**110**	208
Commercial paper investments	**38**	139
Cash and cash equivalents	**422**	864

Of total cash and cash equivalents as of December 31, 2011, $147 million (2010 – $234 million) was held in subsidiaries which have regulatory restrictions, contractual restrictions or operate in countries where exchange controls and other legal restrictions apply and are therefore not available for general use by the Company.

EXHIBIT 5.1 (continued) Thomson Reuters Corporation: Cash Flow Statements and Related Information

NOTE 26: SUPPLEMENTAL CASH FLOW INFORMATION

Details of "Other" in the statement of cash flow are as follows:

	Year ended December 31, 2011	2010
Non-cash employee benefit charges	**161**	206
Employee benefits—past service cost (see note 25)	**72**	–
Embedded derivatives fair value adjustments	**(97)**	72
Net losses (gains) on foreign exchange and derivative financial instruments	**17**	(91)
Losses from redemption of debt securities	**–**	62
Other	**(14)**	191
	139	440

Details of "Changes in working capital and other items" are as follows:

Changes in working capital and other items

	Year ended December 31, 2011	2010
Trade and other receivables	**(164)**	(43)
Prepaid expenses and other current assets	**114**	2
Other financial assets	**2**	9
Payables, accruals and provisions	**(274)**	65
Deferred revenue	**77**	89
Other financial liabilities	**9**	–
Income taxes	**146**	(12)
Other	**(189)**	(148)
	(279)	(38)

The cash flow statement groups cash flows into three categories: cash from operations, financing activities, and investing activities. First, a brief introduction:

1. **Cash from operations (CFO)** is the cash an entity generates or uses in its day-to-day business activities. Money spent or received providing goods and services fits in this category. Generally, CFO includes:

Cash Inflows	Cash Outflows
Amounts received from customers	Payments for inventory
Tax refunds	Payments to other suppliers
Interest received*	Payments to employees
Dividends received*	Taxes paid
	Interest paid*

*Under IFRS, entities can choose to classify interest and dividends received as cash from operations or cash from investing activities and interest and dividends paid as cash from operations or cash used for financing activities.

2. **Cash from investing activities** is the cash spent on buying capital assets and other long-term assets and the cash received from selling those assets. Investing activities include:

Cash Inflows	Cash Outflows
Sale of capital assets	Cash spent on property, plant, and equipment
Collection of principal on loans made by the entity	Cash spent on intangible assets
Proceeds from the sale of securities held for investment by the entity (i.e., stocks and bonds)	Loans made to other entities
Interest received*	Purchase of securities of other entities made for investment purposes
Dividends received*	

*Under IFRS, entities can choose to classify interest and dividends received as cash from operations, or cash from investing activities and interest and dividends paid as cash from operations, or cash used for financing activities.

3. **Cash from financing activities** is the cash raised from and paid to owners and lenders. Financing activities include:

Cash Inflows	Cash Outflows
Proceeds from the sale of the entity's shares	Repayment of debt principal
Proceeds from the issuance of debt	Repayment of bank loans
Proceeds from bank loans	Repurchase of the entity's shares from investors
	Dividends paid to shareholders*
	Interest paid
	Interest paid*

*Under IFRS, entities can choose to classify interest and dividends received as cash from operations, or cash from investing activities and interest and dividends paid as cash from operations, or cash used for financing activities.

In Note 1, Thomson Reuters provides its definition of cash and cash equivalents (see Exhibit 5.1). Note 10 discloses the amount of cash ($249 million) and short-term investments classified as cash equivalents ($422 million) the company had on December 31, 2011.

QUESTION FOR CONSIDERATION

Quick Motors Ltd. (Quick) sells new cars and services cars. Classify the following cash flows of the business as operating, investing, or financing. Explain your reasoning.

a. Purchase of a number of cars and vans for resale for $375,000 cash.
b. Purchase of a courtesy van for customer dropoff and pickup for $40,000 cash.
c. Sale of a car to a customer for $32,000 cash.
d. Repayment of a $500,000 bank loan used to renovate the showroom.
e. Sale of old furniture and computers for $25,000 cash.
f. Sale of infrequently sold auto parts inventory to a dealer specializing in parts for older cars.
g. Sale of cars used by its salespeople to a charitable organization, which is given 12 months to pay for the cars.

ANSWER:

a. Operating: Cars and vans are Quick's inventory so sales of these are its business and an operating item.
b. Investing: This van won't be resold but is a capital asset generating revenue by providing convenience to customers.
c. Operating: Quick's business is selling cars. Cash received from a sale is an operating item.
d. Financing: Repayment of a loan is a financing activity.
e. Investing: Quick's business is cars, not furniture or computers. Furniture and computers support the sale of vehicles.
f. Operating: Sale of auto parts is a regular business activity of a car dealership.
g. None: No cash is involved in this transaction so it doesn't appear on the cash flow statement. Will be an operating cash flow when cash is received.

LO 4, 5

UNDERSTANDING THE CASH FLOW STATEMENT: SPECIFIC ACTIVITIES

Now the details. We'll focus on understanding the cash flow statement. First, we'll look at financing and investing activities and then examine cash from operations

Financing and Investing Activities

Financing Activities Financing activities is cash raised from and paid to owners and lenders. These are cash transactions that affect the financing accounts on the balance sheet (all accounts on the liabilities and equity side except those involving working capital—see Figure 5.3). Financing activities help an entity meet cash needs that can't be met by cash from operations.

New businesses need money to get things started. This money has to come from owners or lenders or a combination of the two. Growing businesses may need cash from external sources if they haven't saved enough to fund the growth. Even stable businesses may need financing to upgrade or modernize existing operations if the money isn't on hand, or they may simply have to refinance existing debt. Cash inflows from financing activities arise from obtaining bank loans, arranging mortgages, issuing bonds and other long-term debt, and issuing preferred and common shares. Financing cash outflows arise from repaying debt and repurchasing shares. Interest and dividend payments can be treated as financing activities since they're costs of financing, but IFRS allows entities to choose to classify them as either financing or operating activities, so you might see both in practice.

Thomson Reuters' financing activities include the addition and repayment of long-term debt, short-term borrowing, repurchase of common shares, and payment of dividends. Thomson Reuters' statement of cash flows shows that in 2011 it repaid $648,000,000 in long-term debt and spent $326,000,000 repurchasing its common shares from investors (this means Thomson Reuters bought its own shares back from shareholders). In addition, the company was able to raise $349,000,000 in cash by issuing new long-term debt to investors and $400,000,000 under short-term loan facilities. Overall, Thomson Reuters had a net cash outflow from financing activities of $1,227,000,000, which means it spent $1,227,000,000 more on financing activities than it raised.

FIGURE 5.3

Link between Cash Flow Statement Categories and Balance Sheet Accounts

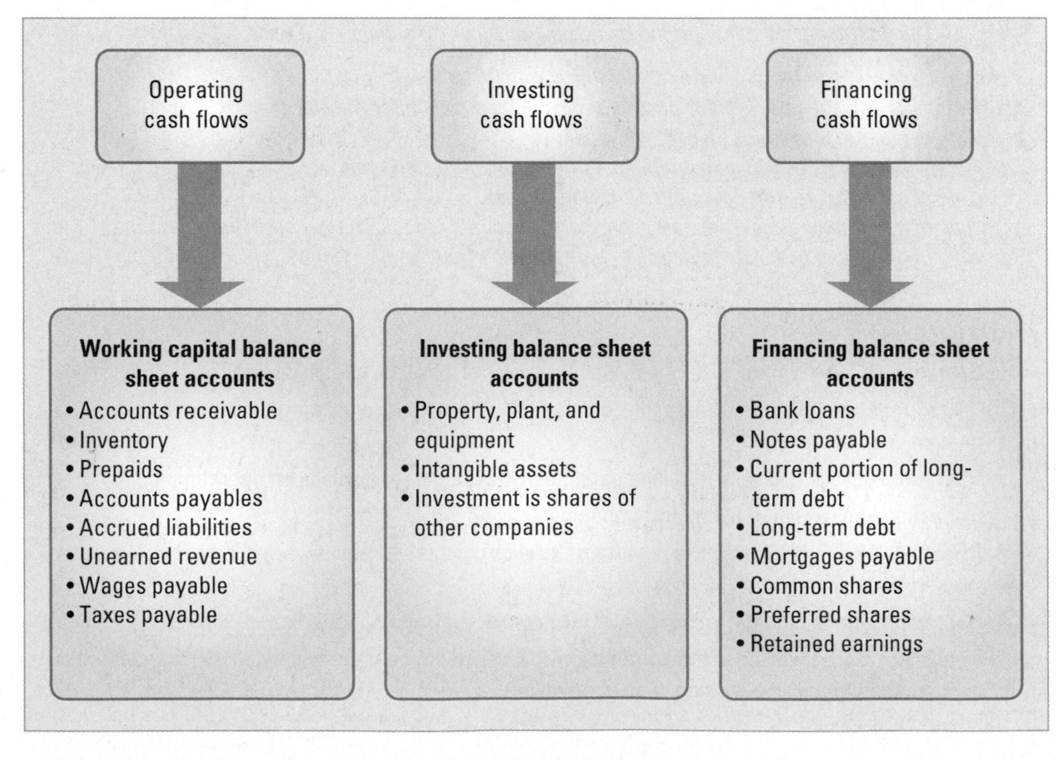

Investing Activities Investing activities is the cash spent on buying capital assets and other long-term assets and the cash received from selling those assets. The investing activities section lists cash transactions involving non-working capital asset accounts on the balance sheet, including plant, property, and equipment; intangible assets; and investments in the equity and debt of other companies. These assets are typically used for more than one period and contribute to the entity earning income, but they aren't sold as part of ordinary business activities.

Entities must spend cash on investing activities to maintain or expand its operations. A stable company must still replace and upgrade its physical resources (buildings, equipment, technology) to ensure that it can operate at existing levels, remain competitive, and maintain efficiency. A growing organization must add resources to meet the demands of its growth. For example, if Thomson Reuters continues to expand and grow it will have to spend cash to acquire existing companies and invest in new computer hardware. Even if Thomson Reuters was satisfied with the existing level of its operations, it would have to continually upgrade its computer hardware and software. A business that is getting smaller (perhaps it's less competitive or there's less demand for its goods or services) may sell off unused assets. A struggling business might sell some of its assets to raise money to help it survive. This is a short-term strategy because, as productive assets are sold, the entity will be less able to generate operating cash flows.

Thomson Reuters' investing activities include cash spent purchasing existing companies and capital assets (mainly computer hardware and software). It received cash from the disposal of investments it had previously made in other companies. Thomson Reuters' 2011 statement of cash flow shows that it spent $1,286,00,000 in cash acquiring companies and $1,041,000,000 on capital expenditures (computer hardware and software). It received $415,000,000 from disposing of companies it had previously purchased. Overall, Thomson Reuters spent $1,807,000,000 more on investing activities than it received.

In essence, the financing and investing sections report changes in the related balance sheet accounts that are due to cash flows. However, if this is all the cash flow statement did, there would be little benefit to having it at all; stakeholders could simply reorganize the information themselves. In fact, the financing and investing activities sections provide additional information by not combining positive and negative changes in the related balance sheet accounts. For example, Thomson Reuters reports separate financing activities for "proceeds from debt" and "repayments of debt." It's sometimes very difficult, if not impossible, to determine these more detailed changes from the balance sheet and notes.

One final point about the cash flow statement is that it only reports transactions involving cash. This may seem obvious but it's important. If a company borrows $100,000 from the bank to buy equipment, the cash flow statement reports $100,000 of financing activities (the bank loan) and $100,000 of investing activities (the equipment purchase). But suppose the company finances the $100,000 equipment purchase directly with the manufacturer. The company receives the equipment and promises to pay the manufacturer $100,000 later, but no cash changes hands. This transaction isn't reported in the cash flow statement because no cash is involved. These two arrangements are essentially the same but they are accounted for differently in the cash flow statement. If the equipment was partially paid in cash and partially financed by the manufacturer, only the cash paid would be reported in the cash flow statement. However, IFRS require disclosure of these financing and investing non-cash transactions in the notes.

Cash from Operations

Cash from operations is the cash an entity generates or uses in its day-to-day business activities. It's the cash left over after all cash payments pertaining to operating activities are deducted from operating cash inflows. Thomson Reuters' cash inflows from operations is the amounts received from customers who purchase its services. Cash outflows from operations include payments to employees and for selling and marketing, telecommunications, maintaining technology, acquisition and creation of data, administration, and so on.

CFO is an important source of liquidity for an entity. It provides cash that can be used to purchase capital assets, grow, retire debt, and pay dividends, reducing the need for external sources of financing. While CFO is usually positive, it can be negative. Negative CFO means that operating cash inflows are less than operating cash outflows, so simply operating the business uses cash. As a result, the entity must have sources of cash to make up the shortfall. In the short run, negative CFO can be covered by drawing on cash reserves, using available lines of credit, borrowing or raising equity capital, or selling assets. Negative CFO is a significant problem in the longer term because external sources of cash aren't inexhaustible.

Negative CFO isn't necessarily bad news. Entities just starting up or in a growth phase can have negative CFO because growth requires investment in current assets such as inventory and accounts receivable. Also, a new or expanding business doesn't reach its maximum sales capacity immediately, and many operating costs have to be incurred regardless of the level of sales, for example, salaries and wages, rent, advertising and promotion, insurance, and interest. As a result, a business may have negative CFO while sales are increasing. Debt and equity investors may be willing to provide cash to new or growing businesses with good prospects. On the other hand, companies may have difficulty raising cash if lenders and equity investors think they are "throwing good money after bad." Lenders will demand higher interest rates to compensate for the risk of lending to a struggling company and equity investors won't pay very much for the shares of companies not offering much promise of a reasonable return on their investment.

There are two ways that CFO can be presented in a cash flow statement:

1. The **indirect method** reconciles net income to CFO by adjusting net income for non-cash amounts and for operating cash flows not included in the calculation of net income.
2. The **direct method** reports CFO by showing cash collections and cash disbursements related to operations during the period.

Thomson Reuters uses the indirect method. If you look at Thomson Reuters' statement of cash flows in Exhibit 5.1 you'll see that the starting point for calculating CFO is net earnings (net loss), followed by a series of adjustments. These adjustments reconcile net earnings to a cash number. In fiscal 2011, Thomson Reuters had CFO of $2,597,000,000.

Exhibit 5.2 provides an example of the direct method from the statement of cash flows of Stantec Inc. (Stantec). Notice that the CFO section lists operating cash inflows and outflows from different sources (Stantec calls CFO "Cash flows from operating activities"). The presentation looks like an income statement prepared on the cash basis. In Note 19 to its financial statements, Stantec also provides CFO, calculated using the indirect method. Compare the two approaches. CFO is the same under both methods, but the presentation is very different.

The appeal of the direct method is that it reports sources and amounts of cash inflows and outflows, important information for evaluating an entity's liquidity and solvency. It's also intuitive because it focuses on an entity's cash flows, which is the purpose of the statement. In practice, the direct method is rarely used. The widespread use of the indirect method is a bit surprising because IFRS encourages the use of the direct method, although it doesn't require it.

The popularity of the indirect method is probably that it highlights the difference between income and cash flow. This allows stakeholders to see the impact of managers' choices on net income. Some stakeholders could, however, be confused or misled by the indirect method because it implies that items like depreciation represent sources of cash, when they're not (we discuss this point further below). The only cash flow information with the indirect method is CFO itself. The two methods are compared schematically in Figure 5.4.

Now we'll examine the indirect method of calculating CFO in detail because it's so widely used and can be difficult to understand. Broadly, when reconciling from net income to CFO there are two types of adjustments that must be made. The first removes transactions and economic events that are included in the calculation of net income but have no effect on cash flow.

An example of this type of adjustment is depreciation expense. Depreciation doesn't involve cash—it's just the allocation of the cost of a depreciable item to expense over its life. Since net income includes depreciation, a non-cash expense, it needs to be removed when reconciling from net income to CFO. The same is true for any transaction or economic event that doesn't involve cash. Because depreciation is a non-cash expense subtracted in the calculation of net income, adding the amount back to net income eliminates it.

EXHIBIT 5.2 Stantec Inc.: Statement of Cash Flows

Consolidated Statements of Cash Flows

Years ended December 31 *(in thousands of Canadian dollars)*	Notes	**2011** **$**	2010 $
CASH FLOWS FROM (USED IN) OPERATING ACTIVITIES			
Cash receipts from clients		**1,611,974**	1,499,392
Cash paid to suppliers		**(496,270)**	(508,637)
Cash paid to employees		**(943,439)**	(821,360)
Interest received		**1,953**	3,111
Interest paid		**(16,604)**	(16,775)
Finance costs paid		**(2,546)**	(1,773)
Income taxes paid		**(50,282)**	(51,548)
Income taxes recovered		**9,800**	9,522
Cash flows from operating activities	33	**114,586**	111,932

33. Cash Flows from (Used in) Operating Activities

Cash flows from (used in) operating activities determined by the indirect method are as follows:

(in thousands of Canadian dollars)	For the year ended December 31 **2011** **$**	 2010 $
CASH FLOWS FROM (USED IN) OPERATING ACTIVITIES		
Net income for the year	**12,662**	94,741
Add (deduct) items not affecting cash:		
Depreciation of property and equipment	**27,933**	25,461
Impairment of goodwill	**90,000**	–
Amortization of intangible assets	**18,395**	17,289
Deferred income tax	**4,281**	(2,397)
Loss on dispositions of investments and property and equipment	**1,298**	586
Share-based compensation expense	**5,575**	2,822
Provision for self-insured liability and claims	**11,463**	10,962
Other non-cash items	**(9,155)**	(5,908)
Share of income from equity investments	**(793)**	(2,209)
Gain on sale of equity investments	–	(7,183)
	161,659	134,164
Trade and other receivables	**11,917**	11.647
Unbilled revenue	**(26,685)**	(1,250)
Prepaid expenses	**(2,166)**	4,055
Trade and other payables	**(15,936)**	(22,975)
Billings in excess of costs	**(7,247)**	(13,158)
Income taxes payable	**(6,956)**	(551)
	(47,073)	(22,232)
Cash flows from operating activities	**114,586**	111,932

Source: Extracted from Stantec Inc.'s 2011 annual report.

FIGURE 5.4

Comparison of the Direct and Indirect Methods of Calculating Cash from Operations

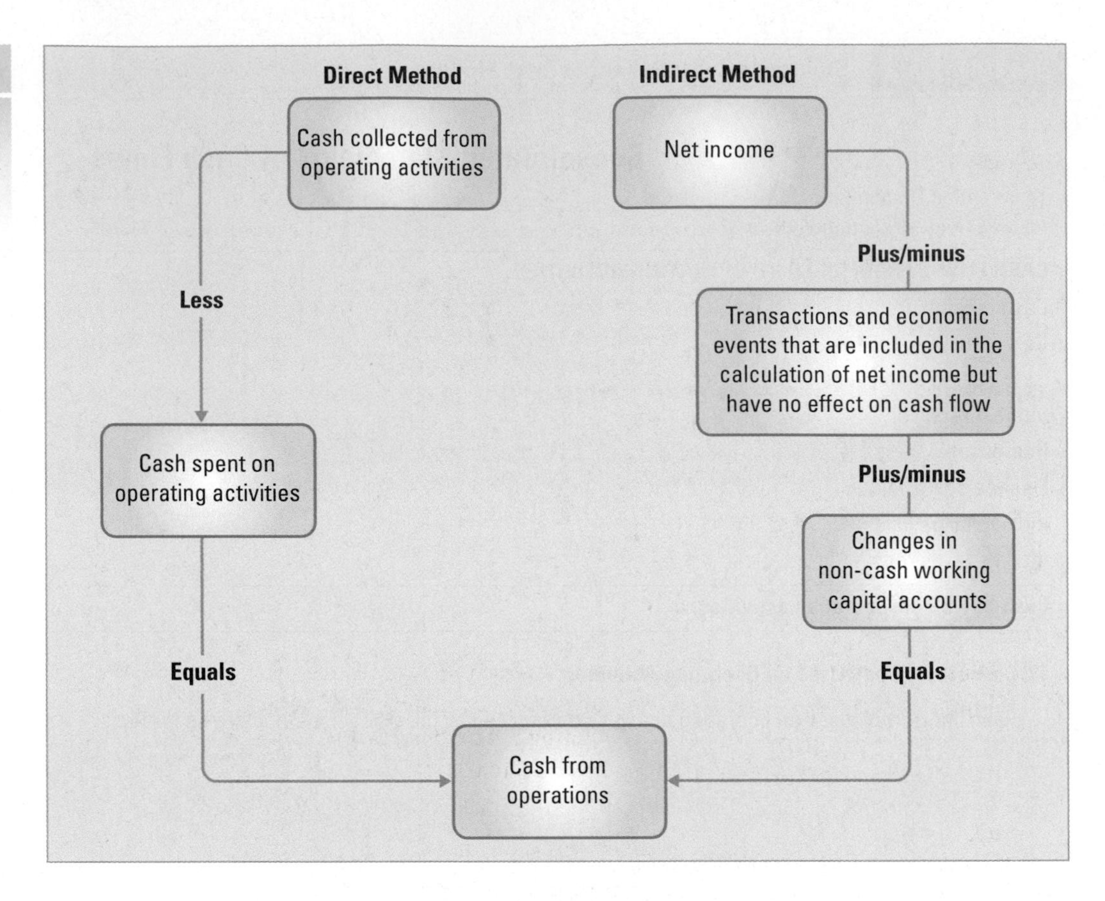

Here's an example. Below is Moose Jaw Company's (Moose Jaw) income statement:

Moose Jaw Company Income Statement For the Year Ended December 31, 2017	
Revenue	$35,000
Expenses	18,000
Depreciation expense	8,000
Net income	$ 9,000

All of Moose Jaw's revenues and expenses are in cash except for depreciation. All of its cash flows are operating cash flows. If you were asked to calculate Moose Jaw's cash from operations it would be a simple matter of subtracting expenses (except for depreciation) from revenue since these were all cash transactions:

Revenue (all cash)	$35,000
Expenses (all cash)	18,000
Cash from operations	$17,000

The depreciation expense would be ignored because it doesn't involve cash. CFO calculated using the direct method would look like this.

The difference between net income and CFO is simply the amount of the depreciation expense. To calculate Moose Jaw's CFO using the indirect method, we adjust net income by adding back the depreciation that was expensed when calculating net income in the first place:

Net income	$ 9,000
Add: Depreciation expense	8,000
Cash from operations	$17,000

Expense	Description	Treatment (add to or subtract from net income when reconciling net income to CFO)
Depreciation/ amortization	Allocation of the cost of a capital asset to expense over its life.	Add
Gains	The amount by which the selling price of an asset is greater than its carrying amount.	Subtract
Losses	The amount by which the selling price of an asset is less than its carrying amount.	Add
Deferred (future) income taxes	Difference between how taxes are calculated for accounting purposes versus how they are calculated for the taxation authorities. Deferred income taxes will be discussed later in the book.	Add or subtract
Writeoffs and writedowns of assets	Occurs when an asset's carrying amount is decreased to reflect a decline in fair value that is not supported by a transaction.	Add

FIGURE 5.5

Non-Cash Items and Their Treatment in CFO Calculation Using the Indirect Method

The thinking is straightforward. If a non-cash item is subtracted when calculating net income (as depreciation is) then it must be added back when reconciling from net income to CFO. Similarly, if a non-cash item is added when calculating net income, then it must be subtracted when reconciling from net income to CFO. When we calculate CFO using the direct approach, we ignore these non-cash items and simply prepare a statement that reflects only operating cash inflows and outflows.

A list of non-cash items that must be adjusted for when calculating CFO using the indirect method is provided in Figure 5.5. (Some of the items on the list won't be discussed in detail until later in the book.)

QUESTION FOR CONSIDERATION

A friend suggests that an entity can increase its CFO by increasing its depreciation expense. The friend reasons that because non-cash expenses such as depreciation are added back to net income when calculating CFO using the indirect method, a larger depreciation expense will result in more CFO. Evaluate your friend's suggestion.

ANSWER: While depreciation is added back to net income when calculating CFO using the indirect method, the amount of depreciation expensed has no effect on CFO. Depreciation is added back to net income because it's a non-cash expense deducted in the calculation of net income. Whether the depreciation expense is large or small has no effect on cash from operations because you would add back the same amount that was subtracted when calculating net income.

The second type of adjustment for calculating CFO using the indirect method adjusts revenues and expenses so only cash flows are reflected. Revenues and expenses are recognized on an accrual basis, which means they can have cash and non-cash components. Remember that cash flows associated with revenues and expenses can occur before, after, or at the same time as recognition on the income statement. We can convert accrual revenues and expenses to cash by adjusting for changes over a period in the non-cash working capital accounts on the balance sheet (such as accounts receivable, inventory, prepaids, accounts payable, wages payable, and accrued liabilities). You can see this type of adjustment on Thomson Reuters' statement of cash flows in Note 26 (the second panel in the note) in Exhibit 5.1. The total shown in this panel can be found in the calculation of CFO in the statement of cash flows on the line named "Changes in working capital and other items."

INSIGHT

Adjusting for Gains and Losses

The treatment of gains and losses when calculating CFO using the indirect method can be confusing. When an asset (not inventory) is sold, a gain or loss is reported on the income statement if the selling price is different from its carrying amount. The gain or loss is the difference between the carrying amount of the asset and the selling price; it's not cash. The cash from the sale is an investing activity. Net income, however, includes the gain or loss. The reconciliation from net income to CFO removes the gain or loss so that a non-cash event isn't included in CFO (gains are subtracted, losses added). If they aren't removed, there would be a double count (i.e., the same amount would be included twice in the statement) because CFO would include the gain or loss and the full amount of the proceeds would be reported as an investing activity—the total would be different from the amount of cash actually received.

For example, Rife Inc. (Rife) sells land with a carrying amount of $10,000 for $25,000 cash. This is the only transaction Rife has for the year. The gain on the sale of the land is $15,000 ($25,000 – $10,000) and net income is also $15,000. CFO is

Cash from operations:	
Net income	$15,000
Less: Gain on sale of land	15,000
Cash from operations	$ 0
Cash from investing activities:	
Sale of land	$25,000

Here's the journal entry for the sale:

Dr. Cash	25,000	
Cr. Land		10,000
Cr. Gain		15,000

The cash flow statement only reflects transactions that affect cash. In this case, cash increased by $25,000, which is reported as an investing activity. If the gain wasn't subtracted from net income when reconciling to CFO, CFO would be $15,000 and cash from investing activities would be $25,000, for total inflow of $40,000. This is clearly wrong, since Rife only received $25,000.

McGraw Hill connect

KNOWLEDGE CHECK 5.2

In 2017, Baltic Ltd. (Baltic) reported net income of $16,000, based on revenues of $100,000; expenses other than depreciation of $70,000; depreciation of $6,000; and a loss on the sale of a piece of land of $8,000. All revenues and expenses (other than depreciation) were for cash.

Calculate Baltic's CFO for 2017 using the indirect method.

Converting accrual net income to CFO is quite straightforward. Understanding why the adjustments are made is more difficult. First, let's look at the mechanics. Figure 5.6 shows the adjustments that must be made when reconciling from net income to CFO. The box in Figure 5.6 entitled "Adjustments for non-cash transactions" represents the first type of adjustment we discussed above. The second type of adjustment is for the changes in the non-cash working capital accounts on the balance sheet. When using the indirect method, increases in working capital asset accounts such as accounts receivable, inventory, and prepaids are subtracted from net income, and decreases are added back. Increases in working capital liability accounts such as accounts payable, wages payable, and accrued liabilities are added to net income, and decreases are

FIGURE 5.6 **Calculating Cash and Operations Using the Indirect Approach**

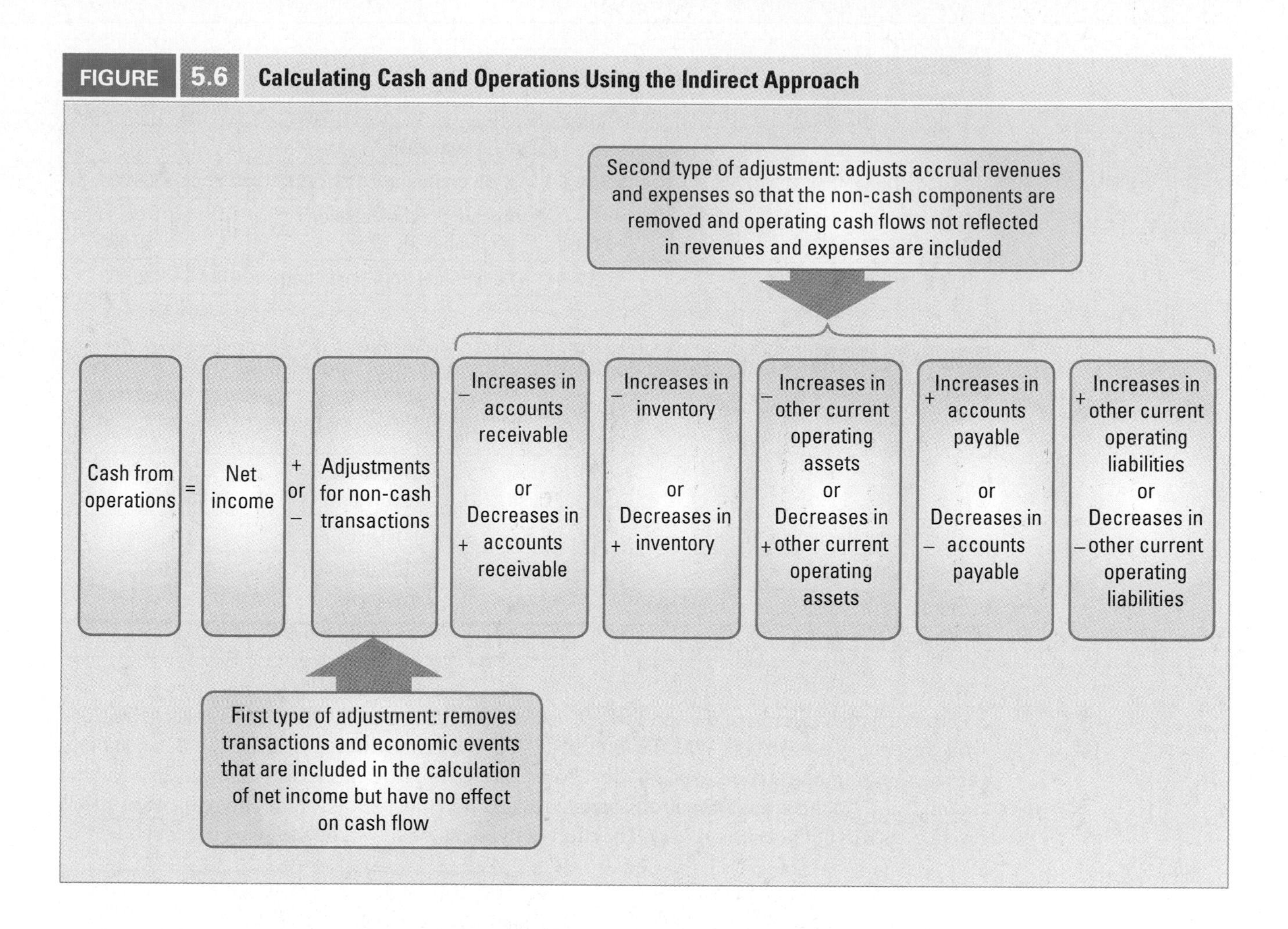

subtracted. At this point, take another look at Thomson Reuters' statement of cash flows and Note 26 in Exhibit 5.1 to see this type of adjustment.

What's the connection between accrual revenues and expenses, non-cash working capital accounts on the balance sheet, and cash flows? When revenues or expenses are recorded at different times than the associated cash flows, the difference appears on the balance sheet as a non-cash working capital item. Consider the following scenarios:

- A sale made on credit doesn't involve cash, so an account receivable is recorded. When cash from the sale is collected, there is no income statement effect, and accounts receivable decreases.
- Purchase of insurance coverage for a future period means cash is expended but there is no expense until the coverage is in effect. The amount paid for the policy is reported as prepaid insurance.

We will show these effects with three examples. The first looks at cash collections and revenue; the second at cash disbursements and wage expense; and the third at cash flow associated with inventory, accounts payable, and cost of goods sold. We will use the accounting equation spreadsheet method introduced in Chapter 3 to show the cash implications for each example. This method is useful because the cash column in the spreadsheet provides all the information we need to understand cash flows.

Example 1: Kamloops Inc. Examine the information for Kamloops Inc. in Table 5.8 and the partial accounting equation spreadsheet in Table 5.9. The spreadsheet summarizes the entries in 2018 regarding revenue, cash, and accounts receivable. Examine the spreadsheet to see how these entries affected revenue in comparison with cash.

TABLE 5.8 Kamloops Inc.: Financial Information

Kamloops Inc. Information about the Year 2018			
Cash on December 31, 2017	$ 70,000	Cash on December 31, 2018	$566,000
Accounts receivable on December 31, 2017	60,000	Accounts receivable on December 31, 2018	89,000
Sales during 2018	525,000	Collections from customers in 2018	496,000

TABLE 5.9 Kamloops Inc.: Partial Accounting Equation Spreadsheet

Kamloops Inc. Partial Spreadsheet for 2018			
	Cash	Accounts receivable	Revenue
Balance on December 31, 2017	70,000	60,000	
During 2018—revenue		**525,000**	525,000
During 2018—collection of receivables	**496,000**	(496,000)	
Balance on December 31, 2018	566,000	89,000	**525,000**

From the cash column of the spreadsheet, you can see that $496,000 of cash was collected in 2018 while revenue was $525,000. Why the difference? There are two reasons: (a) there was $60,000 of receivables outstanding at the end of 2017 that were collected in 2018 (this is cash inflow in 2018 but not revenue) and (b) there was $89,000 of sales in 2018 that were uncollected at the end of the year (this is revenue in 2018 but not cash inflow). The effect of these can be shown by the following equation:

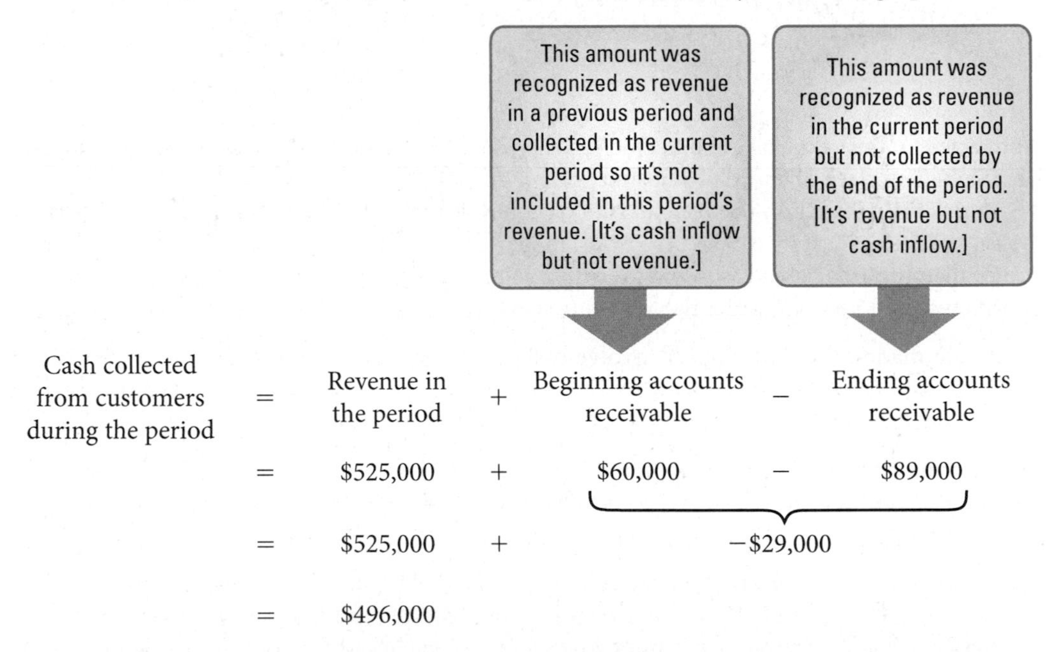

The next point is crucial. Notice that the difference between beginning and ending accounts receivable ($60,000 − $89,000 = −$29,000) is the same as the difference between cash collected during 2018 and revenue in 2018 ($496,000 − $525,000 = −$29,000). This isn't a coincidence! When accounts receivable increase, it means the amount of credit sales in the year that are uncollected as of the year-end is greater than the amount of cash collected from credit sales recognized in a previous year. As a result, revenue will be greater than cash collected by the amount of the difference. When accounts receivable decrease, the opposite is true. This is why an increase in accounts receivable is deducted from net income when calculating CFO using the indirect method and why a decrease is added back.

TABLE 5.10 Yoho Ltd.: Financial Information

Yoho Ltd. Information about the Year 2017			
Cash on December 31, 2016	$98,000	Cash on December 31, 2017	$ 5,000
Wages payable on December 31, 2016	13,000	Wages payable on December 31, 2017	8,000
Wage expense for 2017	88,000	Wages paid to employees during 2017	93,000

TABLE 5.11 Yoho Ltd.: Partial Accounting Equation Spreadsheet

Yoho Ltd. Partial Spreadsheet for 2017			
	Cash	**Wages Payable**	**Wage Expense**
Balance on December 31, 2016	98,000	13,000	
During 2017—wage expense		88,000	**(88,000)**
During 2017—wages paid to employees	**(93,000)**	(93,000)	
Balance on December 31, 2017	5,000	8,000	**(88,000)**

Example 2: Yoho Ltd. For this example, we will examine cash spent on wages. Consider the information about Yoho Ltd. in Table 5.10 and the partial accounting equation spreadsheet in Table 5.11. The spreadsheet summarizes the entries that would have been made in 2017 regarding wage expense, cash, and wages payable. Examine the spreadsheet to see how these entries affected the wage expense account compared with the cash account.

The same logic applied in example 1 applies here. The difference between the wage expense in 2017 and cash spent on wages during 2017 ($88,000 − $93,000 = $ −5,000) is the same as the decrease in wages payable in 2017 ($8,000 − $13,000 = $ −5,000). Once again, this isn't a coincidence. A decrease in wages payable means that the entity paid employees more during the year than it expensed in wages. Therefore, the wage expense is less than cash paid. So, when calculating CFO using the indirect method, a *decrease* in wages payable over the period is subtracted from net income. The relationship is reversed if wages payable increased, in which case an increase would be added to net income. The relationship can be shown in the form of an equation:

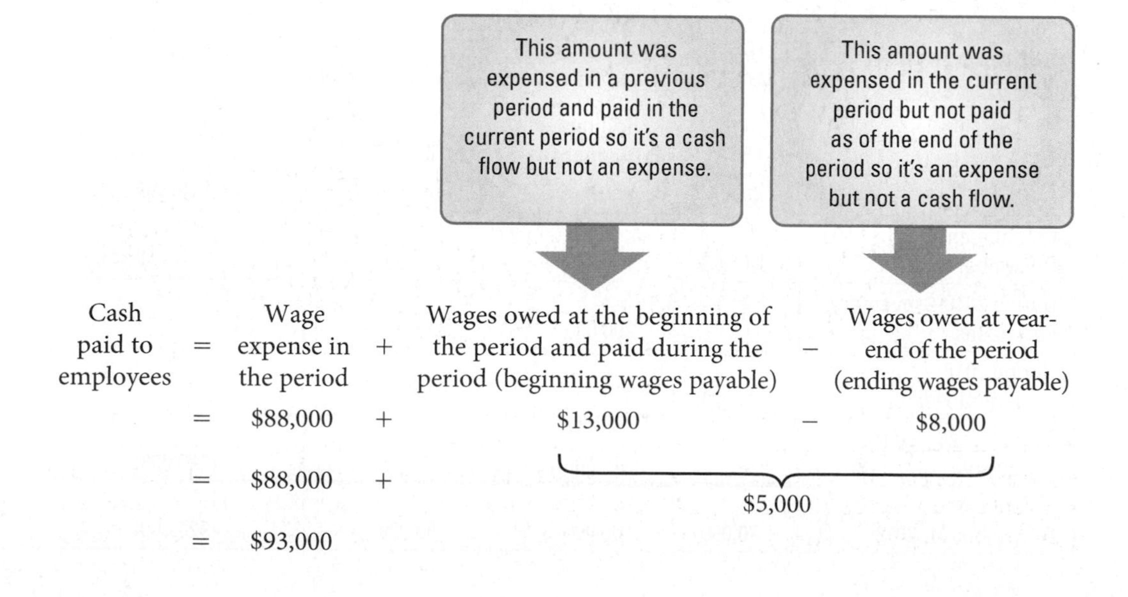

So, for Yoho, we should subtract $5,000 from net income when calculating CFO using the indirect method because $5,000 more cash was paid in wages in 2017 than was expensed.

Example 3: Rollingdam Ltd. For the third example, we will examine cash paid for inventory. Consider the following information about Rollingdam Ltd. (Rollingdam) in Table 5.12 and the partial accounting equation spreadsheet in Table 5.13. The spreadsheet summarizes the entries that would have been made in 2018 regarding cost of goods sold, cash, inventory, and accounts payable. Examine the spreadsheet to see how these entries affected cost of goods sold in comparison with cash. This example is a bit more complicated because cash spent for inventory involves two balance sheet accounts, inventory and accounts payable, not just one. The example assumes accounts payable pertains only to inventory purchases.

First, remember that inventory isn't expensed until it's sold. This is important because if you buy inventory but don't sell it, you're spending money, but there's no effect on the income statement. If inventory is paid for in cash when purchased, a decrease in inventory means less cash is spent on inventory in the year than the amount expensed as cost of goods sold (because you're selling some inventory paid for in previous periods). Therefore, a decrease in inventory should be added to net income when calculating CFO using the indirect method, and an increase in inventory should be subtracted.

Of course, inventory is usually purchased on credit. A decrease in accounts payable means the entity paid more for inventory during the year than it expensed to cost of goods sold. Therefore, the cost of goods sold is less than cash paid. So a decrease in accounts payable should be subtracted from net income when calculating CFO. Similarly, an increase in accounts payable should be added to net income.

TABLE 5.12 Rollingdam Ltd.: Financial Information

Rollingdam Ltd. Information about the Year 2018			
Cash on December 31, 2017	$340,000	Cash on December 31, 2018	$ 70,000
Inventory on December 31, 2017	125,000	Inventory on December 31, 2018	100,000
Accounts payable on December 31, 2017	60,000	Accounts payable on December 31, 2018	90,000
Payments made to inventory suppliers during 2018	270,000	Inventory purchased during 2018 (All inventory is purchased on credit)	300,000
Cost of goods sold during 2018	325,000		

TABLE 5.13 Rollingdam Ltd.: Partial Accounting Equation Spreadsheet

Rollingdam Ltd. Partial Spreadsheet for 2018				
	Cash	**Inventory**	**Accounts Payable**	**Cost of Goods Sold**
Balance on December 31, 2017	340,000	125,000	60,000	
During 2018—inventory purchases		300,000	300,000	
During 2018—payments made for inventory	**(270,000)**		(270,000)	
During 2018—cost of goods sold		(325,000)		**(325,000)**
Balance on December 31, 2018	70,000	100,000	90,000	(325,000)

From Table 5.13, we see that the amount that Rollingdam spent on inventory in 2018 was $55,000 less than its cost of goods sold ($270,000 − $325,000 = −$55,000). We can also see that inventory decreased by $25,000 ($100,000 − $125,000) and accounts payable increased by $30,000 ($90,000 − $60,000). If we add the decrease in inventory and the increase in accounts payable ($25,000 + $30,000), we come up with the same $55,000 difference.

The methods described in this section are intended to help you understand the workings of the calculation of CFO using the indirect method. Next we'll investigate how to interpret and use the cash flow statement.

KNOWLEDGE CHECK 5.3

You are provided with the following information about Ituna Inc. (Ituna) for 2017. Use this information to calculate the amount that net income would be adjusted by (how much would be added to or subtracted from net income) when reconciling from net income to CFO using the indirect method.

Ituna Inc. Information about the Year 2017			
Inventory on December 31, 2016	$ 8,500	Inventory on December 31, 2017	$5,600
Accounts payable on December 31, 2016	6,200	Accounts payable on December 31, 2017	4,900
Cost of goods sold during 2017	47,250		

INTERPRETING AND USING THE CASH FLOW STATEMENT

LO 5

Thomson Reuters' Statement of Cash Flows

We've done a fairly thorough job looking at what's in Thomson Reuters' statement of cash flows but we haven't talked about what it means. Thomson Reuters' cash flow statement (Exhibit 5.1) shows that during fiscal 2011 it generated CFO of $2,597,000,000. CFO is cash that can be used for paying dividends, acquiring assets, paying off liabilities, financing expansion, and so on. CFO is valuable because it provides cash internally—it isn't necessary to go to lenders or prospective shareholders. Thomson Reuters' CFO means that ordinary business activities produced enough cash to meet its operating requirements, with almost $2.6 billion left to apply to other purposes. In 2011, Thomson Reuters used its CFO to acquire companies ($1,286,000,000) and other capital assets ($1,041,000,000), reduce its debt load ($299,000,000) by repaying more debt than it incurred, repurchase common shares ($326,000,000), and pay dividends ($963,000,000). CFO didn't cover all Thomson Reuters' investing and financing activities so its balance of cash and cash equivalents decreased by $442,000,000, leaving the company with cash and equivalents of $422,000,000 on December 31, 2011. This is a fairly significant amount of cash although it's the lowest year-end balance since 2006.

Thomson Reuters' 2011 CFO is about $75 million lower than in 2010, a relatively small decrease (less than 3 percent), yet its net income decreased by $2.325 billion, from $933 million in 2010 to a loss of $1.392 billion in 2011. Why was there so little change in CFO whereas there was such a large decrease in profit? The reason is that in 2011 there was an impairment loss on goodwill of $3.010 billion. This means that the carrying amount of goodwill was determined to be too high—there was less future benefit associated with the goodwill—so the carrying amount was decreased or "written down." Decreasing the carrying amount of an asset has no impact on cash: it simply decreases the amount of the asset on the balance sheet and incurs an expense. The journal entry for the writedown of goodwill would be:

Dr. Goodwill impairment (expense +, equity −)	3,010,000,000	
Cr. Goodwill (asset −)		3,010,000,000

We'll talk about writedowns and impairments later in the book but for now I'll mention that, while there is no cash involved in a writedown or impairment, it doesn't mean that they don't have any economic impact. Writing down an asset means that there is less future benefit associated with the asset—it will generate less cash flow in future.

The cash flow statement also shows that Thomson Reuters paid $399,000,000 in interest to lenders and $511,000,000 in income taxes. Note that these amounts are different than the amounts expensed during the year. The difference is because interest and taxes are expensed on an accrual basis, which will usually be different than the actual amounts paid. The amount of interest and taxes paid are required disclosures under IFRS and ASPE. Thomson Reuters provides this information at the very bottom of the cash flow statement in Exhibit 5.1.

There are other analyses we can do using the information in the cash flow statement. For example, we can compare the amount of cash collected from customers in each of the years shown on the balance sheet. We can do this by using the tools developed in the previous section. We can calculate cash collections by adjusting revenue on the income statement by subtracting the increase in accounts receivable and adding the increase in deferred revenue (see Note 26 in Exhibit 5.1):

Cash collected from customers in 2011	=	Revenue	−	Increase in accounts receivable	+	Increase in deferred revenue
	=	$13,807,000,000	−	$164,000,000	+	$77,000,000
	=	$13,720,000,000				

During 2011, Thomson Reuters collected $13,720,000,000 in cash from customers. For 2010, cash collections were $13,116,000,000 (try this calculation yourself). This shows that in 2011 Thomson Reuters collected slightly less cash than the amount of revenue it reported, whereas in 2010 the amount of cash collected was a bit more than the amount of revenue.

INSIGHT

Liquidity versus Solvency

Stakeholders often use financial statements to assess an entity's liquidity and solvency. Liquidity is a short-term concept that refers to the availability of cash or the ability to convert assets to cash. It's important for evaluating whether an entity can meet its current obligations. Cash, investments in the shares of public companies, and accounts receivable (usually) are liquid. Land, buildings, equipment, and intangible assets are usually not very liquid because they can be difficult to convert to cash quickly.

Solvency refers to an entity's viability in the long-term and its ability to pay its debts as they come due. An entity might be insolvent if its liabilities are greater than its assets or if it's unable to pay its debts. An entity with $1 million in cash may be liquid, but with a $2 million loan coming due in two years and no ability to generate additional cash, it would be considered insolvent.

LO 5 Other Issues

CFO, especially if it's regular and predictable, is an important source of liquidity because it represents a reliable source of cash for meeting obligations. The cash flow statement provides other valuable information about an entity's solvency by indicating whether it will be able to pay liabilities when they mature. In Chapter 2, the current ratio was introduced as a commonly used measure of liquidity. There are limits to the current ratio because it's static—it's based only on balance sheet items. The cash flow statement, CFO in particular, provides a different view of liquidity because it shows cash generated over time. Another measure of an entity's ability to meet its short-term obligations is the operating cash flows to current liabilities ratio a (operating cash flow ratio):

$$\text{Operating cash flows to current liabilities ratio} = \frac{\text{Cash from operations}}{\text{Average current liabilities}}$$

This ratio indicates whether an entity is generating enough cash from operations to meet its current liabilities. A ratio less than one indicates that CFO isn't adequate to meet current liabilities and cash may have to be obtained from other sources or the rate of cash expenditure slowed. Thomson Reuters' operating cash flows to current liabilities ratio is:

$$\begin{aligned}\text{Operating cash flows to current liabilities ratio} &= \frac{\text{Cash from operations}}{\text{Average current liabilities}}\\ &= \frac{\$2{,}597{,}000{,}000}{\$4{,}604{,}000{,}000 + \$5{,}011{,}000{,}000} = \frac{\$2{,}597{,}000{,}000}{\$4{,}807{,}500{,}000}\\ &= 0.54\end{aligned}$$

This means that Thomson Reuters doesn't generate enough cash from operations to cover its average current liabilities for the year. The ratio for 2010 was 0.55, almost identical to 2011. Thomson Reuters' 2011 ratio is actually a bit better than this because about 30 percent of its current liabilities are deferred revenue (obligations to provide services to customers who paid in advance), which are obligations to provide services, not cash. If we adjust current liabilities for deferred revenue, the ratio becomes 0.75, and for 2010, 0.74, slightly better but still below one. However, while this ratio provides a warning flag, the evidence suggests that this is a sustainable situation for Thomson Reuters. The company has successfully operated for many years with its operating cash flow ratio below one. Like most ratios, it's important to evaluate the operating cash flows to current liabilities ratio in relation to benchmarks such as similar companies and over a number of years for Thomson Reuters.

Another way of considering an entity's cash flow is by examining its **free cash flow**, which is defined as

$$\text{Free cash flow} = \text{CFO} - \text{Capital expenditures}$$

An entity must regularly spend on capital assets to maintain its ability to operate. Equipment, buildings, furniture and fixtures, computers, and other capital assets must be replaced as they become old or obsolete. Free cash flow is the cash available after capital expenditures have been made. (A **capital expenditure** is money spent to purchase capital assets.) Free cash flow is available for use at management's discretion; for example, to acquire new companies, expand, reduce debt, or buy back shares. Thomson Reuters' free cash flow for 2011 is

$$\begin{aligned}\text{Free cash flow} &= \text{CFO} - \text{Capital expenditures}\\ &= \$2{,}597{,}000{,}000 - \$1{,}041{,}000{,}000\\ &= \$1{,}556{,}000{,}000\end{aligned}$$

Cash Flow Patterns There can be eight different combinations of cash flows from operations, investing activities, and financing activities and each one tells a different story. For example, a new, fast-growing company could have negative CFO, cash inflows from financing activities, and cash outflows for investing activities because it would be spending cash on growth and would need to raise financing to cover the CFO shortfall and purchase needed capital assets. A stable, mature entity might have positive CFO, negative cash from investing activities (it would be investing in capital assets, presumably replacing assets as required), and negative cash from financing activities (it would be paying down debt and/or paying dividends). A summary of different cash flow patterns is provided in Figure 5.7.

FIGURE 5.7

Cash Flow Patterns

	Cash from Operations	Cash from Investing Activities	Cash from Financing Activities	
1	+	+	+	Entity is building its cash reserves by generating positive cash from operations, selling capital assets and/or investments, and raising capital by issuing debt and/or equity. This is an uncommon pattern—a very liquid entity, possibly looking for acquisition.
2	+	+	–	Entity is using CFO and cash from the sale of capital assets/investments to reduce debt or pay owners. Perhaps a still successful but contracting industry (need to reduce capacity) or entity has excessive debt that must be retired.
3	+	–	+	Entity is using CFO and cash from borrowing and/or sale of equity to expand. This is indicative of a successful growing entity.
4	+	–	–	Entity is using CFO to buy capital assets and reduce debt or pay owners. This may be a mature, successful entity that isn't investing (all) its cash in maintaining operating capacity or growth.
5	–	+	+	Entity's negative CFO is being covered by selling capital assets and/or long-term investments and by borrowing or from equity investments. Entity may be downsizing but investors seem willing to invest.
6	–	+	–	Entity is financing operating cash flow shortages and debt retirement and/or payments to shareholders by selling capital assets and/or investments. Lack of operating success and sell-off of assets suggests downsizing, perhaps in a declining industry.
7	–	–	+	Entity is growing, as indicated by negative CFO (increasing inventories and accounts receivable) and increasing investment in capital assets. Lenders and/or owners are providing capital to finance the growth.
8	–	–	–	Entity is using existing cash reserves to finance operations, purchase capital assets or long-term investments, and reduce debt and/or pay equity investors. This is not sustainable because cash reserves will eventually be exhausted and the entity won't be able to operate.

Source: Adapted from M.T. Dugan, B.E. Gup, and W.D. Samson, "Teaching the Statement of Cash Flow," *Journal of Accounting Education,* Volume 9, 1991, pages 35–52.

Patterns of the components of cash flow for several Canadian firms are shown in Figure 5.8. There are some things to notice in this table:

- Thomson Reuters reports a net loss but has positive CFO. Net losses don't automatically mean a cash flow problem, but they will if they continue.
- Lanesborough Real Estate Investment Trust reports a sizable net income but negative CFO. This situation highlights the importance of not ignoring the cash flow statement. Net income doesn't automatically imply liquidity.

FIGURE 5.8

Cash Flow Patterns of Selected Canadian Corporations

Company and Year-End	Net Income (000)	Cash from Operations (000)	Investing Activities (000)	Financing Activities (000)	Net Change in Cash (000)
Canadian Pacific Railway Limited December 31, 2011	$ 570,000	$ 512,000 +	$(1,044,000) –	$ 217,000 +	$314,000
Crown Gold Corporation December 31, 2011	(1,897.5)	(1,091.1) –	100.0 +	502.5 +	(488.6)
Denison Mines Corp. December 31, 2011	(70,869)	(19,983) –	(85,744) –	62,261 +	(43,466)
Lanesborough Real Estate Investment Trust December 31, 2011	5,0535.2	(383.2) –	4,501.7 +	(4,041.7) –	76.8
Supremex Inc. December 31, 2011	8,314.8	19,005.2 +	2,175.1 +	(18,704.5) –	2,475.8
Thomson Reuters Corporation December 31, 2011	(1,392,000)	2,597,000 +	(1,807,000) +	(1,227,000) –	(442,000)

\+ Indicates a net cash inflow.
– Indicates a net cash outflow.
Cash from operations + cash from investing + cash from financing activities don't necessarily add to the net change in cash because of adjustments not included in the table.

ACCOUNTING STANDARDS FOR PRIVATE ENTERPRISES

IFRS and ASPE have similar requirements for the cash flow statement, although there are some differences:

- ASPE doesn't require a cash flow statement provided the required cash flow information is available from the other financial statements and the notes. IFRS don't provide this option.
- ASPE requires interest paid and collected that is reported in the income statement to be classified as CFO whereas IFRS allows entities to classify interest payments as CFO or financing activities and interest received as CFO or investing activities.
- ASPE requires dividends paid to be classified as financing activities whereas IFRS allows entities to choose between financing activities and CFO. ASPE requires dividends earned to be classified as CFO while IFRS allows a choice between CFO and investing activities.

Let's look at one more cash flow statement, for a company that's in the early stages of its development. Nuvo Research Inc. is a pharmaceutical company that develops pain relief products. Young companies usually require cash in their early years, especially ones investing in researching and developing new products. It can take many years to develop a portfolio of products that allow the company to generate more cash from operations than it consumes. Nuvo isn't a new company; it's been publicly traded since 1997, but it's reported a profit only once, in 2009, and as of December 31, 2011 had accumulated negative retained earnings (deficit) of $208,465,000. The company has never paid a dividend. Yet Nuvo has managed to raise money from lenders and equity investors to finance the development of its products. Exhibit 5.3 provides extracts from Nuvo's statements of cash flow for the years ended December 31, 2006 through 2011. In that period, the company had negative cash from operations of over $43 million and raised over $55 million by issuing common shares to cover its cash requirements. What's important to see in this exhibit is how a company can survive without generating cash from operations. However, if investors decided that the company wasn't likely to eventually make a profit, they would stop investing and the company would fail.

EXHIBIT 5.3 Nuvo Research Inc.: Statements of Cash Flow[2]

Nuvo Research Inc. Statements of Cash Flow December 31,						
	2011	**2010**	**2009**	**2008**	**2007**	**2006**
Cash from operations	$(11,839)	$(12,378)	$16,259	$(9,115)	$(12,268)	$(13,889)
Cash flows from financing activities						
Issuance of common shares (net of costs)	48	84	11,704	1,115	23,854	18,581
Issuance of long-term debt (net of costs)				1,956		1,000
Repayment of long term debt	(3,085)	(77)	(243)	(630)	(675)	(1,492)
Repayment of short-term debt						(1,598)
Miscellaneous				(32)		3,500
Total cash flows from financing activities	(3,037)	7	11,461	2,409	23,179	19,991
Cash flows from investing activities	1,406	(842)	(391)	(123)	(301)	2,165
Increase (decrease) in cash and cash equivalents	(13,545)	(13,833)	26,883	(6,572)	10,578	8,497
Cash and cash equivalents, beginning of period	28,269	42,102	15,219	21,791	11,213	2,716
Cash and cash equivalents, end of period	14,724	28,269	42,102	15,219	21,791	11,213

LO 6

IMPACT OF MANAGER DECISIONS ON CASH FLOW INFORMATION AND THE EFFECT OF ACCRUAL ACCOUNTING CHOICES ON THE CASH FLOW STATEMENT

Throughout the book, we have discussed how managers can use the alternative accounting methods and judgment that are part of accrual accounting to manage financial statement numbers. Some people suggest that one attractive aspect of cash accounting and the cash flow statement is that they can't be managed or manipulated the way accrual information can be.

This isn't true. Cash information can't be managed in the same way as accrual information, where managers decide when to recognize revenue and expenses, but it can be affected by managers' decisions, perhaps in a way that is even more dangerous to the entity. Cash information is "cleaner" in the sense that a transaction has an impact on cash flow only if cash is involved. As a result, managers can't exercise any judgment on the accounting for cash *once a transaction involving cash has occurred*. However, managers can influence the timing and amount of cash flows.

Managers can alter the timing of cash flows by timing when bills are paid or reducing "discretionary" spending on research and development, advertising and promotion, marketing, or maintenance. These spending reductions increase CFO but they may or may not be in the interests of the entity. Take the following examples:

- Reducing maintenance spending on equipment would increase CFO in the short term but could contribute to higher costs in the future. The equipment may eventually require more costly maintenance or even need replacing sooner than if it had been properly maintained. Poorly maintained equipment could also reduce the efficiency of operations or the quality of the goods produced, which would increase costs and reduce revenues.
- Cutting research and development and advertising, marketing, and promotion would increase CFO in the current period but could have negative longer-term consequences by decreasing future sales or competitiveness.

- Increasing CFO by delaying payments to suppliers could affect suppliers' willingness to offer credit in future.
- Increasing cash flow by selling capital assets or other long-term assets would increase cash from investing activities but it could result in the disposal of assets that could generate revenue and profit.

Of course, in all these examples it's difficult to be sure whether management is making good decisions or desperately trying to conserve cash, which makes understanding the cash flow statement numbers more difficult.

Cash flow statement users can overcome the difficulty of preparers who manage the timing of their cash flows by examining cash flow statements for a number of periods. Many of these managerial decisions simply move cash flows among periods, which an alert user can observe by carefully examining a number of cash flow statements.

Comparing cash flow information and accrual information can help identify possible earnings management. For example, if a company is recognizing revenue earlier (for example, on long-term contracts) you might see an increase in revenues and income, but not an increase in cash from operations (since revenue is being recognized but cash isn't being collected).

Accounting policy choices don't affect the cash flows associated with a transaction. For example, how the revenue is recognized doesn't affect when cash is collected. However, the accounting choice may have other cash flow implications. For example, an accounting choice could affect the amount of tax an entity pays or the bonuses managers receive.

Solved Problem

This solved problem is another case analysis that will help you to learn and develop the problem-solving skills introduced in Chapter 4. In this case, a student operating a small business comes to you for an explanation for the business's poor cash position despite a good net income. You should attempt to solve the case on your own before reading the solution.

TRENDY T-SHIRTS INC.

In Spring 2017, Simon Francis decided that instead of working for someone else during the summer, he would start a business of his own to finance his education designing and selling T-shirts to the residents and many vacationers in the area near where he lived.

Simon incorporated a company called Trendy T-Shirts Inc. (Trendy). He decided he would operate the business out of a modified van purchased by Trendy. The van would allow him to move around so he could be where the customers were. Simon used his own computer to create T-shirt designs and purchased equipment to print the designs on the shirts. To start up the business, Simon invested $6,000 of his own money and borrowed $10,000 from his parents. His parents told him they had to be repaid within three years.

Simon thought that Trendy's first year in business was successful. He earned enough money to pay for his schooling and take a nice vacation during the winter. In fact, Simon thought Trendy was so successful he expanded in 2018. For 2018, Simon bought some additional equipment and a second van that was operated by an employee. He also increased the number of designs and the quantity of T-shirts he produced because the previous summer he had run short of shirts. Trendy financed the purchase of the second van and the equipment with a bank loan Simon quickly repaid out of operating cash flows.

It's now October 2018 and Trendy has ceased operations for the year. Simon feels very satisfied with the performance of his business for the year—a net income of $14,250 for the year ended September 30, 2018. However, when Simon got around to looking at Trendy's bank statements (he hadn't bothered to look at them over the summer because he was so busy) he was shocked to see that there was only $2,820 in the bank. There wasn't enough money to pay for school, take another vacation, or repay the remaining bank loan. Trendy's cash flow statements for the last two years (shown in Exhibit 5.4) confirmed his fears—there wasn't enough cash to meet his needs—and Simon can't figure out why.

Required:

a. Use the cash flow statement to explain to Simon how his business can be successful but not give him enough cash to meet his needs. Be sure to consider Trendy's activities and Simon's decisions in both 2017 and 2018.

b. Simon is thinking about going to the bank to borrow $10,000, which would be paid to him as a dividend. If you were the banker, would you lend money to Trendy? Explain.

EXHIBIT 5.4 Cash Flow Statements for Trendy T-Shirts Inc.

Trendy T-Shirts Inc.
Cash Flow Statement for the Years Ended September 30

	2018	2017
Operations		
Net income	$14,250	$ 9,430
Add: Depreciation expense	8,100	3,250
Less: Increase in inventory	3,510	1,250
Cash from operations	18,840	11,430
Financing		
Loan from parents	(6,000)	10,000
Bank loan	7,500	
Van and equipment loan	(18,000)	
Van and equipment loan repayment	18,000	
Common stock issued		6,000
Dividends paid		(12,500)
Cash from financing activities	1,500	3,500
Investing		
Purchase of van	(17,000)	(11,000)
Purchase of equipment	(2,200)	(2,250)
Cash outflows from investing activities	(19,200)	(13,250)
Increase in cash	1,140	1,680
Cash balance at the beginning of the year	1,680	0
Cash balance at the end of the year	$ 2,820	$ 1,680

Solution:

Part (a)

Report to Simon Francis regarding the performance of Trendy T-Shirts Inc.

Dear Simon:

I am writing to help clarify your confusion regarding Trendy T-Shirts Inc.'s cash position compared with its accrual accounting performance. Your business performed well in 2018—earning an income of $14,250—but your cash position is poor—only $2,820 is on hand at the end of the year before paying yourself a dividend. To explain, it is important to understand the difference between accrual accounting and cash flow. Accrual accounting reflects economic flows and economic activity, not just cash and the change in cash. As a result, the amount of income you report does not necessarily match your business's cash flow.

During 2017, Trendy generated cash from operations—the cash an entity generates from selling T-shirts—of $11,430, which could be used for paying off debts, paying dividends, expanding operations, making investments in equipment, and so on. This amount was different from your net income of $9,430 for two reasons. First, in the calculation of net income, a depreciation expense of $3,250 was deducted. This is not cash that was spent; it is simply part of the cost of the van and equipment deducted in calculating net income. The idea is to expense part of the cost of these assets each year because they contribute to your business over many years. (Note that Trendy did spend $13,250 in cash on the van and equipment in 2017. I will have more to say about this shortly.) The second difference between cash from operations and net income was the $1,250 investment in inventory you had at the end of the 2017 season. This inventory had been paid for by the end of 2017 but it had not been expensed because it had not been sold. This means that you had $1,250 in cash tied up in T-shirts you could sell in 2018.

A similar analysis can be provided for 2018. Your cash from operations in 2018 was $18,840, a fair bit higher than in 2017. Trendy's income statement reported $8,100 in non-cash depreciation expense and an additional $3,510 was invested in inventory that was unsold at end of the year. The bottom line is, your business is generating decent cash flow. So why do you not have enough cash on hand to meet your needs?

There are several reasons. First, you spent a significant amount of money purchasing assets that will help you make money over several years, that is, the vans and equipment. So, while your business is generating cash, you have invested a significant amount of money to get your business going. These cash outlays are required when a business starts up or expands. In your first two years, Trendy spent $32,450 on assets. If you do not expand in future years, these assets will contribute to sales without costing you any cash.

Second, Trendy has $4,760 in cash invested in inventory, which seems like a lot. Does this amount represent plain T-shirts or ones that have designs? If it is the latter, will these shirts be salable? Do designs go out of style? If the inventory can't be sold, the income of your business may, in fact, be overstated because the cost of unsalable inventory should be expensed. If the inventory is shirts without designs, then they can be used in future, although it seems like a lot of money to be tied up in items that can be easily purchased at any time. If possible, you could return the T-shirts to free up some cash.

Third, in 2017 Trendy paid a $12,500 dividend, probably one it couldn't afford. In 2017 Trendy was able to pay for the van and equipment ($13,250) and for the dividend ($12,500) by generating cash from operations ($11,430), borrowing ($10,000), and from your own investment ($6,000). But by paying the dividend, there was little cash left to finance expansion. Had Trendy not expanded, paying the dividend probably would not have been a problem.

In 2018, operations generated most of the cash ($18,840) needed to pay for the second van and some additional equipment ($19,200), although a short-term loan ($18,000) was needed to bridge the cash shortage at the beginning of the year. A $7,500 bank loan was used mainly to repay your parents. The problem in 2018 was that Trendy spent about the same amount of money as it generated from all sources. There was nothing left over to pay a dividend. In contrast, the amount of money spent in 2017 before paying the dividend was significantly less than the amount generated from operations and financing activities. However, your dividend in 2017 was paid for by borrowing from your parents and from the money you invested in Trendy to start with, not with cash from operations.

This should be a short-term problem for you. Assuming that your business continues to be as successful as it has been, and if you control your inventory, Trendy should be generating about $20,000 a year in cash from operations. Assuming you don't expand further, that amount will allow you to pay off your $7,500 bank loan in 2019 and have plenty of cash available for your own needs. In the meantime, you'll have to find an alternative source of cash to meet your personal needs this year. Perhaps you can borrow from your parents again or obtain a personal bank loan.

Part (b)

As a banker, I would give serious consideration to providing a $10,000 loan to Trendy on the basis of its operations. Trendy generates a lot of cash and it would be able to support a loan—both the interest and principal—assuming it continues to perform as it did in 2018. That said, T-shirts can be a risky business; what is popular one year might not be popular in the next. On the other hand, over the years, T-shirts have enjoyed sustained popularity so that mitigates some of the risk. Even if the business contracted by 25 percent there would still be adequate cash flow to repay the loan plus interest. Trendy has its two vans and the equipment along with the inventory to use as collateral for a loan. It is not clear, however, how much cash those items would raise if they had to be sold. I would need an estimate of what they are worth.

It is a significant concern that Trendy does not need the cash for the business. Assuming no additional purchases of capital assets are required (no additional expansion is indicated) and little cash is needed for working capital (for example, to purchase inventory and supplies), the main purpose of the loan would be to allow Trendy to pay a dividend. If that is the case, the amount of equity that Simon would have in the business would be $7,180 (initial equity investment + net incomes − dividends = $6,000 + $9,430 + $14,250 − $12,500 − $10,000 [assuming the bank loan of $10,000]). This would be in comparison with liabilities of $21,500 ($4,000 + $7,500 + $10,000 [assuming the bank loan and dividends of $10,000]). This represents a relatively small amount of equity relative to debt (debt-to-equity ratio = $21,500/$7,180 = 2.99). If Simon neglects his business for some reason in the future or chooses not to continue in business, our bank and the other lenders stand to lose much more than Simon does (although Simon's parents will lose $4,000 of their money).

All told, I would be inclined to recommend a loan to Trendy. The business has been able to generate cash in the past and stands to do so in the future. I recommend that, if any assets have not been secured against the other bank loan, we should take those assets as security against our loan. In addition, we should obtain personal guarantees from Simon and his parents, if possible. This will provide the bank with additional protection.

Finally, the terms of the loan should prevent Trendy from purchasing additional equipment and limit payments to Simon until the bank loan has been reduced or paid off. This is necessary because additional purchases will use up cash from operations and reduce or eliminate cash needed to pay off the bank loan. Additional purchases will also result in a repetition of the current situation where Simon is not able to draw enough cash from Trendy to meet his personal needs. In addition, further expansion may add to the bank's risk since future demand for Trendy's products isn't known, and it is not clear whether Simon will be able to effectively manage an expanded business.

INSIGHT

"What If" Scenarios

Notice that the banker's response in part (b) focuses on what will happen, not on what has happened. This is very important to keep in mind. Historical information can sometimes be a useful basis for predicting future cash flows (and earnings), but the future will usually not be the same as the past. As a result, the bank must consider "what if" scenarios. What if sales decrease? What if profit margins decrease? This type of assessment allows the banker to evaluate the risks faced. Also recognize that the banker's response is only one of many possible ones. For example, some bankers might decline to make the loan because it's for personal rather than business reasons. That conclusion would be fine but it would still have to be supported by a similar type of analysis, as in part (b).

SUMMARY OF KEY POINTS

LO 1 Cash is king. Without adequate cash or cash flow, an entity won't be able to operate because it won't be able to pay its bills. If an entity can't generate enough cash from its business activities to meet its needs it will have to raise cash by borrowing, selling shares, or selling assets. Stakeholders sometimes don't give enough attention to cash flow when evaluating an entity. The standard measure of performance under accrual accounting, earnings, isn't designed to reflect flows of cash. Cash flow isn't a better or worse measure than earnings; it's just a different measure of performance; each has its role to play.

LO 2 The cash cycle is the process of how an entity begins with cash, invests in resources, provides goods or services to customers using those resources, and then collects cash from customers. Entities usually have to invest cash in resources before cash is received from customers—there is almost always a lag between the expenditure of cash and the receipt of cash.

LO 3 Entities' cash flows are affected by how their operations are organized. Changing credit terms offered to customers, arranging different payment terms with suppliers, and changing the quantity of inventory held will affect the amount of cash the entity has at any point in time.

LO 4 The cash flow statement provides information about an entity's historical cash flows. Cash flows in the cash flow statement are grouped into three categories: cash from operations (CFO), cash from investing activities, and cash from financing activities.

LO 5 CFO can be calculated and reported in two ways on the cash flow statement. The indirect method reconciles from net income to CFO by adjusting for non-cash amounts and for operating cash flows not included in the calculation of net income. The direct method reports CFO by showing cash collections and cash disbursements related to operations during the period.

LO 6 Some people argue that one of the attractions of cash accounting over accrual accounting is that cash accounting can't be managed or manipulated. It's true that cash accounting information can't be manipulated in the same way as accrual information, where managers must decide when to recognize revenue and expenses, however, managers can manage the timing and amount of cash flows.

FORMULA SUMMARY

$$\text{Operating cash flows to current liabilities ratio} = \frac{\text{Cash from operations}}{\text{Average current liabilities}}$$

$$\text{Free cash flow} = \text{CFO} - \text{Capital expenditures}$$

KEY TERMS

bank overdraft, p. 259
capital expenditure, p. 277
cash cycle, p. 252
cash flow statement, p. 259
cash from financing activities, p. 263
cash from investing activities, p. 262
cash from operations (CFO), p. 262
cash lag, p. 253
direct method (of calculating cash from operations), p. 266
free cash flow, p. 277
indirect method (of calculating cash from operations), p. 266
inventory conversion period, p. 253
inventory self-financing period, p. 253
payables deferral period, p. 253
receivables conversion period, p. 253

SIMILAR TERMS

The left column gives alternative terms that are sometimes used for the accounting terms introduced in this chapter, which are listed in the right column.

statement of cash flows, statement of changes in financial position	**cash flow statement, p. 259**
cash flow from operating activities	**cash from operations, p. 262**

ASSIGNMENT MATERIALS

Questions

Q5-1. Explain the difference between cash accounting and accrual accounting.

Q5-2. Explain why net income isn't equal to cash from operations.

Q5-3. Why is the cash flow statement included in the general purpose financial statement package? Explain your answer fully.

Q5-4. Explain each of the following:
a. Payables deferral period
b. Inventory self-financing period
c. Inventory conversion period
d. Receivables conversion period

Q5-5. What is cash from operations? How is information about cash from operations useful to stakeholders?

Q5-6. If you examine the cash flow statements of most public companies, you'll notice that depreciation appears in the calculation of cash from operations (these would be companies that use the indirect method of calculating cash from operations). Does this mean that depreciation is a source of cash for a company? Explain.

Q5-7. Explain the difference between liquidity and solvency. Which is more important to an entity? Is it possible for an entity to be liquid but not solvent or solvent but not liquid? Explain.

Q5-8. Why is it important for stakeholders to be aware of an entity's liquidity? What are the consequences of not having adequate liquidity? Explain.

Q5-9. Which should be more important to a shareholder of a company, cash flow or net income? Explain your answer.

Q5-10. Why is depreciation added back to net income when cash from operations is calculated using the indirect method?

Q5-11. Why are losses added back to and gains subtracted from net income when cash from operations is calculated using the indirect method?

Q5-12. What does it mean when an entity has negative cash from operations? What circumstances can result in this? Why is it cause for concern? Is it necessarily bad news for an entity? Explain.

Q5-13. Which should be more important to the management of an entity, cash flow or income? Explain your answer.

Q5-14. Explain the three types of cash flows reported in a cash flow statement. Give examples of each type and explain the classification of each example.

Q5-15. New businesses frequently fail because of poor cash flow. Explain why you think new businesses have this problem.

Q5-16. What are the two methods for calculating and reporting cash from operations? Explain how each arrives at cash from operations. As a user of financial statements, which method of calculating cash from operations would you prefer to see in a cash flow statement? Explain.

Q5-17. IFRS allows managers to choose how to classify interest paid in the cash flow statement. What are the alternative classifications allowed? What is the impact on the cash flow statement of these alternatives? What is the impact on the income statement? Which treatment do you prefer? Explain.

Q5-18. What information does the cash flow statement provide to stakeholders that isn't in the income statement?

Q5-19. What is the cash cycle? Describe the cash cycle for a wine maker.

Q5-20. An entity has a very profitable year, yet its cash flow and cash from operations are negative. Explain how this can happen.

Q5-21. An entity reports a loss for the year. Explain how the entity could have positive cash flow and positive cash from operations in that year.

Q5-22. In fiscal 2017, Calstock Inc. decided to shorten the amount of time it allowed customers to pay amounts they owed from 45 days to 30 days. What will the impact of this policy change be on cash from operations in 2017?

Q5-23. Why is the amount expensed for wages during a period usually not the same as the amount paid in wages during that period?

Q5-24. What does the term "cash" in the cash flow statement refer to? Explain.

Q5-25. Assuming inventory is paid for in cash, explain why an increase in accounts receivable means that cash collected during a period is less than the amount of revenue recognized.

Q5-26. Explain why a decrease in inventory means that cash paid for inventory during a period is less than the amount of inventory expensed.

Q5-27. How can managers' decisions affect an entity's cash flow and cash from operations? How are these decisions different from managers' ability to influence accrual financial statements?

Q5-28. Managers often receive bonuses based on the net income of the entities they manage. Do you think it would be better to use cash from operations as a basis to award bonuses rather than net income? Explain your answer.

Q5-29. What objectives of financial reporting does the cash flow statement serve? Explain.

Q5-30. One way for a biotechnology, software, or other high-technology company to increase cash from operations would be to reduce spending on research. Explain why reducing spending on research (which is expensed when incurred according to IFRS) would increase cash from operations. Explain why reducing spending on research is potentially a serious problem for these types of companies. Respond by discussing the business implications of reducing spending on research.

Q5-31. In a recent negotiation between labour and management of a major corporation, management argued that the company's low earnings made it imprudent to grant the requested wage increase. The labour union disagreed, contending the company had significant positive cash flow with which it could meet the union's demands. Do you think the company's ability to pay should be based on its net income, its cash flow, or something else? Explain.

Q5-32. Give examples of the circumstances that could cause cash flow problems for a golf course.

Q5-33. Explain why growing companies sometimes face cash flow problems.

Exercises

E5-1. **(Calculating the cash lag, LO 2)** Dickens Tailor Shop (Dickens) makes tailored-to-measure suits, jackets, and pants for men and women. Customers who are interested in purchasing tailored-to-measure clothing make an appointment with one of Dickens' tailors, at which time the customer decides on the style of clothing he or she wishes to buy, selects an appropriate fabric, and is measured by the tailor. Dickens keeps a large selection of fabrics so customers can see the actual fabric their clothing will be made from. A bolt of fabric is, on average, held in inventory for seven months before it is used to make a garment. Dickens pays for its fabric 30 days from the time it is received from the supplier. The time from a customer's first appointment to the completion and delivery of the garment is, on average, 45 days. Customers receive an invoice when the garment is delivered and payment is received from the customer, on average, 20 days from the time of delivery.

Required:

Calculate the following for Dickens Tailor Shop (assume a month has 30 days):
a. Payables deferral period
b. Inventory self-financing period
c. Inventory conversion period
d. Receivables conversion period
e. Number of days between receiving inventory from suppliers and receiving cash from customers

E5-2. **(Determining the effect of credit policy on cash flow, LO 2)** You are provided the following information about McPherson Inc.:

Purchases by quarter for 2018 were

1st Quarter	2nd Quarter	3rd Quarter	4th Quarter	Total
$360,000	$402,000	$425,000	$485,000	$1,672,000

- Accounts payable at the beginning of the 1st quarter was $204,000. McPherson gets 60 days to pay from its suppliers.
- Assume purchases and payments occur evenly over each quarter and payments are made on the date they are due.

Required:

a. How much cash will McPherson pay its suppliers in each quarter of 2018 and for the entire year of 2018?
b. Suppose McPherson was notified by its suppliers in 2017 that for all purchases made after December 31, 2017, payment would have to be received by the supplier within 30 days of delivery. How much would McPherson pay in each quarter and for the entire year of 2018? (Assume beginning accounts payable is $204,000. This amount would be subject to the 2017 credit terms and would be payable over 60 days.)
c. Explain any differences between the amount paid in a. and b. above.
d. Suppose in 2019 purchases per quarter were exactly the same as in 2018. What amount would be paid to suppliers in 2019? Why is the amount paid in 2019 different from 2018?

E5-3. **(The effect of depreciation on cash from operations, LO 1, 3)** In 2017, Anyox Ltd. (Anyox) reported net income of $200,000. All revenues and expenses were in cash, except for a $30,000 depreciation expense.

Required:

a. Calculate cash from operations for Anyox in 2017.
b. Suppose that instead of a $30,000 depreciation expense in 2017, Anyox expensed $44,000 for depreciation. Assume that all other revenues and expenses remained the same. What would Anyox's net income be in 2017? What would its cash from operations be in 2017? Explain the reasons for any differences or similarities in your answer for when the depreciation expense was $30,000 and when it was $44,000.

E5-4. **(The effect of asset writedowns on cash from operations, LO 1, 5)** In the year ended December 31, 2017, Hexham Inc. (Hexham) reported net income of $7,400,000, which included a writeoff* of $2,000,000 of company assets. During 2017 accounts receivable

*A writeoff is a reduction in the carrying amount of an asset to some measure of its fair value. It's achieved by debiting an expense and crediting the asset.

increased by $200,000, inventory increased by $350,000, and accounts payable decreased by $30,000. Depreciation expense in 2017 was $556,000.

Required:

a. What journal entry did Hexham make to record the writeoff of the assets?
b. Calculate cash from operations using the indirect method.
c. Suppose that at the last minute, Hexham's management decided to delay writing off the assets from its books:
   i. What would Hexham's net income be in 2017?
   ii. What would Hexham's cash from operations be in 2017?
d. Explain the differences you found between the net income Hexham originally reported and the net income you calculated under c(i).
e. Explain the differences you found between the cash from operations numbers you calculated under (b) and (c)(ii).

E5-5. **(Classifying transactions for a cash flow statement, LO 4)** Classify each of the following transactions and economic events as an operating, investing, or financing cash flow; a cash equivalent; or whether the item has no effect on cash flow. Also, indicate whether each item increases or decreases cash flow. State whether the treatment differs between IFRS and ASPE.

a. Equipment is purchased for cash.
b. Capital assets are depreciated.
c. Cash dividends are paid to shareholders.
d. Interest is paid on a bond.
e. Accounts receivable are collected from customers.
f. Land is purchased in exchange for shares in the company.
g. Cash is obtained from a lender in exchange for a long-term note payable.
h. Long-term debt is repaid.
i. Suppliers of inventory are paid in cash.
j. Inventory is purchased on credit.
k. Cash is invested in a GIC that matures in 45 days.
l. A bank loan is obtained.
m. A lender accepts shares of the borrowing company as repayment for the loan.
n. A supplier refunds money because the merchandise received was damaged.
o. A customer makes a deposit for services that will be provided next year.
p. An insurance policy purchased and paid for last year is expensed this year.

E5-6. **(Classifying transactions for a cash flow statement, LO 4)** Ashley Booth owns and operates a movie theatre in a small city. For each of the following, state whether the item should be classified as an operating, financing, or investing cash flow, whether the item represents a cash inflow or outflow, and the amount that would be reported on the cash flow statement. Explain your reasoning. Assume Ashley uses ASPE.

a. Sold $150,000 in snacks at the concession stand for cash.
b. Repaid a $25,000 bank loan.
c. Paid employees $100,000 in wages.
d. Gave $5,000 in refunds for tickets purchased but not used.
e. Expensed $30,000 for depreciation.
f. Sold old equipment for $18,000. The loss on the sale was $5,000.
g. Purchased new projection equipment for $10,000 cash. She also agreed to pay the equipment supplier $5,000 in two years.
h. Purchased advertising in local newspapers during the year for $15,000 cash.
i. Ashley contributed $20,000 in cash for additional shares in the theatre.
j. Paid $10,000 in interest on loans.

E5-7. **(Classifying transactions for a cash flow statement, LO 4)** Basanti Retirement Home Inc. (Basanti) is a privately owned home for seniors who can live independently but prefer the convenience of having meals, cleaning, and nursing assistance available to them. For each of the following, state whether the item should be classified as an operating, financing, or investing cash flow, whether the item represents a cash inflow or outflow, and the amount that would be reported on the cash flow statement. Explain your reasoning. Assume Basanti uses IFRS.

a. Collected $900,000 in rent from residents.
b. Spent $48,000 in cash renovating the dining room.
c. Paid $25,000 in dividends to the owners.
d. Borrowed $100,000 from the bank.
e. Sold some old furniture of $22,000 cash. There was a loss of $3,000 on the sale.
f. Paid $2,500 to have the carpets in the residence cleaned.
g. Paid nursing staff $175,000 cash
h. Purchased new mattresses on credit. Payment will be made in the next fiscal year.
i. Paid for maintenance work done in the previous fiscal year.

E5-8. **(Determining missing information, LO 4)** Calculate the missing information (indicated by shaded areas) from the following cash flow statements:

Cash from (used by)	Company 1	Company 2	Company 3	Company 4	Company 5
Operations	$30,000	($36,000)	$	$48,000	$
Investing activities	(13,500)		1,500	(30,000)	(15,000)
Financing activities		45,000	(30,000)	(18,000)	6,000
Net increase (decrease) in cash	3,000	(15,000)	18,000		(24,000)

E5-9. **(Calculating cash from operations, LO 4, 5)** You are provided the following information about Clarke Inc. (Clarke) for 2018:

Net income	$ 437,500
Accounts receivable on January 1, 2018	1,375,000
Accounts receivable on December 31, 2018	1,562,500
Inventory on January 1, 2018	1,750,000
Inventory on December 31, 2018	1,525,000
Accounts payable on January 1, 2018	1,187,500
Accounts payable on December 31, 2018	1,437,500
Depreciation expense	262,500

Required:

Calculate cash from operations for Clarke for 2018. Provide a brief explanation for the difference between net income and cash from operations.

E5-10. **(Calculating cash from operations, LO 4, 5)** You are provided the following information about Brooks Ltd. (Brooks) for fiscal 2017:

Net income	$ 877,500
Accounts receivable on July 1, 2016	292,500
Accounts receivable on June 30, 2017	375,000
Inventory on July 1, 2016	1,162,500
Inventory on June 30, 2017	1,432,500
Accounts payable on July 1, 2016	675,000
Accounts payable on June 30, 2017	735,000
Unearned revenue on July 1, 2016	1,500,000
Unearned revenue on June 30, 2017	375,000
Depreciation expense for 2017	300,000

Required:

Calculate cash from operations for Brooks for fiscal 2017. Provide a brief explanation for the difference between net income and cash from operations.

E5-11. **(Determining the changes on the balance sheet from the cash flow statement, LO 5)** Examine the following cash from operations section of Comox Ltd. and determine whether the asset and liability accounts shown increased or decreased during the year.

Comox Ltd. Cash from Operations For the year ended December 31, 2018 (000)	
Net income	$1,980
Depreciation	274
Loss on sale of equipment	35
Changes in working capital accounts	
Accounts receivable	62
Inventories	(74)
Accounts payable and accrued liabilities	51
Wages payable	(18)
Other current assets	(11)
Cash from operations	$2,299

E5-12. **(Organize information into a cash flow statement, LO 5)** Use the following information to prepare a well-organized cash flow statement for Quesnel Ltd. for the year ended December 31, 2017. Use the information to calculate net income for the year. Assume Quesnel uses IFRS. If alternatives for any items exist, state the choices you make.

Cash and cash equivalents at the beginning of the year	$120,000
Cash and cash equivalents at the end of the year	350,000
Decrease in accounts payable	28,000
Decrease in prepaids	6,900
Depreciation expense	300,000
Dividends paid	50,600
Increase in accounts receivable	41,400
Increase in inventory	75,900
Increase in wages payable	10,350
Issuance of common shares	184,000
Issuance of long-term debt	287,500
Loss on the sale of land	32,200
Net income	?
New bank loans	575,000
Proceeds from the sale of land	250,000
Purchase of common shares of a public company	115,000
Purchase of new equipment	632,500
Repayment of long-term debt	379,500

E5-13. **(Adjustments to net income when using the indirect method of calculating cash from operations, LO 5)** Tracadie Inc. (Tracadie) uses the indirect method to calculate and report cash from operations in its cash flow statement. For each of the following items indicate whether the item would be added to net income, deducted from net income, or not be relevant when calculating cash from operations. Assume Tracadie uses IFRS. State any other assumptions you make.

a. Loss on the sale of office furniture from Tracadie's executive offices.
b. Dividends paid.
c. Purchase of a building for cash.
d. Increase in accounts payable.
e. Decrease in inventory.
f. Proceeds from the sale of land.

g. Decrease in accrued liabilities.
h. Increase in long-term debt.
i. Gain on the sale of equipment used by Tracadie to provide its services.
j. Increase in accounts receivables.
k. Depreciation expense.

E5-14. **(Interpreting and comparing two cash flow statements, LO 4, 5)** Below are summarized cash flows for two companies. Both companies are mature companies in the same industry and both began and finished the year with the same amount of cash. Evaluate the two companies' situations regarding their cash flows. Which do you think shows a stronger cash flow and liquidity situation?

	Company A	Company B
Cash at the beginning of the year	$550,000	$550,000
Operating cash flows	(28,000)	298,000
Investing cash flows	95,000	(50,000)
Financing cash flows	60,000	(121,000)
Cash at the end of the year	$677,000	$677,000

E5-15. **(Calculate cash from operations using the indirect method, LO 1, 4, 5)** Consider the following income statement and non-cash working capital account information of Yahk Ltd. (Yahk). Assume Yahk uses IFRS.

Yahk Ltd.
Non-cash Working Capital Accounts
As of December 31,

	2017	2016		2017	2016
Accounts receivable	$ 60,000	$ 47,500	Accounts payable	$130,000	$117,500
Inventory	187,500	217,500	Wages payable	22,500	30,000
Prepaids	25,000	20,000	Taxes payable	40,000	25,000
			Interest payable	23,750	32,500
Total current operating assets	$272,500	$285,000	Total current operating liabilities	$216,250	$205,000

Yahk Ltd.
Income Statement
For the Year Ended December 31, 2017

Sales	$815,000
Cost of goods sold	250,000
Gross margin	565,000
Wage expense	150,000
Interest expense	35,000
Depreciation expense	50,000
Other expense	65,000
Loss on sale of equipment	25,000
Tax expense	60,000
Net income	$180,000

Required:

a. Calculate cash from operations for Yahk using the indirect method and prepare the cash from operations section of Yahk's cash flow statement. State any accounting choices you make.
b. Explain why cash from operations is different from net income in 2017.

E5-16. **(Calculate cash flows from operating activities, LO 5)** Use the information about Yahk Ltd. provided in E5-15 and calculate the following. Assume accounts payable pertains only to inventory purchases.

a. Cash collections from customers.
b. Amounts paid to employees.
c. Amount paid in interest.
d. Amount paid in taxes.
e. Amount paid for other expenses.

E5-17. **(Calculate cash collections, LO 5)** In its April 30, 2018 financial statements, Murphy Inc. (Murphy) reported a beginning accounts receivable balance of $363,000 and an ending accounts receivable balance of $456,000. Murphy reported sales for the year ended April 30, 2018 of $4,626,000. All sales are on credit.

Required:

Calculate the amount of cash Murphy collected from customers during fiscal 2018.

E5-18. **(Calculate cash payments, LO 5)** In its May 31, 2017 annual report, Maloneck Ltd. (Maloneck) reported that it had inventory of $175,000 and accounts payable of $104,000 on May 31, 2016, and inventory of $196,000 and accounts payable of $122,000 on May 31, 2017. Maloneck's income statement for the year ended May 31, 2017 reported cost of goods sold of $1,220,000.

Required:

Calculate the amount of cash that Maloneck paid to suppliers for purchases of inventory during fiscal 2017. Assume that accounts payable pertain only to the purchase of inventory on credit.

E5-19. **(Calculate cash payments made to employees, LO 5)** In its August 31, 2017 annual report, Davidson Corp. (Davidson) reported wages payable on August 31, 2016 of $87,500 and wages payable on August 31, 2017 of $112,500. Davidson's income statement reports wages expense of $1,173,000.

Required:

Calculate the amount of cash that Davidson paid in wages to employees in fiscal 2017.

E5-20. **(Calculate cash collections, LO 5)** In its December 31, 2017 financial statements, McEathron Inc. (McEathron) reported a beginning accounts receivable balance of $4,750,000 and an ending accounts receivable balance of $4,498,000. The company also had $315,000 of unearned revenue on December 31, 2016 and $455,000 of unearned revenue on December 31, 2017. McEathron reported sales for the year ended December 31, 2017 of $32,850,000. All sales are on credit.

Required:

Calculate the amount of cash McEathron collected from customers during 2017.

E5-21. **(Impact of the sale of land, LO 1, 5)** Willems Ltd. (Willems) owns a piece of land that cost $100,000. Willems recently sold the land for $75,000. The buyer paid $50,000 in cash and will pay the remainder in 14 months.

Required:

a. What is the gain or loss on the sale of the land?
b. What is the effect of the sale on Willems' cash?
c. How would this transaction affect the cash flow statement? Respond assuming Willems uses (i) the indirect method of calculating CFO and (ii) the direct method of calculating CFO.
d. What would be the effect on CFO if the gain or loss was adjusted for, if Willems used the indirect method?
e. Discuss how the sale of the land is accounted for in the cash flow statement? Can you think of other ways that the transaction could be presented? Which approach do you think is best? Explain.

Problems

P5-1. **(Calculating missing information about balance sheet accounts, LO 5)** The following general equation can be used to determine missing information about balance sheet accounts:

Ending balance in the account	=	Beginning balance in the account	+	Transactions and economic events that increase the balance in the account	−	Transactions and economic events that decrease the balance in the account

Use the equation to determine the missing information in each of the following independent situations. For each case assume that the year-end is December 31. You can also use an accounting equation spreadsheet to determine the missing information.

a. On December 31, 2017 Foxboro Ltd. (Foxboro) owed its employees $44,000. During 2017, Foxboro's employees earned $400,000 and were paid $420,000. How much did Foxboro owe its employees on December 31, 2016?
b. Canora Inc. (Canora) had $1,000,000 and $900,000 of accounts receivable and on January 1 and December 31, 2017 respectively. During 2017, Canora collected $4,900,000 from customers. What amount of credit sales did Canora make during 2017?
c. Sheth Inc. (Sheth) purchases all of its inventory on credit. On January 1, 2016, Sheth had $2,500,000 of inventory on hand and on December 31, 2016 it had $3,000,000 of inventory. Cost of goods sold during 2016 was $10,700,000. The balances in Sheth's accounts payable account on January 1, 2016 and December 31, 2016 were $1,900,000 and $2,200,000 respectively. How much did Sheth pay its suppliers during 2016?
d. On January 1, 2016, Cleaveley Ltd. (Cleaveley) had $350,000 of inventory on hand. During 2016, Cleaveley sold $1,040,000 of inventory and purchased $1,230,000 of inventory. How much inventory did Cleaveley have on December 31, 2016?
e. Dokis Inc. (Dokis) capitalizes certain development costs and amortizes them over five years. On January 1, 2016, the balance in Dokis's development cost account on the balance sheet was $150,000 and on December 31, 2016 the balance was $170,000. During 2016, the amortization expense for development costs was $40,000. What amount of development costs did Dokis capitalize during 2016? Assume that Dokis doesn't have a separate contra-asset account for accumulating amortization for this account.

P5-2. **(Calculating missing information about balance sheet accounts, LO 5)** The following general equation can be used to determine missing information about balance sheet accounts:

Ending balance in the account	=	Beginning balance in the account	+	Transactions and economic events that increase the balance in the account	−	Transactions and economic events that decrease the balance in the account

Use this equation to determine the missing information in each of the following independent situations. For each case, assume that the year-end is June 30. You can also use an accounting equation spreadsheet to determine the missing information.

a. On June 30, 2017, LaSalle Ltd. (LaSalle) owed its employees $456,000. During fiscal 2017, LaSalle's employees earned $3,750,000 and were paid $3,360,000. How much did LaSalle owe its employees on July 1, 2016?
b. On July 1, 2017, Gambo Ltd. (Gambo) had $975,000 of inventory on hand. During fiscal 2018, Gambo sold $980,000 of inventory and purchased $2,445,000 of inventory. How much inventory did Gambo have on June 30, 2018?
c. Norquay Inc. (Norquay) purchases all of its inventory on credit. On July 1, 2017, Norquay had $750,000 of inventory on hand and on June 30, 2018 it had $600,000 of inventory. Cost of goods sold during fiscal 2018 was $2,850,000. The beginning and ending balances in Norquay's accounts payable account on July 1, 2017 and June 30, 2018 were $405,000 and $309,000 respectively. How much did Norquay pay its suppliers during fiscal 2018?

d. On July 1, 2016, Holstein Inc. (Holstein) had $1,110,000 of accounts receivable and on June 30, 2017 it had $1,260,000 of accounts receivable. During fiscal 2017, Holstein collected $6,450,000 from customers. What amount of credit sales did Holstein make during fiscal 2017? Assume all of Holstein's sales were on credit.

e. Kanata Inc. (Kanata) capitalizes the cost of decorating a new store and amortizes them over five years. On July 1, 2017 the balance in Kanata's unamortized store decoration costs account on the balance sheet was $445,000. On June 30, 2018 the balance in the account was $485,000. During fiscal 2018, the amorization expense for store decoration costs was $90,000. What amount of store decoration costs did Kanata capitalize during fiscal 2018? Assume that Kanata doesn't have a separate contra-asset account for accumulating amorization for this account.

P5-3. **(Inferring cash flow patterns, LO 1, 5)** Pasadena Ltd. (Pasadena) is a small manufacturing company. During 2018, Pasadena has been struggling because of a slowdown in the overall economy and in the industry it supplies parts to. Sales are down significantly but the company has been unable to reduce many of its operating costs. To generate cash, Pasadena has been forced to sell off some land it owns at a loss. Even so, cash reserves have decreased by 50 percent. Management has decided to delay all but essential capital expenditures until business conditions have improved. Pasadena also had to repay a large bank loan that came due during the year. Despite extensive negotiations with a number of banks, the company was unable to refinance the loan. Fortunately, late in the year a new equity investor was found who provided new money to repay the bank loan and provide additional working capital. Pasadena didn't pay dividends during the year.

Required:

What pattern of cash flows would you expect to see if you examined Pasadena's cash flow statement for 2018? That is, would you expect operating, investing, and financing cash flows to be positive or negative? Explain your answer fully. Be sure to make reference to business conditions faced by the company.

P5-4. **(Inferring cash flow patterns, LO 1, 5)** Sean McNama is a renowned medical researcher at a large Canadian university. For many years he has been working on a technology that could significantly improve the vision of visually impaired people. In late 2016, Sean incorporated a company, McNama Vision Research Ltd. (MVR), that will further develop the technology and ultimately bring it to market. Shares of MVR were sold to venture capitalists who think the company has a reasonable chance of being hugely successful. In 2017, MVR completed its state-of-the-art research centre near the university. Money was used to buy equipment and renovate the facility so it would be suitable. Money is also being used to provide operating funds (to pay salaries, rent, utilities, and other operating costs) until MVR has developed a product it can bring to market. Sean is hoping to have something to sell by 2020. Equipment continues to be purchased when it's needed.

Required:

What pattern of cash flows would you expect to see if you examined the MVR cash flow statement for 2017? That is, would you expect operating, investing, and financing cash flows to be positive or negative? Explain your answer fully. Be sure to make reference to business conditions faced by the company.

P5-5. **(Interpreting cash flow patterns, LO 1, 5)** Onoway Inc. is a manufacturing company. You have been presented with the following summarized information from Onoway Inc.'s cash flow statement:

Cash from operations	$4,247,500
Cash from investing activities	(1,675,000)
Cash from financing activities	2,098,000

Required:

Examine the cash flow pattern for Onoway Inc. What does the pattern say about the situation the company finds itself in? (That is, consider what type of circumstances would give rise to a situation in which CFO and financing activities would be positive and investing activities would be negative.)

P5-6. **(Interpreting cash flow patterns, LO 1, 5)** You have been presented with the following summarized information from Peachland Ltd.'s cash flow statement:

Cash from operations	$(2,625,000)
Cash from investing activities	3,980,000
Cash from financing activities	(2,225,000)

Required:

Examine the cash flow pattern for Peachland Ltd. What does the pattern say about the situation that the company finds itself in? (That is, consider what type of circumstances would give rise to a situation in which CFO and financing activities would have net cash outflows and investing activities would have a net cash inflow.)

P5-7. **(Interpreting cash flow patterns, LO 1, 5)** You have been presented with the following summarized information from Rimouski Ltd.'s cash flow statement:

Cash from operations	$(3,250,000)
Cash from investing activities	1,500,000
Cash from financing activities	2,000,000

Required:

Examine the cash flow pattern for Rimouski Ltd. What does the pattern say about the situation that the company finds itself in? (That is, consider what type of circumstances would give rise to a situation in which CFO would have a net cash outflow and investing and financing activities would have net cash inflows.)

P5-8. **(Impact of credit policy on cash inflows, LO 3, 6)** Dionne Gifts Inc. is a large Canadian wholesale importer of gift items from around the world. Dionne sells its merchandise to retailers across the country. Gift importing is a competitive business because there are a lot of alternative sources for many items so it's important for importers to be sensitive to the needs of their customers. Currently, Dionne allows its customers up to 60 days to pay for their purchases. The president of the company, Greg Dionne, is considering reducing the amount of time customers have to pay to 30 days. He says that some of his competitors already offer those terms and he thinks doing so will improve the company's cash flow. Greg Dionne has asked for your help assessing the impact of reducing the number of days customers get to pay. He provides you with the following estimate of quarterly sales for the upcoming 2017 fiscal year. He also points out that he expects sales in the fourth quarter of 2016 to be $975,000:

Dionne Gifts Inc. Estimated Sales by Quarter for 2017 (000)			
1st Quarter	**2nd Quarter**	**3rd Quarter**	**4th Quarter**
$1,075	$1,385	$2,100	$1,215

Required:

a. How much will Dionne collect each quarter if it continues to offer customers 60 days to pay? What would accounts receivable be at the end of 2017? (Assume sales occur evenly throughout each quarter.)
b. How much will Dionne collect each quarter if it changes its policy effective January 1, 2017 and offers customers 30 days to pay? (Remember that the amount in accounts receivable represents sales that gave customers 60 days to pay.) What would accounts receivable be at the end of 2017?
c. What is the impact on cash flow of changing the collection period? What is the impact on accounts receivable?

d. Suppose sales in 2017 are exactly the same as in 2018. What would collections in each quarter be in 2018? What's the long-term impact on cash collections of reducing the collection period to 30 days?
e. Do you think it's a good idea for Dionne to change the collection period? Don't just consider cash flow in your answer.

P5-9. **(Cash flow presentation of interest and dividends under different methods allowed by IFRS, LO 4, 5, 6)** Below is a summarized cash flow statement of Thomson Reuters Corporation, the international provider of information. The amounts exclude interest paid and received and dividends paid during 2010 and 2009. IFRS allows companies to choose to include interest and dividends paid an operating or financing cash flow and interest received as either operating or investing cash flows.

Thomson Reuters Corporation Summarized Cash Flow Statements For the years ended December 31, (millions)		
	2010	**2009**
Net cash provided by operations	$3,041	$3,083
Net cash used in investing activities	(1,675)	(1,365)
Net cash used in financing activities	(318)	(144)
Interest paid	393	425
Interest received	7	8
Dividends paid	901	907

Required:

a. Recalculate each category of Thomson Reuters' 2009 and 2010 cash flows under the following assumptions:
   i. Treat dividends, interest received, and interest paid as operating cash flows;
   ii. Treat dividends and interest paid as financing cash flows, and interest received as an investing cash flow;
   iii. Treat dividends as a financing cash flow and interest paid and received as operating cash flows (this is what Thomson Reuters does).
b. Interpret the results you obtained in part (a).
c. What is the economic impact of the different treatments?
d. Which treatment do you think is most useful to stakeholders? Explain your answer.
e. Why do you think Thomson Reuters would choose the approach it used?

P5-10. **(Analyzing cash flows, LO 2)** Simpson Ltd. (Simpson) imports novelty items from Asian manufacturers and sells them to retailers. The company began operations at the beginning of 2018. The following information is available about Simpson's operation:

- Simpson's suppliers allow it 30 days to pay for purchases. Assume purchases are made evenly throughout the year.
- Simpson allows customers 60 days to pay for their purchases. Assume sales occur evenly throughout the year.
- Simpson has a markup on its product of 100 percent. (If a customer purchases merchandise that costs Simpson $1 the customer pays $2.)
- Operating costs, other than the cost of product sold, are $135,000 per quarter. These costs are paid in cash during the quarter.
- Simpson began operations with $235,000 in cash contributed by its shareholders.
- Quarterly information for 2018:

	1st Quarter	2nd Quarter	3rd Quarter	4th Quarter	Total
Sales	$290,000	$320,000	$380,000	$450,000	$1,440,000
Inventory purchases	$300,000	$140,000	$195,000	$250,000	$885,000

Required:

a. Prepare income statements for each quarter of 2018 and for the entire year. (*Hint:* Use the fact that Simpson has a 100 percent markup to calculate cost of goods sold.)
b. Calculate the amount of inventory on hand at the end of each quarter and the end of the year.
c. Calculate the amount of accounts receivable at the end of each quarter and the end of the year.
d. Calculate the amount of accounts payable at the end of each quarter and the end of the year.
e. Calculate the amount of cash on hand at the end of each quarter and the end of the year. What was the net cash flow for each quarter and the year?
f. Explain the difference between net income and net cash flow during 2018. Evaluate Simpson's liquidity during 2018. What could be done to improve Simpson's liquidity?
g. What would net income be if Simpson gave customers 30 days to pay? What would net cash flow be? Discuss your results compared with when customers had 60 days to pay. Are there any business issues to consider in using a 30 day instead of a 60 day collection period?

P5-11. **(Organize information into a cash flow statement, LO 4, 5)** Use the following alphabetical list of information to prepare a well-organized cash flow statement for Winkler Ltd. for the year ended July 31, 2016. The bookkeeper who prepared the information wasn't sure about exactly what information to provide to you so there may be information that shouldn't be included in the cash flow statement.

Accounts receivable	$ 560,000
Cash and cash equivalents at the beginning of the year	450,500
Cash and cash equivalents at the end of the year	64,500
Decrease in accounts payable	44,000
Decrease in accounts receivable	51,000
Decrease in cash	441,000
Depreciation	852,000
Dividends	750,000
Dividends declared but not paid	350,000
Gain on the sale of equipment	225,000
Increase in inventory	96,000
Increase in prepaids	12,000
Increase in taxes payable	77,000
Issuance of common shares	1,000,000
Issuance of long-term debt	3,000,000
Land	1,000,000
Loss on the sale of land	100,000
Net income	750,000
Proceeds from the sale of land	55,000
Proceeds from the sale of property, plant, and equipment	356,000
Purchase of long-term investments	1,355,000
Purchase of property, plant, and equipment for cash	1,750,000
Repayment of bank loans	955,000
Retirement of long-term debt	1,750,000
Shares exchanged for equipment	500,000
Writedown of assets	310,000

P5-12. **(Calculating cash from operations, LO 1, 4, 5, 6)** You are provided with the following balance sheet information and summarized income statement for Rivulet Inc.:

Rivulet Inc. Current Operating Assets and Liabilities As of December 31, 2017 and 2018					
	2018	**2017**		**2018**	**2017**
Accounts receivable	$248,000	$202,000	Accounts payable	$384,000	$434,000
Inventory	550,000	630,000	Accrued liabilities	98,000	64,000

Rivulet Inc. Income Statement For the Year Ended December 31, 2018	
Revenue	$2,150,000
Cost of goods sold	1,064,000
Gross margin	1,086,000
Other expenses	784,000
Depreciation expense	430,000
Loss on sale of capital assets	50,000
Net loss	$ 178,000

All sales are credit sales. Accounts payable pertains exclusively to the purchase of inventory and accrued liabilities pertains exclusively to other expenses.

Required:

a. Prepare Rivulet's cash from operations section of the cash flow statement using the indirect method.
b. Calculate these amounts:
   i. cash collected from customers
   ii. cash paid to suppliers of inventory
   iii. cash paid for other expenses

   Use this information to prepare Rivulet's cash from operations section of the cash flow statement using the direct method.
c. Do you think the direct method or indirect method provides more useful information to stakeholders? Explain. What information is available when the direct method is used that isn't available when the indirect method is used?
d. Explain the difference between net income and cash from operations. Why did Rivulet have a loss on its income statement but positive cash from operations?
e. What are the implications of having a loss on the income statement but positive cash from operations?

P5-13. **(Calculating cash from operations using both the direct and indirect methods, LO 1, 4, 5)** You are provided with the following balance sheet information and summarized income statement for Katrime Ltd.:

Katrime Ltd. Current Operating Assets and Liabilities As of May 31, 2016 and 2017					
	2017	**2016**		**2017**	**2016**
Accounts receivable	$427,000	$278,000	Accounts payable	$392,000	$315,000
Inventory	818,000	566,000	Wages payable	72,000	85,000
Prepaid insurance	72,000	35,000			

Katrime Ltd. Income Statement For the Year Ended May 31, 2017	
Revenue	$1,381,000
Cost of goods sold	735,500
Gross margin	645,500
Wages expense	333,000
Depreciation expense	42,500
Insurance expense	30,000
Other expenses	137,500
Loss on sale of capital assets	27,500
Net income	$ 75,000

All sales are credit sales. Accounts payable pertains exclusively to the purchase of inventory. Other expenses were fully paid in cash during the year.

Required:

a. Prepare Katrime's cash from operations section of the cash flow statement using the indirect method.
b. Calculate these amounts:
   i. cash collected from customers
   ii. cash paid to suppliers of inventory
   iii. cash paid to employees

   Use this information to prepare Katrime's cash from operations section of the cash flow statement using the direct method.
c. Do you think the direct method or indirect method provides more useful information to stakeholders? Explain. What information is available when the direct method is used that isn't available when the indirect method is used?
d. Explain the difference between net income and cash from operations. Why did Katrime have a profit on its income statement but negative cash from operations?
e. What are the implications of showing a profit on the income statement but negative cash from operations?

P5-14. **(Interpreting the cash flow statement, LO 1, 5)** Mankota Ltd. (Mankota) produces precision equipment for the mining industry. The company is private and has two shareholders. Mankota has been hugely successful in the last few years with high demand from mining companies around the world. Its production facility runs at full capacity but it's still unable to keep up with customer demand. The owners want to expand because they're concerned that Mankota won't capitalize on market opportunities and will lose market share to competitors, even those with inferior products. Mankota's sales have increased by almost 300 percent over the last few years and profits have increased from $750,000 in 2015 to $5.9 million in the year ended December 31, 2018. Despite its success, Mankota is using up cash very quickly and management is worried that it won't have enough cash to operate effectively and expand to meet demand. You have been provided with Mankota's cash flow statements for the years ended December 31, 2017 and 2018. Prepare a report to management explaining the reasons for the company's cash problems despite its profitability. Management has also asked for any suggestions you might have to improve the situation.

Required:

Prepare the report.

Mankota Ltd. Statement of Cash Flows For the Years Ended December 31,		
	2018	2017
Cash from operations		
Net income	$5,900,000	$4,700,000
Items not affecting cash: Depreciation	1,525,000	1,155,000
	7,425,000	5,855,000
Changes in non-cash working capital accounts		
Accounts receivable	(1,425,000)	(965,000)
Inventory	(1,958,000)	(785,000)
Prepaids	58,000	(19,500)
Accounts payable and accrued liabilities	985,000	542,000
Cash from operations	5,085,000	4,627,500
Financing activities		
Issue of long-term debt	1,500,000	1,900,000
Bank loans	252,000	550,000
Repayment of long-term debt	(750,000)	(750,000)
Dividends paid	(750,000)	(500,000)
Cash inflows from financing activities	252,000	1,200,000
Investing activities		
Purchase of property, plant, and equipment	(6,350,000)	(5,850,000)
Sale of property, plant, and equipment	375,000	125,000
Cash outflows from financing activities	(5,975,000)	(5,725,000)
Increase in cash and cash equivalents	(638,000)	102,500
Cash and cash equivalents, beginning of year	752,500	650,000
Cash and cash equivalents, end of year	$ 114,500	$ 752,500

P5-15. **(Interpreting the cash flow statement, LO 1, 5)** Iqaluit Water Company Ltd. (Iqaluit) is a bottler and marketer of bottled water. Iqaluit was established many years ago in response to the demand for healthful, refreshing drinks. Iqaluit sells its products to distributors in Canada, the United States, and Europe. In the last few years, Iqaluit's performance has deteriorated significantly in the face of increased competition and high marketing and promotion costs. Management is concerned that the company is in financial distress and may be headed for serious problems that will threaten its survival. Some of Iqaluit's shareholders have approached you for advice about the company's status. The have provided you with Iqaluit's most recent cash flow statements and have asked you to prepare a report that addresses the prospects for the company.

Required:
Prepare the report.

Iqaluit Water Company Ltd. Statement of Cash Flows For the Years Ended July 31,		
	2017	**2016**
Cash from Operations		
Net loss	($ 812,000)	($ 952,000)
Items not affecting cash		
Depreciation	278,500	310,000
(Gain) Loss on disposal of assets	(325,000)	225,000
Writedown of assets	150,000	95,000
	(708,500)	(322,000)
Changes in non-cash working capital accounts		
Accounts receivable	208,000	242,000
Inventory	150,000	90,000
Prepaids	85,000	101,000
Accounts payable and accrued liabilities	(88,000)	(110,000)
Cash from operations	(353,500)	1,000
Financing activities		
Issue of short-term debt	300,000	225,000
Bank loans	425,000	500,000
Repayment of long-term debt	(450,000)	(450,000)
Dividends paid	(1,000,000)	(1,000,000)
Cash outflows from financing activities	(725,000)	(725,000)
Investing activities		
Purchase of plant, property, and equipment	(72,000)	(12,000)
Proceeds from sale of equipment	950,000	485,000
Sale of land*	625,000	
Cash inflows from investing activities	1,503,000	473,000
Decrease in cash and cash equivalents	424,500	(251,000)
Cash and cash equivalents, beginning of year	224,000	475,000
Cash and cash equivalents, end of year	$ 648,500	$ 224,000

*Iqaluit held land as an investment that it decided to sell in 2017. The land was not used in the company's bottling operations.

Required: Prepare the report.

P5-16. **(Evaluating the impact of growth on performance and cash flow, LO 1, 3, 5)** Tofino Ltd. manufactures heavy construction equipment. Until recently, it sold its products almost exclusively in North America. In 2015, management decided to expand its sales activities to more global markets, in particular emerging economies. In late 2016, the new sales strategy began to be effective and in 2017 sales increased by over 25 percent, with almost all the growth coming from non-North American customers. To make these sales, Tofino had to offer very different payment terms than in the past. Most of the new customers are chronically short of cash and want to be able to pay between two and three years after delivery of the equipment. That way, the projects the equipment was being used for would help generate the cash flow to pay for it. Tofino agreed to these terms to achieve growth. Despite the increase in sales, profit in 2017 is down from the previous year. The decrease in net income is mainly due to increased costs associated with the expansion to new markets. More concerning is that cash flow has become a big problem and the company has even struggled to pay some of its bills. The amount of cash on hand is frequently below the minimum amount needed for efficient operations.

You are an analyst for a small investment dealer and you've been asked to do an analysis of some of Tofino's financial statement information to assess and explain its current situation. In particular, there is concern about the deteriorating performance and cash flow problems. You've been also been asked to explain the reasons and the implications of the difference between net income and cash from operations.

Tofino Ltd.
Income Statements
For the Years Ended December 31,
(000)

	2017	2016
Sales	$229,100	$182,550
Cost of sales	185,571	142,389
Gross margin	43,529	40,161
Selling, general, and administrative	17,870	14,969
Depreciation	6,873	6,207
Research and development	1,833	1,351
Interest	9,164	4,564
Income before taxes	7,789	13,070
Income taxes	2,025	3,215
Net income	$ 5,764	$ 9,855

Tofino Ltd.
Cash Flow Statement
For the years ended December 31,
(000)

	2017	2016
Cash from operating activities		
Net income	$ 5,764	$ 9,855
Depreciation	6,873	6,207
Changes in non-cash operating accounts		
Increase in accounts receivable (current and non-current)	(46,550)	(5,215)
Increase in inventory	(3,715)	(1,825)
(Decrease) increase in other current operating assets	215	(86)
Increase in accounts payable and accrued liabilities	(2,685)	(946)
(Decrease) increase in income taxes payable	241	(101)
Increase in other current operating liabilities	(75)	(37)
	(39,932)	7,852
Financing activities		
Issue of long-term debt	21,000	10,000
Repayment of long-term debt	(15,000)	(15,000)
Increase in bank loans	4,250	375
	10,250	(4,625)
Investing activities	(11,582)	(8,275)
(Decrease) increase in cash during the year	(41,264)	(5,048)
Cash at the beginning of the year	72,452	77,500
Cash at the end of the year	$31,188	$72,452

P5-17. **(Analyzing the cash flow statement of a family, LO 5)** The Stadlers are a middle-class family living comfortably in a single-family home in a suburb of Vancouver. Mr. and Mrs. Stadler earn a decent family income, bringing home almost $65,000 after taxes and other deductions. They have two active school-age children. The Stadlers have come to you to assess their family's financial situation. As a starting point you decide to look at their cash flow for 2017. You organize the information they provided you into the traditional cash flow statement format shown below

Stadler Family Cash Flow Statement for 2017	
Cash from operations	
Cash received in salaries	$64,275
Cash spent on household activities	(48,750)
Cash spent on vacations	(3,200)
Cash spent on children and their activities	(15,900)
	(3,575)
Financing activities	
Payments on mortgage (including interest)	(9,650)
Bank loan	15,000
Second mortgage	12,500
Borrowing from parents	5,000
	22,850
Investing activities	
Home renovations	(4,825)
New car	(16,750)
Savings	(500)
	(22,075)
Increase in cash during the year	(2,800)
Cash at the beginning of the year	3,290
Cash at the end of the year	$ 490

Required:

Prepare a report analyzing the Stadler's cash flow statement. How do you think the Stadlers are doing? Do you have any suggestions about any changes they could make? What other information would help you analyze the situation more thoroughly?

P5-18. **(Preparing and interpreting financial statements, LO 1, 5)** Souvenirs-On-The-Go Ltd. (Souvenirs-On-The-Go) is a mobile souvenir stand that moves around the city to be "where the action is." Souvenirs-On-The-Go was started this summer by Evan Shayne as a way to earn money in the summer months to help pay for his education. Evan registered his corporation and contributed $15,000 of his savings to the company in exchange for shares. Souvenirs-On-The-Go borrowed $7,000 from Evan's parents to provide additional cash and purchased a used cart for $15,000 cash. If it's successful, Evan hopes to operate Souvenirs-On-The-Go for four years, until he graduates from university. Souvenirs-On-The-Go obtained a municipal vending licence for $500 that allows the cart to operate in designated areas around the city. The licence is valid for two years.

Over the summer, Souvenirs-On-The-Go sold $22,400 in souvenirs, all for cash. It purchased $12,200 worth of souvenirs, including $1,800 in souvenirs that weren't paid for by the end of the summer. Souvenirs-On-The-Go incurred $1,050 of maintenance and repairs on the cart and $3,100 of miscellaneous expenses during the summer. As of the end of the summer, the maintenance and repairs had been fully paid for and $500 of the miscellaneous expenses was still owed to the suppliers, and unsold souvenirs costing $2,200 remained. However, Evan thinks he will be able to sell them next summer. Souvenirs-On-The-Go also owes Evan's parents $600 in interest.

Required:

The summer is now over and Evan is back at school. Evan hasn't had a chance to evaluate the performance of Souvenirs-On-The-Go and he has asked you to prepare an income statement, balance sheet, and cash flow statement for the summer just ended. Use the financial statements you prepared to assess the financial situation of Souvenirs-On-The-Go. Your assessment should consider information from all of the financial statements. (To prepare the cash flow statement, identify Souvenirs-On-The-Go cash transactions and organize them into the different categories [operating, investing, financing].)

P5-19. **(Assessing the ability to pay a dividend, LO 3, 4, 5)** Newbrook Ltd. is a small public company that operates two mines in northern Canada. The mining industry is highly cyclical, with the success of companies like Newbrook dependent on the price of the commodity they mine. Newbrook's existing mines are well established and produce reliable amounts of resources at a reasonable cost. The company is continuing exploration for new potential mines but its capital expenditures are mainly due to replacing and upgrading assets at the existing mines. At a recent executive management meeting, it was proposed that the company pay a dividend for the first time. The proposal was made because the company was coming off its most successful year in its history in terms of net income and cash flow and the company's cash reserves are at an all-time high. The chief financial officer reminded the group that paying a dividend was a big step and once paid it was unwise to reduce or eliminate a dividend because the stock price would be significantly affected in a negative way. The proposal is to declare an annual dividend of $0.10 per share. The company has 10 million shares outstanding.

You have been asked to examine Newbrook's cash flow statements for the last four years and to prepare a report assessing whether it makes sense to pay a dividend at this time.

Newbrook Ltd.
Summarized Cash Flow Statements
For the Years Ended December 31,

	2017	2016	2015	2014
Operating cash flows	$2,480,000	$ 335,000	$1,750,000	($ 250,000)
Financing cash flows	(250,000)	500,000	(245,000)	350,000
Investing cash flows	(1,300,000)	(990,000)	(872,000)	(1,000,000)
Change in cash for the year	930,000	(155,000)	633,000	(900,000)
Cash at the beginning of the year	1,078,000	1,233,000	600,000	1,500,000
Cash at the end of the year	$2,008,000	$1,078,000	$1,233,000	$ 600,000

Required:

Prepare the report requested by the management executive committee. In your report, consider whether Newbrook can afford a dividend, whether the $0.10 is a reasonable annual dividend or if a dividend should be paid whether the amount should be greater or less than the proposed $0.10 per share.

P5-20. **(Impact of events on income and cash flow, LO 5, 6)** You own 20 percent of Peribonka Ltd., a manufacturing company. You aren't involved in the day-to-day management of the company and you rely on the financial statements for information. You have been examining the 2016 financial statements and note that net income for the year was $215,000 and cash from operations $300,000. You are quite satisfied with these performance measures, which are significantly better than last year's, but you do have some concerns about decisions management has made and their impact on these numbers. You call a friend who is an executive at the company and he provides you with some additional information. He explains the following:

- The production manager decided to delay the major maintenance program that is usually done in December to January to accommodate the unusually tight production schedule and to accommodate vacations during the holiday season. The cost of the maintenance program is about $125,000.
- There was a delay in processing a batch of cheques to suppliers that was supposed to be mailed on December 23 but didn't get prepared and mailed until January 3. The total of the cheques was $210,090.
- Peribonka increased its estimate of the useful lives of certain assets, which decreased the depreciation expense for the year by $30,000.

Required:

a. What would Peribonka's net income and cash from operations have been had the maintenance been done at the usual time, the payables paid on time, and the estimate of the useful lives of the assets not been changed?

b. What are some possible explanations for the changes and treatments described above? What are some possible reasons for management making these choices?

P5-21. **(The effect of accrual accounting policies on the cash flow statement, LO 6)** The chief accountant of Phidias Publications Ltd. (Phidias) is thinking about how accrual accounting policy choices affect the cash flow statement. Phidias publishes a number of newspapers in mid-sized Canadian communities. One of the key success factors of the newspaper business is the circulation of the papers. Phidias spends a significant amount of money recruiting and maintaining subscribers. The accountant thinks that sound arguments can be made for both expensing the cost of recruiting and maintaining subscribers when they are incurred, and capitalizing the costs and amortizing them over a number of years.

The accountant has prepared the following cash flow statement, which is complete except for how to account for the cost of recruiting and maintaining subscribers. During 2017, Phidias spent $54,000 on this.

Phidias Publications Ltd. Cash Flow Statement For the Year Ended December 31, 2017		
Cash from operations		
Cash collected from customers and advertisers	$938,400	
Cash paid to employees	(450,000)	
Cash paid to suppliers	(362,000)	
Cash paid in interest	(20,800)	
Cash from operations		$105,600
Cash from investing activities		
Proceeds from sale of capital assets	44,000	
Purchase of capital assets	(120,000)	
Cash from investing activities		(76,000)
Cash from financing activities		
Dividends paid	(30,000)	
Repayment of bank loan	(70,000)	
Proceeds of long-term debt	130,000	
Cash from financing activities		30,000
Unclassified—recruiting and maintaining subscriber costs		(54,000)
Cash generated during the year		5,600
Cash on hand on December 31, 2016		18,500
Cash on hand on December 31, 2017		$ 24,100

Required:

a. Present arguments for and against the two proposed accounting treatments for the cost of recruiting and maintaining subscribers.
b. Explain the effect of the two accounting alternatives on Phidias' income statement.
c. Complete Phidias's cash flow statement assuming that cash spent on recruiting and maintaining subscribers is expensed when incurred.
d. Complete Phidias's cash flow statement assuming that cash spent on recruiting and maintaining subscribers is capitalized and amortized over three years.
e. Discuss the difference between the statements you prepared in (c) and (d) above. What are the implications of the different treatments to the underlying cash flow and liquidity of Phidias?
f. Which cash flow statement do you think the managers of Phidias would prefer? Explain.

P5-22. **(Accrual and cash flow information analysis, LO 1, 5)** In December 2016, Alexander Bedlam organized Soldit Properties Ltd. (Soldit), a company that sells real estate on behalf of clients. Alexander exchanged $40,000 in cash for 1,000 common shares of Soldit. When business actually began in January 2017, Alexander was very busy—so busy that he didn't bother keeping any records. At the end of the month, Alexander noticed that he had less than the $40,000 in cash that he started business with. He didn't understand how he could have been so busy and still have lost money. Alexander has come to you for help to understand his situation. From your conversation with Alexander, you obtain the following information:

i. During the month, five properties were sold with a sales value of $1,200,000. Soldit earns a commission of five percent of the sales value of the property.
ii. Sales assistants sold three of the five properties sold in January. These three properties had a total sales value of $800,000. Sales assistants receive a commission of four percent of the sales value of the properties they sell.
iii. The commission on one of the properties hasn't been received. The client owes Soldit $16,000.
iv. During January, Soldit made the following payments in cash:

Salaries	$ 4,400
Commissions to sales assistants	32,000
Down payment on car	6,000
Rent (for January)	2,400
Purchase of computer, fax, and copier	4,000
Utilities	1,000

v. Soldit has taken delivery of the car and the computer, fax, and copier. The price of the car was $40,000 and the price of the computer, fax, and copier was $10,000. All these assets have expected useful lives of five years.

Required:

a. Prepare an income statement for January for Soldit.
b. Prepare a cash flow statement for January for Soldit. (To prepare the statement, organize the amounts into the different cash flow categories.)
c. How did Soldit perform in January? How should Alexander interpret these two statements? Did Soldit perform as badly as Alexander seems to think? Explain your answer.

P5-23. **(Interpreting a cash flow statement, LO 1, 5)** Anna Malover is a full-time veterinarian who started her own business five years ago. Anna felt that the market for doggie fashions had a lot of promise, based on her clients' complaints about fashionable doggie clothes being so hard to find. She decided to start a business to design, make, and sell a line of high-fashion doggie clothes, including hats, booties, sweaters, and coordinating accessories under the name Doggie Duds.

Anna wanted to continue her career as a full-time veterinarian and hired a full-time manager to manage Doggie Duds on a day-to-day basis. Anna has never been involved in the daily operations of the company, relying on periodic meetings with the manager and the company's annual financial statements. Since the business started, it has grown to be the number-one provider of dog clothes and accessories in the country, with seven stores across Ontario and Quebec. Anna has come to rely on the cash flow generated by Doggie Duds to support her lifestyle and usually pays herself a significant cash dividend each year.

After seeing the cash flow statement for 2017, Anna was very disappointed that the cash balance had decreased for the first time since the business began. As a result, she fired the manager for his poor performance and hired a new manager, Hue Gego, to "turn around" the company in 2018. Anna offered Hue a bonus based on the increase in total cash from 2017 to 2018.

It's now January 2019. Upon seeing the 2018 financial statements, Anna is very pleased with her decision, noting that cash increased significantly during the year. As a result, Anna was able to increase her dividend for the year to $90,000.

Doggie Duds Inc.
Cash Flow Statement
For the Years Ended December 31,

	2018	2017
Operations		
Net income	$116,020	$133,500
Add: Depreciation expense	27,600	25,300
Less: Gain on sale of land*	150,000	0
Cash from operations	(6,380)	158,800
Financing		
Repayment of bank loan**	0	(85,000)
Dividends	(90,000)	(50,000)
	(90,000)	(135,000)
Investing		
Sale of land	200,000	0
Purchase of new computer system***	0	(40,000)
	200,000	(40,000)
Increase (decrease) in cash	103,620	(16,200)
Cash balance at the beginning of the year	22,200	38,400
Cash balance at the end of the year	$125,820	$ 22,200

*In 2015, Doggie Duds purchased a vacant lot beside one of its stores for $50,000 for future expansion. As of 2018, the land was still vacant and it was sold in 2018 for $200,000.

**In 2016, Doggie Duds borrowed $85,000 from the bank to open its seventh store. The loan was fully repaid in 2017. Doggie Duds has an additional loan of $250,000 still outstanding. The full balance is due on December 31, 2019.

***In 2017, Doggie Duds replaced its aging computer system with a new system that includes integrated sales, accounting and inventory tracking systems, and state-of-the-art registers in all stores. The system is expected to last five years.

Required:

a. Who are the users of the Doggie Duds financial statements? What will they be using the statements for? Discuss the possible objectives of financial reporting for Doggie Duds.
b. Do you think that Anna was justified in firing the manager based on poor performance in 2017? Why or why not?
c. Do you think that the company performed as well as Anna thinks in 2018? Why or why not?
d. Do you think it's wise of Anna to offer a bonus based on the overall increase in cash? Why or why not?

Note: This question was written by Angela Kellett of the University of Ontario Institute of Technology and is used with permission.

P5-24. **(Comparing the direct and indirect methods of calculating CFO, LO 1, 5)** Examine the cash flow statements provided by Stantec Inc. as shown in Exhibit 5.2. Stantec provides calculations of CFO using both the direct and indirect methods. How do the two cash flow statements differ? What information does each statement provide that the other doesn't? Which do you think provides more useful information to stakeholders?

Using Financial Statements

HIGH LINER FOODS INCORPORATED

High Liner Foods Incorporated (High Liner) is a leading North American processor and marketer of prepared, value-added frozen seafood and is North America's largest marketer of prepared frozen seafood products. Its branded products are sold to most grocery and club stores throughout the United States, Canada, and Mexico. The company also sells food service products to restaurants and institutions, and is a major supplier of private-label seafood products to North American food retailers and food service distributors. The company began in 1899 with the founding of W.C. Smith & Company, a salt fish operation in Lunenburg, N.S., the current home of their head office and one of the most modern and diversified food processing plants in the world. High Liner trades on the Toronto Stock Exchange under the symbols HLF and HLF.A.[3]

High Liner's consolidated balance sheets and statements of cash flows and earnings, along with extracts from the notes to the financial statements, are provided in Exhibit 5.5. Use this information to respond to questions FS5-1 to FS5-12.[4]

EXHIBIT 5.5 High Liner Foods Incorporated: Extracts from Financial Statements

High Liner Foods
CONSOLIDATED STATEMENTS OF INCOME
(in thousands of Canadian dollars, except per share information)

	Notes	Fifty-two weeks ended: December 31, 2011	January 1, 2011
Sales		$ 668,589	$ 584,715
Cost of sales		516,659	447,542
Gross profit		151,930	137,173
Distribution expenses		35,021	30,027
Selling, general and administrative expenses		72,086	68,500
Business acquisition, integration and other expenses		11,275	875
Results from operating activities		33,548	37,771
Finance costs		5,983	5,165
Share of income of equity accounted investee (net of income tax)	7	53	(18)
Income before income taxes		27,512	32,624
Income taxes			
Current	20	5,692	6,380
Deferred	20	3,640	6,259
Total income taxes		9,332	12,639
Net income		$ 18,180	$ 19,985

EXHIBIT 5.5 **(continued) High Liner Foods Incorporated: Extracts from Financial Statements**

High Liner Foods
CONSOLIDATED STATEMENT OF FINANCIAL POSITION
(in thousands of Canadian dollars)

	Notes	December 31, 2011	January 1, 2011	January 3, 2010
ASSETS				
Current:				
Cash and cash equivalents		$ 3,260	$ 598	$ 1,953
Accounts receivable	9	84,920	50,452	57,963
Income tax receivable		3,557	701	1,288
Other financial assets	22	1,346	890	1,590
Inventories	8	261,330	131,980	119,308
Prepaid expenses		3,019	1,889	2,024
Total current assets		357,432	186,510	184,126
Non-current:				
Property, plant and equipment	6	99,933	67,269	69,061
Deferred income taxes	20	1,695	2,403	3,628
Other receivables and miscellaneous assets		1,210	814	406
Investment in equity accounted investee	7	275	157	-
Employee future benefits	14	94	91	118
Intangible assets	4,5	103,109	31,239	19,965
Goodwill	4,5	126,787	39,819	35,983
		333,103	141,792	129,161
		$ 690,535	$ 328,102	$ 313,287
LIABILITIES AND SHAREHOLDERS' EQUITY				
Current:				
Bank loans	12	$ 120,980	$ 42,725	$ 23,051
Accounts payable and accrued liabilities	10	108,553	60,065	49,905
Provisions	11	675	550	1,423
Other current financial liabilities	22	793	2,334	3,989
Income taxes payable		1,990	3,230	29
Current portion of long-term debt	13	2,543	4,426	4,582
Current portion of finance lease obligations	13	1,064	972	864
Total current liabilities		236,598	114,302	83,843
Non-current:				
Long-term debt	13	237,438	43,912	49,920
Other long-term financial liabilities	22	–	207	928
Long-term finance lease obligations	22	2,599	3,045	2,700
Deferred income taxes	20	41,099	9,895	5,705
Employee future benefits	14	11,274	9,630	6,991
Total liabilities		529,008	180,991	150,087
Shareholders' Equity				
Common shares	16	78,067	78,326	106,098
Contributed surplus		8,406	8,917	—
Retained earnings		76,770	65,557	59,240
Accumulated other comprehensive loss		(1,716)	(5,489)	(2,138)
Total equity		161,527	147,311	163,200
		$ 690,535	$ 328,302	$ 313,287

EXHIBIT 5.5 (continued) High Liner Foods Incorporated: Extracts from Financial Statements

High Liner Foods
CONSOLIDATED STATEMENTS OF CASH FLOWS
(in thousands of Canadian dollars)

	Notes	Fifty-two weeks ended. December 31, 2011	January 1, 2011
Cash provided by (used in) operations:			
Net income from continuing operations for the period		$ 18,180	$ 19,985
Charges (credits) to income not involving cash from operations:			
Depreciation and amortization		9,734	8,505
Loss on disposal of assets		271	114
Income tax expense		9,332	12,639
Interest expense		5,983	5,165
Share-based payment expense		651	3,095
Payments of employee future benefits different than expense		(131)	309
Share of income of equity accounted investee		53	(18)
Movement of provisions		370	1,642
Unwound foreign exchange gains reclassed from Accumulated Other Comprehensive Income		–	(165)
Unrealized foreign exchange loss		195	(130)
Cash flow from operations before changes in non-cash working capital		44,638	51,141
Net change in non-cash working capital balances		(25,142)	8,063
		19,496	59,204
Interest paid		(5,194)	(4,717)
Income taxes paid		(10,730)	(4,131)
		3,572	50,356
Cash provided by (used in) financing activities:			
Increase in current working capital facilities		78,286	20,674
Proceeds from lease financing		–	668
Proceeds from long-term debt		258,125	–
Repayment of long-term debt		(49,649)	(4,511)
Repayment of finance lease obligations		(893)	(806)
Common share dividends paid		(5,184)	(4,379)
Non-voting common share dividends paid		(707)	(859)
Deferred financing costs		(15,077)	–
Advances to affiliates		–	(5)
Share-based payments exercised		243	32
Share retraction costs		–	(150)
Repurchase of capital stock		(1,221)	(25,480)
		263,923	(14,816)
Cash provided by (used in) investing activities:			
Purchase of property, plant and equipment (net of investment tax credits)		(6,952)	(4,339)
Net proceeds on disposal of assets		143	34
Acquisition of business (net of cash acquired)		(257,778)	(30,952)
Change other receivables and miscellaneous assets		(382)	(1,462)
		(264,969)	(36,719)
Foreign exchange decrease on cash and cash equivalents		136	(176)
Change in cash and cash equivalents during the period		2,662	(1,355)
Cash and cash equivalents, beginning of period		598	1,953
Cash and cash equivalents, end of period		$ 3,260	$ 598

EXHIBIT 5.5 (continued) High Liner Foods Incorporated: Extracts from Financial Statements

3. Significant accounting policies

Cash and cash equivalents

Cash and cash equivalents are cash on hand, demand deposits with initial and remaining maturity of three months or less or short-term, highly liquid investments, also 90 days or less that are readily convertible to known amounts of cash and which are subject to an insignificant risk of changes in value. Cash and cash equivalents do not include any restricted cash.

25. Supplemental information

All amounts in ($000s)

Change in non-cash working capital balances in the consolidated statements of cash flows:

	Fifty-two weeks ended:	
	December 31, 2011	January 1, 2011
Accounts receivable	$ 5,484	$ 9,194
Inventories	(34,828)	(9,501)
Prepaids	(324)	70
Accounts payable and accrued liabilities	4,526	8,300
	$ (25,142)	$ 8,063

FS5-1. What amounts does High Liner report in its December 31, 2011 and January 1, 2011 statements of cash flow for each of the following?
a. Cash provided by (used for) operating activities.
b. Cash provided by (used for) investing activities.
c. Cash provided by (used for) financing activities.

FS5-2. Examine High Liner's statements of cash flows. Explain and interpret the information in the statement and discuss what it tells you about High Liner.

FS5-3. What method does High Liner use to calculate cash flows from operating activities? How can you tell?

FS5-4. High Liner's statement of cash flows uses the term cash and cash equivalents.
a. What does High Liner include in its definition of cash equivalents?
b. Does it make sense to include cash and cash equivalents in a statement of cash flow, or would using cash only make better sense? Explain your answer.
c. How much cash and cash equivalents does High Liner have on December 31, 2011, January 1, 2011, and January 3, 2010? Is the amount of cash on hand a concern? Explain.
d. Is it possible for an entity to have too much cash? Explain.

FS5-5. Compare High Liner's net earnings and cash from operations in fiscal 2011 and 2010. Why are the amounts in each year different? In general, why are net income and cash from operations different?

FS5-6. Examine High Liner's statements of cash flow for the years ended December 31, 2011 and January 1, 2011 and find the following information:
a. Amount of cash spent repaying long-term debt.
b. Amount of cash spent purchasing property, plant, and equipment.
c. Change of cash during each year.
d. Amount of dividends paid on common shares each year.

FS5-7. What pattern of cash flows does High Liner have (are operating, financing, and investing cash flows positive or negative)? What does this pattern tell you about the circumstances of High Liner's business?

FS5-8. Why are depreciation and amortization added back to net income when calculating CFO using the indirect method? How much did High Liner expense for depreciation and amortization in 2011? What would High Liner's net income have been if its depreciation and amortization expense for 2011 was $11,000,000? What would have been its CFO? Explain your results.

FS5-9. How much did High Liner expense for interest in 2010 and 2011? How much did it pay in interest to lenders? Why might these amounts be different?

FS5-10. Note 25 to High Liner's financial statements shows that inventories increased by $34,828,000 in the year ended December 31, 2011. What impact does this increase have on cash from operations? Explain why.

FS5-11. Calculate High Liner's free cash flow for the years ended December 31, 2011 and January 1, 2011. What does the free cash flow tell you about High Liner?

FS5-12. You are an analyst for an investment company. Use the information provided to prepare a report evaluating High Liner's liquidity. Do you think the company has a strong liquidity position? Explain.

ENDNOTES

1. Extracted from Thomson Reuters Corporation's 2011 financial statements, as filed by Thomson Reuters on March 19, 2012 with the Canadian securities regulatory authorities on http://www.sedar.com. Reprinted with the permission of Thomson Reuters Corporation.
2. Extracted from Nuvo Research Inc.'s 2006–2011 financial statements.
3. Adapted from High Liner Foods Incorporated's Web site at http://www.highlinerfoods.com/en/home/abouthighliner/overview.aspx.
4. Extracted from High Liner Foods Incorporated's 2011 audited financial statements.

CHAPTER 6

Cash, Receivables, and the Time Value of Money

LEARNING OBJECTIVES

After studying the material in this chapter you will be able to do the following:

LO 1 Discuss how cash is accounted for in financial statements.

LO 2 Describe the impact on cash reporting of inflation and deflation, and foreign currencies.

LO 3 Recognize the importance of cash management and internal controls over cash.

LO 4 Explain the concept of the time value of money and its relevance to accounting, and do some basic time value of money calculations.

LO 5 Describe accounting for receivables and uncollectible amounts.

LO 6 Explain how returns and discounts are accounted for.

LO 7 Account for long-term receivables including when there is no interest specified.

LO 8 Understand how managers can use accounting estimates to create hidden reserves to manage earnings.

LO 9 Use information about accounts receivable to analyze and interpret financial statements.

Skateboarders are shreddin' and doing ollies at the municipal outdoor skate park in Keswick, Ontario. Some long-time boarders like Derek Therriault, now finishing Grade 12 at Our Lady of the Lake High School, say they love the park because it was built with several features usually found only in street skateboarding.

Courtesy Town of Georgina

"You would find different sets of stairs and rails," explained Therriault, 17, who plans to study business at Ryerson University.

The municipality's official rules for using the facility require skateboarders to wear "appropriate safety equipment including a helmet, knee pads, elbow pads and wrist guards specifically designed for skateboarding," according to the annual recreation guide.

Therriault acknowledges that he and his friends never wear helmets or safety gear, not even after he broke his left wrist while skateboarding there in 2011 and needed surgery.

"I was trying a trick on it," he recalled, saying he got hurt while falling awkwardly on the grass gap beside the rail.

His advice to boarders who want to minimize their risks? "Practise the tricks you know, get comfortable with them, and from that learn new tricks," he suggests.

Therriault follows his own advice most of the time, except, he admits with a chuckle, when his friend Mike Neilson wants to film something new to put on his "Aft3rhours" YouTube channel.

The park opened in 2004 to serve the young people in the town of 45,000, about an hour north of Toronto. Graffiti isn't permitted, and the facility closes after dark in the summer. The town clearly wants to minimize its risks associated with the use of the skateboard park, although it can't completely prevent epic wipeouts by the boarders, cyclists, and scooter riders.

The company that built the park, Premier Landscaping and Design of Richmond Hill, Ontario, also tries to minimize its financial risks when conducting business.

Established in 1990, Premier has won awards for garden design and construction and counts among its clients Juno Award-winning opera singer Ben Heppner. Premier's owner Joe Morello has been interviewed about landscape design on CTV's *The Marilyn Denis Show* and has won awards at the Canada Blooms show for two years in a row.

Q. What exactly did Premier do to build the skate park?

Joe Morello. My brother, landscape architect Pat Morello from LANDinc., designed the park and we did the initial work and then we hired skateboard specialists in cement finishing. We did the excavation and the base work and the forming, and then we did all the reinforcements and the actual casting of the concrete, building the rails and walls and the steps. A local contractor did the landscaping.

Q. Can you tell me more about the accounting process with the skate park—was it milestone based, like your usual landscape projects are?

Joe Morello. The Town of Georgina gave us a 20 percent deposit or a mobilization fee when the design was complete and we agreed upon the budget. Another 20 percent when the excavation was done, another 20 percent when the bowl area was completed, and then 30 percent was for the completion of the park and the final 10 percent was held back for 30 days.

Q. Did you send out physical invoices?

Joe Morello. Yes, Joanne (Morello, Premier's financial manager) wrote them up when an interim payment was required.

Q. How did you make sure the construction went ahead smoothly without much risk?

Joe Morello. We had no accounting issues, but something funny that happened was after we poured fresh concrete. There were kids that wanted to come and jump all over it. So we had to have security on site until the concrete cured. Some kids did manage to get their initials written in it, anyway.

Q. To avoid risk, how do you decide if a client's credit rating is good before you take them on?

Joe Morello. For some clients, it's important to get payment terms and a lot of details in a contract. So we have different types of contracts. Simpler ones, where there shouldn't be any issues, and others, which are very detailed.

If I don't feel good, for whatever reason, we just won't continue on with the estimating process. One example might be if their budgets aren't reasonable. Another red flag would be if I see them having tried some work already and it's not working out, then I don't want to go into anyone else's mistake. A couple of times we had a guy that started and he worked for a week and then he left, so I ask myself "Why did he leave?" and I don't take the job.

And we've been very lucky, actually. For most clients, it's a non-issue. They are happy and they have a personal relationship with me since I am on site often. But don't forget, we can put a lien on their house or we can remove the work we've put in if they don't pay. That's put right in our contract.

Q. Have you been back to the park since it opened?

Joe Morello. I have. It looks great!

–E.B.

INTRODUCTION

In the last chapter, we discussed the importance of cash flow and liquidity. The emphasis there was the cash flow statement and liquidity. In this chapter, we examine some of an entity's most liquid assets—cash and receivables—and consider how to use balance sheet information to evaluate liquidity. Cash, of course, is the most liquid asset and is vital for the effective operation and survival of an entity. Yet, accounting for cash isn't always as straightforward as counting the money in your pocket. Receivables are amounts owed to the entity, usually by customers. Our examination of receivables will show the importance of estimates on the values of assets on the balance sheet and the amount of income an entity reports.

I also introduce a powerful tool used in accounting and financial analysis, "time value of money," which recognizes that money received today is more valuable than the same amount of money received sometime in the future.

LO 1

CASH

Accounting for cash is relatively straightforward and doesn't generate much controversy, although there are some twists and turns.

www.aircanada.com

Exhibit 6.1 shows the asset section of Air Canada's balance sheets from its December 31, 2011 financial statements. Air Canada reported cash and cash equivalents of $1,115 million, $1,090 million, and $848 million on January 1, 2010, December 31, 2010, and December 31, 2011, respectively.[1] Note 3P in Exhibit 6.1 describes what Air Canada includes in cash equivalents. In general, cash equivalents are short-term investments easily and quickly converted into a known amount of cash and include treasury bills, guaranteed investment certificates (GICs), commercial paper, and money market funds. Short-term investments typically must mature within three months to be classified as a cash equivalent. Cash equivalents exclude equity investments such as common and preferred shares because their prices fluctuate daily, which means the amount of cash received from selling them is only certain once they are sold. Cash equivalents can also include bank overdrafts used for short-term cash management purposes (see Chapter 5 for more information).

An interesting item on Air Canada's balance sheet is the account called "restricted cash." Sometimes use of an entity's cash is restricted because of a legal or contractual obligation to use it in a specified way. On December 31, 2011, Air Canada reported $76 million of restricted cash as a current asset, representing money paid in advance for vacation packages (this is a legal requirement of the travel industry—see Note 3R in Exhibit 6.1). Note 3R also explains there is non-current restricted cash included in "Deposits and other assets." This cash is restricted because it's being held by banks as collateral for letters of credit. (A **letter of credit** is a guarantee from a bank that a payment to a supplier will be made.) Note 8 shows that on December 31, 2011 there was $182 million of this restricted cash. Restricted cash is disclosed separately because it can't be used for day-to-day operating purposes, so it isn't a liquid asset and isn't included in cash and cash equivalents in the cash flow statement.

QUESTION FOR CONSIDERATION

Why is it important for an entity to disclose that some of its cash is restricted?

ANSWER: It's normally assumed that cash is a liquid asset available for use as needed by management. Restricted cash has been set aside for a specific use; therefore, it isn't available to meet the liquidity needs of the entity. Stakeholders will be interested in restricted cash because it could affect their evaluation of the entity's liquidity.

EXHIBIT 6.1 Air Canada: Cash and Cash Equivalents; Restricted Cash

Consolidated Financial Statements and Notes 2011

Consolidated Statement of Financial Position

(Canadian dollars in millions)		December 31 2011	December 31 2010	January 1 2010
ASSETS				
Current				
Cash and cash equivalents	Note 3P	$ 848	$ 1,090	$ 1,115
Short-term investments	Note 3Q	1,251	1,102	292
Total cash, cash equivalents and short-term investments		2,099	2,192	1,407
Restricted cash	Note 3R	76	80	78
Accounts receivable		712	641	701
Aircraft fuel inventory		92	67	63
Spare parts and supplies inventory	Note 3S	93	88	64
Prepaid expenses and other current assets		255	279	338
Total current assets		3,327	3,347	2,651
Property and equipment	Note 5	5,088	5,629	6,287
Intangible assets	Note 6	312	317	329
Goodwill	Note 7	311	311	311
Deposits and other assets	Note 8	595	549	547
Total assets		**$ 9,633**	**$ 10,153**	**$ 10,125**

SEE NOTE 8

3. SUMMARY OF SIGNIFICANT ACCOUNTING POLICIES

P) CASH AND CASH EQUIVALENTS

Cash and cash equivalents include $356 pertaining to investments with original maturities of three months or less at December 31, 2011 ($497 as at December 31, 2010 and $323 as at January 1, 2010). Investments include bankers' acceptance and bankers' discount notes, which may be liquidated promptly and have original maturities of three months or less.

R) RESTRICTED CASH

The Corporation has recorded Restricted cash under Current assets representing funds held in trust by Air Canada Vacations in accordance with regulatory requirements governing advance ticket sales, recorded under Current liabilities, for certain travel related activities.

Restricted cash with maturities greater than one year from the balance sheet date is recorded in Deposits and other assets. This restricted cash relates to funds on deposit with various financial institutions as collateral for letters of credit and other items.

8. DEPOSITS AND OTHER ASSETS

		2011	2010
Aircraft related deposits (a)		$ 138	$ 131
Restricted cash	Note 3R	182	140
Prepayments under maintenance agreements	Note 3J	65	65
Investment in Aveos	Note 20	51	51
Other deposits		24	24
Aircraft lease payments in excess of rent expense	Note 3BB	54	52
Deposit related to the Pension and Benefits Agreement	Note 20	20	20
Asset backed commercial paper	Note 18	24	29
Other		37	37
		$ 595	$ 549

LO 2 IS A DOLLAR A DOLLAR?

Chapter 2 introduced the unit-of-measure assumption, a fundamental accounting concept requiring that financial statement information be measurable and stated in monetary units, such as Canadian dollars. A dollar of cash reported on a balance sheet means a dollar in hand. But is a dollar always worth a dollar? In fact, a dollar's value isn't constant over time. While the face value of a dollar stays the same, what a dollar can buy and its value relative to other currencies will change.

LO 2 The Effect of Changes in Purchasing Power

If you hide $10,000 under your mattress, your IFRS financial statements will always show $10,000 in cash, *but* as time passes you will probably become less and less well off. Why? Over time, **inflation**—a period when, on average, prices in the economy are rising—reduces the purchasing power of cash. If prices are rising, you can buy fewer goods and services with your money as time passes, which means the purchasing power of your money is declining even though the face value stays the same. The reverse is true with **deflation**, a period when, on average, prices in the economy are falling. Deflation is a far less common phenomenon than inflation.

Using Canada's inflation rate, $10,000 hidden at the beginning of 2000 would purchase, in mid-2011, what $7,805 would have purchased in 2000. In other words, while the number of dollars you had would be the same in 2000 and 2011, you would be able to buy fewer goods and services in 2011 than in 2000.

Canadian companies use the "nominal dollar" as the unit of measure for financial reporting, which means that no adjustment is made for changes in purchasing power. IFRS requires adjustments for entities in countries with very high levels of inflation, but this isn't a problem in Canada. A decrease in purchasing power could be reflected in financial statements by recording a loss. If an entity held $10,000 cash over a period in which purchasing power decreased by 10 percent, a loss of $1,000 would be reported on the income statement. By doing this, the financial statements would reflect the cost of holding cash in an inflationary period.

LO 2 The Effect of Changing Prices of Foreign Currencies

Canada is a trading nation. Much of its economic activity involves transactions with entities in foreign countries and in foreign currencies. Many Canadian companies have operations in other countries. Transactions involving foreign currencies and foreign operations can impact an entity's financial statements, including the amount of cash it reports.

For example, Quarry Ltd. (Quarry) is a Canadian company with a U.S. dollar bank account. Because of the unit-of-measure assumption, all amounts reported in the financial statements must be stated in a single currency. If Quarry's unit of measure is Canadian dollars, its U.S. cash must be stated in Canadian dollars. Since **exchange rates** of currencies fluctuate, the number of Canadian dollars that a U.S. amount represents will vary. (The exchange rate is the price to buy one currency unit, stated in terms of another currency.)

Suppose that on December 31, 2015, Quarry had US$1,000,000 and the exchange rate was $0.97—that is, US$1 could be exchanged for Cdn$0.97. In its December 31, 2015 financial statements, Quarry would report its US$1,000,000 as $970,000 of Canadian cash (exchange rate × amount of foreign currency = $0.97 × US$1,000,000). The Cdn$970,000 is reported even though the money is still actually in U.S. dollars. If one year later, on December 31, 2016, Quarry's U.S. bank account still had US$1,000,000 but the exchange rate was $0.99, Quarry would report $990,000 of Canadian cash.

Thus, when exchange rates change, the number of Canadian dollars reported changes even though the amount of the foreign currency stays the same. The change in the exchange rate from December 31, 2015 to December 31, 2016 causes Quarry to report $20,000 more in Canadian dollars, even though the number of U.S. dollars hadn't changed.

CASH MANAGEMENT AND CONTROLS OVER CASH

LO 3

It would be easy to conclude that the more cash an entity has, the better, but that's not quite true. Having too little cash, of course, is a potential threat to the survival of an entity. But having too much cash can be a problem as well. While holding cash provides insurance against the unexpected, it's an unproductive asset—it doesn't make money. At best, cash in an interest bearing account or other liquid investments earns a very small return. But a crucial question when examining an entity's financial position is, how much cash is too much? In an economic crisis, when banks are reluctant to lend, having large cash reserves becomes crucial for survival.

Cash management is a key function of an entity's management. Stakeholders use financial statement information to assess whether an entity is maintaining adequate reserves of liquidity and to evaluate management's stewardship of the liquidity.

Management has the important stewardship responsibility of developing and maintaining adequate internal controls. **Internal controls** ensure that an entity achieves its objectives. In an accounting context, internal controls address the reliability of the accounting system's information and protect an entity's assets from loss, theft, or inappropriate use. For example, a retail store may place alarm devices on more expensive inventory items. These devices are an internal control that helps prevent theft. Poor internal controls can lead to significant losses.

External stakeholders should be concerned that an entity's internal controls are adequate. Without them, stakeholders can't rely on the financial statements for decision making or be confident that management is protecting assets from theft or misuse. Canadian public companies must annually disclose the results of senior managers' assessment of the company's internal control over financial reporting. These controls provide assurance of the reliability of financial statement information produced by an entity's accounting system. Any weaknesses identified in the design or effectiveness of internal controls must be described in the annual report, along with plans to resolve the problems. These requirements don't apply to private companies.

Cash is an important asset for an entity to control. It's attractive to thieves because it's easy to hide and it can't be identified once it's stolen. Entities that handle a lot of cash—such as retail stores, casinos, arcades, and laundromats—need special internal controls to protect their cash. There are many ways that cash can be stolen, in addition to being physically taken. Weak internal controls might allow an employee to write cheques to non-existent suppliers and then cash the cheques him- or herself, pay a supplier more than is actually owed, or alter records to cover up a cash theft.

There are many controls that can limit the likelihood that cash will be stolen. One of the most important and effective controls over cash and other assets is **segregation of duties**, which means ensuring that people who handle an asset aren't also responsible for record keeping for that asset. If duties aren't segregated, an employee could steal assets and cover up the theft with fictitious entries to the accounting records. For example, consider a person who receives cheques from customers and deposits them in the bank, and who is also responsible for recording the deposit in the accounting system. That person might deposit some of the cheques in his or her own bank account and cover up the theft with a journal entry writing off accounts receivable in the amount stolen.

An important internal control tool for cash is the **bank reconciliation**, which explains the differences between an entity's accounting records and its bank account.

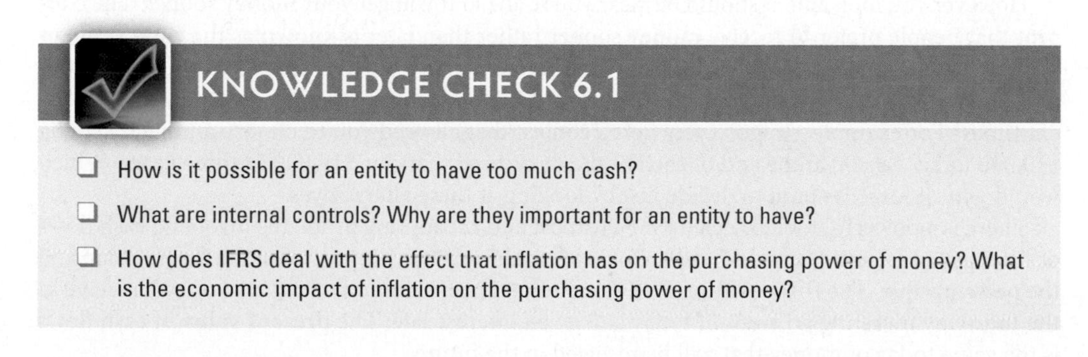

KNOWLEDGE CHECK 6.1

- ❑ How is it possible for an entity to have too much cash?
- ❑ What are internal controls? Why are they important for an entity to have?
- ❑ How does IFRS deal with the effect that inflation has on the purchasing power of money? What is the economic impact of inflation on the purchasing power of money?

QUESTION FOR CONSIDERATION

You purchased a vending machine selling a variety of drinks in a busy suburban mall as an investment. As owner, you are responsible for stocking the machine with drinks, collecting the cash, and maintaining the machine, and you've hired someone living near the mall to take care of these things for you. Explain why internal controls are important in this situation and why hiring one person to handle all those tasks represents weak internal controls. What internal controls would help protect you?

ANSWER: Internal controls are important to protect your assets—in this case, the drinks and the cash. Because you have hired someone to stock the machine and collect the cash, it's possible your employee could steal the drinks, the cash, or both. Without proper controls, it would be difficult to know whether your employee was stealing.

The easiest way to ensure that cash or drinks aren't stolen is to do the jobs yourself. If you can't, control would be stronger if one person stocked the machine and another collected the cash (segregation of duties). That way, you could compare the number of drinks sold as reported by the person stocking the machine with the cash received from the person collecting the cash. Sales and cash collections that didn't match would indicate a problem.

If you must use the same person for both stocking and collection, it's important to keep control of the inventory. Controlling the inventory means your employee would only use inventory supplied by you, so you would know the number of drinks going into the machine and, therefore, the amount of cash you should receive. This is a weak control because there is nothing to prevent the person from buying drinks, placing them in the machine, and keeping the cash from those sales. This kind of theft is very difficult to detect. Another possible control is an electronic counter, not accessible to your employee, to keep track of the number of drinks sold. This would also allow you to compare the number of drinks sold with the cash collected, but you would have to inspect the machine from time to time to check the counter.

LO 4

THE TIME VALUE OF MONEY

Would you rather receive \$1,000 today or \$1,000 a year from now? The answer should be easy: It's better to have cash now rather than the same amount of cash later. Here are some reasons why:

1. Having the money sooner allows you to earn a return. By investing in a one-year investment certificate paying 4 percent interest per year, your \$1,000 would turn into \$1,040 in a year. By waiting a year to receive the \$1,000, you would lose the opportunity to earn that \$40.
2. By getting the money today, you can spend and enjoy it now. A person is likely to prefer having a plasma TV or taking a holiday sooner rather than later, or at least having the option of doing so.
3. As explained earlier, inflation causes the purchasing power of money to decline over time. With inflation of 2 percent, \$1,000 received in a year will only buy what \$980 would buy today.
4. Getting the money sooner reduces the likelihood that you aren't going to be paid.

However you look at it, it should be clear you're ahead if you get your money sooner. The concept that people prefer to receive money sooner rather than later is known as the **time value of money**. While conceptually it makes sense that money today is better than the same amount of money in the future, how do you choose among different amounts that can be received at different times? For example, suppose you won a contest that allowed you to choose among receiving \$10,000 today, \$4,000 at the end of each of the next three years, or \$14,000 in three years. Which would you choose? It's hard to decide just by looking at these alternatives.

There is a powerful tool for evaluating business and accounting problems involving cash flows occurring at different times. We will look at this tool from two perspectives: the future value and the present value. The **future value (FV)** of cash flows is the amount of money you will receive in the future by investing an amount today at a given interest rate. The **present value** of cash flows is the value today of money that will be received in the future.

Future Value

LO 4

Money in a bank account growing over time is an application of the future value concept. If you put \$1,000 in a bank account paying interest of 5 percent per year, in one year you would have earned \$50 in interest and your bank account would have \$1,050 in it. The amount of interest earned is calculated by multiplying the amount in your bank account by the interest rate: $\$1,000 \times 0.05 = \$50$. The amount of money in the bank account at the end of the year is calculated by multiplying the amount in the account by one plus the interest rate $(1 + r)$: $\$1,000 \times 1.05 = \$1,050$. In time-value-of-money terms, the future value of \$1,000 invested at 5 percent for one year is \$1,050.

If you leave your \$1,050 in the bank for another year and continue to receive interest at 5 percent per year, at the end of the second year you would have \$1,102.50 ($\$1,050 \times 1.05$). During the second year you would have earned \$52.50 of interest ($\$1,050 \times 0.05$). You earned more than \$50 in interest in the second year because of **compound interest**—interest earned on the principal amount and on interest accumulated in previous periods. In the second year, interest wasn't only earned on the original \$1,000, but also on the \$50 in interest earned in the first year. In time value of money terms, the future value of \$1,000 invested at 5 percent for two years is \$1,102.50. (If the interest was only calculated on the initial investment of \$1,000, the interest every year would be \$50. Interest paid or earned only on the principal amount is called **simple interest**.)

The formula for calculating the future value of an investment made today is:

$$FV_{n,r} = (1 + r)^n \times \text{Amount invested}$$

FV (future value) is the amount you will receive in the future for an amount invested for n periods at an interest rate of r per period. This formula incorporates the compounding of interest. We can use the formula to calculate the future value of an investment of \$1,000 at 5 percent for two years:

$$\begin{aligned} FV_{2,0.05} &= (1 + 0.05)^2 \times \$1,000 \\ &= 1.1025 \times \$1,000 \\ &= \$1,102.50 \end{aligned}$$

This is the same amount we calculated earlier.

You could find out how much you would have if you invested \$1,000 at 8 percent for 25 years:

$$\begin{aligned} FV_{n,r} &= (1 + r)^n \times \text{Amount invested} \\ FV_{25,0.08} &= (1 + 0.08)^{25} \times \$1,000 \\ &= 6.84848 \times \$1,000 \\ &= \$6,848.48 \end{aligned}$$

The future value technique is very useful and powerful. There are many questions that can be answered by using it. Let's look at a couple of examples.

Example 1: The Mayos In 2017, Mr. and Mrs. Mayo received \$2,500 from Mr. Mayo's parents as a gift in honour of the birth of their first daughter, Ellin. Mr. and Mrs. Mayo plan to invest the money to help pay for Ellin's university education. They would like to know how much Ellin will receive if they invest the \$2,500 in a 20-year investment certificate that earns 6 percent interest per year.

$$\begin{aligned} FV_{n,r} &= (1 + r)^n \times \text{Amount invested} \\ FV_{20,0.06} &= (1 + 0.06)^{20} \times \$2,500 \\ &= \$8,017.84 \end{aligned}$$

Therefore, Ellin will receive \$8,017.84 when the investment certificate matures in 2037. In this example, the periods are years, but periods could be days, weeks, months, or anything else.

However, the interest rate selected must be appropriate to the period used in the analysis (i.e., you would use the annual interest rate only if you were measuring the periods in years).

Example 2: Ms. Secretan Ms. Secretan recently purchased a new car to replace her rusting 13-year-old vehicle. She arranged a $35,000, three-year loan at 0.5 percent per month from the bank to pay for the car, interest compounded monthly. Under the terms of the loan, Ms. Secretan doesn't have to make any payments until the end of the three-year term, at which time she must pay the bank the principal and interest in full. Ms. Secretan would like to know how much she will have to pay in three years when the loan must be repaid.

$$\begin{aligned} FV_{n,r} &= (1 + r)^n \times \text{Amount invested} \\ &= FV_{36,0.005}\,(1 + 0.005)^{36} \times \$35{,}000 \\ &= \$41{,}883.82 \end{aligned}$$

Ms. Secretan will have to pay the bank $41,883.82 in three years. Because the loan is compounded monthly, the number of periods is 36 months, not three years. If three years at an interest rate of 6 percent per year was used, the answer would be different.

KNOWLEDGE CHECK 6.2

- ❑ What reasons explain why it is better to have money today than in the future?
- ❑ What is the difference between simple and compound interest?
- ❑ What is the formula used to determine the future value $1 invested today?

QUESTION FOR CONSIDERATION

Your aunt recently won $100,000 in a lottery and she has come to you for advice on investing her money. She wants to invest for ten years and then retire. Your aunt is only interested in investments she considers safe so she has narrowed her choice to two investments with large banks: a ten-year investment certificate with an interest rate of 8 percent calculated annually and a ten-year certificate with interest calculated and compounded at the rate of 4 percent every six months (this means there are 20 six-month investment periods at 4 percent rather than 10 one-year investment periods at 8 percent).

Which investment would you recommend to your aunt? Explain your answer. Make sure you explain why the quantitative result you obtain occurs.

ANSWER: Your aunt would be better off with the investment that has 4 percent interest calculated and compounded every six months. Quantitatively,

$$\begin{aligned} \text{Investment 1:} \quad FV_{n,r} &= (1 + r)^n \times \text{Amount invested} \\ FV_{10,0.08} &= (1 + 0.08)^{10} \times \$100{,}000 \\ &= \$215{,}892 \end{aligned}$$

$$\begin{aligned} \text{Investment 2:} \quad FV_{n,r} &= (1 + r)^n \times \text{Amount invested} \\ FV_{20,0.04} &= (1 + 0.04)^{20} \times \$100{,}000 \\ &= \$219{,}112 \end{aligned}$$

Investment 2 is more attractive because compounding occurs more often. Even though the interest rate appears to be the same for both investments, more interest is earned with Investment 2. For example, in the first year, your aunt earns 8 percent on $100,000 with Investment 1. But with Investment 2, she earns 4 percent on $100,000 in the first half of the first year ($4,000) and then 4 percent on $104,000 in the second half ($4,160) of that year, which gives a total of $8,160 of interest in the first year. The effect of the more frequent compounding builds over the life of the investment.

Present Value

LO 4

The present-value technique looks at what cash received in the future is worth today. This is another very powerful tool for comparing alternative cash flow arrangements. Consider the $1,102.50 you had in your bank account after two years invested at 5 percent per year (this is the example that introduced the discussion of future values). The question asked in a present value analysis is, "At an interest rate of 5 percent, what is today's equivalent of the $1,102.50 you will receive in two years?" Another way of posing the question is, "How much would you pay or invest today to receive $1,102.50 in two years if the interest rate was 5 percent?" Based on the earlier example, you should guess that the present value of $1,102.50 to be received in two years at 5 percent is $1,000. This result can be confirmed by using the following formula:

$$PV_{n,r} = \frac{1}{(1+r)^n} \times \text{Amount to be received or paid}$$

$$PV_{2,0.05} = \frac{1}{(1+0.05)^2} \times \$1{,}102.50$$

$$= \$1{,}000$$

In this formula, n is the number of periods and r is the interest rate. Note that the term "discount rate" is often used instead of interest rate in a present value analysis. The **discount rate** is the rate used to calculate the present value of future cash flows. Present value is nothing more than the amount that would be received in the future less the interest that would be earned on the money over the investment period.

What the calculation tells us is that at a discount rate of 5 percent, having $1,000 now is equivalent to receiving $1,102.50 in two years. In other words, if you were offered a choice between $1,000 now or $1,102.50 in two years and your discount rate was 5 percent, you would be indifferent—the two amounts are equally valuable to you. However, if you were offered $1,100 in two years instead, you would prefer the $1,000 now. And if you were offered $1,110 in two years, you would prefer the $1,110 to $1,000 now. Remember, when I introduced the time-value-of-money concept, I explained that people preferred receiving money sooner rather than later. However, people are willing to accept money later rather than sooner, but only at a price. That price is a larger amount of money.

Suppose that instead of using a discount rate of 5 percent to determine the present value of $1,102.50 to be received in two years, you decide that 7 percent is the appropriate discount rate. What is the present value of the $1,102.50 in this case?

$$PV_{2,0.07} = \frac{1}{(1+0.07)^2} \times \$1{,}102.50$$

$$= \$962.97$$

At a discount rate of 7 percent, the present value of $1,102.50 to be received in two years is $962.97. This means you would be willing to pay no more than $962.97 today to receive $1,102.50 in two years. Having to pay anything more than $962.97 would be too much. Or, you would prefer receiving any amount more than $962.97 today rather than $1,102.50 in two years. Anything less than $962.97 today would make $1,102.50 in two years preferable.

It's important to recognize the key role that the discount rate plays in determining the present value. The higher the discount rate, the lower the present value of a future amount. This corresponds to the future-value effect whereby the higher the interest rate paid on an investment, the more money received in the future. Discount rate selection is somewhat subjective and many considerations go into the choice, including risk and expected inflation. Further discussion about determining the discount rate is beyond the scope of this book.

Let's look at two examples of the present-value technique.

Example 3: Luiz DeSilva Luiz DeSilva has decided to give his new nephew a gift of a university education. Luiz estimates that it will cost $150,000 for a four-year education at a good school, including tuition and living expenses, when his nephew is ready for university in 18 years. Luiz has an investment opportunity that will earn 8 percent per year. How much must Luiz invest today to have the $150,000 required in 18 years? In other words, what is the present value of $150,000 to be received in 18 years using a discount rate of 8 percent?

$$PV_{n,r} = \frac{1}{(1+r)^n} \times \text{Amount to be received or paid}$$

$$PV_{18,0.08} = \frac{1}{(1+0.08)^{18}} \times \$150{,}000$$

$$= \$37{,}537.35$$

Therefore, if Luiz invested $37,537.35 today at 8 percent, his nephew would have $150,000 in 18 years to pay for his university education.

Example 4: Quyon Ltd. Quyon Ltd. (Quyon) recently purchased a machine for $500,000. The purchase agreement allows Quyon to pay for the machine in three years with no interest. What would be the equivalent price if Quyon had to pay for the machine in cash today if the appropriate discount rate was 6 percent? In other words, what is the present value of $500,000 to be paid in three years using a discount rate of 6 percent?

$$PV_{n,r} = \frac{1}{(1+r)^n} \times \text{Amount to be received or paid}$$

$$PV_{3,0.06} = \frac{1}{(1+0.06)^{3}} \times \$500{,}000$$

$$= \$419{,}809.64$$

Therefore, $419,809.64 is the current cash equivalent of paying $500,000 in three years at a discount rate of 6 percent.

QUESTION FOR CONSIDERATION

You have the option of receiving $1,000 today, $1,500 in four years, or $1,700 in six years. Which would you choose? Assume a discount rate of 6 percent. Explain your choice.

ANSWER: To answer this question, it's necessary to compare the present values of each of the cash flows and select the one with the highest present value because it's the most valuable. Note that the present value of a cash flow to be received or paid now is always the actual amount of the cash flow, regardless of the discount rate:

$$\text{Option 1:} \quad PV_{n,r} = 1\frac{1}{(1+r)^n} \times \text{Amount to be received or paid}$$

$$PV_{0,0.06} = \frac{1}{(1+0.06)^{0}} \times \$1{,}000$$

$$= \$1{,}000$$

$$\text{Option 2:} \quad PV_{4,0.06} = \frac{1}{(1+0.06)^{4}} \times \$1{,}500$$

$$= \$1{,}188.14$$

$$\text{Option 3:} \quad PV_{6,0.06} = \frac{1}{(1+0.06)^{6}} \times \$1{,}700$$

$$= \$1{,}198.43$$

Option 3 is the best one because it has the largest present value.

TABLE 6.1 Option 4: Calculation of Present Value

Calculation of Present Value of Option 4 (receive $250 per year for six years, beginning one year from now, at a discount rate of 6 percent)			
Cash received	**Amount of cash received**	**Discount factor** $\frac{1}{(1 + r)^n}$	**Present value of cash flow**
Now	$ 0		
In one year ($n = 1$)	250	0.9434	$ 235.85
In two years ($n = 2$)	250	0.8900	222.50
In three years ($n = 3$)	250	0.8396	209.90
In four years ($n = 4$)	250	0.7921	198.02
In five years ($n = 5$)	250	0.7473	186.82
In six years ($n = 6$)	250	0.7050	176.24
Totals		4.9174	$1,229.33

Discounting, another term for calculating the present value of a future cash flow, is a very powerful tool because it allows comparisons of cash flows received at different times and in different amounts. So far, we have looked at simple situations involving a single cash flow sometime in the future. The present-value technique can be used in more complex situations. Let's add a fourth option to the three prizes offered in the previous Question for Consideration. Option 4 is that you could receive $250 per year for six years, beginning in one year. How would option 4 stack up against receiving $1,700 in year six, the best option of the first three?

This calculation is a bit more complicated but the concepts and approach are the same. Option 4 requires you to determine the present value of a series of six cash flows occurring at different times. The calculation of the present value of this series of cash flows is shown in Table 6.1.

Since the present value of the cash flows in option 4 is the largest of the four offered, that's the one that should be selected.

Present Value of an Annuity

LO 4

For option 4 in the example above, you would receive a $250 payment at the end of each of the next six years. A series of equal cash flows (inflows or outflows) made at equally spaced time intervals is known as an **annuity**. To calculate the present value of the series of six $250 payments, you would do the following:

1. Find the discount rate for each of the six years.
2. Multiply the cash flow in each year by the appropriate discount rate to determine the present value of the cash flow in each year.
3. Add up the present values from each year to get the present value of the entire series of cash flows.

We followed these three steps in Table 6.1. The present value of an annuity can also be calculated using the following equation:

$$PV_{n,r} = \sum \left[\frac{1}{(1 + r)^n} \right] \times \text{Amount to be received or paid in each period}$$

$$= \frac{1}{r} \times \left[1 - \frac{1}{(1 + r)^n} \right] \times \text{Amount to be received or paid in each period}$$

Applying this formula to option 4 gives us the following:

$$\text{PV of an annuity}_{n,r} = \frac{1}{r} \times \left[1 - \frac{1}{(1+r)^n}\right] \times \text{Amount to be received or paid in each period}$$

$$\text{PV of an annuity}_{6,0.06} = \frac{1}{0.06} \times \left[1 - \frac{1}{(1+0.06)^6}\right] \times \$250$$

$$= \$1,229.33$$

This is the same amount that we calculated in Table 6.1. Note that the n in this formula refers to the number of periods for which the cash flow will be received.

The formula can only be used if the following conditions are met:

- The cash flow is the same in each period.
- The same discount rate is applied to each period's cash flow.
- The cash flow occurs in every period beginning one period from the present.

If *any* of these conditions isn't met, the formula doesn't apply and the individual cash flows must be evaluated on a year-by-year basis. Let's look at an example of an annuity.

Example 5: Tuttle Inc. Tuttle Inc. (Tuttle) can invest in a business opportunity that it estimates will earn $5,000,000 at the end of each of the next five years. Assuming the appropriate discount rate is 12 percent, what is the present value of the payments Tuttle would receive by investing in the opportunity? What is the maximum amount that Tuttle should pay to invest in the business opportunity? The answer can be obtained by applying the formula for the present value of an annuity.

$$\text{PV of an annuity}_{n,r} = \frac{1}{r} \times \left[1 - \frac{1}{(1+r)^n}\right] \times \text{Amount to be received or paid in each period}$$

$$\text{PV of an annuity}_{5,0.12} = \frac{1}{0.12} \times \left[1 - \frac{1}{(1+0.12)^5}\right] \times \$5,000,000$$

$$= \$18,023,881$$

The present value of a series of $5,000,000 payments to be received at the end of each of the next five years at a discount rate of 12 percent is $18,023,881. This means that Tuttle would pay no more than $18,023,881 to invest in this business opportunity. By paying $18,023,881, Tuttle is earning exactly 12 percent on its investment, which is what it requires (that's why the 12 percent discount rate is used). If Tuttle had to pay more than $18,023,881, it would earn less than 12 percent, which wouldn't be acceptable.

Discounting is relevant for a number of accounting issues. For example, if a company makes sales on credit where payment isn't due for a long time and no interest is charged on the debt, discounting helps determine how much revenue should be recognized. Discounting is also relevant for many liabilities, such as leases, pensions, and other long-term obligations. Later in this chapter, we will examine an accounting application of the time value of money.

KNOWLEDGE CHECK 6.3

- ❑ What is the formula used to determine the present value of $1 to be received sometime in the future?
- ❑ What is the present value of $100 to be received in ten years if the discount rate is 9 percent? ($42.24)
- ❑ What is an annuity?

QUESTION FOR CONSIDERATION

A famous professional athlete recently signed a one-year contract with his team for $15,000,000. Because the team was having financial problems, the athlete agreed to accept the $15,000,000 in equal payments of $750,000 per year over the next 20 years. The team stated at a press conference that the $15,000,000 justly rewarded the best player in the game with the highest one-year salary in the history of the sport, exceeding the previous high salary of $9,500,000.

Do you agree with the team's statement that the salary is the highest in the history of the sport? Explain your answer. Assume a discount rate of 10 percent and that payments are received at the end of each year.

ANSWER: If the previous high salary of $9,500,000 was paid in one year, the $15,000,000 salary is nowhere near the previous high. The present value of a series of $750,000 payments received over 20 years is

$$PV_{n,r} = \frac{1}{r} \times \left[1 - \frac{1}{(1+r)^n}\right] \times \text{Amount to be received or paid}$$

$$\text{PV of an annuity}_{20,0.10} = \frac{1}{0.10} \times \left[1 - \frac{1}{(1+0.10)^{20}}\right] \times \$750{,}000$$

$$= \$6{,}385{,}173$$

Because the payments on the contract are spread over 20 years, the present value of the athlete's salary is $6,385,173. Receiving $750,000 over 20 years is equivalent to receiving $6,385,173 today. In nominal dollar terms, the athlete is receiving more money than any athlete before him. However, comparing the present value of the payments made under different contracts is a more legitimate way of comparing the contracts.

RECEIVABLES

Receivables are amounts owing to an entity. Most receivables result from selling goods and services to customers on credit. These are usually called *accounts receivable*. Receivables can also represent amounts owing by shareholders and employees (shareholder/employee loans receivable), tax refunds (taxes receivable), amounts owing from investments (interest and dividends receivable), proceeds due from the sale of capital assets, and so on. Receivables are usually current assets, but if an amount owing is to be received in more than a year it would be classified as non-current. Our discussion will focus on accounts receivable because these are the most common and significant receivables reported on financial statements, but the concepts generally apply to all types of receivables.

Accounts receivable arise when revenue is recognized but payment isn't received. As discussed in Chapter 4, the journal entry to record a credit sale is

Dr. Accounts receivable (asset +)	xxx	
Cr. Revenue (revenue +, owners' equity +)		xxx

When the customer pays the amount owed, the journal entry recorded is

Dr. Cash (asset +)	xxx	
Cr. Accounts receivable (asset −)		xxx

Accounts receivable are essentially loans to customers. Most businesses would probably prefer to do business on a cash basis because selling on credit lengthens an entity's cash cycle and introduces the risk that amounts owed won't be collected. There are also costs to administer the credit program—doing credit checks, processing billings and collections, and pursuing customers that don't pay. However, selling on credit is the normal, practical way of doing business in non-retail transactions.

For most retail businesses, credit is offered through major credit cards such as MasterCard and Visa, but credit can be an important and lucrative business in the retail industry. Companies such as Sears Canada, Home Depot, Canadian Tire, and Hudson's Bay Company offer their own credit cards to customers and earn interest from customers who don't pay for purchases within the allowed period of time.

Financial statements prepared in accordance with IFRS report receivables at their net realizable value (NRV)—the estimated amount that will be collected. When a company sells on credit, a number of events can reduce the amount actually collected:

- Customers might not pay what they owe due to financial problems, disputes over whether the goods or services were delivered or acceptable, or simply because they are dishonest.
- Some customers may receive refunds or price reductions if they aren't satisfied with the goods or services provided.
- Customers may receive a discount if they pay their bills early. For example, an entity may offer a customer a 2 percent discount if the amount owed is paid within 10 days. Thus, if the customer owes $1,000, only $980 has to be paid if payment is made within 10 days. After 10 days, the full amount must be paid.

Under accrual accounting, bad debts, returns, and discounts are costs of doing business in the period the revenue is recognized and the effect of these items is to reduce net income (by reducing sales or increasing expenses) and reduce accounts receivable. It's important to note that management won't know the amount of bad debts, returns, and discounts at the end of a period when financial statements are being prepared so management has to make estimates.

Reporting receivables at NRV makes sense for many stakeholders. NRV is most useful for cash flow prediction and liquidity analysis because it represents an estimate of the amount of cash that will be received. For the stewardship and management evaluation objectives, knowing the actual amount owed by customers and the estimated amount that will be collected are useful for assessing how well receivables, credit and collection, returns, and discounts are being managed.

When a customer makes a purchase using a credit card such as Visa or MasterCard or a debit card, the amount isn't reported as accounts receivable. The credit/debit card payment is equivalent to cash; in most cases the money is transferred electronically to the merchant's bank account. For a credit card, the account receivable belongs to the credit card company. For a debit card, the money is transferred from the customer's bank account to the merchant's. The merchant pays a fee for being able to accept the credit/debit cards for payment. For example, a $100 purchase made using a MasterCard might cost a business 2 percent of the charged amount, or $2. When the merchant receives payment from the bank, it would receive $98 instead of $100. The fees associated with debit cards are much lower than with credit cards.

The credit card transaction would be

Dr. Cash (asset +)	98	
Dr. Card service fee (expense +, owners' equity −)	2	
Cr. Revenue (revenue +, owners' equity +)		100
To record the sale of goods using a credit card at the gross amount		

Accepting credit and debit cards adds costs to running the business, but there are benefits. By accepting credit cards merchants get the cash immediately, don't have to worry about bad debts, and save the cost of operating a credit program. Cards may also encourage customers to buy, or buy more, than if only cash was accepted.

INSIGHT

For private companies that don't follow IFRS or ASPE, the amount reported for accounts receivable could represent gross receivables, net receivables, or receivables net of some estimates (such as bad debts) but not others (such as returns). A stakeholder must be very careful to understand exactly what is represented by the reported numbers. This is especially true for financial statements prepared primarily for tax purposes. Estimates such as returns and discounts can't be deducted when calculating taxable income, so a preparer might not include these estimates in the financial statements. For tax purposes, an allowance for uncollectible amounts can be deducted.

Accounting for Uncollectible Receivables

LO 5

One cost of doing business on credit is that some customers don't pay what they owe. This cost must be accounted for. Accounting for uncollectible receivables must address two effects. First, an expense must be recorded to reflect the cost of amounts not collected. Second, accounts receivable must be decreased by the estimated uncollected amount so the balance sheet reflects the amount that will be collected.

The easiest way to account for uncollectible receivables, or bad debts, is to simply write off the receivable when it becomes clear that a customer won't be paying. In this approach, known as the **direct writeoff method**, an amount owing from a customer is removed from the list of receivables and an expense recorded when management decides it won't be collected. The journal entry would be

Dr. Bad debt expense (expense +, owners' equity −)	xxx	
Cr. Accounts receivables (assets −)		xxx

For example, in September 2015, the management of Killowen Inc. (Killowen) decided that $10,000 owed to it by Fredericton Ltd. wouldn't be paid. The amount had been in dispute for 18 months and management decided that pursuing the matter further wasn't worthwhile. Killowen has a December 31 year-end. If Killowen used the direct writeoff method, it would make the following journal entry in September 2015, when management decided the $10,000 wouldn't be collected:

Dr. Bad debt expense (expense +, owners' equity −)	10,000	
Cr. Accounts receivable (assets −)		10,000
To write off an uncollectible account receivable		

The direct writeoff method is simple and straightforward, but it isn't good matching. In the example, the bad debt expense would be recognized over 18 months after the sale had occurred. Matching requires the cost of bad debts to be expensed in the period when the related revenue is recognized. In other words, if Killowen is using accrual accounting it shouldn't wait until it decides a customer isn't going to pay. Another problem with the direct writeoff method is that it's easily manipulated because management can choose when to write off accounts receivable.

If we are going to expense bad debts in the period in which the related revenue is recognized, an obvious question is, "How do we know which accounts to write off?" Answer: We don't know. If we knew at the time of the transaction that a customer wasn't going to pay, we wouldn't have offered them credit. Under accrual accounting, an estimate of the amount that won't be collected is made without knowing which specific receivables won't be collected.

There are two methods used to estimate the cost of bad debts:

1. the percentage-of-receivables method
2. the percentage-of-credit-sales method

TABLE 6.2 Killowen Inc.: Selected Accounts Receivable

Killowen Inc. Accounts Receivable Ledger December 31, 2018	
Customer	**Account balance**
Charlottetown Inc.	$ 31,200.05
Dartmouth Ltd.	157,000.10
Fredericton Ltd.	25,000.92
Gander Inc.	38,500.68
Moncton Ltd.	22,250.25
Saint John Inc.	117,410.41
St. John's Ltd.	57,200.09
Ending accounts receivable	$1,194,000.00

With either method, the following adjusting journal entry is made each period to account for bad debts:

Dr. Bad debt expense (expense +, owners' equity −)	XXX	
Cr. Allowance for uncollectible accounts (contra-asset +)		XXX

The bad debt expense is a cost of selling on credit. The **allowance for uncollectible accounts** is a contra-asset account to accounts receivable representing the amount of receivables management estimates won't be collected. A contra-asset account is used because it's impossible to identify the specific receivables that won't be collected when the estimate is made. The accounts receivable account is a listing of the amount owed by each customer. An extract from the detailed list for Killowen Inc. is presented in Table 6.2. Taken together, accounts receivable and allowance for uncollectible accounts provide an estimate of the NRV of accounts receivable.

The Percentage-of-Receivables Method With the **percentage-of-receivables method**, managers estimate at the end of the period the amount of receivables that won't be collected. The managers determine the amount that should be in the allowance for uncollectibles account at the end of the period and the amount of debit or credit needed to bring the allowance account to the desired balance. The focus is on estimating the NRV of the ending balance of receivables. The bad debt expense isn't calculated directly—it's simply "the other side of the journal entry" required to adjust the allowance account.

For example, Killowen Inc.'s management estimates that $71,500 of its ending accounts receivable of $1,194,000 on December 31, 2018, won't be collected. The balance in the allowance account before the end-of-period adjusting entry is recorded is a credit of $5,000. (The reason why there might be a balance in the allowance account before the adjusting entry is made will be made clear shortly.) To bring the allowance account to the desired credit balance of $71,500, a credit of $66,500 is required. The following journal entry is recorded:

Dr. Bad debt expense (expense +, owners' equity −)	66,500	
Cr. Allowance for uncollectible accounts (contra-asset +)		66,500
To record the bad debt expense for 2018		

This focus on calculating the balance in the allowance account is why the percentage-of-receivables method is called a *balance sheet approach*. The effect on the accounts involved can be seen in Table 6.3.

TABLE 6.3 Killowen Inc.: Accounts Receivable, Allowance for Uncollectible Accounts, and Bad Debt Expense

Killowen Inc. December 31, 2018			
	Accounts receivable	**Allowance for uncollectible accounts**	**Bad debt expense**
Balances on December 31, 2018, before adjusting entry	$1,194,000	$ (5,000)	$
Adjusting entry		(66,500)	$66,500
Ending balances on December 31, 2018	$1,194,000	$(71,500)	$66,500

The NRV of Killowen's accounts receivable is $1,122,500 ($1,194,000 − $71,500). There is a balance in the allowance account before the adjusting entry is made on December 31, 2018 because management's estimate of the amount of receivables it wouldn't collect during 2018 wasn't correct—the estimate, which was made on December 31, 2017, was $5,000 too high. This isn't surprising. An estimate is a prediction of the future and it's unlikely to be exact. When the adjusting entry is made, management is making an educated guess about the amount of receivables that won't be collected. The actual amount will only be known long after the period ends. As we will see later in this chapter, managers can use estimates as a way of managing financial statement numbers to achieve their reporting objectives.

How does management estimate the amount of receivables that won't be collected? One way is to use an **aging schedule**—a technique that estimates uncollectible accounts receivable based on the length of time they have been unpaid. Current receivables are those that are due within the period the entity allows customers to pay. If the entity allows customers to pay within 30 days, receivables that have been outstanding for 30 days or less are current. The remaining receivables are then classified by how long overdue they are.

Management uses historical information about the proportion of each category of receivables that hasn't been collected in the past, along with current knowledge of factors that might cause those historical percentages to change, to estimate the amount of current accounts receivable that won't be collected. Typically, the older a receivable is, the less likely it is to be collected. Note that historical information might be helpful for making a prediction but you can't assume that the future will be the same as the past. Circumstances such as an economic slowdown or a change in the credit terms an entity offers can weaken the relationship between the past and the future. If important information isn't considered in the estimate, it will be less accurate. An aging schedule for Killowen is shown in Table 6.4.

Based on the aging schedule, Killowen would report gross accounts receivable of $1,194,000, less an allowance for uncollectible accounts of $71,500. Information about bad debts and uncollectible accounts receivable can be used by stakeholders to assess the efficiency and effectiveness of an

TABLE 6.4 Killowen Inc.: Aging Schedule

Killowen Inc. Aging Schedule December 31, 2018					
	Current	**1 to 30 days overdue**	**31 to 90 days overdue**	**Over 90 days overdue**	**Total**
Amount	$950,000	$125,000	$72,000	$47,000	$1,194,000
Percentage estimated to be uncollectible	1%	4%	40%	60%	
Amount estimated to be uncollectible	$ 9,500	$ 5,000	$28,800	$28,200	$ 71,500

entity's credit and collection policies as well as the valuation of the receivables. Companies following IFRS must disclose all changes to the allowance account during the year, so stakeholders can understand the estimates being made.

The aging schedule isn't only an internal device for calculating uncollectible receivables. Banks will usually require this schedule if the receivables are security for a loan and/or the maximum amount to be borrowed is a percentage of receivables. Banks usually won't accept older receivables as security because they have a high risk of being uncollectible.

KNOWLEDGE CHECK 6.4

You have been given the following list of aged accounts receivable for Onward Inc. (Onward) on December 31, 2017:

Current	$175,000
1–30 days overdue	32,000
31–60 days overdue	12,500
61–90 days overdue	5,700
Over 90 days overdue	2,300

Onward's management estimates that it will collect 98 percent of the current accounts receivable, 94 percent of the receivables 1–30 days overdue, 80 percent of those 31–60 days overdue, 65 percent of those 61–90 days overdue, and 30 percent those more than 90 days overdue. Onward uses the percentage-of-receivables method for estimating bad debts. There is a credit balance of $1,025 in allowance for uncollectible accounts on December 31, 2017 before the adjusting entry is made.

Required:

- ❑ How much of each category of accounts receivable does Onward not expect to collect?
- ❑ Prepare the journal entry that Onward should make on December 31, 2017 to record the bad debt expense.

Percentage-of-Credit-Sales Method Managers can estimate the bad debt expense by using a percentage of credit sales recognized in the period. This is called the **percentage-of-credit-sales method.** The logic is that some portion of credit sales won't be collected in each period, and that amount is the bad debt expense. Cash sales aren't considered because, of course, they are 100 percent collected. Again, management bases its estimate on the historical collection rate of credit sales and knowledge of any changes that might cause it to change. If Killowen had credit sales of $9,375,000 during 2018 and management estimated that 0.8 percent wouldn't be collected, the adjusting journal entry on December 31, 2018 would be

Dr. Bad debt expense (expenses +, owners' equity −)	75,000	
Cr. Allowance for uncollectible accounts (contra-asset +)		75,000
To record the bad debt expense for 2018		

Unlike the percentage-of-receivables method, which takes a balance sheet approach, the percentage-of-credit-sales method follows an *income statement approach*. It determines the bad debt expense, an income statement account. The credit to the allowance account isn't calculated directly. This method gives a better matching of costs and benefits because the amount expensed is directly related to the amount of credit sales recognized in the period. Because this method focuses on the income statement, the estimate of the NRV of accounts receivable may not be as accurate as with the percentage-of-receivables approach.

In any year, the estimated bad debts probably won't equal the actual amount of uncollected receivables—that's the nature of estimates. However, the annual bad debt estimate may sometimes be consistently too high or too low; that is, the percentage of credit sales used doesn't reflect the actual amount of bad debts incurred each year. Management may not be changing or be aware of the need to change the assumptions for estimating bad debts in response to a change in the environment. If the bad debt expense is consistently too high, a credit balance builds up in the allowance account and net accounts receivable will be understated (the amount reported will be lower than what is likely to be collected). The opposite is true if the bad debt expense is consistently too low. Eventually, an adjusting entry will be needed to put the allowance account in line with the actual economic situation.

Writing Off Receivables We have examined methods for estimating uncollectible amounts. But what happens when we finally know who isn't going to pay? For both estimation methods, the receivable is removed from the receivables listing when a specific item is identified as being uncollectible. A credit to accounts receivable reduces the balance in the account. The allowance account is reduced by a debit because the specific uncollectible account identified is now a reality instead of an estimate, and the amount is transferred from the "estimate account" (allowance) to the "actual account" (receivables).

LO 5

When Killowen Inc.'s management decides the $10,000 owing from Fredericton Ltd. isn't going to be collected, it would make the following entry:

Dr. Allowance for uncollectible accounts (contra-asset −)	10,000	
Cr. Accounts receivable—Fredericton (asset −)		10,000
To write off a $10,000 account receivable from Fredericton Ltd.		

This entry writes off, or removes from the accounting records, the account receivable from Fredericton Ltd. If we examined the accounts receivable ledger in Table 6.2 after the writeoff, we would find that Fredericton's amount owing is $15,000.92 instead of $25,000.92. A writeoff has no effect on the net amount of accounts receivable (accounts receivable − allowance for uncollectibles). This can be seen by comparing Killowen's receivables before and after the writeoff of the $10,000 owed by Fredericton. The comparison is shown in Table 6.5. The allowance and accounts receivable both decrease by $10,000, but net accounts receivable remains the same.

Recognize that writing off an account receivable has no effect on the income statement. The income statement effect occurs when the adjusting entry to record the bad debt expense and the adjustment to allowance for uncollectible accounts is made.

If at a later time, Fredericton paid the $10,000 that had been written off, the journal entry would be reversed, reinstating the receivable and the allowance. The receivable would then be recorded as collected.

Comparison of the Methods We've looked at three methods of accounting for uncollectible amounts—direct writeoff, percentage-of-receivables, and percentage-of-credit sales. Under accrual accounting, the direct writeoff method isn't acceptable because it doesn't match expenses to revenues. The two estimation methods are used in practice and both provide a bad debt expense and report accounts receivable at NRV. These methods require management judgment to determine the amount of the bad debt expense, the balance in the allowance account, and the decision to write off a specific account receivable. This need for judgment makes estimating bad debts a tool managers can use to "manage the numbers" in the financial statements.

Returns and Discounts Accounts receivable should also be adjusted for estimated returns (goods sold but expected to be returned by customers) and discounts (reductions in the payment if the amount owing is paid promptly).

LO 6

Customers are often allowed to return goods purchased. Merchandise that is returned is like a sale that didn't happen. Thus, adjustments are needed so revenue and accounts receivable aren't overstated (too high). (The impact on inventory and cost of goods sold would also be reversed.)

TABLE 6.5 Killowen Inc.: Accounts Receivable before and after Writeoff

	Before writeoff	After writeoff
Accounts receivable	$1,194,000	$1,184,000
Less: Allowance for uncollectible accounts	71,500	61,500
Accounts receivable, net	$1,122,500	$1,122,500

The accounting is similar to what's done for uncollectibles. Estimated returns are credited to a contra-asset account called allowance for sales returns and debited to a contra-revenue account. Unlike uncollectibles, returns aren't reported as expenses but are netted against revenue (accumulated in contra-revenue accounts).

If Killowen estimated that there should be $30,000 in its allowance for sales returns account on December 31, 2018 (meaning it expected $30,000 of the sales in accounts receivable to be returned), it would record the following journal entry:

Dr. Sales returns (contra-revenue +)	30,000	
Cr. Allowance for sales returns (contra asset +)		30,000
To record estimate sales returns		

When a customer returned merchandise, Killowen would debit the allowance account and credit accounts receivable. Note that estimated refunds on cash sales are debited to sales returns and credited to accrued liabilities.

Accounting for discounts is essentially the same. At the end of a period, management estimates the amount of discount that would be given on the receivables outstanding. Suppose Killowen gives its customers a 2 percent discount if they pay within 10 days of receiving an invoice. At the end of 2018, Killowen has $1,194,000 in receivables outstanding and management estimates that 60 percent of these will pay within 10 days and receive the 2 percent discounts. Therefore, Killowen would require a balance of $14,328 ($1,194,000 × 0.6 × 0.02). If the balance in the allowance account before making the journal entry was zero, Killowen would record the following entry:

Dr. Sales discounts (contra-revenue +)	14,328	
Cr. Allowance for sales discounts (contra asset +)		14,328
To record estimate sales discounts		

LO 5, 6

In Sum Revenue reported on the income statement is normally shown after estimated returns and discounts have been deducted, so a stakeholder doesn't see the amount of returns and discounts (which could be useful information). If estimated sales returns and discounts aren't recorded, accounts receivable and revenue will be overstated. On Killowen's December 31, 2018 financial statements, gross sales would be reduced by $44,328 ($30,000 for returns and $14,328 for discounts) and accounts receivable would be adjusted as follows:

Accounts receivable	$1,194,000
Less: Allowance for uncollectible accounts	71,500
Less: Allowance for sales returns	30,000
Less: Allowance for discounts	14,328
Accounts receivable, net	$1,078,172

LO 7

Long-Term Receivables

Receivables aren't always current assets. Amounts owing from customers or others can be due in more than one year or operating cycle. When payment isn't due for a long time, or if it's spread out over a long period, then the time value of money becomes a consideration. If interest isn't being paid on the long-term receivable or if the interest rate charged is below the market rate, the amount of revenue recognized and the receivable will be too high if the time value of money is ignored.

Let's look at an example. On December 31, 2017, Winnipeg Inc. (Winnipeg) sold goods to Regina Ltd. (Regina) for $200,000. Because of Regina's financial difficulties, Winnipeg agreed to accept payment in full in two years, on January 2, 2020. Regina isn't required to pay interest. Regina's owners have personally guaranteed the debt, so Winnipeg is confident that it will receive its money, and recognized the revenue when the goods were shipped.

How much revenue should Winnipeg recognize when the goods are shipped and how should it account for the receivable? Clearly, Winnipeg hasn't earned $200,000 because the present value of the money it will receive in two years is less than $200,000. Assuming a discount rate of 8 percent we can calculate the present value of $200,000 to be received in two years:

$$PV_{n,r} = \frac{1}{(1+r)^n} \times \text{Amount to be received or paid}$$

$$PV_{2,0.08} = \frac{1}{(1+0.08)^2} \times \$200{,}00$$

$$= \$171{,}468$$

If we consider the time value of money, Winnipeg should recognize $171,468 of revenue in 2017 for the sale to Regina. The journal entry Winnipeg would make in 2017 is

Dr. Long-term receivable (asset +)	171,468	
Cr. Revenue (revenue +, shareholders' equity +)		171,468
To record the sale of goods to Regina Ltd.		

You're probably wondering how we can record a receivable for $171,468 when Winnipeg will be receiving $200,000 in 2020. The difference between the amount Winnipeg recognizes as revenue in 2017 and the cash it will receive in January 2020 is interest. Even though Winnipeg and Regina agreed that there wouldn't be any interest in their deal, accountants would argue that the interest is really there but hidden. So, from an accountant's perspective, there is a sale for $171,468 and $28,532 in interest ($200,000 − $171,468). Over the two-year period, Winnipeg will recognize interest revenue and increase the long-term receivable by the amount of the interest revenue. Winnipeg's journal entry each year would be

Dr. Long-term receivable (asset +)	XXX	
Cr. Interest revenue (revenue +, shareholders' equity +)		XXX
To accrue interest revenue on the long-term receivable from Regina Ltd.		

The effects on the accounts involved in the sale to Regina are shown in Table 6.6.

When the time value of money is considered, the sale to Regina is equivalent to selling the goods for $171,468 cash on the transaction date and then earning $28,532 in interest by financing the sale. Over the two years, $200,000 of revenue is recognized, but the timing and type of revenue changes. Table 6.6 shows that Winnipeg recognizes interest revenue each year, but because it won't be paid until 2020 the amount accrued each year is added to the long-term receivable. Winnipeg's December 31, 2019 balance sheet reports a $200,000 receivable, the amount Regina originally agreed to pay. The amount is classified as a current asset because it's then due within one year.

If Regina was paying interest at the market rate, it would be unnecessary to discount the cash flow. The revenue and receivable would be set up at $200,000 in 2017 and the interest revenue of $16,000 ($200,000 × 8%) would be recorded each year.

Financial Statement Presentation

LO 5, 6

Let's look at an example that reflects some of the concepts covered in the discussion of receivables. Exhibit 6.2 provides extracts from the management discussion and analysis and financial statements from Supremex Inc.'s (Supremex) 2011 annual report. Supremex is Canada's leading manufacturer and marketer of stock and customer envelopes and related products. The company has nine manufacturing facilities in seven provinces.[2] Note the following in the exhibit:

❶ This paragraph explains the credit risk faced by Supremex because of its receivables. It explains the steps the company takes to mitigate the risk of non collection.

❷ Supremex's balance sheet reports $18,740,499 in accounts receivable. Note 6, item ❺, shows that this isn't exclusively amounts owing from customers.

❸ The revenue recognition note explains that revenues are shown net of estimated returns and discounts.

TABLE 6.6 Winnipeg Inc.: Long-Term Receivables

Winnipeg Inc. Partial Spreadsheet							
	Cash	Current accounts receivable	Long-term receivable	Revenue	Interest revenue	Journal entry	
December 31, 2017 (transactional entry)			171,468	171,468		Dr. Long-term receivable 171,468 Cr. Revenue 171,468	Recognition of revenue on sale of goods to Regina Ltd.
Ending balance sheet December 31, 2017			**171,468**				
December 31, 2018 (adjusting entry)			13,717		13,717	Dr. Long-term receivables 13,717 Cr. Interest revenue 13,717	Recognition of interest revenue earned in 2018. Interest is calculated based on the receivable on December 31, 2017. The interest is added to the long-term receivable account. Interest earned = $171,468 × 0.08. Amounts are rounded to the nearest dollar.
Ending balance sheet December 31, 2018			185,185				
December 31, 2019 (adjusting entry)			14,815		14,815	Dr. Long-term receivables 14,815 Cr. Interest revenue 14,815	Recognition of interest revenue earned in 2019. Interest earned = $185,185 × 0.08.
December 31, 2019 (adjusting entry)		200,000	(200,000)			Dr. Accounts receivable 200,000 Cr. Long-term receivable 200,000	To reclassify the receivable as current.
Ending balance sheet December 31, 2019		**200,000**					
January 2, 2020	200,000	(200,000)				Dr. Cash 200,000 Cr. Accounts receivable 200,000	Collection of the $200,000 from Regina Ltd.

❹ Shows the gross and net amount of trade receivables (the amounts due from customers) and the allowance for doubtful accounts.

❺ Shows that some of the accounts receivable reported on the balance sheet aren't due from customers (trade receivables). These could be due from shareholders, employees, or something else.

❻ Describes the credit terms Supremex offers its customers. This is important information for assessing how effective the company's collection process is.

❼ Supremex's aging schedule.

❽ Reconciliation for the opening and closing balances in allowance for doubtful accounts. This information is important for assessing the effectiveness of the company's credit policies and changes that have taken place in the ability of the company to collect amounts owing. The "charge for the period" is the bad debt expense and "utilized" is the amount written off during the period.

❾ Explains the company's credit risk with respect to its accounts receivable.

EXHIBIT 6.2 **Extracts from Supremex Inc.'s 2011 Management Discussion and Analysis and Financial Statements**

MANAGEMENT'S DISCUSSION AND ANALYSIS OF FINANCIAL CONDITION AND RESULTS OF OPERATIONS FOR THE THREE- AND TWELVE-MONTH PERIODS ENDED DECEMBER 31, 2011

Credit

The Company is exposed to credit risk with respect to trade receivables. To mitigate this risk, the Company analyzes and reviews the financial health of its current customers on an ongoing basis. A specific credit limit is established for each customer and reviewed periodically by the Company. Supremex is protected against any concentration of credit risk through its clientele and geographic diversity. ❶ No single customer accounts for more than 10% of consolidated accounts receivable. Supremex's customer base is solidly diversified and consists mainly of large national customers, such as large Canadian corporations, nationwide resellers and governmental bodies, as well as paper merchants and solution and process providers. Historically, the level of bad debt has been low given the nature of the customers. As at December 31, 2011, the maximum credit risk exposure for receivables corresponds to their carrying value.

Supremex Inc.

CONSOLIDATED STATEMENTS OF FINANCIAL POSITION

As at	**Notes**	**December 31, 2011 $**	**December 31, 2010 $**	**January 1, 2010 $**
ASSETS	**15**			
Current assets				
Cash		**2,606,332**	148,874	38,962
❷ Accounts receivable	**6**	**18,740,499**	19,595,945	21,092,867
Inventories	**7**	**13,103,192**	11,939,720	13,921,726
Prepaid expenses		**512,584**	425,193	1,429,144
Assets held for sale	**8**	—	5,568,000	—
Total current assets		**34,962,607**	37,677,732	36,482,699
Assets held for sale	**8**	—	348,048	—
Property, plant and equipment	**9**	**29,528,673**	30,449,945	40,056,241
Intangible assets	**10**	**26,599,029**	32,762,929	38,926,829
Goodwill	**11**	**75,751,125**	75,751,125	75,501,125
Total assets		**166,841,434**	176,989,779	190,966,894
LIABILITIES AND EQUITY				
Current liabilities				
Accounts payable and accrued liabilities	**12**	**19,990,280**	20,111,812	18,534,512
Provisions	**13**	**656,567**	931,297	795,018
Income tax payable		**3,490,996**	745,683	—
Distribution payable	**14**	—	292,978	1,464,888
Current portion of secured credit facilities	**15**	**5,000,000**	14,415,489	7,500,000
Current portion of derivative financial liability		—	—	808,652
Total current liabilities		**29,137,843**	36,497,259	29,103,070
Secured credit facilities	**15**	**49,176,934**	54,654,387	84,379,377
Deferred income tax liabilities	**16**	**2,182,392**	7,376,780	5,665,294
Accrued pension benefit liability	**17**	**19,251,100**	6,984,300	5,487,500
Other post-retirement benefit obligations	**17**	**649,600**	648,300	657,000
Derivative financial liability	**15**	**1,776,293**	—	—

EXHIBIT 6.2 (continued) Extracts from Supremex Inc.'s 2011 Management Discussion and Analysis and Financial Statements

As at	Notes	December 31, 2011 $	December 31, 2010 $	January 1, 2010 $
Equity				
Share capital	18	**10,000,000**	—	—
Fund units	18	—	282,798,322	282,798,322
Contributed surplus		**280,423,746**	7,625,424	7,625,424
Deferred compensation		—	—	(315,079)
Deficit		**(225,680,313)**	(219,511,314)	(224,364,863)
Accumulated other comprehensive loss	19	**(76,161)**	(83,679)	(69,151)
Total equity		**64,667,272**	70,828,753	65,674,653
Total liabilities and equity		**166,841,434**	176,989,779	190,966,894

2. SIGNIFICANT ACCOUNTING POLICIES

Revenue recognition

❸ Revenue is measured at the fair value of the consideration received or receivable, net of estimated returns and discounts, and after eliminating intercompany sales.

Revenue from the sale of goods is recognized when the following criteria are met:

- The risks and rewards of ownership, including managerial involvement, have been transferred to the buyer;
- The amount of revenue can be measured reliably;
- The receipt of economic benefits is probable; and
- Costs incurred or to be incurred can be measured reliably.

6. ACCOUNTS RECEIVABLE

	December 31, 2011 $	December 31, 2010 $	January 1, 2010 $
❹ Trade receivables	**17,727,394**	18,439,189	19,694,737
❹ Less: Allowance for doubtful accounts	**(237,360)**	(62,714)	(45,353)
❹ Trade receivable—net	**17,490,034**	18,376,475	19,649,384
❺ Other receivables	**1,250,465**	1,219,470	1,443,483
	18,740,499	19,595,945	21,092,867

❻ Trade receivables are non-interest bearing and are generally on 30–60 days terms.

❼ The aging analysis of trade receivables at each reporting date was as follows:

	December 31, 2011 $	December 31, 2010 $	January 1, 2010 $
Current	**11,990,422**	12,724,734	13,603,619
31–60 days	**4,411,804**	4,083,148	4,973,185
61–90 days	**910,264**	1,277,228	979,059
91–120 days	**203,123**	298,281	115,850
Over 120 days	**211,781**	55,798	23,024
	17,727,394	18,439,189	19,694,737

EXHIBIT 6.2 **(continued) Extracts from Supremex Inc.'s 2011 Management Discussion and Analysis and Financial Statements**

❽ **Allowance for doubtful accounts**

The changes in the allowance for doubtful accounts were as follows:

	December 31, 2011 $	December 31, 2010 $
Balance, beginning of year	62,714	45,353
Charge for the year	235,527	108,245
Pioneer acquisition [note 5]	—	19,271
Utilized	(61,109)	(109,981)
Impact of foreign exchange gains (losses)	228	(174)
Balance, end of year	237,360	62,714

❾ The Company is exposed to normal credit risk with respect to its accounts receivable and maintains provisions for potential credit losses. Potential for such losses is mitigated because there is no significant exposure to any single customer and because customer credit worthiness is evaluated before credit is extended.

FINANCIAL STATEMENT ANALYSIS ISSUES

LO 8, 9

Earnings Management—Hidden Reserves

LO 8

In principle, errors in estimates aren't a major concern. Predicting the future is difficult, so no one should expect management to get the estimates "right" each time (or anytime, for that matter). But if managers' errors are biased—that is, always higher or always lower than the actual amount—then amounts in the financial statements can be significantly misstated. Making biased estimates (intentional "errors") allows managers to manage earnings.

Hidden reserves are undisclosed accounting choices by which managers can manage earnings and other financial information with the intention of satisfying their self-interests. Using hidden reserves is an abuse of accounting information; it undermines the usefulness and credibility of financial statements. While hidden reserves are inappropriate, the suspected use of them makes it important for stakeholders to understand them. A simple example will show how management can manage earnings by using accounting estimates to move profits from one period to another through the allowance for uncollectible accounts and bad debt expense.

In 2017, Discovery Ltd. (Discovery), a public company, enjoyed its most successful year ever. Its performance exceeded the expectations of management, investors, and stock market watchers. Sales in 2017 were $50,000,000 and net income should have been $3,000,000. However, in late 2017, managers realized that 2018 would be less successful and they feared that the poorer performance in 2018 would have a negative effect on Discovery's stock price and the managers' bonuses.

For its December 31, 2017 financial statements, Discovery's management increased the allowance for uncollectible accounts to 4.5 percent of the ending balance of accounts receivable from the 3 percent it had used in the past, which had proven to be a reasonable estimate. Management justified the change by arguing it was concerned about the collectability of a number of receivables, so a more cautious allowance was appropriate. Because accounting estimates can be very difficult for auditors to verify, you have a situation that managers can use to their advantage. By increasing the percentage-of-receivables that was expected to be uncollectible, Discovery increased its bad debt expense in 2017 from $405,000 to $607,500 and decreased net income by $202,500.

TABLE 6.7 Discovery Ltd.: Extracts from Financial Statements

Discovery Limited Extracts from the December 31, 2017 and 2018 Financial Statements (in thousands)				
	No hidden reserves		Using hidden reserves	
	2017	2018	2017	2018
Revenue	$50,000	$47,000	$50,000	$47,000
Expenses (except bad debts)	46,595	43,800	46,595	43,800
Bad debt expense	405	397.5	607.5	195
Net income	$ 3,000	$ 2,802.5	$ 2,797.5	$ 3,005
Accounts receivable	$13,500	$13,250	$13,500	$13,250
Allowance for uncollectible accounts	405	397.5	607.5	397.5

As expected, in 2018 Discovery's performance wasn't as strong as in 2017. Sales declined to $47,000,000. During 2018, $405,000 of accounts receivable were written off (which turned out to be 3 percent of the December 31, 2017 accounts receivable). At the end of 2018, management decided that the receivables it was "concerned" about a year earlier were no longer a problem and, accordingly, Discovery would return to its usual 3 percent estimate. Because only $405,000 of accounts receivable had to be written off during 2018, there was a credit balance of $202,500 in the allowance account before the 2018 adjusting entry. For the allowance account to have the desired balance of $397,500 at the end of 2018 (representing 3 percent of the 2018 year-end accounts receivable—$13,250,000 × 0.03), it needed to be increased (credited) by $195,000, making the bad debt expense for 2018 only $195,000.

Table 6.7 shows income statements and accounts receivable information comparing when Discovery creates a hidden reserve and when it doesn't. By using a hidden reserve, Discovery is able to report a profit increase of $207,500 ($3,005,000 − $2,797,500) from 2017 to 2018, an increase of over 7 percent instead of a decrease of $197,500 ($2,802,500 − $3,000,000), and a positive earnings trend rather than a negative one. Note that total income over the two years is the same under either scenario but by altering the allowance for uncollectible accounts, Discovery is able to shift income from 2017 to 2018.

This example is set up to make the problem, motivation, and effect of the uncertainty of accounting estimates transparent. It allows you to see how management can use the uncertainties to achieve its reporting objectives. In reality, it's hard to see these hidden choices so it's difficult to know anything unusual is occurring. This is why these types of manipulations are called hidden reserves.

You might be wondering how managers can get away with behaviour that is clearly unethical, violates the spirit of fair presentation of the financial statements, and, as a result, is inconsistent with IFRS. One reason is that it can be difficult to evaluate the reasonableness of estimates. As long as an estimate falls within a reasonable range and managers can provide a satisfactory explanation for it, a change can be difficult to quarrel with. After all, management knows the entity best so is best able to make estimates, and is responsible for the financial statements. Additional disclosures of estimates (e.g., the reconciliation of changes to the allowance account provided by Supremex in Exhibit 6.2) are very helpful.

It's important to emphasize that the problem shown in the example isn't that the estimate of uncollectibles changed. The problem is with the motivation for the change. For financial statement information to be useful it must reflect current economic circumstances. If there is legitimate concern about the collectability of receivables, then increasing the allowance for uncollectibles is appropriate. Unfortunately, it's difficult to tell whether management is providing information or satisfying its self-interests.

INSIGHT

Hidden Reserves

Are hidden reserves a real problem? Back in the late 1990s, Arthur Levitt, then chairman of the U.S. Securities and Exchange Commission, commented on the problems with financial reporting by saying, "Companies stash accruals in 'cookie jar' reserves during the good economic times and reach into them when necessary in the bad times."[3]

Mr. Levitt's comments highlight the problem of entities using the flexibility available in accounting standards to manage the information reported in their financial statements. While many years have passed since Mr. Levitt made his comment, examples continue to arise of managers using hidden reserves to manage the earnings of their companies. The hidden reserve is a problem all stakeholders should be aware of.

The allowance for the uncollectible accounts estimate is only one of many available to management for creating hidden reserves. Estimates for sales returns and warranty liabilities can also be used. The use of hidden reserves isn't limited to public companies. Managers of private companies might also want to have a "rainy day" fund.

Current and Quick Ratios

LO 9

In this chapter we have examined two of an entity's most liquid assets—cash and receivables. We will discuss one other liquid asset, investments in shares and debt of other companies, in Chapter 11. In Chapter 2, I introduced the current ratio, an indicator of whether an entity had adequate resources to meet its current obligations. A problem with the current ratio is that all current assets (which are included in the numerator) may not be liquid.

I'll use the information about Supremex Inc. in Exhibit 6.2 for this discussion. Among Supremex's December 31, 2011 current assets are $13,103,192 of inventory and $512,584 of prepaid expenses. Inventory often converts to cash relatively slowly (look back at the discussion of the cash lag in Chapter 5), calling into question whether inventory is truly a liquid asset. While some inventory can be sold quickly and considered liquid (for example gold and silver), in many cases it isn't very liquid. Prepaid expenses, for instance, include amounts paid in advance for insurance, rent, or services to be received, represent cash already spent so they won't be converted to cash in the ordinary course of business.

To compensate for these not so liquid current assets, the **quick** or **acid test** ratio provides a stricter test of liquidity. It's stricter because it excludes the less liquid assets. The quick or acid test ratio is defined as

$$\text{Quick ratio} = \frac{\text{Quick assets}}{\text{Current liabilities}} = \frac{\text{Cash} + \text{Cash equivalents} + \text{Marketable securities} + \text{Receivables}}{\text{Current liabilities}}$$

Quick assets are assets that are cash or can be realized in cash fairly quickly. Marketable securities are investments such as shares and debt of public companies (particularly investments in public companies). Supremex's quick ratio for 2011 is

$$\text{Quick ratio} = \frac{\$2{,}606{,}332 + \$18{,}740{,}499}{\$29{,}137{,}843}$$
$$= 0.73$$

The ratio means that for every dollar of current liabilities, Supremex has $0.73 of quick assets. Assessing whether this is a reasonable ratio involves comparison. Supremex's quick and current ratios for 2007 through 2011, along with the ratios for two other packaging companies, are provided in Table 6.8.

Both Supremex's current and quick ratios show a declining trend over the five years. The low point for both was 2010, with improvement in 2011. However, both ratios are much lower than in

TABLE 6.8 Supremex Inc. and Comparable Firms, 2007–2011: Current and Quick Ratios

	Current ratio					Quick ratio				
	2011	2010	2009	2008	2007	2011	2010	2009	2008	2007
Supremex	1.20	1.03	1.25	1.62	1.94	0.73	0.54	0.73	0.98	1.20
CCL Industries Inc.	1.66	1.39	1.49	1.47	1.60	1.30	1.09	1.17	1.15	1.31
Winpak Ltd.	4.44	4.56	4.09	4.43	3.32	3.21	3.11	2.63	2.35	1.33

2007. The ratios of the two competitors are much stronger than Supremex's. Of course, current and quick ratios are only two indicators of liquidity. Others, such as the ability to generate cash from operations, should be considered as well.

Quick ratios less than one aren't unusual. Entities that have a lot of inventory often have quick ratios that are less than one because the numerator excludes the inventory but the denominator includes any obligations associated with the inventory.

It's important to recognize that "normal" ratios will vary from industry to industry. If you examine the ratios of firms in different industries, you'll find wide variation in ratios across industries and variation over time within industries. When selecting benchmarks, it's important to choose an appropriate one for the analysis you're undertaking.

LO 9

Accounts Receivable Turnover Ratio

An important responsibility of management is to effectively manage the entity's credit program. The **accounts receivable turnover ratio** is useful for assessing information about an entity's liquidity and how well credit is managed. The ratio is defined as

$$\text{Accounts receivables turnover ratio} = \frac{\text{Credit sales}}{\text{Average accounts receivable}}$$

For receivables, *turnover* means the number of times in a period they are incurred and collected. An accounts receivable turnover ratio of eight means the entity incurs and collects receivables eight times a year. Since credit sales typically aren't reported, total sales are used instead. The ratio provides information on how quickly the entity collects its receivables. It therefore provides insight on both liquidity and on management's handling of its stewardship responsibilities over its credit program. The higher the ratio, the more quickly cash is being collected from customers (thereby shortening the cash lag). Average accounts receivable is calculated by adding the balances in the accounts receivable account at the beginning and end of the year and dividing by two.

A more intuitive measure can be obtained by dividing the accounts receivable turnover ratio into 365 to give the **average collection period of accounts receivable**—the number of days, on average, it takes to collect receivables. The ratio is defined as

$$\text{Average collection period of accounts receivable} = \frac{365}{\text{Accounts receivable turnover ratio}}$$

Table 6.9 shows the accounts receivable turnover ratio and the average collection period of accounts receivable for Supremex for 2007 to 2011.

Table 6.9 shows that Supremex's accounts receivable turnover ratio has been stable over the last three years, but there is a definite downward trend over the five-year period. The stability over the last three years suggests that management is in control of receivables. From ❻ in Exhibit 6.2, we find that Supremex offers customers 30–60-day payment terms and the average collection period is in the middle of that range, which also suggests good control of receivables. Notice that sales and receivables declined steadily over the period. So even though receivables seem to be managed well, the business appears to be contracting. This being the case, the decreasing turnover ratios could be reflecting easier credit terms being offered to customers or credit being offered to customers with lower credit ratings.

TABLE 6.9 Supremex Inc.: Accounts Receivable Turnover Ratio and Average Collection Period of Accounts Receivable

For the year ended December 31,	Sales	Average accounts receivable	Accounts receivable turnover ratio	Average collection period of accounts receivable (in days)
2011	$143,892,199	$19,168,222	7.51	48.62
2010	153,124,398	20,344,406	7.53	48.49
2009	166,233,035	21,883,802	7.60	48.05
2008	182,552,864	22,562,795	8.09	45.11
2007	187,461,997	22,450,853	8.35	43.71

There are some caveats to using this ratio:

- First, correctly applying the ratio requires credit sales, but most financial statements don't report credit and cash sales separately. For entities with significant cash sales (such as retail businesses), using total sales can make the ratio difficult to interpret, especially if the proportion of cash sales varies.
- Second, if an entity operates in a number of industries or offers different credit terms to different customers, the ratio will be affected by the proportion of sales in each business.
- Third, using the year-end accounts receivables balances to calculate average receivables may not provide a good estimate of the year's average. Ratios of businesses that are highly seasonal will be sensitive to how average receivables is calculated.

Despite these limitations, the accounts receivable turnover ratio is a useful tool for assessing an entity's credit management and liquidity. The limitations may make it difficult to compare different entities but examining an entity's trends may be a reasonable way to apply this tool. Changes in the ratio will raise questions for further investigation but won't likely provide any definitive answers.

Other Issues

LO 9

Further examination of the information in Exhibit 6.2 provides additional insights that can be used to analyze and interpret accounts receivable and the financial statements. The numbers below refer to the numbers in Exhibit 6.2:

❼ Examination of an aging schedule gives insight into the condition of the accounts receivable. A decrease in the proportion of current receivables could mean customers are having financial problems that are affecting their ability to pay or management isn't monitor collections carefully enough. Supremex's aging schedule, restated to show the proportion of each category of receivables as a proportion of total receivables, is shown below.

	December 31, 2011	December 31, 2010	January 1, 2010
Current	67.64%	69.01%	69.07%
31–60 days	24.89%	22.14%	25.25%
61–90 days	5.13%	6.93%	4.97%
91–120 days	1.15%	1.62%	0.59%
Over 120 days	1.19%	0.30%	0.12%
	100.00%	100.00%	100.00%

The table shows that a smaller proportion of year-end receivables are current and that the proportion of receivables that are three months or more overdue has increased over the three balance sheet dates shown. This is consistent with the larger bad debt expense recorded in 2011.

❹ and ❽ Changes in allowance for doubtful accounts can give an indication of problems with collections. An increase in the allowance as a proportion of receivables could be the result of customers' financial problems, relaxation of credit terms (easier credit to attract new customers), poor or weakening controls over collections, or changes in accounting policies. Significant unexplained changes could indicate earnings management. The reconciliation of the opening and closing balance in the allowance account (❽) allows stakeholders to see the source of changes and allows them to compare estimates (charges − bad debt expense) with actual amounts (utilized − writeoffs). Repeated estimation errors in the same direction could indicate earnings management. For Supremex, the charge for 2010 (the expense) is significantly greater than the actual amount utilized (the amount deemed uncollectable and written off) in 2011. The amount expensed in 2011 was more than two times greater than the amount expensed in 2010, even though there are less receivables at the end of 2011. The allowance for doubtful accounts as a proportion of trade receivables increased significantly in 2011 from 2010. This suggests that management is expecting more problems collecting the year-end 2011 receivables than it did for 2010's receivables. This is consistent with the information presented in the aging schedule (❼).

One final red flag to be aware of: It's reasonable to expect accounts receivable to remain a constant proportion of sales. In other words, if sales increase by 10 percent, accounts receivable should increase by the same amount. If managers try to increase sales by offering very attractive credit terms or record highly questionable sales, accounts receivable as a proportion of sales will increase.

Solved Problem

The solved problem in this chapter will build on the problem-solving skills developed in Chapter 4. Some of the issues raised in this and similar questions may have actual rules prescribed by IFRS. However, at this stage, you don't need to be aware of the rules. Instead, apply the principles you have learned to come up with sensible responses to accounting issues. Consider the principles and basic definitions developed in the book so far. When reviewing the problem, keep in mind that the objective is to provide a well-reasoned and well-supported set of recommendations that address the accounting issues faced by the entity in the context of the role you are assigned.

SAVOY HEALTH CLUB LTD.

Fred Irving, the founder, owner, and operator of the Savoy Health Club Ltd. (Savoy or "the club") recently agreed in principle to sell Savoy to Jim Floor. The parties have agreed in principle to a purchase price equal to five times net income for the year ended June 30, 2018. The deal can't be finalized until Jim Floor receives and accepts the June 30, 2018 financial statements. In the event that Jim Floor doesn't accept the financial statements, outstanding accounting issues can be submitted to an independent arbitrator for resolution. Until the agreement in principle was signed, Savoy's financial statements were prepared exclusively for tax purposes. Fred Irving is in the process of finalizing the June 30, 2018 financial statements but he is unsure about how to account for a number of issues.

Fred Irving has hired you to prepare a report explaining appropriate accounting treatments for the issues he is concerned about. Fred wants full explanations and justifications for the recommendations you make so he can explain them to Jim Floor and to the arbitrator, if necessary. Your discussions with Fred Irving provide the following information:

1. People join the club by paying a one-time initiation fee of $600. Provincial legislation requires that health clubs allow members to pay their initiation fees in equal instalments over 12 months, which most new members do. Historically, between 30 percent and 35 percent of people who join the club stop paying their initiation fees sometime during the year.

   In addition, members must pay a monthly fee of $80, either on the first day of each month or as a single payment on the renewal date of their contract, in which case they receive a $160 discount. (Members sign a one-year contract each year.) Approximately 40 percent of members pay in a lump sum at the start of the year. Some members who pay their monthly fees each month stop paying sometime during the year.

2. During 2018, Savoy began selling advertising as an additional source of revenue. Businesses can buy space in various parts of the club for a fee. Advertisers supply the ad and they are posted in the agreed part of the club by Savoy's staff. Invoices are sent to advertisers once an ad is posted. Savoy offers a 3 percent discount if the amount owing is paid within 10 days of the invoice date. At year-end, $8,000 was owed by advertisers, of which $5,000 is still eligible for discounts.
3. Normal maintenance work on some of the athletic equipment has been delayed for the last two months due to scheduling problems with the contractor. The work will cost about $4,000 and is now scheduled for July 2018.
4. The club pays monthly rent of $3,000. Rent is paid six months in advance on October 1 and April 1.
5. Fred Irving has never taken a salary.

Required:

Prepare the report requested by Fred Irving.

Comment: *As you examine this solution, it's important to remember that there is no single right answer. There are many wrong answers, but more than one good answer. Good answers are well supported, consistent, and have the role well played. The answer below is prepared as a report to Fred Irving. Comments on the answer, which aren't part of the report itself but provide some additional explanation, are shown in italics.*

Solution:

Mr. Fred Irving
2334 Piché St.
Bordeaux, Québec

Dear Mr. Irving:

Attached is the report you requested recommending accounting treatments for unresolved items in the financial statements of Savoy Health Club Ltd. In preparing this report, I have attempted to provide reasonable, justified alternatives for the outstanding accounting issues. There is often more than one reasonable choice for treating accounting problems. In these situations, I have attempted to choose the alternative that serves the objective of increasing net income, thereby increasing the selling price of Savoy.

In previous years, Savoy's financial statements were prepared primarily for income tax purposes and presumably the accounting choices made served to legitimately reduce Savoy's tax burden. Financial statements prepared for tax purposes meet the requirements of the *Income Tax Act* but are often not appropriate for determining the selling price of a business as they are designed to defer taxes and therefore tend to understate income. Using such statements for determining the selling price of Savoy will unfairly reduce the amount you receive.

Financial statements prepared for determining the selling price of a business should provide a reasonable representation of the ongoing earning ability of the business. Because these financial statements will be used by Mr. Floor, the prospective buyer of Savoy, and potentially by an arbitrator, it is important to use a recognized standard as the basis for preparing the statements. Accordingly, I recommend using International Financial Reporting Standards (IFRS). While IFRS are not necessarily the best criteria for setting the selling price of a business, they are widely known and recognized. It is possible that the buyer will reject some of the accounting choices you incorporate into the financial statements and you may have to concede some issues to come to an agreement. However, all recommendations made in this report are supportable in terms of IFRS, fairness, and accrual accounting.

If you have any questions, please contact me.

Yours truly,

John Friedlan, CA

Comment: *The letter to Fred Irving, the person who engaged the accountant, lays out the accountant's perspective in pursuing the engagement. The letter is an important part of effective role-playing and provides a vehicle for discussing the constraints, facts, and objectives relevant to the case. The objective of preparing financial statements for determining the selling price of Savoy is clearly the most important objective. The accountant's perspective in the report is to work within the constraints and the facts, but, when possible, serving the client's objective of getting a good price for Savoy. Clearly, Savoy's financial statements to date aren't appropriate for the intended purpose. Using them would be unfair to Mr. Irving. Some might contend that it isn't appropriate to change accounting methods because consistency would be violated. However, because the objectives of financial reporting have changed, the change in accounting approach is justifiable. As a result, the accountant should advise Mr. Irving to make accounting choices that produce a fair price for the sale of his business. This isn't to imply that the managers will intentionally misstate the financial statements. Rather, when there are legitimate alternatives, they will select the more favourable. It's reasonable to assume the other parties will take a similar position—that Jim Floor will argue for accounting treatments that will tend to lower the selling price of Savoy. The solution recommends using IFRS but ASPE would also be appropriate.*

REPORT TO FRED IRVING

Terms of Reference

You have asked me to prepare a report recommending appropriate accounting treatments for a number of issues that must be resolved before presenting the financial statements of Savoy Health Club Ltd. (Savoy) to Mr. Jim Floor, who has agreed in principle to purchase Savoy from you. The financial statements, specifically net income, will be used to determine the final selling price of Savoy. I understand that if Mr. Floor does not accept the financial statements as presented to him, you and Mr. Floor will attempt to resolve any differences through negotiations, followed by arbitration if necessary.

My objective in preparing this report is to come up with reasonable and justified treatments for the accounting problems that will result in an income measure that reflects normalized earnings (earnings that can reasonably be expected to repeat in future years). International Financial Reporting Standards will be the basis for my evaluation of the accounting issues.

Comment: *Materiality will be low in this situation. Each dollar change in net income has a five-dollar effect on the price of Savoy. That is, if an accounting choice results in a $1,000 increase in net income, the selling price of Savoy increases by $5,000. Also, disclosure can't be used to resolve any accounting issues. Because the selling price depends on net income, measurement of all accounting events is necessary for them to be relevant.*

Issues

Revenue Recognition There are three revenue recognition issues that must be addressed: initiation fees, monthly membership fees, and advertising fees, as follows:

1. *Initiation fees* There are three possible ways the initiation fees could be recognized:
   (i) when the membership agreement is signed
   (ii) when cash is collected
   (iii) over the life of the membership

Under IFRS, there are five criteria that must be met if revenue is to be recognized. There is no uncertainty about revenues and costs once the contract is signed. New members sign contracts agreeing to pay the $600 initiation fee, so the amount of revenue is known when someone joins. The costs of recruiting new members include advertising, salespeople, promotions, office space for meeting with prospective members, and so on. There are no costs after someone joins, except perhaps the cost of collecting amounts owed.

The key question in this analysis is: What is Savoy providing in exchange for the initiation fee? If the fee represents the right to be a member and actual usage requires additional fees, it can be argued that revenue can be recognized when the agreement is signed. Alternatively, if the initiation fee is really part of the cost of ongoing membership, then recognizing revenue over the life of the membership is appropriate.

In my opinion, the initiation fee is clearly separate from the monthly fee and simply represents the "right to belong." In other words, by signing a membership contract a person earns the right to use the club, provided the monthly fee is paid. Thus, Savoy has delivered what has been promised when the contract is signed (subject to collectability).

Collectability is an issue because most people do not pay their initiation fees in full and 30 to 35 percent stop paying altogether. Revenue can be recognized as long as reasonable estimates of the uncollectible amount can be made. If a reasonable estimate cannot be made, then recognizing revenue when cash is collected makes sense. In my opinion, the 30 to 35 percent range provides a reasonable basis for an estimate and the historical range is not unreasonably large.

I recommend that the initiation fee revenue be recognized when a member signs a contract. An allowance for uncollectible amounts should be set up within the 30 to 35 percent range. At that point, cash has been paid or is owing and Savoy has provided a right to membership. The monthly membership fees cover the actual usage of the facility.

Comment: *The most difficult revenue recognition issue is initiation fees because other alternatives for recognizing the revenue can be defended. For example, a case can be made for recognizing revenue when cash is collected or over the life of the membership. The method I recommended is the best one for Mr. Irving and it's consistent with IFRS. Mr. Floor may object on the basis that the approach makes him pay for uncertain revenue. The key to doing a good job on these types of analyses is to identify a valid accounting alternative that is, when possible, consistent with the interests of your client, and well supported.*

2. *Monthly membership fees* Monthly fees should be recognized during the month to which they pertain. The monthly fee entitles members to use the club for a period of time. This means that revenue is earned as time passes. Therefore, revenue should be accrued to reflect portions of monthly membership fees earned as of the financial statement date. This accounting approach should be used regardless of whether a member pays monthly or at the start of the year. If the member pays in full on the renewal date of the contract, the amount paid should be treated as unearned revenue and an adjusting entry should be prepared to recognize the appropriate amount of revenue when the financial statements are prepared. The amount paid would be spread over the full year.

   There are no legitimate alternatives for recognizing revenue for the monthly fees. Revenue is earned as members have access to the club. The amount of revenue is known because the monthly fee is set in the contract signed by the member. Costs of earning the revenue are known because these are the costs of operating the club. Collection may be an issue for some members, although it should be possible to make an estimate of the amounts that will not be collected, based on past experience.

Comment: *Accounting for the monthly membership fees is an example of a situation where the facts dictate the accounting method. It would be desirable from Mr. Irving's point of view to recognize revenue earlier, say when a member signs the annual contract, because this would place more revenue in the current period. However, these choices wouldn't be appropriate under IFRS (our constraint) because the service hasn't yet been provided (the facts).*

3. *Advertising revenue* Like the monthly membership revenue, advertising revenue is earned over the period that it is posted in the club, so it is appropriate to recognize the revenue with the passage of time, regardless of when cash is received. There are two accounting challenges: the discounts for prompt payment and bad debts. It is likely that some advertisers who owed money at the end of 2018 will pay promptly and receive a discount. As a result, the discount should be recorded in 2018. This treatment will reduce net income and the price Mr. Floor will have to pay. However, this is the only appropriate treatment. Determining the amount of discount to record will not be a problem since the amount of discount on the outstanding receivables will be known within the first ten days of 2018. It is also necessary to record a bad debt expense for amounts owed by advertisers. This will be a more difficult estimate because the advertising is a new business so there is not much history on which to base the estimate. You can use your experience with the advertising payments to date to come up with an estimate. You can also agree with Mr. Floor to adjust the selling price for any uncollected amounts within the first 90 or 120 days of the year.

Comment: *Recognition of the advertising revenue is also dictated by the facts. They key aspect of this is recognizing the challenges with making estimates. It's necessary for discounts and bad debts to be reflected in the 2018 income statements but the exact amounts won't be known on June 30.*

Maintenance Costs Maintenance ensures that the equipment lives up to its operating potential. Without it, the useful life of the equipment will be shorter than expected. While regularly scheduled maintenance is necessary for proper operation of the equipment and for customer satisfaction, management judgment determines whether maintenance is required at a point in time. It is senseless from a business perspective to do maintenance unless it is required.

In this case, we must rely on management's judgment that maintenance was not required at the time and therefore should not be included as an expense in the income statement in the current period. This is not a situation where an expense should be accrued, such as a good or service consumed but not billed, nor is it an expense that should be matched to revenue recognized in the current period but that will not be incurred until a future period (such as a warranty expense). This is an independent transaction that has not taken place. IFRS are a transactions-based accounting system. Since there has been no transaction, it is not appropriate under IFRS to accrue the maintenance costs.

Comment: *Strictly speaking, the maintenance expense should be recorded when it is incurred. There are many uncertainties surrounding this cost, including the amount and whether it will be incurred (perhaps Mr. Floor will decide, should he buy Savoy, that this particular service call isn't necessary). Since IFRS record transactions and economic events that have happened, it's easy to make a case that these maintenance costs shouldn't be accounted for in 2018.*

However, as the accountant explained in the letter to Mr. Irving, the financial statements should be a reasonable representation of the ongoing and continuing earning ability of the business. After all, Mr. Floor is buying future earnings and future cash flows. Maintenance is an ongoing and regular cost of operating the health club. By excluding this particular maintenance cost in fiscal 2018, net income is overstated in relation to ongoing and continuing earnings. So, while the treatment proposed by the accountant is consistent with IFRS, we can question whether it's fair. The accountant's choice is consistent with Mr. Irving's objectives and with the constraints, and perhaps with the facts, and therefore is a reasonable recommendation. Mr. Floor and the arbitrator may see things differently. This demonstrates some of the practical limitations of using IFRS for setting the price of a business.

Rent Clearly, rent should be accrued on a monthly basis. Rent expense should reflect the cost of the space used during the period in question because it is only that cost that contributed to earning revenue. Savoy paid $18,000 to the property owner on April 1, 2018 to cover rent for April 1 to September 30, 2018. A rent expense of $9,000 should be accrued in the June 30, 2018 income statement.

Comment: *This is a clear application of accrual accounting. The rent should be expensed in the period when the space was used, regardless of when the cash is expended.*

Owner's Salary The owner's salary is a non-existent expense. Mr. Irving never took a salary over the life of the business, so it is not appropriate to include it in the calculation of net income. Historical cost financial statements are intended to be representations of what happened. If a salary for Mr. Irving is included, the statements would include something that did not happen.

Comment: *The issue here is whether the selling price should include a cost of management. An owner-manager has the option of removing money from the company as salary or dividend (a question that has significant tax implications), or not at all. From an entity standpoint, the financial statements don't reflect all the costs of operating Savoy because the cost of management is a part of the cost. The method and amount of compensation received by an owner-manager can distort net income for purposes of setting the price of Savoy because the owner-manager can choose to pay himself as much or as little as he wishes. There is no simple solution to this issue. The treatment recommended by the accountant is consistent with IFRS and is the best choice to achieve Mr. Irving's objectives. Ultimately, this issue, along with the accounting for the maintenance cost, may be better resolved through negotiations.*

SUMMARY OF KEY POINTS

LO 1 Cash reported on the balance sheet often includes cash equivalents, which are short-term investments that can be converted into a known amount of cash easily and quickly. Good management requires that there be enough cash available to meet obligations, but not so much as to result in the inefficient use of the entity's resources.

LO 2 Protecting the entity's assets is an important management responsibility. Internal controls are mechanisms ensuring that an entity achieves its objectives. In an accounting context, internal controls work to make information produced by the accounting information system reliable and protect an entity's assets from loss, theft, or inappropriate use.

LO 3 The amount of cash reported on the balance sheet represents the face value of an entity's cash and doesn't reflect changes in the purchasing power of the money. Also, because financial statements are stated in a single currency, cash held in foreign currencies must be translated into Canadian dollars so it can be reported on the balance sheet.

LO 4 The time value of money is the concept that cash received in the future isn't worth as much as the same amount of cash today. The future value is the amount of money you will receive in the future by investing cash today at a given interest rate. The present value of cash flows is the equivalent value today of an amount of money that will be received in the future. Present- and future-value analyses are valuable tools for comparing the values of cash flows that occur at different times and in different amounts. Present value is commonly used as a basis for valuing certain assets and liabilities.

LO 5 Receivables are amounts owing to an entity. Under accrual accounting, receivables should be valued at their net realizable value (NRV). This means that uncollectibles, discounts, and returns can reduce the amount of cash the entity will actually realize. There are three ways to account for uncollectible amounts:

- direct writeoff method
- percentage-of-receivables method
- percentage-of-credit-sales method

The percentage-of-receivables and percentage-of-credit-sales methods are accrual methods that attempt to match the cost of offering credit to customers to the revenue recognized in the period. The direct writeoff method doesn't match costs and revenues. The three methods can lead to different bad debt expenses in a given year, although over the life of an entity the amount expensed will be the same.

LO 6 Returns and discounts are costs of doing business in the period the revenue is recognized. Management must accrue estimated returns and discounts when financial statements are being prepared. Sales for a period are reported net of returns and discounts and they are accrued in contra-sales and contra-accounts receivable accounts.

LO 7 Amounts owing from customers or others that are due in more than one year or operating cycle should be classified as non-current assets. If interest isn't being charged on a long-term receivable or if the interest rate charged is below the market rate, the amount of revenue recognized and the receivable will be too high if the time value of money is ignored.

LO 8 Hidden reserves are undisclosed accounting choices used to manage earnings and other financial information with the intention of satisfying the self-interests of the managers.

LO 9 The current ratio has limitations because some current assets aren't very liquid. The quick or acid test ratio is sometimes used to overcome this problem by including only liquid assets in the numerator. The accounts receivable turnover ratio and the average collection period of accounts receivable provide information on how well management is managing the entity's credit program and on the entity's liquidity.

FORMULA SUMMARY

$$\text{Quick ratio} = \frac{\text{Quick assets}}{\text{Current liabilities}} = \frac{\text{Cash} + \text{Cash equivalents} + \text{Marketable securities} + \text{Receivables}}{\text{Current liabilities}}$$

$$\text{Accounts receivable turnover ratio} = \frac{\text{Credit sales}}{\text{Average accounts receivable}}$$

$$\text{Average collection period of accounts receivable} = \frac{365}{\text{Accounts receivable turnover ratio}}$$

KEY TERMS

accounts receivable turnover ratio, p. 342
acid test ratio, p. 341
aging schedule, p. 331
allowance for uncollectible accounts, p. 330
annuity, p. 325
average collection period of accounts receivable, p. 342
bank reconciliation, p. 319
compound interest, p. 321
deflation, p. 318
direct writeoff method, p. 329
discount rate, p. 323
exchange rate, p. 318
future value (FV), p. 320
hidden reserves, p. 339
inflation, p. 318
internal control, p. 319
letter of credit, p. 316
percentage-of-credit-sales method, p. 332
percentage-of-receivables method, p. 330
present value, p. 320
quick ratio, p. 341
receivables, p. 327
segregation of duties, p. 319
simple interest, p. 321
time value of money, p. 320

SIMILAR TERMS

The left column gives alternative terms that are sometimes used for the accounting terms introduced in this chapter, which are listed in the right column.

interest rate	**discount rate, p. 323**
allowance for doubtful accounts, allowance for bad debts	**allowance for uncollectible accounts, p. 330**

ASSIGNMENT MATERIALS

Questions

Q6-1. What is meant by “internal control”? Why are strong internal controls important to an entity?

Q6-2. What is meant by “segregation of duties”? Why is it important for internal control purposes that people who physically handle an asset aren’t also responsible for accounting for the asset?

Q6-3. Why is cash considered an unproductive asset?

Q6-4. How is it possible that an entity can have too much cash?

Q6-5. In August 2014, you received a birthday gift of $500 in cash from a generous uncle. Your uncle wanted you to have the money so that you could enjoy yourself as you were beginning your studies at university. Unfortunately, you lose the $500 in your very messy room in your residence hall. In June 2018, you find the $500 when you clean out your room to move out after graduating. Are you as well off on the day you found the $500 as you were on the day you received it? Explain your answer.

Q6-6. The unit of measure used in Canadian financial statements is the *nominal* dollar. What is a nominal dollar? What real economic costs are ignored by using a nominal dollar as the unit of measure, rather than using a unit of measure that takes into consideration the changing purchasing power of a dollar?

Q6-7. What does it mean when cash on an entity's balance sheet is classified as restricted? What are the implications of restricted cash for interpreting the financial statements?

Q6-8. Why is an amount of cash today more valuable than the same amount of cash in the future?

Q6-9. What is the difference between compound interest and simple interest? Would you receive more interest from an investment that pays compound interest or from one that pays simple interest? Explain.

Q6-10. Explain the terms *present value* and *future value*. Give an example of when each measurement would be appropriate.

Q6-11. What is a "receivable"? How are receivables classified and valued on a balance sheet? What are some of the different types of receivables an entity can report?

Q6-12. How are the current and quick ratios affected by how an entity recognizes revenue? Explain. Is an entity's liquidity affected by how it recognizes revenue? Explain.

Q6-13. What is the relationship between an account receivable and the income statement? What is the relationship between an account receivable and the revenue recognition criteria discussed in Chapter 4?

Q6-14. What are some of the benefits and drawbacks to a business of offering credit terms to customers? Would a business prefer to do business in cash or on credit? Explain.

Q6-15. Why is the amount reported on a balance sheet for receivables usually not the same as the sum of the amounts that customers and other people who owe the entity money have promised to pay?

Q6-16. You are a bank manager. The owner of a small business has come to see you about a loan. He presents you with the financial statements of his business. The accounts receivable are reported at the amount customers have promised to pay. The owner says he writes off bad debts once he decides the amount won't be collected. Do you have any concerns about how the receivables are reported on the balance sheet? Explain. What information about the receivables would you want?

Q6-17. Explain why, when an entity uses the percentage-of-receivables or percentage-of-credit-sales method of accounting for bad debts, a writedown of a receivable has no effect on the income statement.

Q6-18. Why is the direct writeoff method of accounting for bad debts not appropriate in accrual accounting?

Q6-19. Why is the percentage-of-credit-sales method of accounting for bad debts referred to as an income statement approach, whereas the percentage-of-receivables method is referred to as a balance sheet approach?

Q6-20. If an entity uses the percentage-of-credit-sales method of accounting for uncollectible accounts, what are the effects on the financial statements if the entity consistently uses too low a percentage of credit sales for estimating bad debts? What are the effects on the financial statements if it consistently uses too high a percentage? Consider the effects on both the income statement and the balance sheet.

Q6-21. What is an aging schedule? How is the aging schedule used for calculating the bad debt expense?

Q6-22. How does management decide what percentage of receivables or what percentage of credit sales should be used to calculate the bad debt expense and the balance in the allowance for uncollectables account? Is this a subjective or objective decision? Explain.

Q6-23. How does management decide when to write off an account receivable or some other receivable? Is this an objective or subjective decision? Explain. How can management use its judgment to achieve its financial reporting objectives? Explain.

Q6-24. Verlo Ltd. recently made a $100,000 sale to a customer. The terms of the sale agreement permit the customer to pay the $100,000 in two years. The customer doesn't have to pay any interest. The revenue recognition criteria were met at the time of delivery of the product, so Verlo Ltd. recognized $100,000 of revenue. Evaluate Verlo Ltd.'s accounting for this sale.

Q6-25. What are the costs and benefits of allowing customers to return merchandise? How should returns be accounted for? What is the impact of returns on the income statement and balance sheet?

Q6-26. What is the benefit to a business of giving a discount to customers for paying earlier (say in ten days instead of 30)? What difficulties do accountants face when dealing with discounts at the end of a period?

Q6-27. What is a hidden reserve? Why would management create hidden reserves? Why is it possible for managers to create hidden reserves? Why is the existence of hidden reserves a problem for users of financial statements?

Q6-28. What is the quick ratio? How does the quick ratio differ from the current ratio? What would be a better measure of liquidity for a jewellery store, the quick ratio or the current ratio? Explain. Which would be the better measure of liquidity for a mine holding a large inventory of gold bullion? Explain.

Q6-29. Explain why the accounts receivable turnover ratio is useful for evaluating the liquidity of an entity.

Exercises

E6-1. **(Classifying cash on the balance sheet, LO 1)** For each of the following items, explain whether the amount described should be included in "Cash and cash equivalents" on Kitsault Inc.'s (Kitsault) December 31, 2017 balance sheet:

a. $250 kept in the office to pay for incidentals such as office supplies.
b. $12,500 kept in a savings account at the bank.
c. $7,000 of cheques received from customers in mid-December 2017 but not yet cashed.
d. $144,200 that is owed by a senior executive. The amount is to be paid on January 5, 2018.
e. An investment certificate that will pay $10,000 plus accrued interest on the date it is cashed. The certificate can be cashed at any time by Kitsault.
f. A $500,000 line of credit from the bank that Kitsault uses to provide working capital when it's needed. On December 31, 2017, Kitsault had borrowed $120,000 from the line of credit.
g. $250,000 seized by a foreign government as part of a dispute over a transaction with a company in the foreign country.
h. $25,000 in post-dated cheques. The cheques can be cashed on February 21, 2018.

i. $10,000 held by Kitsault's lawyer for purposes of paying a particular supplier when equipment ordered is delivered. The supplier required that the lawyer hold the money so that it would be assured of payment. The equipment is due to be delivered in February 2018.
j. £3,000 (British pounds) held in an account at a major British bank.
k. Shares in a public company traded on the Toronto Exchange. On December 31, 2017 the shares have a market value of $5,000.

E6-2. **(Calculating future values and the effect of compounding, LO 4)** Calculate the future value in each of the following situations. The interest rates are stated in annual amounts.
a. Invest $100,000 at 4 percent for six years.
b. Invest $100,000 at 4 percent for six years, compounded semi-annually.
c. Invest $100,000 at 4 percent for six years, compounded quarterly.
d. Invest $100,000 at 4 percent for six years, compounded monthly.

E6-3. **(Calculating future values, LO 4)** Calculate the future value in each of the following situations:
a. Mrs. Langer purchases a Canada Savings Bond for $5,000 that pays 3 percent interest per year for eight years, compounded annually. How much will she receive when the bond matures in eight years?
b. Mr. Rhodes purchases a long-term investment for $70,000 that pays 5 percent interest per year for 12 years, compounded semi-annually. How much will he receive when the investment matures in 12 years?
c. Ricer Ltd. borrows $100,000 at 8 percent for four years. Interest and principal must be paid in full in four years, at the end of the term of the loan. How much will Ricer Ltd. have to pay the lender in four years?
d. Ms. Maynes lends her child $25,000 to help finance his education. The loan bears no interest, but must be repaid in six years. How much will Ms. Maynes receive from the child in six years?

E6-4. **(Calculating present values, LO 4)** Calculate the following:
a. Present value of $200,000 to be received in ten years at a discount rate of 14 percent.
b. Present value of the following series of cash payments: $50,000 to be received in one year, $25,000 in three years, and $10,000 in five years, at a discount rate of 6 percent.
c. Present value of the following series of cash payments: $10,000 to be received in one year, $25,000 in three years, and $50,000 in five years, at a discount rate of 6 percent.

E6-5. **(Calculating present values, LO 4)** Answer the following questions. Provide explanations for each:
a. A customer purchases $20,000 of goods. The goods will be paid for in cash in three years. How much revenue should be recorded on the date the goods are delivered, assuming a discount rate of 8 percent?
b. Would you pay $7,000 for an investment opportunity that will pay you $4,000 in one year, $3,000 in two years, and $2,000 in three years, if your discount rate is 12 percent?
c. A "zero coupon bond" is a type of long-term debt that pays no interest, but simply pays a single amount on the date the bond matures. Your broker offers you a zero coupon bond that will pay $5,000 in 20 years. How much would you pay for the bond today, if your discount rate is 10 percent?
d. At a discount rate of 8 percent, what is the maximum you would pay for an investment that will pay you $6,000 in one year, $4,000 in two years, and $8,000 in three years?
e. If your discount rate is 10 percent, would you prefer $10,000 today or $15,000 in five years?

E6-6. **(Calculating the present value of annuities, LO 4)** Answer the following questions. Explain your answers:

a. A contest advertises that the winner wins $1,000,000. The $1,000,000 prize is paid in equal instalments over 25 years, with the first payment being made one year from the date the contest winner is announced. What is the "real" (present) value of the prize? Assume a discount rate of 8 percent.
b. You have the option of receiving $2,000,000 today or $250,000 a year for 15 years, beginning one year from now. If your discount rate is 12 percent, which would you choose?
c. A store allows you to purchase a new computer for $200 down and $50 a month for 36 months. If the appropriate discount rate is 1 percent per month, what would be the equivalent cash price today for the computer?
d. You can purchase an investment that pays interest of $200 per year for ten years plus $2,500 in the tenth year. If your discount rate is 10 percent, what is the maximum amount you should pay for the investment? (When answering, remember that calculating an annuity only applies to equal payments. In this question, the present value of the additional $2,500 received in the tenth year must be determined separately.)

E6-7. **(Calculating the future value, present value, and present value of annuities, LO 4)** Use the tools introduced in this chapter to answer the following questions. You have to decide which tool to use in each case. Explain your conclusions.

a. An investor purchases a $5,000 investment certificate that pays 8 percent interest per year, compounded semi-annually. How much will the investor receive when the certificate matures in five years? Assume the appropriate discount rate is 10 percent.
b. An investor is offered a choice of three possible investments. In each case, the investor must invest $1,000. The first investment will pay the investor $2,500 at the end of year five. The second will pay $500 in one year, $650 in two years, $800 in three years, $200 in four years, and $100 in five years. The third investment will pay $400 at the end of each of the next five years. If the investor's discount rate is 10 percent, which is the most attractive investment?
c. A retiring teacher has the opportunity to receive $10,000 per year for the next 20 years. If the teacher's discount rate is 7 percent, what is the most she should pay for this investment?
d. An entity borrows $50,000 at 9 percent for three years. Interest and principal must be paid in full in three years, at the end of the term of the loan. How much will the entity have to pay the lender in three years? Assume the appropriate discount rate is 10 percent.
e. You are offered a choice of receiving $1,000 today or $1,500 in three years. If your discount rate is 10 percent, which alternative would you prefer? Would your choice change if your discount rate is 15 percent?
f. A contest advertises that the winner wins $50,000,000. The $50,000,000 prize is paid in equal instalments over 25 years, with the first payment being made one year from the date the contest winner is announced. What is the "real" (present) value of the prize? Assume a discount rate of 8 percent.

E6-8. **(Basic journal entries, LO 5)** Prepare the journal entries necessary to record the following transactions and economic events for Magnetawan Ltd. (Magnetawan):

a. During 2018, Magnetawan had cash sales of $175,000 and credit sales of $625,000.
b. During 2018, $405,000 of accounts receivable was collected.
c. Management estimated that 5 percent of credit sales wouldn't be collected.
d. During 2018, Magnetawan wrote off $34,000 of accounts receivables.

E6-9. **(Journal entries for accounts receivable, LO 5)** In early 2018, Pugwash Ltd. (Pugwash) delivered a large order of goods to Ripon Inc. (Ripon), a new customer. In compliance with company policy, Pugwash did a credit check on Ripon and decided to provide it with a credit limit of $7,000. Ripon's order was for $9,500 so $2,500 was paid when the goods were delivered. Due to financial problems, Ripon wasn't able to pay the amount owing and in September Pugwash wrote off the amount owing. In December, Pugwash received a cheque from Ripon for the amount owing along with a letter of apology for the delay in paying the invoice.

Required:

a. Prepare the journal entry to record the sale to Ripon.
b. Prepare the journal entry to record the writeoff of the receivable from Ripon. Assume Pugwash estimates its bad debt expense using the percentage of credit sales method.
c. Prepare the journal entry that would be recorded when Pugwash received the cheque from Ripon in December.

E6-10. **(Writing off an account receivable, LO 5)** Nordegg Ltd. (Nordegg) recently learned that a major customer would be permanently shutting down its operations within 30 days. The reason for the shut-down isn't clear but Nordegg's management assumes there are financial problems underlying the decision. As of Nordegg's year-end, it isn't clear whether it will receive any of the $50,000 owed to it by the customer. Despite the uncertainty regarding collection, Nordegg's management decided it would write off the $50,000 receivable in the current fiscal year.

Required:

a. Prepare the journal entry that Nordegg would prepare if it were using the direct writeoff method of accounting for uncollectible amounts. What would be the effect on net income of the entry?
b. Prepare the journal entry that Nordegg would prepare if it were using the percentage-of-credit-sales method of accounting for uncollectible amounts. What would be the effect of the entry on net income?
c. Prepare the journal entry that Nordegg would prepare if it were using the percentage-of-receivables method of accounting for uncollectible amounts. What would be the effect of the entry on net income?
d. Why do you think that Nordegg decided to write off the receivable in the current fiscal year, even though it didn't know whether it would be paid or not? In your answer, consider accounting principles and the objectives of accounting.

E6-11. **(Accounting for long-term receivables, LO 7)** On May 31, 2017, Debden Ltd., a land development company, sold land to Grindstone Inc. for $16,000,000. The sale agreement required that Grindstone pay $4,000,000 to Debden on May 31, 2017 and then $4,000,000 on each of May 31, 2018, 2019, and 2020. Debden recognized the sale of the land in the year ended May 31, 2017.

Required:

a. How much revenue should Debden recognize as a result of its sale of the land to Grindstone? Prepare the journal entry that Debden should prepare to record the sale. Assume a discount rate of 14 percent.
b. How much interest revenue will be reported on Debden's income statement for the years ended May 31, 2018, 2019, and 2020 as a result of the sale to Grindstone? Prepare the journal entry that should be prepared each year to record the interest revenue.
c. How much would be reported as receivable from Grindstone on Debden's balance sheets for the years ended May 31, 2017, 2018, 2019, and 2020? How would the receivable be classified on each year's balance sheet? Explain your answer.
d. Suppose Debden insisted on recognizing $16,000,000 as revenue in 2017. What would be the implications for users of its financial statements? Why might Debden's management want to report the full $16,000,000 immediately?

E6-12. **(Calculating accounts receivable, LO 5)** Use the following information to calculate accounts receivable on July 31, 2018 and the amount of accounts receivable written off in 2018. Assume that all sales are on credit:

	July 31,	
	2018	**2017**
Accounts receivable	$?	$ 75,800
Allowance for uncollectible accounts	(3,300)	(3,000)
Revenue recognized during 2018	350,000	
Collections of accounts receivable during 2018	375,000	
Bad debt expense for 2018	3,500	
Amount of accounts receivable written off during 2018	?	

E6-13. **(Calculating accounts receivable, LO 5)** Use the following information to calculate accounts receivable on December 31, 2017 and the amount of accounts receivable written off during 2017:

	December 31,	
	2017	**2016**
Accounts receivable	$?	$134,750
Allowance for uncollectible accounts	(8,712)	(7,062)
Unearned revenue	40,040	56,100
Revenue recognized during 2017*	949,300	
Collections of accounts receivable during 2017	847,000	
Bad debt expense for 2017	9,130	
Amount of accounts receivable written off during 2017	?	
Cash received from customers in 2017 for services to be provided during 2018	31,240	

*Includes recognition of revenue classified as unearned in previous periods. All other revenue is on credit.

E6-14. **(Calculating the bad debt expense and the allowance for uncollectible accounts, LO 5)** You are provided with the following information about Eldon Corp.:

i. Accounts receivable on December 31, 2017 = $287,500.
ii. Sales during the year ended December 31, 2017 = $2,262,500 (all sales are on credit).
iii. Accounts receivable written off during 2017 = $39,600.
iv. Balance in allowance for uncollectible accounts on December 31, 2016 = $38,150.
v. Historically, an average of 2 percent of credit sales has been uncollectible.

Required:

Calculate Eldon's bad debt expense for the year ended December 31, 2017 and the allowance for uncollectible accounts on December 31, 2017. Prepare the journal entry required to record the bad debt expense.

E6-15. **(The effect of errors on net income, LO 5)** Innerkip Ltd. (Innerkip) uses the percentage-of-credit-sales method of estimating the bad debt expense. Since 2014, Innerkip has used too low a percentage in calculating the bad debt expense each year. In 2018, management realized the error and decided to make an adjusting entry to correct it. Credit sales every year from 2014 through 2018 were $500,000. Innerkip determined the bad debt expense using 2 percent of revenue each year. Management decides it will use 2.3 percent beginning in 2018 (and should have done since 2014). Innerkip has written off $11,500 of accounts receivable each year from 2014 through 2018. The balance in the allowance account on January 1, 2014 (the first day of Innerkip's fiscal year) was $11,500.

a. What bad debt expense did Innerkip record in each year from 2014 to 2018?
b. What was the effect on net income each year of using too low a bad debt expense estimate?
c. What was the balance in the allowance account at the end of each year?
d. What effect does correcting the error have on net income in 2018?
e. Prepare the journal entry that Innerkip would make in 2018 to correct the error and leave an appropriate balance in the allowance account. Assume the adjusting entry to correct the error is made after the entry to record the 2018 bad debt expense.

E6-16. **(Comparing the percentage-of-receivables and percentage-of-credit-sales methods, LO 5)** The following information has been obtained about Elzevir Inc. (Elzevir) for 2017. The information was obtained before any year-end adjusting entries were made. Elzevir's year-end is March 31:

Accounts receivable on March 31, 2017	$1,575,000
Credit sales for the year ended March 31, 2017	9,361,500
Allowance for uncollectible accounts on March 31, 2017 (credit balance)	11,250

Required:

a. Calculate the bad debt expense that Elzevir would record for the 2017 fiscal year, assuming that management expects that 6 percent of year-end accounts receivable won't be collected. What would be the balance in allowance for uncollectible accounts on March 31, 2017 (after the adjusting entry is recorded)? Prepare the journal entry to record the bad debt expense.
b. Calculate the bad debt expense that Elzevir would record for the 2017 fiscal year, assuming that management expects that 1.5 percent of credit sales during fiscal 2017 won't be collected. What would be the balance in allowance for uncollectible accounts on March 31, 2017 (after the adjusting entry is recorded)? Prepare the journal entry to record the bad debt expense.
c. What would your answers in (a) and (b) be if the balance in allowance for uncollectible accounts on March 31, 2017 (before any year-end adjusting entries) was a debit of $11,250? Explain any differences you find.

E6-17. **(Using an aging schedule to calculate the bad debt expense, LO 5)** Pipestone Ltd. (Pipestone) uses an aging schedule to estimate the amount of receivables that won't be collected. Pipestone allows its customers up to 60 days to pay amounts owed. Any receivable outstanding for more than 60 days is considered overdue. Based on historical information, management estimates that it will collect 97.5 percent of current accounts receivable, 90 percent of receivables overdue by between 1 and 30 days, 75 percent of receivables overdue by between 31 and 90 days, and 40 percent of receivables overdue by more than 90 days. Management has provided you with the following aged receivable schedule:

Account age	Balance on January 31, 2017
Current	$700,000
1–30 days overdue	288,000
31–90 days overdue	128,400
More than 90 days overdue	58,800

The balance in allowance for uncollectible accounts before the period-end adjusting entry is made is a debit of $10,800.

Required:

a. What amount of ending accounts receivable is estimated to be uncollectible on January 31, 2017?

b. Prepare the journal entry required to record the bad debt expense for Pipestone for the year ended January 31, 2017.

E6-18. **(Compute the accounts receivable turnover ratio and the average collection period for accounts receivable, LO 9)** The following information was obtained from Acamac Corp.'s (Acamac) 2018 financial statements:

Sales (all sales are on credit)	$4,150,000
Accounts receivable on March 31, 2018	520,000
Accounts receivable on March 31, 2017	475,000

Required:

a. Calculate Acamac's accounts receivable turnover ratio for 2018.
b. Calculate the average collection period for accounts receivable during 2018.
c. Is Acamac's average collection period for 2018 reasonable? What information would you require to answer this question? Explain.

E6-19. **(Correcting the balance in Allowance for Uncollectible Accounts, LO 5)** Trilby Inc. (Trilby) uses the percentage-of-credit-sales method for estimating its bad debt expense. The percentage that Trilby uses is based on historical information. Trilby's management hasn't revised the percentage for several years, a period during which a number of environmental and business factors have changed. Trilby's management recently realized that over the last three years the percentage of credit sales that the company used was too high. As a result, the balance in allowance for uncollectible accounts is $53,000 higher than it would have been had a better estimate of bad debts been used each year.

Required:

a. Prepare the adjusting journal entry that Trilby must make to have an appropriate balance in allowance for uncollectible accounts.
b. What is the effect of the error in estimating bad debts in each of the years the error is made? What is the effect of the adjusting entry on net income? Answer the question by comparing the reported net income with what net income would have been had the error not been made and the adjusting entry not required.
c. What is the impact of this error and the adjusting entry on the users of the financial statements? Explain fully.

E6-20. **(Accounting for sales returns, LO 6)** In 2018, for the first time, Rumsey Ltd. offered customers a 30-day, no questions asked, returns policy for unused merchandise. For the year ended December 31, 2018, Rumsey's management estimated that $10,000 of merchandise would be returned under the policy during January 2019. Rumsey has $525,000 of accounts receivable on December 31, 2018 before accounting for the estimated returns. Sales for the year before adjusting for sales returns is $4,125,000.

Required:

a. What journal entry should Rumsey record for 2018 for estimated sales returns?
b. What amounts would be reported for accounts receivable and sales after the entry is made?
c. What entry would be recorded if, on January 7, 2019, $2,000 of merchandise was returned?

E6-21. **(Accounting for discounts, LO 6)** Sapawe Inc. offers customers a 2 percent discount if they pay their invoices within 10 days. On December 31, 2017, Sapawe reported accounts receivable of $275,000 (before adjusting for discounts), of which $120,000 is still eligible for the discount. Management estimates that 30 percent of the amount will be paid within the discount period. For the year ended December 31, 2017, Sapawe reported sales of $1,965,000 (before adjusting for discounts).

Required:

a. What journal entry should Sapawe record on December 31, 2017 to account for 2018 estimated discounts?
b. What amounts would be reported for accounts receivable and sales after the entry is made?
c. What entry would be recorded if on January 7, 2018 a cheque for $980 was received in payment of a $1,000 invoice within the discount period?

E6-22. **(Accounting for bad debts, discounts, and returns, LO 5, 6)** Yamaska Ltd., a new clothing manufacturer, has just completed its first year of operations and is in the process of preparing its first set of annual financial statements. You work for Yamaska's accountant and you've been asked to work on accounts receivable. You have been provided with the following information:

- The accounts receivable listing shows that customers owed Yamaska $235,000 on December 31.
- Sales for the year were $1,900,000, all on credit.
- The ages of the accounts receivable are:

• Current	$180,000
• Up to 60 days overdue	40,000
• Over 60 days overdue	15,000

Management expects to collect 98 percent of the current receivables, 80 percent of the receivables that are up to 60 days overdue, and 50 percent of the rest.

- The company offers a 2 percent discount for prompt payment. Of the current receivables, $120,000 is still eligible for the discount. Management expects 40 percent of customers to pay in time to receive the discount.
- The company allows returns under certain circumstances. Management expects that $12,000 of goods will be returned by the end of January.

Required:

a. Prepare all adjusting journal entries required for bad debts, discounts, and returns.
b. Determine the net amount of accounts receivable that will be reported on the December 31, 2018 balance sheet.
c. Determine the amount of net sales that will be reported on the 2018 income statement.
d. How confident should a stakeholder be with the amounts reported in these financial statements? Explain your answer.

E6-23. **(Identifying quick assets, LO 9)** Which of the following assets would you classify as quick assets for purposes of calculating the quick ratio? Explain your reasoning. Remember, the quick ratio should include assets that can quickly and readily be converted to cash.

a. Prepaid insurance
b. Interest receivable
c. A term deposit that matures in one month
d. Account receivable due to be paid in 16 months
e. Current portion of a long-term note receivable
f. Apartment building
g. Investment certificate maturing in 12 months
h. Inventory of gold bars
i. Cash restricted to pay off a loan
j. Inventory of hardware
k. Post-dated cheques—the cheques can be cash 45 days after the year-end
l. Term deposit maturing in one month
m. Shares in a privately owned corporation

E6-24. **(Compute current and quick ratios, LO 9)** Following are the balance sheets for the years ended June 30, 2018 and 2017 for Seahorse Inc.:

Seahorse Inc. Balance Sheets As of June 30					
	2018	2017		2018	2017
Assets			**Liabilities and Shareholders' Equity**		
Current assets			*Current liabilities*		
Cash and cash equivalents	$ 95,000	$ 105,000	Accounts payable	$ 175,000	$ 173,750
			Accrued liabilities	30,000	47,500
Accounts receivable	237,500	145,000	Unearned revenue	25,000	30,000
Inventory	275,000	245,000	Current portion of long-term debt	112,500	150,000
Prepaids	20,250	18,750	Current liabilities	342,500	401,250
Current assets	627,750	513,750			
Capital assets (net)	932,250	1,025,000	Long-term debt	275,000	387,500
			Common shares	412,500	312,500
			Retained earnings	530,000	437,500
Total assets	$1,560,000	$1,538,750	Total liabilities and shareholders' equity	$1,560,000	$1,538,750

Required:

a. Calculate the current ratio and the quick ratio on June 30, 2017 and 2018.
b. Assess the change in the liquidity position of Seahorse Inc.
c. Can you think of any circumstances where a significant increase in the quick ratio could be an indicator of a deteriorating liquidity position?

E6-25. **(Working with the accounts receivable turnover ratio, LO 9)** During 2018, Paynton Inc. (Paynton) reported revenue of $1,592,000. Paynton's accounts receivable turnover ratio for 2018 was 4.92. What was Paynton's average amount of accounts receivable during 2018? What was Paynton's average collection period for accounts receivable during 2018?

E6-26. **(Working with the accounts receivable turnover ratio, LO 9)** During 2018, Kincolith Inc. (Kincolith) reported revenue of $125,125,000. During 2018, the average collection period for accounts receivable was 47 days. Accounts receivable at the end of 2017 was 12 percent greater than at the end of 2018. What was Kincolith's accounts receivable at the end of 2017?

E6-27. **(Calculating and explaining accounts receivable turnover and average collection period, LO 9)** Use the following information about Sunnyside Ltd. to calculate the accounts receivable turnover ratio and the average collection period for 2016 and 2017. Explain what each number means.

	2017	2016	2015
Accounts receivable	$ 275,200	$ 249,800	$244,900
Allowance for uncollectable amounts	8,256	8,243	7,837
Net accounts receivable	266,944	241,557	237,063
Sales	1,845,000	1,552,000	

E6-28. **(Interpreting accounts receivable turnover, LO 9)** Agassiz Inc. (Agassiz) provides commercial cleaning services. The company picks up items needing cleaning and returns them to the business within 48 hours. Agassiz invoices customers monthly and requires payment within 30 days. Over the last few years, the company has been growing fairly rapidly. You are provided with the following information about Agassiz:

	2018	2017	2016	2015
Revenue—year ended June 30	$1,922,720	$1,424,250	$1,076,700	$
Accounts receivable—June 30	261,800	165,624	122,283	93,113

Required:

You are the bank manager responsible for Agassiz's loan. You have decided to have a look at how well the company has been managing its receivables in light of its recent growth. Calculate Agassiz's accounts receivable turnover ratio and the average collection period for accounts receivable and use the information to prepare a report analyzing the situation.

Problems

P6-1. **(Taking discounts, LO 6)** Most of Alix Ltd.'s suppliers offer a 2 percent cash discount on purchases if invoices are paid within 10 days. Otherwise the balance is due in full within 30 days. So for a $1,000 invoice Alix would have to pay $980 within 10 days or the full $1,000 within 30 days. Alix has a policy of paying at the last possible moment. This policy has been in effect for many years, dating back to a time when Alix was having serious cash flow problems. Should Alix change this policy and pay within 10 days and receive the discount? Assume that Alix has a line of credit that allows it to borrow at 10 percent per year. Provide calculations in support of your conclusion.

P6-2. **(Thinking about internal controls, LO 3)** A religious centre collects cash contributions from people who attend services. The cash is stored in the religious centre's office in an unlocked drawer until later in the week, when the volunteer treasurer takes the money and deposits it in the centre's bank account. The office is located near the entrance to the religious centre and visitors to the centre often go to the office. Many of the members of the religious centre know where the money is stored because they have filled volunteer positions and are familiar with the procedures the centre follows.

Required:

Describe what you think are the weaknesses in the internal controls in the scenario and explain the implications of the weaknesses:

P6-3. **(Thinking about internal controls, LO 3)** Trustees of a local school board are given credit cards by the board for charging amounts pertaining to their responsibilities. Statements come to the board office and are reviewed by a staff person who approves them for payment. Occasionally, a trustee will be asked to explain a charge not clearly related to the trustee's work. Trustees are also entitled to receive reimbursement for travel, including $0.50 per kilometre travelled in their own cars. To receive reimbursement, a trustee must submit a form indicating the number of kilometres travelled. Trustees usually submit a travel form every six to eight months.

Required:

Describe what you think are the weaknesses in the internal controls in the scenario and explain the implications of the weaknesses:

P6-4. **(Thinking about internal controls, LO 3)** A travelling amusement park hires people in the towns the park visits to operate the rides on the midway. The person hired is given full responsibility for the ride. Responsibility includes collecting cash from the people who want to take the ride, making sure people get on and off the rides safely, and operating the ride. At the end of the day, the person gives the cash collected from customers to the park manager.

Required:

Describe what you think are the weaknesses in the internal controls in the scenario and explain the implications of the weaknesses:

P6-5. **(Interpreting current and quick ratio data, LO 9)** For most retail businesses the current ratio is significantly higher than the quick ratio. Why do you think this is the case? To answer, think about what the balance sheet of a retail business looks like, particularly the types of current assets that it has.

P6-6. **(Time value of money calculations, LO 4)** For each of the following situations, do the necessary calculations and make a decision:

a. A company purchases equipment for $75,000. It is to pay $15,000 on the delivery date, $22,500 one year from the delivery date, and $37,500 two years from the delivery date. How much should the entity record as the cost of the equipment? The purchase agreement doesn't require the company to pay interest. Assume a discount rate of 10 percent.
b. A woman saving for her retirement invests $50,000 in a long-term investment certificate. The certificate pays 5 percent interest per year compounded annually for 18 years. How much money will the woman receive when she retires in 18 years?
c. An investment promises to pay investors $25,000 per year for 12 years. The first payment will be received one year from the date the investment is made. What is the maximum amount the investor should pay for the investment if her discount rate is 8 percent?
d. A company borrows $500,000 for four years from a group of lenders. The company doesn't have to pay interest each year but must pay the principal and interest at the end of the loan term. Assuming an interest rate of 9 percent, how much will the company have to pay the lenders when the loan comes due in four years?
e. Would you prefer to receive $30,000 today, $50,000 in five years, or $8,000 at the end of each of the next five years? Assume a discount rate of 10 percent.

P6-7. **(Analyzing changes to credit policy, LO 5, 9)** Magundy Inc. (Magundy) imports high-end merchandise from Europe and distributes it to retailers across eastern Canada. Magundy has tended to be very conservative in managing its operations. In late 2016, the shareholders of Magundy decided that they weren't satisfied with the performance and growth of the company, and replaced the president with a younger, more aggressive person who they believed would be better able meet their performance and growth objectives.

In early 2017, the new president decided that Magundy had been too cautious in granting credit to customers so he implemented a new credit policy that significantly increased the number of retailers who would be able to carry Magundy's merchandise. The new president thought the new credit policy would increase sales significantly, which would meet the objectives of the owners. The new credit policy allowed businesses that were considered higher credit risks (customers that were more likely to not pay their debts) to obtain credit from Magundy. The new credit policy also allows all customers more time to pay Magundy for purchases.

By the end of 2017, it appeared that the new president's strategy was working. Sales during the year had increased 20 percent over the previous year, to $2,395,000.

Required:

You have been asked by the shareholders to prepare a report evaluating certain aspects of Magundy's performance during 2017. Your report should consider the following:

a. What should Magundy's bad debt expense for 2017 be? In previous years, Magundy calculated its bad debt expense based on 2 percent of credit sales during the year. Explain your answer.
b. How would you expect Magundy's accounts receivable turnover ratio to change from 2016 to 2017? Explain.
c. How would the new credit strategy affect Magundy's liquidity?
d. Do you think the new president's credit strategy is a good one? What are the risks and benefits of the new strategy?

P6-8 **(Impact of accepting credit cards, LO 6)** Wooler Inc. operates a discount store in a medium-sized Canadian city. At the beginning of 2016, the owner decided to begin accepting major credit cards in the store. Until then, only cash had been accepted. The owner had been advised by a number of business consultants that by accepting credit cards, sales would increase significantly and, therefore, so would profit. The consultants were right about sales—they increased significantly—but profits were flat. The owner has come to you for an explanation for the results. She would like to know why profit has remained low despite the increase in sales. She has provided you with the following information:

	2014	2015	2016	2017
Sales	$215,000	$225,000	$281,000	$301,000
Percentage of sales by credit card	0%	0%	68%	81%
Cost of credit sales (3.5%)	0	0	6,688	8,533
All other expenses	191,350	200,250	250,090	267,890
Net income	$ 23,650	$ 24,750	$ 24,222	$ 24,577

P6-9. **(Comparing the effects of different methods of accounting for bad debts, LO 5)** You have obtained the following information about Plantagenet Inc. (Plantagenet) from its 2018 annual report:

i. Plantagenet's year-end is June 30.
ii. Sales for the year ended June 30, 2018 were $8,470,000; 85 percent of sales are credit sales.
iii. The balance in accounts receivable on June 30, 2018 was $1,220,000.
iv. The balance in allowance for uncollectible accounts on June 30, 2017 was $96,000.
v. During fiscal 2018, Plantagenet wrote off $84,000 of accounts receivable.
vi. The bad debt expense can be estimated as 1.5 percent of credit sales or 9.5 percent of year-end accounts receivable.
vii. Net income for the year ended June 30, 2018, including all revenues and expenses except for the bad debt expense, was $500,000.

Required:

a. Determine the bad debt expense for the year ended 2018, assuming that Plantagenet used:
   i. the direct-writeoff method for accounting for uncollectible accounts.
   ii. the percentage-of-credit-sales method for accounting for uncollectible accounts.
   iii. the percentage-of-receivables method for accounting for uncollectible accounts.
b. What would be the balance in allowance for uncollectible accounts on June 30, 2018 using the three methods identified in (a)?
c. Prepare the journal entry required to record the bad debt expense under each of the three methods identified in (a).
d. What would net income be in 2018 under each of the three methods in (a)?
e. Explain why the three methods in (a) provide different bad debt expenses.
f. Which method of determining the bad debt expense and the allowance for uncollectible accounts is best? Explain.

P6-10. **(Comparing the effects of different methods of accounting for bad debts, LO 5)** You have obtained the following information about Rossburn Inc. (Rossburn) from its 2017 annual report:

i. Rossburn's year-end is September 30.
ii. Sales for the year ended September 30, 2017 were $750,000; 85 percent of sales are credit sales.
iii. The balance in accounts receivable on September 30, 2017 was $145,000.
iv. The balance in allowance for uncollectible accounts on September 30, 2016 was $13,500.

v. During fiscal 2017, Rossburn wrote off $18,000 of accounts receivable.
vi. The bad debt expense can be estimated as 2.5 percent of credit sales or 10 percent of year-end accounts receivable.
vii. Net income for the year ended September 30, 2017, including all revenues and expenses except for the bad debt expense, was $45,000.

Required:

a. Determine the bad debt expense for the year ended 2017, assuming that Rossburn used:
   i. the direct-writeoff method for accounting for uncollectible accounts.
   ii. the percentage-of-credit-sales method for accounting for uncollectible accounts.
   iii. the percentage-of-receivables method for accounting for uncollectible accounts.
b. What would be the balance in allowance for uncollectible accounts on September 30, 2017 using the three methods identified in (a)?
c. Prepare the journal entry required to record the bad debt expense under each of the three methods identified in (a).
d. What would net income be for 2017 under each of the three methods in (a)?
e. Explain why the three methods in (a) provide different bad debt expenses.
f. Which method of determining the bad debt expense and the allowance for uncollectible accounts is best? Explain.

P6-11. **(Observing the effect of errors in estimating the bad debt expense and the allowance of uncollectible accounts on the financial statements, LO 5, 9)** Since 2013, Halkirk Inc. (Halkirk) has estimated that its bad debt expense would be approximately 3 percent of credit sales each year. In late 2014, Halkirk made a number of changes to its internal control procedures that increased the effectiveness of its credit granting and receivables collection. As a result, in 2015 uncollectibles decreased to about 2 percent of credit sales. However, the accounting department never bothered to lower the 3 percent rate that had been implemented in 2013.

The following information is also available about Halkirk's receivables and bad debts:
i. Halkirk's year-end is December 31.
ii. The balance in Halkirk's allowance account on January 1, 2013 was $90,000.
iii. Credit sales and writeoffs by year and accounts receivable on December 31 of each year were:

Year	Credit sales made during the year	Writeoffs during the year	Accounts receivable on December 31*
2013	$3,375,000	$ 88,200	$1,183,500
2014	3,712,500	101,475	1,264,500
2015	4,185,000	80,438	1,381,500
2016	4,725,000	74,016	1,512,000
2017	5,377,500	103,496	1,692,000
2018	5,850,000	107,550	1,813,500

*Accounts receivable is the gross amount, before deducting the allowance for doubtful accounts.

Required:

a. Calculate the bad debt expense Halkirk's accounting department would have made in each year from 2013 through 2018.
b. Calculate the balance in allowance for uncollectible accounts on December 31 of each year, after the adjusting entry recording the bad debt expense for the year recorded.
c. Examine the balance in the allowance account over the period from 2013 through 2018. Explain what is happening to the allowance account as a result of using a percentage of credit sales that is consistently too high. (To answer, it might help to look at the balance in the allowance account as a percentage of accounts receivable.)

d. What is the effect on income each year of using a percentage of credit sales that is consistently too large? Explain.
e. What is the net amount of accounts receivable (accounts receivable—allowance for uncollectibles) on Halkirk's balance sheet on December 31, 2018? Does the amount on the balance sheet represent the net realizable value of the accounts receivable on December 31, 2018? Explain.
f. What would the balance in the allowance account be on December 31, 2018 after the adjusting entry for bad debts is made if Halkirk expensed 2 percent of credit sales as bad debts beginning in 2015?
g. Suppose that in 2018 management become aware of the error it was making estimating bad debts each year by using 3 percent of credit sales instead of 2 percent. What journal entry would Halkirk have to make to reduce the balance in the allowance account to the amount calculated in (f)? What would the effect of this journal entry on net income be in 2018? What are some of the implications of these errors on users of the financial statements?

P6-12. **(Explaining differences in accounts receivable turnover, LO 9)** Tadoussac Inc. and Sturgis Ltd. are plumbing supply companies operating in eastern Canada. Both companies are looking for investment to help with their expansion plans. You work for a small venture capital firm that is considering investing in one of the companies. You've been asked to look at the accounts receivable of the two and provide a report. You have the following information:

	Tadoussac Inc.			Sturgis Ltd.		
	2018	2017	2016	2018	2017	2016
Accounts receivable	$245,000	$225,000	$216,900	$221,000	$212,100	$205,000
Allowance for uncollectable amounts	28,000	26,800	24,900	15,200	14,900	14,000
Net accounts receivable	217,000	198,200	192,000	205,800	197,200	191,000
Sales (all credit)	1,215,000	1,119,000		1,530,000	1,481,000	

Required:

Calculate the accounts receivable turnover ratio and the average collection period for 2017 and 2018. Provide an interpretation of the results and provide some possible explanations for any differences you find. What additional information would you want to understand any differences?

P6-13. **(The effect of transactions on ratios, LO 5, 9)** Indicate whether each of the following transactions and economic events will increase, decrease, or have no effect have on the current ratio, quick ratio, accounts receivable turnover ratio, and the average collection period of accounts receivable. Assume that the current and quick ratios are greater than 1.0 before each of the items is considered and the company uses accrual accounting.

1. Credit sale.
2. Recording a new long-term receivable.
3. Cash sale.
4. Recording the accrual for sales returns.
5. Customer returns merchandise (ignore the impact on inventory and cost of sales).
6. A GIC classified as a cash equivalent matures and cash is received from the bank.
7. Writing off an uncollectible account.

P6-14. **(The effect of transactions on ratios, LO 5, 9)** Indicate whether each of the following transactions and economic events will increase, decrease, or have no effect on the current ratio, quick ratio, accounts receivable turnover ratio, and the average collection period of accounts receivable. Assume that the current and quick ratios are greater than 1.0 before each of the items is considered and the company uses accrual accounting.

1. Recording the bad debt expense.
2. Collection of accounts receivable.
3. Purchase of inventory on credit.
4. A new short-term bank loan.
5. Reclassification of a long-term receivable as current (because it will come due within 12 months).
6. Recording the accrual for discounts for prompt payment

P6-15. **(Determine missing information, LO 9)** Use the information provided to determine the values for the missing information (indicated by shaded boxes):

Current assets on December 31, 2017 = $ ____

Current liabilities on December 31, 2017 = $1,325,000

Current ratio on December 31, 2017 = 1.15

Quick assets on December 31, 2017 = $850,000

Quick ratio on December 31, 2017 = ____

Accounts receivable on December 31, 2017 = $ ____

Accounts receivable on December 31, 2016 = $207,000

Revenues (all on credit) during 2017 = $2,750,000

Accounts receivable turnover ratio for 2017 = ____

Average collection period of accounts receivable for 2017 = 32 days

P6-16. **(Determine missing information, LO 9)** Use the information provided to determine the values for the missing information (indicated by shaded boxes):

Current assets on December 31, 2018 = $275,000

Current liabilities on December 31, 2018 = $ ____

Current ratio on December 31, 2018 = 1.25

Quick assets on December 31, 2018 = $ ____

Quick ratio on December 31, 2018 = 0.85

Accounts receivable on December 31, 2018 = $55,000

Accounts receivable on December 31, 2017 = $45,000

Revenues (all on credit) during 2018 = $ ____

Accounts receivable turnover ratio for 2018 = 5.75

Average collection period of accounts receivable for 2018 = ____

P6-17. **(The effect of transactions and economic events on ratios, LO 5, 9)** Complete the table below by indicating whether the transactions or economic events would increase, decrease, or have no effect on the financial ratios in the period they occur. Assume the entity uses an accrual method for estimating the bad debt expense and the allowance for uncollectibles. Also assume the current and quick ratios are greater than one before each of the events occurs.

	Current ratio	Quick ratio	Accounts receivable turnover ratio	Average collection period of accounts receivable	Debt-to-equity ratio	Profit margin ratio
Writeoff of an account receivable						
Recording the allowance for discounts						
Recording the bad debt expense						
Sale of merchandise on credit; payment due in three years						

P6-18. **(The effect of transactions and economic events on ratios, LO 5, 9)** Complete the table below by indicating whether the transactions or economic events would increase, decrease, or have no effect on the financial ratios in the period they occur. Assume the entity uses an accrual method for estimating the bad debt expense and the allowance for uncollectibles. Also assume that the current and quick ratios are greater than one before each of the events occurs.

	Current ratio	Quick ratio	Accounts receivable turnover ratio	Average collection period of accounts receivable	Debt-to-equity ratio	Profit margin ratio
Recording the allowance for returns						
Collection of a previously written off account receivable						
Sale of merchandise on credit; payment due in 30 days						
Collection of an account receivable						

P6-19. **(The effect of transactions on ratios, LO 5, 9)** For the year ended December 31, 2018, Alpena Inc. (Alpena) had revenues of $2,456,000 (all on credit). Its average collection period of accounts receivable for 2018 was 62 days. Accounts receivable on December 31, 2017 was $420,000. Calculate the effect on the average collection period of accounts receivable and the accounts receivable turnover ratio if the following additional transactions occurred during 2018. Consider the effect of each transaction or economic event separately.

a. Alpena, which uses the percentage-of-credit-sales method of estimating the bad debt expense, wrote off $7,000 of accounts receivable.
b. Alpena collected $80,000 of accounts receivable from customers.
c. Alpena recognized cash revenue of $125,000.
d. Alpena recognized credit revenue of $125,000.
e. Alpena recorded bad debt expense of $5,000.
f. Alpena recorded allowance for sales returns of $7,500

P6-20. **(Accounting for long-term receivables, LO 4, 7)** On March 31, 2016, Bellburn Land Development Ltd. (Bellburn) sold a piece of land to the city for $5,000,000. The company determined that it wouldn't be developing the land so it decided to take advantage of the offer from the city. Management was satisfied that the amount offered represented fair value for the land. The terms of the sale require full payment on April 3, 2018. No interest is specified in the agreement. Despite the fact that Bellburn won't be receiving its cash for two years, it decided to recognize the revenue from the sale during the year ended March 31, 2016 because the revenue recognition criteria were met at the time. The market rate of interest for an arrangement of this type is 10 percent.

Required:

a. How much revenue should Bellburn recognize in the year ended March 31, 2016 from the sale of the land? Prepare the journal entry that Bellburn would make to record the sale.
b. What amount would be reported on Bellburn's March 31, 2016 balance sheet for accounts receivable as a result of the sale of the land? How would the receivable be classified on the balance sheet? Explain your answer.
c. How much interest revenue should Bellburn report on its March 31, 2017 and 2018 income statements from the sale of the land? Prepare the journal entry that Bellburn

would make to record the interest revenue each year. What amount would be shown as receivable on Bellburn's March 31, 2017 and 2018 balance sheets? How would the receivable be classified on the balance sheet each year?

d. What journal entry would Bellburn make when it received payment in full on April 3, 2018?
e. Suppose that instead of being an interest free arrangement, the city agreed to pay 10 percent interest per year, payable on March 31 each year. What amount of revenue should Bellburn recognize in fiscal 2016?

P6-21. **(Using an aging schedule to calculate the bad debt expense, LO 3)** Examine the following information about Weyakwin Inc. (Weyakwin):

i. Ending balance in allowance for uncollectible accounts on April 30, 2017 = $67,800 (credit balance).
ii. Accounts receivable written off during the year ended April 30, 2018 = $58,000.
iii. Aging schedule for accounts receivable outstanding on April 30, 2018:

Account age	Balance on April 30, 2018	Percent estimated to be uncollectible
Current	$288,000	1%
1–30 days overdue	112,000	5%
31–60 days overdue	60,000	15%
61–120 days overdue	40,000	40%
More than 120 days overdue	60,000	75%

Required:

a. What amount of closing accounts receivable is estimated to be uncollectible on April 30, 2018?
b. Prepare the journal entry required to record the bad debt expense for Weyakwin for the year ended April 30, 2018.
c. What are some possible explanations for the change in the allowance account between April 30, 2017 and April 30, 2018?

P6-22. **(Correcting the balance in Allowance for Uncollectible Accounts, LO 3)** Trilby Inc. (Trilby) uses the percentage-of-credit-sales method for estimating its bad debt expense. The percentage Trilby uses is based on historical information. Trilby's management hasn't revised the percentage for several years, a period during which a number of environmental and business factors have changed. Trilby's management recently realized that over the last three years the percentage of credit sales the company has been using is too high. As a result, the balance in allowance for uncollectible accounts is $53,000 higher than it would have been had a better estimate of bad debts been used each year.

Required:

a. Prepare the adjusting journal entry that Trilby must make to have an appropriate balance in allowance for uncollectible accounts.
b. What is the effect of the error in estimating bad debts in each of the years the error was made? What is the effect of the adjusting entry on net income? Answer the question by comparing the reported net income with what net income would have been had the error not been made and the adjusting entry not required.
c. What is the impact of this error and the adjusting entry on the users of the financial statements? Explain fully.

P6-23. **(Managing accounts receivable, LO 5, 9)** You are a financial analyst and you've been asked by your manager to compare the credit management of two companies, Truax Inc. (Truax) and Ilderton Ltd. (Ilderton). The two are in the same industry, but operate in different parts of the country. They don't compete because their services can only be provided in their local markets. Through conversations with representatives of each of the companies, the analyst learned that Truax gives its customers 45 days to pay invoices whereas Ilderton gives 30 days. You obtained the following information about each company. All sales are on credit:

Truax Inc.	2018	2017	2016	2015	2014
Revenue	$2,604,420	$2,480,400	$2,340,000	$2,250,000	$
Accounts receivable at year-end	400,680	364,765	334,286	310,345	302,100
Ilderton Ltd.	**2018**	**2017**	**2016**	**2015**	**2014**
Revenue	$2,257,164	$2,129,400	$2,047,500	$1,950,000	$
Accounts receivable at year-end	235,121	229,214	222,554	216,667	207,000

Required:

a. Calculate the accounts receivable turnover ratio for Truax and Ilderton for 2015–2018.
b. Calculate the average collection period of accounts receivable for Truax and Ilderton for 2015–2018.
c. Prepare a report that discusses how well each company's management is managing receivables.

P6-24. **(Assessing liquidity, LO 9)** Examine the following information about companies A, B, and C and prepare a report explaining the liquidity position of each. Which company do you think has the strongest liquidity position? Which has the poorest? Use the quick and current ratios in your analysis.

	Company A	Company B	Company C
Cash	$ 45,000	$150,000	$100,000
Accounts receivable	310,000	250,000	180,000
Inventory	225,000	180,000	300,000
Prepaids	25,000	25,000	25,000
	$605,000	$605,000	$605,000
Bank loan	$100,000	$100,000	$100,000
Accounts payable	180,000	180,000	180,000
Current portion of long-term debt	250,000	250,000	250,000
	$530,000	$530,000	$530,000

P6-25. **(Creating hidden reserves, LO 8)** The president of Remo Ltd. (Remo) wants to use hidden reserves to "save" income for a year when the company isn't performing very well. To accomplish this objective, the president instructed the accounting department to overestimate the bad debt expense each year. Instead of using the historical norm of 1.5 percent of credit sales, the president suggested using 1.75 percent of credit sales. Remo commenced this "policy" in 2014 and it has continued through 2018, a period in which Remo has been very successful. The following information about Remo is available:

	2014	2015	2016	2017	2018
Credit sales	$5,054,000	$6,317,500	$7,265,126	$8,572,848	$9,858,774
Net income, excluding the bad debt expense	464,968	631,750	690,186	797,274	887,290
Accounts receivable writeoffs	63,000	75,810	94,763	108,777	128,593

The credit balance in Remo's allowance for uncollectible accounts on January 1, 2014 was $63,000.

Required:

a. Prepare a table that shows
   i. Remo's bad debt expense from 2014 through 2018 using the 1.5 percent rate.
   ii. Remo's bad debt expense from 2014 through 2018 using the 1.75 percent rate.
   iii. The allowance for uncollectible accounts at the end of each year using each of the estimates.
   iv. Net income for each year using each of the two estimates.
b. How could the president of Remo justify using the 1.75 percent rate for estimating bad debts?
c. In 2019, Remo's net income fell slightly and the president was concerned about a negative response from shareholders and creditors. He was especially concerned that Remo was planning to approach new equity investors to invest in Remo. Credit sales during 2019 were $5,191,000 and net income for the year, excluding the bad debt expense, was $441,410. At this point, the president "recognized" the error that had been made over the previous five years and decided it was time to correct it. The president instructed the accounting department to reduce the balance in the allowance account to the level that would have existed had Remo used 1.5 percent of credit sales as the basis of calculating the bad debt expense each year.
   i. What journal entry would be prepared to reduce the balance in the allowance account to the desired level?
   ii. What would the effect on net income be of making this journal entry?
d. Why are hidden reserves a serious problem that undermines the integrity and usefulness of accounting information?

P6-26. (Interpreting bad debts for a bank, LO 5, 9) Zbaraz Bank Ltd. (Zbaraz) lends money to borrowers around the world. The major areas of concern to management and stakeholders are what's called the *loan loss provision* (which is equivalent to the bad debt expense for non-banking companies) and the *allowance for loan losses* (which is equivalent to the allowance for uncollectible accounts for non-banking companies). You are provided with the following information about Zbaraz loan situation:

Zbaraz Bank Ltd.
Allowance for Loan Losses

	2017	2016	2015
Beginning balance	$21,138,000	$21,324,000	$22,140,000
Loan losses (writeoffs of loans):			
Consumer loans	6,510,000	6,138,000	4,566,000
Canadian commercial loans	924,000	1,578,000	1,410,000
International commercial loans	396,000	234,000	90,000
Total	7,830,000	7,950,000	6,066,000
Loan loss recoveries:			
Consumer loans	1,332,000	1,386,000	852,000
Canadian commercial loans	930,000	696,000	1,086,000
International commercial loans	162,000	360,000	594,000
Total	2,424,000	2,442,000	2,532,000
Loan loss provision	?	?	?
Ending balance	$21,000,000	$21,138,000	$21,324,000

a. Calculate the loan loss provision for Zbaraz for 2015, 2016, and 2017.
b. Examine the information about Zbaraz's loan losses and the loan loss provision you calculated in (a). Interpret and discuss any trends that you see in the data.

c. At the end of 2017, Zbaraz had a total of $1,002,666,000 of loans in its portfolio and reported on its balance sheet. The loan portfolio was broken down as follows:

Consumer loans	$ 444,654,000
Canadian commercial loans	386,820,000
International commercial loans	171,192,000
Total	$1,002,666,000

Which of the categories of loans is the most risky? Explain. Given the risk of that category, why does Zbaraz lend to this group?

d. The portfolio of loans could be further broken down in countries loaned to, industries, purpose of the consumer loan (car loan, home renovation loan, etc.), and so on. What additional information would you want about Zbaraz's loan portfolio as a stakeholder in the bank? Explain your answer.

Using Financial Statements

CAE INC.

CAE is a global leader in modelling, simulation, and training for civil aviation and defence. The company employs approximately 8,000 people at more than 100 sites and training locations in approximately 30 countries. It offers civil aviation, military, and helicopter training services in more than 45 locations worldwide and trains approximately 100,000 crew members yearly. In addition, the CAE Oxford Aviation Academy offers training to aspiring pilot cadets in 12 CAE-operated flight schools. CAE's business is diversified, ranging from the sale of simulation products to the provision of comprehensive services such as training and aviation services, professional services, in-service support, and crew sourcing. The company applies simulation expertise and operational experience to help customers enhance safety, improve efficiency, maintain readiness, and solve challenging problems. It is now leveraging its simulation capabilities in new markets such as health care and mining.

www.cae.com/en

The company was founded in 1947 and is headquartered in Canada. Its shares are traded on the Toronto and New York stock exchanges (TSX: CAE; NYSE: CAE).[4]

CAE's consolidated balance sheets, statements of income, and statements of cash flow, along with extracts from the notes to the financial statements, are provided in Exhibit 6.3.[5] Use this information to respond to questions FS6-1 to FS6-12.

FS6-1. Find or determine the following amounts in CAE's financial statement information:

a. Cash and equivalents on March 31, 2012.
b. Net amount of accounts receivable on March 31, 2012.
c. Gross amount of accounts receivable on March 31, 2012.
d. Allowance for doubtful accounts on March 31, 2012.
e. Amount of trade receivables that are past due on March 31, 2012.
f. Cash from operations for fiscal 2012.
g. Revenue for fiscal 2012.

FS6-2. How much does CAE report on its balance sheet for accounts receivable on March 31, 2012? What does that amount represent (how would you explain its meaning to a novice user of financial statements)? How much do CAE's customers actually owe it on March 31, 2012? Why are the two amounts different?

FS6-3. Use the information provided in Exhibit 6.3 to make a complete assessment of CAE's liquidity position. Discuss the liquidity on March 31, 2012 and compare it with its liquidity on March 31, 2011.

FS6-4. Calculate CAE's current and quick ratios, and the amount of working capital on hand on March 31, 2012 and 2011. Using the current and quick ratios, the amount of working capital, and the information in the statements of cash flow, provide an assessment of CAE's liquidity position.

EXHIBIT 6.3 CAE Inc.: Extracts from Financial Statements

CAE Inc.

CONSOLIDATED FINANCIAL STATEMENTS

Consolidated Statement of Financial Position

(amounts in millions of Canadian dollars)	Notes	**March 31 2012**	March 31 2011	April 1 2010
Assets			(Note 2)	(Note 2)
Cash and cash equivalents		**$ 287.3**	$ 276.4	$ 312.9
Accounts receivable	5	**308.4**	296.8	238.2
Contracts in progress: assets	11	**245.8**	230.5	205.5
Inventories	6	**153.1**	124.3	126.8
Prepayments		**47.7**	43.5	24.2
Income taxes recoverable		**95.5**	53.5	30.7
Derivative financial assets	29	**10.3**	18.9	27.9
Total current assets		**$ 1,148.1**	$ 1,049.2	$ 966.2
Property, plant and equipment	7	**1,293.7**	1,211.0	1,197.1
Intangible assets	8	**533.2**	375.8	290.4
Deferred tax assets	17	**24.1**	20.7	24.7
Derivative financial assets	29	**7.2**	11.6	15.1
Other assets	9	**177.4**	149.0	97.8
Total assets		**$ 3,183.7**	$ 2,817.3	$2,591.3
Liabilities and equity				
Accounts payable and accrued liabilities	10	**$ 597.6**	$ 551.9	$ 493.0
Provisions	12	**21.6**	20.9	32.1
Income taxes payable		**10.9**	12.9	6.5
Contracts in progress: liabilities	11	**104.6**	125.8	167.4
Current portion of long-term debt	13	**136.0**	86.2	68.5
Derivative financial liabilities	29	**12.7**	12.4	9.3
Total current liabilities		**$ 883.4**	$ 810.1	$ 776.8
Provisions	12	**6.0**	10.4	8.2
Long-term debt	13	**685.6**	574.0	600.9
Royalty obligations	29	**161.6**	161.6	148.0
Employee benefits obligations	15	**114.2**	62.8	81.4
Deferred gains and other non-current liabilities	16	**186.0**	187.6	129.3
Deferred tax liabilities	17	**91.8**	64.5	13.2
Derivative financial liabilities	29	**12.9**	13.4	15.1
Total liabilities		**$ 2,141.5**	$ 1,884.4	$1,772.9
Equity				
Share capital	18	**$ 454.5**	$ 440.7	$ 436.3
Contributed surplus		**19.2**	17.1	14.2
Accumulated other comprehensive (loss) income	19	**(9.8)**	(9.8)	11.4
Retained earnings		**558.0**	466.4	338.5
Equity attributable to equity holders of the Company		**$ 1,021.9**	$ 914.4	$ 800.4
Non-controlling interests		**20.3**	18.5	18.0
Total equity		**$ 1,042.2**	$ 932.9	$ 818.4
Total liabilities and equity		**$ 3,183.7**	$ 2,817.3	$2,591.3

EXHIBIT 6.3 (continued) CAE Inc.: Extracts from Financial Statements

Consolidated Income Statement

Years ended March 31
(amounts in millions of Canadian dollars, except per share amounts)

	Notes	2012	2011
			(Note 2)
Revenue	31	**$1,821.2**	$1,630.8
Cost of sales		**1,221.1**	1,082.0
Gross profit		**$ 600.1**	$ 548.8
Research and development expenses		**62.8**	44.5
Selling, general and administrative expenses		**256.4**	239.9
Other (gains) losses—net	22	**(21.2)**	(18.2)
Operating profit		**$ 302.1**	$ 282.6
Finance income	23	**(6.6)**	(4.4)
Finance expense	23	**69.2**	64.4
Finance expense—net		**$ 62.6**	$ 60.0
Earnings before income taxes		**$ 239.5**	$ 222.6
Income tax expense	17	**57.5**	61.7
Net income		**$ 182.0**	$ 160.9

FS6-5. The second paragraph under accounts receivable in Note 1 explain that CAE is involved in a program in which can sell some of its accounts receivable. What's the maximum amount CAE can receive under the program? Why do you think CAE would sell its receivables rather than just collecting them as they come due? How would the company that buys the receivables make money from owning them?

FS6-6. Read the part of Note 1 on the use of judgements, estimates, and assumptions. Why is this note included in the financial statements and why is it important? (In your answer discuss why estimates are necessary when CAE prepares its financial statements?) Explain why estimates can be difficult for managers to make.

FS6-7. Note 5 to CAE's financial statements shows that the accounts receivable balance shown on the balance sheet isn't exclusively accounts receivable. What other amounts are included in the accounts receivable balance? What proportion of the total do these other amounts represent? What are accounts receivable versus other types of receivables? Do you think knowing the amounts of the different types of receivables is important? Explain.

FS6-8. Calculate CAE's accounts receivable turnover ratio for the years ended March 31, 2012 and 2011. What is the average collection period of accounts receivable for the two years? Do the accounts receivable turnover ratio and the average collection period indicate that CAE is managing its receivables well? Explain.

FS6-9. What amount of CAE's March 31, 2012 accounts receivable are not overdue? What amount is overdue three months or less? What amount is overdue more than three months? Compare the percentages of overdue receivables on March 31, 2012 with the percentages on March 31, 2011 and April 1, 2010. Assess the change over the year.

EXHIBIT 6.3 (continued) CAE Inc.: Extracts from Financial Statements

Consolidated Statement of Cash Flows

Year ended March 31 *(amounts in millions of Canadian dollars)*	Notes	2012	2011
Operating activities			
Net income		**$ 182.0**	$ 160.9
Adjustments to reconcile net income to cash flows from operating activities:			
Depreciation of properly, plant and equipment		**92.3**	85.2
Amortization of intangible and other assets		**33.5**	24.5
Financing cost amortization	23	**1.6**	1.8
Deferred income taxes	17	**36.4**	52.0
Investment tax credits		**(14.5)**	(17.7)
Share-based payments	24	**4.7**	16.2
Defined benefit pension plans	15	**(13.1)**	(12.0)
Amortization of other non-current liabilities		**(12.0)**	(8.7)
Other		**(5.3)**	3.1
Changes in non-cash working capital	25	**(71.7)**	(79.0)
Net cash provided by operating activities		**$ 233.9**	$ 226.3
Investing activities			
Business combinations, net of cash and cash equivalents acquired	3	**$ (126.0)**	$ (71.3)
Joint venture, net of cash and cash equivalents acquired	4	**(27.6)**	(1.9)
Capital expenditures for property, plant and equipment		**(165.7)**	(111.3)
Proceeds from disposal of property, plant and equipment		**34.4**	1.5
Capitalized development costs		**(42.8)**	(22.6)
Enterprise resource planning (ERP) and other software		**(17.3)**	(18.5)
Other		**5.0**	(6.8)
Net cash used in investing activities		**$ (340.0)**	$(230.9)
Financing activities			
Net borrowing under revolving unsecured credit facilities	13	**$ 14.2**	$ –
Net effect of current financial assets program	30	**4.9**	32.2
Proceeds from long-term debt net of transaction costs	13	**195.0**	44.5
Repayment of long-term debt	13	**(36.1)**	(44.2)
Proceeds from finance lease	13	**–**	11.0
Repayment of finance lease	13	**(32.8)**	(33.5)
Dividends paid		**(33.4)**	(37.9)
Common stock issuance	18	**4.4**	2.8
Other		**(0.7)**	(2.8)
Net cash provided by (used in) financing activities		**$ 115.5**	$ (27.9)
Net increase (decrease) in cash and cash equivalents		**$ 9.4**	$ (32.5)
Cash and cash equivalents, beginning of year		**276.4**	312.9
Effect of foreign exchange rate changes on cash and cash equivalents		**1.5**	(4.0)
Cash and cash equivalents, end of year		**$ 287.3**	$ 276.4
Supplemental information:			
Dividends received		**$ 4.7**	$ 6.8
Interest paid		**49.4**	43.5
Interest received		**4.7**	3.7
Income taxes paid		**26.9**	14.9

EXHIBIT 6.3 (continued) CAE Inc.: Extracts from Financial Statements

NOTE 1—NATURE OF OPERATIONS AND SUMMARY OF SIGNIFICANT ACCOUNTING POLICIES

Accounts receivable

Receivables are initially recognized at fair value and are subsequently carried at amortized cost, net of an allowance for doubtful accounts, based on expected recoverability. The amount of the allowance is the difference between the asset's carrying amount and the present value of the estimated future cash flows, discounted at the original effective interest rate. The loss is recognized in income. Subsequent recoveries of amounts previously provided for or written-off are credited against the same account.

The Company is involved in a program in which it sells undivided interests in certain of its accounts receivable and contracts in progress: assets (current financial assets program) to third parties for cash consideration for an amount up to $150.0 million without recourse to the Company. The Company continues to act as a collection agent. These transactions are accounted for when the Company is considered to have surrendered control over the transferred accounts receivable and contracts in progress: assets.

Use of judgements, estimates and assumptions

The preparation of the consolidated financial statements in conformity with IFRS requires the Company's management (management) to make judgements, estimates and assumptions that affect the reported amounts of assets and liabilities and the disclosure of contingent assets and liabilities at the date of the consolidated financial statements, as well as the reported amounts of revenues and expenses for the period reported. It also requires management to exercise its judgement in applying the Company's accounting policies. The areas involving a higher degree of judgement or complexity, or areas where assumption and estimates are significant to the consolidated financial statements, are disclosed below. Actual results could differ from those estimates. Changes will be reported in the period in which they are identified.

NOTE 5—ACCOUNTS RECEIVABLE

Accounts receivable are carried on the consolidated statement of financial position net of allowance for doubtful accounts. This provision is established based on the Company's best estimates regarding the ultimate recovery of balances for which collection is uncertain. Uncertainty of ultimate collection may become apparent from various indicators, such as a deterioration of the credit situation of a given client and delay in collection beyond the contractually agreed upon payment terms. Management regularly reviews accounts receivable, monitors past due balances and assesses the appropriateness of the allowance for doubtful accounts.

Details of accounts receivable were as follows:

(amounts in millions)	**March 31 2012**	March 31 2011	April 1 2010
Past due trade receivables not impaired			
1–30 days	**$ 28.7**	$ 33.0	$ 21.2
31–60 days	**9.8**	22.4	10.7
61–90 days	**8.9**	11.7	9.3
Greater than 90 days	**31.3**	15.2	20.6
Total	**$ 78.7**	$ 82.3	$ 61.8
Allowance for doubtful accounts	**(7.6)**	(6.0)	(5.6)
Current trade receivables	**113.2**	114.8	90.6
Accrued receivables	**45.5**	41.3	34.5
Receivables from related parties	**38.1**	16.6	14.5
Other receivables	**40.5**	47.8	42.4
Total accounts receivable	**$ 308.4**	$ 296.8	$ 238.2

Changes in the allowance for doubtful accounts were as follows:

As at March 31 (amounts in millions)	**2012**	2011
Allowance for doubtful accounts beginning of year	**$ (6.0)**	$ (5.6)
Additions	**(6.2)**	(3.2)
Amounts charged off	**2.4**	0.9
Unused amounts reversed	**2.0**	2.1
Exchange differences	**0.2**	(0.2)
Allowance for doubtful accounts, end of year	**$ (7.6)**	$ (6.0)

EXHIBIT 6.3 (continued) CAE Inc.: Extracts from Financial Statements

NOTE 30—FINANCIAL RISK MANAGEMENT

Credit risk

Credit risk is defined as the Company's exposure to a financial loss if a debtor fails to meet its obligations in accordance with the terms and conditions of its arrangements with the Company. The Company is exposed to credit risk on its accounts receivable and certain other assets through its normal commercial activities. The Company is also exposed to credit risk through its normal treasury activities on its cash and cash equivalents and derivative financial assets.

Credit risks arising from the Company's normal commercial activities are managed in regards to customer credit risk. An allowance for doubtful accounts is established when there is a reasonable expectation that the Company will not be able to collect all amounts due according to the original terms of the receivables (see Note 5). When a trade receivable is uncollectible, it is written-off against the allowance account for trade receivables. Subsequent recoveries of amounts previously written-off are recognized in income.

The Company's customers are primarily established companies with publicly available credit ratings and government agencies, which facilitates risk monitoring. In addition, the Company typically receives substantial non-refundable advance payments for construction contracts. The Company closely monitors its exposure to major airlines in order to mitigate its risk to the extent possible. Furthermore, the Company's trade accounts receivable are not concentrated with specific customers but are held from a wide range of commercial and government organizations. As well, the Company's credit exposure is further reduced by the sale of certain of its accounts receivable and contracts in progress assets to third-party financial institutions for cash consideration on a non-recourse basis (current financial assets program). The Company does not hold any collateral as security. The credit risk on cash and cash equivalents is mitigated by the fact that they are in place with a diverse group of major Japanese, North American and European financial institutions.

The Company is exposed to credit risk in the event of non-performance by counterparties to its derivative financial instruments. The Company uses several measures to minimize this exposure. First, the Company enters into contracts with counterparties that are of high credit quality (mainly A-rated or better). The Company signed *International Swaps & Derivatives Association, Inc.* (ISDA) Master Agreements with the majority of counterparties with whom it trades derivative financial instruments. These agreements make it possible to apply full netting when a contracting party defaults on the agreement, for each of the transactions covered by the agreement and in force at the time of default. Also, collateral or other security to support derivative financial instruments subject to credit risk can be requested by the Company or its counterparties (or both parties, if need be) when the net balance of gains and losses on each transaction exceeds a threshold defined in the ISDA Master Agreement. Finally, the Company monitors the credit standing of counterparties on a regular basis to help minimize credit risk exposure.

The carrying amounts presented in Note 5 and Note 29 represent the maximum exposure to credit risk for each respective financial asset as at the relevant dates.

FS6-10. Examine the aging schedule that CAE provides in Note 5. How does the aging schedule help you assess the company's credit management? What's the importance of separating the amount into different categories of amounts past due? What do you think the impact on the allowance for doubtful accounts would be if the amount of past due accounts increased significantly? Explain.

FS6-11. Examine the table in Note 5 to CAE's financial statements that describes the changes in the allowance for doubtful accounts. By how much did the balance in the account change in fiscal 2012? Why did the balance change? What journal entry would CAE have made to record additions to the allowance account for fiscal 2012? What entry would be made when management determined that a specific amount owing from a customer wasn't going to be collected?

FS6-12. Note 30 discusses credit risk faced by the company. What is the credit risk that CAE faces? What are the economic consequences to CAE of not managing its credit risk well? What steps does (should) the company take to minimize its credit risk? Is it possible to eliminate the credit risk CAE faces? Explain. How does the company account for the existence credit risk?

ENDNOTES

1. Extracted from Air Canada's 2011 financial statements.
2. Extracted from Supremex Inc.'s 2011 annual report.
3. Arthur Levitt, speech to the Financial Executives Institute, New York, New York, November 16, 1998, quoted at the United States Securities and Exchange Commission Web site, http://www.sec.gov/news/speech/speecharchive/1998/spch227.htm (accessed July 4, 2012).
4. Adapted from CAE Inc.'s Web site at http://www.cae.com/en/about.cae/home.asp.
5. Extracted from CAE Inc.'s 2011 audited financial statements.

CHAPTER 7

Inventory

LEARNING OBJECTIVES

After studying the material in this chapter you will be able to do the following:

LO 1 Explain the nature, purpose, and importance of inventory to an entity.

LO 2 Distinguish between the perpetual and periodic methods of inventory control.

LO 3 Distinguish among the different cost formulas used to account for inventory and cost of sales, and understand the impact the different cost formulas have on the amounts reported in the financial statements.

LO 4 Explain the lower of cost and NRV (net realizable value) rule.

LO 5 Explain the concept of conservatism.

LO 6 Describe how biological assets and agricultural produce are accounted for.

LO 7 Describe inventory for service businesses such as accounting and law firms.

LO 8 Identify different types of inventory accounting errors and explain their impact on the financial statements.

LO 9 Discuss the relationship between inventory accounting policy and income tax.

LO 10 Analyze and interpret inventory information in financial statements.

When a server delivers that steaming cup of regular coffee to a customer eating at a Pickle Barrel restaurant in Toronto, that customer may not be aware of the accounting story that got the coffee to the table.

Mountain View Estates Coffee Company

All 12 Pickle Barrel locations serve two kinds of coffee. The regular is called Headstrong. The decaf is Colombian. The beans come from Mountain View Estates Coffee Company, a wholesale business based in Toronto.

Founded in 1997 by brothers Alan, Eric, and Stuart Shabsove, Mountain View sells to specialty coffee shops, restaurants, and corporate coffee stations in lunchrooms across the country. It also runs a fundraising program for schools, hockey teams, and religious organizations.

Alan Shabsove's office is located at back of Mountain View's new warehouse and showroom on Logan Avenue. It opened in the fall of 2011 near the Port of Toronto. Through a set of doors is the warehouse and loading dock. Aside from coffee in bags ranging from 1.75 ounces to 5-pound packages, Mountain View has close to 900 products in their inventory, including tea, cups and lids, stir sticks, cold drinks, soap, take-out containers, and cookies.

How does the company keep track of it all? That's where accounting comes in. According to Shabsove, they keep up to 100 different coffees in stock at all times.

The green (raw) beans are ordered from various suppliers in North America and sometimes come directly from growers in coffee-producing countries like Costa Rica, Peru, and Honduras. Sixty-kilogram sacks of green beans arrive at the company's roasting facility on Clayson Road in North York every two to three weeks. Some beans take only a week for delivery after they're ordered. Other kinds can take a month or more to get to Toronto.

Once a week, Mountain View manually checks its inventory, both the raw materials and the finished products. "Coffee is done by weekly count of green bags purchased and roast quantities roasted by the pound," Shabsove said.

Mountain View uses an accounting software program called Cougar Mountain to handle the sales, paperwork, and purchase orders. This program can also draw down supplies from the inventory information.

"We track volumes of coffees sold by running a velocity report on each coffee so we can tell approximately how much of each blend we will need weekly," Shabsove explained. "That amount is roasted and packed."

Mountain View then transports the roasted coffee beans to the warehouse downtown every day, where it's prepared for delivery.

If the warehouse looks a little short on something, more will be ordered to replenish the inventory. Since the sales can fluctuate, flexibility is needed with the inventory levels.

"Our orders of product are very sporadic. We can have a week where we sell many items of one product and the next week, few of the same. We find it easier just to have a look and gauge what we need," Shabsove said.

Coffee does pose a few special inventory accounting challenges.

When the beans are roasted, they have a 14 to 23 percent shrinkage rate, according to the Coffee Association of Canada's Web site, based on moisture and the type of bean, among other things. This means that 100 kilograms of green coffee beans from the original inventory might produce only 87 kilograms of roasted product.

Shabsove acknowledges they don't bother to collect inventory information about the shrinkage results every time they roast.

"It would be tough to track exactly," he said.

They also don't waste a lot of coffee from the inventory in their operations, except a little during research and development. Their roaster is automatically set to exact time and temperatures. Also, Mountain View has an on-site laboratory to ensure the beans come out with the right colours and consistencies. Quality control technicians use a Photovolt colour spectrometer that compares each roast to the Specialty Coffee Association standards chart.

In Shabsove's view, green beans should be roasted within six months after they arrive in Canada to be at their peak of freshness, although that's not a big worry for his company, because the time lag from roasting to sale is short.

"Coffees are almost certain to be sold within a week," he said.

Luckily for Shabsove, he can keep an eye on all the inventory details of his business and not have to go very far for a coffee break. Mountain View's warehouse recently opened a new street-level retail coffee shop for the neighbourhood, just a few steps up from his office.

–E.B.

INTRODUCTION

For many entities, inventory *is* the business. What's a clothing store without clothes or a car dealership without cars? What's an appliance manufacturer without the parts to build the appliances or a fast food outlet without burgers, fries, or the ingredients to make pizza? In each case, it's the inventory that is directly responsible for revenue generation. Many service businesses also require inventory to provide their services to customers. Auto mechanics require oil. Lawn care companies require fertilizer.

Accounting for inventory can be surprisingly tricky. Our exposure to accounting for inventory so far has been straightforward—we record the inventory at cost and then expense the cost when it's sold. But the real world isn't always that simple. Imagine a company with thousands of identical units of inventory that didn't all cost the same amount. Often the cost of the particular unit that was sold isn't known. However, we still have to determine a cost for the inventory sold so we can prepare the financial statements. This is a challenge accountants face: how to determine the value of inventory on hand and the cost of inventory sold when we don't know the cost of the specific inventory sold or used.

This chapter examines inventory accounting issues and how the resolutions of those issues affect financial statement numbers. The chapter also discusses the close link between accounting and tax. We have already identified tax minimization as an important objective of financial reporting. Here we'll see how the Canadian income tax system affects accounting choices and financial reporting by entities.

LO 1 WHAT IS INVENTORY?

Inventory is assets held for sale or assets used to produce goods that will be sold as part of the entity's normal business activities. It can also include materials and supplies used to provide services to customers. The type of inventory carried depends on what an entity does. Consider inventory in the following businesses:

Business	Inventory
Pizza shop	Pizza ingredients, drinks, dipping sauces, pizza boxes, napkins, plastic utensils, paper cups and plates
Winery	Wine available for sale, aging wine, supplies needed to make wine (grapes, sugar, yeast), other supplies (bottles, labels, corks)
Land development and home builder	Homes completed or under construction, developed and undeveloped land
Forest products company	Lumber, panels, pulp, paper, logs, wood chips, processing materials and supplies

www.canfor.com
www.highlinerfoods.com
www.indigo.ca
www.leons.ca
www.loblaw.ca
www.magna.com
www.timhortons.com
www.westjet.com

We can learn a lot about the nature of a business from the composition of its balance sheet. For example, Indigo Books & Music Inc.'s inventory is 50.6 percent of current assets and 38.8 percent of total assets (see Table 7.1). Indigo requires a huge inventory in its stores and warehouses to meet the demands of in-store and online customers, but because its stores are rented rather then owned it doesn't have a lot of investment in property, and because it's a retail business, accounts receivable are low (retail customers mainly pay by cash or major credit cards). Magna International Inc., an auto parts manufacturer, also has a huge investment in inventory (see Table 7.1), but it has even larger investments in accounts receivable (its sales are on credit) and property, plant, and equipment (land, buildings, machinery, and equipment used to manufacture its products). WestJet Airlines Ltd.'s inventory of spare parts, fuel, and supplies is very important to the operation of its business but makes up a relatively small proportion of its current assets (2.2 percent) and total assets (0.9 percent. Table 7.1 shows the dollar value of the inventory of eight companies in different industries, along with the proportion of current assets and total assets the inventory is.

TABLE 7.1 Amount of Inventory in Different Companies*

Company (year-end in parenthesis)	Type of business	Dollar value of inventory	Inventory as a percentage of current assets	Inventory as a percentage of total assets
Canfor Corporation (12/31/2011)	Forest products	$ 348,300,000	61.3%	14.5%
High Liner Foods Incorporated (12/31/2011)	Food processing	261,330,000	73.1%	37.8%
Indigo Books & Music Inc. (3/31/2012)	Retail	229,706,000	50.6%	38.8%
Leon's Furniture Limited (12/31/2011)	Furniture retail	87,830,000	25.6%	14.8%
Loblaw Companies Limited (12/31/2011)	Grocery retail	2,025,000,000	31.3%	11.6%
Magna International Inc. (12/31/2011)	Auto parts maker	2,045,000,000	25.1%	13.9%
Tim Horton's Inc. (1/1/2012)	Fast food service	136,999,000	22.1%	6.2%
WestJet Airlines Ltd. (12/31/2011)	Airline	31,695,000	2.2%	0.9%

*Magna's inventory amount is stated in U.S. dollars. Information for all companies is prepared in accordance with IFRS, except for Magna International and Tim Hortons, which are prepared in accordance with U.S. generally accepted accounting principles.

Many entities have different categories of inventory, and information about these is disclosed on the balance sheet or in the notes. Companies that manufacture or process inputs into finished goods can break inventory down into three subcategories:

1. **Raw materials** The inputs into the production process. For example, raw materials inventory for a furniture manufacturer includes wood used to build the furniture.
2. **Work-in-process** or **WIP** Inventory that is partially completed on the financial statement date. For a car manufacturer, a partially completed car would be classified as WIP inventory.
3. **Finished goods** Inventory that has been completed and is ready for sale. Also, one entity's inventory is another's equipment, and one entity's finished good is another's raw material. For example, the ovens used to bake bread are equipment for the bakery but finished goods inventory to the company that makes ovens. The flour and sugar used to make bread are the bakery's raw materials but finished goods for the flour mill and the sugar refiner.

WHAT DO IFRS SAY?

LO 1

There are some important questions about accounting for inventory:

- How should inventory be measured in financial statements?
- What costs should be included in inventory?
- How should inventory costs flow through the inventory account on the balance sheet to cost of goods sold on the income statement?
- What information should be disclosed?

Generally, IFRS require inventory to be valued at cost on the balance sheet. When the net realizable value (NRV) of inventory is less than cost, inventory is written down to its NRV. (NRV is the amount the inventory could be sold for, less selling costs.) This is known as the *lower of cost and NRV rule*. There are some types of inventory that are recorded at NRV. These topics will be discussed later in the chapter.

The cost of inventory usually includes more than the amount paid to the supplier. For inventory that's purchased (e.g., inventory acquired by retailers and wholesalers for sale to customers, and raw materials purchased by manufacturers and processors), cost includes all costs incurred to ready the inventory for sale or use: purchase price of the inventory, import duties and other taxes, shipping and handling, and any other costs directly related to the purchase of the inventory.

For manufacturers and processors, determining the cost of inventory is tricky. A manufacturer uses a combination of purchased raw materials, workers, and other assets (e.g., machinery and equipment) to produce finished goods. The cost of inventory should include all the costs incurred to produce the finished inventory. IFRS require that the cost of inventory include the cost of materials used plus the cost of labour directly used to produce the product, plus an allocation of overhead incurred in the production process. **Overhead** is the costs in a manufacturing process other than direct labour and direct materials. Overhead costs can be very difficult to associate directly with the product being made.

Without going into too much detail, let's consider how this costing process works. Consider a small shop that makes handcrafted wood furniture. A skilled worker uses wood, fabric, glue, and nails to make a chair. Clearly, the cost of the materials and the amount the worker is paid while making the chair are included in the cost. But there are other costs: machines to do some of the work, rent for the facility where the work is done, and heat and light for this facility. Others work in the facility; people who supervise the skilled worker, clean up the shop, maintain the equipment, prepare the furniture for shipping, and so on. These other costs are considered overhead and are included in the cost of inventory. Accountants must find ways of attaching these overhead costs to the furniture produced. If the furniture shop produces different types of tables and chairs, along with other kinds of furniture, allocating costs can get complicated.

Mc Graw Hill connect

KNOWLEDGE CHECK 7.1

Again, consider the small shop making handcrafted wood furniture. According to IFRS, which of the following costs would be included in the cost of inventory and which would not? Briefly explain your answers.

- ❑ amount paid to shipping company that delivered a shipment of fabric for a custom order of furniture
- ❑ salary paid to the accountant in the facility
- ❑ cost of varnish used to finish a set of bookcases
- ❑ shop floor supervisor who ensures all projects are proceeding as planned

Even though IFRS require all production costs, including overhead, to be included in the cost of inventory, they don't provide specific directions for determining which costs and how much of them should be included. As a result, different entities can determine the cost of inventory differently, which impairs comparability. IFRS do state that costs not related to producing the inventory and readying it for sale are to be excluded. These costs include storage, administration (head-office costs), selling and marketing, and waste.

Keep in mind that entities that don't have to follow IFRS might approach things differently. For example, an entity whose main objective is to minimize taxes might expense as much of its overhead costs as it can as it's incurred, within the rules of the *Income Tax Act* (ITA), to defer taxes.

A final consideration for this section is what and when items should be included in inventory. It's possible for a business to hold goods that shouldn't be included in inventory and may not have possession of goods that should be. For example, goods on consignment are reported in the inventory of the manufacturer/distributor, not in the inventory of the seller (the party that has possession of the inventory). Goods in transit should be included in the inventory of the buyer if title has transferred—the goods have been sold. If the transfer occurs when the goods are given over to a shipping company—sometimes referred to as *FOB (free on board) shipping point*—then the buyer includes them in inventory when they're shipped. (This requires careful tracking since some goods may be in transit at the end of a period.) If title transfers on delivery—FOB destination—the inventory remains on the books of the seller until they're received by the buyer.

LO 2 PERPETUAL AND PERIODIC INVENTORY CONTROL SYSTEMS

There are two systems for keeping track of or "controlling" transactions affecting inventory in an accounting system: perpetual inventory systems and periodic inventory systems. A **perpetual inventory control system** keeps an ongoing tally of purchases and sales of inventory, and the inventory account is adjusted to reflect changes as they occur. When inventory is purchased or sold the inventory records are immediately debited or credited to record the change. When inventory is sold, cost of sales is debited immediately. A perpetual system can determine cost of sales at any time.

On December 31, 2016, Telkwa Ltd. (Telkwa) had $20,000 of inventory on hand. During 2017, it purchased $100,000 of new inventory and had sales of $210,000. Cost of sales for 2017 was $95,000. On December 31, 2017, Telkwa had inventory of $25,000. The following journal entry records each purchase of inventory in a perpetual inventory control system:

Dr. Inventory (asset +)	www	
Cr. Accounts payable (liability +) or Cash (asset −)		www
To record the purchase of inventory using a perpetual inventory control system		

Each time inventory is sold, Telkwa would record the following journal entries:

Dr. Cash (asset +) or Accounts receivable (asset +)	xxx	
Cr. Revenue (revenue +, owners' equity +)		xxx
To record the sale of inventory		

Dr. Cost of sales (expense +, owners' equity −)	yyy	
Cr. Inventory (asset −)		yyy
To record the sale of inventory in a perpetual inventory control system and the corresponding cost of sales		

With a perpetual system, the cost of the inventory sold is known when the sale occurs and is recorded at that time. Because recording cost of sales occurs when the actual exchange with the customer takes place, the entry is a transactional entry.

With a **periodic inventory control system**, the inventory account isn't adjusted whenever a transaction affects inventory. Inventory purchases aren't recorded directly to inventory but are accumulated in a separate purchases account. The amount of inventory at the end of a period is determined by counting it, not from the accounting system. With a periodic system, cost of sales is determined indirectly using the following equation:

$$\text{Cost of sales} = \text{Beginning inventory} + \text{Purchases} - \text{Ending inventory}$$

The beginning and ending inventory balances are known from the inventory counts and the amount of purchases is available from the purchases account. Because it's necessary to count the inventory to calculate cost of sales, it isn't possible to determine cost of sales from the accounting system before the end of a period.

The following journal entry records each purchase of inventory in a periodic inventory control system:

Dr. Purchases (expense +)	www	
Cr. Accounts payable (liability +), Cash (asset −)		www
To record the purchase of inventory in a periodic inventory control system; the total amount of purchases in 2017 is $100,000 (*Note:* The purchases account is an expense account.)		

Each time inventory is sold, Telkwa would make the following journal entry:

Dr. Cash (asset +)	xxx	
Cr. Revenue (revenue +, owners' equity +)		xxx
To record the sale of inventory (This entry is the same as with the perpetual system. The sale transaction isn't affected by the inventory control system being used.)		

No entry records cost of sales until the end of the period after the inventory has been counted. Because the recording of cost of sales isn't triggered by an external transaction (it isn't triggered by the sale), it's an adjusting entry. Telkwa's cost of sales for 2017 would be calculated as follows:

$$\begin{aligned}\text{Cost of sales} &= \text{Beginning inventory} + \text{Purchases} - \text{Ending inventory}\\ &= \$20{,}000 + \$100{,}000 - \$25{,}000\\ &= \$95{,}000\end{aligned}$$

The following adjusting entry is necessary so that $25,000 of inventory is reported on Telkwa's December 31, 2017, balance sheet and $95,000 of cost of sales is reported on its 2017 income statement:

Dr. Cost of sales (expenses +)	95,000	
Dr. Inventory (assets +)	5,000	
Cr. Purchases (expenses −)		100,000
To record cost of sales for 2017		

connect

KNOWLEDGE CHECK 7.2

- ❑ Describe the three subcategories of inventory usually reported in the financial statements of manufacturing firms.
- ❑ Describe the two inventory control systems used to keep track of inventory transactions. How do the two differ?
- ❑ Trenche Ltd. provides you with the following information about its inventory:

Inventory on December 31, 2017	$ 175,000
Purchases during 2018	1,245,000
Inventory on December 31, 2018	210,000

Trenche uses a periodic inventory control system. Use this information to calculate Trenche's cost of sales for 2018.

LO 2

Internal Control

A perpetual inventory control system doesn't eliminate the need for counting the inventory from time to time. Sales aren't the only way inventory is consumed; it can be stolen, lost, damaged, or destroyed. There can also be accounting errors. A perpetual system only accounts for the cost of inventory actually sold and only a physical count will determine inventory consumed in other ways.

For example, if $5,000 of inventory had been stolen during the year, the perpetual inventory records would show $5,000 more inventory than there actually is because the theft wouldn't be recorded (thieves don't usually report their activities). If the inventory wasn't counted, the inventory amount on the balance sheet would be overstated by $5,000 and expenses would be understated by $5,000. (Stolen inventory is an expense in the period the theft occurs or is discovered.) Differences between the accounting records and the count can also be due to errors in recording transactions. After the count, the accounting records are adjusted to correspond with the actual amount of inventory on hand.

Counting inventory is important for internal control. Differences between the count and the accounting records allow management to identify inventory "shrinkage," allowing it to investigate its cause and implement a plan for reducing or eliminating the problem. For example, if management discovers that inventory is being stolen it can consider steps to better protect it from theft. Information about inventory theft could help stakeholders assess how well management is fulfilling its stewardship responsibilities, but information on stolen inventory is rarely, if ever, reported in financial statements. It's usually included in cost of sales.

With a periodic inventory control system, it isn't possible to determine whether any theft has taken place because there are no records to compare with the physical count. Therefore, the cost of stolen items is included by default, in cost of sales. More important, it isn't possible to tell from the accounting records that there is a problem with stolen inventory. This is a weakness of a periodic system. A periodic system doesn't allow for as effective control over inventory as a perpetual system. The choice between a periodic and perpetual inventory control system is thus an internal control issue, not an accounting issue. Managers choose between periodic and perpetual inventory control systems based on the costs and benefits of the two systems.

Control over inventory is crucial. A survey done by the Centre for Retail Research in its Global Retail Theft Barometer found that worldwide retail shrinkage was over US$107 billion in 2010 with almost 80 percent of the shrinkage due to shoplifting and employee theft.

LO 3

INVENTORY VALUATION METHODS

Now we'll discuss how the amount of ending inventory and cost of sales is determined each period. So far, we've assumed that the actual cost of a unit of inventory when it's used or sold is known, so cost of sales is simply debited and inventory credited for the amount. In fact, the actual cost is often not known. Consider an oil refinery that purchases oil daily on the world market at the prevailing price and stores it in large storage tanks. The price of oil fluctuates day-to-day, even minute-to-minute, so each storage tank will contain oil purchased at many different prices. What is the cost of a barrel of oil removed from the tank to produce gasoline and other petroleum products? It's impossible to know. Once oil of different prices is mixed together, the cost of the individual amounts of oil is lost and it isn't possible to determine the cost of gasoline produced from a barrel of the oil.

Inventories of nails, lumber, seeds, tennis balls, chocolate bars, and plastic furniture—inventory that is relatively low in cost and homogeneous (the items are virtually identical)—have the same problem. Tracking the cost of individual items requires identifying the cost of each individual nail, seed, or tennis ball, which would be difficult, costly, and impractical. But to determine cost of sales for a period and the amount of ending inventory, it's necessary to assign a cost to the inventory used or sold.

To solve the problem, accountants have developed methods called *cost formulas* that move costs through the inventory account to cost of sales without regard for the actual physical movement of the inventory. By using a cost formula, the balance sheet cost of inventory may not be the actual cost of the physical items on hand and cost of sales may not be the actual cost of the physical units sold or used.

IFRS allow three cost formulas:

1. first-in, first-out (FIFO)
2. average cost
3. specific identification

If the inventory is homogeneous or interchangeable, then average cost or first-in, first-out (FIFO) inventory cost formulas are used. IFRS don't state a preference between the two. IFRS require specific identification for inventory items that aren't interchangeable. For example, each car on a dealer's lot has distinctive features that distinguish it from most of the other ones on the lot, so one car isn't necessarily a replacement for another. In addition, each car has a vehicle identification number (VIN).

Before these cost formulas are described in detail, keep the following points in mind:

- The method used has no effect on the underlying economic activity of the entity but, like other accounting choices, it may affect the amounts reported on the balance sheet and income statement, so there may be economic consequences.

QUESTION FOR CONSIDERATION

Thessalon Inc. (Thessalon) manufactures gumballs. Its most popular product is a one-quarter-inch gumball that comes in six colours. This is the gumball size commonly found in dispensers in stores, malls, and so on, as well as in candy stores. Thessalon can have as many as 1,000,000 of these gumballs in inventory at any point in time, depending on the time of year. Once they are made, the gumballs are stored in large containers that hold up to 50,000 gumballs. The gumballs are then packaged into smaller containers for shipment to customers. The cost of gumballs can vary because some of the inputs used in their production are commodities whose price can vary from day to day.

Why is it unlikely that Thessalon would know the exact cost of any particular order of one-quarter-inch gumballs? Why is it likely that Thessalon would use a cost formula to determine the value of its inventory and its cost of sales?

ANSWER: With the cost of gumballs varying because of changing input prices and the vast number of gumballs on hand at any time, it's impossible to determine the cost of any particular gumball under the current storage arrangement unless each gumball was given an identifying mark allowing Thessalon's management to determine its cost. This would be impractical and costly. Because Thessalon is unable to identify the cost of individual gumballs, it's impossible to determine the cost of an order. This is where a cost formula becomes useful. The large amount of low-cost, identical inventory makes using a cost formula cost-effective and practical for Thessalon, rather than trying to determine the exact cost of the gumballs sold.

- Cost formulas allocate cost between ending inventory and cost of sales. The sum of ending inventory and cost of sales is always the same, but different cost formulas allocate the cost differently.
- Cost formulas are a way to move costs from the balance sheet to the income statement in a logical and understandable way. A formula's cost flow doesn't necessarily reflect or affect the physical flow of inventory.
- Cost isn't the only basis for valuing inventory. There are methods that use measures of current market value to value inventory, such as replacement cost and net realizable value. In most cases, these methods aren't acceptable according to IFRS because they aren't based on cost.

LO 3

First-In, First-Out (FIFO)

Under **first-in, first-out (FIFO)**, the cost associated with the inventory that was purchased or produced first is the cost expensed first. For raw materials used in a manufacturing process, the cost associated with the raw materials purchased first is the cost charged to the production process first. With FIFO, the cost of inventory reported on the balance sheet represents the cost of the inventory most recently purchased or produced. The oldest costs are the first ones expensed.

We can conceptualize FIFO by imagining a warehouse with new purchases of inventory entering the warehouse from a loading dock at the back while customers buy and receive the inventory at the front of the warehouse, as shown in Figure 7.1. New inventory purchases coming into the warehouse "push" the inventory purchased earlier toward the front of the warehouse. The inventory gradually moves from the back of the warehouse to the front where it can be sold to customers. The result is that the "oldest" costs (those that entered the accounting system first) are expensed first, while the "newest" costs (those associated with the most recently acquired inventory) remain in inventory at the end of the period. This conceptualization uses a physical flow of goods through a warehouse to show how costs move through a FIFO inventory system, but remember that the cost formulas address the flow of costs, not the physical flow of goods.

FIGURE 7.1

FIFO Inventory System

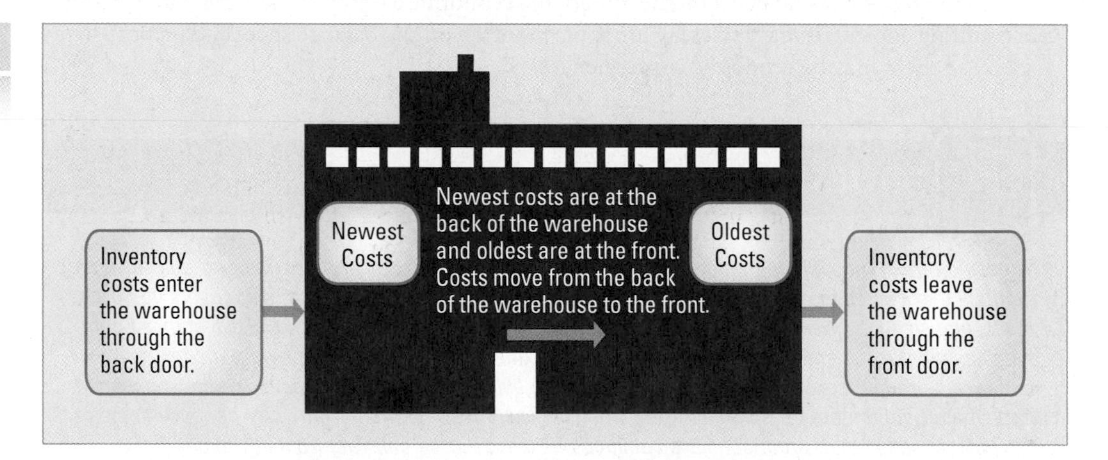

LO 3

Average Cost

With the **average cost method**, the average cost of the inventory on hand during the period is calculated, and that average is used to determine cost of sales and ending inventory. It doesn't attempt to distinguish between units of inventory with different costs or make assumptions about when costs move from inventory to cost of sales (as FIFO does). Instead, the average cost method simply assumes all inventory units have the same cost, and the cost of individual units of inventory is lost.

We can conceptualize the average cost method by considering the refinery discussed earlier. The crude oil is purchased at different market prices and is mixed together in storage tanks. The cost of each litre taken from the tank is an average of the prices that went into the tank in the first place.

Specific Identification

LO 3

The **specific identification method** assigns the actual cost of a particular unit of inventory to that unit of inventory. Unlike average cost and FIFO, when specific identification is used the physical flow of inventory matches the flow of costs in the accounting system. As a result, the inventory cost reported on the balance sheet is the actual cost of the specific items in inventory, and cost of sales is the actual cost of the specific items sold during the period. The specific identification method is suitable for more expensive inventory that is unique (such as works of art or some types of jewellery) or for inventory with relatively distinguishable individual units (such as cars, major appliances, and home entertainment equipment, which have individual serial numbers). As mentioned above, IFRS recommend this method for inventories that aren't interchangeable.

KNOWLEDGE CHECK 7.3

- ❑ What are cost formulas and why are they necessary for inventory accounting?
- ❑ Identify and explain the three cost formulas allowed by IFRS.

Specific identification provides some opportunity for managers to manipulate financial statement information. If there are identical items with different costs in inventory, managers could choose to sell the items that would have a desired effect on the financial statements. For example, a car dealer may have two of the same model car with the same features but purchased for different amounts. Selling the more expensive car will lower net income, and selling the less expensive model will result in a higher net income. By choosing the "appropriate" unit of inventory, the dealer can help achieve an objective of financial reporting. FIFO and average cost don't allow for this type of income management.

Comparison of the Different Cost Formulas

LO 3

Now that the cost formulas have been explained, let's examine an example to see the effects the cost formulas have on the financial statements. Information about the purchases and sales of inventory made by Woolchester Inc. (Woolchester) during October 2017 is shown in Table 7.2. We will use this information and a periodic inventory control system to calculate ending inventory

TABLE 7.2 Woolchester Inc.: Purchases and Sales of Inventory

Woolchester Inc. Information about the Purchases and Sales of Inventory during October 2017			
	Number of units	**Price per unit**	**Total**
Inventory balance on September 30, 2017	0	$ 0	$ 0
Purchases:*			
October 3	100	50	5,000
October 15	125	55	6,875
October 25	75	59	4,425
Sales:**			
October 8	80	125	10,000
October 20	130	125	16,250

*All purchases of inventory are made for cash.
**All sales are for cash.

TABLE 7.3 Woolchester Inc.: Inventory Transactions—FIFO

Woolchester Inc. Inventory Transactions for October 2017 Using FIFO Periodic						
			Cash	**Inventory***	**Revenue**	**Cost of sales**
October 3		Purchase 100 units @ $50	$(5,000)	$ 5,000		
October 8		Sell 80 units @ $125	10,000		$10,000	
October 15		Purchase 125 units @ $55	(6,875)	6,875		
October 20		Sell 130 units @ $125	16,250		16,250	
October 25		Purchase 75 units @ $59	(4,425)	4,425		
October 31		Inventory expensed for October 2017: 100 units @ $50 = $5,000 + 110 units @ $55 = $6,050		(11,050)		$(11,050)
October 31	**Ending balances**		**$ 9,950**	**$ 5,250**	**$26,250**	**$(11,050)**
	Remaining in inventory:	15 units @ $55 = $ 825 75 units @ $59 = $4,425				

*For clarity, in this table purchases are made directly to the inventory account instead of to purchases.

15 units @ $55 = $ 825
+ 75 units @ $59 = $4,425

100 units @ $50 = $5,000
+ 110 units @ $55 = $6,050

on October 31, 2017 and the cost of sales and the gross margin for October 2017. We will also see that cash flow isn't affected by the choice of inventory cost formula and control method.

FIFO These transactions are accounted for in Table 7.3 using FIFO. On October 31, Woolchester has to make the adjusting entry to record cost of sales and inventory used during the period. We determine the costs that should be expensed for October by looking at the units and costs available for sale during the month in the order the inventory was purchased. Woolchester had the following inventory on hand, in order of acquisition, during October:

- 100 units at $50
- 125 units at $55
- 75 units at $59

To record the cost of selling 210 units during October, Woolchester would expense the cost associated with the 100 units at $50 each and the cost associated with 110 units at $55 each. Under FIFO, the total cost of sales for October would be $11,050. Ending inventory would contain the costs associated with the remaining 15 units at $55 and the 75 units at $59 each. It's important to note that if Woolchester had a beginning inventory balance at the start of October, the costs associated with that inventory would be expensed first under FIFO.

Average Cost When the average cost method is used, the average cost of the inventory available for sale is determined when the entry recording cost of sales is made. The average cost is then applied to the inventory sold and the inventory on hand at the end of the period.

The entries for Woolchester for October using average cost periodic are shown in Table 7.4. The table shows

- The average cost per unit of inventory available for sale during October is $54.33 ([(100 units @ $50) + (125 units @ $55) + (75 units @ $59)] ÷ 300 units).
- Cost of sales for October is $11,409.30, the product of the average cost and the number of units sold ($54.33 × 210).
- Ending inventory is $4,890.70, the product of the average cost and the number of units on hand at the end of October ($54.33 × 90). The $54.33 is also the cost associated with each of the 90 units of inventory on hand at the start of the next period.

TABLE 7.4 Woolchester Inc.: Inventory Transactions—Average Cost

Woolchester Inc. Inventory Transactions for October 2017 Using Average Cost Periodic						
			Cash	Inventory*	Revenue	Cost of sales
October 3		Purchase 100 units @ $50	$(5,000)	$ 5,000		
October 8		Sell 80 units @ $125	10,000		$10,000	
October 15		Purchase 125 units @ $55	(6,875)	6,875		
October 20		Sell 130 units @ $125	16,250		16,250	
October 25		Purchase 75 units @ $59	(4,425)	4,425		
October 31		Cost of sales for October 2017: 210 units @ $54.33		(11,409.30)		$(11,409.30)
Average cost = [(100 units @ $50) + (125 units @ $55) + (75 units @ $59)] / 300 units = $54.33						
October 31	Ending balances		$ 9,950	$ 4,890.70	$26,250	$(11,409.30)
	Remaining in inventory: 90 units @ $54.33 = $4,890.70					

*For clarity, in this table purchases are made directly to the inventory account instead of to purchases.

90 units @ $54.33 = $4,890.70

210 units @ $54.33 = $11,409.30

If the perpetual system of inventory control was used, the results for average cost would be different. The inventory control system doesn't affect the amounts with FIFO or specific identification. The mechanics of periodic and perpetual systems are essentially the same, but with a perpetual system the cost of sales and changes to inventory are calculated with each transaction, whereas with a periodic system these calculations are only done at the end of the period.

Specific Identification When the specific identification method is used, the flow of costs and the physical flow of the inventory are the same: cost of sales is the cost of the actual units of inventory sold and the balance in inventory at the end of the period is the actual cost of the units still on hand. As a result, the amount of inventory at the end of the period and cost of sales for the period depend on which units are sold. With FIFO and average cost, ending inventory and cost of sales aren't affected by which physical units are sold.

Woolchester's entries for October using specific identification appear in Table 7.5. With specific identification, the cost of the actual units is tracked. During October, we'll assume that Woolchester sold the following units:

- October 8 sale: 80 units at $50 for $4,000
- October 20 sale: 12 units at $50 and 118 at $55 units for $7,090
- Ending inventory: 8 units at $50, 7 at $55 units, and 75 at $59 units for $5,210

The units sold during October are shown graphically in Figure 7.2.

If on October 20, either by design or by chance, Woolchester sold 124 of the $55 units and only six of the $50 units, cost of sales would be $11,120 instead of $11,090. In this case, ending inventory would be $5,180 instead of $5,210. Simply by changing the actual physical units that were given to customers, amounts reported on the income statement and the balance sheet change. This is how managers can use the specific identification method to manage earnings and other financial statement numbers.

TABLE 7.5 Woolchester Inc.: Inventory Transactions—Specific Identification

Woolchester Inc. Inventory Transactions for October 2017 Using Specific Identification			Cash	Inventory	Revenue	Cost of sales
October 3		Purchase 100 units @ $50	$(5,000)	$ 5,000		
October 8		Sell 80 units @ $125	10,000		$10,000	
October 15		Purchase 125 units @ $55	(6,875)	6,875		
October 20		Sell 130 units @ $125	16,250		16,250	
October 25		Purchase 75 units @ $59	(4,425)	4,425		
October 31		Inventory expensed for October 2017: 80 units @ $50 + 12 units @ $50 +118 units @ $55		(11,090)		$(11,090)
October 31	**Ending balances**		$ 9,950	$ 5,210	$26,250	$(11,090)
	Remaining in inventory:	8 units @ $50 = $ 400 7 units @ $55 = $ 385 75 units @ $59 = $4,425		8 units @ $50 = $ 400 + 7 units @ $55 = $ 385 + 75 units @ $59 = $4,425		80 units @ $50 = $ 4,000 + 12 units @ $50 = $ 600 +118 units @ $55 = $ 6,490

FIGURE 7.2 Woolchester Inc.: Specific Identification—Units Sold

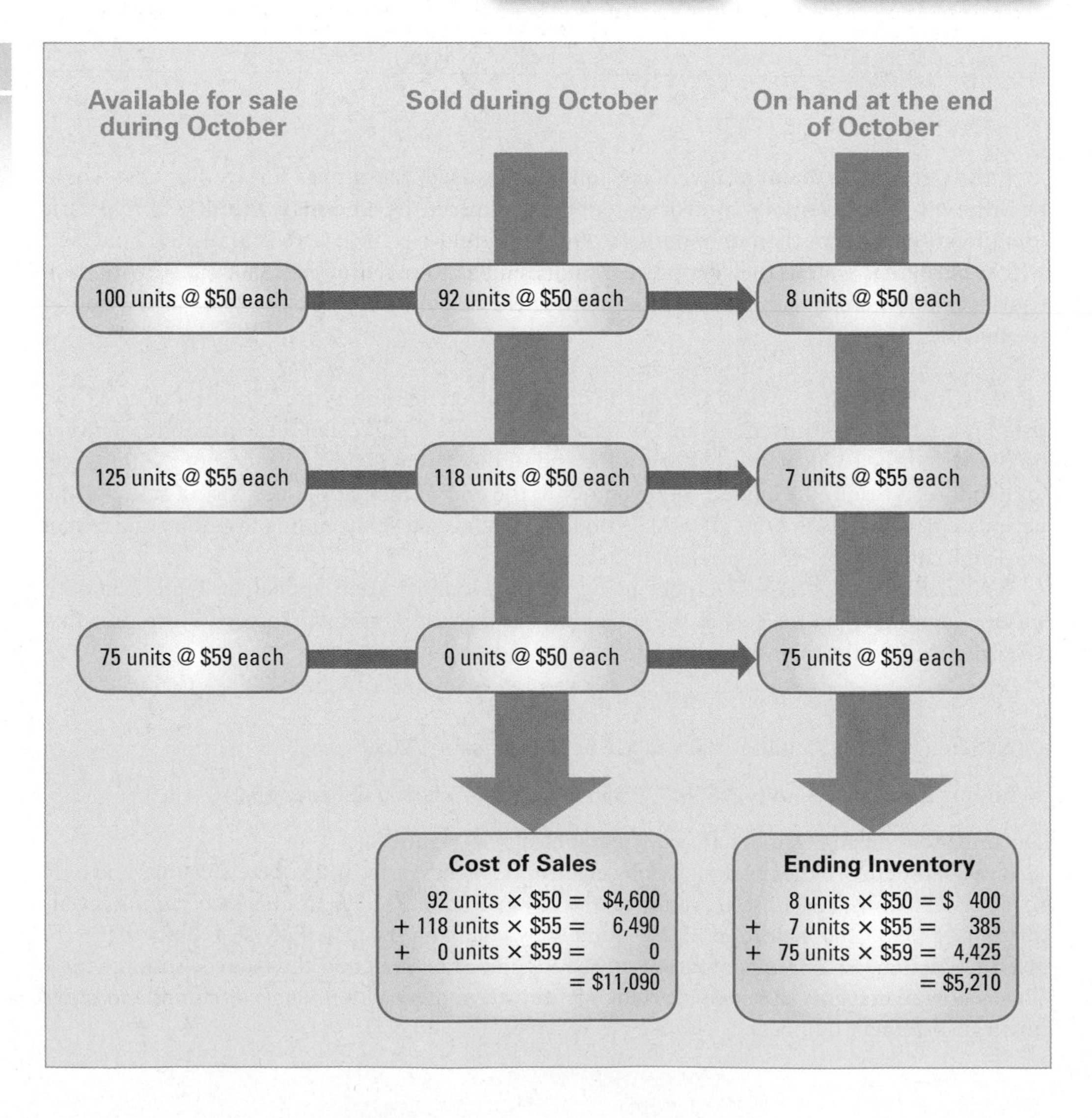

TABLE 7.6 Woolchester Inc.: Summary of Inventory Information under the Cost Formulas

Woolchester Inc. Summary Information on Inventory Transactions for the Month Ended October 31, 2005						
	Revenue	Cost of sales	Gross margin	Gross margin percentage	Cash flow	Ending inventory
FIFO	$26,250	$11,050.00	$15,200.00	57.9%	$9,950	$5,250.00
Average cost	26,250	11,409.30	14,840.70	56.5	9,950	4,890.70
Specific identification	26,250	11,090.00	15,160.00	57.8	9,950	5,210.00

Notice that cash flow is the same for all the cost formulas.

Summary of the Comparison of Different Cost formulas Table 7.6 summarizes the results from each of the cost formulas discussed above and highlights a number of important points:

- Cash flow isn't directly affected by the cost formula used. In all of the situations described, there is a net increase in cash of $9,950 from the purchase and sale of inventory during October (see the cash column in Tables 7.3, 7.4, and 7.5). The choice of cost formula can have secondary effects (the result of measurements in the financial statements) on cash flow because outcomes based on financial statement numbers may be affected. For example, the cost formula used for financial reporting purposes is usually also used for tax purposes. If the cost formula used yields higher cost of sales, and, therefore, lower income before tax, less cash will have to be paid for taxes. Outcomes such as management bonuses, compliance with debt covenants, and selling prices of businesses, among others, may also be affected by the cost formula used.
- Cost of sales and inventory are affected by the choice of cost formula, which affects other numbers in the financial statements. But the underlying economic activity of the entity isn't affected. This means that the number of units sold and purchased during the period and the number of units in inventory at the end of the period are the same regardless of the cost formula used.
- Because the amounts reported for inventory and cost of sales differ under each cost formula, many other financial accounting measures and ratios are also affected. For example, gross margin, gross margin percentage, net income, return on assets and return on equity, profit margin, current ratio, and debt-to-equity ratio will vary. Again, the underlying economic activity of the entity isn't affected but the representation of the activity is affected, which may alter the perceptions, interpretations, and inferences of stakeholders and may have economic consequences (taxes, bonuses, etc.).
- The sum of cost of sales and ending inventory in each case is $16,300. This isn't a coincidence. The different cost formulas affect the balance sheet and income statement allocation of the cost of inventory available for sale during a period but they don't affect the total amount. This relationship can be seen in Figure 7.3. The top box, cost of goods available for sale in a period, is the same under all three cost formulas. What differs is the distribution between cost of goods sold and ending inventory.
- When inventory prices are rising, FIFO cost of sales will always be lower than average cost method cost of sales and FIFO gross margin and net income will always be higher. When inventory prices are rising, FIFO ending inventory will be higher than average cost ending inventory.
- The different cost formulas provide different results only if the cost of inventory is changing. If the cost of inventory remains constant over a period of time, all the methods will yield the same results.

FIGURE 7.3

Distribution of Goods Available for Sale

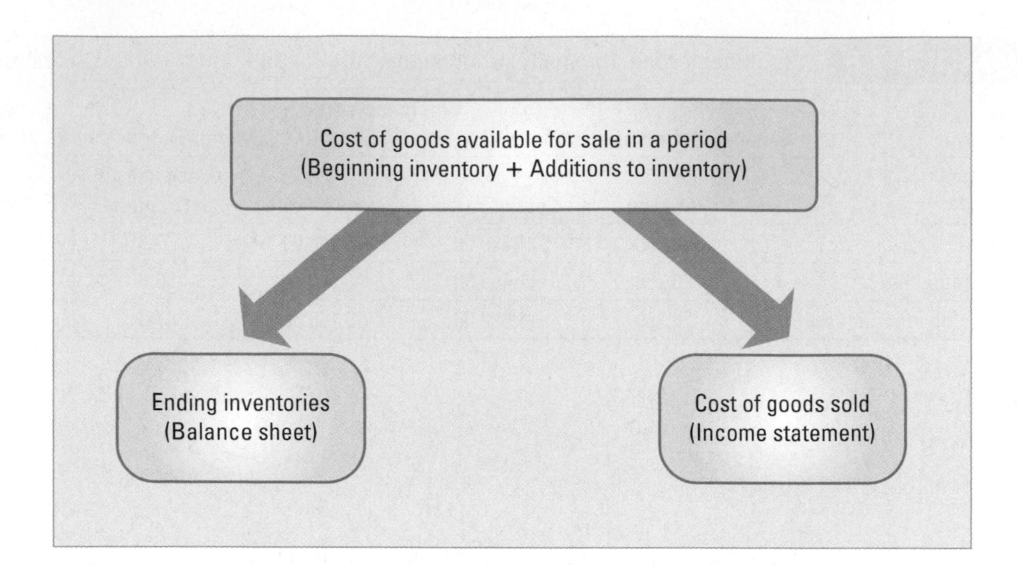

QUESTION FOR CONSIDERATION

Table 7.6 shows that cost of sales and gross margin are different with different cost formulas, but cash flow is the same for each. Explain why this is the case.

ANSWER: The cost formulas are accounting methods for allocating the cost of inventory between the balance sheet and the income statement. They are accrual accounting concepts that involve economic flows, not necessarily cash flows. The cost formula an entity selects has no effect on the amount of cash it pays to suppliers of inventory or for the inputs used to produce inventory. The actual amount of cash paid isn't affected by accrual accounting choices made by the managers. Alternative cost formulas may affect secondary cash flows, such as income tax and bonuses to managers.

LO 3

WHICH METHOD IS BEST?

As I wrote earlier, IFRS require the specific identification method when units of inventory aren't interchangeable. Most entities don't have inventories that justify specific identification so they have to choose between FIFO and average cost. IFRS don't recommend one method over the other and offer no guidance on how to choose between them. Entities may use more than one cost formula but the same formula should be used for similar inventories with similar uses. FIFO and average cost are both widely used in Canada.

It's difficult to provide strong conceptual support for either one of these methods, which is probably why both are acceptable. In many cases, an entity will choose the method used by other similar entities for comparison. Ultimately, what we have to pay attention to is the impact the two methods will have on the financial statements and be aware that companies can use different methods.

When FIFO is used, the inventory costs reported on the balance sheet are most current—they are associated with the inventory purchased or produced most recently. This provides as close an approximation of the replacement cost of the inventory as is possible while still valuing the inventory at cost. (**Replacement cost** is the amount it would cost to replace inventory, or any asset, at current prices.) Stakeholders who are interested in predicting future cash flows might find a FIFO valuation useful because it gives the most current indication of what it would cost to replace the inventory at current prices. When prices are rising, the reported amount for ending inventory will be higher with FIFO than with average cost because the newest (higher) costs are in inventory. As a result, the current ratio will be higher with FIFO. The higher balance-sheet valuation could be beneficial if, for example, the size of an entity's bank loan is related to the amount of inventory (e.g., the bank will lend $0.30 for each $1 of inventory).

On the income statement, the costs associated with the oldest inventory are expensed to cost of sales first under FIFO. This means that the cost of sales is less current—the most current cost of inventory isn't being matched to the current revenue. As a result, gross margin and net income might be poorer indications of actual economic performance than when a more current measure of cost of sales is used. This effect could be misleading to stakeholders attempting to predict future profitability. Future profitability is based on what inventory will cost in the future, not what it cost in the past. If inventory costs are rising and the entity can't raise prices to offset the increase in costs, the gross margin calculated under FIFO isn't as good an indicator of future performance. Consequently, stakeholders who base predictions on an income statement based on FIFO might overestimate future profitability.

Average cost provides a balance sheet measure of inventory that isn't as current as FIFO provides, but cost of sales is more current than with FIFO. In periods when inventory costs are rising, the effects of using FIFO versus average costs are summarized in Table 7.7.

TABLE 7.7 Impact of Using FIFO versus Average Cost When Prices Are Rising

	Ending inventory	Current ratio	Current assets	Total assets	Liabilities	Cost of Sales	Net income
FIFO	Higher	Higher	Higher	Higher	No effect	Lower	Higher
Average cost	Lower	Lower	Lower	Lower	No effect	Higher	Lower

An appeal of FIFO is that in many cases it corresponds with the physical flow of goods. For many products, good inventory management requires that the oldest inventory be sold to customers first or used first.

Because average cost yields an income figure that is lower than FIFO when prices are rising, companies with a tax minimization objective would choose average cost over FIFO. Private companies often prefer average cost because their most important objective is minimizing taxes. However, some private firms may wish to maximize net income and assets to satisfy lenders or because of an upcoming sale of shares.

INSIGHT

Last-In, First-Out (LIFO)—Another Cost Formula

There is a fourth cost formula—**last-in, first-out** or **LIFO**, which first expenses the costs associated with the inventory purchased or produced most recently. With LIFO, the cost of inventory reported on the balance sheet represents the cost of old, sometimes very old, inventory. On the income statement, the cost of inventory sold represents the most recent costs, so the most current inventory costs are matched to revenue.

LIFO isn't allowed under IFRS and can't be used in Canada for tax purposes. In the United States, LIFO can be used both for financial reporting purposes and for tax purposes. If a U.S. company chooses to use LIFO for tax purposes it must also use it for financial reporting purposes. This means that in periods when inventory prices are rising, a company will have to accept lower net income for financial reporting purposes to get the tax benefit. The fact that LIFO is widely used in the U.S. suggests that many companies consider tax reduction an important objective since they are prepared to report lower earnings in their general purpose financial statements for that reason.

INSIGHT

Impact of Inflation on Inventory and Cost of Goods Sold

In inflationary periods, when prices are rising, interpreting inventory and cost of sales can be a bit tricky. Rising prices means the cost of replacing inventory is greater than the amount expensed. This may mean profit is overstated. For example, suppose a company starts operations with an investment by the shareholders of $1. The company uses the $1 to purchases a unit of inventory which it then sells for $1.50, earning a profit of $0.50. The company pays the profit out in a $0.50 dividend to the shareholders. Assuming all this activity involves cash at the end of all of this, the company will have $1 in the bank ($1 − $1 + $1.50 − $0.50). Now suppose that when the company goes to buy a new unit of inventory, the price has gone up to $1.25. The company doesn't have enough money to replace the inventory (the inventory costs $1.25 but there's only $1 in the bank)! When a company uses FIFO, older and lower costs get expensed first, so profit is overstated in the sense that the company has to use some of its profit to replace the inventory sold.

LO 4

THE LOWER OF COST AND NRV RULE

In the fashion business, what's popular today might be virtually unsellable in a couple of months. A clothing chain buys a large supply of fashionable styles for the 2016 fall season, but when the spring 2017 merchandise arrives, the chain may still have fall inventory left that will be hard to sell at the full retail price. From a business standpoint, it makes sense for the chain to sell those fall fashions for whatever it can get—even if it's for less than cost.

But how should the chain account for items that can't be sold for more than they cost? According to IFRS, inventory on hand at the end of a period must be evaluated according to the **lower of cost and net realizable value (LCNRV) rule**, which requires inventory to be recorded at its **net realizable value (NRV)** if NRV is less than cost. NRV is the amount the entity would receive from selling the inventory, less any additional costs to complete production of the product and less costs to complete the sale.

If on the financial statement date the NRV of inventory is less than its cost, the inventory must be written down to NRV. When the NRV of inventory is less than its cost, that means the inventory is impaired. The amount of the writedown is the difference between the inventory's cost and its NRV, and it's reported as a loss or expense on the income statement in the period the impairment is identified, not when the inventory is sold. Remember that if inventory is written down, it's still on hand and can be sold. What has changed is its carrying amount (the carrying amount will be its NRV, not its cost). A **writedown** is a reduction in the carrying amount of inventory (or another asset) to some measure of market value, and it's achieved by debiting an expense and crediting the asset. When an asset is written down to zero, it's called a **writeoff**. If inventory is written down, the following journal entry is recorded:

Dr. Cost of sales or inventory loss (expenses +, owner's equity −)	xxx	
Cr. Inventory (asset −)		xxx
To record a writedown of inventory		

This journal entry reduces the balance in inventory on the balance sheet, increases expenses, and decreases net income. IFRS require disclosure of writedowns in the financial statements. The writedown could be disclosed on a separate line on the income statement or, more likely, included in cost of sales with disclosure in the notes. That some entities only disclose writedowns in the notes emphasizes how important it is to read the notes. If a stakeholder ignores a writedown (or if a company doesn't follow IFRS or ASPE and doesn't disclose it), his ability to interpret the financial statements is impaired. A writedown might distort the gross margin, and without adequate disclosure a stakeholder wouldn't understand why the gross margin percentage might have changed from previous years. Information about the nature and amount of inventory writedowns helps stakeholders assess management performance and predict future earnings.

TABLE 7.8 Sangree Ltd.: Inventory Information

Sangree Ltd. Inventory Information on December 31, 2017							
	1	2	3	4	5	6	7
	Number of units	Cost per unit	NRV* per unit	Total cost	Total NRV	Lower of cost and NRV	Amount of writedown required
Item 1	10,000	$7.23	$6.92	$ 72,300	$ 69,200	$ 69,200	$3,100
Item 2	5,000	4.24	4.48	21,200	22,400	21,200	0
Item 3	10,000	5.20	4.99	52,000	49,900	49,900	2,100
Total				$145,500	$141,500	$140,300	$5,200

*NRV equals selling price less cost to complete the sale.

IFRS require a writedown to be reversed if the NRV of inventory increases in a subsequent period. In this situation, inventory that was previously written down is written back up to its original cost (it wouldn't be written up above its original cost).

The lower of cost and NRV rule is an application of the accounting concept of conservatism, which requires that measurements in financial statements should ensure that assets, revenues, and net income aren't overstated and that liabilities and expenses aren't understated. Conservatism is discussed in detail in the next Insight box.

Let's consider an example showing how the lower of cost and NRV rule works. Sangree Ltd. (Sangree) carries three inventory items. Information about the cost and NRV of Sangree's inventory on December 31, 2017 is shown in Table 7.8.

The lower of cost and NRV rule is applied by comparing the cost and NRV for each item of inventory and using the lower amount to determine the inventory's carrying value. For items 1 and 3, NRV is lower than cost, so NRV is used and included in column 6, while for item 2 cost is lower than NRV so cost is used. The total of column 6 will appear on the balance sheet for inventory. A writedown of $5,200 ($145,500 − $140,300) is required to record the impairment in the value of the inventory. Column 7 shows the amount by which items 1 and 3 must be written down by. Sangree would make the following journal entry to record the inventory writedown:

Dr. Cost of sales or inventory loss (expense +, shareholders' equity −)	5,200	
Cr. Inventory (asset −)		5,200
To record the writedown of inventory to market value		

Now let's suppose that in the first quarter of 2018 the market for inventory item 3 recovers and its NRV was $7 per unit at the end of the quarter. Let's also assume that 4,000 of the units Sangree had on hand on December 31 were still in inventory at the end of the first quarter. Because NRV has increased, Sangree should reverse the writedown recorded for the 4,000 units still on hand. The 4,000 item 3s were written down by a total of $840 (4,000 units × $0.21 ($5.20 − $4.99)) so the following entry is made to reverse the writedown:

Dr. Inventory (asset +)	840	
Cr. Cost of sales or inventory loss (expense −, shareholders' equity +)		840
To reverse the writedown of inventory		

Two things to notice about the reversal are (a) it only applies to inventory that was previously written down, in this case only inventory that was on hand on December 31, 2017 and (b) inventory is only written back up to its cost—even though the NRV at the end of the third quarter was $7, the inventory is only written up to $5.20, its original cost.

In the example, Sangree applied the lower of cost and NRV rule on an item-by-item basis. The rule could also have been applied on the inventory as a whole, in which case the total cost would have been compared to the total NRV. Using this approach, the amount of the writedown required would be $4,000 ($145,500 − $141,500). Notice that the approach used affects the amount of the writedown and the value of ending inventory. In most situations IFRS require that cost and NRV be compared on an item-by-item basis.

There are many circumstances that can cause the NRV of inventory to decline. Changes in fashion styles have already been mentioned, and other reasons include

- technological change (e.g., the selling price of last year's leading-edge computer equipment will usually fall dramatically when faster and more powerful computers come on the market)
- damaged goods
- fluctuations in commodity markets (e.g., lumber, minerals)

LO 5

INSIGHT

Conservatism/Prudence

An important accounting concept used under ASPE/IFRS is conservatism. (IFRS use the term *prudence* to represent this concept.) **Conservatism** requires caution in the exercise of accounting judgments in financial statements to ensure that assets, revenues, and net income aren't overstated and that liabilities and expenses aren't understated. Conservatism doesn't mean there should be a deliberate understatement of assets, revenues, and net income or a deliberate overstatement of liabilities and expenses, but the uncertainty surrounding many economic events makes caution in estimates appropriate. Some examples of conservatism include:

- The lower of cost and NRV rule used for inventory.
- Capital assets written down if impaired.
- Certain losses recorded as soon as they are identified but gains must be realized before recognizing.
- Intangible assets not reported as assets unless purchased.
- Research costs expensed as incurred.
- Revenue recognized late in the earnings process.
- Market values of many assets not recorded in the financial statements.

The reasons for conservatism in accounting aren't entirely clear. A possible explanation is that the managers who are responsible for an entity's financial statements tend to be optimistic about the prospects for the entities they manage, or that they have incentives to act in their self-interest when making accounting choices. Conservatism can serve to dampen the effects of managerial optimism and self-interest.

Some of the examples of conservatism make sense. If capital assets or inventory aren't written down when impaired, then the future benefits associated with these assets would be less than the amount reported on the balance sheet.

An important issue with conservatism is its asymmetry—the treatment of economic events that increase income and assets is sometimes different from events that decrease them. If the market value of assets increases, the gains are typically not recognized until the assets are sold and the increases in value realized. (IFRS allow increases in the market value of capital assets to be recorded in certain circumstances, but this option isn't widely used at this point.)

It's noteworthy that the importance of conservatism has decreased in recent years.

A problem with conservatism is that conservative choices today can result in the opposite effect in later periods. For example, in 2018, Carcajou Ltd. (Carcajou) purchased computer equipment for $210,000. Carcajou's management decides to depreciate the equipment over three years. Carcajou's summarized income statements for the years ended December 31, 2018, 2019, and 2020 are shown in Panel A of Table 7.9. If, instead, Carcajou's management made a more conservative estimate of the equipment's life and depreciated it over two years, net income in the first two years would be lower than with the three-year depreciation period, a more conservative result (see Panel B of Table 7.9). However, in 2020, net income is much higher because there is no depreciation expense. Over the three years, the depreciation expense and net income are the same, but they are distributed differently.

(*continued*)

INSIGHT (CONT.)

TABLE 7.9 Carcajou Ltd.: Income Statements

Panel A

Carcajou Ltd.
Income Statements for the Years Ended December 31

	2018	2019	2020	Total
Revenue	$750,000	$800,000	$825,000	$2,375,000
Expenses	620,000	660,000	680,000	1,960,000
Depreciation of computer equipment*	70,000	70,000	70,000	210,000
Net income	$ 60,000	$ 70,000	$ 75,000	$ 205,000

*Computer equipment cost $210,000 and is depreciated over three years. ($210,000 ÷ 3 years = $70,000)

Panel B

Carcajou Ltd.
Income Statements for the Years Ended December 31

	2018	2019	2020	Total
Revenue	$750,000	$800,000	$825,000	$2,375,000
Expenses	620,000	660,000	680,000	1,960,000
Depreciation of computer equipment*	105,000	105,000	0	210,000
Net income	$ 25,000	$ 35,000	$145,000	$ 205,000

*Computer equipment cost $210,000 and is depreciated over two years. ($210,000 ÷ 2 years = $105,000)

Managers can use conservatism to pursue their self-interests by managing financial statement measurement. Applying conservatism requires judgment by the managers, and these judgments can be highly subjective and open to abuse.

KNOWLEDGE CHECK 7.4

- ❑ In times of rising prices, which inventory cost formula will provide the highest inventory valuation and the highest net income? Which will provide the lowest inventory valuation and net income? Explain.
- ❑ What is the lower of cost and net realizable value rule, and why is it used?
- ❑ Explain the accounting concept of conservatism.

INVENTORY DISCLOSURES IN FINANCIAL STATEMENTS

LO 3, 4

IFRS require that the following information be disclosed about inventory:

- accounting policies adopted, including cost formula used
- carrying amount (book value) of inventories
- carrying amount of inventories carried at fair value less costs to sell (NRV)
- amount of inventory expensed during the period
- amounts of any inventory writedowns and reversals of writedowns
- carrying amount of inventories pledged as security for liabilities

Exhibit 7.1 provides an example of the type of information about inventory that appears in financial statements. Big Rock Brewery Inc. is a Calgary-based brewer of premium craft beer. The company's

www.bigrockbeer.com

EXHIBIT 7.1 Inventory Disclosures—Big Rock Brewery Inc.

CONSOLIDATED STATEMENTS OF FINANCIAL POSITION

Big Rock Brewery Inc.

in thousands of Canadian dollars	December 30, 2011	December 31, 2010	January 1, 2010
ASSETS (note 18)			
Non-current assets			
Property, plant and equipment (note 11)	$ 36,874	$ 38,595	$ 40,889
Intangible assets (note 12)	207	286	344
	37,081	38,881	41,233
Current			
Inventories (note 13)	4,429	3,951	3,333
Accounts receivable (notes 14 and 22)	2,788	1,789	3,617
Prepaid expenses and other (note 15)	217	397	305
Cash	655	769	728
	8,089	6,906	7,983
Total assets	$ 45,170	$ 45,787	$ 49,216

Total amount of inventory

Describes the different categories of inventory.

4.5 Inventories

Big Rock categorizes inventories as raw materials (materials and supplies to be consumed in the production process), brews in progress (in the process of production for sale), finished product (held for sale in the ordinary course of business), consignment product (consigned to provincial warehouses for sale) and resale goods (to be sold in the ordinary course of business in the dry-goods store).

How inventory is valued and cost formula used

Inventories are valued at the lower of cost and net realizable value. Cost is determined using a weighted average cost method.

13. INVENTORIES

The inventories for the Corporation are categorized as follows:

	Dec. 30 2011	Dec. 31 2010	Jan. 1 2010
Raw materials and returnable glass containers	$ 1,087	$ 1,154	$ 1,054
Brews in progress	599	834	657
Finished product	2,636	1,829	1,518
Consignment product	92	97	50
Dry goods store (resale goods)	15	37	54
	$ 4,429	$ 3,951	$ 3,333

Work-in-process

Breakdown of different categories of inventory

Ties to amount on the balance sheet

Amount of inventory written down or off

During the year ended December 30, 2011, charges of $187 (2010–$73) and $221 (2010–$140), respectively, were recorded to net income relating to obsolete, damaged or unsellable packaging inventory and promotional and resale goods, and damaged finished goods inventory.

There were no reversals of amounts previously charged to income in respect of write-downs of inventory for the years ended December 30, 2011 and December 31, 2010.

Finished goods inventory includes $256 (December 31, 2010–$216; January 1, 2010–$nil) of depreciation charges on production equipment used to convert raw materials to finished goods.

balance sheet for the year ended December 31, 2011 reports inventory of $4,429,000, representing about 10 percent of total assets. This single number reports the entire inventory held by Big Rock; however, more information is available in the notes. Note 4.5 describes the different categories of Big Rock's inventory and that it values its inventory at the lower of cost and NRV and uses weighted average cost as its cost formula. Note 13 breaks down the inventory into categories (raw materials and returnable glass containers, brews in progress, finished goods, consignment product, and resale goods). These categories are described in Note 4.5. Note 13 also discloses that an expense of $221,000 was recorded to account for damaged finished goods inventory. The note doesn't report the cost of inventory sold but we can assume that cost of goods sold on the income statement is that amount.[1]

BIOLOGICAL ASSETS AND AGRICULTURAL PRODUCE

LO 6

IFRS have special rules for biological assets and agricultural produce. A **biological asset** is a living animal or plant, for example dairy cows, forests, apple trees and apples on trees, and beef cattle. **Agricultural produce** is the harvested product of biological assets, for example milk from the cows, felled trees from the forest, apples from the apple trees, animal carcasses. Biological assets and agricultural produce (while it's still alive) are valued at fair value less cost to sell on the balance sheet date provided the entity (a) controls the asset as a results of past events; (b) it's probable the entity will receive future economic benefits from the asset; and (c) the fair value can be measured reliably. (Fair value is very similar but not exactly the same as NRV.) If fair value can't be determined, then cost is used. Changes in fair value from period to period are reported on the income statement.

Once a biological asset is harvested (beef cattle are slaughtered) or the produce from a biological asset (milk from dairy cows, fruit from a tree) is harvested, the produce is treated as any other type of inventory. The produce is valued at fair value when it's harvested and that becomes the cost of the inventory for accounting purposes. Agricultural produce isn't fair-valued after it's harvested. Once harvested, the same rules apply to agricultural products as to other types of inventory.

Biological assets and agricultural produce are fairly common in Canada—for example, companies with stands of timber, wineries, and agricultural companies. The best way to see this accounting treatment is with an example. Village Farms International, Inc. is a grower and marketer of hydroponic greenhouse grown produce, including tomatoes, bell peppers, and cucumbers. Its biological assets are its produce on the vines. These are reported at fair value on the balance sheet. Extracts from Village Farms' financial statements are shown and explained in Exhibit 7.2.[2]

EXHIBIT 7.2 Village Farms International, Inc.—Biological Assets and Agricultural Produce

Village Farms International, Inc.
Consolidated Statements of Financial Position
(in thousands of United States dollars)

	December 31, 2011	December 31, 2010	January 1, 2010
ASSETS			
Current assets			
Cash and cash equivalent	$2,865	$9,734	$2,611
Trade receivables	8,579	8,131	9,594
Other receivables	512	510	592
Inventories (note 7)	11,624	10,714	9,753
Assets held for sale (note 6)	407	407	–
Income taxes receivable	–	775	–
Prepaids and deposits	590	801	909
Biological asset (note 8)	5,572	5,223	7,340
Total current assets	30,149	36,295	30,799
Non-current assets			
Property, plant and equipment (note 9)	97,601	62,972	66,599
Deferred tax asset (note 20)	689	2,967	4,549
Intangible assets (note 10)	1,198	1,301	1,404
Other assets (note 11)	1,381	1,125	877
Total assets	$131,018	$104,660	$104,228

This is the produce on the vines at year-end. All of Village's biological assets are current but it's possible for them to be long-term as well.

EXHIBIT 7.2 (continued) Village Farms International, Inc.—Biological Assets and Agricultural Produce

Village Farms International, Inc.
Consolidated Statements of Income and Comprehensive Income
For the Years Ended December 31, 2011 and December 31, 2010
(in thousands of United States dollars, except per share data)

	December 31, 2011	December 31, 2010
Net sales	$164,448	$144,768
Cost of sales (note 18)	(140,627)	(123,632)
Change in biological asset (note 8)	269	(2,018)
Selling, general and administrative expenses (note 18)	(14,594)	(13,199)
Income before interest and other expenses (income)	9,496	5,919
Interest expense	3,033	2,814
Interest income	(17)	(39)
Foreign exchange (gain) loss	(1)	57
Amortization of intangible assets (note 10)	103	103
(Gain) loss on derivatives (note 13)	(1,054)	247
Other income, net	(285)	(1,432)
(Gain) loss on disposal/sale of assets	(14)	339
Income before income taxes	7,731	3,830
Provision for (recovery of) income taxes (note 19)	1,926	(421)
Net income and comprehensive income	$5,805	$4,251

The change in the fair value of biological assets in the period is recognized as income.

2 BASIS OF PRESENTATION AND ADOPTION OF IFRS

Basis of Measurement

The consolidated annual financial statements have been prepared on the historical cost basis except for the following material items in the statement of financial position:

- biological assets are measured at fair value less costs to sell.

This is how biological assets are valued on the balance sheet.

3 SIGNIFICANT ACCOUNTING POLICIES, JUDGMENTS AND ESTIMATION UNCERTAINTY

Inventories

Inventory refers to deferred crop costs which are incurred to date on current production and are not defined as a biological asset. Inventories of Company-grown produce consist of raw materials, labour and overhead costs incurred less costs charged to cost of sales throughout the various crop cycles, which end at various times throughout the year. Growing crops are accounted for in accordance with our policy on "Biological Assets." Cost of sales is based on estimated costs over the crop cycle allocated to both actual and estimated future yields at each period end date.

The carrying value of agricultural produce is its fair value less cost to sell at the date of harvest and is presented with biological asset on the statement of financial position.

The cost of produce inventory purchased from third parties is valued at the lower of cost and net realizable value.

LO 7 INVENTORY AND THE SERVICES INDUSTRY

For the most part in this chapter, the discussion of inventory has focused on entities that sell physical goods to customers. A large part of the Canadian economy is made up of entities providing services. Examples of service businesses include banks, insurance companies, hotels, professional services (e.g., accountants and lawyers), and airlines. The not-for-profit sector also provides many services in the Canadian economy, for example hospitals. One characteristic of service

EXHIBIT 7.2 (continued) Village Farms International, Inc.—Biological Assets and Agricultural Produce

3 SIGNIFICANT ACCOUNTING POLICIES, JUDGMENTS AND ESTIMATION UNCERTAINTY (continued)

Biological Assets

Biological assets consist of the Company's produce on the vines at the year end. Measurement of the biological asset begins six weeks prior to harvest as management at this point has visibility on production and expected sales. Costs related to the crop prior to this point are presented in deferred crop costs (inventory). The produce on the vine is measured at fair value less costs to sell and costs to complete, with any change therein recognized in profit or loss. Costs to sell include all costs that would be necessary to sell the assets, including finishing and transportation costs.

This is what's included in biological assets.

Significant Accounting Judgments and Estimation Uncertainties

iv) Biological asset

The fair value of the biological asset is derived using a discounted cash flow model. Management uses estimates for the expected sales price of produce on the vine and costs to sell and complete, which are determined by considering historical actual costs incurred on a per pound basis. The estimated selling price and costs are subject to fluctuations based on the timing of prevailing growing conditions and market conditions.

8 BIOLOGICAL ASSET

Information about the biological asset presented on the statement of financial position and in the statement of income follows:

	December 31, 2011	December 31, 2010	January 1, 2010
Estimated sales value of biological asset	$9,373	$8,517	$11,210
Less			
Estimated remaining costs relating to the biological asset	3,182	2,714	3,054
Estimated selling costs	619	580	816
Fair value of biological asset less costs to sell	5,572	5,223	7,340
Less actual costs (note 7)	2,176	2,096	
Increase in fair value of biological asset over cost	3,396	3,127	
Fair value over cost of harvested and sold biological asset	3,127	5,145	
Change in biological asset	$269	($2,018)	

businesses is that they don't have inventory to offer customers—their services can't be stored. An empty seat on a plane or an empty hotel room can't be saved for when there is more demand. An hour of an accountant's or lawyer's time can't be stored for the busy season. However, service entities do have inventory that's used to provide their services (hospitals have medical supplies, hotels have toiletries that are provided in the rooms).

However, if you examine the balance sheet of a service provider such as an accounting firm, you will find a kind of inventory: the costs the firm has accumulated providing services to clients. For example, the firm's accounting records would accumulate the cost of employee and partner time spent on an engagement. Travel costs, administration costs, supplies, printing, and any other costs incurred to provide services to the client would be recorded as assets until the revenue earned from the client is recognized, at which time the accumulated costs would be expensed and matched to the revenues. Accumulating costs that are a result of client engagement is important for internal control purposes so that management can have information to base billings, and to assess the profitability of different engagements.

An example of the asset side of the balance sheet of a publicly traded Australian law firm called Slater & Gordon Limited is provided in Exhibit 7.3. The work in progress account represents the firm's "inventory" and is the costs incurred on each of the firm's cases. Notice that some of the work in progress is classified as non-current, meaning that these files won't be closed within a year. Also notice that Slater & Gordon has very few tangible assets. Seventy-five percent of its assets are cash, receivables, and work in progress.[3]

EXHIBIT 7.3 Balance Sheet of Slater & Gordon Limited

SLATER & GORDON LIMITED AND CONTROLLED ENTITIES
ABN 93 097 297 400

CONSOLIDATED STATEMENT OF FINANCIAL POSITION
AS AT 30 JUNE 2011

Work in progress is a law firm's inventory.

Some work in progress isn't current.

	Note	2011 $'000	2010 $'000
Current assets			
Cash and cash equivalents	8	4,032	30,110
Receivables	9	95,804	66,719
Work in progress	10	179,606	111,869
Current tax asset	6	391	–
Other current assets	11	4,836	4,124
Total current assets		**284, 669**	**212,822**
Non-current assets			
Plant and equipment	12	9,943	6,943
Work in progress	10	7,045	7,245
Intangible assets	13	58,352	25,966
Other non-current assets	14	18,401	17,346
Total non-current assets		**93,741**	**57,500**
Total assets		**378,410**	**270,322**

Describes what's included in work in progress.

(h) Work in progress

Work in progress is carried at either cost or it may include profit recognised to date based on the value of work completed. The following are the methodologies adopted for each practice area in determining the value of work in progress:

Non-personal injury

For family law, estate/probate, industrial law, commercial law and funded project litigation matters, time records and historical levels of fees billed are used in determining the value of work completed.

Personal injury

Work in progress for practice areas, other than project litigation matters, that do not calculate the fees due by a client solely by reference to time records is recognised using the percentage of completion method when the stage of completion can be reasonably determined, and the fee per file and probability of success can be reliably estimated, making allowance for the "No Win, No Fee" conditional fee arrangements, under which the Personal Injury practice operates.

ACCOUNTING STANDARDS FOR PRIVATE ENTERPRISES

ASPE and IFRS are very similar in the ways they account for inventory, except that ASPE don't have specific standards for biological assets and agricultural produce so these assets will often be absent from the balance sheet.

INVENTORY ERRORS

LO 8

For a variety of reasons, errors can occur in accounting for inventory. Sources of error include:

- incorrect counting of inventory at the beginning or end of a period
- incorrect entry of inventory data into the accounting system
- excluding items from inventory that should be included (goods on consignment, goods in transit)
- including items in inventory that should be excluded (goods on consignment, goods in transit, goods sold but not shipped)
- errors in costs included in inventory
- failure to make adjustments for lost, stolen, damaged, or obsolete inventory

Inventory errors affect both the income statement and balance sheet in more than one period. They can also occur with both periodic and perpetual inventory control systems. To understand the impact of inventory errors, we'll examine the equation for calculating cost of goods sold under a periodic system:

Cost of goods sold = Beginning inventory + Purchases − Ending inventory

Errors can occur in any component of the equation and the nature of the error will determine how the financial statements are affected. For example, suppose that Alban Ltd. failed to include $5,000 of inventory in its December 31, 2018 year-end count. As a result, ending inventory and total assets are understated by $5,000, cost of goods sold is overstated by $5,000, and net income and retained earnings are understated by $5,000. Let's look at the math to see why. If Alban's beginning inventory was $100,000, during the year it purchased $250,000 of inventory, and the correct ending inventory was $125,000, we see the following:

	No error	Error
Beginning inventory	$100,000	$100,000
+ Purchases	250,000	250,000
− Ending inventory	125,000	120,000
= Cost of goods sold	$225,000	$230,000

If the inventory count had been done correctly, ending inventory would have been $125,000 and cost of goods sold would have been $225,000. Because of the error, ending inventory is $120,000 (understated by $5,000) and cost of goods sold is $230,000 (overstated by $5,000). The error on the income statement flows through to net income and retained earnings. Ratios are also affected; in Alban's case the current ratio, debt-to-equity ratio, return on assets and equity, gross margin percentage, and profit margin would all be affected. Different types of errors will affect the financial statements in different ways. The error would spill over into the next period because beginning inventory would be understated by $5,000 (it would be $120,000 instead of $125,000) and cost of goods sold would therefore be understated by $5,000.

LO 9

INVENTORY ACCOUNTING AND INCOME TAXES

The accounting choices made by managers frequently have tax implications. Often, as we have discussed, managers must choose among accounting alternatives that can lower the entity's tax burden or achieve some other objective of financial reporting. In situations where the *Income Tax Act* doesn't specify a treatment, the method used for financial reporting purposes will often be used for tax purposes. Inventory accounting is an example. The *Income Tax Act* isn't very specific about how to account for inventory for tax purposes so entities will usually use the inventory accounting methods selected for the general purpose financial statements. This means that these accounting choices can have a bearing on the amount of tax an entity pays.

www.cra-arc.gc.ca

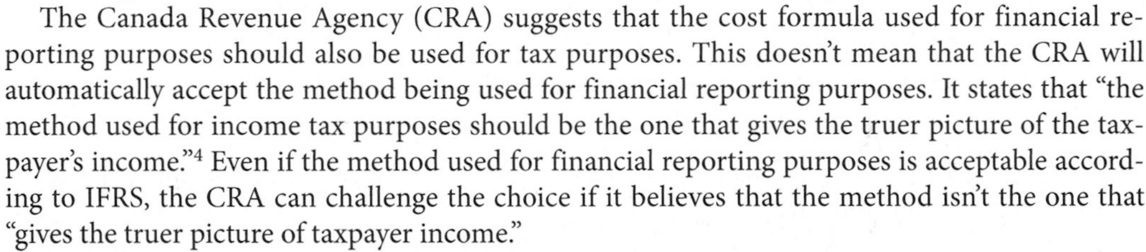

The Canada Revenue Agency (CRA) suggests that the cost formula used for financial reporting purposes should also be used for tax purposes. This doesn't mean that the CRA will automatically accept the method being used for financial reporting purposes. It states that "the method used for income tax purposes should be the one that gives the truer picture of the taxpayer's income."[4] Even if the method used for financial reporting purposes is acceptable according to IFRS, the CRA can challenge the choice if it believes that the method isn't the one that "gives the truer picture of taxpayer income."

The definition of cost for tax purposes is similar to that used for accounting purposes. The CRA explains that cost for inventories of merchandise purchased for resale or of raw materials acquired for a manufacturing process, means laid-down cost. Laid-down cost includes invoice cost, customs and excise duties, transportation and other acquisition costs, and storage costs where they are significant.[5]

Entities are allowed to use the lower of cost and NRV rule for tax purposes. If the fair market value of inventory at the end of a year is less than its cost, the taxpayer can then use fair market value. This treatment allows the taxpayer to reduce income by writing down the value of inventory to fair market value (NRV).

The CRA requires that methods used to account for inventory for tax purposes be applied consistently from period to period. A method used for tax purposes can only be changed with the permission of the Minister of National Revenue. The minister will usually approve a change if the new method (a) is a more appropriate way of determining income, (b) will be used for financial reporting purposes, and (c) will be used consistently in future years.[6] Restrictions on an entity's ability to change how it accounts for inventory limits changes made simply to avoid tax.

LO 10

FINANCIAL STATEMENT ANALYSIS ISSUES

For many businesses, inventory management is a crucial managerial responsibility. Management's effectiveness and efficiency in managing inventory can have a significant impact on company performance. Managing inventory requires careful balance because carrying too much or too little inventory can be costly. The more inventory an entity has, the more cash is tied up and unavailable for other purposes. On the other hand, too little inventory may mean an entity will run out of the products customers need. This means a loss of revenue for that particular transaction. Worse, the customer and the stream of revenue it would have generated may be permanently lost. Thus, the consequence of not carrying enough inventory could be a decline in revenue. If a manufacturing company runs out of the inventory required for its production process, the entire production process may be forced to stop, which would be very costly.

The **inventory turnover ratio (ITO)** provides information on how efficiently inventory is being managed by measuring how quickly the entity is able to sell its inventory. The inventory turnover ratio is defined as

$$\text{Inventory turnover ratio} = \frac{\text{Cost of sales}}{\text{Average inventory}}$$

Average inventory can be calculated by summing the amount of inventory at the beginning and the end of the period and dividing by two. A better measure can be obtained by using quarterly or monthly data if they are available. This is especially important for seasonal businesses. Many retail businesses have their lowest amount of inventory after the Christmas season and the highest amount in the period leading up to Christmas.

The ITO indicates the number of times during a period that the entity is able to purchase and sell its stock of inventory. Usually, a higher ITO ratio is better because it shows that the entity can sell or "turn over" the inventory more quickly. It also shows that the inventory is more liquid because it's sold more quickly and cash is realized sooner than with slower-moving inventory. A decreasing ITO may indicate that inventory isn't selling or is slow moving because it's obsolete or there is low demand for it. In deteriorating economic periods, an entity's ITO should decrease because it will have too much inventory (the amount of inventory increases while sales and cost of sales decrease). On the other hand, a decreasing ITO could indicate that inventory is being built up in anticipation of increasing sales.

As with other financial ratios, it isn't possible to make sense of the inventory turnover ratio in absolute terms. The ratio must be considered in comparison with those of other, similar entities, or for a particular entity over time. Inventory turnover ratios can vary significantly from industry to industry. A distributor of products imported from Asia will need to carry more inventory than a company with a reliable supplier around the corner.

Another way of looking at the efficiency of inventory management is obtained by dividing the ITO into 365 to give the **average number of days inventory on hand**, the average number of days it takes to sell inventory. The average number of days inventory on hand is defined as

$$\text{Average number of days inventory on hand} = \frac{365}{\text{Inventory turnover ratio}}$$

When a company reduces the average number of days it holds its inventory, it improves its efficiency.

If an entity has many types of inventory, the ITO ratio can be difficult to interpret because the different inventories may turn over at different rates. The ITO ratio calculated using the aggregate total reported on the balance sheet will just be an average of the turnover ratios of all the different types of inventory.

Let's look at the ITO and the average number of days of inventory on hand for Leon's Furniture Limited (Leon's) and The Brick Ltd., two large furniture and appliance retailers, for 2007 through 2011. The information is presented in Table 7.10.

The calculation of the 2011 ITO and average number of days inventory on hand for Leon's is as follows:

$$\begin{aligned}\text{Inventory turnover ratio} &= \frac{\text{Cost of sales}}{\text{Average inventory}}\\ &= \frac{\$394{,}099{,}000}{\$87{,}830{,}000 + \$85{,}423{,}000 \div 2}\\ &= 4.55\end{aligned}$$

$$\begin{aligned}\text{Average number of days inventory on hand} &= \frac{365}{\text{Inventory turnover ratio}}\\ &= \frac{365}{4.55}\\ &= 80.2 \text{ days}\end{aligned}$$

Over the period shown, Leon's ITO ratio has been relatively stable, ranging from a low of 4.55 in 2011 to a high of 5.23 in 2008. The 2008 amount seems to have been an outlier. 2011 shows a fairly significant decline that will bear watching. The average number of days has ranged from 69.9 to 80.2 days. There are no definitive trends that show definite improvement

TABLE 7.10 Leon's Furniture Ltd. and The Brick Ltd.: Inventory Turnover Ratio 2007–2011 (in thousands of dollars)

Leon's	2011	2010	2009	2008	2007
Inventory	$87,830	$85,423	$83,957	$92,904	$75,640
Cost of goods sold	394,099	412,379	419,819	440,360	363,261
Inventory turnover ratio	4.55	4.87	4.75	5.23	4.83
Average number of days inventory on hand	80.2	75.0	76.9	69.9	75.5
The Brick	**2011**	**2010**	**2009**	**2008**	**2007**
Inventory	$161,684	$172,844	$170,862	$207,627	$236,703
Cost of goods sold	753,977	782,734	701,893	824,553	850,100
Inventory turnover ratio	4.51	4.55	3.71	3.71	3.80
Average number of days inventory on hand	81.0	80.1	98.4	98.3	96.1

or deterioration in inventory management. Changes in ITO can be due to many factors: more inventory needed to meet the demands of customers and the competition, or the mix of inventory may be changing (each **category** of Leon's inventory may not have the same turnover ratio).

The Brick's information paints a more definitive story. Over the five years, The Brick's ITO ratio has improved so that in 2011 both The Brick's and Leon's ITO ratios were almost identical. Before 2011, The Brick's ITO was consistently and significantly lower than Leon's. In recent years, The Brick's management has taken steps to improve its inventory management. The Brick's 2010 annual report explained that in 2009 the company took steps to "reduce the level of slow moving inventory on hand, to improve in-stock positions for top-selling items, and to improve the logistics of in-transit inventory." As a result, the company can support sales with lower inventory levels.

Another point to note is that a company's management of its inventory affects the ratios and how they are interpreted. For example, some companies use an approach called **just-in-time (JIT)** inventory management. In a JIT inventory system, a manufacturer orders materials or produces parts or finished goods only when they are required. In a non-JIT system, a company maintains stocks of inventory for use in production or for sale. A company using JIT inventory should have lower amounts of inventory and a higher ITO than companies that don't use JIT. With less inventory and faster ITO, the impact of different cost formulas will be less significant. You may discuss JIT inventory systems in detail in your managerial accounting course, but for now the point is to recognize that ratios can be affected by many different management decisions.

Stakeholders need to pay attention to levels and categories of inventory to get an understanding of an entity's situation. The focus of this discussion has been on retail businesses, but manufacturing companies also have significant amounts of inventory. For example, if a manufacturer's raw materials are increasing faster than work-in-process or finished goods, it's an indication that new orders are coming in and additional inventory is required. It could also be due to an anticipated increase in raw material prices.

The existence of inventory doesn't mean that it can be sold. Suppose that at the end of a year you notice that the amount of inventory reported on the balance sheet had increased significantly from previous years. How can you interpret that change? If sales had increased along with inventory, you might conclude that inventory has increased to support the increased level of sales. If there was no increase in sales, you could conclude that management was building up inventory in anticipation of an expansion or to reflect anticipated sales growth. On the other hand, the increase might reflect over-purchasing, slow moving inventory, or obsolete inventory that had not yet been written off.

INSIGHT

It should be clear from the discussion of the different inventory cost formulas that financial analysis and financial ratios for an entity will be affected by the cost formula used. This means that it may be difficult to compare firms in an industry if the amount of inventory and cost of sales differ because they are using different cost formulas or treating similar costs differently. The different treatments can affect the inventory turnover ratio, current ratio, gross margin, and profit margin, to name a few. It's important to remember that while the various accounting methods affect our accounting measures, they don't affect the concept that is being measured. Whether a company uses FIFO or average cost doesn't alter its actual liquidity or profitability.

A Banker's View of Inventory

When an entity borrows money, the lender commonly requests collateral in the event the borrower can't repay the loan. Inventory seems like a sensible asset to use as collateral but, usually, banks don't welcome it because inventory can be difficult to dispose of. After all, if the borrower can't sell the inventory, how will a bank sell it? What would a bank do with large quantities of toasters, shirts, or machine-tooled dies? Banks recover as little as five or ten cents for each dollar of inventory that is reported on the balance sheet if the borrower can't repay a loan.

All the same, many businesses require financing for their inventory. This is especially true for seasonal businesses. Consider a company that produces Christmas decorations. The company would build up its inventory during the year until it began shipping its products as the holiday season approached. Most seasonal businesses won't have a stockpile of cash available to self-finance the inventory buildup so they rely on bank credit to finance this, and banks will lend against inventory, despite their concerns. However, when a bank lends against inventory, it expects the loan to be repaid in full at the end of the entity's operating cycle. In other words, inventory loans aren't permanent. In contrast, when accounts receivable is the collateral, the amount borrowed can remain outstanding permanently, based on the amount of receivables the entity has.

Solved Problem

In 2014, Naomi Krajden developed a computer game called *Zordef of the Deep* (*Zordef*). The game was a big hit among Naomi's friends and they suggested it might be successful commercially. At first, Naomi tried to market *Zordef* online on her Web site. However, it quickly became obvious that this approach wasn't going to work. In the six months Naomi tried to distribute the game on her own, she managed to sell only 154 copies.

In mid-2015, Naomi had a chance meeting with a marketing representative with Wonder Software Ltd. (WS), a company that produces computer software. WS is a privately owned corporation with its head office near Ottawa. Naomi demonstrated *Zordef* to the representative and he offered to bring it to WS's executives for evaluation. After testing and discussions, WS offered to market *Zordef*. Naomi and WS agreed that Naomi would transfer title to the game to WS in exchange for 30 percent of the net income earned on sales of the game. The contract between the parties stipulated that WS could deduct appropriate, reasonable expenses in determining net income. *Zordef of the Deep* was released in November 2016.

Games of this type have lives of about three years. Most sales are generated in the first few months and then tail off quickly. Sales of *Zordef* in the ten months ended August 31, 2017 were \$838,000. WS estimates that sales of *Zordef* for the 12 months ending August 31, 2018, will be about \$420,000, and perhaps \$100,000 in the 12 months after that. WS recently presented Naomi with an income statement for the ten months ended August 31, 2017 and a cheque for \$18,000. The income statement and additional information obtained from WS is shown below:

Zordef of the Deep Computer Game Statement of Income for the Ten Months Ended August 31, 2017		
Sales (Note 1)		$838,000
Cost of goods sold (Note 2)	$304,000	
Selling and administrative costs (Note 3)	252,000	
Packaging design costs (Note 4)	97,000	
Advertising (Note 5)	85,000	
Product development costs (Note 6)	32,000	
Taxes	8,000	778,000
Net income		$ 60,000

Notes:

1. Revenue is recognized when shipped to the customer. The sales figure is net of an allowance for doubtful accounts and returns.
2. Cost of goods sold includes production costs of the game. Approximately $154,000 represents direct costs of production (labour and materials) and an allocation of $115,000 of overhead costs, including depreciation of plant and equipment, supervisory staff, quality control staff, and so on. Also included is $15,000 for games that had to be discarded because they were damaged or not usable and $20,000 for the estimated payment to Naomi.
3. Selling and administrative costs include commissions paid to salespeople, an allocation of salespeople's salaries and an allocation of general office overhead. A special charge of $50,000 was levied against *Zordef of the Deep* to account for senior management's time spent on the game.
4. The charge represents money spent to develop packaging for *Zordef of the Deep*. The packaging was designed by an outside agency and the charge represents the full amount paid for the design.
5. The company spent $40,000 directly advertising and promoting *Zordef of the Deep* to consumers and retailers. The remaining amount is an allocation of the overall corporate advertising budget that includes promotion of the WS full product line.
6. Before *Zordef* was brought to market, WS made modifications to the program. The cost represents the time of WS's programmer charged at the prevailing market rate. This is the rate WS charges outsiders who contract WS to do programming.

Naomi Krajden is disturbed that, despite the amount of sales of the game, the profit figure is very low, and she doesn't think she is being dealt with fairly. She has asked you to prepare a report examining the accounting methods used by WS in calculating *Zordef's* net income. The report will be used in negotiations with WS and potentially in any legal action taken by Naomi.

Required:

Prepare the report to Naomi Krajden.

Comment: *This case takes an aggressive stance on behalf of Naomi Krajden. The response argues that only incremental costs should be charged to* Zordef. *Other approaches are possible and legitimate. WS would likely disagree strongly with this approach and the negotiations would go from there.*

Ms. Naomi Krajden
11242 Joseph Casavant
Montreal, Quebec

Dear Naomi:

I have reviewed the financial statements you have been given by Wonder Software Ltd. (Wonder) that shows the profitability of your *Zordef of the Deep* game, which you sold to Wonder in exchange for 30 percent of the profits. It appears from the information disclosed in the statement that Wonder has done its best to charge as many expenses to the product as possible, presumably with the purpose of minimizing the net income earned by the game and thereby minimizing the payments to you. This is a good strategy for Wonder since it keeps more cash in the company but bad for you because you get paid less.

Comment: *The role is important. You are advising Naomi Krajden who believes she has been disadvantaged by the accounting done by Wonder Software. This means that your response should focus on looking out for Naomi's best interests.*

There are many ways to do accounting. Often, there are reasonable alternative methods that can be justified in a situation. In my analysis below, I will recommend alternative accounting treatments that are in your interests but can be reasonably justified. I will not bind myself to Accounting Standards for Private Enterprises (ASPE) or International Financial Reporting Standards (IFRS). I do not think that limiting choices to ASPE/IFRS will always provide an economically sound outcome. The basis of my approach is that only new costs Wonder incurred by adding *Zordef* to its product line should be charged to *Zordef* for purposes of determining the profit of the game. I will argue that allocated costs should not be included. This approach could be called an incremental cost approach. This is, of course, only one approach to this situation and Wonder will likely use alternatives to make their case. While I am confident the positions I take are compelling, it is important to recognize that good arguments can be made for the alternatives.

It is not always possible to definitively resolve the controversy without additional information. In these situations, I will identify the additional information that is required and why it is required.

1. Revenue recognition describes the point in time an entity records a sale. It is appropriate for Wonder to recognize revenue when the programs are shipped. It is really the only reasonable time available. It is reasonable to allocate the bad debt expense since it is likely very difficult to attribute the costs directly to the sales of individual products. Returns should be based on estimated returns of *Zordef*. However, the bases for allocating the costs and estimating returns should be reviewed to ensure they are reasonable and are applied correctly (so that *Zordef* is not overcharged).
2. The $154,000 of direct materials and labour can be reasonably charged to *Zordef* since they are costs incurred to produce the game. The allocation of overhead is consistent with IFRS but is not, in my opinion, appropriate in this situation ($115,000). The only overhead costs that should be allocated to *Zordef* are incremental ones—new costs that were incurred because of the introduction of *Zordef*. From the information provided, it does not appear that new costs were incurred because of *Zordef*. The $15,000 for production problems should be excluded in the determination of your profit share since it pertains to management and production inefficiencies. There is no reason why you should bear this cost. It is also completely inappropriate to include your profit share in the *Zordef* statement ($20,000). Your payment represents a share of the profit, not a cost of the product. Therefore, *Zordef*'s net income should be increased by $150,000.

   In the event my recommendations above are not accepted (through negotiation or a legal ruling), it will be necessary to verify the amounts allocated to *Zordef*. It will also be necessary to find out the method used to allocate costs and to assess its reasonableness and to determine whether the method has been properly applied. These steps are necessary because Wonder has incentives for overstating the costs allocated to *Zordef*.
3. As described in point 2, allocated costs should not be included in the *Zordef* income statement. Unless a case can be made for incremental general and administrative costs, these should not be charged to *Zordef*. The $50,000 senior management charge is not appropriate since *Zordef* is being charged for the work senior managers are supposed to do. In addition, there may be double counting with the allocation of the general and admin plus the $50,000 for senior management. Only the sales commissions represent a legitimate charge. Therefore expenses must be decreased by $50,000 plus the allocated portion of general office overhead.
4. The cost of developing packaging for *Zordef* should be charged against *Zordef*. However, the full amount of the cost was expensed in fiscal 2017. Since *Zordef* will be sold in fiscal 2018 and 2019, it is appropriate that some of the cost of the packaging be charged against revenue in those years. This is known as matching. If the *Zordef* income statement is to reflect the actual

performance of the product, then it makes economic sense to match costs attributable to sales to the revenue. Instead, Wonder has fully expensed the cost in 2017, which lowers income in the current period and reduces the payment to you. The packaging could be allocated on a straight-line basis over the three years of the expected product life. This treatment will reduce expenses by about $65,000 in the current year ($97,000 ÷ 3 years × 2 years).

5. The $40,000 of direct advertising costs should be charged against *Zordef* since they are direct costs. The remaining costs should not be charged because they are not direct costs and there was likely no increase in the overall advertising budget because of the addition to *Zordef*. Therefore, expenses should decrease by $45,000.
6. It is unreasonable to charge *Zordef* for costs that were not incurred by Wonder. *Zordef* should be charged the actual cost incurred to pay the programmers to do the modifications. If the programmers are on salary and did not get paid more or overtime as a result of *Zordef*, this is not an incremental cost and should not be charged to *Zordef* at all. Charging the market rate for the services provided by in-house programmers does not in any way reflect the economic cost to Wonder for the programming. I suggest that your initial position should be that unless incremental programming costs were incurred there should be no charge to *Zordef*, and in negotiations you can back off to the actual cost of the programmers' time.

Without complete information, it is not possible to determine the exact net income to present to Wonder. However, based on the analysis above, net income should increase by a minimum of $310,000 (which may increase with additional information) and increase the payment to you to $93,000.

Please contact me if you have any questions.

SUMMARY OF KEY POINTS

LO 1 Inventory is goods available for sale by an entity, or goods that will be used to produce goods that will be sold. It can also include materials used in supplying a service to customers. According to IFRS, inventory is valued at the lower of cost and net realizable value, where cost includes all costs incurred to purchase or make the products and get them ready for sale to customers. For inventory that's purchased, cost should include all the costs incurred to ready the inventory for sale or use. For manufacturers and processors, cost of inventory should include the cost of materials used plus the cost of labour directly used to produce the product plus an allocation of overhead incurred in the production process.

LO 2 There are two types of control systems for keeping track of inventory transactions: perpetual systems and periodic systems. A perpetual inventory control system keeps an ongoing tally of purchases and sales of inventory, and the inventory account is adjusted to reflect changes as they occur. With a periodic inventory control system, the balance in ending inventory is determined by counting the inventory on hand and calculating cost of sales indirectly using the equation, cost of sales = beginning inventory + purchases − ending inventory. The choice between a periodic and a perpetual inventory control system is an internal control issue, not an accounting one.

LO 3 Accountants don't usually keep track of the costs associated with individual items of inventory. Instead, they use cost formulas to move costs from inventory to cost of sales, without regard for the actual physical flow of the inventory. There are three cost formulas currently in use in Canada: FIFO, average cost, and specific identification. The choice of cost formula doesn't directly affect the cash flow of the entity, but the amounts reported on the balance sheet and the income statement can be significantly different depending on the cost formula used.

LO 4 According to IFRS (and ASPE), inventory on hand at the end of a period must be reported at the lower of cost and net realizable value (NRV). If the NRV of inventory at the end of a reporting period is lower than its cost, the inventory must be written down to its NRV. The amount of a writedown is expensed in the period of the writedown. Inventory that has been written down can be written back up to its original cost (but not higher than that).

LO 5 Conservatism (prudence) is an accounting concept that says caution should be exercised when making accounting judgments so that assets, revenues, and net income aren't overstated and that liabilities and expenses aren't understated.

LO 6 Biological assets are living plants and animals and agricultural produce is the harvested product of biological assets. Before harvesting, biological assets and agricultural products are valued at fair value and changes in fair value are included in the calculation of net income. Agricultural produce is valued at fair value when it's harvested and that becomes the cost of the inventory for accounting purposes.

LO 7 Services businesses like law firms and accounting firms report on their balance sheets a type of inventory that reflects costs incurred on behalf of clients that haven't been billed to the client.

LO 8 Inventory errors are mistakes made in accounting for inventory. Errors can arise from many sources, including inventory counts and bookkeeping errors. Errors will affect the balance sheet and income statement, may impact more than one period, and will affect many financial ratios.

LO 9 Managers often make accounting choices that have tax implications. When the *Income Tax Act* doesn't specify a treatment, the method used for financial reporting purposes will often be used for tax purposes. The Canada Revenue Agency suggests that the cost formula used for financial reporting purposes should also be used for tax purposes. Entities can apply the lower of cost and NRV rule for tax purposes.

LO 10 Management's effectiveness and efficiency in managing inventory can have a significant impact on entity performance. Managing inventory requires careful balance as carrying too much or too little can be costly. The inventory turnover ratio and the average number of days inventory on hand provide information on how efficiently and effectively inventory is being managed. A low or decreasing inventory turnover ratio can indicate that inventory isn't selling or is slow moving because it's obsolete or there is low demand. Generally, a higher inventory turnover ratio indicates better management of inventory.

FORMULA SUMMARY

$$\text{Inventory turnover ratio} = \frac{\text{Cost of sales}}{\text{Average inventory}}$$

$$\text{Average number of days inventory on hand} = \frac{365}{\text{Inventory turnover ratio}}$$

KEY TERMS

agricultural produce, p. 399
average cost method, p. 386
average number of days inventory on hand, p. 405
biological assets, p. 399
category, p. 406
conservatism, p. 396
finished goods inventory, p. 381
first-in, first-out (FIFO), p. 386
inventory, p. 380
inventory turnover ratio (ITO), p. 404
just-in-time (JIT) inventory, p. 406
last-in, first-out (LIFO), p. 393
lower of cost and net realizable value (LCNRV) rule, p. 394

net realizable value (NRV), p. 394
overhead, p. 381
periodic inventory control system, p. 383
perpetual inventory control system, p. 382
raw materials inventory, p. 381
replacement cost, p. 392
specific identification method, p. 387
work-in-process inventory (WIP), p. 381
writedown, p. 394
writeoff, p. 394

SIMILAR TERMS

The left column gives alternative terms that are sometimes used for the accounting terms introduced in this chapter, which are listed in the right column.

prudence **conservatism, p. 396**

ASSIGNMENT MATERIALS

Questions

Q7-1. Describe the type of inventory you would expect each of the following entities to have:
a. Shoppers Drug Mart Corporation (drug store)
b. Holiday Inn (hotel)
c. Barrick Gold Corporation (gold mining company)
d. Ryerson University (university)
e. Toyota Motor Corporation (car maker)
f. Coca-Cola Company (soft drink maker)
g. Burger King Corporation (fast-food chain)

Q7-2. For each of the following entities, describe what would be included in raw materials, work-in-process, and finished goods inventory:
a. computer producer (company assembles computers from parts it buys from various manufacturers)
b. producer of frozen French fries
c. wood-furniture maker
d. miner and refiner of gold

Q7-3. Explain the concept of conservatism.

Q7-4. When evaluating its year-end inventory at the end of fiscal 2017, a company determines that its inventory is valued $250,000 to $350,000 above NRV. What is the impact on the balance sheet and income statement in 2017 and 2018 if the inventory is written down by $250,000 is 2017? What is the impact if the inventory is written down by $350,000 in 2017? What accounting concept might lead management to use the higher amount for the writedown? Explain. Assume the written-down inventory is sold in 2018.

Q7-5. Explain why it isn't possible to calculate cost of goods sold when a periodic inventory control system is used if the inventory isn't counted.

Q7-6. Explain and give examples of the following types of inventory:
a. raw materials
b. work-in-process
c. finished goods
d. supplies

Q7-7. Why isn't it possible to determine the amount of inventory that was stolen during a period when a periodic inventory control system is used?

Q7-8. Explain the difference between periodic and perpetual inventory control systems. Which do you think is the better system to use? Why?

Q7-9. Why is it often necessary to use a cost formula for valuing inventory and determining cost of sales? Why can't the actual cost of the goods sold be used to calculate cost of sales in these situations?

Q7-10. Regardless of the cost formula being used (FIFO, average cost, specific identification), the sum of cost of sales plus ending inventory will be the same. Explain why.

Q7-11. Explain why a FIFO inventory system gives higher inventory valuation and lower cost of sales than average cost when prices are rising.

Q7-12. Explain how costs flow through the following cost formulas: FIFO versus average cost versus specific identification.

Q7-13. What is the lower of cost and NRV rule? Why is it used?

Q7-14. Why might it be difficult to actually determine the NRV of inventory when applying the lower of cost and NRV rule? Provide some examples of when determining NRV might be difficult.

Q7-15. Why is it necessary to count inventory when a perpetual inventory control system is used? Explain. Why is it necessary to count inventory when a periodic inventory control system is used? Explain.

Q7-16. Explain how the specific identification method of valuing inventory works. Why do most entities not use this method? Under what circumstances is the method useful? Why does this method sometimes make it easy to manipulate the financial statements?

Q7-17. Why is the choice of the inventory cost formula important for tax purposes? Explain.

Q7-18. Why isn't it possible to satisfy a tax minimization objective and an income maximization objective when selecting the inventory cost formula an entity will use?

Q7-19. Onslow Ltd. (Onslow) is a small public company trading on a Canadian stock exchange. Onslow's managers have a bonus plan that is based on net income and the managers believe that the amount of reported earnings is important for maintaining the company's stock price. Assume that whether Onslow uses FIFO or average cost will have a significant effect on reported earnings (FIFO earnings being higher) and the amount of assets it reports on its balance sheet. Discuss the issues that Onslow's management must consider when choosing between FIFO and average cost.

Q7-20. Does it matter which cost formula an entity uses if the price it pays for its inventory is stable? Explain.

Q7-21. How does the choice of cost formula affect financial ratios such as the inventory turnover ratio and the current ratio? Does the choice have any effect on the actual rate at which an entity's inventory turns over or the entity's actual liquidity? Explain.

Q7-22. What is inventory turnover? What does it tell a stakeholder about how the entity is managing its inventory? What could be some reasons for a decreasing inventory turnover ratio? What could be some reasons for an increasing inventory turnover ratio?

Q7-23. Which cost formula for valuing inventory is best? Explain.

Q7-24. Explain why the cash spent on inventory isn't affected by the cost formula used.

Q7-25. What are biological assets? What makes them different from most other types of assets an entity has?

Q7-26. Under ASPE, agricultural produce isn't accounted for any differently than other types of inventory. A farmer has an apple orchard. What amount would be reported on the farm's balance sheet for apples mid-way through the growing season under ASPE?

What would be reported if the balance sheet was prepared according to IFRS? Explain the difference.

Q7-27. Describe the nature of "inventory" that would appear on the balance sheet of an accounting firm? Why does this "inventory" appear on the balance sheet? Why aren't the costs simply expensed as incurred?

Q7-28. At the 2017 year-end inventory count, some inventory is counted twice (the count shows more inventory than is really there). What is the impact of double-counting inventory on the 2017 and 2018 financial statements? Explain.

Exercises

E7-1. **(Effect of an error on the financial statements, LO 8)** Elko Inc. uses a periodic inventory control system. During Elko's inventory count on December 31, 2017, $200,000 of the inventory was counted twice, in error. Elko reported inventory of $1,550,000 on December 31, 2016 and during the year it purchased $4,500,000 of inventory. The count on December 31, 2017 reported $1,900,000 of inventory, including the counting error. What is the effect of the counting error on net income for the year ended December 31, 2017 and on the amount of inventory reported on the balance sheet on December 31, 2017? Explain your answer.

E7-2. **(Determine cost of units sold and cost of units remaining in inventory using different cost formulas, LO 2, 3)** The following information is provided for Heatherton Inc. (Heatherton):

Heatherton Inc. Inventory Information for October 2018		
	Number of units purchased	**Price paid per unit**
Purchased on October 8, 2018	2,200	$ 8
Purchased on October 17, 2018	1,650	$ 9
Purchased on October 25, 2018	1,800	$10

On October 31, 2018, Heatherton sold 4,800 units of inventory to customers.

Required:

Identify which inventory costs would be expensed in October 2018 and which costs would be in inventory on October 31, 2018 using the average cost and FIFO cost formulas. Assume Badger had no inventory on hand at the beginning of October and that it uses a periodic inventory system.

E7-3. **(Calculating cost of sales and ending inventory using different cost formulas, LO 3)** You are provided the following information about Jaffray Ltd. (Jaffray) for June 2017. Assume that Jaffray uses a periodic inventory system and that during June the company sold 500 units of inventory:

Date	Description	Number of units	Cost per unit	Total cost
June 1	Opening inventory	500 units	$10	$ 5,000
June 12	Purchase	350 units	$11	3,850
June 22	Purchase	450 units	$12	5,400
	Total	1,300 units		$14,250

Required:

Calculate cost of goods sold and ending inventory on June 30, 2017 for Jaffray, using the average cost and FIFO cost formulas. How many units of inventory are on hand at the end of June under each cost formula?

E7-4. **(Calculating cost of sales and ending inventory using different flow assumptions, LO 3)** You are provided the following information about Kinistino Inc. (Kinistino) for November 2018. Assume that Kinistino uses a periodic inventory system and that during November the company sold 52,000 units of inventory:

Date	Description	Number of units	Cost per unit	Total cost
November 1	Opening inventory	35,000 units	$4.50	$157,500
November 13	Purchase	21,100 units	4.90	103,390
November 21	Purchase	11,800 units	5.25	61,950
	Total	67,900 units		$322,840

Required:

Calculate cost of goods sold and ending inventory on November 30, 2018 for Kinistino, using the average cost and FIFO cost formulas. How many units of inventory are on hand at the end of November under each cost formula?

E7-5. **(Calculating cost of sales and ending inventory using average cost and FIFO cost formulas, LO 2, 3)** Information is provided for Lucan Ltd. below.

Date	Purchases	Sales	Balance
June 30, 2018			8,500 units @ $8.50
July 5, 2018	2,400 units @ $9.00		
July 8, 2018		4,200 units @ $15.00	
July 15, 2018	4,400 units @ $9.50		
July 20, 2018		7,500 units @ $16.00	
July 22, 2018	6,000 units @ $9.75		
July 29, 2018		5,200 units @ $16.50	
July 31, 2018			4,400 units @ $

Required:

Calculate cost of goods sold and ending inventory for Lucan Ltd., using the average cost and FIFO cost formulas. Assume Lucan uses a periodic inventory system.

E7-6. **(Classifying different types of inventory, LO 1)** Whonock Ltd. (Whonock) is a manufacturer of fine wood furniture. Indicate whether Whonock would classify the costs associated with each of the following types as inventory and if it should be classified as inventory, whether it would be considered raw materials, work-in-process, finished goods, or supplies. Provide a brief explanation for each classification.

a. lumber
b. unpainted furniture
c. furniture makers' tools
d. fabric
e. sandpaper
f. furniture awaiting shipment on the loading dock
g. crates used for packing furniture for shipment
h. storage containers for parts (nails, screws, etc.) used to build the furniture

E7-7. **(Classifying different types of inventory, LO 1)** Clarke's Beach Burgers Inc. (CBB) is a burger joint that claims to have the best burgers in the world. For each of the following items, indicate whether CBB would classify the costs as inventory and, if it should be classified as inventory, how you would classify the inventory. Provide a brief explanation for each classification.

a. wrappers for burgers
b. plastic cutlery
c. brooms and mops
d. oil for cooking the French fries
e. raw meat
f. cooking implements
g. ketchup, mustard, and relish
h. cleaning supplies (soap, disinfectant, etc.)

E7-8. **(Classifying different types of inventory, LO 1)** For each of the following, explain whether the asset can be classified as inventory on the entity's balance sheet. This is a tricky question that requires some careful thought:

Entity	*Asset*
a. bank	cash
b. equipment rental store	chain saw
c. commercial real estate developer	shopping centre

E7-9. **(Using the specific identification cost formula to account for inventory, LO 3)** Explain which of the following businesses would likely use the specific identification cost formula to account for its inventory and which would use FIFO or average cost:
a. customer furniture maker
b. car dealership
c. lumberyard
d. high-end audio-visual store
e. orange juice producer

E7-10. **(Calculating cost of sales and ending inventory using the average cost and FIFO cost formulas when prices are stable, LO 2, 3)** The following information is provided for Clova Ltd. (Clova):

	Number of units	Purchase price per unit	Selling price per unit
Inventory on hand on January 1, 2017	50,000	$5	
Inventory purchases during 2017	200,000	$5	
Inventory purchases during 2018	250,000	$5	
Sales during 2017	190,000		$11
Sales during 2018	270,000		$11

Required:

a. Calculate ending inventory on December 31, 2017 and 2018, and cost of sales and gross margin for the years ended December 31, 2017 and 2018 for Clova, using FIFO and average cost. Assume that Clova uses a periodic inventory control system.
b. Explain the results you obtained in (a). Do you find anything unusual about the amounts you calculated for ending inventory, cost of sales, and gross margin under each of the cost formulas?

E7-11. **(Managing income with specific identification, LO 3)** Fermeuse Motors Ltd. (Fermeuse) is a new car dealership. Fermeuse has four identical vehicles on its lot ready for sale. The cost of the cars and their vehicle identification numbers is:

VIN 2X346782N	$21,200
VIN 3K786281L	19,800
VIN 8T492711K	22,900
VIN 4U787412Q	20,150

Recently, a customer purchased one of the cars for $32,000 and will be picking it up in a few days. The customer will be indifferent to which car he receives.

Required:

a. If Fermeuse wanted to minimize its profit on this sale, which of the cars would it have sold to the customer? Calculate gross margin and ending inventory at the end of the period.
b. If Fermeuse wanted to maximize its profit on this sale, which of the cars would it have sold to the customer? Calculate gross margin and ending inventory at the end of the period.
c. What is the impact on ending inventory of your choices in (a) and (b) above? Under what circumstances might Fermeuse management want to maximize profit? Under what circumstances might it want to minimize profit? In reality, would it be possible for Fermeuse's management to have the opportunity to manage the financial statements in this way? Explain.

E7-12. **(Calculating inventory turnover ratio and the average number of days inventory on hand, LO 10)** You are provided with the following information about Gabarus Inc. (Gabarus):

Cost of sales for the year ended June 30, 2018	$27,050,000
Inventory balance on June 30, 2017	$ 6,900,000
Inventory balance on June 30, 2018	$ 7,800,000

Required:

a. Calculate Gabarus's inventory turnover ratio for the year ended June 30, 2018.
b. What is the average length of time it took Gabarus to sell its inventory in 2018?
c. Is Gabarus's inventory turnover ratio satisfactory? What would you need to know to fully answer this question?

E7-13. **(Lower of cost and NRV, LO 4)** Frobisher Inc. (Frobisher) uses the lower of cost and NRV rule to value its inventory. Frobisher's inventory on February 28, 2017 had a cost of $1,125,000 and a NRV of $1,035,000.

Required:

a. By how much should Frobisher's inventory be written down?
b. Prepare the journal entry Frobisher should prepare to record the writedown.
c. What amount should be reported for inventory on Frobisher's February 28, 2017 balance sheet?

E7-14. **(Lower of cost and NRV, LO 4)** Puvirnituq Ltd. (Puvirnituq) uses the lower of cost and NRV rule to value its inventory. Puvirnituq's inventory on December 31, 2017 had 250,000 units of inventory on hand with an average cost of $4.75 per unit and an NRV $4 per unit. On March 31, 2018, the NRV of the inventory was $4.30 per unit and 70,000 of the units that were on hand at the end of December were still in inventory.

Required:

a. By how much should Puvirnituq's inventory be written down in 2017?
b. Prepare the journal entry Puvirnituq will prepare to record the writedown in 2017.
c. What amount should be reported for inventory on Puvirnituq's December 31, 2017 balance sheet?
d. By how much should Puvirnituq's inventory be written up on March 31, 2018?
e. Prepare the journal entry needed to write up the inventory.
f. What amount should be reported for inventory on Puvirnituq's March 31, 2018 balance sheet? Assume no new inventory was purchased in the first quarter of 2018.

E7-15. **(Working with the inventory turnover ratio and the average number of days inventory on hand, LO 10)** Use the information provided in each row to calculate the missing values (shaded boxes). Each row is an independent situation.

	Cost of sales	Average inventory	Inventory turnover ratio	Average number of days inventory on hand
a.	$ 625,000	$		46.1
b.		4,312,000	4.77	
c.		152,100		11.0
d.	4,875,000	2,900,000		

E7-16. **(Compute missing information, LO 2)** Complete the following table by calculating the missing values (shaded boxes).

	Dec. 31, 2016	Dec. 31, 2017	Dec. 31, 2018	Dec. 31, 2019
Beginning inventory	$100,000	$	$	$
Purchases		775,000	1,200,000	1,300,000
Ending inventory	150,000		200,000	
Cost of sales	900,000	800,000		1,310,000

E7-17. **(The effect of different cost formulas on liquidity, LO 3, 10)** The balances in the current asset and liability accounts for Virden Ltd. (Virden) are provided below. The balances for inventory are provided using the FIFO and average cost formulas.

Cost formula	Inventory balance on December 31, 2018
FIFO	$247,000
Average cost	229,000

Account	Account balance on December 31, 2018
Cash	$140,000
Accounts receivable	367,000
Prepaid assets	25,000
Bank loan	148,000
Accounts payable and accrued liabilities	318,000

Required:

a. Calculate Virden's current ratio on December 31, 2018, using the two cost formulas.
b. How do you explain the results you obtained in (a)?
c. How do the different results you obtained in (a) affect your analysis of Virden Ltd.'s liquidity?
d. Which current ratio provides the best measure of Virden's liquidity? Explain.

E7-18. **(Impact of cost formulas on inventory turnover, LO 3, 10)** Inventory and cost of goods sold information for Lafleche Inc. is provided below:

Cost formula	Inventory balance on December 31, 2017	Inventory balance on December 31, 2018	Cost of goods sold for 2018
FIFO	$595,000	$632,000	$2,475,000
Average cost	558,000	601,000	2,506,000

Required:

a. Calculate the inventory turnover ratio and average number of days in inventory under the two cost formulas.
b. Why are the amounts different under the two cost formulas?
c. Under which cost formula is inventory turning over more quickly?

E7-19. **(Effect of transactions and economic events on ratios, LO 4, 10)** Complete the following table by indicating whether the transactions or economic events would increase, decrease, or have no effect on the financial ratios listed. Assume that the current ratio is greater than 1.0, the quick ratio less than 1.0, and the gross margin percentage was 51 percent before considering the effect of each transaction or economic event.

	Current ratio	Quick ratio	Gross margin percentage	Inventory turnover ratio	Profit margin percentage	Debt-to-equity ratio
a. $10,000 of inventory that was damaged in an accident is written off						
b. Inventory costing $5,000 is sold for $11,000 cash						
c. Inventory on consignment is delivered to the seller						
d. Inventory is purchased for $35,000; payment will be made in 30 days						

E7-20. **(Recording inventory transactions, LO 2, 4)** For each of the following transactions and economic events, prepare the necessary journal entries. Provide a brief explanation for each journal entry and state any assumptions you make. Assume a periodic inventory system is used.

a. Merchandise costing $5,000 is returned by a customer. The inventory can be resold at full price. The customer paid $8,000 for the merchandise.
b. An inventory count reveals the accounting records have $20,000 more inventory more than is physically present.
c. $15,000 of inventory is purchased for cash.
d. Inventory costing $10,000 is sold to a customer for $22,000 cash. The entity uses a periodic inventory control system.
e. Inventory costing $8,000 is sold to a customer on credit for $20,000, with the amount due in 30 days. The entity uses a perpetual inventory control system.
f. Beginning inventory is $25,000, purchases during the year are $200,000, and the year-end inventory count shows $32,000. The company uses a periodic inventory system.
g. Management discovers that the NRV of its inventory is $200,000 and its cost is $215,000.

E7-21. **(Inventory cost formulas when prices are falling, LO 3, 4)** Prespatou Inc. (Prespatou) operates in a part of the computer industry where the cost of inventory has been falling recently. The cost of inventory purchased by Prespatou over the last year is summarized below. Prespatou values its inventory at the lower of cost and net realizable value. Assume that purchases are made at the start of a month before any sales occur during that month and that Prespatou uses a periodic inventory system.

Date	Quantity	Cost per unit	Selling price per unit
Purchases			
Opening inventory	70	$950	
October 1, 2016	144	900	
January 2, 2017	108	860	
April 1, 2017	84	810	
July 2, 2017	170	775	
Sales			
October–December, 2016	162		$1,710
January–March, 2017	116		1,620
April–June, 2017	86		1,550
July–September, 2017	158		1,390

Required:

a. Calculate cost of sales for the year ended September 30, 2017 and ending inventory on September 30, 2017 for Prespatou using the average cost and FIFO cost formulas.
b. Which cost formula is most attractive for an accounting objective of income maximization?
c. Which cost formula is most attractive for an accounting objective of tax minimization?
d. Compare the relative values under the two cost formulas of ending inventory and cost of sales in this situation versus a situation where prices are rising. What is different between the two situations?
e. Apply the lower of cost and NRV rule to the year-end inventory. Assume that Prespatou's selling costs for inventory are $120 per unit.

E7-22. **(Inventory cost formulas and taxes, LO 3, 9)** Warspite Ltd.'s (Warspite) purchases for the year ended June 30, 2017 were:

Date	Quantity purchased	Cost per unit
September 4	16,000	$5.50
December 4	20,000	6.00
March 6	30,000	6.30
June 7	14,000	6.60

The beginning balance in inventory on July 1, 2016 was 24,000 units with a cost of $5 per unit. The inventory count on June 30, 2017 found that there were 22,000 units on hand at the end of the year. Warspite uses a periodic inventory control system. During fiscal 2017, Warspite had revenues of $984,000 and expenses other than the cost of sales and taxes of $400,000. Warspite pays taxes equal to 20 percent of its income before taxes.

Required:

a. Prepare income statements for fiscal 2017 for Warspite, using FIFO and average cost. Your income statements should show the amount of taxes that the company has to pay for the income it earned in fiscal 2017. Taxes are calculated by multiplying income before taxes (revenue—all expenses except taxes) by the tax rate.
b. Which method would you recommend that Warspite use if its primary objective of financial accounting is to minimize taxes? Explain your answer.
c. What are possible explanations as to why Warspite would choose not to use the method you recommended in (b)?

E7-23. **(Examining conservatism, LO 4)** Anvil Ltd. (Anvil) follows IFRS when preparing its financial statements. For each of the following independent situations, explain how Anvil should account for the transaction or economic event. Explain your reasoning. In each case, provide the journal entry that Anvil should prepare.

a. A piece of equipment purchased for $25,000 was destroyed in an accident during initial installation. The equipment had not yet been depreciated.
b. Inventory with a cost of $100,000 has gone out of style and it will have to be sold at a discount. Management estimates that Anvil will be able to sell the inventory for $60,000.
c. Equipment used by one of the divisions of Anvil has become technologically obsolete because there is a new generation of equipment that is more efficient and produces higher quality output. Anvil's existing equipment can still be used (it still functions) but is used infrequently because of the lower quality output it produces.
d. Last year, Anvil loaned $300,000 to a biotechnology company. Last week, the biotechnology company announced it was bankrupt and would be liquidating all of its assets and going out of business. Anvil doesn't expect to receive anything from the biotechnology company for the loan.

E7-24. **(Inventory errors, LO 8)** During its 2017 year-end inventory count, Lamaline Ltd. included inventory it had received on consignment from a supplier. Lamaline uses a periodic inventory control system. Explain the impact of this error on the following:

a. 2017 ending inventory
b. 2017 cost of goods sold
c. 2017 gross margin
d. 2017 net income

E7-25. **(Inventory errors, LO 8)** During 2017, $15,000 of purchases weren't recorded. The company uses a periodic inventory system. Explain the impact of this error on the following:

a. 2017 ending inventory
b. 2017 cost of goods sold
c. 2017 gross margin
d. 2017 net income

E7-26. **(Impact of different accounting methods, LO 1, 10)** IFRS require that companies include overhead in inventory. However, different companies can account for certain overhead costs differently. For example, in 2017, Companies A and B were identical in every respect except for how they accounted for $100,000 of overhead costs. Company A includes the $100,000 in the cost of inventory while Company B expenses the $100,000 as incurred. At the end of 2017, both companies had half the inventory they produced during the year on hand (which for Company A means that half the $100,000 of overhead is in inventory).

What is the impact on the following amounts of the two different treatments of the overhead costs?

a. Inventory at the end of 2017
b. Current assets at the end of 2017
c. Cost of goods sold and expenses in 2017
d. Net income for 2017

E7-27. **(Accounting estimates, LO 8)** Hemlo Inc. is a manufacturing company. Because of the nature of its products it can sometimes be difficult to determine their NRV. In the year ended December 31, 2017 Hemlo's management estimated that the NRV of certain items of inventory was $245,000 while their cost was $400,000 and the inventory was written down to NRV. It turned out that this inventory didn't have to be written down and it was sold in mid-2018 for $425,000. Hemlo's summarized income statement for 2017 is provided below. The writedown of inventory is included in cost of sales:

Hemlo Inc. Summarized Income Statement For the year ended December 31, 2017	
Sales	$3,450,000
Cost of sales	1,207,500
Gross margin	2,242,500
Other expenses	1,897,500
Net income	$ 345,000

Required:

a. How much writedown did Hemlo record in 2017?
b. What is the impact on gross margin, gross margin percentage, net income, and profit margin of the writedown?
c. What would the impact be on 2018's income statement of the sale of the written-down inventory?
d. What would the gross margin have been on that inventory if it had been written down versus if it hadn't been written down in 2017?

Problems

P7-1. **(Calculating cost of sales and ending inventory using average cost and FIFO cost formulas, LO 1, 2, 3)** Adamo Limited (AL) is a wholesaler of machine parts. Jacob Avery, an employee of AL, recently purchased AL from the original owner, Mr. Adam, who is retiring. Mr. Avery has come to you for advice on how to calculate ending inventory and cost of goods sold. He has asked you to explain your reasoning for any choices you make. Mr. Avery provided you with the following example of his inventory costs using Part 17592a.

Inventory Information for Part 17592a				
	Number of units	Date of purchase/sale	Cost per unit	Selling price per unit
Opening inventory	250 units	Various	$13.00	
Purchase	200 units	Nov. 10	13.50	
Sale	160 units	Nov. 12		30.00
Purchase	150 units	Nov. 20	13.75	
Sale	320 units	Nov. 22		60.00
Purchase	180 units	Nov. 25	14.00	

Required:

Calculate ending inventory as at November 30 and cost of goods sold for Part 17592a for November. Provide the explanations requested by Mr. Avery. Mr. Avery will use a periodic inventory system.

P7-2. **(The impact of cost formulas on ratios, LO 3, 10)** Cardigan Corp. (Cardigan) and Huskisson Ltd. (Huskisson) are small distribution companies. They are identical in every respect—amount of sales, quantity of inventory sold, number of employees. Everything is the same except that Cardigan uses FIFO as its cost formula and Huskisson uses average cost.

Balance Sheets as of December 31, 2018		
	Cardigan (FIFO)	Huskisson (Average cost)
Assets		
Cash	$ 142,200	$ 142,200
Accounts receivable	378,000	378,000
Inventory	1,582,500	1,176,750
Other current assets	63,000	63,000
Total current assets	2,165,700	1,759,950
Property, plant, and equipment (net)	2,260,500	2,260,500
Total assets	$4,426,200	$4,020,450
Liabilities and Shareholders' equity		
Bank loan	$ 225,000	$ 225,000
Accounts payable	1,132,500	1,132,500
Other current liabilities	97,500	97,500
Total current liabilities	1,455,000	1,455,000
Long-term debt	393,000	393,000
Other non-current liabilities	75,000	75,000
Total liabilities	1,923,000	1,923,000
Capital stock	300,000	300,000
Retained earnings	2,203,200	1,797,450
Total liabilities and shareholders' equity	$4,426,200	$4,020,450

Income Statements for the Year Ended December 31, 2018		
	Cardigan (FIFO)	**Huskisson (average cost)**
Revenue	$5,310,000	$5,310,000
Cost of sales	2,548,800	2,867,400
Gross margin	2,761,200	2,442,600
Other expenses	2,175,000	2,175,000
Net income	$ 586,200	$ 267,600

You also learn that on December 31, 2017, the balances in inventory for the two companies were

Ending Inventory Balances on December 31, 2017		
	Cardigan (FIFO)	**Huskisson (average cost)**
Inventory	$1,432,650	$1,345,500

Required:

a. Calculate the following ratios for each of the companies:
   i. current ratio
   ii. quick ratio
   iii. inventory turnover ratio
   iv. average number of days inventory on hand
   v. gross margin percentage
   vi. profit margin percentage
b. Which company has the strongest liquidity position?
c. Which company is the most profitable?
d. Which company manages its inventory most effectively?
e. The two companies' bankers lend money based on the amount of accounts receivable and inventory on hand. Which company will be able to obtain the largest loan? From the banks' point of view, is the company that receives the largest loan the best credit risk? Explain.

P7-3. **(The impact of cost formulas on ratios, LO 3, 10)** Weybridge Corp. (Weybridge) and Kennetcook Ltd. (Kennetcook) are small retail stores. They are identical in every respect—amount of sales, quantity of inventory sold, number of employees. Everything is the same except that Weybridge uses FIFO as its cost formula and Kennetcook uses average cost.

Income Statements For the Year Ended December 31, 2017		
	Weybridge (FIFO)	**Kennetcook (average cost)**
Revenue	$885,000	$885,000
Cost of sales	552,240	621,270
Gross margin	332,760	263,730
Other expenses	242,000	242,000
Net income (loss)	$ 90,760	$ 21,730

Balance Sheets as of December 31, 2017		
	Weybridge (FIFO)	Kennetcook (average cost)
Assets		
Cash	$ 23,700	$ 23,700
Accounts receivable	63,000	63,000
Inventory	263,750	196,126
Other current assets	10,500	10,500
Total current assets	360,950	293,326
Property, plant, and equipment (net)	376,750	376,750
Total assets	$737,700	$670,076
Liabilities and Shareholders' equity		
Bank loan	$ 37,500	$ 37,500
Accounts payable	188,750	188,750
Other current liabilities	16,250	16,250
Total current liabilities	242,500	242,500
Long-term debt	65,500	65,500
Other non-current liabilities	12,500	12,500
Total liabilities	320,500	320,500
Capital stock	50,000	50,000
Retained earnings	367,200	299,576
Total liabilities and shareholders' equity	$737,700	$670,076

You also learn that on December 31, 2016 the balances in inventory for the two companies were:

Ending Inventory Balances on December 31, 2016		
	Weybridge (FIFO)	Kennetcook (average cost)
Inventory	$240,000	$241,406

Required:

a. Calculate the following ratios for each of the companies:
   i. current ratio
   ii. quick ratio
   iii. inventory turnover ratio
   iv. average number of days inventory on hand
   v. gross margin percentage
   vi. profit margin percentage
b. Which company has the strongest liquidity position?
c. Which company is most profitable?
d. Which company manages its inventory most effectively?
e. The two companies' bankers lend money based on the amount of accounts receivable and inventory on hand. Which company will be able to obtain the largest loan? From the banks' point of view, is the company that receives the largest loan the best credit risk? Explain.

P7-4. **(Recommending inventory accounting policies, LO 1, 2, 3, 4, 9)** Riondel Inc. is a new company that assembles laptop computers from parts bought from manufacturers around the world. The company makes three different models; except for the computing power and some of the features, all are identical. Riondel keeps its prices as low as possible by continually searching for the lowest cost parts that meet its quality requirements (so the parts that go into each computer change regularly). As a result, the cost of the computers is constantly changing. In addition to the cost of parts, labour and overhead are incurred to build the computers.

Riondel is owned by five friends who graduated from the same university with IT and business degrees. All five are involved in the management of the company and they are all on the board of directors. The company is financed mainly by the equity contributions of the owners. It also has a bank loan, which is personally guaranteed by the five owners. Riondel's first year is coming to an end and the owners are satisfied that it has performed as well as or better than expected. They are considering expanding operations but cash may be a problem.

Required:

Prepare a report to Riondel's management recommending accounting policies for inventory. Your report should fully explain your recommendations.

P7-5. **(Recommending inventory accounting policies, LO 1, 2, 3, 4, 9)** Ormiston Ltd. (Ormiston) is a Canadian manufacturer of wooden shingles. Ormiston purchases lumber from sawmills and manufactures the shingles in one of its two factories. The shingles are used in house construction, mainly in the southern and western United States. Ormiston is planning to go public in the next year or two. Currently, it's owned by a group of investors, including a venture capital firm. Most of the owners aren't involved in the management of the company though some are on the board of directors. Ormiston is managed by a professional management team, which receives salary plus bonuses based on company performance as compensation. Ormiston has a large loan outstanding from the bank. The amount of the loan is based on accounts receivable and inventory outstanding on the last day of each calendar month. Ormiston has usually borrowed the maximum amount allowable under the borrowing agreement. Ormiston pays surplus cash (cash that isn't required for operations and is available after paying of debts) out to its shareholders. Note that lumber prices tend to be quite volatile.

Required:

Prepare a report to Ormiston's management recommending accounting policies for inventory. Management is determining appropriate policies for when it goes public as well as to satisfy its other requirements. Your report should fully explain your recommendations.

P7-6. **(Considering the effect of inventory errors, LO 1, 2, 10)** Grosswerder Ltd. (Grosswerder) is a small manufacturing company. During the fiscal year just ended, a number of errors were made in accounting for inventory. For each of the following errors, indicate their effect on the financial statement elements and ratios shown in the table below. Indicate whether the financial statement element or ratio would be overstated (higher than it would have been had the error not occurred), understated (lower than it would have been had the error not occurred), or not affected by the error. Grosswerder uses a periodic inventory control system. The ratios before considering the adjustments are shown in brackets in the following table.

a. Some of the inventory in Grosswerder's warehouse was counted twice during the year-end inventory count.
b. Certain costs that are normally included in inventory were expensed as incurred (and not included in cost of sales). Some inventory relating to these costs was on hand at the end of the year.
c. Inventory that was being held at a third-party warehouse wasn't included in the inventory count.
d. Damaged inventory that can't be sold was included in the year-end inventory balance.
e. Some inventory wasn't included in the inventory count because it had been shipped to a customer before the year-end. Revenue is recognized when merchandise is delivered to customers.

	Net income	Cost of sales	Total assets	Shareholders' equity	Current ratio [1.65]	Inventory turnover ratio [4.3]	Debt-to-equity ratio [1.25]
a.							
b.							
c.							
d.							
e.							

P7-7. **(Considering the effect of inventory errors, LO 1, 2, 4, 10)** Zealand Ltd. (Zealand) is a distributor of imported products. In the fiscal year just ended, a number of errors were made in accounting for inventory. For each of the following errors, indicate their effect on the financial statement elements and ratios shown in the following table. Indicate whether the financial statement element or ratio would be overstated, understated, or not affected by the error. Zealand uses a periodic inventory control system. The ratios before considering the adjustments are shown in brackets in the table.

a. Some inventory was accounted for as sold even though it wasn't shipped as of the end of the year. The inventory wasn't included in the inventory count. Revenue is normally recognized on delivery.
b. Some inventory wasn't counted.
c. The NRV of previously-written-down inventory recovered but wasn't written back up.
d. Inventory received from a supplier on consignment was included in the inventory count.

	Net income	Cost of sales	Total assets	Shareholders' equity	Current ratio [1.31]	Inventory turnover ratio [2.4]	Debt-to-equity ratio [0.52]
a.							
b.							
c.							
d.							

P7-8. **(Determining the amount of inventory on hand when a periodic inventory control system is used, LO 2, 10)** On August 19, 2017, Enterprise Inc. (Enterprise) suffered a serious fire that destroyed its entire inventory of fine paper products. Enterprise uses a periodic inventory control system and as a result doesn't keep track of the amount of inventory that has been removed from inventory. Enterprise last counted its inventory on June 30, 2017, its year-end. At that time, there was $1,125,000 of inventory on hand. Enterprise's records indicate that sales from July 1 to August 19, 2017 were $980,000 and that during that time additional inventory was purchased for $325,000. Enterprise's usual gross margin percentage on its fine paper is 35 percent.

Required:

Enterprise has insurance that covers it fully for losses suffered by fire, except for a $20,000 deductible. Prepare a report to Enterprise's management that computes the amount of the loss that should be claimed from the insurance company as a result of the fire. Explain any factors that management should be aware of that would change the amount of the claim.

P7-9. **(Determining the amount of inventory on hand when a periodic inventory control system is used, LO 2, 10)** On February 19, 2018, Exploits Inc.'s (Exploits) entire inventory was stolen in a daring daylight robbery. The thieves held warehouse personnel at gunpoint while they methodically loaded trucks with the contents of the warehouse. There were no injuries.

Exploits is fully insured against theft and so must file a claim with its insurance company for the loss suffered. Because Exploits uses a periodic inventory control system, it doesn't know for certain the amount of inventory that was stolen. However, from your discussions with company personnel you have learned that Exploits has two categories of inventory. Category one inventory usually generates a gross margin percentage of 65 percent whereas the category two usually generates a gross margin percentage of 48 percent. Sales of category one since the company's year-end on October 31, 2017 were $610,000. Sales of category two over the same time period were about $595,000. During the period since the year-end, Exploits purchased $300,000 of category one inventory and $285,000 of category two inventory. The financial records show that on October 31, 2017 there was $325,000 of category one inventory and $525,000 of category two inventory on hand.

Required:

Prepare a report to Exploits' management that computes the amount of the loss that should be claimed from the insurance company as a result of the robbery. Explain any factors that management should be aware of that would change the amount of the claim.

P7-10. **(Lower of cost and NRV, LO 4)** Tumbell Corp. (Tumbell) reports its inventory at the lower of cost and net realizable value. Tumbell has five inventory categories. You are provided with the following cost and NRV information about each category:

Inventory category	Cost	Net realizable value
Category 1	$168,000	$187,500
Category 2	346,500	322,500
Category 3	111,750	112,800
Category 4	147,150	117,750
Category 5	220,500	228,000
Total	$993,900	$968,550

Required:

a. What amount should Tumbell report on its balance sheet for inventory? Assume Tumbell applies the lower of cost and NRV rule on an item-by-item basis.
b. What is the amount of writedown that is required?
c. Record any journal entries required to account for the writedown.

P7-11. **(Lower of cost and NRV, LO 4)** Wolverine Corp. (Wolverine) reports its inventory at the lower of cost and NRV. Wolverine has five inventory categories. You are provided with the following cost and NRV information about each category on December 31, 2017, Wolverine's year-end:

Category	Number of units	Average carrying amount per unit	NRV per unit	Total carrying amount*	Net realizable value*
Category 1	20,688	$13.35	$32.86	$ 276,178	$ 679,874
Category 2	46,138	10.41	23.84	480,291	1,099,918
Category 3	39,375	17.40	15.23	685,125	599,760
Category 4	40,300	7.83	18.37	315,549	740,230
Category 5	18,755	9.38	8.59	175,828	161,143
Total*				$1,932,972	$3,280,925

*Totals have been rounded.

You later receive the following information about Wolverine's inventory on March 31, 2018, the end of the company's first quarter:

Category	Total number of units	Number of units that were on hand on December 31, 2017	Average carrying amount per unit	NRV per unit	Total carrying amount*	Net realizable value*
Category 1	24,825	5,412	$13.40	$32.86	$ 332,655	$ 815,849
Category 2	41,524	14,800	10.60	22.15	440,152	919,751
Category 3	43,313	21,520	14.25	18.25	617,203	790,453
Category 4	38,285	4,500	8.00	18.37	306,280	703,219
Category 5	21,568	8,104	7.50	9.10	161,762	196,271
Total*					$1,858,052	$3,425,543

*Totals have been rounded.

Required:

a. What amount should Wolverine report on its balance sheet for inventory on December 31, 2017?
b. What is the amount of writedown required on December 31, 2017?
c. Record any journal entries required on December 31, 2017 to account for the writedown.
d. Are any adjustments needed to inventory on March 31, 2018? Describe and explain any adjustments required and prepare any journal entries that are needed.
e. What amount should Wolverine report on its balance sheet for inventory on March 31, 2018?

P7-12. **(Determine the amount of inventory lost due to theft, LO 1, 2)** Nackawic Ltd. (Nackawic) imports novelty items from China and sells them to dollar stores, novelty shops, and other low-price retailers in eastern Canada. Recently, the manager of Nackawic's warehouse in Fredericton became concerned that a significant amount of goods were being stolen from the warehouse. He wanted to know the extent of the problem so he could take remedial steps, if necessary. He spoke with the company accountant, who told him that if he counted the inventory on hand she could give him an idea of how much inventory was being stolen.

The manager closed the warehouse and had the inventory counted. He advised the accountant that there was $3,066,896 of inventory on hand on the date of the count. The manager also told the accountant that since the last year-end, goods costing $15,688 had been damaged and had to be thrown away. The accountant examined the financial records pertaining to the Fredericton warehouse and found that since the last year-end, goods costing $1,244,550 had been purchased and stored in the warehouse, and that goods costing $1,319,320 had been shipped to customers over the same period. The inventory count at the end of the previous reporting period reported inventory of $3,279,706.

Required:

a. Estimate the amount of novelty items that might have been stolen from the Fredericton warehouse.
b. Is it possible to conclude with certainty the amount you calculated in (a) was due to theft? Explain.
c. Why was it necessary to count the inventory to estimate the amount of inventory that was stolen?

P7-13. **(Determine the amount of inventory shrinkage, LO 1, 2)** Gabriola Audio and Visual Ltd. (Gabriola) is a large retailer of audio-visual equipment and supplies. Recently, the owner read about the large amount of theft that occurred in retail stores in Canada. While she never thought this was much of a problem for her, she wanted an idea of how much was being stolen so she could decide whether it was worthwhile to install theft-prevention equipment or take other steps. Her accountant told her that if she counted the inventory on hand he could give her an idea of the amount of inventory being stolen.

The owner had the inventory counted after store closing one Sunday. According to the count, there was $1,440,000 of inventory on hand. The manager also told the accountant that since the year-end, $81,000 of merchandise had been returned to suppliers. At the last year-end, Gabriola had $1,910,000 of inventory. Since the year-end, the store had purchased $802,500 of inventory and had sales of $1,300,000. The gross margin that Gabriola usually earns is 25%.

Required:

a. Determine the amount that might have been stolen from the store.
b. Is it possible to conclude with certainty that the amount you calculated in (a) was due to theft?
c. Why was it necessary to count the inventory to estimate the amount of inventory that was stolen?
d. If Gabriola had used a perpetual inventory control system, would a count of the inventory have been required to provide the manager with the information she required?

P7-14. **(Consider the effect of different inventories on the inventory turnover ratio, LO 10)** Xena Inc. (Xena) is an importer of gift items from Europe and Asia. Xena classifies its inventory into three categories: porcelain figurines, toys, and linens. Over the years, Xena has found that the success of the three categories has tended to vary, sometimes quite significantly, although, fortunately for the company, poor performance of one category seems to be offset by success in another. On its balance sheet and income statement, Xena doesn't break down its inventory, sales, and cost of sales into the three categories.

For its years ended October 31, 2017 and 2018, Xena reported inventory of $417,500 and $433,250 respectively. For the fiscal year ended October 31, 2018, Xena reported sales of $1,961,000 and cost of sales of $963,625. However, the following breakdown of inventory, sales, and cost of sales has been made available to you:

Category	Inventory balance on October 31, 2017	Inventory balance on October 31, 2018	Sales for the year ended October 31, 2018	Cost of sales for the year ended October 31, 2018
Porcelain figurines	$146,250	$159,500	$862,500	$345,000
Toys	168,750	126,250	692,750	415,750
Linens	102,500	147,500	405,750	202,875

Required:

a. Calculate the gross margin percentage, inventory turnover ratio, and the average number of days inventory on hand for the year ended October 31, 2018 using the aggregated amounts reported for inventory, sales, and cost of sales on Xena's balance sheet and income statement.
b. Calculate the gross margin, inventory turnover ratio, and the average number of days inventory on hand for the year ended October 31, 2018 for each category of inventory that Xena carries.
c. What are the implications of the results you obtained in parts (a) and (b) of the question?
d. How is your ability to analyze Xena affected by the aggregated information presented in the company's balance sheet and income statement versus the information that was made available to you? Explain fully.

P7-15. **(Consider the effect of different inventories on the inventory turnover ratio, LO 10)** Herschel Inc. (Herschel) is a small chain of convenience stores. Herschel classifies its inventory into three categories: perishable items, packaged goods, and household items. On its balance sheet and income statement, Herschel doesn't break down its inventory, sales, and cost of sales into the three categories.

For its years ended December 31, 2016 and 2017, Herschel reported inventory of $671,000 and $873,500 respectively. For the fiscal year ended December 31, 2017, Herschel reported sales of $7,013,000 and cost of sales of $5,575,000. However, the following breakdown of inventory, sales, and cost of sales has been made available to you:

Category	Inventory balance on Dec. 31, 2016	Inventory balance on Dec. 31, 2017	Sales for the year ended Dec. 31, 2017	Cost of sales for the year ended Dec. 31, 2017
Perishable items	$50,000	$42,500	$2,375,000	$2,000,000
Packaged goods	183,500	306,000	2,013,000	1,650,000
Household items	437,500	525,000	2,625,000	1,925,000

Required:

a. Calculate the gross margin percentage, inventory turnover ratio, and the average number of days inventory on hand for the year ended December 31, 2017 using the aggregated amounts reported for inventory, sales, and cost of sales on Herschel's balance sheet and income statement.
b. Calculate the gross margin percentage, inventory turnover ratio, and the average number of days inventory on hand for the year ended December 31, 2017 for each category of inventory that Herschel carries.
c. What are the implications of the results you obtained in parts (a) and (b)? How is your ability to analyze Herschel affected by the aggregated information presented in the company's balance sheet and income statement versus the information that was made available to you? Explain fully.

P7-16. **(Cost formulas, LO 2, 3, 4, 9)** The purchase and sale of inventory by Yearly Inc. (Yearly) during the year ended December 31, 2017 is summarized below. Assume that purchases are made on the first day of each quarter and sales on the last day of each quarter. Yearly pays for all its inventory in cash when it's delivered.

Economic event	Quantity	Purchase price per unit	Selling price per unit
Opening inventory	5,000	$6.00	
Purchases—first quarter	4,000	6.15	
Purchases—second quarter	5,500	6.45	
Purchases—third quarter	9,500	6.60	
Purchases—fourth quarter	3,500	6.80	
Sales—first quarter	6,500		$11.00
Sales—second quarter	5,000		11.00
Sales—third quarter	11,000		11.50
Sales—fourth quarter	2,500		11.50

Required:

a. Determine cost of sales for the year ended December 31, 2017 and ending inventory on December 30, 2017 using FIFO and average cost, assuming that Yearly uses a periodic inventory control system.
b. How much cash was spent on inventory during 2017 under each cost formula? Is the amount of cash spent on inventory under each cost formula the same or different? Explain.
c. Which cost formula would you recommend if Yearly's objective was to minimize taxes? Explain.

d. Which cost formula would you use if you were Yearly's CEO and your bonus were based on net income? Explain.
e. Which cost formula would you recommend if the amount of Yearly's bank loan was a percentage of inventory? Explain.
f. Yearly uses the lower of cost and net realizable value to value its inventory. Suppose that on December 31, 2017, the NRV of Yearly's inventory plummeted to $6.25 per unit. What would you do under each cost formula?
g. Does it matter which cost formula Yearly uses? Explain fully.

P7-17. **(Cost formulas, LO 2, 3, 4, 9)** The purchase and sale of inventory by Ripple Inc. (Ripple) during the year ended April 30, 2018 is summarized below. Assume that sales are made on the first day of each quarter and purchases are made on the last day. Ripple pays for all its inventory in cash when it's delivered.

Economic event	Quantity	Purchase price per unit	Selling price per unit
Opening inventory	150,000	$5.50	
Purchases—first quarter	180,000	7.00	
Purchases—second quarter	102,000	8.00	
Purchases—third quarter	140,000	8.50	
Purchases—fourth quarter	160,000	7.40	
Sales—first quarter	136,000		$16.00
Sales—second quarter	176,000		16.00
Sales—third quarter	110,000		16.00
Sales—fourth quarter	134,000		16.00

Required:

a. Determine cost of sales for the year ended April 30, 2018 and ending inventory on April 30, 2018 using FIFO and average cost, assuming that Ripple uses a periodic inventory control system.
b. How much cash was spent on inventory during 2018 under each cost formula? Is the amount of cash spent on inventory under each cost formula the same or different? Explain.
c. Which cost formula would you recommend if Ripple's objective was to minimize taxes? Explain.
d. Which cost formula would you use if you were Ripple's CEO and your bonus was based on net income? Explain.
e. Which cost formula would you recommend if the amount of Ripple's bank loan was a percentage of inventory? Explain.
f. Ripple uses the lower of cost and net realizable value to value its inventory. Is it necessary to make any adjustments to inventory on April 30, 2018 to ensure compliance with the lower of cost and NRV rule? Explain.
g. Does it matter which cost formula Ripple uses? Explain fully.

P7-18. **(Analyzing inventory problems, LO 10)** Punnichy Ltd. is a rapidly growing distributor of women's fashions. Cedric Punnichy, the company founder and president, has developed a knack for picking the fashions that capture the market's fancy each year. As a result, Punnichy has been approached by more and more retailers to supply clothes to them. In addition, existing customers have increased their purchases from Punnichy. As a result, Punnichy has increased the amount of inventory it carries, reflecting both increased demand and the need to carry a wider range of goods. Cedric Punnichy is concerned that control over the inventory is inadequate. He is also concerned about accounts receivable. Punnichy currently offers customers 30 days to pay. He has approached you to look at some data about the inventory to assess the situation, identify possible areas of weakness, and make recommendations for improvements. Cedric Punnichy has provided you with the following information:

	2017	2016	2015	2014	2013
Sales	$41,072,051	$35,406,941	$31,613,340	$27,731,000	$25,210,000
Cost of sales	26,080,753	22,306,373	19,853,178	17,331,875	15,630,200
Accounts receivable	5,748,969	4,905,259	4,185,098	3,869,256	3,151,250
Inventory	13,632,775	11,206,037	9,072,483	8,191,149	6,252,080

Required:

Prepare a report to Mr. Punnichy addressing his concerns. Provide appropriate analysis of the data in your report.

P7-19. **(Analyzing inventory problems, LO 10)** Champlain Books Ltd. (Champlain) is a small independent book seller in a Canadian city. Book selling is a tough competitive business but Champlain has managed to succeed by providing good service, offering hard-to-find book titles, and building a loyal clientele. The owner of the store, Sam Champlain, has been concerned recently about the store's performance, mainly a declining cash balance, despite increasing sales. Sam has asked you to look at the store's performance over the last five years to see if you can see any problems he should address. He has provided you with the following information:

Champlain Books Ltd. Selected Financial Information for the Year Ended December 31,						
	2018	2017	2016	2015	2014	2013
Sales	$473,664	$459,868	$453,071	$444,188	$431,250	$
Cost of sales	329,695	317,015	311,409	302,928	293,250	
Gross margin	143,969	142,853	141,662	141,260	138,000	
Inventory	148,358	138,651	130,804	124,338	117,300	113,780

Required:

Examine the information provided to you by Sam Champlain and from your analysis prepare a report explaining any problems you identify and the consequences of the problems. Provide possible explanations and solutions that might resolve the problems.

P7-20. **(Analyzing inventory problems, LO 10)** Pincher Creek Mountain Equipment Ltd. (PCME) is an importer and national distributor of high-quality outdoor clothing and equipment. PCME has exclusive Canadian distribution rights for many of the products it purchases from manufacturers. The company orders merchandise throughout the year but must bring in stock in anticipation of the needs of retailers. Retailers place orders several months in advance of the delivery date and PCME must in turn place orders with the manufacturers. However, PCME must assess to what extent it should order more or less inventory than retailers ordered and how much of new products it should bring in. PCME must keep adequate inventory on hand because it's too time-consuming and costly to make special orders in most cases (for example, if a retailer decided that more of a particular item was needed, it wouldn't make sense in most cases for PCME to make the order). PCME normally gives its customer 60 days from the date of delivery to pay. The economy has deteriorated over the last few months. You have been provided with the following extracts from PCME's financial statements:

Pincher Creek Mountain Equipment Ltd. Selected Financial Information for the Year Ended December 31,				
	2017	2016	2015	2014
Sales	$7,716,270	$7,314,000	$6,900,000	$
Cost of sales	4,128,204	4,059,270	3,795,000	
Gross margin	3,588,066	3,254,730	3,105,000	
Cash	$ 138,000	$ 264,000	$ 300,000	$ 258,000
Accounts receivable	1,935,883	1,459,880	1,339,806	1,314,000
Inventory	2,382,000	1,622,400	1,203,600	1,050,000
Other current assets	42,000	32,400	38,400	37,200
Short-term bank loan	1,200,000	900,000	630,000	540,000
Accounts payable and accrued liabilities	3,309,600	2,220,000	1,902,000	1,662,000

Required:

You have been asked to evaluate PCME's liquidity from the information provided. (Be sure to use evaluation tools that have been introduced in this chapter as well as one from previous chapters.) Explain factors that could have given rise to your findings. Consider the following issues in your report:

a. What are the possible ways that PCME could increase its inventory turnover ratio? Do you think these ways could be reasonably achieved?
b. How would an improvement affect the liquidity of the company? Explain.
c. Why is the ITO an important indicator of liquidity?

P7-21. **(Analyzing inventory problems, LO 10)** You are a loan officer for a major Canadian bank. Recently, the bank was approached by Freshwater Ltd. for a large loan. Freshwater is a large producer of widgets. It's the only Canadian company that continues to produce widgets in Canada. The company has been in business for 40 years and continues to be owned by the family that originally started it. Until the early 2000s, Freshwater was the largest widget supplier in the world. Freshwater's market share has declined significantly in recent years. Freshwater is currently managed by the children of the founder. The widget industry has grown increasingly competitive in recent years, with foreign competitors now large players around the world. Freshwater's widgets are known for their high quality and this is the focus of its marketing plan. Despite its struggles, Freshwater has managed to increase sales each year for the last 20 years. However, the company's profits and cash have declined in recent years and management would like a loan to improve its liquidity position. It's asking for a $10 million line of credit, with repayment beginning in the third year. The loan would be paid off in full in 10 years. Management points to its ability to maintain growth in a highly competitive environment as proof of Freshwater's ability to repay the loan.

Required:

Prepare a preliminary report on whether your bank should provide the line of credit requested by Freshwater. Analyze the market conditions, the impact they are having on the company's performance, and the risks for the future.

Using Financial Statements

MCGRAW-HILL RYERSON LIMITED

www.mcgrawhill.ca

McGraw-Hill Ryerson Limited (MHR) publishes and distributes educational and professional products in both print and non-print media. Product offerings include text and professional reference books, multimedia tools, and teaching, assessment, support, and monitoring solutions. The Company is committed to providing Canadians with material of the highest quality for their education and enjoyment.

The Company is structured on a market-focused basis and operates in three primary market areas through the following revenue divisions:

- Higher Education Division: post-secondary education, including universities and community and career colleges.
- School Division: elementary and secondary schools.
- Professional Division: retailers (online and bricks-and-mortar), wholesalers, libraries, and professionals.

McGraw-Hill Ryerson is a public company trading in the TSX under the symbol MHE, operated independently, in close cooperation with various divisions and international subsidiaries of its majority shareholder, The McGraw-Hill Companies, Inc.

MHR's consolidated balance sheets and statements of income and comprehensive income, and cash flows, along with extracts from the notes to the financial statements and extracts from management's discussion and analysis, are provided in Exhibit 7.4.[7] Use this information to respond to questions FS7-1 to FS7-9.

FS7-1. What amount of inventory did MHR report on its December 31, 2011 statement of financial position? What proportion of current assets and what proportion of total assets did inventory make up? How has the proportion of inventory changed over the three balance sheets provided? Interpret the changes. What is included in MHR's inventory? Do you think the inventory can be considered liquid? Explain.

FS7-2. Describe the accounting policies that MHR uses to account for its inventory. What costs are included in the Canadian product inventory? What does the term "net realizable value" mean? How would MHR know the net realizable value of its inventory?

FS7-3. What was the cost of goods sold by MHR in 2011 and 2010? What was the cost of inventory recognized as an expense in each year? Why do the amounts differ? Calculate MHR's gross margin and gross margin percentage for 2011 and 2010. Interpret the changed in the gross margin percentage.

FS7-4. During fiscal 2010 and 2011 MHR reported inventory writedowns. What is a writedown and why was it necessary for MHR to write down some of its inventory? What were the amounts of the writedowns? Where is it reflected in the statements of income and comprehensive income? What impact do writedowns have on MHR's cash flow? Explain. What impact did the writedown have on gross margin for fiscal 2011? What journal entry would MHR have made in 2011 to record the writedown? Do you think inventory writedowns are a major problem in a business like MHR's? Explain.

FS7-5. Examine the operating activities section of MHR's statements of cash flows and Note 15 to the financial statements. What was MHR's cash flow from operations in 2011? Why was cash from operations so different from net income in 2011? By how much did MHR's inventory change in 2011? What was the impact of the change in inventory on cash from operations? Explain why the change has that effect.

FS7-6. Calculate MHR's inventory turnover ratio and the number of days inventory on hand for 2011 and 2010. (The amount of inventory sold in 2011 and 2010 isn't in the income statement—you have to look in the notes for it.) Evaluate the change in turnover over the two-year period.

EXHIBIT 7.4 **MHR Inc.: Extracts from Financial Statements**

Statements of Financial Position

McGraw-Hill Ryerson Limited. Incorporated under the laws of Ontario.

(In thousands of dollars)

As at	December 31, 2011	December 31, 2010	January 1, 2010
Assets			
Current			
Cash and cash equivalents	**41,926**	44,394	35,878
Marketable securities *[note 14]*	**716**	832	821
Trade and other receivables, net *[note 14]*	**11,429**	9,273	11,319
Inventories, net *[note 11]*	**6,123**	5,370	6,052
Due from parent and affiliated companies *[note 10]*	**1,925**	1,403	2,564
Prepaid expenses and other assets	**280**	291	318
Income taxes receivable	**—**	—	2,368
Total current assets	**62,399**	61,563	59,320
Property, plant, and equipment, net *[note 12]*	**14,071**	14,630	15,182
Intangible assets *[note 6]*	**16,439**	18,205	19,214
Deferred tax assets, net *[note 9]*	**494**	812	1,524
Total non-current assets	**31,004**	33,647	35,920
	93,403	95,210	95,240
Liabilities and Equity			
Current			
Trade and other payables	**11,122**	9,949	9,862
Income taxes payable	**713**	6	—
Due to parent and affiliated companies *[note 10]*	**4,784**	4,675	5,893
Total current liabilities	**16,619**	14,630	15,755
Employee future benefits *[note 7]*	**2,281**	2,588	2,555
Long-term payable *[note 5]*	**44**	391	—
Total liabilities	**18,944**	17,609	18,310
Equity			
Issued capital			
Authorized 5,000,000 no par value common shares			
Issued and outstanding 1,996,638 common shares	**1,997**	1,997	1,997
Paid-in capital	**702**	372	104
Retained earnings	**71,760**	75,232	74,829
Total equity	**74,459**	77,601	76,930
	93,403	95,210	95,240

EXHIBIT 7.4 (continued) MHR Inc.: Extracts from Financial Statements

Statements of Income and Comprehensive Income

(In thousands of dollars—except per share data)

Years ended December 31	2011	2010
Revenue		
Sales revenue, less returns	78,953	78,249
Other income	2,496	2,192
Rental income	583	584
Total revenue	82,032	81,025
Cost of goods sold	29,470	30,866
Gross profit	52,562	50,159
Operating expenses *[notes 5, 7, and 8]*	30,224	30,208
Amortization—pre-publication costs *[note 6]*	9,047	7,907
Depreciation—property, plant, and equipment *[note 12]*	949	951
Operating income	12,342	11,903
Finance income *[note 14]*	386	203
Finance costs	(141)	(153)
Foreign exchange loss	(88)	(105)
Income before income taxes	12,499	11,038
Income tax expense *[note 9]*	3,742	3,517
Net income and comprehensive income for the year attributable to equity holders of the Company	8,757	7,521

Statements of Cash Flows

(In thousands of dollars)

Years ended December 31	2011	2010
Operating Activities		
Net income for the year	8,757	7,521
Add (deduct) non-cash items		
Amortization—pre-publication costs *[note 6]*	9,047	7,907
Depreciation—property, plant, and equipment *[note 12]*	949	951
Increase (decrease) in employee future benefits	(307)	33
Deferred taxes *[note 9]*	318	712
	18,764	17,124
Net change in non-cash working capital balances related to operations *[note 15]*	(1,735)	5,654
Cash provided by operating activities	17,029	22,778

EXHIBIT 7.4 (continued) MHR Inc.: Extracts from Financial Statements

Notes to Financial Statements

(All figures in the accompanying notes are in $000's, except per share data or where noted otherwise.)

1 SUMMARY OF BUSINESS AND SIGNIFICANT ACCOUNTING POLICIES

Inventories

Inventories are stated at the lower of cost, on a first-in, first-out basis, and net realizable value. The Canadian product inventory cost consists of paper, print, and binding costs. The inventory cost of imported and agency product is the purchase price of the product. Net realizable value is the estimated selling price in the ordinary course of business, less estimated costs necessary to make the sale. A significant estimate for the Company is the reserve for inventory obsolescence. The reserve is based upon management's assessment of the demand for its products in the market as compared to the number of units currently on hand.

2 SIGNIFICANT ACCOUNTING JUDGMENTS, ESTIMATES, AND ASSUMPTIONS

Estimates and assumptions

The Company makes estimates and assumptions concerning the future. The resulting accounting estimates will, by definition, seldom equal the actual results. The key assumptions concerning the future and other key sources of estimation uncertainty at the reporting date that have a significant risk of causing a material adjustment to the carrying amounts of assets and liabilities within the next financial year are discussed below.

Inventory

The values associated with inventory involve significant estimates and assumptions, including those with respect to estimating obsolescence such as sales forecasts and attrition rates. These significant estimates and assumptions require considerable judgment which could affect the Company's future results, if the current estimates change. These determinations will affect the amount of provision expense on inventory in future periods.

11 INVENTORIES

The cost of inventory recognized as an expense and included in the statements of income and comprehensive income in cost of goods sold for the year ended December 31, 2011 amounted to $21,507 (2010—$23,316). During the year ended December 31, 2011 $765 (2010—$501) of inventory provision was charged to the statements of income and comprehensive income. As at December 31, 2011, none of the inventory was pledged as security, and there was $336 of reversals during the year ended December 31, 2011 (2010—$315) of any write-downs in inventory that were recognized as an expense in prior periods. An unexpected change in sales and sales forecasts for certain items caused the reversals of the write-downs.

15 STATEMENTS OF CASH FLOWS

The net change in non-cash working capital balances related to operations consists of the following:

	2011 $	2010 $
Trade and other receivables	(2,156)	2,046
Inventories	(753)	682
Due from parent and affiliated companies	(522)	1,161
Income taxes receivable	—	2,368
Prepaid expenses and other assets	11	27
Deferred leasing costs	29	28
Trade and other payables	1,173	88
(Decrease) increase in long term payable	(347)	391
Income taxes payable	707	6
Due to parent and affiliated companies	109	(1,219)
Other	14	76
	(1,735)	5,654

FS7-7. An important part of MHR's business is publishing and selling textbooks (like this one). What do you think are some of the challenges MHR faces with respect to managing its textbook inventory? What important decisions must management make regarding its textbook inventory? What are the risks MHR faces regarding its textbook inventory?

FS7-8. Read the financial statement note that discusses accounting estimates. What important information for readers does this note provide? Why is it important for stakeholders to understand this note? What type of estimates do you think MHR's management has to make with respect to inventory?

FS7-9. Is it possible for a company to have too much inventory? What are the consequences to a company like MHR of carrying too much inventory? What types of analytical tools could you suggest that might help determine that the amount of inventory a company is carrying is getting too large?

ENDNOTES

1. Extracted from Big Rock Brewery Inc.'s 2011 annual report.
2. Extracted from Village Farms International, Inc.'s 2011 annual audited financial statements and its Web site at http://www.villagefarms.com.
3. Extracted from Slater & Gordon Limited's 2011 annual report.
4. Interpretation Bulletin IT473R, "Inventory Valuation" (Canadian Customs and Revenue Agency, December 21, 1998); http://www.cra-arc.gc.ca/E/pub/tp/it473r/ it473r-e.html.
5. Ibid.
6. Ibid.
7. Extracted from McGraw-Hill Ryerson Limited's 2011 financial statements.

Practise and learn online with Connect. Connect resources include additional and interactive study exercises, videos, and practice quizzing, as well as additional material you won't find in the printed text.

CHAPTER 8

Capital Assets: Property, Plant, and Equipment, Intangibles, and Goodwill

LEARNING OBJECTIVES

After studying the material in this chapter you will be able to do the following:

LO 1 Define capital assets and recognize their different categories.

LO 2 Explain the strengths and limitations of the different methods for valuing capital assets on the balance sheet.

LO 3 Recognize how to account for the purchase of capital assets.

LO 4 Describe the different methods of depreciating capital assets and understand the implications of the different methods for financial statements and for the users of the statements.

LO 5 Recognize the information about capital assets that is disclosed in financial statements.

LO 6 Discuss the problems with accounting for intangible assets and understand that many of an entity's intangible assets aren't reported on its balance sheet.

LO 7 Explain how to account for disposals of depreciable capital assets and for impairments of capital assets.

LO 8 Explain how the cash flow statement is affected by whether expenditures are expensed or capitalized.

LO 9 Analyze and interpret information about capital assets in financial statements.

LO 10 Differentiate between capital cost allowance for tax purposes and depreciation for financial reporting purposes. (Appendix)

Many passengers on WestJet's fleet of 97 Boeing 737 aircraft like to pass the hours in flight from chilly Canada to their sun and beach destinations by watching live satellite television. They can do that on the screens in the seatback in front of them. WestJet was the first airline in Canada to offer the service, back in 2005, including 24 free Bell channels, and first-run, pay-per-view movies.

WestJet Airlines Ltd.

While WestJet's existing fleet of airplanes will keep the original entertainment systems for now, Marshall Wilmont, the vice-president of product development, told the *Financial Post* in April 2012 that the low-cost airline is looking to offer a more modern screen technology on the airline's new jets. Three of those planes were scheduled to be delivered and start flying in 2012. In these planes, passengers could rent lightweight tablet devices that snap onto their food trays. These sky tablets would come preloaded with 10 movies, 10 hours of television shows, and some games.

All the in-seat entertainment system sets and the 54 airplanes that WestJet owns outright (it leases 43 others) are considered capital assets by the accountants at the company's corporate head office, located at 22 Aerial Place NE near the Calgary International Airport. The airline's annual report for 2011 also lists as capital assets its buildings, spare parts, and ground equipment, among other things.

At the end of 2011, WestJet's property and equipment were valued at $1.91 billion, and, not surprisingly, this is mainly the airplanes that it owns. The company also intends to take delivery of another 37 new owned planes and one leased plane from Boeing by the end of 2018.

Since capital assets can be physical items that get used up over time to help the company do business, WestJet accountants spread the cost of the asset out over a set period of time, usually based on current industry standards. WestJet's management said in the 2011 annual report that an airplane depreciates over 20 years, by which time one of its 737s would be worth just $4 million to $6 million in residual value.

While the fleet size is set to grow to a muscular 135 planes, including owned and leased in the next few years, WestJet is also moving ahead to create a smaller, regional airline by the end of 2013. For that venture, the company announced in May 2012 that it has plans to order 20 turboprop Q400 planes from Bombardier, with an option for 25 more. WestJet president and CEO Gregg Saretsky wouldn't reveal how much WestJet is paying for the small new planes, but the *Toronto Star* pegged the price at less than $30 million each.

–E.B.

LO 1

INTRODUCTION—WHAT ARE CAPITAL ASSETS?

Capital assets are resources that contribute to earning revenue over more than one period by helping an entity produce, supply, support, or make available the goods or services it offers to its customers. Unlike inventory, these assets aren't bought and sold in the ordinary course of business (although they are sometimes bought and sold), but they are essential to any type of entity. In this chapter we will examine three categories of capital assets: property, plant, and equipment; intangibles; and goodwill. These categories are described in Table 8.1.

TABLE 8.1 Categories of Capital Assets

	Definition	Examples
Property, plant, and equipment	Tangible assets used to produce or supply goods or services to customers, rented to customers, or used for administrative purposes	Land, buildings, equipment, vehicles, computers, furniture and fixtures, money spent to find and develop natural resources
Intangible assets	Capital assets without physical substance	Patents, copyrights, trademarks, brand names, computer software, customer lists, broadcast rights, licences, movies
Goodwill	An intangible asset that arises when one business acquires another and pays more than the fair value of the net identifiable assets purchased	

Property, plant, and equipment (PPE) are **tangible assets** because they have physical substance, for example, land, buildings, equipment, and furniture. **Intangible assets** lack physical substance. They can be ideas, rights, or images, like patents, copyrights, brands, trademarks, and software. PPE and intangibles both can have very long lives—like land, which lasts forever, or buildings, which can last for decades. Or they can have relatively short lives—like computer hardware and software. I'll explain goodwill later.

Virtually all entities need some capital assets. Indigo Books & Music Inc.'s capital assets include furniture and fixtures for its stores (shelving, counters, signs, flooring, etc.), the cost of renovating and decorating stores, and computer equipment. Magna International Inc. has land, buildings, and equipment to operate its manufacturing facilities. The amount and percentage of different categories of capital assets for different companies are shown in Table 8.2. In examining Table 8.2, you might be surprised that Loblaw, a retail grocery chain, has such a larger proportion of PPE than Indigo. Both are in the retail business but Loblaw owns its land and buildings whereas Indigo doesn't. A company that has a large proportion of property, plant, and equipment in its assets is known as a capital intensive business.

www.bce.ca
www.highlinerfoods.com
www.indigo.ca
www.loblaw.ca
www.magna.com
www.timhortons.com
www.westjet.com
www.westfraser.com

Capital assets don't have to be owned to be classified as assets on the balance sheet. It's common practice for companies to lease assets instead of buying them. If certain conditions are met, these can be recognized in the financial statements. For example, it's common for airlines to lease their planes. We explore leasing further in Chapter 9, but for now recognize that ownership isn't needed for an asset to be recognized on the balance sheet.

Some of an entity's capital assets don't appear on its balance sheet even though most people, including accountants, would agree they have future benefits. Traditional accounting sometimes

TABLE 8.2 Amount of Capital Assets in Different Companies

Company	Type of business	Dollar value of property, plant, and equipment	Dollar value of intangibles	Dollar value of goodwill	Property, plant, and equipment as a percentage of total assets	Intangibles as a percentage of total assets	Goodwill as a percentage of total assets
BCE Inc. (12/31/2011)	Telecommunications	$18,785,000,000	$8,012,000,000	$7,185,000,000	47.6%	20.3%	18.2%
High Liner Foods Incorporated (12/31/2011)	Food processing	99,933,000	103,109,000	126,787,000	14.5%	14.9%	18.4%
Indigo Books & Music Inc. (3/31/2012)	Retail	67,464,000	22,810,000	0	9.9%	3.3%	0.0%
Loblaw Companies Limited (12/31/2011)	Retail grocery	8,807,000,000	81,000,000	948,000,000	50.5%	0.5%	5.4%
Magna International Inc. (12/31/2011)*	Auto parts maker	4,236,000,000	30,000,000	1,196,000,000	28.9%	0.2%	8.1%
Tim Hortons Inc. (1/1/2012)	Fast food service	1,463,765,000	4,544,000	0	66.4%	0.2%	0.%
WestJet Airlines Ltd. (12/31/2011)	Airline	1,911,227,000	33,793,000	0	55.0%	1.0%	0.0%
West Fraser Timber Co. Ltd. (12/31/2011)	Forest products	935,700,000	563,000,000	263,700,000	36.9%	22.2%	10.4%

*Magna's amounts are stated in US dollars.

Note: Information for all companies is prepared in accordance with IFRS, except for Magna International and Tim Hortons, which are prepared in accordance with United States generally accepted accounting principles.

has difficulty with certain types of capital assets, especially intangibles. For example, many software and biotechnology companies don't report the software and pharmaceuticals they develop as assets. Some of the aircraft flown by airlines aren't reported because they're leased. Many companies' brand names aren't recorded. The investments that entities make in their employees rarely appear as assets.

MEASURING CAPITAL ASSETS AND LIMITATIONS TO HISTORICAL COST ACCOUNTING

LO 2

Most companies following IFRS use historical cost to account for their capital assets (although companies can choose to use fair value). With historical cost, all costs incurred to acquire an asset and get it ready for use are **capitalized**—recorded on the balance sheet as an asset—and this amount forms the basis of its valuation on the company's balance sheet. For example, a piece of land purchased in 1953 for $25,000 would be reported on the 2018 balance sheet at $25,000, even if the market value of the land may have increased to $1,000,000.

One has to wonder about the usefulness of historical cost information. How useful is it today to know that land cost $25,000 when it was purchased in 1953? Historical cost accounting's purpose is to match the cost of capital assets to revenue earned over the life of the asset. But for making projections or other future-oriented decisions it's difficult to understand how the historical cost of capital assets, which are sometimes very old, can be useful.

There are three alternatives to historical cost accounting for capital assets: fair value, replacement cost, and value-in-use. Each alternative provides different information to stakeholders and each has shortcomings of its own. None is ideal for all uses. These methods are summarized in Figure 8.1.

Fair value is the price that would be received to sell an asset in an orderly transaction between market participants. This amount is more useful than historical cost to a bank, for example, which would want to know the current value of collateral being offered as part of a

FIGURE 8.1

Ways to Measure Capital Assets

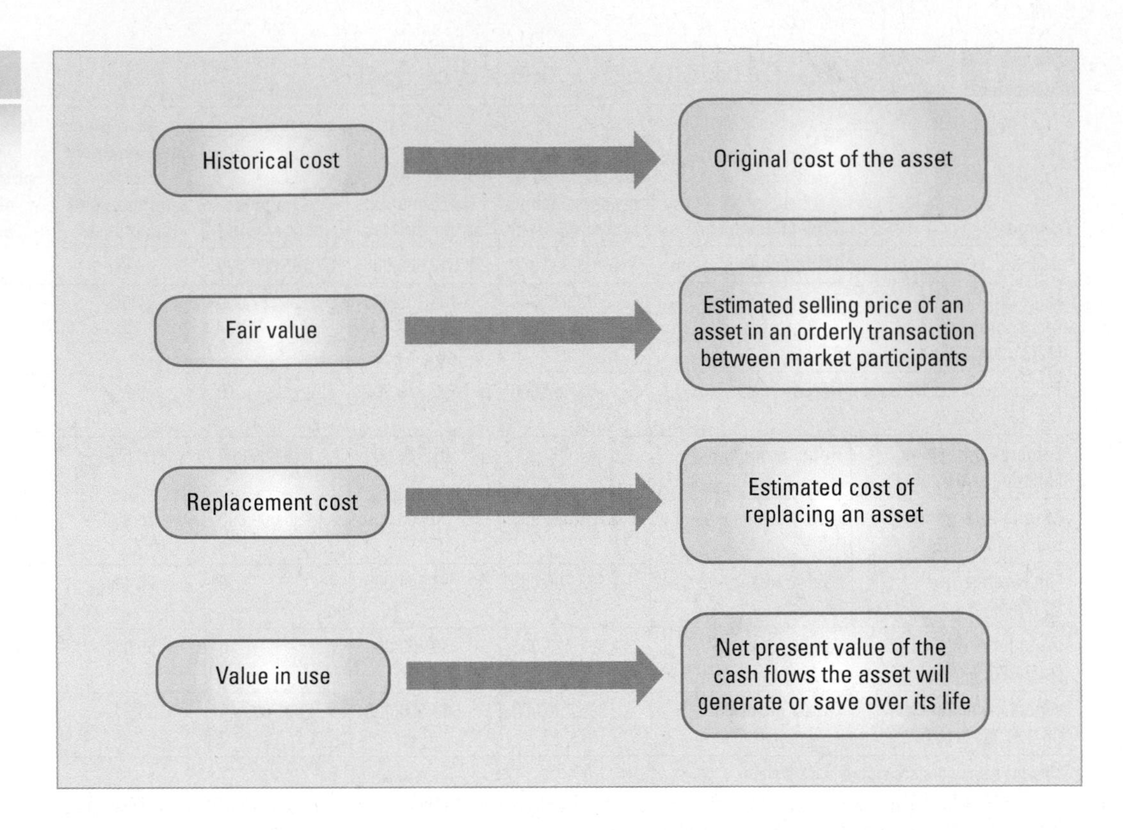

loan agreement. Fair value is less objective and less reliable than historical cost because the amount is an estimate and isn't supported by a transaction. Obtaining a reasonable estimate of fair value can be difficult because many used and even new capital assets aren't bought and sold very often and so there isn't a ready market price. Also, today's fair value doesn't say anything about what the asset could be sold for in the future—it's only an estimate of the current fair value.

Replacement cost is the amount that would have to be spent to replace a capital asset. It can be the cost of a new identical item, or it can be the cost of an equivalent one if, for example, the existing asset is no longer available. Most capital assets have to be replaced from time to time and information on the timing and amounts involved in replacement would be very useful for predicting cash flows. Like fair value, replacement cost is less objective than historical cost because there is no transaction supporting the amount. Also, obtaining replacement costs can be very difficult for some assets, especially if they don't exist anymore, and today's replacement cost doesn't say anything about the cost when the asset is actually replaced.

Another method of valuing capital assets is **value-in-use**, which is the net present value of the cash flow the asset will generate or save over its life (IFRS refers to value-in-use as **entity-specific value**). For example, value-in-use for an apartment building is the present value of rents, less operating costs over the remaining life of the building, plus the amount the building could be sold for at the end of its life. Value-in-use is relevant for many purposes, including for investors trying to figure out the value of a business. However, value-in-use has severe practical limitations. First, individual assets rarely generate cash on their own but instead they interact with other assets to generate cash flows. For example, what is the value-in-use of a computer that contributes to the development of some software? Second, estimating the future cash flows of an asset or group of assets can require many assumptions, making the estimate imprecise and possibly unreliable.

Historical cost also has its uses, although not for future-oriented decisions. It can be used by stakeholders interested in evaluating historical performance, such as calculating return on investment. Historical cost information is also useful for stewardship and tax purposes.

QUESTION FOR CONSIDERATION

For each of the following situations, specify which measurement basis—historical cost, fair value, replacement cost, or value-in-use—is most appropriate for the purpose described. Provide a brief explanation for each choice.

a. Determine the amount of fire insurance needed for a building.
b. Determine the value of the assets of an entity going out of business.
c. Evaluate the price that should be paid for a business.

SOLUTION:

Situation	Measurement basis	Explanation
a. Determine the amount of fire insurance needed for a building.	Replacement cost	Fire insurance is intended to allow the insured to replace a building destroyed by fire. Therefore, the replacement cost of the building is the appropriate measurement basis.
b. Determine the value of the assets of an entity going out of business.	Fair value	An entity that is going out of business will likely be looking to sell its assets to satisfy its creditors and/or allow the owners to receive cash from the liquidation. Fair value gives the current selling prices of assets.
c. Evaluate the price that should be paid for a business.	Value-in-use	The value of a business is the present value of the future net cash flows that will be obtained from operating it.

WHAT IS COST?

LO 3

When a capital asset is acquired, it's always recorded on the balance sheet at cost (cost is considered the fair value on the date the asset is acquired). Cost should include all the costs incurred to purchase (or build) the asset and get it ready for use. Amounts that can be included are the purchase price; architectural design and engineering fees; taxes (non-refundable); delivery costs; transportation insurance costs; duties, testing and preparation charges; installation costs; and legal costs, as well as any and all costs related to getting the asset up and running. Employee costs to ready the asset for use, including wages, should also be capitalized. Costs that aren't necessary or related to the acquisition, such as unnecessary work or repairs caused by poor planning, should not be capitalized.

Interest can be capitalized until an asset is ready for use, after which it is expensed. Capitalizing interest is most common when an entity is building an asset itself. For example, an entity using its own employees to build an extension to its warehouse capitalizes the interest incurred to finance the project up until it's complete and ready for use.

Determining whether certain costs should be capitalized can be difficult, and treatment of the costs requires judgment. This need for judgment introduces the possibility that different managers will account for similar costs differently. Any time ambiguity exists, managers' choices may be influenced by self-interest. For example, if tax minimization is an entity's main objective, it may expense as much and as many of the costs of acquiring the asset as it reasonably can. On the other hand, if the entity prefers to maximize current income it will capitalize as much as it can to defer expensing costs. Figure 8.2 provides a graphic example of the costs that could be included in the cost of a new machine.

FIGURE 8.2

Cost of a Capital Asset

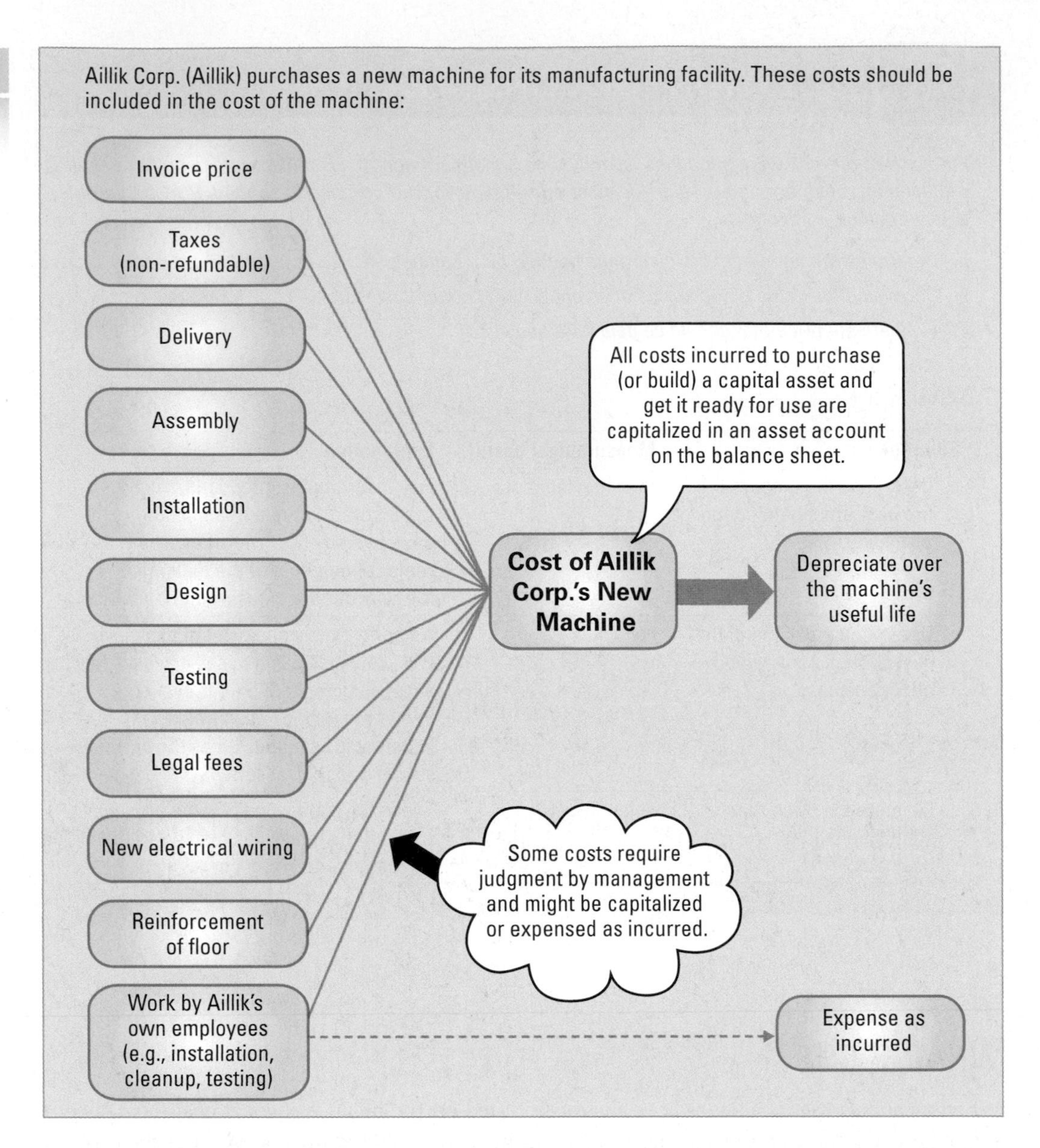

Expenditures enabling an asset to do what it's designed to do are classified as **repairs** or **maintenance** and should be expensed when incurred. Changing a car's oil regularly doesn't make the car better—it allows it to operate as intended by the manufacturer. If an entity spends money on an existing asset and the expenditure meets the definition of an asset—it provides a future benefit to the entity and it's probable the benefit will be enjoyed, the benefit is controlled, is the result of a past transaction, and is measurable—the amount should be capitalized. This type of expenditure is sometimes called a **betterment** because it makes the existing asset better. The cost of rebuilding an engine so that it's more powerful and efficient should be capitalized, because the vehicle can now do more work (carry heavier loads) and use less fuel, both of which benefit the entity.

While some expenditures can easily be classified as betterments or maintenance, the treatment isn't always obvious. As a result, managers' choices may be motivated by their reporting objectives. If management is most concerned with the current bottom line, it will be inclined to capitalize as much of the outlays as possible. Treating an expenditure as a betterment spreads the cost over a number of years because it's capitalized and depreciated over the remaining life of the asset. Treating it as a repair or as maintenance increases expenses and reduces income by the full amount of the expenditure in the period in which it's incurred. Generally, expenditures on existing capital assets are much more likely to be repairs or maintenance than betterments.

QUESTION FOR CONSIDERATION

Meadow Inc. (Meadow) recently acquired a new computer server for its head-office network. The server had a list price of $50,000 but the head of the computing department negotiated a price of $46,900. HST was $6,097 and delivery was $2,000. Replacing the cables in the offices to meet the needs of the new server cost $8,000. A planning error by Meadow's management made it necessary for most of the cabling work to be redone, which cost an additional $2,100. Installing the server was $3,000, but once it was installed, management realized that the ventilation wasn't adequate. Moving and reinstalling the server cost an additional $2,600. Meadow purchased a three-year insurance policy for the server for $3,600.

Calculate the amount that should be capitalized for the purchase of the new server. Also, indicate which cost items shouldn't be included in the capitalized amount. Explain your reasoning.

SOLUTION:

Cost	Amount capitalized	Explanation
Purchase price	$46,900	The only price that is relevant is the amount actually paid. The list price doesn't matter.
Taxes	Not capitalized	HST is a refundable tax so it isn't capitalized. Taxes that aren't refunded would be included in the cost.
Delivery	2,000	Delivery costs are necessary to get the server ready for use.
Cabling	8,000	Cabling costs are necessary to get the server ready for use. The server can't do its job without adequate cabling.
Cabling required due to error	Not capitalized	The additional costs were incurred due to a mistake. They weren't required to get the server ready for use and don't add anything to the value of the server. These costs should be expensed when incurred.
Installation	3,000	Installation costs are necessary to get the server ready for use. It can't serve its purpose if it isn't installed.
Reinstallation	Not capitalized	Reinstallation was required because of poor planning. The cost wasn't necessary and doesn't provide future benefit.
Insurance	Not capitalized	Insurance isn't a cost to get the server ready for use. It is insurance protection for the server when it's operating. It should be recorded as a prepaid asset and expensed as it's used.
Total amount to be capitalized for acquisition of the server	$59,900	

Basket Purchases

LO 3

Sometimes an entity will purchase a "basket" or bundle of assets at a single price where the prices of individual assets won't be known. Basket purchases raise the problem of how to allocate the total cost among the assets in the bundle. Good accounting requires that the purchase price be allocated in proportion to the market values of each of the assets. The allocation is important because the different assets in the bundle may be accounted for differently, and different allocations will result in different financial statement effects (as we will see below).

For example, suppose that Pockwock Ltd. (Pockwock) purchases land and a building for $25,000,000. If the land was worth 40 percent of the total cost and the building 60 percent, the journal entry would be

Dr. Land (asset +)	10,000,000	
Dr. Building (asset +)	15,000,000	
Cr. Cash (asset −)		25,000,000
To record the basket purchase of land and building		

In practice, it's difficult to know exactly what the market values of the land and building are as separate assets. Consequently, as long as the amount assigned to each is reasonable, managers have the flexibility to make the allocation as it suits their reporting objectives. If the main concern is minimizing taxes, managers will allocate more of the cost to the building because buildings can be deducted to reduce taxes whereas land can't. If management is more concerned about increasing net income, it could allocate more of the cost to land, which isn't depreciated.

If Pockwock obtained an independent appraisal estimating the value of the land at between $9,000,000 and $12,000,000, it could justifiably assign any amount between those two values to the land. If Pockwock's reporting objective was minimizing tax, it would allocate $9,000,000 of the purchase price to land and $16,000,000 to the building. This would maximize the amount of expense, thereby permanently reducing the tax Pockwock would have to pay. The downside is that net income would be lower. If instead management wanted to minimize the effect on income, it would allocate $12,000,000 to the cost of the land and $13,000,000 to building, which would minimize the amount to be depreciated.

The choice being made here isn't arbitrary. Both treatments can be justified because they are within the range of the independent appraisal. A reader might be suspicious of any management choice in these circumstances, but it's important to keep in mind that it's usually not possible to know what the "truth" is. The actual individual market values of the land and building can't be known unless they are sold separately. The portion of cost assigned to each asset is an informed estimate.

LO 4 DEPRECIATION

Most capital assets get used up. A machine, a mine, even an idea, doesn't last forever. The machine no longer produces goods effectively and has to be replaced. The resource in the mine is exhausted and the patent for the idea expires. Because capital assets get used up while helping to earn revenue, it makes sense for the cost to somehow be matched to the revenues they help earn. Expensing the cost of a capital asset is conceptually the same as expensing the cost of inventory when it's sold or salaries when the work is done. It's an application of matching. The hard part is figuring out how to do it. Because capital assets contribute to earning revenue over more than one period, the cost must be expensed in a reasonable way over the life of the asset.

Different terms are used for the process of allocating the cost of a capital asset to expense over time. IFRS uses the term **depreciation** for the process of allocating the cost of property, plant, and equipment to expense and **amortization** for intangible assets. A third term, **depletion**, is used for natural resources. The categories of capital assets and the terms applied to each are summarized in Figure 8.3. I use the term depreciation for the general concept of allocating the cost of a capital asset to expense over its useful life.

As I said, the hard part about expensing the cost of a capital asset is figuring out a way of doing it. There is little authoritative or specific guidance. IFRS say the cost of an asset less its **residual value** (the amount that would be received today from selling the asset if it was at the end of its useful life) should be depreciated or amortized over its useful life in a "systematic" way. There are many questions: What is a systematic way of depreciating the cost? What is the useful life? What is the residual value?

Managers must use their knowledge and judgment to answer these questions, and stakeholders must recognize that there are different reasonable treatments. Any choice within a reasonable range is likely acceptable. For example, could anyone strongly argue that the useful life of a car is

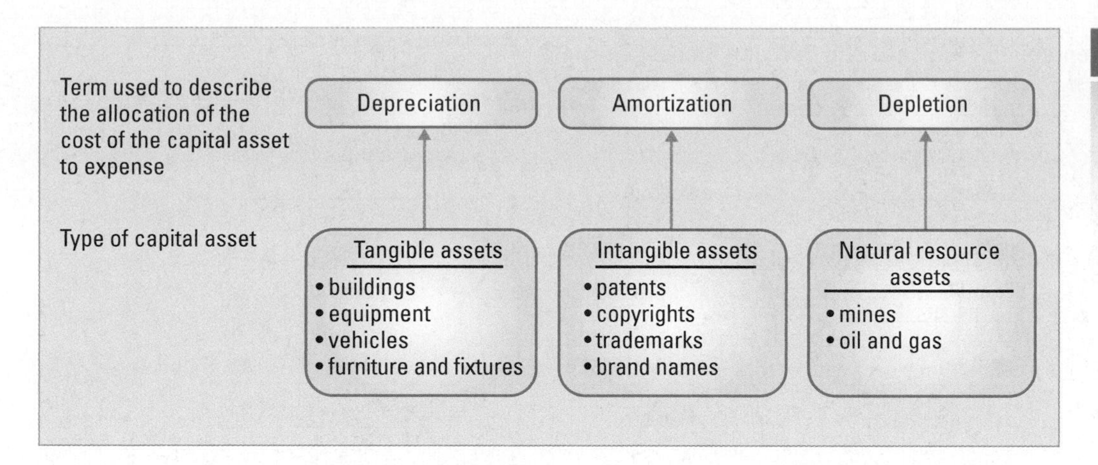

FIGURE 8.3

Summary of Types of Capital Assets and Terms Used to Describe the Allocation of the Cost

three, five, or seven years? An asset doesn't come with a tag advising owners how long it will last or what its residual value is. The useful life, residual value, and how an asset contributes to earning revenue depend on how it's used, what it's used for, and how it's cared for.

There are two main reasons why capital assets are depreciated: physical use and obsolescence. Physical use refers to the effects that the passage of time, wear and tear, and exposure to the elements have on the capital asset's ability to help earn revenue. As a machine gets older and is used, it will break down more often, use more energy to operate, and produce less and lower-quality output. Eventually, the machine must be replaced.

Assets become obsolete because of changes in technology and shifts in the business environment. Most computers purchased three or more years ago can probably still do what they did when they were new. However, these computers may now be too slow, lacking memory or multimedia capabilities, or unable to handle some current software applications. They have less to contribute to the money-making activities of the business than state-of-the-art equipment would. Advances in technology render many older computers obsolete.

Not all assets are depreciated. Land is usually not depreciated because it doesn't wear out or become obsolete. The buildings on a piece of land will come and go but the land will always be there. An exception to this treatment is land mined for its natural resources. In that case, the cost of the land is expensed as the land is mined because it's "used up" as the resource is removed. Intangible assets aren't amortized when there are no factors limiting their useful lives. For example, the licences bought by wireless companies for the right to use airwaves for wireless communications aren't amortized. Goodwill also isn't amortized.

Depreciation and Market Values

Depreciation allocates the cost of a capital asset to expense. The carrying amount of the asset (cost less depreciation to date) isn't an estimate of its market value. Resist the temptation to think that it is.

Depreciation Methods

Now let's look at how capital assets are depreciated. Three methods are generally accepted according to IFRS and ASPE. Each method allocates the cost of a capital asset to expense in a different way and, as a result, each will provide a different net income and carrying amount in each year of the asset's life. These methods can be grouped into three major categories:

1. straight-line
2. accelerated
3. usage-based

At the beginning of fiscal 2017, Vermilion Corp. (Vermilion) purchased equipment for $1,200,000. Management estimated a residual value of $200,000 and a useful life of four years. Panel A of Figure 8.4 plots the annual depreciation expense over the useful life of the asset under

FIGURE 8.4 Depreciation Expense and Carrying Amount Example

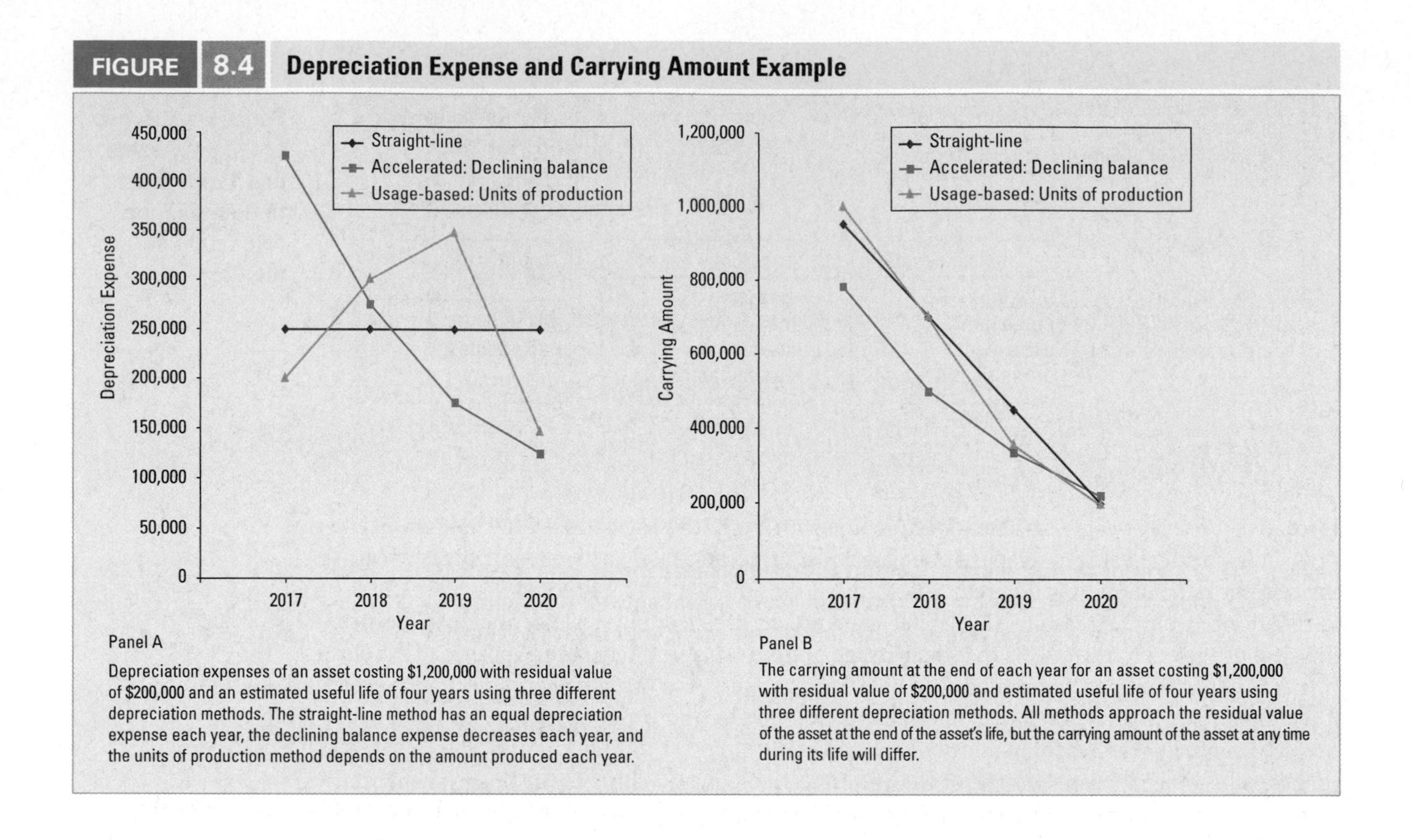

Panel A

Depreciation expenses of an asset costing $1,200,000 with residual value of $200,000 and an estimated useful life of four years using three different depreciation methods. The straight-line method has an equal depreciation expense each year, the declining balance expense decreases each year, and the units of production method depends on the amount produced each year.

Panel B

The carrying amount at the end of each year for an asset costing $1,200,000 with residual value of $200,000 and estimated useful life of four years using three different depreciation methods. All methods approach the residual value of the asset at the end of the asset's life, but the carrying amount of the asset at any time during its life will differ.

each of the three methods. The decline of the asset's carrying amount under each method is shown in Panel B. Refer to Figure 8.4 when you study the following discussion of each method.

When the asset is purchased, the following journal entry is made:

Dr. Capital assets—equipment (assets +)	1,200,000	
Cr. Cash (assets −) or Liability (liability +)		1,200,000
To record the purchase of a capital asset		

Under any depreciation method, the following journal entry will be made each period to record the depreciation expense:

Dr. Depreciation expense (expense +, owners' equity −)	xxx	
Cr. Accumulated depreciation (contra-asset +)		xxx
To record the depreciation expense and the increase in the accumulated depreciation account for the year		

The depreciation expense is the portion of the equipment's cost that is expensed during the period. The credit entry reduces the carrying amount of the equipment on the balance sheet. Notice that the credit is to a contra-asset account, not to the equipment account itself. Recall from Chapter 3 that a contra-asset account accumulates reductions in a related asset account. That means the equipment remains in its account at full cost while depreciation accumulates in the contra-asset accumulated depreciation account. The carrying amount of the equipment equals the amount in the equipment account less the amount in the associated accumulated depreciation account.

Straight-Line Depreciation Straight-line depreciation is straightforward and simple to use, which makes it appealing. With **straight-line depreciation**, the depreciation expense is the same in each period, implying that the contribution to revenue generation by the capital asset is the same each period. This assumption probably isn't entirely valid because over time the capability of most assets declines, repairs and maintenance increase, and sales tend to vary. However, since it's so difficult to estimate the asset's contribution in each period, this approach is reasonable (or as reasonable as any other). The equation for calculating depreciation using the straight-line method is

$$\text{Depreciation expense} = \frac{\text{Cost} - \text{Estimated residual value}}{\text{Estimated useful life}}$$
$$= \frac{\text{Depreciable amount}}{\text{Estimated useful life}}$$

The **depreciable amount** is the amount of a capital asset that will be depreciated. For Vermilion's machine, the depreciable amount is \$1,000,000 (\$1,200,000 − \$200,000) and the annual depreciation expense is \$250,000 (\$1,000,000 ÷ 4 years).

$$\text{Depreciation expense} = \frac{\$1{,}200{,}000 - \$200{,}000}{4\text{ years}}$$
$$= \$250{,}000\text{ per year}$$

Figure 8.5 shows the depreciation schedule for the life of the asset.

		Balance Sheet		Income Statement
	Column 1	Column 2	Column 3	Column 4
Year	Cost	Accumulated depreciation on December 31	Carrying amount on December 31 (cost − depreciation)	Depreciation expense for the year ended December 31
2017	$1,200,000	$ 250,000	$950,000	$ 250,000
2018	1,200,000	500,000	700,000	250,000
2019	1,200,000	750,000	450,000	250,000
2020	1,200,000	1,000,000	200,000	250,000
Total				$1,000,000

FIGURE 8.5 Depreciation Schedule Using Straight-Line Depreciation

The annual depreciation expense will change as estimates of the asset's useful life and residual value change. If we changed the estimated useful life to five years and the residual value to \$150,000, the annual depreciation expense becomes \$210,000. If everything else stays the same, these changes will result in net income being \$40,000 higher in each of the first four years compared with our original estimates. These changes have no direct economic impact on the entity, but they may affect the outcome of contracts based on net income and other financial statement measures. This example shows how management's estimates may influence perceptions of the entity, affect decisions a stakeholder makes, and have economic consequences. As I discuss in the appendix to this chapter, the choice of depreciation method has no tax implications.

Accelerated Depreciation **Accelerated depreciation** methods allocate more of the cost of a capital asset to expense in the early years of its life and less in the later years. When an asset's revenue-generating ability is greater in the early part of its life, an accelerated method of depreciation makes sense. Accelerated depreciation is appropriate for assets sensitive to obsolescence, such as computers, and assets that clearly lose efficiency and/or effectiveness over time. Look at Figure 8.4 to see the pattern of accelerated depreciation in graphic form.

The most common accelerated depreciation method used in Canada is the **declining balance** method. This method applies a depreciation rate to the carrying amount of the asset at the beginning of the period to calculate the depreciation expense, that is,

$$\text{Depreciation expense} = |\text{Cost} - \text{Accumulated depreciation at the beginning of the period}| \times \text{Rate}$$
$$= \text{Carrying amount at the beginning of the period} \times \text{Rate}$$

Because a fixed rate is being applied to a declining balance, an asset is never depreciated to zero. That is a reason why the residual value is usually ignored with this method.

The depreciation schedule for Vermilion's equipment is shown in Figure 8.6. A rate of 35 percent is applied to this asset. The depreciation expense in the first year is $420,000 ($1,200,000 × 0.35). In the second year, it's $273,000 ([$1,200,000 − $420,000] × 0.35). Notice how the depreciation expense decreases each year. You can also see that at the end of year 4, only $985,793 of the cost has been depreciated. Since the residual value of the equipment is $200,000, the remaining $14,207 would also be expensed in year 4.

Depreciation expense equals the depreciation rate of 35% times the carrying amount on January 1 or column 3 × 35%.

Equals column 2 + column 4.

Equals column 1 − column 2.

Depreciation expense decreases over time.

Equals column 3 − column 4.

FIGURE 8.6 Depreciation Schedule Using Accelerated Depreciation

	Column 1	Column 2	Column 3	Column 4	Column 5	Column 6
Year	Cost	Accumulated depreciation on January 1	Carrying amount on January 1	Depreciation expense for the year ended December 31	Carrying amount on December 31	Accumulated depreciation on December 31
2017	$1,200,000	0	$1,200,000	$420,000	$780,000	$420,000
2018	1,200,000	$420,000	780,000	273,000	507,000	693,000
2019	1,200,000	693,000	507,000	177,450	329,550	870,450
2020	1,200,000	870,450	329,550	115,343	214,207	985,793
Total				$985,793		

Accumulated depreciation is the sum of the depreciation expenses. This column shows the account balance at the beginning of the year.

For managers who are concerned about their company's level of income, accelerated depreciation is less attractive than straight-line depreciation because in the first years of an asset's life the depreciation expense is larger, which makes net income lower. In later years, however, the accelerated depreciation expense is lower than with straight-line depreciation, and net income will be higher. This effect can be seen in the plots in Panel A of Figure 8.4. However, if an entity is growing and continually purchasing and replacing capital assets, the depreciation expense using straight-line depreciation will almost always be lower than with declining balance. If an entity isn't growing, declining balance eventually produces lower depreciation expenses.

There are other accelerated depreciation methods, but these are rarely used in Canada and won't be discussed.

Usage-Based Depreciation: Units of Production If an asset's consumption can be readily associated with its use and not to the passage of time or obsolescence, then a usage-based depreciation method can be used. One of the more common usage-based methods is units of production. To use the **units-of-production** method, the manager must be able to estimate the number of units that the asset will produce over its life. The year's depreciation expense is the proportion of units produced in the year to total estimated units to be produced over the asset's life. In our example, if the asset's estimated production over its useful life is 200,000 units and 40,000 are produced in the first year, the depreciation expense in the first year would be

$$\text{Depreciation expense} = \frac{\text{Number of units produced in the period}}{\text{Estimated number of units}} \times (\text{Cost} - \text{Estimated residual value})$$

$$= \frac{40{,}000 \text{ units}}{200{,}000 \text{ units}} \times (\$1{,}200{,}000 - \$200{,}000)$$

$$= \$200{,}000$$

The depreciation schedule using this method is shown in Figure 8.7. Note that it's assumed that the asset's actual lifetime production will equal the estimated production. In practice, this assumption will often not be true.

Equals column 1 − column 2.

Accumulated depreciation is the sum of the depreciation expenses.

The proportion of estimated total output produced in the year. Equals column 4 ÷ total of column 4.

Equals the depreciable amount ($1,000,000) times column 4.

	Balance Sheet					Income Statement
	Column 1	Column 2	Column 3	Column 4	Column 5	Column 6
Year	Cost	Accumulated depreciation	Carrying amount	Percentage of total production in year	Production	Depreciation expense
1	$1,200,000	$ 200,000	$1,000,000	20%	40,000	$ 200,000
2	1,200,000	500,000	700,000	30	60,000	300,000
3	1,200,000	850,000	350,000	35	70,000	350,000
4	1,200,000	1,000,000	200,000	15	30,000	150,000
Total				100%	200,000	$1,000,000

FIGURE 8.7

Depreciation Schedule Using Units-of-Production Depreciation

The units-of production method is widely used in Canada by companies in natural resource industries such as mining, oil and gas, and forestry. In these industries, it's possible to estimate the amount of resource available. The estimated amount is the basis for depreciating the costs of discovering and developing the mine, oil and gas reserve, or forest (costs such as the purchase of the land or land rights, finding the resource, and developing it).

One could imagine other usage-based measures of asset to use. For example, the number of kilometres a delivery truck travels and the number of hours that equipment runs are possibilities. However, there are some difficulties with applying a depreciation method based on actual use:

- It's difficult to make a reasonable estimate of the capacity of many assets, but the estimate is crucial for determining the depreciation expense for a period. For example, estimating that a truck will travel 200,000 kilometres rather than 150,000 will have a significant effect on the depreciation expense.
- Usage-based depreciation isn't appropriate for many types of assets. For example, this method doesn't work well for buildings or office equipment as there is no obvious unit of measurement that could be applied.

If reasonable measures of usage can be obtained, the usage-based depreciation methods result in good matching; there is a direct association between the amount of depreciation and the consumption of the asset. Unfortunately, the difficulties described above limit the usefulness of the method.

Comparing Methods

LO 4

We'll now expand the Vermilion example to see how different depreciation methods affect the financial statements. Vermilion has no capital assets other than the machine it purchased in 2017. Table 8.3 shows summarized income statements, year-end capital assets, and total assets for the years 2017 through 2020, using the three different depreciation methods. Note the following when examining Table 8.3:

- Vermilion began operations in 2017 with $1,500,000 in cash.
- Vermilion's revenues and expenses, other than the depreciation expense, are identical regardless of the method of depreciation.

- The tax expense is based on the actual rules stated in the *Income Tax Act* and is the same under all three methods.
- The undepreciated portion of the equipment under the declining balance method is fully expensed in 2020.
- All production is sold in the year it's produced.

Notice the significant effect the depreciation method has on Vermilion's net income, net capital assets, and total assets. In 2017, for example, net income ranges from a loss of $117,936 to a profit of $102,064. What does this tell a stakeholder? Is Vermilion doing well, as suggested by the $102,064 profit, or poorly, as indicated by the loss? These questions aren't easy to answer because while the numbers are different in each income statement, the underlying economic position of Vermilion is the same. Accounting choices affect the appearance of the statements but not the underlying economic activity.

Although income in individual years differs under the three depreciation methods, notice that total net income for the four years is the same for all the methods (see Panel E of Table 8.3). The cumulative income statements highlight the fact that the different accounting choices affect the timing of revenues and expenses but not the totals.

Does this mean that accounting choice doesn't matter? It can matter very much, but whether it does or not depends on who is using the financial statements, how they're being used, and for what reason. Only the most unsophisticated financial statement user would be misled by a company's depreciation policy. Research shows that changing depreciation methods to report a higher income doesn't result in a higher stock price. However, if a contract depends on the financial statement numbers, the depreciation method could make a difference.

If Vermilion's managers had a bonus plan based on net income, they might prefer units-of-production depreciation because their bonus would be higher in the first year. If a loan was needed, managers might be reluctant to use the declining balance method because of the loss it produces in the first year. The managers may believe that lenders are less willing to invest in an unprofitable entity. For tax purposes, none of these methods is appropriate because the *Income Tax Act* specifies how depreciation must be calculated (as will be discussed in the appendix to this chapter).

Mc Graw Hill connect

KNOWLEDGE CHECK 8.1

Dragon Ltd. (Dragon) is a small, privately owned company. A professional manager manages the company, and the shareholders aren't involved in day-to-day management. Recently, Dragon began to manufacture products it had previously purchased and sold to its customers.

- ❑ What decisions must Dragon's manager make regarding the accounting for the new equipment before she can calculate the depreciation expense for the current year?
- ❑ Using the following assumptions, calculate each year's depreciation expense and ending balance in accumulated depreciation expense using the straight-line, declining balance, and units-of-production depreciation methods. For declining balance, use a rate of 50 percent.
    - i. The cost of buying and getting the equipment operating was $800,000 ($750,000 cost + $50,000 in delivery, set-up, and ancillary costs).
    - ii. The residual value of the equipment is estimated to be $80,000.
    - iii. The useful life of the equipment is three years.
    - iv. The equipment will produce 20,000 units in the first year, 32,000 in the second year, and 28,000 units in the third year.
- ❑ Prepare the journal entries that would be required for each of the three years for the straight-line method.

TABLE 8.3 Vermilion Corp.: Summarized Financial Statement Information Using Three Different Depreciation Methods

Panel A — Vermilion Corp. 2017

	Straight line	35% declining balance	Units of production
Revenue	$ 680,000	$ 680,000	$ 680,000
Expenses	360,400	360,400	360,400
Depreciation expense	250,000	420,000	200,000
Operating income	69,600	(100,400)	119,600
Taxes	17,536	17,536	17,536
Net income	$ 52,064	($ 117,936)	$ 102,064
Equipment (at cost)	1,200,000	1,200,000	1,200,000
Accumulated depreciation	(250,000)	(420,000)	(200,000)
Equipment (net)	950,000	780,000	1,000,000
Total assets	$1,552,064	$1,382,064	$1,602,064

Panel B — Vermilion Corp. 2018

	Straight line	35% declining balance	Units of production
Revenue	$1,020,000	$1,020,000	$1,020,000
Expenses	540,600	540,600	540,600
Depreciation expense	250,000	273,000	300,000
Operating income	229,400	206,400	179,400
Taxes	21,264	21,264	21,264
Net income	$ 208,136	$ 185,136	$ 158,136
Equipment (at cost)	1,200,000	1,200,000	1,200,000
Accumulated depreciation	(500,000)	(693,000)	(500,000)
Equipment (net)	700,000	507,000	700,000
Total assets	$1,760,200	$1,567,200	$1,760,200

Panel C — Vermilion Corp. 2019

	Straight line	35% declining balance	Units of production
Revenue	$1,190,000	$1,190,000	$1,190,000
Expenses	630,700	630,700	630,700
Depreciation expense	250,000	177,450	350,000
Operating income	309,300	381,850	209,300
Taxes	53,452	53,452	53,452
Net income	$ 255,848	$ 328,398	$ 155,848
Equipment (at cost)	1,200,000	1,200,000	1,200,000
Accumulated depreciation	(750,000)	(870,450)	(850,000)
Equipment (net)	450,000	329,550	350,000
Total assets	$2,016,048	$1,895,598	$1,916,048

Panel D — Vermilion Corp. 2020

	Straight line	35% declining balance	Units of production
Revenue	$ 510,000	$ 510,000	$ 510,000
Expenses	270,300	270,300	270,300
Depreciation expense	250,000	129,550	150,000
Operating income	(1 0,300)	110,150	89,700
Taxes	3,428	3,428	3,428
Net income	($ 13,728)	$ 106,722	$ 86,272
Equipment (at cost)	1,200,000	1,200,000	1,200,000
Accumulated depreciation	(1,000,000)	(1,000,000)	(1,000,000)
Equipment (net)	200,000	200,000	200,000
Total assets	$2,002,320	$2,002,320	$2,002,320

Panel E — Vermilion Corp. 2017–2020

	Straight line	35% declining balance	Unit of production
Revenue	$3,400,000	$3,400,000	$3,400,000
Expenses	1,802,000	1,802,000	1,802,000
Depreciation expense	1,000,000	1,000,000	1,000,000
Operating income	598,000	598,000	598,000
Taxes	95,680	95,680	95,680
Net income	$ 502,320	$ 502,320	$ 502,320
Equipment (at cost)	1,200,000	1,200,000	1,200,000
Accumulated depreciation	(1,000,000)	(1,000,000)	(1,000,000)
Equipment (net)	200,000	200,000	200,000
Total assets	$2,002,320	$2,002,320	$2,002,320

Revenue and expenses (except for depreciation) are the same under all three methods.

Net income varies significantly from method to method because the depreciation expense is different under each method.

The carrying amount of the equipment, accumulated depreciation, and the amount of total assets at the end of the year depend on the depreciation method used.

Over Vermilion's four-year life, the income statements are identical.

INSIGHT

Depreciation: An Arbitrary Allocation?

Practically speaking, no depreciation method can be justified over all others because in almost all cases it's impossible to know how a capital asset contributes to earning revenue. Indeed, some people have argued that the choice of depreciation method is arbitrary—one method of depreciation can't be proven to be superior to any other. It can also be difficult to estimate the useful life of an asset or its residual value with any precision. As long as an estimate is reasonable under the circumstances, it's acceptable. As a result, managers have considerable leeway in choosing the depreciation methods, useful lives, and residual values for their entity's capital assets. Their decisions can be influenced by their knowledge of how the assets are actually used, the methods used by other firms in the industry, the information needs of stakeholders, and their own interests.

LO 4

Summary

In summary, there are several depreciation issues you need to be aware of:

1. There are a number of different, acceptable methods of depreciating capital assets, with little restriction on which can be used. None of the methods stand out clearly as the best for all situations.
2. Because it's difficult to estimate the useful life or residual value of an asset, there will be variation in managers' choices. Estimates depend on how the asset is used and how it's cared for, and these can be difficult to figure out from financial statements.
3. As a result of points 1 and 2, managers can make choices that serve their reporting objectives.
4. Depreciation has no effect on cash flow.
5. Managers' choices can have economic consequences; for example, they will affect contracts such as management bonuses and debt covenants that depend on accounting measurements.

Because of these issues, similar entities might use different depreciation methods and make different assumptions regarding useful life and residual value. As a result, it can be difficult to compare financial statements. Stakeholders must pay careful attention to entities' accounting choices to understand whether differences between them reflect actual differences in economic activity or simply differences in how the accounting is done.

Figure 8.8 shows the useful lives of the capital assets of three Canadian airlines: Air Canada, WestJet, and Transat A.T. Inc. All use straight-line depreciation, but notice the differences in the useful lives of the assets. Air Canada depreciates its planes over 20 to 25 years, Transat over 7 to 10 years, and WestJet over 20 years. Although there might be economic reasons for the differences, they may simply reflect different judgments by management. These methods are significantly different and as a result make it difficult to compare the financial statements.

FIGURE 8.8 Differences in Depreciation Policies and Estimates among Canadian Airlines

	Company		
Category of asset	**Air Canada**	**WestJet**	**Transat A.T.**
Airframe , engines, and landing gear	20–25 years	20 years	7–10 years
Cabin interior equipment	5 years	Not disclosed separately	Not disclosed separately
Buildings	Maximum 50 years	40 years	10–45 years
Ground and other equipment	3–25 years	5–25 years	Not disclosed separately
Spare engines and related parts	Average remaining useful life of the fleet	20 years	
Leaseholder improvements	Lesser of the lease term or five years	Term of lease	Term of lease

Componentization of Assets

LO 4

IFRS requires **componentization** of assets. When an item of property, plant, and equipment is made up of parts or components for which different useful lives or depreciation methods are appropriate, IFRS requires each component to be accounted for separately. For example, the engines, fuselage, electronics, seats, etc. of an airplane have different useful lives so the cost of the plane must be allocated among the components and each component depreciated separately. The alternative would be to consider the airplane as a single asset and depreciate it over its useful life. Because this asset is usually purchased for a single price, management has to decide how to allocate the cost among the components. As a result, management has some flexibility here, and that can be used to achieve reporting objectives.

ACCOUNTING STANDARDS FOR PRIVATE ENTERPRISES

Strictly speaking, Accounting Standards for Private Enterprises requires componentization like IFRS. But accounting for components in this way hasn't been practised in Canada. As a result, the depreciation expense in any given year will likely be different under IFRS and ASPE.

VALUING CAPITAL ASSETS AT FAIR VALUE

LO 2

Property, plant, and equipment: So far our discussion has assumed that entities will account for their capital assets at cost. Most entities do use cost but IFRS provides the option of valuing certain capital assets at fair value. Property, plant, and equipment can be reported at fair value if the fair value can be measured reliably. Intangibles can be valued at fair value if there is an active market for them. Intangibles tend to be unique so this requirement makes revaluation of them very unusual. A taxi licence or tradable pollution rights are examples of intangibles that could meet the requirement.

Let's demonstrate the accounting with an example. At the beginning of 2017, Restoule Ltd. purchased a building with an estimated life of 25 years for $5 million. On December 31, 2017 and 2018, Restoule recorded depreciation expenses of $200,000 ($5,000,000 ÷ 25 years) and on December 31, 2018 the building had a carrying amount of $4,600,000 ($5,000,000 − [$200,000 × 2]). At the end of 2018, Restoule elects to value the building at its fair value of $6 million. By revaluing the building at fair value, the carrying amount on December 31, 2018 becomes $6,000,000. The revaluation could be presented on Restoule's balance sheet in two ways:

	Gross method	Proportional method
Building (gross carrying amount)	$6,000,000	$6,521,739*
Accumulated depreciation	0	521,739
Carrying amount	$6,000,000	$6,000,000

*To obtain the gross amount of the building, divide the revalued carrying amount of the building ($6,000,000) by the percentage of the building that hasn't been depreciated under the cost model (0.92 = 4,600,000 ÷ $5,000,000) or $6,000,000 ÷ 0.92.

The gross method simply records the asset at its revalued amount and eliminates accumulated depreciation. With the proportional method, the ratio of accumulated depreciation to gross carrying amount of the asset must be the same before and after the revaluation, and the carrying amount must equal the market value. At the time of the revaluation, Restoule's building was 8 percent depreciated ($400,000 ÷ $5,000,000), so after the revaluation accumulated depreciation must be 8 percent of the gross carrying amount of the building and the carrying amount must be $6,000,000. These requirements mean the gross carrying amount at the end of 2018 must be $6,521,739, and accumulated depreciation $521,739. The key point is that the building is reported on the balance sheet at $6 million, its fair value.

Since assets increased by $1,400,000 ($6,000,000 − $4,600,000), another adjustment is needed to keep the accounting equation in balance. This adjustment is reported in "other comprehensive income" in the statement of comprehensive income and as "accumulated other comprehensive income—revaluation surplus" in the equity section of the balance sheet. (Comprehesive income is the change in equity during a period from transactions and economic events that involve non-owners [remember that revenue and expenses affect equity]). Restoule's statement of comprehensive income and the equity section of its balance sheet might appear as follows (all numbers shown are assumed except for the increase in the value of the building):

Restoule Ltd. Statement of Comprehensive Income For the Year Ended December 31, 2018	
Net income	$5,300,000
Other comprehensive income—revaluation surplus	1,400,000
Comprehensive income	$6,700,000

Restoule Ltd. Balance Sheet—Shareholders' Equity As of December 31, 2018	
Common shares	$17,250,000
Retained earnings	35,550,000
Accumulated other comprehensive income—revaluation surplus	1,400,000
Total shareholders' equity	$54,200,000

If, instead, the fair value of Restoule's building decreased to $4 million at the end of 2018, the carrying amount on the balance sheet would become $4,000,000. However, the decrease in value would be reported as a loss on the income statement (not in other comprehensive income), and there would be no accumulated other comprehensive income–revaluation surplus account on the balance sheet. In other words, losses are recognized in the calculation of net income whereas gains are included in other comprehensive income, not in the calculation of net income, because they aren't realized.

IFRS requires that revaluations be done often enough so the difference between the carrying amount and market value isn't significant. It also requires an entity to account for similar assets in the same way. Treatment of changes in valuation after the first one can get complicated, so I'll leave coverage of that to a higher-level accounting course.

Evidence shows that very few companies elect to use the market value approach for valuing capital assets. Fair value can also be used for other categories of capital assets, including:

- *Investment properties*: Investment property is land and buildings held to earn rent or for capital appreciation. The definition excludes land and building used to produce or supply goods or services, used for administrative purposes, or held for sale as part of the normal business activities of the company. Companies must make an accounting policy choice to value investment properties at cost (and depreciate over their useful lives) or at fair value. If the fair value approach is used, changes in fair value are reported in the calculation of net income. (Note that this is a little different from the revaluation model for property, plant, and equipment where increases in value are reported in other comprehensive income.)
- *Biological assets*: In Chapter 7, I mentioned special rules for biological assets and agricultural produce. That discussion was in the context of inventory. Here I'll briefly mention biological assets from the perspective of capital assets. A biological asset is a living animal or plant. What distinguishes a biological asset from other assets is that it grows, reproduces, and produces. IFRS requires that biological assets be valued at the end of each reporting period at fair value less costs to sell. The change in fair value is included in the calculation of net income.

ACCOUNTING STANDARDS FOR PRIVATE ENTERPRISES

Accounting Standards for Private Enterprises doesn't allow valuation of capital assets at fair value.

INSIGHT

Implications of Valuing Capital Assets at Fair Value

Recent research has shown that relatively few companies fair-value their capital assets, and those that do tend to be companies in the real estate business. Some things to keep in mind about using fair values:

- Fair-valuing makes income (or comprehensive income) more volatile because changes in value are recognized even if an asset isn't sold.
- For many capital assets, it may be difficult to determine a precise fair value, which provides flexibility to management to manage earnings.
- Fair values may provide more relevant information for stakeholders because the assets are valued at current rather than historical values.

Financial Statement Disclosure

LO 5

Companies that adhere to IFRS are required to disclose the following information about their capital assets:

- measurement basis for determining the carrying amount (cost or fair value)
- depreciation method and useful lives of each major category of capital assets
- gross carrying amount and accumulated depreciation at the beginning and end of the period
- a reconciliation of the carrying amount at the beginning and end of the period
- depreciation expense

Exhibit 8.1 provides an example of capital asset disclosure for West Fraser Timber Co. Ltd. (West Fraser), an integrated forest products company producing lumber, wood chips, fibreboard, plywood, pulp, and newsprint.[1] West Fraser's balance sheets only provide a small part of its capital asset story, showing only the net amount (cost less accumulated depreciation) of the company's PPE, timber licences, goodwill, and intangible assets. The notes must be examined to get the full story about these assets. Connect the references in Exhibit 8.1 to the following explanations of the information West Fraser provides about its capital assets.

www.westfraser.com

❶ Net amount of PPE, timber licences, and goodwill and other intangibles (balance sheet). The notes to the financial statements must be examined to get more detail about these amounts.

❷a Reconciliation from December 31, 2010 to December 31, 2011 for each category of PPE and in total. Note that the bottom number in the total column corresponds with the amount for PPE on the balance sheet. (Note 7.)

❷b Gross amount, accumulated amortization (depreciation), and net amount for each category of PPE and in total. Net amount in the total column corresponds with the amount on the balance sheet. (Note 7.) **❷a** and **❷b** provide additional detail over what's on the balance sheet.

❸a Reconciliation from December 31, 2010 to December 31, 2011 for timber licences, goodwill, and other intangibles. Note that the bottom number in the timber licences and goodwill and other intangibles columns corresponds with amounts on the balance sheet. (Note 8.)

❸b Gross amount, accumulated amortization, and net amount for timber licences, goodwill, and other intangibles. Net amount in total corresponds with the amount on the balance sheet. (Note 8.) **❸a** and **❸b** provide additional detail over what's on the balance sheet.

❹ Amortization (depreciation) expense for 2010 and 2011 (statement of earnings). If you add together the amortization lines in Notes 7 and 8, you'll come up with the total for 2011 that's on the statement of earnings.

EXHIBIT 8.1 West Fraser Timber Co. Ltd.: Disclosures about Capital Assets

Consolidated Balance Sheets

(in millions of Canadian dollars)

	December 31, 2011	December 31, 2010	January 1, 2010
Assests			
Current assets			
Cash and short-term investments	$ 67.8	$ 163.1	$ 12.0
Receivables (note 24)	266.7	246.0	200.6
Income taxes receivable	4.4	—	67.6
Inventories (note 6)	397.8	372.4	407.7
Prepaid expenses	8.6	7.6	11.2
	745.3	789.1	699.1
❶ **Property, plant and equipment** (note 7)	935.7	924.7	1,031.9
Timber licences (note 8)	490.1	509.6	499.7
Goodwill and other intangibles (note 8)	336.6	345.4	354.0
Other assets (note 9)	29.6	41.5	29.1
	$ 2,537.3	$ 2,610.3	$ 2,613.8

Consolidated Statement of Earnings and Comprehensive Earnings

For the years ended December 31, 2011 and 2010
(in millions of Canadian dollars)

	2011	2010
Sales	$ 2,762.1	$ 2,885.9
Costs and expenses		
Cost of products sold	1.916.6	1,787.0
Freight and other distribution costs	460.3	441.2
Export taxes	57.7	59.7
❹ Amortization	167.7	185.0
Selling, general and administration	104.7	107.0
Equity-based compensation	(2.7)	31.4
	2,704.3	2,611.3
Operating earnings	57.8	274.6
Interest expense (note 16)	(20.1)	(27.7)
Exchange gain (loss) on long-term debt	(6.7)	16.9
Other income (expense) (note 17)	13.9	(8.5)
Earnings from continuing operations before tax provision	44.9	255.3
Tax provision (note 18)	(18.1)	(73.5)
Earnings from continuing operations	26.8	181.8
Earnings from discontinued operations (note 20)	45.9	4.6
Earnings	$ 72.7	$ 186.4

EXHIBIT 8.1 (continued) West Fraser Timber Co. Ltd.: Disclosures about Capital Assets

Notes to Consolidated Financial Statements

For the years ended December 31, 2011 and 2010

(in millions of Canadian dollars, except where indicated)

3. Significant accounting policies

Property, plant and equipment

❺ Property, plant and equipment are stated at cost, less accumulated amortization and impairment losses. Expenditures for additions and improvements are capitalized. Borrowing costs are capitalized when the asset construction period exceeds 12 months and the borrowing costs are directly attributable to the asset. Expenditures for maintenance and repairs are charged to earnings. Upon retirement, disposal or destruction of an asset, the cost and related amortization are removed from the accounts and any gain or loss is included in earnings.

Property, plant and equipment are amortized on a straight-line basis over their estimated useful lives as follows:

❻

Buildings	10–30 years
Manufacturing equipment and machinery	6–20 years
Fixtures, mobile and other equipment	3–10 years
Roads	Not exceeding 40 years
Major maintenance shutdowns	12 to 36 months

Timber licences and other intangibles

❼ Timber licences and other intangible assets are stated at historical cost, less accumulated amortization and impairment losses, and are amortized on a straight-line basis over their estimated useful lives as follows:

❽

Timber licences	40 years
Power purchase agreement	Over the life of the agreement
Software	3–5 years
Non-replaceable timber rights	As timber is logged

❾ **Impairment of property, plant, equipment, timber licences and other intangibles**

The Company reviews property, plant, equipment, timber licences and other intangible assets for impairment whenever events or changes in circumstances indicate that the carrying amount may not be fully recoverable. For the purpose of impairment testing, property, plant, equipment, timber licences and other intangible assets are separated into cash generating units ("CGU"). The Company has identified each of its mills as a CGU for impairment testing of property, plant, equipment and other intangibles. Timber licences are tested for impairment by combining CGUs within the economic area of the related licence.

Recoverability is assessed by comparing the CGU carrying amount to the discounted estimated net future cash flows the assets are expected to generate. If the carrying amount exceeds the discounted estimated net future cash flows, the assets of the CGU are written down to the higher of fair value less costs to sell and value in use (being the present value of the estimated net future cash flows of the relevant asset or CGU).

Estimated net future cash flows are based on several assumptions concerning future circumstances including selling prices of products, U.S./Canadian dollar exchange rates, production rates, input costs and capital requirements. The estimated net future cash flows are discounted at rates based on management's estimate of the Company's weighted average cost of capital.

Where an impairment loss subsequently reverses, the carrying amount of the asset or CGU is increased to the lesser of the revised estimate of its recoverable amount and the carrying amount that would have been recorded had no impairment loss been previously recognized.

❿ **Goodwill**

Goodwill represents the excess of the purchase price paid for an acquisition over the fair value of the net assets acquired. Goodwill is not amortized, but is subject to an impairment test annually or more frequently if events or circumstances indicate that it may be impaired.

Goodwill impairment is assessed by comparing the fair value of its CGU to the underlying carrying amount of the CGU's net assets, including goodwill. When the carrying amount of the CGU exceeds its fair value, the fair value of the CGU's goodwill is compared with its carrying a mount to measure the amount of impairment loss, if any.

EXHIBIT 8.1 (continued) West Fraser Timber Co. Ltd.: Disclosures about Capital Assets

7. Property, plant and equipment

		Manufacturing plant, equipment & machinery	Construction-in-progress	Roads and bridges	Other	Total
❷a	As at December 31, 2010	$ 847.1	$ 12.8	$ 34.4	$ 30.4	$ 924.7
	Additions	101.0	43.6	8.3	0.2	153.1
	Disposals	(0.1)	(0.2)	—	(2.0)	(2.3)
	Amortization[1]	(133.8)	—	(7.7)	(0.7)	(142.2)
	Foreign exchange	2.2	—	—	0.2	2.4
	Transfers	11.0	(11.3)	—	0.3	—
	As at December 31, 2011	$ 827.4	$ 44.9	$ 35.0	$ 28.4	$ 935.7
❷b	**As at December 31, 2011**					
	Cost	$ 2,581.7	$ 44.9	$ 89.5	$ 34.7	$ 2,750.8
	Accumulated amortization	(1,754.3)	—	(54.5)	(6.3)	(1,815.1)
	Net	$ 827.4	$ 44.9	$ 35.0	$ 28.4	$ 935.7

1. Amortization by function is $140.0 million cost of products sold and $2.2 million selling, general and administration (2010—$154.3 million and $2.6 million, respectively).

8. Timber licences, goodwill and other intangibles

		Timber licences	Goodwill	Power purchase agreement	Other	Goodwill and other intangibles
❸a	As at December 31, 2010	$ 509.6	$ 263.7	$ 73.2	$ 8.5	$ 345.4
	Additions	—	—	—	1.1	1.1
	Disposals	—	—	—	(0.7)	(0.7)
	Amortization[1]	(16.3)	—	(7.3)	(1.9)	(9.2)
	Adjustment	(3.2)	—	—	—	—
	As at December 31, 2011	$ 490.1	$ 263.7	$ 65.9	$ 7.0	$ 336.6
	As at December 31, 2011					
❸b	Cost	$ 651.0	$ 263.7	$ 115.2	$ 24.3	$ 403.2
	Accumulated amortization	(160.9)	—	(49.3)	(17.3)	(66.6)
	Net	$ 490.1	$ 263.7	$ 65.9	$ 7.0	$ 336.6

1. Amortization by function is $24.1 million cost of products sold and $1.4 million selling, general and administration [2010—$25.8 million and $1.8 million respectively).

❺ Explains how PPE is accounted for.

❻ Describes the method used to depreciate PPE (straight line) and the estimated useful lives of the main categories of PPE.

❼ Explains how timber licences and other intangibles are accounted for.

❽ Describes the method used to depreciate timber licences and other intangibles (straight line) and the estimated useful lives of the timber licences and other intangibles.

❾ Describes how impairment of PPE, timber licences, and other intangibles is determined. Identifies the assumptions required to estimate future cash flows (value-in-use).

❿ Describes how goodwill arises and how it's accounted for, including how it's determined if goodwill is impaired.

West Fraser's financial statements provide some context for understanding the accounting it uses for capital assets but the information doesn't give an idea about whether the accounting methods are reasonable or appropriate. That insight comes from familiarity with the business. Managers have considerable discretion for deciding how to present details about their entities' capital assets, and West Fraser provides fairly detailed information about its capital assets.

QUESTION FOR CONSIDERATION

Some people argue that depreciation of the cost of capital assets is arbitrary. Explain.

SOLUTION: The purpose of depreciation is to match the cost of capital assets to the revenues they help generate. But what is the relationship between a delivery vehicle and revenue, a lawn mower and revenue, a computer and revenue, or a machine and revenue? Clearly, these capital assets make contributions to earning revenue, but it's impossible to know exactly what they are. Nevertheless, accrual accounting requires that capital assets be depreciated, so it's necessary to develop methods to do this. As a result, different depreciation methods can be justified in terms of the facts, as long as they are reasonable. It's impossible to argue that one method allocates the cost of capital assets to expense better than any other method. In other words, the choice is arbitrary.

NATURAL RESOURCES

Natural resource industries, mining and oil and gas, play a major role in the Canadian economy, so it's important to note some of the accounting issues these companies face. They spend a lot of money and a lot of time trying to find resources they can extract and sell. IFRS are as yet not very clear on which costs incurred developing a resource should be capitalized. Also, companies must bear failures as part of the cost of being successful. For example, in the oil and gas industry, companies often have to drill a number of wells to find ones that provide oil and gas. One question accountants deal with is, should all the costs incurred finding oil in a particular area, say a country, be capitalized and depleted, regardless of whether the wells have oil or not? Or should only the costs associated with wells that produce oil be capitalized? Then there is the question of when costs should start being capitalized (until the starting time, costs would be expensed as incurred). These are very complicated accounting issues. At this stage, it's worthwhile being familiar with them, even though the answers are unclear, even within IFRS.

INTANGIBLE ASSETS

LO 6

Intangible assets, including knowledge assets or intellectual capital, are capital assets with no physical qualities. Intangible assets can't be seen, touched, or felt like a machine, building, or table, but they are often crucial to the success of an entity. Intangible assets include patents, copyrights, trademarks, franchise rights, brand names, customer lists, software, licences, movies, human resources, and goodwill.

Accounting for intangible assets under IFRS is similar to accounting for property, plant, and equipment, although there are differences, as we'll see. Generally, to be recognized as an intangible asset, an item must meet the following conditions:

- It must be separately identifiable (be able to sell or license it).
- It must have future benefits.
- The future benefits must be controlled by the entity.
- The cost must be reliably measurable.
- Alternatively, an intangible asset can be recognized if it represents a contractual or legal right.

If these criteria aren't met, the costs involved must be expensed when incurred.

Intangible assets are amortized over their useful lives. However, if the period over which the intangible is expected to provide benefits isn't limited, it's considered to have an indefinite life and doesn't have to be amortized. For example, Exhibit 8.2 shows the accounting treatment of BCE Inc.'s intangible assets.[2] Software, customer relationships, and program and feature films have finite lives and are amortized. The brand name, spectrum and other licences, and broadcast licences aren't amortized because management believes these have indefinite lives. Connect the references in Exhibit 8.2 to the following explanations of the information BCE provides about its program rights and broadcast licences.

www.bce.ca

❶ Carrying amount of all of BCE`s intangibles (except goodwill), net of accumulated amortization. Details on the different types of intangibles are provided in Note 14.

❷ Amortization expense for intangible assets with finite lives. Details on the amount of amortization associated with each type of intangible are provided in Note 14.

❸ This note describes the different categories of finite-life intangible assets and explains how they are accounted for. The three categories described are software, customer relationships, and program and feature film rights. Amounts associated with these categories are provided in Note 14.

EXHIBIT 8.2 BCE Inc.: Accounting for Intangible Assets

CONSOLIDATED STATEMENTS OF FINANCIAL POSITION

	(IN MILLIONS OF CANADIAN DOLLARS)	NOTE	DECEMBER 31, 2011	DECEMBER 31, 2010	JANUARY 1, 2010
	ASSETS				
	Current assets				
	Cash		130	129	195
	Cash equivalents		45	642	489
	Trade and other receivables	11	3,119	2,885	2,779
	Current tax receivable		43	139	118
	Inventory	12	427	431	442
	Prepaid expenses		262	224	290
	Other current assets		152	205	138
	Total current assets		4,178	4,655	4,451
	Non-current assets				
	Property, plant and equipment	13	18,785	17,775	17,347
❶	Intangible assets	14	8,013	6,201	6,347
	Deferred tax assets	9	329	501	401
	Investments in associates and joint ventures		307	303	260
	Other non-current assets	15	629	652	855
	Goodwill	16	7,185	5,806	5,774
	Total non-current assets		35,248	31,238	30,984
	Total assets		39,426	35,893	35,435

EXHIBIT 8.2 (continued) BCE Inc.: Accounting for Intangible Assets

CONSOLIDATED INCOME STATEMENTS

FOR THE YEAR ENDED DECEMBER 31 (IN MILLIONS OF CANADIAN DOLLARS, EXCEPT SHARE AMOUNTS)	NOTE	2011	2010
Operating revenues	3	19,497	18,069
Operating costs	5	(11,868)	(10,884)
Severance, acquisition and other costs	6	(409)	(262)
Depreciation	13	(2,538)	(2,388)
❷ Amortization	14	(723)	(737)
Finance costs			
Interest expense	7	(842)	(685)
Interest on employee benefit obligations	20	(984)	(992)
Interest on fund unit liability		—	(370)
Expected return on pension plan assets	20	1,032	898
Other income	8	129	173
Earnings before income taxes		3,294	2,822
Income taxes	9	(720)	(632)
Net earnings		2,574	2,190
Net earnings attributable to:			
Common shareholders		2,221	2,083
Preferred shareholders		119	112
Non-controlling interest		234	(5)
Net earnings		2,574	2,190

NOTE 2 | SIGNIFICANT ACCOUNTING POLICIES

❸ *INTANGIBLE ASSETS*

FINITE-LIFE INTANGIBLE ASSETS

Finite-life intangible assets are carried at cost less accumulated amortization and accumulated impairment losses, if any.

Software

We record internal-use software at historical cost. Cost includes expenditures that *are* attributable directly to the acquisition or development of the software, including the purchase cost, labour and overhead

Research costs are expensed as incurred. Software development costs are capitalized when all the following conditions are met:

- technical feasibility can be demonstrated
- management has the intent and the ability to complete the asset for use or sale
- it is probable that economic benefits will be generated
- costs attributable to the asset can be measured reliably.

Customer Relationships

Customer relationship assets are acquired through business combinations and are recorded at fair value at the date of acquisition.

Program and Feature Film Rights

We account for program and feature film rights as intangible assets when these assets are acquired for the purpose of broadcasting. Program and feature film rights, which include producer advances and licence fees paid in advance of receipt of the program or film, are stated at acquisition cost less accumulated amortization and accumulated impairment losses. Programs and feature films under licence agreements are recorded as assets and liabilities for rights acquired and obligations incurred when:

- the company receives a broadcast master and the cost is known or reasonably determinable for new program and feature film licences
- the licence term commences for licence period extensions or syndicated programs.

Programs and feature films are classified as non-current assets with related liabilities classified as current or non-current, based on the payment terms. Amortization of program and feature film intangible assets is recorded in *Operating costs* in the income statements.

❹ INDEFINITE-LIFE INTANGIBLE ASSETS

Brand assets, mainly comprised of the Bell and Bell Media brands, and broadcast licences are acquired through business combinations and are recorded at fair value at the date of acquisition. Wireless spectrum licences are recorded

EXHIBIT 8.2 (continued) BCE Inc.: Accounting for Intangible Assets

at acquisition cost, including borrowing costs when the time to build or develop the related network is in excess of one year.

Currently there are no legal, regulatory, competitive or other factors that limit the useful lives of our brands or spectrum licences.

❻ *IMPAIRMENT OF NON-FINANCIAL ASSETS*

Goodwill and indefinite-life intangible assets are tested for impairment annually or when there is an indication that the asset may be impaired. Property, plant and equipment and finite-life intangible assets are tested for impairment if events or changes in circumstances, assessed quarterly, indicate that their carrying amount may not be recoverable. For the purpose of impairment tests, assets are grouped at the lowest level for which there are separately identifiable cash inflows.

Impairment losses are recognized and measured as the excess of the carrying value of the assets over their recoverable amount. An asset's recoverable amount is the higher of its fair value less costs to sell and its value in use. Previously recognized impairment losses, other than those attributable to goodwill, are reviewed for possible reversal at each reporting date and, if the asset's recoverable amount has increased, all or a portion of the impairment is reversed.

❺ *DEPRECIATION AND AMORTIZATION*

We depreciate property, plant and equipment and amortize finite-life intangible assets on a straight-line basis over their estimated useful lives. We review our estimates of useful lives on an annual basis and adjust depreciation and amortization on a prospective basis, if needed. Land and assets under construction or development are not depreciated.

	ESTIMATED USEFUL LIFE
Property, plant and equipment	
Network infrastructure and equipment	2 to 50 years
Buildings	10 to 50 years
Finite-life intangible assets	
Software	2 to 7 years
Customer relationships	5 to 30 years
Program and feature film rights	Up to 5 years

NOTE 14 | INTANGIBLE ASSETS

YEAR ENDED DECEMBER 31, 2011	FINITE LIFE					INDEFINITE-LIFE				
	SOFTWARE	CUSTOMER RELATIONSHIPS	OTHER	PROGRAM AND FEATURE FILM	TOTAL	BRAND	SPECTRUM AND OTHER LICENCES	BROADCAST LICENCES	TOTAL	TOTAL INTANGIBLE ASSETS
COST ❼										
January 1, 2011	5,210	846	218	—	6,274	2,024	1,687	—	3,711	9,985
Additions	244	—	—	330	574	—	—	—	—	574
Acquisition through business combinations	70	—	65	416	551	218	—	1,293	1,511	2,062
Transfers	336	3	(5)	—	334	—	—	—	—	334
Retirements and disposals	(72)	(2)	—	—	(74)	—	—	—	—	(74)
Amortization included in operating costs	—	—	—	(382)	(382)	—	—	—	—	(382)
December 31, 2011	5,788	847	278	364	7,277	2,242	1,687	1,293	5,222	12,499
ACCUMULATED AMORTIZATION ❽										
January 1, 2011	3,505	224	55	—	3,784	—	—	—	—	3,784
Amortization for the year	656	50	17	—	723	—	—	—	—	723
Retirements and disposals	(70)	(2)	—	—	(72)	—	—	—	—	(72)
Other	49	2	—	—	51	—	—	—	—	51
December 31, 2011	4,140	274	72	—	4,486	—	—	—	—	4,486
NET CARRYING AMOUNT ❾										
January 1, 2011	1,705	622	163	—	2,490	2,024	1,687	—	3,711	6,201
December 31, 2011	1,648	573	206	364	2,791	2,242	1,687	1,293	5,222	8,013

4. Identifies the types of intangible assets with indefinite lives (brand names and broadcast and spectrum licences) and explains how they are accounted for.
5. Describes amortization method used for finite-life intangible assets (straight line) and their estimated useful lives.
6. Describes when and how impairment of different categories of capital assets is determined and how impairment losses are accounted for.
7. Reconciliation of changes during the year to each category of intangible assets.
8. Reconciliation of changes during the year to the accumulated amortization associated with each category of intangible asset.
9. Carrying amount of each category of intangible asset (cost − accumulated amortization). The totals in the right-hand column are the amounts that appear on the balance sheet.

Like property, plant, and equipment, an entity can elect to value intangibles at cost or fair value, but fair value can only be used if there is an active market for it, to provide a value. The accounting treatment of intangible assets, particularly internally generated ones, is one of the greatest challenges currently facing the accounting profession. In the "new economy" of the 21st century, entities invest significant resources in the creation of knowledge assets and intellectual capital they use rather than sell. Regardless of how valuable they might be, costs associated with internally generated brands, customer lists and loyalty, information, and similar types of items, as well as training costs, advertising and promotion costs, and so on must be expensed as incurred. The accounting for intangible assets that are purchased is significantly different. When an intangible asset is purchased, in many situations it's recorded at cost, classified as an asset on the balance sheet, and amortized over its useful life (or treated as having an indefinite life). The accounting for purchased versus internally developed intangible assets is compared in Figure 8.9.

It's difficult to argue that internally generated intangibles aren't assets, at least conceptually. There is no doubt that these investments provide an expectation of future benefits. Without ongoing research, technology companies would quickly become worthless as their products became obsolete. Successful brand names, customer lists, and skillful personnel clearly provide future benefits to an entity. There are reasons why contemporary accounting fails to recognize knowledge assets and intellectual capital. One is that IFRS's recognition criteria states that for an item to be recognized as an asset there must be probable future benefits associated with it. It's very uncertain if there will be a future benefit to expenditures of these types. Measurability is also a problem since the relation between an expenditure and a future benefit is often unclear. Another

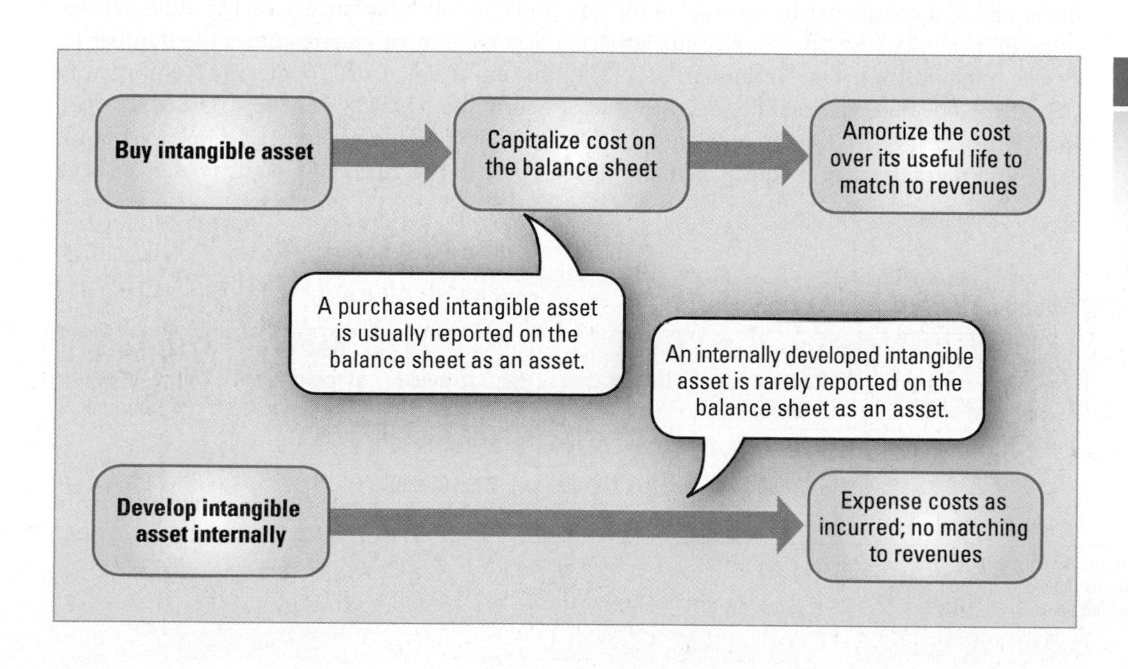

FIGURE 8.9 **Accounting for Purchased versus Internally Developed Intangible Assets**

part of the problem is that many knowledge assets are developed internally by entities over time, and in many or most cases it isn't at all clear that a valuable resource will ultimately emerge. In contrast, most tangible capital assets are purchased in a completed form—ready or almost ready for use.

The fact that investments in knowledge assets are expensed when they are incurred has significant implications for the financial statements. For instance, the economic costs incurred to earn revenue aren't expensed in the period the benefits are earned. As a result, net income as a measure of performance is weakened. For example, a pharmaceutical company will expense all expenditures in developing a new drug. By the time the new drug has been developed, tested, and approved by Health Canada and other regulators around the world, many years will have passed. When the drug finally makes it to market, most of the costs incurred to develop it have been expensed. What does profit mean if many of the costs incurred to earn the revenues aren't reported in the period the revenues are recognized? Clearly, net income won't be the performance measure we typically think it is. This is similar to expensing the cost of a retailer's inventory when it's purchased rather than when it's sold.

Many financial ratios are adversely affected by the accounting treatment used for knowledge assets. Gross margin, profit margin, return on assets (net income ÷ total assets), return on equity (net income ÷ shareholders' equity), and many others are distorted as a result of the accounting used for intangibles. Research has shown that return on assets and return on equity would both tend to be higher if knowledge assets were capitalized.

Let's look at Research In Motion Limited's (RIM) spending on research and development (R&D) to get an idea of the magnitude of the issue. RIM is the designer and maker of the BlackBerry wireless device. In the year ended March 3, 2012, RIM spent $1.159 billion on research and development, representing 113.9 percent of net income for the year and 8.5 percent of revenue. (RIM spent $1.351 billion and $965 million in 2011 and 2010 respectively on R&D.) These investments create and develop the products and technologies of the future, but the amounts are being expensed as incurred, not when the products are ultimately sold. If RIM's investment in R&D has future benefit, there is a clear and significant mismatching of revenues and expenses resulting in net income and assets being lower than they should be. If the $3.875 billion that RIM spent on research and expensed in 2010 through 2012 had been capitalized instead of expensed, total assets and net income would have been significantly higher than reported (because the expenditure on R&D has been increasing). For example, if RIM capitalized its R&D spending and amortized it over three years, net income in fiscal 2012 would have been about $267 million or 23 percent higher. Figure 8.10 provides information on the amount and impact of R&D spending by three Canadian companies. Notice the significant impact that R&D spending has on net income.

Another way to consider assets missing from the balance sheet is to compare the book value of the equity of a company (the amount in the equity section of its balance sheet) and the market value of its equity (the price on the stock market of the company's shares times the number of shares outstanding). On December 31, 2011, the book value of Google Inc.'s equity was US$58,145,000,000 whereas the market value of equity was US$208,712,395,751 ($642.40 per share times 324,894,763 shares outstanding). The huge $151 billion difference between the book value and market value of equity is due at least in part to the fact that Google's balance sheet

FIGURE 8.10 R&D Spending by Canadian Companies

	Revenues (000s)	Net income (000s)	R&D expense (000s)	R&D as a percentage of revenue	R&D as a percentage of net income
Research In Motion Limited*	$18,435,000,000	$1,164,000,000	$1,559,000,000	8.5%	133.9%
BCE†	19,497,000,000	2,574,000,000	229,000,000	1.2%	8.9%
Valeant Pharmaceuticals International, Inc.‡	2,463,450,000	159,559,000	65,687,000	2.7%	41.2%

*U.S. dollars, U.S. GAAP, year-end March 3, 2012.
†Canadian dollars, IFRS, year-end December 31, 2011.
‡U.S. dollars, U.S. GAAP, year-end December 31, 2011.

doesn't report the full value of many of its intangible assets, such as its technology. Another example: Coca-Cola is one of the best-known brand names in the world, yet if you examine its balance sheet there is no mention of this valuable asset. On December 31, 2011, the book value of Coca-Cola's shareholders' equity was US$31.921 billion whereas the market value of its equity was over US$158 billion, a difference of over $126 billion. A large measure of this difference is likely due to the missing value of the Coca-Cola brand name.

Goodwill

LO 6

Most intangible or knowledge assets, regardless of how they are accounted for, can be identified. An entity will own a patent, a copyright, a franchise, a licence, and so on. Goodwill, probably the most commonly seen intangible asset on balance sheets, is different: it doesn't really represent anything in particular. To understand this point, we need to understand how goodwill arises.

Goodwill arises when one company purchases all or a majority of the shares of another company and pays more for it than the fair value of the assets and liabilities of the purchased company. The purchaser must determine the fair value of each asset and liability on the purchase date. **Goodwill** is the amount paid over and above the fair value of the purchased entity's identifiable assets and liabilities on the date of purchase. That is,

Goodwill = Purchase price − Fair value of identifiable assets and liabilities purchased

Identifiable assets and liabilities are tangible and intangible assets and liabilities that can be specifically identified. Identifiable assets include cash, inventory, land, buildings, patents, copyrights, and research and development.

For example, assume that Rushoon Inc. (Rushoon) purchased 100 percent of the outstanding shares of Molanosa Ltd. (Molanosa) for $12,000,000. The fair value of Molanosa's identifiable net assets (assets − liabilities) on the date of the purchase was $10,500,000. The goodwill that arose as a result of the purchase of Molanosa's shares by Rushoon is

Goodwill = Purchase price − Fair value of identifiable net assets
= $12,000,000 − $10,500,000
= $1,500,000

Why would Rushoon pay $1,500,000 more than the fair value of Molanosa's identifiable net assets? What does the goodwill actually represent? Well, it's hard to be sure because goodwill is a residual—the amount left over after the identifiable net assets have been valued. It's assumed that if a purchaser paid more than the fair value of the identifiable assets and liabilities for a company, the extra amount paid is for something of value, even if it isn't clear exactly what. Goodwill is often attributed to things such as management ability, location, synergies created by the acquisition, customer loyalty, reputation, and benefits associated with the elimination of a competitor—all things that should lead to higher profits but are very difficult to specifically identify and measure. Of course, it's also possible the buyer paid too much. However, it would probably be imprudent for a manager to admit that too soon after the purchase!

It's interesting to note that assets such as management skill, location, reputation, and so on that are considered goodwill all exist before a company is purchased. However, internally generated goodwill never appears on the balance sheet. Goodwill is recognized only when one company purchases another. It's much too difficult to determine if there are future benefits associated with expenditures that give rise to goodwill, so the amounts are expensed as incurred.

IFRS say that goodwill isn't amortized. Instead, management must estimate the fair value of the goodwill each year to determine if it's impaired. If the fair value is less than the carrying amount, the goodwill must be written down to its fair value. The writedown amount is expensed in the income statement in the year. IFRS provide guidelines for estimating the fair value of goodwill. However, because of its nature, the estimate is very subjective and requires judgment, so management has considerable leeway in deciding the timing and amount of any writedown.

Goodwill can represent a significant proportion of a company's assets. Return to Table 8.2 and notice that goodwill represented over 18 percent of BCE Inc.'s and High Liner Foods Incorporated's assets. But goodwill on the balance sheet doesn't tell stakeholders very much. It provides information about the amount that was spent for an investment, but nothing about what the goodwill represents, or if it represents anything at all. Stakeholders can only speculate as to whether it represents a wise expenditure of company resources.

QUESTION FOR CONSIDERATION

Why is it difficult to say for sure what goodwill is? Do you think goodwill meets the definition of an asset under IFRS? (See Chapter 2 for the criteria for an asset.)

SOLUTION: It's difficult to say for sure what goodwill is because it's a residual—the amount left over after identifiable assets and liabilities have had fair values assigned to them. Therefore, it isn't possible to determine what the goodwill reported on the balance sheet represents. Also, other than faith in IFRS's requirement to estimate the fair value of goodwill, it isn't possible to know whether an entity's goodwill really has any future benefit because it's hard to assess future benefit if you don't know what it is you are assessing.

In Chapter 2, the following criteria for an asset were identified:

- Provide a future benefit to the entity that it's probable the entity will enjoy.
- Be controlled by the entity that will obtain the benefits.
- Be the result of a transaction or event that has already occurred.
- Be measurable.

The first and fourth criteria pose the biggest problems. If we don't really know what goodwill is, how can we be reasonably sure there is a future benefit and reasonably measure it? The second criterion is met since the buying entity controls the company that was purchased, so it controls the goodwill. The third criterion is met because goodwill is recorded only when another company is purchased. Goodwill is measurable when it's purchased, although very imprecisely, since the goodwill itself isn't measured—it's the portion of the purchase price not assigned to specific assets and liabilities. One can question whether the cost of goodwill can actually be determined.

LO 7 SALE OF CAPITAL ASSETS

In Chapter 4, we discussed the gains and losses that arise on the sale of capital assets. When an entity sells an asset not usually sold in the ordinary course of its business for an amount that's different from its carrying amount, a gain or a loss arises. In Chapter 4, the examples were limited to situations where land, an asset that isn't depreciated, was sold. In this section, we look at depreciable assets.

When a depreciable asset is sold, the cost of the asset and its accumulated depreciation must both be removed from the books. A gain or loss arises when the asset is sold for an amount that's different from its carrying amount. If the amount received is greater than the carrying amount, a gain is recorded. If the amount received is less than the carrying amount, there is a loss.

Let's look at an example. At the beginning of 2011, Ycliff Inc. (Ycliff) purchased equipment for $1,200,000. Management estimated the equipment would have a residual value of $200,000 and useful life of 10 years. Ycliff depreciated the equipment on a straight-line basis. At the end of 2017, the carrying amount of the asset was $500,000:

Cost	$1,200,000
Accumulated depreciation	
([$1,200,000 − $200,000] ÷ 10 years × 7 years)	700,000
Carrying amount	$ 500,000

In 2018, one-quarter of the way through the year, Ycliff sold the equipment for $400,000 in cash. Since the sale occurred one-quarter of the way into 2018, a depreciation expense of $25,000 is necessary for 2018. (The depreciation expense to the date of sale of the asset is required at the time of sale. Otherwise, the depreciation expense will be understated and the gain or loss on sale will be misstated.)

Dr. Depreciation expense (expense +, shareholders' equity −)	25,000	
Cr. Accumulated depreciation (contra-assets +)		25,000
To record the part-year depreciation expense for equipment sold during 2018 ([(\$1,200,000 − 200,000) ÷ 10] × 0.25)		

On the date of the sale, accumulated depreciation on the equipment was \$725,000 (\$700,000 + \$25,000) and the carrying amount was \$475,000 (\$1,200,000 − \$725,000). The journal entry to record the sale is as follows:

Dr. Cash (asset +)	400,000	
Dr. Accumulated depreciation (contra-asset −)	725,000	
Dr. Loss on sale of equipment (income statement − , shareholders' equity −)	75,000	
Cr. Equipment (asset −)		1,200,000
To record the sale of equipment at a loss		

The journal entry removes the cost of \$1,200,000 and the accumulated depreciation of \$725,000 from the books. The gain or loss is equal to the proceeds from the sale of the asset, less its carrying amount. In the example,

Proceeds from sale	\$400,000	
− Carrying amount	− 475,000	(\$1,200,000 − \$725,000)
Loss	(\$ 75,000)	

In this scenario, there is a loss because the sale proceeds are less than the carrying amount. Recognize that the amount of gain or loss is determined by the carrying amount, which is determined by how the asset is accounted for: the amount initially capitalized, depreciation method, useful life, residual value, and the choice of the cost or revaluation models.

If, for example, Ycliff depreciated the equipment over 12 years instead of ten, the carrying amount of the equipment would have been \$595,833 (\$1,200,000 − {[(\$1,200,000 − \$200,000) ÷ 12] × 7.25}) and the loss would have been \$195,833 (\$400,000 − \$595,833). Any changes affecting the carrying amount of an asset will change the amount of gain or loss reported (assuming the selling price is a constant). In some cases, a manager's decision to sell an asset may be affected by the amount of any gain or loss. For example, if an entity requires higher net income to meet the requirements of a loan covenant, the manager may be unwilling to sell a capital asset at a loss or may sell one to generate a gain.

Exhibit 8.3 shows the financial statement presentation of a loss on the disposal of capital assets. In 2011, Supremex Inc. (Supremex), Canada's largest manufacturer and marketer of a broad range of high-quality stock and custom envelopes, labels, and related mailing products, reported a loss of \$400,165 on the disposal of property, plant, and equipment.[3] The equipment was sold for \$336,611 (see the investing section of Supremex's statements of cash flow in Exhibit 8.3). The separate disclosure (rather than including the amount in revenue or other production costs) is important because it allows stakeholders to see the impact of transactions that aren't a main part of the company's business.

KNOWLEDGE CHECK 8.2

Mc Graw Hill connect

Suppose that in the Ycliff example the company had sold the equipment for \$750,000 instead of \$400,000.

- ☐ How much depreciation would be recorded on the asset for 2018?
- ☐ What would be the gain or loss that Ycliff would report for the sale of the equipment in 2018?
- ☐ Prepare the journal entry required to record the sale.

EXHIBIT 8.3

Supremex Inc.: Presentation of a Loss on Disposal of Capital Assets

www.supremex.com

Supremex Inc.

CONSOLIDATED STATEMENTS OF EARNINGS

Years ended December 31	Notes	2011 $	2010 $
Revenue		**143,892,199**	153,124,398
Operating expenses	7, 20	**96,209,379**	102,935,634
Selling, general and administrative expenses	20	**18,144,751**	17,000,754
Operating earnings before amortization, write-down, loss on disposal of property, plant and equipment, acquisition costs and restructuring expenses		**29,538,069**	33,188,010
Amortization and write-down of property, plant and equipment	8, 9	**4,397,561**	6,661,624
Amortization of intangible assets	10	**6,163,900**	6,163.900
Amortization of deferred compensation		—	315,079
Loss on disposal of property, plant and equipment		**400,165**	340,169
Acquisition costs	5	—	152,070
Restructuring expenses	13	**1,089,401**	2,054,519
Operating earnings		**17,487,042**	17,500,649
Financing charges	15	**5,974,751**	4,720,981
Earnings before income taxes		**11,512,291**	12,779,668
Income tax expense	16	**3,197,417**	2,961,850
Net earnings		**8,314,874**	9,817,818

Supremex Inc.

CONSOLIDATED STATEMENTS OF CASH FLOW

Years ended December 31	Notes	2011 $	2010 $
INVESTING ACTIVITIES			
Business acquisition	5	**109,623**	(1,739,920)
Acquisition, of property, plant and equipment	9	**(3,998,290)**	(3,234,037)
Proceeds from sale of property, plant and equipment		**336,611**	507,847
Proceeds from sale of assets held for sale	8	**5,727,170**	—
Net cash flows from (used in) investing activities		**2,175,114**	(4,466,110)

LO 7

IMPAIRMENT OF CAPITAL ASSETS

Sometimes the value of capital assets becomes impaired. Impairment means that the carrying amount of a capital asset is greater than its future benefits. Examples of impaired capital assets include a building destroyed by fire, a plant that is no longer productive, and reductions in the earnings expected from a mine. When capital assets become impaired they should be written down. A writedown reduces the carrying amount of the capital asset and reduces income.

According to IFRS, a capital asset is impaired if its recoverable amount is less than its carrying amount. **Recoverable amount** is the greater of the fair value less cost to sell and value-in-use (defined as the present value of the asset's future cash flows). If an asset is impaired, the amount of the writedown equals

Carrying amount − Recoverable amount

Under IFRS, writedowns of capital assets can be reversed if the recoverable amount increases in a later period, except for writedowns of goodwill.

Note that capital assets aren't evaluated for impairment in the same way as inventory, which uses the lower of cost and net realizable value rule. For inventory, cost is compared with NRV at the end of each period, and if NRV is less than cost, the inventory must be written down. The assessment of capital assets takes a longer-term perspective—cash flows over the entire life of an asset are considered, not a short-term measure of market value. A short-term decline in fair value or a short-term reduction in net cash flows isn't enough to trigger the writedown of a capital asset.

Let's consider the example of Overflow Ltd. (Overflow), which owns a small office building. The building is recorded at its cost of $12,000,000 less accumulated depreciation of $5,000,000. In recent years, the neighbourhood has deteriorated, and as a result the rents Overflow can obtain have declined. Management now estimates the building will generate net cash flows with a present value of $5,000,000 (this is the value-in-use) over its remaining life. In addition, an independent real estate appraisal estimates the fair value of the building to be $2,500,000. Since the value-in-use is greater than fair value, we use the value-in-use as the recoverable amount. Since the recoverable amount is less than the carrying amount, Overflow must write down the building to its recoverable amount of $5,000,000, a writedown of $2,000,000 ($7,000,000 − $5,000,000).

Dr. Loss due to impairment of building (income statement −, shareholders' equity −)	2,000,000	
Cr. Accumulated depreciation (contra-asset +)		2,000,000
To write down the building to its recoverable amount		

The writedown is credited to accumulated depreciation, which decreases the carrying amount of the asset. Notice from the journal entry that cash isn't affected. A writedown decreases the carrying amount of assets, but cash isn't involved. (Of course, there will ultimately be cash flow consequences since the building will be generating less in rent than in the past.)

While the rules for determining whether a capital asset is impaired are clear, actually determining the impairment is very subjective and requires a lot of judgment in deciding the timing and amount of a writedown. For many assets, the future cash flows, present value of future cash flows, and fair value are highly uncertain. There is ample evidence that managers will time writedowns of capital assets to accomplish reporting objectives.

For example, managers might write down capital assets as part of a big bath (introduced in Chapter 4) when the company is facing hard times. During a big bath, assets are written down, resulting in large expenses now, but paving the way for higher earnings in the future because there is less carrying amount of assets to depreciate (assets written off in the big bath don't have to be depreciated in the future). A company must be able to justify a big bath—assets can't be written off on the whim of management, but management can usually provide a "reasonable" justification, particularly if the company isn't performing well.

ACCOUNTING STANDARDS FOR PRIVATE ENTERPRISES

According to Accounting Standards for Private Enterprises, a capital asset is impaired if the undiscounted net cash flow an asset is expected to generate over its remaining life, including its residual value, is less than its carrying amount. When this condition exists, the carrying amount of the asset is compared with its fair value. If the fair value is less than the carrying amount, the asset is written down to its fair value. ASPE doesn't allow writedowns to be reversed if the fair value increases in a later period.

LO 8 DOES THE WAY CAPITAL ASSETS ARE ACCOUNTED FOR AFFECT THE CASH FLOW STATEMENT?

It may come as a surprise, but how certain expenditures are accounted for can affect the cash flows reported in the cash flow statement. Accounting choices don't affect the actual amount of cash entering and leaving an entity, but they can affect how cash flows are classified. An expenditure that is capitalized appears as an investing activity in the cash flow statement. If that same expenditure is expensed when incurred, it's included in cash from operations (CFO).

Suppose that in 2017, Balaclava Ltd. (Balaclava) spends $1 million in cash on the development of a new product. If the expenditure is capitalized, Balaclava records an intangible asset called new product development costs. If the company amortizes the development costs over four years, there will be an annual amortization expense of $250,000 in 2017 through 2020. If, instead, Balaclava expenses the new product costs when incurred (the decision to capitalize or expense product development costs requires a lot of judgment), there would be an expense of $1 million in 2017.

Panel A of Table 8.4 provides summarized income statements for Balaclava Ltd. for 2017 and 2018, for both capitalizing and expensing the new product development costs. These income statements assume that revenues and expenses other than the amortization expense are cash. If the expenditure is capitalized, net income is reduced by $250,000 in 2017 through 2020, the amount of the amortization expense, because the $1,000,000 is being amortized over four years. If the product development costs are expensed when incurred, income is reduced by $1,000,000 in 2017 and there is no income statement effect in the following years.

Panel B of Table 8.4 provides summarized cash flow statements for Balaclava Ltd. for 2017 and 2018 under the two scenarios. If the $1,000,000 is capitalized, the outlay is classified as an

TABLE 8.4
Balaclava Ltd.

Panel A: Summarized Income Statements

Balaclava Ltd.
Income Statement for the years ended December 31, 2017 and 2018

	December 31, 2017		December 31, 2018	
	Capitalize	**Expense**	**Capitalize**	**Expense**
Revenues	$25,000,000	$25,000,000	$25,000,000	$25,000,000
Expenses	15,000,000	15,000,000	15,000,000	15,000,000
Amortization of product development costs	250,000		250,000	
Product development expense		1,000,000		
Net Income	$ 9,750,000	$ 9,000,000	$ 9,750,000	$10,000,000

Panel B: Summarized Cash Flow Statements

Balaclava Ltd.
Cash Flow Statements for the Years Ended December 31, 2017 and 2018

	December 31, 2017		December 31, 2018	
	Capitalize	**Expense**	**Capitalize**	**Expense**
Cash Flow Operations				
Net income	$ 9,750,000	$ 9,000,000	$ 9,750,000	$10,000,000
Add back:				
Amortization of product development costs	250,000	0	250,000	0
Cash from operations	10,000,000	9,000,000	10,000,000	10,000,000
Investing activities:				
Product development	1,000,000	0	0	0
Increase in cash	$ 9,000,000	$ 9,000,000	$10,000,000	$10,000,000

investing activity and the $250,000 amortization expense is added back to net income in the calculation of CFO using the indirect method. If the cost is expensed in full in 2017, it's classified as CFO. (With this alternative, the cost doesn't appear explicitly in the cash flow statements because it's in the calculation of net income.)

Notice how the accounting choice affects the cash flow statement. In 2017, there is a $9,000,000 overall increase in cash under both methods, but CFO is $10,000,000 when the product development costs are capitalized and $9,000,000 when they are expensed as incurred. If the costs are capitalized, investing activities are $−1,000,000, whereas if the costs are expensed, there are no investing activities. In 2018, CFO and investing activities are the same under both alternatives because the only financial statement impact of the new product development costs is amortization, which has no effect on cash.

Even the cash flow statement, a statement designed to neutralize the effects of accounting choices by managers, is affected by accounting choices. In evaluating CFO, a stakeholder has to consider the accounting policies used by similar companies because some will capitalize certain outlays while others will expense them, which impairs comparability.

INSIGHT

Why Accounting Choice?

It's difficult for accounting students to understand why there is so much choice available to managers. Accounting choice is a double-edged sword. It allows managers to present information in ways that are useful to stakeholders, but it also provides them the means to achieve their own reporting objectives. It isn't always possible for stakeholders to see how the managers are using flexible accounting rules. This is a danger stakeholders face.

The issue of dealing with accounting policy choice has no easy answer. A system that allows choice opens itself up for abuse by managers. A system with no choice reduces the likelihood for abuse but may render financial statements useless by not allowing accounting choices that reflect an entity's actual economic activity. IFRS allow a lot of choice and emphasize the exercise of judgment. Stakeholders should recognize the opportunity for abuse and use accounting information cautiously. Thus far, we have seen the effect the choice of revenue recognition method, inventory cost formula, and depreciation method, along with many estimates managers make, has on the financial statements. With these choices alone, a wide range of numbers could appear in an entity's financial statements, all representing the identical underlying economic activity.

Accounting plays a very important role in communicating information about an entity. For the efficient and effective operation of the economy, it's essential that managers and any external accountants (including auditors) behave ethically. If stakeholders can't use accounting information with confidence, the costs of doing business will increase and economic performance will decline.

FINANCIAL STATEMENT ANALYSIS ISSUES

LO 9

Despite the importance of capital assets to many entities, there are limits to the insights about an entity that can be gained from analyzing historical cost information about them. First, as we discussed earlier, the usefulness of historical cost information about capital assets for many decisions is questionable. Second, even under IFRS there is extensive choice about how to account for capital assets, and how it's done significantly affects the numbers in the financial statements. The following policy and estimate choices will affect expenses, net income, assets, and retained earnings, and any ratios that depend on these measures:

- what costs get capitalized
- depreciation method used
- estimates of useful life and residual value

- existence of unrecorded assets (especially intangible assets)
- impairment of capital assets

With that in mind, a ratio often used to measure the performance and operating efficiency of an entity is **return on assets (ROA)**, defined as

$$\text{Return on assets} = \frac{\text{Net income} + \text{After-tax interest expense}}{\text{Average total assets}}$$

The numerator is a measure of how the entity has performed—in this case, net income with the after-tax interest expense added back. After-tax interest expense is the cost of interest after taking into consideration the fact the government picks up part of the cost of borrowing because interest is deductible for tax purposes. That is, if an entity incurs $10,000 in interest and its tax rate is 25 percent, the actual cost of interest is $7,500 ($10,000 × [1 − tax rate] = $10,000 × [1 − 0.25]). That is because the entity pays $2,500 less in taxes, since the interest expense is deductible. After-tax interest expense is added back so the ROA is independent of how the assets are financed. If the interest expense isn't deducted, the ROA would be affected by the amount of debt the entity had.

The denominator is the investment—in this case, the entity's investment in assets. It can be expressed as average assets for the year or year-end assets. Both the numerator and denominator introduce some problems. The ratio will be affected by management's accounting choices, as well as by when the assets were purchased. Assets purchased at different times will have different costs. As a result, comparing the ROA of different entities must be done with a great deal of caution.

This ratio can be thought of in the same way as a bank account. The denominator—the investment or the assets invested in—is the amount of money in your bank account. The numerator—the return—is the interest the bank pays you over the year. The return on assets is the interest rate the bank account earned. If you invested $1,000 in a bank account and over the following year the bank paid you $50 in interest, your return would be 5 percent ($50 ÷ $1,000).

ROA is a measure of how efficiently an entity uses its assets to generate a profit. A company can improve its ROA in two ways: lower its asset base or increase its profits. For example, if a company is able to reduce its inventory or increase its accounts receivable turnover without affecting profits, ROA will increase. If an entity has capital assets it isn't using, selling them will increase its ROA.

As an example, we'll look at WestJet Airlines Ltd. (WestJet). Relevant information from WestJet's financial statements for the period 2007 through 2011 is summarized in Table 8.5. ROA is shown in the last row. Note that this analysis combines financial statement numbers prepared under old Canadian GAAP (2007–2009) and amounts prepared under IFRS (2010–2011). Strictly speaking, the amounts prepared under the different standards aren't comparable. This analysis is shown for learning purposes.

TABLE 8.5 WestJet Airlines Ltd.: Return on Assets*

	2011	2010	2009	2008	2007	2006
Net income	$148,702,000	$90,197,000	$98,178,000	$178,506,000	$192,833,000	
Interest expense	60,911,000	70,914,000	67,706,000	76,078,000	75,749,000	
Tax expense	59,304,000	43,268,000	38,618,000	76,243,000	43,924,000	
Tax rate	0.2851	0.3242	0.2823	0.2993	0.1855	
Total assets	$3,473,678,000	$3,383,980,000	$3,493,702,000	$3,268,702,000	$2,984,222,000	$2,726,527,000
ROA	5.61%	4.02%	4.34%	7.41%	8.91%	

*Information for 2011 and 2010 is prepared in accordance with IFRS. Information for 2006–2009 is prepared in accordance with Canadian generally accepted accounting principles in effect at the time.

The calculation of ROA for 2011 is as follows:

$$\text{Return on assets} = \frac{\text{Net income} + \text{After-tax interest expense}}{\text{Average total assets}}$$
$$= \frac{\$148{,}702{,}000 + [\$60{,}911{,}000 \times (1 - 0.2851)]}{[(\$3{,}473{,}678{,}000 + \$3{,}383{,}980{,}000) \div 2]}$$
$$= \frac{\$192{,}247{,}274}{\$3{,}428{,}829{,}000}$$
$$= 5.61\%$$

The tax rate is calculated by dividing the tax expense by income before taxes:

$$\text{Tax rate} = \frac{\text{Tax expense}}{\text{Income before taxes (Net income + Income tax expense)}}$$
$$= \frac{\$59{,}304{,}000}{\$208{,}006{,}000}$$
$$= 28.51\%$$

WestJet's ROA declined from 2007 through 2010 but has increased in 2011 (although not to as high a level as in 2007 and 2008). Over the five years, WestJet's ROA has been fairly steady. Comparisons can also be made with other companies. Table 8.6 shows ROA for three airlines.[4]

TABLE 8.6 Comparison of Return on Assets for Canadian Airlines and the Transportation Industry

	2011	2010	2009	2008	2007	5-year average
WestJet Airlines Ltd.	5.61%	4.02%	4.34%	7.41%	8.91%	6.40%
Transat A.T. Inc.	–0.80%	5.95%	5.58%	–3.63%	8.46%	3.11%
Air Canada	0.70%	3.52%	2.62%	–6.35%	5.07%	1.11%

WestJet outperformed Air Canada in all years and Transat in three of the five years. WestJet's five-year average is much higher than the other two. The variation of WestJet's ROA is much lower than Air Canada and Transat over the five years.

A ratio that can be used to examine the efficiency of use of property, plant, and equipment is the fixed asset turnover ratio. This ratio measures the number of dollars of sales generated by each dollar invested in property, plant, and equipment. A higher ratio implies a more efficient use of assets (more sales per dollar of property, plant, and equipment). The fixed asset turnover ratio is calculated as:

$$\text{Fixed asset turnover ratio} = \frac{\text{Revenue}}{\text{Average PPE}}$$

For WestJet for 2011 the calculation is:

$$\text{Fixed asset turnover ratio} = \frac{\text{Revenue}}{\text{Average PPE}}$$
$$= \frac{\$3{,}071{,}540{,}000}{[(\$1{,}911{,}227{,}000 + \$1{,}989{,}522{,}000) \div 2]}$$
$$= 1.57$$

Table 8.7 provides a comparison of the fixed asset turnover ratio for three Canadian airlines.

The results suggest that Transat is much more efficient than its competitors in using its property, plant, and equipment. However, the ratio must be analyzed carefully, and this is

TABLE 8.7 Comparison of Fixed Asset Turnover for Canadian Airlines

	2011	2010	2009	2008	2007
WestJet Airlines Ltd.	1.57	1.21	1.00	1.14	0.97
Transat A.T. Inc.	41.83	33.12	25.57	21.01	0.17
Air Canada	2.17	1.81	1.42	1.44	1.53

especially true for airlines. The age of the fleet of planes will affect the turnover ratio. An older fleet will have a lower carrying value than a newer one (because there is less accumulated depreciation) and therefore the fixed asset turnover ratio will be higher. (On the other hand, an older fleet might have higher maintenance costs.) Also, as we've discussed, leasing of aircraft is common in the industry and an airline that uses leases more extensively will have a higher ratio (because the airline will be generating revenues without any corresponding planes on the balance sheet). Of course, care must also be exercised when comparing ratios of different industries. One would expect a lower ratio for companies in more capital intensive industries.

To illustrate the effect of policy choices on financial statement analysis, we will examine how using different depreciation methods affects two financial ratios, profit margin and ROA, for Vermilion Corp. Vermilion's financial statements are found in Table 8.3. For simplicity, we assume that Vermilion incurred no interest expense and that total assets at the beginning of 2017 are $1,500,000. The two ratios are calculated using straight-line and declining balance depreciation. The results are shown in Table 8.8.

Observe how different the ratios are in each year. For example, in 2017 the profit margin with straight-line depreciation is 7.7 percent whereas with declining balance it's −17.3 percent. The ROA using straight-line depreciation ranges from a low of −0.7 percent to a high of 13.6 percent, while for declining balance the lowest value is −8.2 percent and the highest is 19 percent.

TABLE 8.8 Vermilion Inc.: Effect of Straight-Line and Declining Balance Depreciation Methods on Profit Margin and ROA

		2017	2018	2019	2020
Profit margin	Straight line	7.7%	20.4%	21.5%	–2.7%
	Declining balance	–17.3	18.2	27.6	20.9
Return on assets	Straight line	3.4	12.6	13.6	–0.7
	Declining balance	–8.2	12.6	19.0	5.5

Although the different accounting choices don't affect an entity's economic situation, ratios can paint a variety of pictures. The conclusions we draw about an entity will vary with accounting choices so we need to be aware of their impact. Financial analysis must be based on an understanding of the accounting choices that went into the financial statements. If comparisons are being made between entities, or for a particular entity over time, it's important to ensure that like things are being compared.

Solved Problem

This chapter's solved problem is a case analysis in an unusual setting. It gives readers an opportunity to apply the material covered thus far in the book. The case is challenging and readers should not be discouraged if they struggle in places. Take the time to do a complete and thorough analysis before reading the solution.

HIGH-TECH INDUSTRIES INC.

High-Tech Industries Inc. (High-Tech) develops and manufactures highly sophisticated technical equipment for mining companies and has gained a worldwide reputation for the quality and reliability of its products. For many years, High-Tech was the only company in this market but recently a number of competitors have entered the industry. All these competitors have been supported by their national governments. In the last three years, High-Tech has seen its profits and its margins decline drastically in the face of the new competition. In its most recent fiscal year, High-Tech reported a loss of $42,000,000.

The management of High-Tech has approached government officials for financial support to "level the playing field" with its competitors. High-Tech has suggested that without adequate support it may be forced to move some or all of its operations to another country and it has asked for immediate subsidies of between $50 and $75 million.

A government committee is examining whether High-Tech should receive government funding. Although the government itself and many members of the committee seem to support High-Tech, there is at least one member of the committee who strongly believes that governments should not be subsidizing private businesses. The dissenting committee member has asked you to evaluate whether High-Tech's financial information provides a reasonable picture of its financial position. Your report will be used by the dissenting member to present his side of the story to the committee, so it's important that you clearly detail any problems that you identify with the accounting information. Your report should also discuss alternative treatments for the problems you identify and consider their quantitative impact.

The committee member has supplied you with a summarized income statement and explanatory notes that High-Tech prepared especially for the committee. This information is available in Figure 8.11.

Required:

Prepare the report requested by the dissenting committee member.

Comment: *This is another user-oriented case. Your task is to assist the committee member by providing an analysis of the income statement that supports him. The role requires you to identify areas where the accounting used by High-Tech doesn't reasonably indicate a need for government support. In other words, you must assess whether High-Tech's income statement is appropriate for the stated purpose.*

Your report should make clear that High-Tech has incentives to understate its performance and it should identify situations where High-Tech has taken advantage of accounting to present a poor situation. The report must establish some criteria for assessing High-Tech's performance. It could be cash flow (low income doesn't necessarily mean poor liquidity or financial problems), it could be accrual income adjusted for unusual items, or some other measure of performance. Some criteria are necessary so that there is a context for interpreting financial statements.

An important aspect of this case is that IFRS (or ASPE) don't necessarily have a role to play. It might be necessary for High-Tech to prepare IFRS financial statements, but these statements may not provide the information needed for the intended purpose. Because of IFRS's rules, it's possible that High-Tech's income statement doesn't reasonably reflect its need for a subsidy. Remember that managers preparing the financial statements may be constrained by IFRS but stakeholders may adjust and modify financial statements to whatever form they please. If IFRS's rules don't provide information that is appropriate, then those rules shouldn't be followed. This doesn't imply a free-for-all. Any basis of accounting must be supported and supportable. Each choice must be well explained and justified so that it will be convincing to other committee members and to High-Tech's representatives.

Solution:

Report on High-Tech Industries Inc.

I have examined the income statement and explanatory information provided by High-Tech Industries Inc. In my opinion, that statement is not appropriate for evaluating the economic condition of High-Tech for the purpose of determining whether it should receive a government subsidy. The statement tends to understate the actual economic performance of the company because of

FIGURE 8.11 Additional Information about High-Tech Industries Inc.

1. High-Tech is a private company. Normally, its financial statements are not publicly available, but to support its position High-Tech has provided the government committee with a summarized income statement for its 2017 fiscal year.

High-Tech Industries Inc. Summarized Income Statement for the Year Ended October 31, 2017		
Revenue		$225,000,000
Cost of sales		106,000,000
Gross margin		119,000,000
Expenses:		
Salaries and benefits	$59,000,000	
Selling, general, marketing, and administration	25,000,000	
Loss on sale of technology	22,000,000	
Research and development	40,000,000	
Depreciation and amortization	15,000,000	161,000,000
Net loss		($ 42,000,000)

2. High-Tech normally uses the percentage-of-completion method for recognizing revenue on its long-term contracts.
3. In 2017, the company entered into a large contract with an Asian company to develop mining equipment. The equipment is similar to equipment High-Tech has developed for other customers. Work has begun on the project and it's expected to be completed in 2019. Because of economic problems in the Asian country, High-Tech is recognizing revenue on a zero-profit basis for this contract. Management believes there is a higher than normal probability that the customer will be unable to pay in full for the equipment.

   The contract will generate $33,000,000 in revenue and incur estimated costs of $17,000,000. To date, $6,900,000 of costs have been incurred and the customer has already made payments of $7,000,000 to High-Tech. The project is currently on budget and all payments have been made on schedule. In addition, High-Tech expensed the costs of obtaining the contract in its 2017 income statement.
4. The majority shareholder of High-Tech owns a company that provides testing and other consulting advice to High-Tech. During 2017, High-Tech paid $18,000,000 to that company.
5. In 2014, High-Tech purchased the rights to a technology developed by a British company. The technology proved not to be useful to High-Tech and in 2017, it sold those rights to another company at a loss of $22,000,000.
6. High-Tech invests heavily in research and development. These expenditures have been increasing significantly in each recent year and the trend is expected to continue. Research and development costs are expensed when they are incurred.

the measurement conventions used. The statement takes a conservative approach to reporting and includes at least one item that is not representative of ongoing performance. In addition, the statement is not a good indication of whether High-Tech actually needs cash. The statement is prepared on what is known as accrual accounting, which measures economic flows rather than cash flows.

The usual basis for preparing financial statements in Canada is International Financial Reporting Standards (IFRS) or Accounting Standards for Private Enterprises (ASPE). The information provided does not state which set of standards, if any, the company follows but it appears High-Tech has adhered to IFRS to some extent. While IFRS provide a useful set of standards for preparing financial statements, they are not useful for all decisions in all situations. In the case of High-Tech, application of IFRS served to understate its income in the current period, as IFRS are inherently conservative. In my analysis below, I suggest treatments that may deviate from IFRS as those treatments do not give a reasonable view of the economic situation of the company. Overall, I will use accrual accounting as the basis for evaluating High-Tech's performance, although not necessarily IFRS-based accrual accounting. I think it is also important to assess High-Tech's liquidity.

My review of the statements assesses the information provided. However, considerable additional information is needed to fully assess High-Tech. Thus, my conclusions are only preliminary. Additional information that should be requested includes: comparative financial statements, cash flow statements, balance sheets, and notes to the financial statements. I have provided my analysis in the absence of a more complete set of information so you can participate in the upcoming committee meeting in an informed way.

Use of Zero-Profit Method The impact of the zero-profit method is to reduce income by deferring profits to 2019 when the contract is completed. There is no theoretical problem with using different revenue recognition methods for different contracts, provided that the facts justify the different treatments. That is, the circumstances surrounding the contract with the Asian country must be such that the revenue or costs are difficult to reasonably estimate or collection of cash is questionable.

In this situation, it does not appear that the zero-profit method is justified. High-Tech contends that cash collection is quite uncertain, but High-Tech has already collected \$7,000,000, which suggests willingness and ability to pay. As well, payments are being made on schedule. Therefore, there does not seem to be good reason to deviate from the percentage-of-completion method. Since the contract spans three years, I suggest using the percentage-of-completion method and recognizing one-third of the revenue and related expenses in 2017. This treatment will add almost \$6.5 million $\left([\$33{,}000{,}000 - \$17{,}000{,}000] \times \frac{\$6{,}900{,}000}{\$17{,}000{,}000}\right)$ to income during the year. (The exact amount may change pending additional information on the amount of work done through the end of 2017.)

Related-Party Transactions High-Tech does business with a company owned by its majority shareholder. These "related-party transactions" are a concern because the shareholder could influence the terms of transactions between the companies. If the services provided have an actual market value of \$18,000,000 and were required by High-Tech, then recording them at their transaction value is acceptable. However, it is impossible to determine what the market value of the services actually is or indeed whether they were needed or provided. The majority shareholder is in a position to overstate the value of the services provided, with the purpose of understating High-Tech's income to make its financial situation look worse. There are no negative economic consequences to the major shareholder because she has an economic interest in both transacting entities. It is necessary to know extensive details about the services provided to High-Tech and even to confirm the actual existence of them. I recommend that these costs be completely removed from the income statement until additional information is provided. This treatment will reduce the reported loss by \$18,000,000.

Loss on Sale of Purchased Technology During 2017, High-Tech sold technology at a significant loss, which represented more than half of the reported net loss for the year. A number of issues arise from this loss:

- The loss is likely not to recur in future periods. Therefore, if everything else stayed exactly the same as this year, the loss in 2017 would be \$20,000,000 instead of \$42,000,000.

- The loss is an accounting loss, not a cash loss. High-Tech paid for this technology a few years ago and the sale does not leave the company out of pocket in the current period. In fact, by selling the technology it is actually $22,000,000 better off in a cash sense.
- When did the economic loss actually occur? While the loss was recognized in 2017, the actual economic loss may have been suffered in a previous period, which means the loss should have been recognized earlier.
- Should taxpayers be subsidizing a company for its poor decisions?

I recommend that this loss be disregarded when evaluating the company's income statement. Instead, the analysis should focus on earnings before non-recurring items. This treatment would reduce High-Tech's loss by $22,000,000.

Research and Development Costs Research and development (R&D) is an investment by an entity in future revenue-generating resources. Standard accounting practice (IFRS) expenses research and most development costs when they are incurred. While no one would dispute that R&D is, conceptually, an asset, the future benefits associated with these expenditures are highly uncertain, which is why they are expensed. By expensing R&D currently, High-Tech understates its current income because expenses are not being matched to the revenues they will help earn, presumably sometime in the future.

It makes better sense to capitalize the R&D costs and amortize them over some (probably short) period of time (say four years). That means that only $10,000,000 of the year's expenditures should be expensed this year. This adjustment will increase income by $30,000,000. However, for consistency, R&D expensed in previous years should be capitalized and amortized. Given that R&D spending is increasing, the net effect of these adjustments will be to increase income in the current period. However, it is not possible to state an amount that should be amortized in the current period.

Summary

Net loss as reported	($42,000,000)
Add:	
Adjustment to percentage-of-completion method	6,500,000
Loss on sale of technology	22,000,000
Non-arm's-length transactions	18,000,000
Research and development costs	30,000,000
Deduct: Amortization of previous years' R&D	?
Revised net income	$34,500,000

Revised net income shows that High-Tech was profitable in 2017. Even with additional adjustments for R&D amortization and for the related-party transactions, income will likely be positive. This approach is also more representative of its ongoing economic performance.

Please contact me if you have any questions about my report and if you require assistance at the upcoming hearing.

Comment: *A good analysis should have included the following:*

- *effective role playing*
- *an indication of a basis for evaluating whether High-Tech should receive a subsidy*
- *a solid discussion of the accounting issues and recommendations on appropriate treatments*
- *an attempt to quantify the impact of the proposed accounting changes*

Remember that this analysis represents only one approach. Different ones are possible. The preceding problem is intended to give an idea how this case could be approached, not to serve as the definitive answer.

SUMMARY OF KEY POINTS

LO 1 Most companies using IFRS use historical cost to account for their capital assets. There are three alternatives to historical cost for valuing capital assets: fair value, replacement cost, and value-in-use. A main objection to these alternatives is that the measures aren't as reliable as historical cost. None of these measurement bases is ideal for all purposes. IFRS provides entities with the option of valuing certain capital assets at fair value.

LO 2 Most companies following IFRS use historical cost to account for their capital assets. With historical cost, all costs incurred to acquire an asset and get it ready for use are *capitalized*—recorded on the balance sheet as an asset—and this amount forms the basis of its valuation on the company's balance sheet. There are three alternatives to historical cost accounting for capital assets: fair value, replacement cost, and value-in-use. Each provides different information to stakeholders and has shortcomings of its own. None is ideal for all uses.

LO 3 The cost of an asset reported on an entity's balance sheet should include all the costs associated with purchasing the asset and getting it ready for use. Costs incurred by employees of the purchasing entity, including wages, should also be capitalized. Costs incurred to improve an existing asset should be capitalized and depreciated whereas costs incurred to maintain an asset should be expensed when incurred.

LO 4 The process of allocating the cost of a capital asset to expense over time to reflect its use is known as depreciation. IFRS say the cost of an asset, less its residual value, should be depreciated over its useful life in a "systematic" way. There are three major methods of depreciation: straight-line, accelerated, and usage-based. All of the methods result in the same amount of depreciation over the life of the asset. Only the timing of the expense is affected. Different depreciation methods don't affect an entity's cash flow, but the method used can have economic consequences because of the effect on financial statement numbers.

LO 5 Companies that adhere to IFRS are required to disclose the following information about their capital assets:

- measurement basis for determining the carrying amount (cost or fair value)
- depreciation method and useful lives for each major category of capital assets
- gross carrying amount and accumulated depreciation at the beginning and end of the period
- a reconciliation of the carrying amount at the beginning and end of the period
- depreciation expense

LO 6 Intangible assets, including knowledge assets and intellectual capital, are capital assets that have no physical substance. Most internally generated intangible assets aren't reported as assets on the balance sheet because the recognition criteria for assets aren't met. Instead, the money spent developing intangible assets is expensed when incurred. Expensing investments in knowledge assets and intellectual capital when they are incurred has significant implications for the financial statements, including violation of the matching principle, and impairs the meaningfulness of net income.

LO 7 When a depreciable asset is sold, the cost of the asset and the accumulated depreciation associated with it must be removed from the accounting records. If the proceeds received on disposal are different from the asset's carrying amount, a gain or loss is reported on the income statement. The amount of the gain or loss is a function of how the capital asset is accounted for.

Sometimes capital assets become impaired. Under IFRS, a capital asset is impaired when its recoverable amount is greater than its carrying amount. When a capital asset is impaired, it must be written down to its recoverable amount. Management has considerable discretion in deciding the timing and amount of a writedown because determining the impairment is very subjective.

LO 8 How expenditures on capital assets are accounted for affects presentation of cash flows reported in the cash flow statement. Accounting choices don't affect the actual amount of cash that enters and leaves an entity, but they can affect the amount reported as cash from operations

(CFO) and investing activities. If an expenditure is capitalized, the outlay is reported in the cash flow statement as an investing activity. If that same expenditure is expensed when incurred, the expenditure is included in CFO.

LO 9 Despite the importance of capital assets to many entities, there are limits to the insights about an entity that can be gained from analyzing the historical cost information about them in the financial statements. Despite the limitations, return on assets is a ratio often used to measure the performance and operating efficiency of an entity.

LO 10 (Appendix). The *Income Tax Act* (ITA) uses the term capital cost allowance (CCA) to describe depreciation for tax purposes. The mechanics of CCA are the same as they are for financial accounting—the cost of capital assets is somehow expensed over time—but the ITA is very detailed about the method and rate that must be used for each type of asset. For most assets, the ITA requires the declining balance method, though straight line is used for some assets. There is no choice or discretion available to the managers—the rules in the ITA must be followed exactly.

LO 10

APPENDIX: DEPRECIATION AND TAXES

The *Income Tax Act* (ITA) is very specific about how capital assets can be depreciated for tax purposes. The ITA uses the term **capital cost allowance (CCA)** to describe depreciation for tax purposes. The mechanics of CCA are the same for tax as they are for financial accounting—the cost of capital assets is somehow expensed over time—but the ITA is very detailed about the method and rate that must be used for each type of asset. For most assets, the ITA requires the declining balance method, though straight line is required for some assets. Examples of CCA classes are provided in Figure 8.12. There is no choice or discretion available to the managers—the rules in the ITA must be followed exactly. Managers can do whatever they please for financial reporting purposes, but when the entity's income tax return is prepared, the depreciation expense in the general purpose financial statements is replaced with CCA.

FIGURE 8.12 Examples of CCA Classes and Rates

CCA class	Example	CCA rate
Class 1	Buildings acquired after 1987	4% declining balance
Class 9	Aircraft, including furniture, fittings, or equipment attached, and their spare parts	25% declining balance
Class 10	Automobiles, vans, trucks, buses, computers, and system software	30% declining balance
Class 16	Automobiles for lease or rent, taxis, and coin-operated video games or pinball machines	40% declining balance

Although the CCA rules would be acceptable for financial reporting purposes for many assets, in some cases they might not satisfy the IFRS requirement that depreciation must be done in a systematic way. The government might use the ITA to achieve policy objectives. For example, the government might try to encourage investment by allowing entities to expense certain assets quickly. This treatment may make sense for tax purposes but it may not reflect how an asset's future benefits are used up.

Another example is the **half-year rule**, which allows an entity to only deduct for tax purposes one-half the allowable amount of CCA in the year an asset is purchased. If an entity purchases a vehicle for $20,000, it should be allowed to deduct 30 percent of the cost for tax purposes, or $6,000 ($20,000 × 0.3), in the first year (vehicles are a CCA class that allows a 30 percent declining balance rate). The half-year rule allows the entity to only deduct $3,000 ($20,000 × 0.3 × 0.5). The half-year rule prevents entities from getting the full tax benefit from a new capital asset if the asset is purchased late in the year.

INSIGHT

It's easy to make the mistake of thinking that a depreciation policy that minimizes income for financial reporting purposes will minimize taxes. However, depreciation for financial reporting purposes is irrelevant for tax. If an entity uses different methods and rates for financial reporting than those specified in the ITA, an adjustment is required when preparing the entity's tax return. Some companies will use the CCA methods for financial reporting, especially private companies that use their financial statements mainly for tax purposes, to reduce their bookkeeping costs. The irrelevance of depreciation for tax purposes contrasts with the ITA treatment of inventory. Because the ITA doesn't specify how to account for inventory for tax purposes, the accounting method selected for the general purpose financial statements is usually used for tax purposes.

FORMULA SUMMARY

$$\text{Depreciation expense (straight line)} = \frac{\text{Cost} - \text{Estimated residual value}}{\text{Estimated useful life}}$$

$$\text{Depreciation expense (declining balance)} = \text{Carrying amount at the beginning of the period} \times \text{Rate}$$

$$\text{Depreciation expense (unit of production)} = \frac{\text{Number of units produced in the period}}{\text{Estimated number of units to be produced over the asset's life}} \times (\text{Cost} - \text{Estimated residual value})$$

$$\text{Goodwill} = \text{Purchase price} - \text{Fair value of identifiable assets and liabilities purchased}$$

$$\text{Return on assets} = \frac{\text{Net income} + \text{After-tax interest expense}}{\text{Average total assets}}$$

$$\text{Tax rate} = \frac{\text{Tax expense}}{\text{Income before taxes (Net income} + \text{Tax expense)}}$$

$$\text{Fixed asset turnover ratio} = \frac{\text{Revenue}}{\text{Average property, plant, and equipment}}$$

KEY TERMS

accelerated depreciation, p. 449
amortization, p. 446
betterment, p. 444
capital asset, p. 440
capital cost allowance, p. 482
capitalize, p. 441
componentization, p. 455
declining balance, p. 449
depletion, p. 446
depreciable amount, p. 449
depreciation, p. 446
entity-specific value, p. 442
fair value, p. 441
goodwill, p. 467
half-year rule, p. 482
identifiable assets and liabilities, p. 467
intangible asset, p. 440
maintenance, p. 444
recoverable amount, p. 470
repair, p. 444
residual value, p. 446
return on assets (ROA), p. 474
straight-line depreciation, p. 448
tangible asset, p. 440
units-of-production depreciation, p. 450
value-in-use, p. 442

SIMILAR TERMS

The left column gives alternative terms that are sometimes used for the accounting terms introduced in this chapter, which are listed in the right column.

fixed asset, long-lived asset	**capital asset, p. 440**
knowledge asset, intellectual capital	**intangible asset, p. 440**
diminishing balance	**declining balance, p. 449**
entity-specific value	**value-in-use, p. 442**

ASSIGNMENT MATERIALS

Questions

Q8-1. Describe the types of capital assets you would expect each of the following entities to have:

a. gas station
b. university
c. convenience store
d. hotel
e. dairy farm
f. electric utility
g. golf course

Q8-2. What is an intangible asset? How do intangible assets differ from tangible ones? Give examples of each.

Q8-3. What is goodwill? How does it arise?

Q8-4. Why are capital assets depreciated?

Q8-5. What characteristics distinguish capital assets from inventory?

Q8-6. What effect does depreciation have on an entity's cash flow? Why is depreciation added back to net income when the indirect method of calculating cash from operations is used?

Q8-7. Academic research has shown that the stock price of a public company isn't affected by the depreciation method an entity uses. Why do you think this is the case? Does the depreciation method an entity uses ever matter? Explain.

Q8-8. What does it mean when a capital asset is impaired? Provide two examples of how a capital asset could become impaired.

Q8-9. Why is the selection of a depreciation method not a concern if tax minimization is the main objective of financial reporting?

Q8-10. Why is accounting for knowledge assets and intellectual capital such a difficult problem under IFRS?

Q8-11. To make room for new equipment that it was installing, Sandwich Inc. had to knock down a wall. The cost of knocking down the wall was $32,000. While the installation was in progress, another wall was accidentally knocked down. The cost of replacing that wall was $44,000. Which, if any, of these costs should be capitalized? Explain.

Q8-12. Explain why repairs are expensed whereas betterments are capitalized.

Q8-13. Explain why gains and losses on the sale of capital assets are affected by management's estimates of the useful life and residual value of the assets.

Q8-14. What effect does a writedown of capital assets have on cash flow? Explain.

Q8-15. What is a writedown of a capital asset? Why are writedowns required? How does the approach to writing down capital assets differ from the approach used for writing down inventory?

Q8-16. For each business identified below, explain how the capital asset contributes to generating revenue by the business:

Business	Asset
a. Lawn care	Lawn mower
b. Arena	Zamboni machine
c. Jewellery store	Display cases
d. Doctor's office	Waiting room furniture
e. Auto parts manufacturer	Warehouse

Q8-17. Why does judgment by the managers who prepare financial statements play such an important role in determining an entity's depreciation expense? Be specific.

Q8-18. A cow owned by a dairy farm has a calf. If the calf wasn't fair valued at the end of each reporting period (the cost method was used instead), how would the calf be reported on the farm's balance sheet?

Q8-19. Explain how accounting policies can affect the cash from operations an entity reports when we know that different accounting policies have no effect on cash flow.

Q8-20. Explain the following bases for valuing capital assets. Provide examples of how each might provide useful information to a user:

a. historical cost
b. replacement cost
c. fair value
d. value-in-use

Q8-21. Company A owns a world-renowned trademark, but it doesn't appear on its balance sheet. Company B owns a world-renowned trademark, which is valued on the company's balance sheet at $125,000,000. Explain why this difference might arise.

Q8-22. Wisdom Inc. tries to use conservative accounting methods. For example, it tends to make conservative estimates of the useful lives of capital assets (shorter lives rather than longer ones) and residual value (lower estimates of residual value).

a. What is the impact of these conservative accounting policies on income? Explain.
b. How could these conservative policies have unconservative effects when Wisdom Inc. disposes of capital assets? Explain.

Q8-23. What is capital cost allowance? How does capital cost allowance differ from depreciation for financial reporting purposes?

Q8-24. Define and explain the use of the following terms. Provide examples of when each would be used:

a. amortization
b. depreciation
c. depletion

Q8-25. Is it possible for an entity to use a capital asset that is completely depreciated? Explain. What would be the carrying amount of such an asset?

Q8-26. Esk Ltd. (Esk) recently purchased a fully equipped restaurant at an auction for $500,000. The restaurant included all the equipment, furniture, and fixtures. The building itself is rented. Now Esk must allocate the purchase price to the items purchased. Explain how Esk should allocate the purchase price to the specific items. Why is it necessary for the purchase price to be allocated to the specific items? What motivations might influence the allocations that Esk makes?

Exercises

E8-1. **(Accounting for acquisition costs, LO 3)** Ayr Ltd. is a small manufacturing company located near Montreal. The company recently purchased a new machine to satisfy the increasing demand for its products. For each of the following, explain whether the expenditure would be capitalized or expensed:

a. The equipment cost $100,000, plus $14,975 in HST and $50,000 was paid in cash with the remainder due in 30 days.

b. To fit the machine into the existing shop space it was necessary to reorganize the layout of existing equipment. The reorganization cost $12,500.
c. It was necessary to knock down a wall to get the machine into place. The work cost $6,700.
d. During the installation mistakes by workers damaged the electrical system in the shop. Repairs cost $8,000.

E8-2. **(Straight-line depreciation, LO 3, 4, 7)** Namaka Inc. (Namaka) recently purchased new display cases for its retail stores. The display cases cost $150,000, taxes were $22,000 (of which $19,500 is refundable), delivery cost $5,000, and set-up cost $8,000. Namaka's management expects to use the display cases for five years, at which time they will be replaced. Management uses straight-line depreciation on assets of this type and estimates that the new display cases have a residual value of $5,000.

Required:

a. Prepare the journal entry to record the purchase of the new display cases.
b. Prepare a depreciation schedule showing the depreciation expense for each of the five years Namaka expects to keep the display cases and the carrying amount of the machine at the end of each year. Assume that the display cases were purchased midway through the fiscal year and only a half-year's depreciation is to be expensed in the first year.
c. Suppose the display cases sold at the end of the third year for $25,000. Prepare the journal entry to record the sale and any other journal entries required with respect to the display cases in the third year.

E8-3. **(Accelerated depreciation, LO 3, 4, 7)** Examine the information provided in E8-2 and respond to parts (a), (b), and (c) assuming Namaka will use declining balance depreciation at a rate of 40 percent for the display cases.

E8-4. **(Accelerated depreciation, LO 3, 4, 7)** In early 2017, Olds Ltd. (Olds) purchased new computer equipment. Olds does cutting-edge graphic design work and requires highly sophisticated computer hardware and software. The new equipment cost $400,000 plus $20,000 in taxes (all of which is refundable), $25,000 for installation, $65,000 for training, and $75,000 for a three-year service contract on the equipment.

Olds's management expects to be able to use the computer equipment for about four years, although with the passage of time the equipment will likely be less useful for more sophisticated work because better equipment becomes available very quickly. Accordingly, management has decided to amortize the equipment using the declining balance method at a rate of 50 percent per year. Management has indicated that it hopes to be able to sell the equipment at the end of four years for $35,000.

Required:

a. Prepare the journal entry to record the purchase of the new equipment.
b. Prepare a depreciation schedule showing the depreciation expense for each of the four years Olds expects to use the computer equipment and the carrying amount of the equipment at the end of each year.
c. Suppose the computer equipment was sold at the end of 2019 for $55,000. Prepare the journal entry to record the sale and any other journal entries required with respect to the computer equipment in 2019.

E8-5. **(Straight-line depreciation, LO 3, 4, 7)** Examine the information provided in E8-4 and respond to parts (a), (b), and (c) assuming that Olds Ltd. will use straight-line depreciation for the computer equipment.

E8-6. **(Units-of-production depreciation, LO 3, 4, 7)** Kyuquot Corp. (Kyuquot) produces fad toys for children. In 2017, Kyuquot purchased a new stamping machine to produce the latest fad toy. The machine cost $60,000 plus taxes of $10,000 ($7,800 of the taxes is refundable), and delivery and installation of $4,000. Kyuquot's management estimates that the market for the toy is about 500,000 units and demand for the toy will last no more than four years. Management expects that it will be able to produce and sell 60,000 units in 2017, 300,000 units in 2018, 130,000 units in 2019, and 10,000 units in 2020. Once the fad dies, the machine won't be useful for any purpose and will have to be sold for scrap, about $4,000. Kyuquot will use unit-of-production amortization for the machine.

Required:

a. Prepare the journal entry to record the purchase of the new machine.
b. Prepare a depreciation schedule showing the depreciation expense for each year and the carrying amount of the machine at the end of each year.
c. Suppose that at the end of 2019, Kyuquot's management realized the fad had died more quickly than expected and there was no more demand for the toy. Prepare the journal entry to record the sale and any other journal entries required with respect to the machine in 2019. Assume that Kyuquot produced and sold 75,000 units in 2019 and received $2,000 from a scrap dealer for the machine.

E8-7. **(Straight-line depreciation, LO 3, 4, 7)** Examine the information provided in E8-6 and respond assuming that Kyuquot will use straight-line depreciation for the machine.

E8-8. **(Accelerated depreciation, LO 3, 4, 7)** Examine the information provided in E8-6 and respond, assuming that Kyuquot will use declining balance depreciation at a rate of 50 percent for the machine. Evaluate the appropriateness of the rate Kyuquot will use to depreciate the machine.

E8-9. **(Determining impairment, LO 7)** For each of the following capital assets, determine if the asset is impaired according to IFRS and, if necessary, the amount of the writedown required. Remember to determine the recoverable amount first:

	Asset	Carrying amount	Value in use	Fair value less cost to sell
a.	Apartment building	$18,000,000	$23,000,000	$20,500,000
b.	Patent	7,000,000	3,250,000	2,500,00
c.	Assembly line	25,000,000	12,750,000	18,000,000
d.	Service centre	4,500,000	6,000,000	6,250,000

E8-10. **(Accounting for a basket purchase, LO 3, 4)** In January 2018, Klemtu Inc. purchased two pieces of used equipment for $175,000. A discussion with a used equipment broker determined that the first piece of equipment was worth about $75,000. Management estimates that the first piece will have a useful life of five years and the second piece a useful life of eight years. Management has decided to use straight-line depreciation.

Required:

Prepare the journal entries that Klemtu would make to record the purchase of the two pieces of equipment. What entry would be made to record the depreciation expense for the year ended December 31, 2018?

E8-11. **(Capital expenditure or expense, LO 1)** Steinbach Veterinary Hospital Inc. provides health care for pets and farm animals in a Manitoba community. During 2017, Steinbach made the following expenditures. Indicate whether each expenditure should be capitalized or expensed. Briefly explain your reasoning:

a. Purchased a new operating table for the clinic.
b. Paid for advertising on radio and in community newspapers.
c. Paid to have the clinic's lawn cut.
d. Purchased a supply of syringes.
e. Purchased original Native art for the waiting room area.
f. Payment for malpractice insurance for the year for the veterinarians.
g. Payment for replacing windows broken during a storm.

E8-12. **(Determining the gain or loss on the sale of land, LO 7)** In 2015, Chin Corp. purchased a piece of land for $2,500,000. In 2018, the land was sold for $3,500,000.

Required:

Prepare the journal entry to record the sale of Chin Corp's land.

E8-13. **(Determining the gains or loss on the sale of capital assets, LO 7)** For each of the following situations, calculate any gain or loss that would arise on the sale of the asset and prepare the journal entries that would be required at the time of the sale. Assume that in each case the assets were depreciated on a straight-line basis and that a full year's depreciation was expensed in the year the asset was acquired. All sale transactions occur in the fiscal year ended December 31, 2017.

a. Equipment purchased in 2012 for $100,000 is sold on June 30, 2017 for $37,000. When the equipment was acquired it was estimated to have a 10-year life and residual value of $8,000.
b. A building purchased in 2003 for $5,000,000 is sold on March 31, 2017 for $7,500,000. When the building was purchased, it was estimated to have a 25-year life and a residual value of $1,000,000.
c. A delivery van purchased in 2015 for $60,000 is sold on December 31, 2017 for $30,000. When the van was purchased, it was estimated to have a five-year life and a residual value of $10,000.

E8-14. **(Classifying capital assets, LO 6)** Indicate whether the following assets would be considered tangible or intangible. Explain your reason for the classification.

a. unique design for office furniture
b. office furniture
c. right to enter another entity's property to access a lake
d. land
e. exclusive right to open and operate Tim Hortons stores in a city
f. building that houses a Tim Hortons store

E8-15. **(Calculation of goodwill, LO 6)** On December 31, 2017, Resolute Inc. (Resolute) purchased 100 percent of the common shares of Uno Ltd. (Uno) for $22,000,000. At the time of the purchase, Resolute's management made the following estimates of the fair values of Uno's assets and liabilities:

Assets	$25,000,000
Liabilities	6,000,000

Required:

Calculate the amount of goodwill that Resolute would report on its December 31, 2017 consolidated balance sheet as a result of its purchase of Uno.

E8-16. **(Calculate the amount of goodwill, LO 6)** On April 15, 2016, Oderin Inc. (Oderin) purchased 100 percent of the common shares of Bellburn Ltd. (Bellburn) for $16,000,000. At the time of the purchase, Oderin's management made the following estimates of the fair values of Bellburn's assets and liabilities:

Current assets	$7,000,000
Tangible capital assets	17,000,000
Patents	3,500,000
Current liabilities	4,750,000
Long-term debt	10,250,000

Required:

a. Calculate the amount of goodwill that Oderin recorded when it purchased Bellburn on April 15, 2016.
b. In fiscal 2020, management determined that the goodwill associated with the purchase of Bellburn was impaired and that it should be written down to $2,500,000. Prepare the journal entry that Oderin would make to record the impairment of the goodwill. What amount would be reported on the fiscal 2020 balance sheet for goodwill and what expense would be reported in the income statement?

E8-17. **(Calculation of gains and losses on sale of capital assets, LO 4, 7)** On July 4, 2017, Sydney Inc. purchased new equipment for its print shop. The equipment cost $102,000.

Sydney's accountant estimated that the useful life of equipment would be five years and the residual value $12,000. Assume that Sydney took a full year of depreciation for the equipment in the year ended June 30, 2018.

Required:

a. Prepare a depreciation schedule for the new equipment, assuming the use of straight-line depreciation. Set up your depreciation schedule like Figure 8.5 in the chapter.
b. Prepare a depreciation schedule for the new equipment assuming the use of declining-balance depreciation using a depreciation rate of 35 percent. Set up your depreciation schedule like Figure 8.6 in the chapter.
c. Assume that on June 30, 2021, after the depreciation expense had been recorded for the year, Sydney sold the equipment for $45,000. Prepare the journal entry that is required to record the sale assuming that
   i. The depreciation schedule in (a) was used.
   ii. The depreciation schedule in (b) was used.
d. Explain the reason for the different income statement effects for the journal entries you recorded in (c).

E8-18. **(Preparing depreciation schedules, LO 4)** In July 2017, Dogwood Inc. purchased new equipment for $200,000. Dogwood's management estimates that the equipment's useful life will be eight years and that its residual value will be $10,000. Dogwood's year-end is June 30.

Required:

a. Prepare a depreciation schedule for each year of the new piece of equipment's life using
   i. straight-line depreciation
   ii. declining balance depreciation (30 percent)
   iii. units-of-production method

   Your depreciation schedule should show the depreciation expense for each year and the carrying amount of the equipment and accumulated depreciation at the end of each year. For the units-of-production method, assume that 10 percent of the production is produced in each of fiscal 2018, 2019, 2024, and 2025, and 15 percent in each of the remaining years.
b. Which method do you think Dogwood's managers would prefer if the company was planning on going to the bank for a loan? Explain.

E8-19. **(Repairs and maintenance, or betterments, LO 3)** For each of the following independent items, indicate whether the expenditure should be capitalized or expensed. Provide your reasoning.

a. A courier company changes the oil, oil filters, spark plugs, and air filters of the trucks in its delivery fleet.
b. An airline paints its aircraft with its new colours.
c. An office building replaces broken windows.
d. An office suite is rewired to allow for more phone lines to be installed so customer service can be improved.
e. The CPUs of 12 computers are replaced because of a defect.
f. The carpets in a law office are cleaned.
g. An extension is added to a building.
h. Staff is sent on a training program to develop their customer service skills.

E8-20. **(Choosing a depreciation period, LO 4)** Eskasoni Inc. (Eskasoni) recently replaced the roof on its 32-year-old building. The roofing company guarantees the roof for 15 years and advised Eskasoni's management that the roof should last 25 years with no problems. Eskasoni is depreciating the building on a straight-line basis over 40 years and it is expected that the building will have to be demolished and replaced before it is 45 years old.

Required:

How should Eskasoni depreciate the new roof (method, useful life, and residual value)? Explain your answer fully.

E8-21. **(Determine the cost of a capital asset, LO 3)** The Nameless Cove Hotel (Nameless Cove) is a luxury resort in Atlantic Canada. Recently, Nameless Cove built a new, Olympic-size swimming pool on its grounds. The pool was constructed by Deep and Sure Pool Company (Deep and Sure). The following costs were incurred to build the pool:

i.	Building permits	$ 1,000
ii.	Design costs	8,000
iii.	Redesign costs required to make changes that Nameless Cove wanted after construction began	5,000
iv.	Cost of clearing the land of trees and bushes	12,000
v.	Amount paid to Deep and Sure for construction of the pool	150,000
vi.	Damage and repairs to an adjacent property caused when heavy equipment was brought onto the site to do the excavation	22,000
vii.	Cost of meals served to workers	2,000
viii.	Penalties paid to Deep and Sure because Nameless Cove did not want construction to be done on certain regular working days	9,000
ix.	Damage and repair of underground telephone lines that Nameless Cove neglected to advise Deep and Sure about	5,500
x.	Construction of a patio	45,000
xi.	Electrical wiring installed for pool equipment and lighting around the patio	15,000
xii.	Cost of new plants for the patio	9,200

Required:

Determine the amount that should be capitalized as part of the cost of the pool. Explain your reasoning for including or excluding each item in the capitalized cost.

E8-22. **(Effect of transactions and economic events on ratios, LO 6, 7, 9)** Complete the table below by indicating whether the transactions or economic events would increase, decrease, or have no effect on the financial ratios listed in the period they occur in. Assume the current ratio is greater than 1.0 before considering each of the situations.

	Return on assets	Profit margin percentage	Current ratio	Debt-to-equity ratio	Fixed-asset turnover ratio
a. Writedown of a machine.					
b. A company that follows IFRS decides that it will account for its building at fair value. It determines that the fair value of the land has increased from $1 million to $4 million. Changes in fair value are included in net income.					
c. Equipment is purchased during the year. A full year of depreciation is expensed in the year of purchased.					
d. Capitalize development costs. Costs were incurred in cash and depreciation will begin in a future period.					

E8-23. **(Effect of transactions and economic events on ratios, LO 6, 7, 9)** Complete the table below by indicating whether the transactions or economic events would increase, decrease, or have no effect on the financial ratios listed in the period they occur. Assume the current ratio is greater than 1.0 before considering each of the situations.

	Return on assets	Profit margin percentage	Current ratio	Debt-to-equity ratio	Fixed-asset turnover ratio
a. Sale of a building. The buyer promises to pay in full in three years. The carrying amount of the building is less than the selling price.					
b. A company following IFRS owns a factory with a carrying amount of $25 million. The value-in-use of the factory is estimated to be $37 million and the fair value is $21 million.					
c. An intangible asset was acquired for cash and it was determined that no factors limit its useful life.					
d. Expense research costs. Costs were incurred in cash.					

E8-24. **(Effect of transactions and economic events on accounting measures, LO 6, 7, 8, 9)** Complete the following table by indicating whether the transactions or economic events would increase, decrease, or have no effect on the financial ratios listed in the period they occur.

	Net income	Gross margin	Total assets	Owners' equity	Cash from operations	Investing cash flows (in the cash flow statement)	Total cash flow
a. An intangible asset was acquired for cash and it was determined that no factors limit its useful life.							
b. Capitalize development costs. Costs were incurred in cash and depreciation will begin in a future period.							
c. Purchase equipment on credit. Depreciation expense is recorded in the year of purchase.							
d. Spend cash to repair a damaged piece of equipment.							
e. A company that follows IFRS accounts for its investment property at fair value. The fair value of the building has increased from $1 million to $4 million. (Changes in fair value are included in net income.)							

E8-25. (Computing fixed asset turnover, LO 10) Use the following information to calculate the fixed asset turnover ratio for Alonsa Ltd. for the years ended December 31, 2017 and 2018. Interpret your results:

Property, plant, and equipment on January 1, 2017	$ 5,250,000
Property, plant, and equipment on December 31, 2017	6,125,000
Property, plant, and equipment on December 31, 2018	5,925,000
Sales in 2017	12,525,000
Sales in 2018	16,750,000

E8-26. (Evaluating the effect of the sale of a capital asset on the cash flow statement, LO 4, 7, 8) In 2014, Triangle Corporation purchased a piece of heavy equipment for $450,000. The equipment was estimated to have an eight-year life and it was depreciated on a straight-line basis. Residual value was estimated to be zero. In 2018 (after four years of depreciation was recorded), the equipment was sold for $210,000 in cash. What journal entry would be made to record the sale of the equipment? How would the sale be reflected in the cash flow statement? Would there be any effect on the calculation of cash from operations?

E8-27. (Evaluating the effect of the sale of a capital asset, LO 4, 7) In 2013, Cariboo Ltd. purchased a piece of specialized machinery for $1,500,000. The machinery was estimated to have a seven-year life and it was depreciated on a straight-line basis. Residual value was estimated to be $100,000. At the beginning of 2018 (after five years of depreciation was recorded), the machinery was sold for $425,000 in cash. What was the gain or loss on the sale? What journal entry would be made to record the sale of the machinery?

Suppose that instead Cariboo used the declining-balance method of depreciation using a rate of 25 percent. What would be the gain or loss on the sale of the machinery when it was sold in 2018? What journal entry would be needed to record the sale? Explain the difference between the two depreciation approaches? What is the economic difference between the two? What would be the impact on cash from operations of the two methods of depreciating the machinery?

E8-28. (Impact of capital asset transactions on the cash flow statement, LO 8) For each of the following items, indicate whether it would appear on the cash flow statement as cash from operations, an investing cash flow, or a financing cash flow, or that it wouldn't have an effect on cash flows:

a. Gain on the sale of furniture and fixtures
b. Purchase equipment in exchange for a long-term note payable
c. Payment of cash to add an extension to an existing building
d. Amortization of an intangible asset
e. Proceeds from the sale of land that's sold at a loss
f. Research costs
g. Writedown of equipment
h. Capitalization of development costs
i. Borrow money from the bank that's used to purchase new equipment

E8-29. (CCA versus depreciation, LO 10, Appendix) On January 3, 2017, Acme Inc. (Acme) purchased new equipment to process fresh fruit into jams and jellies for retail sale. The equipment cost $25,000, fully installed, and the amount was capitalized for accounting and tax purposes. Management estimates a residual value of zero. Acme's equipment is classified as class 43, which has a CCA rate of 30 percent declining balance. Acme's year-end is December 31.

Required:

a. What is the maximum amount of CCA that could be claimed for tax purposes in 2017? Explain.
b. What is the maximum amount of CCA that could be claimed for tax purposes in 2018? Explain.
c. If Acme decides to depreciate the equipment on a straight-line basis over 15 years, what would the depreciation expense be in 2017?

d. How does the useful life estimated by Acme's management affect the amount of CCA that can be claimed? Explain.
e. Why are the amounts calculated in (a) and (c) likely different? Explain.

E8-30. **(Revaluing capital assets to market, LO 4)** Tagish Ltd. is a small public company located in eastern Canada. Tagish's management has decided to report its land and building at fair value as allowed by IFRS for its December 31, 2018 year-end. The land was acquired 15 years ago for $4,000,000. The building was built six years ago at a cost of $12,000,000. The building is being depreciated over 25 years on a straight-line basis with a residual value of zero. A recent appraisal valued the land at $7,500,000 and the building at $10,500,000. Assume that Tagish's net income for 2018 was $5,750,600 and common shares and retained earnings on December 31, 2018 were $10,000,000 and $15,000,000 respectively.

Required:

a. What amount would Tagish report on its December 31, 2018 balance sheet for land and building if it carries them at fair value?
b. If Tagish uses the proportional method to present its capital assets, what would be the balance in the accumulated depreciation account for the building on December 31, 2018?
c. How would the change in the value of the land and building be reported in the statement of income and comprehensive income and balance sheet in 2018?
d. What do you think the benefits and problems for stakeholders are of a company reporting its capital assets at market value?

Problems

P8-1. **(Establishing a depreciation policy, LO 4)** You are the accountant for a chain of diners in pizza and Italian food restaurants. The company is owned by the founder plus ten other investors who aren't involved in the management of the chain. These investors rely on the financial statements to evaluate how the company is doing. The chain has recently started a home delivery service for its pizza so that people could enjoy hot and fresh gourmet style restaurant pizza in their homes. After a trial period, the chain purchased ten cars to make deliveries. You have to prepare the year-end financial statements for the restaurant and have to decide how to depreciate the car. What depreciation method, useful life, and residual value would you assign to the cars? Explain your decision fully and discuss the factors you considered. Assume the restaurant prepares its financial statements in accordance with IFRS. The cars cost $200,000.

P8-2. **(Interpreting a writedown, LO 5, 7, 9)** Fiscal 2017 was an outstanding year for Esterhazy Inc. (Esterhazy). For a variety of reasons, the company's sales surged and net income was going to exceed financial analysts' expectations by more than 20 percent or $13,000,000. Esterhazy's management recognized that the high earnings for the year were due to some unusual business circumstances and weren't likely to be repeated in the foreseeable future.

Before finalizing its financial statements, Esterhazy's management evaluated the company's assets and determined that several were overvalued. As a result, Esterhazy's assets were written down by a total of $12,000,000 so that the assets wouldn't be overstated on the balance sheet. All of the assets written down were being depreciated and their remaining useful lives ranged between five and eight years. Esterhazy is a public company that is traded on a Canadian stock exchange.

Required:

a. Explain the effect of the writedown on the 2017 financial statements as well as the implications for subsequent years' financial statements.

b. Explain how users of the financial statements would be affected by the writedown and how the financial statements should be interpreted as a result of recording the writedown.
c. Why do you think Esterhazy chose to write down the assets?
d. Does it matter that Esterhazy wrote down these assets? Explain.

P8-3. **(Interpreting a writedown, LO 5, 7, 9)** In fiscal 2017, Plumas Technologies Inc. (Plumas) purchased a company that owned a technology Plumas believed was extremely valuable for its future success. Plumas paid $900,000,000 for the company. Among the assets Plumas obtained by purchasing the company was "technologies under development," which Plumas estimated to have a fair value of $350,000,000. This means that Plumas estimated that the technologies under development would generate net revenues of at least $350,000,000.

Plumas decided to expense the technologies under development in full in fiscal 2017. As an alternative, Plumas could have treated the technologies under development as an asset and amortized them over 10 years. Plumas is a public company that is traded on a Canadian stock exchange.

Required:

Explain the effect on the current year's financial statements, as well as the implications for future years' financial statements, of fully expensing the technologies under development. Also, explain how users of the financial statements would be affected by how Plumas accounted for the acquired technologies and how the financial statements should be interpreted as a result of how the acquired technologies were accounted for. Why do you think Plumas chose to account for the technologies in the way it did?

P8-4. **(Determining cost, LO 3, 4)** Mr. Bogan operates a dairy farm in Quebec. Recently, one of his cows gave birth to a female calf that will eventually join the dairy herd that produces the milk Mr. Bogan sells. When the calf was born, Mr. Bogan had the veterinarian check the calf. At first the calf drinks its mother's milk, but later it will graze on grass in the pasture. During the winter, the calf will eat hay that Mr. Bogan grows on another part of his farm. Eventually the calf will be a milk-producing cow.

Required:

a. According to IFRS, how would the calf (and then the producing cow) be valued on the farm's balance sheet?
b. According to ASPE, how would the calf (and then the producing cow) be valued on the farm's balance sheet?
c. Compare the two approaches. Which do you think provides more useful information to stakeholders? What are some of the problems with each of the methods?

P8-5. **(Changing accounting estimates, LO 3)** Wishart Ltd. owns and operates several landfills. The company is owned by a group of investors, most of who aren't involved in the day-to-day operations. As a result, the financial statements are an important source of information for the shareholders. The company also has a large amount of long-term debt borrowed from several lenders. In late 2017, Wishart's management determined that it would need an infusion of additional capital to finance and expand two of the landfills and to upgrade the equipment at several others. However, the company has been struggling financially of late and management is concerned that it might get a frosty response from prospective shareholders or creditors. In a recent executive meeting. the CFO proposed increasing the useful lives of several of the company's landfills. He argued that the initial estimates were conservative and that based on recent estimates of the amount of garbage that would be produced by Wishart's customers, the landfills would be able to operate 15 to 20 percent longer than estimated. The CFO said he would study the proposal further, but there was general agreement among the executive that this would be a good and reasonable strategy.

Required:

a. What effect would the change proposed by the CFO have on accounting measures such as revenue, expenses, net income, property, plant, and equipment, total assets, and shareholders' equity?
b. What would the impact be on ratios such as profit margin, return on assets, fixed asset turnover, and debt-to-equity ratio?
c. What would be the real economic impact of the proposed change?
d. How is it possible that a change in the life of the landfill by such a significant amount?
e. As a prospective lender to Wishart, how would your evaluation of the company be affected by the increase in the useful life of the landfills?

P8-6. **(Repairs, maintenance, and betterments, LO 3)** In January 2012, Klemtu Inc. (Klemtu) purchased a new piece of equipment that was expected to increase the efficiency of the company's production process and the quality of its output. The equipment cost $150,000. The equipment was estimated to have a six-year useful life and a residual value of $15,000. In February 2016, Klemtu paid $98,000 to overhaul the equipment. The overhaul upgraded the technology of the equipment and extended its useful life by an additional two years. In May 2016, the equipment broke down and required servicing to get it to operate properly. The servicing cost $10,000. Klemtu's year-end is December 31. The estimated residual value remained $15,000 throughout the period.

Required:

a. Provide the journal entry to record the purchase of the equipment in March 2012.
b. How would you account for the overhaul done in February 2016? Explain your reasoning.
c. How would you account for the servicing done in May 2016? Explain.
d. What effect would the events in (b) and (c) have on Klemtu's depreciation expense?
e. What would be the depreciation expense in each year of the equipment's life, assuming that Klemtu uses straight-line depreciation?

P8-7. **(Calculate missing information, LO 3, 4, 7)** Use the following information and determine the carrying amount of the property, plant, and equipment of Manotick Inc. on December 31, 2017, the company's year-end. (An accounting equation spreadsheet, journal entries, or T-accounts may help you answer this question.)

i. On January 1, 2017, the cost of Manotick's property, plant, and equipment was $1,125,000 and the accumulated depreciation was $337,500.
ii. During fiscal 2017, Manotick sold property, plant, and equipment with a cost of $165,000 at a loss of $30,000. Manotick received $45,000 for the assets.
iii. During fiscal 2017, Manotick sold land, which is included in property, plant, and equipment, for $217,500 cash, which generated a gain for accounting purposes of $60,000.
iv. During fiscal 2017, property, plant, and equipment were purchased for $285,000 cash plus long-term debt of $337,500.
v. During fiscal 2017, Manotick wrote down property, plant, and equipment by $48,000.
vi. Manotick recorded a depreciation expense of $127,500 for fiscal 2017.

P8-8. **(Calculate missing information, LO 3, 4, 7)** Use the following information and determine the carrying amount of the property, plant, and equipment of Havelock Ltd. on July 1, 2017, the first day of its 2018 fiscal year. (An accounting equation spreadsheet, journal entries, or T-accounts may help you answer this question. *Hint:* You are calculating the account balance at the beginning of the year.)

i. On June 30, 2018, the cost of Havelock's property, plant, and equipment was $1,125,000 and the accumulated depreciation was $512,500.
ii. During fiscal 2018, Havelock purchased property, plant, and equipment for $237,500 in cash plus $100,000 in notes payable.

iii. During fiscal 2018, Havelock sold property, plant, and equipment with a cost of $135,000 at a gain of $30,000. Havelock received $50,000 cash for the assets.
iv. During fiscal 2018, Havelock sold land, which is included in property, plant, and equipment, for $107,500 cash. The sale produced a loss for accounting purposes of $40,000.
v. During fiscal 2018, Havelock wrote down property, plant, and equipment by $41,500.
vi. Havelock recorded a depreciation expense of $115,000.

P8-9. **(Impact of accounting errors, LO 3, 4, 9)** For each of the following errors, indicate its effect on the financial statement elements and ratios shown in the table below. Indicate whether the financial statement element or ratio would be overstated (higher than it would have been had the error not occurred), understated (lower than it would have been had the error not occurred), or not affected by the error in the year the error occurred (except for item (d)).

a. New equipment is purchased but is expensed immediately rather than being capitalized and depreciated.
b. Advertising costs are capitalized instead of being expensed as incurred.
c. A building's useful life is estimated to be 10 years instead of 25 years. What is the impact in the first year of the building's life?
d. A building's useful life is estimated to be 10 years instead of 25 years. What is the impact in the 15th year of the building's life?
e. A piece of land is depreciated over 25 years, the life of the building that is on the land.

	Net income	Total assets	Owners' equity	Current ratio [1.65]	Return on assets	Debt-to-equity ratio [1.25]	Fixed asset turnover ratio
a.							
b.							
c.							
d.							
e.							

P8-10. **(Comparing income statements, LO 3, 4, 9)** You have been provided with the following financial statements of two companies, Aguanish Ltd. (Aguanish) and Lanigan Inc. (Lanigan).

	Aguanish Ltd. Income statement for the year ended December 31, 2018	Lanigan Inc. Income statement for the year ended December 31, 2018
Sales	$1,275,000	$1,275,000
Cost of sales	465,000	465,000
Selling, general, and administrative expenses	375,000	375,000
Depreciation expense	210,000	325,000
Interest expense	52,000	52,000
Income tax expense	51,000	51,000
Net income	$ 122,000	$ 7,000

The two companies are identical in every respect, except for how they account for their capital assets. Aguanish depreciates its assets on a straight-line basis while Lanigan depreciates its assets using the declining balance method.

Required:

a. Examine the financial statements of the two companies. Which would be a better investment? Explain.
b. Why do you think the two companies would use different depreciation methods?
c. Does it matter that the companies use different depreciation methods? Explain.

P8-11. **(Effect of capitalizing versus expensing R&D costs, LO 4, 6, 8, 9)** Mirror Inc. is a global telecommunications company based in Canada. It's a world leader in business telecommunications and is always on the leading edge of new technology. Technology changes rapidly and to maintain its competitive position, Mirror must invest heavily in research and development to ensure it has the next great breakthrough under development.

Mirror prepares its financial statements in accordance with IFRS, so it expenses all research costs and any development costs that don't meet the criteria for capitalization. To date, none of Mirror's development costs have met the criteria for capitalization. The company has incurred no interest expense. The following information has been summarized from Mirror's financial statements:

Mirror Inc.
Extracts from Financial Statements
(in millions)

	2018	2017	2016	2015	2014
Summarized from the income statement					
Revenue	$1,593.9	$ 995.5	$ 671.0	$ 187.0	$ 5.5
Expenses*	1,217.2	977.8	592.1	271.1	165.0
R&D expenditures	490.0	270.0	190.0	115.0	110.0
Net loss	$ (113.3)	$ (252.3)	$ (111.1)	$(199.1)	$(269.5)
Summarized from the balance sheet					
Total assets	$2,777.5	$2,471.7	$2,321.1	$ 715.0	$ 308.0
Total liabilities	1,083.2	889.8	812.4	300.3	138.6
Total shareholders' equity	1,694.3	1,581.9	1,508.7	414.7	169.4
Summarized from the cash flow statement					
Cash from operations	$ 137.5	$ (198.0)	$ (90.2)	$(154.0)	$(330.0)
Cash expended on investing activities	(220.1)	(271.7)	(1,177.0)	(385.0)	(209.0)

*Includes all expenses incurred by Mirror except for research and development.

Required:

a. Recalculate net income for 2016 through 2018 assuming that R&D costs were capitalized and expensed over three years using straight-line amortization beginning in 2014.
b. What would total assets be at the end of 2016 through 2018 if R&D costs were capitalized and amortized over three years?
c. What would shareholders' equity be at the end of 2016 through 2018 if R&D costs were capitalized and amortized over three years?
d. What would cash from operations and cash expended on investing activities be if R&D costs were capitalized and amortized over three years?
e. What would the following ratios be assuming that (1) R&D costs were expensed as incurred and (2) R&D costs were capitalized and amortized over three years? Assume that Mirror didn't have an interest expense over the period 2014–2018.
   i. return on assets
   ii. debt-to-equity ratio
   iii. profit margin percentage

f. How would your interpretation of Mirror differ depending on how R&D costs are accounted for? Which accounting approach do you think is more appropriate? Explain. Your answer should consider the objectives of the stakeholders and the managers who prepare the accounting information, as well as the accounting concepts discussed throughout the book.

P8-12. **(Effect of capitalizing versus expensing R&D costs, LO 4, 6, 8, 9)** Florze Software Inc. (Florze) is a software development company located in Kanata, Ontario. Software is a highly competitive industry and the life of a software product is usually quite short. To remain competitive, companies must invest heavily in research and development to keep their existing products up to date and to develop new ones. Florze expenses all research costs and any development costs that don't meet the criteria for capitalization. Florze has never capitalized any development costs. Florze has incurred no interest expense over the past five years. The following information has been summarized from Florze's financial statements:

Florze Software Inc.
Extracts from Financial Statements

	2017	2016	2015	2014	2013
Summarized from the income statement					
Revenue	$8,983,800	$5,611,000	$3,782,000	$ 1,054,000	$ 899,000
Expenses*	4,105,950	3,262,750	2,805,500	2,123,500	2,084,750
R&D expenditures	3,487,500	2,712,500	1,550,000	581,250	387,500
Net income (loss)	$1,390,350	$ (364,250)	$ (573,500)	$(1,650,750)	$(1,573,250)
Summarized from the balance sheet					
Total assets	$9,784,375	$8,707,125	$8,176,250	$ 2,518,750	$ 1,085,000
Total liabilities	4,011,595	3,047,495	2,452,875	730,438	271,250
Total shareholders' equity	5,772,780	5,659,630	5,723,375	1,788,313	813,750
Summarized from the cash flow statement					
Cash from operations	$ 465,000	$ (775,000)	$ (232,500)	$(1,085,000)	$(2,325,000)
Cash expended on investing activities	(1,395,000)	(1,085,000)	(5,425,000)	(1,550,000)	(883,500)

*Includes all expenses incurred by Florze except for research and development.

Required:

a. Recalculate net income for 2015 through 2017, assuming that R&D costs were capitalized and amortized over three years using straight-line amortization beginning in 2013.
b. What would total assets be at the end of 2015 through 2017 if R&D costs were capitalized and amortized over three years?
c. What would shareholders' equity be at the end of 2015 through 2017 if R&D costs were capitalized and amortized over three years?
d. What would cash from operations and cash expended on investing activities be for 2015 through 2017 if R&D costs were capitalized and amortized over three years?
e. What would the following ratios be assuming that (1) R&D costs were expensed as incurred and (2) R&D costs were capitalized and expensed over three years? Assume that Florze didn't have an interest expense over the period 2013–2017.
   i. return on assets
   ii. debt-to-equity ratio
   iii. profit margin percentage

f. How would your interpretation of Florze differ depending on how R&D costs are accounted for? Which accounting approach do you think is more appropriate? Explain. Your answer should consider the objectives of the stakeholders and the managers who prepare the accounting information, as well as the accounting concepts discussed throughout the book.

P8-13. **(Recommending a depreciation policy, LO 3, 4, 9)** Early in 2017, Mr. Peribonka purchased a machine for $80,000 to produce a new gadget he designed. Mr. Peribonka invested $50,000 of his own money to buy the machine and borrowed the remainder from the bank. Mr. Peribonka figures the machine will last six years, after which it will be worthless. He has sold 25,000 gadgets this year and thinks he can sell 60,000 in 2018; 100,000 in 2019 and 2020; 30,000 in 2021; and 15,000 in 2022.

Mr. Peribonka needs to prepare financial statements for the year ended December 31, 2017. He needs the statements for tax purposes, the bank, and for his own information. He has most of the information put together but he isn't sure what to do about depreciation and has come to you for advice. For tax purposes the machine is in class 43, which has a declining balance CCA rate of 30 percent.

Required:

Provide the advice Mr. Peribonka has requested. Explain in detail your thinking, your alternatives, and your recommendations.

P8-14. **(Impaired asset, LO 4, 7)** In January 2015, Coaticook Inc. (Coaticook) purchased a patent for a pharmaceutical designed to help bald people to grow hair. The drug behind the patent was considered revolutionary at the time and Coaticook's management thought that purchasing the patent would provide it with a product that would reinvigorate sales and the company's stock price. Coaticook purchased the patent for $125 million. At the time of the purchase, the patent had 10 years left before it expired and it was being amortized on a straight-line basis. At purchase, management estimated the patent would generate an average of $22 million in net revenue (revenue less the cost of producing and selling the drug) per year over its remaining life. In 2015 and 2016, net revenues significantly exceeded expectations, but in mid-2017 a competing product came to market that was more effective than Coaticook's product, with fewer side effects. As a result, management slashed its estimate of the net revenues by 50 percent. A present value analysis of the estimated future cash flows produced an estimated value-in-use of the product in mid-2017 of $42 million. Management thinks it might be able to sell the patent for about $7 million.

Required:

It's July 2017. Coaticook's management has approached you for advice on how it should account for, if at all, the change in market conditions for its product in its June 30, 2017 second quarter financial statements. Management would like you to fully explain your reasoning and to provide any journal entries required to deal with the problem. They would also like your opinion on what effect this information will have on the company's stock price and on its performance for the year.

P8-15. **(Effect of a recording error on the financial statements, LO 3, 4, 8, 9)** In 2014, Rigolet Ltd. purchased a small delivery truck for $36,000. In error, Rigolet's bookkeeper recorded the purchase as an expense rather than classifying it as an asset. The error went unnoticed until late in 2017, when the truck was sold for $6,000 and no record could be found of it in the accounts.

Required:

a. Show the entry that Rigolet's bookkeeper made to record the purchase of the truck. Show the entry that should have been made.
b. Rigolet uses straight-line depreciation for its vehicles and the useful life assigned to similar vehicles is five years with a $5,000 residual value. What would have been the effect of the error on net income and total assets (amount and direction of the error) in 2014, 2015, and 2016?

c. What would be the effect of the error on net income and total assets (amount and direction of the error) in 2017, the year the truck was sold?
d. What would be the effect of the error on the cash flow statement in each of years 2014 through 2017?
e. Assuming the error is material, what would the implications of this error be for users of the financial statements? Explain.

P8-16. **(Effect of a recording error on the financial statements, LO 3, 4, 8, 9)** In 2017, We-Non-Cha Woodworking Ltd. (We-Non-Cha) purchased and installed a new state-of-the-art lathe line in its woodworking shop in British Columbia. The new lathe line cost $1,750,000 to purchase and install, all of which was capitalized. The line is being depreciated on a declining balance basis at 20 percent per year. We-Non-Cha used its own employees to install the line. Because of errors made by We-Non-Cha's employees, it was necessary to remove parts of the lathe line after they were already installed to reinforce the building to meet safety standards. The extra work added $200,000 to the cost of the lathe line and is included in the $1,750,000 cost.

Required:

a. How should the cost of the extra work have been accounted for? Explain.
b. What would be the effect of capitalizing the cost of the extra work instead of expensing it on net income and total assets (amount and direction of the error) in 2017, 2018, and 2019? Explain your reasoning.
c. What would be the effect of capitalizing the cost of the extra work instead of expensing it on the cash flow statement in each of years 2017 through 2019?
d. Assuming the effect is material, what would be the implications of capitalizing the cost of the extra work instead of expensing it for users of the financial statements? Explain.

P8-17. **(Effect of accounting on business decisions, LO 7, 9)** Judge Ltd. (Judge) operates a small chain of auto supply shops. The company has been in business for many years and for most of that time it was owned and operated by the Judge family. In recent years Judge has been in financial difficulty and management has been turned over to a team of professional managers. The managers own 10 percent of Judge's shares and the Judge family owns the remainder. Judge has agreed to a number of strict accounting-based covenants with its creditors, including that its debt-to-equity ratio not go above 1.5:1 at the end of any quarter over the term of either its bank loan or long-term debt. If the covenant is violated, all loans become payable in full in 30 days.

Judge owns a piece of land and a building that used to be one of its shops but hasn't been used for four years. The building is in very poor condition and isn't in a very good part of town. Judge hasn't been able to find a tenant or a buyer in over two years. The land and building have a carrying amount of $3,370,000 and Judge has now received an offer of $2,000,000 for them. The offer is attractive, especially because it would provide some urgently needed cash. The offer expires on June 30, 2017, the last day of Judge's fiscal year, and it's not likely to be renewed.

It's now June 27, 2017. Judge's management estimates that net income for the year will be about $450,000. Management also projects that on June 30, 2017 current liabilities will be $1,150,000 and long-term debt will be $3,350,000. Common shares on June 30, 2017 will be $1,600,000 and retained earnings on June 30, 2016 was $1,450,000.

You have been asked by Judge's president to prepare a report discussing all the business and accounting issues relevant to the land and building.

Required:

Prepare the report requested by Judge's president.

P8-18. **(Basket purchase, LO 3, 4, 10)** Quabbin Corp. (Quabbin) is a small manufacturing company in Regina. It's owned by five shareholders, two of whom manage the company. The other three are silent investors who invested when the company was struggling financially. Quabbin has significant borrowings from the bank and it anticipates that it will have to request a significant increase in its line of credit in the next few months.

Recently, Quabbin purchased some land, a building, and a number of pieces of used equipment from a bankrupt company. The total cost of the bundle of goods was $5,200,000. For accounting purposes, Quabbin estimates that the building will last about 12 years and the equipment should last about five years. It's expected that neither the building nor the equipment will have any residual value. For tax purposes, CCA on the building can be charged at 4 percent per year on a declining balance basis. CCA on the equipment is 30 percent per year declining balance. CCA can't be claimed on the land.

The land, building, and equipment were appraised by Quabbin to ensure it was getting a good deal before they were purchased. The land was appraised at between $950,000 and $1,300,000, the building at between $2,100,000 and $2,800,000, and the equipment at between $1,500,000 and $2,000,000.

You have been asked for advice by Quabbin's controller about how to account for the purchase of the land, building, and equipment. The controller has requested that you explain your recommendation fully so that he can in turn explain the situation to the managers. Your report should also provide the journal entry that Quabbin would make to record its purchase of the land, building, and equipment.

Required:

Prepare the report.

P8-19. **(Preparing depreciation schedules, LO 3, 4, 5, 8)** In July 2017, Hanna Palladium Mines Inc. (Hanna), a public company, began operation of its new palladium mine. Geologists estimate that the mine contains about 310,000 ounces of palladium. Hanna incurred the following capital costs in starting up the mine:

Exploration and development	$25,000,000
Mine extraction equipment	18,000,000
Buildings	5,000,000

The exploration and development costs were incurred to find the mine and prepare it for operations. The mine extraction equipment should be useful for the entire life of the mine and Hanna should be able to sell the equipment for $3,500,000 when the mine is exhausted in ten years. The buildings are expected to last much longer than the ten-year life of the mine, but they won't be useful once the mine is shut down.

The production engineers estimate that all the palladium can be removed from the mine over ten years. They estimate the following year-by-year production for the mine:

2018	5,000 ounces
2019	25,000 ounces
2020–2025	40,000 ounces
2026	30,000 ounces
2027	10,000 ounces

Hanna's year-end is June 30.

Required:

a. Show the journal entries necessary to record the purchase of the extraction equipment and the construction of the buildings.
b. Prepare depreciation schedules using the straight-line, declining balance (20 percent per year), and units-of-production methods for the three types of capital costs.
c. Which method would you recommend that Hanna use to depreciate its capital assets? Explain. Do you think the same method should be used for each type of capital asset? Explain.
d. The mine is viable as long as the cash cost of extracting the platinum remains below the price Hanna can obtain for its platinum. If the price falls below the cash cost of extraction, it may be necessary to close the mine temporarily until prices rise. What would be the effect on depreciation if the mine were temporarily shut down?

e. Under some circumstances, it may become necessary to shut the mine permanently. How would you account for the capital assets if the mine had to be shut down permanently? Show the journal entries you would make in regard to the capital assets in this event. State any assumptions you make.

P8-20. **(Observing the effects of accounting choices on the cash flow statement, LO 6, 8)** Barkway Inc. (Barkway) is in the process of finalizing its cash flow statement for 2018. The statement has been completely prepared except for the new product development costs that the controller hasn't decided how to account for. The controller has been examining IAS 38 on intangible assets and realizes that considerable judgment is needed in accounting for product development costs. The controller's interpretation of the facts suggests that capitalizing or expensing the development costs could be supported. Preliminary net income, *before* accounting for the development costs, is $242,500. The product development costs for the year are $205,000. Barkway's preliminary cash flow statement is shown below (the product development costs aren't reflected in the cash flow statement):

Barkway Inc. Cash Flow Statement for the Year Ended August 31, 2018	
Cash from operations	
Net income	$
Add: Depreciation	92,500
Add: Net decrease in non-cash working capital	52,500
Add: Loss on sale of capital assets	87,500
Cash from operations	
Investing activities	
Proceeds from the sale of capital assets	122,500
Purchase of capital assets	(245,000)
Cash from (used for) investing activities	
Financing activities	
Increase in long-term debt	187,500
Repayment of mortgage loan	(62,500)
Dividends	(25,000)
Cash from (used for) financing activities	
Change in cash during 2018	
Cash and equivalents, beginning of the year	55,000
Cash and equivalents, end of the year	

Required:

a. Complete the cash flow statement (shaded boxes) assuming that
   i. the new product development costs are capitalized and amortized; assume that if the product development costs are capitalized, it isn't necessary to depreciate any of the costs in 2018.
   ii. the new product development costs are expensed as incurred
b. Compare the two cash flow statements. How do they influence your evaluation of Barkway?
c. How are the balance sheet and income statement affected by the different accounting treatments for the new product development costs?
d. If Barkway's management received bonuses based on net income, which treatment for the product development costs do you think they would prefer? Explain.

P8-21. (Observing the effects of accounting choices on the cash flow statement, LO 6, 8) Okotoks Ltd. (Okotoks) is in the process of finalizing its cash flow statement for 2017. The statement has been completely prepared except for some costs that the controller isn't sure whether certain costs should be capitalized or expensed. Normally relatively minor, this year these costs were significant and the classification will have an impact on the financial statements. The preliminary net loss, *before* accounting for these costs, is $12,500. The repair/betterment costs for the year are $105,000. The nature of the costs is ambiguous so the controller will likely be able to capitalize or expense them. The costs aren't reflected in the preliminary cash flow statement shown below:

Okotoks Ltd. Cash Flow Statement for the Year Ended April 30, 2017	
Cash from operations	
Net loss	$
Add: Depreciation	137,500
Less: Gain on sale of capital assets	47,5000
Less: Net increase in non-cash working capital	56,000
Cash from operations	
Investing activities	
Proceeds from the sale of capital assets	155,000
Purchase of capital assets	(662,500)
Cash from (used for) investing activities	
Financing activities	
Increase in long-term debt	500,000
Repayment of long-term loan	(375,000)
Sale of common stock	525,000
Cash from (used for) financing activities	
Change in cash during 2017	
Cash and equivalents, beginning of the year	49,000
Cash and equivalents, end of the year	$

Required:

a. Complete the cash flow statement (shaded boxes) assuming that
   i. the costs are capitalized
   ii. the costs are expensed

   Assume that if the costs are capitalized it will be necessary to depreciate $30,000 in 2017.

b. Compare the two cash flow statements. How is your evaluation of Okotoks influenced by them?

c. How are the balance sheet and income statement affected by the different accounting treatments for the costs?

d. Assuming that the controller is correct in her belief that the costs can be reasonably classified as either repairs or betterments, what factors would you advise the controller to consider in making her decision? Explain.

P8-22. (Understanding the relationship between the balance sheet and the cash flow statement, LO 3, 8, 9) Albanel Ltd. (Albanel) is a manufacturing company. On December 31, 2017, Albanel reported property, plant, and equipment, net of accumulated depreciation, of $4,750,000. Below is Albanel's cash flow statement for the year ended December 31, 2018. All purchases and sales of property, plant, and equipment were for cash.

Albanel Ltd. Cash Flow Statement for the Year Ended December 31, 2018	
Net income	$275,000
Depreciation expense	310,000
Gain on sale of land	(75,000)
Gain on sale of equipment	(32,000)
Loss on sale of building	110,000
Increase in non-cash working capital	(70,000)
	518,000
Investing Activities	
Purchase of land and building	(487,000)
Purchase of equipment	(315,000)
Proceeds from sale of building	780,000
Proceeds from sale of land	225,000
Proceeds from sale of equipment	100,000
	303,000
Financing Activities	
Repayment of long-term debt	(800,000)
Increase in cash during the year	21,000
Cash at beginning year	82,000
Cash at end of year	$103,000

Required:

a. What were the carrying amounts of the property, plant, and equipment sold by Albanel during 2018?
b. What amount would Albanel report for property, plant, and equipment, net of accumulated depreciation, on its December 31, 2018 balance sheet?

P8-23. **(Evaluating and interpreting the effects of a writedown, LO 6, 7)** Mildmay Ltd. (Mildmay) is a public company that manufactures machine parts. In its most recent financial statements, Mildmay wrote down $175,000,000 of its assets, which it will continue to use. The new president and CEO of Mildmay announced that the writedowns were the result of competitive pressures and the poor performance of the company in the last year. They were reported separately in Mildmay's income statement as required by IFRS and the notes said that the circumstances giving rise to the writedown were unusual and not expected to recur. Mildmay doesn't include the writeoff in its calculation of operating income.

Mildmay's summarized income statement for the year ended December 31, 2017 is (amounts in millions of dollars):

Revenue		$ 625
Operating expenses:		
Cost of goods sold	$470	
Depreciation	87	
Selling, general, and administrative costs	82	639
Operating income		(14)
Other expenses:		
Non-recurring item	175	
Interest expense	33	
Income tax expense	(53)	155
Net income		($169)

The writedowns will reduce the depreciation expense by $16,500,000 per year for each of the next eight years. After the announcement and release of the income statement, analysts revised their forecasts of earnings for the next three years to

Year ended December 31, 2018	$11,000,000
December 31, 2019	35,000,000
December 31, 2020	71,000,000

Required:

a. What would net income be in each of 2017 through 2020 had Mildmay not written off the assets and continued to depreciate them? Assume that the operations of Mildmay don't change regardless of the accounting method used.
b. Why do you think the new management might have made the decision to write off the assets?
c. As an investor trying to evaluate the performance and predict future profitability, what problems do asset writedowns of this type create for you? Consider how the writeoff is reflected in the income statement and use the Mildmay case as a basis for your discussion.

P8-24. **(Case analysis, uses concepts from the book so far, LO 9)** Wanda's Fashions is a small tailor's shop located in the centre of a medium-sized community. The shop is owned and operated by Wanda, who alters clothing, tailors clothing to the specification of customers, and carries a line of ready-made clothing that she designs and makes herself. Wanda also makes all the uniforms worn by the employees of her brother Wendel's businesses. Wanda has been in business for over 20 years and has a list of over 200 people who use her services regularly, both for tailoring new clothes and for repairing and altering clothes.

The store owns several sewing machines, pressing equipment, mannequins, and furniture and fixtures in the showroom portion of the store. There is also a large sign in front of the store. All capital assets are depreciated using the rates required by the *Income Tax Act*. Wanda has a large quantity of fabrics in stock so she can provide a wide selection to customers who wish to have clothes made for them.

Wanda operates the store on her own. She has two tailors who work for her part-time, based on how busy she is. Her children, Wendy and Webster, sometimes work in the store when it's busy. Webster also helps his mother do alterations and some of the tailoring. The children aren't paid for their work but Wanda pays for their university tuition fees and last year bought them a car.

The shop is located in a three-storey building owned by Wanda and her husband Willie. In addition to Wanda's shop, the building houses three other storefront businesses (a fruit store, a butcher shop, and a video store) and has two businesses and three apartments on the second floor. Each of the tenants (except Wanda's Fashions) pays a monthly rent. Wanda, Willie, and their children live on the third floor of the building.

Wanda and Willie prepare a single set of financial statements for tax purposes. The statements encompass all income and expenses generated by the business activities (all of which are unincorporated), including Wanda's Fashions, building operations, and some of Willie's unincorporated business ventures.

Wolfgang Wondergarment has expressed interest in purchasing Wanda's shop. Wolfgang is an experienced tailor who arrived in Canada three years ago. He has been working as a tailor for a major chain but he feels he is ready to have his own business. He will be meeting with Wanda next week to discuss the sale. Wanda has said that she will provide any information that is required.

Required:

Wolfgang Wondergarment has asked you for help in preparing for the meeting. Wolfgang would like a report outlining the information that should be requested from Wanda, including questions and concerns he should have about the financial statements that Wanda will show him. Wolfgang believes that Wanda's accountant (actually her cousin Wesley) will be present, so Wolfgang wants full explanations of what is needed and why it's required.

Using Financial Statements

TELUS CORPORATION

TELUS Corporation is a leading national telecommunications company in Canada, with $10.4 billion of annual revenue and 12.7 million customer connections including 7.3 million wireless subscribers, 3.6 million wireline network access lines and 1.3 million Internet subscribers, and more than 500,000 TELUS TV customers. TELUS provides a wide range of communications products and services including wireless, data, Internet protocol (IP), voice, television, entertainment and video. TELUS trades on the TSX and the New York Stock Exchange.[5]

TELUS' statements of income and extracts from the balance sheets, statements of cash flows, and notes to the financial statements are provided in Exhibit 8.4.[6] Use this information to respond to questions FS8-1 to FS8-12.

FS8-1. Find or determine the following from the information provided about TELUS:

a. What amount of property, plant, and equipment does TELUS report on its December 31, 2011 balance sheet?
b. What amount of goodwill does TELUS report on December 31, 2011?
c. What amount of property, plant, and equipment was disposed of or retired during fiscal 2011? What amount of accumulated depreciation was associated with the property, plant, and equipment that was disposed of or retired?
d. What amount did TELUS expense for depreciation and amortization during 2011?
e. What is the cost and carrying amount (net book value) of TELUS' network assets on December 31, 2011? What is the amount of accumulated depreciation associated with TELUS' network assets?
f. Over what period is TELUS depreciating its wireless site equipment?
g. How much cash did TELUS spend on the purchase of capital assets in 2011?
h. How much was TELUS' amortization expense for software in 2011?

FS8-2. What was TELUS' net income for fiscal 2011? What was its cash from operations (CFO)? How do you explain the difference between net income and CFO? Based on your assessment of net income and CFO, did TELUS have a good year or a bad year in 2011? Based on the information provided, are you concerned about TELUS' liquidity position? Explain.

FS8-3. What amount of property, plant, and equipment does TELUS report on its December 31, 2011 balance sheet? What does the amount on the balance sheet represent (how would you explain what the amount means to a novice user of financial statements)? What proportion of TELUS' assets are capital assets? Why do you think the proportion and amount is so large? (When you answer, consider the nature of the business.) What was the net realizable value of TELUS' property, plant, and equipment on December 31, 2011?

FS8-4. How much property, plant, and equipment has TELUS contractually committed to purchase through 2013? How are these assets reflected on the December 31, 2011 balance sheet? Do you think this is an appropriate way to account for the prospective assets?

FS8-5. What amount of property, plant, and equipment does TELUS have that is fully depreciated but still in use? What is the carrying amount of this property, plant, and equipment? How is it possible that TELUS can still be using assets that are fully depreciated?

FS8-6. What is goodwill? How does it arise? How much goodwill did TELUS report on December 31, 2011? How does TELUS amortize its goodwill? How much new goodwill did TELUS add in 2011? Is it possible that TELUS has goodwill that isn't reported on its balance sheet? Explain.

FS8-7. What are intangible assets? How much of intangible assets did TELUS report on its December 31, 2011 balance sheet? What are the largest categories of TELUS' intangible assets? How are these intangible assets amortized? Why are some of TELUS' intangible assets not amortized?

EXHIBIT 8.4 TELUS Corporation: Extracts from the Financial Statements

CONSOLIDATED STATEMENTS OF FINANCIAL POSITION

(in millions)	Note	**December 31, 2011**	December 31, 2010 (adjusted–Note 25(d))	January 1, 2010 (Note 25(d))
Assets				
Current assets				
Cash and temporary investments, net		**$ 46**	$ 17	$ 41
Accounts receivable	24(a)	**1,428**	1,318	1,195
Income and other taxes receivable		**66**	62	16
Inventories	24(a)	**353**	283	270
Prepaid expenses		**144**	113	105
Derivative assets	4(h)	**14**	4	1
		2,051	1,797	1,628
Non-current assets				
Property, plant and equipment, net	15	**7,964**	7,831	7,832
Intangible assets, net	16	**6,153**	6,152	6,166
Goodwill, net	16	**3,661**	3,572	3,572
Other long-term assets	24(a)	**81**	235	286
Investments		**21**	37	41
		17,880	17,827	17,897
		$19,931	$19,624	$19,525
Liabilities and Owners' Equity				
Current liabilities				
Short-term borrowings	18	**$ 404**	$ 400	$ 500
Accounts payable and accrued liabilities	24(a)	**1,419**	1,477	1,336
Income and other taxes payable		**25**	6	174
Dividends payable	12	**188**	169	150
Advance billings and customer deposits	24(a)	**655**	658	530
Provisions	19	**88**	122	299
Current maturities of long-term debt	20	**1,066**	847	549
Current portion of derivative liabilities	4(h)	**—**	419	62
		3,845	4,098	3,600
Non-current liabilities				
Provisions	19	**122**	204	91
Long-term debt	20	**5,508**	5,209	5,623
Other long-term liabilities	24(a)	**1,343**	649	1,334
Deferred income taxes		**1,600**	1,683	1,522
		8,573	7,745	8,570
Liabilities		**12,418**	11,843	12,170
Owners' equity				
Common Share and Non-voting Share equity	21	**7,513**	7,759	7,334
Non-controlling interests		**—**	22	21
		7,513	7,781	7,355
		$19,931	$19,624	$19,525
Commitments and Contingent Liabilities	22			

The accompanying notes are an integral part of these consolidated financial statements.

EXHIBIT 8.4 (continued) TELUS Corporation: Extracts from the Financial Statements

CONSOLIDATED STATEMENTS OF INCOME AND OTHER COMPREHENSIVE INCOME

Years ended December 31 (millions except per share amounts)	Note	2011	2010
			(adjusted—Note 25(c))
Operating Revenues			
Service		**$ 9,606**	$ 9,131
Equipment		**719**	611
		10,325	9,742
Other operating income	6	**72**	50
		10,397	9,792
Operating Expenses			
Goods and services purchased		**4,726**	4,236
Employee benefits expense	7	**1,893**	1,906
Depreciation		**1,331**	1,339
Amortization of intangible assets		**479**	402
		8,429	7,883
Operating Income		**1,968**	1,909
Financing costs	8	**377**	522
Income before Income Taxes		**1,591**	1,387
Income taxes	9	**376**	335
Net Income		**1,215**	1,052
Other Comprehensive Income	10		
Items that may subsequently be reclassified to income			
Change in unrealized fair value of derivatives designated as cash flow hedges		**6**	54
Foreign currency translation adjustment arising from translating financial statements of foreign operations		**4**	—
		10	54
Item never subsequently reclassified to income			
Employee defined benefit plans actuarial gains (losses)		**(851)**	(214)
		(841)	(160)
Comprehensive Income		**$ 374**	$ 892
Net Income (Loss) Attributable To:			
Common Shares and Non-voting Shares		**$ 1,219**	$ 1,048
Non-controlling interests		**(4)**	4
		$ 1,215	$ 1,052
Total Comprehensive Income (Loss) Attributable To:			
Common Shares and Non-voting Shares		**$ 378**	$ 888
Non-controlling interests		**(4)**	4
		$ 374	$ 892

EXHIBIT 8.4 **(continued) TELUS Corporation: Extracts from the Financial Statements**

CONSOLIDATED STATEMENTS OF CASH FLOWS

Years ended December 31 (millions)	Note	2011	2010
			(adjusted—Note 25)
Operating Activities			
Net income		**$ 1,215**	$ 1,052
Adjustments to reconcile net income to cash provided by operating activities:			
Depreciation and amortization		**1,810**	1,741
Deferred income taxes		**205**	217
Share-based compensation	13	**(12)**	(30)
Net employee defined benefit plans expense	14(b)–(c)	**(32)**	(9)
Employer contributions to employee defined benefit plans		**(298)**	(140)
Gain on 51% Transactel (Barbados) Inc. interest re-measured at acquisition-date fair value and subsequent adjustment to contingent consideration	6, 16(e)	**(17)**	—
Other		**(66)**	(42)
Net change in non-cash operating working capital	24(b)	**(255)**	(119)
Cash provided by operating activities		**2,550**	2,670
Investing Activities			
Capital expenditures	5,15,16	**(1,847)**	(1,721)
Acquisitions and other	16(e)	**(110)**	—
Proceeds from the sale of property and other assets		**4**	10
Other		**—**	4
Net change in non-cash investing working capital		**(15)**	(24)
Cash used by investing activities		**(1,968)**	(1,731)
Financing Activities			
Non-voting Shares issued		**24**	15
Dividends paid to holders of Common Shares and Non-voting Shares	12(a)	**(642)**	(473)
Issuance and repayment of short-term borrowing	18	**4**	(100)
Long-term debt issued	20, 24(b)	**4,068**	3,725
Redemptions and repayment of long-term debt	20, 24(b)	**(3,946)**	(4,119)
Acquisition of additional equity interest in subsidiary from non-controlling interest	16(e)	**(51)**	—
Dividends paid by a subsidiary to non-controlling interest		**(4)**	(3)
Other		**(6)**	(8)
Cash used by financing activities		**(553)**	(963)
Cash Position			
Increase (decrease) in cash and temporary investments, net		**29**	(24)
Cash and temporary investments, net, beginning of period		**17**	41
Cash and temporary investments, net, end of period		**$ 46**	$ 17
Supplemental Disclosure of Cash Flows			
Interest (paid)	24(b)	**$ (378)**	$ (479)
Interest received		**$ 1**	$ 3
Income taxes (inclusive of Investment Tax Credits) (paid), net	9	**$ (150)**	$ (311)

The accompanying notes are an integral part of these consolidated financial statements.

EXHIBIT 8.4 (continued) TELUS Corporation: Extracts from the Financial Statements

1 SUMMARY OF SIGNIFICANT ACCOUNTING PRINCIPLES

Summary review of accounting policies and principles and the methods used in their application by the Company

(b) Use of estimates and judgements

The preparation of financial statements in conformity with generally accepted accounting principles requires management to make estimates, assumptions and judgements that affect: the reported amounts of assets and liabilities at the date of the financial statements; the disclosure of contingent assets and liabilities at the date of the financial statements; and the reported amounts of revenues and expenses during the reporting period. Actual results could differ from those estimates.

Estimates

Examples of significant estimates and assumptions include:

- the allowance for doubtful accounts;
- the allowance for inventory obsolescence;
- the estimated useful lives of assets;
- the recoverability of tangible assets;
- the recoverability of intangible assets with indefinite lives:
- the recoverability of goodwill;
- the recoverability of long-term investments;
- the amount and composition of income tax assets and income tax liabilities, including the amount of unrecognized tax benefits; and
- certain actuarial and economic assumptions used in determining defined benefit pension costs, accrued pension benefit obligations and pension plan assets.

Judgements

Examples of significant judgements, apart from those involving estimation, include:

- The Company's choice to depreciate and amortize its property, plant, equipment and intangible assets subject to amortization on a straight-line basis as it believes that this method reflects the consumption of resources related to the economic lifespan of those assets better than an accelerated method and is more representative of the economic substance of the underlying use of those assets.
- The Company's view that its spectrum licences granted by Industry Canada will likely be renewed by Industry Canada; that the Company intends to renew them; and that the Company believes it has the financial and operational ability to renew them and, thus, they are deemed to have an indefinite life, as discussed further in Note 16(c).

(g) Cost of acquisition and advertising costs

Costs of acquiring customers, that are expensed as incurred, include the total cost of hardware sold to customers, commissions, advertising and promotion related to the initial customer acquisition. Costs of acquiring customers, that are capitalized as incurred, include Company-owned hardware situated at customers' premises and associated installation costs. Costs of acquisition that are expensed are included in the Consolidated Statements of Income and Other Comprehensive Income as a component of Goods and services purchased except for commissions paid to Company employees, which are included as Employee benefits expense. Costs of advertising production, advertising airtime and advertising space are expensed as incurred.

(h) Research and development

Research and development costs are expensed except in cases where development costs meet certain identifiable criteria for capitalization. Capitalized development costs are amortized over the life the commercial production, or in the case of serviceable property, plant and equipment, are included in the appropriate property group and are depreciated over its estimated useful life.

(j) Depreciation, amortization and impairment

Depreciation and amortization

Assets are depreciated on a straight-line basis over their estimated useful lives as determined by a continuing program of asset life studies. Depreciation includes amortization of assets under finance leases and amortization of leasehold improvements. Leasehold improvements are normally amortized over the lesser of their expected average service life or the term of the lease. Intangible assets with finite lives (intangible assets subject to amortization) are amortized on a straight-line basis over their estimated lives; estimated lives are reviewed at least annually and are adjusted as appropriate.

Estimated useful lives for the majority of the Company's property, plant and equipment subject to depreciation are as follows:

	Estimated useful lives
Network assets:	
Outside plant	17 to 40 years
Inside plant	4 to 16 years
Wireless site equipment	6.5 to 8 years
Balance of depreciable property, plant and equipment	3 to 40 years

(1) The composite depreciation rate for the year ended December 31, 2011, was 5.0% (2010—5.1%). The rate is calculated by dividing depreciation expense by an average gross book value of depreciable assets for the reporting period. One result of this methodology is that the composite depreciation rate will be lower in a period that has a higher proportion of fully depreciated assets remaining in use (Note 15).

EXHIBIT 8.4 (continued) TELUS Corporation: Extracts from the Financial Statements

Estimated useful lives for the majority of the Company's intangible assets subject to amortization are as follows:

	Estimated useful lives
Wireline subscriber base	40 years
Customer contracts, related customer relationships and leasehold interests	6 to 10 years
Software	3 to 5 years
Access to rights-of-way and other	8 to 30 years

Impairment—general

Impairment testing compares the carrying values of the assets or cash-generating units being tested with their recoverable amounts (recoverable amounts being the greater of the assets' or cash-generating units' values in use or their fair values less costs to sell). Impairment losses are immediately recognized to the extent that the asset or cash-generating unit carrying values exceed their recoverable amounts. Should the recoverable amounts for previously impaired assets or cash-generating units subsequently increase, the impairment losses previously recognized (other than in respect of goodwill) may be reversed to the extent that the reversal is not a result of "unwinding of the discount" and that the resulting carrying value does not exceed the carrying value that would have been the result if no impairment losses had been previously recognized.

(r) Property, plant and equipment; intangible assets

General

Property, plant and equipment and intangible assets are recorded at historical cost and, with respect to self-constructed property, plant and equipment, include materials, direct labour and applicable overhead costs. With respect to internally developed, internal-use software, recorded historical costs include materials, direct labour and direct labour-related costs. Where property, plant and equipment construction projects are of a sufficient size and duration, an amount is capitalized for the cost of funds used to finance construction. The rate for calculating the capitalized financing costs is based on the Company's weighted-average cost of borrowing experienced during the reporting period.

When property, plant and/or equipment are sold by the Company, the net book value is netted against the sale proceeds and the difference, as set out in Note 6, is included in Consolidated Statements of Income and Other Comprehensive Income as Other operating income.

Asset retirement obligations

Provisions for liabilities, as set out in Note 19, are recognized for statutory, contractual or legal obligations, normally when incurred, associated with the retirement of property, plant and equipment (primarily certain items of outside plant and wireless site equipment) when those obligations result from the acquisition, construction, development and/or normal operation of the assets. The obligations are measured initially at fair value, determined using present value methodology, and the resulting costs are capitalized into the carrying amount of the related asset. In subsequent periods, the liability is adjusted for the accretion of discount, for any changes in the market-based discount rate and for any changes in the amount or timing of the underlying future cash flows. The capitalized asset retirement cost is depreciated on the same basis as the related asset and the discount accretion, as set out in Note 8, is included in the Consolidated Statements of Income and Other Comprehensive Income as a component of Financing costs.

FS8-8. TELUS is a fairly well-known brand name in Canada, yet it's not included among the company's intangible assets. Why not? Do you think the TELUS brand name should be reported as an asset? What would some of the problems be with recording the brand name as an asset? Can a brand name ever appear as an asset on a balance sheet? Explain how and why.

FS8-9. Accounting for property, plant, and equipment, intangible assets, and goodwill requires many estimates and the exercise of judgment by a company's management. What are some of the estimates and judgments that TELUS' management must make with respect to these assets? What are the challenges that TELUS' managers face when making these estimates and judgments (be specific—consider TELUS' business in your answer)? Is there any way that the judgment required could be reduced? What impact do estimates and judgment have on an entity's financial statements?

FS8-10. How does TELUS account for purchases of new property, plant, and equipment on its balance sheet? What method(s) does TELUS use to depreciate its property, plant, and equipment? What was TELUS' depreciation expense for property, plant, and equipment in 2011? How much depreciation had been accumulated against property, plant, and equipment on December 31, 2011? Why does TELUS depreciate its property, plant, and equipment (aside from the fact it's required by IFRS)? What does the carrying amount of TELUS' property, plant, and equipment tell you about what it could be sold for? What does the carrying amount tell you about what these assets are "worth" to TELUS?

EXHIBIT 8.4 (continued) TELUS Corporation: Extracts from the Financial Statements

15 PROPERTY, PLANT AND EQUIPMENT

Summary schedule of items comprising property, plant and equipment

(millions)	Network assets	Buildings and leasehold improvements	Assets under finance lease	Other	Land	Assets under construction	Total
	(adjusted—Note 25(d))						
At cost							
As at January 1, 2010	$22,141	$2,244	$13	$1,644	$ 49	$431	$26,522
Additions(1)	443	15	10	35	—	840	1,343
Dispositions, retirements and other	(568)	(13)	(2)	(182)	—	—	(765)
Reclassifications	675	105	—	53	—	(833)	—
As at December 31, 2010	22,691	2,351	21	1,550	49	438	27,100
Additions(1)	**502**	**19**	**1**	**41**	**7**	**887**	**1,457**
Additions arising from business acquisitions (Note 16(e))	—	**11**	—	**7**	—	—	**18**
Dispositions, retirements and other	**(206)**	**(7)**	**1**	**(51)**	**(1)**	—	**(264)**
Reclassifications	**779**	**99**	—	**75**	—	**(953)**	—
As at December 31, 2011	**$23,766**	**$2,473**	**$23**	**$1,622**	**$ 55**	**$372**	**$28,311**
Accumulated depreciation							
As at January 1, 2010	$16,040	$1,333	$ 9	$1,308	$—	$—	$18,690
Depreciation	1,088	118	2	131	—	—	1,339
Dispositions, retirements and other	(573)	(8)	(1)	(178)	—	—	(760)
As at December 31, 2010	16,555	1,443	10	1,261	—	—	19,269
Depreciation	**1,091**	**121**	**2**	**117**	—	—	**1,331**
Dispositions, retirements and other	**(218)**	**(4)**	**8**	**(39)**	—	—	**(253)**
As at December 31, 2011	**$17,428**	**$1,560**	**$20**	**$1,339**	**$—**	**$—**	**$20,347**
Net book value							
As at January 1, 2010	$ 6,101	$ 911	$ 4	$ 336	$ 49	$431	$ 7,832
As at December 31, 2010	$ 6,136	$ 908	$11	$ 289	$ 49	$438	$ 7,831
As at December 31, 2011	**$ 6,338**	**$ 913**	**$ 3**	**$ 283**	**$ 55**	**$372**	**$ 7,964**

(1) For the year ended December 31, 2011, additions include $15 (2010—$12) in respect of asset retirement obligations.

The gross carrying amount of fully depreciated property, plant and equipment that was still in use as at December 31, 2011, was $3.0 billion (December 31, 2010—$3.0 billion; January 1, 2010—$2.6 billion).

As at December 31, 2011, the Company's contractual commitments for the acquisition of property, plant and equipment were $188 million over a period through to 2013 (December 31, 2010—$170 million over a period through to 2013).

EXHIBIT 8.4 (continued) TELUS Corporation: Extracts from the Financial Statements

16 INTANGIBLE ASSETS AND GOODWILL

Summary schedule of items comprising intangible assets, including goodwill and review of reported fiscal year acquisitions from which goodwill arose

(a) Intangible assets and goodwill, net

	Intangible assets subject to amortization						Intangible assets with indefinite lives					
(millions)	Subscriber base	Customer contracts, related customer relationships and lease-hold interests	Software	Access to rights-of-way and other	Assets under construction	Total	Spectrum licences	Acquired brand	Total	Total intangible assets	Goodwill[1]	Total intangible assets and goodwill
							(adjusted – Note 25(d))					
At cost												
As at January 1, 2010	$245	$137	$2,408	$104	$ 158	$3,052	$4,867	$ 7	$4,874	$ 7,926	$3,936	$11,862
Additions	—	—	38	8	344	390	—	—	—	390	—	390
Dispositions, retirements and other	—	—	(213)	—	—	(213)	—	—	—	(213)	—	(213)
Reclassifications	—	—	262	—	(262)	—	—	—	—	—	—	—
As at December 31, 2010	245	137	2,495	112	240	3,229	4,867	7	4,874	8,103	3,936	12,039
Additions	—	—	**39**	**4**	**347**	**390**	—	—	—	**390**	—	**390**
Additions arising from business acquisitions (e)	—	**60**	**1**	—	—	**61**	—	—	—	**61**	**110**	**171**
Dispositions, retirements and other	—	—	**(256)**	**(23)**	—	**(279)**	—	—	—	**(279)**	**(21)**	**(300)**
Reclassifications	—	—	**422**	—	**(422)**	—	—	—	—	—	—	—
As at December 31, 2011	**$245**	**$197**	**$2,701**	**$ 93**	**$ 165**	**$3,401**	**$4,867**	**$ 7**	**$4,874**	**$ 8,275**	**$4,025**	**$12,300**
Accumulated amortization												
As at January 1, 2010	$ 52	$ 27	$1,605	$ 76	$ —	$1,760	$ —	$—	$ —	$ 1,760	$ 364	$ 2 124
Amortization	6	14	378	4	—	402	—	—	—	402	—	402
Dispositions, retirements and other	—	—	(211)	—	—	(211)	—	—	—	(211)	—	(211)
As at December 31, 2010	58	41	1,772	80	—	1,951	—	—	—	1,951	364	2,315
Amortization[2]	**6**	**19**	**431**	**4**	—	**460**	—	—	—	**460**	**19**	**479**
Dispositions, retirements and other	—	—	**(267)**	**(22)**	—	**(289)**	—	—	—	**(289)**	**(19)**	**(308)**
As at December 31, 2011	**$ 64**	**$ 60**	**$1,936**	**$ 62**	**$ —**	**$2,122**	**$ —**	**$—**	**$ —**	**$ 2,122**	**$ 364**	**$ 2,486**
Net book value												
As at January 1, 2010	$193	$110	$ 803	$ 28	$ 158	$1,292	$4,867	$ 7	$4,874	$ 6,166	$3,572	$ 9,738
As at December 31 2010	$187	$ 96	$ 723	$ 32	$ 240	$1,278	$4,867	$ 7	$4,874	$ 6,152	$3,572	$ 9,724
As at December 31, 2011	**$181**	**$137**	**$ 765**	**$ 31**	**$ 165**	**$1,279**	**$4,867**	**$ 7**	**$4,874**	**$6,1 53**	**$3,661**	**$ 9,814**

(1) Accumulated amortization of goodwill is amortization recorded prior to 2002.

(2) Includes a goodwill impairment relating to an immaterial Wireline segment subsidiary classified as held for sale at, and disposed of subsequent to, December 31, 2011.

EXHIBIT 8.4 (continued) TELUS Corporation: Extracts from the Financial Statements

The gross carrying amount of fully amortized intangible assets subject to amortization that were still in use as at December 31, 2011, was $662 million (December 31, 2010—$772 million; January 1, 2010—$752 million).

(b) Intangible assets subject to amortization

Estimated aggregate amortization expense for intangible assets subject to amortization, calculated for such assets held as at December 31, 2011, for each the next five fiscal years is as follows:

Years ending December 31 (millions)	
2012	$406
2013	248
2014	104
2015	44
2016	32

As at December 31, 2011, the Company's contractual commitments for the acquisition of intangible assets were $142 million over a period through to 2018 (December 31, 2010—$134 million over a period thought to 2018).

(c) Intangible assets with indefinite lives—spectrum licences

The Company's intangible assets with indefinite lives include spectrum licences granted by Industry Canada. Industry Canada's spectrum licence policy terms indicate that the spectrum licences will likely be renewed. The Company's spectrum licences are expected to be renewed every 20 years (December 31, 2010—every 5 years or every 10 years; January 1, 2010—every 5 years or every 10 years) following a review by Industry Canada of the Company's compliance with licence terms. In addition to current usage, the Company's licensed spectrum can be used for planned and new technologies. As a result of the combination of these significant factors, the Company's spectrum licences are currently considered to have indefinite lives.

FS8-11. What was TELUS' return on assets for the years ended December 31, 2011 and 2010? Interpret the ratios you calculated.

FS8-12. By simply looking at TELUS' balance sheet, do you think that it would be easy to get into its business? Explain why or why not.

ENDNOTES

1. Extracted from West Fraser Timber Co. Ltd.'s 2011 annual financial statements.
2. Extracted from BCE Inc.'s 2011 audited financial statements.
3. Extracted from Supremex Inc.'s 2011 annual financial statements.
4. Data obtained from "Financial Post Industry Report," at the Financial Post Web site, http://www.fpdata.finpost.com/suite/autologreports.asp.
5. Adapted from TELUS Corporation's Web site and reproduced with permission from TELUS Corporation.
6. Extracted from TELUS Corporation's 2011 annual financial statements and reproduced with permission from TELUS Corporation.

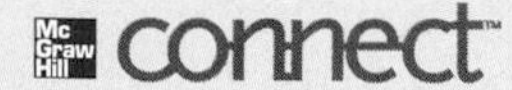

Practise and learn online with Connect. Connect resources include additional and interactive study exercises, videos, and practice quizzing, as well as additional material you won't find in the printed text.

CHAPTER 9

Liabilities

LEARNING OBJECTIVES

After studying the material in this chapter you will be able to do the following:

LO 1 Explain what liabilities are and how they are valued.

LO 2 Describe the nature and type of current liabilities and how they are accounted for.

LO 3 Recognize the characteristics of bonds, mortgages, and other forms of long-term debt. Determine the value of bonds and understand how they are accounted for. Calculate mortgage payments and the amount of interest and principal paid each period.

LO 4 Explain the fundamentals of leasing and how leases are accounted for and reported in the financial statements.

LO 5 Characterize the basics of pensions and pension accounting.

LO 6 Recognize the nature of contingencies, commitments, and subsequent events, and understand the reporting issues surrounding them.

LO 7 Analyze and interpret information about liabilities in financial statements.

LO 8 Describe deferred income taxes and explain how they arise (Appendix).

Dollarama Inc.

Some shoppers say walking into a Dollarama store can be dangerous . . . to their wallets!

With an average of 4,000 products in every store, it's nearly impossible for some customers not to be tempted to add a couple of everyday household items like ponytail elastics and a new glass cutting board for the kitchen to their shopping cart, even though the original reason for visiting the store was just to pick up some Mother's Day cards.

The Quebec-based retail giant now counts over 720 stores across Canada, and is opening a new store every week. Despite the $1 Loonie symbol on the company's green and yellow signs, in 2009 management decided to expand their price range upwards and now sells items for up to $2. In June 2012, Dollarama announced the gradual introduction of items at $2.50 and $3 price points.

Though spending a little bit of extra money at Dollarama once in a while might not cause too serious a problem for customers at the end of the month, overdoing it could put some of them in debt. Company officials at head office in Montreal are also very careful how they manage their corporate debt.

Financial statements released by Dollarama in April 2012 show that the company's total debt for the 2012 fiscal year was $275 million, an improvement from $366 million in fiscal 2011.

The company explained that the debt was mainly money borrowed from banks and a syndicate of private equity companies. Dollarama used the money from the loan to expand, including buying inventory. In fiscal 2012, it opened 52 new stores.

The loan doesn't all have to be paid back right away: the company negotiated an extension until 2015, and obtained lower interest rates on the money.

Dollarama has other liabilities that it must account for, besides debt:

- Dollarama employs over 14,000 employees around the country, plus over 300 head office employees on Royalmount Avenue and at several Montreal-area warehouses.
- Dollarama also offers a pension plan to its workers, a plan its Web site calls "one of best available in the industry," into which the company pays up to $3,000 a year per person, depending on the person's salary.

- When customers pay for their purchases, they also have to pay provincial or federal sales taxes. Dollarama has to fork over the money it collected in taxes and send it to government revenue departments.
- Since Dollarama sometimes buys its products, including batteries, magnets and school supplies, on credit, its liabilities also include $31 million in outstanding invoices still payable.
- Dollarama's liability for leases was nearly $650 million in 2012.

This is one item that isn't on the balance sheet, but is still a sizable commitment.

Most of Dollarama's stores are located in strip malls, and the company prefers to rent the premises, rather than buy its own real estate. It gives them flexibility to close or move if business conditions change. The same goes for head office and the warehouses and distribution centre. Dollarama typically enters into store leases with base terms of ten years and options to renew for one or more periods of five years each.

—E.B.

LO 1

INTRODUCTION: WHAT ARE LIABILITIES?

Liabilities are obligations to provide cash, goods, or services to customers, suppliers, employees, governments, lenders, and anyone else an entity "owes something to." Liabilities can be classified as current—for example, wages owed to employees or payments that must be made to suppliers for recently delivered goods or services—or long-term; for example, Rogers Communications Inc. has $400 million in notes that don't have to be paid until 2041. Many liabilities are straightforward to understand and measure; for example, amounts owed to suppliers and creditors can be traced back to invoices or loan agreements. Other liabilities are very complex. There are also obligations that aren't recorded on the balance sheet at all.

Liabilities are a significant part of most entities' balance sheets. Although not all companies use debt to finance their operations, virtually all will have some liabilities simply because not all purchases are for cash. Table 9.1 shows the amount and proportion of liabilities of a number of Canadian companies. Notice how much the ratio of liabilities to assets varies. Magna International Inc. finances its assets with about 44 percent debt whereas High Liner Foods' debt is

TABLE 9.1 Amount of Liabilities in Different Companies

Company	Type of business	Dollar amount of current liabilities	Dollar amount of non-current liabilities	Liabilities as a proportion of assets	Current liabilities as a proportion of total liabilities
High Liner Foods Incorporated (12/31/2011)	Food processing	$ 236,598,000	$ 292,410,000	76.6%	44.7%
Indigo Books & Music Inc. (3/31/2012)	Retail	229,503,000	7,401,000	34.7%	96.9%
Loblaw Companies Limited (12/31/2011)	Grocery retail	4,718,000,000	6,703,000,000	65.5%	41.3%
Magna International Inc. (12/31/2011)*	Auto parts maker	5,724,000,000	753,000,000	44.1%	88.4%
Tim Hortons Inc. (1/1/2012)	Fast food service	476,650,000	572,867,000	47.6%	45.4%
WestJet Airlines Ltd. (12/31/2011)	Airline	941,857,000	1,161,604,000	60.6%	44.8%

*Magna's inventory amount is stated in U.S. dollars.

Note: Information for all companies is prepared in accordance with IFRS, except for Magna International and Tim Hortons, which are prepared in accordance with U.S. generally accepted accounting principles.

almost 77 percent. The relative amount of current liabilities also varies. Almost all of Indigo's liabilities are current; it has very little long-term debt, whereas about 41 percent of Loblaw's liabilities are current.

An entity's liquidity and solvency are assessed using information about its liabilities. Liabilities are claims on an entity's cash and other resources, so stakeholders may need to know whether there are adequate resources to meet these claims. In the longer term, they need to assess whether an entity will be able to meet its obligations as they come due (in other words, is the entity solvent?). Liabilities are usually not negotiable—they have to be paid regardless of whether an entity is doing well or poorly. If an entity can't meet its obligations it will likely face legal and/or economic consequences.

The IFRS definition of a liability is straightforward: liabilities are obligations arising from past transactions or economic events that require sacrificing economic resources to settle. But don't be deceived by the simplicity of this definition. Accounting for some liabilities involves applying very complex rules; accounting for leases, pensions, and deferred income taxes are among the most difficult accounting topics.

Let's apply the IFRS definition to three different obligations.

1. An amount owed to a supplier for inventory purchased—an account payable.
   - Obligation: The entity must pay for the inventory purchased from the supplier.
   - Past transaction or economic event: The supplier has provided the inventory.
   - Economic sacrifice: The supplier has to be paid, most likely with cash.
2. A customer pays in advance for a service to be delivered at a later date—unearned revenue.
   - Obligation: The entity must provide the goods or services already paid for by the customer.
   - Past transaction or economic event: The customer has paid.
   - Economic sacrifice: The entity must provide the paid-for goods or services.
3. A customer is given a two-year warranty on a purchased item—an accrued liability/provision.
   - Obligation: Provide warranty service as required to the customer.
   - Past transaction or economic event: Purchase of the warrantied item by the customer.
   - Economic sacrifice: Warranty service must be provided.

You should be able to apply this definition to each type of liability we examine in the chapter to understand why it's considered a liability.

In principle, liabilities are valued at their present value. (Suggestion: Review time value of money in Chapter 6.) For most liabilities, the timing and amount of the cash flows are known or can be estimated. It's also possible to identify an appropriate discount rate. Long-term liabilities are valued at the present value of the cash flows they will pay. However, not all liabilities are discounted to their present value. Current liabilities aren't discounted because the impact is usually immaterial. (That is, the present value of an account payable to be paid in 30 days would be almost the same as the undiscounted amount.) Also, liabilities that don't represent an actual amount of money to be paid aren't discounted; for example, unearned revenue isn't discounted because it represents an obligation to deliver goods and services, not cash.

CURRENT LIABILITIES

LO 2

Current liabilities are obligations that will be satisfied in one year or one operating cycle. Information about current obligations is important for assessing the short-term liquidity of an entity. As I mentioned, current liabilities are usually not discounted to their present value. In this section, we will look at a number of different types of current liabilities and discuss the issues that affect accounting for them.

Bank and Other Current Loans

Loans are reported as current liabilities if the amount must be repaid within the next year or operating cycle. Many bank loans are classified as current even if there is no specific requirement for payment within a year or an operating cycle. These **demand loans** are classified as current because the lender can ask for repayment at any time, even though it may have no intention of doing so, and the loans remain on the books for a long time. Entities can also have short-term borrowing arrangements to meet day-to-day operating needs. A **line of credit** from a lender allows an entity to borrow up to a specified maximum amount whenever it requires the money. A line of credit is only classified as a liability if money is actually borrowed.

Accounts Payable

Accounts payable are amounts owed to suppliers for goods and services. Goods and services include anything the entity uses in the course of its operations, including inventory, supplies, utilities, cleaning services, and labour. We have seen numerous examples of recording and settling accounts payable throughout this book. Measuring the amount of accounts payable is usually not difficult because the recording is triggered by an invoice from the supplier. On most balance sheets, accounts payable is highly aggregated, capturing all amounts owed to suppliers.

Collections on Behalf of Third Parties

Most entities act as tax collectors for various government taxation authorities. For example, when we purchase merchandise in a store, the GST (goods and services tax) and provincial sales tax in some provinces, or the HST (harmonized sales tax), is added to the purchase price. Employers withhold amounts from their employees' pay for income taxes, employment insurance, and Canada or Quebec Pension Plans. Employers also withhold amounts for items such as employee shares of benefits, union dues, pension plan contributions, and charitable donations.

The money withheld doesn't belong to the entity. The amounts must be sent to the appropriate government agency, union, pension plan, and so on, and a liability reflects the obligation. For example, suppose a shopper in Alberta buys a plasma TV at Future Shop for $2,200. In addition to charging $2,200 for the TV, Future Shop also collects $110 of GST. This entry would be made to record the sale (assuming the purchase paid for in cash):

Dr. Cash (assets +)	2,310	
Cr. Revenue (revenue +, shareholders' equity +)		2,200
Cr. GST payable (liabilities +)		110
To record the sale of merchandise and collection of GST		

The $110 is a liability because the money doesn't belong to Future Shop; it belongs to the government. The GST isn't included in revenue. When Future Shop remits the money to the government, it would make the following entry:

Dr. GST payable (liabilities −)	110	
Cr. Cash (assets −)		110
To record remittance of GST to the government		

An entity must also record liabilities when it withholds money from an employee's pay, again because the money withheld doesn't belong to the employer. For example, Mr. Barrows is a crane operator for Eyremore Inc. (Eyremore). Mr. Barrows earned $7,000 in May. From his May paycheque, Eyremore withheld $2,000 for income taxes, $240.40 for Canada Pension Plan (CPP), $195.50 for Employment Insurance (EI), and $90 in union dues.

The journal entry that Eyremore would make to record Mr. Barrows' wages and the withholdings is:

Dr. Wages expense (expenses +, shareholders' equity −)	7,000.00	
Cr. Income taxes payable—employee (liabilities +)		2,000.00
Cr. CPP payable (liabilities +)		240.40
Cr. EI payable (liabilities +)		195.50
Cr. Union dues payable (liabilities +)		90.00
Cr. Cash (assets −)		4,474.10
To record wages and employee withholdings		

Of his $7,000 in wages, Mr. Barrows receives $3,868. The rest is collected and distributed on his behalf. When Eyremore sends the money owed to the appropriate parties, it would make the following entry:

Dr. Income taxes payable—employee (liabilities −)	2,000.00	
Dr. CPP payable (liabilities −)	240.40	
Dr. EI payable (liabilities −)	195.50	
Dr. Union dues payable (liabilities −)	90.00	
Cr. Cash (assets −)		2,525.90
To record remittance of payroll withholdings		

Amounts collected on behalf of third parties are usually not disclosed separately but would be included in accounts payable.

Income Taxes Payable

Canadian businesses pay tax on their income to both the federal and provincial governments. Most businesses pay instalments based on the estimated amount of tax they will owe for the year. A corporation pays taxes on its income and must file a tax return within six months of its fiscal year-end. An unincorporated business's income is included in the proprietor or partner's tax return. In an entity's financial statements, the amount of income taxes owed is accrued. The amount accrued is the difference between the estimated amount of income tax for the year and the amount already paid.

Dividends Payable

Dividends payable is an obligation to pay the corporation's shareholders a dividend that has been declared. Once the board of directors has declared a dividend, the amount of the dividend is classified as a liability until it's paid.

Accrued Liabilities and Provisions

An accrued expense and liability are recorded (with an adjusting journal entry) when an entity incurs an expense with no external event such as receipt of an invoice to trigger recording it. A **provision** is similar to this, except there is more uncertainty about the timing and amount of the liability. Examples of accrued liabilities and provisions include

- wages and salaries for employees unpaid at the end of a period (accrued liability)
- interest costs incurred but not payable until a later period (accrued liability)
- goods and services acquired but not invoiced (and not recorded) (accrued liability)
- warranty liabilities (provision)
- liabilities for affinity programs (e.g., airline frequent flyer programs) (provision)
- liabilities to redeem coupons (e.g., discount coupons for grocery products, Canadian Tire money) (provision)

All of these examples require management to estimate the amount of the expense and associated liability. Accrued liabilities can be estimated fairly accurately. For example, accrued wages and salaries can be based on the number of hours worked or proportion of salary earned from the end of the last pay period to the end of the reporting period.

Provisions are more difficult to estimate. For example, managers must estimate the average cost of warranty service. For frequent flyer programs, it's necessary to estimate the number of outstanding miles that will be redeemed and the cost of the rewards the customer will receive. For coupon distributions, it's necessary to estimate the coupon redemption rate. In all of these examples there is the potential for significant errors. Accrued liabilities and

EXHIBIT 9.1 RONA Inc.: Provisions

RONA Inc.
Consolidated Statements of Financial Position
as at December 25, 2011, December 26, 2011 and December 28, 2009
(in thousands of Canadian dollars)

	2011 December 25	2010 December 26	2009 December 28
Liabilities			
Current			
Bank loans	**$ 4,377**	$ 1,943	$ 5,211
Trade and other payables	**487,864**	454,166	409,764
Dividends payable	**2,527**	9,119	–
Current tax liabilities	**–**	3,379	–
Derivative financial instruments (Note 25)	**691**	1,653	776
Provisions (Note 20)	**6,947**	4,625	7,002
Instalments on long-term debt (Note 18)	**20,257**	21,151	9,996
Current liabilities	**522,663**	496,036	432,749
Non-current			
Long-term debt (Note 18)	**232,073**	444,333	430,524
Other non-current liabilities (Note 19)	**33,653**	30,601	27,859
Provisions (Note 20)	**3,606**	4,539	10,762
Deferred tax liabilities (Note 7)	**32,759**	34,314	27,724
Total liabilities	**824,754**	1,009,823	929,618

3. Significant accounting policies

(o) Provisions, contingent liabilities and contingent assets

Provisions are recognized when the Corporation has a present legal or constructive obligation as a result of past events for an amount that can be estimated reliably, and it is likely than an outflow of economic resources will be required to settle the obligation. Provisions that expire in more than 12 months are determined by discounting expected future cash flows if the effect of discounting is material, at a pre-tax rate that reflects market assessment of the time value of money and the risks specific to the liability.

A provision for an onerous contract is recognized when the economic benefits expected to be received under the contract are less than the unavoidable costs of meeting the obligations under the contract. The provision is measured at the present value of the lower of the expected cost of terminating or performing the contract. Before establishing a provision, the Corporation recognizes any impairment loss that has occurred on the assets dedicated to that contract.

provisions can have non-current as well as current components. Carmakers, for instance, offer warranties of three or more years on their vehicles. The warranty cost must be estimated for each year.

Exhibit 9.1 provides an example of a provision reported in RONA Inc.'s[1] financial statement. Note 3(o) explains the nature and measurement of provisions. Note 20 provides a table that reconciles the three categories of provisions—litigation, onerous contracts, and product warranties—from December 26, 2010 to December 25, 2011. The nature of the litigation and onerous contracts are described at the bottom of Note 20. The reconciliation shows the amount of the provision added to the balance during the period (called "provisions created") and the amount of provision used. Provisions are reversed when management removes a provision from the financial statements that it believes won't be incurred. The total column in Note 20 corresponds with the amounts shown as liabilities on the balance sheet.

www.rona.ca

EXHIBIT 9.1 (continued) RONA Inc.: Provisions

A provision for restructuring costs is recognized when the Corporation has established a detailed formal plan for the restructuring and the Corporation has started to implement or has publicly announced the restructuring. There is no provision for future operating losses.

A guarantee provision is recognized when the related goods or services are sold. The provision is based on historical data on guarantees.

Provisions are reviewed at the end of each reporting period and are adjusted to reflect the best estimates at that date.

Total provisions equals the sum of current and non-current provisions on the balance sheet.

20. Provisions and contingent liabilities

	Litigation	Onerous contracts	Product warranties	Total
Balance, December 26, 2010	$ 3,222	$ 5,757	$ 185	$ 9,164
Provisions created during the period	3,006	368	1,153	4,527
Provisions used during the period	(1,098)	(638)	(59)	(1,795)
Provisions reversed during the period	(1,338)	–	(228)	(1,566)
Accretion expense	–	223	–	223
Balance, December 25, 2011	3,792	5,710	1,051	10,553
Current	3,792	2,104	1,051	6,947
Non-current	–	3,606	–	3,606
	$ 3,792	$ 5,710	$ 1,051	$ 10,553

Corresponds with provisions classified as non-current on the balance sheet.

Corresponds with provisions classified as non-current on the balance sheet.

Litigation

Various claims and litigation arise in the course of the Corporation's activities and its insurers have taken up the Corporation's defence in some of these cases.

The litigation period depends on the negotiation procedures. Provisions are recognized based on best estimates of the resolution of the litigation. Management does not expect that the outcome of these claims and litigation will have a material and adverse effect on the Corporation's results and deemed its allowances adequate in this regard.

Onerous contracts

In 2008, the Corporation's management approved a detailed closure plan for two stores in the retail and commercial segment. One store was closed during 2008 and the second during the second quarter of 2009. Following the closure, a provision for onerous contracts was recognized for non-cancellable operating leases for commercial stores which are no longer used at a 4.65% discount rate (5.50% in 2010). The provisions were estimated using market data and contractual obligations at the time of initial recognition. In 2010, an agreement was reached with one lessor to cancel the lease. The lease still in effect expires in 2024.

INSIGHT

Accounting Estimates

Estimating is integral to accounting. Simply because some amounts are difficult to estimate doesn't mean they shouldn't be made, or that they don't provide useful information to stakeholders. It is, however, important to be aware that estimates are imprecise and that they do affect financial statement numbers. In addition, because the actual amounts are uncertain, difficult-to-estimate accruals are attractive for earnings management. Remember in Chapter 6 we discussed how managers can use hidden reserves to manage earnings. Managers can also use estimates of warranty costs or coupon usage in this way. For example, to smooth their income over time, managers could make slightly higher warranty or coupon expenses in years where net income was higher (to lower income) and make slightly lower warranty or coupon expenses in years where net income was lower (to increase income). Management can do this because it's very difficult to be precise with many of the estimates that must be made.

Unearned Revenue

When an entity receives cash in advance of providing goods or services, it has an obligation to provide those goods or services. Since cash is in hand but revenue hasn't been recognized, a liability for the amount received is required. Examples of unearned revenue include

- advance rent payments received by a property owner
- deposits for future goods and services
- tickets purchased for upcoming sporting events, concerts, and the theatre
- gift cards

For example, on December 4, 2017, Mr. Wayne purchased a $100 gift card at Dromore Books Ltd. (Dromore) for his daughter. The gift card entitles the holder to purchase books worth up to $100 but can't be exchanged for cash. Dromore would make the following entry to record the sale:

Dr. Cash (assets +)	100	
Cr. Unearned revenue—gift card (liabilities +)		100
To record the sale of a gift card on December 4, 2017		

When Mr. Wayne's daughter uses the gift card, Dromore would make the following entry:

Dr. Unearned revenue—gift card (liabilities −)	100	
Cr. Revenue (revenue +, shareholders' equity +)		100
To record the use of a $100 gift card		

www.chapters.indigo.ca

Since the gift card can be used at any time, the liability is classified as current even though it might not be used in the next year. An interesting problem with gift cards is how to deal with the fact that not all gift cards sold are redeemed. Exhibit 9.2 shows how Indigo Books & Music deals with this problem.[2] Indigo estimates the amount of gift cards that won't be redeemed (called breakage) and includes the amount in revenue (the journal entry debits liabilities and credits revenue).

Disclosure

IFRS's disclosure requirements for current liabilities are quite general and the financial statements of public companies show a wide variation in classification and detail provided. Current liabilities must be segregated by main class (i.e., bank loans, accounts payable and accrued liabilities, taxes payable, unearned revenue, current portion of long-term debt, and so on). Detailed disclosure on provisions, similar to RONA's in Exhibit 9.1, is also required. Most entities segregate current and non-current liabilities, although IFRS allow entities to present assets and liabilities in order of liquidity without classifying them as current or non-current, in certain circumstances.

KNOWLEDGE CHECK 9.1

- ❑ According to IFRS, what is the definition of a liability?
- ❑ What is a current liability? Why might stakeholders want to know the amount of current liabilities?
- ❑ Explain why amounts owing to employees should be considered a liability.

EXHIBIT 9.2

Indigo Books & Music Inc.: Accrued Liabilities

Consolidated Balance Sheets

(Unaudited)

(thousands of Canadian dollars)	As at December 31, 2011	As at January 1, 2011	As at April 2, 2011
LIABILITIES AND EQUITY			
Current			
Accounts payable and accrued liabilities	241,553	256,432	180,899
Unredeemed gift card liability	60,959	57,094	40,991
Provisions	–	33	–
Deferred revenue	12,110	12,639	11,528
Income taxes payable	310	–	657
Notes payable (note 16)	5,224	–	–
Current portion of long-term debt	1,163	1,302	1,290
Liabilities associated with assets held for sale (note 17)	114,400	–	–
Total current liabilities	435,719	327,500	235,365
Long-term accrued liabilities	4,820	6,822	6,284
Long-term debt	1,327	2,081	1,995
Total liabilities	441,866	336,403	243,644

Gift cards

The Company sells gift cards to its customers and recognizes the revenue as gift cards are redeemed. The Company also recognizes revenue from unredeemed gift cards ("gift card breakage") if the likelihood of gift card redemption by the customer is considered to be remote. The Company determines its average gift card breakage rate based on historical redemption rates. Once the breakage rate is determined, the resulting revenue is recognized over the estimated period of redemption based on historical redemption patterns, commencing when the gift cards are sold. Gift card breakage is included in revenues in the Company's consolidated statements of earnings and comprehensive earnings.

BONDS AND OTHER FORMS OF LONG-TERM DEBT

LO 3

www.westjet.com

Debt is amounts borrowed and owed by an entity. Debt can be long-term (**non-current**) or current. Exhibit 9.3 provides information about the long-term debt of WestJet Airlines Ltd. On December 31, 2011, WestJet reported long-term debt of $828,712,000, of which $158,832,000 was classified as current because it was due to be repaid within the next year.[3] Many entities use long-term debt to finance their businesses. WestJet uses debt mainly to finance aircraft purchases.

Debt comes in all shapes and sizes. Money can be borrowed from banks. Debt can be issued to the public at large or to private organizations such as insurance companies or pension funds. Borrowers can provide receivables, inventory, equipment, buildings, or land to lenders as collateral for loans. The **collateral** is protection for the lenders should the borrower not repay the loan. In that event, the lenders get the collateral or the proceeds from its sale. The interest rate on debt can be fixed or it can vary with changes in interest rates in the economy. The interest rate of a **variable-rate loan** varies with market conditions while the rate of a **fixed-rate loan** doesn't change. The period the debt is outstanding can be long or short. In sum, a debt arrangement includes whatever terms the borrowers and lenders agree on. Note 10 in Exhibit 9.3 describes the terms of WestJet's long-term debt.

The following are examples of debt instruments:

- **bond**—a formal borrowing arrangement in which a borrower agrees to make periodic interest payments to lenders as well as repay the principal at a specified time in the future
- **debenture**—a bond with no collateral provided to the lenders
- **mortgage**—a loan that provides the borrower's property as collateral
- **note payable**—a formal obligation signed by the borrower, promising to repay a debt

EXHIBIT 9.3 WestJet Airlines Ltd.: Long-Term Debt

Consolidated Statement of Financial Position
(Stated in thousands of Canadian dollars)

	Note	December 31 2011	December 31 2010	January 1 2010
Liabilities and shareholders' equity				
Current liabilities:				
Accounts payable and accrued liabilities	20	307,279	287,710	228,911
Advance ticket sales	20	432,186	336,926	297,720
Non-refundable guest credits	20	43,485	36,381	63,164
Current portion of long-term debt	10	158,832	178,337	165,111
Current portion of obligations under finance leases	11	75	108	744
		941,857	839,462	755,650
Non-current liabilities:				
Maintenance provisions	9	151,645	113,206	97,722
Long-term debt	10	669,880	848,465	1,028,165
Obligations under finance leases	11	3,174	3,249	3,358
Other liabilities	20	10,449	8,958	9,517
Deferred income tax	12	326,456	266,407	223,509
Total liabilities		2,103,461	2,079,747	2,117,921

Notes to Consolidated Financial Statements

For the years ended December 31, 2011 and 2010
(Stated in thousands of Canadian dollars, except share and per share amounts)

10. Long-term debt

	December 31 2011	December 31 2010	January 1 2010
Term loans—purchased aircraft [(i)]	828,104	985,571	1,142,304
Term loan—purchased aircraft [(ii)]	–	25,729	33,207
Term loan—flight simulator [(iii)]	–	5,575	6,392
Term loan—live satellite television equipment [(iv)]	–	41	493
Term loan—Calgary hangar facility [(v)]	–	8,707	9,202
Term loan—Calgary hangar facility [(vi)]	608	1,179	1,678
	828,712	1,026,802	1,193,276
Current portion	158,832	178,337	165,111
	669,880	848,465	1,028,165

(i) 52 individual term loans, amortized over a 12-year term, repayable in quarterly principal instalments totaling $40,676, at an effective weighted average fixed rate of 5.96%, maturing between 2014 and 2020. These facilities are guaranteed by Ex-Im Bank and secured by one 800-series aircraft, 38 700-series aircraft and 13 600-series aircraft.

(ii) US dollar denominated term loan paid in full in November 2011. Total amount settled was US $21,804 which consisted of US $21,571 in aggregate outstanding principal of the loan and US $233 in transaction costs on the loan accrued to the scheduled payoff date. This facility was secured by one 800 series aircraft.

(iii) Five-year term loan matured in September 2011 with a final payment of $5,123. This facility was secured by one flight simulator.

(iv) Five-year term loan matured in January 2011 with a final payment of $41. This facility was for the purchase of live satellite television equipment, was guaranteed by the Ex-Im Bank and was secured by certain 700-series and 600-series aircraft.

(v) Ten-year term loan matured in April 2011 with a final payment of $8,575. This facility was secured by the Calgary hangar.

(vi) Term loan repayable in monthly instalments of $50, including floating interest at the bank's prime rate plus 0.50%, with an effective interest rate of 3.50% as at December 31, 2011, maturing April 2013, secured by the Calgary hangar facility.

EXHIBIT **9.3** **(continued) WestJet Airlines Ltd.: Long-Term Debt**

Future scheduled repayments of long-term debt as at December 31, 2011 are as follows:

Within 1 year	158,832
1–3 years	319,100
3–5 years	222,194
Over 5 years	128,586
	828,712

Held within the special-purpose entities, as identified in note 1, Summary of significant accounting policies, are liabilities of $842,976 (December 31, 2010—$1,005,719; January 1, 2010—$1,168,907) related to the acquisition of the 52 purchased aircraft and live satellite television equipment, which are included above in the long-term debt balances.

17. Financial instruments and risk management

(a) Fair value of financial assets and financial liabilities

The Corporation's financial assets and liabilities consist primarily of cash and cash equivalents, accounts receivable, derivatives both designated and not designated in an effective hedging relationship, deposits, accounts payable and accrued liabilities, long-term debt and obligations under finance leases. The following tables set out the Corporation's classification and carrying amount, together with the fair value, for each type of financial asset and financial liability as at December 31, 2011 and 2010, and January 1, 2010:

	Fair value		Amortized cost		Totals	
December 31, 2011	Through profit or loss	Derivatives	Loans and receivables	Other financial liabilities	Carrying amount	Fair value
Asset (liability):						
Cash and cash equivalents (i)	1,291,946	–	–	–	1,291,946	1,291,946
Accounts receivable	–	–	34,122	–	34,122	34,122
Foreign exchange derivatives (ii)	–	4,662	–	–	4,662	4,662
Fuel derivatives (iii)	–	7,611	–	–	7,611	7,611
Interest rate derivatives (iv)	–	(532)	–	–	(532)	(532)
Deposits (v)	28,386	–	–	–	28,386	28,386
Accounts payable and accrued liabilities (vi)	–	–	–	(284,902)	(284,902)	(284,902)
 Long-term debt (vii)	–	–	–	(828,712)	(828,712)	(937,336)
Obligations under finance leases (viii)	–	–	–	(3,249)	(3,249)	(3,249)
	1,320,332	11,741	34,122	(1,116,863)	249,332	140,708

18. Commitments

(c) Letters of guarantee

As at December 31, 2011, the Corporation has available two revolving letter of credit facilities with a Canadian charter bank totaling $38,000 (December 31, 2010—$38,000; January 1, 2010—$38,000). One facility is unsecured for $8,000 and the other is a facility for $30,000 that requires funds to be assigned and held in cash security for the full value of letters of guarantee issued by the Corporation. As at December 31, 2011 $6,610 (December 31, 2010—$6,691; January 1, 2010—$12,491) of letters of guarantee were issued under these facilities with restricted cash of $6,610 (December 31, 2010—$6,691; January 1, 2010—$4,491).

(d) Operating line of credit

The Corporation has available a three-year revolving operating line of credit with a syndicate of three Canadian banks. The line of credit is available for up to a maximum of $76,500 (December 31, 2010—$80,750; January 1, 2010—$85,000) and is secured by the Corporation's campus facility. The line of credit bears interest at prime plus 0.50% per annum, or a banker's acceptance rate at 2.0% annual stamping fee or equivalent, and is available for general corporate expenditures and working capital purposes. The Corporation is required to pay a standby fee of 15 basis points, based on the average unused portion of the line of credit for the previous quarter, payable quarterly. As at December 31, 2011, no amounts were drawn (December 31, 2010—$nil; January 1, 2010—$nil).

EXHIBIT 9.3 (continued) WestJet Airlines Ltd.: Long-Term Debt

(b) Operating leases and commitments

The Corporation has entered into operating leases and commitments for aircraft, land, buildings, equipment, computer hardware, software licenses and satellite programming. As at December 31, 2011 the future payments in US dollars, where applicable, and Canadian dollar equivalents under operating leases and commitments are as follows:

	USD	CAD
Within 1 year	191,462	219,271
1–3 years	371,634	400,588
3–5 years	262,846	279,747
Over 5 years	215,642	261,441
	1,041,584	1,161,047

As at December 31, 2011, the Corporation is committed to lease one additional 737-800 aircraft for a term of eight years in US dollars. This aircraft has been included in the above totals.

In this section, we will focus our attention on bonds, but other forms of long-term debt have similar characteristics.

An entity can be financed either through debt or equity. This is consistent with the accounting equation where assets equal liabilities plus shareholders' equity. Equity represents ownership in the entity while debt is liabilities that have to be repaid. Each form of financing has advantages and disadvantages. Interest on debt is tax-deductible, which means the actual cost of borrowing is lower than the interest rate stated in the loan. (I'll explain the tax-deductibility of interest later in the chapter.) However, debt holders don't have a say in the entity's management; only equity investors (the owners) do. Debt is riskier for the issuing entity because the interest and principal payments have to be made as specified in the loan agreement regardless of how well the entity is doing. Defaulting on these payments (failing to make them when they are due) can have significant and costly economic and legal consequences for an entity. On the other hand, debt is less risky for investors because debt investors must be fully repaid before equity investors get anything if an entity goes out of business. Because debt is less risky for investors, it's a less costly way to finance an entity (the higher the risk investors face, the higher the return they expect).

Characteristics of Bonds

A bond is a formal borrowing arrangement in which a borrower agrees to make periodic interest payments to the lenders and to repay the principal at a specified time in the future. The essentials of a bond are as follows:

- **face value**—the amount the bondholder will receive when the bond matures
- **maturity date**—the date on which the borrower has agreed to pay back the principal (the face value of the bond) to the bondholders
- **coupon rate**—the percentage of the face value the issuer pays to investors each period

A bond with a $1,000 face value, annual coupon rate of 5 percent, and maturity of September 15, 2020 pays the bondholder $50 per year in interest and will repay the $1,000 principal on September 15, 2020.

The **proceeds** of a bond—the amount the issuer receives from the sale of the bond—aren't necessarily the same as its face value. The proceeds are determined by the **effective interest rate**—the real or market rate of interest required by investors to invest in the bond. If the coupon rate is different from the effective interest rate, the bond's selling price must allow investors to earn the effective interest rate. If the coupon rate is lower than the effective interest rate, the bond is sold at a discount and the proceeds are less than the face value. If the coupon rate is greater than the effective interest rate, the bond is sold at a premium and the proceeds are greater than the face value. Only if the coupon rate and effective interest rate are the same will the proceeds equal the face value.

A bond can have features in addition to the basic ones described above, but these are bells and whistles added on to meet the needs of the lenders and borrowers. The additional features come at a price—a change in the interest rate. If a feature is beneficial to investors (lenders), the issuing entity (the borrower) should be able to offer a lower interest rate. If a feature is beneficial to the issuing entity, then investors will require a higher interest rate. The following are some examples of features bonds can have:

- **callable bond**—the bond issuer has the option to repurchase the bond from investors at a time other than the maturity date. This feature is attractive to the issuer because if interest rates fall, the issuer can call the bond and make another issue at a lower interest rate. That isn't attractive to investors as they lose an investment paying a higher-than-market rate of interest, so a callable bond will have a higher market interest rate than an equivalent bond without the call feature.
- **convertible bond**—may be exchanged by the investor for other securities of the issuing entity, such as common stock.
- **retractable bond**—gives investors the option of cashing in the bond before the maturity date, under certain conditions.

A bond agreement can also impose restrictions on the issuer's activities. These restrictions are intended to reduce the investor's risk and reduce the cost of borrowing. Many restrictions are stated in accounting terms; for example, a maximum debt-to-equity ratio or a minimum current ratio. Restrictions may prohibit the payment of dividends if retained earnings falls below a certain amount. Violating restrictive covenants can have significant economic consequences for the entity, including an increase in the interest rate on the debt, an increase in the collateral required, additional covenants, or immediate repayment of the bond. Because violating restrictive covenants is costly, managers will take steps, including operating decisions or accounting choices, to avoid it.

Pricing of Bonds

The present value tools discussed in Chapter 6 are used to determine the price of a bond or other long-term debt. The price of a bond is equal to the present value of the cash flows that will be paid to the investor, discounted at the effective interest rate. The effective interest rate of a bond is determined by market forces and depends on the bond's risk; the riskier the bond, the higher the effective interest rate. The risk for bond investors is whether they will receive their interest and principal.

Let's consider an example of the pricing of long-term debt. Bardal Ltd. (Bardal) plans to issue a bond to raise about $5,000,000 to finance a major expansion. The bond has a face value of $5,000,000 and will be issued on October 1, 2017. It carries a coupon rate of 5 percent, with interest paid annually on September 30, and maturity in five years, on September 30, 2022. Each interest payment will be $250,000 ($5,000,000 × 0.05). For a bond of this type (risk, features, maturity), the effective interest rate is 6 percent. Therefore, the discount rate used to value the cash flows from this bond is 6 percent. (This is important! The appropriate discount rate is the effective interest rate, not the coupon rate on the bond.) Bardal's year-end is September 30. The cash flows from the bond are shown in Figure 9.1.

The proceeds from this bond issue are the present value (discounted at 6 percent) of (a) a series of five annual payments of $250,000 and (b) a payment of $5,000,000 on September 30, 2022,

FIGURE 9.1 Interest and Principal Payments for Bardal's $5,000,000 Bond Issue

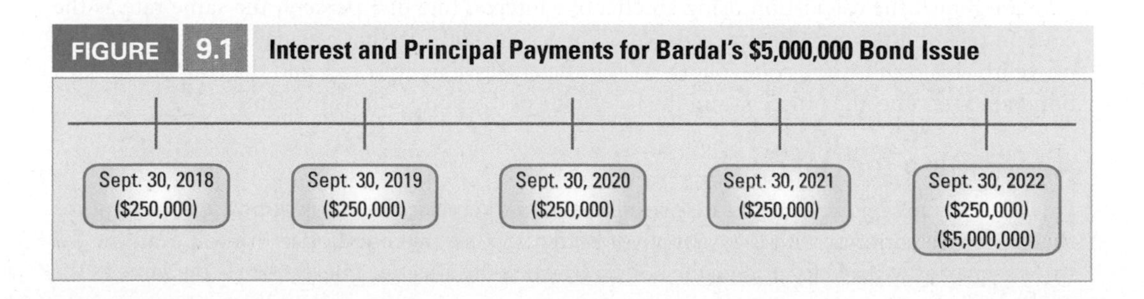

the maturity date of the bond. We use the formula for the present value of an annuity to calculate the present value of the interest payments:

$$\text{PV of an annuity}_{n,r} = \frac{1}{r} \times \left[1 - \frac{1}{(1+r)^n}\right] \times \text{Amount to be paid each period}$$

$$\text{PV of an annuity}_{5,0.06} = \frac{1}{0.06} \times \left[1 - \frac{1}{(1+0.06)^5}\right] \times \$250{,}000$$

$$= \$1{,}053{,}091$$

We use the formula for the present value of a single payment to be received in the future to calculate the present value of the principal that will be repaid on September 30, 2022:

$$\text{PV}_{n,r} = \frac{1}{[1+r]^n} \times \text{Amount to be paid}$$

$$\text{PV}_{5,0.06} = \frac{1}{[1+0.06]^5} \times \$5{,}000{,}000$$

$$= \$3{,}736{,}291$$

The proceeds from the bond are the sum of these two present value calculations:

Proceeds from bond issue	=	Present value of interest payments	+	Present value of principal repayment
	=	$1,053,091	+	$3,736,291
	=	$4,789,382		

Bardal's bond will sell at a discount of $210,618 ($5,000,000 − $4,789,382). Once the terms of the bond have been set (coupon rate, maturity, other features), the proceeds are a function of the effective interest (discount) rate that is used. If we assume an effective interest rate for Bardal's bond of 4 percent instead of 6 percent, the proceeds would be:

$$\text{PV of an annuity}_{n,r} = \frac{1}{r} \times \left[1 - \frac{1}{(1+r)^n}\right] \times \text{Amount to be paid each period}$$

$$\text{PV of an annuity}_{5,0.04} = \frac{1}{0.04} \times \left[1 - \frac{1}{(1+0.04)^5}\right] \times \$250{,}000$$

$$= \$1{,}112{,}956$$

$$\text{PV}_{n,r} = \frac{1}{[1+r]^n} \times \text{Amount to be paid}$$

$$\text{PV}_{5,0.04} = \frac{1}{[1+0.04]^5} \times \$5{,}000{,}000$$

$$= \$4{,}109{,}635$$

Proceeds from bond issue	=	PV of interest payments	+	PV of principal repayment
	=	$1,112,956	+	$4,109,635
	=	$5,222,591		

If we repeat the calculation using an effective interest rate of 5 percent, the same rate as the coupon rate on the bond, the proceeds would be $5,000,000. Try that calculation on your own to prove it! This result isn't a coincidence. When the effective interest rate and the coupon rate of a bond are the same, the proceeds and the face value of the bond will be the same.

Accounting for Bonds

Now that we've seen how bonds are priced in the marketplace, let's look at how we account for them. We will continue with the example of Bardal's $5,000,000 bond offer. We will examine the three scenarios we used for pricing the bonds: (i) when the effective interest rate is the same as the coupon rate on the bond, (ii) when the effective interest rate is greater than the coupon rate, and (iii) when the effective interest rate is less than the coupon rate.

Scenario 1: Selling Bonds at Face Value When the effective rate of interest is the same as the coupon rate, the bonds sell at their face value and Bardal receives $5,000,000 from the offering. Bardal would make the following journal entry on October 1, 2017 to record the issue of the bonds:

Dr. Cash (asset +)	5,000,000	
Cr. Long-term debt—bonds (liability +)		5,000,000
To record the issue of bonds on October 1, 2017		

On September 30 of each year from 2018 through 2022, Bardal would make the following journal entry to record the payment of interest and the interest expense:

Dr. Interest expense (expense +, shareholders equity −)	250,000	
Cr. Cash (asset −)		250,000
To record the interest expense on the $5,000,000 bond offering		

On September 30, 2022, when the bond matures, Bardal would make the following journal entry to derecognize the bond. **Derecognition** occurs when a bond or other liability is removed from the balance sheet, in this case when the bond is retired by paying the principal to the investors.

Dr. Long-term debt—bonds (liability −)	5,000,000	
Cr. Cash (asset −)		5,000,000
To record derecognition of the bonds on September 30, 2022		

The accounting in this scenario is straightforward. The bonds are reported as a $5,000,000 non-current liability on Bardal's balance sheet. On the September 30, 2021 balance sheet, they are reclassified as a current liability because the bond would be payable in the next fiscal year. The income statement would show an interest expense of $250,000 each year over the life of the bond.

Scenario 2: Selling Bonds at a Discount In this scenario the effective interest rate for Bardal's bonds is greater than the coupon rate. Investors expect a return of 6 percent on a bond like Bardal's, but Bardal's coupon rate is only 5 percent. As a result, Bardal has to sell its bonds for less than their face value so that investors can earn the 6 percent effective interest rate. Recall that the price for Bardal's bond with an effective interest rate of 6 percent is $4,789,382. This means investors earn a 6 percent return by investing $4,789,382 for five $250,000 annual interest payments plus a $5,000,000 payment at the end of five years. (If Bardal tries to sell the bond for more than $4,789,382 no one will buy it.)

When bonds are sold for less than their face value, they are said to have been sold at a **discount**. The discount is the difference between the face value of the bonds and the proceeds, in this case $210,618 ($5,000,000 − $4,789,382). The discount is recorded in a contra-liability account. Bardal would make the following entry to record the issue of its bonds:

Dr. Cash (asset +)	4,789,382	
Dr. Bond discount (contra-liability +)	210,618	
Cr. Long-term debt—bonds (liability +)		5,000,000
To record the issue of bonds on October 1, 2017 at a discount		

The carrying amount of the bonds (the face value of the bonds less the bond discount) is the net present value of bonds discounted using the effective interest rate. The discount can be thought of as interest that investors must receive to earn the effective interest rate and represents compensation for the low coupon rate. The discount of $210,618 is amortized over the life of the bonds and is included as part of the interest expense each year.

The bonds would be reported on Bardal's October 1, 2017 balance sheet shown in Table 9.2. The discount is classified as a contra-liability account, which is netted against the face value of the bonds.

TABLE 9.2 Methods of Reporting Bond Discount

Bardal Ltd. Extracts from the October 1, 2017, Balance Sheet	
Long-term debt—Bonds payable	$5,000,000
Unamortized discount on October 1, 2017	210,618
Carrying amount of long-term debt—Bonds payable	$4,789,382

There are two methods for amortizing the discount: straight-line method and effective interest rate method. IFRS require the effective interest rate method. The key point to understand is that the discount is amortized over the life of the bond and the amortized portion is included in the interest expense. The effective interest rate method is a bit complicated but because it's required by IFRS, I will introduce it. Follow the discussion by referring to Table 9.3. With the effective interest rate method, the annual interest expense is calculated as the amount of liability outstanding at the beginning of the period times the effective interest rate. For Bardal, for fiscal 2018 the expense would be $287,363 ($4,789,382 [the carrying amount of the bond on October 1, 2017] × 0.06 [the effective interest rate]). The amount of discount that's amortized in a period is the difference between the interest expense (calculated using the effective interest rate) and the amount of interest paid (based on the coupon rate). For fiscal 2018 $37,363 of discount is amortized (interest expense − interest paid = $287,363 − $250,000). The entry for fiscal 2018 is:

Dr. Interest expense (expense +, shareholders' equity −)	287,363	
Cr. Bond discount (contra-liability −)		37,363
Cr. Cash (asset −)		250,000

Notice that the interest expense has two components: the cash payment (or accrued amount) of $250,000 and the amortization of the bond discount of $37,363. IFRS require the effective rate because it gives a constant interest rate over the life of the bond. It's important to understand that at the end of the bond's life the discount is fully amortized and the liability on the maturity date is equal to the amount that has to be paid to the bondholders. At maturity, Bardal would derecognize the bond with the same entry as in Scenario 1. The discount would be completely amortized by then. Table 9.3 shows how the discount decreases over the life of the bond and how the carrying amount of the bond increases, reaching its face value at maturity. Carefully review Table 9.3 and the notes to understand how the method works.

TABLE 9.3 Amortization of Bond Discount and Carrying Amount of Bonds

	Column 1	Column 2	Column 3	Column 4	Column 5	Column 6	Column 7
Year-end date	Carrying amount of the bond at the beginning of the period	Bond discount at the beginning of the period	Interest expense ❶	Interest paid ❷	Discount amortized ❸	Bond discount at the end of the period ❹	Carrying amount of the bond at end of the period ❺
September 30, 2018	$4,789,382	$210,618	$287,363	$250,000	$ 37,363	$173,255	$4,826,745
September 30, 2019	4,826,745	173,255	289,605	250,000	39,605	133,650	4,866,350
September 30, 2020	4,866,350	133,650	291,981	250,000	41,981	91,669	4,908,331
September 30, 2021	4,908,331	91,669	294,500	250,000	44,500	47,169	4,952,831
September 30, 2022	4,952,831	47,169	297,170	250,000	47,169	0	5,000,000

❶ Column 1 × effective interest rate. For 2018: $4,789,382 × 0.06 = $287,363.
❷ Specified in the bond agreement. $5,000,000 × 0.05.
❸ Column 3 − Column 4: Interest expense − interest paid. For 2018: $287,363 − $250,000 = $37,363.
❹ Column 2 − Column 5.
❺ Column 1 + Column 5.

Note: Numbers sometimes don't add up exactly due to rounding.

INSIGHT

Straight-Line Method of Amortizing Discounts and Premiums

Companies following ASPE can choose either the effective interest rate or straight-line methods for accounting for bond discounts and premiums. The straight-line method is much easier to apply because it allocates an equal amount of premium or discount to each period. To determine the amount of amortization each period, divide the initial amount of premium or discount by the number of periods until maturity. The interest expense for each period is the same: the amount of discount or premium amortized plus the amount of interest the bond pays for each period. The formulas can be stated as follows:

Discount/premium amortization for the period	=	Amount of premium/discount when bond is issued	÷	Number of periods bond will be outstanding

Interest expense for the period	=	Interest paid or payable for the period discount/premium amortization for the period	+	Discount/premium amortization for the period

With the straight-line method, the interest expense each period is the same. For the Bardal bond, the amount of the discount amortized each year is:

Amount of discount amortization each year = \$210,618 ÷ 5 years
= \$42,123.60

Interest expense each year = \$250,000 + \$42,123.60
= \$292,123.60

KNOWLEDGE CHECK 9.2

On January 1, 2017, Krydor Inc. (Krydor) issued a two-year, \$1,000,000 bond with a 10 percent coupon, with interest paid annually on December 31. The bond matures on December 31, 2018. The effective interest rate for this bond is 11 percent.

- ❑ What price will Krydor sell the bond for?
- ❑ What journal entry will Krydor make to record the issue of the bond?
- ❑ Record journal entries that would be made on December 31, 2017 and 2018, to record the interest expense for the year (use straight-line method).
- ❑ What journal entry will Krydor make when the bond is derecognized and the investors are repaid the principal? Don't include the interest portion of the entry.

Scenario 3: Selling Bonds at a Premium In this scenario, the bonds are sold to investors for more than their face value; that is, the bonds are sold at a **premium**. This will happen when the coupon rate is greater than the effective interest rate. When Bardal's bond had a coupon rate of 5 percent and the effective interest rate was 4 percent, it sold for \$5,222,591 and had a premium of \$222,591 (\$5,222,591 − \$5,000,000). The premium is the difference between the proceeds and the face value of the bonds. Bardal would make this entry to record the issue of the bonds at a premium:

Dr. Cash (asset +)	5,222,591	
Cr. Bond premium (contra-liability +)		222,591
Cr. Long-term debt—bonds (liability +)		5,000,000
To record the issue of bonds on October 1, 2017 at a premium		

Accounting for a premium is the same as for a discount, except that the bond premium account carries a credit balance (for a discount it's a debit balance) and the amortization of the premium decreases the interest expense (instead of increasing it, as with a discount). When investors pay a premium for a bond, they are, in effect, repaying in advance the interest they will collect that is over and above the amount required by the effective interest rate.

As with a discount, a premium is amortized over the life of the bonds using the straight-line method or effective interest method. The entry for fiscal 2018 using the effective interest rate method is:

Dr. Interest expense (expense +, shareholders' equity −)	208,904	
Dr. Bond premium (contra-liability −)	41,096	
Cr. Cash (asset −)		250,000

At maturity, Bardal would make the same entry to derecognize the bond as in Scenario 1. The premium would be completely amortized by then. Table 9.4 shows how the premium decreases over the life of the bond and how the carrying amount of the bond decreases, reaching its face value at maturity.

TABLE 9.4 Amortization of Bond Premium and Carrying Amount of Bonds

	Column 1	Column 2	Column 3	Column 4	Column 5	Column 6	Column 7
Year-end date	Carrying amount of the bond at the beginning of the period	Bond premium at the beginning of the period	Interest expense ❶	Interest paid ❷	Premium amortized ❸	Bond premium at the end of the period ❹	Carrying amount of the bond at end of the period ❺
September 30, 2018	$5,222,591	$222,591	$208,904	$250,000	$41,096	$181,495	$5,181,495
September 30, 2019	5,181,495	181,495	207,260	250,000	42,740	138,754	5,138,755
September 30, 2020	5,138,755	138,754	205,550	250,000	44,450	94,305	5,094,305
September 30, 2021	5,094,305	94,305	203,772	250,000	46,228	48,077	5,048,077
September 30, 2022	5,048,077	48,077	201,923	250,000	48,077	0	5,000,000

❶ Column 1 × effective interest rate. For 2018: $5,222,591 × 0.04 = $208,904.
❷ Specified in the bond agreement. $5,000,000 × 0.05.
❸ Column 4 − Column 3: Interest expense − interest paid. For 2018: $250,000 − $208,904 = $41,096.
❹ Column 2 − Column 5.
❺ Column 1 + Column 5.

Note: Numbers sometimes don't add up exactly due to rounding.

INSIGHT

Some Perspective on Technical Complexity

Accounting can be very complex; some liability topics are especially so. The effective interest rate method is an example. It's important to put this complexity in perspective at this point in your accounting studies. The emphasis in this book is for you to understand what the numbers in financial statements mean so you can use them intelligently and effectively. To this end, the details of how premiums and discounts are amortized is less important than understanding how the price of bonds is determined, why premiums and discounts arise, and what impact premiums and discounts have on the interest expense.

Accruing Interest on Long-Term Debt

What happens if an entity's year-end isn't the same as the date the interest is paid? With accrual accounting, it's necessary to accrue the interest expense at the end of the period so the cost of borrowing is recognized in the appropriate period, even though the interest isn't paid until later. This is the accrued expense/accrued liability adjusting entry we discussed in Chapter 3.

In Bardal's first quarter statements for the three months ended December 31, an adjusting entry is required to accrue the interest expense for October 1 to December 31. We'll use the facts from Scenario 1 to show this adjusting entry (there is no premium or discount in Scenario 1). For the period October 1 through December 31, 2019, Bardal incurs three months of interest that should be expensed in the first quarter of fiscal 2020 (fiscal 2020 is the year ended September 30, 2020), so on December 31, 2019, the following adjusting entry is required:

Dr. Interest expense (expense +, shareholders' equity −)	62,500	
Cr. Interest payable (liability +)		62,500

The amount is one-quarter of the interest cost for a year ($250,000 × 0.25)

On September 30, 2020, when Bardal actually pays the interest, it would record the following entry (the same entry would be required at the end of the second and third quarters of fiscal 2020):

Dr. Interest expense (expense +, shareholders' equity −)	62,500	
Dr. Interest payable (liability −)	187,500	
Cr. Cash (asset −)		250,000

This entry records the following:

1. the interest expense for the fourth quarter of fiscal 2020
2. the reduction in the interest payable liability that was accrued on December 31, 2019, March 31, 2020, and June 30, 2020
3. the cash payment to investors

Early Retirement of Debt

Entities sometimes retire their long-term debt before it matures. For example, lower market interest rates can make it worthwhile to retire existing high-interest-rate debt and then issue new debt at a lower rate. This can be done relatively easily, if the debt includes an option for the issuer to redeem it. Alternatively, an entity could repurchase its debt on the open market, if it's publicly traded.

Accounting for the early retirement of debt requires removing any unamortized discount or premium from the books—the remaining unamortized premium or discount is included in the income statement when the debt is retired. A gain arises if the cost of retiring the debt is less than its carrying amount, and a loss occurs if the cost of retiring the debt is greater than its carrying amount.

For example, on December 31, 2018, Aklavik Ltd. (Aklavik) retired some bonds by paying $1,250,000 to investors. The bonds had a face value of $1,000,000 and there was an unamortized discount of $58,000 at the time the bonds were retired. Aklavik would record the following journal entry to derecognize (retire) the bonds (*Note:* This entry assumes that the interest expense for the period ended December 31, 2018 was recorded before the bonds were retired):

December 31, 2018

Dr. Long-term debt—bonds (liability −)	1,000,000	
Dr. Loss on redemption of bond (income statement +, shareholders' equity −)	308,000	
Cr. Bond discount (contra-liability−)		58,000
Cr. Cash (asset −)		1,250,000

To record the early retirement of bonds on December 31, 2018

A similar approach would be used if there was an unamortized premium recorded on the date the bonds were retired. If there was no unamortized discount or premium, the gain or loss would be the difference between the face value of the bonds and the amount paid to retire them.

Disclosure

The balance sheet itself usually only reveals the total amount of long-term debt outstanding and the amount that is maturing within the next year. The totals might provide some information about the riskiness of the entity, but stakeholders need more information to estimate future cash flows, funding requirements, and earnings, and to evaluate the management and stewardship of the entity.

Return to Exhibit 9.3 and examine the information on WestJet's long-term borrowing. The table at the beginning of Note 10 lists its long-term borrowing arrangements. For each loan the purpose and the amount outstanding is stated. Most of the borrowing is for purchasing aircraft. The footnotes below the table describe the terms of the loans. For example, footnote (vi) describes the terms of the loan to purchase aircraft:

- On December 31, 2011, $608,000 was outstanding.
- Repayable in monthly instalments of $50,000, including interest.
- Floating interest rate at the bank's prime rate plus 0.50 percent, with an effective interest rate as of December 31, 2011 of 3.50 percent.
- Matures April 2013.
- Secured by the Calgary hangar facility.

The table at the end of Note 10 discloses the principal repayments WestJet is scheduled to make over the next five years and thereafter on its long-term debt. This information is important for assessing future cash flows, cash requirements, and financing needs. According to this disclosure, WestJet's repayments seem relatively smooth over the next few years.

Note 18 on commitments and contingencies describes credit resources available to WestJet. Note 18(c) explains that the company has two letters of credit totaling $38,000,000 available from a Canadian chartered bank. A **letter of credit** is a guarantee from a bank that a customer will pay amounts owed to a seller. One of the letters is unsecured (there is no specific collateral for the arrangement) and the other requires that money be held by the bank in the full amount of the amount guaranteed. On December 31, 2011, letters of credit of $6,610,000 had been issued, meaning that the banks had guaranteed payment for purchases of $6,610,000. The letters of credit are secured by a general agreement against company assets (which means that bank has a broad claim against company assets). In addition, there is $6,610,000 in restricted cash (which means $6,610,000 is on deposit with the bank that isn't available for general purposes by WestJet).

Note 18(d) describes the terms of an operating line of credit WestJet has available. It provides up to $76.5 million in borrowing, secured against WestJet's campus facility. It's a source of liquidity that isn't reflected in the financial statements until the money is actually borrowed. The note describes the interest rate that applies, the allowable purposes for the money (general expenses and working capital), and that WestJet must pay 0.15 percent per quarter on the unused portion of the line of credit. On December 31, 2011, none of the line of credit had been utilized.

Private companies may provide less information than WestJet because stakeholders don't require, or have access to, the information in other ways.

Fair Value of Debt

Under IFRS, bonds and other forms of long-term debt are valued at the present value of the cash payments to investors, discounted using the effective interest rate on the date the bond is issued. Interest rate changes over the life of a bond cause the market value of a bond to change (if interest rates go up, the market value decreases and vice versa), but financial statements don't reflect these changes. By ignoring changes in interest rates, financial statements don't reflect real economic gains and losses on long-term debt.

These gains and losses aren't recognized under IFRS, but disclosure of the market value of debt must be made in the notes to the financial statements. For example, in Exhibit 9.3, Note 17(a) shows that the fair value of WestJet's long-term debt on December 31, 2011 was $937,336,000 versus a carrying amount of $828,712,000. This represents a loss of $108,624,000 that isn't reflected in the financial statements. The fair value and carrying amount of the long-term debt are different because interest rates have changed since the debt was originally issued.

QUESTION FOR CONSIDERATION

Because of an increase in competition in the industry, a respected bond-rating agency recently downgraded its rating on Quaw Inc.'s (Quaw) corporate bonds, which means that the bonds are considered riskier. What do you think the effect of the downgrade would be on the carrying amount of Quaw's bonds? What do you think the impact would be on the market value of the bonds? Explain your answers.

ANSWER: The carrying amount would be unchanged and the amount of interest Quaw would have to pay would be the same until the bond matured. Under IFRS, an entity's own bonds are recorded at the transaction value, so changes in the effective rate of interest don't affect the carrying amount. The downgrade causes the effective rate of interest of the bonds to increase and the market value of the bonds to fall, so that investors will receive the rate of return they require.

Mortgages

A common borrowing arrangement is with a mortgage. When people buy homes, they usually finance them with a mortgage. A mortgage is a loan for which the borrower provides real property—for example, land, equipment, or buildings—as security. If the borrower can't make its loan payments, the lender can have the real property sold and the proceeds used to satisfy the loan. Many mortgages feature blended payments. The borrower agrees to make equal period payments over the mortgage term made up of interest and principal. Over the life of the mortgage, the payments stay the same but the amount of principal and interest changes. As time passes, the amount of principal paid each period increases and the amount of interest decreases. This makes sense because as time passes the amount of principal outstanding decreases, so the amount of interest will decrease. This arrangement is different than bonds, where the borrower agrees to pay interest periodically and repay the principal at the end of the loan period.

Let's look at an example to see how mortgages work. On January 2, 2017, Ardrossan Ltd. arranged a $5,000,000, five-year mortgage at an interest rate of 5 percent per year. Payments are made annually at the end of each year. (Mortgage payments are usually made monthly or even bi-weekly. Ardrossan's year-end is December 31. To make the example simpler, I'm using annual payments.) The first thing we have to do is calculate the annual payment Ardossan will have to make each year over the term of the mortgage. The annual payment is calculated by dividing the amount borrowed by the present value of annuity factor (see Chapter 6).

$$\text{Mortgage payments} = \frac{\text{Amount borrowed}}{\text{Present value of an annuity}} = \frac{\text{Amount borrowed}}{\frac{1}{r} \times \left[1 - \frac{1}{(1+r)^n}\right]}$$

where r is the interest rate and n is the number of periods. For this example the interest rate is 5 percent and the term is five years, so annual payment would be:

$$\text{Mortgage payments} = \frac{\text{Amount borrowed}}{\frac{1}{r} \times \left[1 - \frac{1}{(1+r)^n}\right]} = \frac{\$5{,}000{,}000}{\frac{1}{0.05} \times \left[1 - \frac{1}{(1+0.05)^5}\right]} = \$1{,}154{,}873.99$$

TABLE 9.5 Ardrossan Ltd.: Mortgage Payment Schedule

	Column 1	Column 2	Column 3	Column 4	Column 5
Year-end date	Mortgage principal owing at the beginning of the period	Annual payment	Interest payment (expense)	Principal payment	Mortgage principal owing at the end of the period
December 31, 2018	$5,000,000.00	$1,154,873.99	$250,000.00	$904,873.99	$4,095,126.01
December 31, 2019	4,095,126.01	1,154,873.99	204,756.30	950,117.69	3,145,008.32
December 31, 2020	3,145,008.32	1,154,873.99	157,250.42	997,623.57	2,147,384.75
December 31, 2021	2,147,384.75	1,154,873.99	107,369.24	1,047,504.75	1,099,879.99
December 31, 2022	1,099,879.99	1,154,873.99	54,994.00	1,099,879.99	0.00

Note that if payments were to be monthly, r would be 0.00417 (0.05/12 months) and n would be 60 months.

Now let's look at the payment schedule (Table 9.5). Column 2 is the annual payment we just calculated. The payment has to be broken into interest (Column 3) and principal (Column 4). The interest payment each year is the mortgage balance at the beginning of the period times the interest rate (Column 1 × 0.05). The amount of principal repaid each year is the annual payment minus the interest payment (Column 2 − Column 3).

Ardrossan would make the following journal entry to record the mortgage:

Dr. Cash (asset +)	5,000,000	
Cr. Mortgage (liability +)		5,000,000
To record the mortgage		

The payment on December 31, 2017 would be recorded as:

Dr. Interest expense (expense +)	250,000.00	
Dr. Mortgage (liability −)	904,873.99	
Cr. Cash (Asset −)		1,154,873.99
To record the mortgage payment on December 31, 2017		

The payment on December 31, 2022 would be recorded as:

Dr. Interest expense (expense +)	54,994.00	
Dr. Mortgage (liability −)	1,099,879.99	
Cr. Cash (Asset −)		1,154,873.99
To record the mortgage payment on December 31, 2022		

LO 4 LEASES

Suppose an entity needs a new truck but doesn't have the money to pay for it, so it borrows from a bank. When an asset purchase is financed this way, the balance sheet will show the truck as an asset and the bank loan as a liability. Now suppose the entity finds someone with a truck who will let the entity use it for a few years in exchange for a monthly payment. In this case, what should appear on the balance sheet? This is the issue of leasing. A **lease** is a contract in which one entity, the lessee, agrees to pay another entity, the lessor, a fee for the use of an asset. A **lessee** is the entity that leases an asset from its owner and a **lessor** is the entity that leases assets it owns to other entities. In a lease, the lessor owns the asset but the lessee has certain rights and obligations, which are defined in the lease agreement.

Leasing is a very common way for entities to obtain the use of assets without actually buying and owning them. For example, airlines often lease airplanes. On December 31, 2011, WestJet had a fleet of 97 aircraft of which 41 were leased and Air Canada leased 99 of its fleet of 205 planes. There are a number of reasons why entities might prefer to lease assets instead of buying them:

- With a lease, an entity doesn't have to obtain separate financing for the purchase. This can be important when there is already a lot of debt and lenders such as banks are reluctant to lend more.
- Leasing allows for financing of 100 percent of the cost of the asset. Lenders will often lend only a portion of a purchase amount.
- Leases can provide flexibility to lessees. For example, a lease agreement could allow the exchange of leased computer equipment for more up-to-date equipment during the term of the lease. This gives the lessee some protection from technological obsolescence.
- Leasing is attractive for entities that don't need certain assets continuously. For example, a company may require heavy equipment only at certain stages of a project. A lease allows the entity to use the equipment without the cost of owning assets that are idle for significant amounts of time.

Leasing has accounting implications. Before accounting standards for leasing were introduced, creative managers were able to use leases to do **off-balance-sheet financing**—when an entity incurs an obligation without reporting a liability on its balance sheet. Initially, accounting rules required a lessee to simply record a lease or rent expense when payment to the lessor was paid or payable. The lessee could have used the leased asset in much the same way a purchaser would, but neither the leased asset nor the lease liability had to be reported on the balance sheet.

Off-balance-sheet financing allows an entity to incur a liability without the balance sheet consequences, such as a higher debt-to-equity ratio. This can be attractive to entities in danger of violating debt-to-equity covenants or for simply limiting the amount of debt the entity appears to have. Also, since the debt-to-equity ratio is a measure of an entity's risk, off-balance-sheet financing makes an entity appear less risky. Of course, an entity's risk isn't affected by the accounting treatment, but the tools for measuring it are.

As leasing became more common, accounting standard setters recognized that many of these leasing contracts were actually purchases in disguise. Rules were established requiring leased assets and associated liabilities to be reported on the lessee's balance sheet if the lease resulted in the transfer of the risks and rewards of ownership to the lessee. Effectively, a lease is accounted for in the same way as a purchase, if certain criteria are met.

There are two categories of leases: capital or finance leases and operating leases. A **capital** or **finance lease** transfers the risks and rewards of ownership to the lessee. At the beginning of a capital lease, the leased asset and a liability are recorded on the lessee's balance sheet at the present value of the lease payments to be made over the life of the lease. The leased asset is accounted for in the same way as an owned asset, including being depreciated over its useful life (or the term of the lease if that is shorter than the useful life). In most cases, the lessor treats the lease as a sale, removes the leased asset from its books, and reports a receivable equal to the present value of lease payments to be received. For a lessee, a lease should be classified as a capital lease if any of the following three criteria are met:

1. It's likely the lessee will get ownership of the asset by the end of the lease.
2. The lease term is long enough that the lessee receives most of the economic benefits of the asset.
3. The present value of the lease payments is equal to most of the fair value of the leased asset.

Deciding if any of these criteria are met is a matter of professional judgment. IFRS don't provide any quantitative guidelines, so there are no rules for managers and accountants to follow.

If the risks and rewards of ownership aren't transferred to the lessee but are retained by the lessor, then it's an **operating lease**. With an operating lease, the lessee doesn't record the leased assets or the associated liability on its balance sheet. Instead, the lessee recognizes an expense when a payment to the lessor is paid or payable, and the lessor recognizes revenue from the lease when payments are received or receivable. When a lease is classified as an operating lease, the lessee has off-balance-sheet financing.

Let's look at an example to see how lease accounting works. On December 31, 2017, Outram Inc. (Outram) signed an agreement to lease 200 computers from Cheekye Computer Leasing Corp. (Cheekye) for its new head office and distribution centre in Edmonton. The lease is for four years and Outram agreed to pay Cheekye $80,000 on December 31 of each year, beginning in 2018. Outram took delivery of the computers on January 1, 2018. At the end of the lease, Outram can purchase the computers for $1 each. Outram is responsible for maintaining, repairing, and insuring the computers. If Outram had purchased the computers, they would have cost $265,000. Outram's year-end is December 31.

Let's apply the criteria to this lease arrangement:

- Outram is likely to gain title of the computers at the end of the lease because it can purchase them for $1 each. At such a low price, Outram would certainly purchase them if they could still be used or if they could be sold for more than $1.
- We don't know the useful life of these computers, but it's hard to imagine they'd have a life much longer than four years. Given the nature of computer equipment, it's reasonable to conclude that Outram will derive most of the economic benefits from them.
- Outram pays $80,000 a year for four years under the terms of the lease. The present value of a series of four payments of $80,000 beginning in 2018 is $253,589 ($1/0.10 \times [1-1/(1+0.10)^4] \times$ $80,000). Assuming a discount rate of 10 percent, the present value of the lease payments is over 95 percent ($253,589 ÷ $265,000) of the purchase price of the computers and very close to the fair value of the equipment.

Outram should account for this as a capital lease because it appears that all three criteria are met. Remember, if any of the criteria are met the lease would be accounted for as a capital lease. Outram should capitalize an amount equal to the present value of the lease payments it will make over the life of the lease, which is $253,589. The journal entry to record the acquisition of the computers by a capital lease is

Dr. Assets under capital lease (asset +)	253,589	
Cr. Lease liability (liability +)		253,589
To record the acquisition of 200 computers under a capital lease		

After the initial recording of the leased asset and lease liability, the asset and liability are accounted for separately. (The accounting effects are summarized in the complicated-looking Table 9.6.) Leased capital assets are accounted for in much the same way as any capital asset—depreciated over their useful lives. Depreciation does present some interesting issues, though. If the term of the capital lease is shorter than the useful life of the asset and the lessee isn't likely to take title of the asset at the end of the lease, the asset should be depreciated over the term of the lease.

Since Outram will likely own the computers at the end of the lease, depreciating them over an estimated five-year life is reasonable (although it does seem a bit long for computers). If Outram uses straight-line depreciation, the annual depreciation expense will be $50,718 ($253,589 ÷ 5, column B), assuming no residual value. The carrying amount of the computers on January 1 and December 31 of each year is shown in columns A and C respectively (the carrying amount of the computers decreases by $50,718 each year, the amount of the depreciation expense). The journal entry to record the depreciation expense each year is

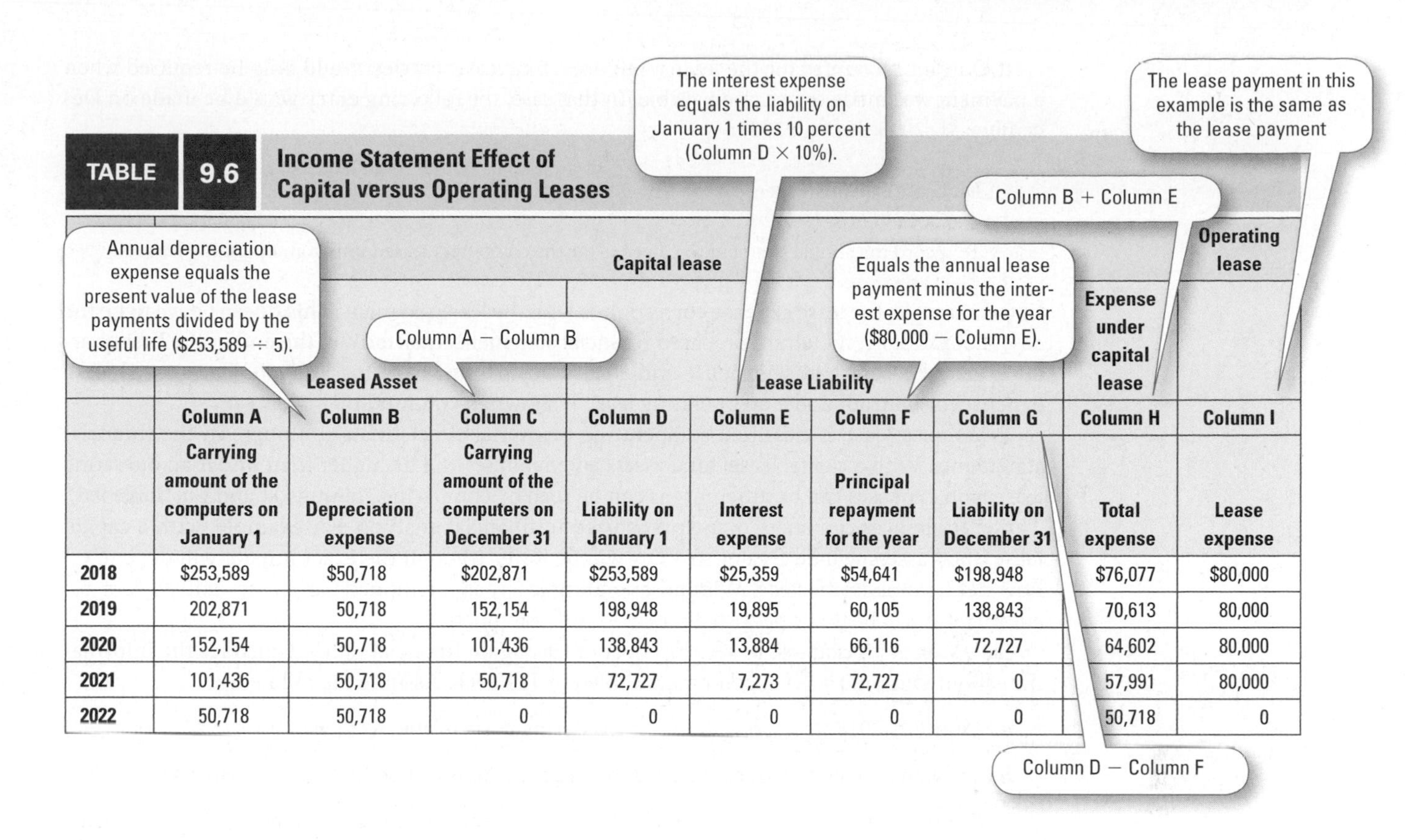

TABLE 9.6 Income Statement Effect of Capital versus Operating Leases

	Capital lease								Operating lease
	Leased Asset			Lease Liability				Expense under capital lease	
	Column A	Column B	Column C	Column D	Column E	Column F	Column G	Column H	Column I
	Carrying amount of the computers on January 1	Depreciation expense	Carrying amount of the computers on December 31	Liability on January 1	Interest expense	Principal repayment for the year	Liability on December 31	Total expense	Lease expense
2018	$253,589	$50,718	$202,871	$253,589	$25,359	$54,641	$198,948	$76,077	$80,000
2019	202,871	50,718	152,154	198,948	19,895	60,105	138,843	70,613	80,000
2020	152,154	50,718	101,436	138,843	13,884	66,116	72,727	64,602	80,000
2021	101,436	50,718	50,718	72,727	7,273	72,727	0	57,991	80,000
2022	50,718	50,718	0	0	0	0	0	50,718	0

Dr. Depreciation expense (expense +, shareholders' equity −)	50,718	
Cr. Accumulated depreciation (contra-asset +)		50,718
To record the depreciation of leased computers		

The interest expense is calculated by multiplying the liability outstanding at the beginning of the year by the interest rate. Lease agreements typically don't state the interest rate so the rate has to be assumed. Here we use the same rate, 10 percent, that was used to calculate the present value of the lease payments. Remember though, the interest rate will affect the financial statement numbers and managers have some flexibility in choosing the rate.

Throughout 2018, Outram's liability was $253,589 (column D), so the interest expense for 2018 is $25,359 ($253,589 × 0.10, column E). The portion of the $80,000 payment that's not interest is repayment of principal, which reduces the liability. In 2018, the liability is reduced by $54,641 ($80,000 − $25,359, column F), so the liability on December 31, 2018, is $198,948 ($253,589 − $54,641, column G). For 2019, the interest expense is calculated on the $198,948 liability that is outstanding for the entire year.

Over time, the interest portion of the annual payment decreases and the principal portion increases. This happens because, as the liability decreases, less interest is paid and more of the payment is applied to the liability. This effect can be seen in columns D, E, and F of Table 9.6. The journal entry to record the lease payment in 2018 is

Dr. Interest expense (expenses +, shareholders' equity −)	25,359	
Dr. Lease liability (liability −)	54,641	
Cr. Cash (asset −)		80,000
To record the lease payment to Cheekye for 2018		

Column H in Table 9.6 shows the total amount expensed in each year because of the lease. The amount of the expense is the depreciation expense plus the interest expense. If you add the expenses over the five years, you'll find that the total expense is $320,000, the sum of the annual lease payments.

If Outram accounted for the lease as an operating lease, entries would only be required when a payment was made or became payable. In that case, the following entry would be made on December 31, 2018 through 2021:

Dr. Lease expense (expense +, shareholders' equity −)	80,000	
Cr. Cash (asset −)		80,000

To record the annual payment to Cheekye for the computers leased under an operating lease

In the example, the lease expense corresponds with the lease payment. This doesn't have to be the case. For example, if Outram prepared financial statements quarterly, at the end of the first quarter it would record a lease expense and a lease payment payable for $20,000. The annual lease expense for Outram under an operating lease is shown in column I of Table 9.6.

Whether a lease is classified as operating or capital affects many numbers in the financial statements. With a capital lease, total assets and liabilities will be higher than under an operating lease, and expenses can be different (as can be seen by comparing columns H and I in Table 9.6). These differences can affect many ratios used in financial analysis. For example, with a capital lease, total assets will be greater so ROA will be lower (though the exact impact will depend on how net income is affected). With an operating lease, as mentioned earlier, an entity's debt-to-equity ratio will be lower because there are fewer liabilities.

Let's look at an example to see the effect of leasing on financial ratios. Consider the information about Outram's lease of computers shown in Table 9.6. Assume the following:

a. Outram's 2018 net income before considering costs related to the lease was $425,000.

b. Outram's interest expense for 2018, before considering lease interest was $50,000.

c. Total assets on December 31, 2017, before considering the effect of the lease were $2,250,000.

d. Total assets on December 31, 2018, before considering the effect of the lease were $2,500,000.

e. Outram's tax rate is 20 percent (the amount of tax Outram pays isn't affected by the classification of the lease).

Outram's ROA for 2018 using each of the two leasing arrangements are

	Capital lease	Operating lease
Total assets, December 31, 2017	$2,503,589[1]	$2,250,000[2]
Total assets, December 31, 2018	2,702,871[3]	2,500,000[2]
Net income for fiscal 2018	348,923[4]	345,000[5]

[1] $2,250,000 + $253,589 (carrying amount of the computers on December 31, 2017—from column A in Table 9.6).
[2] Total assets aren't affected if the lease is classified as an operating lease.
[3] $2,500,000 + $202,871 (carrying amount of the computers on December 31, 2018—from column A in Table 9.6).
[4] $425,000 − $76,077 (lease related expenses—column H in Table 9.6).
[5] $425,000 − $80,000 (lease expense—column I in Table 9.6).

$$\text{ROA} = \frac{\text{Net income} + \text{After-tax interest expense}}{\text{Total assets}}$$

$$\text{ROA}_{\text{capital lease}} = \frac{\$348{,}923 + [\$75{,}359 \times (1 - 0.2)]}{\frac{(\$2{,}702{,}871 + \$2{,}503{,}589)}{2}}$$

$$= 15.7\%$$

$$\text{ROA}_{\text{operating lease}} = \frac{\$345{,}000 + [\$50{,}000 \times (1 - 0.2)]}{\frac{(\$2{,}500{,}000 + \$2{,}250{,}000)}{2}}$$

$$= 16.2\%$$

EXHIBIT 9.4 WestJet Airlines Ltd.: Lease Disclosures

Notes to Consolidated Financial Statements
For the years ended December 31, 2011 and 2010
(Stated in thousands of Canadian dollars, except share and per share amounts)

1. Statement of significant accounting policies

(j) Property and equipment

Property and equipment is stated at cost and depreciated to its estimated residual value. Assets under finance leases are initially recorded at the present value of minimum lease payments at the inception of the lease. Expected useful lives and depreciation methods are reviewed annually.

Asset class	Basis	Rate
Aircraft, net of estimated residual value	Straight-line	20 years
Engine, airframe and landing gear overhaul	Straight-line	8 to 15 years
Live satellite television equipment	Straight-line	10 years/Term of lease
Ground property and equipment	Straight-line	5 to 25 years
Spare engines and rotables, net of estimated residual value	Straight-line	20 years
Buildings	Straight-line	40 years
Leasehold improvements	Straight-line	Term of lease
 Assets under finance leases	Straight-line	Term of lease

Estimated residual values of the Corporation's aircraft range between $4,000 and $6,000 per aircraft. Spare engines have a residual value equal to 10% of the original purchase price. Residual values, where applicable, are reviewed annually against prevailing market rates at the consolidated statement of financial position date.

Major overhaul expenditures are capitalized and depreciated over the expected life between overhauls. All other costs relating to the maintenance of fleet assets are charged to the consolidated statement of earnings on consumption or as incurred.

(n) Leases

The determination of whether an arrangement is, or contains, a lease is made at the inception of the arrangement based on the substance of the arrangement and whether (i) fulfillment of the arrangement is dependent on the use of a specific asset and (ii) whether the arrangement conveys a right to use the asset.

The ROA with a capital lease is slightly lower than with an operating lease because average total assets are greater. The numerator is also larger, which offsets part of the impact of the larger denominator.

IFRS require extensive disclosure about an entity's lease arrangements. For operating leases, an entity should disclose the minimum lease payments in the next five years and beyond. For capital leases, an entity should disclose the amount of assets it has under capital leases, along with accumulated depreciation associated with those assets, and information about capital lease liabilities.

In Exhibit 9.3, you can see the information about finance lease liabilities on WestJet's statement of financial position. On December 31, 2011, WestJet had current finance (capital) lease obligations of $75,000 and non-current ones of $3,174,000. Exhibit 9.4 provides the following disclosures about its leases:[4]

www.westjet.com

- Accounting policies applied to finance (capital) leases are shown in Notes 1(j) and (n).
- Note 7 shows the carrying amount of assets under capital lease. There are $3,105,000 of leased assets included in property, plant, and equipment on the December 31, 2011 balance sheet.
- Note 18(b) gives a breakdown of the payments to be made for operating leases over the next five years and thereafter. This is important information because it gives insight into the amount of off-balance-sheet financing the company has.

EXHIBIT 9.4 (continued) WestJet Airlines Ltd.: Lease Disclosures

Finance leases transfer substantially all the risks and rewards incidental to ownership. Finance leases are recognized as assets and liabilities on the consolidated statement of financial position at the fair value of the leased property or, if lower, the present value of the minimum lease payments, each determined at the inception of the lease. Any costs directly attributable to the finance lease are added to the cost of the leased asset. Minimum lease payments are apportioned between a finance charge, which produces a constant rate of interest on the outstanding liability, and a principal reduction of the lease liability. Depreciation of finance lease assets follows the same methods used for other similar owned assets over the term of the lease.

Operating leases do not result in the transfer of substantially all risks and rewards incidental to ownership. Non-contingent lease payments are recognized as an expense in the consolidated statement of earnings on a straight-line basis over the term of the lease.

7. Property and equipment

	January 1 2011	Net additions	Depreciation[i]	Transfers	December 31 2011
Aircraft [ii]	1,616,263	32,164	(149,021)	15,227	1,514,633
Ground property and equipment	60,298	9,669	(10,843)	539	59,663
Spare engines and rotables	72,952	18,904	(6,305)	4,865	90,416
Deposits on aircraft	98,344	23,880	–	(11,979)	110,245
Buildings	122,662	6	(3,432)	–	119,236
Leasehold improvements	6,617	2,648	(761)	2,851	11,355
Assets under finance leases	3,243	–	(138)	–	3,105
Assets under development	9,143	4,934	–	(11,503)	2,574
	1,989,522	92,205	(170,500)	–	1,911,227

December 31, 2011	Cost	Accumulated depreciation	Net book value
Aircraft	2,510,811	(996,178)	1,514,633
Ground property and equipment	130,543	(70,880)	59,663
Spare engines and rotables	130,675	(40,259)	90,416
Deposits on aircraft	110,245	–	110,245
Buildings	135,822	(16,586)	119,236
Leasehold improvements	15,462	(4,107)	11,355
Assets under finance leases	4,221	(1,116)	3,105
Assets under development	2,574	–	2,574
	3,040,353	(1,129,126)	1,911,227

18. Commitments

(b) Operating leases and commitments

The Corporation has entered into operating leases and commitments for aircraft, land, buildings, equipment, computer hardware, software licenses and satellite programming. As at December 31, 2011 the future payments in US dollars, where applicable, and Canadian dollar equivalents under operating leases and commitments are as follows:

	USD	CAD
Within 1 year	191,462	219,271
1–3 years	371,634	400,588
3–5 years	262,846	279,747
Over 5 years	215,642	261,441
	1,041,584	1,161,047

As at December 31, 2011, the Corporation is committed to lease one additional 737-800 aircraft for a term of eight years in US dollars. This aircraft has been included in the above totals.

KNOWLEDGE CHECK 9.3

- ❑ Explain the difference between finance (capital) and operating leases. How does each affect the financial statements?
- ❑ On January 1, 2017, a company enters into a 10-year lease for some equipment. The lease requires annual payments of $25,000 on December 31 of each year. If the appropriate discount rate for the lease is 7 percent, how much would be recorded on the balance sheet for the equipment if the lease was classified as a capital lease?

QUESTION FOR CONSIDERATION

Explain why companies might prefer to have their leases classified as operating leases instead of capital leases. Explain why and how companies are able to arrange their leases to satisfy this preference under IFRS.

ANSWER: The disadvantage of a capital lease is that a liability equal to the present value of the lease payments must be reported on the balance sheet. This increases the amount of debt reported, which may affect the entity's perceived risk and perceived ability to carry additional debt. Measurements such as the debt-to-equity ratio increase when leases are capitalized, which may have economic consequences if there exists a covenant limiting the debt-to-equity ratio, or similar measures. Operating leases, on the other hand, have no effect on liabilities. They allow the entity to keep its lease liabilities "off the balance sheet."

A lease is classified as a capital lease if the risks and rewards of ownership are transferred to the lessee. IFRS don't clearly define risks and rewards of ownership, but they provide criteria for guiding managers, so judgment plays an important role in determining the classification.

ACCOUNTING STANDARDS FOR PRIVATE ENTERPRISES

ASPE provide quantitative guidelines to help managers classify leases. A lease for more than 75 percent of its useful life or with a present value of lease payments of more than 90 percent of the fair value of the asset indicate a capital lease. These guidelines are often interpreted as rules by managers. As a result, classifying a lease according to ASPE requires less judgment than IFRS (although the ASPE standard isn't intended to be used that way).

A private company might choose not to follow ASPE for leases. It may make sense for small businesses to avoid the complexities of lease accounting if their stakeholders don't require it.

PENSIONS AND OTHER POST-RETIREMENT BENEFITS

LO 5

As part of their compensation packages, many employees receive pensions and other benefits after they retire. A **pension** is income provided after retirement. Pensions are provided to Canadians by employers, by government, through the Canada and Quebec Pension Plans, and through personal savings in registered retirement savings plans (RRSPs). Retired employees can also receive benefits such as extended medical (medical costs not covered by a provincial health

TABLE 9.7 Benefit Plan Information for Some Large Canadian Companies

Company	Fair value of benefit plan assets	Estimated benefit obligation	Unfunded amount (difference between plan assets and estimated benefits)
BCE Inc.	$16,591,000,000	$19,357,000,000	($2,766,000,000)
Canadian National Railway Company	14,719,000,000	15,111,000,000	(392,000,000)
Canfor Corporation	529,900,000	806,100,000	(276,200,000)
Loblaw Companies Limited	1,330,000,000	1,906,000,000	(576,000,000)
Rogers Communications Inc.	684,000,000	817,000,000	(133,000,000)

plan), dental, vision, and prescription coverage. Employee pensions and other post-retirement employee benefits are negotiated between an employer and its employees.

Post-retirement benefits are an extremely important issue in Canada, for both economic and accounting reasons. The amounts involved in benefit plans give an idea of their economic significance. Table 9.7 gives the fair value of the assets in a number of Canadian companies' benefit plans and the estimated benefits that employees are entitled to as of the end of their 2011 fiscal years. Notice that for all of the companies shown, the benefits promised exceed the value of the assets in the plans, sometimes by huge amounts (like over $2.7 billion for BCE Inc.). This means the plans are underfunded—there aren't enough assets to meet the current obligations to the employees.

Accounting for pensions and post-retirement benefits is complex and the information reported in the financial statements can be confusing. Most of the issues in pension and post-retirement benefits accounting are beyond the scope of this book. However, because of the subject's economic significance and its prominence in many entities' financial statements, an introduction to it is appropriate.

Employees earn their benefits while they are working even though they receive them after they retire. In effect, instead of giving full compensation in cash while working, the employer funds a pension plan that provides benefits to employees after retirement. The benefits are part of employees' compensation so the cost is expensed over the employee's working career. In other words, it's a question of matching.

There are two types of pension plans: defined-contribution plans and defined-benefit plans. In a **defined-contribution plan** the employer makes contributions to the plan as specified in the pension agreement with the employees. For example, the employer's contribution might be a percentage of each employee's wage or salary. Employees often make contributions as well. The pension benefits an employee receives depend on the amount contributed to the plan by the employer and the employee and on the performance of the investments in the pension plan.

Accounting for defined-contribution plans is fairly straightforward. The employer's contribution is the pension expense for the year. A pension liability is reported on the employer's balance sheet if the full contribution isn't made by the end of the period. For example, under its defined-contribution pension plan, Nojack Ltd. (Nojack) is required to contribute $250,000 to the plan in 2017. On December 15, 2017, Nojack's treasurer wrote a cheque for $200,000 to the plan. The remaining $50,000 is to be paid in 2018. The entry that Nojack would make to record its contribution in 2017 is

Dr. Pension expense (expense +, shareholders' equity −)	250,000	
Cr. Cash (asset −)		200,000
Cr. Pension liability (liability +)		50,000

To record the contribution to the employee defined-contribution pension plan for 2017

The $50,000 pension liability would be reported on Nojack's December 31, 2017 balance sheet.

In a **defined-benefit plan**, the employer promises to provide employees with specified benefits in each year they are retired. For example, a defined-benefit plan might provide employees with a pension equal to 2.5 percent of the final year's salary for each year worked for the entity. An employee who worked for 30 years and had a salary in the last year of $125,000 would receive an annual pension of $93,750 ($125,000 × 0.025 × 30 years).

The crucial difference between defined-contribution and defined-benefit plans is risk. With a defined-benefit plan, employers bear the risk because they promise specified benefits to employees, regardless of how the investments in the pension plan perform. If there isn't enough money in the plan to pay the pensions, the employer must make up the difference. In a defined-contribution plan, the employer only promises a contribution. The pension the retired employee receives depends on the performance of the pension fund. As a result, the employee bears the risk.

With a defined-benefit pension plan, there are two decisions an entity must make. The first is the accounting question—what should the annual pension expense be? The second is the funding question—what should the annual contribution to the plan be? The pension expense and the amount contributed are often separate calculations, and the amounts don't have to be, and usually aren't, the same.

Determining the amount to expense and the amount to fund are complex present-value problems. The objective of a defined-benefit plan is to provide an employee with regular payments of a specified amount (an annuity) for the rest of the employee's life after retirement. The calculation itself is relatively straightforward, but the assumptions required are difficult. For example, consider the employee described previously who is to receive an annual pension of $93,750. Conceptually, the pension plan must have enough money on hand when the employee retires to purchase an annuity that will pay the employee $93,750 a year for life. If the employee is expected to live for 15 years after retirement and the appropriate discount rate is 8 percent, the plan would need $802,451.13 ($1/0.08 \times [1 - 1/(1 + 0.08)^{15}] \times$ $93,750) to purchase an annuity that guaranteed an annual payment of $93,750 for 15 years. Two crucial assumptions have been made: the number of years that the employee would live after retirement and the appropriate discount rate. If either of these assumptions changes, the amount that must be available in the retirement year to purchase the annuity would change, possibly dramatically.

We also have to determine the amount to invest in the pension plan each year over the employee's working life so the $802,451 will be in the plan when the employee retires. Then consider that we have to figure this out for an entire workforce, and the process becomes very complicated. The whole exercise is dependent on a set of assumptions:

- the number of years employees will work for the employer
- the number of employees who will qualify for benefits
- the number of employees who will die before they retire
- the age at which employees will retire
- the salary employees will earn in the year or years on which the pension is based
- the number of years employees will live after retirement
- the return the money in the pension fund will earn (the higher the expected return, the less money needs to be invested in the pension fund by the employer)

Now remember that funding pension plans and calculating pension expenses is based on events that will take place over the many years until an employee retires—20, 25, 30, or even more years into the future! These assumptions and the time span involved make pension accounting complex.

Accounting for other post-retirement benefits (other than pensions) is similar to the accounting for pensions. However, unlike pensions, companies aren't required to fund non-pension post-retirement benefits, and most pay for these benefits as they occur. The obligations can be significant and will likely grow as the number of retired employees grows.

An example of pension and benefits disclosure is provided in Exhibit 9.5 for Canfor Corporation, an integrated Canadian forest products company.[5] The numbered references below refer to the relevant parts of Exhibit 9.5.

www.canfor.com

EXHIBIT 9.5 Canfor Corporation: Pension and Other Benefit Plan Disclosures

3. Significant Accounting Policies

The following accounting policies have been applied to the financial information presented.

❶ ***Employee benefits***

Defined Contribution Plans

A defined contribution plan is a post-employment benefit plan under which an entity makes contributions to a separate entity and has no legal or constructive obligation to pay further amounts. Obligations for contributions to defined contribution pension plans are recognized as an employee benefit expense in net income when they are due.

Defined Benefit Plans

A defined benefit plan is a post-employment benefit plan other than a defined contribution plan. Canfor has various defined benefit plans that provide both pension and other retirement benefits to most of its salaried employees and certain hourly employees not covered by forest industry union plans. Canfor also provides certain health care benefits and pension bridging benefits to eligible retired employees.

13. Employee Future Benefits

Canfor has several funded and unfunded defined benefit plans, as well as defined contribution plans, that provide pension, other retirement and post-employment benefits to substantially all salaried employees and certain hourly employees. The defined benefit plans are based on years of service and final average salary. Canfor's other post-retirement benefit plans are non-contributory and include a range of health care and other benefits. Canfor also provides pension bridge benefits to certain eligible former employees.

Total cash payments for employee future benefits for 2011 were $71.9 million (2010—$64.5 million), consisting of cash contributed by Canfor to its funded pension plans, cash payments directly to beneficiaries for its unfunded other benefit plans, cash contributed to its defined contribution plans, and cash contributed to forest industry union defined benefit plans.

Defined benefit plans

Information about Canfor's defined benefit plans, in aggregate, is as follows:

Defined Benefit Plan Assets

	2011		2010	
(millions of Canadian dollars)	**Pension Benefit Plans**	**Other Benefit Plans**	Pension Benefit Plans	Other Benefit Plans
Fair market value of plan assets				
Beginning of year	**$ 513.5**	**$ –**	$ 466.8	$ –
Actual return on plan assets	**10.2**	**–**	45.6	–
Canfor contributions	**48.3**	**5.5**	38.7	5.1
Employee contributions	**0.8**	**–**	0.9	–
Benefit payments	**(42.9)**	**(5.5)**	(38.5)	(5.1)
❷ End of year	**$ 529.9**	**$ –**	$ 513.5	$ –

❶ The significant accounting policy for employee future benefits explains how the company accounts for its employee future benefits.

❷ The fair value of the assets in the pension plan is $529,900,000.

❸ The $631,600,000 is the pension benefits that employees have earned and that have been accounted for. The $174,500,000 is the non-pension benefits that have been accrued. Important: The assets and obligations of the pension fund itself don't appear in Canfor's balance sheet. The pension fund is a separate entity.

EXHIBIT 9.5 **(continued) Canfor Corporation: Pension and Other Benefit Plan Disclosures**

Defined Benefit Plan Obligations

	2011		2010	
(millions of Canadian dollars)	**Pension Benefit Plans**	**Other Benefit Plans**	Pension Benefit Plans	Other Benefit Plans
Accrued benefit obligation				
Beginning of year	**$ 608.0**	**$ 150.8**	$ 553.6	$ 123.7
Current service cost	**10.2**	**1.8**	8.8	1.7
Interest cost	**32.7**	**8.3**	33.7	8.0
Employee contributions	**0.8**	–	0.9	–
Benefit payments	**(42.9)**	**(5.5)**	(38.5)	(5.1)
Actuarial loss (gain)	**21.5**	**19.2**	49.5	22.0
Other	**1.3**	**(0.1)**	–	0.5
❸ End of year	**$ 631.6**	**$ 174.5**	$ 608.0	$ 150.8

Reconciliation of Funded Status of Benefit Plans to Amounts Recorded in the Financial Statements

	December 31, 2011		December 31, 2010		January 1, 2010	
(millions of Canadian dollars)	**Pension Benefit Plans**	**Other Benefit Plans**	Pension Benefit Plans	Other Benefit Plans	Pension Benefit Plans	Other Benefit Plans
Fair market value of plans assets	**$ 529.9**	**$ –**	$ 513.5	$ –	$ 466.8	$ –
Accrued benefit obligation	**(631.6)**	**(174.5)**	(608.0)	(150.8)	(553.6)	(123.7)
❹ Funded status of plans—surplus (deficit)	**$ (101.7)**	**$ (174.5)**	$ (94.5)	$ (150.8)	$ (86.8)	$ (123.7)
Unamortized past service costs	–	**0.1**	–	–	–	0.1
Effect of limit on recognition of asset	–	–	(4.1)	–	(3.8)	–
Accrued benefit liability	**$ (101.7)**	**$ (174.4)**	$ (98.6)	$ (150.8)	$ (90.6)	$ (123.6)
Pension bridge benefits	**(16.8)**	–	(18.4)	–	(15.9)	–
Other pension plans	**(2.4)**	–	(1.0)	–	0.8	–
Total accrued benefit liability, net	**$ (120.9)**	**$ (174.4)**	$ (118.0)	$ (150.8)	$ (105.7)	$ (123.6)

Significant assumptions

The actuarial assumptions used in measuring Canfor's benefit plan provisions and benefit costs are as follows:

	December 31, 2011		December 31, 2010		January 1, 2010	
	Pension Benefit Plans	**Other Benefit Plans**	Pension Benefit Plans	Other Benefit Plans	Pension Benefit Plans	Other Benefit Plans
❺ Accrued benefit obligations at reporting date:						
Discount rate	**5.00%**	**5.30%**	5.50%	5.75%	6.25%	6.75%
Rate of compensation increases	**3.00%**	**n/a**	3.00%	n/a	3.00%	n/a
Benefit costs for year ended December 31:						
Discount rate	**5.50%**	**5.75%**	6.25%	6.75%	n/a	n/a
Expected return on plan assets	**7.00%**	**n/a**	7.50%	n/a	n/a	n/a
Future salary increases	**3.00%**	**n/a**	3.00%	n/a	n/a	n/a

❹ This is the difference between the obligation to employees (❸) and the fair value of the assets in the plan (❷). There are some additional adjustments (beyond the scope of the book) that aren't shown in the exhibit that are needed to get to the exact amount that is reported on the balance sheet.

❺ These assumptions went into the calculations. They are very important because the results are only as good as the underlying assumptions. By disclosing them, stakeholders can assess whether they are reasonable.

Information about pensions and other post-retirement benefits is important to many stakeholders. These benefits can represent very significant obligations to an entity and may even affect its solvency. Increasingly, entities are questioning their ability to meet the commitments they have made to their employees and some have attempted to reduce the size of their commitments. Stakeholders want to assess the impact benefits have on the entity's ability to survive, compete, and be profitable. Employees and retired employees would clearly have an interest in information about the benefit plans since it affects the quality of their lives after retirement. The pension plan's condition provides information about an entity's cash flow requirements.

There is one final point about pension accounting. The complexity of the assumptions required to calculate the pension expense cause managers to exercise considerable judgment. Some critics contend that some managers have made unrealistic assumptions and that by doing so they have significantly understated the pension expense and pension liability.

LO 6

CONTINGENCIES

Suppose an entity realizes that it might incur a gain or a loss as the result of an event, but the amount of that gain or loss, or even if there will be one at all, is uncertain and won't be known until some future event occurs. What, if anything, should the impact on the financial statement be?

For example, in 2017, Rosyth Ltd. (Rosyth) was sued for $10,000,000. As of the end of fiscal 2018, the case hadn't been resolved so the amount (if anything) Rosyth will ultimately have to pay is unknown. The lawsuit could be accrued, disclosed in the notes, or ignored for financial reporting purposes. If accrued, the financial statements will reflect the economic impact of the lawsuit, but does it make sense to accrue contingencies that have a low probability of being realized? For example, a frivolous lawsuit launched by a disgruntled employee? Recognition would affect the financial statements, but would it result in a reasonable representation of the company's economic situation? It's not known what the cost will actually be, even though the suit is for $10,000,000. After all, just because someone sues you for $10,000,000 doesn't mean they're going to get $10,000,000. On the other hand, ignoring an event like this deprives stakeholders of important information about risks the entity faces and could open entities and their auditors to lawsuits for failing to provide important information. Disclosure provides information about existence and significance but doesn't affect the financial statement numbers, so outcomes such as bonus payments or covenants that depend on financial statement numbers aren't affected.

IFRS identify economic events called **contingent liabilities**, which have the following characteristics:

- a possible obligation whose existence has to be confirmed by a future event beyond the control of the entity (e.g., a judge's ruling in a lawsuit)
- an obligation with uncertainties about the probability that payment will be made or about the amount of payment (it doesn't meet the definition of a provision)

A contingent liability isn't recognized in the financial statements but is disclosed in the notes, unless the probability of having to pay is remote. If it's recognized, it's classified as a provision (discussed earlier in the chapter).

A contingent asset is an asset whose existence is uncertain. Contingent assets aren't recognized in the financial statements, but they are disclosed in the notes if realization is probable (IFRS define probable as "more likely than not"). If realization of the asset becomes virtually certain, the asset is recognized in the financial statements and no longer referred to as a contingent asset.

EXHIBIT 9.6 Canfor Corporation: Contingencies

27. Contingencies

On January 18, 2011, the U.S. triggered the arbitration provision of the 2006 Softwood Lumber Agreement ("SLA") by delivering a Request for Arbitration. The U.S. claims that the province of British Columbia ("BC") has not properly applied the timber pricing system grandparented in the SLA. The U.S. also claims that subsequent to 2006, BC made additional changes to the timber pricing system which had the effect of reducing timber prices. The claim focuses on substantial increases in Grade 4 (non sawlog or low grade) volumes commencing in 2007. It is alleged that timber was scaled and graded as Grade 4 that did not meet the criteria for that grade, and was accordingly priced too low.

As the arbitration is a state-to-state international dispute under the SLA, Canada is preparing a defence to the claim with the assistance of the BC provincial government and the BC lumber industry. In August 2011, the U.S. filed a detailed statement of claim with the arbitration panel, which Canada responded to in November 2011. The U.S. subsequently filed a reply, to which Canada filed a response in early February 2012. A hearing before the arbitration panel is currently expected before the end of the first quarter of 2012. It is not possible at this time to predict the outcome or the value of any final claim, and accordingly no provision has been recorded by the Company.

Canfor has other contingent liabilities in respect of legal claims arising in the ordinary course of business. It is not anticipated that any material liabilities will arise from such contingent liabilities.

Application of these accounting standards requires considerable judgment because it's necessary to estimate the probability of a contingency being realized and its amount.

Exhibit 9.6 provides the contingency note from Canfor Corporation's 2011 financial statements.[6] The note pertains to a long-standing trade dispute regarding the importation of Canadian lumber into the United States. Essentially, the U.S. is claiming that the price of Canadian lumber is too low, which is damaging to the U.S. lumber industry. The note explains the issue and concludes that it's not possible to predict the outcome of the dispute and the financial impact on Canfor, if any. As a result, no provision is recorded.

www.canfor.com

COMMITMENTS

LO 6

A **commitment** is a contractual agreement to enter into a future transaction. Agreements committing an entity to future purchases of goods or services aren't reported as liabilities, according to IFRS. These arrangements are called executory contracts. When neither party to a contract has performed its part of the bargain, neither the liability to pay nor the asset representing the good or service to be received is recorded. For example, it's common in professional sports for athletes to sign long-term, high-value, guaranteed contracts. Neither the liability to pay the athlete nor the team's right to the athlete's services are reported on the team's balance sheet. Signing the contract doesn't trigger recognition of the liability; performance by the athlete does. Once the athlete has played (assuming that he or she wasn't paid in advance), a liability for wages can be set up.

The IFRS approach isn't the only way of accounting for executory contracts. An alternative would be to record the asset and liability associated with the contract (perhaps only when it isn't possible for either party to cancel the contract). For example, in December 2017, Chopaka Inc. (Chopaka) signed a contract to purchase $400,000 of lumber for construction of new homes. The lumber is to be delivered over the period March through October 2018. The contract isn't cancellable by either Chopaka or the supplier. Under IFRS, this contract wouldn't be reflected in the financial statements. However, if executory contracts were recognized, Chopaka would report a $400,000 asset representing the lumber to be delivered and a $400,000 liability to pay for the lumber when it's delivered. There are no income statement effects of this treatment, but it increases assets and liabilities.

While IFRS generally don't allow for recognition of executory contracts, information about an entity's significant commitments can be important to stakeholders, so disclosure of them is appropriate. If Chopaka followed IFRS, it might disclose its contract to purchase lumber if it was significant. This decision is a judgment call made by the managers.

EXHIBIT 9.7 WestJet Airlines Ltd.: Commitments

Notes to Consolidated Financial Statements
For the years ended December 31, 2011 and 2010
(Stated in thousands of Canadian dollars, except share and per share amounts)

18. Commitments

(a) Purchased aircraft

As at December 31, 2011, the Corporation is committed to purchase 35 737-700 and two 737-800 aircraft for delivery between 2012 and 2018. The remaining estimated amounts to be paid in deposits and purchase prices for the 37 aircraft in US dollars and Canadian dollar equivalents are as follows:

	USD	CAD
Within 1 year	99,550	101,240
1–3 years	421,238	428,392
3–5 years	703,952	715,907
Over 5 years	386,466	393,030
	1,611,206	1,638,569

Exhibit 9.7 provides an example of commitment disclosure. Note 18(a) shows that WestJet Airlines Ltd. has committed to spend approximately $1.64 billion in 2012 and beyond to purchase new aircraft. Notice that the table in Note 18(a) shows how much money is committed in the different time periods. This information is helpful for predicting future cash requirements and financing needs. Purchase commitments are another example of off-balance-sheet obligations a company can have.

LO 6 EVENTS AFTER THE REPORTING PERIOD/SUBSEQUENT EVENTS

What happens if a significant economic event occurs after the end of an entity's fiscal year? Strictly speaking, events that didn't occur during the reporting period should be ignored. On the other hand, any information that is potentially useful to stakeholders should be provided on a timely basis, and IFRS recognize this. An **event after the reporting period**, or **subsequent event**, is an economic event that occurs after an entity's year-end but before the financial statements are released to stakeholders.

There are two subsequent event categories:

1. events that provide information about circumstances that existed at the year-end
2. events that happened after the end of the period

For the first type of subsequent event, the financial statements are adjusted to reflect the new information. The new information allows managers to make better estimates than they could at the financial statement date. Here are some examples of subsequent events that could lead to adjustments to the financial statements:

- A customer files for bankruptcy after the year-end; the estimated uncollectible accounts receivable might be adjusted.
- Sale of inventory after the end of the period; this could provide information about the NRV of the inventory at year-end.
- Settlement of a lawsuit after the year-end; a liability could be accrued rather than just disclosed in the notes.

EXHIBIT 9.8 Examples of Subsequent Event Notes

WestJet Airlines Ltd. (year-end December 31, 2011)

21. Subsequent events

(a) Aircraft financing

On February 2, 2012, the Ex-Im Bank authorized a final commitment of $77,559 to support the financing of the two 737-800 aircraft to be delivered in February and June of 2012. The final commitment is drawn down at the time the Corporation takes delivery of the aircraft. Upon delivery of the second aircraft, any unused portion of the final commitment will be cancelled. In conjunction with the final commitment, the Corporation secured two new term credit facilities with a Canadian chartered bank. The facilities will be financed in Canadian dollars and amortized over a 12-year term, each repayable in fixed principal instalments plus a floating rate of interest equal to the three month Canadian dealer offer rate plus 75 basis points. As disclosed in note 17, the Corporation has entered into swap contracts to fix the interest rate over the 12 year term of the loans at a rate of 2.89% and 2.99%, respectively, inclusive of the 75 basis points.

(b) Normal course issuer bid

On February 7, 2012, the Corporation filed a notice with the TSX to make a normal course issuer bid to purchase outstanding shares on the open market. As approved by the TSX, the Corporation is authorized to purchase up to 6,914,330 common voting shares and variable voting shares (representing approximately 5 per cent of the Corporation's issued and outstanding shares at the time of the bid) during the period February 10, 2012 to February 9, 2013, or until such time as the bid is completed or terminated at the Corporation's option. Any shares purchased under this bid will be purchased on the open market through the facilities of the TSX at the prevailing market price at the time of the transaction. Common voting shares and variable voting shares acquired under this bid will be cancelled.

Shoppers Drug Mart Corporation (year-end December 31, 2011)

31. SUBSEQUENT EVENTS

On January 20, 2012, $250,000 of three-year medium-term notes (the "Series 3 Notes"), were repaid in full, along with all accrued and unpaid interest owing on the final semi-annual interest payment. The repayment was financed through the combination of available cash and commercial paper issued under the Company's commercial paper program. The net debt position of the Company remained substantially unchanged as a result of these refinancing activities.

On February 9, 2012. the Board of Directors declared a dividend of 26.5 cents per common share payable April 13, 2012 to shareholders of record as of the close of business on March 30, 2012.

No information about these adjustments is disclosed in the notes. The information is used to revise the numbers in the statements.

www.westjet.com
www1.shoppersdrugmart.ca

The second type of subsequent event is events that took place after the end of the period and are unrelated to circumstances that existed at year-end. These events only appear in the notes—the financial statements aren't adjusted. Of course, many events occur after the year-end and virtually none of them are disclosed as subsequent events. What should be disclosed isn't well defined. IFRS say that events that will have a significant or material effect on the entity should be disclosed. In many cases, managers have flexibility as to whether and how an event occurring after the year-end will be reported in the financial statements.

For public companies, most events of any consequence would be disclosed to the public by newspaper reports or press releases long before the financial statements are released. For private companies, especially those that get little public attention, disclosure of the second type of event would much more likely to be "news" to stakeholders.

Information about subsequent events, regardless of how a stakeholder learns about them, is useful for forecasting future earnings or cash flows. Exhibit 9.8 provides some examples of subsequent event disclosures. The examples are about WestJet's arrangement of financing for the purchase of new aircraft and notice of the company's intention to repurchase some of its shares and Shoppers Drug Mart Corporation's announcements that it has repaid a note that was outstanding on December 31, 2011 and the declaration of a dividend.[7]

INSIGHT

Debt and Taxes

Earlier, we briefly discussed the tax implications of debt. Entities are allowed to deduct interest when calculating taxable income. (**Taxable income** is the measure of income, as defined by the *Income Tax Act*, that is used to calculate the amount of tax an entity must pay.) This means the actual cost of borrowing money is less than the amount paid to the lender. In effect, taxpayers pay for part of the cost of borrowing. The **after-tax cost of borrowing** is the interest rate an entity pays after taking into consideration the savings that come from being able to deduct interest in the calculation of taxable income. It's calculated using the following formula:

$$\text{After-tax cost of borrowing} = \text{Stated interest rate} \times (1 - \text{Tax rate})$$

Estmere Inc. (Estmere) has a $10,000,000 long-term bond outstanding that has an interest rate of 6 percent. Estmere pays the bondholder $600,000 in interest on December 31 of each year and its tax rate is 30 percent. Estmere's after-tax cost of borrowing is as follows:

$$\begin{aligned}\text{After-tax cost of borrowing} &= \text{Stated interest rate} \times (1 - \text{Tax rate})\\ &= 6\% \times (1 - 0.3)\\ &= 6\% \times 0.7\\ &= 4.2\%\end{aligned}$$

Since Estmere is able to reduce its income by $600,000 each year because it can deduct the interest cost, it has to pay $180,000 ($600,000 × 0.3) less tax than it would if the cost of borrowing weren't deductible.

LO 7

FINANCIAL STATEMENT ANALYSIS ISSUES

Analyzing an entity's liabilities provides important information about its financial situation and its prospects, and it can also provide insight into its financial management. For example, creditors can obtain information allowing them to assess the amount they would be willing to lend the entity; the terms of the loan, including interest rate and amount and type of collateral; and restrictive covenants. In addition, the evaluation of liabilities provides important information about an entity's liquidity. We looked at tools for evaluating liquidity in previous chapters. Below, tools for analyzing risk, capital structure, and the ability to carry debt are discussed.

Debt-to-Equity Ratio

The debt-to-equity ratio is a measure of the amount of debt relative to the equity an entity uses for financing. The ratio gives an indication of the entity's risk and ability to carry more debt. More debt makes an entity riskier. As explained earlier in the chapter, debt is riskier for an entity because interest and principal payments on debt must be made regardless of how well the entity is doing. An entity that has relatively little debt (compared with industry norms) is able to assume more.

It's important to recognize that debt isn't necessarily a bad way to finance an entity. Debt is less costly than equity and interest on debt is tax-deductible whereas dividends paid to shareholders aren't. However, debt becomes riskier for lenders as the amount of it increases because the likelihood of non-payment increases with the amount of debt. As a result, debt becomes costlier for borrowers because lenders are paid higher interest rates as compensation for accepting more risk. An entity should have a balance between debt and equity, but the appropriate mix depends on the nature of the entity. The debt-to-equity ratio is an important tool for evaluating an entity's debt load and its capital structure. (**Capital structure**, the amount of debt and equity the entity has, is the term used to describe how an entity is financed.)

TABLE 9.8 Debt-to-Equity Ratios of Canadian Airlines*

Debt-to-equity ratio	2011	2010	2009	2008	2007
WestJet	1.54	1.59	1.72	2.02	2.14
Air Canada†	−3.40	−8.88	−6.01	13.91	3.85
Air Transat	1.88	1.71	2.07	2.70	2.88

*WestJet's and Air Canada's ratios for 2011, 2010, and 2009 are based on information prepared in accordance with IFRS. WestJet's and Air Canada's ratios for 2007–2008 and Air Transat's ratios for all years are based on information prepared in accordance with Canadian GAAP in effect at the time.
†Air Canada's debt-to-equity ratio is negative in some years because equity was negative in those years.

The debt-to-equity ratio is defined as

$$\text{Debt-to-equity ratio} = \frac{\text{Total liabilities}}{\text{Total shareholders' equity}}$$

WestJet's debt-to-equity ratio on December 31, 2011 is calculated as

$$\begin{aligned}\text{Debt-to-equity ratio} &= \frac{\text{Total liabilities}}{\text{Total shareholders' equity}}\\ &= \frac{\$2{,}103{,}461}{\$1{,}370{,}217}\\ &= 1.54\end{aligned}$$

WestJet's debt-to-equity ratio of 1.54 means it has $1.54 of liabilities for every $1 of equity. Is that too much? It isn't possible to answer without a context. Determining whether a ratio is too high depends on many factors, including industry and circumstances. Entities that have highly reliable cash flows can carry more debt because they can be confident that the cash flows will be available to make interest and principal payments. WestJet's ratio has steadily declined since 2007 (see Table 9.8). The decline is due to decreasing the amount of long-term debt the company is carrying and increasing retained earnings (due to net income). The ratios of Air Canada and Air Transat are also provided in Table 9.8 for comparison. Note that in the period shown, Air Canada went through significant financial crises that resulted in the company filing for bankruptcy protection.

Interest Coverage Ratio

The **interest coverage ratio** is one of a number of coverage ratios that measure an entity's ability to meet its fixed financing charges. In particular, the interest coverage ratio indicates how easily an entity can meet its interest payments from its current income. The interest coverage ratio is defined as

$$\text{Interest coverage ratio} = \frac{\text{Net income} + \text{Interest expense} + \text{Income tax expense}}{\text{Interest expense}}$$

The larger the ratio, the better able the entity is to meet its interest payments. The ratio is limiting in that it ignores the fact that entities have financing charges other than interest. These include debt repayment and payments on operating leases. This ratio can be modified to include these other charges, but the interest coverage ratio is appropriate to this introductory discussion.

The interest coverage ratio for WestJet for the year ended December 31, 2011 is calculated as

$$\begin{aligned}\text{Interest coverage ratio} &= \frac{\text{Net income} + \text{Interest expense} + \text{Income tax expense}}{\text{Interest expense}}\\ &= \frac{\$148{,}702{,}000 + \$60{,}911{,}000 + \$59{,}304{,}4000}{\$60{,}911{,}000}\\ &= 4.41\end{aligned}$$

TABLE 9.9 Interest Coverage Ratios for Canadian Airlines[8]

Interest coverage ratio	2011	2010	2009	2008	2007	2006
WestJet	4.41	2.88	3.02	4.35	4.08	3.17
Air Canada	0.22	0.94	0.95	n.m.*	2.66	1.04
Air Transat	n.m.	21.32	13.70	n.m.	15.32	12.33

*n.m. means the ratio isn't meaningful, usually because of negative income.

The interest coverage ratio of 4.41 means that WestJet's income before taxes and interest expense covers its interest costs over four times. Of course, earnings and cash flows can be volatile and coverage ratios can change dramatically from period to period. Also, net income isn't cash.

WestJet's interest coverage ratio for the period 2006 through 2011 is shown in Table 9.9, along with the ratios for Air Canada and Air Transat. WestJet has consistently had a higher ratio than Air Canada but a much lower one than Air Transat, in the last five years (except in 2008 and 2011 when Air Transat reported losses).

LO 7

THE IMPACT OF OFF-BALANCE-SHEET LIABILITIES

So far in this chapter we have encountered a number of off-balance-sheet liabilities. Leases, pensions, contingencies, and commitments can give rise to obligations not classified as liabilities on the balance sheet, even if the entity is in compliance with accounting standards. In this section, we'll look at the impact that off-balance-sheet liabilities can have on the balance sheet.

www.westjet.com

Exhibit 9.9 provides the commitments and contingencies note from WestJet's 2011 financial statements and a table of contractual obligations taken from the management discussion and analysis.[9] Refer also to the liabilities and shareholders' equity side of WestJet's 2011 balance sheet in Exhibit 9.3. On December 31, 2011, WestJet reported liabilities of $2,103,461,000. In addition, it had commitments to spend $1,638,569,000 on new aircraft in 2012 and beyond, and $1,161,047,000 in operating leases and other commitments from 2012 forward. Discounting these amounts using a rate of 20 percent gives a present value for these off-balance-sheet items of about $900,000,000, which would increase liabilities on December 31, 2011, to $3,003,461,000—an amount about 43 percent greater than the amount actually reported. As a result, the debt-to-equity ratio (total liabilities ÷ shareholders' equity) would increase from 1.54 to 2.19. There are some important points to keep in mind when thinking about this analysis:

- The off-balance-sheet items have a significant effect on an important measure of capital structure and risk, and it's important to consider them when analyzing the financial statements. Misleading conclusions can be drawn if they aren't considered. If an entity makes extensive use of operating leases, liabilities and the debt-to-equity ratio will be understated.
- Off-balance-sheet obligations can impair comparability if companies use different approaches to acquiring assets (purchase versus lease).
- WestJet's accounting for these off-balance-sheet items is legitimate and appropriate.
- WestJet's actual risk isn't affected by including the off-balance-sheet items in a debt-to-equity analysis, but risk measurement is affected.

This situation is not unique to WestJet. Many companies have significant off-balance-sheet obligations. For example, Magna International Inc. had US$1.608 billion in operating lease commitments on December 31, 2011. Air Canada had commitments of almost $5 billion to purchase new aircraft and over $2 billion in operating lease commitments. Clearly, it's very important to pay attention to these off-balance-sheet obligations to get a complete view of an entity's situation. One has to wonder whether IFRS should recognize all these items on the balance sheet to achieve a complete picture of a company's obligations.

EXHIBIT 9.9 WestJet Airlines Ltd.: Off-Balance-Sheet Liabilities

18. Commitments

(a) Purchased aircraft

As at December 31, 2011, the Corporation is committed to purchase 35 737-700 and two 737-800 aircraft for delivery between 2012 and 2018. The remaining estimated amounts to be paid in deposits and purchase prices for the 37 aircraft in US dollars and Canadian dollar equivalents are as follows:

	USD	CAD
Within 1 year	99,550	101,240
1–3 years	421,238	428,392
3–5 years	703,952	715,907
Over 5 years	386,466	393,030
	1,611,206	1,638,569

(b) Operating leases and commitments

The Corporation has entered into operating leases and commitments for aircraft, land, buildings, equipment, computer hardware, software licenses and satellite programming. As at December 31, 2011 the future payments in US dollars, where applicable, and Canadian dollar equivalents under operating leases and commitments are as follows:

	USD	CAD
Within 1 year	191,462	219,271
1–3 years	371,634	400,588
3–5 years	262,846	279,747
Over 5 years	215,642	261,441
	1,041,584	1,161,047

From WestJet's Management Discussion and Analysis

Contractual obligations and commitments

At December 31, 2011, our contractual obligations, which do not include commitments for goods and services required in the ordinary course of business, are indicated in the following table:

($ in thousands)	Total	Within 1 year	1–3 years	3–5 years	Over 5 years
Long-term debt repayments	828,712	158,832	319,100	222,194	128,586
Obligations under finance leases	5,596	245	490	490	4,371
Operating leases and commitments (i)	1,161,047	219,271	400,588	279,747	261,441
Purchase obligations (ii)	1,638,569	101,240	428,392	715,907	393,030
Total contractual obligations	3,633,924	479,588	1,148,570	1,218,338	787,428

(i) Relates to operating leases and commitments for aircraft, land, buildings, equipment, computer hardware, software licenses and satellite programming. Included within the amounts are US dollar obligations, converted at the period exchange rate of 1.0169 Canadian dollars to one US dollar, of: within one year—US $191,462; 1–3 years—US $371,634 (2013—US $186,694 and 2014—US $184,940); 3–5 years—US $262,846 (2015—US $150,010 and 2016—US $112,836) and Over 5 years—US $215,642.

(ii) Relates to purchased aircraft. The purchase obligations in US dollars, converted at the period exchange rate of 1.0169 Canadian dollars to one US dollar are: within one year—US $99,550; 1–3 years—US $421,238 (2013—US $220,525 and 2014—US $200,713); 3–5 years—US $703,952 (2015—US $363,251 and 2016—US $340,701) and Over 5 years—US $386,466.

Solved Problem

The solved problem for this chapter is another example of a user-oriented case. This case will give you more experience with and exposure to situations where you have to work with the financial statements provided so you can learn to look critically at what is done and to apply your knowledge to satisfy your client.

BENITO CORP.

In October 2017, the Benito family sold its 100 percent interest in Benito Corp. (BC) to a corporation wholly owned by the Nampa family. Because the two families couldn't agree on an exact selling price, the contract of purchase and sale required that the purchaser pay an amount equal to four times BC's audited net income before taxes for the fiscal year ended September 30, 2018. When BC was purchased, the Nampa family replaced the company's senior management. The new CEO of BC is the son of the head of the Nampa family, Shayne Nampa. Shayne has explained that acquiring BC is an important step in the growth of the Nampa family's corporate holdings, and an important objective is to minimize the income taxes.

On October 25, 2018, Ellin Benito approached you for advice. She explained that the Benito family had received BC's financial statements and they were very concerned about some aspects of them. They believe that Shayne Nampa isn't acting in good faith and is trying to cheat the Benito family of money that is rightfully owed to them. Ms. Benito has asked you for a detailed report analyzing aspects of the financial statements the Benito family find questionable. She would like thorough explanations of the issues and recommendations for alternative treatments you think are more appropriate. Ms. Benito wants you to provide clear explanations and support for your positions so she will be able to explain her concerns when she meets Mr. Nampa. The outstanding items are described below:

a. During fiscal 2017 (before BC was sold), BC management began planning to offer its products online. Shayne Nampa continued the development of the new e-business and expects that it will be launched mid-way through fiscal 2019. Through the end of fiscal 2018, BC spent $476,000 developing the new e-business. Costs were incurred for Web site design, market surveys, and so on. The costs incurred in 2017 had been capitalized but BC expensed the full amount in fiscal 2018.

b. In May 2018, BC signed a contract with Fong Inc. for a $200,000 order of specially designed products. Fong Inc. didn't want to take delivery until the order was complete, so BC agreed to deliver the products in September 2018. Representatives of Fong Inc. monitored production to ensure that all finished goods met Fong Inc.'s specifications. Fong Inc. agreed to pay BC as production proceeded and as a result, by August 2018 Fong Inc. had paid 80 percent of the agreed price. The remaining 20 percent was to be paid on final delivery. The products were ready for shipping in the first week of September 2018. However, Ms. Benito learned from a BC employee that BC requested and obtained permission to delay shipping until mid-October. The products were finally delivered on October 13, 2018 and revenue was recognized at that time. BC normally recognizes revenue on delivery. The cost of the order was $110,000.

c. In August 2018, BC signed a $40,000 contract with Cashtown Maintenance Ltd. to do major repairs and maintenance to some of its equipment. The work began in late October and is expected to be completed sometime in November. BC paid Cashtown $15,000 when the agreement was signed, with the remainder due when the work is complete. BC expensed the full $40,000 when the contract was signed and recorded an accounts payable for the amount that was owing.

d. During fiscal 2018, a manager who had been with the company for many years was fired by Shayne Nampa after it became clear to Mr. Nampa that they wouldn't be able to work together. The manager was offered a small settlement but she declined and has filed a $500,000 wrongful dismissal lawsuit against BC. BC has accrued a provision of $300,000 just in case they have to pay.

Required:

Prepare the report requested by Ellin Benito.

REPORT TO ELLIN BENITO ON THE SEPTEMBER 30, 2018 FINANCIAL STATEMENTS OF BENITO CORP.

Dear Ms. Benito:

Thank you for engaging me to examine the September 30, 2018 financial statements of Benito Corp. (BC). Based on the information you provided, it appears that Shayne Nampa is using International Financial Reporting Standards (IFRS) to his advantage and to your detriment. You may find it surprising, but IFRS are quite flexible and often require judgment, and managers can sometimes use that for their own economic benefit. Since the final selling price for Benito Corp. depends on the company's income for fiscal 2018, it is in Mr. Nampa's interest to report as low a net income as he can justify. I will look at each of the issues in turn:

New e-business: BC expensed all the costs incurred ($476,000) for its proposed e-business in fiscal 2018. By expensing the amount rather than treating it as an asset, management is saying that the money spent has no future benefit, or that the future benefit is very uncertain. It is not acceptable under IFRS to overstate assets but that doesn't mean that you can write off any costs incurred. If there is a case for supporting a future benefit for the amounts spent then it is appropriate to capitalize the costs and amortize them when revenue is being earned; that is, match the costs to the revenue. One could look at this the same way as research and development costs. Early stage costs (research) should be expensed but development costs should be capitalized if they result in future benefits (profitability). The key question is, what are the revenue prospects for the new e-business? Mr. Nampa is continuing with development, which suggests that he thinks it will be successful. If there is reasonable evidence that the investment will be recovered from its operation, then the costs should be capitalized. It is not possible to provide a definitive conclusion at this point, but it is also not necessary to accept the treatment used in BC's financial statements.

Comment: *IFRS can often be reasonably interpreted in different ways. Just because the managers who prepared the financial statements have made certain choices doesn't mean you shouldn't or can't question those choices. To serve the needs of your client, you need to consider alternative ways of accounting. However, it's essential that you provide valid support for your alternative. An alternative shouldn't be proposed just because it's better for your client. It should be proposed because it's better for your client and it can be supported with the constraints and facts.*

Sale to Fong Inc.: It is my opinion that BC rearranged the terms of the contract with Fong Inc. to avoid recognizing the revenue in fiscal 2018. BC normally recognizes revenue on delivery, and by delaying delivery until after the year-end it was able to defer this revenue and income. This delay violates the spirit of the agreement made with the Benito family. As of September 30, 2018, all the conditions necessary for recognizing revenue had been achieved: production was complete, Fong representatives were satisfied that the goods met specifications, the goods were ready for shipment, and 80 percent of the agreed price had been paid. In essence, the risks and rewards of ownership had been transferred even though BC had physical custody of the goods. Delivery had not occurred, but the delay was at BC's request. Revenue should be recognized on the Fong sale in the year ended September 30, 2018.

Comment: *This situation is an excellent example of how acceptable accounting according to IFRS leads to an undesirable outcome for a stakeholder. The revenue recognition criteria are designed to discourage entities from recognizing their revenue too early. For the sale of BC, the conservative nature of the criteria serves the purposes of the new owners. Further, revenue should be recognized at the earliest time revenue recognition is achieved; in the sale to Fong, that would be in September 2018. Further, simply following IFRS doesn't automatically make a treatment appropriate in the circumstances. From the information provided, it's clear that BC modified the terms of the contract to reduce income and the amount it would pay the Benito family. As an advisor to Ms. Benito, it's appropriate to call into question the structure of and accounting for the transaction.*

Expensing of repairs and maintenance in fiscal 2018: No expense should have been recorded in 2018 for this work. The work was not done until fiscal 2019 so there was no reason to record an expense in 2018—the work should be matched to the period in which it was performed or, if it meets the definition of an asset, should be capitalized at the time the work is done. The payment made in

August 2018 should have been recorded as a prepaid. There is no liability at the end of 2018 because there is no present obligation at the end of fiscal 2018. The liability would arise when the work is done. This is an executory contract for the unpaid portion since neither party has performed.

Accrual of provision in wrongful dismissal suit: This seems more like a contingent liability than an event for which a provision should be recorded. More information about the specifics of the case are required but it is likely difficult to determine the actual amount the fired employee will receive or if anything will be received. It seems that BC was aggressive in recognizing the expense and the liability to lower net income and the selling price. It is appropriate to record a provision if a payout for the lawsuit is probable, and in a case like this it seems quite possible that BC should pay. However, any amount recorded should be reasonable.

The impact on the income of these adjustments can be summarized as follows:

New e-business	$476,000
Sale to Fong Incorporated	90,000
Repairs and maintenance	40,000
Wrongful dismissal	300,000
Total increase in net income before taxes	$906,000

If all these adjustments are made there would be an increase in the selling price of BC of $3,624,000 ($906,000 × 4).

Again, thank you for using my services. If you have any questions, please do not hesitate to contact me.

Sincerely,

John Friedlan, CA

SUMMARY OF KEY POINTS

LO 1 Liabilities are obligations to provide cash, goods, or services to customers, suppliers, employees, governments, lenders, and any other creditors. According to IFRS, liabilities are obligations arising from past transactions or economic events that an entity must sacrifice economic resources to satisfy. In principle, liabilities should be valued at their present value, and in many cases they are. However, there are some exceptions.

LO 2 Current liabilities are obligations that will be satisfied in one year or one operating cycle. Information about current obligations is important for assessing the short-term liquidity of an entity. Current liabilities are usually not discounted to their present value. There are many different types of current liabilities, including loans, accounts payable, collections on behalf of third parties, accrued liabilities, and unearned revenue.

LO 3 A bond is a formal borrowing arrangement in which a borrower agrees to make periodic interest payments to the lenders, as well as to repay the principal at a specified time in the future. The essential characteristics of a bond are its face value, maturity date, and coupon rate. The price of bonds and other long-term debt are determined by discounting the interest and principal payments to investors using the effective interest rate.

If a bond's coupon rate is different from the effective interest rate, a premium or discount arises, which is amortized over the life of the debt. The amount amortized each period is included in the interest expense for the period. Once a bond is recorded, its value isn't adjusted for changes in market interest rates. If the end of the reporting period doesn't correspond with the date interest payments are made, the interest expense and interest payable must be accrued. When debt is retired early, any premium or discount must be removed from the books immediately, and a gain or a loss may arise from this.

LO 4 A lease is a contractual arrangement whereby a lessee agrees to pay a lessor a fee in exchange for the use of an asset. There are two types of leases: capital or finance leases and operating leases. A capital/finance lease transfers the risks and rewards of ownership to the lessee. Assets associated with a capital/finance lease are capitalized on the balance sheet of the lessee, along with a liability equal to the present value of the lease payments to be made over the life of the lease. An important accounting and reporting benefit of capital/finance leases is that they overcome off-balance-sheet financing. If the risks and rewards of ownership aren't transferred to the lessee, then it's an operating lease. Under an operating lease, the lessee recognizes an expense when the payment to the lessor is paid or payable.

LO 5 A pension provides income to a person after retirement. Employees earn their pensions and other post-retirement benefits while they are working, even though they receive the benefits after they retire. There are two types of pension plans: defined contribution and defined benefit. Accounting for defined-contribution plans is relatively straightforward, but accounting for defined-benefit plans is complex because it's necessary to estimate and accrue the cost of benefits that won't be received for many years.

LO 6 A contingent liability is a possible obligation whose existence has to be confirmed by a future event that isn't in the control of the entity, or it's an obligation with uncertainties about the probability that payment will be made or the amount of payment (it doesn't meet the definition of a provision). A contingent liability isn't recognized in the financial statements but it is disclosed in the notes, unless the probability of having to pay is remote.

A commitment is a contractual agreement to enter into a transaction in the future. Agreements that commit an entity to purchase goods or services in the future aren't reported as liabilities, according to IFRS. Significant commitments should be disclosed in the notes to the financial statements.

A subsequent event is an economic event that occurs after an entity's year-end, but before the financial statements are released to stakeholders. When a subsequent event provides additional information about circumstances that existed at the year-end, the financial statements should be adjusted to reflect the new information. Subsequent events unrelated to circumstances at year-end should only be disclosed in the notes to the financial statements if they are material or significant.

LO 7 Analysis of an entity's liabilities can provide important information about its financial situation and prospects. This analysis can also provide insight into the financial management of the entity. Two tools for analyzing liabilities are the debt-to-equity ratio and the interest coverage ratio. In addition, the evaluation of liabilities provides important information about an entity's liquidity.

LO 8 (Appendix) Future income taxes arise because the accounting policies used to prepare general purpose financial statements are sometimes different from the rules entities must follow to determine the amount of income tax they must pay. The differences that give rise to future income taxes are temporary and eventually reverse. Future income taxes don't represent money owed to or owed by the government.

APPENDIX: DEFERRED INCOME TAXES/FUTURE INCOME TAXES

LO 8

Perhaps one of the most confusing and misunderstood topics in accounting is *deferred income taxes* or *future income taxes* (you'll see both terms used in financial statements). Table 9.10 shows the deferred income tax asset or liability of four Canadian companies. With numbers this big it's important to understand where they come from and what they mean.

TABLE 9.10 Deferred Income Tax Assets and Liabilities of Some Canadian Companies

Company (year-end shown in brackets)	**Deferred income tax asset**	**Percentage of total assets**	**Deferred income tax liability**	**Percentage of total liabilities**
Indigo Books & Music (3/31/2012)	$48,633,000	8.2%		
Encana Corporation (12/31/2011)			US$4,086,000,000	23.2%
Canfor Corporation (12/31/2011)	18,100,000	0.7%	103,300,000	9.9%
WestJet Airlines Ltd. (12/31/2011)			326,456,000	15.5%

Note: Information for all companies is prepared in accordance with IFRS.

EXHIBIT 9.10 WestJet Airlines Ltd.: Income Statement

Consolidated Statement of Earnings
For the years ended December 31
(Stated in thousands of Canadian dollars, except per share amounts)

	Note	2011	2010
Revenues:			
Guest		2,790,299	2,390,887
Other		281,241	216,407
		3,071,540	2,607,294
Expenses:			
Aircraft fuel		915,878	674,608
Airport operations		421,561	388,112
Flight operations and navigational charges		344,442	325,582
Sales and distribution		273,364	255,732
Marketing, general and administration		209,880	194,481
Depreciation and amortization		174,751	170,462
Aircraft leasing		165,571	143,381
Maintenance		146,260	117,057
Inflight		139,478	124,303
Employee profit share		23,804	22,222
		2,814,989	2,415,940
Earnings from operations		256,551	191,354
Non-operating income (expense):			
Finance income	16	15,987	9,910
Finance costs	16	(60,911)	(70,914)
Gain on foreign exchange		2,485	2,579
(Loss) gain on disposal of property and equipment		(54)	570
Loss on derivatives		(6,052)	(34)
		(48,545)	(57,889)
Earnings before income tax		208,006	133,465
Income tax expense:	12		
Current		1,236	1,573
Deferred		58,068	41,695
		59,304	43,268
Net earnings		148,702	90,197

www.westjet.com

Deferred income taxes have two sides. They appear as assets and liabilities on the balance sheet and they are reported on the income statement as part of the income tax expense. Examine WestJet's income statement in Exhibit 9.10 and notice that the *income tax expense* is split into two parts: current expense and deferred expense.[10] The current expense is the income taxes WestJet must pay now—the amount calculated on WestJet's tax return and cash paid or is currently payable to government. For the year ended December 31, 2011, WestJet had to pay income taxes of $1,236,000 and its deferred income tax expense was $58,068,000. WestJet's income tax expense for 2011 was $59,304,000 ($1,236,000 + $58,068,000). Also look at WestJet's balance sheet in Exhibit 9.3 and notice the deferred income tax liability of $326,456,000.

The first thing to recognize is that deferred income taxes have nothing to do with the amount of income tax an entity has to pay. **Deferred (future) income tax assets and liabilities** and the **deferred (future) income tax expense** arise because the accounting methods used to prepare

TABLE 9.11 **Temporary and Permanent Differences between Tax and Financial Reporting**

Issue	Type of difference	Tax	Financial reporting
Depreciation of assets	Temporary	CCA (capital cost allowance) at prescribed rates	Depreciate in a "systematic" way over an asset's useful life
Revenue recognition	Temporary	Percentage of completion for contracts lasting more than two years	Completed-contract or zero-profit methods allowed if consistent with the facts
Warranty costs	Temporary	Deduct when the warranty cost is incurred	Accrue the expense when the revenue is recognized
Discounts and premiums on long-term debt repaid	Temporary	Recognized when the principal is repaid	Amortized over the term of the debt
Pension costs	Temporary	Deduct when money contributed to the pension fund	Expense based on accounting estimate of the pension obligation
Meals and entertainment expenses	Permanent	Only 50 percent of the amount spent is deductible	100 percent is expensed
Interest and penalties on late payment of taxes	Permanent	Not deductible	Expensed

general purpose financial statements are sometimes different from the methods used to calculate the income tax an entity must pay. When the *Income Tax Act* (ITA) specifies how an entity must account for particular transactions and economic events, that method must be used for tax purposes, but a different accounting method can be used for financial reporting purposes.

There are many revenues and expenses that are recognized for both tax and financial reporting purposes, but recognition happens at different times. These differences in timing are called **temporary differences** and they give rise to deferred income taxes. **Permanent differences** are revenues and expenses recognized for tax purposes but not for financial reporting purposes, or recognized for financial reporting purposes but not for tax purposes. These are referred to as permanent because they never reverse. Examples of temporary and permanent differences are shown in Table 9.11.

Deferred income taxes arise because certain assets and liabilities are measured differently for tax and financial reporting purposes. The amount of deferred income tax associated with an asset or liability at a point in time is calculated using the following formula (this is the amount that would appear on the balance sheet at the end of a period):

$$\text{Future income tax}_{\text{end of period}} = \left[\begin{matrix}\text{Tax basis of an} \\ \text{asset or liability}\end{matrix} - \begin{matrix}\text{Accounting basis of} \\ \text{an asset or liability}\end{matrix}\right] \times \text{Tax rate}$$

The tax basis of an asset or liability is its carrying amount for tax purposes. For a capital asset the tax basis would be the cost of the asset less the amount of capital cost allowance deducted since it was acquired. The accounting basis of an asset or liability is the carrying amount for financial reporting purposes. It's the amount reported on a general purpose balance sheet.

The amount of deferred income tax expense for a period related to an asset or liability is calculated as follows:

$$\begin{matrix}\text{Deferred income tax on} \\ \text{the balance sheet}_{\text{end of period}}\end{matrix} - \begin{matrix}\text{Deferred income tax on} \\ \text{the balance sheet}_{\text{beginning of period}}\end{matrix} = \text{Deferred income tax expense}$$

This calculation is done for every asset and liability for which there is a difference between the tax basis and accounting basis, to obtain the deferred income tax amounts on the balance sheet and income statement.

To see how this works, we'll examine a common source of temporary differences: CCA versus depreciation expense. For tax purposes, a company must follow the CCA rules in the ITA, while

TABLE 9.12 Comparison of Tax Basis and Accounting Basis for Askilton Inc.'s Machine

	Tax			Financial reporting			Deferred income taxes		
	Tax basis, January 1 [1]	CCA for the year [2]	Tax basis, December 31 [3]	Accounting basis (carrying amount), January 1 [4]	Depreciation expense [5]	Accounting basis (carrying amount), December 31 [6]	Tax basis − Accounting basis [7]	Deferred income tax asset (liability) [8]	Deferred income tax expense [9]
2017	$200,000	$30,000	$170,000	$200,000	$20,000	$180,000	($10,000)	($ 2,000)	(2,000)
2018	170,000	51,000	119,000	180,000	20,000	160,000	(41,000)	(8,200)	(6,200)
2019	119,000	35,700	83,300	160,000	20,000	140,000	(56,700)	(11,340)	(3,140)

for financial reporting purposes depreciation is calculated to match the cost of capital assets to the revenues they help earn.

On January 1, 2017, Askilton Inc. (Askilton) purchased a new machine for $200,000. For tax purposes, the machine has a CCA rate of 30 percent declining balance. For accounting purposes, management is depreciating the machine straight-line over ten years with no residual value. Askilton's tax rate is 20 percent. Table 9.12 compares the tax and financial reporting bases for Askilton's machine, and shows the calculation of deferred income tax amounts.

[1] Tax basis of the asset at the beginning of the year: equals the tax basis at the end of the previous year.

[2] Amount of CCA for the year: equals the tax basis at the beginning of the year times 30%, except for 2017 where the amount is $200,000 × 30% × 50% (half-year rule).

[3] Tax basis of the asset at the end of the year: equals the tax basis at the beginning of the year, less CCA for the year.

[4] Accounting basis of the asset at the beginning of the year: equals the accounting basis at the end of the previous year.

[5] Depreciation expense for the year (cost ÷ useful life [$200,000 ÷ 10 years]).

[6] Accounting basis of the asset at the end of the year: equals the accounting basis at the beginning of the year less the depreciation expense for the year.

[7] Column [3] − column [6]: difference between the tax basis and accounting basis for the machine at the end of the year.

[8] Column [7] × tax rate (20%): deferred income tax liability associated with the machine at year-end.

[9] Amount by which the deferred income tax liability changed during the year: The balance in the deferred income tax liability account on December 31, 2017 is ($2,000). The required balance on December 31, 2018 is ($8,200). To reach the required balance an adjustment of ($6,200) is needed. In journal entry terms, a credit to deferred income tax liability and a debit to deferred income tax expense for $6,200 are needed.

Table 9.13 shows different situations that give rise to deferred income tax assets and liabilities. In the case of Askilton's machine (an asset), the tax basis of the machine is less than the accounting basis (column 1 < column 4 in Table 9.12) on December 31 of each year, so there is a deferred

TABLE 9.13 Tax Basis, Accounting Basis, and Deferred Income Tax Balance

			Deferred income tax balance
Tax basis of an asset	>	Accounting basis of an asset	Asset
Tax basis of an asset	<	Accounting basis of an asset	Liability
Tax basis of a liability	>	Accounting basis of an liability	Liability
Tax basis of a liability	<	Accounting basis of an liability	Asset

income tax liability. What the deferred income tax liability means is that more of the cost of the machine has been expensed for tax purposes than for financial reporting purposes (the amount of CCA claimed is greater than the amount of depreciation expensed on the machine).

The other piece of the puzzle is the amount of tax Askilton has to pay. Calculating taxes can be very complicated and won't be discussed here. To show the presentation in the financial statements, we'll assume the following:

	Income before taxes	Current income tax expense
2017	$65,000	$10,000
2018	78,000	9,400
2019	70,000	11,460

The income tax expense in Askilton's income statement would be reported as shown in Table 9.14. (It's assumed that the only source of deferred income taxes is Askilton's machine.) Financial statements must disclose the current and deferred portions of the income tax expense. The amount can be shown in the income statement, as in Table 9.14, or in the notes to the financial statements. The balance sheet presentation is shown in Table 9.15.

TABLE 9.14 Financial Statement Presentation of Deferred Income Taxes

Askilton Inc.
Income Statement Extracts
December 31,

	2017	2018	2019
Income before taxes	$65,000	$78,000	$70,000
Income tax expense:			
Current expense	10,000	9,400	11,460
Deferred expense (benefit)	2,000	6,200	3,140
	12,000	15,600	14,600
Net income	$53,000	$62,400	$55,400

TABLE 9.15 Financial Statement Presentation of Deferred Income Taxes

Askilton Inc.
Balance Sheet Extracts
December 31,

	2017	2018	2019
Non-current liabilities:			
Deferred income taxes	$2,000	$8,200	$11,340

A simpler approach to accounting for income taxes is called the **taxes payable method**, in which the tax expense equals the amount of tax an entity must pay for the year. There are no deferred income taxes with this method because temporary differences are ignored. The taxes payable approach makes earnings more variable, which can make an entity look riskier. Askilton's tax expense using the taxes payable method is shown in Table 9.16. Companies using ASPE can use the taxes payable approach.

TABLE 9.16 Net Income Calculated Using the Taxes Payable Method

Askilton Inc.
Income Statement Extracts
December 31,

	2017	2018	2019
Income before taxes	$65,000	$78,000	$70,000
Income tax expense	10,000	9,400	11,460
Net income	$55,000	$68,600	$58,540

Believe it or not, the Askilton example is a straightforward one. In practice, things can get a lot more complicated. But here we're interested in a basic understanding of what deferred income taxes tell us. Here are some points to consider:

www.westjet.com

- Look at WestJet's income statement in Exhibit 9.10 and notice that the company paid only $1,236,000 in tax—that's a remarkably low tax rate of 0.6 percent. Stakeholders could get the wrong impression about how much tax WestJet has to pay if they only consider the current income tax expense. The low tax rate is due to temporary differences, mainly differences between WestJet's depreciation expense and the amount of CCA it's allowed to claim. Eventually, over WestJet's life, those temporary differences will reverse and WestJet will pay higher taxes. As we'll see in Exhibit 9.11, WestJet's actual tax rate is 28.51 percent.

EXHIBIT 9.11 WestJet Airlines Ltd.: Income Taxes[11]

Notes to Consolidated Financial Statements
For the years ended December 31, 2011 and 2010
(Stated in thousands of Canadian dollars, except share and per share amounts)

12. Income taxes

(a) Reconciliation of total tax expense

The effective rate on the Corporation's earnings before income tax differs from the expected amount that would arise using the combined Canadian federal and provincial statutory income tax rates. A reconciliation of the difference is as follows:

	2011	**2010**
Earnings before income tax	208,006	133,465
❶ Combined Canadian federal and provincial income tax rate	27.26%	29.46%
❷ Expected income tax provision	56,702	39,319
Add (deduct):		
Non-deductible expenses	3,344	2,380
❸ Non-deductible share-based payment expense	3,430	4,534
Effect of tax rate changes	(4,539)	(3,726)
Other	367	761
Actual income tax provision	59,304	43,268
❹ Effective tax rate	28.51%	32.42%

(c) Deferred tax

Components of the net deferred tax liability are as follows:

	December 31 2011	**December 31 2010**	**January 1 2010**
Deferred tax liability:			
Property and equipment	(278,003)	(280,899)	(274,853)
❺ Deferred partnership income	(67,473)	(43,437)	(11,913)
Net unrealized gain on derivatives designated in a hedging relationship	(1,062)	–	–
Deferred tax asset:			
Share issue costs	747	1,143	1,561
❻ Net unrealized loss on effective portion of derivatives designated in a hedging relationship	–	919	2,120
Non-capital losses[(i)]	7,348	45,010	50,200
Credit carry forwards[(ii)]	11,987	10,857	9,376
	(326,456)	(266,407)	(223,509)

(i) Non-capital losses will begin to expire in 2014.
(ii) Credit carry forwards recognized for unused corporate minimum tax credits will begin to expire in 2013.

- The temporary differences giving rise to deferred income taxes are often not very temporary. For example, if an entity is growing, the temporary differences due to differences between the CCA deducted and the depreciation expensed will usually grow as well, resulting in a deferred income tax liability that increases year after year. This is why capital-intensive businesses often have huge future income tax liabilities.
- Deferred income tax liabilities aren't discounted. As a result, amounts reported on the balance sheet are overstated because the time value of money is ignored. If deferred income tax balances won't be decreasing for a long time, some of them can actually be relatively small in present value terms.
- Deferred income taxes are affected by the accounting policies used. For example, changing the method of depreciation or the useful life of an asset will change the amount of deferred income taxes but not the amount of taxes paid.
- Deferred income taxes have long been misinterpreted and abused. Every now and then the media or politicians point to future or deferred income tax liabilities as evidence that corporations aren't paying "their fair share" of taxes. This interpretation is wrong as deferred income taxes don't represent money owed to government—they are the result of differences between financial reporting and tax. If entities used the taxes payable method, deferred income taxes would disappear but they would pay exactly the same amount of income tax.
- Only the current portion of the income tax expense on the income statement represents a current cash flow. The deferred portion represents a non-cash accrual. As a result, deferred income tax accounting reduces the association between earnings and cash flows.

Finally, have a look at Exhibit 9.11 for an example of the disclosures about income taxes provided in the notes to the financial statements. In the note, WestJet discloses the following information:

❶ The tax rate that WestJet's income is subject to (as established by the government).

❷ The expected income tax expense (tax rate times accounting income before taxes).

❸ Permanent differences between tax and financial reporting explaining why the income tax expense isn't equal to the tax rate times income for accounting purposes.

❹ The effective tax rate is the rate determined by dividing earnings before taxes by the tax expense (current plus deferred portions).

❺ Sources of the deferred income tax liability. Most of the liability is timing differences associated with plant and equipment (CCA versus depreciation expense).

❻ Sources of the deferred income tax asset.

CANADIAN GAAP FOR PRIVATE ENTERPRISES

Companies that follow Canadian GAAP for Private Enterprises can choose to use the taxes payable method.

FORMULA SUMMARY

$$\text{PV of an annuity}_{n,r} = \frac{1}{r} \times \left[1 - \frac{1}{(1+r)^n}\right] \times \text{Amount to be paid in each period}$$

$$\text{PV}_{n,r} = 1 - \frac{1}{(1+r)^n} \times \text{Amount to be paid in each period}$$

$$\text{Proceeds from bond issue} = \text{Present value of interest payments} + \text{Present value of principal repayment}$$

$$\text{ROA} = \frac{\text{Net income} + \text{After-tax interest expense}}{\text{Total assets}}$$

$$\text{After-tax cost of borrowing} = \text{Stated interest rate} \times (1 - \text{Tax rate})$$

$$\text{Debt-to-equity ratio} = \frac{\text{Total liabilities}}{\text{Total shareholders' equity}}$$

$$\text{Interest coverage ratio} = \frac{\text{Net income} + \text{Interest expense} + \text{Income tax expense}}{\text{Interest expense}}$$

$$\text{Deferred income tax}_{\text{end of period}} = \left(\text{Tax basis of an asset or liability} - \text{Accounting basis of an asset or liability}\right) \times \text{Tax rate}$$

$$\text{Deferred income tax expense} = \text{Deferred income tax on the balance sheet}_{\text{end of period}} - \text{Deferred income tax on the balance sheet}_{\text{beginning of period}}$$

KEY TERMS

after-tax cost of borrowing, p. 552
bond, p. 523
callable bond, p. 527
capital lease, p. 537
capital structure, p. 552
collateral, p. 523
commitment, p. 549
contingent liability, p. 548
convertible bond, p. 527
coupon rate, p. 526
debenture, p. 523
debt, p. 523
deferred (future) income tax assets and liabilities, p. 560
deferred (future) income tax expense, p. 560
defined-benefit plan, p. 545
defined-contribution plan, p. 544
demand loan, p. 517
derecognition, p. 529
discount (on debt), p. 529
effective interest rate, p. 526
event after the reporting period, p. 550
face value of a bond, p. 526
finance lease, p. 537
fixed-rate loan, p. 523
interest coverage ratio, p. 553
lease, p. 537
lessee, p. 537
lessor, p. 537
letter of credit, p. 534
line of credit, p. 518
maturity date of a bond, p. 526
mortgage, p. 523
non-current debt, p. 523
note payable, p. 523
off-balance-sheet financing, p. 537
operating lease, p. 538
pension, p. 543
permanent differences, p. 561
premium (on debt), p. 531
proceeds, p. 526
provision, p. 519
retractable bond, p. 527
subsequent event, p. 550
taxable income, p. 552
taxes payable method, p. 563
temporary differences, p. 561
variable-rate loan, p. 523

SIMILAR TERMS

The left column gives alternative terms that are sometimes used for the accounting terms introduced in this chapter, which are listed in the right column.

long-term debt	**non-current debt, p. 523**
future income tax expense	**deferred income tax expense, p. 560**
security	**collateral, p. 523**
event after the reporting period	**subsequent event, p. 550**
finance lease	**capital lease, p. 537**
capital lease	**finance lease, p. 537**

ASSIGNMENT MATERIALS

Questions

Q9-1. Use the definition of a liability to explain why taxes payable is a liability.

Q9-2. What is a liability? According to IFRS, what are the characteristics of a liability? Do you think these characteristics capture every obligation an entity has? Explain.

Q9-3. What is a current liability? Why is it important to know the amount of current liabilities an entity has? Why is the distinction between current and non-current liabilities important for some stakeholders?

Q9-4. Why is the current portion of long-term debt classified separately as a current liability? What would the impact on users of the financial statements be if the current portion wasn't reported separately?

Q9-5. A retail store sells merchandise for $100 plus HST of $113. How much should the store record as revenue? Explain why. If any part of the $113 is not included in revenue, how is it accounted for?

Q9-6. Why is it necessary to estimate many liabilities? Provide some examples of liabilities that must be estimated.

Q9-7. When a business sells a gift card, why is the amount recorded as a liability instead of revenue?

Q9-8. What is an accrued liability? What is a provision? Distinguish among an accrued liability, provision, and accounts payable? Under what circumstances are accrued liabilities and provisions required?

Q9-9. What are the characteristics of debt that make it risky? Why do these characteristics make debt risky?

Q9-10. Explain the following terms as they relate to bonds:

a. effective rate of interest
b. coupon rate
c. maturity date
d. proceeds
e. face value

Q9-11. Hyannas Inc. has recently arranged financing for its planned expansion. The $5,000,000 bank loan is secured against inventory, receivables, and certain capital assets while the second loan for $2,000,000 is unsecured. Which loan would you expect to have a higher interest rate? Explain.

Q9-12. Why would recording an "interest-free" loan at its face value result in the overstatement of net income for the borrower?

Q9-13. What are bond discounts and premiums? Why are bonds sometimes sold at a discount or premium?

Q9-14. What are restrictive covenants? Why are restrictive covenants sometimes included as part of debt agreements? How does a borrower benefit from a restrictive covenant? Why would a borrower prefer to avoid having restrictive covenants in loan agreements, assuming no changes in the other terms of the loan?

Q9-15. How do bond discounts and premiums affect an entity's interest expense? Explain.

Q9-16. Why do gains and losses arise when an entity redeems its bonds before they mature? How are the gains and losses calculated?

Q9-17. What are off-balance-sheet liabilities? Why do some entities find keeping some liabilities off-balance-sheet attractive? How do off-balance-sheet liabilities affect stakeholders' ability to interpret financial statements? Why is it possible to keep some liabilities off-balance-sheet?

Q9-18. Why do managers sometimes have incentives to understate liabilities? What are the implications for the financial statements of understating liabilities? Provide examples of how managers can understate liabilities.

Q9-19. Explain the difference between a capital (finance) lease and an operating lease. Explain how each type of lease is accounted for and the effect each has on the balance sheet and income statement.

Q9-20. What amount is reported on a lessee's balance sheet at the start of a capital (finance) lease for a leased asset and the associated liability? Why do the amounts reported for the asset and liability differ for balance sheets prepared after the start of the lease?

Q9-21. Identify and explain the criteria that IFRS provide to assist in the classification of leases. What are the problems and benefits of providing preparers of the financial statements with these criteria?

Q9-22. Why do IFRS require disclosure of operating lease obligations and significant purchase commitments?

Q9-23. Distinguish between a defined-benefit pension plan and defined-contribution pension plan. Which plan is more attractive for employees? Explain. Which plan is less risky for employers? Explain.

Q9-24. Why are the assets in a pension plan not reported on the balance sheet of the entity sponsoring the pension plan? Does this treatment result in an understatement of the sponsoring entity's assets?

Q9-25. Because it's so difficult to estimate the cost of providing defined-benefit pensions to employees, it would make more sense, and result in more accurate financial statements, to simply expense pension costs as employees receive their pension. Discuss this statement. In your discussion, address relevant accounting concepts and the impact of the proposed approach on the financial statements.

Q9-26. What is a subsequent event? How are subsequent events accounted for?

Q9-27. What is a commitment? How are commitments accounted for?

Q9-28. According to IFRS, what is a contingent liability? How do IFRS require contingent liabilities to be accounted for? What happens if a contingent liability becomes measurable?

Q9-29. What is the interest coverage ratio? What information does the interest coverage ratio provide?

Q9-30. Why is the actual cost of borrowing usually lower than the stated rate of interest that the borrower pays to a lender such as a bank? Can you think of a situation where the actual cost of borrowing wouldn't be lower than the stated rate of interest?

Q9-31. In its most recent balance sheet, Vosburg Inc. reported a debt-to-equity ratio of 1.85 to 1. This ratio has increased slightly from the previous year when the ratio was 1.55 to 1. Assess Vosburg Inc.'s debt-to-equity ratio and the change in the ratio over the last year.

Q9-32. **(Appendix).** A labour union leader said at a recent rally that there would be plenty of money for health care, education, and other social programs if governments simply collected the deferred (future) income taxes that corporations owe and report on their balance sheets. A friend of yours asked you, in response to the union leader's comments, how it is that businesses can avoid paying their taxes whereas working people can't.

Required:

Respond to your friend.

Q9-33. **(Appendix).** What are future income taxes and what circumstances cause them to appear on an entity's balance sheet?

Q9-34. **(Appendix).** Distinguish the future income tax method of accounting for income taxes from the taxes payable method.

Q9-35. **(Appendix).** Entities that use future income tax accounting show two components of the income tax expense: the current expense and the future expense. Explain these two components.

Exercises

E9-1. **(Determining the proceeds from a bond, LO 3)** On July 15, 2018, Capstick Inc. will be making a $40,000,000 bond issue to public investors. The bond matures in seven years on July 14, 2025, has a coupon rate of 4 percent, and pays interest annually on July 14. Determine how much Capstick will receive in proceeds from its bond if the effective interest rate when the bond is issued is

a. 3 percent
b. 4 percent
c. 5 percent

E9-2. **(Determining the proceeds from a bond, LO 3)** On December 1, 2017, Exlou Inc. will be making a $15,000,000 bond issue to public investors. The bond matures in 12 years on November 30, 2029 and pays interest annually on November 30. The effective interest rate on December 1, 2017 is expected to be 9 percent. How much will Exlou receive in proceeds from its bond if the coupon rate on the bond is

a. 10 percent?
b. 9 percent?
c. 8 percent?

E9-3. **(Preparing journal entries, LO 2, 3)** Provide the journal entries needed for each of the following situations:

a. On October 1, 2017, Utopia Ltd. arranges a $50,000 six-month working capital loan from a commercial lender. The money is deposited in Utopia's bank account. On March 1, 2018 Utopia repays the loan by paying the bank $51,250.
b. Tesseralik Inc. issues a $10,000,000 long-term bond. The company receives $9,950,000.
c. Risteen Corp. has a $500,000 loan secured against some property. The loan requires monthly payments of $10,750. For July 2017 $8,212 of the payment is interest and the remainder principal.

E9-4. **(Accruing interest expense, LO 3)** Quesnel Inc. has a number of outstanding loans. For each of the following situations, record the adjusting journal entry that would be required at year-end to accrue the interest expense. In each case, assume that the year-end is December 31:

a. A $100,000 bank loan with an annual interest rate of 5 percent, interest payable on July 31 and January 31.
b. A $25,000 five-year note payable with annual interest of 6 percent per year, payable annually on October 31.
c. An 8 percent, $1,000,000 loan from a shareholder with interest payable quarterly on December 31, March 31, June 30, and September 30.
d. A 7 percent, $700,000 bank loan with interest payable quarterly on January 2, April 2, July 2, and October 2.

E9-5. **(Accounting for gift cards, LO 2, 7)** Juno Boutique Inc. (Juno) operates a chain of fashion boutiques. In 2017, Juno began offering gift cards for sale to customers. The cards can be exchanged for any merchandise in Juno's stores, but they can't be redeemed for cash. During 2017, gift cards worth $62,000 were sold. By the end of the year, $24,000 of the gift cards had been redeemed by customers who purchased merchandise that cost Juno $15,000.

Required:

a. Prepare the journal entry required to record the sale of the gift cards.
b. Prepare the journal entry required to record the redemption of the gift cards.
c. How would the unused gift cards be reported in Juno's financial statements?
d. What effect does the sale of gift cards have on Juno's current ratio?
e. Why is sale a gift card not considered revenue for Juno?

E9-6. **(Accounting for gift cards, LO 2, 7)** Pages Books Inc. (Pages) operates a national chain of book stores in Canada. Pages offers gift cards for sale for customers who would like to give a gift of books but who aren't sure what titles they should buy. The cards can be exchanged for any merchandise in Pages' stores or online, but can't be redeemed for cash. At the beginning of 2017, Pages had $4,275,000 in its unredeemed gift card liability account. During 2017, gift cards worth $4,875,000 were sold and $4,189,000 were redeemed to purchase merchandise costing $3,375,000. Pages estimates that about 4 percent of gift cards outstanding at the end of the year won't be redeemed.

Required:

a. For the year ended December 31, 2017, prepare all journal entries (transactional and adjusting) Pages must make.
b. How would the unused gift cards be reported in Pages' financial statements?
c. What effect does the sale of gift cards have on Pages' current ratio? What impact does using a gift card have on the current ratio?
d. Why is the sale of a gift card not considered revenue for Pages?

E9-7. **(Classifying liabilities, LO 2, 3)** How would each of the following items be classified on Maniwaki Forestry Corp.'s (Maniwaki) September 30, 2017 balance sheet? Explain your reasoning.

a. A $2,500,000 20-year mortgage on Maniwaki's land and building. The mortgage requires annual equal payments of $293,650.
b. $125,200 withheld from employee paycheques for income taxes.
c. A $2,500 deposit received for lumber to be delivered in March 2018.
d. $300,000 owed to a supplier for equipment delivered in December 2017; $150,000 of the amount owed is due on December 15, 2017 and the remainder on November 1, 2018.
e. A $325,000 demand loan from the bank.
f. A three-year warranty provision for finished fine lumber. The total provision is $3 million with the obligation spread evenly over the three years.

E9-8. **(Valuing liabilities, LO 1, 3)** On March 31, 2017, Etzikom Inc. (Etzikom) purchased a corporate jet from the manufacturer for $3,750,000. Etzikom paid $250,000 in cash to the manufacturer and received a four-year, $3,500,000, interest-free loan for the remainder of the purchase price. The terms of the loan require Etzikom to pay the manufacturer $875,000 on March 31 of each of the next four years, beginning on March 31, 2018. Assume a discount rate of 5 percent when responding to the following questions.

Required:

a. Prepare the journal entry that Etzikom should make to record the purchase of the jet. Explain the amount you have recorded for the jet on the balance sheet.
b. Prepare the journal entries that Etzikom should make on March 31, 2017 through 2021 to record payments on the loan.
c. How much should Etzikom report as a liability for the loan on its balance sheet on March 31, 2017 through 2021?
d. Could Etzikom record the liability at $3,500,000 on March 31, 2017? What are the problems of accounting for the liability this way?

E9-9. **(Collections on behalf of third parties, LO 2)** For the following two independent situations, prepare the journal entry that Durrell Ltd., an Alberta retail business, should record. Record the entry for both the amounts collected or withheld and for the remittances.

a. During November 2017, Durrell sold and delivered $145,000 of services to customers. In addition, customers were charged and paid 5 percent GST. Durrell remits the GST it collects from customers on the tenth day of the following month.
b. During November, Durrell's employees earned $42,000. From this amount, Durrell withheld $13,000 for income taxes, $4,105 for Canada Pension Plan (CPP), $1,860 for Employment Insurance (EI), $750 in union dues, $1,450 for employee contributions to the company pension plan, $1,000 for long-term disability insurance, and $200 in contributions to local charities. Durrell remits the withholdings on the tenth day of the following month.

E9-10. **(Classifying liabilities as current and non-current, LO 2, 3)** The accountant of Hantsport Ltd. (Hantsport) is currently preparing the December 31, 2017 financial statements. She has asked you to help her classify the following items:

a. During December 2017, Hantsport withheld $4,000 from employees for their contributions to the company pension plan. The company is required to remit the contributed amount to the pension fund manager within 10 days of collection.
b. As of the end of December, Hantsport owed suppliers $68,000 for inventory purchases during November and December 2017.
c. The company has a $50,000 note payable coming due in March. Hantsport has arranged a three-year, $50,000 loan from the bank that will be used to repay the loan.
d. Hantsport has received $10,000 in advances for goods that will be delivered during 2018.
e. Hantsport has $100,000 outstanding with a private lender. $25,000 is scheduled to be repaid in 2018.
f. Hantsport declared a $120,000 cash dividend on December 21, 2017. The dividend is to be paid on January 15, 2018.
g. Hantsport has a $300,000 loan from the bank that has been outstanding for three years. The bank can demand repayment at any time.

Required:

Classify each of the items as a current or non-current liability (note that some may classified partially as current and partially as non-current). Provide your reasoning for each item.

E9-11. **(Assessing loan safety, LO 7)** You are provided the following information about two companies, Naicam Ltd. and Riverton Inc.

	Naicam Ltd.	Riverton Inc.
Total assets	$2,758,000	$8,750,000
Total liabilities	1,950,000	4,875,000
Total shareholders' equity	808,000	3,875,000
Net income	352,000	1,015,000
Income tax expense	62,118	179,118
Interest expense	175,000	221,000

Required:

a. Calculate the debt-to-equity ratio and the interest coverage ratio for each company.
b. Which company do you think would be considered a safer investment by a long-term lender? Explain.

E9-12. **(Assessing loan safety, LO 7)** You are provided the following information about two companies, Lombardy Ltd. and Savona Inc.

	Lombardy Ltd.	Savona Inc.
Total assets	$9,250,000	$12,358,000
Total liabilities	3,450,000	7,100,000
Total shareholders' equity	5,800,000	5,258,000
Net income	400,000	1,250,000
Income tax expense	70,588	220,588
Interest expense	161,000	331,333

a. Calculate the debt-to-equity ratio and the interest coverage ratio for each company.
b. Which company do you think would be considered a safer investment by a long-term lender? Explain.

E9-13. **(Accounting entries for a defined-contribution pension plan, LO 5)** Iskut Inc. (Iskut) provides its employees with a defined-contribution pension plan. Each year the company is required to contribute $1,000 to an investment fund for each employee. In the year ended December 31, 2017, Iskut contributed $200,000 on behalf of its 230 employees.

Required:

a. What journal entry would Iskut make to record the contribution to the pension plan?
b. What other entries would be necessary? Explain. What would appear on the balance sheet about the pension plan on December 31, 2017?

E9-14. **(Accounting entries for a defined-benefit pension plan, LO 5)** Brigus Corp. (Brigus) provides its employees with a defined-benefit pension plan. The plan was instituted three years ago. During the year ended March 31, 2017, Brigus contributed $150,000 to the plan. An evaluation of the plan as of the end of fiscal 2017 found that contributions of $250,000 were required in 2017 to have enough money in the plan to provide the benefits promised to employees when they retire.

Required:

a. What journal entry would Brigus have made in fiscal 2017 to record the cash it contributed to the pension plan?
b. How much pension liability should be reported on Brigus' balance sheet on March 31, 2017? Explain what this amount represents.

E9-15. **(Classifying transactions and economic events, LO 6)** Classify the following transactions and economic events for Sayabec Ltd. as commitments, subsequent events, or contingent liabilities. Some may fit more than one classification. Indicate how each should be reflected in the December 31, 2017 financial statements and explain your reasoning. In responding, consider the usefulness of the information to different stakeholders.

a. On December 15, 2018, Sayabec signed a three-year contract with a supplier to provide raw materials. The contract is the largest ever agreed to by Sayabec. The contract goes into effect in May 2018.
b. In May 2017, Sayabec guaranteed a $1,000,000 bank loan made to a company owned by a major shareholder. Sayabec is responsible for paying the principal and any outstanding interest in case the company is unable to make its payments. So far, the company has made all payments as required.
c. On January 10, 2018, a large customer declared bankruptcy. The customer had been in financial difficulty for some time. Sayabec expects to receive no more than 25 per cent of the amount owed by the customer.
d. On January 20, 2018, Sayabec announced that the board of directors had declared a dividend of $0.25 per share. The dividend is 20 percent higher than the last dividend.
e. In November 2017, Sayabec was notified by the Canada Revenue Agency that it owed $459,000 in taxes related to the taxation years 2014 and 2015. Sayabec's accountants say that the reassessment has no basis in fact. Sayabec is appealing the reassessment and plans to take it to court if necessary.

E9-16. **(Classifying transactions and economic events, LO 6)** Classify the following transactions and economic events for Langham Ltd. (Langham) as commitments, subsequent events, or contingent liabilities. Some may fit more than one classification. Show how each should be reflected in the December 31, 2017 financial statements and explain your reasoning. In responding, consider the usefulness of the information to different stakeholders.

a. In January 2018, signed a contract with a supplier that will provide Langham with an important raw material over the next five years. Langham will pay prevailing market prices for the guaranteed supply.
b. In May 2017, Langham filed a $10,000,000 claim against a competitor for theft of intellectual property rights. The claims statement was that the competitor profited from the use of Langham's patents without obtaining the rights to use them.
c. On November 15, 2017, Langham signed a contract for new heavy equipment. The equipment is in the development phase by the manufacturer and is expected to be delivered in late 2020. The contract specifies the price Langham will pay. Payment is due on delivery.
d. On January 18, 2018, one of Langham's customer's production facilities was destroyed in a fire. As a result, the customer declared bankruptcy. Langham doesn't expect to receive any of the amount owed by the customer.

E9-17. **(Interest-free loans, LO 1, 3)** On December 31, 2017, Chauvin Inc. purchased land and building from a developer for $22 million. Chauvin paid $6 million in cash when the deal closed and the developer financed the remainder by giving Chauvin a four-year, $16 million interest-free loan. Under the terms of the loan, Chauvin is required to pay $4 million on December 31 of each of the next four years. Assume the market rate of interest on financing of this type is 5 percent.

Required:

a. How much should Chauvin report as a liability for the loan on its balance sheet on December 31, 2017 through 2021? What would the interest expense be each year?
b. Why isn't it appropriate to record the liability initially at $16 million? What is the impact on the financial statements of recording the liability at this amount?

E9-18. **(Accounting for bonds, LO 3)** On November 1, 2017, Nordin Inc. (Nordin) issued a $5,000,000 bond with a 6 percent coupon rate and a maturity date of October 31, 2022. Interest is paid semi-annually on April 30 and October 31. The effective interest rate for a bond of this type on November 1, 2017 was 8 percent. Nordin's year-end is October 31.

Required:

a. What will the proceeds from the bond issue be?
b. Prepare the journal entry to record the issue of the bond on November 1, 2017.
c. Prepare an amortization schedule using the effective interest rate method for any premium or discount that arose on issue of the bond.
d. Prepare the journal entry required to record the interest expense on April 30 and October 31, 2018 and 2020.
e. Prepare the journal entry required to record the retirement of the bond on maturity.

E9-19. **(Accounting for bonds, LO 3)** On September 1, 2017, Yone Ltd. issued a $2,000,000 bond with a 9 percent coupon rate and a maturity date of August 31, 2023. Interest is paid annually on August 31. The effective interest rate for a bond of this type on September 1, 2017 was 7 percent. Yone's year-end is August 31.

Required:

a. What will be the proceeds from the bond issue?
b. Prepare the journal entry to record the issue of the bond on September 1, 2017.
c. Prepare an amortization schedule using the effective interest rate method for any premium or discount that arose on issue of the bond.
d. Prepare the journal entry required to record the interest expense on August 31, 2018, 2019, and 2022.
e. Prepare the journal entry required to record the retirement of the bond on maturity.

E9-20. **(Accounting for bonds, LO 3)** On February 1, 2017, Jura Corp. (Jura) issued an $8,000,000 bond with a 7 percent coupon rate and a maturity date of January 31, 2023. Interest is paid annually on January 31. The effective interest rate for a bond of this type on February 1, 2017 was 7 percent. Jura's year-end is January 31.

Required:

a. What will the proceeds from the bond issue be?
b. Prepare the journal entry to record the issue of the bond on February 1, 2017.
c. Prepare an amortization schedule using the effective interest rate method for any premium or discount that arose on issue of the bond.
d. Prepare the journal entry required to record the interest expense on January 31, 2018, 2020, and 2022.
e. Prepare the journal entry required to record the retirement of the bond on maturity.

E9-21. **(Early retirement of bonds, LO 3)** In fiscal 2017, Ruthilda Inc. (Ruthilda) decided to exercise its option to redeem its outstanding bond issue before the maturity date in 2024. The bonds had a face value of $6,000,000 and Ruthilda paid $6,400,000 to redeem them. The bonds were originally issued at a premium of $300,000 and at the time the bonds were redeemed, $120,000 of the premium had been amortized.

Required:

a. Prepare the journal entry to record the early retirement of the bonds.
b. What would the entry be if Ruthilda was able to redeem the bonds on the open market at a cost of $5,600,000?
c. What is the economic significance of a gain or loss on the redemption of bonds? How do you think the gain or loss should be reported in the financial statements? Explain. In responding, consider the information needs of the stakeholders.

E9-22. **(Early retirement of bonds, LO 3)** In fiscal 2017, Hurette Inc. (Hurette) decided to exercise its option to redeem its outstanding bond issue before the bonds matured in 2022. The bonds had a face value of $10,000,000 and Hurette paid $10,500,000 to redeem them. The bonds were originally issued at a discount of $500,000 and at the time the bonds were redeemed $200,000 of the discount had been amortized.

Required:

a. Prepare the journal entry to record the early retirement of the bonds.
b. What would the entry be if Hurette were able to redeem the bonds on the open market at a cost of $9,500,000?
c. What is the economic significance of a gain or loss on the redemption of bonds? How do you think the gain or loss should be reported in the financial statements? Explain. In responding, consider the information needs of users of the financial statements.

E9-23. **(Cost of borrowing, LO 3)** For each of the following situations, determine the entity's after-tax cost of borrowing:

a. A corporation has a $5,000,000 bond with a coupon rate of 8 percent. The corporation has a tax rate of 25 percent.
b. A small business has a three-year, $500,000, 5 percent note payable with a supplier. The small business has a tax rate of 13 percent.
c. A not-for-profit organization, which doesn't have to pay tax, has a $125,000 bank loan at the prime lending rate plus 2.5 percent. For the year just ended, the prime lending rate was 3 percent.
d. How is an entity's after-tax cost of borrowing affected by its tax rate? Is it more desirable for an entity to have a higher tax rate so that it can lower its after-tax cost of borrowing? Explain.

E9-24. **(Accounting for leases, LO 4)** On February 1, 2017, Berwyn Ltd. signed a four-year lease for four delivery trucks. Under the terms of the lease, Berwyn must make annual lease payments of $87,500 beginning on February 1, 2017 and on each January 31 for the next three years. The interest rate that applies to the lease is 8 percent.

Required:

a. Assume Berwyn's lease was accounted for as an operating lease:
   i. What amount would be recorded as an asset for the trucks on February 1, 2017?
   ii. Prepare the journal entries that would have to be made in fiscal 2018 and fiscal 2020 to account for the lease.
b. Assume Berwyn's lease was accounted for as a capital (finance) lease:
   i. What amount would be recorded as an asset for the trucks on February 1, 2017?
   ii. What journal entry would be required on February 1, 2017 to record the lease and the initial payment?
   iii. What journal entries would be required on January 31, 2018 to record the lease payment?
   iv. What journal entry would be required on January 31, 2018 to record the depreciation of the trucks (assume straight-line depreciation and no residual value)?
   v. What would the carrying amount of the trucks and the lease liability be on Berwyn's January 31, 2018 and 2020 balance sheets?

E9-25. **(The effect of interest rates on capital leases, LO 4)** On June 1, 2017, Zealand Corp. (Zealand) signed a six-year lease for heavy equipment. The lease requires Zealand to make annual lease payments of $200,000 on May 31 of each year beginning in 2018. The lease is to be treated as a capital (finance) lease.

Required:

a. Indicate the amount that would be recorded for heavy equipment and for the lease liability on June 1, 2017, assuming the appropriate interest rate for the lease was:
   i. 8 percent
   ii. 10 percent
   iii. 12 percent
b. Indicate the annual depreciation expense for the heavy equipment, assuming straight-line depreciation over six years and assuming the appropriate interest rate for the lease was:
   i. 8 percent
   ii. 10 percent
   iii. 12 percent

c. Indicate the interest expense pertaining to the lease in the fiscal year ended May 31, 2018, assuming the appropriate interest rate for the lease was:
   i. 8 percent
   ii. 10 percent
   iii. 12 percent

E9-26. **(The effect of bond transactions on the cash flow statement, LO 3)** Wivenhoe Ltd. (Wivenhoe) includes a cash flow statement in the financial statement package it prepares for the bank. Wivenhoe uses the indirect method for calculating cash from operations. For each of the following items, indicate whether it would be reported in Wivenhoe's cash flow statement as an operating, financing, or investing activity. Indicate how each item would be shown in reconciling from net income to cash from operations using the indirect method.

a. Amortization of a bond premium.
b. Proceeds from the issue of a bond.
c. Interest payment to lenders.
d. Repayment of a bond on maturity.
e. Loss on early retirement of a bond.
f. Amortization of a bond discount.

E9-27. **(Lease accounting and financial ratios, LO 4, 7)** Zeballos Inc. (Zeballos) has arranged to lease new equipment for its distribution centre. The terms of the lease require Zeballos to pay $475,000 per year for the next eight years. The interest rate for the lease is 6 percent. The lease comes into effect on December 31, 2017, the last day of the current fiscal year and the first payment is to be made on that day. Subsequent payments are due on December 31 of each year through 2024. Zeballos has provided you with the following balance sheet information on December 31, 2017, before accounting for the new lease.

Current assets	$ 628,000
Non-current assets	4,204,000
Current liabilities	496,800
Non-current liabilities	3,400,000
Shareholders' equity	935,200

Required:

a. Calculate the current ratio and debt-to-equity ratio for Zeballos, assuming the lease is accounted for as an operating lease (ignore the effect of the lease payments).
b. Calculate the current ratio and debt-to-equity ratio for Zeballos, assuming the lease is accounted for as a capital (finance) lease. *Hint:* When accounting for the lease payment cash is reduced and under the operating lease treatment, there is a corresponding increase in prepaid lease payment, which is a current asset and equal to the cash payment.
c. Which calculations provide a better representation of Zeballos' liquidity and underlying risk? Explain.
d. Does it matter how Zeballos accounts for its lease (IFRS notwithstanding)? Explain.

E9-28. **(Accounting for bonds, LO 3)** On June 1, 2017, Joffre Inc. (Joffre) issued a $6,000,000, 10-year bond with an 8 percent coupon rate. Proceeds from the bond issue were $6,421,415. Interest is to be paid annually on May 31. Joffre's year-end is December 31. Assume that Joffre uses the effective interest rate method to amortize any bond premiums or discounts.

Required:

a. Prepare the journal entry to record the issue of the bond on June 1, 2017.
b. Prepare the journal entry to accrue the interest expense on December 31, 2017.
c. Prepare the journal entry to record the payment of interest to bondholders on May 31, 2018.

E9-29. **(Future income taxes, LO 8)** Use the following information to calculate the balance in the future income tax account for a machine owned by the entity:

Cost of the machine when it was purchased	$5,000,000
Total amount of CCA deducted since the machine was purchased	2,305,000
Total amount of depreciation expensed since the machine was purchased	1,787,500
Tax rate	45%

E9-30. **(Future income taxes, LO 8)** Use the following information to calculate the balance in the future income tax account for a building owned by the entity:

Cost of the machine when it was purchased	$1,400,000
Total amount of CCA deducted since the machine was purchased	820,000
Total amount of depreciation expensed since the machine was purchased	1,150,000
Tax rate	20%

E9-31. **(Future income taxes, LO 8)** For the fiscal year ended November 30, 2017, Vibank Ltd. (Vibank) has income before taxes of $2,250,000. Vibank's tax return shows taxable income of $2,475,000 for that year. The tax basis of Vibank's assets exceeded the accounting basis by $400,000 on November 30, 2017 and the balance in the future income tax account on November 30, 2016 was a credit of $150,000. All temporary differences pertain to non-current assets. Vibank has a tax rate of 25 percent.

Required:

a. What amount should Vibank report for future income taxes on its November 30, 2017 balance sheet?
b. What is Vibank's net income for fiscal 2017?
c. What would Vibank's net income be if it used the taxes payable method?
d. Explain the difference between (b) and (c).
e. Prepare the journal entry required to record Vibank's income tax expense for fiscal 2017, using the deferred (future) income tax method.

E9-32. **(Future income taxes, LO 8)** For the fiscal year ended December 31, 2018, Rossland Ltd. (Rossland) has income before taxes of $650,000. Rossland's tax return shows taxable income of $550,000 for the year. The accounting basis of Rossland's assets exceeded the tax basis by $150,000 on December 31, 2018 and the balance in the future income tax account on December 31, 2017 was a credit of $20,000. All temporary differences pertain to non-current assets. Rossland has a tax rate of 15 percent.

Required:

a. What should Rossland report for future income taxes on its December 31, 2018 balance sheet?
b. What is Rossland's net income for fiscal 2018?
c. What would Rossland's net income be if it used the taxes payable method?
d. Explain the difference between (b) and (c).
e. Prepare the journal entry required to record Rossland's income tax expense for fiscal 2018, using the deferred (future) income tax method.

E9-33. **(The effect of different depreciation methods on future income taxes, LO 8)** Caycuse Inc. (Caycuse) completed its first year of operations on December 31, 2017. The company owns a single asset that cost $200,000 and has no residual value. For tax purposes, Caycuse can deduct $30,000 in CCA in calculating its taxable income in 2017. Assume that Caycuse's tax rate is 16 percent.

Required:

a. Determine the future income tax asset or liability on December 31, 2017 if Caycuse depreciates its asset on a straight-line basis over 10 years.
b. Determine the future income tax asset or liability on December 31, 2017 if Caycuse depreciates its asset on a straight-line basis over five years.
c. Determine the future income tax asset or liability on December 31, 2017 if Caycuse depreciates its asset on a declining balance basis at 30 percent per year.
d. Determine the future income tax asset or liability on December 31, 2017 if Caycuse depreciates its asset on a declining balance basis at 15 percent per year..
e. According to the IFRS characteristics for determining whether a liability exists, is a future income tax liability really a liability? Should a future income tax asset be considered an asset? How would you interpret the future income tax assets or liabilities that you calculated in parts (a) through (d) above?

Problems

P9-1. **(Determining whether certain economic events are liabilities, LO 1)** Explain whether each of the following would be considered a liability according to IFRS (using the criteria from the chapter) on December 31, 2017. Intuitively, would you consider each of these items a liability, regardless of how it's accounted for according to IFRS? Explain.

a. The cost of providing warranty services to a customer who purchased a product in 2017. The warranty covers parts and labour for three years from the date of purchase.
b. A company borrows $950,000 on January 8, 2018. The loan bears an annual interest rate of 7.5 percent and must be renewed each year.
c. A small business signs a two-year, non-cancellable lease on office space in a downtown building in December 2016. The lease requires the business to pay $10,000 in rent over the two years of the lease.

P9-2. **(Determining whether certain economic events are liabilities, LO 1)** Explain whether each of the following would be considered a liability according to IFRS (using the criteria from the chapter) on December 31, 2017. Intuitively, would you consider each of these items a liability, regardless of how it's accounted for according to IFRS? Explain.

a. Interest on a bank loan outstanding on December 31, 2017. Interest isn't payable until the loan is repaid on September 30, 2018.
b. A $1,000,000 loan from a shareholder that bears no interest and has no scheduled repayment date.
c. The cost of cleaning up the site of a factory when it closes, as required by environmental laws. The factory is expected to close in 25 years.

P9-3. **(Effect of transactions and economic events on ratios, LO 2, 3, 4, 6, 7)** The president of Oskelaneo Ltd. (Oskelaneo) wants to know the effect a number of transactions and economic events will have on several financial measures for the company's fiscal year ended September 30, 2017. Complete the following table by showing whether the listed transactions or economic events would increase, decrease, or have no effect on the financial measures listed. Explain your reasoning and state any assumptions that you make. Consider each item independently.

Ratio/amount before taking the transaction/economic event into effect	Debt-to-equity ratio	Current ratio	Interest coverage ratio	Cash from operations	Return on assets
	1.25:1	1.25	2.5	$425,000	4.3%
a. On September 30, 2017, Oskelaneo accrued interest on a bank loan. The interest will be paid in December 2017.					
b. Oskelaneo signed a new capital lease on September 30, 2017.					
c. A fire destroyed a small building owned by Oskelaneo on October 4, 2017.					
d. Oskelaneo received cash from a customer for services that will be provided in February 2018.					
e. A customer sued Oskelaneo in January 2017 for negligence. A decision by the court isn't expected for at least two years. The company's lawyers state that it is unlikely the company will lose the lawsuit.					

P9-4. **(Effect of transactions and economic events on ratios, LO 3, 4, 5, 6, 7)** The president of Ruskin Inc. (Ruskin) wants to know the effect a number of transactions and economic events will have on several financial measures for the company's fiscal year ended April 30, 2017. Complete the following table by indicating whether the listed transactions or economic events would increase, decrease, or have no effect on the financial measures listed. Explain your reasoning and state any assumptions that you make. Consider each item independently.

Ratio/amount before taking the transaction/economic event into account	Debt-to-equity ratio	Current ratio	Interest coverage ratio	Cash from operations	Return on assets
	0.75:1	0.85	5.2	$3,500,000	8.5%
a. Ruskin signed a contract in January 2017 to purchase raw materials beginning in fiscal 2018 at an agreed-to price.					
b. Ruskin provided services to a customer that had been paid for in the previous fiscal year.					
c. Ruskin made its annual contribution to its defined-contribution pension plan in April 2017.					
d. In March 2017, Ruskin repaid a bond that was classified as the current portion of long-term debt.					
e. In November 2016, Ruskin paid $1,000,000 to settle a lawsuit that was launched three years ago. The amount owed had been accrued as a current liability earlier.					

P9-5. **(Buy or lease?, LO 4)** Like hospitals in many communities, Mortlach General Hospital is chronically short of the cash it needs to provide all the services required by its community. Management is continually looking for ways to save money or improve efficiencies. The hospital recently decided to add a new operating room to meet increasing demand. The cost of the new room is estimated to be about $500,000. The hospital foundation could provide the $500,000 needed. The foundation has the money on hand but since this was an unanticipated proposal, it would take money away from other purposes. An alternative proposal from a member of the board of directors with connections to commercial lenders would have a private lender finance the construction of the new operating room and lease it to the hospital. The lease would be for five years and would require monthly payments of $12,000. The hospital foundation would fundraise to cover the cost of the monthly lease payments. After five years, the hospital would own the operating room. Management considers an appropriate discount rate to be about 5 percent.

Required:

Prepare a report to management that explains fully whether Mortlach General Hospital should pay for the operating room in cash or accept the lease arrangement.

P9-6. **(Assessing personal financial situation, LO 7)** Dan and Sarah Kula earn $108,000 after tax. They have a mortgage on their home that has four years left until it must be paid off (they would arrange a new mortgage at that time). The monthly mortgage payment is $2,000 per month. In addition, the Kulas have a car lease on which they pay $600 per month. The lease has three more years left until the Kulas must buy the car or arrange a new lease. It costs the Kulas $5,200 per month to operate their household. (Dan and Sarah have three children. Their household costs include childcare.) Dan and Sarah spend about $8,000 a year on vacations and they try to save $10,000 per year for retirement, the kids' educations, and any emergencies that might arise. Currently, they have $35,000 in savings, including cash of $7,000. The Kulas currently have a $5,000 balance on their credit cards, which carry an interest rate of 15 percent per year.

Dan and Sarah recently learned that they are going to have another child. Their house is too small for another child so they are looking to sell the existing house and buying a new one in the same neighbourhood. The Kulas estimate that it will cost them $10,000 in cash to move and cause their mortgage payments increase to $2,400 per month. The new baby will add about $500 a month to household expenses.

Required:

Assess the Kulas' financial situation. Do you think they can afford to move? What steps could they take to make moving a reasonable step?

P9-7. **(Impact of covenants, LO 3, 7)** In late 2017, Bedeque Ltd. (Bedeque) arranged a long-term loan of $1,000,000 from a local bank to provide $250,000 in needed working capital and $750,000 to finance the purchase of some new equipment. The loan would be repayable in four years. However, the terms of a previous loan require that the company maintain a current ratio greater than 1.5 and a debt-to-equity ratio of less than 1. If either of these restrictions isn't met, the loan would have to be repaid within 30 days. The previous loan agreement also states that for Bedeque to pay dividends, retained earnings must be greater than $1,700,000 after the dividend.

Bedeque's controller has asked you to figure out how the new loan will affect the restrictions on the December 31, 2017 balance sheet. Bedeque's shareholders are expecting a dividend in early 2018 so the controller also wants to know how much can be paid. The controller has provided you with a projected balance sheet for December 31, 2017. The balance sheet takes into consideration all expected economic activity through the end of the year (including the closing entry), except for the impact of the new loan.

Bedeque Inc. **Projected Balance Sheet as of December 31, 2017**			
Current assets	$ 720,000	Current liabilities	$ 600,000
Non-current assets	5,250,000	Non-current liabilities	1,500,000
		Common shares	2,000,000
		Retained earnings	1,870,000
Total assets	$5,970,000	Total liabilities and shareholders' equity	$5,970,000

Required:

Prepare a report that provides the information the controller wants. Explain your findings and reasoning.

P9-8. **(Accounting for possible unexpected warranty costs, LO 6)** Nouvelle Ltd. (Nouvelle) is a privately owned industrial-products manufacturer located in Sherbrooke, Quebec. The president of Nouvelle owns 25 percent of the shares of the company and three investors who aren't active in managing the company own the rest. The company has a large demand loan outstanding. The terms of the loan require that Nouvelle maintain a current ratio of greater than 1.2 and a debt-to-equity ratio of 1.3 to 1 or less. Nouvelle's senior executives have an employment contract that entitles them to share a bonus pool equal to 10 percent of the company's net income. The financial statements are also used for tax purposes.

On December 21, 2017, Nouvelle's quality control engineer presented a report to the president where she expressed concern about problems with a new product line. The engineer believes these new products were rushed into production with some technical flaws that haven't been corrected. The engineer says service calls required on the new products are about 20 percent higher than other company products and she expects repairs will increase dramatically once the products have been used by customers for more than 2,500 hours, which should occur 12 to 18 months from the date of purchase. She estimates that the cost of repairing these products will be $1,500,000 higher than the amount originally budgeted. Repair costs to date on the new product line are about $125,000 higher than budgeted. The engineer bases her concerns on extensive tests she has carried out in the quality control laboratory.

Nouvelle's product design engineer, who was responsible for developing the products, has stated flatly that there are no technical flaws and that the increase in service calls is reasonable for a new product line.

On December 15, 2017, Nouvelle's vice-president of finance provided the president with the following estimates of the December 31, 2017 financial statements:

Net income	$ 1,270,000
Current assets	11,150,000
Current liabilities	9,100,000
Non-current liabilities	28,750,000
Shareholders' equity	31,400,000

Required:

Prepare a report to Nouvelle's president discussing the accounting and financial reporting issues regarding the treatment of the concerns raised by the quality control engineer. Your report should identify alternative ways to treat the possible future costs and explain the implications of the alternatives. The president would also like your supported recommendations on what should be done.

P9-9. **(Assessing debt load, LO 3, 6, 7)** Yarm Ltd. (Yarm) recently released its December 31, 2017 financial statements. In a press release announcing the results, Yarm's management proudly stated that the company had maintained its debt load well below the industry average of 2.5 to 1. Yarm's summarized balance sheet for the years ended December 31, 2016 and 2017, along with extracts from the notes to the financial statements, are provided below.

Required:

Assess Yarm's debt position. Do you think management should be as proud of its financial situation as it is? Explain your thinking. (For discounting, an appropriate rate is 10 percent.)

Yarm Ltd. Balance Sheets for the Years Ended December 31 (in thousands of dollars)					
	2017	2016		2017	2016
Cash	$ 350	$ 275	Accounts payable and accrued liabilities	$1,820	$1,700
Accounts receivable	750	720	Current portion of long-term debt	200	200
Inventory	1,300	1,210		2,020	1,900
Other	350	310	Long-term debt	1,200	1,400
	2,750	2,515	Other non-current liabilities	250	275
				3,470	3,575
Property, plant, and equipment (net)	1,970	2,010			
Intangible assets (including goodwill)	1,750	1,850	Common shares	1,800	1,800
			Retained earnings	1,200	1,000
Total assets	$6,470	$6,375	Total liabilities and shareholders' equity	$6,470	$6,375

Extracts from Yarm's financial statements:

- The company leases most of its production equipment. The leases are generally for four to five years and all are classified as operating leases. Minimum annual lease payments for the next five years are:

2018	$750,000
2019	$775,000
2020	$810,000
2021	$850,000
2022	$800,000

- The company has long-term binding commitments to purchase supplies from a Korean company. The commitments require a minimum purchase of $500,000 for the next three years.
- On January 15, 2018, the company signed an agreement to borrow $750,000 from a local bank. The annual interest rate on the loan will be 6 percent for a term of three years. The loan comes into effect on February 19, 2018.

P9-10. **(Accounting for frequent travel plans, LO 1, 2, 6, 7)** Intercity Bus Lines (Intercity) is a Canadian company that provides bus transportation between communities throughout Canada. In recent years, bus travel and the company's revenues have declined significantly and it's looking for ways to build its customer base. The marketing manager has observed that frequent flyer programs are very successful for airlines and has suggested a similar program for Intercity. She suggests that for every mile of travel on an Intercity bus a traveller would receive one point. The points could be redeemed for travel on Intercity buses. She proposes that levels be established; for example, for 500 points a customer might receive a trip of 250 miles or less.

At a recent planning meeting, Intercity's CFO raised some questions about the frequent travel programs. He wondered if there would be any impact on the company's financial statements. After the meeting, the CFO asked you to prepare a report discussing the proposed program and the financial reporting impact it would have. He asked you to consider the following:

- Would frequent travel points be considered liabilities?
- If they are liabilities, how are they measured?

- What effect would the plan have on the financial statements and should management be concerned about these impacts?
- What types of concerns should management have in operating such a program?

Required:

Prepare the report requested by the CFO.

P9-11. **(Accounting for a rebate promotion, LO 1, 2, 6)** Urling Inc. (Urling) is a small public company that produces packaged consumer foods. Urling began operations about 22 years ago and has been a public company for eight years. The company is managed by professional managers, who own about 10 percent of Urling's stock. About 30 percent of the shares are owned by members of the family who originally founded the company and the rest are widely held by private and institutional investors. Urling stock has struggled in recent years. The company has failed to meet earnings targets for the last two fiscal years. For the current fiscal year, management has projected earnings of $2,500,000, which is about a 2 percent increase from last year.

Recently, Urling introduced a new line of upscale frozen entrées to satisfy the tastes and lifestyles of busy baby boomers. For the first time, Urling's management decided to promote sales by offering rebates to customers. In the past, the company had promoted its products through advertising and in-store price reductions. The new promotion entitles customers to a $5 rebate if they purchase four entrées and mail in the bar codes from the packages. Urling used special packaging highlighting the promotion, provided in-store signs, and advertised in newspaper and magazines. Since the promotion began several months ago, approximately 250,000 entrées have been sold and sales of an additional 70,000 are expected by year-end. Approximately 1,500 customers have already mailed in their requests for rebates.

Because Urling has never used this type of promotion before, its marketing manager isn't sure how to account for it. The marketing manager has indicated that the number of rebate claims can be very difficult to estimate, especially because it's a new promotion and a new product. The manager has indicated that the number of claims can range between 2 percent and 25 percent of the product sold. Urling's controller has projected that net income before accounting for the new promotion will be about $2,555,000. Because projected earnings are so close to the forecast, the president is quite uneasy about the effect the new promotion will have.

Required:

a. Prepare a report to Urling's president outlining the accounting issues and problems with the new rebate promotion. Provide recommendations on how the promotion should be accounted for and provide support for your recommendations that can be used in any discussions with the company's auditors. Indicate how the rebate promotion will be reported in the financial statements.
b. Prepare a journal entry that will account for the rebate promotion in the current fiscal year.

P9-12. **(Accounting for a possible loss, LO 6)** Hoselaw Ltd. (Hoselaw) is a privately owned manufacturing company in eastern Ontario. The company is owned by five shareholders, three of whom aren't active in the management of the business. The company has a large demand loan outstanding at the bank.

The government recently informed Hoselaw's management that seepage from a dumpsite on its property might have polluted the groundwater used by a local community. The company has denied responsibility but the community has launched a $2,000,000 lawsuit against Hoselaw to compensate it for additional costs of obtaining fresh water and for cleaning up the contamination. The lawyers for the community and the company have met to discuss possible settlement terms, but little progress has been reported. Hoselaw's net income over the last five years has averaged $725,000, and its assets, as reported on the most recent balance sheet, have a carrying amount of $3,750,000.

Required:

Prepare a report to Hoselaw's president discussing the issues surrounding how to account for the environmental incident and the lawsuit. Your report should include a discussion of the alternative accounting treatments available and the implications of each.

P9-13. **(Accounting for a possible loss, LO 6)** In May 2017, a child was injured at a play area at the Kakisa Design Furniture Shoppe. The play area was provided so parents could leave their children while they shopped in the store. The parents of the child thought the injury was due to poor supervision and poor maintenance, so they are suing Kakisa for $1 million. As of December 31, 2017 (Kakisa's year-end), the lawsuit hasn't been settled. Kakisa's lawyers believe that the company will probably lose the lawsuit if it goes to trial. The lawyers think that Kakisa stands to lose somewhere between $75,000 and $350,000.

Kakisa is a family-owned business but no family members are involved in the management of the store. The financial statements are used by the members of the Kakisa family, for tax purposes, and by the store's banker. In January 2019, the lawsuit was finally settled, with Kakisa paying the family of the injured child $150,000.

Required:

a. Prepare a report to Kakisa's president explaining the accounting issues that must be considered in deciding how to account for the lawsuit in the December 31, 2017 financial statements. Provide a recommendation on how the lawsuit should be accounted for and explain your reasoning fully.
b. What are the accounting issues that would have to be considered when the December 31, 2018 financial statements are prepared?

P9-14. **(Accounting for leases, LO 4)** Vista Inc. (Vista) is a new manufacturing company that was formed in January 2017 to supply certain specialized machine parts to a large public company. Vista's managers decided to arrange long-term leases for the company's equipment, rather than to arrange financing and buy the equipment. Had Vista purchased the equipment, it would have cost about $2,000,000. Instead, Vista signed a ten-year lease for the equipment in January 2017 that required it to make annual payments of $300,000 on December 31, the company's year-end. At the end of the lease, Vista has the option to purchase the equipment at its fair market value at the time. However, Vista's management thinks it's unlikely it will exercise the option because after ten years the equipment will be technologically out of date. The interest rate appropriate for this lease is 9 percent.

On December 31, 2017, Vista had total liabilities (before accounting for the lease obligation) of $1,600,000, common shares of $1,000,000, and income, before lease-related expenses and taxes, of $700,000. Vista's tax expense for 2017 is estimated to be $80,000 (including the effect of the lease).

Required:

a. What are some of the reasons that Vista might have leased rather than purchased the equipment?
b. Should the lease be accounted for as a capital (finance) lease or an operating lease? Explain.
c. What journal entry would be required when the lease agreement was signed if the lease was considered a capital (finance) lease? What entry would be required if it was classified as an operating lease?
d. Prepare a schedule showing the principal and interest components of each annual payment over the life of the lease, assuming the lease is treated as a capital (finance) lease. Prepare the journal entries that Vista would make on December 31, 2017 and December 31, 2020 to record the lease payment. What would the entries be if the lease were classified as an operating lease?
e. What amount would be reported on Vista's balance sheet for the machinery when the lease was signed in January 2017? What does this amount represent?

f. Over what period of time should the equipment be depreciated? Explain. Prepare the journal entry to record the depreciation expense for the year ended December 31, 2017. Assume Vista uses straight-line depreciation.
g. How would Vista's debt-to-equity ratio be affected by accounting for the lease as a capital (finance) lease? Compare the debt-to-equity ratio on December 31, 2017, when the lease is classified as a capital (finance) lease versus an operating lease.
h. Compare the effect on the income statement of classifying the lease as a capital (finance) lease versus an operating lease. Make the comparison for the years ended December 31, 2017 and 2020, and in total over the term of the lease.
i. What steps could Vista take to have the lease classified as an operating lease? Why might Vista prefer that classification?
j. For purposes of determining a bonus for Vista's managers, do you think it's more appropriate to treat the lease as a capital (finance) lease or an operating lease? In answering, focus on determining management's bonus, not how IFRS would require the lease to be classified.

P9-15. **(Accounting for leases, LO 4)** On May 1, 2018, Isachsen Inc. (Isachsen) signed a four-year lease with an office supply company to supply Isachsen with all required office equipment over the lease period. Had Isachsen purchased the office equipment, it would have cost about $250,000. The lease requires Isachsen to make annual lease payments of $75,000 on April 30 of each year. Isachsen made the first payment on April 30, 2019. At the end of the lease, Isachsen will own the equipment. Isachsen's management believes the office equipment will be useful for between six and eight years. The interest rate appropriate for this lease is 11 percent.

On April 30, 2019, Isachsen had total liabilities (before accounting for the lease obligation) of $1,375,000, common shares of $750,000, and retained earnings of $450,000. Isachsen's income before lease related-expenses and taxes for the year ended April 30, 2019 was $275,000. Isachsen's tax expense for fiscal 2019 is estimated to be $80,000 (including the effect of the lease).

Required:

a. What are some of the reasons that Isachsen might have leased rather than purchased the office equipment?
b. Should the lease be accounted for as a capital (finance) lease or an operating lease? Explain.
c. What journal entry would be required when the lease agreement was signed if the lease was considered a capital (finance) lease? What entry would be required if it were classified as an operating lease?
d. Prepare a schedule showing the principal and interest components of each annual payment over the life of the lease, assuming the lease is treated as a capital (finance) lease. Prepare the journal entries that Isachsen would make on April 30, 2019 and April 30, 2021 to record the lease payment. What would the entries be if the lease was classified as an operating lease?
e. What amount would be reported on Isachsen's balance sheet for the equipment when the lease was signed in May 1, 2018? What does this amount represent?
f. Over what period of time should the equipment be depreciated? Explain. Prepare the journal entry to record the depreciation expense for the year ended April 30, 2019. Assume Isachsen uses straight-line depreciation.
g. How would Isachsen's debt-to-equity ratio be affected by accounting for the lease as a capital (finance) lease? Compare the debt-to-equity ratio on April 30, 2019 when the lease is classified as a capital (finance) lease versus an operating lease.
h. Compare the effect on the income statement of classifying the lease as a capital (finance) lease versus an operating lease. Make the comparison for the years ended April 30, 2019 and 2021, and in total over the term of the lease.
i. What steps could Isachsen take to have the lease classified as an operating lease? Why might Isachsen prefer that classification?
j. Suppose you were considering buying all the shares of Isachsen. Which balance sheet and income statement would be more useful to you in assessing the company—statements where the lease was classified as a capital (finance) lease or as an operating lease?

P9-16. **(Effect of inaccurate accruals, LO 7)** In 2017, Ogoki Ltd. announced a major restructuring of its operations. The restructuring was in response to several years of poor performance and declining net income, the result of increased competition from Asia. The company announced that it would be downsizing its production facilities and reducing its workforce by 20 percent. Management estimated that the cost of reducing the workforce would be about $75 million. The reduction in the workforce and the related costs are to take place in 2018.

In 2018, Ogoki carried out its restructuring. When it was completed, the actual cost of reducing the workforce was $50 million. All of these costs were related to severance packages paid to and retraining of employees. Ogoki's year-end is December 31.

Required:

a. Provide the journal entry that Ogoki would make in 2017 to record the estimated cost of reducing the workforce. Why do you think the entry would be made in 2017 when the reduction in the workforce was actually to take place in 2018? How would the amount be shown on the income statement? Explain.
b. What entry would be made to record the $50 million in cash costs incurred in 2018 to reduce the workforce? What effect would this entry have on the income statement in 2018? Explain.
c. What additional entry or entries would be needed in 2018 to adjust for the fact that management estimated the cost of reducing the workforce to be $75 million whereas the actual cost proved to be only $50 million? What is the effect of this difference on the financial statements in 2017 and 2018? Provide some possible explanations for the error in the estimate in 2017. When answering, consider the managers' financial reporting objectives.

P9-17. **(The effects of buying versus leasing on the financial statements, LO 4)** Winterton Rail Ltd. (Winterton) is considering obtaining some new locomotives. The purchase price of the locomotives is $59,724,975. Winterton is considering whether it should purchase the locomotives or lease them directly from the manufacturer. If Winterton buys the locomotives, it would borrow the full purchase price from a large institutional lender and repay the loan by making an annual payment of $7,500,000 on the last day of each of the next 20 years. If Winterton leases the locomotives, it would make annual lease payments of $7,500,000 to the manufacturer on the last day of each of the next 20 years.

Required:

a. Prepare the journal entries Winterton would make if it borrowed the money and purchased the locomotives.
b. Prepare the journal entries Winterton would make when the lease agreement is signed if it leased the locomotives and the lease was considered a capital (finance) lease.
c. Prepare the journal entries Winterton would make when the lease agreement is signed if it leased the locomotives and the lease was considered an operating lease.
d. Compare the three alternatives in (a), (b), and (c). Explain the similarities and differences among them. Under what circumstances might one of the alternatives be preferred over the others? Explain.

P9-18. **(Lease accounting and financial ratios, LO 4, 7)** Kincaid Airlines Ltd. is a small airline in western Canada. Recently, Kincaid decided to add new planes to its fleet. Kincaid's summarized balance sheet on December 31, 2017 is shown below. The non-current liabilities entry is a bond that matures in 2028. The terms of the bond stipulate that Kincaid must maintain a current ratio greater than 1.0 and a debt-to-equity ratio of less than 1.3. If either of these covenants is violated, the term note becomes payable immediately.

Instead of purchasing the new aircraft, Kincaid arranged 20-year leases with the manufacturer. The terms of the lease require annual payments of $4.2 million, beginning on January 1, 2018. The lease goes into effect on January 1, 2018.

Kincaid Corp. Balance Sheet as of December 31, 2017			
Assets:		Liabilities and shareholders' equity:	
Current assets	$ 18,950,000	Current liabilities	$ 13,990,000
Capital assets and other non-current assets	83,550,000	Non-current liabilities	39,100,000
			53,090,000
		Shareholders' equity	49,410,000
Total assets	$102,500,000	Total liabilities and shareholders' equity	$102,500,000

Required:

a. Calculate the current ratio and debt-to-equity ratio on December 31, 2017.
b. Calculate the current ratio and debt-to-equity ratio on January 1, 2018 if the new lease is accounted for as an operating lease. Assume no changes to the balance sheet from December 31, 2017, except for the accounting for the lease.
c. Calculate the current ratio and debt-to-equity ratio on January 1, 2018, if the new lease is accounted for as a capital (finance) lease. Assume that the appropriate interest rate that should be applied to the lease is 12 percent. Assume no changes to the balance sheet from December 31, 2017, except for the accounting for the lease. Remember that the first payment is due on January 1, 2018.
d. You are Kincaid's controller. The president of the company has just informed you of his plan to lease the new aircraft. Write a memo to the president raising any concerns you have with the plan and providing advice and recommendations as to how he should proceed.

P9-19. (Accounting for bonds, LO 3) On March 1, 2017, Glaslyn Inc. (Glaslyn) issued a $10,000,000 bond with a 4 percent coupon rate and a maturity date of February 28, 2023. Interest will be paid semi-annually on August 31 and February 28. Glaslyn's year-end is December 31. The effective interest rate for a bond of this type on March 1, 2017 was 5 percent.

Required:

a. What will the proceeds be from the bond issue?
b. Prepare the journal entry to record the issue of the bond on March 1, 2017.
c. Prepare an amortization schedule using the effective interest rate method for any premium or discount that arose from the issue of the bond.
d. Prepare the journal entry required to accrue the interest expense and interest payable on December 31, 2017. Make the entry assuming the effective interest rate method of amortization.
e. Prepare the journal entry required to record the interest expense on March 31, 2018 (the end of the first quarter). Assume Glaslyn uses the effective interest rate amortization method.
f. Prepare the journal entry required to record the retirement of the bond on maturity. Include the interest expense and amortization of any bond premium or discount in the entry.
g. Assume that Glaslyn's bond agreement allowed it to redeem the bond on February 28, 2020 for $11,000,000. Prepare the journal entry required to record early retirement of the bond.
h. Assume the role of a shareholder in Glaslyn. How would you interpret the gain or loss that would be reported on Glaslyn's income statement as a result of the early retirement of the bond? Explain.

P9-20. (Accounting for bonds, LO 3) On June 1, 2016, Hamiota Inc. (Hamiota) issued a $250,000,000 bond with a 5 percent coupon rate and a maturity date of May 31, 2026. Interest will be paid annually on May 31. Hamiota's year-end is December 31. The appropriate interest rate for a bond of this type on June 1, 2016 was 4.5 percent.

Required:

a. What will the proceeds be from the bond issue?
b. Prepare the journal entry to record the issue of the bond on June 1, 2016.
c. Prepare an amortization schedule using the effective interest rate method for any premium or discount that arose from the issue of the bond.
d. Prepare the journal entry required to accrue the interest expense and accrued interest payable on December 31, 2016 and 2017.
e. Prepare the journal entry required to record the payment to investors on May 31, 2017 and 2018.
f. Prepare the journal entry required to record the retirement of the bond on maturity. Include the interest expense and amortization of any bond premium or discount in the entry. Use the effective interest rate method.
g. On May 31, 2021, Hamiota was able to buy back all the outstanding bonds on the open market for $241,000,000. Prepare the journal entry required to record early retirement of the bond. Assume the entry to record the interest expense to May 31, 2021 has already been recorded.
h. Do you think that the decision to buy back the bonds early was a good one? Explain.

P9-21. **(Future income taxes, LO 8)** Noggle Inc. (Noggle) processes fresh apples that it purchases from local farmers into apple juice and applesauce. All of Noggle's processing equipment was purchased in 2017 for $900,000. For accounting purposes, Noggle is depreciating the equipment on a straight-line basis over 10 years. For tax purposes, the asset is in a CCA class that allows Noggle to deduct 30 percent of the capital cost of the asset on a declining-balance basis. Because of the half-year rule, Noggle can deduct only one-half of the allowable amount (15 percent) of the cost in 2017. Noggle has an income tax rate of 18 percent and its income before depreciation and taxes is $300,000 in each year from 2017 through 2019. Noggle has no temporary differences between tax and financial reporting except for the difference between depreciation and CCA on the processing equipment, and there are no permanent differences.

Required:

a. Calculate Noggle's taxable income in 2017 through 2019.
b. Calculate the amount of income tax that Noggle must pay in 2017 through 2019.
c. Calculate the accounting and tax bases of the processing equipment in 2017 through 2019.
d. Calculate the future tax asset or liability that would be reported on Noggle's balance sheet at the end of 2017 through 2019.
e. Prepare the journal entry that Noggle would make each year to record its income tax expense in 2017 through 2019.
f. Calculate Noggle's net income in 2017 through 2019.
g. What would Noggle's net income be in 2017 through 2019 if it used the taxes payable method?
h. As a banker, which measure of net income is more useful to you? Explain.

Using Financial Statements

CANADIAN TIRE CORPORATION LIMITED

Canadian Tire Corporation, Limited (Canadian Tire) is one of the leading retailers in Canada. The company, aided by associate dealers, franchisees, and agents, operates the flagship Canadian Tire chain, which includes more than 450 stores from coast to coast. These stores offer a wide selection of automotive parts, accessories, and services; sports and leisure products; and household goods. The company also offers online shopping and runs the 40-unit Part Source automotive parts specialty chain. Canadian Tire Petroleum is the nation's leading independent retailer of gasoline, with about 250 gasoline filling stations. Canadian Tire Financial Services finances and manages the Canadian Tire Options MasterCard program; markets insurance and warranty products; and offers emergency roadside assistance through the Canadian Tire Auto Club. The company also owns Mark's Work Wearhouse, operator of over 370 men's and women's clothing stores, and the Forzani Group, the largest national sporting goods retailer in Canada, which operates banners that include Sport Chek and Sports Experts. Canadian Tire trades on the TSX under the symbols CTC and CTC.A.[12]

Canadian Tire's consolidated balance sheets and statements of earnings as well as extracts from the statements of cash flows and notes to the financial statements from its 2011 annual report are provided in Exhibit 9.12.[13] Use this information to respond to questions FS9-1 to FS9-11.

FS9-1. Use the information in Exhibit 9.12 to respond to the following questions:

a. What amount of current liabilities did Canadian Tire have on December 31, 2011 and January 1, 2011? What amount of non-current liabilities did it have?
b. How much did Canadian Tire report as trade and other payables December 31, 2011 and January 1, 2011? How much of that amount was classified as trade payables and accrued liabilities?
c. What was Canadian Tire's debt-to-equity ratio on December 31, 2011 and January 1, 2011? Interpret the ratios you calculated.
d. Which liabilities on Canadian Tire's balance sheet are valued at their present value?
e. What was Canadian Tire's interest coverage ratio for the years ended December 31, 2011 and January 1, 2011?
f. Calculate Canadian Tire's current and quick ratios on December 31, 2011 and January 1, 2011. What is your assessment of the company's liquidity? What other factors might you consider in assessing the company's liquidity?
g. What is Canadian Tire's cash from operations for fiscal 2011 and 2010? Why is cash from operations so different from net earnings?
h. What amount of long-term debt did Canadian Tire report on December 31, 2011 and January 1, 2011? What amount of the long-term debt was classified as current?

FS9-2. Examine Note 23 to Canadian Tire's financial statements.

a. What is a contingent liability? How are contingent liabilities accounted for?
b. Explain the information in the first paragraph of the note. Do you find this information useful? Explain. Why do you think the information is provided in this very general way?
c. Describe the situation in the second paragraph of Note 23. What would the impact on the financial statements be had the $24.4 million referred to been accrued on the financial statements? How would it affect you as a prospective investor that the amount wasn't accrued, provided that it was disclosed in the notes? (*Note:* "The Bank" referred to in the note is the Canadian Tire bank, which is owned by Canadian Tire.)

FS9-3. The following questions pertain to Canadian Tire's long-term debt:

a. How much long-term debt was outstanding on December 31, 2011? How much of that long-term debt was classified as current? What does it mean when long-term debt is classified as a current liability? What is the purpose of classifying long-term debt as current?
b. How much did Canadian Tire have outstanding from its Series 2008-1 senior notes on December 31, 2011? When does this debt mature? What is the interest rate on the debt? Why is it important and useful for stakeholders to know the maturity and interest rate associated with a loan obligation?
c. What was Canadian Tire's interest expense in fiscal 2010 and 2011? How much interest did Canadian Tire pay in those years? Why are the interest expense and the amount of interest paid different?
d. How much is scheduled to be repaid to lenders in each of the next five years? In examining the scheduled repayments, do you have any concerns? Explain.
e. In Note 26, Canadian Tire states, "The Company has provided covenants to certain of its lenders. The Company was in compliance with all of its covenants in 2011 and 2010." Why is this statement provided and do you find it useful?

EXHIBIT 9.12 Canadian Tire Corporation, Limited: Extracts from the Financial Statements

Consolidated Balance Sheets

As at (C$ in millions)	December 31, 2011	January 1, 2011 (Note 44)	January 3, 2010 (Note 44)
ASSETS			
Cash and cash equivalents (Note 9)	$ 325.8	$ 568.9	$ 885.8
Short-term investments (Note 10)	196.4	196.7	60.9
Trade and other receivables (Note 11)	829.3	673.9	853.8
Loans receivable (Note 12)	4,081.7	4,051.0	4,008.7
Merchandise inventories	1,448.6	901.0	933.0
Income taxes recoverable	–	99.3	94.7
Prepaid expenses and deposits	44.3	37.6	41.1
Assets classified as held for sale (Note 13)	30.5	20.8	15.0
Total current assets	6,956.6	6,549.2	6,893.0
Total assets	$ 12,338.8	$ 11,048.5	$ 11,407.2
LIABILITIES			
Bank indebtedness (Note 9)	$ 124.8	$ 118.0	$ 83.7
Deposits (Note 20)	1,182.3	615.6	863.4
Trade and other payables (Note 21)	1,640.9	1,179.9	1,192.9
Provisions (Note 22)	191.9	196.2	220.9
Short-term borrowings (Note 24)	352.6	100.6	163.0
Loans payable (Note 25)	628.7	687.0	757.4
Income taxes payable	3.9	–	–
Current portion of long-term debt (Note 26)	27.9	354.2	690.6
Total current liabilities	4,153.0	3,251.5	3,971.9
Long-term provisions (Note 22)	55.1	25.1	26.7
Long-term debt (Note 26)	2,347.7	2,365.4	2,441.1
Long-term deposits (Note 20)	1,102.2	1,264.5	1,196.9
Deferred income taxes (Note 19)	66.1	–	–
Other long-term liabilities (Note 27)	205.7	137.1	127.5
Total liabilities	7,929.8	7,043.6	7,764.1
SHAREHOLDERS' EQUITY			
Share capital (Note 29)	710.5	711.6	720.4
Contributed surplus	1.1	0.3	0.2
Accumulated other comprehensive income (loss)	11.0	(32.3)	(38.6)
Retained earnings	3,686.4	3,325.3	2,961.1
Total shareholders' equity	4,409.0	4,004.9	3,643.1
Total liabilities and shareholders' equity	$ 12,338.8	$ 11,048.5	$ 11,407.2

EXHIBIT 9.12 (continued) Canadian Tire Corporation, Limited: Extracts from the Financial Statements

Consolidated Statements of income

For the years ended (C$ in millions except per share amounts)	December 31, 2011	January 1, 2011
		(Note 44)
Revenue (Note 32)	$ 10,387.1	$ 9,213.1
Cost of producing revenue (Note 33)	(7,326.4)	(6,422.1)
Gross margin	3,060.7	2,791.0
Other income	18.4	1.1
Operating expenses		
Distribution costs	(329.2)	(296.3)
Sales and marketing expenses	(1,286.3)	(1,090.4)
Administrative expenses	(701.5)	(682.9)
Total operating expenses (Note 34)	(2,317.0)	(2,069.6)
Operating income	762.1	722.6
Finance income	23.0	32.4
Finance costs	(155.2)	(168.1)
Net finance costs (Note 36)	(132.2)	(135.7)
Income before income taxes	629.9	586.8
Income taxes (Note 37)	(162.9)	(142.6)
Net income	$ 467.0	$ 444.2

FS9-4. The following questions pertain to Canadian Tire's income taxes:

a. What amount did Canadian Tire report as its income tax expense in the years ended December 31, 2011 and January 1, 2011? What portion was classified as a current expense and what portion was a deferred income tax expense? How much did Canadian Tire owe government for income taxes on December 31, 2011? How much did the company actually pay in income taxes to government during 2011? Why is this amount different from the current income tax expense?

b. What amount does Canadian Tire report on its December 31, 2011 balance sheet for deferred income taxes? What does this amount represent?

c. What was Canadian Tire's combined statutory income tax rate in fiscal 2010 and 2011? What is Canadian Tire's actual (effective) income tax rate based on the income tax expense in fiscal 2010 and 2011? What is Canadian Tire's tax rate based on its current income tax expense in fiscal 2010 and 2011?

FS9-5. Examine the part of Note 41 to Canadian Tire's financial statement that describes its other commitments:

a. What is a commitment?

b. What types of commitments has Canadian Tire entered into?

c. What is the dollar amount associated with the commitments?

d. How has Canadian Tire accounted for its commitments? Why are commitments accounting for this way?

e. What is the impact on the financial statements of accounting for commitments in this way?

f. Are the disclosures about Canadian Tire's commitments important? Explain.

EXHIBIT 9.12 (continued) Canadian Tire Corporation, Limited: Extracts from the Financial Statements

Consolidated Statements of Cash Flows

For the years ended (C$ in millions)	December 31, 2011	January 1, 2011 (Note 44)
Cash generated from (used for):		
Operating activities		
Net income	$ 467.0	$ 444.2
Adjustments for:		
Impairment on loans receivable (Note 12)	352.0	347.0
Depreciation on property and equipment and investment property	229.8	223.8
Income tax expense	162.9	142.6
Net finance costs	132.2	135.7
Amortization of intangible assets	66.3	50.3
Changes in fair value of derivative instruments	(3.1)	(16.0)
Other	3.4	10.3
Gain on revaluation of shores (Note 8)	(10.4)	–
	1,400.1	1,337.9
Changes in working capital and other (Note 38)	219.6	(293.1)
Cash generated from operating activities before interest and taxes	1,619.7	1,044.8
Interest paid	(176.6)	(190.5)
Interest received	26.1	6.7
Income taxes paid	(63.7)	(131.5)
Cash generated from operating activities	1,405.5	729.5
Financing activities		
Issuance of long-term debt	–	264.5
Issuance of short-term borrowings	2,676.8	1,160.3
Repayment of short-term borrowings	(2,666.7)	(1,222.7)
Issuance of loans payable	129.3	248.4
Repayment of loans payable	(187.6)	(318.8)
Issuance of share capital (Note 29)	11.6	16.7
Repurchase of share capital (Note 29)	(11.9)	(25.4)
Repayment of long-term debt and finance lease liabilities	(355.6)	(690.8)
Dividends paid	(89.6)	(68.5)
Payment of transaction costs related to long-term debt	–	(1.7)
Cash used for financing activities	(493.7)	(638.0)
Cash used in the year	(249.6)	(351.7)
Cash and cash equivalents, net of bank indebtedness, beginning of year	450.9	802.1
Effect of exchange rate fluctuations on cash held	(0.3)	0.5
Cash and cash equivalents, net of bank indebtedness, end of year (Note 9)	$ 201.0	$ 450.9

EXHIBIT 9.12 (continued) Canadian Tire Corporation, Limited: Extracts from the Financial Statements

3. Significant Accounting Policies

Provisions

A provision is recognized if, as a result of a past event, the Company has a present legal or constructive obligation that can be estimated reliably and it is probable that an outflow of economic benefits will be required to settle the obligation. The amount recognized as a provision is the best estimate of the consideration required to settle the present obligation at the end of the reporting period, taking into account risks and uncertainty of cash flow. Where the effect of discounting is material, provisions are determined by discounting the expected future cash flows at a pre-tax rate that reflects current market assessments of the time value of money and the risks specific to the liability. Where the future cash flow estimates have been adjusted for the risks specific to the liability, the discount rate does not reflect the risks specific to the liability. The unwinding of the discount is reflected in finance costs in the Consolidated Statements of Income.

When a portion or all of the economic benefits required to settle a provision are expected to be recovered from a third party, a receivable is recognized as an asset if it is virtually certain that the Company will receive the reimbursement and the amount can be reliably measured.

Warranties and returns

A provision or warranties and returns is recognized when the underlying products or services are sold. The provision is based on historical warranty and returns data and is discounted to present value.

Site restoration and decommissioning

Legal or constructive obligations associated with the removal of underground fuel storage tanks and site remediation costs on the retirement of certain property and equipment, and the termination of certain lease agreements are recognized in the period in which they are incurred when it is probable that an outflow of resources embodying economic benefits will be required and a reasonable estimate of the amount of the obligation can be made. The obligations are initially measured at the Company's best estimate, using an expected value approach, and are discounted to present value. An amount equal to that of the initial obligation is added to the capitalized costs of the related asset. Over time, the discounted obligation amount accretes to the expected fair value of the cost to restore/decommission the location. This accretion amount is reflected in finance costs in the Consolidated Statements of Income for the period. The initial costs are depreciated over the useful lives of the related property and equipment in accordance with the depreciation rate outlined in the property and equipment note above.

Customer loyalty programs

The Company maintains customer loyalty programs in promoting our interrelated businesses. The Company issues paper-based "Canadian Tire Money" to Dealers and to consumers whenever they make cash or debit card purchases at the Company's Petroleum gas bars. The Company also issues electronic-based "Canadian Tire Money on the Card" whenever consumers make a Canadian Tire Options MasterCard purchase from any location in the World. Both the paper-based and the electronic-based "Canadian Tire Money" can only be redeemed at the Canadian Tire Retail stores for merchandise at the option of the consumer.

An obligation arises from the above customer loyalty program when the Dealers pay the Company to acquire paper-based "Canadian Tire Money," as the Dealers retain the right to return Canadian Tire Money to the Company for refund in cash. An obligation also arises when the Company issues electronic-based "Canadian Tire Money on the Card." These obligations are measured at fair value by reference to the fair value of the awards for which they could be redeemed based on the estimated probability of their redemption and are expensed to sales and marketing expenses in the Consolidated Statements of Income.

21. Trade and Other Payables

(C$ in millions)	**December 31, 2011**	January 1, 2011	January 3, 2010
Trade payables and accrued liabilities	**$ 1,598.6**	$ 1,095.1	$ 1,074.6
Deferred revenue	**39.5**	37.6	36.5
Derivatives (Note 39)	**2.8**	47.2	81.8
	$ 1,640.9	$ 1,179.9	$ 1,192.9

Deferred revenue consists mainly of unearned insurance, premiums, unearned Roadside Assistance Club memberships and unearned revenue related to gift certificates and gift cards.

The average credit period on trade payables is five to ninety days (2010—five to sixty days).

EXHIBIT 9.12 (continued) Canadian Tire Corporation, Limited: Extracts from the Financial Statements

22. Provisions

The following table presents the changes to the Company's provisions:

(C$ in millions)	Warranties and returns	Site restoration and decommissioning	Onerous contracts	Customer loyalty	Other	Total
Balance at January 1, 2011	$ 109.7	$ 24.8	$ 6.8	$ 65.3	$ 14.7	$ 221.3
Assumed in a business combination	–	0.1	0.7	–	30.2	31.0
Charges net of reversals	245.1	5.3	1.1	(111.2)	3.1	368.6
Utilizations	(242.9)	(7.5)	(1.5)	114.0	(16.2)	(379.3)
Unwinding of discount	1.2	0.5	–	–	–	17
Change in discount rate	0.1	3.6	–	–	–	3.7
Balance at December 31, 2011	**$ 113.2**	**26.8**	**7.1**	**68.1**	**31.8**	**$ 247.0**
Less: Current portion	107.9	7.4	2.1	68.1	6.4	191.9
Long-term portion	$ 5.3	$ 19.4	$ 5.0	$ –	$ 25.4	$ 55.1

Warranties and returns

The provision for warranties and returns relates to the Company's obligation to stores within its Dealer network for defective goods in their current inventories and defective goods sold to customers throughout its store operations that have yet to be returned, as well as after sales and service for replacement parts. The Company undertakes to make good, by repair, replacement or refund any manufacturing defects that become apparent within one year from the date of sale unless stated otherwise. The provisions are based on estimates made from actual historical experience and data associated with similar products and services. The Company expects to incur substantially all of the liability over the next year.

The Company is reimbursed for defective goods from either the suppliers the products were purchased from or its Dealer network as part of its agreement with its Dealers.

Site restoration and decommissioning

In the normal course of business, the Company leases property and has a legal or constructive obligation to return the sites to their original or agreed upon state at the end of the lease term. The Company accrues tor these costs based on reasonable estimates of the fair value and discounts based on the timing of expected outflows, where applicable.

The Company accrues for environmental restoration related to the treatment or removal of contaminated soil and site decommissioning related primarily to tank removal costs and building/canopy demolition. The Company accrues for these costs based on reasonable estimates of the fair value and discounts based on the timing of expected outflows, where applicable. Environmental reserves are expected to be paid out over five years and decommissioning reserves are expected to be paid out over 40 years as the sites are closed. In certain cases the actual outflow may be shorter or longer than the estimated life span.

Customer loyalty

The Company maintains a provision related to its loyalty programs, including paper-based "Canadian Tire Money" issued at Petroleum gas bars and issued to Dealers, "Electronic Canadian Tire Money on-the-Card" issued whenever consumers make a Canadian Tire Options MasterCard purchase from any location in the World, and Canadian Tire coins issued to customers at Dealers. The provisions are measured at fair value by reference to the fair value of the awards for which they can be redeemed multiplied by the estimate of the probability of their redemption. The Company expects to discharge substantially all of the liability over the next year.

23. Contingencies

Legal matters

The Company and certain of its subsidiaries are party to a number of legal proceedings. The Company has determined that each such proceeding constitutes a routine legal matter incidental to the business conducted by the Company and that the ultimate disposition of the proceedings will not have a material effect on its consolidated earnings, cash flows, or financial position.

The Bank is the subject of two class action proceedings regarding allegations that certain fees charged on the Bank issued credit cards are not permitted under the Quebec Consumer Protection Act. The Bank has determined that it has a solid defense to both actions on the basis that banking and cost of borrowing disclosure is a matter of exclusive federal jurisdiction. Accordingly, no provision has been made for amounts, if any, that would be payable in the event of an adverse outcome. If adversely decided, the total aggregate exposure to the Company would have been approximately $24.4 million at December 31, 2011.

EXHIBIT 9.12 **(continued) Canadian Tire Corporation, Limited: Extracts from the Financial Statements**

24. Short-Term Borrowings

Short-term borrowings include commercial paper notes and bank line of credit borrowings. The commercial paper notes are short-term notes issued with varying original maturities of one year or less, typically 90 days or less, at interest rates fixed at the time of each renewal. The notes may bear interest payable at maturity or be sold at a discount and mature at face value. Commercial paper notes issued by the Company are recorded at amortized cost.

25. Loans Payable

Franchise Trust, a legal entity sponsored by a third party bank, originates loans to Dealers. Loans payable are the loans that Franchise Trust has incurred to fund the loans to Dealers. These loans are not direct legal liabilities of the Company, but have been consolidated in the accounts of the Company as the Company effectively controls the silo of Franchise Trust containing the Dealer loan program.

Loans payable is recorded at fair value and are due within one year.

26. Long-Term Debt

Long-term debt is measured at amortized cost, using the effective interest method, and includes the following:

	December 31, 2011		January 1, 2011		January 3, 2010	
(C$ in millions)	**Face value**	**Carrying amount**	Face value	Carrying amount	Face value	Carrying amount
Senior notes[1]						
Series 2005-1, 4.187%, November 19, 2010	**$ –**	**$ –**	$ –	$ –	$ 341.7	$ 341.7
Series 2006-1, 4.271%, November 18, 2011	**–**	**–**	300.0	300.0	300.0	299.7
Series 2006-2, 4.405%, May 20, 2014	**238.7**	**238.7**	238.7	238.7	238.7	238.4
Series 2008-1, 5.027%, February 20, 2013	**600.0**	**598.3**	600.0	598.3	600.0	597.4
Series 2010-1, 3.158%, November 20, 2015	**250.0**	**248.8**	250.0	248.7	–	–
Subordinated notes[1]						
Series 2005-1, 4.507%, November 19, 2010	**–**	**–**	–	–	20.1	20.1
Series 2006-1, 4.571%, November 13, 2011	**–**	**–**	17.5	17.5	17.5	17.5
Series 2006-2, 4.765%, May 20, 2014	**13.9**	**13.9**	13.9	13.9	13.9	13.9
Series 2008-1, 6.027%, February 20, 2013	**34.9**	**34.8**	34.9	34.8	34.9	34.8
Series 2010-1, 4.128%, November 20, 2015	**14.6**	**14.5**	14.6	14.5	–	–
Medium-term notes						
5.22% due October 1, 2010	**–**	**–**	–	–	300.0	299.8
4.95% due June 1, 2015	**300.0**	**299.4**	300.0	299.2	300.0	299.0
5.65% due June 1, 2016	**200.0**	**198.6**	200.0	198.3	200.0	202.5
6.25% due April 13, 2028	**150.0**	**149.4**	150.0	149.3	150.0	149.3
6.32% due February 24, 2034	**200.0**	**199.1**	200.0	199.1	200.0	199.0
5.61% due September 4, 2035	**200.0**	**199.2**	200.0	199.1	200.0	199.1
Finance lease obligations	**176.4**	**176.4**	193.0	193.0	202.5	202.5
Promissory note	**4.5**	**4.5**	15.2	15.2	17.0	17.0
Total debt	**$ 2,383.0**	**$ 2,375.6**	$ 2,727.8	$ 2,719.6	$ 3,136.3	$ 3,131.7
Current	**$ 27.9**	**$ 27.9**	$ 354.2	$ 354.2	$ 690.6	$ 690.6
Non-current	**2,355.1**	**2,347.7**	2,373.6	2,365.4	2,445.7	2,441.1
Total debt	**$ 2,383.0**	**$ 2,375.6**	$ 2,727.8	$ 2,719.6	$ 3,136.3	$ 3,131.7

[1] *Senior and subordinated notes are those of GCCT.*

EXHIBIT 9.12 (continued) Canadian Tire Corporation, Limited: Extracts from the Financial Statements

The carrying value of long-term debt is net of debt issuance costs of $6.6 million (January 1, 2011—$7.2 million; January 3, 2010—$8.0 million), and the benefit of the effective portion of the cash flow hedges of $0.8 million (January 1, 2011—benefit of $1.0 million; January 3, 2010—cost of $3.4 million).

Debt covenants

The Company has provided covenants to certain of its lenders. The Company was in compliance with all of its covenants in 2011 and 2010.

Summary of debt repayment by year

(C$ in millions)	2012	2013	2014	2015	2016	Thereafter	Total
Senior notes	$ –	$ 600.0	$ 238.7	$ 250.0	$ –	$ –	$ 1,088.7
Subordinated notes	–	34.9	13.9	14.6	–	–	63.4
Medium-term notes	–	–	–	300.0	200.0	550.0	1,050.0
Finance lease obligations	23.6	20.7	14.6	13.3	11.3	92.9	176.4
Promissory note	4.3	0.2	–	–	–	–	4.5
	$ 27.9	$ 655.8	$ 267.2	$ 577.9	$ 211.3	$ 642.9	$ 2,383.0

37. Income Taxes

The following are the major components of the income tax expense:

(C$ in millions)	**2011**	2010
Current tax expense		
Current period	**$ (185.7)**	$ (178.3)
Adjustments in respect of prior years	**16.4**	45.3
	$ (169.3)	$ (133.0)
Deferred tax expense		
Deferred income tax expense relating to the origination and reversal of temporary differences	**$ 6.4**	$ (9.6)
Deferred income lax expense (benefit) resulting from change in tax rate	**–**	–
	$ 6.4	$ (9.6)
Income tax expense	**$ (162.9)**	$ (142.6)

Reconciliation of income tax expense

Income taxes in the Consolidated Statements of Income vary from amounts that would be computed by applying the statutory income tax rate for the following reasons:

(C$ in millions)	**2011**	2010
Income before income taxes	**$ 629.9**	$ 586.8
Income taxes based on the applicable tax rate of 28.08% (2010—30.49%)	**(176.9)**	(179.0)
Adjustment to income taxes resulting from:		
Prior years' tax settlements	**7.6**	42.0
Change in legislation relating to stock options	**(1.8)**	(8.0)
Adjustments of prior years' tax estimates	**9.0**	3.4
Lower income tax rates on earnings of foreign subsidiaries	**0.4**	1.9
Other	**(1.2)**	(2.9)
Income tax expense	**$ (162.9)**	$ (142.6)

The applicable tax rate is the aggregate of the Canadian federal income tax rate of 16.5% (2010—18.0%) and Canadian provincial income tax rate of 11.58% (2010—12.49%). The decrease in the applicable tax rate from 2010 is primarily due to federal and provincial legislative rate reductions enacted by the respective governments.

EXHIBIT 9.12 (continued) Canadian Tire Corporation, Limited: Extracts from the Financial Statements

40. Operating Leases

The Company as lessee

The Company leases a number of retail stores, distribution centres, Petroleum sites, facilities and office equipment under operating leases with termination dates extending to 2043. Generally, the leases have renewal options, primarily at the Company's option.

The annual lease payments for property and equipment under operating leases are as follows:

(C$ in millions)	**2011**	2010
Less than one year	$ 290.6	$ 197.6
Between one and five years	910.8	674.7
More than five years	908.9	884.4
	$ 2,110.3	$ 1,756.7

The following amounts recognized as an expense in the Consolidated Statements of Income are as follows:

(C$ in millions)	**2011**	2010
Minimum lease payments	**$ 215.2**	$ 167.3
Contingent rent	**1.7**	1.9
Sub-lease payments received	**(0.8)**	–
	$ 216.1	**$ 169.2**

Due to the redevelopment or replacement of existing properties, certain leased properties are no longer needed for business operations. Where possible, the Company sub-leases these properties to third parties, receiving sub-lease payments to reduce costs. In addition, the Company has certain premises where it is on the head lease and sub-leases the property to franchisees. The total future minimum sublease payments expected to be received under these non-cancellable sub-leases is $94.8 million as at December 31, 2011 (2010—$ 0.9 million). The Company has recognized a provision of $4.8 million (2010—$4.9 million) in respect of these leases (Note 22).

FS9-6. Examine the information provided in Note 40 to Canadian Tire's financial statements on operating leases.

a. What is an operating lease and how is it accounted for?
b. What is the dollar amount of the operating leases Canadian Tire has entered into?
c. Suppose the operating lease payments reported in Note 40 were to be reported as capital leases:
   i. What would the journal entry be on December 31, 2011 to record these leases as capital (finance) leases, assuming the leases went into effect on that date? Assume a discount rate of 10 percent and assume the payments to be made "thereafter" are evenly distributed over 2018 through 2025.
   ii. What effect would classifying these leases as capital (finance) leases have on Canadian Tire's debt-to-equity ratio? Explain and show your calculations.
   iii. Do you think that treating all leases as capital (finance) leases gives a better indication of an entity's debt load? Explain.

FS9-7. What is a guarantee? Describe the nature of the guarantee described in Note 41. Does the guarantee meet the definition of a liability (see Chapter 2). Under what circumstances are guarantees reported as liabilities? If a guarantee isn't reported as a liability, why is it reported in the notes to the financial statements? Is information about guarantees useful to stakeholders? Explain.

EXHIBIT 9.12 (continued) Canadian Tire Corporation, Limited: Extracts from the Financial Statements

41. Guarantees and Commitments

Guarantees

In the normal course of business, the Company enters into numerous agreements that may contain features that meet the definition of a guarantee. A guarantee is defined to be a contract (including an indemnity) that contingently requires the Company to make payments to the guaranteed party based on (i) changes in an underlying interest rate, foreign exchange rate, equity or commodity instrument, index or other variable that is related to an asset, a liability or an equity security of the counterparty, (ii) failure of another party to perform under an obligating agreement, or (iii) failure of a third party to pay its indebtedness when due.

The Company has provided the following significant guarantees to third parties:

Third party debt agreements

The Company has guaranteed the debt of certain Dealers. These third party debt agreements require the Company to make payments if the Dealer fails to make scheduled debt payments. The majority of these third party debt agreements have expiration dates extending to January 28, 2012. The maximum amount that the Company may be required to pay under these debt agreements is $50.0 million (2010—$50.0 million), of which $38.8 million (2010—$36.8 million) has been issued at December 31, 2011. No amount has been accrued in the consolidated financial statements with respect to these debt agreements.

Other commitments

As at December 31, 2011, the Company had other commitments. The Company has not recognized any liability relating to these commitments:

The Company has obtained documentary and standby letters of credit aggregating $25.8 million (2010—$25.2 million) relating to the importation of merchandise inventories and to facilitate various real estate activities for the Company's merchandise operations.

The Company has entered into agreements to buy back franchise-owned merchandise inventory should the banks foreclose on any of the franchisees. The terms of the guarantees range from less than a year to the lifetime of the particular underlying franchise agreement. The Company's maximum exposure is $69.9 million (2010—$11.9 million).

The Company has committed to pay $9.2 million (2010—$8.2 million) for various commitments and contingent liabilities including a customs bond and the obligation to buy back two franchise stores.

The Company has committed to pay $68.4 million (2010—$91.2 million) in total to third parties for credit card processing and information technology services mainly in support of the Company's credit card and retail banking services for periods up to 2016.

43. Subsequent Event

On February 9, 2012 the Company's Board of Directors declared a dividend of $0.30 per share payable or June 1, 2012 to shareholders of record as of April 30, 2012.

FS9-8. What are subsequent events and why are they reported in financial statements? Describe the subsequent event Canadian Tire reported in its 2011 statements. What is the relevance of this event to stakeholders? Do you think the event when reported in the financial statement would be "news" to any stakeholder who was very interested in Canadian Tire? Explain. Why was the event described in the note disclosed and not recorded in the financial statements?

FS9-9. Canadian Tire has one of the oldest, most well-known loyalty programs in Canada, Canadian Tire money. Examine Notes 3 and 22 regarding customer loyalty and answer the following questions:

a. Why do companies have loyalty programs?
b. What is the obligation that Canadian Tire has as a result of issuing paper and electronic Canadian Tire Money?
c. What is the amount of Canadian Tire's provision for customer loyalty on December 31, 2011?
d. How does Canadian Tire estimate the amount of the provision?

FS9-10. Canadian Tire provides warranties on products it sells and allows customers to return goods after purchase. Examine Notes 3 and 22 regarding provisions for warranties and returns and answer the following questions:

a. What is a warranty and why does Canadian Tire provide them for goods it sells? Why does Canadian Tire allow customers to return merchandise?
b. When are costs associated with providing warranty service recorded? Why are they recorded at this time?
c. How does Canadian Tire estimate its warranty costs and returns? Why are estimates necessary?
d. What amount does Canadian Tire report as a provision for warranties and returns on December 31, 2011? What portion of this amount is non-current? Why has the amount changed from the beginning of the year to the end of the year?
e. What adjusting journal entry does Canadian Tire record at end of a period to record the provision for warranties and returns?

FS9-11. Examine Notes 3 and 22 to Canadian Tire's financial statements on provisions and answer the following questions:

a. What is a provision and why are they necessary under IFRS?
b. What are site restoration and decommissioning costs and why are they necessary?
c. What was the balance in the site restoration and decommissioning provision on January 1, 2011 and on December 31, 2011? What caused the balance to change during the year? What are the current and long-term portions on December 31, 2011?
d. Why is part of the balance current and part long-term?
e. Do you think it's easy or difficult to determine the amount of this provision? Explain.
f. Do you think information about the asset retirement obligation is important and useful to stakeholders? Explain.

ENDNOTES

1. Extracted from RONA Inc.'s fiscal 2011 annual report.
2. Extracted from Indigo Books & Music Inc.'s fiscal 2011 third-quarter report.
3. Extracted from WestJet Airlines Ltd.'s 2011 annual report.
4. Ibid.
5. Extracted from Canfor Corporation's 2011 audited annual financial statements.
6. Ibid.
7. Extracted from WestJet Airlines Ltd.'s and Shoppers Drug Mart Corporation's 2011 audited financial statements.
8. Data obtained from "Financial Post Industry Report," at the Financial Post Web site, http://www.fpdata.finpost.com/suite/autologreports.asp (accessed July 2012).
9. Extracted from WestJet Airlines Ltd.'s 2011 annual report.
10. Ibid.
11. Ibid.
12. Adapted from Reference for Business's Canadian Tire profile available at http://www.referenceforbusiness.com/history/Ca-Ch/Canadian-Tire-Corporation-Limited.html.
13. Extracted from Canadian Tire Corporation Limited's 2011 annual report.

Practise and learn online with Connect. Connect resources include additional and interactive study exercises, videos, and practice quizzing, as well as additional material you won't find in the printed text.

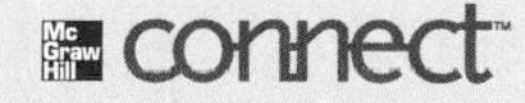

CHAPTER

10 Owners' Equity

LEARNING OBJECTIVES

After studying the material in this chapter you will be able to do the following:

LO 1 Recognize the differences among proprietorships, partnerships, corporations, and not-for-profit organizations and be familiar with accounting and reporting differences among these different types of entities.

LO 2 Characterize equity and the different types of equity securities, and explain the accounting for the issuance and repurchase of shares.

LO 3 Describe the transactions and economic events affecting retained earnings, accumulated other comprehensive income, and contributed surplus.

LO 4 Recognize the implications of changing accounting policies and accounting estimates.

LO 5 Define leverage and explain the effects it has on the return on equity and on the profitability of an entity.

LO 6 Discuss the nature and purpose of employee stock options, and the accounting issues and controversy surrounding them.

LO 7 Explain how and why accounting information has economic consequences.

LO 8 Analyze and interpret information about equity provided in financial statements.

A popular television commercial for Tim Hortons® features Canadian hockey superstar Sidney Crosby sitting in a municipal rink dressing room, and reminiscing about learning to play the nation's most important sport.

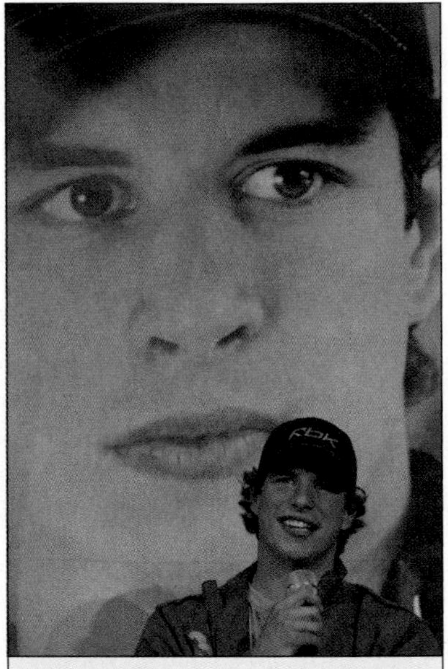

Tim Hortons Inc.

When Crosby was a preschooler in 1993, he played centre for a Timbits house league hockey team in Cole Harbour, N.S. The commercial shows old footage of him from his early days, celebrating after scoring a goal, and telling a TV interviewer how much he loved hockey.

"Hockey is that thought inside your head saying 'Wouldn't it be amazing, getting up every day and playing and doing something that you love to do?'" the youngster gushed.

Beginning in 2006, Crosby became an official ambassador for the Timbits minor hockey program run by the Canadian coffee and donuts chain. It provides team jerseys and medals to some 65,000 boys and girls every year across Canada.

It's not widely known how much money Crosby earns from his Tim Hortons' endorsement, nor from his other sponsors, which include Gatorade, Reebok, and Canada Bread.

But some star athletes like Crosby earn plenty from endorsements and appearance fees on top of their pay for showing up to play their games. According to Forbes.com, basketball star LeBron James earned $40 million from his deals with Nike, Dunkin' Donuts, Coca-Cola, and McDonald's in one year, on top of his $13 million salary.

Crosby's side deals are in addition to the $104.4 million contract he negotiated in 2012 with the Pittsburgh Penguins franchise. His new agreement will pay him about $12 million US per year for the first few years he plays, then progressively less each year for the remaining nine years of the contract.

Crosby got a $5 million signing bonus when he accepted his previous contract with Pittsburgh in 2007.

The CEO of Tim Hortons, Paul D. House, may not be a household name, despite running an $8 billion dollar company. But the businessman and "Sid the Kid" do have something in common when it comes to their paycheques: their regular salary isn't their only source of income.

House's base annual salary was $772,500 in 2012, according to company proxy documents. And, like Crosby, the CEO is eligible for a bonus.

House, a Canadian who worked for Dairy Queen until he joined Tim Hortons in 1985, was on track for a $1 million annual performance bonus if the company met its earnings targets in 2012.

Many Canadian corporate execs also get parts of the company equity in their overall compensation packages. House currently holds 170,000 common shares of the company, which are valued at about $9 million, should he cash them in. House could also benefit from over $2 million more in company shares in 2012.

He also gets an annual allowance for a company car worth $20,450. Then there is the $17,000 in company contributions annually for his life insurance and his pension plan.

If House were to be fired, Tim Hortons would have to pay him $6,982,437 in severance pay.

As executive salaries go, House's package ranked him 62nd on a recent list of the 100 highest paid Canadian executives.

According to a June 2012 *Globe and Mail* list, top spot among CEOs went to J. Michael Pearson, of Valeant Pharmaceuticals, whose total annual haul was $36 million in 2011.* That amount includes a base salary of $1.56 million, a bonus of $2.96 million, and combined stock options, shares, and other benefits worth $31 million.

Please note: The information presented in this article relating to Tim Hortons Inc. is correct only to the time of publication, and may no longer be accurate.

*www.theglobeandmail.com/report-on-business/careers/management/executive-compensation/executive-compensation-rankings-for-canadas-top-earners/article4243534.

–E.B.

INTRODUCTION

Entities finance their assets from two sources: debt and equity. These two sources of financing are seen in the structure of the accounting equation:

Assets = Liabilities + Owners' (shareholders') equity

Liabilities represent assets financed by debt while equity represents assets financed by the owners. Owners' investments can be direct or indirect. Direct investment is purchasing an ownership interest from an entity in exchange for cash or other assets. Indirect investments occur when an entity reinvests the profits it earns into its own activities, instead of distributing them to owners as dividends or *distributions.*

We can rearrange the accounting equation to provide a different view of equity: equity as the residual interest of owners:

Assets − Liabilities = Owners' (shareholders') equity

In this view, equity is what's left over after the entity's assets have been used to satisfy the creditors. As we will see, the equity section of the balance sheet represents the owners' interest as measured by accountants; it doesn't represent the market value of the entity.

CORPORATIONS, PARTNERSHIPS, AND PROPRIETORSHIPS

LO 1

We will begin the discussion with a look at the different types of entities in our economy. Our focus throughout most of the book has been on corporations, so let's begin there. A corporation is a separate legal and taxable entity. The owners of a corporation are its shareholders. One of the main attractions of a corporation is the limited liability provided by its corporate status. Shareholders aren't liable for the corporation's obligations and losses beyond the amount they have invested.

This limited liability is especially important for public companies, where most shareholders have little involvement in the management and operation of the entity. If the owner of 1,000 shares of a large public corporation was liable for obligations the corporation couldn't meet—for example, paying off a bank loan—that shareholder would probably be reluctant to invest. After all, how many people would want to hold shares in public companies if it included the risk of losing their savings, houses, or cars?

In some circumstances, shareholders might agree to waive the limited liability protection of a corporation. For example, lenders may demand that the shareholders of private corporations personally guarantee to repay amounts borrowed by the corporation in the event it isn't able to repay.

Corporations divide the shareholders' equity section of their balance sheets into four categories:

Share capital	Money and other assets from the sale of shares by the corporation directly to shareholders. Represents direct investments by shareholders.
Contributed surplus	A catch-all category that captures equity transactions not included in the other categories.
Retained earnings	Accumulated earnings not distributed to the shareholders. Represents indirect investment by shareholders.
Accumulated other comprehensive income	Accumulated amounts reported as other comprehensive income in the statement of comprehensive income. This category doesn't exist in ASPE.

It's important to separate direct and indirect investment on the balance sheet because shareholders need to know whether the money distributed to them is due to the profits earned by the corporation or if it's just a return of the money they invested. A dividend paid because the corporation has been profitable shares the success of the corporation with the shareholders. A dividend paid from amounts directly invested simply returns the money the shareholders have invested. (Investments that use investors' money to provide returns to the investor are known as Ponzi schemes. Financial statements showing where the payouts are coming from can help expose them.)

Proprietorships and, usually, partnerships aren't incorporated and don't pay income taxes. A proprietorship's income is included in the personal tax return of the proprietor and the income of a partnership is divided among the partners, who include it in their tax returns. Partnerships and proprietorships don't have limited legal liability, which means that partners and proprietors are personally liable for any obligations a partnership or proprietorship is unable to meet. **Limited partnerships** provide limited liability protection to some partners. There are two types of partners in a limited partnership:

- **Limited partners** have the same limited liability protection as they would if the entity was a corporation—they aren't personally liable for the debts and obligations of the partnership.
- **General partners** don't have limited liability and are liable for all debts and obligations of the partnership. A limited partnership must have at least one general partner.

Limited partnerships are useful when a partnership is preferred but some of the investors aren't actively involved and aren't prepared to accept the risk associated with unlimited liability. Limited partners can't be involved in the management of the partnership or they risk losing their limited liability. There are tax benefits associated with using limited partnerships.

Another form of partnership, commonly used by professionals such as accountants and lawyers, is the **limited liability partnership (LLP)**. A LLP is an ordinary partnership where partners aren't personally liable for claims against the firm arising from negligence or other forms of malpractice by other partners. The assets of the partnership are at risk but not the personal assets of an innocent partner. If you look at the Web sites of Canadian accounting and law firms, you will see that most have "LLP" after their names.

Most accounting for partnerships and proprietorships isn't very different from that of corporations, although there are no legal requirements for partnerships or proprietorships to use IFRS or ASPE. These could be used if, for example, a lender demanded it. Publicly traded partnership units prepare financial statements in accordance with IFRS.

The equity sections of partnerships' and proprietorships' balance sheets are structured differently from those of corporations. For example, Exhibit 10.1 shows the balance sheet, statement of partners' equity, and Notes 6 and 16 of the financial statements of Assiniboia Farmland Limited Partnership (Assiniboia), a limited partnership formed for the purposes of purchasing, selling, owning, leasing, developing, managing, and cultivating crop and other farmlands.[1]

In the equity section of Assiniboia's balance sheet, there is a single line called partners' capital (equity). The statement of changes in partners' capital provides additional detail about the partners' capital. Notice that the partners' direct investment isn't separated from the retained earnings of the partnership, as it is in a corporation. In a partnership, an equity account is kept for each partner showing the capital contributed, the portion of the earnings that is attributable to, and the distributions to, each partner. (Distributions are amounts taken out of the partnership.) This breakdown by partner isn't shown in Assiniboia's statement of changes in partners' capital.

EXHIBIT 10.1 Assiniboia Farmland Limited Partnership: Financial Statement Extracts

Assiniboia Farmland Limited Partnership

STATEMENTS OF FINANCIAL POSITION

AS AT DECEMBER 31, 2011 AND 2010 AND JANUARY 1, 2010

	Note	December 31, 2011	December 31, 2010	January 1, 2010
LIABILITIES				
Current liabilities				
Accounts payable	14	$ 933,165	$ 941,149	$ 608,634
Non-current liabilities				
Long-term debt	15	19,414,493	20,783,200	16,718,943
		20,347,658	21,724,349	17,327,577
PARTNERS' CAPITAL				
Partners' capital	16	43,753,575	37,133,841	26,685,819
		$ 64,101,233	$ 58,858,190	$ 44,013,396

Assiniboia Farmland Limited Partnership

STATEMENTS OF PARTNERS' CAPTIAL

FOR THE YEARS ENDED DECEMBER 31, 2011 AND 2010

	Note	Number of units	Amount
Balance at January 1, 2010	16	1,111,147	$ 26,685,819
Private placements of units		390,861	11,880,638
Issuance costs related to private placements		–	(555,296)
Partners' distributions		–	(843,411)
Comprehensive income (loss) for the period		–	(33,909)
Balance, December 31, 2010		1,502,008	$ 37,133,841
Private placement of units		183,119	7,507,879
Issuance costs related to private placements		–	(472,784)
Partners' distributions		–	(869,663)
Comprehensive income (loss) for the period		–	454,302
Balance, December 31, 2011		1,685,127	$ 43,753,575

EXHIBIT 10.1 (continued) Assiniboia Farmland Limited Partnership: Financial Statement Extracts

Assiniboia Farmland Limited Partnership

NOTES TO THE FINANCIAL STATEMENTS

FOR THE YEARS ENDED DECEMBER 31, 2011 and 2010

16. Partners' capital

The Limited Partnership Agreement provides that the capital of the Limited Partnership be comprised of up to 2,000,000 limited partnership units. At December 31, 2011 there are 1,685,127 (December 31, 2010—1,502,008) limited partnership units outstanding. During the year ended December 31, 2011, the Limited Partnership issued the following units:

i) On December 16, 2011, the Limited Partnership issued 183,119 limited partnership units through a private placement at $41.00 per unit, for total proceeds of $7,507,879.

During the year ended December 31, 2010, the Limited Partnership issued the following units:

i) On June 30, 2010, the Limited Partnership issued 49,503 limited partnership units through a private placement at $30.30 per unit, for total proceeds of $1,499,941.

ii) On December 21, 2010, the Limited Partnership issued 341,358 limited partnership units through a private placement at $30.41 per unit, for total proceeds of $10,380,697.

Under the terms of the Limited Partnership agreement, the limited partners do not have the ability to retract their units nor is interest earned on the partners' capital account balance. The General Partner has complete discretion over the amount of semi-annual distributions and determines the amount of distributions based on available cash flow. No distinction is made, on distribution, between original capital investment and share of earnings as the partners' capital contributions are not considered to be separate from cumulative share of earnings.

The Limited Partnership Agreement provides that the net loss of the Limited Partnership, if any, for each fiscal period will be allocated at the end of the fiscal period solely to the General Partner.

Net profits of the Limited Partnership, if any, for each fiscal period are allocated to the General and Limited Partners as follows:

a) First to the Limited Partners, to the extent of the Limited Partners' 8.0% Preferred Return, including any amount accumulated but unallocated from the prior fiscal periods,

b) Second to the General Partner, an amount of net income which is sufficient to offset the net losses previously allocated to the General Partner; and

c) Any remaining amount shall be allocated 80% to the Limited Partners and 20% to the General Partner.

Alliance Pipeline Limited Partnership

NOTES TO THE FINANCIAL STATEMENTS

(thousands of Canadian dollars, unless otherwise noted)

6. Partners' Equity

Alliance is authorized to issue an unlimited number of Class A and B units. The Class A and B units are voting and participate equally in profits, losses and capital distributions of the Partnership. The Class A and B units are held equally by the Partnership's limited partners, Enbridge Income Partners Holdings Inc. and Fort Chicago Pipelines (Canada) Ltd.

UNITS

There were 556,207.2 Class A units and 73,557.9 Class B units outstanding during 2011 and 2010. At December 31, 2011, Class A units were recorded at $490.0 million (December 31, 2010—$520.9 million) and Class B units were recorded at $75.9 million (December 31, 2010—$80.0 million). Changes are due to current net income and distributions paid.

The General Partner does not hold any units. It manages the operations of Alliance, and has a 1% interest in the profits and capital of Alliance.

Any units issued by Alliance must be first offered to the Partners in proportion to their ownership interests.

The Class A Units and the Class B Units are equal with respect to all rights, benefits, obligations and limitations provided under the limited partnership agreement.

GENERAL PARTNER

At December 31, 2011, the General Partner account was $9.6 million (December 31, 2010—$10.0 million). Changes are due to current year net income and distributions paid.

CONTRIBUTED SURPLUS

At December 31, 2011, the contributed surplus account was $21.8 million (December 31, 2010—$21.0 million). Changes are due to requirements for funding of capital projects during the year.

An example of a statement of partners' equity with a column for each partner is shown in Table 10.1.

TABLE 10.1 Statement of Partners' Equity for a Partnership with Three Partners

Statement of Partners' Equity For the year ended December 31, 2017				
	Partner 1	Partner 2	Partner 3	Total
Capital on January 1, 2017	$85,000	$117,000	$49,000	$251,000
Share of net income	22,000	31,000	15,000	68,000
Distributions	(15,000)	(8,000)	(6,000)	(29,000)
Capital on December 31, 2017	$92,000	$140,000	$58,000	$290,000

Not-for-profit organizations (NFPO) are economic entities whose objective is to provide services, not to make a profit. NFPOs don't have owners or ownership shares that can be traded or sold. Any "net income" earned by the NFPO is reinvested in the organization. Because NFPOs aren't organized to earn a profit, it isn't appropriate to use the term net income when discussing them. Usually the "bottom line" on an NFPO's statement of operations (the term sometimes used for an NFPO's "income statement") is called the *excess of revenues over expenses*. This terminology indicates that the NFPO produced revenues greater than expenses, or vice versa.

For NFPOs such as charities, revenues shouldn't be thought of in the same way as revenues earned by a business. For charities, revenues come from donations, contributions, and grants and the money is spent providing services to people in need, not to earn revenue. For example, the Canadian Cancer Society provides support to cancer patients across Canada. The services are paid for by contributors to the Cancer Society, not by patients. Thus, the relationship that exists between expenses and revenues in a for-profit organization doesn't exist for many NFPOs.

www.cancer.ca
www.heartandstroke.ca

Because an NFPO doesn't have owners, it won't have an owners' or shareholders' equity section in its balance sheet. However, the difference between assets and liabilities must somehow be referred to on the balance sheet. Different NFPOs use different terms; for example, the Heart and Stroke Foundation of Ontario refers to its "equity" as *net assets*, while the Canadian Cancer Society uses the term *resources*.

Most Canadian universities are not-for-profit organizations. The University of Ontario Institute of Technology's (UOIT) statement of financial position and statement of operations are presented in Exhibit 10.2.[2] Accounting for NFPOs is somewhat specialized and we won't go into detail here. However, notice the net assets section of Exhibit 10.2. These are resources obtained by the university from sources other than creditors. UOIT classifies its net assets—its assets less its liabilities—into the following categories:

- *invested in capital assets*: the amount UOIT has invested in capital assets, less the amount financed by long-term debt and capital contributions
- *internally restricted*: funds whose use has been restricted by the university, in this case for academic and research purposes
- *endowments:* donations to the university; only income generated from endowed funds can be used, not the principal donated
- *unrestricted:* resources that can be used in whatever way UOIT chooses

Notice that the bottom line of UOIT's statement of operations is called "excess/(deficiency) of revenue over expenses." Also notice the sources of UOIT's revenue: over $78 million comes from government grants. In a business, revenue comes from the customers who buy the business's goods and services. About 53 percent of UOIT's revenue comes from government. The students who benefit from their university education provide about 27 percent of revenue through their tuition fees.

EXHIBIT 10.2 University of Ontario Institute of Technology: Financial Statements

UNIVERSITY OF ONTARIO INSTITUTE OF TECHNOLOGY
Consolidated Statement of Financial Position
March 31, 2011

	2011	2010
ASSETS		
CURRENT		
Cash	$ –	$ 2,069,790
Grant receivable	12,732,986	6,742,602
Other accounts receivable	8,228,119	7,075,758
Inventories	292,584	293,470
Prepaid expenses and deposits	491,379	537,736
	21,745,068	16,719,356
INVESTMENTS (Note 2)	13,320,203	11,227,413
CAPITAL ASSETS (Note 3)	437,538,308	348,928,803
OTHER ASSETS (Note 4)	6,831,815	6,831,815
TOTAL ASSETS	$ 479,435,394	$ 383,707,387
LIABILITIES		
CURRENT		
Bank indebtedness (Note 5)	$ 6,399,001	$ –
Accounts payable and accrued liabilities	34,535,302	27,599,096
Deferred revenue (Note 6)	12,407,991	11,323,739
Current portion of other long term debt (Note 7)	232,292	5,978,047
Current portion of obligations under capital lease (Note 8)	186,281	–
Current portion of long term debenture debt (Note 9)	3,738,314	3,511,742
	57,499,181	48,412,678
OTHER LONG TERM DEBT (Note 7)	1,663,251	1,383,340
LONG TERM OBLIGATIONS UNDER CAPITAL LEASE (Note 8)	37,699,849	–
LONG TERM DEBENTURE DEBT (Note 9)	198,137,279	201,875,594
DEFERRED CAPITAL CONTRIBUTIONS (Note 10)	182,866,270	147,035,946
	477,865,830	398,707,558
NET ASSETS/(DEFICIT)		
UNRESTRICTED	(30,248,898)	(21,695,267)
ENDOWMENTS (Note 14)	12,482,659	11,229,931
INVESTED IN CAPITAL ASSETS (Note 12)	13,014,772	(10,855,866)
INTERNALLY RESTRICTED (Note 13)	6,321,031	6,321,031
	1,569,564	(15,000,171)
Contingencies and Contractual Commitments (Note 19)		
Guarantees (Note 20)		
TOTAL LIABILITIES AND NET ASSETS	479,435,394	383,707,387

EXHIBIT 10.2 **(continued) University of Ontario Institute of Technology: Financial Statements**

UNIVERSITY OF ONTARIO INSTITUTE OF TECHNOLOGY
Consolidated Statement of Operations
For the year ended March 31, 2011

	2011	2010
REVENUE		
Grants	**$ 78,303,278**	$ 53,532,470
Donations	**3,196,361**	3,976,889
Student tuition fees	**40,208,041**	32,810,949
Student ancillary fees	**15,151,417**	16,742,539
Other income	**6,509,096**	4,885,812
Amortization of deferred capital contributions	**2,924,104**	2,591,571
Interest revenue	**75,014**	54,954
Unrealized gain on investments	**913,111**	–
	147,280,422	114,595,184
EXPENSES		
Salaries and benefits	**57,948,567**	48,772,914
Supplies and expenses	**29,140,204**	24,554,006
Purchased Services	**13,156,780**	13,712,572
Professional fees	**795,141**	776,653
Interest expense	**14,852,827**	14,291,396
Amortization of capital assets	**16,197,377**	14,536,429
Gain/Loss on disposal of assets	**(241,181)**	(346,750)
Unrealized loss on investments	**–**	26,450
	131,849,715	116,323,670
Excess/(deficiency) of revenue over expenses	**$ 15,430,707**	$ (1,728,486)

CHARACTERISTICS OF EQUITY

LO 2

Unlike debt, equity offers no promises. When a corporation borrows money, the rate of interest, the timing of payments, and other terms of the loan are usually laid out in a contract. If the corporation is unable to meet the terms of the contract, it faces potentially significant economic and legal consequences. In contrast, a shareholder isn't entitled to dividends or any other type of payments, and return of principal isn't guaranteed. The rights of shareholders come after those of debt holders. If a corporation goes bankrupt, the debt holders must be paid what they are owed before shareholders receive anything. From the corporation's standpoint, issuing equity is less risky than debt because equity doesn't commit the corporation to any payments at any time. The corporation has more flexibility to manage, particularly through difficult times.

However, there are drawbacks to issuing equity. New shareholders have a voice in the corporation—not necessarily a say in its day-to-day affairs, but certainly the right to be heard and vote on certain issues. In other words, new shareholders dilute the power of existing ones. Consider a small business operated by a single entrepreneur who needs money for expansion and finds an investor willing to invest in exchange for a 50 percent interest in the corporation. The new shareholder owns 50 percent of the corporation and is able to participate in the key decisions of the company, so the entrepreneur can no longer act alone. The new shareholder is also entitled to half the value of the company.

Also, dividends aren't deductible for tax purposes, which raises the cost of equity relative to debt. Dividends aren't expensed for accounting purposes because they aren't a cost of doing business—they are a distribution of company assets to the shareholders. Interest payments, in contrast, are expensed in the calculation of net income and are deductible for tax.

When a corporation is formed, it must file articles of incorporation with the appropriate government agency. The articles of incorporation define the terms of reference of the new corporation. Any changes to these terms of reference must be approved by the shareholders. The articles of incorporation define the types and characteristics of the shares the corporation can issue. The maximum number of each type of share that can be issued is the **authorized capital stock** of the corporation.

Exhibit 10.3 provides equity information about Potash Corporation of Saskatchewan.[3] I will refer to this exhibit several times in the chapter. Refer to the reference numbers in the exhibit to see the information presented in the financial statements. Note 15 shows that Potash Corporation has authorized an unlimited number of common shares ❶. This means that Potash Corporation's board of directors can issue new shares whenever new capital is required, without consulting the shareholders. Other companies have a limit on the number of shares that can be issued—for example, High Liner Foods Inc. has 200 million common shares authorized.

The number of shares that have been distributed to shareholders is the **issued shares** of the corporation. The **outstanding shares** of a corporation are the number of shares currently in the hands of shareholders. The number of shares outstanding may differ from the number of shares issued because shares are sometimes repurchased by a corporation and held for resale. On December 31, 2011, Potash Corporation had 858,702,991 common shares outstanding ❷.

Corporation or company acts are federal and provincial laws that govern companies incorporated in particular jurisdictions. For example, the ***Canada Business Corporations Act*** is the federal legislation governing federally incorporated companies. These laws give shareholders certain rights and privileges, regardless of whether their investments are large or small. For example, a corporation's shareholders are entitled to attend its annual general meeting, where they can ask questions. Shareholders can usually vote on the composition of the board of directors, the appointment of auditors, amendments to the corporation's articles of incorporation, and other matters. For smaller shareholders, the annual general meeting of a public company may be the only place their voices can be heard.

Even though every shareholder has the right to attend the annual general meeting, smaller shareholders have a limited ability to exert influence. For example, a shareholder who owns 1,000 shares of Potash Corporation owns about 0.00012 percent of the votes, based on the 858,702,991 shares outstanding on December 31, 2011.

KNOWLEDGE CHECK 10.1

- ❑ What is a not-for-profit organization (NFPO)? Why don't NFPOs have "owners' equity"?
- ❑ What characteristics distinguish equity from debt?
- ❑ Explain the terms *authorized capital stock* and *outstanding shares.*

LO 2

Common and Preferred Shares

Broadly speaking, there are two types of shares a corporation can issue: common and preferred. Because these shares can have various features added to them, many different varieties of shares are possible.

Common Shares **Common shares** represent residual ownership in an entity. Common shareholders are entitled to whatever earnings and assets are left after obligations to debt holders and preferred shareholders have been satisfied. For example, consider a one-year venture into which common shareholders invest $50,000 and creditors lend $50,000 at 10 percent interest for the year. No matter how much the venture makes, the creditors receive $5,000 in interest plus the $50,000 principal amount. If the venture earns $20,000, the shareholders are entitled to the full amount: the creditors receive $55,000—they don't share in the profits. If the venture loses money, the creditors would still get their interest plus principal, whereas the equity investors would lose some of their initial investment.

Common shares don't have a specified dividend associated with them. Boards of directors declare dividends at their discretion. A corporation has no obligation to pay a dividend at any

EXHIBIT 10.3 Potash Corporation of Saskatchewan: Equity Information

Consolidated Statements of Financial Position

As at — In millions of US dollars

Notes		December 31, 2011		December 31, 2010	January 1, 2010
	Shareholders' Equity				
Note 15	Share capital	1,483		1,431	1,430
	Contributed surplus	291	❼	308	273
	Accumulated other comprehensive income	816	❺	2,394	1,798
	Retained earnings	5,257		2,552	2,804
	Total Shareholders' Equity	7,847		6,685	6,305
	Total Liabilities and Shareholders' Equity	$ 16,257		$ 15,547	$ 12,842

Consolidated Statements of Comprehensive Income

For the years ended December 31 (Net of related income taxes)		In millions of US dollars 2011	2010
Net Income		$ 3,081	$ 1,775
Other comprehensive (loss) income			
Net (decrease) increase in net unrealized gains on available-for-sale investments[1]		(1,581)	663
Net actuarial losses on defined benefit plans[2]		(136)	(25)
Net losses on derivatives designated as cash flow hedges[3]		(38)	(119)
Reclassification to income of net losses on cash flow hedges[4]		47	53
Other		(6)	(1)
Other Comprehensive (Loss) Income	❻	$ (1,714)	$ 571
Comprehensive Income		$ 1,367	$ 2,346

❽ Consolidated Statements of Changes in Equity

In millions of US dollars

	Equity Attributable to Common Shareholders[1]								
			Accumulated Other Comprehensive Income						
	Share Capital	**Contributed Surplus**	Net unrealized gains on available-for-sale investments	Net unrealized losses on derivatives designated as cash flow hedges	Net actuarial losses on defined benefit plans	Other	**Total Accumulated Other Comprehensive Income**	**Retained Earnings**	**Total Equity**
Balance—January 1, 2010	$ 1,430	$ 273	$ 1,900	$ (111)	$ –[2]	$ 9	$ 1,798	$ 2,804	$ 6,305
Net income	–	–	–	–	–	–	–	1,775	1,775
Other comprehensive income (loss)	–	–	663	(66)	(25)	(1)	571	–	571
❹ Share repurchase	(69)	(47)	–	–	–	–	–	(1,884)	(2,000)
Effect of share-based compensation	–	96	–	–	–	–	–	–	96
Dividends declared	–	–	–	–	–	–	–	(118)	(118)
Issuance of common shares	70	(14)	–	–	–	–	–	–	56
Transfer of actuarial losses on defined benefit plans	–	–	–	–	25	–	25	(25)	–
Balance—December 31, 2010	$ 1,431	$ 308	$ 2,563	$ (177)	$ –[2]	$ 8	$ 2,394	$ 2,552	$ 6,685
Net income	–	–	–	–	–	–	–	3,081	3,081
Other comprehensive (loss) income	–	–	(1,581)	9	(136)	(6)	(1,714) ❻	–	(1,714)
Effect of share-based compensation	–	(9)	–	–	–	–	–	–	(9)
Dividends declared	–	–	–	–	–	–	–	(240)	(240)
Issuance of common shares	52	(8)	–	–	–	–	–	–	(44)
Transfer of actuarial losses on defined benefit plans	–	–	–	–	136	–	136	(136)	–
Balance—December 31, 2011	$ 1,483	$ 291 ❼	$ 982	$ (168)	$ –[2]	$ 2	$ 816 ❺	$ 5,257	$ 7,847

EXHIBIT 10.3 (continued) Potash Corporation of Saskatchewan: Equity Information

NOTE 15 SHARE CAPITAL

Authorized

❶ The company is authorized to issue an unlimited number of common shares without par value and an unlimited number of first preferred shares. The common shares are not redeemable or convertible. The first preferred shares may be issued in one or more series with rights and conditions to be determined by the Board of Directors. No first preferred shares have been issued.

Issued

	Number of Common Shares	Consideration
Balance, January 1, 2010	887,926,650	$ 1,430
Issued under option plans	7,339,116	68
Issued for dividend reinvestment plan	46,947	2
❸ Repurchased	(42,190,020)	(69)
Balance, December 31, 2010	853,122,693	$ 1,431
Issued under option plans	5,490,335	48
Issued for dividend reinvestment plan	89,963	4
Balance, December 31, 2011	❷ 858,702,991	$ 1,483

NOTE 22 NET INCOME PER SHARE

	2011	2010
Basic net income per share[1]		
❾ Net income available to common shareholders	$ 3,081	$ 1,775
Weighted average number of common shares	855,677,000	886,371,000
Basic net income per share	$ 3.60	$ 2.00
Diluted net income per share[1]		
Net income available to common shareholders	$ 3,081	$ 1,775
Weighted average number common shares	855,677,000	886,371,000
Dilutive effect of stock options	20,960,000	24,722,000
Weighted average number of diluted common shares	876,637,000	911,093,000
Diluted net income per share	$ 3.51	$ 1.95

[1]Net income per share calculations are based on dollar and share amounts each rounded to the nearest thousand.

Diluted net income per share is calculated based on the weighted average number of shares issued and outstanding during the year, incorporating the following adjustment. The denominator is: (1) increased by the total of the additional common shares that would have been issued assuming exercise of all stock options with exercise prices at or below the average market price for the year; and (2) decreased by the number of shares that the company could have repurchased if it had used the assumed proceeds from the exercise of stock options to repurchase them on the open market at the average share price for the year. For performance-based stock option plans, the number of contingently issuable common shares included in the calculation is based on the number of shares, if any, that would be issuable if the end of the reporting period were the end of the performance period and the effect were dilutive.

Excluded from the calculation of diluted net income per share were weighed average options outstanding of 2,519,300 relating to the 2011 and 2008 Performance Option Plans (2010—1,441,050 relating to the 2008 Performance Option Plan) as the options' exercise prices were greater than the average market price of common shares for the year.

time and the board can eliminate or reduce dividends if it chooses. Public companies don't like to cut their dividends because it suggests the company is in serious trouble and usually the share price falls dramatically as a result.

There can be more than one class of common shares. Some corporations issue common shares with different voting rights and different dividends. For example, Rogers Communications Inc. has two classes of common shares, Class A voting common shares and Class B non-voting common shares. The Class A common shares have 50 votes per share while the Class B shares have no votes. This difference in voting power allows the Rogers family to control the company without owning more than 50 percent of the company's common shares. This is a fairly common arrangement in Canada; other examples include Bombardier Inc., Celestica Inc., and Onex Corporation.

Some shares have a **par value**—a value assigned to each common share in the articles of incorporation. The *Canada Business Corporations Act* and the corporations acts of a number of provinces don't permit par value shares, so they are quite rare in Canada (shares that don't have a par value are called **no par value shares**). The financial statement impact of par value shares is that the selling price of the share is split between the common shares account (credited for the par value of the shares issued) and contributed surplus (credited for rest).

Though equity is usually sold for cash, it doesn't have to be. An investor can exchange property or expertise for an equity interest. In that situation, the challenge is determining the amount that should be recorded for the property received and the shares issued. This is problematic for private companies since their shares aren't actively traded. In situations where the market value of the shares or property isn't available, estimates or appraisals have to be made, in which case a wide range of valuations is possible.

Preferred Shares **Preferred shares** are shares with rights that must be satisfied before those of common shareholders. Preferred share dividends must be paid before any are paid to common shareholders. If the corporation is liquidated, preferred shareholders recover their investment before the common shareholders receive anything. Preferred shares often have characteristics of debt, such as a specified dividend payment. However, unlike debt holders, preferred shareholders can't take any action against the corporation if the dividend isn't paid. Dividends on preferred shares aren't guaranteed, and if management decides that it won't pay a dividend then the preferred shareholders are out of luck.

There are five different types of preferred shares:

- **Cumulative** If a company doesn't pay the dividend on preferred shares in current or previous years, all unpaid dividends must be paid before the common shareholders can receive any dividends. This means that if a preferred dividend is missed, dividends on common shares can't be paid until all missed preferred dividends have been paid. This requirement reduces the risk that preferred shareholders won't receive their dividends.
- **Convertible** Shareholders can exchange preferred shares for a specified number of common shares for each preferred share that they convert.
- **Redeemable** The issuer can repurchase the preferred shares from the shareholders if it chooses, according to specified terms.
- **Retractable** Shareholders can require the issuer to purchase the preferred shares from them, if they choose, according to specified terms.
- **Participating** The amount of the preferred share dividend increases above the stated amount if certain conditions are met. The amount is often tied to the dividend paid on the common shares.

One of the attractions of preferred shares is that investors can expect to receive periodic payments (as they would with debt), but preferred dividends are taxed at a lower rate than interest. On the other hand, corporations can't deduct preferred dividends for income tax purposes. Private companies sometimes use preferred shares for tax and estate-planning purposes.

INSIGHT

Treasury Stock

In most jurisdictions in Canada, shares that are repurchased must be retired or cancelled immediately, meaning the shares no longer exist. In some jurisdictions in Canada, and in other countries, entities are allowed to own shares that were previously sold to investors and repurchased but not retired. These are called **treasury stock**. Treasury stock can't vote or receive dividends but it's available for resale by the entity.

Preferred shares are known as **hybrid securities**, a category of securities with characteristics of both debt and equity. (Convertible debt, debt that can be converted to equity, is another example.) IFRS require hybrid securities to be classified according to their economic nature, not simply by what they are called. Applying this accounting standard is complicated and beyond the scope of this book. Generally, the classification depends on whether a security has a mandatory payment associated with it and has to be repaid or converted by contract or at the option of the security holder.

The journal entry to record issuance of preferred shares is similar to the one made to record issuance of common shares. The credit is made to a preferred shares account instead of the common shares account.

LO 2

Share Repurchases

Sometimes a corporation will buy its own common shares from the shareholders. For example, during 2010, Potash Corporation repurchased 42,190,020 of its common shares for $200 million ❸. The journal entry to record the repurchase is shown below. The amount of the debit to share capital (common shares) is the average price paid per share by investors (share capital ÷ number of shares outstanding) times the number of shares repurchased. The amount paid over the average price is debited to retained earnings and contributed surplus. You can see the impact on the components of equity in Potash Corporation`s statement of changes in equity in Exhibit 10.3 ❹:

Dr. Retained earnings (shareholders' equity −)	1,884,000,000	
Dr. Share capital (shareholders' equity −)	69,000,000	
Dr. Contributed surplus (shareholders' equity −)	47,000,000	
Cr. Cash (assets −)		200,000,000
To record the repurchase of 42,190,020 common shares		

Why an entity repurchases its shares isn't entirely clear, but some explanations have been suggested and investigated:

- If an entity has excess cash, repurchasing shares is a way of distributing the cash to investors without establishing a precedent of paying regular or higher dividends.
- It increases the earnings per share (net income ÷ average number of common shares outstanding during the period) and should increase share price, assuming that the operating activity of the entity isn't affected by the repurchase, because ownership is divided among fewer shares.
- It is a way for management to communicate to the market that it thinks the market is understating the value of its shares.

When an entity repurchases its shares, there is no effect on the income statement. The accounting for share repurchases reduces cash and shareholders' equity.

INSIGHT

Exchanges between Investors

www.tsx.ca

Remember that when an entity issues shares to or repurchases shares from shareholders, an entry is made in the accounting records only. For public companies, the vast majority of purchase and sale transactions of shares take place between individual investors in a secondary market, for example, on the Toronto Stock Exchange (TSX). The entity whose shares are being exchanged isn't a party to these transactions and the transactions have no financial statement effect.

That isn't to say that an entity's managers aren't keenly interested in its share price. The entity's share price can have an effect on the managers' wealth (their compensation is sometimes related to share price and they are often shareholders), on their job prospects (managers of entities whose share price isn't doing well will sometimes be fired or may have fewer opportunities in the job market), and because market price provides information about how the entity is seen to be performing.

RETAINED EARNINGS, DIVIDENDS, AND STOCK SPLITS

LO 3

Retained Earnings

Retained earnings represents the accumulated earnings of an entity less all dividends paid to shareholders over its entire life. Retained earnings can be thought of as profits that have been reinvested in the entity by the shareholders. It represents an indirect investment by shareholders—indirect, because investors don't decide for themselves to make the investment. Although net income or loss and dividends are the most common economic events affecting retained earnings, some others are shown in Table 10.2 while still others are beyond the scope of this book.

TABLE 10.2 Transactions and Economic Events That Affect Retained Earnings

Economic event	Description
Net income or net loss	A measure of how the owners' wealth has changed over a period.
Dividends	Distributions of earnings to shareholders.
Correction of errors	Accounting errors made in a previous period should be corrected retroactively by adjusting retained earrings.
Retroactive application of an accounting policy	When an entity changes an accounting policy, the financial statements are restated as if the new accounting policy had always been used.
Share retirement	When an entity repurchases its shares from shareholders and pays more than the average price shareholders paid for them.

Correction of errors affects retained earnings when an error made in a previous period is discovered. The prior years' financial statements are restated so they appear in their corrected form. For example, in 2015 Auld Ltd. (Auld) purchased land for $700,000. The cost of the land was incorrectly expensed instead of capitalized. The error wasn't discovered until 2017. To correct the error, Auld would make the following journal entry in 2017:

Dr. Land (assets +)	700,000	
Cr. Retained earnings (shareholders' equity +)		700,000
To correct an error in accounting for the purchase of land in 2015		

The credit to retained earnings is required because when the land was incorrectly expensed in 2015, net income was $700,000 lower than it should have been (tax effects are ignored). As a result, at the end of 2015 retained earnings was $700,000 too low. The entry shown above restates retained earnings with the balance as it would have been had the error not occurred.

Changes of accounting policies are discussed later in this chapter, but when an entity changes an accounting policy the financial statements are restated so it appears as if the entity has always been using the new accounting policy. This means that current amounts in balance sheet accounts, including retained earnings, are restated to reflect the new policy.

Throughout the book, I have emphasized that managers have considerable latitude, even under IFRS, in deciding how to account for many transactions and economic events. The effects of these differences accumulate in retained earnings. Over an entity's entire life, retained earnings won't be affected by different accounting choices, but at any point in time retained earnings can vary significantly, depending on the accounting choices made.

Dividends

Dividends are distributions of a corporation's earnings to its shareholders. They are discretionary and must be declared by the board of directors. Dividends are declared on a per share basis and every share of a specific class must receive the same dividend. If, for example, an entity has a single class of common shares, it isn't possible to pay some of the shareholders a dividend and not others. Once a dividend is declared, it's classified as a liability on the balance sheet until it's paid.

Corporations don't have an unlimited ability to pay dividends, and there are legal limitations against paying them. The *Canada Business Corporations Act* prohibits payment of dividends if it's reasonable to believe the corporation would be unable to pay its liabilities as a result. There can also be contractual restrictions, such as a lending agreement, against paying dividends. For example, TransCanada Pipelines Limited (TCPL) states that some of its preferred share and debt securities limit its ability to declare dividends on preferred and common shares (see Exhibit 10.4).[4]

www.transcanada.com

EXHIBIT 10.4 TransCanada Pipelines Limited: Restrictions on Dividends

NOTE 17 COMMON SHARES

Restriction on Dividends

Certain terms of the Company's preferred shares and debt instruments could restrict the Company's ability to declare dividends on preferred and common shares. At December 31, 2011, approximately $2.7 billion (2010—$3.6 billion; 2009—$2.6 billion) was available for the payment of dividends on common and preferred shares.

For accounting purposes, there are three important dates pertaining to dividends:

- **date of declaration**: The date when the board of directors of a corporation declares a dividend.
- **date of record**: The registered owner of shares on the date of record receives the dividend. If a shareholder sells shares after the date of declaration but before or including the date of record, the new shareholder is entitled to receive the dividend. If a shareholder sells shares after the date of record, the previous shareholder receives the dividend.
- **date of payment**: The date when the dividends are actually paid to shareholders.

The accounting implications of these points are discussed below. There are three types of dividends: cash, property, and stock.

Cash Dividends A **cash dividend** is a cash payment from the corporation to its shareholders. These are the most common type. Let's look at an example to see how the accounting is done. On December 15, 2017 Bankeir Inc. (Bankeir) declared a $0.10 quarterly dividend on its common shares. On the date of declaration, Bankeir had 500,000 common shares. It paid the dividend on January 12, 2018. The company's year-end is December 31. The following journal entries are required to record the declaration and payment of the dividends:

December 15, 2017

Dr. Retained earnings (shareholders' equity −)	50,000	
Cr. Dividend payable on common shares (liability +)		50,000
To record the declaration of a $0.10 per common share dividend on December 15, 2017		

January 12, 2018

Dr. Dividend payable on common shares (liability −)	50,000	
Cr. Cash (asset −)		50,000
To record payment of the common share dividends on January 12, 2018		

The first entry records the declaration of the dividend by reducing retained earnings and recognizing a liability to pay the dividend to shareholders. The second entry records the payment to the shareholders and removes the liabilities from the balance sheet. Bankeir's December 31, 2017 balance sheet would report the dividend payable as a current liability. Note that no entry is required on the date of record. That date determines who receives the dividend payment.

People sometimes say that dividends are "paid out of retained earnings." This means retained earnings decreases when dividends are declared. However, if a corporation doesn't have cash or access to cash, it can't pay a cash dividend no matter how much retained earnings there is. Also, a dividend can be paid if there is a deficit in retained earnings (the balance is negative).

Property Dividends **Property dividends** are paid with property instead of cash. In theory, the payment can be any property the entity has: inventory, capital assets, investments, etc. In practice, for public companies or for private companies with many shareholders, property dividends are impractical. Since every share of the same class must receive the same dividend, the entity must have property that can be distributed equally. One type of property that can be readily used for this is shares of a corporation owned by the issuing entity (not its own shares).

If an entity pays a property dividend, the dividend is recorded at the property's fair value on the date the dividend is declared. If the fair value of the property isn't equal to its carrying amount on that date, a gain or loss is reported on the income statement. For example, Drook Corp. (Drook) decided to distribute the shares it owned of Rylstone Inc. as a dividend. The carrying amount of the shares was $5,000,000 and their fair value on the date the dividend was declared was $7,200,000. The journal entries that Drook would make to record the property dividend are

Dr. Investment in Rylstone (assets +)	2,200,000	
Cr. Gain on disposal of investments (income statement +, shareholders' equity +)		2,200,000
To record the gain on the shares of Rylstone being distributed to shareholders as a property dividend		

Dr. Retained earnings (shareholders' equity −)	7,200,000	
Cr. Property dividend payable (liability +)		7,200,000
To record the declaration of a property dividend		

Dr. Property dividend payable (liability −)	7,200,000	
Cr. Investment in Rylstone (assets −)		7,200,000
To record payment of the property dividend		

The first entry adjusts the value of the property to its fair value on the date the dividend was declared. Because the fair value of the dividend was greater than its carrying amount, a gain is recognized on the income statement. The second entry records the declaration of the dividend. The amount of the property dividend is the fair value of the property on the date the dividend is declared. The third entry records the actual payment of the dividend—Drook's shareholders receive the actual shares of Rylstone when the dividend is paid.

Stock Dividends In a **stock dividend**, shareholders receive company shares as the dividend. The number of shares received depends on how many shares a shareholder owned on the date of declaration. For example, if Hylo Ltd. (Hylo) declared a 5 percent stock dividend, a shareholder that owned 1,000 shares would receive 50 shares of Hylo stock and then have 1,050 shares of Hylo stock. If Hylo had 100,000 shares outstanding before the stock dividend, there would be 105,000 shares afterwards. Each shareholder would own exactly the same proportion of Hylo before and after the dividend. The market price of Hylo's shares should fall by 5 percent as a result because nothing about the entity has changed except for the number of shares outstanding. Thus, the value of Hylo is spread over a larger number of shares (so the value of each share is less), but the total value of Hylo's shares should be the same.

A stock dividend decreases retained earnings and increases common shares, but there is more than one acceptable method of assigning an amount to the shares distributed. The shares can be valued at either their market value just before they are issued or the board of directors can assign a value to the shares; for example, the average amount paid by shareholders for the shares already outstanding.

Returning to the Hylo example, suppose that Hylo declared and distributed its stock dividend on June 23, 2017, when the market price of its common shares was $10. It would make the following entry if it valued the shares at their market value:

Dr. Retained earnings (shareholders' equity −)	50,000	
Cr. Common shares (shareholders' equity +)		50,000
To record declaration and distribution of a 5 percent stock dividend		

The form of the journal entry would be the same if a different value was assigned to the share, only the amount would change. Note that no matter how the shares are valued, only the shareholders' equity section of the balance sheet is affected. There is no effect on assets, liabilities, or the income statement.

LO 3

Stock Splits

A **stock split** divides an entity's shares into a larger number of units, each with a smaller value. A stock split is really nothing more than a big stock dividend. A **reverse stock split** reduces the number of shares. A stock split might split an entity's existing shares two for one, which means that a shareholder that previously had 1,000 shares would have 2,000 after the split. A three-for-two split means that a shareholder with 1,000 shares would have 1,500 after the split. In a one-for-two reverse stock split a shareholder who had 1,000 shares would have 500 after the split.

Unlike a stock dividend, there is no accounting effect of a stock split—the amounts in the retained earnings and common shares accounts are unchanged. No journal entries are required to record a stock split. The number of shares outstanding changes, so any measurements based on the number of shares will change. For example, if an entity's shares split three for one, retained earnings will be unchanged, but earnings per share will be one-third of what it was before the split.

Various explanations have been offered for stock dividends and splits. One is that it allows shareholders to receive "something" when the entity is unable or unwilling to pay a cash dividend. Another explanation is that it lowers the price of a stock into a range that makes it accessible to more investors. Some companies don't split their stock even though the price of their common shares is very high. For example, Berkshire Hathaway Inc.'s (the company run by Warren Buffet) shares have traded at prices over US$120,000 per share and the company has specifically rejected calls to split its stock to lower the price.

In January 2011, Potash Corporation of Saskatchewan announced a three-for-one stock split that went into effect on February 15, 2011. The split was reported as a subsequent event in the 2010 financial statements and the impact was reflected in that year's statements.

KNOWLEDGE CHECK 10.2

- ❑ What is retained earnings? Why is retained earnings considered an indirect investment in an entity?
- ❑ What economic events affect retained earnings?
- ❑ What is a stock dividend? Is an investor better off when he or she receives a stock dividend?

INSIGHT

The reality is that both stock splits and stock dividends are a bit of sleight of hand. Neither has any real economic significance—they merely divide the entity into a different number of pieces. In other words, there are more pieces of pie, not more pie. Stock dividends and stock splits have no effect on the assets, liabilities, or net income of an entity, and they don't change the underlying value of a shareholder's interest in an entity. There is no evidence to suggest that shareholders are better off after a stock dividend or split than they were before.

QUESTION FOR CONSIDERATION

Several years ago a friend of yours received 1,000 shares of a public company as a gift from her uncle. Recently, the company shares split four for one and now she has 4,000 shares. Your friend isn't sure what this means, but she is concerned that the shares that were trading for $104 per share before the split are now trading for around $26 per share.

Explain the meaning of a stock split and its economic significance to your friend. Should she be concerned about the decrease in the share price?

ANSWER: A stock split is the division of a company's shares into a larger number of units, each with a smaller value. A stock split doesn't really have any economic significance. It's like cutting a pie into six pieces, and then cutting it into 12 pieces when you realize that you will have more than six guests. You have the same amount of pie, just more pieces. One slice from a pie cut into six pieces is the same as two pieces of a pie cut into 12 pieces if the pies are the same size.

The same is true for a stock split. You have 4,000 shares instead of 1,000, but there are also four times as many shares outstanding. You own exactly the same percentage of the outstanding shares. The decrease in the share price makes perfect sense because after the split each share represents 25 percent of what it did before the split. The market value of your shares is the same before and after the split. Before the split the shares were worth $104,000 (1,000 × $104), and after the split they were worth $104,000 (4,000 × $26).

ACCUMULATED OTHER COMPREHENSIVE INCOME

LO 3

Comprehensive income was introduced in our initial examination of the financial statements in Chapter 2. Over the years, accounting standard setters excluded certain transactions and economic events from the calculation of net income and these were debited or credited to equity directly. **Comprehensive income** was created to be an all-inclusive measure of performance capturing all transactions and economic events, even ones excluded from the calculation of net income, that don't involve owners. Comprehensive income is

Comprehensive income = Net income + Other comprehensive income

Comprehensive income has two components: net income as it is usually calculated and **other comprehensive income**, which is revenues, expenses, gains, and losses that aren't included in the calculation of net income. There are only a few events classified as other comprehensive income:

- gains and losses on certain costs pertaining to pensions and other post-retirement benefits
- gains and losses on certain investment securities (discussed in Chapter 11)
- gains and losses from translation of companies owned that are stated in foreign currencies
- gains from writing up property, plant, and equipment using the revaluation method (discussed in Chapter 8)

Examine the shareholders' equity section of Potash Corporation of Saskatchewan Inc.'s (Potash Corp.) balance sheet in Exhibit 10.3 and notice the account called "Accumulated other comprehensive income ❺." In the same way, retained earnings accumulates net incomes over an entity's life, **accumulated other comprehensive income** (or **loss**) accumulates other comprehensive incomes (not comprehensive incomes). When the books are closed, the amount of other comprehensive income in the statement of comprehensive income is added to accumulated other comprehensive income in the equity section, as shown in Figure 10.1.

FIGURE 10.1
Comprehensive Income

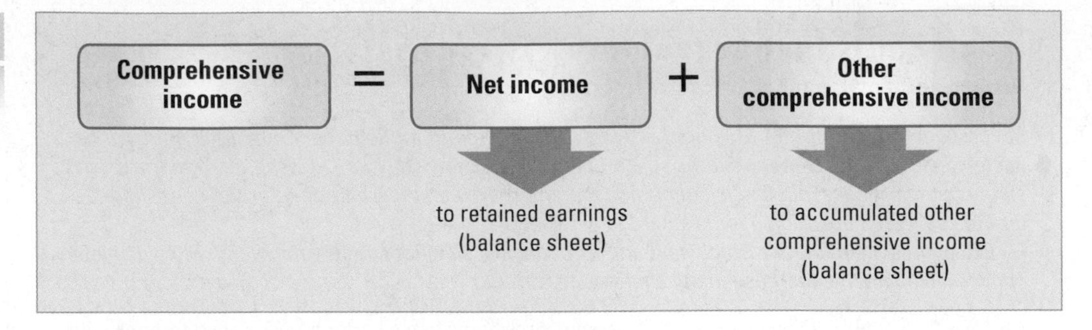

Exhibit 10.3 shows information about comprehensive income in Potash Corp.'s financial statements. Note the following as you examine the exhibit:

- Potash Corp.'s consolidated statement of comprehensive income provides the items that are included in other comprehensive income for the year. Other comprehensive income for 2011 was ($1,714,000,000) ❻. This amount can also be found in the statement of changes in equity.
- The consolidated statement of changes in equity provides a reconciliation for the year for the accumulated other comprehensive loss account. The balance in this account on December 31, 2011 is ($816,000,000) ❺. The amount can also be found on the balance sheet.
- Other comprehensive income is closed to accumulated other comprehensive loss on the balance sheet.

LO 3 CONTRIBUTED SURPLUS

There is one more account in the equity section we need to mention: contributed surplus. **Contributed surplus** captures equity transactions that don't fit into the other equity accounts:

- amounts paid for company shares in excess of the par value
- receipt of donated assets
- equity component of some hybrid securities
- repurchase of shares for more than the average per share cost
- employees' stock-based compensation (discussed later in the chapter)

The equity section of Potash Corp.'s December 31, 2011 balance sheet and the statement of changes in equity in Exhibit 10.3 shows contributed surplus of $291,000,000 ❼. The statement of changes in equity shows that the changes to contributed surplus during 2011 were due to stock-based compensation and the issuance of common shares. In 2010, contributed surplus was also affected by the share repurchase.

LO 3 STATEMENT OF CHANGES IN EQUITY

The statement of shareholders' equity provides a summary of changes during a year in each of an entity's equity accounts. This statement captures the impacts we have discussed in each of the preceding sections. Exhibit 10.3 provides Potash Corp.'s statement of shareholders' equity ❽.

LO 4 ACCOUNTING CHANGES—POLICIES AND ESTIMATES

Consistency in applying accounting choices is an important principle. If an entity changed its accounting on a whim, the integrity and usefulness of the financial statements would be undermined and it would be much more difficult for users to understand and interpret the statements. However, this doesn't mean that an entity can never change its accounting. New accounting standards implemented in IFRS might require a change. Or an entity may decide that an alternative way of accounting provides better information to stakeholders. Or the reporting objectives of the entity have changed, making a different way of accounting appropriate. IFRS allow changes in accounting policies only if they make financial statement information more relevant and reliable. Of course, whether information is more relevant and reliable is a judgment call.

There are two types of accounting changes—changes in policies and changes in estimates. **Accounting policies** are methods an entity selects for financial reporting. They include the revenue recognition method, inventory cost formula, and capitalization policies. **Accounting estimates** are judgments about uncertain future events that managers must make to complete accrual accounting financial statements. Accounting estimates include the useful lives and residual values of capital assets, bad debt expenses, warranty expenses, and many more. We've discussed these often in the book.

What happens if an entity decides to change an accounting policy or estimate? The two types of changes are dealt with differently. If a company changes an accounting policy—for example, switching from FIFO to average cost—the change is applied retroactively. That is, previous years' financial statements are restated as if the new accounting method had always been used. This treatment also means that retained earnings has to be restated to adjust for the difference between the old and new methods.

Changes in accounting estimates are treated differently. If management decides an accounting estimate has to be revised—for example, if the initial estimate of an asset's useful life was too long—the change is reflected from the time of management's decision. Previous years aren't revised.

Let's look at an example. In 2014, Aubigny Ltd. (Aubigny) purchased an asset for $48,000. Management used straight-line depreciation and assumed a zero residual value and a useful life of eight years. In each of years 2014, 2015, and 2016, Aubigny expensed $6,000 for depreciation ($48,000 ÷ 8 years). In 2017, it became clear the asset would only last for six years. As a result, Aubigny would have to depreciate the remaining carrying amount of the asset over three years rather than five. The $30,000 ($48,000 − $18,000) carrying amount of the equipment at the beginning of 2017 would be depreciated over the remaining three years on a straight-line basis, so the depreciation expense in 2017, 2018, and 2019 would be $10,000 ($30,000 ÷ 3). Retained earnings isn't adjusted because the depreciation expense in previous years isn't restated. The year-by-year depreciation expense and accumulated depreciation for each year is shown in Table 10.3.

TABLE 10.3 Aubigny Ltd.: Change in Accounting Estimate

	2014	2015	2016	2017	2018	2019
Depreciation expense	$6,000	$ 6,000	$ 6,000	$10,000	$10,000	$10,000
Accumulated depreciation	$6,000	$12,000	$18,000	$28,000	$38,000	$48,000
				↑ Current year		

IFRS require disclosure of changes in accounting policies and estimates. This type of information is very important for stakeholders' understanding of financial statements because it helps explain statement changes that aren't the result of operations.

LEVERAGE

LO 5

Leverage is the use of debt in the capital structure of an entity. Leverage can increase the returns earned by the owners because profits earned from investing borrowed money, above the cost of borrowing, go to the owners. Leverage also adds risk because interest on borrowed money must be paid regardless of how well or poorly the entity performs.

Let's look at an example. Four Friends Partnership (FFP) was formed to operate a one-year business venture. The four friends decide that $100,000 of invested capital is required to safely launch the venture, but they aren't sure how much debt and how much equity to use. They are considering three possible financing arrangements:

1. one hundred percent equity financing: $100,000 of their own money and no bank borrowing
2. fifty percent debt and 50 percent equity: $50,000 of their own money and $50,000 borrowed from the bank
3. ninety percent debt and 10 percent equity: $90,000 borrowed from the bank and $10,000 of their own money

The friends have predicted two possible outcomes for their venture: a good news outcome where revenues will be $80,000 and expenses $60,000 (excluding interest), and a bad news outcome where revenues will be $50,000 and expenses $48,000 (excluding interest). If the friends decide to borrow, the bank will charge an interest rate of 10 percent. At the completion of the venture, the friends will have to repay any money borrowed from the bank.

We will examine the effect of leverage by using return on equity (ROE). ROE was introduced in Chapter 3 and is defined as

$$\text{Return on equity} = \frac{\text{Net income} - \text{Preferred dividends}}{\text{Average common shareholders' equity}}$$

ROE is a measure of an entity's profitability and effectiveness in using the assets provided by the owners to generate net income. The effects of leverage on FFP's venture are shown in Table 10.4. When 100 percent equity is used, the friends simply earn what the venture earns. If the good news outcome occurs, they earn $20,000, which is a 20 percent ROE ($20,000 ÷ $100,000). If the bad news outcome occurs, they earn $2,000, a 2 percent ROE ($2,000 ÷ $100,000). With both outcomes, the friends get their original investment back.

If FFP borrows to finance its venture, it must pay interest on the borrowed money, but anything earned in excess of the interest cost belongs to the partners. When 50 percent debt is used, FFP must pay $5,000 ($50,000 × 10%) in interest, so net income is $15,000 in the good news outcome (see Table 10.4). FFP earned 20 percent or $10,000 on the borrowed money, of which $5,000 was paid in interest, leaving $5,000 for the friends. In other words, the friends earned an extra $5,000 without having to invest their own money (they also made $10,000 on their investment of $50,000). As a result, the ROE increases to 30 percent, even though the income of the venture decreased (the friends earned $15,000 on their investment of $50,000). With ROE, we look at the return on the equity investment. In this situation, the friends invested half as much money but profit decreased by only 25 percent. This is the effect of leverage: using "someone else's" money can increase equity investors' returns.

But there's a dark side to leverage. While leverage makes good news better, it also makes bad news worse. If the bad news outcome occurs on their 100 percent equity, the four friends earn a small return of 2 percent. The friends take home $2,000 in profit and recover their initial $100,000 investment. With the 50 percent equity, 50 percent debt financing option, the cost of borrowing is more than what FFP earned. The four friends must pay $3,000 of their own money to cover the interest. (The venture earned $2,000 before interest, so that over $3,000 of the friends' money is used to pay the bank.) The $3,000 loss means that the friends lose some of their initial investment. In this scenario, the ROE is −6 percent (−$3,000 ÷ $50,000).

The effect of leverage in the 10 percent equity, 90 percent debt alternative is more dramatic. In the good news outcome, the four friends have an ROE of 110 percent on their $10,000 investment. (FFP earns $11,000 [$20,000 − $9,000 in interest]). In the bad news outcome, the ROE is −70 percent. FFP owes the bank $9,000 in interest ($90,000 × 10%) but the venture only earned $2,000 so the remaining $7,000 is paid out of the partners' original investment. The loss on the venture is $7,000, and 70 percent of the friends' original $10,000 investment is lost.

How, you might ask, can the friends' return be increasing when the net income of the venture is decreasing? The amount of income being earned as a proportion of the equity investment is increasing, even though the actual dollar amount of net income is decreasing. The friends will have more profit from the venture if only equity is used, but if the bank finances part of the venture, the friends will have a higher return and be able to keep some of their money for other purposes.

TABLE 10.4 Scenarios Showing the Effect of Leverage on Performance

Four Friends Partnership (FFP) Information regarding new venture			
Financing alternatives			
	100% equity	**50% debt and 50% equity**	**90% debt and 10% equity**
Debt	$ 0	$50,000	$90,000
Equity	100,000	50,000	10,000
Projected performance outcomes			
Good news outcome			
Revenue	$80,000	$80,000	$80,000
Expenses	60,000	60,000	60,000
Operating income	20,000	20,000	20,000
Interest expense	0	5,000	9,000
Net income	$20,000	$15,000	$11,000
Return on equity	20%	30%	110%
Bad news outcome			
Revenue	$50,000	$50,000	$50,000
Expenses	48,000	48,000	48,000
Operating income	2,000	2,000	2,000
Interest expense	0	5,000	9,000
Net income	$ 2,000	$ (3,000)	$(7,000)
Return on equity	2%	−6%	−70%

Amount invested by debt (the bank) and equity (the friends) investors. Total amount required for the venture is $100,000.

Operating income is the amount the venture makes before considering the cost of financing. It's the same under all financing alternatives.

Interest expense: the cost of financing. Equals the borrowed amount times the interest rate.

ROE is the return on the owners' investment. The ROE increases even though net income decreases because the amount the owners invested decreases with the amount of debt financing. With no debt the friends make $20,000 on a $100,000 investment while with 90 percent debt they make $11,000 on a $10,000.

Net income is the amount earned by the four friends (the owners) after deducting financing costs (interest). Net income decreases as the amount of debt increases because the amount of interest increases.

From a practical perspective, leverage is useful for a variety of reasons: (a) it allows for more investment or a larger venture; (b) it allows investors to diversify—instead of investing all their money in one project, investors can "spread the money around," which reduces risk; and (c) it allows a project to go ahead even if the investors don't have enough of their own money.

It's important to recognize that the difference in net income of each scenario is due to the cost of financing. In all three financing alternatives, the performance of the business activity itself, the operating income, is the same. (Operating income is $20,000 in the good news outcome and $2,000 in the bad news outcome.) What differs in the income statements is the amount of interest. When analyzing financial statements, separating an entity's business performance from the cost of financing it can provide valuable insights. Entities that go into bankruptcy protection are often viable if the debts are reorganized.

It's important to remember that there are limits to the amount of money that an entity can borrow. It's possible that if FFP wanted to borrow $90,000 when the owners were investing only $10,000, the bank might charge a higher interest rate or not lend at all because of the investment's risk.

Also note that the FFP example ignores income taxes. This approach is sensible because FFP is a partnership and partnerships don't pay taxes. Taxes are important, though. The tax implications of any decisions must be taken into consideration. Finally, an entity's balance sheet is an important source of information about leverage. Examination of the debt-to-equity ratio gives insight into the amount of leverage an entity has and is a basis for evaluating the risk the entity is taking on.

connect

KNOWLEDGE CHECK 10.3

- ❑ What is leverage?
- ❑ What are the advantages and disadvantages of using leverage when financing a business?
- ❑ For a given total amount of debt and equity financing, why does the return on equity to the owners increase as the proportion of equity financing and the amount of net income decrease?

LO 6

EMPLOYEE STOCK OPTIONS

Employees can be compensated in many ways. Salary, bonus, shares in the company, and stock options are common ones. In this section, we will describe employee stock options and discuss the accounting issues surrounding this form of compensation.

Let's begin by covering some stock option basics:

- An **employee stock option** is the right to purchase a specified number of shares of the employer's stock at a specified price over a specified period of time. Employee stock options represent the right to purchase shares, not shares themselves.
- The price at which the employee may purchase the shares is called the **exercise price**. For tax reasons, the exercise price of a stock option is usually the same as or greater than the market price of the shares on the date it's granted.
- The final date an option can be exercised is called the **expiry date**. If the employee has not exercised or used the option by its expiry date, it can't be used to purchase shares. An employee will exercise an option only if the exercise price is less than the market price because otherwise they would be buying shares for more than they are worth in the open market.

Stock options can be an attractive way of compensating employees because they don't cost the entity any cash. This can be very important for entities that are short of cash or are trying to conserve cash, as is common in growing or new businesses. Stock options give employees the opportunity to make lots of money if the company is successful. However, don't interpret the fact that stock options don't cost the entity any cash to mean that they aren't costly. In fact, stock options have a significant economic cost. They are exercised when the exercise price is below the market value of the shares, which dilutes the value of the shares of other shareholders. This means that the wealth of existing shareholders is transferred to the employees exercising the options.

The significance of stock options as a form of compensation for senior executives can be seen in Table 10.5, which shows the compensation earned by the CEOs of nine Canadian companies.[5] The table breaks down the CEOs' compensation into salary, bonus, other, share-based awards, option-based awards, and pension value. Aside from the fact that these CEOs earn a lot of money, notice how significant a role stock options play in compensation of many CEOs.

Exhibit 10.5 describes the stock option plan of WestJet Airlines Ltd.[6] The first part of the note provides some basic terms of the plan. There are limits on the number of shares that can be reserved for any person or to employees in total. Also, the number of shares issuable in a year can't be greater than 10 percent of the issued and outstanding voting shares. The expiry period, exercise price, and vesting period are described. (The vesting period is the time an employee must remain with the company to be entitled to exercise the options.) The rest of the note provides details on the plan. Note the following:

- At the end of 2011, there were 7,350,756 options outstanding with an average exercise price of $14.17. Of these, 5,044,598 could be exercised at the end of 2011 at an average exercise price of $14.03. The price of WestJet's shares on December 31, 2011 was $11.76.
- During 2011, over 1.5 million options with an average exercise price of $16.32 expired. This occurred because the exercise price of the options was greater than the market price. Over one million options with an average exercise price of $12.56 were exercised during 2011. These

TABLE 10.5 Compensation of CEOs of Major Canadian Companies

Company	Executive	Salary	Bonus	Other	Share-based awards	Option-based awards	Pension value	Total
Bank of Montreal	William Downe	$1,026,250	$1,150,000	$ 12,069	$5,400,000	$2,300,000	$1,531,923	$11,420,242
Canadian Tire Corp.	Stephen Wetmore	1,250,000	1,314,562	306,032	1,249,989	2,499,989	–	6,620,572
Dollarama Inc.	Larry Rossy	500,000	1,375,000	–	–	515,360	3,000	2,393,360
Loblaw Companies Ltd.	Galen G. Weston	1,000,000	1,134,324	36,223	–	1,507,494	–	3,678,041
Potash Corp. of Saskatchewan Inc.	William Doyle	1,169,406	1,226,788	153,055	–	3,782,717	1,045,301	7,377,267
Shaw Communications Inc.	Bradley Shaw	2,393,940	4,675,000	191,426	825,000	–	7,765,970	15,851,336
Rogers Communications Inc.	Nadir Mohamed	1,200,000	1,468,500	84,300	2,481,242	2,482,340	463,980	8,180,362
Tim Hortons Inc.	Paul House	583,069	645,107	153,595	2,900,000	–	16,407	4,298,178
Valeant Pharmaceuticals International Inc.	Michael Pearson	1,561,643	2,964,894	13,802,664	12,038,730	5,950,910	–	36,318,841

EXHIBIT 10.5 WestJet Airlines Ltd.: Stock Option Plan

Notes to Consolidated Financial Statements

For the years ended December 31, 2011 and 2010
(Stated in thousands of Canadian dollars, except share and per share amounts)

13. Share capital

(c) Stock option plan

The Corporation has a stock option plan, whereby at December 31, 2011, 11,520,284 (2010—11,693,868) voting shares were reserved for issuance to officers and employees of the Corporation, subject to the following limitations:

(i) the number of common voting shares reserved for issuance to any one optionee will not exceed 5% of the issued and outstanding voting shares at any time;

(ii) the number of common voting shares reserved for issuance to insiders shall not exceed 10% of the issued and outstanding voting shares; and

(iii) the number of common voting shares issuable under the stock option plans, which may be issued within a one-year period, shall not exceed 10% of the issued and outstanding voting shares at any time.

In May 2011, the Board approved amendments to the stock option plan to extend the maximum permitted expiry date from five years to seven years for all new option granted. Stock options are granted at a price equal to the five day weighted average market value of the Corporation's voting shares preceding the date of grant and vest completely or on a graded basis on the first, second and third anniversary from the date of grant.

EXHIBIT 10.5 (continued) WestJet Airlines Ltd.: Stock Option Plan

(c) Stock option plan (continued)

Changes in the number of options, with their weighted average exercise prices, are summarized below:

	2011		2010	
	Number of options	Weighted average exercise price	Number of options	Weighted average exercise price
Stock options outstanding, beginning of year	8,083,431	14.21	11,521,844	13.42
Granted	1,856,471	14.85	2,024,143	12.78
Exercised	(1,033,254)	12.56	(5,100,279)	11.83
Forfeited	(21,564)	13.36	(32,607)	12.58
Expired	(1,534,328)	16.32	(329,670)	14.77
Stock options outstanding, end of year	7,350,756	14.17	8,083,431	14.21
Exercisable, end of year	5,044,598	14.03	3,348,164	16.49

Under the terms of the Corporation's stock option plan, with the approval of the Corporation, option holders can either (i) elect to receive shares by delivering cash to the Corporation in the amount of the exercise price of the options, or (ii) choose a cashless settlement alternative, whereby they can elect to receive a number of shares equivalent to the market value of the options over the exercise price. For the year ended December 31, 2011, option holders exercised 1,030,565 options (2010—5,056,288 options) on a cashless settlement basis and received 170,895 shares (2010—697,023 shares). For the year ended December 31, 2011, 2,689 options were exercised on a cash basis and received 2,689 shares (2010—43,991 options and 43,991 shares, respectively).

The following table summarizes the options outstanding and exercisable as at December 31, 2011:

	Outstanding options			Exercisable options	
Range of exercise prices	Number outstanding	Weighted average remaining life (years)	Weighted average exercise price	Number exercisable	Weighted average exercise price
$11.00–$12.50	2,017,450	1.58	12.48	1,992,745	12.48
$12.51–$15.50	3,572,614	4.46	13.88	1,291,161	12.79
$15.51–$19.99	1,760,692	0.35	16.69	1,760,692	16.69
	7,350,756	2.69	14.17	5,044,598	14.03

The fair value of the options is expensed over the service period, with an offsetting entry to equity reserves. The fair value of each option grant is estimated on the date of grant using the Black-Scholes option pricing model. Upon the exercise of stock options, consideration received, together with amounts previously recorded in equity reserves, is recorded as an increase to share capital.

The fair value of options granted during the years ended December 31, 2011 and 2010, and the assumptions used in their determination are as follows:

	2011	2010
Weighted average fair value per option	4.30	4.02
Weighted average risk-free interest rate	2.3%	2.5%
Weighted average expected volatility	38%	38%
Expected life of options (years)	4.0	3.6
Weighted average dividend yield	1.4%	0.02%

would have been exercised when the market price was greater than the exercise price. During 2011, the price of WestJet's stock ranged from $10.41 to 15.40.

- Exercise prices of outstanding options range from $11.00 to $19.99. A table in the note breaks the options into different exercise price categories, including 3,572,614 options with an average exercise price of $13.88. If these options were exercised, WestJet would receive $49,587,882.32 (3,572,614 × $13.88) in cash in exchange for 3,572,614 WestJet shares. If the market price per share on the date they were exercised was $15, WestJet would be giving up shares worth $53,589,210 ($15 × 3,572,614) for $49,587,882.32. The difference of $4,001,327.68 is the cost borne by the existing shareholders.

Now, how should employee stock options be accounted for? For many years the treatment was to ignore them, and no expense was recorded for stock options granted to or exercised by employees. IFRS require that the value of stock options granted to employees be expensed as part of the compensation expense. The calculation of the compensation expense for stock options is complex and won't be discussed here, but in 2011 WestJet expensed $8,506,000 for stock option compensation.

This treatment makes good economic sense. Some people argue that, since stock options are usually issued at an exercise price that is less than the market value when they are granted, they have no value. This is clearly false. As long as there is time before the stock option expires, it has an economic value. Indeed, if stock options have no value, why would employees negotiate for and accept them as compensation? The entity granting the option is giving something valuable: the opportunity to purchase stock at below-market prices.

A main objection to expensing the value of stock options is that doing so would significantly lower net income. As has been mentioned several times in the book, accounting has economic consequences and people will respond when they see themselves being disadvantaged by an accounting standard (or anything else). Some readers may find it surprising, but accounting standard setting can be very political and occurs in an environment of conflicting interests.

ECONOMIC CONSEQUENCES

LO 7

Accounting matters. The discussion in the previous section about employee stock options and the controversy surrounding how to account for them emphasizes that. If accounting didn't matter, why would people get so excited about new accounting standards?

But why does accounting matter? This theme has been emphasized throughout the book. Accounting matters because it has economic consequences for an entity and its stakeholders. Economic consequences mean the wealth of an entity's stakeholders is affected by how the entity accounts for various transactions and economic events. Many decisions and outcomes, such as those following, can be affected by an entity's choices in how it represents its economic circumstances in the financial statements:

- management compensation
- compliance with debt covenants based on accounting measurements
- selling price of an entity when the price is based on net income or other accounting measurements
- amount of tax an entity pays
- rate changes for regulated companies when the rate is based on accounting measurements
- ability of an entity to receive subsidies from government
- ability of an entity to raise capital (some entities have argued that their ability to raise capital has been adversely affected by certain accounting standards)

This list doesn't include the effect accounting choices might have on decisions made by individual stakeholders—such as buying shares of a particular entity, selling shares already owned, or lending money. But remember, while different accounting choices have economic consequences for stakeholders, the underlying economic activity isn't affected by how an entity accounts.

Whether employee stock options are accrued, disclosed, or ignored doesn't change the economic cost of those options. What is affected is the representation of that economic activity in the financial statements.

LO 8

FINANCIAL STATEMENT ANALYSIS ISSUES

Price-to-Book Ratio

The equity section of an entity's balance sheet represents the book value of its equity. **Book value** (or carrying amount) is the amount recorded in the accounting records for the assets, liabilities, and equities—it's the accounting value of these elements. The **book value of equity** is the balance sheet or accounting value of an entity's equity and is equal to assets minus liabilities as reported on the balance sheet. It's also referred to as the net assets or net worth of the entity.

The book value of equity isn't a measure of its market value. As we have discussed throughout the text, there are many reasons why book values and market values don't correspond. One is that IFRS rely on historical cost to measure many assets and liabilities—they aren't designed or intended to measure market values. For example, property, plant, and equipment is recorded at its cost and isn't adjusted for changes in market value (although IFRS allows the use of fair value), and not all assets are even recorded on the balance sheet (e.g., research and development, advertising, and human resources). However, book value is sometimes viewed as what would be left over for shareholders if a company shut down its operations, paid off all of its creditors, collected from all of its debtors, and liquidated itself. From this view, book value can be seen as the minimum amount an entity is worth. This interpretation makes more sense for entities that reflect most of their assets on the balance sheet (like manufacturers and retailers) but less sense for knowledge-based entities that have many unrecorded assets.

The **market value of equity** is the market price of an entity's shares multiplied by the number of common shares outstanding. For public companies, the shares trade publicly so a market price is readily available. There is no readily available market price for private companies.

The **price-to-book ratio** (PB ratio) is often examined by investors and analysts when considering a stock's desirability. The PB ratio is a measure of the stock market's valuation of a company's equity relative to its book value and it indicates if the shares are reasonably valued. If the market expects a company to have higher earnings, its PB ratio will rise because the market value of the equity will increase.

The PB ratio can be stated as

$$\text{Price-to-book ratio} = \frac{\text{Market value of equity}}{\text{Book value of equity}}$$

A lower PB ratio could indicate that a stock is undervalued and, therefore, an attractive investment. It could also indicate significant problems with the company. Like most of the ratios we have considered in the book, how meaningful a particular amount is varies with the industry. For example, one would expect a software company to have a higher PB ratio than a steelmaker or bank because the software company has many assets that aren't captured on the balance sheet, such as internally generated patents, copyrights and human capital.

For example, the market value of Potash Corporation's equity on December 31, 2011 was \$35,447,259,468 (\$41.28 per share × 858,702,991 shares) and its book value on December 31, 2011 was \$7,847,000,000 (see Potash Corporation's balance sheet in Exhibit 10.3) for a PB ratio of 4.52. Table 10.6 provides the PB ratios for the same period for some of the companies we've discussed in the book.

Earnings per Share

One of the most often quoted financial ratios is **earnings per share (EPS)**. EPS is the amount of net income attributable to each individual common share. The investing public pays close attention to and anxiously awaits the announcement of companies' quarterly and annual earnings and EPS. Analysts project EPS, and whether an entity has had a successful quarter or year is often measured by whether it met the analysts' forecasts.

TABLE 10.6 Price-to-Book Ratios for Selected Companies, 2009–2011*

Company (year-end)	2011	2010	2009
Indigo Books & Music Inc. (March 31, 2011/April 2, 2010/April 4, 2009)	1.23	1.73	1.17
Leon's Furniture Limited (December 31)	2.03	2.53	1.97
Potash Corporation of Saskatchewan Inc. (December 31)	4.52	4.92	4.85
WestJet Airlines Ltd. (December 31)	1.19	1.54	1.45

*Financial statement information for these calculations was prepared in accordance with IFRS.

EPS comes in a number of variations. We will look at two of them. The first and most straightforward is **basic earnings per share (basic EPS)**, which is calculated using the following formula:

$$\text{Basic EPS} = \frac{\text{Net income} - \text{Preferred dividends}}{\text{Weighted-average number of common shares outstanding during the period}}$$

Preferred dividends are deducted from net income in the numerator because they aren't available to common shareholders, but they aren't deducted when net income is calculated. The denominator is the weighted-average number of shares that were outstanding during the year, which is the average number of shares outstanding during the period, taking into consideration when changes in the number of shares outstanding occurred during the period. An example of how to calculate the weighted-average number of shares outstanding is available on Connect®.

We can calculate basic EPS for Potash Corporation's from the information in Exhibit 10.3. See ❾ in the exhibit:

$$\text{Basic EPS} = \frac{\text{Net income} - \text{Preferred dividends}}{\text{Weighted-average number of common shares outstanding during the period}}$$

$$= \frac{\$3{,}081{,}000{,}000 - 0}{855{,}677{,}000}$$

$$= \$3.60$$

EPS is usually reported at the bottom of income statement. A second EPS measure called *diluted EPS* is also reported by companies complying with IFRS. In this chapter and in Chapter 9, we discussed securities such as convertible bonds, convertible preferred shares, and stock options that can be converted into or exchanged for common shares. If these securities are converted or exercised, they may dilute an entity's earnings—they will increase the number of common shares, thereby lowering EPS because earnings would be spread over a larger number of shares. **Diluted earnings per share** is designed to show the effect these dilutive securities would have on EPS if all of the securities had been converted or exchanged for common shares during the year. The actual calculations can get complicated and won't be shown here, but diluted EPS can be thought of as a worst-case scenario of EPS. You can find Potash Corporation's diluted EPS in Note 22 in Exhibit 10.3.

Despite all the attention it receives in the media, EPS has significant limitations:

- Like any ratio, EPS has no inherent meaning and must be considered in relation to some benchmark. For example, current EPS could be compared with previous years' EPS to observe trends, or compared with analysts' forecasts of EPS.
- EPS depends on the accounting policies and estimates used in the financial statements.
- EPS may be affected by changes in the number of shares outstanding during a period. For example, if an entity repurchases some of its shares, EPS will increase.
- EPS gives no indication of the entity's ability or willingness to pay dividends. It is simply the earnings attributable to each common share. It doesn't mean cash is on hand.

- It can be very difficult to compare the EPS figures of different entities. Aside from the effect of different accounting choices, EPS is also affected by financing. Entities with identical assets and operating performance will have different EPS if they are financed differently—that is, if they have different proportions of debt and equity.

ACCOUNTING STANDARDS FOR PRIVATE ENTERPRISES

Accounting Standards for Private Enterprises doesn't require companies to report earnings per share.

Dividend Payout Ratio and Dividend Yield

Investors earn returns from equity investments in two ways: appreciation of the price of shares owned and dividends. I will briefly add a couple of additional ratios for evaluating the dividends companies pay. The **dividend payout ratio** measures the percentage of net income that's paid out in dividends. The ratio can be calculated as:

$$\text{Dividend payout ratio} = \frac{\text{Common annual cash dividends declared}}{\text{Net income}}$$

Potash Corporation's dividend payout ratio for 2011 is calculated as:

$$\begin{aligned}\text{Dividend payout ratio} &= \frac{\text{Common annual cash dividends declared}}{\text{Net income}} \\ &= \frac{\$240{,}000{,}000}{\$308{,}100{,}000} \\ &= 7.79\%\end{aligned}$$

This means that in 2011, Potash Corporation paid out 7.79 percent of its net income for the year in dividends.

A high ratio means a large proportion of earnings is paid out to shareholders while a relatively small amount is reinvested in the company. A payout ratio that's not too high suggests that an existing dividend is relatively safe (the company can maintain the dividend even if earnings drop) and there's room to increase the dividend in future. A ratio that's too high can be a source of concern because if the company doesn't perform as well it may not be able to maintain the dividend. The dividend payout ratio will be affected by the accounting choices the company makes. The dividend payout ratio can also be calculated on a per share basis by dividing earnings per share by cash dividends declared per share.

Dividend yield provides similar information except that it's based on the company's share price and not on its earnings. The dividend yield formula is:

$$\text{Dividend yield} = \frac{\text{Common annual cash dividends per share}}{\text{Current share price}}$$

Potash Corporation's dividend yield on December 31, 2011 was:

$$\begin{aligned}\text{Dividend yield} &= \frac{\text{Common annual cash dividends per share}}{\text{Current share price}} \\ &= \frac{\$0.28}{\$41.28} \\ &= 0.68\%\end{aligned}$$

This means that using the share price on December 31, 2011 the dividend yield on Potash Corporation's shares was 0.68 percent. (This calculation is based on share price as stated in U.S. dollars because Potash Corporation reports in U.S. dollars.) Note that the dividend yield changes on a day-to-day basis as the share price changes.

Since share prices respond immediately to new information the dividend yield is a more current indicator of the dividend performance of a company. A higher dividend yield means a higher return to investors. However, a dividend yield that's "too" high must be viewed cautiously. When the share price falls, the dividend yield increases. However, a falling share price may indicate problems for the company—it may not be able to sustain the dividend and the company may have to cut the dividend to conserve cash. A low dividend yield isn't an indication of bad news. Growing companies may not pay dividends because they require the cash to fund their growth. For these companies, investors will earn their return through the appreciation in the value of the shares.

Table 10.7 provides the dividend payout ratio and dividend yield for some selected companies:

TABLE 10.7 Dividend Payout Ratio and Dividend Yield 2008–2011*

	Dividend payout ratio				Dividend yield			
Company	2011	2010	2009	2008	2011	2010	2009	2008
Indigo Books & Music Inc. (March 31, 2012/April 2, 2011/April 4, 2010)	16.76%	56.48%	0.00%	0.00%	3.42%	2.21%	0.00%	0.00%
Leon's Furniture Limited (December 31)	64.18%	35.54%	59.70%	42.39%	4.19%	2.16%	4.57%	4.22%
Potash Corporation of Saskatchewan Inc. (December 31)	7.79%	6.65%	12.03%	3.53%	0.68%	0.25%	1.12%	1.67%
WestJet Airlines Ltd. (December 31)	18.73%	7.92%	0.00%	0.00%	1.70%	0.36%	0.00%	0.00%

*Financial statement information for these calculations was prepared in accordance with IFRS for 2011 and 2010 and in accordance with Canadian GAAP in effect at the time for 2009 and 2008.

INSIGHT

In Canada, the activities and performance of public companies get a lot of attention. This is understandable, as many members of the public have an interest in these companies, either directly or indirectly through pension plans and mutual funds.

However, most corporations and businesses in Canada are private. That means there is no market price on which to base a reasonable estimate of their market values. This is one of the reasons why accounting information is so important for evaluating an entity. For example, how much would you pay to buy a small business in your community? How much would you pay to join a partnership of accountants? Without a market-determined measure of value, it's difficult to know. That's why accounting information is relied on for determining the value of a private company for purposes of a purchase and sale, or in a divorce.

Return on Shareholders' Equity

In Chapter 8, **return on assets (ROA)** was introduced as a measure of the performance and operating efficiency of an entity. ROA provides a measure of the return the entity earns regardless of how it's financed. **Return on equity (ROE)** is a measure of return earned by resources invested only by common shareholders.

$$\text{Return on equity} = \frac{\text{Net income} - \text{Preferred dividends}}{\text{Average common shareholders' equity}}$$

Because ROE measures return to the common shareholders, preferred dividends are deducted from net income. These dividends aren't available to the common shareholders, but the amount isn't deducted in the calculation of net income. The denominator, average common shareholders' equity, excludes equity contributed by the preferred shareholders. As was discussed in the section in this chapter on leverage, ROE will be affected by how the entity is financed. The more leverage or debt that an entity uses, the more volatile ROE will be.

For Potash Corporation, ROE for 2011 was

$$\text{Return on equity} = \frac{\text{Net income} - \text{Preferred dividends}}{\text{Average common shareholders' equity}}$$
$$= \frac{\$3{,}081{,}000{,}000 - \$0}{(\$7{,}847{,}000{,}000 + \$6{,}685{,}000{,}000) \div 2}$$
$$= \frac{\$3{,}081{,}000{,}000}{\$7{,}266{,}000{,}000}$$
$$= 42.40\%$$

Potash Corporation's common shareholders earned a 42.4 percent return on their investment in the company. Investors can compare the ROEs of different entities as part of their evaluation of investment alternatives.

Higher ROEs mean an investment is more attractive, but risk must be considered as well. Generally, the higher the risk of an investment, the higher the return investors expect. Thus, a higher return may indicate more risk, and investors must decide if they willing to accept the additional risk in exchange for the higher return. This risk–return relationship, the trade-off between risk and return, explains why interest rates that banks pay to depositors are low, whereas expected returns on speculative investments tend to be high.

Table 10.8 provides ROEs for some of the companies we have examined so far in the book. Like other ratios, notice the variation across companies and over time. Leon's ROE has a definite downward trend although the range of values is fairly narrow. Potash Corporation's ROE is consistently high, but is fairly stable outside of 2011 and 2008.

TABLE 10.8 Return on Equity for Selected Companies, 2005–2011*

Company	2011	2010	2009	2008	2007	2006	2005
Indigo Books & Music Inc. (March 31, 2012/April 2, 2011/April 4, 2009)	21.34%	−7.78%	14.10%	29.96%	22.69%	24.78%	12.82%
Leon's Furniture Limited (December 31)	13.56	16.11	15.61	18.77	19.19	19.56	19.19
Potash Corporation of Saskatchewan Inc. (December 31)	42.40	27.33	17.81	65.90	25.08	25.72	24.03
WestJet Airlines Ltd. (December 31)	11.12	6.70	7.97	17.62	21.96	15.54	3.81

*Financial statement information for these calculations was prepared in accordance with IFRS for 2011 and 2010 and in accordance with Canadian GAAP in effect at the time for 2005 through 2009.

Solved Problem

This case is designed to make you think about financial statements from the perspective of a particular stakeholder. The main theme is the problems a buyer of a small business has with a set of financial statements for that business. As usual, you should try to work through the case before looking at the solution.

KENASTON CONVENIENCE STORE

The Kenaston Convenience Store (KCS) is located near a subdivision in Regina. KCS offers food staples, basic household goods, newspapers and magazines, candy, drinks, and snacks. KCS opened several years ago and is owned and operated by the Wu family. The store has been very successful and now that the neighbourhood has matured and the population is large enough, a major chain of convenience stores, Community Mart Ltd. (CML), is interested in buying KCS to establish a presence in the area. It's CML's usual practice to only move into an area once the population density has reached a certain level. It prefers to buy out an existing convenience store in an area because it gets the benefit of an established location and eliminates a competitor.

You are CML's location evaluator. It's your job to make contact with the owners of established convenience stores and evaluate their suitability for acquisition. Your preliminary evaluation of KCS is that it's a potential candidate for acquisition and your initial discussions with Mr. Wu were favourable. Mr. Wu has agreed to allow you to look at KCS's most recent income statements. The income statements are presented below:

Kenaston Convenience Store **Income statements for the years ended March 31,**		
	2017	**2016**
Revenue	$417,250	$368,425
Cost of sales	279,968	251,476
Gross margin	137,282	116,949
Expenses		
Depreciation of property and equipment	22,000	21,600
Interest	10,150	11,200
Utilities	14,700	13,900
Other	7,500	4,200
Advertising and promotion	6,200	4,500
Salaries and wages	2,000	2,200
Repairs and maintenance	1,150	750
Income before taxes	73,582	58,599
Income taxes	11,773	9,376
Net income	$ 61,809	$ 49,223

In addition, you obtained the following information from your discussion with Mr. Wu and from observing the business:

- KCS is located in a two-storey, 30-year-old building at the edge of the new subdivision. The building cost $300,000 and there is a $210,000 mortgage on it. The Wu family lives in a spacious apartment above the store. Mortgage payments and all utilities and property taxes for the entire building are included in KCS's income statements.
- KCS is one of three convenience stores in the area. KCS has been in business the longest. The Wu family is well liked in the area and KCS has provided a lot of support over the years for various community activities such as children's sports teams, picnics, and holiday events.
- The store is open seven days a week from 7 a.m. to 11 p.m. The store is always staffed by Mr. or Mrs. Wu or one of their children. All work in the store is also done by family members. No one gets paid for the work they do but money is provided as it is needed, often just taken from the cash register.
- The financial statements are prepared for the bank, which has provided a small loan in addition to the mortgage on the building, and for tax purposes.
- KCS depreciates its property and equipment on the same basis as is required for tax purposes, using the rates specified in the *Income Tax Act*.
- All sales are for cash (no credit sales) and are recorded on the cash register. Not all sales are rung up on the register.

- In late 2017, there was a power failure. KCS's backup generator failed and perishable food items with a value of $4,500 had to be thrown away.
- Inventory is counted on the last day of the year. Cost of goods sold is calculated by adding the opening inventory to purchases made during the year and then subtracting ending inventory. Family members often take store items for their own use.

Required:

Prepare a report for your manager, the vice-president of acquisitions, outlining your evaluation of the KCS's income statements. In your report, identify and discuss whether the statements are representative of KCS's activity and whether they give a good indication of how the store would perform if CML purchased and operated it. Be sure to identify and discuss any adjustments you would recommend to make the financial statements more useful.

Report to the controller:

I have examined the income statements for the Kenaston Convenience Store (KCS) and additional information related to the potential purchase of the business. There are many complications with using these income statements as an indicator of the profit our company will earn as operators of the store. I propose that we revise these income statements to approximate ones that would have resulted had the store been owned and operated by our company for the last two years. This will be most useful for determining an appropriate price to pay for KCS. For some of the issues, the amount of adjustment needed is fairly clear but for others further information is needed. I will indicate how each issue should be handled.

1. The fact that the business has been almost exclusively staffed by family members without explicit compensation means that the wage expenses are significantly understated and profitability overstated. It should be easy to estimate the staffing costs based on our experience and given the level of sales. The staff costs should include at least one employee at the manager level in accordance with our normal staffing policies.
2. KCS's building is owned by the Wus, which means CML has to purchase the building or be the Wu's tenants. If we rent, the income statements should reflect a fair rent for the building. It is possible that the building depreciation expense offsets rent, but the amount has to be confirmed. If we buy the building, we must consider the purchase price and any financing costs, as well as any rent earned from the apartment unit. We also need to determine the building's market value. Since CML is purchasing KCS's location, it is important for the store to remain where it is.
3. The cost of merchandise sold is overstated as the family consumed some goods for personal use. An expense is recorded but there is no corresponding revenue for these items.
4. The revenues reported on the income statement are understated because some sales aren't rung up, presumably to avoid paying income taxes. Estimating the amount of the understatement will be challenging. We could estimate sales by determining KCS's inventory purchases during the year and applying an appropriate margin. However, this is impeded by the fact that cost of sales is also misstated through the Wu's personal use of inventory. Assuming that the personal use inventory is small compared to the inventory actually sold, we can use this estimation technique.
5. The amounts reported for utilities and supplies on the income statements are too high because they include the electricity, heat, and telephone costs for the family home as well as those of the business. We will have to estimate the business's portion of the costs. Of course, if CML buys the building then some of the costs pertaining to the apartment will continue, so those need to be included as well.
6. The advertising and promotion budget may be a fairly accurate representation of the costs incurred but aren't relevant since our approach to promotion may be quite different. Again, we are better served by estimating the budget we would normally follow for a store of this size.
7. The depreciation of capital assets has been based on CCA rates and may not be relevant for our purposes. We should revise the estimated depreciation cost to reflect our normal depreciation policies, based on the market values of the assets required to operate this business. That may

require replacement of some equipment and fixtures that aren't in good condition. Our inventory management and reporting requirements may require more sophisticated cash registers and other computers, costs that need to be taken into consideration when estimating the possible profit of acquiring this company.

8. The loss caused by the power failure is an event that should not recur in future and so should be excluded from the analysis of the expected future performance of KCS.
9. We need to find out what "other expenses" are. These may or may not be incurred under our ownership. They could represent personal expenses or legitimate business expenses. The amount in 2017 may include the loss due to the power failure.
10. Interest costs likely apply to the entire building, and bank loans may be personal as well as business. We need to determine the purpose of the loans. The cost of the debt we will incur to operate the business needs to be included in the income statement.
11. The Wus have generated goodwill in the neighbourhood through their support of community activities. It's possible that this goodwill may not transfer to CML, as a corporate face may not have the same impact. I think that CML should continue the community support if it buys KCS and there is likely to be minimal impact on sales.

In summary, KCS's income statements are a good starting point for analysis, but significant adjustments are needed to make them representative of how the store will perform if owned by CML. Our experience in the industry may help us overcome the problems with the sales and cost of sales, though there is significant room for error. The maximum price we are willing to pay for the business should be based on the expected future profits and the value we place on eliminating the competition.

SUMMARY OF KEY POINTS

LO 1 A corporation is a separate legal and taxable entity. The shareholders of a corporation aren't liable for the obligations of and losses suffered by the corporation, beyond what they have invested.

Partnerships and proprietorships aren't incorporated. They don't pay income tax or file tax returns—earnings are taxed in the hands of the proprietor or partners. Partners have limited liability only in the case of limited and limited liability partnerships. The equity section of a partnership has a separate account for each partner, to keep track of the capital contributed by, the share of the partnership's earnings of, and the drawings made by each partner.

Not-for-profit organizations (NFPOs) are economic entities whose objective is to provide services, not to make a profit. NFPOs don't have owners or ownership shares that can be traded or sold.

LO 2 Common shares represent the residual ownership in an entity. They are entitled to whatever earnings and assets are left after obligations to creditors and preferred shareholders have been satisfied. Preferred shareholders' rights pertaining to the payment of dividends and/or to the distribution of assets must be satisfied before common shareholders' rights in the event of liquidation. Dividends aren't deductible for tax purposes or expensed for accounting purposes. Shareholders aren't entitled to dividends or any other type of payments from the corporation and return of principal isn't guaranteed.

LO 3 Retained earnings is the accumulated earnings of an entity over its entire life, less all dividends paid to shareholders over the entity's life. Retained earnings is an indirect investment by shareholders. Dividends are distributions of a corporation's earnings to its shareholders. There are three types of dividends: cash, property, and stock. Dividends are discretionary and are declared by the board of directors. They are declared on a per share basis and every share of a specific class must receive the same dividend. When a dividend is declared, it's classified as a liability on the balance sheet. Contributed surplus captures equity transactions that don't fit into the other equity accounts. A stock split divides an entity's shares into a larger number of units, each with a smaller value.

LO 4 There are two categories of accounting changes—changes in policies and changes in estimates. A change in an accounting policy is applied retroactively. A change in an accounting estimate is adjusted from the period of the change forward.

LO 5 Leverage is the use of debt to attempt to increase the return earned on an equity investment. Leverage is attractive because any profits earned from investing borrowed money, above the cost of borrowing, go to the owners. It's risky because the cost of borrowing must be paid, regardless of how well or how poorly the entity performs.

LO 6 Employee stock options give employees the right to purchase a specified number of shares of the employer's stock at a specified price over a specified period of time. Stock options are an important way of compensating employees. In Canada, the economic value of stock options on the date they are granted to employees must be estimated and the amount expensed as a compensation expense.

LO 7 Accounting matters because it has economic consequences for an entity and its stakeholders. Economic consequences mean the wealth of an entity's stakeholders is affected by how the entity accounts for various transactions and economic events.

LO 8 The equity section of an entity's balance sheet represents the book value of its equity. The book value of equity is the balance sheet or accounting value of equity and is equal to assets minus liabilities as reported on the balance sheet. It isn't a measure of the market value of the equity. The price-to-book ratio is a measure of the stock market's valuation of a company's equity relative to its book value. The dividend payout ratio and dividend yield provide information about the amount of dividends being paid.

Earnings per share is the amount of net income attributable to each individual common share. Basic earnings per share equals net income less preferred dividends divided by the weighted-average number of common shares outstanding during the period. Diluted EPS shows the effect that dilutive securities would have on EPS if the securities were converted or exchanged for common shares. Return on equity provides a measure of the return earned by resources invested by the common shareholders.

FORMULA SUMMARY

$$\text{Assets} = \text{Liabilities} + \text{Owners' (shareholders') equity}$$

$$\text{Comprehensive income} = \text{Net income} + \text{Other comprehensive income}$$

$$\text{Basic EPS} = \frac{\text{Net income} - \text{Preferred dividends}}{\text{Weighted-average number of common shares outstanding during the period}}$$

$$\text{Return on equity} = \frac{\text{Net income} - \text{Preferred dividends}}{\text{Average common shareholders' equity}}$$

$$\text{Price-to-book ratio} = \frac{\text{Market value of equity}}{\text{Book value of equity}}$$

$$\text{Dividend payout ratio} = \frac{\text{Common annual cash dividends declared}}{\text{Net income}}$$

$$\text{Dividend yield} = \frac{\text{Common annual cash dividends per share}}{\text{Current share price}}$$

KEY TERMS

accounting estimates, p. 619
accounting policies, p. 619
accumulated other comprehensive income/loss, p. 617
authorized capital stock, p. 608
basic earnings per share (basic EPS), p. 627
book value, p. 626
book value of equity, p. 626
Canada Business Corporations Act, p. 608
cash dividend, p. 614
common shares, p. 608
comprehensive income, p. 617
contributed surplus, p. 618
convertible preferred share, p. 611
cumulative preferred share, p. 611
date of declaration of a dividend, p. 614
date of payment of a dividend, p. 614
date of record of a dividend, p. 614
diluted earnings per share, p. 627
dividend payout ratio, p. 628
dividend yield, p. 628
earnings per share (EPS), p. 626
employee stock option, p. 622
exercise price, p. 622
expiry date, p. 622
general partner, p. 602
hybrid security, p. 612
issued shares, p. 608
leverage, p. 619
limited liability partnership (LLP), p. 602
limited partner, p. 602
limited partnership, p. 602
market value of equity, p. 626
no par value share, p. 611
other comprehensive income, p. 617
outstanding shares, p. 608
par value, p. 611
participating preferred share, p. 611
preferred shares, p. 611
price-to-book ratio, p. 626
property dividend, p. 615
redeemable preferred share, p. 611
retractable preferred share, p. 611
return on assets (ROA), p. 629
return on equity (ROE), p. 629
reverse stock split, p. 616
stock dividend, p. 615
stock split, p. 616
treasury stock, p. 611

SIMILAR TERMS

The left column gives alternative terms that are sometimes used for the accounting terms introduced in this chapter, which are listed in the right column.

additional paid-in capital	**contributed surplus, p. 618**
authorized share capital, authorized shares	**authorized capital stock, p. 608**
distributions	**dividends, p. 50**
dividend in kind	**property dividend, p. 615**
net assets, net worth	**book value of equity, p. 626**

ASSIGNMENT MATERIALS

Questions

Q10-1. Explain the difference between common and preferred shares. Which type of share is less risky to an investor? Explain.

Q10-2. What does it mean when an entity uses leverage to finance itself? What are the advantages and disadvantages of using leverage?

Q10-3. Explain why it's difficult to finance a new business by using a large amount of debt. What concerns would a lender have if they were asked to provide a loan that would represent 90 percent of the company's financing?

Q10-4. Describe and explain the characteristics that distinguish corporations from partnerships and proprietorships.

Q10-5. Why are common shares said to represent the residual interest in an entity?

Q10-6. Explain the differences between debt and equity. What are the advantages and disadvantages of each? Which do you think is preferable for an entity to use? Explain.

Q10-7. What is a not-for-profit organization? If their objective is not to make a profit, what is it? Why is a traditional income statement not appropriate for a not-for-profit organization?

Q10-8. Explain why not-for-profit organizations don't have an owners' equity section on their balance sheets. What do they have instead? What does that section of the balance sheet represent? How should it be interpreted?

Q10-9. What is a limited partnership? What is the difference between limited partners and general partners? Why must a limited partnership have at least one general partner?

Q10-10. What are dividends? Why are dividends not expensed when calculating net income whereas interest is expensed?

Q10-11. What does par value mean? How does the entry to record the issuance of common shares differ depending on whether the shares have a par value? Provide an example.

Q10-12. Grosvenor Ltd. has the following securities outstanding:
i. $1,000,000 bond with 10 percent coupon rate.
ii. $1,000,000 of cumulative preferred shares with a 6.5 percent dividend rate.
What effect would the interest on the bond and preferred dividend have on the income statement? What would the net cash cost of each security be? Assume that Grosvenor has a tax rate of 30 percent.

Q10-13. Over the last six months, the price of Ixworth Inc.'s (Ixworth) shares has fallen from a high of $32 per share to its current price of $18. Ixworth doesn't plan to issue common shares in the foreseeable future, yet management has expressed concern about the falling share price. Explain why Ixworth's management might be concerned about its share price.

Q10-14. How are changes in the price of a company's shares traded on stock exchanges such as the TSX reflected in the company's own financial statements?

Q10-15. Distinguish between stock splits and stock dividends. How is each accounted for? What is the economic significance of each?

Q10-16. What is retained earnings? What transactions and economic events have an effect on retained earnings? Why is retained earnings considered an indirect investment in an entity?

Q10-17. What are property dividends? How are they accounted for?

Q10-18. What is accumulated other comprehensive income (AOCI)? Where does it appear in the balance sheet? What causes it to change in a period?

Q10-19. You are a shareholder in a public company. The company is proposing to introduce an employee stock option program for its senior executives. Do you think that this proposal is a good idea? In your response, focus on the incentives the stock option plan would create for the executives.

Q10-20. Why do employee stock options impose a cost on shareholders?

Q10-21. Car prices tend to increase over time. One car manufacturer has offered students the opportunity to lock in the price of a new car for when they graduate. By paying $500 today, a student can purchase any car made by the manufacturer at today's price at any time over the next three years. The $500 fee isn't refundable.

Required:

Do you think it's worthwhile to spend $500 to lock in the price of a car for three years? Explain. What are the risks associated with purchasing this price guarantee? Suppose you could sell the price guarantee to somebody else. What would happen to the amount you could sell the price guarantee for if the price of cars increased? What if the price of cars decreased? Explain.

Q10-22. What is meant by the term "economic consequences"? Why does accounting have economic consequences?

Q10-23. Since the underlying economic activity of an entity isn't affected by accounting choices such as when revenue is recognized or how capital assets are depreciated, why does anyone care what accounting choices an entity makes?

Q10-24. Distinguish between the book value and market value of equity. Why are the two amounts usually different? How is book value per share calculated?

Q10-25. A business owner shows you his balance sheet and points out that the total amount of equity is $4,567,000. He says that is the price a buyer should pay for the business. Do you agree? Explain.

Q10-26. Corporations disclose the number of shares authorized and the number of shares outstanding. Explain what these terms mean.

Q10-27. How are preferred shares "preferred"? Are dividends on preferred shares guaranteed? If the preferred shares have a cumulative feature, are the dividends guaranteed? Explain.

Q10-28. Would you rather receive a cash dividend or a stock dividend from a corporation? Explain.

Q10-29. Why do most companies not pay out 100 percent of their earnings each year in dividends?

Q10-30. Why are preferred dividends deducted from net income when calculating earnings per share? Explain. Does earnings per share give an indication of the amount of dividends shareholders can expect to receive? Explain.

Q10-31. What is the impact on earnings per share if a company buys back some of its shares from investors? What is the economic impact on the company?

Q10-32. Explain the dividend yield of a share and a company's dividend payout ratio. What does it mean if the dividend yield and dividend payout are zero? Is this a bad situation if both are zero?

Q10-33. Explain why changes in accounting policies and corrections of errors have an effect on retained earnings.

Q10-34. Why might a loan agreement limit or prevent the payment of dividends by the borrower?

Q10-35. Why do you think property dividends are accounted for at their market value instead of their carrying amount? Why are property dividends relatively uncommon?

Q10-36. Explain the difference between a change in accounting policy and a change in accounting estimate. How is each accounted for in the financial statements?

Exercises

E10-1. **(Business form, LO 1)** Jason Wong and Mohammed Ismail are in the process of setting up a painting business. For a number of years, the two friends had summer jobs doing interior house painting and they thought it would be fun to have their own business. Jason and Mohammed have asked your advice on whether they should organize the business as a partnership or a corporation.

Required:

Prepare a report to Jason and Mohammed advising them about the benefits and drawbacks of the two business forms. Provide a recommendation as to which one you think would be best for them. Consider the needs of the friends as well as other stakeholders (customers, prospective creditors) in the report.

E10-2. **(Preparing journal entries, LO 2, 3, 5, 6)** For each of the following transactions or economic events, prepare the journal entry that would be required. Assume the year-end in each case is December 31:

a. On April 2, 2017, Barthel Inc. issued 200,000 common shares for $4,500,000.
b. On May 17, 2017, Cayley Corp. announced a three-for-one stock split. On the day before the split, Cayley had 1 million shares outstanding, $2.5 million in the common shares account, and $8 million in retained earnings.
c. On December 9, 2017, Duro Ltd. declared a $0.25 per share cash dividend. The dividend was paid on February 11, 2018. Duro Ltd. had 1,000,000 shares outstanding on December 9, 2017.
d. On August 17, 2017, Gullies Inc. issued 300,000 common shares with a par value of $0.01 for $6,000,000.
e. On April 21, 2017, Quimper Corp. declared and distributed a 5 percent common stock dividend. On April 20, 2017 (just before the dividend was declared), Quimper had 25,000,000 common shares outstanding and the market price per share was $2.75. The balance in the common shares account on April 20, 2017 was $20,000,000.
f. On December 4, 2017, Yarrow Ltd. declared a property dividend of some of the company's products. Each shareholder received an identical case of products that was taken directly from inventory. The carrying amount of the inventory on December 4, 2017 was $1,200,000 and its market value, based on the most recent selling price to customers, was $2,100,000. The dividend was distributed to the shareholders on December 21, 2017.

E10-3. **(Accounting for equity transactions and preparing the shareholders' equity section of the balance sheet, LO 2, 3)** You are provided with the following information from the equity section of Aurora Ltd.'s balance sheet on December 31, 2017:

Preferred stock—Authorized, 200,000 shares; outstanding 60,000 shares	$1,500,000
Common shares—Authorized, unlimited; outstanding 400,000 shares	1,200,000
Retained earnings	9,110,000

During the year ended December 31, 2018 the following occurred (events are listed in the order they occurred during the year):

i. Semi-annual dividend on common shares of $0.50 per share was declared and paid.
ii. 100,000 shares of common shares were issued for $30 per share.
iii. 20,000 shares of preferred shares were issued for $50 per share.
iv. 20,000 shares of common shares were issued in exchange for patent. The shares traded for the patent had a fair value on the date of the transaction of $380,000.
v. Preferred dividends were declared and paid, $2.50 per share.
vi. 10 percent stock dividend was declared on the outstanding common shares.

vii. Semi-annual dividend on common shares of $0.50 per share was declared. The dividend will be paid in January 2019.
viii. Net income was $1,250,000.

Required:

a. Prepare the journal entries required to record the above events.
b. Prepare the shareholders' equity section of Aurora balance sheet on December 31, 2018.

E10-4. **(Accounting for equity transactions and preparing the shareholders' equity section of the balance sheet, LO 2, 3)** You are provided with the following information from the equity section of Tingwick Ltd.'s balance sheet on December 31, 2016:

Preferred shares—authorized, 5,000,000 shares; outstanding 2,000,000 shares	$ 40,000,000
Common shares—authorized, 400,000,000; outstanding 125,000,000 shares	425,000,000
Accumulated other comprehensive income (loss)	(1,750,000)
Retained earnings	195,500,000

During the year ended December 31, 2017, the following occurred (events are recorded in the order they occurred during the year):

i. Semi-annual dividend on common shares of $0.60 per share was declared and paid.
ii. Issued 3,000,000 common shares for $8 per share.
iii. Issued 750,000 preferred shares for $10 per share.
iv. Issued 3,000,000 common shares in exchange for all the common shares of another company. The estimated value of the acquired company was $25 million.
v. Preferred dividends of $1 per share were declared and paid.
vi. Declared a 2 percent stock dividend on the outstanding common shares.
vii. Net income was $31,000,000.
viii. Comprehensive income for 2017 was $31,200,000.
ix. Semi-annual dividend on common shares of $0.65 per share was declared. The dividend will be paid in January 2018.

Required:

Prepare the shareholders' equity section of Tingwick balance sheet on December 31, 2017.

E10-5. **(Correction of an accounting error, LO 3)** In fiscal 2017, Upshall Ltd. (Upshall) purchased land for $250,000. For some reason, the land was expensed when it was purchased. A new employee in the accounting department who was asked to review the company's property, plant, and equipment discovered the error in 2019. Retained earnings on December 31, 2018, Upshall's last year-end, was $3,250,000.

Required:

Prepare the journal entry that must be made in Upshall's books to correct the error. What would retained earnings be on December 31, 2019 after the error had been corrected? Explain why the error is corrected in this way.

E10-6. **(Correction of an accounting error, LO 3)** In fiscal 2013, Minaki Inc. (Minaki) purchased machinery for $3,500,000. The machinery was supposed to be depreciated over 10 years on a straight-line basis, but for some reason, it wasn't. Minaki's new controller discovered the error in late 2017. Retained earnings on December 31, 2016, Minaki's last year-end, was $17,800,000.

Required:

Prepare the journal entry that must be made in Minaki's books to correct the error. What would retained earnings be on December 31, 2017 after the error had been corrected? Explain why the error is corrected in this way.

E10-7. **(Accumulated other comprehensive income, LO 3)** For the year ended December 31, 2017, Redvers Ltd. issued the following summarized statement of comprehensive income. Use the information in the statement to determine accumulated other comprehensive income on December 31, 2017. Accumulated other comprehensive income on December 31, 2016 was $245,000.

Redvers Ltd. Summarized Statement of Comprehensive Income For the year ended December 31, 2017	
Net income	$925,000
Other comprehensive income	(95,000)
Comprehensive income	$830,000

E10-8. **(Equity section amounts, LO 3)** Determine the missing amounts in 2015 through 2018 for the shaded areas in the table below:

	2014	2015	2016	2017	2018
Net income	$	$	$195,000	$101,000	$155,000
Other comprehensive income					
Comprehensive income			210,000		145,000
Retained earnings	512,000	425,000	550,000	525,000	
Accumulated other comprehensive income	16,850	5,700		(8,000)	
Dividends		45,000			155,000

E10-9. **(Equity transactions, LO 2, 3, 8)** The shareholders' equity section of Fogo Ltd.'s balance sheet is shown below:

Fogo Ltd. Extracts from the December 31, 2017 balance sheet	
Shareholders' equity	
Preferred stock (authorized 100,000; outstanding 25,000)	$1,250,000
Common shares (authorized 1,000,000; outstanding 500,000)	1,800,000
Retained earnings	6,880,000
Total shareholders' equity	$9,930,000

During 2018, the following occurred:

i. On January 31, 50,000 common shares were issued for $200,000.
ii. On July 31, 75,000 common shares were issued for $350,000.
iii. Dividends on preferred stock of $100,000 were declared and paid.
iv. Dividends on common shares of $400,000 were declared and paid.
v. Net income for 2018 was $1,950,000.

Required:

a. Calculate the weighted-average number of common shares outstanding during 2018.
b. Calculate basic earnings per share for the year ended December 31, 2018.
c. Calculate return on shareholders' equity for the year ended December 31, 2018.
d. Prepare the shareholders' equity section for Fogo's December 31, 2018 balance sheet.

E10-10. **(Calculating earnings per share, LO 8)** For each of the following situations, calculate basic earnings per share for the year ended December 31, 2018:

	Situation A	Situation B	Situation C	Situation D	Situation E
Shares outstanding on December 31, 2017	100,000	250,000	1,000,000	800,000	10,000,000
Shares issued on June 30, 2018	0	0	0	0	2,000,000
Shares repurchased on June 30, 2018	0	50,000	0	0	0
Net income for 2018	$100,000	$525,000	($200,000)	$250,000	$25,000,000
Preferred dividends declared and paid during 2018	0	50,000	0	100,000	1,000,000

E10-11. **(Accounting for equity transactions, LO 2, 3)** During the year ended December 31, 2017, Roxana Corp. (Roxana) had the following equity-related transactions and economic events. On December 31, 2016, the balance in Roxana's common shares account was $4,000,000 with 1,000,000 shares outstanding, the balance in its preferred shares account was $0 with no shares outstanding, and retained earnings was $2,375,000.

i. On January 2, Roxana issued 200,000 common shares for $1,000,000.
ii. On February 28, Roxana issued 50,000 preferred shares for $1,250,000.
iii. On June 30, Roxana paid a dividend of $0.10 per common share.
iv. On September 30, Roxana declared a reverse stock split whereby the number of shares outstanding was reduced by half. A shareholder that had 1,000 shares before the reverse stock split would have 500 after the split.
v. On December 31, Roxana paid dividends to preferred shareholders of $2 per share.
vi. On December 31, Roxana paid a dividend of $0.10 per common share.
vii. Net income for 2017 was $1,150,000.

Required:

a. Prepare the journal entries required to record items (i) through (vi).
b. Prepare the equity section of Roxana's balance sheet on December 31, 2017 and provide comparative information for December 31, 2016.
c. Show the equity section of Roxana's balance sheet as it would have been reported in the December 31, 2016 financial statements. Explain the difference between the equity section for 2016 as reported in the 2017 annual report versus the 2016 annual report.
d. Calculate earnings per share and return on shareholders' equity for the year ended December 31, 2017. If earnings per share for 2016 had been reported as $1.75 per share, what amount would be reported for the year ended December 31, 2016 in the 2017 annual report?
e. How did the reverse stock split affect the performance of Roxana?

E10-12. **(Reporting shareholders' equity and assessing the ability to pay dividends, LO 2, 3, 8)** Kamsack Inc. (Kamsack) was formed in July 2017 to distribute imports from China. During its first year Kamsack had the following equity transactions:

i. Issued 100,000 common shares to its two shareholders for $10 per share.
ii. Issued 50,000 common shares to the owner of a Chinese company for the exclusive distribution rights in Canada for certain products made by companies she owned. The value of the shares and the exclusive rights is estimated to be about $400,000.
iii. Issued 1,500 preferred shares for $100 each. The preferred shares pay no dividends but must be repurchased by Kamsack within five years for $150 per share.
iv. For the year ended June 30, 2018, Kamsack reported a net loss of $50,000.

Required:

a. Prepare the journal entries need to recorded events (i), (ii), and (iii).
b. Prepare Kamsack's equity section as it should be reported on its June 30, 2018 balance sheet.
c. Can Kamsack pay a dividend on June 30, 2018? Explain your answer. (Think carefully; this question is tricky.)

E10-13. **(Accounting for equity transactions, LO 2, 3)** On June 30, 2017, Utusivik's equity section was as follows:

Preferred shares (500,000 shares authorized, 25,000 outstanding)	$ 2,000,000
Share capital (5,000,000 shares authorized, 1,000,000 outstanding)	8,000,000
Accumulated other comprehensive income	85,000
Retained earnings	11,900,000

During the year ended June 30, 2018, Utusivik Inc. (Utusivik) had the following equity-related transactions and economic events.

i. On August 1, 2017, Utusivik issued 500,000 common shares for $22 each.
ii. On November 30, 2017, Utusivik issued 50,000 preferred shares for $80 each.
iii. On December 31, 2017, Utusivik declared and paid a dividend of $0.75 per common share.
iv. On April 30, 2018, Utusivik declared a three-for-one stock split.
v. On June 29, 2018, Utusivik obtained the rights to a patent in exchange for 60,000 Utusivik common shares. The market value of Utusivik stock on June 30, 2018 was $16 per share.
vi. On June 30, 2018, Utusivik declared and paid a dividend to preferred shareholders of $1.50 per share.
vii. On June 30, 2018, Utusivik declared and paid a dividend of $0.85 per common share.
viii. Net income for 2018 was $4,500,000.
ix. Comprehensive income for 2018 was $4,600,000.

Required:

a. Prepare the journal entries required to record items (i) through (vii).
b. Prepare the equity section of Utusivik's balance sheet on June 30, 2018 and provide comparative information for June 30, 2017.
c. Show the equity section of Utusivik's balance sheet as it would have been reported in the June 30, 2017 annual report. Explain the difference between the equity section for 2017 as reported in the 2018 annual report versus the 2017 annual report.
d. Calculate earnings per share and return on shareholders' equity for the year ended June 30, 2018. If earnings per share for 2017 had been reported as $1.80 per share, what amount would be reported for 2017 in the 2018 annual report?
e. How did the stock split affect the performance of Utusivik?

E10-14. **(Calculating earnings per share, LO 2, 3, 8)** For the year ended December 31, 2017 Savory Inc. (Savory) reported net income of $750,000. On December 31, 2016, Savory had the following capital stock outstanding:

Preferred shares, no par, $5 annual dividend, cumulative, authorized 50,000 shares and 50,000 shares outstanding	$ 750,000
Common shares, no par, authorized 800,000 shares; issued and 400,000 shares outstanding	3,000,000

On May 31, 2017, Savory issued 40,000 common shares for $480,000 and on September 30, 2017 it issued 50,000 common shares for $750,000. On September 30, 2017, Savory declared and paid the dividend on the preferred shares. No common share dividends were paid in the year.

Required:

a. Calculate Savory's basic earnings per share for the year ended December 31, 2017.
b. How much of a dividend should Savory's shareholders expect to receive in 2018?

E10-15. **(Calculating earnings per share, LO 2, 3, 8)** For the year ended December 31, 2017, Wabush Inc. (Wabush) reported net income of $11,700,000. On December 31, 2016, Wabush had the following capital stock outstanding:

Preferred shares, no par, $2.50 annual dividend, cumulative, authorized 5,000,000 shares, and 1,000,000 shares outstanding	$ 25,000,000
Common shares, no par, authorized: 150,000,000 shares; issued and outstanding: 75,000,000 shares	185,000,000

On June 30, 2017, Wabush repurchased 5,000,000 common shares for $7.50 per share. Preferred dividends were paid during the year. No dividends in common shares were paid during the year.

Required:

a. Calculate Wabush's basic earnings per share for the year ended December 31, 2017.
b. How much of a dividend should Wabush's shareholders expect to receive in 2018?

E10-16. **(Impact of equity transactions on the statement of cash flows, LO 2, 3, 8)** Indicate if each of the following transactions and economic events would appear in the cash flow statement. If it does appear in the cash flow statement, would it be reported as cash from operations, an investing cash flow, or a financing cash flow? Explain your reasoning.

a. Conversion of preferred shares into common shares
b. Issuance of common shares for capital assets
c. Stock split of 3:1
d. Payment of cash dividends on common shares
e. Payment of cash dividends on preferred shares
f. Declaration of cash dividends on common shares
g. Issuance of common shares for cash
h. Issuance of preferred shares for cash
i. Distribution of a stock dividend
j. Payment of a property dividend
k. Repurchase of common shares for cash
l. Exercise of stock options by employees

E10-17. **(The difference between par and no par value shares, LO 2, 8)** What is the required journal entry for each of the following transactions?

a. 25,000 shares of no par value shares are issued for $30 per share.
b. 25,000 shares of $0.10 par value shares are issued for $30 per share.
c. 25,000 shares of $1.00 par value shares are issued for $30 per share.
d. What effect does par value have on the financial statements? Does par value affect any ratios or the interpretation of the financial statements? Explain.

E10-18. **(Accounting for dividends, LO 3, 8)** Gogama Ltd. (Gogama) is planning on declaring a dividend for its common shareholders and is considering three alternatives. The dividend would be declared on December 31:

i. Declare a cash dividend of $5 per share.
ii. Declare a property dividend. Shareholders would receive two common shares of Judson Inc. (Judson) for each share of Gogama stock owned. Judson's common shares have a market value of $2.50 per share and were originally purchased by Gogama for $1 per share.
iii. Declare a 5 percent stock dividend. Shareholders would receive one Gogama common share for each 20 shares of Gogama stock owned. The current market value of Gogama's stock is $100.

Gogama's year-end is December 31. The balances in the common shares and retained earnings accounts on December 31, 2017 are $7,500,000 and $12,500,000 respectively, after accounting for net income for the year but before accounting for the dividend. Gogama currently has 500,000 common shares outstanding and net income for 2017 is $1,750,000.

Required:

a. Prepare the journal entries required to record each of the dividends. State any assumptions you make.
b. How would the equity section of Gogama's December 31, 2017 balance sheet be affected by the three dividends? Show the effect of each dividend separately.
c. What would basic earnings per share be under each dividend alternative?
d. What difference does it make which dividend alternative Gogama chooses? Is there an economic difference among the three? Explain. Under what circumstances might one dividend alternative be preferred by Gogama over the others?
e. Suppose that instead of paying a property dividend, Gogama sold its shares in Judson and used the proceeds of the sale to pay a cash dividend. Prepare the journal entries required to record the sale of the Judson shares and the declaration and payment of the dividend. What is the difference between paying a property dividend and selling the shares and using the proceeds to pay a dividend?

E10-19. (Calculating dividend payout ratio and dividend yield, LO 8) Havelock Ltd. is a small public company. You are provided with the following information for the years ended December 31, 2016 and 2017:

	2016	2017
Net income	$ 1,800,000	$ 2,100,000
Earnings per share	$0.18	$0.21
Common dividends per share	$0.09	$0.09
Market value per share on December 31	$2.25	$2.75
Common shares outstanding during the year	10,000,000	10,000,000
Note: There was no change in the number of common shares outstanding from January 1, 2016 to December 31, 2017.		

Required:

a. What are the dividend payout ratio and dividend yield in each year? Explain what each amount means.
b. Why did the dividend payout ratio and dividend yield change from 2016 to 2017?
c. Havelock's net income and EPS increased in 2017.Why didn't the dividend paid increase as well?
d. Are high dividend payout ratio and dividend yield always attractive to investors?

E10-20. (Calculating ratios, LO 8) Ioco Ltd. is a public company. You are provided with the following information for the years ended December 31, 2016 and 2017:

	2016	2017
Net income	$125,000,000	$125,000,000
Earnings per share	$1.25	$1.25
Common dividends per share	$0.25	$0.25
Market value per share on December 31	$6.25	$7.10
Common shares outstanding during the year	100,000,000	100,000,000
Note: There was no change in the number of common shares outstanding from January 1, 2016 to December 31, 2017.		

Required:

a. What are the dividend payout ratio and dividend yield in each year? Explain what each amount means.
b. Why did the dividend yield change from 2016 to 2017 while the dividend payout ratio stayed the same?
c. What is preferred by investors, high or low dividend payout ratios and dividend yields?

E10-21. (Calculating dividend payout ratio and dividend yield, LO 8) Abney Ltd. is a public company. You are provided with the following information for the years ended December 31, 2015–2017. Amounts are in thousands of dollars, except for per share amounts:

	2017	2016	2015
Common dividends declared	$1,109,000	$1,015,000	$833,000
Cash dividends declared per common share	1.61	1.56	1.46
Net income	1,227,000	1,374,000	1,440,000
Common shareholders' equity	15,503,000	15,220,000	12,898,000
Market price per share on December 31	37.99	36.19	33.17
Weighted average number of shares outstanding	689,326	651,185	569,170

Required:

a. Calculate Abney's dividend payout ratio, dividend yield, basic earnings per share, and return on equity for 2015 through 2017. Assume that shareholders' equity on December 31, 2014 was $9,785,000.
b. Interpret the amounts you calculated in part (a).

E10-22. (Impact of stock dividends and stock splits, LO 3, 8) On December 31, 2017, Nehpton Ltd. reported $3 million of common shares and $6 million of retained earnings. On that date, the company had five million shares authorized and two million outstanding. Management is considering a 10 percent stock dividend or a two-for-one stock split and would like to know the impact on the equity section of the two transactions.

Required:

a. Prepare the equity section of Nehpton's balance sheet under the following conditions:
   i. As originally reported;
   ii. If management declared a 10 percent stock dividend;
   iii. If management declared a two-for-one stock split.
b. Explain how earnings per share would be affected in each case. Which situation would be most attractive to the shareholders?

E10-23. (Accounting for a partnership, LO 1) In July 2017, Mr. Irving and Ms. Ruth formed a partnership to offer consulting services. Mr. Irving contributed $40,000 in cash to the partnership and Ms. Ruth contributed non-cash assets with a market value of $100,000. During its first year of operations, the partnership earned revenues of $184,000 and incurred expenses of $100,000. Mr. Irving and Ms. Ruth agreed to divide the profits of the partnership in proportion to the value of their initial contributions. During the year, Mr. Irving withdrew $10,000 in cash from the partnership and Ms. Ruth withdrew $14,000 in cash. The partnership's first year-end is December 31, 2017.

Required:

a. Record the journal entries required for formation of the partnership.
b. Prepare the statement of partners' capital on December 31, 2017.

E10-24. **(Change in accounting estimate, LO 4)** On November 12, 2013, Josselin Inc. purchased a new front-end loader for $275,000 cash. Management estimated that the loader would have a useful life of 10 years and a residual value of $25,000. Near the end of fiscal 2017, management reassessed the useful life of the loader and decided that because the workload of the loader was much heavier than originally expected, its useful life would probably be about eight years and the residual value about $35,000. Josselin's year-end is October 31 and the company uses straight-line depreciation for this type of asset.

Required:

a. Prepare the journal entry to record the purchase of the loader in 2013.
b. What journal entry would be made in 2017 to reflect the change in the estimated useful life of the loader?
c. What would the depreciation expense for the loader be in fiscal 2014? Prepare the journal entry to record the depreciation expense.
d. What would the depreciation expense for the loader be in fiscal 2018? Prepare the journal entry to record the depreciation expense.
e. Suppose the loader was sold in on January 31, 2020 for $42,000. Prepare the journal entry to record the sale.

E10-25. **(Units-of-production depreciation and change in accounting estimate, LO 4)** Grindstone Corp. (Grindstone) produces fad toys for children. In 2015, Grindstone purchased a new stamping machine to produce the latest fad toy. The machine cost $30,000 plus non-refundable taxes of $2,100, and delivery and installation of $1,000. Grindstone's management estimates that the market for the toy is about 250,000 units and demand for the toy will last no more than four years. Management expects that it will be able to produce and sell 30,000 units in 2015, 150,000 units in 2016, 65,000 units in 2017, and 5,000 units in 2018. Once the fad dies, the machine won't be useful for any purpose and will have to be sold for scrap, about $2,000. Grindstone will use units-of-production depreciation for the machine.

Required:

a. Prepare the journal entry to record the purchase of the new machine.
b. Prepare a depreciation schedule showing the depreciation expense for each year and the carrying of the machine at the end of each year.
c. Suppose that early in 2017, Grindstone's management realized that the fad would last longer than expected and that it would be able to sell 100,000 units in 2017, 50,000 in 2018, and 10,000 in 2019, at which time the machine would be scrapped and Grindstone would receive $1,000. Prepare a depreciation schedule showing the depreciation expense for 2017, 2018, and 2019, and the carrying costs of the machine at the end of each year.

E10-26. **(Calculate financial ratios, LO 8)** Utterson Inc. (Utterson) is a small manufacturing company in northern Ontario. Utterson's owner has approached you to take an equity position in the company. The owner has provided the balance sheets for the last two years. In addition, you have learned that net income in 2017 was $35,000, interest expense was $11,000, $5,000 in dividends was paid on the preferred shares, and $10,000 was paid on the common shares on December 31. Utterson's tax rate is 18 percent. The estimated market value of Utterson's shares on December 31, 2017 was $15 per share, the weighted-average number of shares outstanding during 2017 was 20,000, and there were 25,000 shares outstanding on December 31, 2017.

Utterson Inc. Balance sheets as of December 31,					
	2017	2016		2017	2016
Assets			**Liabilities and Shareholders' Equity**		
Current assets	$100,000	$ 90,000	Current liabilities	75,000	$ 73,000
Non-current assets	264,000	240,000	Long-term debt	110,000	127,000
			Preferred shares	25,000	25,000
			Common shares	70,000	50,000
			Accumulated other comprehensive income	5,000	(4,000)
			Retained earnings	79,000	59,000
Total assets	$364,000	$330,000	Total liabilities and shareholders' equity	$364,000	$330,000

Required:

Calculate the following ratios for 2017: current ratio, debt-to-equity ratio, return on assets, return on equity, basic earnings per share, dividend payout ratio, dividend yield, and price-to-book ratio.

Problems

P10-1. **(Effect of transactions and economic events on ratios, LO 2, 3, 5, 6, 8)** Complete the following table by indicating whether the listed transactions or economic events would increase, decrease, or have no effect on the financial ratios listed. Explain your reasoning and state any assumptions that you make.

	Debt-to-equity ratio	Return on equity	Dividend payout ratio	Price-to-book ratio
	1.2:1	12.4%	25%	2.1
Stock dividend				
Payment of a cash dividend that was declared in a previous period				
Issue of common shares for land				
Purchase by the company of its own shares for cash				
Declaration and payment of a cash dividend; the dividend was higher than last year and net income is unchanged				

P10-2. **(Effect of transactions and economic events on ratios, LO 2, 3, 5, 6, 8)** Complete the following table by indicating whether the listed transactions or economic events would increase, decrease, or have no effect on the financial ratios listed. Explain your reasoning and state any assumptions that you make.

	Return on assets	Basic earnings per share	Current ratio	Dividend yield
	6.9%	$1.72	1.23	3.1%
Issue of common shares for cash				
Conversion of long-term debt to common shares				
Two-for-one stock split				
Declaration of a cash dividend				
Increase in the market value of common shares				

P10-3. **(Effect of transactions and economic events on ratios, LO 2, 3, 5, 6, 8)** Complete the following table by indicating whether the listed transactions or economic events would increase, decrease, or have no effect on the financial ratios listed. Explain your reasoning and state any assumptions that you make.

	Return on assets	Basic earnings per share	Current ratio	Dividend yield
	6.9%	$1.72	1.23	3.1%
Stock dividend				
Payment of a cash dividend the was declared in a previous period				
Issue of common shares for land				
Purchase by the company of its own shares for cash				
Declaration and payment of a cash dividend; the dividend was higher than last year and share price is unchanged				

P10-4. **(Effect of transactions and economic events on ratios, LO 2, 3, 5, 6, 8)** Complete the following table by indicating whether the listed transactions or economic events would increase, decrease, or have no effect on the financial ratios listed. Explain your reasoning and state any assumptions that you make.

	Debt-to-equity ratio	Return on equity	Dividend payout ratio	Price-to-book ratio
	1.2	12.4%	25%	2.1
Issue of common shares for cash				
Conversion of long-term debt to common shares				
Two-for-one stock split				
Declaration of a cash dividend				
Increase in the market value of common shares				

P10-5. **(The effects of leverage, LO 5)** Chitek Inc. (Chitek) is an oil and gas exploration company operating in northern Canada. Chitek has not yet begun extracting oil or gas from the ground, but it's close to that stage. When Chitek was formed about 18 months ago, shareholders contributed $10,000,000 in exchange for 7,500,000 common shares in the company. Chitek now requires $15,000,000 of additional capital to exploit the resources it believes it has discovered.

Chitek's CEO is considering two options: sell additional shares in the company or borrow the required funds. If the company borrows, it will have to pay 8 percent interest per year. If it uses equity, it will have to sell 2,500,000 shares to raise the money.

Oil and gas exploration is a risky business. Performance is subject to many factors, including the quantity of oil and gas that can be economically extracted, the market price of the resource, and the ability to control costs. Chitek's CEO has projected two possible outcomes: a good outcome and a poor outcome. Under the good outcome, the CEO estimates that income from operations (income before financing costs) will be $3,500,000 in the first year. Under the poor outcome, the CEO estimates that income from operations will be $500,000 in the first year.

Assume Chitek has a tax rate of 16 percent, that all tax effects are reflected in operating income except for the tax effect of the additional debt or equity, and that the debt/equity is issued at the beginning of the year.

Required:

a. Prepare partial income statements for Chitek, assuming:
   i. Equity financing of the additional $15,000,000 and the good outcome.
   ii. Equity financing of the additional $15,000,000 and the poor outcome.
   iii. Debt financing of the additional $15,000,000 and the good outcome.
   iv. Debt financing of the additional $15,000,000 and the poor outcome.
b. Calculate basic earnings per share and return on shareholders' equity for the four scenarios described in (a).
c. Explain the advantages and disadvantages of Chitek using debt and the advantages and disadvantages of using equity.
d. If you were a prospective lender, would you lend $15,000,000 to Chitek? Explain.
e. Would you advise Chitek to use debt or equity to raise the additional $15,000,000? Explain.

P10-6. **(The effects of leverage, LO 5)** Thomas Macdiarmid is a successful entrepreneur. He recently sold off a successful venture and pocketed $6 million in cash. Thomas is now considering a new venture. He has an opportunity to purchase a rundown strip mall in a large city. The mall would cost about $3 million and the needed renovations would cost an additional $3 million. Since Thomas has the $6 million in cash, he could use his own money to finance the entire project but he's thinking that it might be a less risky strategy to diversify, invest only half the money in the mall project and put the rest in other investments. This would require borrowing the other $3 million. Thomas has already spoken with a prospective lender who said she would be prepared to lend the $3 million at 9 percent per year on a three-year term (the principal would have to be paid back in three years). Interest would have to be paid annually. Thomas estimates that the renovations would take about three months and the mall would be in full operation one month later.

Thomas recognizes that this is a fairly risky venture and he has come up with two possible estimates for the mall, a good news outcome and a bad news outcome. Under the good news outcome, the mall would generate $1,125,000 in operating income (income before interest) in each year once the renovations were complete. Under the bad news outcome, the mall would generate $250,000 in operating income (income before interest). Assume that the project would have a tax rate of 15 percent, and that all tax effects are reflected in operating income except for the tax effect of the additional debt or equity.

a. How much profit would the strip mall earn under each financing alternative and each outcome? What would Macdarmid's return on shareholders' equity for the four scenarios be?
c. Explain to Macdiarmid the advantages and disadvantages of using debt and the advantages and disadvantages of using equity.
d. If you were a prospective lender, would you lend $3 million to Macdiarmid? Explain.
e. Would you advise Macdiarmid to use debt or equity to raise the additional $3 million? Explain.

P10-7. **(Effect of employee stock options, LO 6, 8)** At its annual meeting in March 2017, the shareholders of Jasper Inc. (Jasper) approved a plan allowing the company's board of directors to grant stock options to certain employees as part of their compensation packages. During the year ended December 31, 2017, the board granted 200,000 options to its senior executives. The stock options were issued when Jasper's shares had a market price of $22 per share. The exercise price of the options is $24 per share.

During fiscal 2017, Jasper earned revenues of $37,345,000 and had cost of sales of $18,525,000; selling, general, and administrative expenses of $4,560,000; interest expense of $3,535,000; other expenses of $5,700,000; and an income tax expense of $1,340,000. The economic value of the stock options when they were issued was $1,200,000.

On December 31, 2017, the equity section showed the following:

Capital stock (unlimited number of common shares authorized; 7,000,000 outstanding)	$21,500,000
Retained earnings	18,950,000

During fiscal 2017, Jasper didn't issue or repurchase any common shares. Dividends of $0.10 were declared and paid during the year.

Required:

a. Prepare Jasper's income statement for the year ended December 31, 2017, assuming both that the value of the stock options is expensed when granted and assuming it isn't expensed.
b. Calculate basic earnings per share and return on shareholders' equity, assuming the value of the stock options is expensed when granted and assuming they aren't expensed.
c. What effect do the two treatments for employee stock options have on cash flow?
d. Which accounting approach do you think Jasper's managers would prefer? Explain.
e. Which approach do you think gives a better representation of Jasper's economic performance?
f. If Jasper didn't accrue the cost of the options in its financial statements, what information would you want disclosed about them? Explain.

P10-8. **(Effect of employee stock options, LO 6, 8)** At its annual meeting in June 2016, the shareholders of Rusylvia Ltd. (Rusylvia) approved a plan allowing the company's board of directors to grant stock options to certain employees as part of their compensation packages. During the year ended March 31, 2017, the board granted 200,000 options to its senior executives. The stock options were issued when Rusylvia's shares had a market price of $10 per share. The exercise price of the options is $10.25 per share.

During fiscal 2017, Rusylvia earned revenues of $34,500,000, and had cost of sales of $15,200,000; selling, general, and administrative expenses of $4,800,000; interest expense of $3,500,000; other expenses of $5,900,000; and an income tax expense of $1,220,000. The estimated value of the stock options when they were issued was $1,800,000.

On March 31, 2016, the equity section showed the following:

Preferred shares (unlimited number authorized; 400,000 outstanding, $3 annual dividend, cumulative)	$16,000,000
Common shares (unlimited number authorized; 8,000,000 outstanding)	9,000,000
Retained earnings	14,850,000

In March 2017, Rusylvia declared and paid the dividend on the preferred shares and declared and paid a cash dividend of $0.25 per share on the common shares.

Required:

a. Prepare Rusylvia's income statement for the year ended March 31, 2017,
   i. assuming that the options are expensed.
   ii. assuming that the options aren't expensed.
b. Calculate basic earnings per share and return on shareholders' equity, assuming both that the value of the stock options is expensed when granted, and assuming it isn't expensed.
c. What effect do the two treatments for employee stock options have on cash flow?
d. Which accounting approach do you think Rusylvia's managers would prefer? Explain.
e. Which approach do you think gives a better representation of Rusylvia's economic performance?
f. If Rusylvia didn't accrue the cost of the options in its financial statements, what information would you want disclosed about them? Explain.

P10-9. **(Stock splits and dividends, LO 3, 8)** During the year ended December 31, 2017, Liberty Inc. reported the following equity events:

March 31, 2017	10 percent stock dividend
April 15, 2017	$1 cash dividend per share
June 30, 2017	Three-for-one stock split
October 15, 2017	$0.60 cash dividend per share

The equity section of Liberty's balance sheet on December 31, 2016 was as follows:

Common shares (unlimited number of shares 10,000,000 authorized, 1,000,000 issued and outstanding)	$ 5,750,000
Retained earnings	12,450,000

Net income for fiscal 2017 was $3,500,000. In previous years, Liberty paid its shareholders annual dividends of $2.50 per share.

Required:

a. Prepare Liberty's shareholders' equity section on December 31, 2017.
b. Calculate basic earnings per share for 2017. What would EPS have been if the stock split and stock dividend had not occurred?
c. As a Liberty shareholder, what is your reaction to the reduction in the per share dividend from $2.50 per share to $1.60 per share?
d. The market value of Liberty's shares on December 31, 2017 was $18.20 per share. What do you estimate the market price of the shares would have been had the stock dividend and stock split not occurred? Explain your answer.
e. Calculate Liberty's price-to-book ratio on December 31, 2017. What would the price-to-book ratio have been had the stock split and stock dividend not occurred?
f. What would Liberty's dividend payout ratio be for 2017 and the dividend yield on December 31, 2017? How would these amounts be affected by the stock dividend and stock split?

P10-10. (Stock splits and dividends, LO 3, 8) During the year ended November 30, 2017 Aguanish Inc. (Aguanish) reported the following equity events:

March 15, 2017	10 percent stock dividend
May 15, 2017	Annual preferred dividend of $3 per share
July 15, 2017	Four-for-one stock split
August 15, 2017	$1 dividend per common share

The equity section of Aguanish's balance sheet on November 30, 2016, was as follows:

Preferred shares (authorized, issued, and outstanding: 200,000)	$ 4,000,000
Common shares (unlimited number of shares authorized; 2,000,000 issued and outstanding)	18,500,000
Retained earnings	23,450,000

Net income for fiscal 2017 was $6,500,000. In previous years, Aguanish paid its common shareholders annual dividends of $5 per share.

Required:

a. Prepare Aguanish's shareholders' equity section on November 30, 2017.
b. Calculate basic earnings per share for fiscal 2017. What would EPS have been had the stock split and stock dividend not occurred?
c. As an Aguanish shareholder, what is your reaction to the reduction in the per share dividend from $5 per share to $1 per share?
d. The market value of Aguanish's shares on November 30, 2017 was $120 per share. What do you estimate the market price of the shares would have been had the stock dividend and stock split not occurred? Explain your answer.
e. Calculate Aguanish's price-to-book ratio on November 30, 2017. What would the price-to-book ratio have been had the stock split and stock dividend not occurred? Explain your answer.
f. From a shareholder's perspective, what are the benefits and drawbacks of the stock dividend and stock split?

P10-11. (Hybrid securities, LO 2) In May 2017, Kugluktuk Ltd. (Kugluktuk) sold $200,000 in convertible bonds to investors. The bonds have a coupon rate of 9 percent and mature in May 2027. The bonds are convertible into common shares at the option of the company. The terms of the bond agreement make it highly likely that the bonds will be converted before they mature. Kugluktuk's summarized balance sheet just before the convertible bonds were sold is shown:

Kugluktuk Ltd. Summarized balance sheet (just before the sale of convertible bonds)			
Assets	$2,400,000	Liabilities	$1,000,000
		Shareholders' equity	1,400,000
Total assets	$2,400,000	Total liabilities and shareholders' equity	$2,400,000

Required:

a. Do you think that the convertible bonds are debt or equity? Explain. (Consider the characteristics of debt and equity in your response.)
b. Prepare the journal entry to record the issuance of the convertible bond and calculate the resulting debt-to-equity ratio, assuming that the bonds are classified as debt.
c. Prepare the journal entry to record the issuance of the convertible bond and calculate the resulting debt-to-equity ratio, assuming that the bonds are classified as equity.
d. How do you think Kugluktuk's management would want to classify the convertible bonds for accounting purposes? Explain.

e. How do you think Kugluktuk's management would want to classify the convertible bonds for tax purposes? Explain.
f. How do you think Kugluktuk's management would account for the convertible bonds if the classification for tax purposes had to be the same as the classification for accounting purposes?
g. Does it matter how the convertible bonds are classified? Explain.

P10-12. **(Hybrid securities, LO 2)** In August 2017, Ethelbert Ltd. (Ethelbert) issued 10,000 shares of cumulative, redeemable preferred shares to investors for $500,000. The preferred shares pay an annual dividend of $4 per share and are redeemable beginning in 2019. Ethelbert must redeem the preferred shares before September 1, 2031. Ethelbert's summarized balance sheet just before the preferred shares were sold is shown:

Ethelbert Ltd. Summarized balance sheet (just before the sale of preferred shares)			
Assets	$4,400,000	Liabilities	$2,000,000
		Shareholders' equity	2,400,000
Total assets	$4,400,000	Total liabilities and shareholders' equity	$4,400,000

Required:
a. Do you think that the preferred shares are really debt or equity? Explain. (Consider the characteristics of debt and equity in your response.)
b. Prepare the journal entry to record the issuance of the preferred shares and calculate the resulting debt-to-equity ratio, assuming that the shares are classified as debt.
c. Prepare the journal entry to record the issuance of the preferred shares and calculate the resulting debt-to-equity ratio, assuming that the shares are classified as equity.
d. How do you think Ethelbert's management would want to classify the preferred shares for accounting purposes? Explain.
e. How do you think Ethelbert's management would want to classify the preferred shares for tax purposes? Explain.
f. How do you think Ethelbert's management would account for the preferred shares if the classification for tax purposes had to be the same as the classification for accounting purposes?
g. Does it matter how the preferred shares are classified? Explain.

P10-13. **(Analyzing the effects of different financing alternatives, LO 2, 8)** Owakonze Inc. (Owakonze), a privately owned corporation, is in need of $5,000,000 to finance an expansion of its operations. Management is considering three financing alternatives:

i. Issue 250,000 common shares to a group of private investors for $20 per share. In recent years, dividends of $0.75 per share have been paid on the common shares.
ii. Issue 50,000 cumulative preferred shares with an annual dividend of $6 per share for $100 per share. The preferred shares are redeemable after eight years for $112 per share.
iii. Issue a $5,000,000 bond with a coupon rate of 8.5 percent per year and maturity in 12 years.

It's now late July 2017. Owakonze's year-end is July 31. Owakonze plans to raise the needed money at the beginning of its 2018 fiscal year, but management wants to know the financial statement effects and implications of each alternative. Owakonze's accounting department has provided the right-hand side of the balance sheet as of July 31, 2017 and a summarized projected income statement for the year ended July 31, 2018. The projected statements don't reflect any of the proposed financing alternatives. One of Owakonze's existing loans has a covenant that requires the debt-to-equity ratio be below 1:1. Owakonze has a tax rate of 15 percent.

Owakonze Ltd. Summarized projected income statement for the year ended July 31, 2018	
Revenue	$ 5,600,000
Expenses	4,600,000
Income tax expense	150,000
Net income	$ 850,000

Owakonze Ltd. Liabilities and shareholders' equity as of July 31, 2017	
Liabilities	$ 7,500,000
Shareholders' equity:	
Preferred shares (200,000 shares authorized, 0 issued)	0
Common shares (unlimited number of shares authorized, 1,000,000 outstanding)	8,500,000
Retained earnings	7,000,000
Total liabilities and shareholders' equity	$23,000,000

Required:

a. Calculate projected net income for Owakonze under the three financing alternatives.
b. Calculate basic earnings per share and return on shareholders' equity under the three financing alternatives.
c. Prepare a report to Owakonze's management explaining the effect of each of the financing alternatives on the financial statements. Include in your report a discussion of the pros and cons of each financing alternative. Also, make a recommendation as to which alternative it should choose. Support your recommendation.

P10-14. (Different ways of looking at income, LO 2, 8) In the traditional approach to financial reporting in Canada, net income is thought of as the increase of wealth that belongs to the owners of the entity. In this view, interest is an expense, whereas dividends are a reduction of retained earnings. However, this is only one way to view an entity and its financial statements. Net income could also be calculated by expensing both interest and dividends. An alternative wouldn't treat interest, dividends, or income taxes as expenses.

During the year ended December 31, 2017, Atnarko Ltd. (Atnarko) had revenues of $2,450,000, expenses of $1,400,000, and income taxes of $115,000. In addition, Atnarko incurred interest costs of $170,000, and it declared and paid preferred share dividends of $75,000 and common share dividends of $150,000.

Required:

a. Prepare an income statement for Atnarko using the traditional approach. Explain why the measure of income is useful from the perspective of shareholders.
b. Devise three alternative measures of net income and prepare income statements on these bases. Explain which users of the income statement would find your alternative measures useful.

P10-15. (Assessing the payment of dividends, LO 8) Kintore Biotech Ltd. (Kintore) is a publicly traded generic pharmaceuticals company. Extracts from the last five years' financial statements are shown below.

Kintore completed an upgrade of its facilities in 2015 that was financed by a share issuance made in late 2014. Management believes that cash from operations should now be fairly stable and that net cash outflows on investing activities should range between $450,000 and $750,000 per year. Kintore's business is fairly stable, although there are significant uncertainties, such as the impact of new patent-protected drugs being introduced that are considered superior to Kintore's generic products. Kintore has access to a $1,000,000 line of credit secured against accounts receivable that it hasn't used to date. After two years of satisfactory and steady performance since the upgrade was completed, the board of directors is considering a proposal to implement an annual common share dividend. Kintore has never paid dividends before.

	2017	2016	2015	2014	2013
Assets					
Cash	$ 256,000	$ 187,500	$ 215,000	$ 950,000	$ 87,500
All other assets	4,454,000	3,855,000	3,387,500	2,250,000	1,525,000
Total assets	$4,710,000	$4,042,500	$3,602,500	$3,200,000	$1,612,500
Liabilities	$1,450,000	$1,300,000	$1,200,000	$1,100,000	$ 700,000
Shareholders' equity					
Capital stock (unlimited number of common shares authorized, 20,000,000 outstanding)	1,882,500	1,812,500	1,780,000	1,712,500	600,000
Retained earnings	1,377,500	930,000	622,500	387,500	312,500
Total shareholders' equity	3,260,000	2,742,500	2,402,500	2,100,000	912,500
Total liabilities and shareholders' equity	$4,710,000	$4,042,500	$3,602,500	$3,200,000	$1,612,500
Extracts from the cash flow statement					
Cash from operations	$ 565,000	$ 487,500	$ (125,000)	$ (37,500)	$ 112,500
Cash spent on investing activities	(382,500)	(300,000)	(775,000)	(600,000)	(450,000)

Required:

It's now early 2018. The chair of Kintore's board of directors has asked you to prepare a report assessing the pros and cons of implementing an annual common share dividend. Identify additional information needed to make a definitive decision. If you recommend that a dividend should be paid, what amount per share should be paid? Provide support for your positions.

P10-16. (Assessing leverage, LO 5, 8) Ferland Air Ltd. (Ferland) is a regional airline in western Canada. The company started up to provide air service to communities across the region and expanded quickly to meet the demand for service. Ferland borrowed heavily to finance the expansion but in recent years its growth has been more controlled and it hasn't needed to borrow. You are a financial analyst for a bank. You have been asked to prepare a report that examines Ferland's financial situation to assess how the company is financed (the amount of debt and equity) and evaluate its use of leverage. Your bank has been asked to consider whether it would provide financing for a possible expansion. Ferland is considering borrowing one to two million dollars so it can service some new centres and would like to know whether the balance sheet can support additional loans. Summarized liabilities and shareholders' equity from the last five years' balance sheets are provided below:

Ferland Air Ltd.
Summarized Liabilities and Shareholders' Equity
For the years ended December 31,

	2017	2016	2015	2014	2013
Current operating liabilities	$ 8,104,788	$ 7,278,350	$ 7,171,600	$ 5,215,488	$ 3,880,100
Current portion of long-term debt	2,297,363	2,149,588	2,076,450	2,167,088	1,925,950
Long-term debt	10,834,313	13,148,900	14,836,188	15,720,425	16,157,738
Common share capital	8,877,138	8,807,225	6,413,475	6,330,713	6,123,800
Retained earnings	10,099,725	8,740,025	7,639,638	5,692,063	3,951,538

Required:

Prepare the report.

P10-17. (Assessing financing alternatives, LO 2, 5, 8) Bindloss Ltd. is a small manufacturing company in Alberta that produces products needed by companies in the oil and gas industry. With the oil patch booming, Bindloss is looking for financing for a planned expansion. The company is currently owned by Harry Bindloss, who owns 100 percent of the outstanding shares of the company. The oil and gas industry is cyclical, so although Bindloss has been successful for the last few years it's likely that there will be years where the company doesn't do well. Harry Bindloss is considering two financing alternatives for the expansion: a $750,000 five-year, 9 percent term loan with equal principal repayments due at the end of each year ($150,000 of principal must be repaid each year) and interest payments due monthly. Alternatively, Harry has located an investor who would provide $750,000 of equity financing in exchange for a 25 percent interest in the company. The liabilities and shareholders' equity side of Bindloss's balance sheet as of its most recent year-end, along with a summarized income statement, is provided below.

Bindloss Ltd Summarized Liabilities and Shareholders' Equity As of December 31, 2017	
Bank loans	$ 100,000
Accounts payable and accrued liabilities	275,000
Current portion of long-term debt	75,000
Total current liabilities	450,000
Long-term debt	250,000
	700,000
Common share capital	250,000
Retained earnings	750,000
	1,000,000
Total liabilities and shareholders' equity	$1,700,000

Bindloss Ltd Summarized Income Statement For the year ended December 31, 2017	
Revenue	$2,150,000
Expenses	1,700,000
Interest expense	30,000
Net income	$ 420,000

During 2017, the company paid Mr. Bindloss $195,000 in dividends or $0.26 per share on his 750,000 shares.

Required:

Harry Bindloss would like you to prepare a report analyzing the pros and cons of each financing alternative. He would like you to explain the impact each alternative would have on the company's balance sheet, its income statement, and on measures of performance.

P10-18. **(Accounting changes, LO 4, 8)** On October 1, 2014, Independent Manufacturing Inc. (Independent) purchased a state-of-the-art mould-casting machine for $4,100,000. Independent's management estimated that the machine would be useful for five years and had a residual value of $250,000. Independent uses straight-line depreciation on all its capital assets. In September 2017, management realized that the useful life of the machine was going to be seven years. The estimated residual value is $175,000. Independent's year-end is September 30.

Required:

a. What depreciation expense would Independent have originally reported in fiscal 2015 and 2016 for the machine? What would the carrying amount of the machine have been on September 30, 2016?

b. What depreciation expense would Independent have reported in fiscal 2015 and 2016 for the machine after the accounting change had been made?
c. What depreciation expense will Independent report for the machine for the year beginning ended September 30, 2017, assuming the residual value remains $175,000? What would the carrying amount of the machine be on September 30, 2017?
d. What is the economic significance of this change? How are accounting ratios affected by the change? What are the implications of this change to users of the financial statements? Explain.
e. Do you think this type of change can be objectively made? Explain. What possible motivations could Independent's managers have for making the change? Explain.

P10-19. **(Earnings per share, LO 8)** Nisku Inc. (Nisku) and Grimsby Ltd. (Grimsby) are similar companies. You are considering investing in one of them and have received information about each for the year ended December 31, 2017.

	Nisku Inc. income statement	Grimsby Ltd. income statement
	For the year ended December 31, 2017	For the year ended December 31, 2017
Revenue	$3,125,000	$3,125,000
Cost of sales	1,187,500	1,187,500
Gross margin	1,937,500	1,937,500
Other expenses	1,406,250	1,406,250
Income before taxes	531,250	531,250
Income tax expense	79,687	79,687
Net income	$ 451,563	$ 451,563
	Shareholders' equity Common shares: Authorized: unlimited Outstanding: 1,000,000	*Shareholders' equity* Common shares: Authorized: unlimited Outstanding: 4,000,000
Share capital*	$ 625,000	$ 625,000
Retained earnings	3,375,000	3,375,000
Shareholders' equity	$4,000,000	$4,000,000

*During 2017, no new shares were issued during the year and each company paid dividends of $187,500.

Required:

Calculate EPS and ROE for both companies and decide which one you would invest in. Explain your conclusion.

P10-20. **(Comparing performance on a per share basis, LO 2, 8)** Kepenkeck Ltd. and Opeongo Inc. are Canadian public companies. You are provided with the following information for the years ended December 31, 2017:

	Kepenkeck Ltd.	Opeongo Inc.
Current liabilities	$12,785,000	$ 12,785,000
Non-current liabilities	35,250,000	35,250,000
Shareholders' equity	72,052,500	72,052,500
Net income	23,750,000	23,750,000
Cash dividends declared and paid	8,000,000	8,000,000
Market value of shares on December 31	15.00	7.50
Weighted-average number of common shares outstanding	50,000,000	100,000,000

Required:

a. Calculate earnings per share and dividends per share for the two companies along with the dividend payout ratio and the dividend yield.
b. Use the information you calculated in a. to compare the performance of the two companies. Explain any differences you found. Which company performed better? Explain.

Using Financial Statements

HUSKY ENERGY INC.

Husky Energy Inc. (Husky) is an integrated energy company operating primarily in Canada and the United States. It operates in three segments: Upstream, Midstream, and Downstream. The Upstream segment explores for, develops, and produces crude oil, bitumen, natural gas, and natural gas liquids. The Midstream segment markets crude oil, bitumen, natural gas, natural gas liquids, sulphur, and petroleum coke; pipeline transportation and processing of crude oil and natural gas; storage of crude oil, diluents, and natural gas; and cogeneration of electrical and thermal energy. The Downstream segment upgrades heavy crude oil feedstock into synthetic crude oil; markets refined petroleum products; and refines crude oil. As of December 31, 2011, the company had 549 independently operated Husky- and Mohawk-branded petroleum product outlets. Husky is headquartered in Calgary, Alberta, and is publicly traded on the Toronto Stock Exchange under the symbols HSE and HSE.PR.A.[7]

Husky's consolidated balance sheets, statements of income and comprehensive income and shareholders' equity, and extracts from the statements cash flows and the notes to the financial statements are provided in Exhibit 10.6. Use this information to answer questions FS10-1 to FS10-8.[8]

EXHIBIT 10.6 Husky Energy Inc.

CONSOLIDATED FINANCIAL STATEMENTS

Consolidated Balance Sheets

(millions of dollars)	December 31, 2011	December 31, 2010	January 1, 2010
Liabilities and Shareholders' Equity			
Current liabilities			
Accounts payable and accrued liabilities *(note 13)*	2,867	2,506	1,941
Income taxes payable	–	–	270
Asset retirement obligations *(note 16)*	116	63	29
Long-term debt due within one year *(note 14)*	407	–	–
	3,390	2,569	2,240
Long-term debt *(note 14)*	3,504	4,187	3,229
Other long-term financial liabilities *(note 22)*	–	102	96
Other long-term liabilities *(note 15)*	342	289	284
Contribution payable *(notes 8, 22)*	1,437	1,427	1,500
Deferred tax liabilities *(note 17)*	4,329	3,767	3,705
Asset retirement obligations *(note 16)*	1,651	1,135	738
Commitments and contingencies *(note 20)*			
Total Liabilities	14,653	13,476	11,792
Shareholders' equity			
Common shares *(note 18)*	6,327	4,574	3,585
Preferred shares *(note 18)*	291	–	–
Retained earnings	11,097	10,012	10,099
Other reserves	58	(12)	32
Total Shareholders' Equity	17,773	14,574	13,716
Total Liabilities and Shareholders' Equity	32,426	28,050	25,508

EXHIBIT 10.6 (continued) Husky Energy Inc.

Consolidated Statements of Income

Year ended December 31 (millions of dollars, except share data)	2011	2010
Gross revenues	24,489	18,085
Royalties	(1,125)	(978)
Revenues, net of royalties	23,364	17,107
Expenses		
Purchases of crude oil and products	14,264	10,580
Production and operating expenses	2,518	2,309
Selling, general and administrative expenses	428	291
Depletion, depreciation, amortization and impairment *(note 7)*	2,519	1,992
Exploration and evaluation expenses *(note 6)*	470	438
Other—net	(189)	(15)
	20,010	15,595
Earnings from operating activities	3,354	1,512
Financial items *(note 14)*		
Net foreign exchange gains (losses)	10	(49)
Finance income	86	79
Finance expenses	(310)	(325)
	(214)	(295)
Earnings before income taxes	3,140	1,217
Provisions for income taxes *(note 17)*		
Current	354	188
Deferred	562	82
	916	270
Net earnings	2,224	947
Earnings per share *(note 18)*		
Basic	2.40	1.11
Diluted	2.34	1.05
Weighted average number of common shares outstanding *(millions)*		
Basic	923.8	852.7
Diluted	932.0	852.7

The accompanying notes to the consolidated financial statements are an integral part of these statements.

Consolidated Statements of Comprehensive Income

Year ended December 31 (millions of dollars)	2011	2010
Net earnings	2,224	947
Other comprehensive income (loss)		
Derivatives designated as cash flow hedges, net of tax *(note 22)*	–	6
Actuarial losses on pension plans, net of tax *(note 19)*	(20)	(14)
Exchange differences on translation of foreign operations, net of tax	88	(91)
Hedge of net investment, net of tax *(note 22)*	(18)	41
Other comprehensive income (loss)	50	(58)
Comprehensive income	2,274	889

EXHIBIT 10.6 (continued) Husky Energy Inc.

Consolidated Statements of Changes in Shareholders' Equity

	Attributable to Equity Holders					
				Other Reserves		
(millions of dollars)	Common Shares *(note 18)*	Preferred Shares *(note 18)*	Retained Earnings	Foreign Currency Translation *(note 22)*	Hedging *(note 22)*	Total Shareholders' Equity
Balance as at January 1, 2010	3,585	–	10,099	40	(8)	13,716
Net earnings	–	–	947	–	–	947
Other comprehensive income (loss)						
Derivatives designated as cash flow hedges (net of tax of $2 million)	–	–	–	–	6	6
Actuarial losses on pension plans (net of tax of $6 million)	–	–	(14)	–	–	(14)
Exchange differences on translation of foreign operations (net of tax of $16 million)	–	–	–	(91)	–	(91)
Hedge of net investment (net of tax of nil)	–	–	–	41	–	41
Total comprehensive income (loss)	–	–	933	(50)	6	889
Transactions with owners recognized directly in equity						
Issue of common shares	1,000	–	–	–	–	1,000
Share issue costs	(12)	–	–	–	–	(12)
Exercise of options	1	–	–	–	–	1
Dividends declared on common shares *(note 18)*	–	–	(1,020)	–	–	(1,020)
Balance as at December 31, 2010	4,574	–	10,012	(10)	(2)	14,574
Net earnings	–	–	2,224	–	–	2,224
Other comprehensive income (loss)						
Derivatives designated as cash flow hedges (net of tax of less than $1 million)	–	–	–	–	–	–
Actuarial losses on pension plans (net of tax of $8 million)	–	–	(20)	–	–	(20)
Exchange differences on translation of foreign operations (net of tax of $14 million)	–	–	–	88	–	88
Hedge of net investment (net of tax of $3 million)	–	–	–	(18)	–	(18)
Total comprehensive income (loss)	–	–	2,204	70	–	2,274
Transactions with owners recognized directly in equity						
Issue of common shares	1,200	–	–	–	–	1,200
Share issue costs	(27)	–	–	–	–	(27)
Issue of preferred shares	–	300	–	–	–	300
Share issue costs	–	(9)	–	–	–	(9)
Stock dividends paid	580	–	–	–	–	580
Dividends declared on common shares *(note 18)*	–	–	(1,109)	–	–	(1,109)
Dividends declared on preferred shares *(note 18)*	–	–	(10)	–	–	(10)
Balance as at December 31, 2011	6,327	291	11,097	60	(2)	17,773

EXHIBIT 10.6 (continued) Husky Energy Inc.

Consolidated Statements of Cash Flows

Year ended December 31 (millions of dollars)	2011	2010
Operating activities		
Net earnings	2,224	947
Items not affecting cash:		
Accretion *(note 14)*	79	57
Depletion, depreciation, amortization and impairment *(note 7)*	2,519	1,992
Exploration and evaluation expenses *(note 6)*	68	200
Deferred income taxes *(note 17)*	562	82
Foreign exchange	14	30
Stock-based compensation *(note 18)*	(1)	(13)
Gain on sale of assets	(261)	(2)
Other	(6)	(221)
Settlement of asset retirement obligations *(note 16)*	(105)	(60)
Income taxes paid	(282)	(784)
Interest received	12	1
Change in non-cash working capital *(note 9)*	269	(7)
Cash flow—operating activities	5,092	2,222
Financing activities		
Long-term debt issuance	5,054	6,108
Long-term debt repayment	(5,434)	(5,028)
Debt issue costs	(5)	(12)
Proceeds from common share issuance, net of share issue costs *(note 18)*	1,173	988
Proceeds from preferred share issuance, net of share issue costs *(note 18)*	291	–
Dividends on common shares *(note 18)*	(495)	(1,020)
Dividends on preferred shares *(note 18)*	(7)	–
Interest paid	(143)	(181)
Capitalized interest paid	(86)	(51)
Other	324	49
Change in non-cash working capital *(note 9)*	238	232
Cash flow—financing activities	910	1,085
Investing activities		
Capital expenditures	(4,800)	(3,379)
Proceeds from asset sales *(note 10)*	179	9
Other	(115)	(150)
Change in non-cash working capital *(note 9)*	316	67
Cash flow—investing activities	(4,420)	(3,453)
Increase (decrease) in cash and cash equivalents	1,582	(146)
Effect of exchange rates on cash and cash equivalents	7	6
Cash and cash equivalents at beginning of year	252	392
Cash and cash equivalents at end of year	1,841	252

EXHIBIT 10.6 (continued) Husky Energy Inc.

Note 3 Significant Accounting Policies

k) Share Capital

Preferred shares are classified as equity since they are cancellable and redeemable only at the Company's option and dividends are discretionary and payable only if declared by the Board of Directors. Incremental costs directly attributable to the issuance of shares and stock options are recognized as a deduction from equity, net of tax. Common share dividends are paid out in common shares or in cash, and preferred share dividends are paid in cash. Both common and preferred share dividends are recognized as distributions within equity.

v) Earnings per Share

The number of basic common shares outstanding is the weighted average number of common shares outstanding for each period. Shares issued during the period are included in the weighted average number of shares from the date consideration is receivable. The calculation of basic earnings per common share is based on net earnings attributable to common shareholders divided by the weighted average number of common shares outstanding.

The number of diluted common shares outstanding is calculated using the treasury stock method, which assumes that any proceeds received from in-the-money stock options would be used to buy back common shares at the average market price for the period. The calculation of diluted earnings per share is based on net earnings attributable to common shareholders divided by the weighted average number of common shares outstanding adjusted for the effects of all dilutive potential common shares, which are comprised of share options granted to employees. Stock options granted to employees provide the holder with the ability to settle in cash or equity. For the purposes of the diluted earnings per share calculation, the Company must adjust the numerator for the more dilutive effect of cash-settlement versus equity-settlement despite how the stock options are accounted for in net earnings. As a result, net earnings reported based on accounting of cash-settled stock options may be adjusted for the results of equity-settlements for the purposes of determining the numerator for the diluted earnings per share calculation.

Note 18 Share Capital

Common Shares

The Company is authorized to issue an unlimited number of no par value common shares.

Changes to issued common share capital were as follows:

($ millions)	Number of Shares	Amount
January 1, 2010	849,860,935	3,585
Common shares issued, net of share issue costs	40,816,326	988
Options exercised	31,534	1
December 31, 2010	890,708,795	4,574
Common shares issued, net of share issue costs	44,362,214	1,173
Stock dividends	22,461,089	580
Options exercised	5,000	–
December 31, 2011	**957,537,098**	**6,327**

On December 7, 2010, Husky issued 11.9 million common shares at a price of $24.50 per share for total gross proceeds of $293 million via an overnight-marketed public offering. The Company also issued a total of 28.9 million common shares to the principal shareholders, L.F. Investments (Barbados) Limited and Hutchison Whampoa Luxembourg Holdings S.à.r.l. at a price of $24.50 per share for total gross proceeds of $707 million. The public offering was conducted under the Company's universal base shelf prospectus filed November 26, 2010 with the securities regulatory authorities in all provinces of Canada.

On June 29, 2011, Husky issued approximately 37 million common shares at a price of $27.05 per share for total gross proceeds of approximately $1.0 billion through a public offering, and a total of approximately 7.4 million common shares at a price of $27.05 per share for total gross proceeds of $200 million through a private placement to L.F. Investments (Barbados) Limited and Hutchison Whampoa Luxembourg Holdings S.à.r.l. The public offering was conducted under the Company's universal base shelf prospectus filed November 26, 2010 with the securities regulatory authorities in all provinces of Canada, the Company's universal base shelf prospectus filed June 13, 2011 with the Alberta Securities Commission and the U.S. Securities and Exchange Commission and the respective accompanying prospectus supplements.

Amendments to Common Share Terms

At the special meeting of shareholders held on February 28, 2011, the Company's shareholders approved amendments to the common share terms, which provide shareholders with the option to receive dividends in common shares or in cash. Quarterly dividends may be declared in an amount expressed in dollars per common share and paid by way of issuance of a fraction of a common share per

EXHIBIT 10.6 (continued) Husky Energy Inc.

outstanding common share determined by dividing the dollar amount of the dividend by the volume weighted average trading price of the common shares on the principal stock exchange on which the common shares are traded. The volume weighted average trading price of the common shares would be calculated by dividing the total value by the total volume of common shares traded over the five trading day period immediately prior to the payment date of the dividend on the common shares.

During the year ended December 31, 2011, the Company declared dividends payable of $1.20 per common share (2010—$1.20 per common share) resulting in dividends of $1.1 billion (2010—$1.0 billion). At December 31, 2011, $287 million was payable to shareholders on account of dividends declared on November 3, 2011.

Preferred Shares

The Company is authorized to issue an unlimited number of no par value preferred shares.

($ millions)	Number of Shares	Amount
January 1, 2011	–	–
Cumulative Redeemable Preferred Shares, Series 1 issued, net of share issue costs	12,000,000	291
December 31, 2011	**12,000,000**	**291**

On March 18, 2011, Husky issued 12 million Cumulative Redeemable Preferred Shares, Series 1 (the "Series 1 Preferred Shares") at a price of $25.00 per share for aggregate gross proceeds of $300 million. Net proceeds after share issue costs were $291 million. The Series 1 Preferred Shares were offered by way of a prospectus supplement under the short form base shelf prospectus filed November 26, 2010 with the securities regulatory authorities in all provinces of Canada.

Holders of the Series 1 Preferred Shares are entitled to receive a cumulative quarterly fixed dividend yielding 4.45% annually for the initial period ending March 31, 2016 as declared and when declared by the Company's Board of Directors. Thereafter, the dividend rate will be reset every five years at a rate equal to the 5-year Government of Canada bond yield plus 1.73%. Holders of Series 1 Preferred Shares will have the right, at their option, to convert their shares into Cumulative Redeemable Preferred shares, Series 2 (the "Series 2 Preferred Shares"), subject to certain conditions, on March 31, 2016 and on March 31 every five years thereafter. Holders of the Series 2 Preferred Shares will be entitled to receive cumulative quarterly floating rate dividends at a rate equal to the three-month Government of Canada Treasury Bill yield plus 1.73%.

In the event of liquidation, dissolution or winding-up of the Company, the holders of the Series 1 Preferred Shares will be entitled to receive $25 per share. All accrued unpaid dividends will be paid before any amounts are paid or any assets of the Company are distributed to the holders of any other shares ranking junior to the Series 1 Preferred Shares. The holders of the Series 1 Preferred Shares will not be entitled to share in any further distribution of the assets of the Company.

During the year ended December 31, 2011, the Company declared dividends payable of approximately $0.87 per Series 1 Preferred Share (2010—nil). An aggregate of $7 million was paid for the year ended December 31, 2011 and $3 million representing approximately $0.28 per Series 1 Preferred Share (2010—nil), was payable as dividends on the Series 1 Preferred Shares at December 31, 2011.

Stock Option Plan

Pursuant to the Incentive Stock Option Plan (the "Option Plan"), the Company may grant from time to time to officers and employees of the Company options to purchase common shares of the Company. The term of each option is five years and it vests one-third on each of the first three anniversary dates from the grant date. The Option Plan provides the option holder with the right to exercise the option to acquire one common share at the exercise price or surrender the option for a cash payment. The exercise price of the option is equal to the weighted average trading price of the Company's common shares during the five trading days prior to the grant date. For options granted up to 2009, when the option is surrendered for cash, the cash payment is the difference between the weighted average trading price of the Company's common shares on the trading day prior to the surrender date and the exercise price of the option. For options granted after 2009, when the option is surrendered for cash, the cash payment is the difference between the weighted average trading price of the Company's common shares for the five trading days following the surrender date and the exercise price of the option.

Certain options granted under the Option Plan and henceforth referred to as performance options vest only if certain shareholder return targets are met. The ultimate number of performance options that vest will depend upon the Company's performance measured over three calendar years. If the Company's performance is below the specified level compared with its industry peer group, the performance options awarded will be forfeited. If the Company's performance is at or above the specified level compared with its industry peer group, the number of performance options exercisable shall be determined by the Company's relative ranking. Stock compensation expense related to the performance options is accrued based on the price of the common shares at the end of the period and the anticipated performance factor. This expense is recognized over the three-year vesting period of the performance options. Performance options are no longer granted and the last grant was on August 7, 2009.

EXHIBIT 10.6 (continued) Husky Energy Inc.

Included in accounts payable and accrued liabilities and other long-term liabilities on the consolidated balance sheet at December 31, 2011 was $17 million (December 31, 2010—$19 million; January 1, 2010—$33 million) representing the estimated fair value of options outstanding. The total recovery recognized in selling, general and administrative expenses on the consolidated statements of income for the Option Plan for the year ended December 31, 2011 was $2 million (2010—recovery of $13 million). At December 31, 2011, stock options exercisable for cash had an intrinsic value of nil (December 31, 2010—nil; January 1, 2010—$1 million).

The following options to purchase common shares have been awarded to officers and certain other employees:

	2011		2010	
	Number of Options *(thousands)*	**Weighted Average Exercise Prices**	**Number of Options** *(thousands)*	**Weighted Average Exercise Prices**
Outstanding beginning of year	29,541	$ 37.04	28,399	$ 40.78
Granted[1]	9,618	$ 28.80	8,870	$ 27.95
Exercised for common shares	(5)	$ 28.19	(31)	$ 24.14
Surrendered for cash	–	$ –	(39)	$ 23.24
Expired or forfeited	(5,817)	$ 37.30	(7,658)	$ 40.50
Outstanding end of year	33,337	$ 34.62	29,541	$ 37.04
Exercisable end of year	18,486	$ 39.50	17,325	$ 41.20

[1]Options granted during the year ended December 31, 2011 were attributed a fair value of $4.41 per option (2010—$4.80) at grant date.

	Outstanding Options			Options Exercisable	
Range of Exercise Price	**Number of Options** *(thousands)*	**Weighted Average Exercise Prices**	**Weighted Average Contractual Life** *(years)*	**Number of Options** *(thousands)*	**Weighted Average Exercise Prices**
$24.96–$29.99	17,504	$ 28.45	4	2,792	$ 28.06
$30.00–$34.99	816	$ 31.25	2	677	$ 31.16
$35.00–$39.99	210	$ 39.97	1	210	$ 39.97
$40.00–$42.99	12,917	$ 41.60	–	12,917	$ 41.60
$43.00–$45.02	1,890	$ 45.02	2	1,890	$ 45.02
December 31, 2011	33,337	$ 34.62	2	18,486	$ 39.50

Earnings per Share

	2011	2010
Net earnings—basic *($ millions)*	2,214	947
Net earnings—diluted *($ millions)*	2,184	898
Weighted average common shares outstanding—basic *(millions)*	923.8	852.7
Weighted average common shares outstanding—diluted *(millions)*	932.0	852.7
Earnings per share—basic	$ 2.40	$ 1.11
Earnings per share—diluted	$ 2.34	$ 1.05

For the purposes of calculating net earnings–basic, net earnings were adjusted for dividends declared on preferred shares of $10 million for the year ended December 31, 2011 (2010—nil). Net earnings–diluted was calculated by adjusting net earnings–basic for the more dilutive effect of stock compensation expense based on cash-settlement versus equity-settlement of stock options. For the purposes of determining net earnings–diluted, stock compensation recovery was $2 million based on cash-settlement for the year ended December 31, 2011 (2010—recovery of $3 million). Stock compensation expense of $28 million for the year ended December 31, 2011 (2010—$36 million) was used to determine net earnings–diluted based on equity-settlement.

The diluted weighted average common shares outstanding was adjusted for 8.2 million common shares that were declared as stock dividends for the year ended December 31, 2011 (2010—nil). For the year ended December 31, 2011, 26 million tandem options and 7 million tandem performance options (2010—20 million tandem options and 10 million tandem performance options) were excluded from the calculation of diluted earnings per share as these options were anti-dilutive.

FS10-1. Examine the information provided in Exhibit 10.6 and find the following information:

a. Retained earnings on December 31, 2010 and 2011.
b. Dividends paid on common and preferred shares in 2010 and 2011.
c. Total shareholders' equity on December 31, 2010 and 2011.
d. Net income for the years ended December 31, 2010 and 2011.
e. Net assets on December 31, 2010 and 2011.
f. Comprehensive income for 2010 and 2011.
g. Number of common shares outstanding on December 31, 2010 and 2011.
h. Number of shares issues as stock dividends paid in 2011.
i. Other comprehensive income (loss) for the years ended December 31, 2010 and 2011.
j. Number of stock options granted in 2010 and 2011.
k. Amount reported for preferred shares on December 31, 2010 and 2011.

FS10-2. Use the information provided in Exhibit 10.6 and calculate the following ratios for the years ended December 31, 2010 and 2011. Interpret and explain your findings:

a. Earnings per share
b. Return on shareholders' equity
c. Debt-to-equity ratio

FS10-3. Answer the following questions about Husky's preferred shares:

a. What are the terms of the preferred shares?
b. How much did Husky raise by issuing preferred shares? What was the price per share? What were the costs associated with issuing the shares?
c. How many preferred shares did Husky issue?
d. How much was paid to preferred shareholders as dividends in 2011?
e. Why aren't preferred shares included in the calculation of earnings per share?

FS10-4. How much did Husky pay in cash as dividends to common shareholders in 2011? How much did it declare in dividends in 2011? Why are the amounts different? Why are dividends not included in the calculation of net income?

FS10-5. Use the information in Exhibit 10.6 to answer the following questions:

a. How many common shares did Husky sell during fiscal 2011 (excluding shares issued as part of the stock dividend and shares issued from the exercise of stock options)?
b. How much was each share sold for? How much did Husky receive after paying share issue costs?
c. What is the journal entry that Husky would have made to record the issue of shares in fiscal 2011?
d. What do you think the impact of repurchasing shares would have on the share price of the remaining outstanding shares?
e. Why do companies sell new shares to investors?

FS10-6. Examine the information in Note 18 to Husky's financial statements pertaining to the company's stock option plan and answer the following questions:

a. Describe the terms of the stock option plan.
b. How many employee stock options were outstanding on December 31, 2011? How many of the stock options could be exercised on December 31, 2011?
c. How many options were granted during fiscal 2011? What was the average exercise price of the options granted during fiscal 2011?
d. How many options were exercised during fiscal 2011? What was the average price paid for the shares purchased by the employees? Why do you think so few options were exercised?
e. How many options expired during fiscal 2011? Why would an employee allow an option to expire without exercising it?
f. What amount did Husky expense in fiscal 2011 as a result of granting stock options to employees? Why is the stock option expense added back to net income in the calculation of cash from operations?
g. What does it "cost" shareholders when a manager exercises a stock option?
h. What do you think is the purpose of Husky's share compensation plan?

FS10-7. Examine the information in Exhibit 10.6 and answer the following questions:

a. What was Husky's comprehensive income in fiscal 2010 and 2011?
b. What are the sources of the other comprehensive loss in 2011?
c. What is "other reserves" (accumulated other comprehensive income (loss)) on December 31, 2010 and 2011?
d. Why do you think other comprehensive income isn't just included in the calculation of net income?

FS10-8. During 2011, Husky issued a stock dividend. Answer the following questions about the stock dividend.

a. How many shares did Husky issue as the stock dividend?
b. What amount did Husky attribute to the stock dividend?
c. If you owned 10,000 Husky shares, how many new shares would you have received as a dividend?
d. What effect did the stock dividend have on the financial statements?
e. What journal entry would Husky have recorded to account for the stock dividend?
f. What impact, if any, do you think the stock dividend would have on Husky's earnings per share? Explain.
g. What impact, if any, do you think the stock dividend would have had on Husky's stock price? Explain.
h. As a Husky shareholder, would you be happy to receive the stock dividend (would the dividend make you better off)?

ENDNOTES

1. Extracted from Assiniboia Farmland Limited Partnership's 2011 financial statements.
2. Extracted from the University of Ontario Institute of Technology's 2011 financial statements.
3. Extracted from Potash Corporation of Saskatchewan's 2011 financial statements.
4. Extracted from TransCanada Pipelines Limited's 2011 annual report.
5. Extracted from *The Globe and Mail*, June 8, 2012 and http://www.theglobeandmail.com/report-on-business/careers/management/executive-compensation/executive-compensation-rankings-for-canadas-top-earners/article4243534.
6. Extracted from WestJet Airlines Ltd.'s 2011 annual report.
7. Adapted from Yahoo! Finance at http://finance.yahoo.com/q/pr?s=HSE.TO.
8. Extracted from Husky Energy Inc.'s 2011 audited financial statements.

CHAPTER

11

Investments in Other Companies

LEARNING OBJECTIVES

After studying the material in this chapter you will be able to do the following:

LO 1 Understand why companies invest in other companies.

LO 2 Describe how corporations account for their subsidiaries.

LO 3 Discuss the accounting for investments where there is significant influence.

LO 4 Explain the accounting for passive investments.

LO 5 (Appendix) Recognize the issues affecting financial statements in periods after a subsidiary is purchased.

Nineteen sweaty women in exercise gear are pumping their arms forward and doing a two-step to the beat of Latin dance music on a sunny June morning in Vaughan, Ontario, while the instructor, Elena, calls out "Four more!"

Onex Corporation

The Zumba cardio fitness class is being held at the new Schwartz-Reisman Centre north of Toronto, a recreation complex. Gerald Schwartz, who is president and CEO of the public Canadian equity firm Onex Corporation, together with his wife, Heather Reisman, who runs the Indigo Books and Music chain, donated $12 million to help build the new facility.

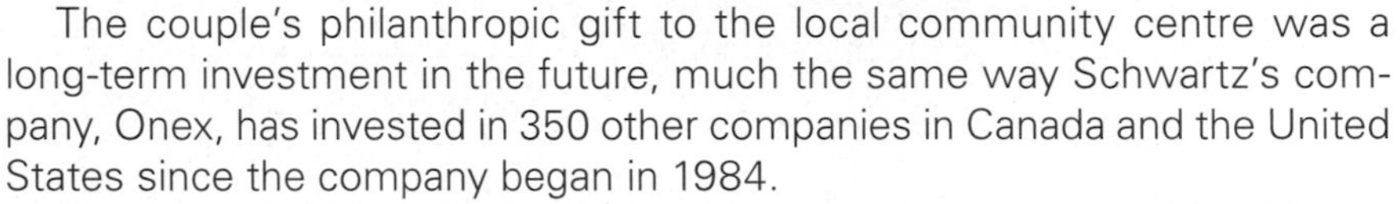

The couple's philanthropic gift to the local community centre was a long-term investment in the future, much the same way Schwartz's company, Onex, has invested in 350 other companies in Canada and the United States since the company began in 1984.

From the Tropicana Casino in Las Vegas, to aerospace and healthcare manufacturers, the investment strategy adopted by Onex has made Schwartz a billionaire: buying struggling businesses in diverse sectors, making them healthier, and selling them at a profit.

"We focus on businesses with considerable cost-saving opportunities to generate EBITDA growth as well as strong free-cash-flow characteristics to pay down debt. Our goal is to build market leaders and ultimately create value for our investors," reads the 2011 second-quarter earnings report.

Onex has stakes in many North American companies, both directly with the company's own money, including money from its own managers, and usually also with outside investors as partners.

Onex operates its own investment funds, such as Onex Partners, and ONCAP, Onex Real Estate, and Onex Credit Partners. The company Web site says that over the years, Onex has made back its money and more, pulling in three times its original investments, and boasting an annual compound return on investment of 29 percent.

Aside from the money Onex makes from buying and selling companies, it receives a committed stream of annual management fees and the opportunity to share in the profits of its third-party investors through carried interest participation.

Onex typically acquires a control position in its businesses, which enables it to exercise the rights of ownership, particularly the ability to make strategic decisions. It does not get involved in the daily operating decisions of the businesses.

While not all of the companies in Onex's portfolio are household names, it did have some high-profile targets in the past, such Air Canada in 1999, although the deal fell through. A hostile takeover of Labatt Breweries in 1995 also fizzled. Onex did take over Cineplex in 2002, selling most of its stake by 2009.

More recently, Onex bought Spirit AeroSystems in 2005, which was spun off from Boeing and still makes parts for both Boeing and Airbus. Back then, Onex spent $134 million on the deal. According to the Onex company Web site, to date, through sales of some of its Spirit shares, and a turnaround in the company, Onex has "realized" $828 million. Onex still owns 4 percent of the company.

–E.B.

INTRODUCTION

One of the first things I pointed out when we looked at Leon's Furniture Limited's financial statements in Chapter 2 was that the statements are consolidated. This means that the single set of statements is an aggregation of more than one corporation's financial information. The financial statements of most public companies are consolidated. Consolidated financial statements are required under IFRS when one company (the parent) controls other companies (subsidiaries). For example, the consolidated financial statements of Rogers Communications Inc. aggregate those of several separate, well-known companies, including Rogers Wireless, Rogers Sportsnet, and the Toronto Blue Jays. An overview of the Rogers' corporate group is shown in Figure 11.1.[1]

FIGURE 11.1 Rogers Communications Inc.: Corporate Organization

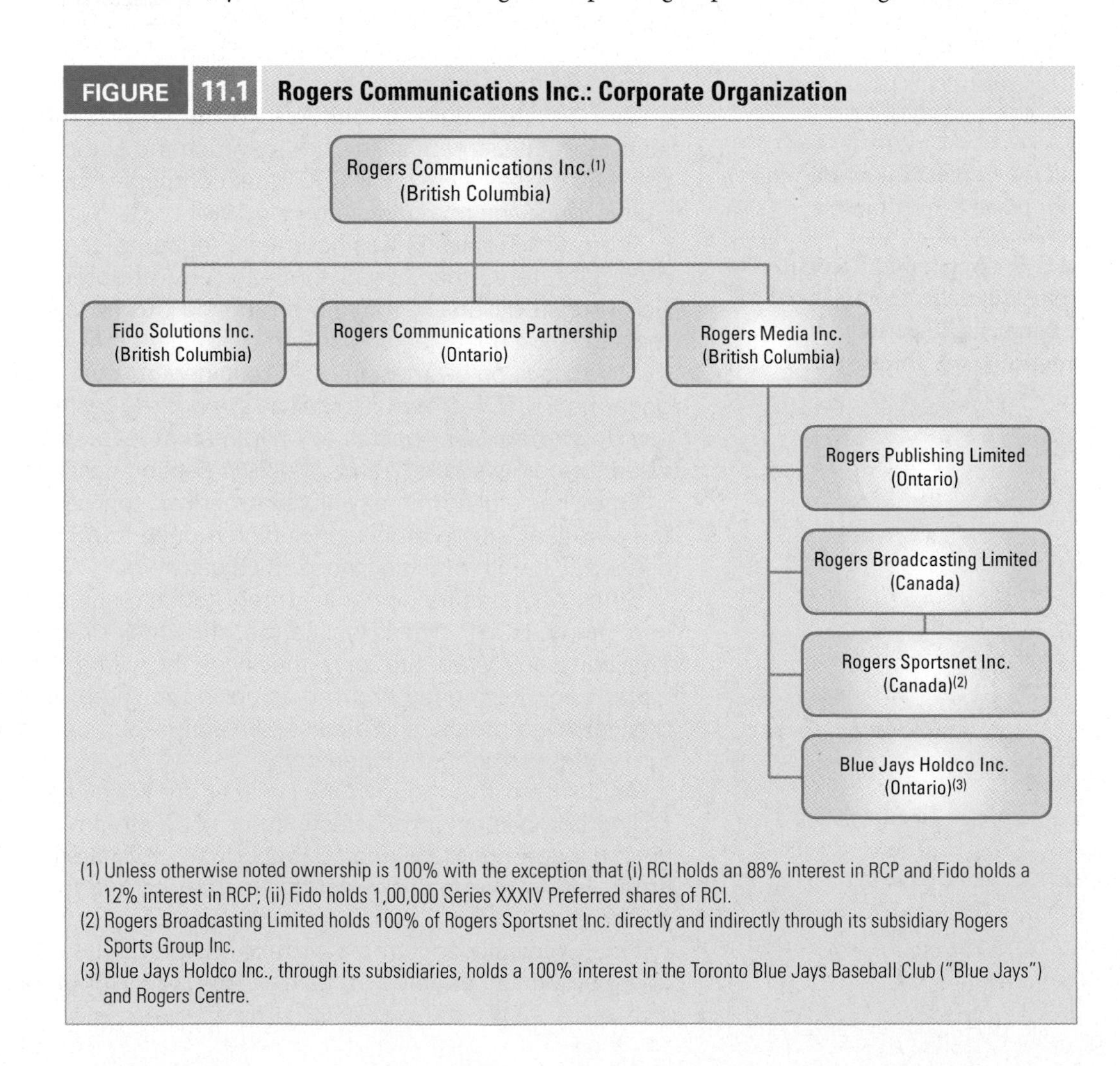

(1) Unless otherwise noted ownership is 100% with the exception that (i) RCI holds an 88% interest in RCP and Fido holds a 12% interest in RCP; (ii) Fido holds 1,00,000 Series XXXIV Preferred shares of RCI.

(2) Rogers Broadcasting Limited holds 100% of Rogers Sportsnet Inc. directly and indirectly through its subsidiary Rogers Sports Group Inc.

(3) Blue Jays Holdco Inc., through its subsidiaries, holds a 100% interest in the Toronto Blue Jays Baseball Club ("Blue Jays") and Rogers Centre.

The idea behind consolidated financial statements is to provide financial information about an entire economic entity, rather than just about the individual pieces. While the concept of consolidated financial statements is straightforward, it's among the most complicated topics in accounting. People studying to become accountants can spend an entire course on the subject.

Gaining control of another company is only one outcome of investment by one corporation in another. Some investments allow the investing corporation to influence the decisions of those companies, but not to control them. Other investments, usually small ones, give the investing corporation no more influence than any small investor would have. These investments, with their different degrees of influence, are each accounted for differently.

In many ways, this topic, particularly consolidation itself, is beyond the scope of an introductory accounting course. However, because consolidated financial statements are encountered so frequently, and because investment-related accounts like goodwill and non-controlling interest are so commonly seen in financial statements, it's important, even for the accounting novice, to be familiar with the subject. To that end, this chapter will provide a discussion of how corporations account for investment in other corporations and how those investments affect the financial statements. The intent is to provide just enough insight into accounting for investments that you can understand and interpret financial statement information relating to it. The appendix to this chapter will address some of the more complex aspects of this topic.

WHY DO COMPANIES INVEST IN OTHER COMPANIES?

LO 1

There are many reasons why one company invests in another. The reason can be as simple as needing to find a place to invest a temporary surplus of cash. For example, seasonal businesses may have excess cash during certain times of the year. Companies may be accumulating cash for future expansion or acquisitions and invest to earn a reasonable return on it in the meantime. This can be achieved by purchasing the debt or equity of other companies. These investments might provide opportunities to earn dividend, interest, and capital gains income for the investing company.

Other investments are strategic. Companies might purchase competing companies to reduce competition and expand their presence in a market. They might purchase their customers to provide markets for their products or their suppliers to ensure the availability of inputs.

For example, in May 2011 Microsoft purchased Skype of US$8.56 billion in cash, an acquisition that could provide Microsoft advantages in the tablet market and improve its video conferencing services. In the largest acquisition in Canada in 2011, Barrick Gold Corp., the largest gold company in the world, purchased Equinox Minerals Ltd., an Australian-based copper producer, for US$7.8 billion. By purchasing Equinox, Barrick increased its presence in the copper mining sector and expanded its portfolio of mining properties.

www.microsoft.com
www.skype.com
www.barrick.com
www.rogers.com
www.onex.com

Companies might also purchase all or part of other companies to diversify. Some businesses are cyclical—their performance depends on where the economy is in the business cycle. Cyclical businesses will be profitable in some years and not in others. By diversifying their investments in different businesses and geographic areas, companies try to mitigate the effect of the business cycle. For example, Onex Corporation has major investments in health care, entertainment, electronics, and financial services.

ACCOUNTING FOR INVESTMENTS IN OTHER CORPORATIONS: INTRODUCTION

LO 2, 3

How an **investor corporation**, or *investor* (a corporation with an investment in another corporation), accounts for its investment in an **investee corporation**, or *investee* (a corporation in which an investor corporation has invested), depends on the influence it has over the investee corporation. For accounting purposes, there are three levels of influence:

1. Control—An investor controls an investee and can make all its important decisions. An investee that is controlled is called a subsidiary of the investor, and the financial statements of the investor and investee are aggregated into a single set of consolidated financial statements.

FIGURE 11.2

Types of Investments in Other Corporations

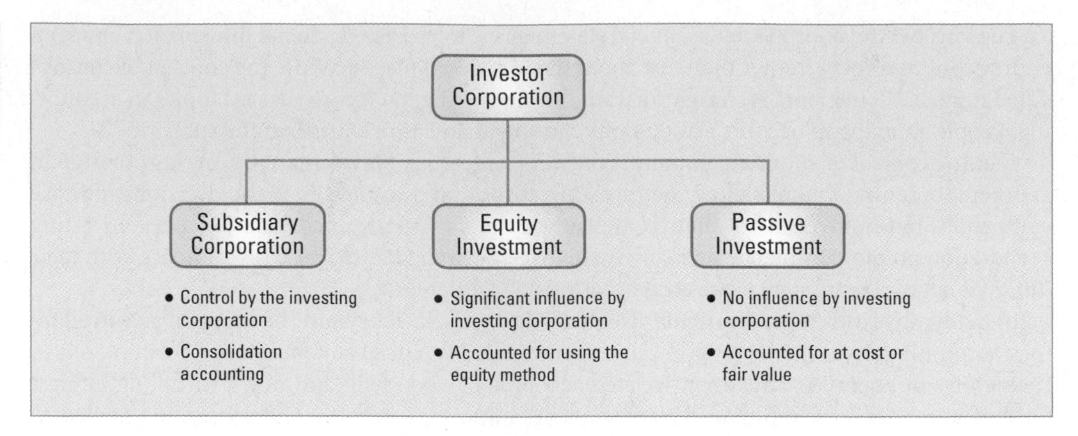

2. Significant influence—The investor doesn't control an investee but can affect its important decisions. The investor corporation should use the equity method of accounting.
3. Passive investment—The investor has no influence over the decision making of the investee (or at least no more influence than any other small investor). The investment is accounted for at cost or fair value, depending on the type of investment.

These different types of investments in other corporations are summarized in Figure 11.2. We will discuss the methods of accounting for investments in other corporations in detail in the following sections.

LO 2

CONTROL: ACCOUNTING FOR SUBSIDIARIES

An investor is said to **control** an investee if it's able to make the important decisions of the investee and determine its strategic operating, financing, and investing policies on an ongoing basis without the support of other shareholders. In other words, the managers of the investor can set the key policies of the investee.

Control usually means the investor owns more than 50 percent of the votes of the investee. Note that 50 percent of votes isn't necessarily the same as 50 percent of common shares. For example, Onex Corporation (Onex) controls a number of companies, despite owning less than 50 percent of the common shares of each. Onex owns 9 percent of the outstanding common shares of Celestica Inc. but has 71 percent of the votes. This is because each of Onex's common shares has 25 votes, whereas those held by other shareholders have only one vote each. Exhibit 11.1 lists the companies that Onex controls, the percentage of the common shares that it owns, and the percentage of the votes that it has.[2] This type of arrangement is quite common in Canada but is less so in other countries.

An investor with control is referred to as the **parent corporation** (parent) and the investee is called a **subsidiary corporation** (subsidiary). IFRS require parent corporations to prepare **consolidated financial statements**, which aggregate the accounting information of a parent corporation and all of its subsidiaries into a single set of statements. This means that each line in the consolidated financial statements reflects the assets, liabilities, revenues, expenses, and cash flows of the parent and all its subsidiaries. Look again at Exhibit 11.1. Onex controls all of the companies listed and their accounting information is rolled into the single set of consolidated financial statements prepared by Onex. Note that for companies that Onex doesn't own 100 percent, the regular financial statements of the investee are available to the other (non-controlling) shareholders. For example, Celestica's financial statements are available to any interested party because it's a public company.

www.onexcorp.com
www.celestica.com

Consolidated statements are intended to provide stakeholders interested in the parent—for example, shareholders—with a single set of financial statements that reflect the assets, liabilities, equity, revenues, and expenses of all the corporations controlled by the parent.

As we proceed through this discussion, it's important to keep in mind that consolidated financial statements are an accounting creation. The individual subsidiaries and the parent are all separate

EXHIBIT 11.1 Onex Corporation: Ownership and Voting of Investee Companies

	December 31, 2011			December 31, 2010		
	Onex Ownership	Onex and Limited Partners Ownership	Voting	Onex Ownership	Onex and Limited Partners Ownership	Voting
Investments made through Onex						
Celestica Inc. ("Celestica")	9%	9%	71%	9%	9%	71%
SITEL Worldwide Corporation ("Sitel Worldwide")	68%	68%	88%	68%	68%	88%
Investments made through Onex and Onex Partners I						
Center for Diagnostic Imaging, Inc. ("CDI")	19%	81%	100%	19%	81%	100%
Emergency Medical Services Corporation ("EMSC")[(a)]	–	–	–	12%	31%	82%
Skilled Healthcare Group, Inc. ("Skilled Healthcare Group")	9%	40%	89%	9%	40%	89%
Spirit AeroSystems, Inc. ("Spirit AeroSystems")	5%	16%	64%	7%	23%	74%
Investments made through Onex and Onex Partners II						
Allison Transmission, Inc. ("Allison Transmission")	15%	49%	(b)	15%	49%	(b)
Carestream Health, Inc. ("Carestream Health")	37%	95%	100%	38%	97%	100%
Hawker Beechcraft Corporation ("Hawker Beechcraft")	19%	49%	(b)	19%	49%	(b)
RSI Home Products, Inc. ("RSI")	20%	50%	50%[(b)]	20%	50%	50%[(b)]
TMS international Corp. ("TMS International")	24%	60%	85%	36%	91%	100%
Investments made through Onex, Onex Partners I, and Onex Partners II						
Husky International Ltd. ("Husky")[(a)]	–	–	–	36%	98%	100%
The Warranty Group, Inc. ("The Warranty Group")	29%	92%	100%	29%	92%	100%
Investments made through Onex and Onex Partners III						
JELD-WEN Holding, Inc. ("JELD-WEN")[(c)]	20%	59%	59%	–	–	–
Tomkins Limited ("Tomkins")	14%	56%	50%[(b)]	14%	56%	50%[(b)]
Tropicana Las Vegas, Inc. ("Tropicana Las Vegas")	17%	76%	76%	16%	74%	74%
Investments made through Onex, Onex Partners I and Onex Partners III						
Res-Care, Inc. ("ResCare")	20%	98%	100%	20%	98%	100%
Other investments						
ONCAP II Fund ("ONCAP II")	46%	100%	100%	46%	100%	100%
ONCAP III Fund ("ONCAP III")	29%	100%	100%	–	–	–
Onex Real Estate Partners ["Onex Real Estate"]	88%	88%	100%	86%	86%	100%

(a) EMSC and Husky were sold during the second quarter of 2011, as described in note 3.

(b) Onex exerts significant influence over these investments, which are designated at fair value through earnings, through its right to appoint members of the boards of directors of these entities.

legal entities; each has its own limited legal liability and each must file its own tax return. The consolidated group isn't a legal entity and doesn't file a tax return.

In the consolidated balance sheet, a subsidiary's assets and liabilities are recorded at the amount the parent paid for them on the date the subsidiary was purchased. This is no different than if the parent had purchased the assets and liabilities separately. What's different is that the subsidiary continues to own the assets and liabilities and to report them on its own balance sheet so that these assets and liabilities are reported in two places—the subsidiary's balance sheet and the consolidated balance sheet. The amounts reported for the same assets and liabilities may be different on the two balance sheets. Assets and liabilities accounted for at cost (e.g., inventory; property, plant, and equipment; and unearned revenue) are reported on the subsidiary's balance sheet at their cost when the subsidiary purchased them and recorded on the consolidated balance sheet at the cost to parent when the subsidiary was purchased. For example, a piece of land purchased by the subsidiary for $1,000 in 1995 but valued at $2,000 when the subsidiary was acquired by the parent in 2017 would be reported on the subsidiary's balance sheet at $1,000 and on the consolidated balance sheet at $2,000. If fair value is used instead of cost, the valuations could be the same. Because the valuations on the subsidiary and consolidated balance sheets may be different, preparing consolidated statements involves more than adding together the statements of the parent and its subsidiaries.

We will examine the accounting for the purchase of a subsidiary with an example. Throughout this chapter, the examples assume the investor invests with cash. Investments can also involve shares of the parent, debt, and non-cash assets. On June 30, 2017, Pefferlaw Ltd. (Pefferlaw) bought 100 percent of the shares of Schuler Corp. (Schuler) from its shareholders for $20,000,000. Pefferlaw would make the following journal entry in its accounting records (not the consolidated statements) to record the investment in Schuler:

Dr. Investment in Schuler (asset +)	20,000,000	
Cr. Cash (asset −)		20,000,000

To record the purchase of 100 percent of the shares of Schuler Corp on June 30, 2017

The investment has no effect at all on Schuler's accounting records or its financial statements because Pefferlaw purchased the shares from Schuler's shareholders, not from the corporation itself.

To prepare consolidated financial statements, Pefferlaw must identify the assets and liabilities it purchased and determine the amount it paid for each. This can be difficult because Pefferlaw purchased the entire company so the purchase price must be allocated to the individual assets and liabilities. To accomplish this, the fair values of all of Schuler's identifiable assets and liabilities must be determined as of the date of the purchase. These are the amounts that are reported in the consolidated financial statements. **Identifiable assets and liabilities** are tangible and intangible assets and liabilities that can be specifically identified and reasonably measured. Remember that an asset or liability's cost is its fair value on the date it was acquired. Also remember from Chapter 9 that amounts paid over the fair value of the identifiable assets less identifiable liabilities is classified as goodwill.

This process of determining the fair value of the assets and liabilities of a subsidiary occurs only once—when the subsidiary is purchased. From that point on, the consolidated financial statements are based on the amounts determined as of the date of the purchase. Of course, assets and liabilities normally valued at fair value would be restated each time the consolidated statements are prepared. Table 11.1 summarizes the book and fair values of Schuler's assets and liabilities on June 30, 2017.

TABLE 11.1 Schuler Corp.: Net Asset Fair Values and Carrying Amounts

	Fair value on June 30, 2017	Carrying amount on June 30, 2017	Difference
Current assets	$ 5,500,000	$ 5,000,000	$ 500,000
Capital assets	21,500,000	14,000,000	7,500,000
Liabilities	(9,000,000)	(8,000,000)	(1,000,000)
	$18,000,000	$11,000,000	$7,000,000

There are a couple of things to notice in Table 11.1:

- First, there are two measurements of Schuler's assets and liabilities. The carrying amounts appear in Schuler's own financial statements. The fair values on June 30 are the amounts Pefferlaw paid for Schuler's assets and liabilities. The fair values appear on Pefferlaw's consolidated balance sheet.
- Second, only $18,000,000 of the purchase price has been attributed to specific assets and liabilities. The remaining $2,000,000 is **goodwill**. (Remember that goodwill = purchase price − fair value of identifiable net assets purchased [identifiable net assets = fair value of identifiable assets − fair value of identifiable liabilities].)

KNOWLEDGE CHECK 11.1

- ❑ Identify and explain the three levels of influence that an investor corporation can have over an investee corporation.
- ❑ What are consolidated financial statements and under what circumstances are they prepared?
- ❑ In consolidated financial statements, what is the basis of valuing a subsidiary's assets and liabilities?

The Consolidated Balance Sheet on the Date the Subsidiary Is Purchased

LO 2

We now have the information needed to prepare Pefferlaw's consolidated balance sheet on June 30, 2017, the date Pefferlaw purchased the shares of Schuler. Pefferlaw's consolidated balance sheet includes the following:

a. The amounts reported on Pefferlaw's own balance sheet on June 30, 2017.

b. The fair value of Schuler's assets and liabilities (not the amounts on Schuler's own balance sheet) on June 30, 2017.

c. The goodwill from the acquisition of Schuler.

Pefferlaw's consolidated balance sheet *doesn't* include these items:

a. The "investment in subsidiary account" on the parent's balance sheet, which is replaced by the actual assets and liabilities of the subsidiary.

b. The shareholders' equity of the subsidiary, which is reflected in the shareholders' equity of the parent.

The contents of Pefferlaw's consolidated balance sheet on June 30, 2017, the date Pefferlaw purchased the shares of Schuler, are shown in Table 11.2.

- Column 1 shows Pefferlaw's balance sheet (this information hasn't been shown before). Notice that this isn't the same as Pefferlaw's consolidated balance sheet. Unconsolidated financial statements for the parent alone are also prepared. In its unconsolidated balance sheet, all that is reported about a parent's subsidiaries is the single line, investment in the subsidiaries (the investment in Schuler account). These unconsolidated statements are required for tax purposes and may be provided to other stakeholders, such as bankers, but aren't usually widely distributed.
- Column 2 shows the fair value of Schuler's assets and liabilities on June 30, 2017. These are the amounts included on the consolidated balance sheet, but *not* on Schuler's own balance sheet (shown in Table 11.1). Schuler's common shares and retained earnings aren't shown because they aren't included in consolidated shareholders' equity.

TABLE 11.2 Pefferlaw Ltd.: Consolidated Balance Sheet

	Column 1	Column 2	Column 3
	Balance sheet of Pefferlaw Ltd., June 30, 2017	Fair value of Schuler Corp.'s assets and liabilities, June 30, 2017	Consolidated balance sheet, June 30, 2017
Current assets	$ 29,000,000	$ 5,500,000	$ 34,500,000
Capital assets	52,000,000	21,500,000	73,500,000
Investment in Schuler	20,000,000		
Goodwill		2,000,000	2,000,000
	$101,000,000	$29,000,000	$110,000,000
Liabilities	$ 38,000,000	$ 9,000,000	$ 47,000,000
Common shares	22,000,000		22,000,000
Retained earnings	41,000,000		41,000,000
	$101,000,000		$110,000,000

The fair value of Schuler's assets and liabilities on the date of purchase, not the carrying amounts on Schuler's own balance sheet, are used in the consolidated balance sheet.

Notice that the fair value of Schuler's $20,000,000 net assets (assets − liabilities = $29,000,000 − $9,000,000) is the same amount as in the Investment in Schuler account. Schuler's net assets replace the investment account in the consolidated statements.

The shareholders' equity section of the subsidiary's balance sheet isn't included in the consolidated financial statements.

- Column 3 is the consolidated balance sheet. The goodwill only appears on the consolidated balance sheet. Goodwill is calculated as

$$\text{Goodwill} = \text{Purchase price} - \text{Fair value of identifiable assests}$$
$$\$2{,}000{,}000 = \$20{,}000{,}000 - \$18{,}000{,}000$$

The purchase of Schuler doesn't affect the consolidated income statement for the year ended June 30, 2017 because the purchase took place on the last day of Schuler's fiscal year. The revenues and expenses of a subsidiary are incorporated into the consolidated income statement only after the date of the purchase. The income statement effects of consolidation are discussed in the appendix.

QUESTION FOR CONSIDERATION

When an entity purchases a subsidiary, the amounts included in the consolidated balance sheet are the fair value of the subsidiary's assets and liabilities on the date of the purchase, not the amounts reported in the subsidiary's own balance sheet. Explain why this treatment isn't a violation of historical cost accounting.

ANSWER: Recording a subsidiary's assets and liabilities at their fair values in the consolidated balance sheet on the date of the purchase isn't a violation of the historical cost accounting because the subsidiary's assets and liabilities are purchased when the parent purchases the subsidiary. Assigning fair values to these assets and liabilities occurs only once—when the subsidiary is actually purchased. The fair values assigned on that date form the basis of valuing those assets and liabilities in the consolidated financial statements from then on.

Non-controlling Interest

LO 2

When a parent controls a subsidiary but owns less than 100 percent of it, "non-controlling interest" (or minority interest) accounts appear in the consolidated financial statements. IFRS require that the consolidated balance sheet include 100 percent of the fair value of a subsidiary's assets and liabilities, even if the parent owns less than 100 percent of them. IFRS also require the consolidated income statements to include 100 percent of the revenues and expenses of a subsidiary, even if it isn't 100 percent owned.

The rationale for this approach is that even if it doesn't own 100 percent of the subsidiary's net assets, the parent nevertheless controls 100 percent of them, and the consolidated statements should report what the parent controls. The problem is that the consolidated statements then contain assets, liabilities, revenues, and expenses that don't belong to the parent's shareholders. What's to be done with the amounts not owned by the parent?

The answer is **non-controlling interest**. On the consolidated balance sheet, non-controlling interest is reported in the equity section that represents the net assets of a subsidiary that are owned by the non-parent shareholders of the subsidiary. On the consolidated income statement, non-controlling interest represents the portion of net income of the subsidiary that belongs to the non-parent shareholders. Net income is calculated as it normally is and then allocated between the parent's shareholders and the non-controlling shareholders. The parent's share of net income goes to retained earnings, and the non-controlling interest's share is closed to non-controlling interest on the balance sheet.

Exhibit 11.2 shows the disclosures about non-controlling interest by Onex Corporation in its financial statements.[3]

INSIGHT

Non-controlling Interest

Non-controlling interest only appears in consolidated financial statements because 100 percent of a subsidiary's net assets, revenues, and expenses are reported even if the parent owns less than 100 percent of the subsidiary. If only the percentage of the subsidiary's net assets, revenues, and expenses owned by the parent was included, there would be no non-controlling interest.

EXHIBIT 11.2 Onex Corporation: Non-controlling Interest in the Income Statement and Balance Sheet

CONSOLIDATED BALANCE SHEETS

(in millions of U.S dollars)	As at December 31, 2011	As at December 31, 2010	As at January 1, 2010
Equity			
Share capital (note 18)	360	373	381
Non-controlling interests	3,862	3,638	3,329
Retained earnings and accumulated other comprehensive earnings	1,460	131	374
	5,682	4,142	4,084
	$ 29,446	$ 28,107	$ 24,024

This represents the equity of the non-controlling shareholders in Onex's net assets

EXHIBIT 11.2 (continued) Onex Corporation: Non-controlling Interest in the Income Statement and Balance Sheet

CONSOLIDATED STATEMENTS OF EARNINGS

Year ended December 31 *(in millions of U.S. dollars except per share data)*	2011	2010
Revenues	$ 24,642	$ 19,734
Cost of sales (excluding amortization of property, plant and equipment, intangible assets and deferred charges)	(19,725)	(15,492)
Operating expenses	(2,921)	(2,306)
Interest income	32	34
Amortization of property, plant and equipment	(462)	(403)
Amortization of intangible assets and deferred charges	(311)	(284)
Interest expense of operating companies (note 20)	(488)	(342)
Unrealized increase in value of investments in associates at fair value, net (note 8)	501	448
Foreign exchange loss	(14)	(8)
Stock-based compensation expense (note 21)	(133)	(186)
Other gains, net (note 22)	–	99
Other items (note 23)	(146)	(221)
Impairment of goodwill, intangible assets and long-lived assets, net (note 24)	(197)	(14)
Limited Partners' Interests charge (note 17)	(627)	(831)
Earnings before income taxes and discontinued operations	151	228
Provision for income taxes (note 16)	(237)	(239)
Loss from continuing operations	(86)	(11)
Earnings from discontinued operations (note 3)	1,715	208
Net Earnings for the Year	$ 1,629	$ 197
Net Earnings (Loss) Attributable To:		
Equity holders of Onex Corporation	$ 1,327	$ (167)
Non-controlling interests	302	364
Net Earnings for the Year	$ 1,629	$ 197

Notice how net income is divided between Onex's shareholders and the non-controlling shareholders.

KNOWLEDGE CHECK 11.2

- ☐ What is goodwill and how is it calculated?
- ☐ What is non-controlling interest and why does it appear in some entities' consolidated financial statements?

Are Consolidated Financial Statements Useful?

LO 2

Now that we've looked at the basics of accounting for subsidiaries (which aren't all that basic!), we should consider the usefulness of consolidated financial statements. Consolidated statements provide, in a single set of financial statements, information about a group of corporations under the control of a parent. This information might be useful to stakeholders who want stewardship information about the entire economic entity or to evaluate the performance of the corporate group as a whole. Consolidated financial statements may be an effective way for a corporate group to communicate the "big picture" to various stakeholders. With control the parent controls the operations of its subsidiaries and can move assets from corporation to corporation. For example, a parent company that is short of cash could have a subsidiary declare a dividend, make a loan, or pay management fees to the parent to help it meet its cash needs. Consolidated statements allow users to see all the resources available to the corporate group.

Consolidated financial statements don't include transactions and profits generated among entities in the corporate group. This means that revenue and profit from exchanges between a parent and a subsidiary, or among the subsidiaries in a consolidated group, aren't included in the consolidated financial statements (this topic is explored in the appendix to this chapter). These **intercompany transactions** and profits aren't meaningful (it would be like selling your computer to yourself and saying you have revenue and profit) and they can be misleading because they make it look like there is more economic activity than there really is. The financial statements of the individual corporations in a consolidated group do include intercompany transactions.

For many stakeholders, however, consolidated financial statements are an obstacle to effective decision making because they aggregate information about the individual corporations in the consolidated group. The details about the different businesses of the parent and its subsidiaries are lost in consolidated financial statements; it's virtually impossible to determine the companies, lines of business, and geographical areas in the group that are doing well and those are doing poorly.

The interests of financial analysts and other sophisticated stakeholders who want to use financial statements as a starting point for predicting future earnings or cash flows may not be served by consolidated statements. For example, the statements can significantly limit the usefulness of ratio analysis. Combining the accounting information of several companies, often those in different industries, results in ratios that aren't representative of any industry. Onex Corporation, mentioned earlier, controls businesses in electronics manufacturing, aerostructures, health care, financial services, customer support services, and metal services. What sense can be made of financial ratios that comprise information about companies in all these very different industries?

IFRS try to help stakeholders by requiring that public companies provide information about the different business activities and the different geographic areas they operate in. This disaggregation of information by types of products and services, geographic location, and major customers is called **segment disclosure**. Onex Corporation's segment information note is shown in Exhibit 11.3. Onex identifies seven industry segments and five geographic segments. For each industry segment, a complete income statement is provided, along with selected information from the balance sheet (to simplify the presentation in the exhibit, I have removed some of the detail from the income statement). Revenue and selected balance sheet information is provided for each geographic segment. A complete set of financial statements for each segment is not. Stakeholders can gain some very useful insights from the segment disclosure. Onex's segment information can be used to determine which segments generate the most revenue, which is the most profitable, and which require the largest investment in assets.

For some stakeholders, even consolidated financial statements with segment information aren't adequate. Lenders are concerned that the legal entities they lend to can make interest and principal payments. The lender might be interested in consolidated statements if a loan is being made to the parent, or if the parent is guaranteeing a loan to a subsidiary. Otherwise, a lender needs the financial statements of the corporation actually borrowing the money.

Consolidated financial statements are intended for stakeholders of the consolidated entity and are of little interest to the non-controlling shareholders or those of a subsidiary. The non-controlling interest on the consolidated statements provides little useful information to stakeholders interested in subsidiaries, who would want to see the financial statements of the

EXHIBIT 11.3 Onex Corporation: Segment Disclosure

2011 Industry Segments

Onex's industry segments.

	Electronics Manufacturing Services	Aerostructures	Healthcare	Financial Services	Customer Care Services	Metal Services	Building Products	Other	Consolidated Total
Revenues	$ 7,213	$ 4,864	$ 5,030	$ 1,184	$ 1,416	$ 2,661	$ 774	$ 1,500	$ 24,642
Cost of sales (excluding amortization of property, plant and equipment, intangible assets and deferred charges)	(6,645)	(4,124)	(3,446)	(579)	(921)	(2,467)	(660)	(883)	(19,725)
Operating expenses	(234)	(178)	(918)	(429)	(377)	(59)	(118)	(608)	(2,921)
Net earnings (loss) for the year	195	224	494	62	(58)	24	(89)	777	1,629
Total assets	$ 2,970	$ 4,978	$ 4,194	$ 4,877	$ 631	$ 1,045	$ 2,581	$ 8,170	$ 29,446
Long-term debt[a]	$ –	$ 1,157	$ 2,670	$ 203	$ 652	$ 377	$ 481	$ 1,421	$ 6,961
Property, plant and equipment additions	$ 60	$ 275	$ 96	$ 3	$ 32	$ 75	$ 13	$ 120	$ 674
Intangible assets with indefinite life	$ –	$ –	$ 258	$ 16	$ 36	$ –	$ 257	$ 376	$ 943
Goodwill additions from acquisitions	$ 34	$ –	$ 41	$ –	$ –	$ –	$ 119	$ 278	$ 472
Goodwill	$ 48	$ 3	$ 911	$ 304	$ 118	$ 239	$ 120	$ 691	$ 2,434

Summarized balance sheet information

Net earnings (loss) attributable to:

	Electronics Manufacturing Services	Aerostructures	Healthcare	Financial Services	Customer Care Services	Metal Services	Building Products	Other	Consolidated Total
Equity holders of Onex Corporation	$ 17	$ 35	$ 512	$ 59	$ (39)	$ 17	$ (60)	$ 786	$ 1,327
Non-controlling interests	$ 178	$ 189	$ (18)	$ 3	$ (19)	$ 7	$ (29)	$ (9)	$ 302
Net earnings (loss) for the year	$ 195	$ 224	$ 494	$ 62	$ (58)	$ 24	$ (89)	$ 777	$ 1,629

Geographic Segments

	2011					
	Canada	U.S.	Europe	Asia and Oceania	Other	Total
Revenue(1)	$ 1,264	$ 15,323	$ 4,181	$ 2,968	$ 906	$ 24,642
Property, plant and equipment	$ 345	$ 3,539	$ 694	$ 408	$ 116	$ 5,102
Intangible assets	$ 238	$ 2,028	$ 223	$ 94	$ 16	$ 2,599
Goodwill	$ 184	$ 1,790	$ 279	$ 148	$ 33	$ 2,434

subsidiary itself. Shareholders are entitled to receive financial statements of the subsidiaries in which they own shares.

Consolidated financial statements are also not relevant for tax purposes. Each individual corporation is required to file tax returns with the Canada Revenue Agency and provincial taxation authorities. This means that each corporation must prepare financial statements for tax purposes regardless of ownership.

INSIGHT

Accounting for subsidiaries provides managers with significant opportunities to make choices that will influence the consolidated financial statements for many years. When a new subsidiary is acquired, management must allocate the purchase price to the identifiable assets and liabilities and to goodwill. Because the process of assigning fair values is imprecise, management can make choices that satisfy its reporting objectives. Different managers could come up with very different reasonable amounts of goodwill for the same acquisition, and different reasonable valuations for the same identifiable assets and liabilities. Because goodwill doesn't have to be amortized, managers concerned about net income might allocate less of the purchase price to depreciable assets and inventory so that more would be included in goodwill.

SIGNIFICANT INFLUENCE

LO 3

When an investor corporation has **significant influence**, it can affect the strategic operating, investing, and financing decisions of the investee corporation, even though it doesn't have control. IFRS suggest that owning between 20 percent and 50 percent of the votes of an investee company is an indication of significant influence. However, judgment must be used to determine whether significant influence exists in a particular situation. An investor corporation could own 30 percent of the voting shares of an investee but not have significant influence because another investor has control. On the other hand, an investment of less than 20 percent could provide significant influence if, for example, the investor represented on the investee corporation's board of directors.

When a corporation has significant influence over another entity, the equity method of accounting should be used. The **equity method of accounting** is almost the same as the consolidation method of accounting for subsidiaries; however, the information appears in the financial statements in a very different way. Instead of aggregating the financial statement of the investee line by line, information about investees subject to significant influence is presented on a single line on the balance sheet and a single line on the income statement.

Using the equity method, an investment is initially recorded on the investor's balance sheet at cost. The balance sheet amount is then adjusted each period by the investor's share of the investee's net income, less dividends declared by the investee. The income statement reports the investor's share of the investee's net income, which is determined by multiplying the investee's net income by the percentage of the investee that the investor owns. The amount is then adjusted for intercompany transactions and other adjustments.

The rationale for using the equity method is that a significant investor can influence important policies of the investee, such as the timing and amount of dividends, which can allow the investor to manage its own earnings. Under the equity method, dividends from an investment aren't considered income, and thus this type of income manipulation isn't possible. A few points about the equity method of accounting are worth noting:

1. Though an equity investment account changes to reflect the earnings of an investee and the dividends it declares, the amount reported on the balance sheet doesn't reflect the market value of the investment. The changes to the balance sheet amount are based on IFRS net income, not on changes in the investee's fair value.
2. The income reported from an investment accounted for using the equity method isn't an indication of the amount of dividends or cash that will be forthcoming from the investee.

It is simply an allocation of the investor's share of the investee's income. An equity investment may not be very liquid and the investor may be limited in its ability to obtain cash from the investee.

3. The equity investment account on the investor's balance sheet provides virtually no information about the investee corporation. Information about investments the investor has significant influence over is usually not included in the segment disclosures described earlier. If the investee corporation is public, the financial statements of the investee can be examined. If the investee is private, then little will be known about it.

www.brookfield.com

An example of equity accounting can be seen in Exhibit 11.4, which shows how Brookfield Asset Management Inc. reports its investments accounted for using the equity method.[4] Equity-accounted investments are called "associates" in Brookfield's financial statements and the amount invested in associates is included on its balance sheet under "Investments" and shown in Note 7. Brookfield's associates include General Growth Properties and Transelec S.A. Note 7 shows the ownership interest Brookfield has in each associate. On the income statement, Brookfield reports $2,205,000,000 in income from equity investments.

ACCOUNTING STANDARDS FOR PRIVATE ENTERPRISES

Consolidation and equity accounting are mostly relevant for public companies. Companies that follow ASPE can elect not to consolidate or equity account even if they control or have significant influence over an investee corporation. These companies can record subsidiaries using the equity method or simply at cost, and they can account for investees over which they have significant influence at cost. Accounting at cost means the investment remains on the balance sheet at the original amount paid until it's sold. Private companies may choose to avoid consolidation and equity accounting because it's costly and in many cases doesn't provide useful information to stakeholders.

EXHIBIT 11.4 Brookfield Asset Management Inc.: Equity Accounting

CONSOLIDATED FINANCIAL STATEMENTS

CONSOLIDATED BALANCE SHEETS

(MILLIONS)	Note	Dec. 31, 2011	Dec. 31, 2010
Assets			
Cash and cash equivalents	28	**$ 2,027**	$ 1,713
Other financial assets	4	**3,773**	4,419
Accounts receivable and other	5	**6,723**	7,869
Inventory	6	**6,060**	5,849
Investments	7	**9,401**	6,629
Investment properties	8	**28,366**	22,163
Property, plant and equipment	9	**22,832**	18,520
Timber	10	**3,155**	2,834
Intangible assets	11	**3,968**	3,805
Goodwill	12	**2,607**	2,546
Deferred income tax asset	13	**2,118**	1,784
Total Assets		**$ 91,030**	$ 78,131

Includes equity-accounted investments.

EXHIBIT 11.4 Brookfield Asset Management Inc.: Equity Accounting

CONSOLIDATED STATEMENTS OF OPERATIONS

YEARS ENDED DECEMBER 31 (MILLIONS, EXCEPT PER SHARE AMOUNTS)	Note	2011	2010
Total revenues	20	$ **15,921**	$ 13,623
Asset management and other services	20	**388**	365
Revenues less direct operating costs			
Property	20	**1,678**	1,495
Renewable power	20	**740**	748
Infrastructure	20	**756**	221
Private equity	20	**538**	628
Equity-accounted income	7	**2,205**	765
Investment and other income	20	**328**	503
		6,633	4,725
Expenses			
Interest		**2,352**	1,829
Operating costs		**481**	417
Current income taxes	13	**97**	97
		3,703	2,382
Other Items			
Fair value changes	21	**1,286**	1,651
Depreciation and amortization		**(904)**	(795)
Deferred Income taxes	13	**(411)**	(43)
Net Income		$ **3,674**	$ 3,195
Net income attributable to:			
Shareholders		$ **1,957**	$ 1,454
Non-controlling interests		**1,717**	1,741
		$ **3,674**	$ 3,195
Net income per share:			
Diluted	19	$ **2.89**	$ 2.33
Basic	19	$ **3.00**	$ 2.40

Income from equity-accounted investments

2. SIGNIFICANT ACCOUNTING POLICIES

b) Basis of Presentation

ii. Associates

Associates are entities over which the company exercises significant influence. Significant influence is the power to participate in the financial and operating policy decisions of the investee but not control or joint control over those policies. The company accounts for investments over which it has significant influence using the equity method, and they are recorded in Investments on the Consolidated Balance Sheets. Interests in investments accounted for using the equity method are initially recognized at cost. If the cost of the associate is lower than the proportionate share of the investment's underlying fair value, the company records a gain on the difference between the cost and the underlying fair value of the investment in net income. If the cost of the associate is greater than the company's proportionate share of the underlying fair value, goodwill relating to the associate is included in the carrying amount of the investment. Subsequent to initial recognition, the carrying value of the company's interest in an investee is adjusted for the company's share of comprehensive income and distributions of the investee. Profit and losses resulting from transactions with an associate are recognized in the consolidated financial statements based on the interests of unrelated investors in the associate.

EXHIBIT 11.4 (continued) Brookfield Asset Management Inc.: Equity Accounting

7. INVESTMENTS

The following table presents the ownership interests and carrying values of the company's investments in associates and equity-accounted joint ventures:

AS AT (MILLIONS)	Investment Type	Ownership Interest Dec. 31 2011	Ownership Interest Dec. 31 2010	Carrying Value Dec. 31 2011	Carrying Value Dec. 31 2010
Property					
General Growth Properties	Associate	**23%**	10%	**$ 4,099**	$ 1,014
245 Park Avenue	Joint Venture	**51%**	51%[3]	**619**	580
Grace Building[1]	Joint Venture	**41%**	–	**618**	–
U.S Office Fund[1]	–	–	47%	–	1,806
Other properties[2]	Various	**20 –75%[3]**	20–51%[3]	**1,578**	1,466
Renewable power					
Bear Swamp Power Co. LLC	Joint Venture	**50%**	50%	**130**	95
Other power	Various	**50%**	50%	**228**	171
Infrastructure					
Natural gas pipeline	Associate	**26%**	26%	395	384
Transelec S.A.	Associate	**28%**	28%	**584**	373
Other infrastructure assets	Various	**30–50%**	30–50%	719	513
Other	Various	**25–50%**	25–50%	**431**	227
Total				**$ 9,401**	$ 6,629

1. The company acquired a controlling interest in the U.S. Office Fund on August 9, 2011, resulting in the consolidation of the U.S. Office Fund and its equity-accounted investments, as described in Note 3.
2. Other properties include investments in Darling Park Trust and E&Y Centre Sydney which represent investments in joint ventures where control is either shared or does not exist resulting in the investment being equity-accounted.
3. Investments in which the company's ownership interest is greater than 50% are in equity-accounted joint ventures.

The following table presents the change in the balance of investments in associates and equity-accounted joint ventures:

(MILLIONS)	2011	2010
Balance at beginning of year	**$ 6,629**	$ 4,466
Additions, net of disposals	**(100)**	638
Acquisitions through business combinations[1]	**685**	922
Share of net income	**2,205**	765
Share of other comprehensive income (loss)	**193**	(16)
Distributions received	**(204)**	(374)
Foreign exchange	**(7)**	228
Balance at end of year	**$ 9,401**	$ 6,629

1. The company acquired a controlling interest in the U.S. Office Fund on August 9, 2011, resulting in the consolidation of the U.S Office Fund and its equity-accounted investments, as described in Note 3.

Ties to balance sheet amount.

Ties to balance sheet amount.

PASSIVE INVESTMENTS

LO 4

Financial instruments are assets and liabilities that represent the contractual rights or obligations of the entity to receive or pay cash or other financial assets. We have discussed several financial instruments so far in the book, including accounts receivable, accounts payable, bank loans, and bonds. In this section, we'll discuss a category of investments we can call **passive investments**—investments the investor corporation can't influence the strategic decision making of the investee corporation. These investments don't give the investor corporation control or significant influence.

All investments in non-voting securities—securities such as debt, preferred shares, or non-voting common shares—are classified as passive investments because without voting power it isn't possible to have influence. Voting shares are passive investments when the investor corporation holds a relatively small proportion of the investee's shares. IFRS suggest that holding less than 20 percent of the votes of an investee is a passive investment; however, 20 percent is only a guideline. A 10 percent investment that includes representation on the board of directors could give the investor corporation significant influence.

We'll classify passive investments by how they're accounted for. Under IFRS, there are three ways to account for passive investments. By and large, it is IFRS's objective to value passive investments at fair value:

- Amortized cost (allowed for certain debt investments only)
- Fair value through other comprehensive income (FVTOCI) (allowed for certain equity investments only)
- Fair value through profit and loss (FVTPL)

Figure 11-3 shows how these methods are applied. We'll look at the three methods in turn:

- **Amortized cost**: Amortized cost is used for bonds and other debt instruments. It should be used if (i) the investment is part of management's plan to hold the investment to receive the

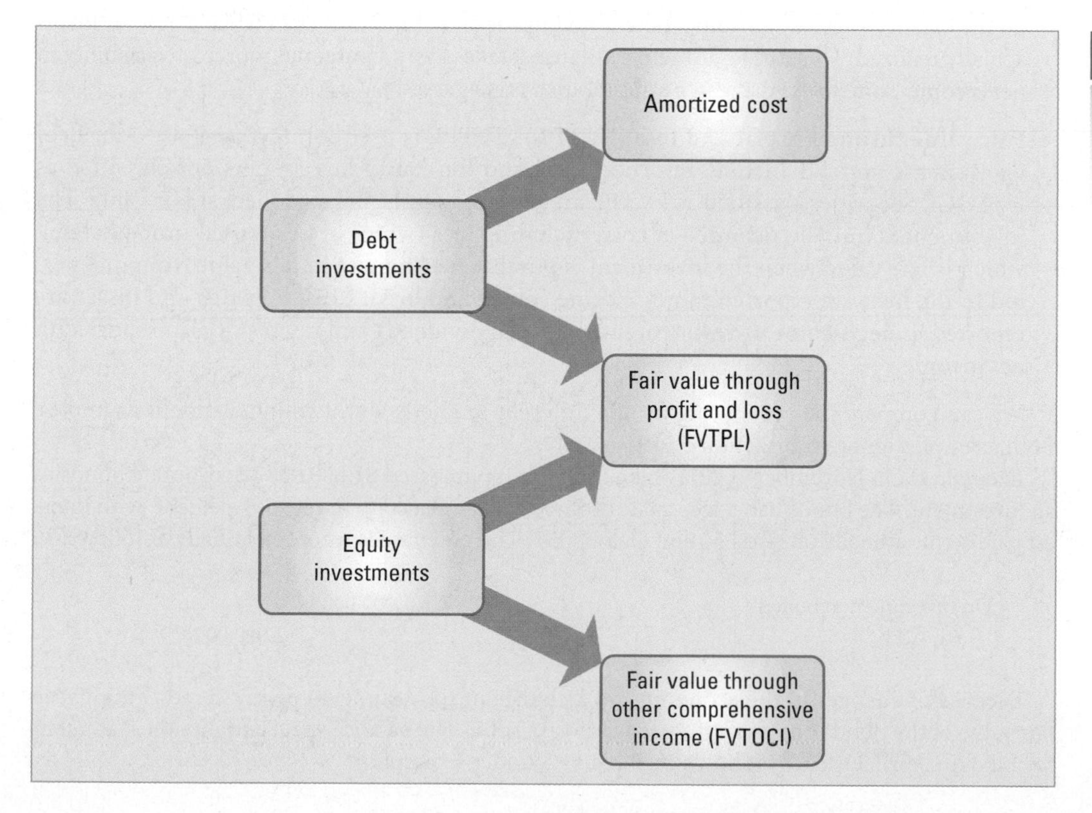

FIGURE 11.3 **Accounting Methods for Passive Investments**

cash flows (interest and principal)—not to actively trade it and (ii) the investment has contractual terms that give rise to interest and principal payments on specified dates. It's because of this second requirement that equity investments can't be accounted for using amortized cost (equity investments don't have specified cash flows).

Amortized cost investments are recorded at cost, including any costs or fees incurred to complete the transaction (which is fair value when they are acquired). They are carried at cost while they are owned unless they become impaired. Changes in fair value after acquisition are ignored. Gains and losses are recognized on the income statement when an investment is sold (the gain or loss is the difference between the proceeds from sale and the carrying amount). Interest income is reported in the income statement as investment income when it's earned. If the investment is purchased at a discount or premium, the discount or premium must be amortized to investment income over the period to maturity using the effective interest rate method. If an investment becomes impaired, it must be written down. Impairment occurs if the cash flows associated with the investment are at increased risk. The higher risk may be indicated by bankruptcy, financial difficulty, and failure to make interest and principal payments. If an investment is impaired, it's written down to fair value and the loss is reported in the income statement. Impairment losses can be reversed if circumstances change.

- **Fair value through other comprehensive income (FVTOCI)**: FVTOCI can only be used for equity securities that are so designated by management when the investment is acquired. Once made, the classification can't be changed. Securities classified as FVTOCI are reported on the balance sheet at fair value. The investment is initially recorded at cost, including fees, which is fair value when the investment is purchased. Changes in fair value from one period to the next are reported in other comprehensive income (OCI), not in net income. At the end of each period, any fair value changes reported in OCI are closed to accumulated other comprehensive income in the equity section of the balance sheet. When an investment is sold, the realized gain or loss (the difference between the proceeds from sale and the original cost) can either be left in accumulated OCI or be transferred to retained earnings. Dividend income from the shares is reported in net income in the period it's earned (not in OCI).

  The most important characteristic of FVTOCI is that, even though the shares are reported on the balance sheet at fair value there is no impact on net income, even when a gain or loss is actually realized. This can be attractive because it takes away a potential source of variability in net income, something that can be desirable to managers.

- **Fair value through profit and loss (FVTPL)**: FVTPL is used for anything else—for debt investments not classified as amortized cost and for equity investments not classified as FVTOCI. Securities classified as FVTPL are reported on the balance sheet at fair value. The investment is initially recorded at cost, excluding fees (which are expensed immediately), which is fair value when the investment is purchased. Changes in fair value from one period to the next are reported in net income (profit and loss). Realized gains and losses are reported in net income. Investment income from dividends and interest is also reported in net income.

We can compare the accounting for the different methods with two independent examples. Both examples ignore transaction costs:

Example 1: On November 1, 2017, Elko Inc. (Elko) purchased $1,000,000 in corporate bonds as an investment. The bonds had a face value of $1,000,000 and a coupon rate of 7 percent, with interest paid semi-annually on April 30 and October 31. The purchase is recorded initially as follows:

Dr. Investment in bonds	1,000,000	
Cr. Cash		1,000,000

Because of changes in the economy and a change in the issuing company's credit rating, the fair value of the bonds on April 30, 2018 was $1,025,000. The balance sheet and income statement for Elko on April 30, 2018 is shown in Table 11.3 under Example 1.

TABLE 11.3 Elko Inc.: Financial Statements

Elko Inc. Balance sheet as of April 30, 2018				
	Example 1 Debt Investment		Example 2 Equity Investment	
	Amortized cost	Fair value through profit and loss	Fair value through OCI	Fair value through profit and loss
Assets				
All other assets	$11,500,000	$11,500,000	$11,500,000	$11,500,000
Investments:				
Bonds	1,000,000	1,025,000		
Shares			1,025,000	1,025,000
	$12,500,000	$12,525,000	$12,525,000	$12,525,000
Liabilities and Shareholders' Equity				
All liabilities	$ 7,000,000	$ 7,000,000	$ 7,000,000	$ 7,000,000
Shareholders' equity:				
Common shares	2,000,000	2,000,000	2,000,000	2,000,000
Retained earnings	3,500,000	3,525,000	3,500,000	3,525,000
Accumulated other comprehensive income: unrealized holding gains			25,000	
Total shareholders' equity	5,500,000	5,525,000	5,525,000	5,525,000
	$12,500,000	$12,525,000	$12,525,000	$12,525,000

Elko Inc. Income statement for the year ended April 30, 2018				
	Example 1 Debt Investment		Example 2 Equity Investment	
	Amortized cost	Fair value through profit and loss	Fair value through OCI	Fair value through profit and loss
Revenue	$ 8,000,000	$ 8,000,000	$ 8,000,000	$ 8,000,000
Expenses	6,870,000	6,870,000	6,870,000	6,870,000
Investment income:				
Interest	70,000	70,000		
Dividends			70,000	70,000
Unrealized holding gain on investment		25,000		25,000
Net income	$ 1,200,000	$ 1,225,000	$ 1,200,000	$ 1,225,000
Other comprehensive income: unrealized holding gains on available for trade investments			25,000	
Comprehensive income	$ 1,200,000	$ 1,225,000	$ 1,225,000	$ 1,225,000

Example 2: On November 1, 2017, Elko Inc. (Elko) purchased shares in a public company for $1,000,000. The purchase is recorded initially as follows:

Dr. Investment in shares	1,000,000	
Cr. Cash		1,000,000

On April 30, 2018, the fair value of the shares was $1,025,000. In addition, on April 1, 2018, the shares paid a dividend of $70,000.

Notice that the balance sheet valuation of Elko's investments is fair value if they are classified as FVTPL or FVTOCI, and cost if they are classified as amortized cost. The unrealized gain is reported in net income and closed to retained earnings if classified as FVTPL. If the investment is classified as FVTOCI, the gain is then reported in other comprehensive income and closed to accumulated other comprehensive income in the equity section of Elko's balance sheet. Under amortized cost, a gain is only recognized if the investment is actually sold.

KNOWLEDGE CHECK 11.3

- ❑ What are the three methods of accounting for passive investments and under what circumstances is each used?
- ❑ What is the basis of valuation on the balance sheet for each method of accounting for passive investments?
- ❑ For each method of accounting for passive investments, explain how unrealized gains and losses are accounted for.

ACCOUNTING STANDARDS FOR PRIVATE ENTERPRISES

ASPE requires equity investments that are publicly traded to be valued at fair value on the balance sheet. There is no option to account for unrealized gains and losses in other comprehensive income because comprehensive income doesn't exist in ASPE. An entity can elect to measure any other investment at fair value. When fair value is used, unrealized gains and losses are included in net income. Otherwise, equity investments are carried at cost less any impairment loss, and debt investments are carried at amortized cost. Interest and dividend income and gains and losses are included in the calculation of net income.

Solved Problem

Tecumseh Inc. (Tecumseh) is a small diversified company in eastern Canada. The company is owned and operated by the Doh family. Tecumseh operates a restaurant in Moncton, New Brunswick, a potato farm in Prince Edward Island, a fish processing plant in Newfoundland, and a trucking company operating throughout the Maritime provinces. The president of Tecumseh, Mark Doh, has approached your Aunt Meaghan for a $250,000 loan to update the potato farm's operations. Your aunt recently won a lottery and she has set up an investment fund to invest in small Canadian businesses. She thinks it would be fun to be involved in these businesses and hopes that it will be a good way for her to make some money from her winnings.

As part of the preliminary investigation, Tecumseh has provided a consolidated balance sheet for the two years ended December 31, 2018. The balance sheet consolidates all of Tecumseh's activities. This is the first time your aunt has ever seen a consolidated balance sheet (the other companies she has considered were not consolidated) and she's not sure what to make of it. She has asked you to write a report identifying the key aspects of the consolidated balance sheet she should be aware of when deciding whether to grant the loan to the potato farm. She would also like any other general observations you can make about the balance sheet. Tecumseh's consolidated balance sheets and some additional information are provided below.

Tecumseh Inc.					
Consolidated balance sheets for the years ended December 31					
	2018	2017		2018	2017
Cash	$ 55,000	$ 85,000	Bank loan	$ 125,000	$ 25,000
Accounts receivable	1,250,000	850,000	Accounts payable	1,110,000	985,000
Inventory	850,000	800,000	Unearned revenue	125,000	99,000
Other current assets	35,000	45,000		1,360,000	1,109,000
	2,190,000	1,780,000	Long-term debt	2,300,000	1,900,000
Plant, property, and equipment	4,285,000	4,021,000	Future income taxes	310,000	275,000
Goodwill	900,000	900,000		3,970,000	3,284,000
			Share capital	2,000,000	2,000,000
			Accumulated other comprehensive income	(25,000)	5,000
			Retained earnings	1,180,000	1,137,000
			Non-controlling interest	250,000	275,000
Total assets	$7,375,000	$6,701,000	Total liabilities and shareholders' equity	$7,375,000	$6,701,000

Additional Information

- Tecumseh Inc. has four operations: a restaurant, a potato farm, a fish processing plant, and a trucking company. Each operation is organized as a separate corporation.
- The non-controlling interest relates to the potato farm. The farmer who operates the farm owns 25 percent of the shares of the farm.
- The goodwill arose when Tecumseh purchased the trucking company.

Solution:

Dear Aunt Meaghan:

Thank you for the opportunity to prepare this report for you. Based on my review of Tecumseh's balance sheets for the years ended December 31, 2018 and 2017, I offer the following points for your consideration:

1. The first and most important point to remember is that you are being asked to lend money to the potato farm and these financial statements apply to the entire corporate group. That is, the assets and liabilities reported in the balance sheet belong to all of Tecumseh's operations, not just to the potato farm, which is a separate legal entity. This balance sheet doesn't give you much insight into the assets and liabilities of the farm itself. You must obtain the financial statements of the potato farm. Will your loan be guaranteed by the parent company or will the obligation to repay be limited to the farm? If only the farm is on the hook then the relevance of these consolidated statements is limited.
2. The goodwill on the balance sheet is a large asset but it is not clear what it represents. The goodwill arose when Tecumseh bought the trucking company and means it paid $900,000 more than could be attributed to specifically identifiable net assets. Thus, you can't tell what the goodwill represents or if it represents anything at all. In addition, this goodwill is not related to the potato farm, the company to which you are being asked to lend.
3. The non-controlling interest on the liability side of the balance sheet represents the fact that Tecumseh does not own 100 percent of the potato farm. The consolidated balance sheet reports 100 percent of the net assets controlled by Tecumseh, even though it doesn't own 100 percent of the farm's net assets. The additional information states that 25 percent of the farm is owned by

the potato farmer. The non-controlling interest account reflects this fact. This account doesn't mean that money, goods, or services are owed to a third party but simply show the potato farmer's "equity" in the assets and liabilities reported in the consolidated balance sheet.

4. The non-controlling interest does provide a small clue about how the potato farm is doing. The non-controlling interest decreased from 2017 to 2018, which means that the farm suffered a loss in 2018 (or dividends paid were greater than net income). You will have to get financial statements for the farm itself before making a decision about whether to make a loan to it, but this piece of information gives some insight into what to expect.
5. In general, the ability to analyze consolidated financial statements is quite limited. Tecumseh's balance sheet combines the assets and liabilities of four very different types of businesses, so it's very difficult to make much sense of any type of ratio analysis.
6. I notice from the balance sheet that Tecumseh's overall debt has increased significantly in 2018 over 2017. Long-term debt increased by $400,000 and the bank loan by $100,000. As a result, the debt-to-equity ratio has increased from 0.96 to 1.17—not alarming (though consideration of the individual business lines is necessary), but you should investigate the need for such a large increase in debt, especially in light of a much smaller increase in property, plant, and equipment. In addition, you should find out whether the new debt is for the farm or for another part of the operation. You should also find out what security has been provided for the existing debt and whether the owners have personally guaranteed it. This is important information because it will give you some insight into how much protection (through collateral and personal guarantees) you can obtain if you decided to lend money to the farm.
7. Liquidity on the consolidated balance sheet seems strong (the current ratio is 1.61, which is about the same as in 2017), but I am very concerned about the large increase in accounts receivable. Not much analysis of receivables is possible without the income statement and other information, but this could be a concern if the increase does not correspond with an increase in revenues. Tecumseh may be having trouble collecting its receivables, or perhaps there is a receivable to a manager or shareholder in the reported balance. Once again, you need to find out whether this increase in receivables pertains to the farm.
8. As I have indicated throughout this report, you do not have nearly enough information to make a lending decision. You need the farm's financial statements and you must obtain additional information. It is always important to remember that these are historical financial statements; they report past transactions. Ultimately, a lending decision should be based on the ability of an entity to generate cash flows to pay the interest on the loan and the principal.

Best wishes and thanks for letting me do this report for you.

Your nephew,
John

APPENDIX

LO 5 The Consolidated Financial Statements in Periods after a Subsidiary Is Purchased

In periods after the acquisition of a subsidiary, the consolidated financial statements are more than the sum of the lines on the income statements and balance sheets of the parent and subsidiaries. Three adjustments are described below.

Fair Value Adjustments Remember that consolidated financial statements report the assets and liabilities of the subsidiary at their fair values on the date the subsidiary was acquired. This treatment has consequences for later periods. When the inventory that was on hand at acquisition is sold, cost of goods sold is the cost of the inventory as reported on the consolidated balance sheet, not the cost on the subsidiary's balance sheet. Similarly, the depreciation and amortization of capital assets is calculated using their fair values on the acquisition date (if the revaluation model isn't used). Recall the Pefferlaw-Schuler example from the main part of the chapter. In that example, the $21.5 million fair value of Schuler's capital assets included in Pefferlaw's consolidated balance sheet is what is depreciated (see Table 11.2). It doesn't matter that these same assets are recorded at $14 million on Schuler's own balance sheet. For the purpose of preparing the consolidated financial statements, it's the $21.5 million that matters. It isn't even necessary for the same depreciation method to be used on both the consolidated and subsidiary's statements.

Remember, the fair value of a subsidiary's assets and liabilities isn't determined each time consolidated financial statements are prepared (unless fair-valuing is the accounting policy). Fair-valuing is done once, when the subsidiary is acquired, and those values become the historical costs for use in the preparation of future consolidated financial statements.

Goodwill As mentioned earlier, goodwill doesn't have to be amortized. Management must regularly evaluate the goodwill and write it down if it's impaired. A writedown reduces the amount of goodwill on the consolidated balance sheet and the reduction is expensed on the consolidated income statement.

Intercompany Transactions For the most part, a consolidated income statement can be prepared by adding together the income statements of the parent and the subsidiaries. Some adjustments are needed, two of which we just discussed. It may also be necessary to adjust the consolidated financial statements for intercompany transactions. Intercompany transactions are economic activities among entities in a corporate group and are eliminated when consolidated financial statements are prepared.

It's important and useful that intercompany transactions are eliminated. This means that revenues and expenses and changes in the value of assets and liabilities that result from transactions between subsidiaries and with the parent aren't reflected in the consolidated statements. These have no economic significance to the consolidated entity. Only transactions with entities external to the consolidated group have economic significance. Transactions between corporations within the group are recorded in the financial statements each corporation prepares but are eliminated on consolidation. After all, are the shareholders of a consolidated entity better off if a subsidiary sells merchandise to its parent at a profit? If sales among entities in a corporate group aren't eliminated, revenues and expenses in the consolidated income statement will be overstated, and receivables, inventory, and payables on the balance sheet may also be overstated.

Let's use an example to examine the effect of intercompany transactions. Seech Inc. (Seech) is a 100-percent-owned subsidiary of Pitaga Ltd. (Pitaga). During the year ended December 31, 2017, Seech sold merchandise costing $2,000,000 to Pitaga for $4,500,000. This is the only transaction that Pitaga and Seech entered into during 2017 (either with each other or anyone else). Seech recorded the sale with the following journal entries:

Dr. Accounts receivable (asset +)	4,500,000	
Cr. Revenue (revenue +, shareholders' equity +)		4,500,000
To record the sale of merchandise to Pitaga		
Dr. Cost of sales (expense +, shareholders' equity −)	2,000,000	
Cr. Inventory (asset −)		2,000,000
To record the cost of the merchandise sold to Pitaga		

Pitaga recorded its purchase of the merchandise from Seech with the following journal entry:

Dr. Inventory (asset +)	4,500,000	
Cr. Accounts payable (liability +)		4,500,000
To record the purchase of merchandise from Seech		

Notice the effect of this transaction. Seech has earned a profit of $2,500,000 ($4,500,000 − $2,000,000) and the inventory it sold to Pitaga is now valued at $4,500,000 on Pitaga's balance sheet. There are receivables and payables of $4,500,000. In the context of transactions-based accounting, nothing has happened to justify reporting the revenue and profit and the increase in the value of inventory, accounts receivable, and accounts payable in the consolidated statements. From the perspective of the consolidated entity, this is like recognizing a profit, increasing the value of inventory, and reporting payables and receivables when moving goods from one warehouse to another. Table 11.4 sets out the effect of intercompany transactions between Pitaga and Seech.

TABLE 11.4 Effect of Intercompany Transactions: Scenario 1 (Seech's sale of merchandise to Pitaga—merchandise held by Pitaga at year-end)

	Column 1		Column 2	Column 3
	Accounting information for the year ended December 31, 2017		Pitaga Ltd. consolidated statements (intercompany transactions not eliminated)	Pitaga Ltd. consolidated statements (intercompany transactions eliminated)
	Pitaga Ltd.	Seech Inc.		
Revenue	$ 0	$4,500,000	$4,500,000	$ 0
Cost of sales	0	2,000,000	2,000,000	0
Net income	$ 0	$2,500,000	$2,500,000	$ 0
Accounts receivable	$ 0	$4,500,000	$4,500,000	$ 0
Inventory	$4,500,000	$ 0	$4,500,000	$2,000,000
Accounts payable	$4,500,000	$ 0	$4,500,000	$ 0

- Column 1 shows the summarized income statements and extracts from the balance sheets of the two companies. (These statements would be used for tax purposes and perhaps by a banker who loaned money to these entities.)
- Column 2 shows Pitaga's consolidated financial statements if the intercompany transactions aren't eliminated. In this column, Pitaga appears to be an active, perhaps successful enterprise, with sales of $4,500,000 and net income of $2,500,000. It isn't possible to tell from these statements that no real economic activity has occurred.
- Column 3 shows the consolidated statements if the intercompany transactions are eliminated. These statements show no activity: no revenues, no expenses, inventory reported at its cost to Seech, and no receivables or payables.

This example demonstrates how intercompany transactions can affect the financial statements and the potential difficulties for stakeholders who interpret and analyze financial statements that include intercompany transactions. When the financial statements (not the consolidated financial statements) of a subsidiary are being examined, it's important to be aware that intercompany transactions can have a significant effect.

QUESTION FOR CONSIDERATION

Explain why including intercompany transactions in consolidated financial statements can make those statements misleading to users.

ANSWER: If intercompany transactions aren't eliminated from consolidated financial statements, a number of problems exist that can mislead stakeholders:

1. Revenue from sales by one member of the consolidated entity to another will be included in consolidated revenue. This will overstate the economic activity of the entity, making it appear the entity is generating more revenue than it really is.
2. If an entity purchases inventory from another entity in the consolidated group at a profit, the value of the inventory on the balance sheet is increased, even though there hasn't been economic activity to justify the increase.
3. If the transactions between the corporations in the consolidated entity aren't settled in cash, receivables and payables will be increased by the amounts owing between the entities, thereby overstating current assets and current liabilities by the amounts owing between the entities.
4. As a result of the effects in (1) to (3), financial ratios will be distorted, and thus different from the amounts that would be reported if intercompany transactions were eliminated.

SUMMARY OF KEY POINTS

LO 1 There are many reasons why one company invests in another: earning a return on idle cash; strategic moves such as purchasing a competitor, supplier, or customer; and to diversify.

LO 2 When an investor has control of an investee, the investor prepares consolidated financial statements. Consolidated financial statements aggregate the accounting information of a parent corporation and all of its subsidiaries into a single set of financial statements. On the consolidated balance sheet, the assets and liabilities of a subsidiary are reported at their fair value on the date the subsidiary was purchased.

Goodwill arises when a parent pays more than the fair value of the subsidiary's identifiable assets and liabilities on the date the subsidiary is purchased. Goodwill isn't amortized.

Non-controlling interest arises when a parent company owns less than 100 percent of the shares of a subsidiary it controls. It arises because the consolidated balance sheet includes 100 percent of a subsidiary's assets and liabilities and the income statement includes 100 percent of its revenues and expenses, even though the parent owns less than 100 percent of those assets and liabilities.

LO 3 When one corporation has significant influence on the decision making of another, the equity method of accounting is used. The equity method is essentially the same as accounting for subsidiaries using the consolidation method, except that the information about equity-accounted-for investments is presented on a single line on the balance sheet and a single line on the income statement. An investment accounted for using the equity method is initially recorded on the investor's balance sheet at cost. The balance sheet amount is then adjusted each period by the investor's share of the investee's net income, less dividends declared by the investee.

LO 4 Passive investments are those for which the investor corporation can't influence the strategic decision making of the investee corporation. All investments in non-voting securities are passive. Voting shares are accounted for as passive investments when the investing company holds a relatively small proportion of the voting shares.

Passive investments can be accounted for by amortized cost, fair value through profit and loss (FVTPL), or fair value through other comprehensive income (FVTOCI). Amortized cost and FVTPL can be used for debt investments whereas FVTPL and FVTOCI are available for equity investments. Investment income is always reported in the calculation of net income.

LO 5 (Appendix) In periods after the acquisition of a subsidiary, the consolidated financial statements are more than the sum of the lines on the income statements and the balance sheets of the parent and subsidiaries. Three adjustments that must be considered are fair value adjustments of assets and liabilities, possible impairment of goodwill, and the elimination of intercompany transactions.

KEY TERMS

amortized cost, p. 683
consolidated financial statement, p. 670
control, p. 670
equity method of accounting, p. 679
fair value through other comprehensive income, p. 684
fair value through profit and loss, p. 684
financial instruments, p. 683
goodwill, p. 673
identifiable assets and liabilities, p. 672
intercompany transaction, p. 677
investee corporation, p. 669
investor corporation, p. 669
non-controlling interest, p. 675
parent corporation, p. 670
passive investment, p. 683
segment disclosure, p. 677
significant influence, p. 679
subsidiary corporation, p. 670

SIMILAR TERMS

The left column gives alternative terms that are sometimes used for the accounting terms introduced in this chapter, which are listed in the right column.

minority interest	**non-controlling interest, p. 675**

ASSIGNMENT MATERIALS

Questions

Q11-1. What is goodwill? Under what circumstances is it recorded on financial statements?

Q11-2. Why is understanding the extent to which one corporation influences another important for accounting purposes? What impact does an entity's degree of influence have on the accounting for investments?

Q11-3. Explain the following degrees of influence that one corporation can have over another and the implications of each for financial reporting:
a. control
b. significant influence
c. no influence

Q11-4. What are consolidated financial statements? What are some of their benefits and limitations?

Q11-5. Why do companies invest in other companies?

Q11-6. What are intercompany transactions? Why are the effects of intercompany transactions eliminated when consolidated financial statements are prepared?

Q11-7. What is a subsidiary? How are subsidiaries accounted for? Explain.

Q11-8. What is meant by "non-controlling interest"? What does the non-controlling interest on a company's balance sheet represent? What does it represent on the income statement?

Q11-9. Explain how a non-controlling shareholder in a subsidiary would use the non-controlling interest accounts on the parent's consolidated balance sheet and income statement.

Q11-10. When a subsidiary is acquired, the managers of the parent must allocate the purchase price to the subsidiary's identifiable assets and liabilities. Because the subsidiary's assets and liabilities are bought as a bundle, management has some flexibility in how it allocates the purchase price. Given this flexibility, how do you think the objectives of financial reporting would affect management's allocation of the purchase price? Explain.

Q11-11. What is segment disclosure? Why is segment information required in the financial statements of public companies?

Q11-12. Explain the usefulness of the consolidated financial statements of a parent corporation for the following stakeholders:
a. shareholder of the parent corporation
b. major supplier of one of the subsidiaries
c. Canada Revenue Agency (for income tax determination)

Q11-13. What are the two methods for accounting for debt investments? Explain how the methods differ in valuing investments on the balance sheet. Explain how the methods differ in their treatment of gains and losses.

Q11-14. What are the two methods for accounting for passive equity investments? Explain how the methods differ in valuing investments on the balance sheet. Explain how the methods differ in their treatment of gains and losses. How is dividend income treated under the two methods?

Q11-15. Explain why consolidated financial statements aren't just the sum of the amounts reported on the parent's and subsidiaries' financial statements.

Q11-16. Explain the following terms:
a. investor corporation
b. investee corporation
c. parent corporation
d. subsidiary corporation

Q11-17. When the equity method of accounting for investments is used, dividends received from the investee corporation reduce the balance in the investment account on the investor's balance sheet and aren't treated as investment income on the income statement. Explain.

Q11-18. Explain the difference between the parent's consolidated financial statements and the financial statements of the parent alone.

Exercises

E11-1. **(Accounting for different types of investments in securities, LO 2, 3, 4)** How should an investor corporation account for the following investments?
a. Ownership of 51 percent of the voting shares of a company.
b. Ownership of 20 percent of the outstanding common shares of a company. These common shares represent 60 percent of the votes.
c. Ownership of 25 percent of the shares of a company.
d. Ownership of 0.05 percent of the shares of a company.

E11-2. **(Accounting for different types of investments in securities, LO 2, 3, 4)** State how the investor corporation would account for the following investments. Explain your choice.
a. Purchase of $1,000,000 of bonds that management intends to hold until they mature in three years.
b. Investment in non-voting shares of a private corporation. Management hopes to sell the shares within six months.
c. Investment representing 15 percent of the voting shares of a private corporation. One person owns the remainder.
d. Investment in 52 percent of the voting shares of a private corporation. One person owns the remaining shares.
e. Investment in 30 percent of the voting shares of a public corporation. The investor corporation is the largest single investor in the public corporation and it has five representatives on its board of directors. The board has 15 members.

E11-3. **(Non-controlling interest, LO 2)** On December 31, 2017, Kootuk Inc. (Kootuk) purchased 75 percent of the common shares of Grimmer Ltd. (Grimmer) for $3,500,000. At the time of the purchase, Kootuk's management made the following estimates of the fair values of Grimmer's assets and liabilities:

	Carrying amount of Grimmer's assets and liabilities on December 31, 2017	Fair value of Grimmer's assets and liabilities on December 31, 2017
Assets	$5,000,000	$6,000,000
Liabilities	2,000,000	2,400,000

Required:

a. Calculate the amount of non-controlling interest that Kootuk would report on its December 31, 2017 consolidated balance sheet as a result of its purchase of Grimmer.
b. What amount would be included in the assets and liabilities on the Kootuk's December 31, 2017 consolidated balance sheet as a result of the purchase of Grimmer?

E11-4. **(Non-controlling interest, LO 2)** On August 31, 2018, Hoselaw Inc. (Hoselaw) purchased 60 percent of the common shares of Upsalquitch Ltd. (Upsalquitch) for $8,000,000. At the time of the purchase, Upsalquitch's management made the following estimates of the fair values of Hoselaw's assets and liabilities:

	Carrying amount of Upsalquitch's assets and liabilities on August 31, 2018	Fair value of Upsalquitch's assets and liabilities on August 31, 2018
Current assets	$1,000,000	$1,250,000
Tangible capital assets	3,000,000	3,600,000
Patents	100,000	1,000,000
Current liabilities	875,000	900,000
Long-term debt	2,125,000	2,000,000

Required:

a. Calculate the amount of non-controlling interest that Hoselaw would report on its August 31, 2018 consolidated balance sheet as a result of its purchase of Upsalquitch.
b. What amount would be included in each asset and liability account on the August 31, 2018 consolidated balance sheet as a result of the purchase of Upsalquitch?
c. What does non-controlling interest on the balance sheet represent? Explain why it appears. How should users of financial statements interpret non-controlling interest?

E11-5. **(Accounting for passive investments, LO 4)** Chockpish Inc. (Chockpish) has provided you with the following list of transactions and economic events that involved its passive investment portfolio in 2018. For each of the items, prepare any journal entries required. Explain your entries fully. Chockpish's year-end is December 31.

a. On January 15, 2,000, shares of Inwood Corp. were purchased at $37 per share.
b. On February 12, a cheque for $10,000 was received from Guthrie Inc. for dividends.
c. At the close of trading on December 31, bonds of Hydraulic Corp. were priced $980 per thousand-dollar bond. Chockpish's 100 bonds have a carrying amount of $1,000 per bond. The company invests in this type of bond for the cash flow it generates.
d. At the close of trading on December 31, shares of Kynoch Ltd. were priced at $12 per share. Chockpish's 5,000 shares of Kynoch Ltd. have a carrying amount of $15 per share. Chockpish designated these shares as fair value through other comprehensive income.
e. At the close of trading on December 31, shares of Jobrin Inc. were priced at $19 per share. Chockpish's 3,000 shares of Jobrin have a carrying amount of $22 per share. Chockpish accounts for these shares as fair value through profit and loss.

E11-6. **(Consolidation accounting, LO 2)** To expand its market penetration in the retail clothing market, Balmoral Designs Ltd. (Balmoral) purchased 100 percent of the outstanding shares of Chipman Fine Clothiers Inc. (Chipman). Balmoral paid $4,200,000 cash for the shares and its management determined that at the time of acquisition the fair value of Chipman's identifiable assets and liabilities was $2,400,000. The following information was obtained as of the date Chipman was acquired and was prepared before the purchase occurred:

	Balmoral	Chipman (carrying amounts)	Chipman (fair values)		Balmoral	Chipman (carrying amounts)	Chipman (fair values)
Current assets	$ 7,000,000	$1,900,000	$2,400,000	Current liabilities	$ 5,000,000	$ 750,000	$750,000
Non-current assets	5,000,000	1,050,000	1,170,000	Non-current liabilities	2,000,000	400,000	420,000
				Shareholders' equity	5,000,000	1,800,000	
Total assets	$12,000,000	$2,950,000		Total liabilities and shareholders' equity	$12,000,000	$2,950,000	

Required:

Calculate the amounts that would appear on Balmoral's consolidated balance sheet on the date it acquired Chipman.

E11-7. **(Consolidation accounting, LO 2)** To expand its product line, Dorchester Manufacturing Ltd. (Dorchester) purchased 100 percent of the outstanding shares of Hardisty Inc. (Hardisty). Dorchester paid $3,500,000 cash for the shares. The following information was obtained as of the date Hardisty was acquired and was prepared before the purchase occurred:

	Dorchester	Hardisty (carrying amounts)	Hardisty (fair values)		Dorchester	Hardisty (carrying amounts)	Hardisty (fair values)
Current assets	$ 4,250,000	$1,500,000	$1,900,000	Current liabilities	$ 3,250,000	$1,250,000	$1,350,000
Non-current assets	16,250,000	5,000,000	6,000,000	Non-current liabilities	9,000,000	3,150,000	3,550,000
				Shareholders' equity	8,250,000	2,100,000	
Total assets	$20,500,000	$6,500,000		Total liabilities and shareholders' equity	$20,500,000	$6,500,000	

Required:

Calculate the amounts that would appear on Dorchester's consolidated balance sheet on the date it acquired Hardisty.

E11-8. **(The equity method of accounting, LO 3)** On January 1, 2017, Fletwode Corp. (Fletwode) purchased 2,250,000 common shares of Irvine Ltd. (Irvine) for $10,000,000. The investment represents a 30 percent interest in Irvine and gives Fletwode significant influence over Irvine. For 2017, Fletwode's share of Irvine's net income was $390,000, and during the year Irvine paid dividends of $100,000 to all shareholders. Both companies have December 31 year-ends.

Required:

a. Prepare Fletwode's journal entry to record its investment in Irvine.
b. What amount would be reported on Fletwode's December 31, 2017 balance sheet for this investment? How much would Fletwode report on its December 31, 2017 income statement from its investment in Irvine?

E11-9. **(The equity method of accounting, LO 3)** On June 1, 2017, Wostok Corp. (Wostok) purchased 1,000,000 common shares of Griffin Ltd. (Griffin) for $2,000,000. The investment represents a 40 percent interest in Griffin and gives Wostok significant influence. During fiscal 2018, Wostok's share of Griffin's net income was $440,000. Also, Griffin paid dividends during the year of $0.50 per share. Both companies have May 31 year-ends.

Required:

a. Prepare Wostok's journal entry to record its investment in Griffin.
b. How much would Wostok report on its May 31, 2018 income statement from this investment?
c. What amount would be reported on Wostok's May 31, 2018 balance sheet for its investment in Griffin?

E11-10. **(Consolidated income statement, LO 2, 5)** Explain how the following items would affect consolidated net income in the year a subsidiary is purchased and in the year after:

a. Impairment of the value of goodwill.
b. Land with a carrying amount of $2,000,000 on the subsidiary's balance sheet on the date the subsidiary was purchased has a fair value of $5,000,000.
c. Equipment with a carrying amount of $1,000,000 on the subsidiary's balance sheet on the date the subsidiary was purchased has a fair value of $1,500,000. The equipment had a remaining useful life of five years on the date of acquisition.
d. Inventory with a carrying amount of $200,000 on the subsidiary's balance sheet on the date the subsidiary was purchased has a fair value of $230,000.
e. Dividends paid by the subsidiary to the parent.
f. Services sold at a profit by the subsidiary to the parent.
g. The subsidiary is 80 percent owned by the parent.

Problems

P11-1. **(Fair value through profit and loss versus fair value through other comprehensive income, LO 4)** In June 2016, Jolicure Inc. (Jolicure) and Horsefly Inc. (Horsefly) each began operations. Each company was formed with an initial capital contribution of $100,000. During the years ended May 31, 2017 and 2018, each company had revenue of $225,000 and total expenses of $175,000, before accounting for passive investments. During fiscal 2017, each company purchased 3,000 shares of Nictaux Ltd. (Nictaux), a public company, for $12 per share. On May 31, 2017 and 2018 respectively the fair value of Nictaux's shares was $20 and $15. On May 31, 2017, each company had total assets (excluding the shares in Nictaux) of $200,000 and total liabilities of $50,000. On May 31, 2018, each company had total assets (excluding the shares in Nictaux) of $275,000 and total liabilities of $75,000. Jolicure accounts for the shares as fair value through profit and loss while Horsefly accounts for them as fair value through other comprehensive income.

Required:

a. Prepare summarized balance sheets and income statements for Jolicure and Horsefly as of May 31, 2017 and 2018.
b. Which company performed better in each year? What is the impact of using fair value through profit and loss versus fair value through other comprehensive income on the reported performance of the company?

P11-2. **(Accounting for passive investments, LO 4)** On August 1, 2017, Lourdes Inc. (Lourdes) purchased 20,000 preferred shares of Matagami Ltd. for $120 per share. The shares have a dividend of $12 per share and the shares must be repurchased by Matagami on or before November 30, 2023 for $120 per share. On December 31, 2017, Lourdes' year-end, the fair value of the shares was $95 per share. On December 31, 2017, Lourdes had total assets (excluding the investment in the preferred shares) of $35 million, total liabilities of $25 million and share capital of $4 million. In addition, Lourdes' revenues and expenses for 2017 (excluding all income statement effects related to the preferred shares) were $8,200,000 and $6,100,000 respectively. Retained earnings on January 1, 2017 was $6,060,000. The preferred dividends were paid on November 15, 2017.

Required:

a. Prepare a summarized balance sheet and income statement on December 31, 2017, assuming that Lourdes accounts for the shares as a (i) fair value through profit and loss, (ii) fair value through other comprehensive income, and (iii) amortized cost, and that Lourdes owned the shares on December 31, 2017.
b. Prepare a summarized balance sheet and income statement on December 31, 2017, assuming that Lourdes accounts for the shares as a (i) fair value through profit and loss, (ii) fair value through other comprehensive income, and (iii) amortized cost, assuming that Lourdes sold the shares on December 31, 2017, for $95 per share.

P11-3. **(Preparation of a consolidated balance sheet on the date a subsidiary is purchased, LO 2)** On August 31, 2017, Pacquet Inc. (Pacquet) purchased 100 percent of the common shares of Schwitzer Ltd. (Schwitzer) for $2,000,000 cash. Pacquet's and Schwitzer's balance sheets on August 31, 2017 just before the purchase are as shown in the following table.

Balance Sheets as of August 31, 2017		
	Pacquet Inc.	**Schwitzer Ltd.**
Current assets	$3,500,000	$ 625,000
Capital assets	3,250,000	1,250,000
Total assets	$6,750,000	$1,875,000
Current liabilities	$1,350,000	$ 375,000
Non-current liabilities	1,250,000	500,000
Common shares	2,000,000	250,000
Retained earnings	2,150,000	750,000
Total liabilities and shareholders' equity	$6,750,000	$1,875,000

Management determined that the fair values of Schwitzer's assets and liabilities were as follows:

	Fair value of Schwitzer's identifiable assets and liabilities on August 31, 2017
Current assets	$ 875,000
Capital assets	1,950,000
Current liabilities	375,000
Non-current liabilities	550,000

Required:

a. Prepare Pacquet's balance sheet immediately following the purchase.
b. Calculate the amount of goodwill that would be reported on Pacquet's consolidated balance sheet on August 31, 2017.
c. Prepare Pacquet's consolidated balance sheet on August 31, 2017.
d. Calculate the current ratios and debt-to-equity ratios for Pacquet, Schwitzer, and for the consolidated balance sheet on August 31, 2017. Interpret the differences between the ratios. When calculating the ratios, use Pacquet and Schwitzer's balance sheets after the purchase had been made and recorded.
e. You are a lender who has been asked to make a sizeable loan to Schwitzer. Which balance sheets would you be interested in viewing? Explain. How would you use Pacquet's consolidated financial statements in making your lending decision?

P11-4. **(Preparation of a consolidated balance sheet on the date a subsidiary is purchased, LO 2)** On January 31, 2018, Paju Inc. (Paju) purchased 100 percent of the common shares of Shellmouth Ltd. (Shellmouth) for $6,250,000 in cash. Paju's and Shellmouth's balance sheets on January 31, 2018, just before the purchase are shown in the following table.

Balance Sheets as of January 31, 2018		
	Paju Inc.	Shellmouth Ltd.
Current assets	$ 7,500,000	$5,625,000
Capital assets	14,687,500	1,875,000
Total assets	$22,187,500	$7,500,000
Current liabilities	$ 1,500,000	$1,875,000
Non-current liabilities	7,500,000	625,000
Common shares	9,375,000	3,750,000
Retained earnings	3,812,500	1,250,000
Total liabilities and shareholders' equity	$22,187,500	$7,500,000

Management determined that the fair values of Shellmouth's assets and liabilities were as follows:

	Fair value of Shellmouth's identifiable assets and liabilities on January 31, 2018
Current assets	$4,875,000
Capital assets	2,375,000
Current liabilities	2,000,000
Non-current liabilities	937,500

Required:

a. Prepare Paju's balance sheet immediately following the purchase.
b. Calculate the amount of goodwill to be reported on Paju's consolidated balance sheet on January 31, 2018.
c. Prepare Paju's consolidated balance sheet on January 31, 2018.
d. Calculate the current ratios and debt-to-equity ratios for Paju, Shellmouth, and for the consolidated balance sheet on January 31, 2018. Interpret the differences between the ratios you calculated. When calculating the ratios, use Paju's and Shellmouth's balance sheets after the purchase has been made and recorded.
e. You are a potential investor who has been asked to purchase a 25 percent equity interest in Shellmouth (you would purchase the shares from Shellmouth, not from Paju). Which balance sheets would you be interested in viewing? Explain. How would you use Paju's consolidated financial statements in making your investment decision? What concerns would you have about making an equity investment in Shellmouth?

P11-5. **(Preparation of a consolidated balance sheet on the date a subsidiary is purchased when less than 100 percent of the subsidiary is purchased, LO 5, Appendix)** On March 31, 2018, Popkum Inc. (Popkum) purchased 65 percent of the common shares of Saguay Ltd. (Saguay) for $1,200,000. Popkum's and Saguay's balance sheets on March 31, 2018 just before the purchase were:

Balance Sheets as of March 31, 2018		
	Popkum Inc.	Saguay Ltd.
Current assets	$2,625,000	$ 468,750
Capital assets	2,437,500	937,500
Total assets	$5,062,500	$1,406,250
Current liabilities	$1,012,500	$ 281,250
Non-current liabilities	937,500	375,000
Common shares	1,500,000	187,500
Retained earnings	1,612,500	562,500
Total liabilities and shareholders' equity	$5,062,500	$1,406,250

Management determined that the fair values of Saguay's assets and liabilities were as follows:

	Fair value of Saguay's identifiable assets and liabilities on March 31, 2018
Current assets	$ 656,250
Capital assets	1,462,500
Current liabilities	281,250
Non-current liabilities	412,500

Required:

a. Calculate the amount of goodwill to be reported on Popkum's consolidated balance sheet on March 31, 2018.
b. Calculate the amount of non-controlling interest to be reported on the consolidated balance sheet on March 31, 2018.
c. Prepare Popkum's consolidated balance sheet on March 31, 2018.
d. Calculate the current ratios and debt-to-equity ratios for Popkum, Saguay, and for the consolidated balance sheet on March 31, 2018. Interpret the differences between the ratios.
e. Explain what the non-controlling interest on the balance sheet represents. How would you interpret it from the perspective of a shareholder of Popkum? How would you interpret it from the perspective of a shareholder in Saguay? How would you interpret it from the perspective of a lender?

P11-6. **(Preparation of a consolidated balance sheet on the date a subsidiary is purchased when less than 100 percent of the subsidiary is purchased, LO 5, Appendix)** On October 31, 2017, Pahonan Inc. (Pahonan) purchased 75 percent of the common shares of Seebe Ltd. (Seebe) for $1,500,000. Pahonan's and Seebe's balance sheets on October 31, 2017, just before the purchase are shown:

Balance Sheets as of October 31, 2017		
	Pahonan Inc.	Seebe Ltd.
Current assets	$2,000,000	$2,250,000
Capital assets	6,875,000	750,000
Total assets	$8,875,000	$3,000,000
Current liabilities	$ 600,000	$ 750,000
Non-current liabilities	3,000,000	250,000
Common shares	3,750,000	1,500,000
Retained earnings	1,525,000	500,000
Total liabilities and shareholders' equity	$8,875,000	$3,000,000

Management determined that the fair values of Seebe's assets and liabilities were as follows:

	Fair value of Seebe's assets and liabilities on October 31, 2017
Current assets	$1,950,000
Capital assets	950,000
Current liabilities	800,000
Non-current liabilities	375,000

Required:

a. Prepare the journal entry that Pahonan would make to record its purchase of Seebe's shares.

b. Prepare the journal entry that Seebe would make to record its purchase by Pahonan, if any.
c. Calculate the amount of goodwill to be reported on Pahonan's consolidated balance sheet on October 31, 2017.
d. Calculate the amount of non-controlling interest to be reported on the consolidated balance sheet on October 31, 2017.
e. Prepare Pahonan's consolidated balance sheet on October 31, 2017.
f. Calculate the current ratios and debt-to-equity ratios for Pahonan and Seebe, and for the consolidated balance sheet on October 31, 2017. Interpret the differences between the ratios you calculated.
g. Explain what the non-controlling interest on the balance sheet represents. How would you interpret it from the perspective of a shareholder of Pahonan? How would you interpret it from the perspective of a shareholder in Seebe? How would you interpret it from the perspective of a lender?

P11-7. **(Intercompany transactions, LO 5, Appendix)** Vonda Inc. (Vonda) is a 100-percent-owned subsidiary of Atik Ltd. (Atik). During the year ended March 31, 2017, Vonda sold to Atik, on credit, merchandise costing $500,000 for $1,000,000. These were the only transactions that Atik and Vonda entered into during fiscal 2017 (with each other or with third parties) and no other costs were incurred.

Required:

a. Prepare an income statement for Vonda for the year ended March 31, 2017.
b. What amount of accounts receivable would Vonda report on its March 31, 2017 balance sheet?
c. What amount of inventory and accounts payable would Atik report on its March 31, 2017 balance sheet?
d. Prepare Atik's March 31, 2017 consolidated income statement assuming that intercompany transactions aren't eliminated. How much would be reported for accounts receivable, inventory, and accounts payable on the March 31, 2017 consolidated balance sheet?
e. Prepare Atik's March 31, 2017 consolidated income statement, assuming that intercompany transactions are eliminated. How much would be reported for accounts receivable, inventory, and accounts payable on the March 31, 2017 consolidated balance sheet?
f. Discuss the differences in the information you prepared in parts (d) and (e). Which information is more useful to stakeholders? Explain.

P11-8. **(Intercompany transactions, LO 5, Appendix)** Guilds Inc. (Guilds) is a 100-percent-owned subsidiary of Nutak Ltd. (Nutak). During the year ended August 31, 2017, Guilds sold merchandise costing $300,000 to Nutak for $750,000. These were the only transactions that Nutak and Guilds entered into during 2017 (with each other or with third parties) and there were no other costs incurred. The sale was on credit.

Required:

a. Prepare an income statement for Guilds for the year ended August 31, 2017.
b. What amount of accounts receivable would Guilds report on its August 31, 2017 balance sheet?
c. What amount of inventory and accounts payable would Nutak report on its August 31, 2017 balance sheet?
d. Prepare Nutak's August 31, 2017 consolidated income statement assuming that intercompany transactions aren't eliminated. How much would be reported for accounts receivable, inventory, and accounts payable on the August 31, 2017 consolidated balance sheet?
e. Prepare Nutak's August 31, 2017 consolidated income statement assuming that intercompany transactions are eliminated. How much would be reported for accounts receivable, inventory, and accounts payable on the August 31, 2017 consolidated balance sheet?
f. Discuss the differences in the information you prepared in parts (d) and (e). Which information is more useful to stakeholders? Explain.

P11-9. **(Intercompany transactions, LO 5, Appendix)** Dozois Inc. (Dozois) is a 100-percent-owned subsidiary of Yarbo Ltd. (Yarbo). During the year ended July 31, 2018, Dozois sold merchandise costing $1,100,000 to Yarbo for $1,500,000. During fiscal 2018, Yarbo sold, on credit, the merchandise it had purchased from Dozois to third parties for $1,600,000. These were the only transactions that Yarbo and Dozois entered into during 2018 (with each other or with third parties) and no other costs were incurred.

Required:

a. Prepare an income statement for Dozois for the year ended July 31, 2018.
b. What amount of accounts receivable would Dozois report on its July 31, 2018 balance sheet?
c. What amount of inventory and accounts payable would Yarbo report on its July 31, 2018 balance sheet?
d. Prepare Yarbo's July 31, 2018 consolidated income statement assuming that intercompany transactions aren't eliminated. How much would be reported for accounts receivable, inventory, and accounts payable on the July 31, 2018 consolidated balance sheet?
e. Prepare Yarbo's July 31, 2018 consolidated income statement assuming that intercompany transactions are eliminated. How much would be reported for accounts receivable, inventory, and accounts payable on the July 31, 2018 consolidated balance sheet?
f. Discuss the differences in the information you prepared in parts (d) and (e). Which information is more useful to stakeholders? Explain.

P11-10. **(Passive investments, LO 4)** In July 2017, Roddickton Ltd. (Roddickton) purchased 50,000 shares of Kola Inc. (Kola), a publicly traded company, for $22 per share. Roddickton received dividends of $1.10 per share from its investment in Kola. On December 31, 2017, the closing price for Kola's shares was $29. There were 100,000,000 shares of Kola's common stock outstanding during 2017.

Required:

a. Prepare the journal entry that would be made to record the purchase of the shares.
b. Prepare the journal entry to record the dividends received by Kola during 2017.
c. How would you classify this investment for financial reporting purposes? How would you decide? Does it matter how the investment is accounted for?
d. If the investment in Kola were classified as fair value through other comprehensive income, what amount would be reported on Roddickton's December 31, 2017 balance sheet? Explain. Would there be any impact on the income statement/statement of comprehensive income? Explain.
e. If the investment in Kola were classified as fair value through profit and loss, what amount would be reported on Roddickton's December 31, 2017 balance sheet? Explain. Would there be any impact on the income statement/statement of comprehensive income? Explain.
f. Do you think a management cares whether its investments are classified as fair value through other comprehensive income or fair value through profit and loss? Explain.

Using Financial Statements

BROOKFIELD ASSET MANAGEMENT INC.

Brookfield Asset Management Inc. (Brookfield) is a global alternative asset manager with approximately $150 billion in assets under management. The Company focuses on property, renewable power, infrastructure and private equity. It operates and manages: hydroelectric power generating facilities, as well as a range of wind farms; commercial real estate, which includes office and retail properties in addition to investments in real estate, financial lending and office and retail developments; infrastructure, focused on utilities, transport, energy and timber sectors;

private equity, which includes restructuring and special situations, as well as residential and agricultural development. The company is listed on the New York and Toronto stock exchanges under the symbols BAM and BAM-A.TO.[5]

Brookfield's consolidated balance sheets, statements of operations, and extracts from the statements of cash flows, notes to the financial statements, and annual information form are provided — see Exhibit 11.5 here and Exhibit 11.4 earlier in the chapter (the statements of operations and Note 7 can be found in Exhibit 11.4). Use this information to respond to questions FS11-1 to FS11-6.[6]

FS11-1. Examine the information in Exhibits 11.5 and 11.4 and determine the following information:

a. Amount of non-controlling interests in net assets on December 31, 2011.
b. Amount reported as investments on December 31, 2011.

EXHIBIT 11.5 Brookfield Asset Management Inc.: Financial Statement Extracts

CONSOLIDATED FINANCIAL STATEMENTS

CONSOLIDATED BALANCE SHEETS

(MILLIONS)	Note	Dec. 31, 2011	Dec. 31, 2010
Assets			
Cash and cash equivalents	28	$ 2,027	$ 1,713
Other financial assets	4	3,773	4,419
Accounts receivable and other	5	6,723	7,869
Inventory	6	6,060	5,849
Investments	7	9,401	6,629
Investment properties	8	28,366	22,163
Property, plant and equipment	9	22,832	18,520
Timber	10	3,155	2,834
Intangible assets	11	3,968	3,805
Goodwill	12	2,607	2,546
Deferred income tax asset	13	2,118	1,784
Total Assets		$ 91,030	$ 78,131
Liabilities and Equity			
Accounts payable and other	14	$ 9,266	$ 10,334
Corporate borrowings	15	3,701	2,905
Non-recourse borrowings			
Property-specific mortgages	16	28,415	23,454
Subsidiary borrowings	16	4,441	4,007
Deferred income tax liability	13	5,817	4,970
Capital securities	17	1,650	1,707
Interests of others in consolidated funds	18	333	1,562
Equity			
Preferred equity	19	2,140	1,658
Non-controlling interests in net assets	19	18,516	14,739
Common equity	19	16,751	12,795
Total equity		37,407	29,192
Total Liabilities and Equity		$ 91,030	$ 78,131

EXHIBIT 11.5 (continued) Brookfield Asset Management Inc.: Financial Statement Extracts

CONSOLIDATED STATEMENTS OF CASH FLOWS

YEARS ENDED DECEMBER 31 (MILLIONS)	Note	2011	2010
Operating activities			
Net income		**$ 3,674**	$ 3,195
Adjusted for the following items			
Equity accounted income		**(2,205)**	(765)
Fair value changes		**(1,286)**	(1,651)
Depreciation and amortization		**904**	795
Deferred income taxes		**411**	43
		1,498	1,617
Investment in residential development		**(543)**	(14)
Net change in non-cash working capital balances and other		**(279)**	(183)
		676	1,420

2. SIGNIFICANT ACCOUNTING POLICIES

b) Basis of Presentation

i. Subsidiaries

The consolidated financial statements include the accounts of the company and its consolidated subsidiaries, which are the entities over which the company has control. Subsidiaries are consolidated from the date the company obtains control, and continue to be consolidated until the date when control is lost. Control exists when the company has the power, directly or indirectly, to govern the financial and operating policies of an entity so as to obtain benefit from its activities. Non-controlling interest in the equity of the company's subsidiaries are included within equity on the Consolidated Balance Sheets. All intercompany balances, transactions, unrealized gains and losses are eliminated in full. Changes in the company's ownership interest of a subsidiary that do not result in a loss of control are accounted for as equity transactions and are recorded within Ownership Changes as a component of equity.

The following is a list of the company's principal consolidated subsidiaries indicating the jurisdiction of incorporation or formation and the percentage of voting securities owned, or over which control or direction is otherwise exercised directly or indirectly, by the company:

	Jurisdiction of Formation	Voting Control (%)
Property		
Brookfield Office Properties Inc.	Canada	50.8%
Brookfield Canada Office Properties REIT	Canada	83.3%
Renewable Power		
Brookfield Renewable Energy Partners L.P.	Bermuda	100.0%
Infrastructure		
Brookfield Infrastructure Partners L.P.	Bermuda	100.0%
Other		
Brookfield Multiplex Australia	Australia	100.0%
Brookfield Residential Properties Inc.	Ontario	72.5%
Norbord Inc.	Ontario	52.4%
Brookfield Brasil, S.A.	Brazil	100.0%

ii. Associates

Associates are entities over which the company exercises significant influence. Significant influence is the power to participate in the financial and operating policy decisions of the investee but not control or joint control over those policies. The company accounts for investments over which it has significant influence using the equity method, and they are recorded in Investments on the Consolidated Balance Sheets.

EXHIBIT 11.5 (continued) Brookfield Asset Management Inc.: Financial Statement Extracts

Interests in investments accounted for using the equity method are initially recognized at cost. If the cost of the associate is lower than the proportionate share of the investment's underlying fair value, the company records a gain on the difference between the cost and the underlying fair value of the investment in net income. If the cost of the associate is greater than the company's proportionate share of the underlying fair value, goodwill relating to the associate is included in the carrying amount of the investment. Subsequent to initial recognition, the carrying value of the company's interest in an investee is adjusted for the company's share of comprehensive income and distributions of the investee. Profit and losses resulting from transactions with an associate are recognized in the consolidated financial statements based on the interests of unrelated investors in the associate.

27. SEGMENTED INFORMATION

The company's presentation of reportable segments is based on how management has organized the business in making operating and capital allocation decisions and assessing performance. The company has five reportable segments:

a) Property operations include office properties retail properties, real estate finance, opportunistic investing and office developments located primarily in major North American, Australian, Brazilian and European cities;

b) Renewable power operations, which are predominantly hydroelectric power generating facilities on river systems in North America and Brazil;

c) Infrastructure operations, which are predominantly utilities, transport and energy and timberland operations located in Australia, North America, Europe and South America;

d) Private equity operations include the company's special situations investments, residential development and agricultural development;

e) Assets management services and other, corporate non-operating assets, liabilities and related revenues, cash flows and net income (loss) are presented as asset management services, corporate and other.

The following table disaggregates revenue, net income (loss), assets and liabilities by reportable segments:

AS AT AND FOR THE YEARS ENDED (MILLIONS)	Dec. 31, 2011 Revenue	Net Income	Assets	Liabilities	Dec. 31, 2010 Revenue	Net Income	Assets	Liabilities
Property	$ 2,760	$ 3,682	$ 40,497	$ 19,757	$ 2,589	$ 1,870	$ 31,572	$ 16,211
Renewable power	1,140	(458)	16,826	9,213	1,161	406	14,738	9,902
Infrastructure	1,690	482	14,007	7,756	867	538	13,695	8,446
Private equity	6,770	(23)	13,284	8,241	6,011	276	13,029	7,258
Asset management services, corporate and other	3,561	(9)	6,416	8,656	2,995	105	5,097	7,122
	$ 15,921	$ 3,674	$ 91,030	$ 53,623	$ 13,623	$ 3,195	$ 78,131	$ 48,939

Revenues, assets and liabilities by geographic segments are as follows:

AS AT AND FOR THE YEARS ENDED (MILLIONS)	Dec. 31, 2011 Revenue	Assets	Liabilities	Dec. 31, 2010 Revenue	Assets	Liabilities
United States	$ 4,715	$ 38,192	$ 24,442	$ 5,069	$ 28,122	$ 18,100
Canada	2,809	19,848	11,453	2,607	17,440	12,053
Australia	3,470	15,066	9,308	2,034	16,813	10,028
Brazil	2,519	12,202	5,799	1,688	11,483	6,453
Europe	1,364	4,359	2,246	1,283	3,348	1,937
Other	1,044	1,363	375	942	925	368
	$ 15,921	$ 91,030	$ 53,623	$ 13,623	$ 78,131	$ 48,939

c. Amount of equity accounted income for the year ended December 31, 2011.

d. Amount of net income attributable to shareholders and non-controlling interests for the year ended December 31, 2011.

FS11-2. Examine Notes 2(b)(ii) and 7 (Note 7 is in Exhibit 11.4) to Brookfield's financial statements. What is an associate company and how are "associate" companies accounted for?

What companies does Brookfield account for as associates? Which associate company had the highest carrying value on December 31, 2011 and what was its carrying value? Is it possible for an associate company to have an ownership interest greater than 50 percent? Explain. Why is equity-accounted income deducted from net income when calculating cash from operations?

FS11-3. Examine Note 27 to Brookfield's financial statements and answer the following questions on segmented information:

a. Identify the business segments in which Brookfield operates. Which segment has the most revenues? Which has the most assets? Which has the most income?
b. Identify the geographic segments that Brookfield reports in Note 27. Which segment has the most revenues? Which has the most assets? Why do you think segment income information isn't provided for the geographic segments?
c. Why is segment disclosure required under IFRS? As a user of Brookfield's annual report, how would your ability to use the financial statements be impaired by not having the segmented information?
d. What are the limitations of Brookfield's segment disclosure?

FS11-4. The following questions pertain to Brookfield's non-controlling interest:

a. What is non-controlling interest and why is it reported in Brookfield's financial statements?
b. What amount of non-controlling interest is reported on Brookfield's December 31, 2011 balance sheet? What does this amount represent?
c. What amount of Brookfield's net income is attributable to non-controlling interest for the year ended December 31, 2011? What does this amount represent?
d. Which companies in Brookfield's portfolio gave rise to the non-controlling interest?
e. If you were a non-Brookfield investor in Brookfield Properties Corporation, a company 50.8 percent owned by Brookfield, how would you use the non-controlling interest information included in Brookfield's financial statements?

FS11-5. The following questions pertain to Brookfield's accounting for its subsidiaries:

a. What is a subsidiary and how are subsidiaries accounted for? What are the benefits and limitations of accounting for subsidiaries in this way?
b. In what countries does Brookfield have subsidiaries?
c. What are the implications on the consolidated financial statements when a company has less than 100 percent of the voting control of the subsidiary?

FS11-6. What are the problems and limitations of analyzing financial ratios based on Brookfield's consolidated financial statements? Explain your reasons.

ENDNOTES

1. Extracted from Rogers Communications Inc.'s 2011 annual information form. Used with permission of Rogers Communications Inc. All rights reserved.
2. Extracted from Onex Corporation's 2011 audited annual financial statements.
3. Ibid.
4. Extracted from Brookfield Asset Management Inc.'s 2011 audited annual financial statements.
5. Adapted from http://www.reuters.com/finance/stocks/companyProfile?symbol=BAM.
6. Extracted from Brookfield Asset Management Inc.'s 2011 annual report.

Practise and learn online with Connect. Connect resources include additional and interactive study exercises, videos, and practice quizzing, as well as additional material you won't find in the printed text.

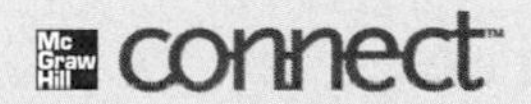

CHAPTER

12

Analyzing and Interpreting Financial Statements

LEARNING OBJECTIVES

After studying the material in this chapter you will be able to do the following:

LO 1 Explain why stakeholders want to analyze financial statements, and identify non-financial information stakeholders might want when analyzing financial statements. Before examining the financial statements themselves, it's valuable to have good knowledge of the entity being examined.

LO 2 Distinguish between permanent and transitory earnings, and discuss the concept of earnings quality.

LO 3 Restate financial statements using vertical and horizontal analysis to remove the effect of size.

LO 4 Use financial ratios to analyze performance.

LO 5 Use financial ratios to analyze liquidity.

LO 6 Use financial ratios to analyze solvency and leverage.

LO 7 Use financial ratios to analyze market measures and dividends of entities.

LO 8 Recognize the limitations of financial statements and ratio analysis in evaluating an entity.

LO 9 Understand how the flexibility of accounting rules, even under IFRS or ASPE, allows managers to manage the earnings of their entities and thereby affect the numbers reported and information disclosed in the financial statements.

Just a few weeks after furniture retailer The Brick Ltd. released its first-quarter financial results in May 2012, BMO Capital Markets equity research analyst Stephen MacLeod reiterated his "outperform" rating on the stock. He also raised his estimate of how much the shares would be worth in one year, increasing his target price to $5 from $4.

Stephen MacLeod

MacLeod earned his MBA from the Rotman School of Management (University of Toronto), and is a Chartered Financial Analyst. Aside from The Brick, he follows at least a dozen publicly traded consumer retail and "special situation" companies, including Leon's, Rogers Sugar, CCL Industries, and The North West Company, which runs stores in remote locations in northern Canada, Alaska, the Carribean, and the South Pacific, along with the Giant Tiger stores in western Canada.

So how does MacLeod come up with his opinions on The Brick and all the companies he must track for the investment bank he works for?

MacLeod, based in Toronto, carries out financial statement analysis. Among other things, he looks closely at the numbers that these companies release to the public in the following key documents: the income statement, the balance sheet, and the cash flow statement.

With Leon's, for example, MacLeod looked at a checklist of important statistics to judge the health of the company: same-store sales growth, total sales, gross margin, occupancy costs, operating expenses, EBITDA (earnings before interest, taxes, depreciation, and amortization), and EPS (earnings per share). (See Chapter 2 for a related story.)

Analysts like MacLeod often also study some key ratios to judge the company's financial situation: these could include ratios to measure things such as liquidity, profitability, debt, operating performance and cash flow.

All those numbers are then compared with results from previous quarters, and also to similar businesses in the same industry.

It may seem like a lot of work, but MacLeod feels his financial statement analysis offers a tremendous value to the public, and, of course, to BMO's private clients.

"If you walk in and buy a piece of furniture and Leon's goes bankrupt a week later it's not going to impact you," MacLeod said. "But if you're a stakeholder like an analyst or an investor or maybe you're leasing [a space] to

Leon's, you might say 'Before I enter into a two-year lease with you let me make sure you have the financial wherewithal to continue paying me for two years.'"

By checking the statements, MacLeod saw that Leon's had a nice big cash position, and strong free-cash-flow generation. He also looked back at Leon's earnings for the last 10 or 20 years and saw that even during the last two recessions, while earnings may have fluctuated, "Leon's was pretty stable over the grand scheme of things and that might tell you that 'OK this is a good credit, someone I'm willing to lend to.'"

Some of MacLeod's detailed research reports on retailers are posted on the BMO Web site and available to the general public. Business journalists writing for *The Globe and Mail* and other news organizations also quote him regularly. StarMine named him one of Canada's top stock analysts in 2009, due to the success of his stock recommendations.

–E.B.

INTRODUCTION

After working your way through 11 chapters of this book, you should have a good idea about how to read and interpret financial statement information. But now what? This chapter pulls together what's been covered so far. A useful analogy is to compare reading a set of financial statements to a mystery. The reader of financial statements, like the reader of a good mystery, must sort through clues, interpret and analyze information, exercise judgment, decide which information is relevant and which should be ignored, and use the information to come to a conclusion. Solving an accounting mystery requires detective work. The numbers tell a story, but it's usually necessary to read between the lines. Some of the questions a stakeholder might ask are shown in Figure 12.1.

This chapter begins with some perspectives on how different stakeholders approach the task of analyzing financial statements. The section discusses the importance of having a good understanding of an entity and explains the concepts of permanent and transitory earnings, which are valuable for understanding how current earnings is useful for predicting future earnings.

Throughout the book, I have introduced tools for analyzing and interpreting financial statements. This chapter reviews those analytical tools and offers some new ones. Two of the new tools are techniques for restating financial statement numbers as proportions and eliminating the

FIGURE 12.1 Analyzing Financial Statements Helps Stakeholders Make Decisions

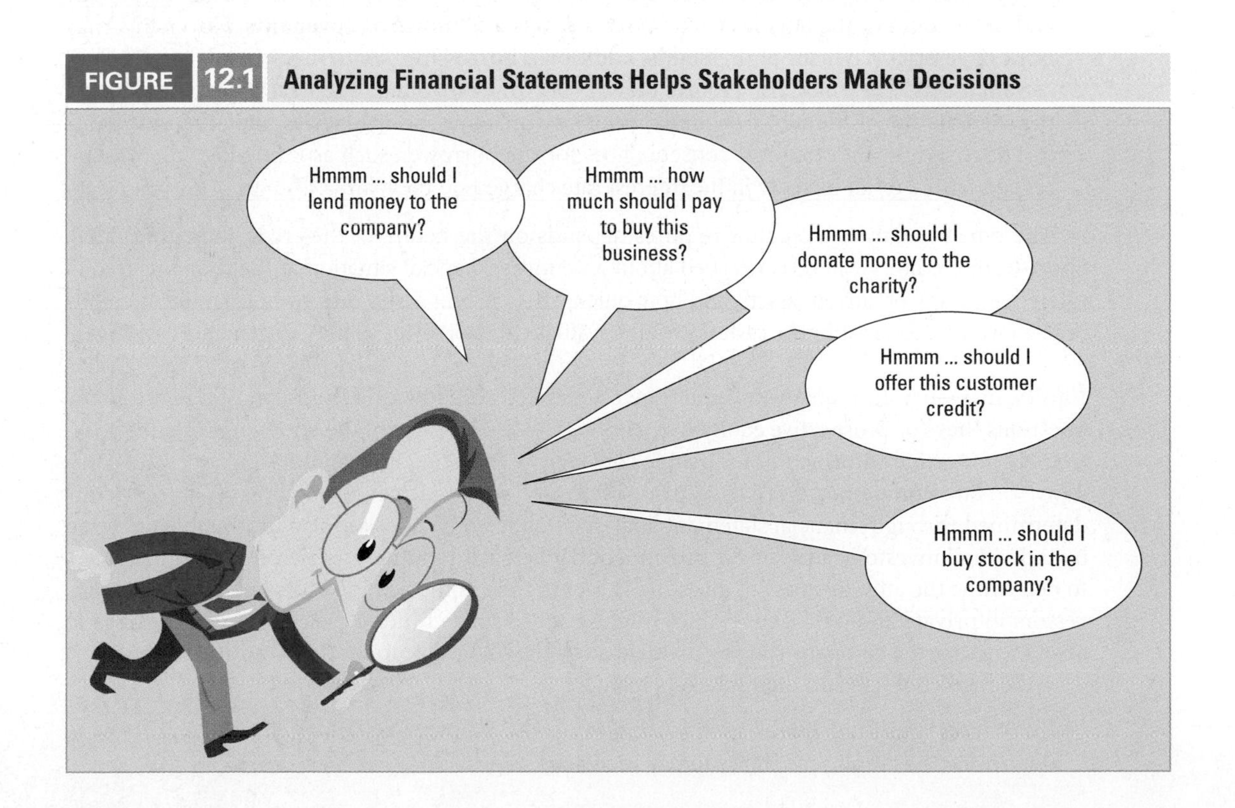

impact of size: common size financial statements and trend statements. The analytical tools and ratios are grouped into four themes:

1. evaluating performance
2. liquidity
3. solvency and leverage
4. other common ratios

In this chapter, I'll use two companies as the main focus of the discussions. The two, WestJet and Leon's, are companies we've examined many times in the book.

LO 1 WHY ANALYZE AND INTERPRET FINANCIAL STATEMENTS?

Analysis and interpretation of financial information isn't an end in itself. People analyze financial statements to help them make decisions. The type of analysis done by stakeholders depends on the decisions they have to make. Different stakeholders need to answer different questions. As a result, each stakeholder group will approach their analysis differently. Let's look at financial statement analysis from the perspective of creditors and investors.

Creditors Creditors come in many shapes and sizes. They may be suppliers that get paid some time (usually in a short time) after supplying the goods or services. They may be banks providing short-term or permanent working capital loans, or long-term lenders through notes payable, bonds, debentures, or mortgages. Creditors may be public or private investors.

Creditors have three broad concerns:

- *Ability to pay.* To assess this concern, creditors consider the resources the entity has and the reliability, timing, and stability of its future cash flows. Creditors are particularly concerned about a borrower's ability to make payments as economic conditions change; for example, if the economy enters a recession.
- *Value of security.* Security is assets an entity can sell to raise cash if it's unable to meet its obligations. For this reason, a creditor will want to know the net realizable value of the assets provided as security.
- *Compliance with covenants.* Lending agreements sometimes place restrictions on the actions and behaviours of the borrower. These restrictions are known as **covenants**. Covenants may limit or restrict payment of dividends, additional borrowing, some investments, and sale of certain assets. They may also require that the borrower maintain financial ratios, for example the current ratio or the debt-to-equity ratio, above or below specified levels. Violating covenants can have significant economic consequences for the borrower, such as immediate repayment, renegotiation, or an increase in the interest rate charged on the loan.

The type of analysis a creditor requires depends on the nature of the credit being provided. Short-term creditors will be concerned about an entity's financial situation at the time the credit's offered, liquidity of current assets, and how quickly the current assets turn over. Long-term creditors will want to forecast future cash flows and evaluate the borrower's ability to generate earnings.

Equity Investors In many ways, equity investors need to know everything and there are many questions they (or prospective equity investors) can ask. The value of the entity or its shares is extremely important information for people considering investing in or purchasing a private company. Private companies don't have prices set on a stock exchange, so a reasonable price is determined through financial statement analysis. Public companies are also thoroughly analyzed by individual investors, analysts for investment bankers, and mutual and pension fund managers to determine the attractiveness of investing in a particular company. Investors and prospective investors in private and public companies might want to predict future cash flows and earnings to assess whether the company can pay dividends or if it will be able to meet upcoming liabilities.

Other stakeholders and their interests include:

- Employees and their representatives analyzing the financial statements of the employer to determine the employer's ability to pay increased wages.

- The Canada Revenue Agency (CRA) analyzing financial statements to assess the reasonableness of amounts reported in tax returns.
- Regulators using financial information to evaluate requests by regulated companies for permission to increase their prices.
- Donors and prospective donors to not-for-profit organizations analyzing financial statements to determine whether money is needed or if donated money is being used efficiently.

There are other stakeholders as well. But remember, while stakeholders use financial statements in their decision making, in most cases the statements don't present the answers to their questions "on a silver platter." Usually, the information in the financial statements must be analyzed, massaged, evaluated, and interpreted before it can provide any insights.

KNOW THE ENTITY

LO 1

Financial statements are only one source of information about an entity, albeit an important one. The successful analysis of an entity can't be achieved only by examining its financial statements. In fact, the analysis of an entity shouldn't even begin with the financial statements.

Financial statements are nothing more than numbers on pages. An understanding of what those numbers are saying requires an understanding of the entity's business, industry, and environment. Information can be obtained from many sources: the media, brokerage firms, and online services such as Globeinvestor.com, Bloomberg.com, Morningstar.ca, and The Motley Fool (www.fool.com).

What does one need to know about an entity, its industry, and environment? The list could be endless and much depends on the entity being investigated. Some possible questions are listed in Figure 12.2.

FIGURE 12.2 **Questions about an Entity**

• What does the entity do—what business or businesses is it in and how does it make money?	• How do economic conditions and changes in economic conditions affect the entity?
• What strategies does the entity use to make money?	• Is the entity regulated? How does regulation affect the way it can conduct business?
• What are the key success factors?	• What are the risks faced by the entity?
• What is the competitive environment? (Are there many competitors? Is it easy for new competitors to enter the market?)	• What are the economic conditions in the industry?
• What are the entity's competitive advantages?	• How does the entity produce, market, and distribute its products?
• Who are the managers? What experience do they have? How ave they performed in the past?	• What are the key inputs and how are they obtained? What are the conditions in the supplier market?
• Who are the customers?	

While one should examine sources besides the annual report to learn about an entity, its industry, and its environment, the sections of annual reports of public companies beyond the financial statements and notes can provide considerable useful information. One valuable section is the **management discussion and analysis (MD&A)**, something that all publicly traded companies, but not private ones, must provide. The MD&A is prepared by an entity's managers and gives them the opportunity to discuss its financial results, position, and future prospects. The MD&A is intended to provide readers with a view of the entity through the eyes of management.

Although the MD&A can provide valuable information, it's important to remember that management prepares it. This is an interesting paradox. Management is, for the most part, the best source of information and insight about the entity. But management is likely biased in how it presents information about the entity. That's not to say that the information it provides is false. Rather, management is likely to focus on the positive aspects of the entity, its performance, and its prospects, and provide favourable and optimistic interpretations of events.

Private companies aren't required to provide a MD&A. In general, one can expect to find far less information about private companies than about public ones, both from the companies themselves and from other sources. Private companies aren't required to disclose their financial statements to the public and the investment community has little interest in them (since there is no opportunity to invest in them).

Of course, stakeholders should evaluate all information for its usefulness and credibility. Just because information is provided by a source other than the entity itself doesn't mean it's unbiased. For example, information from industry associations might support the interests of that industry. Also, research by brokerages and investment bankers may not want to offend companies that might use their services in the future, so they may be reluctant to make negative statements about potential future clients. There are many Internet discussion boards where investors exchange information about investment opportunities. Information from these sources is highly unreliable since it's usually very difficult to verify.

LO 2

PERMANENT AND TRANSITORY EARNINGS AND EARNINGS QUALITY

Permanent versus Transitory Earnings

One of the themes emphasized throughout this book is that net income isn't an absolute or true number, it is a representation of the entity's underlying economic performance. We have seen that measuring economic performance is extremely complex. As a result, it isn't possible to determine an entity's "true" net income. The amount of income an entity reports is a function of the accounting policies it chooses and the estimates it makes. Despite all the difficulties that exist in measuring income, it's important because it provides stakeholders essential information for decision making.

Many stakeholders need to estimate entities' future earnings as part of their decision making. But financial statements prepared in accordance with IFRS or ASPE aren't predictions; they mainly report events that have already happened. The discussion of the qualitative characteristic of relevance in Chapter 2 explains that information is relevant if it helps stakeholders make predictions, even though financial statements themselves aren't predictions.

To forecast future earnings, historical earnings can be used as a starting point. An important aspect of interpreting historical earnings is determining the components of earnings that can be expected to recur in future periods. These **permanent earnings**—earnings that are expected to be repeated in the future—are an indicator of future earnings. In contrast, **transitory earnings** are earnings that aren't expected to be repeated. An entity's net income can have both permanent and transitory components.

The distinction between permanent and transitory earnings and their impact on forecasting future earnings can be shown with an example. In mid-2017, Rusagonis Ltd. (Rusagonis) signed a $100,000 contract with a customer. After considering all costs, Rusagonis's management expects to earn $31,000 from the contract. If the revenue and earnings associated with this contract are to repeat year after year, the contract will increase permanent earnings. Measuring the value of a company as the present value of its future earnings, we would expect the value of Rusagonis to increase by the present value of a series of $31,000 payments to be received for the foreseeable future. As a result of the new contract, lenders would conclude that Rusagonis could support more debt, shareholders might anticipate increased dividends, and unions and employees might argue for increased wages and salaries.

In contrast, if the contract is just a one-time event, Rusagonis is clearly better off, but only by $31,000. A stakeholder would ignore the contract when estimating future earnings because it wouldn't be relevant—it was simply a one-time event and the effect on earnings is transitory. Everything else being equal, earnings would be expected to return to the pre-2017 level in 2018.

This discussion should highlight the importance to stakeholders of understanding the sources of an entity's earnings and the reason for changes in earnings. Permanent and transitory earnings should be interpreted differently, and financial statements should provide information that helps stakeholders distinguish them.

IFRS provide some help by requiring disclosure of events when they are significant and necessary for fair presentation. The language in the accounting standards is somewhat vague, so whether a transaction or economic event should be separately disclosed in the income statement or notes can be a matter of judgment. Managers may have incentives to highlight bad news as unusual and non-recurring and to emphasize good news as "usual" or recurring, because unusual items are more likely to be interpreted as transitory. For public companies, a transitory event should have less of an effect on the stock price, so managers might prefer to classify bad news as unusual. If managers' bonuses are based on earnings before unusual items, there would be incentives for them to classify bad news as unusual and good news as part of "ordinary" operations.

Examples of events that could be disclosed separately include:

- restructuring costs
- impairments, writedowns, and writeoffs of assets
- gains and losses on the disposal of capital assets and long-term investments
- litigation settlements.

An example of a possible unusual item is shown in Exhibit 12.1. In 2010 and 2011, Torstar Corporation reported restructuring and other charges of over $52 million over the two years.[1] If a stakeholder believes that these costs won't occur in the future, then they should be ignored when forecasting earnings. If these expenses aren't excluded when making a forecast, the estimated future earnings would significantly understated. However, stakeholders must exercise caution. It's important to analyze the nature of an expense even if the way it's presented in the income statement suggests it's non-recurring. Note 15 in the exhibit provides some information on the restructuring costs.

EXHIBIT 12.1 Transitory Earnings—Torstar Corporation

Torstar Corporation
Consolidated Statement of Income

(thousands of Canadian dollars except per share amounts)

	Year ended December 31	
	2011	2010
Operating revenue	**$1,548,757**	$1,483,768
Salaries and benefits	**(511,083)**	(501,729)
Other operating costs	**(795,425)**	(731,706)
Amortization and depreciation	**(33,165)**	(31,492)
Restructuring and other charges (note 15)	**(19,411)**	(32,648)
Operating profit	**189,673**	186,193
Interest and financing costs (note 12(d))	**(16,629)**	(24,135)
Adjustment to contingent consideration (note 15)	**630**	
Foreign exchange	**(3,477)**	4,805
Loss of associated businesses (note 7)	**(2,157)**	(28,343)
Other income (note 21)	**19,055**	3,461
Gain on sale of assets (note 22)		4,088
CTV Inc.—gain on sale/remeasurement (note 7)	**74,590**	115,533
Investment write-down (note 23)	**(544)**	(773)
	261,141	260,829
Income and other taxes (note 5)	**(43,000)**	(50,100)
Net income	**$ 218,141**	$ 210,729

EXHIBIT 12.1 (continued) Transitory Earnings—Torstar Corporation

15. PROVISIONS

Restructuring

During the year ended December 31, 2011, the Company recorded restructuring and other charges of $19.4 million, of which $18.8 million was recorded in the Media Segment and $0.6 million in the Book Publishing Segment.

The Media Segment restructuring provisions include $15.6 million relating to staff reductions and a $3.2 million charge for rented spaces that were vacated as reduced staff counts allowed for space consolidation. The $3.2 million charge represents the discounted shortfall between the remaining obligation under the existing leases and the amounts to be received through sublease arrangements. The non-current restructuring provisions are expected to be paid out from 2012 through 2028 within the Media Segment.

The $0.6 million recorded in the Book Publishing Segment relate to staff reductions in the North American Retail business and are all classified as current provisions.

During the year ended December 31, 2010, the Company recorded restructuring and other charges of $32.6 million. This included restructuring provisions of $28.2 million related to staff reductions in the Media Segment, and other charges of $4.4 million.

The other charges of $4.4 million included $2.8 million related to transaction costs for the Company's bid to purchase the newspaper and digital businesses of Canwest Limited Partnership and its related entities; a $1.2 million adjustment to a provision for litigation in the Media Segment; and $0.4 million related to transaction costs from Harlequin's acquisition of the other half of the German publishing business.

QUESTION FOR CONSIDERATION

Explain the difference between transitory and permanent earnings. Why is it important for users of financial statements to distinguish between the two?

ANSWER: Permanent earnings are expected to be repeated in the future, whereas transitory earnings aren't. Forecasting future earnings and cash flows depends on distinguishing between permanent and transitory earnings. For example, a lender trying to determine whether a prospective borrower will be able to meet interest and principal payments will want information about the entity's earnings and cash flows that are likely to occur in the future. Permanent earnings provide information in this regard, whereas transitory earnings don't. This isn't to say that transitory earnings aren't important—they can provide useful insights about the performance of the entity and management—but truly transitory events aren't useful for predictive purposes.

INSIGHT

Our discussion in this section has focused on the reporting requirements of IFRS. It's important to recognize that the interpretation of transactions and other economic events as permanent or transitory isn't just an IFRS issue. Regardless of the accounting basis being used, stakeholders should distinguish events that are permanent and transitory. Stakeholders should also be aware of any information that will affect their predictions. Information about commitments, contingencies, subsequent events, off-balance-sheet financing, and environment changes such as the economy, labour issues, regulation, competition, and so on should also be taken into consideration.

LO 2 Earnings Quality

Earnings quality is another indicator of the usefulness of current earnings for predicting future earnings. Earnings quality is high if current and future earnings are highly correlated and low if current and future earnings aren't correlated. For example, earnings quality is low if there are a lot of transitory earnings in the income statement that can't be easily identified. Earnings quality is high if earnings are mainly permanent or it's easy to separate permanent and transitory earnings.

But earnings quality is much more than separating permanent and transitory earnings. Managers affect earnings quality with their accounting policies, estimates, and accruals. Earnings quality is affected by earnings management when managers move earnings among periods to achieve their reporting objectives. So any accounting choices that distort the relationship between current and future earnings lowers earnings quality and impairs the usefulness of the financial statements for predicting earnings and cash flow. The consequence of low earnings quality is poor forecasts.

As we know, accounting doesn't affect an entity's cash flows (at least not directly, although there can be secondary cash flow effects caused by taxes, bonus plans, and so on). Earnings during a period can be thought of as compriseing two elements: cash flow and accruals. These components can be expressed as an equation:

$$\text{Earnings} = \text{Cash from operations} + \text{Accruals}$$

Cash from operations is real. An entity collects and spends a specific number of dollars during the period. Accounting can do nothing to change that. Accruals represent the non-cash part of earnings. Accruals include things like depreciation, bad debt expense, accrued liabilities, provisions, writedowns of assets, and allowances for returns, to name a few. Accruals require judgment as managers must estimate accrual amounts because the actual amounts aren't usually known.

Consider the bad debt expense. An accrual of a little too much bad debt expense this year means that, at some time in the future, a little bit less of an expense will be required. In other words, if managers make accruals that lower earnings in one period, earnings will be higher in another period to compensate. At the end of the life of an entity, collections are known with certainty, but during an entity's life they have to be estimated. And estimates are inherently uncertain. Managers can use the uncertainty surrounding estimates and accruals to shift earnings among periods and thus lower earnings quality.

Earnings quality can also be affected by an entity's operating decisions—the timing of its actual transactions. For example, if an entity wants to increase its income in a period, it can defer discretionary expenditures to a later period. Expenditures on items such as research and development, advertising, and repairs and maintenance are candidates for this type of treatment. However, cutting these expenditures just to boost the bottom line can be counterproductive, because though the cuts may provide a short-term increase to net income, they may reduce future earnings. An accounting impact of this is that the relationship between current and future earnings is weakened and earnings quality is reduced.

There are a number of ways to evaluate discretionary spending. One way is to look at an expenditure in relation to the sales of the entity. For example, for research and development costs, the following ratio could be calculated:

$$\text{Ratio of research and development expense to sales} = \frac{\text{Research and development expense}}{\text{Sales}}$$

Similar ratios can be calculated for other discretionary expenses. A significant decrease in the ratio in a period could indicate an attempt by management to bolster earnings by cutting discretionary spending. But there could also be legitimate business reasons for the decrease. Remember, the ratios usually give clues, not definite answers.

Earnings management will be further discussed later in the chapter, once the different analytical tools have been discussed. However, below are some additional points to consider:

- Disclosure is one of the most effective ways of achieving understanding of the effects of an entity's accounting choices on its financial statements. If stakeholders are informed about the impact of accounting choices and estimates, they would be better able to assess the quality of an entity's earnings and then make better forecasts and assessments about the quality of information that management is providing. Disclosure requirements have been improving but isn't practical to disclose every detail of an entity's economic activity, so there will always be limitations to comprehensive analyses.
- Accounting choices often have implications beyond the period of the choice. For example, when an entity takes a big bath by writing off or writing down some of its assets, earnings in later periods will be higher than they would have been had the big bath not occurred because there are

fewer costs to expense. If an entity wrote down equipment with a carrying amount of $10,000,000 to $4,000,000, income would be reduced by $6,000,000, but then there would be $6,000,000 less equipment to depreciate over the remaining useful life. The big bath itself would likely be interpreted as a transitory item, but the effect in subsequent years could be viewed as permanent.

connect

KNOWLEDGE CHECK 12.1

- ❑ Why is it useful to stakeholders for entities to provide separate information about non-recurring items?
- ❑ What is meant by the term *earnings quality*? Give examples of how managers' accounting choices and operating decisions can affect an entity's earnings quality.

LO 3, 4, 5, 6, 7

USING RATIOS TO ANALYZE ACCOUNTING INFORMATION

Throughout this book, we have discussed using financial statement information to analyze entities. In most chapters, ratios and other analytical tools were introduced. In this chapter, some of the same ratios and analytical tools are discussed, but they are grouped into four analytical themes:

1. evaluating performance
2. liquidity
3. solvency and leverage
4. other common ratios

The material from earlier chapters isn't repeated in its entirety here, so you may find it helpful to review the earlier part of the book where the ratio or tool was initially introduced. Table 12.1 summarizes the financial statement analysis material covered in each chapter.

Before we begin our discussion, here are a few points to keep in mind:

- There are no accounting standards for ratio or financial statement analysis; a person can modify or create any ratios appropriate for the analysis. What's important is making sure that the right tool is used.
- Although many of the topics, ratios, and tools are presented separately, they can't be considered independently. Integrating information from different analyses will give the most informed insights.
- Financial information has to be integrated with information from other sources for a more complete picture of the entity and its circumstances.
- Materiality is important. Small percentage changes in some accounts (such as gross margin) can be very significant whereas large percentage changes in other accounts may be unimportant.
- Financial statement information can't be interpreted in a vacuum; it must be compared to previous years' information for the same entity and information for other entities, industry standards, forecasts, and other benchmarks.

LO 3

Vertical and Horizontal Analysis

Interpreting raw numbers—the numbers presented in a set of financial statements—can be challenging. It can be difficult to make sense of trends and relationships among the numbers in the statements. It can also be difficult to compare the raw numbers of different entities or compare the raw numbers of an entity year to year. In this section, I will introduce two tools that make this type of analysis easier:

- vertical analysis or common size financial statements
- horizontal analysis or trend financial statements

These tools eliminate the impact of size from the financial statement numbers by restating them as proportions. They also create many of the ratios we examine.

TABLE 12.1 Summary of Financial Statement Analysis Coverage in Chapters 2 through 11

Chapter	Coverage
Chapter 2	• Current ratio, pages 49–50. • Debt-to-equity ratio, pages 50–51.
Chapter 3	• Profit margin ratio, pages 122–123. • Return on equity, page 122.
Chapter 4	• The effect of accounting choices on financial statement numbers, pages 194–204.
Chapter 5	• Interpreting the cash flow statement, pages 275–280. • The effect of accrual accounting choices on the cash flow statement, pages 280–284.
Chapter 6	• Hidden reserves, pages 339–341. • Quick ratios and limitations of the current ratio for measuring liquidity, pages 341–342. • Accounts receivable turnover ratio and average collection period of accounts receivable—limitations of these measures, pages 342–343.
Chapter 7	• Inventory turnover ratio and average number of days inventory on hand—evaluation of inventory management, pages 402–404. • A banker's view of inventory, page 405.
Chapter 8	• Limitations to using historical information about capital assets for decision making, pages 439–440. • The effect of accounting policy choices on the cash flow statement, pages 470–471. • The effect of accounting policy choice on ratios, pages 471–474. • Return on assets—measurement of performance and operating efficiency of an entity, pages 472–473. • Fixed asset turnover ratio, pages 473–474.
Chapter 9	• Debt-to-equity ratio—measure of risk and debt carrying ability, pages 550–551. • Interest coverage ratio—ability to cover fixed financing charges, pages 551–552. • After-tax cost of borrowing, page 550.
Chapter 10	• Leverage, pages 617–620. • Carrying amount versus market value of equity—why the accounting value of equity can differ from the market value, page 624. • Earnings per share (basic and diluted)—summary measure of performance, page 625. • Return on shareholders' equity—measure of return earned by common shareholders, pages 627–629. • Dividend payout ratio, pages, 626–627. • Dividend yield, pages, 626–627.
Chapter 11	• Limitations of consolidated financial statements for ratio analysis, page 677.

Vertical Analysis or Common Size Financial Statements **Vertical analysis** or **common size financial statements** express the amounts on the balance sheet and income statement as percentages of other elements in the same year's statements. On the balance sheet, the amounts are stated as a percentage of total assets and on the income statement they are a percentage of revenue.

If the balance sheet amounts are percentages of total assets, the common size balance sheet will show the percentage each item is of total assets. This gives a good view of the asset and liability composition of the entity and how it has changed over time. Similarly, if income statement amounts are stated as percentages of revenues, the stakeholder can see what proportion of sales each expense represents. This type of analysis shows the relative importance of different expenses and allows comparisons over time and with other entities. For example, comparing common size income statements allows stakeholders to see the percentage of each sales dollar spent on advertising, research and development, or wages. Examining the common size financial statements over a number of years may make it possible to explain things like changes in profitability. It might also help identify problem areas by highlighting expenses that have changed significantly relative to sales.

Table 12.2 provides partial balance sheet (Panel A) and complete income statement (Panel D) information about WestJet Airlines Ltd. Panels B and E provide a vertical analysis (common size information) for the balance sheet and income statement. The common size amounts on the

TABLE 12.2 WestJet Airlines Ltd.: Vertical and Horizontal Analysis

Panel A—WestJet Airlines Ltd.: Selected balance sheet accounts on December 31 ($000s),

	2011	2010	2009	2008	2007
Assets					
Cash and cash equivalents (includes restricted cash)	$1,291,946	$1,187,899	$1,005,181	$ 820,214	$ 653,558
Property and equipment	1,911,227	1,989,522	2,108,351	2,269,790	2,213,063
Total assets	3,473,638	3,383,930	3,350,097	3,268,702	2,984,222
Liabilities and shareholders' equity					
Current liabilities:					
Accounts payable and accrued liabilities	307,279	$ 287,710	$ 228,911	$ 249,354	$ 168,171
Advance ticket sales	432,186	336,926	297,720	251,354	194,929
Current portion of long-term debt	158,832	178,337	165,111	165,721	172,992
Long-term debt	669,880	848,465	1,028,165	1,186,182	1,256,526

[*Note:* 2009–2011 balance sheet information is prepared in accordance with IFRS. 2007 and 2008 balance sheet information is prepared in accordance with Canadian GAAP in effect at the time.]

Panel B—WestJet Airlines Ltd.: Common size balance sheets for selected accounts on December 31,

	2011	2010	2009	2008	2007
Assets					
Cash and cash equivalents (includes restricted cash)	0.372	0.351	0.300	0.251	0.219
Property and equipment	0.550	0.588	0.629	0.694	0.742
Total assets	1.000	1.000	1.000	1.000	1.000
Liabilities and shareholders' equity					
Current liabilities:					
Accounts payable and accrued liabilities	0.088	0.085	0.068	0.076	0.056
Advance ticket sales	0.124	0.100	0.089	0.077	0.065
Current portion of long-term debt	0.046	0.053	0.049	0.051	0.058
Long-term debt	0.193	0.251	0.307	0.363	0.421

Panel C—WestJet Airlines Ltd.: Trend analysis balance sheets for selected accounts on December 31,

	2011	2010	2009	2008	2007
Assets					
Current assets:					
Cash and cash equivalents (includes restricted cash)	1.977	1.818	1.538	1.255	1.000
Property and equipment	0.864	0.899	0.953	1.026	1.000
Liabilities and shareholders' equity					
Current liabilities:					
Accounts payable and accrued liabilities	1.827	1.711	1.361	1.483	1.000
Advance ticket sales	2.217	1.728	1.527	1.289	1.000
Current portion of long-term debt	0.918	1.031	0.954	0.958	1.000
Long-term debt	0.533	0.675	0.818	0.944	1.000

TABLE 12.2 (continued) WestJet Airlines Ltd.: Vertical and Horizontal Analysis

Panel D—WestJet Airlines Ltd.: Consolidated statement of earnings for the years ended December 31 (Cdn$000s),

	2011	2010	2009	2008 (Restated)	2007 (Restated)
Revenues					
Guest revenues	$2,790,299	$2,390,887	$2,067,860	$2,301,301	$1,899,159
Charter and other revenues	281,241	216,407	213,260	248,205	227,997
	3,071,540	2,607,294	2,281,120	2,549,506	2,127,156
Expenses					
Aircraft fuel	915,878	674,608	570,569	803,293	503,931
Airport operations	421,561	388,112	352,333	342,922	299,004
Flight operations and navigational charges	344,442	325,582	298,762	280,920	258,571
Sales and distribution	273,364	255,732	172,326	170,693	149,638
Marketing, general and administration	209,880	194,481	208,316	211,979	177,393
Depreciation and amortization	174,751	170,462	141,303	136,485	127,223
Aircraft leasing	165,571	143,381	103,954	86,050	75,201
Maintenance	146,260	117,057	96,272	85,093	74,653
Inflight	139,478	124,303	112,054	105,849	85,499
Employee profit share	23,804	22,222	14,675	33,435	46,705
Loss on impairment of property and equipment					31,881
Total expenses	2,814,989	2,415,940	2,070,564	2,256,719	1,829,699
Earnings from operations	256,551	191,354	210,556	292,787	297,457
Non-operating income (expense)					
Finance income	15,987	9,910	5,601	25,485	24,301
Finance costs	(60,911)	(70,914)	(67,706)	(76,078)	(75,749)
Gain on foreign exchange	2,485	2,579	(12,306)	30,587	(12,750)
Gain (loss) on disposal of property and equipment	(54)	570	(1,177)	(701)	54
Loss on derivatives	(6,052)	(34)	1,828	(17,331)	
Total non-operating income (expense)	(48,545)	(57,889)	(73,760)	(38,038)	(64,144)
Earnings before income tax	208,006	133,465	136,796	254,749	233,313
Income tax expense					
Current	1,236	1,573	2,690	2,549	2,149
Deferred	58,068	41,695	35,928	73,694	42,116
	59,304	43,268	38,618	76,243	44,265
Net earnings	$ 148,702	$ 90,197	$ 98,178	$ 178,506	$ 189,048

[*Note:* 2010–2011 income statements are prepared in accordance with IFRS. 2007–2009 income statements are prepared in accordance with Canadian GAAP in effect at the time.]

balance sheet are calculated by dividing each line by that year's total assets so that each amount is stated as a proportion of the total. For example, property and equipment for 2011 on the common size balance sheet is calculated as

$$
\begin{aligned}
\text{Common size property and equipment}_{2011} &= \text{Property and equipment}_{2011} \div \text{Total assets}_{2011} \\
&= \frac{\$1,911,227,000}{\$3,473,638,000} \\
&= 0.550 \\
&= 55.0\%
\end{aligned}
$$

TABLE 12.2 (continued) WestJet Airlines Ltd.: Vertical and Horizontal Analysis

Panel E—WestJet Airlines Ltd.: Common size income statement for the years ended December 31,	2011	2010	2009	2008	2007
Revenues					
Guest revenues	0.908	0.917	0.907	0.903	0.893
Charter and other revenues	0.092	0.083	0.093	0.097	0.107
	1.000	1.000	1.000	1.000	1.000
Expenses					
Aircraft fuel	0.298	0.259	0.250	0.315	0.237
Airport operations	0.137	0.149	0.154	0.135	0.141
Flight operations and navigational charges	0.112	0.125	0.131	0.110	0.122
Sales and distribution	0.089	0.098	0.076	0.067	0.070
Marketing, general and administration	0.068	0.075	0.091	0.083	0.083
Depreciation and amortization	0.057	0.065	0.062	0.054	0.060
Aircraft leasing	0.054	0.055	0.046	0.034	0.035
Maintenance	0.048	0.045	0.042	0.033	0.035
Inflight	0.045	0.048	0.049	0.042	0.040
Employee profit share	0.008	0.009	0.006	0.013	0.022
Loss on impairment of property and equipment	0.000	0.000	0.000	0.000	0.015
Total expenses	0.916	0.927	0.908	0.885	0.860
Earnings from operations	0.084	0.073	0.092	0.115	0.140
Non-operating income (expense)					
Finance income	0.005	0.004	0.002	0.010	0.011
Finance costs	(0.020)	(0.027)	(0.030)	(0.030)	(0.036)
Gain on foreign exchange	0.001	0.001	(0.005)	0.012	(0.006)
Gain (loss) on disposal of property and equipment	(0.000)	0.000	(0.001)	(0.000)	0.000
Loss on derivatives	(0.002)	(0.000)	0.001	(0.007)	0.000
Total non-operating income (expense)	(0.016)	(0.022)	(0.032)	(0.015)	(0.030)
Earnings before income tax	0.068	0.051	0.060	0.100	0.110
Income tax expense					
Current	0.000	0.001	0.001	0.001	0.001
Deferred	0.019	0.016	0.016	0.029	0.020
	0.019	0.017	0.017	0.030	0.021
Net earnings	0.048	0.035	0.043	0.070	0.089

Panel F—WestJet Airlines Ltd.: Trend income statement for the years ended December 31,	2011	2010	2009	2008	2007
Revenues					
Guest revenues	1.469	1.259	1.089	1.212	1.000
Charter and other revenues	1.234	0.949	0.935	1.089	1.000
	1.444	1.226	1.072	1.199	1.000
Expenses					
Aircraft fuel	1.817	1.339	1.132	1.594	1.000
Airport operations	1.410	1.298	1.178	1.147	1.000
Flight operations and navigational charges	1.332	1.259	1.155	1.086	1.000
Sales and distribution	1.827	1.709	1.152	1.141	1.000
Marketing, general and administration	1.183	1.096	1.174	1.195	1.000
Depreciation and amortization	1.374	1.340	1.111	1.073	1.000
Aircraft leasing	2.202	1.907	1.382	1.144	1.000
Maintenance	1.959	1.568	1.290	1.140	1.000
Inflight	1.631	1.454	1.311	1.238	1.000
Employee profit share	0.510	0.476	0.314	0.716	1.000
Loss on impairment of property and equipment	0.000	0.000	0.000	0.000	1.000
Total expenses	1.538	1.320	1.132	1.233	1.000
Earnings before income tax	0.892	0.572	0.586	1.092	1.000
Income tax expense					
Current	0.575	0.732	1.252	1.186	1.000
Deferred	1.379	0.990	0.853	1.750	1.000
	1.340	0.977	0.872	1.722	1.000
Net earnings	0.787	0.477	0.519	0.944	1.000

This means that on December 31, 2011, property and equipment represented 55 percent of WestJet's assets. The same approach is used for the income statement except that the denominator is the year's sales. For example, for aircraft fuel for 2011,

$$\text{Common size aircraft fuel}_{2011} = \text{Aircraft fuel}_{2011} \div \text{Total revenue}_{2011}$$
$$= \frac{\$915{,}878{,}000}{3{,}071{,}540{,}000}$$
$$= 0.298$$
$$= 29.8\%$$

Aircraft fuel made up almost 30 percent of WestJet's revenues in 2011.

INSIGHT

Financial Analysis in an IFRS World

The first few years after the 2011 conversion to IFRS will be very challenging for financial analysts. In the first year that a company reports under IFRS, it will have to provide balance sheets prepared under IFRS for three years and income statements for two. That means that for a company with a December 31 year-end it will provide IFRS balance sheets as of December 31, 2010 and 2011 and January 1, 2010 and IFRS income statements for the years ended December 31, 2010 and 2011. IFRS information for earlier periods won't be available. This means that it will not be possible to compare IFRS financial statements with ones from earlier periods. It will be challenging for financial analysts, who usually like to look at a number of periods when analyzing a company. Fortunately, this will be a short-lived problem since new data will be available with each passing year.

In this chapter, I prefer to give several periods of data to provide a realistic approach to financial analysis, but I am limited in the same way real-world analysts are. Since the skills you are learning in this chapter will be valuable beyond the IFRS transition period, I will continue to provide multi-period data and discussions even though the data may not be comparable. Keep this in mind as you work through the rest of the chapter.

Before reading on, take a few minutes to examine the common size statements and try to interpret them.

The common size statements make year-to-year comparisons very convenient. By comparing each row, we see how each amount has changed over time. For example, the common size income statements show that in 2011 fuel expense, as a proportion of sales, increased from 25.9 percent to 29.8 percent. It's difficult to see this just from looking at WestJet's actual statements of earnings.

Some items stand out from the five-year analysis:

- Cash and cash equivalents as a proportion of total assets have increased over the period and, on December 31, 2011, 37.2 percent of assets are cash and cash equivalents.
- Advance ticket sales (tickets paid for but not yet used) have increased steadily as a percentage of sales over the 2008 to 2011 period.
- Aircraft fuel is the largest expense and it increased significantly in 2011 as a percentage of sales. The change is by far the largest of all the expenses. The size of the change and the significance of the expense mean that the impact on net income is large.
- Inflight services expense has increased in dollar amount from 2009 through 2011, but as a percentage of revenue the amount expensed has decreased.

Though I've made this point many times in the book, it bears repeating: *Financial statement analysis may help identify problems, but it won't usually explain them.* For jet fuel, it's easy to conclude that the price increased in 2011. But a challenge the stakeholders have if they want to predict WestJet's income in the future is estimating the cost of jet fuel. This information wouldn't be available in the financial statements, would take a lot of work to estimate, and any estimate would be highly uncertain.

Common size financial statements allow stakeholders to compare entities that are different in size by eliminating the effects of size and presenting the financial statement components on a common basis. Of course, differences between entities have to be interpreted carefully because they can be due to different accounting choices as well as to differences in the economic performance and nature of the entities.

Horizontal Analysis or Trend Statements **Horizontal analysis**, or **trend statements**, is another analytical tool that eliminates the effects of size from financial statements. Trend statements restate the financial statements with each account amount presented as a percentage of a base year amount. This shows the change in each account over time. To construct trend statements, it's first necessary to specify a base year.

Panel C of Table 12.2 provides WestJet's 2007 through 2011 trend amounts for selected balance sheet accounts, and Panel F provides trend income statements. The general formula for calculating trend amounts is

$$\text{Trend statement amount} = \frac{\text{Current year amount}}{\text{Base year amount}} \times 100\%$$

For sales in 2011, the calculation is

$$\begin{aligned}\text{Horizontal analysis revenue} &= \text{Revenue}_{2011} \div \text{Revenue}_{2007} \\ &= \frac{\$3{,}071{,}540{,}000}{\$2{,}127{,}156{,}000} \times 100\% \\ &= 144.4\%\end{aligned}$$

This means that WestJet's revenue sales in 2011 were 144.4 percent of sales in 2007. In other words, sales grew by 44.4 percent between 2007 and 2011. The trend data allow the user to see the change in each account over time relative to the base year.

Notice that for calculating trend data, a base year is chosen for each line in the financial statements and the amounts for other years are stated as a percentage of the base. If trend aircraft fuel for 2011 was calculated, the numerator would be "aircraft fuel in 2011" and the denominator would be "aircraft fuel in 2007." When the trend statement amount is calculated for another line on the financial statements, the amounts from that line are used. To see the percentage change from a time other than the selected base year, the calculation must be redone with a different denominator.

An examination of WestJet's trend data yields some observations:

- Sales have grown steadily over the five years (144.4 percent) but total operating expenses have increased by a greater percentage (153.8 percent).
- Some expenses grew much more quickly than revenues, including aircraft fuel, sales and distribution, aircraft leasing, and maintenance.
- Marketing, general, and administrative expense grew much more slowly than revenues.
- The amount of long-term debt held by WestJet has decreased by almost half since 2007.

Some interpretational issues associated with using trend statements should be noted:

- When the balance in an account changes from positive to negative, or from negative to positive, the change can't be interpreted simply by looking at the percentage change relative to the base year.
- If the balance in an account in the base year is zero, it isn't possible to calculate a trend number for subsequent years. In addition, very small balances in the base year can result in huge percentage changes that may not be meaningful.
- Trend information gives no perspective on materiality. Without reference to the actual numbers, it's possible to spend time worrying about accounts that aren't material.

Evaluating Performance

LO 4

Many stakeholders want to evaluate the performance of entities. This can be challenging because performance is a multi-faceted concept that can be measured in different ways, and different performance indicators can often tell conflicting stories about how an entity is doing. In this section, we discuss different ways of evaluating the performance of an entity. As we do, remember that we can't claim that IFRS or any accounting system can provide an entity's true income. Accounting measurements are representations of an entity's economic activity and are subject to the accounting policies and estimates the managers make. Thus, while there might be a "true" income or economic reality out there, it isn't possible to know what it is. At the same time, while there are many problems with measuring performance, those problems don't take away the need to measure it so that stakeholders can make decisions about how to invest their resources, evaluate how well managers have done their jobs, and address many other performance-related questions. How then does one approach this task?

A logical place to start is with the income statement. In accrual accounting, an income statement shows an entity's economic benefits (revenues) and the economic sacrifices (expenses) that were incurred to generate those benefits. Net income represents the net economic benefit or sacrifice of the owners of the entity over a period. We can also look at subtotals within the income statement to get different indicators of performance. Gross margin (sales − cost of sales), operating income, and income before taxes are examples of different, potentially informative measures that are reported on an income statement. Ratios are among the most commonly used tools for analyzing financial statements and examining the relationships between the numbers. Also, like common size financial statements and trend statements, ratios eliminate the effect of size from the data. Let's examine some common income statement performance measures.

Gross Margin Gross margin is the difference between sales and cost of sales. It's often stated as a percentage of sales and called the gross margin percentage, which is the percentage of each dollar of sales that is available to cover other costs and return a profit to the entity's owners. Gross margin and gross margin percentage are relevant to companies that sell goods. Service providers don't have cost of sales or cost of goods sold. The gross margin percentage is defined as

$$\text{Gross margin percentage} = \frac{\text{Sales} - \text{Cost of sales}}{\text{Sales}} \times 100\% = \frac{\text{Gross margin}}{\text{Sales}} \times 100\%$$

Let's consider Leon's Furniture Ltd. to examine gross margin. (I use Leon's here because WestJet is a service provider so it doesn't have cost of sales.) Relevant data for Leon's are provided in Table 12.3.

TABLE 12.3 Leon's Furniture Ltd. Gross Margin

	December 31, 000s				
	2011	2010	2009	2008	2007
Revenue	$682,836	$710,435	$703,180	$740,376	$637,456
Cost of sales	394,099	412,379	419,819	440,360	363,261
Gross profit (gross margin)	288,737	298,056	283,361	300,016	274,195
Gross margin percentage	42.3%	42.0%	40.3%	40.5%	43.0%

For 2011, Leon's gross margin was $288,737,000 and its gross margin percentage was 42.3 percent. Leon's gross margin percentages can be found in Table 12.3. Leon's gross margin slipped in 2008 and 2009, but in 2010 and 2011 it moved back toward the higher ratio reported in 2007.

An entity's gross margin percentage can be improved in two ways:

1. Increase the price charged for goods or services. It isn't always possible for a business to raise its prices without sales decreasing. Some companies might be willing to accept lower sales for higher margins whereas others accept small margins and try to make money on volume (the gross margin *percentage* will be lower but increased sales will provide a higher gross margin).

TABLE 12.4 Gross Margin Percentages for Selected Companies

Company	Industry	2011	2010
Canfor Corporation (December 31)	Forestry	32.7%	37.7%
High Liner Foods Inc. (December 31, 2011/January 1, 2011)	Food processing	22.7%	23.5%
Indigo Books & Music Inc. (March 31, 2012/April 2, 2011)	Book retailing	41.7%	43.2%
Leon's Furniture Limited (December 31)	Furniture retailing	42.3%	42.0%
Loblaw Companies Limited (December 31/January 1, 2011)	Grocery retailer	23.5%	23.7%
Research In Motion Limited (March 3, 2012/February 26, 2011)	Computer hardware	35.7%	44.3%
The Brick Ltd. (December 31)	Furniture retailing	44.2%	43.1%
Tim Hortons Inc. (January 1, 2012/January 2, 2011)	Food service	37.8%	39.8%

2. Cost control and efficiency. If an entity can obtain the inputs it requires at a lower cost, or use those inputs more efficiently, the entity will have a higher gross margin percentage.

Gross margin percentages can vary dramatically from entity to entity and industry to industry as is seen in Table 12.4. Notice that The Brick Ltd., which is in the same industry as Leon's, has a better gross margin in 2010 and 2011. Some companies, like Loblaw Companies Limited, have relatively "thin" or small margins. This doesn't mean those companies don't perform well. It's important to consider the nature of the business. For example, some businesses make a small amount of money on each transaction but earn a profit by having a lot of sales. Research In Motion struggled in 2011 and its much lower gross margin reflects those problems.

Profit Margin Ratio The profit margin ratio is a bottom-line measure of performance. It indicates the percentage of each sales dollar that the entity earns in profit. The ratio is defined as

$$\text{Profit margin ratio} = \frac{\text{Net income}}{\text{Sales}} \times 100\%$$

A higher profit margin ratio indicates greater profitability because a larger proportion of each dollar of sales is profit. WestJet's profit margin for the fiscal year ended December 31, 2011 is calculated as

$$\begin{aligned}\text{Profit margin ratio} &= \frac{\text{Net income}}{\text{Sales}} \times 100\% \\ &= \frac{\$148{,}702{,}000}{\$3{,}071{,}540{,}000} \times 100\% \\ &= 4.8\%\end{aligned}$$

The profit margin ratio of 4.8 percent means that WestJet made $0.048 for every dollar of sales. WestJet's profit margin in 2010 was 3.5 percent.

There are some variations of the profit margin ratio. We create these variations by moving up the income statement a bit. For example, operating profit margin is income before financing costs (interest), unusual items, and other non-operating costs. This is a measure of performance for the actual business activities of the entity. These variations provide measures of profitability that reflect ongoing operations rather than overall profitability.

Table 12.5 shows the profit margin ratios for some Canadian companies for the years 2010 and 2011, illustrating that there is variation of profit margin among companies.

Return on Investment Our discussion of performance to this point has focused on the income statement. We have looked at two measures of performance, each calculated as a percentage of sales. These provide some insight into an entity's profitability, but they ignore the cost to generate those sales and earn those profits. An entity could have a high gross margin and profit margin, but the amount of investment required to earn those margins—the amount of assets or equity required—might indicate that performance wasn't very good. In other words, a profit of

TABLE 12.5 Profit Margin Ratios for Selected Canadian Companies

Company (year-end)	Profit margin for:	
	2011	2010
Canfor Corporation (December 31)	0.4%	7.1%
High Liner Foods Inc. (December 31, 2011/January 1, 2011)	2.7%	3.4%
Indigo Books & Music Inc. (March 31, 2012/April 2, 2011)	7.1%	(2.0%)
Leon's Furniture Limited (December 31)	6.8%	8.9%
Research In Motion Limited (March 3, 2012/February 26, 2011)	6.3%	17.1%
The Brick Ltd. (December 31)	3.7%	2.5%
Tim Hortons Inc. (January 1, 2012/January 2, 2011)	13.5%	25.5%
WestJet Airlines Ltd. (December 31)	4.8%	3.5%

$1,000,000 will be evaluated differently depending on whether the investment required to earn it was $5,000,000 or $50,000,000.

This is where the measures of return on investment come in. Earlier in the book, two measures of return on investment—return on assets (ROA) and return on equity (ROE)—allowed us to assess the performance of an entity in relation to the investment made. They differ in the investment base that each uses. ROA uses all investment, debt and equity, to determine the return. It measures the entity's performance independent of how its assets were financed. In contrast, ROE determines the common equity investor's return on the investment. Both are valid and widely used measures. Here are the definitions of ROA and ROE in equation form:

$$\text{Return on assets} = \frac{\text{Net income} + \text{After-tax interest expense}}{\text{Average total assets}} = \frac{\text{Net income} + \text{Interest expense} \times (1 - \text{Tax rate})}{\text{Average total assets}}$$

$$\text{Return on equity} = \frac{\text{Net income} - \text{Preferred dividends}}{\text{Average common shareholders' equity}}$$

The numerator in ROA has after-tax interest expense added back because the ratio is a measure of return that is independent of how the assets are financed. If the interest expense wasn't added back in the numerator, ROA would be affected by the amount of debt because the interest expense would increase with the amount of debt.

When calculating ROE, preferred dividends are deducted from net income because it's a measure of return to the common shareholders; preferred dividends are paid to the preferred shareholders. ROA and ROE for the companies we've been focusing on in this chapter are shown in Table 12.6. Leon's ROA was better than The Brick's in both years, but The Brick's ROA increased from 2010 to 2011 as Leon's decreased. It's not possible to compare the ROEs of the companies because in 2010 The Brick's average shareholders' equity was negative and in 2011 it was small, giving rise to a large ROE. Air Canada's ROE isn't measureable because its shareholders' equity is negative.

Keep in mind that these measures of return on investment are affected by managers' accounting choices. This means that comparisons among firms may not be valid, though it might be possible to interpret trends among different firms. Also, remember that returns are related to risk; the higher the risk, the higher the return should be. Therefore, differences in returns may reflect differences in risk as well as different performance levels.

It's common to break down ROA into components—profit margin and asset turnover—to understand how an entity is generating its returns and to help identify how its performance can be improved. ROA can then be stated as

$$\begin{aligned}\text{Return on assets} &= \text{Asset turnover ratio} \times \text{Profit margin ratio} \times 100\% \\ &= \frac{\text{Sales}}{\text{Average total assets}} \times \frac{\text{Net income} + \text{Interest expense} \times (1 - \text{Tax rate})}{\text{Sales}} \times 100\% \\ &= \frac{\text{Net income} + \text{Interest expense} \times (1 - \text{Tax rate})}{\text{Average total assets}} \times 100\%\end{aligned}$$

TABLE 12.6 Return on Assets and Return on Equity for Leon's, The Brick, WestJet, Air Canada, and Air Transat

		2011	2010
Furniture Retail			
Leon's	ROA	9.8%	11.6%
(December 31)	ROE	13.6%	16.1%
The Brick	ROA	7.7%	0.9%
(December 31)	ROE	43.4%	n.m.
Airlines			
WestJet	ROA	5.6%	4.1%
(December 31)	ROE	11.1%	7.1%
Air Canada	ROA	0.7%	3.5%
(December 31)	ROE	n.m.	n.m.
Air Transat	ROA	(0.6%)	6.3%
(October 31)	ROE	(2.8%)	16.3%

n.m: Not measurable because equity is negative.

Note: ROE and ROA calculated using financial statement information prepared in accordance with IFRS, except for Transat, which is prepared using Canadian GAAP.

Remember that profit margin indicates the amount of each sales dollar the entity earns as profit. **Asset turnover** is a measure of how effectively an entity can generate sales from its asset base. The more sales an entity can generate from its asset base, the higher its asset turnover ratio and the higher its ROA. An entity that produces the same amount of sales but carries less inventory than its competitors, everything else being equal, will have a higher asset turnover ratio and a higher ROA.

An entity can generate a given ROA through different combinations of profit margin and asset turnover. The objective for any entity is to maximize its ROA. It's up to management to design strategies that achieve this objective. A business or industry might pursue a strategy of accepting a low profit margin but compensate by having a high asset turnover ratio—make a small amount of money on each sale, but make a lot of sales. Those with a relatively low asset turnover ratio would try to compensate with a higher profit margin.

In Table 12.8, three combinations for earning an 8 percent ROA are shown. Company A generates its ROA with a relatively high profit margin (8 percent) but a relatively low asset turnover ratio (1 percent). Company C does the opposite: its profit margin ratio is very small but its assets turn over quickly. Company B is in between.

By breaking down ROA into its components, it's possible to identify the sources of an entity's performance problems. A low profit margin requires different corrective steps than a low asset turnover ratio. An entity with a low profit margin might focus on product pricing (it might try to increase its prices) or find ways of controlling or reducing costs. A company with a low asset turnover ratio might look for unproductive or idle assets that could be sold, or for assets that could be managed more efficiently and effectively (inventory or receivables levels that could be lowered).

TABLE 12.7 Combinations of Profit Margin and Asset Turnover for Generating a Specific ROA

	Company A	Company B	Company C
Sales	$8,000,000	$1,000,000	$4,000,000
Net income	640,000	20,000	40,000
Average assets	8,000,000	250,000	500,000
Profit margin ratio	8%	2%	1%
Asset turnover ratio	1	4	8
Return on assets	8%	8%	8%

Of course, there are limits to the improvements management can make. If an entity is already performing well in either profit margin or asset turnover, there is only so much the managers can do to make improvements. Also, the nature of an industry imposes limits on these ratios. For example, industries requiring very large capital investments tend to have lower asset turnover ratios.

Now let's examine the components of WestJet's ROA. The information needed from WestJet's financial statements to do the analysis is shown in Table 12.8.

TABLE 12.8 Financial Statement Information for WestJet Airlines Ltd., 2008–2011

	2011	2010	2009	2008	2007
Revenue	$3,071,540	$2,607,294	$2,281,120	$2,549,506	$
Net income (loss)	148,702	90,197	98,178	178,506	
Total assets	3,473,678	3,383,980	3,493,702	3,268,702	2,984,222
Interest expense	60,911	70,914	67,706	76,078	
Tax rate	28.51%	32.42%	28.23%	29.93%	

Note: 2011 and 2010 information was prepared in accordance with IFRS. 2009 and preceding years' information was prepared in accordance with Canadian GAAP in effect at the time.

For 2011, the breakdown of ROA is calculated as follows:

$$\begin{aligned}\text{Return on assets}_{2011} &= \text{Asset turnover ratio} \times \text{Profit margin} \times 100\% \\ &= \frac{\text{Sales}}{\text{Average total assets}} \times \frac{\text{Net income} + [\text{Interest expense} \times (1 - \text{Tax rate})]}{\text{Sales}} \times 100\% \\ &= \frac{\$3{,}071{,}540{,}000}{\$3{,}428{,}829{,}000} \times \frac{\$148{,}702{,}000 + [\$60{,}911{,}000 \times (1 - 0.285)]}{\$3{,}071{,}540{,}000} \times 100\% \\ &= 0.90 \times 6.26\% \\ &= 5.61\end{aligned}$$

Note that in this calculation we use profit margin after adding back the after-tax cost of interest. This makes the calculation consistent with the definition of return on assets. We can use the information in Table 12.8 to calculate return on assets and its components for the fiscal years 2010 and 2011. The results are shown in Table 12.9.

TABLE 12.9 Return on Assets for WestJet, 2008–2011

	Return on assets	=	Asset turnover ratio	×	Profit margin percentage
2011	5.61%	=	0.90	×	6.26%
2010	4.10%	=	0.77	×	5.30%
2009	4.34%	=	0.67	×	6.43%
2008	7.41%	=	0.82	×	9.09%

Note: 2011 and 2010 information was prepared in accordance with IFRS. 2009 and 2008 information was prepared in accordance with Canadian GAAP in effect at the time.

Earnings per Share Earnings per share (EPS) is the amount of net income that is attributable to each individual share of common stock. The most straightforward form is basic EPS, which is calculated using the following formula:

$$\text{Basic EPS} = \frac{\text{Net income} - \text{Preferred dividends}}{\text{Weighted average of common shares outstanding during the period}}$$

Preferred dividends are deducted from net income in the numerator because the amount isn't available to common shareholders, but they aren't deducted in the calculation of net income. The denominator is the weighted-average number of shares that were outstanding during the year. Basic EPS is affected by the number of shares the company has outstanding and the accounting choices of management so it's very difficult to compare EPS amounts between different companies.

Another EPS measure is **fully diluted earnings per share**, which shows the effect that dilutive securities (convertible bonds, convertible preferred shares, and stock options that can be converted into common stock) would have on EPS if they were converted or exchanged for common stock. Fully diluted EPS can be thought of as a worst-case scenario of EPS. EPS is given because predicting future earnings is an important use of financial statements.

ACCOUNTING STANDARDS FOR PRIVATE ENTERPRISES

ASPE doesn't require companies to calculate and present earnings per share.

INSIGHT

Financial Ratios and Market Values

IFRS allows companies to value certain capital assets at their fair value. This will create problems interpreting many ratios (including return on assets and equity and debt-to-equity ratio). Comparability will be impaired unless all the companies being compared use the same valuation method. Also, if the fair value of the assets being revalued fluctuates by a significant amount the ratios will also fluctuate. This situation adds another challenge for stakeholders evaluating financial statements.

McGraw Hill connect™

KNOWLEDGE CHECK 12.2

- ❑ What is gross margin? What is gross margin percentage? What does gross margin percentage mean?
- ❑ Distinguish return on assets from return on equity. How is each calculated?

LO 5

Liquidity

Liquidity is the availability of cash and near-cash resources, which are necessary for making payments as they come due. Lenders and creditors assess an entity's liquidity to ensure it will be able to pay amounts owed. If there is concern that the entity won't be able to meet its obligations, lenders and creditors may not want to provide credit, or they may attach terms to any credit offered that will reflect the level of risk associated with the entity.

In Chapter 6, the current and quick (acid test) ratios were discussed. The current ratio is a measure of the resources an entity has to meet its short-term obligations. The higher the current ratio, the more likely an entity will be able to meet its current obligations. The current ratio also indicates the entity has greater protection in the event the entity's cash flow somehow becomes impaired. The ratio assumes that inventory, receivables, and other current assets can be converted to cash on a timely basis. The current ratio is defined as

$$\text{Current ratio} = \frac{\text{Current assets}}{\text{Current liabilities}}$$

The quick ratio is a stricter test of an entity's ability to meet its obligations because it excludes less liquid current assets such as inventory and prepaids. Inventory can take a fairly long time to convert into cash because it has to be sold and the amount owed by the customer collected before cash is realized. For businesses in which inventory turns over relatively slowly, a lot of time can pass before the inventory is realized in cash. In these cases, inventory can't be considered very liquid. Other current assets (e.g., prepaids) will never be realized in cash, so it makes sense to exclude them from an assessment of liquidity. The quick or acid test ratio is defined as follows:

$$\text{Quick ratio acid test ratio} = \frac{\text{Quick assets*}}{\text{Current liabilities}}$$

*Quick assets include cash, temporary investments, accounts receivable, and any other current assets that can be quickly converted to cash.

A major problem with both the current and quick ratios is that they are static measures. They reflect the existing current resources available to meet existing obligations but say nothing about the entity's ability to generate cash flow. Ultimately, an entity's liquidity depends on its ability to generate cash flows, so paying attention to cash from operations is important. As long as an entity has a steady and reliable flow of cash coming in, a low current ratio isn't a concern. However, if cash flow is unpredictable—for example, if an entity is sensitive to economic changes or competitive changes in the industry—then the current ratio indicates an entity's ability to weather any cash flow disturbances in the short term. A higher current (or quick) ratio means an entity has more insurance in the event that cash flow becomes impaired.

It's important to understand that many liquidity problems arise because of changes in the environment. If an entity's environment remains stable and predictable, it's unlikely to face liquidity problems (assuming that it doesn't already have liquidity problems). However, a changing environment can create significant liquidity pressures. Change can take many forms. It can be economy-wide (an economic slowdown) or specific to the entity (growth) or to an industry (competition). Change in the environment can affect the timing and amount of cash flows. An economic slowdown might reduce an entity's sales, force a reduction in prices, increase the amount of uncollectible accounts receivable, increase the time it takes to collect receivables, and make inventory less saleable. Regardless of these problems, suppliers still have to be paid the full agreed-upon amount.

The turnover of receivables and inventory gives additional insight into an entity's liquidity. Receivables and inventory can be important parts of the cash cycle, so understanding how long it takes to realize them in cash can help a stakeholder predict cash flows and identify liquidity problems. The accounts receivable turnover ratio indicates how quickly an entity collects its receivables. The larger the ratio, the more quickly receivables are being collected. The average collection period is the number of days, on average, it takes to collect receivables. A decrease in the receivables turnover ratio (or an increase in the average collection period) relative to previous years or a deterioration relative to similar firms or industry benchmarks may suggest a liquidity problem. Receivables may have become less collectable (uncollectibles increase) and/or the period of time it takes to collect receivables has increased. As a result, the entity has less cash to meet its obligations. The following are formulas for the accounts receivable turnover ratio and the average collection period for accounts receivable:

$$\text{Accounts receivable turnover ratio} = \frac{\text{Credit sales}}{\text{Average accounts receivable}}$$

$$\text{Accounts collection period of accounts receivable} = \frac{365}{\text{Accounts receivable turnover ratio}}$$

The inventory turnover ratio indicates the number of times during a period the entity is able to purchase and sell (or use) its stock of inventory. The average number of days inventory on hand indicates the number of days, on average, it takes to sell or use inventory. A high turnover rate (or low average number of days inventory on hand) indicates a more liquid inventory that is sold more quickly so less cash is invested in inventory. A decreasing inventory turnover ratio (or increasing average number of days inventory on hand) relative to previous years, or one that is deteriorating relative to similar firms or industry benchmarks, may suggest a liquidity problem. Inventory may not be selling well or some inventory could be obsolete. Following are the formulas for the inventory turnover ratio and the average number of days inventory on hand:

$$\text{Inventory turnover ratio} = \frac{\text{Cost of sales}}{\text{Average inventory}}$$

$$\text{Average number of days inventory on hand} = \frac{365}{\text{Inventory turnover ratio}}$$

A third turnover ratio can be added, one we haven't examined before. The **accounts payable turnover ratio** provides information about how quickly an entity pays its accounts payable. This ratio is calculated using the following formula:

$$\text{Accounts payable turnover ratio} = \frac{\text{Credit purchases}}{\text{Average accounts payable}}$$

IFRS requires disclosure of the cost of inventory expensed during the year so purchases can be estimated using the following equation:

$$\text{Purchases} = \text{Cost of sales} - \text{Beginning inventory} + \text{Ending inventory}$$

This ratio focuses on the amounts owed to suppliers of inventory. The fact that accounts payable usually includes amounts owed to many different types of suppliers, including employees, is a problem. A better ratio would be to consider all purchases on credit and all amounts owed to all suppliers, but this information is typically not available.

In its December 31, 2017 financial statements, Bawlf Ltd. (Bawlf) reported beginning inventory of $190,000, ending inventory of $225,000, and cost of sales of $1,100,000. Accounts payable on December 31, 2016 and 2017 were $127,000 and $135,000, respectively. All of Bawlf's accounts payable pertain to the purchase of inventory. The first step is to calculate the amount of inventory purchased during 2017:

$$\begin{aligned}\text{Purchases} &= \text{Cost of inventory expensed} - \text{Beginning inventory} + \text{Ending inventory}\\ &= \$1{,}100{,}000 \quad - \quad \$190{,}000 \quad + \quad \$225{,}000\\ &= \$1{,}135{,}000\end{aligned}$$

$$\begin{aligned}\text{Accounts payable turnover ratio} &= \frac{\text{Credit purchases}}{\text{Average accounts payable}}\\ &= \frac{\$1{,}135{,}000}{[(\$127{,}000 + \$135{,}000) \div 2]}\\ &= 8.66\end{aligned}$$

The accounts payable turnover ratio can also be stated as the number of days the entity takes to pay its accounts payable. This ratio, the **average payment period for accounts payable**, is calculated as follows:

$$\text{Average payment period for accounts payable} = \frac{365}{\text{Accounts payable turnover ratio}}$$

Bawlf's average payment period for accounts payable can be calculated:

$$\text{Average payment period for accounts payable} = \frac{365}{\text{Accounts payable turnover ratio}} = \frac{365}{8.66} = 42.1 \text{ days}$$

This amount means that, on average, Bawlf takes just over 42 days to pay its suppliers.

Examining accounts payable turnover over time for an entity may provide some useful insights. A decreasing accounts payable turnover ratio or increasing average payment period may indicate that the entity is having cash flow problems and extending the time it takes to pay its accounts payable.

Taken together, these three turnover ratios, when expressed in number of days, give an idea of how well operating cash inflows and outflows are matched. Recall that in Chapter 5 we discussed the lag that exists between the expenditure of cash and the receipt of cash. The three turnover ratios allow us to estimate the lag using the following equation:

$$\text{Cash lag} = \frac{\text{Average collection period of}}{\text{accounts receivable}} + \frac{\text{Average number of}}{\text{days inventory on hand}} - \frac{\text{Average payment period}}{\text{for accounts payable}}$$

The larger the cash lag, the longer the period of time the entity must self-finance its inventory and accounts receivable. The lag length will likely increase during periods of financial distress. This information can be important to stakeholders such as lenders, who want to predict cash flows and assess the risk associated with a loan.

However, analyzing liquidity isn't only a matter of using ratios. The notes to the financial statements often provide information that is useful, information that isn't reflected in the financial statements themselves. For example, many entities have access to lines of credit that they can borrow from as needed. If the available lines of credit have not yet been fully used, the unused amount isn't reported on the balance sheet. That available credit can be an important source of liquidity for the entity and should be taken into consideration when its liquidity position is analyzed.

Exhibit 12.2 provides part of Note 18 from WestJet's financial statements, which describes credit available to the company to use as it's needed.[2] WestJet can borrow up to $76.5 million under the terms of the borrowing arrangement. As of the end of 2011, the line of credit hasn't been used. Notice that WestJet has to pay 0.15 percent on the unborrowed portion of the line.

www.westjet.com

EXHIBIT 12.2 WestJet Airlines Ltd.: Operating Line of Credit

Notes to Consolidated Financial Statements
For the years ended December 31, 2011 and 2010
(Stated in thousands of Canadian dollars, except share and per share amounts)

18. Commitments

(d) Operating line of credit

The Corporation has available a three-year revolving operating line of credit with a syndicate of three Canadian banks. The line of credit is available for up to a maximum of $76,500 (December 31, 2010—$80,750; January 1, 2010—$85,000) and is secured by the Corporation's campus facility. The line of credit bears interest at prime plus 0.50% per annum, or a banker's acceptance rate at 2.0% annual stamping fee or equivalent, and is available for general corporate expenditures and working capital purposes. The Corporation is required to pay a standby fee of 15 basis points, based on the average unused portion of the line of credit for the previous quarter, payable quarterly. As at December 31, 2011, no amounts were drawn (December 31, 2010—$nil; January 1, 2010—$nil).

Therefore, WestJet's cost of the line of credit for 2011 was $114,750 ($76.5 million × 0.15%) even though nothing was borrowed.

Entities sometimes make commitments that require them to make cash payments in the future. These were described earlier in the book as executory contracts—contract arrangements for which neither party has performed its side of the arrangement, so there are no financial statement effects. These commitments, such as payments required under operating leases, have implications for an entity's liquidity because they commit an entity to expend cash.

Mc Graw Hill connect

KNOWLEDGE CHECK 12.3

- ❑ What is liquidity? Why are creditors very interested in the liquidity of entities they provide credit to?
- ❑ Explain the difference between the quick ratio and the current ratio. How is each calculated?

LO 6

Solvency and Leverage

In the last section, liquidity was defined as the availability of cash and near-cash resources to meet obligations as they come due. In contrast, **solvency** refers to its ability to meet its long-term obligations—the financial viability of an entity.

One of the important sources of insight into an entity's solvency is its capital structure. **Capital structure** refers to an entity's sources of financing—its relative proportions of debt and equity. This is important in assessing solvency because the more debt an entity has, the more risk there is to its long-term solvency. A common tool for evaluating capital structure is the debt-to-equity ratio.

The debt-to-equity ratio is a measure of the relative amount of debt to equity an entity is using. It indicates the riskiness of the entity and its ability to carry more debt. More debt increases risk because if interest and principal payments aren't made when required, the entity faces significant economic and legal consequences.

There are many variations of the debt-to-equity ratio. The debt-to-equity ratio discussed so far in the book is defined as

$$\text{Debt-to-equity ratio} = \frac{\text{Total liabilities}}{\text{Total shareholders' equity}}$$

This ratio includes all liabilities and all equity. Other variations on the debt-to-equity ratio include

$$\text{Long-term-debt-to-equity ratio} = \frac{\text{Long-term debt}}{\text{Total shareholders' equity}}$$

$$\text{Debt-to-total-assets ratio} = \frac{\text{Total liabilities}}{\text{Total liabilities} + \text{Total shareholders' equity}} = \frac{\text{Total liabilities}}{\text{Total assets}}$$

We won't discuss these alternatives further, but recognize that, although they are measuring slightly different things, these are different ways of measuring the same concept. For example, the long-term-debt-to-equity ratio excludes working capital (which is used to finance operations) and focuses on the long-term financing of the entity.

Simply using the numbers on the balance sheet to calculate the debt-to-equity ratio can provide misleading results and interpretations. Leases, pensions, and future income taxes can all impair the interpretation of the debt-to-equity ratio and other ratios that incorporate liabilities. If an entity uses operating leases extensively, a form of off-balance-sheet financing, then liabilities and the debt-to-equity ratio will be understated. If this is the case, stakeholders might want to incorporate the operating lease "liability" into their assessment of the entity's capital structure.

Because interest has to be paid regardless of whether an entity is performing well or poorly, debt makes an entity riskier. That doesn't mean entities should carry no debt. Though debt does add risk, it offers some benefits as well:

- Debt is usually less costly than equity because the payments to debt holders are specified and debt holders are entitled to be paid before equity investors. The lower risk means a lower expected return.
- Interest on debt is tax-deductible whereas dividends to shareholders are not.

The amount of debt and equity financing is a crucial management question. Too much debt may result in an inability to pay obligations. Also, debt becomes more expensive as the relative amount of it increases because lenders charge higher interest rates as their risk increases. An entity's optimal amount of debt depends on the entity. An entity with reliable cash flows can afford to carry more debt than one with less predictable cash flows. Factors affecting the reliability of cash flows include competition, threat of technological change, sensitivity to economic cycles, and predictability of capital expenditures.

An entity's solvency can also be assessed by its ability to generate cash from operations. An entity that can reliably generate cash is best equipped to meet its obligations. Earnings are often used instead of cash flow to assess cash flow generating ability. While earnings aren't cash flow and the two can differ significantly in the short term, earnings tend to be a good indicator of long-term cash flow. A reliable flow of earnings or cash assures creditors that the entity will be able to meet its obligations.

The **interest coverage ratio (accrual basis)** is one of a number of ratios designed to measure the ability of an entity to meet its fixed financing charges—its interest payments in particular. The interest coverage ratio is defined as

$$\text{Interest coverage ratio (accrual basis)} = \frac{\text{Net income} + \text{Interest expense} + \text{Tax expense}}{\text{Interest expense}}$$

The larger the ratio, the better able the entity is to meet its interest payments. However, the interest coverage ratio is limiting in that it ignores the fact that entities have fixed charges other than interest. Other fixed charges can include debt repayment and lease payments on operating leases. This ratio can be modified to include these other charges.

Some stakeholders prefer a cash-based interest coverage ratio because debt holders have to be paid in cash, not in earnings. The **interest coverage ratio (cash basis)** shows the number of dollars of cash from operations for each dollar of interest that had to be paid and is calculated as

$$\text{Interest coverage ratio (cash basis)} = \frac{\text{Cash from operations excluding interest paid}}{\text{Interest paid}}$$

In Chapter 9, we calculated the accrual interest coverage ratio for WestJet. Here we'll do the cash-basis interest coverage ratio calculation for WestJet for the year ended December 31, 2011:

$$= \frac{\text{Cash from operations} + \text{Interest paid}}{\text{Interest paid}}$$

$$= \frac{\$506{,}384{,}000 + \$51{,}722{,}000}{\$51{,}722{,}000}$$

$$= 10.79$$

This means that WestJet generated $10.79 of cash from operations for every dollar of interest paid. Thus, lenders can have some confidence that WestJet will be able to make its interest payments. A summary of the accrual and cash basis interest coverage ratios for WestJet for 2010 and 2011 is shown in Table 12.10. The cash-basis measures are higher than the accrual ones but they both increase from 2010 to 2011. This suggests that WestJet's credit risk has

TABLE 12.10 Accrual and Cash-Basis Interest Coverage Ratios for WestJet Airlines Ltd.

WestJet Airlines Ltd.: December 31,	2011	2010
Accrual basis	4.41	2.88
Cash basis	10.79	7.83

improved in 2011. (*Note:* WestJet's cash flow statement isn't provided here. If you want to see the statement, go to www.sedar.com and view WestJet's 2011 financial statements or its annual report.)

The interest coverage ratio and other measures of an entity's ability to meet its fixed charges are important indicators for creditors. A higher coverage ratio is more assurance that creditors will be paid. The level of a coverage ratio considered acceptable depends on the entity. A creditor can accept a lower coverage ratio for an entity with more reliable earnings and cash flows, and it would want a higher level for an entity in a cyclical industry or with highly variable earnings and cash flows.

It's important to remember that the interest coverage and similar ratios are historical measures showing what has happened, not necessarily what will happen. Examining historical trends can help give insight into an entity's ability to generate adequate earnings to cover current and future obligations, but it's also important to consider any changes that may affect that ability. For example, increasing competition or changing economic conditions could impair an entity's ability to generate earnings and cash flow in the future, despite its historical success in doing so.

Let's pull together some of WestJet's solvency and leverage information and do a quick assessment of its situation. This information is provided in Table 12.11.

TABLE 12.11 Solvency and Leverage Information for WestJet Airlines Ltd.*

WestJet Airlines Ltd.: December 31,	2011	2010	2009
Interest coverage ratio: Accrual basis	4.41	2.88	3.02
Interest coverage ratio: Cash basis	10.79	7.83	5.69
Debt-to-equity ratio	1.54	1.59	1.52
Cash from operations	$506,384	$ 418,766	$ 318,661
Total long-term debt plus obligation under finance leases	831,961	1,030,159	1,197,378
Interest expense	60,911	70,914	67,706

*2011 and 2010 calculations are based on financial statements prepared in accordance with IFRS. 2009 calculations are based on financial statements prepared in accordance with Canadian generally accepted accounting principles in effect at the time.

An examination of Table 12.11 shows that WestJet is reducing its reliance on debt in its capital structure. The amount of long-term debt has decreased (current and non-current portion of long-term debt and obligation under finance (capital) leases). Consistent with this, the debt-to-equity ratio has also decreased. The interest coverage ratios have also improved. Cash from operations is strong and increasing, and the cash basis interest coverage ratio is very high. This analysis ignores the impact of off-balance-sheet items (operating leases and commitments) and the effect of the conversion to IFRS (2011 and 2010 are IFRS amounts and 2009 is Canadian GAAP).

www.domtar.com

Accounting ratios are often used as covenants in loan agreements. Exhibit 12.3 provides an extract from the long-term debt note of Domtar Corporation, a paper producing company, that describes covenants under a credit agreement.[3] The covenants mentioned are an interest coverage ratio of not less than 3.0 and a leverage ratio not greater than 3.75. The exact definitions of these measures aren't given and it would be necessary to review the agreement to find out. The note states that the company is in compliance with the agreement as of the end of the quarter.

EXHIBIT 12.3 Domtar Corporation: Covenants

DOMTAR CORPORATION
NOTES TO CONSOLIDATED FINANCIAL STATEMENTS
DECEMBER 31, 2011
(IN MILLIONS OF DOLLARS, UNLESS OTHERWISE NOTED)

NOTE 19.

LONG-TERM DEBT

BANK FACILITY

On June 23, 2011, the Company entered into a new Credit Agreement (the "Credit Agreement"), among the Company and certain of its subsidiaries as borrowers (collectively, the "Borrowers") and the lenders and agents party thereto. The Credit Agreement replaced the Company's existing $750 million revolving credit facility that was scheduled to mature March 7, 2012.

The Credit Agreement contains customary covenants for transactions of this type, including the following financial covenants: (i) an interest coverage ratio (as defined under the Credit Agreement) that must be maintained at a level of not less than 3.0 to 1 and (ii) a leverage ratio (as defined under the Credit Agreement) that must be maintained at a level of not greater than 3.75 to 1. At December 31, 2011, the Company was in compliance with its covenants and no amounts were borrowed (December 31, 2010—nil). At December 31, 2011, the Company had outstanding letters of credit amounting to $29 million under this credit facility (December 31, 2010—$50 million).

Other Common Ratios

LO 7

Price-to-Earnings Ratio It's common to hear discussion of an entity's **price-to-earnings** or **P/E ratio**. Stock market listings in newspapers and online usually provide entities' P/E ratios. The P/E ratio is defined as

$$\text{P/E ratio} = \frac{\text{Market price per share}}{\text{Earnings per share}}$$

Conceptually, the P/E ratio indicates how the market values an entity's earnings and what it sees as its growth prospects. The higher the P/E ratio, the more the market expects earnings to grow. Another way of thinking about this is that the higher an entity's P/E ratio, the more sensitive its share price is to changes in earnings. For example, a P/E ratio of 10 means that a $1 increase in EPS will result in a $10 increase in share price.

The P/E ratio is also an indicator of the risk associated with future earnings. The higher an entity's risk, the lower its P/E ratio will be for a given level of earnings. (The reason for this is that when risk is higher, future cash flows are discounted at a higher rate to reflect the risk.)

The P/E ratio must be interpreted carefully for a number of reasons. Remember from our discussion of earnings quality that earnings in any given period will contain both permanent and transitory components. These will have different effects on the market price of shares, which in turn will have implications for the P/E ratio.

Also, the market price of a share represents the present value of the cash flows that will be received by shareholders—a future-oriented perspective. Earnings, on the other hand, is largely a historically focused measure. As a result, the link between earnings and share price isn't perfect. Current information is immediately reflected in the entity's share price; earnings won't be affected until the next set of financial statements is issued.

If an entity has very low but positive earnings in a period, the P/E ratio will be very large. In that case, the P/E ratio is simply the mathematical result of division by a small number. In addition, a P/E ratio isn't meaningful if an entity has a loss, and it isn't possible to determine the P/E ratios of private companies because the market price for their shares isn't readily available. Finally, earnings are affected by the accounting choices an entity makes, so the P/E ratio will vary with different accounting choices for the same underlying economic activity.

Recent P/E ratios for some of the companies we've examined throughout the book are shown in Table 12.12.[4] Notice in the table that Leon's, a better performer than The Brick, has earnings that are more valued by investors (Leon's P/E ratio is higher).

TABLE 12.12 Average P/E Ratios for Selected Companies

Company (year-end)	2011	2010	2009
Air Canada (December 31)	n.m.	n.m.	n.m.
Indigo Books & Music Inc. (March 31, 2012/April 2, 2011/April 3, 2010)	2.40	n.m.	12.72
Leon's Furniture Limited (December 31)	15.31	16.44	13.13
Research In Motion Limited (March 3, 2012/Feb. 26, 2011/Feb. 27, 2010.)	6.21	10.38	16.29
Transat A.T. Inc. (October 31)	n.m.	9.40	7.82
The Brick (December 31)	7.70	n.m.	n.m.
WestJet Airlines Ltd. (December 31)	11.09	22.69	16.74

Note: The P/E ratio is calculated using the share price on the trading day closest to the company's fiscal year-end and net income for the fiscal year.

n.m.: not measurable because net income was negative.

Dividend Payout Ratio and Dividend Yield The dividend payout ratio and dividend yield provide information to investors about the dividends they receive. These ratios were introduced in Chapter 10. The dividend payout ratio shows the proportion of earnings being paid to common shareholders as dividends and is defined as

$$\text{Dividend payout ratio} = \frac{\text{Common dividends declared}}{\text{Net income}}$$

A dividend payout ratio of 0.25 means that 25 percent of earnings is paid in dividends; the rest is retained. An entity with a net loss can still pay a dividend. If the losses continue, however, it's likely that eventually it won't have the resources to sustain the dividend. To pay dividends, it is necessary to have cash. With a net loss, the dividend payout ratio isn't meaningful. A dividend payout ratio greater than 1.0 is also possible.

The dividend yield indicates the return from dividends investors are receiving from their investment. It's defined as:

$$\text{Dividend yield} = \frac{\text{Common annual cash dividends per share}}{\text{Current share price}}$$

For many investors, dividends are a crucial consideration when making investment decisions. Investors who want cash flow from their investments may want to invest in companies that have reliable annual dividends. Canadian banks are attractive investments in this way. The dividend payout ratio and dividend yield for WestJet are:

$$\begin{aligned}\text{Dividend payout ratio} &= \frac{\text{Common annual cash dividends declared}}{\text{Net income}}\\ &= \frac{\$27{,}852{,}000}{\$148{,}702{,}000} \times 100\%\\ &= 18.7\%\end{aligned}$$

$$\begin{aligned}\text{Dividend yield} &= \frac{\text{Common annual cash dividends per share}}{\text{Current share price}}\\ &= \frac{\$0.20}{\$15.30} \times 100\%\\ &= 1.7\%\end{aligned}$$

This means that for 2011, WestJet paid out 18.7 percent of its earnings in dividends and the dividend yield based on the December 31, 2011 stock price of $11.52 was 1.7 percent.

QUESTION FOR CONSIDERATION

Zehner Ltd. (Zehner) is a publicly traded Canadian company. On December 31, 2017, the last day of its fiscal year, Zehner's management signed a new, long-term contract with a customer. The contract will increase Zehner's revenue significantly and management and financial analysts agree that the contract, to begin mid-2018, will be very profitable.

REQUIRED: How do you think Zehner's share price will be affected by the announcement of the new contract? How will Zehner's December 31, 2017 earnings be affected? Explain.

ANSWER: Zehner's share price should increase. The new contract is expected to be very profitable, which means the company is now more valuable. Higher earnings mean investors can expect more cash in the future. In contrast, the announcement will have no effect on Zehner's December 31, 2017 earnings because earnings represent economic activity that has already occurred. As of December 31, 2017, Zehner has earned no revenue and would report no profits as a result of the new contract. Earnings will only be affected when the contract comes into effect in the middle of 2018, so the full effect won't be reflected in earnings until 2019.

SOME LIMITATIONS AND CAVEATS ABOUT FINANCIAL STATEMENTS AND FINANCIAL STATEMENT ANALYSIS

LO 8

Financial ratios are powerful tools for analyzing and evaluating entities, providing valuable insights into their performance and prospects. However, ratio analysis has limitations, some of them quite severe. Analysis of IFRS-based information is largely constrained by the limitations of the information itself. The existence of these limitations and caveats doesn't mean that financial statement and ratio analysis isn't useful or shouldn't be done. But to get the most out of financial statement and ratio analysis, it's important to understand the strengths and limitations of these tools. Let's examine some of the limitations and the caveats associated with financial statement and ratio analysis.

- *IFRS financial statements are historical.* In most cases, financial statements can be used as a starting point of an analysis, but the user has to incorporate his or her own future-oriented information to project the future.
- *IFRS financial statements have limitations because things change.* Economic conditions, technology, and the marketplace change. Entities themselves change. As a result, the future may be different from the past, which may limit the usefulness of historical financial statements analyses (especially in industries subject to rapid and unpredictable change such as entities in high-technology industries).
- *Managers prepare financial statements.* This is both good and bad news. Managers are the best equipped to prepare financial statements because they are the ones who know and understand the entity best. However, managers' self-interests can influence the accounting choices they make. Also, because an entity can only prepare one set of general purpose financial statements, managers often have to choose among the competing information needs of the different stakeholders when deciding how to orient the financial statements.
- *Financial statements are not comprehensive.* Financial statements don't reflect all of an entity's assets and liabilities, or all of its economic activity. Many valuable resources and important obligations aren't reported. For example, spending on human resources and on research is expensed as incurred, not classified as assets. There are also off-balance-sheet obligations such as commitments and operating leases that aren't reported as liabilities. In addition, while IFRS allows a wider use of fair values, cost is still heavily relied on as the basis of measurement.

- *Accounting policy choices and estimates affect ratios.* Entities can often choose from alternative acceptable accounting policies, so different policies used for similar economic activity can result in different financial statements. To know if differences among entities are due to real economic activity or accounting policy choices, it's important to carefully read the note describing the significant accounting policies. Also, accrual accounting requires managers to make estimates of future, uncertain events when they prepare their financial statements, which requires judgment. All accounting choices can be affected by the assumptions, information, biases, and self-interests of the managers.
- *Comparing financial statements can be difficult to do.* Accounting is used to compare entities. Tools such as common size financial statements and financial ratios allow these comparisons. However, comparisons should be done cautiously and steps should be taken to ensure that comparisons are valid (e.g., by adjusting for differences in accounting policies and estimates).
- *Financial statements are not the only source of information.* It isn't possible to analyze an entity only by its financial statements. A comprehensive analysis will integrate information from many sources.
- *Financial analysis is a diagnostic tool. It doesn't necessarily provide explanations for problems that are identified.* Accounting information reflects the economic activity of an entity—the entity's strategies, management, operations, and environment. Problem areas identified through financial analysis reflect these factors, but understanding the root of a problem requires knowledge of the entity's strategies, operations, and environment.

LO 9 EARNINGS MANAGEMENT

This last section returns to one of the themes we examined throughout the book: earnings management. Managers often have choices when deciding how to account for, disclose, and present information in their financial statements. These choices can create significant economic consequences for stakeholders.

The term *earnings management* isn't limited to making choices that affect net income. It also applies to choices that affect other lines on the income statement and the balance sheet, and it applies to how management discloses information in the notes to the financial statements.

The flexible nature of accounting rules gives managers the ability to manage accounting numbers. The economic consequences of accounting information offer them the motivation. The earnings of public companies are carefully studied by investors and analysts, and the managers of these companies are under pressure to meet investors' expectations and to maintain the stock price. Managers can help achieve these objectives by using accounting choices to increase or smooth earnings. Also, managers' compensation, opportunities in the job market, and job security, can be affected by the results reported in the financial statements. Managers may also have an incentive to pursue any number of objectives: sell company shares for as high a price as possible, obtain the best terms for a loan, avoid violation of debt covenants, obtain financial support from government, minimize taxes, or generally influence the outcome of decisions that rely on accounting information.

Many accounting scandals are the result of using accounting rules to achieve management objectives. Some are clear cases of fraud. However, it's a mistake to think that most or even many earnings management situations are fraudulent. In fact, most cases of earnings management occur within the rules. For example, when a manager decides that the useful life of a new piece of equipment is ten years rather than eight years, she is making a choice that will affect assets, net income, and any ratios that rely on these measures (e.g., profit margin or return on assets). But there is nothing fraudulent about her choice, unless ten years isn't a reasonable estimate of the equipment's useful life. However, just because the choices managers make can be said to be "within the rules" doesn't make this approach to financial reporting right, but it's reality.

Table 12.13 identifies some of the techniques that managers have to manage earnings. The table shows the different financial accounting reporting areas and identifies the techniques as policies, estimates, or other. All of the techniques in the table have been addressed in this book.

TABLE 12.13 Earnings Management Opportunities

	Policies	Estimates	Other
Revenue recognition	• When to recognize revenue	• Bad debts • Returns • Discounts	
Inventory	• Inventory valuation method (FIFO, average cost, specific identification) • Costs included in inventory	• Writedowns of obsolete and damaged inventory	
Capital assets	• Which assets are capitalized	• Depreciation method • Useful lives • Timing and amount of writedowns and writeoffs	
Liabilities	• Leases	• Warranty provisions • Pensions • Accrued liabilities	
Assets versus expenses	• Capitalization policies		
Other			• Big baths • Income statement classifications as ordinary versus unusual • Off-balance-sheet financing • Non-recurring items • Disclosure of commitments and contingencies

A FINAL THOUGHT

Accounting is often characterized as dull and boring. And it can be—if all you think about is the mechanics: journal entries, preparing financial statements in good form, and getting the calculations right. But you've now seen what makes accounting interesting. Accounting is about high-level thinking skills, about human nature, and about judgment. If you've worked with the material presented in the book, you should be on your way to being a sophisticated and savvy user of financial statements.

Good luck!

Solved Problem

Esperanza Stores Corp. (Esperanza) operates two small retail stores in malls in Charlottetown. The two stores were opened in late 2011 and, according to Minh Tran, the president and majority shareholder, they have grown spectacularly over the last few years. To provide customers with the merchandise they want, Esperanza has moved into larger locations and further increased the floor space of its stores by taking over adjacent retail space as it became available. Ms. Tran is currently thinking about opening additional stores.

Ms. Tran has approached the bank for an expanded line of credit. Esperanza's current line of credit is $30,000 and as of December 31, 2017 the line of credit has almost been fully used. Ms. Tran has provided the bank with Esperanza's financial statements for 2014 through 2017. The statements are available in Table 12.14. Additional information provided by Ms. Tran accompanies the financial statements.

TABLE 12.14 Esperanza Stores Corp.: Financial Statements

Esperanza Stores Corp.
Balance Sheets as of December 31,

	2017	2016	2015	2014
Assets				
Cash	$ 10,000	$ 25,000	$ 50,000	$ 75,000
Inventory	200,000	160,000	125,000	78,000
Other current assets	16,298	17,322	8,440	6,000
Total current assets	226,298	202,322	183,440	159,000
Capital assets	182,000	151,000	110,000	75,000
Accumulated depreciation	(75,530)	(60,400)	(41,800)	(22,500)
	$332,768	$292,922	$251,640	$211,500
Liabilities and shareholders' equity				
Bank loan	$ 29,371	$ 23,821	$ 11,966	$ 0
Accounts payable	101,000	81,500	65,000	45,000
Other payables	3,000	13,000	19,000	24,000
Current portion of long-term debt	20,000	5,000	5,000	5,000
Total current liabilities	153,371	123,321	100,966	74,000
Long-term debt	20,000	40,000	45,000	50,000
Common shares	50,000	50,000	50,000	50,000
Retained earnings	109,397	79,601	55,674	37,500
	$332,768	$292,922	$251,640	$211,500

Esperanza Stores Corp.
Income Statements for the years ended December 31,

	2017	2016	2015	2014
Revenue	$535,000	$485,000	$450,000	$350,000
Cost of sales	299,600	264,325	238,500	182,000
Gross margin	235,400	220,675	211,500	168,000
Selling, general, and administrative costs	180,000	170,000	165,000	140,000
Interest expense	6,200	6,000	5,200	5,000
Other expenses	11,000	14,000	18,000	20,000
Income before taxes	38,200	30,675	23,300	3,000
Income taxes	8,404	6,748	5,126	660
Net income	$ 29,796	$ 23,927	$ 18,174	$ 2,340

Ms. Tran provides additional information:

- All sales of merchandise to customers are for cash or major credit card. No credit terms are offered. Esperanza recognizes revenue at the time of sale.
- All inventory is purchased on credit.
- The long-term loan is from a private lender and must be repaid in full by 2015. Esperanza has been making payments on the loan since cash has been available to do so.
- Esperanza has never paid dividends.

Required:

You are Ms. Tran's banker. Review the information provided and prepare a report for your manager assessing whether Esperanza should receive a larger credit line.

Solution:

Comment: *The response below attempts to analyze and interpret the information provided by Esperanza from the perspective of a lender. The analysis relies exclusively on tools introduced in this chapter and elsewhere in the book. In an actual analysis of this type, additional information about the entity, the economy, and the market place would be available and incorporated in the report.*

Report on Esperanza Stores Corp.

I have completed my examination of Esperanza Stores Corp. (Esperanza) and while, on the surface, the stores appear to be performing well, I have some concerns. In essence, it appears that Esperanza is facing a serious liquidity problem and may have difficulty generating the cash flows to support a significant loan. This is not to say that Esperanza is a lost cause, and some improvements could make Esperanza a more viable candidate for a loan. As my report details, there are many positive accomplishments. The data I refer to in my report are presented in Tables 12.15 through 12.18.

Performance

Esperanza has performed well over the last four years. Net income has significantly improved each year, from $2,340 in 2014 to $29,796 in 2017. In addition, Esperanza's profit margin (Table 12.17), return on assets (Table 12.17), and return on equity (Table 12.17) have all increased in each reported year. Sales have also been growing, with 2017 results almost 53 percent greater than they were in 2014. In absolute numbers, sales have grown from $350,000 in 2014 to $535,000 in 2017. Clearly, the company has done a good job building its business.

On the other hand, gross margin percentage (Table 12.17) has declined steadily from 48 percent in 2014 to 44 percent in 2017—a significant and alarming drop. Had Esperanza been able to maintain its 48 percent gross margin in 2017, net income would have been more than $21,000 higher and there would have been significantly more cash coming in.

Further information is needed to explain the decline. Is it due to increased competition or a pricing strategy that tried to increase sales by lowering prices? And what is the gross margin percentage likely to be in future, as this will have significant implications for cash flows?

Despite the decline in the gross margin percentage, the gross margin has increased each year because of the increase in sales. Also, despite the gross margin percentage decline, the profit margin percentage has increased each year. Esperanza has achieved this improvement through cost control. Selling, general, and administrative costs have increased at a much slower rate than sales, and the proportion of these costs as a percentage of revenue has fallen over the four-year period.

An important question is whether spending has been permanently reduced or only deferred. Also, will the reduction in spending will have implications for Esperanza's ability to maintain and increase sales in the future.

Overall, Esperanza has performed well. The company has grown its business with sales, profits, and improving profitability. The company's liquidity is another matter.

Liquidity

While Esperanza's performance has been fine, I have serious concerns about its liquidity. All liquidity indicators have been deteriorating over the past four years and the company is in danger of running out of cash. The current ratio decreased from 2.15 in 2014 to 1.48 in 2017. While a current ratio of 1.48 in and of itself isn't a problem, the significant decline is.

The current ratio also masks the fact that an increasing proportion of Esperanza's assets is inventory. Since 2014, the proportion of total assets represented by inventory has increased from 36.9 percent to 60.1 percent. In addition, the amount of inventory on hand has increased much more rapidly than revenues. While one would expect inventory to grow at a rate similar to sales, over the period 2014 to 2017 the amount of inventory on hand has increased 256 percent, while revenues have grown by only about 53 percent. It's possible Esperanza may be carrying significant amounts of unsalable inventory. If the inventory cannot be sold or can only be sold at a discount, the current ratio overstates the company's liquidity. Other possible explanations for the large increase in inventory are failure to meet expected sales forecasts or a wider range of merchandise being carried in the stores. The increase could also be the result of poor inventory management.

The quick ratio, the availability of very liquid current assets to cover current liabilities, supports a liquidity problem. Esperanza's only quick asset is cash, and over the last four years the amount of cash it's holding has declined significantly—only $10,000 as of December 31, 2017. If, for example, the current portion of long-term debt had to be paid immediately, Esperanza wouldn't have the resources to do so.

The inventory turnover and accounts payable turnover ratios raise similar concerns. Since 2014, Esperanza has been taking much longer to sell its inventory and to pay suppliers. The average number of days inventory is held before being sold has increased by over 40 percent, from 155 days in 2015 to 219 days in 2017. The average number of days the company takes to pay its suppliers has increased from 70 days in 2015 to 98 days in 2017. This suggests that Esperanza is responding to its liquidity problems by delaying payments to suppliers for as long as possible. Taking the average number of days inventory and the average payment period for accounts

TABLE 12.15 Common Size Financial Statements

Esperanza Stores Corp.
Common Size Balance Sheets as of December 31,

	2017	2016	2015	2014
Cash	0.030	0.085	0.199	0.355
Inventory	0.601	0.546	0.497	0.369
Other current assets	0.049	0.059	0.034	0.028
Total current assets	0.680	0.691	0.729	0.752
Capital assets	0.547	0.515	0.437	0.355
Accumulated depreciation	(0.227)	(0.206)	(0.166)	(0.106)
	1.000	1.000	1.000	1.000
Bank loan	0.088	0.081	0.048	0.000
Accounts payable	0.304	0.278	0.258	0.213
Other payables	0.009	0.044	0.076	0.113
Current portion of long-term debt	0.060	0.017	0.020	0.024
Total current liabilities	0.461	0.421	0.401	0.350
Long-term debt	0.060	0.137	0.179	0.236
Common shares	0.150	0.171	0.199	0.236
Retained earnings	0.329	0.272	0.221	0.177
	1.000	1.000	1.000	1.000

Esperanza Stores Corp.
Common Size Income Statements for the Years Ended December 31,

	2017	2016	2015	2014
Revenue	1.000	1.000	1.000	1.000
Cost of sales	0.560	0.545	0.530	0.520
Gross margin	0.440	0.455	0.470	0.480
Selling, general, and administrative costs	0.336	0.351	0.367	0.400
Interest expense	0.012	0.012	0.012	0.014
Other expenses	0.021	0.029	0.040	0.057
Income before taxes	0.071	0.063	0.052	0.009
Income tax expense	0.016	0.014	0.011	0.002
Net income	0.056	0.049	0.040	0.007

TABLE 12.16 Trend Financial Statements

Esperanza Stores Corp. Trend Balance Sheets as of December 31,				
	2017	**2016**	**2015**	**2014**
Cash	0.133	0.333	0.667	1.000
Inventory	2.564	2.051	1.603	1.000
Other current assets	2.716	2.887	1.407	1.000
Total current assets	1.423	1.272	1.154	1.000
Capital assets	2.427	2.013	1.467	1.000
Accumulated depreciation	3.357	2.684	1.858	1.000
	1.573	1.385	1.190	1.000
Bank loan	n/a	n/a	n/a	n/a
Accounts payable	2.244	1.811	1.444	1.000
Other payables	0.125	0.542	0.792	1.000
Current portion of long-term debt	4.000	1.000	1.000	1.000
Total current liabilities	2.073	1.667	1.364	1.000
Long-term debt	0.400	0.800	0.900	1.000
Common shares	1.000	1.000	1.000	1.000
Retained earnings	2.917	2.123	1.485	1.000
	1.573	1.385	1.190	1.000

Esperanza Stores Corp. Trend Income Statements for the Years Ended December 31,				
	2017	**2016**	**2015**	**2014**
Revenue	1.529	1.386	1.286	1.000
Cost of sales	1.646	1.452	1.310	1.000
Gross margin	1.401	1.314	1.259	1.000
Selling, general, and administrative costs	1.286	1.214	1.179	1.000
Interest expense	1.240	1.200	1.040	1.000
Other expenses	0.550	0.700	0.900	1.000
Income before taxes	12.733	10.225	7.767	1.000
Income tax expense	12.733	10.225	7.767	1.000
Net income	12.733	10.225	7.767	1.000

payable together, the period over which Esperanza is self-financing its inventory has increased from 85 days in 2015 (155 – 70) to 121 days in 2017 (219 – 98).

From the information provided, I constructed cash flow statements for 2015 through 2017. These statements are rough because of missing information, particularly the depreciation expense. It seems likely that, given the small change in accumulated depreciation year to year, some capital assets were sold over these years. Therefore, using change in the accumulated depreciation account as an estimate of the depreciation expense may be in error. If assets are actually being sold, actual cash from operations is likely greater than I calculated.

Cash from operations in each of the three years has been positive and growing, but it's still quite small. Depending on sales in 2018, the company might not have enough cash to make its planned payment on the long-term debt. The company's operating cash flow is crucial for assessing a loan. While the current and quick ratios suggest liquidity problems, the problems could be mitigated with enough cash flow. At this point, the cash flow statement and my interpretation of the turnover ratios do not relieve my uneasiness. Even so, Esperanza has been able to reduce its long-term debt over the last three years, although it was achieved by increasing its bank loan each year.

TABLE 12.17 Financial Ratios

Esperanza Stores Corp. Selected Financial Ratios				
	2017	2016	2015	2014
Current ratio	1.475	1.641	1.817	2.149
Quick ratio	0.065	0.203	0.495	1.014
Inventory turnover ratio	1.664	1.855	2.350	
Average number of days inventory on hand	219.3	196.8	155.3	
Accounts payable turnover ratio	3.722	4.086	5.191	
Average payment period for accounts payable	98.1	89.3	70.3	
Purchases (cost of sales − beginning inventory + ending inventory)	$339,600	$299,325	$285,500	
Gross margin percentage	0.440	0.455	0.470	0.480
Profit margin percentage*	0.065	0.059	0.049	0.018
Asset turnover	1.710	1.781	1.943	
Return on assets	0.111	0.105	0.096	
Return on equity	0.206	0.203	0.188	
Debt-to-equity ratio (liabilities ÷ shareholders' equity)	1.088	1.260	1.381	1.417

*Profit margin is calculated as net income + after-tax cost of interest/sales.

TABLE 12.18 Cash Flow Statements

Esperanza Stores Corp. Cash Flow Statements for the Years Ended December 31,			
	2017	2016	2015
Net income	$29,796	$23,927	$18,174
Add: Depreciation expense	15,130	18,600	19,300
	44,926	42,527	37,474
Adjustments for changes in current operating accounts:			
Increase in inventory	(40,000)	(35,000)	(47,000)
Decrease/(increase) in other current assets	1,024	(8,882)	(2,440)
Increase in accounts payable	19,500	16,500	20,000
(Decrease) in other payables	(10,000)	(6,000)	(5,000)
Cash from operations	15,450	9,145	3,034
Investing activities—purchase of capital assets	(31,000)	(41,000)	(35,000)
Financing activities			
Repayment of long-term debt	(5,000)	(5,000)	(5,000)
Bank loan	5,550	11,855	11,966
	550	6,855	6,966
Decrease in cash during year	(15,000)	(25,000)	(25,000)
Cash balance at beginning of year	25,000	50,000	75,000
Cash balance at end of year	$10,000	$25,000	$50,000

There is also potential for trouble if suppliers more aggressively try to collect amounts owing to them or if they stop providing credit. If this happens, any loan our bank makes could be in jeopardy. Esperanza has little to offer in the way of security. There are no receivables, and it's probable that capital assets and inventory will not produce much cash if they had to be sold.

Because of expansion over the last three years, Esperanza has made significant investments in capital assets. An important question is whether additional expenditures for capital assets will be required. The depletion of the company's cash can be largely attributed to the purchases of capital assets each year.

Overall, Esperanza seems to be an attractive and successful business. Its challenge is to survive its liquidity problems. At this point I do not recommend extending additional credit to the company. I think that Esperanza should take immediate steps to reduce its inventory levels to free up cash and reduce its investment in working capital. Also, the company should limit its spending on capital assets until its liquidity position becomes more solid.

SUMMARY OF KEY POINTS

LO 1 Analysis and interpretation of financial information isn't an end in itself. People analyze financial statements to help them make decisions. The type of analysis done by stakeholders depends on the decisions they have to make. Before examining the financial statements themselves it's valuable to have good knowledge of the entity being examined. A source of information about publicly traded companies is the management discussion and analysis.

LO 2 Current income is important for forecasting future earnings. Permanent earnings are expected to repeat in the future and are a useful indicator of future earnings. Earnings that aren't considered permanent are called transitory. An entity's net income can have both permanent and transitory components. IFRS require disclosure of information that is helpful for understanding the components of earnings.

Earnings quality refers to the usefulness of current earnings for predicting future earnings. Earnings quality is high if there is a close relationship between current earnings and future earnings and low if that relationship isn't close. Another way of thinking about earnings quality is the extent to which reported earnings are permanent. Managers lower earnings quality when they manage earnings through their accounting policies, estimates, and accruals, and through the timing of actual transactions, such as discretionary expenditures and sales.

LO 3 Vertical and horizontal analysis are useful devices for simplifying the analysis of financial statements by eliminating the impact of size. Vertical analysis (common size financial statements) expresses the amounts on the balance sheet and income statement as percentages of other elements in the same year's statements. Horizontal analysis (trend statements) restates the financial statements with each account amount presented as a percentage of a base year amount.

LO 4 Performance is a question of how an entity "did" or performed. Tools for evaluating performance include: gross margin, profit margin, return on assets and equity, and earnings per share.

LO 5 Liquidity is the availability of cash and near-cash resources, which are necessary for meeting payments as they come due. Lenders and creditors assess an entity's liquidity to ensure it will be able to pay amounts owed. Liquidity ratios include: current and quick ratios, accounts receivable, inventory, and accounts payable turnover ratios.

LO 6 Solvency refers to an entity's ability to meet its long-term obligations—its financial viability. One of the important sources of insight into an entity's solvency is its capital structure. Two ratios used to assess solvency and leverage are the debt to equity ratio and the interest coverage ratio.

LO 7 There are many other ratios that can be used to analyze an entity. Three of the ratios examined in the chapter are the price/earnings ratio, the dividend payout ratio, and the dividend yield.

LO 8 Financial ratios are a powerful and informative tool for analyzing and evaluating entities. However, ratio analysis has limitations, some of them quite severe. To get the most out of financial statement analysis, it's important to understand the strengths and limitations of the tools being used. The limitations include the following:

- IFRS financial statements are mainly historical.
- Managers prepare financial statements.
- Financial statements are not comprehensive.
- Accounting policy choices and estimates affect ratios.
- Comparing financial statements can be difficult to do.
- Financial statements are not the only source of information.
- Financial analysis is a diagnostic tool. It doesn't necessarily provide explanations for problems that are identified.

LO 9 Managers often have choices when deciding how to account for, disclose, and present information about their entity's transactions and economic events. These choices can have a significant impact on the numbers and disclosures in the financial statements and notes, which in turn can have economic consequences for stakeholders. The economic consequences of accounting information provide managers with incentives to make particular accounting choices that will allow them to meet their objectives of financial reporting—something known as earnings management.

FORMULA SUMMARY

$$\text{Common size amount}_{t\text{ year}} = \frac{\text{Income statement account}_{t\text{ year}}}{\text{Sales}_{t\text{ year}}}$$

$$\text{Common size amount}_{t\text{ year}} = \frac{\text{Balance sheet account}_{t\text{ year}}}{\text{Total assets}_{t\text{ year}}}$$

Performance

$$\text{Trend statement amount}_{\text{current year}} = \frac{\text{Current year amount}}{\text{Base year amount}} \times 100\%$$

$$\text{Gross margin percentage} = \frac{\text{Sales} - \text{Cost of sales}}{\text{Sales}} \times 100\% = \frac{\text{Gross margin}}{\text{Sales}} \times 100\%$$

$$\text{Profit margin ratio} = \frac{\text{Net income}}{\text{Sales}} \times 100\%$$

OR

$$\text{Profit margin ratio} = \frac{\text{Net income} + \text{Interest expense} \times (1 - \text{Tax rate})}{\text{Sales}}$$

$$\text{Return on assests} = \frac{\text{Net income} + \text{After-tax interest expense}}{\text{Average total assets}} \times 100\% = \frac{\text{Net income} + \text{Interest expense} \times (1 - \text{Tax rate})}{\text{Average total assets}} \times 100\%$$

OR

$$\text{Return on assets} = \text{Asset turnover ratio} \times \text{Profit margin ratio} \times 100\%$$

$$\text{Return on equity} = \frac{\text{Net income} - \text{Preferred dividends}}{\text{Average common shareholders' equity}} \times 100\%$$

$$\text{Basic EPS} = \frac{\text{Net income} - \text{Preferred dividends}}{\text{Weighted average of common shares outstanding during the period}}$$

Liquidity

$$\text{Current ratio} = \frac{\text{Current assets}}{\text{Current liabilities}}$$

$$\text{Quick ratio (acid test ratio)} = \frac{\text{Quick assets}}{\text{Current liabilities}}$$

$$\text{Accounts receivable turnover ratio} = \frac{\text{Credit sales}}{\text{Average accounts receivable}}$$

$$\text{Average collection period of accounts receivable} = \frac{365}{\text{Accounts receivable turnover ratio}}$$

$$\text{Inventory turnover ratio} = \frac{\text{Cost of sales}}{\text{Average inventory}}$$

$$\text{Average number of days inventory on hand} = \frac{365}{\text{Inventory turnover ratio}}$$

$$\text{Average payable turnover ratio} = \frac{\text{Credit purchases}}{\text{Average accounts payable}}$$

$$\text{Average payment period for accounts payable} = \frac{365}{\text{Accounts payable turnover ratio}}$$

$$\text{Cash lag} = \begin{matrix}\text{Average collection}\\ \text{period of accounts}\\ \text{receivable}\end{matrix} + \begin{matrix}\text{Average number}\\ \text{of days inventory}\\ \text{on hand}\end{matrix} - \begin{matrix}\text{Average payment}\\ \text{period for accounts}\\ \text{payable}\end{matrix}$$

Solvency and Leverage

$$\text{Debt-to-equity ratio} = \frac{\text{Total liabilities}}{\text{Total shareholders' equity}}$$

$$\text{Interest coverage ratio (accrual basis)} = \frac{\text{Net income} + \text{Interest expense} + \text{Tax expense}}{\text{Interest expense}}$$

$$\text{Interest coverage ratio (cash basis)} = \frac{\text{Cash from operations excluding interest paid}}{\text{Interest paid}}$$

Other Common Ratios

$$\text{P/E ratio} = \frac{\text{Market price per share}}{\text{Earnings per share}}$$

$$\text{Dividend payout ratio} = \frac{\text{Common dividends declared}}{\text{Net income}}$$

$$\text{Dividend yield} = \frac{\text{Common annual cash dividends per share}}{\text{Current share price}}$$

KEY TERMS

accounts payable turnover ratio, p. 728
asset turnover, p. 724
average payment period for accounts payable, p. 728
capital structure, p. 730
common size financial statement (vertical analysis), p. 715
covenant, p. 708
earnings quality, p. 712
fully diluted earnings per share, p. 726
horizontal analysis (trend statements), p. 720
interest coverage ratio (accrual basis), p. 731
interest coverage ratio (cash basis), p. 731
management discussion and analysis (MD&A), p. 709
permanent earnings, p. 710
price-to-earnings (P/E) ratio, p. 733
solvency, p. 730
transitory earnings, p. 710
trend statements (horizontal analysis), p. 720
vertical analysis (common size financial statement), p. 715

SIMILAR TERMS

The left column gives alternative terms that are sometimes used for the accounting terms introduced in this chapter, which are listed in the right column.

horizontal analysis	**trend statements, p. 720**
sustainable earnings, recurring earnings, core earnings, persistent earnings	**permanent earnings, p. 710**
vertical analysis	**common size financial statements, p. 715**

ASSIGNMENT MATERIALS

Questions

Q12-1. Which stakeholder is the most important to an entity? Respond from the perspective of the entity and a stakeholder.

Q12-2. What is net income? Provide an explanation that would be understandable to a person who doesn't have a good understanding of accounting.

Q12-3. You're at a party and another guest comments that one way to overcome many of the accounting scandals would be to eliminate choice from IFRS. Provide a response to the guest.

Q12-4. What is the difference between permanent and transitory earnings? Why is it important to distinguish between these types of earnings if you're predicting future earnings?

Q12-5. Suppose you were considering making an investment in one of Canada's major grocery chains, Loblaw Companies Ltd. or Sobeys Inc. As part of your research, you obtained each company's annual report. What concerns would you have in comparing the information presented in each company's financial statements when making your decision? What steps could you take to overcome these concerns?

Q12-6. Why is it important to learn as much as you possibly can about an entity when doing an analysis of it? Explain.

Q12-7. Is it advisable to make a decision to lend money to an entity by looking only at its financial statements? Explain.

Q12-8. Identify and explain the limitations and caveats associated with using financial ratio analysis on IFRS-based financial statements.

Q12-9. What are the implications for financial statement analysis of the fact that managers can often choose among different, acceptable accounting methods? Provide examples of some of the accounting choices that managers have to make.

Q12-10. Is it possible for an entity to be too liquid? Explain.

Q12-11. Explain why the quick ratio might be a better indicator of an entity's liquidity than the current ratio.

Q12-12. Describe a situation where a user of a private corporation's financial statements would be interested in segregating permanent and transitory earnings. Explain why the separation of the two types of earnings would be important in that situation.

Q12-13. Explain the concept of quality of earnings. What distinguishes high-quality earnings from low-quality earnings?

Q12-14. Explain how each of the following would affect the quality of an entity's earnings:

a. Management decides to increase advertising in the current period as part of a special event. Management expects the increase to occur only in the current year and spending levels to return to historical levels in the future.
b. Management increases the estimated useful life of some of the entity's capital assets.
c. Management decides to write down certain capital assets to reflect changes in market conditions.

Q12-15. What are common size financial statements? Explain why they can be useful in analyzing an entity over and above the actual financial statements of the entity.

Q12-16. What are trend financial statements? Explain why they can be useful for analyzing an entity over and above the actual financial statements of the entity.

Q12-17. What is liquidity? Why are suppliers concerned about the liquidity of an entity?

Q12-18. Why are the accounts receivable turnover and inventory turnover ratios helpful with the assessment of liquidity?

Q12-19. Why isn't it adequate for stakeholders to focus their analyses of entities only on the financial statements? What type of information about an entity that's not included in financial statements might be useful for a stakeholder? What other sources of information might a stakeholder turn to?

Q12-20. What are covenants? Why are covenants sometimes included in lending agreements? What purpose do they serve? Why are covenants often stated in accounting terms?

Q12-21 You are a lender. A company has approached you about a loan. The company has offered to maintain a minimum current ratio and a maximum debt-to-equity ratio as well as to not pay dividends over the term of the loan. How would these covenants affect your decision to lend to the company and the interest rate you would offer?

Q12-22. Explain the three broad concerns that creditors have about the credit they provide to entities. Describe the different types and sources of information that creditors require to evaluate these concerns.

Q12-23. What is the difference between short-term and long-term creditors? Why would each approach financial statement analysis differently? What type of information would each require for making a decision to supply credit to a prospective borrower? Explain.

Q12-24. In many ways, equity investors need to know everything. Explain why this is true.

Q12-25. Would information about each of the following be useful to a prospective long-term creditor of an entity? Would information about each item be available from the financial statements? Explain your answers.

a. competitive advantages and disadvantages
b. risks faced by the entity
c. source of supplies and conditions in the supplier market
d. regulatory environment

Q12-26. Would information about each of the following be useful to a prospective equity investor in an entity? Would information about each item be available from the financial statements? Explain your answers.

a. quality, experience, and performance of the managers
b. strategies for making money
c. competitive environment
d. lines of business

Q12-27. What is the management discussion and analysis (MD&A)? Why do you think public companies are required to provide an MD&A whereas private companies are not?

Q12-28. Contrast the benefits and limitations of information provided to stakeholders by management versus information from a financial analyst who is independent of the entity.

Q12-29. What are the characteristics of accrual accounting that allow managers to manage earnings? Why do these characteristics allow earnings to be managed?

Q12-30. Explain the difference between return on assets and return on equity. Which measure is a more useful measure of the performance of an entity? Explain.

Q12-31. Why is it necessary to evaluate financial ratios on a comparative basis rather than in absolute terms? What bases of comparison can be used?

Q12-32. You have been asked to do an in-depth analysis of a company's financial statements but you haven't been told what the purpose of the analysis is—that is, what decision needs to be made. Is it possible for you to effectively proceed with this assignment? Explain.

Exercises

E12-1. **(Classifying transactions and economic events as permanent or transitory, LO 2)** Would you classify each of the following as transitory or permanent in the entity's financial statements? Explain your reasoning.

a. A warehouse suffers flood damage. The warehouse is on the banks of a river known for periodically overflowing its banks.
b. An airline disposes two older aircraft at a loss. They were replaced by the newest generation of fuel-efficient planes.
c. A clothing chain marks down fall fashions at the end of the season to substantially lower the price so they can be sold.
d. The market price of an important raw material increases by a significant amount.

E12-2. **(Classifying transactions and economic events as permanent or transitory, LO 2)** Would you classify each of the following as transitory or permanent in the entity's financial statements? Explain your reasoning.

a. A company makes a payment to a competitor to settle an industrial espionage law suit.
b. A company makes a large payment in support of a charity event.
c. Revenues and expenses at a division a company will be selling within two months.
d. A company reduces its prices because its competitors' prices have decreased.

E12-3. **(Usefulness of information for decision making, LO 1)** For each of the following situations, explain why IFRS financial statements would be of limited use in predicting the entity's future performance:

a. During the year, a company had a six-month strike that shut down its manufacturing facility.
b. A pharmaceutical company just received final approval for a new drug that's expected to revolutionize the treatment of a serious illness.
c. A restaurant opened for business eight months ago.
d. An Ontario-based retail chain just opened ten new stores in Alberta and B.C. as part of Western expansion.

E12-4. **(Preparing common size financial statements, LO 3)** Examine the summarized income statements for Goglin Ltd. for 2014–2016. Prepare common size (vertical analysis) and trend (horizontal analysis) income statements for the periods shown. Interpret the results you obtain.

Goglin Ltd.
Summarized Income Statements
For the years ended December 31,

	2016	2015	2014
Revenue	$1,250,000	$950,000	$650,000
Cost of sales	640,000	455,000	300,000
Gross margin	610,000	495,000	350,000
Other expenses	455,000	390,000	300,000
Net income	$ 155,000	$105,000	$ 50,000

E12-5. **(Preparing common size financial statements, LO 3)** Examine the balance sheets and income statements for Fairplay Inc.

Fairplay Inc.
Balance Sheets
As of December 31,

	2018	2017	2016
Assets			
Cash	$ 18,000	$ 24,000	$ 20,000
Accounts receivable	105,200	92,800	70,000
Inventory	118,500	92,000	90,000
Other current assets	24,000	22,000	16,000
Total current assets	265,700	230,800	196,000
Capital assets (net of amortization)	510,000	420,000	370,000
Total assets	$775,700	$650,800	$566,000
Liabilities and shareholders' equity			
Bank loans	$ 96,620	$ 54,800	$ 46,000
Accounts payable and accrued liabilities	91,800	82,000	76,000
Total current liabilities	188,420	136,800	122,000
Long-term liabilities	140,000	124,000	100,000
Common shares	250,000	250,000	250,000
Retained earnings	197,280	140,000	94,000
Total liabilities and shareholders' equity	$775,700	$650,800	$566,000

Fairplay Inc.
Income Statements
For the Years Ended December 31,

	2018	2017	2016
Revenue	$1,040,256	$963,200	$860,000
Cost of sales	492,134	457,800	420,000
Gross margin	548,122	505,400	440,000
Selling, general, and administrative expenses	251,790	231,000	220,000
Depreciation	60,000	56,000	46,000
Other expenses	126,490	117,120	96,000
Interest expense	30,000	24,000	16,000
Income before taxes	79,842	77,280	62,000
Income tax expenses	17,566	20,000	16,000
Net income	$ 62,276	$ 57,280	$ 46,000

Additional information:

- All sales are on credit.
- All purchases of inventory are on credit.
- Fairplay must begin repaying its long-term debt in 2020.

Required:

a. Prepare common size (vertical analysis) balance sheets and income statements for 2016, 2017, and 2018.
b. Analyze and interpret the common size financial statements you prepared.

c. How are these common size statements more useful than the statements originally prepared by Fairplay?
d. Why would it be unwise to examine the common size financial statements without considering the financial statements originally prepared by Fairplay?

E12-6. **(Preparing trend financial statements, LO 3)** Use the financial statements for Fairplay Inc. provided in E12-5 to respond to the following:

a. Prepare trend (horizontal analysis) balance sheets and income statements for 2016, 2017, and 2018. Use 2016 as the base year.
b. Analyze and interpret the trend financial statements you prepared.
c. How are these trend statements more useful than the statements originally prepared by Fairplay?
d. Why would it be unwise to examine the trend financial statements without considering the financial statements originally prepared by Fairplay?

E12-7. **(Calculating liquidity ratios, LO 5)** Use the information provided about Fairplay Inc. in E12-5 to respond to the following.

a. Calculate the following for 2017 and 2018:
   i. current ratio
   ii. quick ratio
   iii. accounts receivable turnover ratio
   iv. average collection period of accounts receivable
   v. inventory turnover ratio
   vi. average number of days inventory on hand
   vii. accounts payable turnover ratio
   viii. average payment period for accounts payable
   ix. cash lag
b. Assume the role of an important new supplier to Fairplay. Use the amounts calculated in (a) to prepare a report assessing whether Fairplay should be granted credit terms for purchases from your company. Explain the conclusions you make.

E12-8. **(Assessing liquidity, LO 5)** Atluck Ltd. is a small manufacturing company in Nova Scotia. You have been provided with the following information from the company's most recent balance sheet:

Cash	$ 92,500
Accounts receivable	359,325
Inventory	162,675
Prepaids	72,000
Non-current assets	1,008,875
Current liabilities	292,725
Non-current liabilities	628,650
Total shareholders' equity	774,000

Required:

Calculate Atluck's current and quick ratios using the information from the most current balance sheet. If you were a prospective supplier to Atluck, would you be prepared to offer credit up to $10,000? Provide your reasons.

E12-9. **(Using common size and trend statements to evaluate performance, LO 3, 5)** The income statements of Kronau Corp. for the years ended March 31, 2015 through 2017 are shown below:

Kronau Corp.
Income Statements
For the Years Ended March 31,

	2017	2016	2015
Sales	$2,875,000	$2,612,500	$2,425,000
Cost of sales	1,575,000	1,375,000	1,280,500
Gross margin	1,300,000	1,237,500	1,144,500
Selling, general, and administrative expenses	675,000	575,000	555,500
Depreciation expense	129,000	105,000	95,000
Interest expense	150,000	137,500	130,000
Non-recurring expense	250,000	—	—
Income before income taxes	96,000	420,000	364,000
Income tax expense	18,000	80,000	75,000
Net income	$ 78,000	$ 340,000	$ 289,000

Required:

a. Prepare common size and trend financial statements for Kronau. (For the trend statements, use 2015 as the base year.)
b. Use the information from (a) to evaluate the performance of Kronau. Explain fully. Your evaluation should include a comparison of Kronau's performance from year to year.
c. How does the non-recurring expense affect your ability to evaluate Kronau's performance and to interpret your common size and trend financial statements?

E12-10. **(Calculating accounts payable turnover, LO 5)** You have been provided with the following information from the balance sheets and income statements of Batchawana Inc. (Batchawana). Accounts payable and inventory are from the balance sheet as of December 31 of the stated year and cost of sales is for the stated year ended December 31. Assume that all purchases of inventory are made on credit and cost of sales includes only the cost of inventory sold.

Batchawana Inc.
Financial Statement Information

	2017	2016	2015	2014
Accounts payable	$ 2,509,200	$ 2,132,820	$1,919,538	$1,535,630
Inventory	3,261,960	3,156,574	2,898,502	2,272,732
Cost of sales	10,112,076	10,416,692	9,623,028	7,227,290

Required:

a. Calculate the accounts payable turnover ratio for 2017, 2016, and 2015.
b. Calculate the average payment period for accounts payable for 2017, 2016, and 2015.
c. Interpret your results from (a) and (b).
d. What circumstances could explain a declining accounts payable turnover ratio (or increasing average payment period for accounts payable)?

E12-11. **(Determining the effects of transactions on ratios, LO 3, 4, 5, 6, 7)** Complete the following table by indicating whether the transactions or economic events would increase, decrease, or have no effect on the financial ratios listed. Consider each item independently. State any assumptions you make. Explain your reasoning.

	Quick ratio	Inventory turnover ratio	Return on assets	Profit margin percentage	Debt-to-equity ratio
Ratio before the transactions/ economic events	**0.85**	**3.5**	**12%**	**8%**	**1.5:1**
a. Early retirement of long-term debt (classified as long-term when retired) for cash at a loss					
b. Accrual of a current warranty liability					
c. Declaration of a cash dividend					
d. Sale of common shares for cash					
e. Arrangement of a capital lease on the last day of the fiscal year					

E12-12. **(Determining the effects of transactions on ratios, LO 3, 4, 5, 6, 7)** Complete the following table by indicating whether the transactions or economic events would increase, decrease, or have no effect on the financial ratios listed. Consider each item independently. State any assumptions you make. Explain your reasoning.

	Interest coverage ratio	Accounts receivable turnover	Price-to-earnings ratio	Return on equity	Dividend yield
Ratio before the transactions/ economic events	**4.12**	**4.75**	**22.7**	**12%**	**3.1%**
a. Unexpected announcement by a public company of a new long-term contract with a new customer. Contract goes into effect next year.					
b. Writedown of impaired property, plant, and equipment					
c. 2 for 1 stock split					
d. Payment of an amount owing to a supplier					
e. Credit sale of merchandise to a customer					

E12-13. **(Determining the effects of transactions on ratios, LO 3, 4, 5, 6, 7)** Complete the following table by indicating whether the transactions or economic events would increase, decrease, or have no effect on the financial ratios listed. Consider each item independently. State any assumptions you make. Explain your reasoning.

	Current ratio	Average payment period for accounts payable	Return on assets	Gross margin percentage	Earnings per share
Ratio before the transactions/ economic events	**1.3**	**38**	**12.5%**	**48%**	**$1.75**
a. Accrual of wages owed to employees at the end of a period; amount included in accounts payable					
b. Writedown of inventory to net realizable value; amount included in cost of goods sold					
c. Payment of a previously declared dividend					
d. Purchase of land in exchange for a long-term note payable					
e. Repurchase of common shares for cash					

E12-14. **(Evaluating performance, LO 4)** Dyce Ltd. is an auto parts manufacturer. The auto parts industry has gone through difficult times in recent years due to the challenges faced by the auto industry. You are provided with summarized income statements for Dyce for the last seven years:

Dyce Auto Parts Ltd. Summarized income statements for the years ended December 31, (000)							
	2017	**2016**	**2015**	**2014**	**2013**	**2012**	**2011**
Revenues	$7,448	$5,945	$7,588	$8,399	$8,226	$8,287	$8,061
Cost of goods sold	6,466	5,373	6,716	7,281	7,216	7,205	6,907
Gross margin	982	572	872	1,118	1,010	1,082	1,154
All other expenses	681	740	849	904	830	850	884
Net income	301	(168)	23	214	180	232	270

Required:

a. Calculate the gross margin percentage and profit margin percentage for 2011–2017.
b. Analyze the information provided and your calculation in (a).

E12-15. **(Evaluating accounts receivable, LO 5)** Oungre Inc. is a small printing business that provides a wide range of printing services to retail and commercial clients. Retail customers pay cash, while Oungre offers its commercial customers 30 days from the delivery date to pay amounts owing. You have been provided with the following information from Oungre's accounting records (Oungre's year-end is December 31):

	2015	**2016**	**2017**	**2018**
Accounts receivable (on December 31)	$67,500	$ 75,000	$ 85,000	$ 93,750
Sales (for the year ended)		950,000	1,006,250	1,093,750
Percentage of sales to commercial customers		60.0%	66.0%	75.0%

Required:

a. Calculate Oungre's accounts receivable turnover ratio and average collection period of accounts receivable for 2016, 2017, and 2018.
b. Assess how well Oungre managed its accounts receivable over the three-year period.

c. What are some possible explanations for why Oungre's collection isn't less than 30 days? What steps might Oungre's management take to reduce the collection period?
d. Suppose you didn't know what the proportion of Oungre's sales to commercial customers was. How would your calculation of the accounts receivable turnover ratio and the average collection period of accounts receivable be affected? How would your interpretation of the performance of Oungre's management be affected?

E12-16. **(Evaluating inventory management, LO 5)** Zawale Ltd. is a wholesaler of fresh fruits and vegetables. Zawale purchases fruits and vegetables from growers and supplies them to small grocery stores. You have been provided with the following information from Zawale's accounting records (Zawale's year-end is December 31):

	2014	2015	2016	2017
Inventory (on December 31)	$48,750	$ 54,750	$ 60,750	$ 97,500
Cost of sales (for the year ended)		3,150,000	3,622,500	3,441,375

Required:

a. Calculate Zawale's inventory turnover ratio and average number of days inventory on hand for 2015, 2016, and 2017.
b. Evaluate how well Zawale's management is managing the inventory. Explain.
c. What are some possible explanations for the results you found in (a) and (b)?
d. What are the implications for Zawale's performance of the results you found in (a)? Explain.

E12-17. **(Evaluating accounts payable management, LO 5)** Guisachan Books Inc. is a small book retailer. Guisachan has approached your company, a large publishing house, requesting credit terms on purchases. Guisachan has never purchased from your company. If credit is approved, Guisachan would be given 60 days to pay outstanding amounts. You have been provided with the following information from Guisachan's accounting records (Guisachan's year-end is March 31):

	2014	2015	2016	2017
Accounts payable (on March 31)	$67,200	$ 72,800	$ 85,400	$100,800
Credit purchases (for the year ended)		448,000	462,000	455,000

Required:

a. Calculate Guisachan's accounts payable turnover ratio and average payment period for accounts payable for 2015, 2016, and 2017.
b. Assume that you are the publishing house credit manager. How would you interpret the information about Guisachan's accounts payable? How would this information influence your decision about offering credit to Guisachan? Explain. What additional information would you request before making a final decision? Explain.
c. What effect will the results you calculated in (a) have on Guisachan's cash from operations? Explain. Is this a good situation? Explain. How might Guisachan's suppliers respond? Explain.

E12-18. **(Calculating EPS, price-to-earnings ratio, and dividend ratios, LO 4, 7)** Tantallon Inc. is a publicly traded company. During its year ended December 31, 2018, Tantallon reported net income of $11,879,500. During fiscal 2018, Tantallon declared and paid dividends of $0.08 per share on its 100,000,000 outstanding common shares. During the year, no shares were issued and none were repurchased from investors. In addition, Tantallon paid $500,000 in preferred dividends. On December 31, 2018, Tantallon's common share price was $5.75.

Required:

Calculate the following ratios for 2018. Explain and interpret the meaning of each ratio:

a. basic earnings per share for the year ended December 31, 2018
b price-to-earnings ratio on December 31, 2018
c. dividend payout ratio for the year ended December 31, 2018
d. dividend yield on December 31, 2018

E12-19. **(Calculating EPS, price-to-earnings ratio, and dividend ratios, LO 4, 7)** Kovach Ltd. is a publicly traded company. During its year ended December 31, 2017 Kovach reported a net loss of $37,500,000. During fiscal 2017 Kovach declared and paid four quarterly dividends of $0.05 per share on its 24,000,000 outstanding common shares. During the year no shares were issued and none were repurchased from investors. In addition, Kovach paid $5,000,000 in preferred dividends. On December 31, 2017 Kovach's share price was $6.75.

Required:

a. Calculate the following ratios for 2017. Explain and interpret the meaning of each ratio:
   i. basic earnings per share for fiscal 2017
   ii. price-to-earnings ratio on December 31, 2017
   iii. dividend payout ratio for fiscal 2017
   iv. dividend yield on December 31, 2017
b. Explain how it's possible for Kovach to pay a dividend when it reported a loss during fiscal 2017.
c. Explain why Kovach would have a share price greater than zero when the company is losing money. Why is its dividend yield positive even though the company is losing money?

E12-20. **(Examining the effect of debt covenants on debt and dividends, LO 6)** During fiscal 2017, Husavick Inc. borrowed $250,000 from a private lender. The loan agreement requires that Husavick's debt-to-equity ratio not exceed 2:1 at any time. The loan is repayable in 2023. You have been provided with the following information from Husavick's accounting records:

Husavick Inc. Summarized Balance Sheet For the Year Ended July 31, 2017	
Assets:	
Current assets	$150,000
Non-current assets	615,000
Total assets	$765,000
Liabilities and shareholders' equity:	
Current liabilities	$115,000
Non-current liabilities	375,000
Shareholders' equity	275,000
Total liabilities and shareholders' equity	$765,000

Required:

a. Calculate Husavick's debt-to-equity ratio on July 31, 2017.
b. How much additional debt could Husavick have borrowed without violating the debt covenant on July 31, 2017?
c. How much could Husavick have paid in dividends during fiscal 2017 without violating the debt covenant?
d. What would be the effect on Husavick's debt-to-equity ratio if it declared a $25,000 dividend on July 31, 2017 that was to be paid on August 15, 2017?

E12-21. (Computing ratios, LO 4, 5, 6, 7, 8) Hurstwood Wineries Ltd. (Hurstwood) produces and markets wines from its vineyards in Ontario and B.C. You have been provided with the following income statements and balance sheets for Hurstwood:

Hurstwood Wineries Ltd.
Income Statements
For the Years Ended March 31
(in thousands of dollars)

	2017	2016
Sales	$87,333	$86,865
Cost of goods sold	55,463	54,816
Gross profit	31,870	32,049
Selling and administration	22,561	21,294
Earnings before interest and amortization	9,309	10,755
Interest	1,435	1,563
Depreciation	2,700	2,481
Earnings before unusual items	5,174	6,711
Unusual items	(667)	4,739
Earnings before income taxes	4,507	11,450
Provision for (recovery of) income taxes:		
Current	2,168	3,634
Future	(295)	463
	1,873	4,097
Net earnings for the year	2,634	7,353
Retained earnings—beginning of year	39,395	33,970
Dividends on common shares	1,928	1,928
Retained earnings—end of year	$40,101	$39,395

Hurstwood Wineries Ltd.
Balance Sheets
As of March 31
(in thousands of dollars)

	2017	2016
Assets		
Current assets:		
Accounts receivable	$ 7,542	$ 7,844
Inventories	30,736	31,241
Prepaid expenses	702	557
	38,980	39,642
Capital assets and goodwill	43,884	38,844
Investment	3,565	3,565
	$86,429	$82,051
Liabilities		
Current liabilities:		
Bank indebtedness	$17,883	$13,665
Accounts payable and accrued liabilities	8,548	6,862
Dividends payable	482	482
Income and other taxes payable	928	2,009
Current portion of long-term debt	1,552	1,370
	29,393	24,388
Long-term debt	11,346	12,384
Future income taxes	2,716	3,011
	43,455	39,783
Shareholders' equity		
Common shares (weighted-average number of shares outstanding during 2017 was 3,953,050 and during 2016 was 3,875,200)	2,873	2,873
Retained earnings	40,101	39,395
	42,974	42,268
	$86,429	$82,051

Required:

a. Compute the following ratios and amounts for Hurstwood for 2017 and 2016:
   i. gross margin percentage
   ii. profit margin percentage
   iii. earnings per share
   iv. working capital
   v. current ratio
   vi. quick ratio
   vii. debt-to-equity ratio
   viii. interest coverage ratio
   ix. dividend payout ratio

b. Compute the following ratios and amounts for Hurstwood for 2017:
   i. asset turnover
   ii. return on equity
   iii. return on assets
   iv. inventory turnover ratio
   v. average number of days inventory on hand
   vi. accounts receivable turnover ratio
   vii. average collection period of accounts receivable
   viii. accounts payable turnover ratio
   ix. average payment period for accounts payable
   x. cash lag

c. How do the unusual items reported on the 2017 and 2016 income statements affect your ability to predict Hurstwood's future performance?

d. Comment on Hurstwood's liquidity, based on amounts you calculated in (a) and (b). Be sure to consider the nature of Hurstwood's business in your response.

E12-22. **(Understanding return on assets, LO 4)** You are provided with the following information about Unwin Corp. (Unwin), a small manufacturing company:

	2017	2016	2015	2014	2013
Sales	$1,309,440	$1,223,776	$1,165,500	$1,050,000	$
Net income	156,306	151,398	144,290	136,750	
Total liabilities (at year-end)	346,274	326,674	294,300	272,500	250,000
Shareholders' equity (at year-end)	381,680	325,376	273,976	229,688	192,938
Interest expense	58,500	51,000	42,500	61,500	
Tax rate	18%	18%	18%	18%	

Required:

a. Calculate Unwin's return on assets by determining its profit margin and asset turnover ratio for 2014–2017.

b. Calculate Unwin's return on equity for 2014–2017.

c. Assess the Unwin's profitability. In your response, explain the reasons for any changes in it.

E12-23. **(Understanding return on assets, LO 4)** You are provided with the following information about Wha Ti Inc. (Wha Ti), a small engine service company.

	2018	2017	2016	2015	2014
Sales	$957,264	$854,700	$763,125	$687,500	
Net income	33,504	32,479	30,525	28,875	
Total liabilities (at year-end)	159,535	151,938	144,703	137,813	131,250
Shareholders' equity (at year-end)	318,623	285,119	252,641	222,116	193,241

Required:

a. Calculate Wha Ti's return on assets for 2015–2018 by determining its profit margin and asset turnover ratio. Assume that profit margin equals net income divided by sales.
b. Calculate Wha Ti's return on equity for 2015–2018.
c. Assess the profitability of Wha Ti. In your response, explain the reasons for any changes in Wha Ti's profitability.

E12-24. (Interpreting ratios, LO 5) You have been provided with the following ratios for two retail businesses. Use the ratios to evaluate and compare the liquidity situations of the two businesses.

	Business A	Business B
Current ratio	1.26	1.75
Quick ratio	0.75	0.38
Inventory turnover ratio	3.1	2.60
Accounts payable turnover ratio	4.56	3.65

E12-25. (Interpreting ratios, LO 4) You have been provided with the following ratios for two retail businesses. Use the ratios to evaluate and compare the performance of the two businesses.

	Business A	Business B
Gross margin	40.0%	33.0%
Profit margin	5.0%	6.2%
Return on assets	3.1%	5.1%

Problems

P12-1. (Find the missing information, LO 4, 5, 6, 7) Use the information provided about Kynocks Inc. to determine the missing information from its December 31, 2017 balance sheet and for the income statement for the year ended December 31, 2017. For all final amounts determined for the balance sheet and income statement, round to the thousands of dollars.

Kynocks Inc.
Balance Sheets
As of December 31,

	2017	2016
Cash	$ ______	$110,000
Accounts receivable	______	105,000
Inventory	______	248,000
Capital assets (net)	______	146,000
Total assets	$ ______	$609,000
Accounts payable	$ ______	$184,000
Long-term debt	______	100,000
Common shares	______	75,000
Retained earnings	______	250,000
Total liabilities and shareholders' equity:	$ ______	$609,000

Kynocks Inc.
Income Statement
For the Year Ended December 31, 2017

Revenue	$ ______
Cost of sales	1,500,000
Gross margin	______
Selling, general, and administrative expenses	______
Interest expense	______
Income before taxes	______
Income tax expense	______
Net income	$ ______
Number of common shares outstanding during 2017	______

Additional information:

- No dividends were paid during the year.
- There are no preferred shares outstanding.
- All sales and purchases of inventory are on credit.
- No new common shares were issued during the year and no common shares were repurchased during the year.
- Tax rate = 20.63%.
- Gross margin percentage = 40%.
- Profit margin percentage = 20%.
- Interest coverage ratio = 6.2085.
- EPS = $0.40.
- ROA = 9.85.
- Inventory turnover ratio = 5.474.
- Accounts receivable turnover ratio = 21.739.
- Accounts payable turnover ratio = 7.589.
- Debt-to-equity ratio = 0.733.
- Current ratio = 2.222.

P12-2. **(Find the missing information, LO 4, 5, 6, 7)** Use the information provided about Voligny Inc. (Voligny) to determine the missing information from its December 31, 2017 balance sheet and for the income statement for the year ended December 31, 2017. For all final amounts determined for the balance sheet and income statement, round to thousands of dollars.

Voligny Inc. **Balance Sheets** **As of December 31,**		
	2017	**2016**
Cash	$ ______	$ 25,000
Accounts receivable	______	125,000
Inventory	______	185,000
Capital assets (net)	______	925,000
Total assets	$ ______	$1,260,000
Accounts payable	______	$ 70,000
Long-term debt	______	450,000
Common shares	______	200,000
Retained earnings	______	540,000
Total liabilities and shareholders' equity	$ ______	$1,260,000

Voligny Inc. **Income Statement** **For the Year Ended December 31, 2017**	
Revenue	$ ______
Cost of sales	______
Gross margin	______
Selling general and administrative expenses	______
Interest expense	______
Income before taxes	______
Income tax expense	______
Net income	$ 100,000

Additional information:

- No dividends were paid during the year.
- There are no preferred shares outstanding.
- All sales and purchases of inventory are on credit.
- No new common shares were issued during the year and no common shares were repurchased during the year.
- Tax rate = 20%.
- Gross margin percentage = 45%.
- Profit margin percentage = 10%.
- Interest coverage ratio = 4.906
- EPS = $0.75.
- Inventory turnover ratio = 2.716.
- Accounts receivable turnover ratio = 7.547.
- Accounts payable turnover ratio = 7.222.
- Debt-to-equity ratio = 0.586.
- Current ratio = 4.293.

P12-3. **(Considering the current ratios of different industries, LO 5)** Consider the following industries and indicate whether you think each would have a low or high current ratio (e.g., above or below 1.25). Explain your thinking.

a. telecommunications (like Rogers Communications)
b. airline (like WestJet)
c. retail furniture store (like Leon's)
d. software developer
e. real estate developer (builds and operates apartment buildings)
f. car manufacturer (like General Motors)

P12-4. **(Evaluating the effect of R&D accounting on financial statement analysis, LO 2, 3, 4, 5, 6, 8)** One controversial accounting issue is accounting for research costs. IFRS require research costs to be expensed as incurred. Some people argue that research is a legitimate asset and expensing it results in an understatement of assets and income, violates matching, making companies that invest heavily in research appear less successful than they actually are.

Chortitz Ltd. (Chortitz) is a large and successful software development company. You have been provided with Chortitz's summarized balance sheets for 2014 through 2017 and income statements for 2015 through 2017. Chortitz expensed (and expended) $15,812,000 for research in 2014 and $13,224,000 in 2013.

Chortitz Ltd.
Summarized Balance Sheet Information
As of June 30,
(000s)

	2017	2016	2015	2014
Current assets	$ 95,906	$103,126	$ 82,204	$ 69,630
Total assets	210,432	190,872	170,094	141,178
Current liabilities	64,308	66,440	44,466	37,138
Non-current liabilities	23,100	18,480	12,376	8,662
Shareholders' equity	123,024	105,952	113,252	95,378

Chortitz Ltd. Income Statements For the Years Ended June 30, (000s)			
	2017	2016	2015
Revenues	$ 243,704	$ 186,360	$ 152,686
Cost of revenues:			
License and networking	9,698	4,430	3,002
Customer support	12,592	9,456	5,200
Service	41,192	37,950	24,510
Total cost of revenues	63,482	51,836	32,712
	180,222	134,524	119,974
Operating expenses:			
Research and development	40,114	29,276	18,766
Sales and marketing	84,674	70,832	60,128
General and administrative	21,766	32,722	9,770
Depreciation	10,356	9,172	8,450
Total operating expenses	156,910	142,002	97,114
Income (loss) from operations	23,312	(7,478)	22,860
Interest expense	2,010	1,530	996
Income before income taxes	21,302	(9,008)	21,864
Provision for (recovery of) income taxes	4,230	(1,708)	3,990
Net income for the year	$ 17,072	($ 7,300)	$ 17,874
Weighted average number of common shares outstanding during the year	40,064,184	44,698,536	41,828,730

Required:

a. Recalculate Chortitz's net income in 2015, 2016, and 2017, assuming research is capitalized and amortized over three years. Also calculate total assets and shareholders' equity, assuming research is capitalized and amortized. What amount would be reported on the balance sheet for research in this case? (Assume that one-third of the amount expended on research is expensed each year, including the year of the expenditure, and that the accounting for research and development has no effect on income taxes.)
b. Calculate Chortitz's profit margin ratio, interest coverage ratio, earnings per share, debt-to-equity ratio, ROA, and ROE for 2015, 2016, and 2017 using the information as presented in the company's financial statements. Calculate the same ratios, assuming that Chortitz capitalizes and amortizes its research costs over three years.
c. Evaluate the performance and solvency of Chortitz under the "expense" and "capitalize" scenarios. What are the implications of the differences between the two scenarios? Do you think there is merit in the criticisms some people have expressed about the current IFRS treatment of research costs? Explain fully.

P12-5. **(Evaluating performance, LO 4)** Nywening Ltd. (Nywening) operates in a highly competitive industry. Price is very important to most customers and it's very difficult for small operators such as Nywening to differentiate themselves on product quality. It's possible to differentiate based on service, but most competitors offer reasonably comparable service packages.

The president of Nywening is reviewing the company's performance in 2017. During 2017, sales increased by 15 percent to $875,000. Average total assets for the year were $487,500, net income was $50,000, and interest expense was $15,000. Nywening's tax rate is 20 percent.

The president believes that Nywening can improve its performance in 2018. She would like to see a 12 percent growth in sales in 2018 and a return on assets of 20 percent. The president estimates that it will be necessary for the average amount of assets to increase by 10 percent in 2018. The president doesn't think that any additional borrowing will be required, and as a result, the interest expense for 2018 will be the same as for 2017.

Required:

a. Calculate Nywening's profit margin, asset turnover, and return on assets for 2017.
b. What asset turnover ratio is required in 2018 to achieve the president's objectives? What net income is needed to achieve her objectives? What would the profit margin be if the objectives are achieved? For the purposes of this question, use net income plus the after tax cost of interest to calculate profit margin.
c. Do you think the president's objectives are reasonable?

P12-6. **(Impact of strategy on gross margin and profit, LO 4)** Vita Ltd. manufactures and distributes board games. The company has been in business for many years and has been successful. Performance has been squeezed in recent years by other forms of entertainment. The CEO is giving some thought to different pricing strategies for his products and wants to know the impact of the choices. One of the ideas is to reduce the selling price by 5 percent on all products. He thinks that by doing this sales volume will increase by 18 percent. During 2017, Vita produced and sold 500,000 games for $20 each. The cost of producing each game was $12.50 (cost of sales). All other costs of operating the business were $3,550,000. Cost of sales per unit would remain the same ($12.50) under the new pricing strategy and the other costs would remain $3,550,000.

Required:

a. If the CEO implemented the new strategy and his estimates were correct, determine the following using the 2017 as the basis for your calculations,
   i. Sales in dollars and quantity
   ii. Cost of sales
   iii. Gross margin
   iv. Net income
   v. Gross margin percentage
   vi. Profit margin percentage
b. Explain why Vita could make more money even though it has a lower gross margin.
c. Do you think Vita should undertake the proposed strategy? Explain. Do you see any drawbacks?

P12-7. **(Impact of improving receivables collections and inventory holding period on cash, LO 5)** The general manager of Liberty Inc. issued a challenge to his managers. He wanted to decrease the collection period for accounts receivable and the holding period for inventory. Liberty is a wholesale distributor of low cost items that it imports from producers in Asia. Its customers include retailers in Ontario and Quebec. For the year ended December 31, 2017, the collection period for receivables was 48.2 days and the holding period inventory was 145 days. Liberty normally provides 30 days to its customers to pay its bills. Relevant financial statement information is as follows:

Liberty Inc. Financial Statement Information December 31, 2017	
Cash	$ 65,000
Average accounts receivable	375,000
Average inventory	610,000
Revenue	2,839,730
Cost of sales	1,535,517

Required:

Suppose that Liberty's managers were able to decrease the collection period for receivables to 42 days and the holding period for inventory to 130 days. What would have been the impact on the company's cash on December 31, 2017? (Determine the average amount of inventory and accounts receivable that would be needed in 2017 to achieve the targets.) What would be some methods Liberty could use to achieve the targets set by the general manager?

P12-8. **(Evaluating liquidity, LO 5)** You have been provided with the following information about Everell Inc. (Everell).

	2015	2016	2017	2018
Accounts receivable	$ 300,000	$ 315,000	$ 330,750	$ 347,288
Inventory	200,000	210,000	220,500	231,526
Accounts payable	150,000	157,500	165,376	173,644
Revenue	2,000,000	2,100,000	2,310,000	2,541,000
Cost of sales	1,100,000	1,155,000	1,282,050	1,423,076

Required:

a. Calculate the accounts receivable, inventory, and accounts payable turnover ratios for 2016 through 2018.
b. Calculate the average collection period of accounts receivable, average number of days inventory on hand, and average payment period for accounts payable for 2016 through 2018.
c. Determine Everell's cash lag for 2016 through 2018.
d. Interpret the results you obtained in parts (a) through (c). What do these results tell you about Everell's liquidity over the last three years?
e. What are some possible explanations for the results?
f. Suppose you are a banker that Everell's management has approached about an expanded line of credit. How would the results you obtained in parts (a) through (c). affect your decision? Explain.

P12-9. **(Evaluating liquidity, LO 5)** You have been provided with the following information about Altario Ltd. (Altario).

	2014	2015	2016	2017
Accounts receivable	$ 2,868,750	$ 3,098,250	$ 3,253,163	$ 3,415,822
Inventory	5,625,000	5,850,000	6,142,500	5,835,375
Accounts payable	725,000	738,920	760,351	707,883
Revenue	22,500,000	23,625,000	23,152,500	21,994,875
Cost of sales	9,000,000	9,402,750	9,168,622	8,666,640

Additional information:

- Altario gives its customers 30 days to pay for their purchases. After 30 days interest is charged.
- Most of Altario's suppliers allow 30 days for payment. Most offer discounts if payment is received within 10 days.

Required:

a. Calculate the accounts receivable, inventory, and accounts payable turnover ratios for 2015 through 2017.
b. Calculate the average collection period of accounts receivable, average number of days inventory on hand, and average payment period for accounts payable for 2015 through 2017.

c. Determine Altario's cash lag for 2015 through 2017.
d. Interpret the results you obtained in (a) through (c). What do these results tell you about Altario's liquidity over the last three years? What are some possible explanations for the results? Make recommendations for improving the management of receivables, inventory, and payables.
e. Suppose you are a banker that Altario's management approached about an expanded line of credit. How would the results you obtained in (a) through (c) affect your decision? Explain.

P12-10. **(The effect of leverage on ROA and ROE, LO 4)** Three companies, Company A, Company B, and Company C, are identical in every respect except for how they are financed. You are provided with the following information about each company.

	Company A			Company B			Company C		
	Jan. 1, 2017	Dec. 31, 2017	Dec. 31, 2018	Jan. 1, 2017	Dec. 31, 2017	Dec. 31, 2018	Jan. 1, 2017	Dec. 31, 2017	Dec. 31, 2018
Income before interest and taxes		$22,400	$ 2,400		$22,400	$ 2,400		$22,400	$ 2,400
Interest expense		0	0		2,400	2,400		5,600	5,600
Income tax expense (recovery)		4,928	528		4,400	0		3,696	(704)
Net income		17,472	1,872		15,600	0		13,104	(2,496)
Dividends paid (on common stock)		8,000	4,368		6,128	2,496		3,632	0
Total assets	80,000	89,472	86,976	80,000	89,472	86,976	80,000	89,472	86,976
Shareholders' equity	80,000	89,472	86,976	56,000	65,472	62,976	24,000	33,472	30,976
Tax rate		22%	22%		22%	22%		22%	22%

Required:

a. Calculate ROA and ROE for each company for the years ended December 31, 2017 and 2018.
b. Explain the differences in performance among the three companies.
c. Explain the effect of leverage on the performance measures.
d. Which company is the best investment? Explain.

P12-11. **(Interpreting dividend and stock price information, LO 7)** Embro Inc. is a Canadian publicly traded company. A friend of yours has been watching the stock for some time and feels that now would be a good time to buy. The friend said the company has paid a $1 dividend for the last four years and so provides a steady source of cash that she needs. She wants to go ahead with the purchase but she first wants your opinion on the status of the company. You have the following information about Embro:

	2017	2016	2015	2014
EPS	$ 0.98	$ 1.45	$ 2.25	$ 2.45
Dividend per share	1.00	1.00	1.00	1.00
Market price per share	11.10	18.50	24.25	27.55

Required:

a. Calculate Embro's dividend payout ratio and the dividend yield. Assume that the number of shares outstanding during the period didn't change and calculate the dividend payout ratio on a per share basis (dividends per share ÷ EPS.) Write an email to your friend explaining, based on the information you have, whether she should go ahead and purchase Embro shares. Explain your reasoning.
b. What additional information would you want to help you assess the situation?

P12-12. **(The effect of leasing on ratios, LO 4, 5, 6, 9)** Fodhia Inc. (Fodhia) is a small manufacturing company operating in eastern Canada. Fodhia is a public company. In 2016, Fodhia's management decided to acquire additional manufacturing equipment to be able to meet the increasing demand for its products. However, instead of purchasing the equipment, Fodhia arranged to lease it. The lease came into effect on January 1, 2017. In its 2017 financial statements Fodhia accounted for the leases as operating leases. You have obtained Fodhia's summarized balance sheets and income statements for 2016 and 2017.

Fodhia Inc.
Summarized Balance Sheets
As of December 31,

	2017	2016
Cash	$ 159,000	$ 206,250
Accounts receivable	521,250	456,000
Inventory	1,368,750	1,160,250
Capital assets (net)	2,171,250	1,989,000
Other non-current assets	281,250	331,500
Total assets	$ 4,501,500	$ 4,143,750
Current liabilities	$ 1,296,000	$ 1,367,250
Long-term debt	742,500	712,500
Common shares (750,000 shares outstanding)	900,000	900,000
Retained earnings	1,563,000	1,163,250
Total liabilities and shareholders' equity	$ 4,501,500	$ 4,143,750

Fodhia Inc.
Income Statements
For the Years Ended December 31,

	2017	2016
Revenue	$12,937,500	$10,875,000
Cost of sales	7,163,250	5,997,000
Selling, general, and administrative expenses	4,884,000	4,162,500
Depreciation expense	232,500	206,250
Lease expense for equipment	56,250	
Interest expense	69,000	64,500
Income tax expense	132,750	111,000
Net income	$ 399,750	$ 333,750

Had Fodhia accounted for the equipment leases as capital leases, the following differences would have occurred in the 2017 financial statements:

- No lease expense would have been recorded.
- The leased equipment would have been recorded on the balance sheet as capital assets for $345,000. The equipment would have been depreciated straight line over 12 years.
- A liability of $345,000 would have been recorded at the inception of the lease. On December 31, 2017, the current portion of the liability would have been $23,925. The interest expense arising from the lease in fiscal 2017 would have been $34,500. On December 31, 2017, the remaining liability, including the current portion, would have been $323,250.
- There would be no effect on the tax expense for the year.

Required:

a. Prepare revised financial statements for 2017 assuming that Fodhia treated the leases as capital leases instead of as operating leases.
b. Calculate the following ratios for 2017, first using the financial statements as initially prepared by Fodhia and then using the revised statements you prepared in part (a):
   i. debt-to-equity ratio
   ii. return on assets
   iii. return on equity
   iv. profit margin ratio
   v. current ratio
   vi. asset turnover
   vii. earnings per share
   viii. interest coverage ratio
c. Discuss the differences between the two sets of ratios you calculated in part (b). Why are the ratios different? How might users of the financial statements be affected by these differences? Which set of ratios gives a better perspective on the performance, liquidity, and leverage of Fodhia? Explain.

P12-13. (Determining the effect of a big bath on future earnings, LO 2, 4, 9) Quirpon Inc. (Quirpon) is a large mining company. In 2014, Quirpon wrote down $20,000,000 in costs that it incurred finding and developing certain mining properties. If Quirpon had not written down the $20,000,000 in costs, $4,000,000 in depreciation would have been expensed in each year from 2014 through 2018. The summarized financial statement information for the years 2014 through 2017 is:

Quirpon Inc.
Summarized Financial Statement Information
(in thousands of dollars)

	2013	2014	2015	2016	2017
Revenue		$61,000	$56,000	$62,000	$ 66,000
Operating expenses		24,000	22,000	26,000	29,000
Depreciation expense		14,000	14,400	14,800	15,600
Interest expense		2,400	2,400	2,400	2,400
Income tax expense		5,150	4,300	4,700	4,750
Net income		$15,450	$12,900	$14,100	$ 14,250
Total assets	$74,000	$69,450	$82,350	$96,450	$110,700
Total shareholders' equity	$50,000	$45,450	$58,350	$72,450	$ 86,700

Additional information:

- Quirpon has no preferred shares outstanding.
- The depreciation expense doesn't include the depreciation of the written-down assets and the write-down is not reflected in the presented information.
- Quirpon's tax rate is 25 percent.
- Assume that the writedown and any additional amortization expense do not affect Quirpon's tax expense.

Required:

a. Determine Quirpon's net income for 2014 through 2017, assuming that the $20,000,000 write-down (i) occurred and (ii) did not occur. For (ii) depreciation of the assets must be expensed each year.
b. Calculate Quirpon's profit margin, return on assets, and return on equity, assuming that the writedown (i) occurred and (ii) did not occur.

c. Should the writedown be considered permanent or transitory earnings? Explain.
d. As an equity investor in Quirpon, how would your evaluation of the company be affected by whether the writedown occurred versus whether the assets were amortized over their remaining life? In responding, you should consider permanent versus transitory earnings.

P12-14. **(Forecasting future earnings, LO 1, 2, 4, 5, 6)** You have been presented with Kelliher Ltd.'s income statement for the year ended September 30, 2017.

Kelliher Ltd. **Income Statement** **For the Year Ended September 30, 2017**	
Sales	$5,100,000
Cost of sales	2,295,000
Gross margin	2,805,000
Expenses:	
Salaries and wages	1,101,600
Depreciation	394,800
Selling and administrative	580,000
Interest	200,000
Other	130,000
Unusual items—lawsuit revenue	400,000
Income before income taxes	798,600
Income tax expense	239,580
Net income	$ 559,020

In addition, you have learned the following:

- Cost of sales in 2017 includes a write-down of inventory of $118,000. The amount of the write-down is about three times larger than the amount usually written down each year to account for non-salable inventory or inventory that will have to be sold at a deep discount.
- Sales include $500,000 for a one-time-only sale to the government of a foreign country. The gross margin percentage on this sale was 60 percent, which is significantly higher than what Kelliher normally experiences.
- Selling and administrative costs includes a $80,000 retirement bonus paid to the former CEO.
- Kelliher signed a contract with its employees that goes into effect on October 1, 2017. The contract increases union employees' wages and benefits by 4 percent. Wages to employees covered by the contract represent 70 percent of salaries and wages expense in 2017. Wages to other employees are not expected to change during 2018.
- During 2017, Kelliher won a lawsuit against a former employee for divulging confidential information to her new employer. The employee and her new employer are required to pay damages to Kelliher of $400,000.
- Sales (excluding the one-time sale note above) are expected to grow by 7 percent during 2018. Inventory costs are expected to increase by 8 percent, selling and administrative expenses are expected to decrease by 2 percent, interest expense isn't expected to change, depreciation expense is expected to increase by 3 percent, and other expenses are expected to increase by 5 percent.

Required:

a. Use Kelliher's 2017 income statement and the additional information to forecast an income statement for 2018.
b. Explain and interpret Kelliher's actual performance in 2017 and the performance that you forecast for 2018.
c. Discuss the difficulties that can occur with forecasting the future performance of an entity and the problems with using IFRS or ASPE financial statements for forecasting.

P12-15. **(Evaluating liquidity and solvency, LO 3, 4, 5, 6)** High Fashion Ltd. is a chain of high-end retailers of women's fashions. The chain currently has five locations in top malls in Toronto. High Fashion has been very popular because of its ability to get unique designer fashions not available at any other Canadian store. The success of High Fashion is largely due to the entrepreneur who began the chain, Ellin Bessner, who is very skilled at identifying the tastes of her target market and getting exclusive deals with international and domestic designers. Since 2015, High Fashion has been growing, including adding one new store each year in 2015, 2016, and 2017. Ellin has invested more money in the business to finance the growth but she is almost out of her own money.

Recently, Ellin approached the venture capital firm Dragon's Lair Inc. for a large loan. Ellin would like the money to expand her existing stores and expand into Montreal and Ottawa. Ellin has supplied financial statements for the last four years. Dragon's Lair is interested in investing in High Fashion. It's willing to lend the money but one of the terms of the loan agreement is that Dragon's Lair could convert the loan into a 20 percent stake in High Fashion within five years if it chooses to.

You are an analyst with Dragon's Lair. One of the principals of the firm has asked you to do an analysis of High Fashion's financial statements, evaluating its performance and liquidity over the last four years and assessing its suitability for a loan.

High Fashion Ltd.
Balance Sheets as of December 31,

	2017	2016	2015	2014
Assets				
Cash	$ 85,556	$ 124,678	$ 277,986	$ 375,000
Inventory	725,100	598,852	501,428	390,000
Other current assets	97,000	86,610	72,200	30,000
Total current assets	907,656	810,140	851,614	795,000
Capital assets	1,300,000	948,000	550,000	375,000
Accumulated depreciation	(415,000)	(291,000)	(190,000)	(112,500)
	$1,792,656	$1,467,140	$1,211,614	$1,057,500
Liabilities and Shareholders' equity				
Bank loan	$ 120,411	$ 102,321	$ 66,966	$ 25,000
Accounts payable	438,960	354,000	295,000	225,000
Other payables	15,000	65,000	95,000	120,000
Current portion of long-term debt	100,000	25,000	25,000	25,000
Total current liabilities	674,371	546,321	481,966	395,000
Long-term debt	175,000	275,000	300,000	325,000
Common shares	390,000	325,000	250,000	250,000
Retained earnings	553,285	320,819	179,648	87,500
	$1,792,656	$1,467,140	$1,211,614	$1,057,500

High Fashion Ltd. Income Statements for the Years Ended December 31,				
	2017	2016	2015	2014
Revenue	$2,898,000	$2,520,000	$2,250,000	$1,750,000
Cost of sales	1,556,226	1,340,640	1,186,875	910,000
Gross margin	1,341,774	1,179,360	1,063,125	840,000
Selling, general, and administrative costs	972,279	907,200	834,750	682,500
Interest expense	31,000	30,000	26,000	25,000
Other expenses	55,000	70,000	90,000	100,000
Income before taxes	283,495	172,160	112,375	32,500
Income taxes	51,029	30,989	20,227	5,850
Net income	$ 232,466	$ 141,171	$ 92,148	$ 26,650

Ms. Bessner provides additional information:

- All sales of merchandise to customers are for cash or major credit card. No credit terms are offered. High Fashion recognizes revenue at the time of sale.
- All inventory is purchased on credit.
- The long-term loan is from a private lender and must be repaid in full by 2020. High Fashion has been making payments on the loan since cash has been available to do so.
- High Fashion has never paid dividends.

Required:

Prepare the reported requested by the principal.

P12-16. **(Evaluating liquidity and solvency, LO 1, 2, 4, 5, 6, 7)** Bonanza Inc. (Bonanza) is a small manufacturer of home environmental products such as humidifiers, air cleaners, and ionizers. Bonanza's products are sold in retail stores across Canada and in the United States. Bonanza's product line has been well received by consumers over the years, although many products haven't changed for many years. The president is concerned that the company cash position has been deteriorating in recent years and she has approached your organization for a significant loan to provide the company with additional working capital, as well as to purchase capital assets that need to be replaced. The president has provided income statements and balance sheets for the most recent years.

Bonanza Inc. Income Statements For the Years Ended July 31,			
	2017	2016	2015
Sales	$3,704,000	$3,963,280	$3,923,646
Cost of sales	2,077,944	2,199,620	2,150,158
Selling, general, and administrative expenses	1,304,108	1,341,516	1,312,422
Depreciation	220,000	204,000	196,000
Research and development	90,000	176,000	250,000
Gain on sale of investment	(126,000)	0	0
Income tax expense	26,000	6,000	2,000
Net Income	$ 111,948	$ 36,144	$ 13,066

Bonanza Inc.
Balance Sheets
As of July 31,

	2017	2016	2015	2014
Cash	$ 11,158	$ 53,210	$ 11,066	$ 80,000
Receivables	550,000	430,000	360,000	290,000
Inventory	630,000	420,000	364,000	330,000
Prepaid expenses	102,000	56,000	162,000	30,000
Current assets	1,293,158	959,210	897,066	730,000
Capital assets (net of depreciation)	1,298,000	1,220,000	1,080,000	820,000
Investment, at cost	0	150,000	150,000	0
	$2,591,158	$2,329,210	$2,127,066	$1,550,000
Bank loans	$ 250,000	$ 184,000	$ 94,000	$ 0
Accounts payable and accrued liabilities	700,000	616,000	540,000	420,000
Current liabilities	950,000	800,000	634,000	420,000
Long-term debt	350,000	350,000	350,000	0
Common shares	1,000,000	1,000,000	1,000,000	1,000,000
Retained earnings	291,158	179,210	143,066	130,000
	$2,591,158	$2,329,210	$2,127,066	$1,550,000

Additional information:

- The long-term debt is due to be repaid in early 2019. The amount is owed to a large bank and is secured against certain capital assets.
- Capital asset purchases are paid for in cash.
- Bonanza has a $260,000 line of credit available from its bank. Bank loans represent the amount borrowed against the line of credit.
- All sales to customers and purchases of inventory are made on credit.
- Interest expense is included in selling, general, and administrative expenses. Interest expense was $115,000 in 2017, $102,000 in 2016, and $48,000 in 2015.

Required:

Prepare a report to the corporate lending department evaluating the liquidity and solvency of Bonanza. Provide a preliminary recommendation on whether the loan should be made. Provide support for your recommendation. What additional information would you want before reaching a final decision on the loan application? In your analysis, consider Bonanza's cash flow.

P12-17. **(Evaluating an equity investment, LO 1, 2, 4, 5, 6, 7)** Refer to the information about Bonanza provided in Problem P12-16. You are an investment analyst for Remigny Venture Capital. Remigny raises capital from individual investors and invests in promising small businesses, with the expectation that the businesses will grow and that it will ultimately be able to sell the investments at a profit. The president of Bonanza has approached your organization to make a significant equity investment in the company.

Required:

Prepare a report to Remigny's executive board analyzing Bonanza's performance over the last few years and assessing its attractiveness as an investment. What additional information would you want before reaching a final decision on whether to invest? In your analysis consider Bonanza's cash flow.

P12-18. **(Assessing inventory and performance, LO 1, 2, 3, 4, 5, 6, 7)** Bold! Ltd. is a men and women's retail clothing chain with stores located across Canada. The company is looking for new equity investment to help finance a major expansion. A private investment fund is looking to place some money in the Canadian retail industry and is considering Bold! Ltd. You are an analyst for a private investment fund and your manager has asked you to analyze some the company's information for trends and insights. You have information relevant to inventory and Bold!'s performance for the last seven years as well as other financial statement information that might be useful.

Periods ended:	**2017**	**2016**	**2015**	**2014**	**2013**	**2012**	**2011**
	$000s	**$000s**	**$000s**	**$000s**	**$000s**	**$000s**	**$000s**
Operating revenue	$65,420	$63,240	$59,340	$66,540	$71,246	$70,195	$71,991
General and administrative expenses	28,971	27,911	28,696	27,868	29,776	28,558	25,678
Cost of sales	34,946	31,826	30,781	33,145	36,024	35,515	36,839
Net income	5,157	661	(2,201)	(74)	(2,839)	2,158	4,290
Cash and equivalents	7,953	8,232	4,733	8,477	9,200	2,902	1,511
Inventories	10,962	11,424	12,939	11,612	11,966	14,812	15,465
Accounts receivable	302	290	161	238	254	240	194
Accounts payable and accrued liabilities	3,938	3,755	4,283	3,268	3,770	4,224	4,189

Note: All purchases and sales are on credit.

Required:

Prepare the report requested by your manager. Provide any ratios that you think appropriate. Be sure to interpret your results and explain the tools that you use to do the analysis.

Using Financial Statements

THE RONA GROUP LTD.

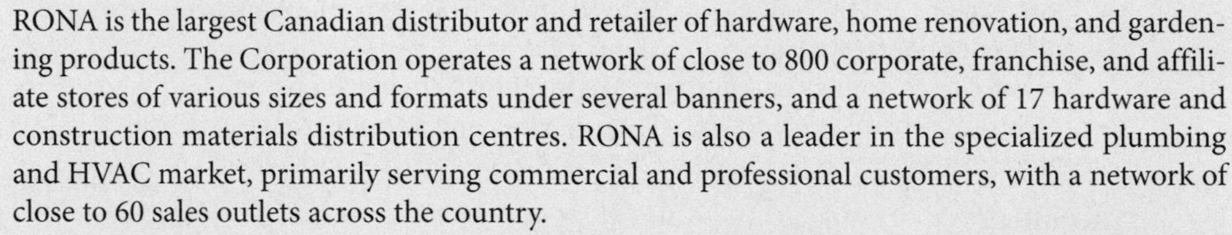

www.rona.ca

RONA is the largest Canadian distributor and retailer of hardware, home renovation, and gardening products. The Corporation operates a network of close to 800 corporate, franchise, and affiliate stores of various sizes and formats under several banners, and a network of 17 hardware and construction materials distribution centres. RONA is also a leader in the specialized plumbing and HVAC market, primarily serving commercial and professional customers, with a network of close to 60 sales outlets across the country.

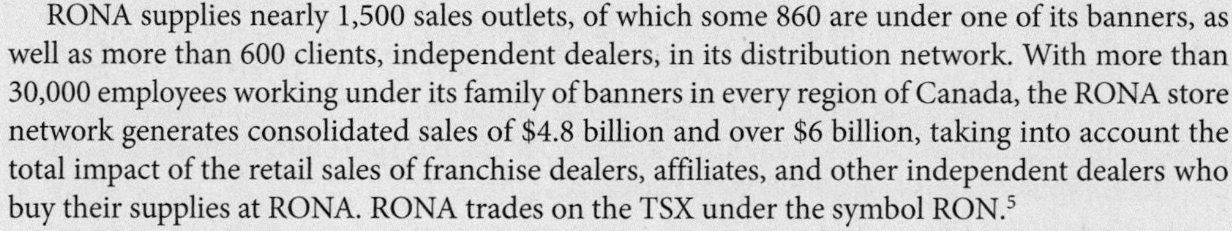

RONA supplies nearly 1,500 sales outlets, of which some 860 are under one of its banners, as well as more than 600 clients, independent dealers, in its distribution network. With more than 30,000 employees working under its family of banners in every region of Canada, the RONA store network generates consolidated sales of $4.8 billion and over $6 billion, taking into account the total impact of the retail sales of franchise dealers, affiliates, and other independent dealers who buy their supplies at RONA. RONA trades on the TSX under the symbol RON.[5]

RONA's consolidated balance sheets, statements of operations, comprehensive earnings, and cash flows, and extracts from the notes to the financial statements are provided in Exhibit 12.4.[6] Use this information to respond to questions FS12-1 to FS12-11.

FS12-1. Prepare common size and trend statements from RONA's balance sheets for fiscal 2009 through 2011 and from its income statements for fiscal 2010 and 2011. Analyze the statements you prepared to identify any issues you think might require additional explanation. Explain why you identified these issues.

FS12-2. Compute and interpret the following ratios for RONA for fiscal years 2010 and 2011. Use these ratios to assess RONA's liquidity. Be sure to use the information provided from RONA's December 28, 2009 balance sheet.

a. current ratio
b. quick ratio
c. accounts receivable turnover ratio
d. average collection period of accounts receivable
e. inventory turnover ratio
f. average number of days inventory on hand

g. accounts payable turnover ratio
h. average payment period for accounts payable

FS12-3. Compute and interpret the following ratios for RONA for fiscal 2010 and 2011. Use these ratios to assess RONA's performance:
a. gross margin
b. profit margin
c. return on assets
d. return on equity

EXHIBIT 12.4 The RONA Group Ltd.: Extracts from the Financial Statements

RONA Inc.
Consolidated Income Statements and Other Comprehensive Income
Years ended December 25, 2011 and December 26, 2010
(in thousands of Canadian dollars, except per share amounts)

Consolidated Income Statements		**2011**		2010
Revenues (Note 4)	**$**	**4,804,584**	$	4,819,589
Operating profit before goodwill impairment and restructuring costs, impairment of non-financial assets and other charges (Note 5.1)		**156,900**		223,205
Goodwill impairment (Note 14)		**(117,000)**		–
Restructuring costs, impairment of non-financial assets and other charges (Notes 5.4 and 32)		**(71,343)**		–
Operating profit (loss)		**(31,443)**		223,205
Finance income (Note 25)		**5,262**		4,394
Finance costs (Note 25)		**(34,729)**		(24,061)
		(29,467)		(19,667)
Income (loss) before income tax expense		**(60,910)**		203,538
Income tax expense (Note 7)		**(13,863)**		(60,717)
Net income (loss)	**$**	**(74,773)**	$	142,821
Net income (loss) attributable to:				
Owners of RONA Inc.	**$**	**(78,382)**	$	137,356
Non-controlling interests		**3,609**		5,465
	$	**(74,773)**	$	142,821
Net income (loss) per share attributable to owners of RONA Inc. (Note 29)				
Basic	**$**	**(0.66)**	$	1.06
Diluted	**$**	**(0.66)**	$	1.05
Consolidated Statements of Other Comprehensive Income				
Net income (loss)	**$**	**(74,773)**	$	142,821
Other comprehensive income (loss) net of taxes:				
Cash flow hedges				
– Loss for the year		**(920)**		(1,490)
– Reclassification to income or loss		**1,632**		273
Actuarial losses (Note 26)		**(2,775)**		(2,352)
Total other comprehensive income (loss)		**(2,063)**		(3,569)
Total comprehensive income (loss)	**$**	**(76,836)**	$	139,252

EXHIBIT 12.4 (continued) The RONA Group Ltd.: Extracts from the Financial Statements

RONA Inc.
Consolidated Statements of Cash Flows
as at December 25, 2011 and December 26, 2010
(in thousands of Canadian dollars)

	2011	2010
Operating activities		
Income (loss) before income tax expense	$ (60,910)	$ 203,538
Adjustments:		
Depreciation, amortization and impairment of non-financial assets (Note 5.2)	149,736	108,718
Change in fair value of derivative financial instruments	(159)	(1,078)
Net gains on disposal of assets	(1,123)	(2,921)
Goodwill impairment (Note 14)	117,000	–
Stock-based compensation expense (recovery) (Note 23)	(2,684)	4,588
Difference between amounts paid for post employment benefits and current period expenses	(2,855)	(3,921)
Other	3,308	2,078
	202,313	311,002
Net change in working capital (Note 8)	66,682	(132,479)
	268,995	178,523
Interest received	3,898	2,819
Income taxes paid	(42,648)	(43,270)
Cash flow from operating activities	230,245	138,072
Investing activities		
Business acquisitions (Note 9)	(47,707)	(80,275)
Acquisition of property, plant and equipment (Note 12)	(70,198)	(104,924)
Acquisition of intangible assets (Note 15)	(39,225)	(41,359)
Acquisition of other financial assets	(6,049)	(2,527)
Proceeds on disposal of property, plant and equipment	10,216	4,950
Proceeds on disposal of other financial assets	4,765	10,031
Interest received	1,365	1,575
Cash flow from investing activities	(146,833)	(212,529)
Financing activities		
Bank loans	(326)	(7,172)
Other long-term debt	92,112	1,899
Financing costs	(2,541)	
Repayment of other long-term debt	(33,886)	(30,433)
Repurchase of debentures (Note 18)	(283,171)	
Proceeds from issue of common shares	4,406	3,713
Proceeds from issue of preferred shares	172,500	–
Fees related to issue of preferred shares	(5,484)	–
Repurchase of common shares (Note 22)	(31,768)	(31,609)
Cash dividends paid by a subsidiary to non-controlling interests	(3,920)	(2,450)
Dividends on common shares	(18,253)	–
Dividends on preferred shares	(5,458)	
Interest paid	(26,051)	(23,171)
Cash flow from financing activities	(141,840)	(89,223)
Net decrease in cash	(58,428)	(163,680)
Cash, beginning of period	75,577	239,257
Cash, end of period	$ 17,149	$ 75,577

EXHIBIT 12.4 (continued) The RONA Group Ltd.: Extracts from the Financial Statements

RONA Inc.
Consolidated Statements of Financial Position
as at December 25, 2011, December 26, 2010 and December 28, 2009
(in thousands of Canadian dollars)

	2011 December 25	2010 December 26	2009 December 28
Assets			
Current			
Cash	$ 17,149	$ 75,577	$ 239,257
Trade and other receivables (Note 10)	370,094	299,889	248,201
Other financial assets (Note 11)	1,468	2,245	2,644
Current tax assets	7,616	–	2,436
Inventory (Note 6)	840,287	905,467	725,810
Prepaid expenses	20,836	17,955	18,114
Current assets	1,257,450	1,301,133	1,236,462
Non-current			
Other financial assets (Note 11)	13,617	9,644	11,118
Property, plant and equipment (Note 12)	874,246	885,044	827,883
Non-current assets held for sale (Note 13)	10,455	16,474	11,080
Goodwill (Note 14)	426,968	529,094	455,572
Intangible assets (Note 15)	126,968	128,223	106,157
Other non-current assets (Note 16)	5,435	3,245	4,406
Deferred tax assets (Note 7)	65,239	48,763	51,830
Total assets	$ 2,780,378	$ 2,921,620	$ 2,704,508
Liabilities			
Current			
Bank loans	$ 4,377	$ 1,943	$ 5,211
Trade and other payables	487,864	454,166	409,764
Dividends payable	2,527	9,119	–
Current tax liabilities	–	3,379	–
Derivative financial instruments (Note 25)	691	1,653	776
Provisions (Note 20)	6,947	4,625	7,002
Instalments on long-term debt (Note 18)	20,257	21,151	9,996
Current liabilities	522,663	496,036	432,749
Non-current			
Long-term debt (Note 18)	232,073	444,333	430,524
Other non-current liabilities (Note 19)	33,653	30,601	27,859
Provision (Note 20)	3,606	4,539	10,762
Deferred tax liabilities (Note 7)	32,759	34,314	27,724
Total liabilities	824,754	1,009,823	929,618
Equity			
Share capital (Note 22)	793,416	632,614	603,756
Retained earnings	1,115,801	1,233,454	1,125,235
Contributed surplus	11,386	11,137	13,138
Accumulated other comprehensive income	(505)	(1,217)	–
Total equity attributable to owners of RONA Inc.	1,920,098	1,875,988	1,742,129
Non-controlling interests	35,526	35,809	32,761
Total equity	1,955,624	1,911,797	1,774,890
Total liabilities and equity	$ 2,780,378	$ 2,921,620	$ 2,704,508

EXHIBIT 12.4 (continued) The RONA Group Ltd.: Extracts from the Financial Statements

RONA Inc.

Notes to Consolidated Financial Statements

as at December 25, 2011 and December 26, 2010
(in thousands of Canadian dollars)

2. Basis of presentation

(e) Fiscal year

The Corporation's fiscal year includes 52 weeks and ends on the last Sunday of December.

3. Significant accounting policies

The accounting policies described below were applied consistently by all of the Corporation's entities.

(c) Revenue recognition

Revenue from the sale of goods is measured at the fair value of the consideration received or receivable, net of returns, rebates and trade and quantity discounts. The Corporation recognizes revenue at the time of sale in stores or upon delivery of the merchandise, when the sale is accepted by the customer and when collection is reasonably assured.

Revenue also includes various services provided by the Corporation, such as product installation and delivery. Revenue from the rendering of services is measured at the fair value of the consideration received or receivable. The Corporation recognizes revenue when the commercial obligations have been fulfilled, the services have been accepted by the customer and collection is reasonably assured.

Revenue also includes royalties received from franchised stores. Royalties are measured as a percentage of revenue and are recognized as earned and when collection is reasonably assured.

Interest income and expenses relating to receivables and loans and advances are reported on an accrual basis using the effective interest method.

(d) Inventory valuation

Inventory is valued at the lower of cost and net realizable value. Cost is determined using the weighted average cost method.

The cost of inventories comprises all costs of purchase and other costs incurred in bringing the inventory to its present location and condition, including realized gains or losses on qualifying cash flow hedges of foreign currency inventory purchases. Inventory is comprised mainly of finished goods.

Net realizable value is the estimated selling price in the ordinary course of business less any applicable estimated selling expenses.

Estimating the impact of certain factors on the net realizable value of inventory, such as obsolescence and losses of inventory, requires a high level of judgment. Inventory quantities, age and condition are measured and assessed regularly throughout the year.

4. Revenues

	2011	2010
Sales of goods	**$ 4,739,484**	$ 4,748,872
Rendering of services	**41,027**	44,725
Royalties received	**24,073**	25,992
Total revenues	**$ 4,804,584**	$ 4,819,589

EXHIBIT 12.4 (continued) The RONA Group Ltd.: Extracts from the Financial Statements

5. Supplemental information on income and charges

5.1 Operating profit before goodwill impairment and restructuring costs, impairment of non-financial assets and other charges

	2011	2010
Revenues	**$ 4,804,584**	$ 4,819,589
Cost of sales (Note 6)	**(3,455,301)**	(3,447,768)
Gross profit	**1,349,283**	1,371,821
Selling, general and administrative expenses	**(1,214,082)**	(1,172,222)
Net gains on disposal of assets	**1,123**	3,250
Other income	**20,576**	20,356
Operating profit before goodwill impairment and restructuring costs, impairment of non-financial assets and other charges	**$ 156,900**	$ 223,205

5.2 Depreciation, amortization and impairment of non-financial assets

	2011	2010
Depreciation of property, plant and equipment	**$ 80,348**	$ 79,837
Depreciation of leasehold property included in property, plant and equipment	**1,860**	1,711
Amortization of intangible assets	**23,831**	26,213
Amortization of other non-current assets	**877**	957
Impairment of non-financial assets (Note 5.4)	**42,820**	–
Total depreciation, amortization and impairment of non-financial assets	**$ 149,736**	$ 108,718

5.3 Employee benefits expense

	2011	2010
Salaries	**$ 486,928**	$ 445,966
Defined benefit expense (Note 26)	**892**	640
Defined contribution expense (Note 26)	**10,473**	10,283
Stock-based compensation expense (recovery) (Note 23)	**(2,684)**	4,588
Other fringe benefits	**$ 105,037**	$ 95,851
Total employee benefits expense	**600,646**	557,328

6. Inventory

For the year ended December 25, 2011, an amount of $3,455,301 in inventory was expensed in the consdidated income statement ($3,447,768 in 2010).

For the year ended December 25, 2011, an inventory write-down charge of $49,363 ($24,306 in 2010) of which $18,700 is included in restructuring costs (Note 5.4) was recognized in the consolidated income statement. No reversal of previous write-downs was recognized.

10. Trade and other receivables

	2011 As at December 25	2010 As at December 26	2009 As at December 28
Trade accounts			
Retail and commercial customers	**$ 260,319**	$ 219,345	$ 161,879
Affiliated and franchised stores	**93,927**	74,894	73,963
Joint ventures	**3,510**	3,711	5,475
	357,756	297,950	241,317
Other accounts receivable	**12,338**	1,939	6,884
	$ 370,094	$ 299,889	$ 248,201

EXHIBIT 12.4 (continued) The RONA Group Ltd.: Extracts from the Financial Statements

17. Bank loans

a) Other subsidiaries

Bank loans are secured by an assignment of certain assets, notably trade and other receivables, inventory and property, plant and equipment, in the amount of $32,423 ($32,570 in 2010). These bank loans bear interest at rates varying from prime rate to prime rate plus 0.50% and are renewable annually. As at December 25, 2011, the interest rates varied from 3.00% to 3.50% (3.00% to 3.50% in 2010). The amount authorized for these credit facilities is $19,060 ($16,660 in 2010) and the amount used is $4,795 ($1,500 in 2010).

18. Long-term debt

	2011 As at December 25	2010 As at December 26	2009 As at December 28
Debentures, unsecured, par value $116,829, rate of 5.40%, maturing in 2016[(a)]	**$ 116,068**	$ 396,967	$ 396,564
Credit facilities, at a weighted average rate of 2.47%, maturing in 2016	**91,249**	–	–
Mortgage loans, secured by assets having a non-depreciated cost of $90,943 ($101,190 in 2010 and $66,300 in 2009), rates varying from prime rate less 0.25% to 8.50% in 2011 (prime rate less 0.25% to 8.50% in 2010 and 2009), maturing on various dates until 2020	**26,107**	42,391	33,561
Obligations under finance leases, rates varying from 4.19% to 10.60% (3.97% to 12.40% in 2010 and 2.90% to 12.40% in 2009), maturing on various dates until 2017	**1,592**	3,557	6,953
Balances of purchase prices, varying from 0.00% to 6.00% (0.00% to 6.00% in 2010, prime rate less 1.00% to 3.00% in 2009), payable on various dates until 2015	**16,314**	20,569	442
Shares issued and fully paid 1,000,000 Class D preferred shares (2,000,000 shares in 2010 and 3,000,000 shares in 2009)[(b)]	**1,000**	2,000	3,000
	252,330	465,484	440,520
Instalments due within one year	**20,257**	21,151	9,996
	$ 232,073	$ 444,333	$ 430,524

(a) Effective rate of 5.55%.

(b) During the year, the Corporation redeemed 1,000,000 shares (1,000,000 shares in 2010 and 2009) for cash consideration of $1,000 ($1,000 in 2010 and 2009).

Revolving credit

On December 23, 2011, the Corporation concluded the renewal of its existing credit facility for a five-year period. This facility, which was to mature in 2012, has been renewed to 2016 and the total available amount has been increased from $650,000 to $950,000. The premium on the base interest rate and borrowing costs varies in accordance with the credit rating assigned to the unsecured debentures.

Credit facilities can be used to issue letters of guarantee and credit letters for imports. As at December 25, 2011, the letters of guarantee issued amount to $1,216 ($1,309 in 2010). For the year 2011, the weighted average interest rate on the revolving credit is 2.2% (2.9% in 2010).

The Corporation is required to meet certain financial ratios. During the years ended December 25, 2011 and December 26, 2010 as well as at the 2011 and 2010 financial year-ends, the Corporation is in compliance with these requirements.

EXHIBIT 12.4 (continued) The RONA Group Ltd.: Extracts from the Financial Statements

Letters of credit

The Corporation also has an unsecured credit facility up to an amount of $55,000, utilized for the issuance of letters of credit for imports. The terms and conditions to be respected are the same as for the revolving credit. As at December 25, 2011, the amount used is $40,046 ($32,360 in 2010).

Maturities for obligations under finance leases are as follows:

				2011		
	Future minimum lease payments		Interest		Value of the future minimum lease payments	
Less than 1 year	$	851	$	91	$	760
Between 1–5 years		925		122		803
Over 5 years		30		1		29
	$	1,806	$	214	$	1,592

The instalments on other long-term debt and share repurchases for the next years are as follows:

	2011 As at December 25		2010 As at December 26		2009 As at December 28	
Less than 1 year	$	17,881	$	19,227	$	6,395
Between 1–5 years		135,860		34,815		26,155
Over 5 years		5,748		410,918		404,663
	$	159,489	$	464,960	$	437,213

21. Guarantees, commitments and contingencies

Guarantees

In the ordinary course of business, the Corporation reaches agreements that could meet the definition of "guarantees."

The Corporation guarantees mortgages for an amount of $1,257. The terms of these loans extend until 2012 and the net carrying amount of the assets held as security, which mainly include land and buildings, is $5,389.

Pursuant to the terms of inventory repurchase agreements, the Corporation is committed towards financial institutions to buy back the inventory of certain customers at an average of 64% of the cost of the inventories to a maximum of $44,961. In the event of recourse, this inventory would be sold in the ordinary course of the Corporation's operations. These agreements have undetermined periods but may be cancelled by the Corporation with a 30-day advance notice. In the opinion of management, the likelihood that significant payments would be incurred as a result of these commitments is low.

Commitments

The Corporation has entered into operating lease agreements expiring until 2021 which call for lease payments of $59,781 for the rental of automotive equipment, computer hardware, distribution equipment, a warehouse and the building housing the head office and the distribution centre in Quebec.

The Corporation has also entered into operating lease agreements expiring until 2030 for corporate store space for minimum lease payments of $931,880.

As part of the operation of big-box stores with dealer-owners, the Corporation is initially involved as a primary tenant and then signs a subleasing agreement with the dealer-owners. In this respect, the Corporation is committed under agreements expiring until 2023 which call for minimum lease payments of $56,851 for the rental of premises and land on which the Corporation erected a building. In consideration thereof, the Corporation has signed subleasing agreements for an equivalent amount.

During 2011, the Corporation signed a three-year partnership with Canucks Sport & Entertainment wherein the Corporation has committed to pay $3,470 due in 2014.

EXHIBIT 12.4 (continued) The RONA Group Ltd.: Extracts from the Financial Statements

The minimum lease payments and minimum amounts receivable under operating lease agreements and other commitments for the next years are as follows:

		2011		
		Minimum lease payments		Minimum amounts receivable
Less than 1 year	$	**139,813**	$	**8,856**
Between 1–5 years		**465,248**		**27,598**
Over 5 years		**446,921**		**20,680**
	$	**1,051,982**	$	**57,134**

		2010		
		Minimum lease payments		Minimum amounts receivable
Less than 1 year	$	125,411	$	10,077
Between 1–5 years		413,031		35,368
Over 5 years		510,364		26,501
	$	1,048,806	$	71,946

The Corporation leases several buildings for its stores as operating leases, the majority of which are non-cancellable. The leases are usually for a term of 20 years and have a renewal clause at the market rates prevailing at that time.

In 2005, the Corporation entered into an eight-year partnership agreement for Olympic and Paralympic sponsorship valued at $60,000. Moreover, in 2006 the Corporation committed an additional amount of $7,000 to financial support programs for athletes. As at December 25, 2011, the balance due on these agreements is $1,900, payable in 2012.

Contingencies

Various claims and litigation arise in the course of the Corporation's activities and its insurers have taken up the Corporation's defence in some of these cases. In addition, upon the acquisition of Réno-Dépôt Inc., the vendor committed to indemnify the Corporation for litigation which the Corporation assumed in the course of this acquisition.

Management does not expect that the outcome of these claims and litigation will have a material and adverse effect on the Corporation's results and deemed its allowances adequate in this regard.

FS12-4. Compute and interpret the following ratios for RONA for fiscal years 2010 and 2011. Use these ratios to assess RONA's solvency and liquidity. Don't restrict your evaluation to the ratios you are required to calculate.

a. debt-to-equity ratio
b. interest coverage ratio (earnings-based)
c. interest coverage ratio (cash-based)

FS12-5. Calculate RONA's gross margin for fiscal 2010 and 2011. Assuming that all other expenses remain the same, what would RONA's net income or loss before taxes have been if it had the same gross margin in 2011 as in 2010? What would net income before taxes have been had the 2010 gross margin been the same as in 2011?

FS12-6. Does RONA have any off-balance-sheet liabilities? Describe these liabilities. What impact do the off-balance-sheet liabilities have on your ability to evaluate RONA's capital structure and risk? Calculate RONA's debt-to-equity ratio on December 25, 2011 using only the amounts reflected in the balance sheet, and compare that amount with the ratio taking into consideration the off-balance-sheet amounts. Don't forget to discount the amounts where appropriate. Assume a discount rate of 15 percent.

FS12-7. RONA's cash position is significantly lower at the end of fiscal 2011 than the year before. Explain the reason for the decrease. Is this something you are concerned about? Explain. Why is RONA's cash from operations so much greater than its net income?

FS12-8. In fiscal 2011, RONA lost almost $75 million whereas in 2010 it made almost $143 million. Analyze RONA's income statements, Note 5.1, and any other information you think is relevant in Exhibit 12.4 and explain the poorer performance in fiscal 2011.

FS12-9. You are the credit analyst for a company that RONA has approached to become a major supplier of lumber. Prepare a report to the manager of the credit department assessing the credit-worthiness of RONA and recommending whether the company should extend credit. Be sure to consider the information provided in the notes to the financial statements provided in Exhibit 12.4.

FS12-10. You are considering purchasing some of RONA's common shares. Use the information provided in Exhibit 12.4 to assess the attractiveness of such an investment. What additional information would you want to make a decision?

FS12-11. Internet research question: What industry is RONA in? What are its competitors? What differentiates RONA from its competitors? Find the financial statements of at least one of its major competitors and compare the two companies' performance.

ENDNOTES

1. Extracted from Torstar Corporation's 2011 audited financial statements.
2. Extracted from WestJet Airlines Ltd.'s 2011 annual report.
3. Extracted from Domtar Corporation's 2011 annual report.
4. Data from the *Financial Post*, "2012 Industry Reports," at http://www.fpinfomart.ca (accessed May 2012).
5. Adapted from RONA Inc.'s Web site at http://www.rona.ca/content/profile_profile_investor-relations.
6. Adapted from RONA Inc.'s 2011 annual report.

Practise and learn online with Connect. Connect resources include additional and interactive study exercises, videos, and practice quizzing, as well as additional material you won't find in the printed text.

APPENDIX

COMPREHENSIVE CASES

CASE 1: ALEXANDER ELECTRONICS LTD.

Alexander Electronics Ltd. (AEL) is a retailer of home electronics, software, music, and video games in a medium-sized Canadian city. The store has been in business for many years and has grown along with the community. Recently, AEL's owner has decided to sell the store because he felt he was too old for the rigours of operating it. Ryan Evans has expressed interest in buying AEL and he and the current owner have been negotiating for several months. Mr. Evans has worked for AEL as a marketing manager and he is confident it will continue to be successful. Buying AEL will also fulfill a lifelong ambition of Mr. Evans to own his own business. The current owner and Mr. Evans have agreed in principle to base the selling price on AEL's net income before unusual items for the year ended December 31, 2017.

It's late January 2018. Mr. Evans has just received AEL's 2017 financial statements. For the most part, he's satisfied with the statements but he has some concerns and has approached you for advice about them. He would like a report evaluating the appropriateness of the treatments used in AEL's 2017 income statements for purposes of determining the price he should pay.

1. AEL has been given exclusive distribution rights in the region for a new video game called *Zordef of the Deep* (*Zordef*). *Zordef* is scheduled to be released on February 5, 2018. When AEL learned in early December 2017 that it would have exclusive distribution rights, it set up a program that would allow people to guarantee themselves a copy of *Zordef* as soon as it was released. Under the program, a customer would purchase the game in advance by paying the full retail price. The customer would then receive a certificate that could be exchanged for *Zordef* when it was released. As of December 31, 2017, over 4,000 people had signed up and paid $69.99 for *Zordef*. AEL's cost per copy will be $45.00. AEL will have to pay the manufacturer of *Zordef* 30 days after the game is delivered to the store. AEL recognized the revenue when a customer signed up for the program, paid for the game, and received their certificate.
2. During 2017, AEL began offering service contracts to customers who wanted support with any technical problems they had with their electronic equipment. Customers can buy one-, two-, or three-year service contracts. Payment must be made in full at the beginning of the contract and the price is discounted for the longer-term arrangements. Customers can cancel their contracts at the end of the first year (for two- and three-year contracts) and receive a refund for the unused portion. AEL recognized the revenue when customers signed up and paid for their contracts.
3. In previous years, AEL's current owner took an annual salary of between $75,000 and $100,000 per year. In 2017, he received no salary, opting instead to receive a dividend of $65,000.
4. In November, AEL launched a major advertising campaign in the city. The campaign ran until just before Christmas. The purpose of the campaign was to promote AEL for the Christmas season as well as to create awareness of the store in parts of the city that historically had not shopped at AEL. AEL capitalized the costs and is amortizing them over 12 months.
5. In February 2017, AEL sold a piece of land for $635,000. The land originally cost $210,000 and was purchased in 2009 when the current owner was thinking that a new, modern, standalone location might eventually be needed to allow AEL to grow to meet the needs of its customers. The owner sold the land because he received an offer that was "too good to refuse" and he didn't think there would be a need for a new location in the foreseeable future.

Required:

Prepare the report requested by Mr. Evans.

CASE 2: ATHINA BUILDING SUPPLIES LTD.

Athina Building Supplies Ltd. (Athina) is a retail and commercial building supply dealer. Until recently, Athina was part of a national chain of stores, but the chain decided to sell off stores that weren't in its core business. Several local investors purchased Athina. The purchasers believe that Athina will be successful, but that it wasn't well managed by the chain. The new investors paid $1,000,000 in cash for Athina. Athina will also pay 25 percent of net income before unusual or non-recurring items that Athina earns in excess of $500,000 for each of the next three years (including fiscal 2017), as reported in Athina's general purpose financial statements.

It's now late January 2018. Athina has just provided its financial statements for the fiscal year ended December 31, 2017 to the national chain as required by the agreement of purchase and sale. The CFO of the company that sold Athina has asked you to examine the financial statements, discuss any issues with Athina's new management, and identify any problems that might affect net income and the amount the national chain is due as part of the agreement. In your review, you identified the following issues:

1. Athina reported net income before unusual or non-recurring items of $510,000 for the year ended December 31, 2017.
2. Athina's business with most customers is transacted in cash or on credit cards. Athina offers credit terms to builders and contractors, allowing them up to 90 days to pay. The revenue on these sales is recognized at the time of the exchange. Athina has also given extended credit terms to a number of struggling home builders in its community. The builder began construction of new homes, but sales have been slower than expected. Athina has agreed to accept payment each time a builder sells one of its homes. To date, none of these builders have defaulted on any amounts they owe. Athina recognizes these sales on collection of cash from a builder. As of the end of December 31, 2017, these builders owe $275,000. The costs associated with these sales are $150,000. These costs were expensed as incurred.
3. During 2017, Athina's management discovered that certain assets purchased several years ago hadn't been depreciated. The amount of depreciation that should have been expensed to date on these assets, $175,000, was fully expensed in 2017.
4. In mid-2013, Athina obtained an exclusive dealership for a line of high-quality kitchen cabinets. The dealership rights were for an initial five-year period, with five-year renewals possible at the option of the manufacturer. At the time of signing the initial agreement, Athina was assured that a renewal was virtually certain. Athina spent $210,000 to set up displays to promote the line. These costs were capitalized and are being amortized over 10 years. In December 2017, Athina learned that the exclusive dealership arrangement won't be renewed because it's no longer part of the national chain. Athina won't be able to sell the products beyond April 2018. Athina wrote off the unamortized portion of the costs in 2017.
5. Athina purchased some heavy equipment for use in the lumberyard at an auction for $225,000. The equipment was fairly old and in poor condition and required $125,000 to get it in working condition. Athina's management believes the equipment will be usable for at least 10 years. Athina capitalized the purchase price of the equipment and expensed the $125,000 as a repair cost.
6. In May 2017, Athina opened a large plumbing department. Because management had little expertise in plumbing but wanted to provide for customers' plumbing needs, it contracted with J. Alexander & Sons Plumbing Ltd. (J. Alexander) to own and operate the plumbing department. J. Alexander paid Athina a $200,000 non-refundable fee on July 15, 2017 and will pay 5 percent of net sales (sales after returns and bad debts) per year. Alexander is getting the plumbing department ready for business. The contract between J. Alexander and Athina is for 10 years. Athina capitalized the $200,000 fee as a long-term deposit and will recognize it as revenue over the term of the contract on a straight-line basis.

Required:

Prepare a report to your CFO on your findings and recommendation regarding Athina.

CASE 3: COOK CORP.

In October 2016, the Cook family sold its 100 percent interest in Cook Corp. to a corporation wholly owned by the Ngo family. Because the two families could not agree on an exact selling price, the contract of purchase and sale required that the corporation that purchased Cook Corp. pay an amount equal to 50 percent of Cook Corp.'s audited net income for the fiscal year ending September 30, 2017. When Cook Corp. was purchased, the Ngo family replaced the senior management of the company. The new CEO of Cook Corp. is the son of the head of the Ngo family, Bic Ngo. Bic Ngo has explained that the acquisition of Cook Corp. is an important step in the growth of the Ngo family's corporate holdings. He said that an important objective of the family is to minimize the amount of tax that must be paid.

On October 25, 2017, Denise Cook, a member of the Cook family, approached you for advice. She explained that the Cook family had received Cook Corp.'s financial statements and they were very concerned about some aspects of the statements. The Cook family believes that Mr. Ngo isn't acting in good faith and is trying to cheat the Cook family of money that is rightfully owed to them. Denise Cook has asked you for a detailed report that analyzes aspects of the financial statements that the Cook family find questionable. She would like thorough explanations of the issues and recommendations of alternative treatments that you think are more appropriate. Denise wants you to provide clear explanations and support for your positions so that she will be able to explain her concerns when she meets Mr. Ngo. The outstanding items are described below:

a. During fiscal 2016 (before Cook Corp. was sold), management began planning to offer its products online. Bic Ngo continued the development of the new e-business and expects that it will be launched mid-way through fiscal 2018. During fiscal 2017, Cook Corp. spent $476,000 developing the new e-business. The costs were incurred for Web site design, market surveys, and so on. The full amount was expensed in Cook Corp.'s financial statements.

b. In May 2017, Cook Corp. signed a contract with Wong Inc. for a large order of specially designed products. Wong Inc. did not want to take delivery of the products until the order was complete so Cook Corp. agreed to deliver the products in September 2017. Representatives of Wong Inc. monitored production to ensure that all finished goods met Wong Inc.'s specifications. Wong Inc. agreed to pay Cook Corp. as production of the product progressed. As a result, when production of the products was completed on schedule in August 2017 Wong Inc. had paid 80 percent of the agreed price. The remaining 20 percent was to be paid on final delivery of the products. The products were ready for shipping in the first week of September 2017. However, Denise learned from an employee of Cook Corp. that Cook Corp. had requested and obtained permission from Wong Inc. to delay shipping until mid-October. The products were finally delivered to Wong Inc. on October 13, 2017 and revenue was recognized at that time.

c. During fiscal 2017, Cook Corp. wrote down by a significant amount the book value of some of the company's manufacturing equipment. Cook Corp. explained in the notes to the financial statements that upon review the equipment was becoming technologically obsolete, and as a result the net book value exceeded the net recoverable amount associated with equipment. The equipment is still being used on the main production line of Cook Corp.'s manufacturing facility.

Required:

Prepare the report requested by Denise Cook.

CASE 4: DAPHNE'S CATERING LTD.

Daphne's Catering Ltd. (DCL) provides catering services to people living in Durham region and the eastern part of Metro Toronto. The company is owned and operated by Daphne Flatt, who founded the business in 1998. DCL can provide meals for groups as small as two and as large as 500. DCL operates out of its state-of-the-art commercial kitchen in Ajax. The meals are prepared in the kitchen and delivered to the site of the event. DCL's kitchen is adjacent to a banquet hall it also owns. DCL also generates revenue by renting out the banquet hall for functions and catering them.

The company has been very successful over the years and Daphne has made a lot of money. Recently, Daphne decided that she would like to slow down the pace of her life and has decided to sell her shares (she owns 100 percent of the company). Joe Insalacco has expressed interest in buying DCL and he has been in negotiations with Daphne for several months. The parties have agreed that Joe will purchase Daphne's shares for $550,000 plus five times average net income for the last two fiscal years.

Two days ago, Daphne couriered DCL's September 30, 2017 year-end financial statements to Joe for his review. Joe is not very knowledgeable about accounting matters so he has engaged you to examine the statements and raise any issues of concern as they pertain to his agreement to buy DCL. You review the financial statements, have a conversation with Joe, and a brief chat with Daphne, and discover the following:

a. DCL's net income for the years ended September 30, 2017 and 2016 respectively was $275,000 and $160,000.

b. In October 2016, DCL printed several thousand brochures for distribution to businesses and homes in certain areas in Durham and Toronto. The brochures were designed to promote DCL's services over the 2016 Christmas and New Year's period. The brochures were specially designed to emphasize the 2016 holiday and appropriate holiday meals. Because of bad weather and problems with the distributor, only about 40 percent of the brochures were distributed. The brochures remain safely stored at the DCL kitchen. A prepaid expense for $19,000 is reported on the September 30 balance sheet for the undistributed brochures.

c. A large corporate function scheduled for September 18, 2017 had to be cancelled on short notice by the customer. The customer asked whether the event could be rescheduled for October 2, 2017. DCL's banquet hall was available on October 2 and DCL was happy to reschedule. On August 31, the customer paid $45,000 (75 percent of the agreed price) as the original contract stipulated. DCL recognized the amount received in August as revenue in its 2017 fiscal year. The customer paid the remaining $15,000 owing on October 4, 2017. Costs incurred for meals, entertainment, and labour were $44,000 and these were expensed at the time of the event.

d. Each year during the last week of September, DCL has a major program of maintenance on its kitchen and banquet hall. Late September is usually a quiet time and Daphne has found it more efficient to do all the maintenance work at once. The banquet hall is closed for several days and the kitchen can have only limited operations. This year, the maintenance program was delayed into October because of the corporate function held on October 2. The cost of the maintenance program in 2017 was $18,000. In 2016, the maintenance program was carried out and completed in late September.

e. DCL is in the process of developing a line of packaged foods for sale in grocery stores. The idea is to allow customers to bring the taste and convenience of a high-quality catered meal to their homes. Over the last 18 months, DCL has invested $55,000 in the development of the product. Daphne is confident that the product will be successfully and profitably brought to grocery stores but she realizes there are significant development, production, and marketing obstacles that will have to be overcome before that occurs. The $55,000 is reported on the balance sheet as a product development cost on September 30, 2017.

Joe has asked you to prepare a report discussing issues pertaining to the purchase of DCL. He would like full explanations of your recommendations and the reasoning behind them so that he can have a full understanding when he meets with Daphne. He would also like you to quantify the impact of the any adjustments you make on the final selling price of DCL.

Required:

Prepare the report requested by Joe Insalacco.

CASE 5: DISCOUNT STORES LIMITED

Discount Stores Limited (Discount) is a chain of retail stores with locations in several medium-sized Ontario communities. Discount sells a wide range of clothing and household items that it obtains at discounts from wholesalers and jobbers. Discount's strategy has long been to provide low prices and good value to customers. The company is wholly owned by Ruth and Irving

Bogan, who founded it many years ago. In recent years, the Bogans have not been involved in managing the company but have hired professional managers. The Bogans currently live in Arizona and rely on the cash flow generated by Discount to live on.

Two years ago, the Bogans hired Harry Highpaid as the chief executive officer of the company to help turn the company around after a number of unprofitable years. At the time Harry was hired, the Bogans were worried that Discount would go bankrupt and they would lose their main source of income. Harry was well known as an excellent manager, and the Bogans were prepared to pay for someone who could reverse the fortunes of their business. The Bogans agreed to pay Harry a salary plus 25 percent of income after taxes in each year of a three-year contract. In his first year with Discount, Harry made significant improvements in the business, but it suffered a small loss. This year, the company has continued to improve, and the Bogans once again feel confident about the viability of Discount.

Harry has just presented the financial statement for the current year to the Bogans for their approval. The Bogans are pleased about Discount's profitability, but they are concerned about some accounting treatments that appear to have contributed to the significant increase in net income.

1. Harry launched an extensive advertising campaign to improve the image of Discount and to attract new customers. According to Harry, the campaign has been a success and as a result Discount has been able to increase its profit margins and has increased the flow of customers through all stores. Harry has capitalized 50 percent of the advertising costs and is amortizing them over five years, arguing that they will benefit the firm over a number of years. In the past, Discount has expensed all advertising costs as they were incurred.
2. Discount has had a policy of writing off slow-moving inventory at the end of each fiscal period. Slow-moving inventory is defined as merchandise that has been on hand for six months or more. Harry has changed the policy and now only writes off inventory that he believes can't be sold.
3. To attract more customers, Harry has begun offering credit to customers. He has not, however, recorded an allowance for bad debt or a bad debt expense for the period.
4. Until this year, Discount depreciated improvements to its leased stores (leasehold improvements) over one lease term, usually five years. However, Discount's leases usually have options that allow the company to extend the lease for an additional five years and in the past the company has always exercised that option. This year, Harry changed the depreciation period for leasehold improvements to ten years for all leases that give Discount the option to extend.

Ruth Bogan has come to you for advice on the above accounting issues. She is concerned that Harry's accounting choices will result in him receiving a bonus that doesn't reflect his actual performance as CEO and unreasonably reduce the amount of money that she and Irving receive from Discount.

Required:

Prepare a report for the Bogans providing them with the advice they seek.

CASE 6: DRINFELD MANUFACTURING LIMITED

Drinfeld Manufacturing Limited (Drinfeld) is a small manufacturer of appliances. Its products are manufactured under the brand names of the stores that buy from Drinfeld. (Drinfeld doesn't sell any appliances under its own brand name.) The company is wholly owned and managed by Liidia and Ilya Drinfeld, a married couple. Recently, the Drinfelds decided to retire and they have been negotiating with a prospective buyer, Jon Karpoff. Mr. Karpoff has received Drinfeld's recent financial statements and he is unsure of the appropriateness of the accounting policies the company uses to assess its performance. Liidia Drinfeld explained that the statements are prepared primarily for tax purposes.

In your discussion with Mr. Karpoff, you learn the following:

1. Drinfeld manufactures several different types of household appliances. It usually carries enough inventory so that it's able to respond to most orders quickly. When a store places an order with Drinfeld for these products, the goods are shipped within days.

2. Drinfeld also carries a significant inventory of parts and supplies used in the production of the appliances. Mr. Drinfeld observed on a recent examination of the inventory that there was some stock (both input materials and finished goods) that has been on hand for some time, including some relating to products that are no longer made.
3. Drinfeld allows retailers to return up to 20 percent of the appliances purchased for any reason.
4. Drinfeld offers a two-year warranty on the appliances it makes. Appliances requiring repairs are returned to the retailer, which ships them to Drinfeld for repair. All costs are paid by Drinfeld.
5. Drinfeld uses CCA rates, the rates prescribed in the *Income Tax Act*, to calculate depreciation.
6. One of Drinfeld's major suppliers is a sheet metal manufacturer that is owned by the Drinfelds' son.
7. Recently, Drinfeld agreed to produce a significantly modified version of an existing product for a chain of appliance stores. The chain promised to purchase a minimum of 7,000 appliances per year for three years. Drinfeld incurred $75,000 in costs modifying the design of the existing appliance. Production of the new product is scheduled to begin in about a month.
8. The Drinfelds pay themselves enough to cover their living requirements. Payments are a combination of wages and dividends.

Mr. Karpoff has come to you requesting advice on the accounting policies that would be best for evaluating Drinfeld's performance and future prospects. He said he will use the recommendations to help him set a price he would be prepared to pay for Drinfeld.

Required:

Prepare the report requested by Mr. Karpoff.

CASE 7: FEDERAL DAIRY LIMITED

Federal Dairy Limited (Federal) is a medium-sized dairy operating in Atlantic Canada. The company's founder, Morden Shapiro, owns 60 percent of the shares. Four private individuals, who have very little involvement in operating decisions, each own 10 percent. Federal produces milk, yogurt, ice cream, etc. that it sells through grocery stores and chains throughout the Maritimes.

Over the years, labour and management have had an acrimonious relationship. Over the past ten years, the union representing Federal's employees have made significant wage concessions to avoid job losses. In the last contract negotiations, Federal and the union agreed that the union would have access to the company's financial statements. The upcoming negotiation will be the first time the union will receive the financial statements.

You have been hired by the union representing Federal's employees to prepare a report on how to account for a number of controversial issues that arose on the union's review of Federal's December 31, 2017 financial statements and its preliminary discussions with Federal's management. The union will use your report in its assessment of Federal's financial position and performance, and its ability to pay higher wages and benefits to employees. The union leader has asked for your report to fully explain your recommendations, discuss arguments that Federal's management might use to counter your recommendations, and identify and discuss alternative treatments that Federal might present for the outstanding issues:

1. In September 2017, Federal signed an agreement with a health organization that provided its "seal of approval" on certain products. The seal of approval provides assurance to consumers that the products meet the health standards of the organization and allows Federal to use the health organization's logo on the products. As part of the agreement, Federal donated $312,000 to the health organization. The amount was paid in October 2017. Federal is allowed to use the seal of approval for four years. Federal expensed the amount when it paid the health organization.
2. In November 2015, the company signed an agreement a well-known professional athlete to endorse the Federal product line. In September 2017, the athlete was found to be a user of performance-enhancing drugs and has been suspended from his sport for at least two years. Federal has decided not to use the athlete's endorsement anymore, although the company's lawyer advises

that the contract doesn't provide any way to avoid paying the agreed $12,000 per month until December 31, 2019. Federal expensed the full amount of the contract owing, $288,000, in 2017.

3. On December 31, 2017, Federal shipped a large order to a customer. Normally, Federal recognizes revenue on delivery to the customer. The goods shipped weren't included in the year-end inventory count. Federal uses a periodic inventory control system. The goods were delivered on January 2, 2018.
4. Federal operates several retail outlets that sell ice cream cones, sundaes, and other take-out products in addition to the other dairy products that the company produces. In 2016, the company added a line of novelty items such as T-shirts, sweatshirts, coffee mugs, with clever sayings that use the Federal names and logo. The line has not been successful. In fact, only 25 percent of the merchandise purchased has been sold and Federal hasn't ordered any new merchandise since February 2017. As of December 31, 2017, Morden determined the following information related to the remaining inventory:

Total retail price of all remaining stock	$300,000
Original invoice cost of the remaining stock	140,000

   Morden asked Atlantic Liquidators, which specializes in purchasing unwanted inventories, for an estimate of what they would pay Federal for the souvenir merchandise. Their offer, which Morden is seriously considering, was $65,000. Federal wrote off the remaining novelty inventory in 2017.
5. Federal increased estimates of certain items including returns, inventory obsolescence, and volume discounts. Management says that these revised estimates reflect current business conditions.
6. Early in 2017, Morden loaned Federal $250,000 to provide the cash to purchase needed capital assets. The loan is to be paid back in 2020. Federal expense $40,000 in interest on the loan in 2017.
7. In January 2018, a large customer suffered a catastrophic fire that may put the customer out of business. Federal doesn't expect to collect any of the $65,000 it's owed by the customer and accrued an additional expense for the amount in 2017.

Required:

Provide the report to the head of the union.

CASE 8: INTERNATIONAL TECHNOLOGIES LTD.

International Technologies Ltd. (ITL) provides "technology solutions" to manufacturing companies. ITL is a wholly owned subsidiary of Global World International Inc. (GWI), a publicly owned conglomerate. In 2014, ITL was performing poorly and GWI considered selling the company for the best offer. As a last resort, GWI hired turnaround specialist Jane Bowen to more effectively manage and salvage ITL. Ms. Bowen's employment contract specifies that in addition to an annual salary she would receive a $10 million cash bonus after the end of the 2017 fiscal year if ITL meets a number of performance objectives over the 2015 to 2017 period. For 2015 and 2016, Ms. Bowen achieved the objectives. To meet the performance objectives for 2017, ITL must report net income in excess of $30 million.

It is now January 25, 2018. ITL's financial statements for the year ended December 31, 2017 have been received at GWI's corporate offices. ITL's net income for 2017 is reported to be $30,550,000. GWI's CFO has examined the financial statements and is satisfied with most aspects of them but is concerned with the reporting of some transactions and economic events. The issues of concern are described in the following Exhibit A. The CFO has asked you, an accountant in GWI's finance department, to prepare a report evaluating the issues. Ms. Bowen has already called the CFO to arrange a meeting to discuss the financial statements and the payment of the bonus. The CFO wants your report to explain the problem in each issue, identify reasonable alternatives, and provide full support for your recommendations.

Required:

Prepare the report requested by the CFO.

EXHIBIT A Issues Identified on Your Review of ITL's 2011 Financial Statements

1. On July 29, 2017, the company made a payment of $250,000 to a computer hacker who obtained access to the computer code to ITL's proprietary software that is used to produce some of ITL's products. The hacker had given the company ten days to pay or she would sell the information to a competitor. Management believed that if the information was obtained by a competitor it would have significant negative consequences for the company. ITL has capitalized the amount of the payment and is amortizing it over the remaining life of the related assets.
2. ITL has always shut down for one week in late December for routine maintenance of the company's equipment. The annual maintenance is essential to ensure that the equipment can meet the precise specifications of customers. For the past three years, maintenance has been completed by the end of December. The annual maintenance originally scheduled for December 2017 was delayed until the first week of January 2018 because of scheduling problems with the company that does the maintenance and because ITL had a number of contracts it wanted to complete by the end of December. The last maintenance was done in December 2016. ITL paid $425,000 for the January 2018 maintenance work.
3. In the last week of December 2017, ITL shipped a $1,250,000 order to a new customer. The customer has been having financial difficulties, so ITL provided special financing terms that gave the customer four months to pay instead of the usual 30 days. Payment is guaranteed by the company that owns the customer. The items sold come with a six-month warranty, the standard warranty offered to all customers. The product is a standard item with only minor modifications to meet the needs of the customer. The order was scheduled to be shipped in early January, but because of an opening in the production schedule ITL was able to complete the order several weeks early. Once the order was completed, it was shipped to the customer. The customer agreed to accept early delivery before ITL shipped the order. The cost of the order was $500,000. The goods were received by the customer on December 31, 2017. ITL recognized revenue when the goods were delivered, as it normally does.

CASE 9: KELLETT LTD.

Kellett Ltd. (Kellett) produces leading-edge pollution control equipment for industrial and commercial use. The company was founded several years ago by Angela Kellett. Ms. Kellett recently decided that she would like to sell ownership of her company and found an interested buyer in Acme Pollution Control Inc., an industry leader. After lengthy negotiations, Ms. Kellett agreed to sell her company to Acme for $25 million plus an additional $10 million if Kellett Ltd.'s net income before taxes, determined using IFRS, was in excess of $5.35 million in the year ended December 31, 2017. The deal closed on January 31, 2017.

It's now early February 2018. Angela Kellett recently received the financial statements for Kellett Ltd. for the year ended December 31, 2017. Audited income before taxes is $4.95 million. As permitted by the agreement of purchase and sale, Angela's representative has gathered additional information from discussions with employees of Kellett Ltd. and a preliminary review of company documents. For the most part, everything reported in the statements appeared in order, except for a number of transactions described below.

You are Angela's representative. Prepare a report addressing the issues you found in your meeting with employees and your preliminary review. Your report should discuss the impact and the appropriateness of the accounting treatments used in the determination of net income before taxes.

a. On December 1, 2017, Kellett Ltd. shipped a $500,000 order for new product to a new customer in Europe. The product was based on a new technology that the company developed. The product has been extensively tested by Kellett Ltd. and has received approval from a number of independent environmental testing labs. Management is very confident that it will meet the needs of customers and global environmental standards. Since this is a new product, the company has assured the customer that it will send technicians to the site to resolve any problems at Kellett Ltd.'s expense. The buyer must be satisfied with the product before it must pay. However, management is satisfied that any additional costs it incurs will be insignificant because of the testing. Kellett Ltd. checked the country's credit rating and found it to be high. The shipment was received in good order by the customer on December 20, 2017. Testing of the product is ongoing and is expected to be completed by the end of January. The cost of the goods sold was $225,000. Kellett will recognize revenue when the customer determines the equipment is satisfactory.

b. In December 2017, Kellett Ltd. signed a $400,000 contract with Dryden Environmental Ltd. to do a cleanup of Kellett's production facility as required by a recent ruling by the provincial environment agency. The work began in late January 2018 and is expected to be completed sometime in early March. Kellett Ltd. paid Dryden $75,000 when the agreement was signed, with the remainder due when the work is complete. The company expensed the full $400,000 when the contract was signed and recorded an accounts payable for the amount owing to Dryden.

c. In December 2017, an order to a customer in the United States was returned. The product delivered didn't meet the specifications of the customer. This situation is a rare occurrence but sometimes it's difficult to determine whether a product will meet the customer's needs. The sale was for $320,000 and the cost of the inventory was $145,000. Kellett Ltd. incurred $12,000 in costs to recondition the returned products. Management decided to write down the inventory value to zero when it was returned to storage for resale. The company originally recorded the revenue on delivery in July 2017.

CASE 10: KONOPASKI IMPORTING INC.

Konopaski Importing Inc. (Konopaski) imports products to Canada from countries around the world. The company has been owned and operated by Michael Konopaski since it began business 25 years ago. Michael has decided to sell the business to Jacob Adessky and the two parties are negotiating the final terms of the deal. Jacob has agreed to $1.5 million for Konopaski plus the carrying amount of inventory on the day before the deal closes, determined using International Financial Reporting Standards. Inventory is by far the largest asset on Konopaski's balance sheet. Konopaski's year-end is December 31 and the deal is to close on March 31.

Jacob has asked for your advice about how to deal with a number of inventory transactions that he thinks may have an impact on the carrying amount of the inventory and the amount he will pay for Konopaski. Jacob has provided you with the following information about Konopaski's inventory:

- Konopaski uses FIFO (first-in, first-out) as its cost formula for inventory.
- Konopaski last counted its inventory on December 31. Michael Konopaski wants to use the accounting records to update the December 31 count to the March 31 closing date.
- Michael Konopaski uses the inventory control system to track inventory and determine the timing and amount of new orders. When Michael determines that an item is slow-moving, he lowers the price until he can find buyers who will purchase it. These items are accounted for when they are sold.
- On March 31, Konopaski recorded a sale to a major customer. The customer was to pick up the goods before the end of business on March 31 but was unable to do so because of mechanical problems with their truck. The goods were picked up on April 1.
- Konopaski often receives discounts from suppliers when it buys large quantities over the course of a year. When a discount is received, Konopaski reduces accounts payable and cost of goods sold in the period the discount is granted.
- Konopaski usually has $10,000 to $20,000 of inventory held on consignment by customers.

Required:

Prepare a report to Jacob Adessky explaining how you think the inventory issues should be accounted for. Be sure to explain the impact the existing treatment will have on the carrying amount of the inventory and the impact your recommendation will have.

CASE 11: PREMIER CLOTHING LTD.

Premier Clothing Ltd. (Premier) is a manufacturer of women's outerwear. Most of Premier's merchandise in manufactured in Canada. Although production costs are higher in Canada, the company finds that the high quality of the clothes allows it to remain profitable. Premier was founded in 2004 by Evan Shayne and Katelyn Menard. Each shareholder owns 50 percent of the shares of the company. In late 2017, Evan and Katelyn had a major disagreement on the direction of the company and they have not spoken since. Evan is no longer involved in the day-to-day operations of the company and any input he provides is done through his lawyer. In April 2018, Evan and Katelyn agreed (through their lawyers) that Katelyn would buy Evan's shares at fair market value, where fair market value would equal three times net income for the year ended December 31, 2018, with the financial statements prepared in accordance with Accounting Standards for Private Enterprises (ASPE) consistently applied.

You are Evan's long-time accountant and financial advisor. On February 15, 2019, Evan storms into your office in a rage. He has just received the 2018 financial statements from Katelyn and they showed that net income was $142,000, well below the average reported in recent years. Evan blasts that this is "a complete and utter ripoff" because he's not going to get nearly enough for his shares, and he isn't going to stand for it.

You tell Evan to calm down and he gives you the financial statements to examine. Evan points out a number of issues he is concerned about and you tell him you will analyze them and prepare a report explaining any problems with the accounting treatments used and the impact on the agreement. The issues are described in Exhibit A, which follows.

Required:

Prepare the report for Evan Shayne.

EXHIBIT A Issues Identified on Your Review of Premier's 2018 Financial Statements

1. In November 2018, Premier purchased a two-year licence to produce garments with the logos of professional sports teams. The licence goes into effect on January 1, 2019 (meaning that Premier can begin selling products with the logos starting on January 1, 2019). Premier paid the sports leagues a non-refundable fee of $100,000 when the agreement was signed in November 2018 and agree to pay a royalty of 3 percent of sales for each item sold with the logo on it. Premier expensed the $100,000 non-refundable fee in 2018.
2. In November 2018, Premier received an order from an outerwear distributor in Chile. The goods were produced, and shipped on December 15. This is the first time Premier has shipped to this distributor and the first time it has shipped outside of North America. Premier's credit department received a report from a credit rating agency in Chile that indicated the customer had a credit rating of "good." The goods shipped are standard models that have been modified to meet the tastes of the Chilean market. These designs have always been popular in the North American market. The customer isn't allowed to return any of the goods but Premier has agreed to provide a rebate of 30 percent of the price the customer paid for any goods that it is unable to sell. Premier has not recognized the revenue as of December 31, 2018 because it's waiting until the goods are sold by the Chilean distributor.
3. In 2014, Premier took advantage of an opportunity to buy large supply fasteners (buttons and zippers) from a supplier that was going out of business. At the time, Evan and Katelyn estimated that the supply of fasteners purchased would last about four years. Since then, styles and technology have changed so that the items purchased in 2014 can only be used on lower-quality items and/or on the less-stylish garments Premier makes. Katelyn now thinks that this supply of fasteners can be used, but that it will take much longer than originally thought. Katelyn has been trying to sell the fasteners but has only managed to dispose of about 30 percent of the remaining amount. For accounting purposes, Katelyn has written off the remaining unsold inventory in the year ended December 31, 2018.

CASE 12: STURDY FURNITURE LTD.

Sturdy Furniture Ltd. is a Canadian manufacturer of public site furniture products. Sturdy's products are designed for use in public places such as parks, malls, town squares—high-traffic locations that require high-quality, durable, and attractive furniture. Sturdy's products include benches, bike racks, planters, recycling bins, and trash containers. Sturdy has a loan outstanding from the Bank of Ontario and is looking to increase the loan to help finance its ongoing expansion.

It's late October 2017. You are an accountant with the Bank of Ontario's regional office in Durham Region. You received a call from the loan officer responsible for the Sturdy loan regarding its 2017 third-quarter unaudited financial statements (the end of the quarter was September 30). The loan agreement requires that Sturdy maintain a current ratio greater than 1.25 and a debt-to-equity ratio below 1.6 at the end of each quarter. Sturdy is onside with the ratios, but just by a small amount. If Sturdy violates either of the covenants, the terms of the loan will be subject to renegotiation and perhaps repayment. In addition, violation would make it significantly less likely that the bank would provide Sturdy with the additional financing it's looking for.

The loan officer expressed some concern to you about Sturdy's accounting for three transactions and the impact on the covenants. She asked you to prepare a report that reviews the transactions and assesses the accounting Sturdy used. She would like full explanations of whether the accounting used was appropriate or inappropriate.

The loan officer provided you with the following information:

1. Summarized balances at the end of Sturdy's third quarter:

Current assets	$ 6,500,000
Non-current assets	23,500,000
Current liabilities	5,100,000
Non-current liabilities	13,100,000
Shareholders' equity	11,800,000

2. Though Sturdy has been very successful in Canada, it hasn't had much success in foreign markets, particularly the United States. This year, Sturdy tried a different strategy. It made arrangements with a well-established U.S. distributor who agreed to market and distribute its products in the southern United States. In late July 2016, (during the third quarter) Sturdy shipped $250,000 worth of furniture to the U.S. distributor. The distributor agreed to pay $400,000 for the furniture. The distributor isn't required to pay for the furniture until it sells it to a customer. The distributor is also allowed to return up to 75 percent of the furniture at no cost. Sturdy recognized the revenue from this sale in the 3rd quarter.
3. During the third quarter, Sturdy completed a deal with one of the Canadian territories to supply outdoor recycling bins. The final design is based on an existing Sturdy product that has been modified to meet the rigours of the cold Canadian winters in the far north. No Sturdy product has ever been used under these conditions but the company tested the product extensively in the extreme-weather facility at the University of Ontario Institute of Technology, and management is confident that the product is well designed for the conditions. Sturdy has provided the territory a two-winter guarantee that it will replace any bins that are broken or damaged due to weather conditions. The contract price is $750,000 and the bins cost $475,000. The revenue was recognized in the third quarter. Sturdy expects payment for the bins within 60 days of the end of the quarter.
4. During the third quarter Sturdy spent $125,000 trying to win a large contract to supply a city in Mexico. The $125,000 includes costs for executives to meet and entertain representatives of the city, development of a sophisticated marketing campaign, and preparation of information packages for politicians in the city. A final decision is expected in late October, but the information being received from Sturdy's advisor in the city isn't favourable. It appears that the city is going to select a Mexican producer. Sturdy recorded the $125,000 as a non-current asset and is amortizing it over three years, beginning after the contract result is announced.

Required:

Prepare a report to the bank lending officer.

CASE 13: THE DIVORCE OF JOANNE AND LAWRENCE APPEL 1

In November 2017, Joanne and Lawrence Appel decided to divorce after 20 years of marriage. Among the assets owned by the couple is a business, Commercial Printing Limited (Commercial), that they organized together in 2003. The Appels are equal shareholders in Commercial but Joanne operates it. The Appels agree that Joanne will purchase the shares of Commercial from Lawrence at fair market value. Since the shares aren't traded on an exchange, no market price is available, so they agree that fair market value will be equal to five times average net income for the past three years, including the fiscal year ending December 31, 2017. Joanne and Lawrence also agree that the accounting policies should be reasonable for determining representative net income for the business. They also recognize that adjustments to the final selling price might be necessary so adjustments to the final selling price can be made to take specific circumstances into consideration.

You obtain the following information about Commercial:

1. Commercial produces printed materials and makes copies for customers.
2. Commercial has used its financial statements primarily for tax purposes. The company writes off any expenditures it makes that can be justified for tax purposes, regardless of whether they have any future benefit.
3. Most transactions are on a cash basis. Commercial offers credit terms for its larger customers.
4. Commercial has $100,000 in loans from the shareholders. The loans are interest-free.
5. The company owns a small building in the north end of the city. Its offices occupy the ground floor of the building and the rest of the building is leased to tenants. Since the building was acquired, its market value has increased from $2.5 million to $3.0 million. The building is recorded on Commercial's balance sheet at cost less CCA.
6. The Appels have charged many personal expenses to the business.
7. Joanne Appel took a salary of $200,000 during the year. A manager doing Joanne's work at a competitor's company would be paid about $65,000.
8. During the summer of 2017, Lawrence Appel negotiated a long-term contract with a customer on behalf of Commercial to produce instruction manuals for its products. The contract begins in January 2018. In exchange for lower printing rates, the customer has guaranteed a minimum of $200,000 of work over two years. The customer will pay as the work is done. Any shortfall from the $200,000 will be paid at the end of the contract term.

Required:

Joanne and Lawrence have asked you to prepare a report that they can use to determine the selling price of Lawrence's shares. The report should state the accounting policies that should be used for preparing the financial statements. These will be used to set the selling price of Commercial. It should also state any adjustments that should be made to the final price because of other information and concerns you have. Since this divorce is less than friendly, you should explain your reasoning fully so that lawyers for the respective parties will have a basis for discussion.

CASE 14: THE DIVORCE OF JOANNE AND LAWRENCE APPEL 2

Use the information provided in "The Divorce of Joanne and Lawrence Appel 1." You have been engaged by Lawrence Appel's lawyer to prepare a report that she can use in his negotiations with Joanne's lawyer. The report should state the accounting policies that should be used for preparing the financial statements that will be used to set the selling price of Commercial, as well as any adjustments that should be made to the final price because of other information and concerns you have. The report should explain your reasoning fully so that Lawrence's lawyer can understand your recommendations and any alternatives Joanne's lawyer might propose.

CASE 15: THE DIVORCE OF JOANNE AND LAWRENCE APPEL 3

Use the information provided in "The Divorce of Joanne and Lawrence Appel 1." You have been engaged by Joanne Appel's lawyer to prepare a report that he can use in his negotiations with Lawrence's lawyer. The report should state the accounting policies that should be used for preparing the financial statements that will be used to set the selling price of Commercial, as well as any adjustments that should be made to the final price because of other information and concerns you have. The report should explain your reasoning fully so that Joanne's lawyer can understand your recommendations and any alternatives Lawrence's lawyer might propose.

GLOSSARY

Accelerated depreciation (page 449) Allocates more of the cost of a capital asset to expense in the early years of its life and less in the later years.

Account (page 109) A category of asset, liability, owners' equity, revenue, or expense.

Accounting (page 3) A system for producing information about an entity and communicating that information to people who want or need the information for making decisions.

Accounting cycle (page 102) The process by which data about economic events are entered into an accounting system, processed, organized, and used to produce information such as financial statements.

Accounting equation (page 44) The conceptual foundation of accounting that states assets = liabilities + owners' equity.

Accounting estimates (pages 132, 619) Estimated amounts that must be made when preparing financial statements because the actual amounts pertaining to many economic events and transactions are not known with certainty at the time. Examples include the amount of accounts receivable that will not be collected, the useful lives of capital assets, and the cost of warranty services that have not yet been provided.

Accounting policies (pages 61, 619) The methods, principles, and practices used by an entity to report its financial results.

Accounting Standards for Private Enterprises (ASPE) (page 13) The broad principles and conventions that provide guidance to accountants and managers for making accounting choices as well as rules and procedures that are established as accepted accounting practices at a particular time for private companies in Canada.

Accounts payable turnover ratio (page 728) A ratio that provides information about how quickly an entity pays its accounts payable; defined as credit purchases ÷ average accounts payable.

Accounts receivable turnover ratio (page 342) A measure of how well an entity's credit program is being managed. Indicates how quickly the entity is collecting its receivables. The ratio is defined as credit sales divided by average receivables.

Accrual accounting (page 52) A system of accounting that measures the economic performance of an entity rather than just its cash flows. Under the accrual system, revenue is recognized when it is earned and expenses matched to revenue, regardless of when the cash is received or spent.

Accrued expense (page 129) An expense that is recognized and recorded in the financial statements before the cash payment is made.

Accrued liability (page 129) A liability that is recognized and recorded in the financial statements but the recording is not triggered by an external event such as receipt of a bill or invoice.

Accrued revenue (page 130) Revenue that is recorded before cash is received.

Accumulated other comprehensive income (or loss) (pages 57, 615) An equity account that accumulates other comprehensive income from the statement of comprehensive income.

Acid test ratio (page 341) A measure of an entity's liquidity. Defined as an entity's most liquid assets (cash, cash equivalents, temporary investments, receivables) divided by current liabilities.

Adjusting entry (page 124) Journal entries recorded at the end of a reporting period that reflect economic changes that may have occurred during the period but that have not been recorded in the accounting system. Adjusting entries are not triggered by exchanges with outside entities.

After-tax cost of borrowing (page 552) The effective interest rate an entity pays after taking into consideration the tax-deductibility of interest. The after-tax cost of borrowing is calculated as: actual interest rate × (1 − tax rate).

Aging schedule (page 331) A schedule that classifies accounts receivable by the length of time they have been outstanding.

Agricultural produce (page 399) The harvested product of biological assets—for example, cows' milk, felled trees from the forest, apples from apple trees, animal carcasses.

Allowance for uncollectible accounts (page 330) A contra asset account to accounts receivable or other receivables account that represents the portion of the receivables that management estimates will not be collected.

Amortization (page 446) The process of allocating the cost of intangible asset to expense over time.

Amortized cost (page 683) A method of accounting for passive investments; used for bonds and other debt instruments. It should be used if (1) the investment is part of management's plan to hold the investment to receive the cash flows (interest and principal)—not to actively trade it and (2) the investment has contractual terms that give rise to interest and principal payments on specified dates.

Annuity (page 325) A series of equal cash flows (inflows or outflows), made at equally spaced time intervals.

Asset turnover (page 724) A measure of how effectively an entity can generate sales from its asset base; defined as sales ÷ average total assets.

Asset (page 44) Economic resources, for carrying out its business activities, that provide future benefits to an entity.

Authorized capital stock (page 608) The maximum number of each type of share that can be issued by a corporation.

Average collection period of accounts receivable (page 342) A measure of how well an entity's credit program is being managed by giving the average number of days receivables are outstanding before they are collected. The average collection period of accounts receivable is calculated by dividing the accounts receivable turnover ratio into 365.

Average cost method (page 386) An inventory cost flow assumption that determines the average cost of all goods on hand during the period and uses that average to calculate cost of sales and the balance in ending inventory.

Average number of days inventory on hand (page 405) A ratio used to evaluate the efficiency of inventory management. The average number of days inventory on hand ratio indicates the number of days it takes an entity to sell its inventory. The ratio is defined as 365 divided by the inventory turnover ratio.

Average payment period for accounts payable (page 728) The average number of days that the entity takes to pay its accounts payable.

Balance sheet (page 44) The financial statement that provides information about the financial position of an entity—its assets, liabilities, and owners' equity—at a moment in time.

Bank overdraft (page 259) Occurs when an entity removes more money from its bank account than there is in the bank account, effectively creating an amount owing to the bank. The amount of the overdraft is treated as a liability.

Bank reconciliation (page 319) Reconciles the differences between an entity's cash account in the accounting records and its bank account.

Basic earnings per share (basic EPS) (page 627) Net income minus preferred share dividends divided by the weighted-average number of shares outstanding during the period.

Betterment (page 444) An expenditure made that improves an existing capital asset, thereby making it more valuable to the entity. A betterment might increase a capital asset's useful life or improve its efficiency.

Big bath (page 211) The expensing of a significant amount of assets that would normally have been depreciated or otherwise expensed in future periods.

Biological assets (page 399) A living animal or plant—for example, dairy cows, forests, apple trees and apples on trees, beef cattle.

Bond (page 523) A formal borrowing arrangement in which a borrower agrees to make periodic interest payments to lenders as well as repay the principal at a specified time in the future.

Book value (page 626) The amount shown in the accounting records for an asset, liability, or equity item.

Book value of equity (page 626) The value of equity as reported in the balance sheet and which is equal to assets – liabilities from the balance sheet. Book value of equity is also referred to as the *net assets* or *net worth of the entity*.

Callable bond (page 527) A bond that gives the bond issuer the option to repurchase the bond from investors at a time other than the maturity date under conditions specified in the bond agreement.

Canada Business Corporations Act (page 608) The federal legislation that governs federally incorporated companies.

Canada Revenue Agency (CRA) (page 8) The Canadian government department responsible for administration and enforcement of the Canadian federal tax laws.

Capital assets (pages 46, 440) Resources that contribute to the earning of revenue over more than one period by helping an entity to produce, supply, support, or make available the goods or services it offers to its customers. Capital assets are not bought and sold in the ordinary course of business.

Capital cost allowance (page 482) Depreciation for tax purposes.

Capital expenditure (page 277) Money spent to purchase capital assets.

Capital lease (page 537) A lease that transfers the risk and rewards of ownership to the lessee. Assets under a capital lease are capitalized on the balance sheet of the lessee along with a liability equal to the present value of the lease payments to be made over the life of the lease.

Capital structure (pages 552, 730) The term used to describe how an entity is financed—the amount of debt and equity the entity has.

Capitalize (page 441) An amount expended or accrued that is recorded on the balance sheet as an asset.

Carrying amount (page 127) The amount recorded in the accounting records for an asset, liability, or equity item.

Cash accounting (page 52) A system of accounting where revenue is recognized when cash is received and expenses recognized when cash is spent.

Cash cycle (page 252) The cycle by which an entity begins with cash, invests in resources, provides goods or services to customers using those resources, and then collects cash from customers.

Cash dividend (page 614) A distribution in cash of a corporation's earnings to its shareholders.

Cash flow statement (page 259) The financial statement that shows how cash was obtained and used during a period and classifies cash flows as operating, investing, or financing.

Cash from/used in financing activities (pages 58, 263) The cash an entity raises and pays to equity investors and lenders.

Cash from/used in investing activities (pages 58, 262) The cash an entity spends buying capital and other long-term assets and receives from selling those assets.

Cash from/used in operations (CFO) (pages 58, 262) The cash an entity generates from or uses in its regular business activities.

Cash lag (page 253) The delay between the expenditure of cash and the receipt of cash.

Category (page 406) Type of good held in inventory; each category of inventory may not have the same turnover ratio.

Closing journal entry (page 139) The journal entry required for resetting temporary account balances to zero and transferring the balances in the temporary accounts to retained earnings or owners' equity.

Collateral (page 523) Goods held as protection for a lender should the borrower not repay a loan. In that event, the lenders take ownership of the collateral or the proceeds from its sale.

Commitment (page 549) A contractual agreement to enter into a transaction in the future.

Common shares (pages 50, 608) Shares representing the residual ownership in an entity. Common shareholders are entitled to whatever earnings and assets are left after obligations to debt holders and preferred shareholders have been satisfied.

Common size financial statement (vertical analysis) (page 715) An analytical tool in which the amounts in the balance sheet and income statement are expressed as percentages of other elements in the same year's statements

Comparability (page 37) The qualitative characteristic of accounting information under Canadian GAAP that states that users should be able to compare the accounting information provided by different entities and the information of a particular entity from period to period.

Completed-contract method (page 201) A revenue recognition method on long-term contracts that recognizes revenue in full when a contract is completed. Only allowed by ASPE.

Componentization (page 455) When a capital asset acquired is made up of parts or components for which different useful lives or depreciation methods are appropriate, IFRS require each component to be accounted for separately.

Compound interest (page 321) Interest that is calculated on the principal amount and on interest accumulated from previous periods.

Comprehensive income (pages 56, 617) The change in equity from transactions and economic events from all sources that don't involve owners.

Conservatism (page 396) A fundamental accounting concept that serves to ensure that assets, revenue, and net income are not overstated and that liabilities and expenses are not understated. The implication is that when preparers are faced with reasonable alternative accounting treatments, they should choose the one that is more conservative.

Consignment sale (page 194) A transaction in which the producer or distributor of goods transfers the goods to another entity for sale but for which risk and rewards of ownership do not transfer. The producer or distributor recognizes revenue when the other entity actually sells the merchandise to somebody else.

Consolidated financial statements (pages 39, 670) A single set of financial statements that aggregate the accounting information of a parent corporation and all of its subsidiaries.

Contingent liability (page 548) A possible obligation whose existence has to be confirmed by a future event beyond the control of the entity or an obligation with uncertainties about the probability that payment will be made or about the amount of payment.

Contra-asset account (page 127) An account that is used to accumulate subtractions from a related asset account.

Contributed surplus (page 618) A shareholders' equity account that shows amounts received by the entity from the sale of shares that are greater than the par value of the shares.

Control (page 670) When an investor is able to make the important decisions of an investee and determine its strategic operating, financing, and investing policies on an ongoing basis, without the support of other shareholders.

Convertible bond (page 527) May be exchanged by the investor for other securities of the issuing entity, such as common stock.

Convertible preferred shares (page 611) Preferred shares that shareholders can choose to exchange for a specified number of common shares.

Corporation (page 7) A separate legal entity created under the corporation laws of Canada or of a province. A corporation has many of the rights and responsibilities of an individual.

Cost of sales (page 54) The cost of an entity's inventory that was sold during a period.

Cost-benefit trade-off (page 4) The concept of comparing the benefits of an action with the costs of the action, and taking action only if the benefits exceed the costs.

Cost-recovery method (page 201) Revenue in a period that is recognized up to the amount of costs incurred during the period (except for the last year of the project).

Coupon rate (page 526) The percentage of the face value that the issuer pays to investors each year as interest.

Covenant (page 708) Restrictions that impose limits on the actions of borrowers.

Credit (page 110) An entry to an account that has the effect of decreasing assets and expenses, and increasing liabilities, owners' equity, and revenues.

Creditor (page 44) An entity to whom the reporting entity has an obligation to provide cash or other assets in the future.

Critical-event approach (page 189) A revenue recognition approach where an entity recognizes revenue at a specified instant in the earnings process called the critical event. When the critical event occurs, 100 percent of the revenue is recognized.

Cumulative preferred shares (page 611) Preferred shares that require payment of any dividends on the shares that have not been paid, in respect of the current year or previous years, before the common shareholders can receive any dividends.

Current assets (page 47) Assets that will be used up, sold, or converted to cash within one year or one operating cycle.

Current liability (page 47) Liabilities that will be paid or satisfied within one year or one operating cycle.

Current ratio (page 49) A measure of an entity's liquidity; defined as current assets divided by current liabilities.

Date of declaration of a dividend (page 614) The date when the board of directors of a corporation declares a dividend.

Date of payment of a dividend (page 614) The date when the dividends are actually paid to shareholders.

Date of record of a dividend (page 614) The registered owner of shares on the date of record is entitled to receive a dividend declared by a corporation.

Debenture (page 523) A bond with no collateral provided to the lenders.

Debit (page 110) An entry to an account that has the effect of increasing assets and expenses, and decreasing liabilities, owners' equity, and revenues.

Debit card (page 115) A method of payment that allows a customer to pay for goods and services by transferring money directly from the customer's bank account to the vendor's bank account. Payment by debit card is equivalent to payment by cash.

Debt (page 523) Amounts borrowed and owed by an entity.

Debt-to-equity ratio (page 50) A ratio that provides a measure of the amount of debt relative to equity an entity uses for financing. The ratio gives an indication of the riskiness of the entity and its ability to carry more debt; defined as total liabilities ÷ total shareholders' equity.

Declining balance (page 449) An accelerated method of depreciation. The method applies a rate to the carrying amount of the asset at the beginning of the period to calculate the depreciation expense.

Deferred expense (page 121) Assets that are acquired in one period but not expensed, at least in part, until a later period.

Deferred (future) income tax assets and liabilities (page 560) Assets and liabilities that arise because the accounting methods used to prepare the general purpose financial statements are different from the methods used to calculate taxable income and the amount of income tax an entity must pay.

Deferred (future) income tax expense (page 560) Also called *deferred income tax*. The temporary difference between the accounting value of assets and liabilities and the tax value of assets and liabilities on the balance sheet date, multiplied by the entity's tax rate.

Deficit (page 50) When retained earnings is negative.

Defined-benefit plan (page 545) A pension plan in which the employer promises to provide employees certain specified benefits in each year they are retired.

Defined-contribution plan (page 544) A pension plan in which the employer makes contributions to the employee pension fund as specified in the agreement with the employees. The pension benefits received at retirement depend on the amount contributed on behalf of the individual (by the employer and the employee) and on how well investments made with the funds in the fund perform.

Deflation (page 318) A period when, on average, prices in the economy are falling.

Demand loan (page 517) A loan that must be repaid whenever the lender requests or demands repayment.

Depletion (page 446) The term used to describe the depreciation of the cost of natural resources.

Depreciable amount (page 449) The amount of a capital asset that will be depreciated.

Depreciation expense (pages 53, 446) The expensing of the cost of capital assets in a period.

Derecognition (page 529) When a bond or other liability is removed from the balance sheet.

Diluted earnings per share (page 627) A financial ratio designed to show the effect that dilutive securities—securities converted or exercised that dilute an entity's earnings by increasing the number of common shares, lowering EPS because earnings are spread over more shares—would have on EPS if all of the securities had been converted or exchanged for common shares during the year.

Direct method (of calculating cash from operations) (page 266) A method of calculating/reporting cash from operations by showing cash collections and cash disbursements from operations during the period.

Direct writeoff method (page 329) A method of accounting for uncollectible receivables where the receivable is removed from the list of accounts receivable and an expense is recorded when management decides that a receivable will not be collected.

Discount (on debt) (page 529) When a bond is sold to investors for less than its face value. This occurs when the coupon rate is greater than the effective rate of interest for the bond.

Discount rate (page 323) The interest rate used to calculate the present value of future cash flows.

Dividend (page 50) Distributions of a corporation's earnings to shareholders.

Dividend payout ratio (page 628) The proportion of earnings that is being paid to common shareholders as dividends.

Dividend yield (page 628) A financial ratio that provides similar information to dividend payout ratio, except that it's based on the company's share price and not on its earnings. Its formula is: dividend yield = common annual cash dividends per share ÷ current share price.

Double-entry bookkeeping (page 107) An accounting system in which each transaction or economic event is recorded in at least two places in the accounts.

Earnings management (page 125) Managers' use of accounting choices to achieve their own objectives.

Earnings per share (EPS) (page 626) The amount of net income that is attributable to each individual share of common stock.

Earnings quality (page 712) The usefulness of current earnings for predicting future earnings.

Economic consequences (page 4) The effect of actions and decisions on people's wealth.

Effective interest rate (page 526) The real or market rate of interest.

Employee stock option (page 622) A right granted to an employee to purchase a specified number of shares of the employer's stock at a specified price over a specified period of time.

Enhancing qualitative characteristics (page 36) In the IFRS framework, qualitative characteristics that enhance the usefulness of accounting information that's relevant and faithfully represented.

Entity (page 3) An economic unit such as an individual, proprietorship, partnership, corporation, government, not-for-profit organization, etc. In the accounting environment, an entity is an economic unit that a stakeholder wants accounting information about.

Entity concept (page 38) Assumes that information can be provided for an entity of interest (corporation, partnership, proprietorship, division of a corporation, etc.), separate from the owners or other entities.

Entity-specific value (page 442) The net present value of the cash flow the asset will generate or save over its life or the net present value of the cash the asset would allow the entity to avoid. Also known as value-in-use.

Equity method of accounting (page 679) An investment accounted for using the equity method is initially recorded on the balance sheet at cost. The balance sheet amount is adjusted each period for the investor's share of the investee company's income, less dividends declared. The income statement reports the investor company's share of the investee's net income.

Event after the reporting period (page 550) An economic event that occurs after an entity's year end, but before the financial statement are approved by the board of directors.

Exchange rate (page 318) The price to buy one currency stated in terms of another currency.

Executory contract (page 115) An exchange of promises where one party promises to supply goods or services and the other party promises to pay for them, but neither side has fulfilled its side of the bargain.

Exercise price (page 622) The price at an employee holding an employee stock option is allowed to purchase the shares.

Expense (page 53) Economic sacrifices made to earn revenue. Sacrifices can be the result of using up an asset or incurring a liability. Expenses result in a decrease in owners' equity.

Expiry date (page 622) The final date that an option can be exercised. After an option expires, it cannot be used to purchase shares.

External audit (page 12) The process of examining, on behalf of stakeholders who are external to the entity, an entity's financial statements and the data supporting the information in the financial statements for the purpose of determining whether the statements adhere to principles such as fairness and IFRS/ASPE.

External auditors (page 12) The people who examine entities' financial information on behalf of stakeholders who are external to the entity.

Face value of a bond (page 526) The amount that the holder of the bond, the investor, will receive when the bond matures.

Fair value (page 441) The price that would be received to sell an asset in an orderly transaction between market participants.

Fair value through other comprehensive income (FVTOCI) (page 684) Used when changes in fair value of securities from one period to the next are reported in other comprehensive income rather than net income.

Fair value through profit and loss (page 684) Used when changes in fair value of securities from one period to the next are reported in net income (profit and loss).

Faithful representation (page 37) In financial statements, representation of the underlying economic activity of an entity. Representationally faithful statements must capture the economic activity of an entity; this means that all the assets, liabilities, revenues, and expenses must be reflected. Accounting information is a faithful representation if it's complete, neutral, and free from error.

Financial accounting (page 16) The field of accounting that provides information to people who are external to an entity—people who do not have direct access to an entity's information.

Finance lease (page 537) A lease that transfers the risks and rewards of ownership to the lessee. Assets associated with a capital lease are capitalized on the balance sheet of the lessee along with liability equal to the present value of the lease payments to be made over the life of the lease.

Financial instruments (page 683) Assets and liabilities that represent the contractual rights or obligations of the entity to receive or pay cash or other financial assets.

Finished goods inventory (page 381) Inventory that has been completed and is ready for sale.

First-in, first-out (FIFO) (page 386) An inventory cost flow formula in which the cost of inventory that is purchased or produced first is expensed first. With a FIFO system, the cost of inventory reported on the balance sheet represents the cost of inventory that was purchased or produced most recently.

Fiscal year (page 41) The 12-month period over which performance is measured and at the end of which a balance sheet is prepared.

Fixed-rate loan (page 523) A loan whose interest rate does not change.

Free cash flow (page 277) Cash from operations less cash spent on capital expenditures.

Fully diluted earnings per share (page 726) An earnings per share measure that reflects the effect that dilutive securities would have on basic EPS if the dilutive securities were converted to or exchanged for common shares.

Fundamental qualitative characteristics (page 36) In the IFRS framework, qualitative characteristics that are required if information is to be useful—that is, relevance and faithful representation.

Future income tax assets and liabilities (page 558) Assets and liabilities that arise because the accounting methods used to prepare the general purpose financial statements are different from the methods used to calculate taxable income and the amount of income tax an entity must pay.

Future income tax expense (page 558) Also called *deferred income tax*. The temporary difference between the accounting value of assets and liabilities and the tax value of assets and liabilities on the balance sheet date, multiplied by the entity's tax rate.

Future value (FV) (page 320) The amount of money you will receive in the future by investing it today at a given interest rate.

General journal (page 133) The chronological record of the journal entries that have been entered into the accounting system.

General ledger (page 135) A record of all the accounts of an entity.

General partner (page 602) Member of a limited partnership who does not have limited liability and is liable for all debts and obligations of the partnership. A limited partnership must have at least one general partner.

General purpose financial statements (page 39) Financial statements that are prepared for a wide range of stakeholders, but not necessarily tailored to the needs of any or all of them.

Going concern (page 38) The assumption that entity that will be continuing its operations for the foreseeable future.

Goodwill (pages 467, 673) The amount that a parent pays for a subsidiary over and above the fair value of the subsidiary's identifiable assets and liabilities on the date the subsidiary is purchased.

Gradual approach (page 189) A revenue recognition approach that results in revenue being recognized gradually over a period of time.

Gross margin (page 55) Sales minus cost of goods sold.

Gross margin percentage (page 55) Gross margin divided by sales.

Half-year rule (page 482) A requirement in the *Income Tax Act* that allows an entity to deduct for tax purposes, in the year an asset is purchased, only one-half the amount of CCA that would otherwise be allowable.

Hidden reserves (page 339) Undisclosed accounting choices used to manage earnings and other financial information with the intention of satisfying the self-interests of the preparers.

Horizontal analysis (trend statement) (page 720) An analytical tool in which the amounts in the balance sheet and income statement are expressed as percentages of a base year set of financial statements.

Hybrid securities (page 612) Securities that have characteristics of debt and equity.

Identifiable assets and liabilities (pages 467, 672) Tangible or intangible assets and liabilities that can be specifically identified and measured with some reliability.

Income statement (page 51) The financial statement that provides a measure of the economic performance of an entity over a period of time. The income statement summarizes an entity's revenues and expenses for a period.

Indirect method (of calculating cash from operations) (page 266) A method of calculating/reporting cash from operations by reconciling from net income to cash from operations by adjusting net income for non-cash amounts that are included in the calculation of net income and for operating cash flows that are not included in the calculation of net income.

Inflation (page 318) A period when, on average, prices in the economy are rising.

Intangible asset (page 440) A capital asset that does not have physical substance, such as patents, copyrights, trademarks, brand names and goodwill.

Intercompany transactions (page 677) Transactions among the corporations in a consolidated group. Intercompany transactions are eliminated when preparing consolidated financial statements.

Interest (page 51) The cost of borrowing money.

Interest coverage ratio (page 553) One of a number of coverage ratios that measure an entity's ability to meet its fixed financing charges.

Interest coverage ratio (accrual basis) (page 731) A ratio that measures the ability of an entity to meet its fixed financing charges. Defined as (net income + interest expense + income tax expense) ÷ interest expense.

Interest coverage ratio (cash basis) (page 731) A ratio that measures the ability of an entity to meet its fixed financing charges. Defined as cash from operations excluding interest paid ÷ interest paid.

Internal control (page 319) The processes that management implements to provide reasonable assurance that an entity will be able to achieve its objectives regarding the reliability of financial reporting, the effectiveness and efficiency of its operations, and compliance with relevant laws and regulations.

International Financial Reporting Standards (IFRS) (page 13) A set of globally accepted, high-quality accounting standards produced by the International Accounting Standards Board and mandatory for Canadian public companies.

Inventory (page 380) Goods that are available for sale by an entity, or goods that will be used to produce goods that will be sold when they are completed. Inventory can also include materials used in supplying a service to customers.

Inventory conversion period (page 253) The average length of time between receiving inventory from a supplier and selling it to a customer.

Inventory self-financing period (page 253) The average number of days between date inventory is paid for and the date cash is collected from the customer.

Inventory turnover ratio (ITO) (page 404) Provides information on how efficiently inventory is being managed by measuring how quickly the entity is able to sell its inventory. The inventory turnover ratio is defined as cost of sales divided by average inventory.

Investee corporation (page 669) A corporation that an investor corporation has invested in.

Investor corporation (page 669) A corporation that has an investment in another company.

Issued shares (page 608) The number of authorized shares that have been distributed to shareholders.

Journal entry (page 109) The method used to enter information about economic events into the accounting system.

Just-in-time (JIT) inventory (page 406) A system where the manufacturer orders materials or produces parts or finished goods only when they are required rather than holding stock of items for production or sale.

Last-in, first-out (LIFO) (page 393) An inventory cost flow assumption in which the cost of inventory that was purchased or produced most recently is matched to revenue first. For raw materials that are used in a manufacturing process, the cost of the raw materials that were purchased most recently is the cost that is used in the production process first.

Lease (page 537) A contractual arrangement where one entity (the lessee) agrees to pay another entity (the lessor) a fee in exchange for the use of an asset.

Lessee (page 537) An entity that leases an asset from the asset's owner.

Lessor (page 537) An entity that leases assets that it owns to other entities.

Letter of credit (pages 316, 534) A guarantee from a bank that a customer will pay amounts owed to a seller.

Leverage (page 619) The use of debt to increase the return earned on the equity investment of the owners.

Liability (page 44) Obligations an entity has to pay debts or provide goods or services. A liability must be the result of a past transaction or economic event and require an economic sacrifice to settle.

Limited liability (page 7) Shareholders of a corporation are not liable for the obligations of and losses suffered by the corporation.

Limited liability partnership (LLP) (page 602) An ordinary partnership in which innocent partners are shielded from personal liability for malpractice liabilities of the firm. An individual partner of the LLP would not be liable for claims against the firm arising from negligence or other forms of malpractice unless the partner was personally involved in the negligence or malpractice.

Limited partners (page 602) Members of a limited partnership who have limited liability protection and as a result are not personally liable for the debts and obligations of the partnership.

Limited partnerships (page 602) Partnerships in which some of the partners have limited liability protection.

Line of credit (page 518) An arrangement with a lender that allows an entity to borrow up to a specified maximum amount when and if the entity requires the money.

Liquidity (page 48) The availability of cash and near-cash reserves, needed to meet obligations as they come due.

Lower of cost and net realizable value (LCNRV) rule (page 394) Requires that when the NRV of inventory at the end of a reporting period is lower than its cost, the inventory must be reported on the balance sheet at its NRV. The amount of the write-down, the difference between the cost of the inventory and its NRV, is reported as a loss in the income statement. The loss is recorded in the period the inventory decreases in value, not when the inventory is sold.

Maintenance (page 444) Expenditures that allow an asset to operate as intended—to do what it is designed to do. Maintenance costs should be expensed when incurred.

Management discussion and analysis (MD&A) (page 709) Prepared by an entity's managers, it provides them the opportunity to discuss its financial results, position, and future prospects. It is intended to provide readers with a view of the entity through the eyes of management.

Managerial accounting (page 16) The field of accounting that provides information to the managers of the entity and others decision makers who work for the entity, to assist them in making decisions related to operating the entity.

Market value of equity (page 626) The market price of an entity's shares multiplied by the number of shares outstanding.

Matching (matching concept) (page 106) The process of recording and reporting expenses in the period that the revenue those expenses help earn is recorded and reported.

Materiality (page 43) The significance of financial information to stakeholders. Information is material if its omission or misstatement would affect the judgment of a user of the information.

Maturity date of a bond (page 526) The date that the borrower or bond issuer has agreed to pay back the principal (the face value of the bond) to the bondholders.

Mortgage (page 523) A loan that provides the borrower's property as collateral.

Net assets (page 53) Assets minus liabilities.

Net realizable value (NRV) (page 394) The amount of cash that is expected to be received from the sale or realization of an asset after taking into consideration any additional costs to ready the asset for sale.

Non-controlling interest (page 675) An account on a consolidated balance sheet that represents the net assets of a subsidiary that are owned by entities other than the shareholders of the parent corporation.

Non-current assets (page 47) Assets that will not be used up, sold, or converted to cash within one year or one operating cycle.

Non-current debt (page 523) Debt that is long-term.

Non-current liability (page 47) Liabilities that will be paid or satisfied in more than one year or one operating cycle.

No par value share (page 611) Shares that do not have a par value assigned to them.

Note payable (page 523) A formal obligation signed by the borrower promising to repay a debt.

Not-for-profit organization (page 8) An entity whose objective is to provide services and not to make a profit. Examples include hospitals, charities, churches, mosques and synagogues, unions, clubs, daycare centres, and universities.

Off-balance-sheet financing (page 537) A financing arrangement that occurs when an entity can incur obligations without a liability appearing on its balance sheet.

Operating cycle (page 47) The time it takes from the initial investment an entity makes in goods and services until cash is received from customers.

Operating lease (page 538) A lease that does not transfer the risks and rewards of ownership to the lessee. Assets associated with an operating lease remain on the books of the lessor, the lessor recognizes revenue from the lease when payments are received or receivable, and the lessee recognizes an expense when the payment to the lessor is paid or payable.

Other comprehensive income (pages 57, 617) Transactions and economic events that involve non-owners and affect equity but that remain, for various reasons, excluded from the calculation of net income.

Outstanding shares (page 608) The number of shares of a corporation currently in the hands of shareholders.

Overhead (page 381) The costs in a manufacturing process other than direct labour and direct materials. Overhead costs are more difficult or even impossible to associate directly with the product being made.

Owners' equity (page 44) The investment the owners of an entity have made in the entity.

Parent corporation (page 670) An investor corporation that controls an investee corporation.

Participating preferred shares (page 611) The amount of the preferred share dividend increases above the stated amount if certain conditions are met. The amount of the preferred dividend is often tied to the dividend paid on the common shares.

Partner (page 8) An entity that is one of two or more owners of a partnership.

Partners' equity (page 50) Owners' equity of a partnership.

Partnership (page 8) An unincorporated business owned by two or more entities. (Partners can be corporations or individuals.) A partnership is not legally separate from the partners who own it.

Par value (page 611) A value assigned to each share of common stock in the articles of incorporation. The *Canada Business Corporations Act* and the corporations acts of a number of provinces do not permit par value shares.

Passive investments (page 683) Investments in which the investor corporation cannot influence the strategic decision making of the investee corporation.

Payables deferral period (page 253) The average number of days between receipt of goods or services from a supplier and payment of the supplier.

Pension (page 543) Income provided to a person after they retire.

Percentage-of-completion method (page 200) A method of revenue recognition used with the gradual approach. It allocates revenues and related expenses among more than one reporting period based on a measure of the effort completed in each period.

Percentage-of-credit-sales method (page 332) A method of estimating uncollectible receivables that is based on management's estimate of the percentage of credit sales that will not be collected.

Percentage-of-receivables method (page 330) An amount of uncollectible receivables based on management's estimate of the percentage of period ending receivables balance that will not be collected.

Period costs (page 205) Costs that are expensed in the period that in which they are incurred.

Periodic inventory control system (page 383) An inventory control system where the inventory account is not adjusted whenever a transaction affects inventory. The balance in the inventory account at the end of period and cost of goods sold for the period are determined by counting the inventory on hand on the period ending date.

Periodic-reporting assumption (page 38) A basic assumption that states that meaningful financial information about an entity can be provided for periods of time that are shorter than the life of an entity.

Permanent accounts (page 139) Balance sheet accounts. These are carried forward from one period to the next.

Permanent differences (page 561) Revenues and expenses that are recognized for tax purposes but never recognized for financial reporting purposes, or are recognized for financial reporting purposes but never recognized for tax purposes.

Permanent earnings (page 710) Earnings that are expected to be repeated in the future.

Perpetual inventory control system (page 382) A system of inventory control that keeps an ongoing record of purchases and sales of inventory. When inventory is purchased or sold, the inventory account is immediately debited or credited to record the change. When inventory is sold, cost of sales is immediately debited.

Posting (page 135) The process of transferring each line of a journal entry to the corresponding account in the general ledger.

Preferred shares (page 611) Shares of a corporation that have rights that must be satisfied before those of common shareholders.

Premium (on debt) (page 531) When a bond is sold to investors for more than its face value. Occurs when the coupon rate is greater than the effective rate of interest for the bond.

Prepaid expenses (page 126) Assets that are acquired in one period but not expensed, at least in part, until a later period or periods.

Preparers (page 10) The people responsible for deciding what, how, and when information is going to be presented in an entity's financial statements. The preparers are the people who make the decisions—senior managers such as controllers, chief financial offers and even chief executive officers—not to the people who do the physical preparation of the statements.

Present value (page 320) The worth today of money that will be received in the future.

Price-to-book ratio (page 626) A measure of the stock market's valuation of a company's equity relative to its book value. Used as an indication of whether the shares are reasonably valued.

Price-to-earnings (P/E) ratio (page 733) Conceptually, the P/E ratio gives an indication of how the market values an entity's earnings. It is seen as indicator of the growth prospects of an entity. Defined as market price per share ÷ earnings per share.

Principal (page 51) The amount borrowed from a lender.

Private corporation (page 7) A corporation whose shares and other securities are not available for purchase without agreement with the private corporation or its shareholders.

Proceeds (page 526) The amount of money a bond issuer receives from selling bonds to investors.

Product costs (page 205) Costs that can be matched to specific revenues and that are expensed when the revenue they help generate is recognized.

Profit margin ratio (page 122) A measure of how effective the entity is at controlling expenses and reflects the amount of income earned for each dollar of sales. Equal to net income/revenue.

Property dividend (page 615) Dividends paid with property instead of cash.

Property, plant, and equipment (page 46) Tangible capital assets that are used on an ongoing basis to earn revenue, but that are not sold in the ordinary course of business.

Proprietor (page 7) A person who owns a proprietorship.

Proprietor's equity (page 50) Owners' equity of a proprietorship.

Proprietorship (page 7) An unincorporated business owned by one person. Not legally separate from the person who owns it.

Prospectus (page 197) A legal document that provides detailed information about a company that is offering its shares for public sale.

Provision (page 519) A liability of uncertain timing and amount.

Prudence (page 394) A fundamental accounting concept that serves to ensure that assets, revenue, and net income are not overstated and that liabilities and expenses are not understated. The implication is that when preparers are faced with reasonable alternative accounting treatments, they should choose the one that is more conservative.

Public corporation (page 7) A corporation whose shares or other securities are available for purchase by any entity that has an interest in owning the securities and money to buy them. The securities of public corporations are usually traded on a stock exchange.

Quick ratio (page 341) A measure of entity's liquidity. Defined as an entity's most liquid assets (cash, cash equivalents, temporary investments, receivables) divided by current liabilities.

Raw materials inventory (page 381) The inputs into the production process of a manufacturer or processor.

Receivables (page 327) Amounts owed to an entity. The amounts can be due from customers (accounts receivable), taxation authorities (taxes receivable), investments (interest and dividends receivable), shareholders or employees (shareholder/employee loans receivable), etc.

Receivables conversion period (page 253) The average length of time between delivery of goods to a customer and receipt of cash.

Recognition (page 206) The process whereby any financial statement element—asset, liability, equity, expense or revenue—is entered into the accounting system and reported in the financial statements.

Recoverable amount (page 470) The greater of the net realizable value (NRV) less cost to sell and value-in-use (defined as the present value of the asset's future cash flows).

Redeemable preferred shares (page 611) Preferred shares that that the issuer can purchase back from investors if it chooses, according to specified terms.

Relevance (page 36) The qualitative characteristic of accounting information under IFRS/ASPE that states that the information provided to users must be relevant or useful for the decisions they have to make. Relevance means the information has predictive and feedback value.

Repairs (page 444) Expenditures that allow an asset to operate as intended—to do what it is designed to do. Repair costs should be expensed when incurred.

Replacement cost (page 392) The current price that would have to be paid to purchase an identical or equivalent asset.

Representational faithfulness (page 37) In financial statements, representation of the underlying economic activity of an entity. Representationally faithful statements must capture the economic activity of an entity; this means that all the assets, liabilities, revenues, and expenses must be reflected. Accounting information is a faithful representation if it's complete, neutral, and free from error.

Residual value (page 446) The amount a capital asset can be sold for at the end of its useful life.

Retained earnings (page 50) A balance sheet account that shows the amount of earnings a corporation has earned over its life less the amount of dividends paid to shareholders over the corporation's life.

Retractable bond (page 527) A bond that gives the investor the option to cash in the bond before the maturity date under certain conditions.

Retractable preferred shares (page 611) Preferred shares that shareholders can require the issuer to purchase the preferred shares from them, if they choose, according to specified terms.

Return on assets (ROA) (pages 474, 629) A measure of the performance and operating efficiency of an entity. Defined as net income + after tax interest expense/total assets.

Return on equity (ROE) (pages 122, 629) A measure of the profitability of an entity and its effectiveness in using the assets provided by the owners of the entity to generate net income. Equal to (net income – preferred dividends) ÷ average common shareholders' equity.

Revenue (page 53) Economic benefits earned by providing goods or services to customers. Revenue results in an increase in owners' equity.

Revenue recognition (page 104) The point in time when revenue is recorded in the accounting system and is reported in the income statement.

Reverse stock split (page 616) A reduction in the number of shares.

Segment disclosure (page 677) Disaggregations of information about an entity by types of products and services, and geographic location.

Segregation of duties (page 319) An internal control procedure that requires that people who handle an asset should not be responsible for the record keeping for the asset.

Share (page 7) A unit of ownership in a corporation.

Shareholder (page 7) An entity that owns shares of a corporation and that is therefore an owner of the corporation.

Shareholders' equity (page 59) The owners' equity of a corporation.

Significant influence (page 679) An ownership interest in an investee corporation that allows the investor corporation to affect the strategic operating, investing, and financing decisions of the investee corporation even though it does not have control.

Simple interest (page 321) Interest that is paid or earned on the principal amount only.

Solvency (page 730) The financial viability of an entity—its ability to meet its long-term obligations.

Special purpose report (page 63) Accounting reports that are prepared to meet the needs of specific stakeholders and/or a specific purpose.

Specific identification method (page 387) An inventory valuation method that assigns the actual cost of a unit of inventory to that unit of inventory.

Stakeholder (page 9) A group or individual that is interested in or has a "stake" in an entity.

Statement of cash flows (page 58) The financial statement that shows how cash was obtained and used during a period and classifies cash flows as operating, investing, or financing.

Statement of changes in equity (page 57) A financial statement that shows changes in each account in the equity section of the balance sheet during a period.

Statement of retained earnings (page 57) The financial statement that summarizes the changes to retained earnings during a period. Required by ASPE.

Statement of changes in shareholders' equity (page 57) Presents changes during a period in each account in the equity section of the balance sheet.

Stock dividend (page 615) The distribution of a corporation's own shares to its existing shareholders as a dividend.

Stock exchange (page 7) A place (physical or virtual) where entities can trade securities of publicly traded entities.

Stock split (page 616) The division of an entity's shares into a larger number of units, each with a smaller value.

Straight-line depreciation (pages 119, 448) The method that depreciates an equal amount of the cost of an asset each period.

Subsequent event (page 550) An economic event that occurs after an entity's year-end, but before the financial statement are approved by the board of directors.

Subsidiary corporation (page 670) An investee corporation that is controlled by an investor corporation.

T-account (page 135) An accounting textbook device used to represent general ledger accounts. Each T-account corresponds with a general ledger account.

Tangible asset (page 440) A capital asset with physical substance, such as land, buildings, equipment, vehicles, and furniture.

Taxable income (page 552) The measure of income that is used, as defined by the *Income Tax Act*, to calculate the amount of tax an entity must pay.

Taxes payable method (page 563) A simpler approach to accounting for income taxes, in which the tax expense equals the amount of tax an entity must pay for the year; there are no deferred income taxes because temporary differences are ignored. This approach makes earnings more variable, which can make an entity look riskier.

Temporary account (page 139) Accounts whose balances are reset to zero at the end of a period by closing them to retained earnings or owners' equity. All income statement accounts are temporary. The balances in temporary accounts are not carried forward from one period to the next.

Temporary differences (page 561) Revenues and expense that are fully recognized for both tax and financial reporting purposes, but the recognition happens at different times.

Timeliness (page 37) A characteristic of accounting information that is available to stakeholders in time to influence their decisions.

Time value of money (page 320) The concept that people would prefer to receive a given amount of money sooner rather than later.

Transactional entry (page 125) An entry that is triggered by an exchange with another entity.

Transitory earnings (page 710) Earnings that are not expected to be repeated in future periods.

Treasury stock (page 611) Shares that were previously sold to investors and that the issuing corporation has repurchased but not retired.

Trend statements (horizontal analysis) (page 720) An analytical tool in which the amounts in the balance sheet and income statement are expressed as percentages of a base year set of financial statements.

Trial balance (page 137) A listing of all the accounts in the general ledger by their balances. The main purpose of the trial balance is to ensure that the debits equal the credits.

Unearned revenue (page 129) A liability that results from receiving cash before the recognition of revenue.

Understandability (page 37) A characteristic of accounting information that is able to be understood by stakeholders.

Unit-of-measure assumption (page 38) A basic assumption that states that economic activity of an entity can be effectively stated in terms of a single unit of measure. The unit of measure that is almost always used is money, and in Canada the monetary unit used is usually the Canadian dollar.

Units-of-production depreciation (page 450) A usage-based method of depreciation used when consumption can be readily associated with an assets use, not to the passage of time or obsolescence.

Value-in-use (page 442) The net present value of the cash an asset will generate over its life or the net present value of the cash the asset will allow the entity to avoid. Also known as *entity-specific value*.

Variable-rate loan (page 523) A loan whose interest rate changes with market conditions.

Verifiability (page 37) A characteristic of accounting information that is independent and similar to what knowledgeable observers can come up with for measuring an attribute.

Vertical analysis (common size financial statements) (page 715) An analytical tool in which the amounts in the balance sheet and income statement are expressed as percentages of other elements in the same year's statements.

Warranty (page 193) A promise by a seller or producer of a product to correct specified problems with the product.

Working capital (page 48) Current assets minus current liabilities.

Working capital ratio (page 49) A measure of an entity's liquidity. Defined as current assets divided by current liabilities.

Work-in-process inventory (WIP) (page 381) Inventory that is partially completed on the financial statement date.

Writedown (page 394) A reduction in the carrying amount of an asset to some measure of the market value of the asset. A writedown is achieved by debiting an expense and crediting the asset.

Writeoff (page 394) The writedown of an asset to zero.

Zero-profit method (page 201) Revenue in a period that is recognized up to the amount of costs incurred during the period (except for the last year of the project).

INDEX

T